MySQL®

Fourth Edition

Developer's Library

ESSENTIAL REFERENCES FOR PROGRAMMING PROFESSIONALS

Developer's Library books are designed to provide practicing programmers with unique, high-quality references and tutorials on the programming languages and technologies they use in their daily work.

All books in the *Developer's Library* are written by expert technology practitioners who are especially skilled at organizing and presenting information in a way that's useful for other programmers.

Key titles include some of the best, most widely acclaimed books within their topic areas:

PHP & MySQL Web Development
Luke Welling & Laura Thomson
ISBN 978-0-672-32916-6

MySQL
Paul DuBois
ISBN-13: 978-0-672-32938-8

Linux Kernel Development
Robert Love
ISBN-13: 978-0-672-32946-3

Python Essential Reference
David Beazley
ISBN-13: 978-0-672-32862-6

Programming in Objective-C
Stephen G. Kochan
ISBN-13: 978-0-321-56615-7

PostgreSQL
Korry Douglas
ISBN-13: 978-0-672-33015-5

Developer's Library books are available at most retail and online bookstores, as well as by subscription from Safari Books Online at **safari.informit.com**.

Developer's Library
informit.com/devlibrary

MySQL.

Fourth Edition

Paul DuBois

✦ Addison-Wesley

Upper Saddle River, NJ • Boston • Indianapolis • San Francisco
New York • Toronto • Montreal • London • Munich • Paris • Madrid
Cape Town • Sydney • Tokyo • Singapore • Mexico City

MySQL®
Fourth Edition

Copyright © 2009 by Pearson Education, Inc.

ISBN-13: 978-0-672-32938-8
ISBN-10: 0-672-32938-7

Library of Congress Cataloging-in-Publication Data

DuBois, Paul, 1956-

  MySQL / Paul DuBois. — 4th ed.

    p. cm.

  Includes index.

  ISBN 978-0-672-32938-8 (pbk.)

  1. SQL (Computer program language) 2. MySQL (Electronic resource) 3. Database management. I. Title.

  QA76.73.S67D588 2009

  005.13'3—dc22

                2008030855

Printed in the United States of America

Fifth Printing April 2011

Trademarks

Warning and Disclaimer

Bulk Sales

Pearson offers excellent discounts on this book when ordered in quantity for bulk purchases or special sales. For more information, please contact

U.S. Corporate and Government Sales
1-800-382-3419
corpsales@pearsontechgroup.com

For sales outside of the U.S., please contact

International Sales
international@pearson.com

Acquisitions Editor
Mark Taber

Development Editor
Michael Thurston

Managing Editor
Kristy Hart

Project Editor
Jovana
San Nicolas-Shirley

Indexer
Cheryl Lenser

Proofreaders
Leslie Joseph
Water Crest
Publishing

Technical Editors
Stephen Frein
Tim Boronczyk

**Publishing
Coordinator**
Vanessa Evans

Cover Designer
Gary Adair

Compositor
Jake McFarland

Contents at a Glance

Note: *Appendixes G, H, and I are located online and are accessible either by registering this book at **informit.com/register** or by visiting **www.kitebird.com/mysql-book**.*

Table of Contents

IV: Appendixes

Note: *Appendixes G, H, and I are located online and are accessible either by registering this book at **informit.com/register** or by visiting **www.kitebird.com/mysql-book**.*

About the Author

Paul DuBois is a writer, database administrator, and leader in the open source and MySQL communities. He has contributed to the online documentation for MySQL and is the author of *MySQL and Perl for the Web* (New Riders), *MySQL Cookbook, Using csh and tcsh*, and *Software Portability with imake* (O'Reilly). He is currently a technical writer with the MySQL documentation team at Sun Microsystems.

Acknowledgments

Acknowledgments are presented here by edition.

Fourth Edition

My technical reviewers, Stephen Frein and Tim Boronczyk, identified many points that needed correction or clarification. Ulf Wendel and Johannes Schlüter made comments and corrections on the PHP material. My thanks to each of them.

The staff at Pearson responsible for this edition were Mark Taber, Acquisitions Editor; Michael Thurston, Development Editor; Jovana San Nicolas-Shirley, Project Editor; Jake McFarland, Compositor; Cheryl Lenser, Indexer; and Gary Adair, Cover Designer.

To my wife Karen, my continued thanks and gratitude for her encouragement and support throughout this effort.

Third Edition

The third edition enjoyed careful technical review by Zak Greant and Chris Newman. Their efforts improved the manuscript at many points. Monty and the developers at MySQL AB also provided insight in response to my questions.

The people at Pearson responsible for this edition were Shelley Johnston, Acquisitions Editor; Damon Jordan, Development Editor; and Andy Beaster, Project Editor.

I am happy to recognize that my wife Karen again deserves special credit for her support during yet more revision and rewriting.

Second Edition

For the second edition, the technical reviewers once again played a crucial role in finding errors and making corrections and clarifications. Hang Lau and Shane Kirk served as reviewers. I'd also like to thank Monty Widenius, Alexander Barkov, Jani Tolonen, and the other MySQL developers for patiently enduring my many questions and supplying answers that made their way into these pages.

The New Riders staff that brought this edition to life were Stephanie Wall, Associate Publisher; Chris Zahn, Development Editor; Lori Lyons, Senior Project Editor; Pat Kinyon, Copy Editor; Cheryl Lenser, Indexer; and Stacey Richwine-DeRome, Compositor.

And, as always, my wife Karen provided the behind-the-scenes support that readers do not see, but without which this book would be much poorer.

First Edition

This book benefited greatly from the comments, corrections, and criticisms provided by the technical reviewers: David Axmark, Vijay Chaugule, Chad Cunningham, Bill Gerrard, Jijo George John, Fred Read, Egon Schmid, and Jani Tolonen. Special thanks goes to Michael "Monty" Widenius, the principal MySQL developer, who not only reviewed the manuscript, but also fielded hundreds of questions that I sent his way during the course of writing the book. Naturally, any errors that remain are my own. I'd also like to thank Tomas Karlsson, Colin McKinnon, Sasha Pachev, Eric Savage, Derick H. Siddoway, and Bob Worthy, who reviewed the initial proposal and helped shape the book into its present form.

The staff at New Riders are responsible first for conceiving this book and then for turning my scribblings into the finished work you hold in your hands. Laurie Petrycki acted as Executive Editor. Katie Purdum, Acquisitions Editor, helped me get under way and took the heat when I missed deadlines. Leah Williams did double duty not only as Development Editor but as Copy Editor; she put in many, many late hours, especially in the final stages of the project. Cheryl Lenser and Tim Wright produced the index. John Rahm served as Project Editor. Debra Neel proofread the manuscript. Gina Rexrode and Wil Cruz, Compositors, laid out the book in the form you see now. My thanks to each of them.

Most of all, I want to express my appreciation to my wife, Karen, for putting up with another book, and for her understanding and patience as I disappeared, sometimes for days on end, into "the writing zone." Her support made the task easier on many occasions, and I am pleased to acknowledge her contribution; she helped me write every page.

We Want to Hear from You!

As the reader of this book, *you* are our most important critic and commentator. We value your opinion and want to know what we're doing right, what we could do better, what areas you'd like to see us publish in, and any other words of wisdom you're willing to pass our way.

You can email or write me directly to let me know what you did or didn't like about this book—as well as what we can do to make our books stronger.

Please note that I cannot help you with technical problems related to the topic of this book, and that due to the high volume of mail I receive, I might not be able to reply to every message.

When you write, please be sure to include this book's title and author as well as your name and phone or email address. I will carefully review your comments and share them with the author and editors who worked on the book.

Email: feedback@developers-library.info
Mail: Mark Taber
         Associate Publisher
         Pearson Education
         800 East 96th Street
         Indianapolis, IN 46240 USA

Reader Services

Visit our website and register this book at informit.com/register for convenient access to any updates, downloads, or errata that might be available for this book.

Introduction

A relational database management system (RDBMS) is an essential tool in many environments, from traditional uses in business, research, and educational contexts, to applications such as powering search engines on the Internet. However, despite the importance of a good database system for managing and accessing information resources, many organizations have found them to be out of reach of their financial resources. Historically, database systems have been an expensive proposition, with vendors charging healthy fees both for software and for support. Also, because database engines often had substantial hardware requirements to run with any reasonable performance, the cost was even greater.

The situation is different now, on both the hardware and software sides of the picture. Small desktop systems and servers are inexpensive but powerful, and there is a thriving movement devoted to writing high-performance operating systems for them. These operating systems are available free over the Internet or at the cost of an inexpensive CD. They include several BSD Unix derivatives (FreeBSD, NetBSD, OpenBSD) as well as various distributions of Linux (Fedora, Debian, Gentoo, SuSE, to name a few).

Production of free operating systems has proceeded in concert with—and to a large extent has been made possible by—the development of freely available tools like gcc, the GNU C compiler. These efforts to make software available to anyone who wants it are part of the Open Source movement. Open Source projects have produced many important pieces of software. For example, Apache is the most widely used Web server on the Internet. Perl, Python, and Ruby are well-established general-purpose scripting languages, and PHP is a language that is popular due largely to the ease with which it enables dynamic Web pages to be written. These all stand in contrast to proprietary solutions that lock you into high-priced products from vendors that don't even provide source code.

Database software has become more accessible, too, and Open Source database systems are freely available. One of these is MySQL, a SQL client/server relational database management system originating from Scandinavia. MySQL includes an SQL server, client programs for accessing the server, administrative tools, and a programming interface for writing your own programs.

MySQL's roots begin in 1979, with the UNIREG database tool created by Michael "Monty" Widenius for the Swedish company TcX. In 1994, TcX began searching for an RDBMS with an SQL interface for use in developing Web applications. They tested some commercial servers, but found all too slow for TcX's large tables. They also took a look at mSQL, but it lacked certain features that TcX required. Consequently, Monty began developing a new server. The programming interface was explicitly designed to be similar to the one used by mSQL because several free tools were available for mSQL, and by using a similar interface, those same tools could be used for MySQL with a minimum of porting effort.

In 1995, David Axmark of Detron HB began to push for TcX to release MySQL on the Internet. David also worked on the documentation and on getting MySQL to build with the GNU `configure` utility. MySQL 3.11.1 was unleashed on the world in 1996 in the form of binary distributions for Linux and Solaris. Today, MySQL works on many more platforms and is available in both binary and source form. The company MySQL AB was formed to provide distributions of MySQL under both Open Source and commercial licenses, and to offer technical support, monitoring services, and training. In 2008, Sun Microsystems acquired MySQL AB and the commitment to Open Source remains strong (Sun was already moving in the direction of making many of its products available under Open Source licensing).

Initially, MySQL became widely popular because of its speed and simplicity. But there was criticism, too, because it lacked features such as transactions and foreign key support. MySQL continued to develop, adding not only those features but others such as replication, subqueries, stored procedures, views, and triggers. These capabilities take MySQL into the realm of enterprise applications. As a result, people who once would have considered only "big iron" database systems for their applications now give serious consideration to MySQL.

MySQL is portable and runs on commercial operating systems (such as Mac OS X, HP-UX, and Windows) and on hardware all the way up to enterprise servers. Furthermore, its performance rivals any database system you care to put up against it, and it can handle large databases with billions of rows. In the business world, MySQL's presence continues to increase as companies discover it to be capable of handling their database needs at a fraction of what they are used to paying for commercial licensing and support.

MySQL lies squarely within the picture that unfolds before us: freely available operating systems running on powerful but inexpensive hardware, putting substantial processing power and capabilities in the hands of more individuals and businesses than ever before, on a wider variety of systems than ever before. This lowering of the economic barriers to computing puts powerful database solutions within reach of more people and organizations than at any time in the past. Organizations that once could only dream of putting the power of a high-performance RDBMS to work for them now can do so for very little cost. This is true for individuals as well. For example, I use MySQL with Perl, PHP, and Apache on my Apple laptop running Mac OS X. This enables me to carry my work with me anywhere. Total cost: the cost of the laptop.

Why Choose MySQL?

If you're looking for a free or low-cost database management system, several are available from which to choose, such as MySQL, PostgreSQL, or SQLite. When you compare MySQL with other database systems, think about what's most important to you.

Performance, support, features (such as SQL conformance or extensions), licensing conditions and restrictions, and price all are factors to take into account. Given these considerations, MySQL has many attractive features to offer:

- **Speed.** MySQL is fast. Its developers contend that MySQL is about the fastest database system you can get. You can investigate this claim by visiting http://www.mysql.com/why-mysql/benchmarks/, a performance-comparison page on the MySQL Web site.

- **Ease of use.** MySQL is a high-performance but relatively simple database system and is much less complex to set up and administer than larger systems.

- **Query language support.** MySQL understands SQL (Structured Query Language), the standard language of choice for all modern database systems.

- **Capability.** The MySQL server is multi-threaded, so many clients can connect to it at the same time. Each client can use multiple databases simultaneously. You can access MySQL interactively using several interfaces that let you enter queries and view the results: command-line clients, Web browsers, or GUI clients. In addition, programming interfaces are available for many languages, such as C, Perl, Java, PHP, Python, and Ruby. You can also access MySQL using applications that support ODBC and .NET (protocols developed by Microsoft). This gives you the choice of using prepackaged client software or writing your own for custom applications.

- **Connectivity and security.** MySQL is fully networked, and databases can be accessed from anywhere on the Internet, so you can share your data with anyone, anywhere. But MySQL has access control so that one person who shouldn't see another's data cannot. To provide additional security, MySQL supports encrypted connections using the Secure Sockets Layer (SSL) protocol.

- **Portability.** MySQL runs on many varieties of Unix and Linux, as well as on other systems such as Windows and NetWare. MySQL runs on hardware from high-end servers down to small personal computers (even palmtop devices).

- **Small size.** MySQL has a modest distribution size, especially compared to the huge disk space footprint of certain other database systems.

- **Availability and cost.** MySQL is an Open Source project available under multiple licensing terms. First, it is available under the terms of the GNU General Public License (GPL). This means that MySQL is available without cost for most in-house uses. Second, for organizations that prefer or require formal arrangements or that do not want to be bound by the conditions of the GPL, commercial licenses are available.

- **Open distribution and source code.** MySQL is easy to obtain; just use your Web browser. If you don't understand how something works, are curious about an algorithm, or want to perform a security audit, you can get the source code and examine it. If you think you've found a bug, please report it; the developers want to know.

What about support? Good question; a database system isn't much use if you can't get help for it. This book is one form of assistance, and I like to think that it's useful in that regard. (The fact that the book has reached its fourth edition suggests that it accomplishes that goal.) There are other resources open to you as well, and you'll find that MySQL has good support:

- The MySQL Reference Manual is included in MySQL distributions, and also is available online and in printed form. The Reference Manual regularly receives good marks in the MySQL user community. This is important, because the value of a good product is diminished if no one can figure out how to use it.
- Technical support contracts, monitoring services, and training classes are available from Sun.
- There are several active MySQL mailing lists to which anyone may subscribe. These lists have many helpful participants, including several MySQL developers. As a support resource, many people find these lists invaluable.

The MySQL community, developers and nondevelopers alike, is very responsive. Answers to questions on the mailing lists often arrive within minutes. When bugs are reported, the developers generally fix them quickly, and fixes become available daily over the Internet. Contrast this with the often-frustrating experience of navigating the Byzantine support channels of big vendors. You've been there? Me, too.

If you are in the database-selection process, MySQL is an ideal candidate for evaluation. You can try MySQL with no risk or financial commitment. If you get stuck, you can use the mailing lists to get help. An evaluation costs some of your time, but that's true no matter what database system you're considering—and it's a safe bet that your installation and setup time for MySQL will be less than for many other systems.

Already Running Another RDBMS?

If you're currently running another database system but feel constrained by it, you definitely should consider MySQL. Perhaps performance of your current system is a concern, or it's proprietary and you don't like being locked into it. Perhaps you'd like to run on hardware that's not supported by your current system, or your software is provided in binary-only format but you want to have the source available. Or maybe it just costs too much! All of these are reasons to look into MySQL. Use this book to familiarize yourself with MySQL's capabilities, contact the MySQL sales crew, ask questions on the mailing lists, and you'll find the answers you need to make a decision.

One thing to keep in mind is that although all major database engines support SQL, each supports a somewhat different dialect. Check the chapters in this book that deal with MySQL's SQL dialect and data types. You may decide that the version of SQL supported by your current RDBMS is too different and that porting your applications would involve significant effort.

Part of your evaluation should be to try porting a few examples, of course. This will give you valuable experience in making an assessment. There is an ongoing commitment by the MySQL developers to an increasing conformance to standard SQL. That has the practical consequence of eliminating porting roadblocks as time goes on, so your porting effort may turn out to be easier than you expect.

Tools Provided with MySQL

MySQL distributions include the following tools:

- **An SQL server.** This is the engine that powers MySQL and provides access to your databases.

- **Client and utility programs.** These include an interactive client program that enables you to enter queries directly and view the results. Also available are several administrative and utility programs that help you run your site: One allows you to monitor and control the server; others let you import data, perform backups, check tables for problems, and more.

- **A client library for writing your own programs.** You can write client programs in C because the library is in C, but the library also can be linked into other language processors such as Perl, PHP, or Ruby to provide the basis for MySQL interfaces in those languages.

In addition to the software provided with MySQL itself, MySQL is used by many talented and capable people who like writing software to enhance their productivity and who are willing to share that software. The result is that you have access to a variety of third-party tools that make MySQL easier to use or that extend its reach into areas such as Web site development.

What You Can Expect from This Book

By reading this book, you'll learn how to use MySQL effectively so that you can get your work done more productively. You'll be able to figure out how to get your information into a database, and you'll learn how to get it back out by formulating queries that give you the answers to the questions you want to ask of that data.

You don't need to be a programmer to understand or use SQL. This book will show you how it works. But there's more to understanding how to use a database system properly than knowing SQL syntax. This book emphasizes MySQL's unique capabilities and shows how to use them.

You'll also see how MySQL integrates with other tools. The book shows how to use MySQL with Perl and PHP to generate dynamic Web pages created from the result of database queries. You'll learn how to write your own programs that access MySQL databases. All of these enhance MySQL's capabilities to handle the requirements of your particular applications.

If you'll be responsible for administering a MySQL installation, this book will tell you what your duties are and how to carry them out. You'll learn how to create user accounts, perform database backups, set up replication, and make sure your site is secure.

Road Map to This Book

This book is organized into four parts. The first concentrates on general concepts of database use. The second focuses on writing your own programs that use MySQL. The third is aimed at those readers who have administrative duties. The fourth provides a set of reference appendixes.

Part I: General MySQL Use

- Chapter 1, "Getting Started with MySQL." Discusses how MySQL can be useful to you, provides a tutorial that introduces the interactive MySQL client program, covers the basics of SQL, and demonstrates MySQL's general capabilities.

- Chapter 2, "Using SQL to Manage Data." Every major RDBMS now available understands SQL, but every database engine implements a slightly different SQL dialect. This chapter discusses SQL with particular emphasis on those features that make MySQL distinctive.

- Chapter 3, "Data Types." Discusses the data types that MySQL provides for storing your information, the properties and limitations of each type, when and how to use them, how to choose between similar types, expression evaluation, and type conversion.

- Chapter 4, "Stored Programs." Discusses how to write and use SQL programs that are stored on the server side. Types of programs available to you are stored functions and procedures, triggers, and events.

- Chapter 5, "Query Optimization." Discusses how to make your queries run more efficiently.

Part II: Using MySQL Programming Interfaces

- Chapter 6, "Introduction to MySQL Programming." Discusses some of the application programming interfaces (APIs) available for MySQL and provides a general comparison of the APIs that the book covers in detail.

- Chapter 7, "Writing MySQL Programs Using C." Discusses how to write C programs using the API provided by the MySQL C client library.

- Chapter 8, "Writing MySQL Programs Using Perl DBI." Discusses how to write Perl scripts using the DBI module. Covers standalone command-line scripts and scripts for Web site programming.

- Chapter 9, "Writing MySQL Programs Using PHP." Discusses how to use the PHP scripting language and the PHP Data Objects (PDO) database-access extension to write dynamic Web pages that access MySQL databases.

Part III: MySQL Administration

- Chapter 10, "Introduction to MySQL Administration." An overview of the database administrator's duties and what you should know to run a MySQL site successfully.

- Chapter 11, "The MySQL Data Directory." An in-depth look at the organization and contents of the data directory, the area under which MySQL stores databases, logs, and status files.

- Chapter 12, "General MySQL Administration." Discusses how to make sure your operating system starts and stops the MySQL server properly when your system comes up and shuts down. Also includes instructions for setting up MySQL user accounts, and discusses log maintenance, configuring storage engines, tuning the server, and running multiple servers.

- Chapter 13, "Access Control and Security." Discusses what you need to know to make your MySQL installation safe from intrusion, both from other users on the server host and from clients connecting over the network. Explains the structure of the grant tables that control client access to the MySQL server. Describes how to set up your server to support secure connections over SSL.

- Chapter 14, "Database Maintenance, Backups, and Replication." Discusses how to reduce the likelihood of disaster through preventive maintenance, how to back up your databases, how to perform crash recovery if disaster strikes in spite of your preventive measures, and how to set up replication servers.

Part IV: Appendixes

- Appendix A, "Obtaining and Installing Software." Discusses where to get and how to install the major tools and sample database files described in the book.

- Appendix B, "Data Type Reference." Explores the characteristics of MySQL's data types.

- Appendix C, "Operator and Function Reference." The operators and functions that are used to write expressions in SQL statements are discussed.

- Appendix D, "System, Status, and User Variable Reference." Describes each variable maintained by the MySQL server, and how to use your own variables in SQL statements.

- Appendix E, "SQL Syntax Reference." Describes each SQL statement supported by MySQL.
- Appendix F, "MySQL Program Reference." Explores the programs provided in the MySQL distribution.

Note

The following Appendices are located online. Go to www.informit.com/title/ 9780672329388 to register your book and access these files. Or, please visit www.kitebird.com/mysql-book to access these files.

- Appendix G, "C API Reference" (online). Explores the data types and functions in the MySQL C client library.
- Appendix H, "Perl DBI API Reference" (online). Discusses the methods and attributes provided by the Perl DBI module.
- Appendix I, "PHP API Reference" (online). Discusses the methods provided for MySQL support in PHP by the PDO extension.

How to Read This Book

Whichever part of the book you happen to be reading at any given time, it's best to try the examples as you go along. That means you should do two things:

- If MySQL isn't installed on your system, you should install it or ask someone to do so for you.
- You should get the files needed to set up the sampdb sample database to which we'll be referring throughout the book.

Appendix A indicates where you can obtain all the necessary components and has instructions for installing them.

If you're a complete newcomer to MySQL or to SQL, begin with Chapter 1. This provides you with a tutorial introduction that grounds you in basic MySQL and SQL concepts and brings you up to speed for the rest of the book. Then proceed to Chapter 2, Chapter 3, and Chapter 4 to find out how to describe and manipulate your own data so that you can exploit MySQL's capabilities for your own applications.

If you already know some SQL, you should still read Chapter 2 and Chapter 3. SQL implementations vary, and you'll want to find out what makes MySQL's implementation distinctive in comparison to others with which you may be familiar.

If you have experience with MySQL but need more background on the details of performing particular tasks, use the book as a reference, looking up topics on a need-to-know basis. You'll find the appendixes especially useful for reference purposes.

If you're interested in writing your own programs to access MySQL databases, read the API chapters, beginning with Chapter 6. If you want to produce a Web-based front end to your databases for easier access to them, or, conversely, to provide a database back end for your Web site to enhance your site with dynamic content, check out Chapter 8 and Chapter 9.

If you're evaluating MySQL to find out how it compares to your current RDBMS, several parts of the book will be useful. Read the SQL syntax and data type chapters in Part I to compare MySQL to the version of SQL that you're used to, the programming chapters in Part II if you need to write custom applications, and the administrative chapters in Part III to assess the level of administrative support a MySQL installation requires. This information is also useful if you're not currently using a database but are performing a comparative analysis of MySQL along with other database systems for the purpose of choosing one of them.

Versions of Software Covered in This Book

The first edition of this book covered MySQL 3.22 and the beginnings of MySQL 3.23. The second edition expanded that range to include MySQL 4.0 and the first release of MySQL 4.1. The third edition covered MySQL 4.1 and the initial releases of MySQL 5.0.

For this fourth edition, the baseline for coverage is MySQL 5.0. That is, the book covers MySQL 5.0 and 5.1, and the early releases of MySQL 6.0. Most of this book still applies if you have a version older than 5.0, but differences specific to older versions usually are not explicitly noted.

The MySQL 5.0 series has reached General Availability status, which means that it is considered stable for use in production environments. There were a lot of changes in earlier pre-production 5.0 releases, and I recommend that you use the most recent version if possible. The current 5.0 version as I write is 5.0.64. The MySQL 5.1 series is in Release Candidate development (currently at 5.1.25) and should reach General Availability status soon. You'll need MySQL 5.1 if you want to try features such as the event scheduler or XML support.

If you're using a version of MySQL older than 5.0, be aware that the following features discussed in this book will not be available to you:

- MySQL 5.0 adds stored functions and procedures, views, triggers, strict input handling, true VARCHAR, and INFORMATION_SCHEMA.
- MySQL 5.1 adds the event scheduler, partitioning, log tables, and XML support.

For information about older versions, check the MySQL Web site at http://dev.mysql.com/doc/, where you can access the Reference Manual for each version.

I also draw your attention to some topics that are not covered in this book:

- The MySQL Connectors, which provide client access for Java, ODBC, and .NET programs.

- The NDB storage engine and MySQL Cluster, which provide in-memory storage, high availability, and redundancy. See the MySQL Reference Manual for details.

- The graphical user interface (GUI) tools such as MySQL Administrator and MySQL Query Browser. These tools help you use MySQL in a windowing environment.

To download any of these products or see their documentation, visit http://www.mysql.com/products/ or http://dev.mysql.com/doc/.

For the other major software packages discussed in the book, any recent versions should be sufficient for the examples shown. (Note that the PDO database-access extension requires PHP 5; PHP 4 will not work.) The current versions are shown in the following table.

Package	Version
Perl DBI module	1.601
Perl DBD::mysql module	4.007
PHP	5.2.6
Apache	2.0.63/2.2.8
CGI.pm	3.29

All software discussed in this book is available on the Internet. Appendix A provides instructions for getting support for MySQL, Perl DBI, PHP and PDO, Apache, and CGI.pm onto your system. The appendix also contains instructions for obtaining the `sampdb` sample database that is used in examples throughout the book and that contains the programs that are developed in the programming chapters.

If you are using Windows, I assume that you have a relatively recent version such as Windows 2000, XP, 2003, or Vista. Some features covered in this book such as named pipes and Windows services are not available in older versions (Windows 95, 98, or Me).

Conventions Used in This Book

This book uses the following typographical conventions:

- `Monospaced font` indicates hostnames, filenames, directory names, commands, options, and Web sites.

- **`Bold monospaced font`** is used in command examples to indicate input that you type.

- *`Italic monospaced font`* is used in commands to indicate where you should substitute a value of your own choosing.

For interactive examples, I assume that you enter commands by typing them into a terminal window or console window. To provide context, the prompt in command examples indicate the program from which you run the command. For example, SQL statements that are issued from within the `mysql` client program are shown preceded by the `mysql>` prompt. For commands that you issue from your command interpreter, the `%` prompt usually is used. In general, this prompt indicates commands that can be run either on Unix or Windows, although the particular prompt you see will depend on your command interpreter. (The command interpreter is your login shell on Unix, or `cmd.exe` or `command.com` on Windows.) More specialized command-line prompts are `#`, which indicates a command run on Unix as the `root` user via `su` or `sudo`, and `C:\>` to indicate a command intended specifically for Windows.

The following example shows a command that should be entered from your command interpreter. The `%` indicates the prompt, which you do not type. To issue the command, you'd enter the boldface characters as shown, and substitute your own username for the italic word:

```
% mysql --user=user_name sampdb
```

In SQL statements, SQL keywords and function names are written in uppercase. Database, table, and column names appear in lowercase.

In syntax descriptions, square brackets (`[]`) indicate optional information. In lists of alternatives, vertical bar (`|`) is used as a separator between items. A list enclosed within `[]` is optional and indicates that an item may be chosen from the list. A list enclosed within `{}` is mandatory and indicates that an item must be chosen from the list.

Additional Resources

If you have a question that this book doesn't answer, where should you turn? Useful documentation resources include the Web sites for the software you need help with, shown in the following table.

Package	Primary Web Site
MySQL	http://dev.mysql.com/doc/
Perl DBI	http://dbi.perl.org/
PHP	http://www.php.net/
Apache	http://httpd.apache.org/
CGI.pm	http://search.cpan.org/dist/CGI.pm/

Those sites provide information such as reference manuals, frequently asked-question (FAQ) lists, and mailing lists:

- **Reference manuals.** The primary documentation included with MySQL itself is the Reference Manual. It's available in several formats, including online and downloadable versions.

  PHP's manual comes in several forms, too.

- **Manual pages.** Documentation for the DBI module and its MySQL-specific driver, DBD::mysql, can be read from the command line with the `perldoc` command. Try `perldoc DBI` and `perldoc DBD::mysql`. The DBI document provides general concepts. The MySQL driver document discusses capabilities specific to MySQL.

- **FAQs.** There are frequently asked-question lists for DBI, PHP, and Apache.

- **Mailing lists.** Several mailing lists centering around the software discussed in this book are available. It's a good idea to subscribe to the ones that deal with the tools you want to use. It's also a good idea to use the archives for those lists that have them. When you're new to a tool, you will have many of the same questions that have been asked (and answered) many times, and there is no reason to ask again when you can find the answer with a quick search of the archives.

  Instructions for subscribing to the mailing lists vary. The following table indicates where you can find the necessary information.

Package	Mailing List Instructions
MySQL	http://lists.mysql.com/
Perl DBI	http://dbi.perl.org/support/
PHP	http://www.php.net/mailing-lists.php
Apache	http://httpd.apache.org/lists.html

- **Ancillary Web sites.** Besides the official Web sites, some of the tools discussed here have ancillary sites that provide more information, such as sample source code or topical articles. Check for a "Links" area on the official site you're visiting.

Getting Started with MySQL

This chapter provides an introduction to the MySQL relational database management system (RDBMS), and to the Structured Query Language (SQL) that MySQL understands. It lays out basic terms and concepts you should understand, describes the `sampdb` sample database that we'll use for examples, and serves as a tutorial that shows you how to use MySQL to create a database and interact with it.

Begin here if you are new to database systems and perhaps uncertain whether you need one or can use one. You should also read the chapter if you don't know anything about MySQL or SQL and need an introductory guide to get started. Readers who have experience with MySQL or other database systems might want to skim through the material. However, everybody should read Section 1.2, "A Sample Database," to become familiar with the purpose and contents of the `sampdb` database that is used throughout the book.

1.1 How MySQL Can Help You

This section describes situations in which the MySQL database system is useful. This will give you an idea of the kinds of things MySQL can do and the ways in which it can help you. If you don't need to be convinced about the usefulness of a database system—perhaps because you've already got a problem in mind and just want to find out how to put MySQL to work helping you solve it—you can proceed to Section 1.2, "A Sample Database."

A database system is essentially a high-powered way to manage lists of information. The information can come from a variety of sources. It might be research data, business records, customer requests, sports statistics, sales reports, personal information, personnel records, bug reports, or student grades. However, although database systems can deal with a wide range of information, you don't use such a system for its own sake. If a job is easy to do already, there's no reason to drag a database into it just to use one. A grocery list is a good example: You write down the items to get, cross them off as you do your shopping, and then throw the list away. It's highly unlikely that you'd use a database for this. Even if you have a palmtop computer, you'd probably keep track of a grocery list using its notepad function rather than its database capabilities.

The power of a database system comes into play when the information you want to organize and manage is so voluminous or complex that your records become more burdensome than you care to deal with by hand. Clearly this is the case for large corporations processing millions of transactions a day; a database is a necessity under such circumstances. But even small-scale operations involving a single person maintaining information of personal interest might require a database. It's not difficult to think of scenarios in which a database can be beneficial, because you needn't have huge amounts of information before that information becomes difficult to manage. Consider the following situations:

- Your carpentry business has several employees. You need to maintain employee and payroll records so that you know who you've paid and when, and you must summarize those records so that you can report earnings statements to the government for tax purposes. You also need to keep track of the jobs your company has been hired to do and which employees you've scheduled to work on each job.

- You run a network of automobile parts warehouses and need to be able to tell which ones have any given part in their inventory so that you can fill customer orders.

- That pile of research data you've been collecting over the course of many years needs to be analyzed for publication. You want to boil down large amounts of raw data to generate summary information, and to pull out selected subsets of observations for more detailed statistical analysis.

- You're a teacher who needs to keep track of grades and attendance. Each time you give a quiz or a test, you record every student's grade. It's easy enough to write down scores in a gradebook, but using the scores later is a tedious chore. You'd rather avoid sorting the scores for each test to determine the grading curve, and you'd really rather not add up each student's scores when you determine final grades at the end of the grading period. Counting each student's absences is no fun, either.

- The organization for which you serve as the secretary maintains a directory of members. (The organization could be anything—a professional society, a club, a symphony orchestra, or an athletic booster club.) You generate a printed directory each year for the members, based on a word processor document that you edit as membership information changes. You're tired of maintaining the directory that way because it limits what you can do with it. It's difficult to sort the entries in different ways, and you can't easily select just certain parts of each entry (such as a list consisting only of names and phone numbers). Nor can you easily find a subset of members, such as those who need to renew their memberships soon—if you could, it would eliminate the job of looking through the entries each month to find those members who need to be sent renewal notices. You've heard about the "paperless office" that's supposed to result from electronic record-keeping, but you haven't seen any benefit from it. The membership records are electronic, but, ironically, aren't in a form that can be used easily for anything *except* generating paper by printing the directory!

These scenarios range from situations involving small amounts to large amounts of information. Their common characteristic is that they involve tasks that can be performed manually but that could be performed more efficiently by a database system.

What specific benefits should you expect to see from using a database system such as MySQL? It depends on your particular needs and requirements, and as illustrated by the preceding examples, those can vary quite a bit. Let's look at a type of situation that occurs frequently and is fairly representative of database use. Database management systems are often employed to handle tasks such as those for which people use filing cabinets. Indeed, a database is like a big filing cabinet in some ways, but one with a sophisticated built-in filing system. There are some important advantages of electronically maintained records over records maintained by hand. For example, if you work in a dentist's office setting in which client records are maintained, here are some of the ways MySQL can help you in its filing system capacity.

Reduced record filing time. You don't have to look through drawers in cabinets to figure out where to add a new record. You just hand it to the filing system and let it put the record in the right place for you.

Reduced record retrieval time. When you're looking for records, you don't search through each one yourself to find the ones containing the information you want. If you want to send out reminders to all patients who haven't been in for their checkup in a while, you ask the filing system to find the appropriate records for you. Of course, you do this differently than if you were talking to another person, with whom you'd say, "Please determine which patients haven't visited within the last six months." With a database, you invoke a strange incantation:

```
SELECT last_name, first_name, last_visit FROM patient
WHERE last_visit < DATE_SUB(CURDATE(), INTERVAL 6 MONTH);
```

That can be pretty intimidating if you've never seen anything like it before, but the prospect of getting results in a second or two rather than spending an hour shuffling through your records should be attractive. (In any case, you needn't worry. That odd-looking bit of gobbledygook won't look strange for long. In fact, you'll understand exactly what it means by the time you've finished this chapter.)

Flexible retrieval order. You needn't retrieve records according to the fixed order in which you store them (by patient's last name, for example). You can tell the filing system to pull out records sorted in any order you like: by last name, insurance company name, date of last visit, and so forth.

Flexible output format. After you've found the records in which you're interested, there's no need to copy the information manually. The filing system can generate a list for you. Sometimes you might just print the information. Other times you might want to use it in another program. For example, after you generate the list of patients who are overdue on their dental visits, you might feed this information into a word processor that prints out notices that you can send to those patients. Or you might be interested only in summary information, such as a count of the selected records. You don't have to count them yourself; the filing system can generate the summary for you.

Simultaneous multiple-user access to records. With paper records, if two people want to look up a record at the same time, the second person must wait for the first one to put the record back. MySQL gives you multiple-user capability so that both can access the record simultaneously.

Remote access to and electronic transmission of records. Paper records require you to be where the records are located, or for someone to make copies and send them to you. Electronic records open up the potential for remote access to the records or electronic transmission of them. If your dental group has associates in branch offices, those associates can access your records from their own locations. You don't need to send copies by courier. If someone who needs records doesn't have the same kind of database software you do but does have electronic mail, you can select the desired records and send their contents electronically.

If you've used database management systems before, you already know about the benefits just described, and you may be thinking about how to go beyond the usual "replace the filing cabinet" applications. The manner in which many organizations use a database in conjunction with a Web site is a good example. Suppose that your company has an inventory database that is used by the service desk staff when customers call to find out whether you have an item in stock and how much it costs. That's a relatively traditional use for a database. However, if your company puts up a Web site for customers to visit, you can provide an additional service: a search page that enables customers to determine item pricing and availability. This gives customers the information they want, and the way you provide it is by searching the inventory information stored in your database for the items in question—automatically. The customer gets the information immediately, without being put on hold listening to annoying canned music or being limited by the hours your service desk is open. And for every customer who uses your Web site, that's one less phone call that needs to be handled by a person on the service desk payroll. (Perhaps the Web site can pay for itself this way?)

But you can put the database to even better use than that. Web-based inventory search requests can provide information not only to your customers, but to your company as well. The queries tell you what customers are looking for, and the query results tell you whether you're able to satisfy their requests. To the extent you don't have what they want, you're probably losing business. So it makes sense to record information about inventory searches: what customers were looking for, and whether you had it in stock. Then you can use this information to adjust your inventory and provide better service to your customers.

So how does MySQL work? The best way to find out is to try it for yourself, and for that we'll need a database to work with.

1.2 A Sample Database

This section describes the sample database that we'll use throughout the rest of this book. It provides a source of examples for you to try as you learn to put MySQL to work. We'll draw examples primarily from two of the situations described earlier:

- The organizational secretary scenario. Our organization has these characteristics: It's composed of people drawn together through an affinity for United States history (called, for lack of a better name, the U.S. Historical League). The members renew their membership periodically on a dues-paying basis. Dues go toward League expenses such as publication of a newsletter, "Chronicles of U.S. Past." The League also operates a small Web site; it hasn't been developed very much, but you'd like to change that.

- The grade-keeping scenario. You are a teacher who administers quizzes and tests during the grading period, records scores, and assigns grades. Afterward, you determine final grades, which you turn in to the school office along with an attendance summary.

Now let's examine these situations more closely in terms of two requirements:

- You must decide what you want to get out of the database—that is, what goals you want to accomplish.

- You must figure out what you're going to put into the database—that is, what data you will keep track of.

Perhaps it seems backward to think about what comes out of the database before considering what goes in. After all, you must enter your data before you can retrieve it. But the way you use a database is driven by your goals, and those are more closely associated with what you want to get from your database than with what you put into it. Presumably you're not going to waste time and effort putting information into a database unless you plan to use it for something later.

1.2.1 The U.S. Historical League

The scenario here is that you as League secretary maintain the membership list using a word processing document. That works reasonably well for generating a printed directory but limits what else you can do with the information. You have these objectives in mind:

- You want to produce output from the directory in different formats, using information appropriate to the application. One goal is to generate the printed directory each year—a requirement the League has had in the past that you plan to continue to carry out. You can think of other uses for the information in the directory, too— for example, to provide the current-member list for the printed program distributed to attendees of the League's annual meeting. These applications involve different sets of information. The printed directory uses the entire contents of each member's entry. For the meeting program, you need to pull out only member names (something that hasn't been easy using a word processor).

- You want to search the directory for members who satisfy various criteria. For example, you want to know which members must renew their memberships soon. Another application that involves searching arises from the list of keywords you maintain for each member. These keywords describe areas of U.S. history in which each member is particularly interested (for example, the Civil War, the Depression, civil rights, or the life of Thomas Jefferson). Members sometimes ask you for a list of other members with interests similar to their own, and you'd like to be able to satisfy these requests.

- You want to put the directory online at the League's Web site. This would benefit both the members and yourself. If you can convert the directory to Web pages by some reasonably automated process, an online version of the directory would be always up to date, something not true of the printed version. And if the online directory can be made searchable, members could easily look for information themselves. For example, a member who wants to know which other members are interested in the Civil War could find that out without waiting for you to perform the search, and you wouldn't need to find the time to do it yourself.

I'm well aware that databases are not the most exciting things in the world, so I'm not about to make any wild claims that using one stimulates creative thinking. Nevertheless, when you stop thinking of information as something you must wrestle with (as you do when using your word processing document) and begin thinking of it as something you can manipulate relatively easily (as you hope to do with MySQL), it has a certain liberating effect on your ability to come up with new ways to use that information:

- If the information in the database can be moved to the Web site in the form of an online directory, you might also be able to make information flow the other way. Suppose that members could edit their own entries online to provide updates for the database. Then you wouldn't have to do all the editing yourself, and it would make the information in the directory more accurate. You'd really like to avoid doing all the directory editing yourself, but the society doesn't have much of a budget, and hiring someone is out of the question.

- If you store email addresses in the database, you could use them to send email to members that haven't updated their entries in a while. The messages could show members the current contents of their entry, ask them to review it, and indicate how to make any needed modifications using the facilities provided on the Web site.

- A database might help make the Web site more useful in ways not even related to the membership list. The League's newsletter, "Chronicles of U.S. Past," has a children's section containing a history-based quiz in each issue. Some of the recent issues have focused on biographical facts about U.S. presidents. The Web site could have a children's section, too, where the quizzes are put online. Perhaps this section could even be made interactive, by putting the information from which quizzes are drawn in the database and having the Web server query the database for questions to present to visitors.

Well! At this point the number of uses for the database that you're coming up with make you realize you might be getting a little carried away. After pausing to come back down to earth, you start asking some practical questions:

- Isn't this a little ambitious? Won't it be a lot of work to set this up?

  Anything's easier when you're just thinking about it and not doing it, of course, and I won't pretend that all of these ideas are trivial to implement. Nevertheless, by the end of this book you'll have done everything we've just outlined. Just keep one thing in mind: It's not necessary to do everything all at once. We'll break the job into pieces and tackle it a piece at a time.

- Can MySQL be used to accomplish all these goals?

  No, it can't, at least not by itself. For example, MySQL has no built-in Web-programming facilities. But you can combine MySQL with other tools that work with it to complement and extend its capabilities.

  We'll use the Perl scripting language and the Perl DBI (database interface) module to write scripts that access MySQL databases. Perl has excellent text-processing capabilities, which allow for manipulation of query results in a highly flexible manner to produce output in a variety of formats. For example, we can use Perl to generate the directory in Rich Text Format (RTF), which can be read by all kinds of word processors, and in HTML format for Web browsers.

  We'll also use PHP, another scripting language. PHP is particularly adapted to writing Web applications, and it interfaces easily with databases. This enables you to initiate MySQL queries from Web pages and to generate new pages that include the results of database queries. PHP can be used with several Web servers (including Apache, the most popular server in the world), making it easy to do things such as presenting a search form and displaying the results of the search.

  MySQL integrates well with these tools and gives you the flexibility to choose how to combine them to achieve the ends you have in mind. You're not locked into some all-in-one suite's components that have highly touted "integration" capabilities but that actually work well only with each other.

- And, finally, the big question: How much will all this cost? The League has a limited budget, after all.

  This might surprise you, but it probably won't cost anything. If you're familiar with the usual ken of database systems, you know that they're generally pretty pricey. By contrast, MySQL often can be used for free. Even in enterprise settings where you need guaranteed support and maintenance arrangements, MySQL is relatively inexpensive as database systems go. (Visit www.mysql.com for details.) The other tools

we'll use (Perl, DBI, PHP, Apache) are free, so, all things considered, you can put together a useful system quite inexpensively.

The choice of operating system for developing the database is up to you. Virtually all
the software we'll discuss runs under both Unix (which I use as an umbrella term that includes BSD Unix, Linux, Mac OS X, and so forth) and Windows. The few exceptions
tend to be shell or batch scripts that are specific to either Unix or Windows.

1.2.2 The Grade-Keeping Project

Now let's consider the other situation for which we'll be using the sample database. The
scenario here is that as a teacher, you have grade-keeping responsibilities. You want to
convert the grading process from a manual operation using a gradebook to an electronic
representation using MySQL. In this case, the information you want to get from a database is implicit in the way you already use your gradebook now:

- For each quiz or test, you record the scores. For tests, you put the scores in order so
  that you can look at them and determine the cutoffs for each letter grade (A, B, C,
  D, and F).
- At the end of the grading period, you calculate each student's total score, and then
  sort the totals and determine grades based on them. The totals might involve
  weighted calculations because you probably want to count tests more heavily than
  quizzes.
- You provide attendance information to the school office at the end of the grading
  period.

The objectives are to avoid manually sorting and summarizing scores and attendance
records. In other words, you want MySQL to sort the scores and perform the calculations
necessary to compute each student's total score and number of absences when the grading
period ends. To accomplish these goals, you'll need the list of students in the class, the
scores for each quiz and test, and the dates on which students are absent.

1.2.3 How the Sample Database Applies to You

If you're not particularly interested in the Historical League or in grade-keeping, you
might be wondering what either of these scenarios have to do with you. The answer is
that they aren't an end in themselves. They simply provide a vehicle by which to illustrate
what you can do with MySQL and tools that are related to it.

With a little imagination, you'll see how example database queries apply to the particular problems you want to solve. Suppose that you're working in that dentist's office I
mentioned earlier. You won't see many dentistry-related queries in this book, but you will
see that many of the queries you find here apply to patient record maintenance, office
bookkeeping, and so forth. For example, determining which Historical League members
need to renew their memberships soon is similar to determining which patients haven't

visited the dentist for a while. Both are date-based queries, so once you learn to write the membership-renewal query, you can apply that skill to writing the delinquent-patient query in which you have a more immediate interest.

1.3 Basic Database Terminology

You may have noticed that you're already several pages into a database book and still haven't seen a whole bunch of jargon and technical terminology. In fact, I still haven't said anything at all about what "a database" actually looks like, even though we have a rough specification of how our sample database will be used. However, we're about to design that database, and then we'll begin implementing it, so we can't avoid terminology any longer. That's what this section is about. It describes some terms that come up throughout the book so that you'll be familiar with them. Fortunately, many relational database concepts are really quite simple. Much of the appeal of relational databases stems precisely from the simplicity of their foundational concepts.

1.3.1 Structural Terminology

Within the database world, MySQL is classified as a relational database management system (RDBMS). That phrase breaks down as follows:

- The database (the "DB" in RDBMS) is the repository for the information you want to store, structured in a simple, regular fashion:
    - The collection of data in a database is organized into tables.
    - Each table is organized into rows and columns.
    - Each row in a table is a record.
    - Records can contain several pieces of information; each column in a table corresponds to one of those pieces.

- The management system (the "MS") is the software that lets you use your data by enabling you to insert, retrieve, modify, or delete records.
- The word "relational" (the "R") indicates a particular kind of DBMS, one that is very good at relating (that is, matching up) information stored in one table to information stored in another by looking for elements common to each of them. The power of a relational DBMS lies in its capability to pull data from those tables conveniently and to join information from related tables to produce answers to questions that can't be answered from individual tables alone. (Actually, "relational" has a formal definition that differs from the way I am using it. However, with apologies to purists, I find that my definition is more helpful for conveying the usefulness of an RDBMS.)

Here's an example that shows how a relational database organizes data into tables and relates the information from one table to another. Suppose that you run a Web site that includes a banner-advertisement service. You contract with companies that want their ads displayed when people visit the pages on your site. Each time a visitor hits one of your pages, you serve an ad embedded in the page that is sent to the visitor's browser and assess the company a small fee. This is an ad "hit." To represent this information, you maintain three tables (see Figure 1.1). One table, company, has columns for company name, number, address, and telephone number. Another table, ad, lists ad numbers, the number for the company that "owns" the ad, and the amount you charge per hit. The third table, hit, logs each ad hit by ad number and the date on which the ad was served.

Some questions can be answered using the information in a single table. To determine the number of companies you have contracts with, you need count only the rows in the company table. Similarly, to determine the number of hits during a given time period, only the hit table need be examined. Other questions are more complex, and it's necessary to consult multiple tables to determine the answers. For example, to determine how many times each of the ads for Pickles, Inc. was served on July 14, you'd use all three tables as follows:

1. Look up the company name (Pickles, Inc.) in the company table to find the company number (14).

2. Use the company number to find matching records in the ad table so that you can determine the associated ad numbers. There are two such ads, 48 and 101.

3. For each of the matched records in the ad table, use the ad number in the record to find matching records in the hit table that fall within the desired date range, and then count the number of matches. There are three matches for ad 48 and two matches for ad 101.

Sounds complicated! But that's just the kind of thing at which relational database systems excel. The complexity actually is somewhat illusory because each of the steps just described really amounts to little more than a simple matching operation: You relate one table to another by matching values from one table's rows to values in another table's rows. This same simple operation can be exploited in various ways to answer all kinds of questions: How many different ads does each company have? Which company's ads are most popular? How much revenue does each ad generate? What is the total fee for each company for the current billing period?

Now you know enough relational database theory to understand the rest of this book, and we don't have to go into Third Normal Form, Entity-Relationship Diagrams, and all that kind of stuff. (If you want to read about such things, I suggest you begin with the works of C.J. Date or E.F. Codd.)

1.3.2 Query Language Terminology

Communication with MySQL takes place via SQL (Structured Query Language). SQL is today's standard database language, and all major database systems understand it (although each implementation has vendor-specific aspects). SQL supports many different kinds of

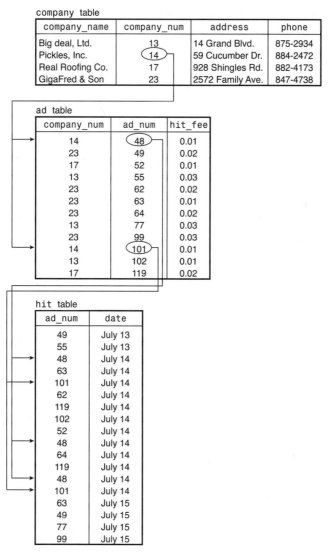

Figure 1.1   Banner advertisement tables.

statements, all designed to make it possible to interact with your database in interesting and useful ways.

As with any language, SQL can seem strange while you're first learning it. For example, to create a table, you need to tell MySQL what the table's structure should be. You and I might think of the table in terms of a diagram or picture. MySQL doesn't, so you create the table by telling MySQL something like this:

```
CREATE TABLE company
(
  company_name  CHAR(30),
  company_num   INT,
  address       CHAR(30),
  phone         CHAR(12)
);
```

Statements like that can be somewhat imposing when you're new to SQL, but you need not be a programmer to learn how to use SQL effectively. As you gain familiarity with the language, you'll look at CREATE TABLE in a different light—as a powerful ally that helps you describe your information, not as a weird bit of gibberish.

1.3.3 MySQL Architectural Terminology

When you use MySQL, you're actually using at least two programs, because MySQL operates using a client/server architecture. The first program is the MySQL server, mysqld. The server runs on the machine where your databases are stored. It listens for client requests coming in over the network and accesses database contents according to those requests to provide clients with the information they ask for. The other programs are client programs; they connect to the database server and issue queries to tell it what information they want.

Most MySQL distributions include the database server and several client programs. (If you use RPM packages on Linux, there are separate server and client RPM packages, so you should install both.) You use the clients according to the purposes you want to achieve. The one most commonly used is mysql, an interactive client that lets you issue queries and see the results. Two administrative clients are mysqldump, a backup program that dumps table contents into a file, and mysqladmin, which enables you to check on the status of the server and performs other administrative tasks such as telling the server to shut down. MySQL distributions include other clients as well. If you have application requirements for which none of the standard clients is suited, MySQL also provides a client-programming library so that you can write your own programs. The library is usable directly from C programs. If you prefer a language other than C, interfaces are available for several other languages—Perl, PHP, Python, Java, and Ruby, to name a few.

The client programs I discuss in this book all are used from the command line. If you'd like to try tools that use a graphical user interface (GUI) and provide point-and-click capabilities, visit http://www.mysql.com/products/tools/.

MySQL's client/server architecture has certain benefits:

- The server provides concurrency control so that two users cannot modify the same record at the same time. All client requests go through the server, so the server sorts out who gets to do what, and when. If multiple clients want to access the same table at the same time, they don't all have to find and negotiate with each other.

They just send their requests to the server and let it take care of determining the order in which the requests are performed.

- You don't have to be logged in on the machine where your database is located. MySQL understands how to work in a networked environment, so you can run a client program from wherever you happen to be, and the client can connect to the server over the network. Distance isn't a factor; you can access the server from anywhere in the world. If the server is located on a computer in Australia, you can take your laptop computer on a trip to Iceland and still access your database. Does that mean anyone can get at your data, just by connecting to the Internet? No. MySQL includes a flexible security system, so you can allow access only to people who should have it. And you can make sure that those people are able to do only what they should. Perhaps Sally in the billing office should be able to read and update (modify) records, but Phil at the service desk should be able only to look at them. You can set each person's privileges accordingly. If you do want to run a self-contained system, set the access privileges so that clients can connect only from the host on which the server is running.

In addition to the usual `mysqld` server that is used in a client/server setting, MySQL makes the server available as a library, `libmysqld`, that you can link into programs to produce standalone MySQL-based applications. This is called the "embedded server library" because it's embedded into individual applications. Use of the embedded server contrasts with the client/server approach in that no network is required. This makes it easier to create and package applications that can be distributed on their own with fewer assumptions about their external operational environment. On the other hand, it should be used only in situations where the embedded application is the only one that needs access to the databases managed by the server.

> ### The Difference Between "MySQL" and "`mysql`"
>
> To avoid confusion, I should point out that "MySQL" refers to the entire MySQL RDBMS and "`mysql`" is the name of a particular client program. They sound the same if you pronounce them, but they're distinguished here by capitalization and typeface differences.
>
> Speaking of pronunciation, MySQL is pronounced "my-ess-queue-ell." We know this because the MySQL Reference Manual says so. On the other hand, depending on who you ask, SQL is pronounced "ess-queue-ell" or "sequel." This book assumes the pronunciation "ess-queue-ell," which is why it uses constructs such as "an SQL query" rather than "a SQL query."

1.4 A MySQL Tutorial

You have all the background you need now. It's time to put MySQL to work!

This section will help you familiarize yourself with MySQL by providing a tutorial for you to try. As you work through it, you will create a sample database and some tables, and then interact with the database by adding, retrieving, deleting, and modifying information

in the tables. During the process of working with the sample database, you will learn the
following things:

- The basics of the SQL language that MySQL understands. (If you already know
  SQL from having used some other RDBMS, it is a good idea to skim through this
  tutorial to see whether MySQL's dialect of SQL differs from the version with
  which you are familiar.)
- How to communicate with a MySQL server using a few of the standard MySQL
  client programs. As noted in the previous section, MySQL operates using a
  client/server architecture in which the server runs on the machine containing the
  databases and clients connect to the server over a network. This tutorial is based
  largely on the `mysql` client program, which reads SQL queries from you, sends
  them to the server to be executed, and displays the results so that you can see what
  happened. `mysql` runs on all platforms supported by MySQL and provides the most
  direct means of interacting with the server, so it's the logical client to begin with.
  Some examples use `mysqlimport` or `mysqlshow` instead.

This book uses `sampdb` as the sample database name, but you might need to use a different name as you work through the material. For example, someone else on your system
already might be using the name `sampdb` for their own database, or your MySQL administrator might assign you a different database name. In either case, substitute the actual
name of your database for `sampdb` whenever you see the latter in examples.

Table names can be used exactly as shown in the examples, even if multiple users on
your system have their own sample databases. In MySQL, it doesn't matter if other people
use the same table names, as long as each of you uses your own database. MySQL prevents
you from interfering with each other by keeping the tables in each database separate.

1.4.1 Obtaining the Sample Database Distribution

This tutorial refers at certain points to files from the "sample database distribution" (also
known as the `sampdb` distribution, after the name of the `sampdb` database). These files
contain queries and data that will help you set up the sample database. See Appendix A,
"Obtaining and Installing Software," for instructions on getting the distribution. When
you unpack it, it creates a directory named `sampdb` containing the files you'll need.
I recommend that you change location into that directory whenever you're working
through examples pertaining to the sample database.

To make it easier to invoke MySQL programs no matter which directory is your current location, you should add the MySQL `bin` directory that contains those programs to
your command interpreter's search path. To do this, add the directory pathname to your
PATH environment variable setting using the instructions in Appendix A.

1.4.2 Preliminary Requirements

To try the examples in this tutorial, a few preliminary requirements must be satisfied:

- You must have the MySQL software installed.
- You need a MySQL account so that you can connect to the server.
- You need a database to work with.

The required software includes the MySQL clients and a MySQL server. The client programs must be located on the machine where you'll be working. The server can be located on your machine, although that is not required. As long as you have permission to connect to it, the server can be located anywhere. If you need to get MySQL, see Appendix A for instructions. If your network access comes through an Internet service provider (ISP), find out whether the provider offers MySQL as a service. If not and your ISP won't install it, choose a different provider that does offer MySQL.

In addition to the MySQL software, you'll need a MySQL account so that the server will allow you to connect and create your sample database and its tables. (If you already have a MySQL account with the server, you can use that, but you might want to set up a separate account for use with the material in this book.)

At this point, we run into something of a chicken-and-egg problem: In order to set up a MySQL account to use for connecting to the server, it's necessary to connect to the server. Typically, you do this by connecting as the MySQL root user on the host where the server is running and issuing CREATE USER and GRANT statements to create a new MySQL account and give it database privileges. If you've installed MySQL on your own machine and the server is running, you can connect to it as root and set up a new sample database administrator account with a username of sampadm and a password of secret as follows (change the name and password to those you want to use, here and throughout the book):

```
% mysql -p -u root
Enter password: ******
mysql> CREATE USER 'sampadm'@'localhost' IDENTIFIED BY 'secret';
Query OK, 0 rows affected (0.04 sec)
mysql> GRANT ALL ON sampdb.* TO 'sampadm'@'localhost';
Query OK, 0 rows affected (0.01 sec)
```

The mysql command includes a -p option to cause mysql to prompt for the root user's MySQL password. Enter the password where you see ****** in the example. I assume that you have already set up a password for the MySQL root user and that you know what it is. If you haven't yet assigned a password, just press Enter at the Enter password: prompt. However, having no root password is insecure and you should assign one as soon as possible. More information on the CREATE USER and GRANT statements, setting up MySQL user accounts, and changing passwords can be found in Chapter 12, "General MySQL Administration."

The statements just shown are appropriate if you'll be connecting to MySQL from the same machine where the server is running. They enable you to connect to the server using the name `sampadm` and the password `secret`, and give you complete access to the `sampdb` database. However, `GRANT` doesn't create the database (you can grant privileges for a database before it exists). We'll get to database creation a bit later.

If you plan to connect to the MySQL server from a host different from the one where the server is running, change `localhost` to the name of the machine where you'll be working. For example, if you will connect to the server from the host `asp.snake.net`, the statements should look like this:

```
mysql> CREATE USER 'sampadm'@'asp.snake.net' IDENTIFIED BY 'secret';
mysql> GRANT ALL ON sampdb.* TO 'sampadm'@'asp.snake.net';
```

If you don't have control over the server and cannot create an account, ask your MySQL administrator to set up an account for you. Then substitute the MySQL username, password, and database name that the administrator assigns you for `sampadm`, `secret`, and `sampdb` throughout the examples in this book.

1.4.3 Establishing and Terminating Connections to the MySQL Server

To connect to your server, invoke the `mysql` program from your command prompt (that is, from your Unix shell prompt, or from a console window prompt under Windows). The command looks like this:

```
% mysql options
```

I use `%` throughout this book to indicate the command prompt. That's one of the standard Unix prompts; another is `$`. Under Windows, you will see a prompt that looks something like `C:\>`. (When you enter commands shown in examples, do not type the prompt itself.)

The `options` part of the `mysql` command line might be empty, but more likely you'll have to issue a command that looks something like this:

```
% mysql -h host_name -p -u user_name
```

You might not need to supply all those options when you invoke `mysql`, but you'll probably have to specify at least a name and password. Here's what the options mean:

- `-h host_name` (alternative form: `--host=host_name`)

  The host where the MySQL server is running. If this is the same as the machine where you are running `mysql`, this option typically can be omitted.

- `-u user_name` (alternative form: `--user=user_name`)

  Your MySQL username. If you're using Unix and your MySQL username is the same as your login name, you can omit this option; `mysql` will use your login name as your MySQL username.

  Under Windows, the default username is ODBC, which is unlikely to be a useful default for you. Either specify a `-u` option on the command line, or add a default to your environment by setting the USER variable. For example, you can use the following set command to specify a username of sampadm:

```
C:\> set USER=sampadm
```

If you set the USER environment variable by using the System item in the Control Panel, it takes effect for each console window and you won't have to issue it at the prompt.

- -p (alternative form: --password)

  This option tells mysql to ask you for your MySQL password by displaying an Enter password: prompt. For example:

  ```
  % mysql -h host_name -p -u user_name
  Enter password:
  ```

  When you see the Enter password: prompt, type in your password. (The password won't be echoed to the screen, in case someone's looking over your shoulder.) Note that your MySQL password is not necessarily the same as the password that you use to log in to Unix or Windows.

  If you omit the -p option, mysql assumes that you don't need one and doesn't prompt for it.

  Another way to specify this option is to indicate the password value directly on the command line by typing the option as -pyour_pass (alternative form: --password=your_pass). However, for security reasons, it's best not to do that. The password becomes visible to others that way.

  If you do decide to specify the password on the command line, note particularly that there is *no space* between the -p option and the following password value. This behavior of -p is a common point of confusion, because it differs from the -h and -u options, which are associated with the word that follows them regardless of whether there is a space between the option and the word.

Suppose that your MySQL username and password are sampadm and secret. If the MySQL server is running on the same host where you are going to run mysql, you can leave out the -h option and the mysql command to connect to the server. It looks like this:

```
% mysql -p -u sampadm
Enter password: ******
```

After you enter the command, mysql prints Enter password: to prompt for your password, and you type it in (the ****** indicates where you type secret).

If all goes well, mysql prints a greeting and a mysql> prompt indicating that it is waiting for you to issue queries. The full startup sequence looks something like this:

```
% mysql -p -u sampadm
Enter password: ******
Welcome to the MySQL monitor.  Commands end with ; or \g.
```

```
Your MySQL connection id is 13762
Server version: 5.0.60-log

Type 'help;' or '\h' for help. Type '\c' to clear the buffer.

mysql>
```

To connect to a server running on some other machine, it's necessary to specify the host-name using an -h option. If that host is cobra.snake.net, the command looks like this:

```
% mysql -h cobra.snake.net -p -u sampadm
```

In most of the examples that follow that show a mysql command line, I'm going to leave out the -h, -u, and -p options for brevity and assume that you'll supply whatever options are necessary. You'll also need to use the same options when you run other MySQL programs, such as mysqlshow.

After you've established a connection to the server, you can terminate your session any time by typing quit:

```
mysql> quit
Bye
```

You can also quit by typing exit or \q. On Unix, Control-D also quits.

When you're just starting to learn MySQL, you'll probably consider its security system to be an annoyance because it makes it harder to do what you want. (You must have per-mission to create and access a database, and you must specify your name and password whenever you connect to the server.) However, after you've moved beyond the sample database used in this book to entering and using your own records, your perspective will change radically. Then you'll appreciate the way that MySQL keeps other people from snooping through (or worse, destroying!) your information.

There are ways to set up your working environment so that you don't have to specify connection parameters on the command line each time you run mysql. These are dis-cussed in Section 1.5, "Tips for Interacting with mysql." The most common method for simplifying the connection process is to store your connection parameters in an option file. You might want to check that section right now to see how to set up such a file.

1.4.4 Executing SQL Statements

After you're connected to the server, you're ready to issue SQL statements for the server to execute. This section describes some general principles about interacting with mysql that you should know.

To enter a statement in mysql, just type it in. At the end of the statement, type a semi-colon character (';') and press Enter. The semicolon tells mysql that the statement is complete. After you enter a statement, mysql sends it to the server to be executed. The server processes it and sends the result back to mysql, which displays the result to you.

The following example shows a simple statement that asks for the current date and time:

```
mysql> SELECT NOW();
```

```
+---------------------+
| NOW()               |
+---------------------+
| 2008-03-21 10:51:23 |
+---------------------+
1 row in set (0.00 sec)
```

Another way to terminate a statement is to use \g ("go") rather than a semicolon:

```
mysql> SELECT NOW()\g
+---------------------+
| NOW()               |
+---------------------+
| 2008-03-21 10:51:28 |
+---------------------+
1 row in set (0.00 sec)
```

Or you can use \G, which displays the results in "vertical" format, one value per line:

```
mysql> SELECT NOW(), USER(), VERSION()\G
*************************** 1. row ***************************
    NOW(): 2008-03-21 10:51:34
   USER(): sampadm@localhost
VERSION(): 5.0.60-log
1 row in set (0.03 sec)
```

For a statement that generates short output lines, \G is not so useful, but if the lines are so long that they wrap around on your screen, \G can make the output much easier to read.

mysql displays the statement result and a line that shows the number of rows the result consists of and the time elapsed during statement processing. In subsequent examples, I usually will not show the row-count line.

Because mysql waits for the statement terminator, you need not enter a statement all on a single line. You can spread it over several lines if you want:

```
mysql> SELECT NOW(),
    -> USER(),
    -> VERSION()
    -> ;
+---------------------+-------------------+------------+
| NOW()               | USER()            | VERSION()  |
+---------------------+-------------------+------------+
| 2008-03-21 10:51:37 | sampadm@localhost | 5.0.60-log |
+---------------------+-------------------+------------+
```

Observe how the prompt changes from mysql> to -> after you enter the first line of the statement. That tells you that mysql thinks you're still entering the statement, which is important feedback: If you forget the semicolon at the end of a statement, the changed prompt helps you realize that mysql is still waiting for something. Otherwise, you'll be

waiting impatiently, wondering why it's taking MySQL so long to execute your statement, and `mysql` will be waiting patiently for you to finish entering your statement!
(`mysql` has several other prompts as well; they're all discussed in Appendix F, "MySQL
Program Reference").

If you've begun entering a multiple-line statement and decide that you don't want to
execute it, type `\c` to clear (cancel) it:

```
mysql> SELECT NOW(),
    -> VERSION(),
    -> \c
mysql>
```

Notice how the prompt changes back to `mysql>` to indicate that `mysql` is ready for a
new statement.

The converse of entering a statement over several lines is to enter multiple statements
on a single line, separated by terminators:

```
mysql> SELECT NOW();SELECT USER();SELECT VERSION();
+---------------------+
| NOW()               |
+---------------------+
| 2008-03-21 10:52:31 |
+---------------------+
+-------------------+
| USER()            |
+-------------------+
| sampadm@localhost |
+-------------------+
+------------+
| VERSION()  |
+------------+
| 5.0.60-log |
+------------+
```

For the most part, it doesn't matter whether you enter statements using uppercase,
lowercase, or mixed case. These statements all retrieve the same information (although the
column headings displayed for the result will differ in lettercase):

```
SELECT USER();
select user();
SeLeCt UsEr();
```

The examples in this book use uppercase for SQL keywords and function names, and
lowercase for database, table, and column names.

When you invoke a function in a statement, it is best to have no space between the
function name and the following parenthesis. In some cases, a space can cause a syntax
error to occur.

You can store statements in a file to create an SQL script and tell `mysql` to read state-ments from the file rather than from the keyboard. Use your shell's input redirection facil-ities for this. For example, if I have statements stored in a file named `myscript.sql`, I can execute its contents with this command (remember to specify any required connection parameter options):

```
% mysql < myscript.sql
```

You can call the file whatever you want. I use the `.sql` suffix as a convention to indi-cate that the file contains SQL statements.

Invoking `mysql` this way to execute statements in a file is something that comes up again in Section 1.47, "Adding New Rows," when we enter data into the `sampdb` data-base. It's a lot more convenient to load a table by having `mysql` read `INSERT` statements from a file than to type in each statement manually.

The remainder of this tutorial shows many SQL statements that you can try for your-self. These are indicated by the `mysql>` prompt before the statement, and such examples are usually accompanied by the output of the statement. You should be able to type in these statements as shown, and the resulting output should be the same. Statements that are shown without a prompt are intended simply to illustrate a point, and you need not execute them. (You can try them if you like. If you use `mysql` to do so, remember to in-clude a terminator such as a semicolon at the end of each statement.)

1.4.5 Creating a Database

We'll begin by creating the `sampdb` sample database and the tables within it, populating its tables, and performing some simple queries on the data contained in those tables. Using a database involves several steps:

1. Creating (initializing) the database
2. Creating the tables within the database
3. Manipulating the tables by inserting, retrieving, modifying, or deleting data

Retrieving existing data is easily the most common operation performed on a database. The next most common operations are inserting new data and updating or deleting exist-ing data. Less frequent are table creation operations, and least frequent of all is database cre-ation. However, we're beginning from scratch, so we must begin with database creation, the least common thing, and work our way through table creation and insertion of our initial data before we get to where we can do the really common thing—retrieving data.

To create a new database, connect to the server using `mysql`. Then issue a `CREATE DATABASE` statement that specifies the database name:

```
mysql> CREATE DATABASE sampdb;
```

You'll need to create the `sampdb` database before you can create any of the tables that will go in it or do anything with the contents of those tables.

You might expect that creating the database would also make it the default (or current) database, but it doesn't. You can see this by executing the following statement to check what the default database is:

```
mysql> SELECT DATABASE();
+------------+
| DATABASE() |
+------------+
| NULL       |
+------------+
```

NULL means "no database is selected." To select sampdb as the default database, issue a USE statement:

```
mysql> USE sampdb;
mysql> SELECT DATABASE();
+------------+
| DATABASE() |
+------------+
| sampdb     |
+------------+
```

Another way to select a default database is to name it on the command line when you invoke mysql:

```
% mysql sampdb
```

That is, in fact, the usual way to select the database you want to use. If you need any connection parameters, specify them on the command line. For example, the following command enables the sampadm user to connect to the sampdb database on the local host (the default when no host is named):

```
% mysql -p -u sampadm sampdb
```

If you need to connect to a MySQL server running on a remote host, specify that host on the command line:

```
% mysql -h cobra.snake.net -p -u sampadm sampdb
```

Unless otherwise indicated, all following examples assume that when you invoke mysql, you name the sampdb database on the command line to make it the default database. If you invoke mysql but forget to name the database on the command line, just issue a USE sampdb statement at the mysql> prompt.

1.4.6 Creating Tables

In this section, we'll build the tables that are needed for the sampdb sample database. First, we'll consider the tables needed for the Historical League, and then those for the grade-keeping project. This is the part where some database books start talking about Analysis and Design, Entity-Relationship Diagrams, Normalization Procedures, and other such stuff. There's a place for all that, but I prefer just to say we need to think a bit about what our database will look like: what tables it should contain, what the contents of each table should be, and some of the issues involved in deciding how to represent the data.

The choices made here about data representation are not absolute. In other situations, you might well elect to represent similar data in a different way, depending on the requirements of your applications and the uses to which you intend to put your data.

1.4.6.1 Tables for the U.S. Historical League

Table layout for the Historical League is pretty straightforward:

- A `president` table. This contains a descriptive record for each U.S. president. We'll need this for the online quiz on the League Web site (the interactive analog to the printed quiz that appears in the children's section of the League's newsletter).
- A `member` table. This is used to maintain current information about each member of the League. It'll be used for creating printed and online versions of the member directory, sending automated membership renewal reminders, and so forth.

1.4.6.1.1 The `president` Table

The `president` table is simpler, so let's discuss it first. This table will contain some basic biographical information about each United States president:

- Name. Names can be represented in a table several ways. For example, we could have a single column containing the entire name, or separate columns for the first and last name. It's certainly simpler to use a single column, but that limits you in some ways:
    - If you enter the names with the first name first, you can't sort on last name.
    - If you enter the names with the last name first, you can't display them with the first name first.
    - It's harder to search for names. For example, to search for a particular last name, you must use a pattern and look for names that match the pattern. This is less efficient and slower than looking for an exact last name.

    To avoid these limitations, our `president` table will use separate columns for the first and last names.

    The first name column will also hold the middle name or initial. This shouldn't break any sorting we might do because it's not likely we'll want to sort on middle name (or even first name). Name display should work properly, too, because the middle name immediately follows the first name regardless of whether a name is printed in "Bush, George W." or in "George W. Bush" format.

    There is another slight complication. One president (Jimmy Carter) has a "Jr." at the end of his name. Where does that go? Depending on the format in which names are printed, this president's name is displayed as "James E.

Carter, Jr.," or "Carter, James E., Jr." The "Jr." doesn't associate with either first or last name, so we'll create another column to hold a name suffix. This illustrates how even a single value can cause problems when you're trying to determine how to represent your data. It also shows why it's a good idea to know as much as possible about the data values you'll be working with before you put them in a database. If you have incomplete knowledge of what your values look like, you might have to change your table structure after you've already begun to use it. That's not necessarily a disaster, but in general it's something you want to avoid.

- Birthplace (city and state). Like the name, this too can be represented using a single column or multiple columns. It's simpler to use a single column, but as with the name, separate columns enable you to do some things you can't do easily otherwise. For example, it's easier to find rows for presidents born in a particular state if city and state are listed separately. We'll use separate columns for the two values.

- Birth date and death date. The only special problem here is that we can't require the death date to be filled in because some presidents are still living. The special value NULL means "no value," so we can use that in the death date column to signify "still alive."

1.4.6.1.2 The `member` Table

The `member` table for the Historical League membership list is similar to the `president` table in the sense that each row contains basic descriptive information for a single person. But each `member` row contains more columns:

- Name. We'll use the same three-column representation as for the `president` table: last name, first name, and suffix.

- ID number. This is a unique value assigned to each member when membership first begins. The League hasn't ever used ID numbers before, but now that the records are being made more systematic, it's a good time to start. (I am anticipating that you'll find MySQL beneficial and that you'll think of other ways to apply it to the League's records. When that happens, it'll be easier to associate rows in the `member` table with other member-related tables that you create if you use numbers rather than names.)

- Expiration date. Members must renew their memberships periodically to avoid having them lapse. For some applications, you might store the start date of the most recent renewal, but this is not suitable for the League's purposes. Memberships can be renewed for a variable number of years (typically one, two, three, or five years), and a date for the most recent renewal wouldn't tell you when the next renewal must take place. Therefore, we will store the end date of the membership. In addition, the League allows lifetime memberships. We could represent these with a date far in the future, but NULL seems more appropriate because "no value" logically corresponds to "never expires."

- Email address. Publishing email addresses will make it easier for those members that have them to communicate with each other more easily. For your purposes as League secretary, these addresses will enable you to send out membership renewal notices electronically rather than by postal mail. This should be easier than going to the post office, and less expensive as well. You'll also be able to use email to send members the current contents of their directory entries and ask them to update the information as necessary.

- Postal address. This is needed for contacting members who don't have email (or who don't respond to it). We'll use columns for street address, city, state, and ZIP code.

  I'm assuming that all League members live in the United States. For organizations with a membership that is international in scope, that assumption is an oversimplification. If you want to deal with addresses from multiple countries, you'll run into some sticky issues having to do with the different address formats used for different countries. For example, ZIP code is not an international standard, and some countries have provinces rather than states.

- Phone number. Like the address columns, this is useful for contacting members.

- Special interest keywords. Every member is assumed to have a general interest in U.S. history, but members probably also have some special areas of interest. This column records those interests. Members can use it to find other members with similar interests. (Strictly speaking, it would be better to have a separate table for keywords that has rows consisting of one keyword and the ID for the associated member. But that is a complication I do not want to deal with here.)

1.4.6.1.3 Creating the Historical League Tables

Now we're ready to create the Historical League tables. For this we use the CREATE TABLE statement, which has the following general form:

```
CREATE TABLE tbl_name (column_specs);
```

tbl_name indicates the name you want to give the table. *column_specs* provides the specifications for the columns in the table. It also includes definitions for indexes, if there are any. Indexes make lookups faster; we'll discuss them further in Chapter 5, "Query Optimization."

For the president table, write the CREATE TABLE statement as follows:

```
CREATE TABLE president
(
    last_name   VARCHAR(15) NOT NULL,
    first_name  VARCHAR(15) NOT NULL,
    suffix      VARCHAR(5) NULL,
    city        VARCHAR(20) NOT NULL,
    state       VARCHAR(2) NOT NULL,
    birth       DATE NOT NULL,
    death       DATE NULL
);
```

You can execute this statement a couple of ways. Either enter it manually by typing it in, or use the prewritten statement that is contained in the `create_president.sql` file of the `sampdb` distribution.

If you want to type in the statement yourself, invoke `mysql`, making `sampdb` the default database:

```
% mysql sampdb
```

Then enter the CREATE TABLE statement as just shown, including the trailing semi-colon so that `mysql` can tell where the statement ends. Indentation doesn't matter, and you need not put the line breaks in the same places. For example, you can enter the statement as one long line if you want.

To create the `president` table using a prewritten description, use the `create_president.sql` file from the `sampdb` distribution. This file is located in the `sampdb` directory that is created when you unpack the distribution. Change location into that directory, and then run the following command:

```
% mysql sampdb < create_president.sql
```

Whichever way you invoke `mysql`, specify any connection parameters you might need (hostname, username, or password) on the command line after the command name.

Now let's look more closely at the CREATE TABLE statement. Each column specification in the statement consists of the column name, the data type (the kind of values the column will hold), and possibly some column attributes.

The two data types used in the `president` table are VARCHAR and DATE. VARCHAR(*n*) means the column contains variable-length character values, with a maximum length of *n* characters each. That is, they contain strings that might vary in size, but with an upper bound on their length. You choose the value of *n* according to how long you expect your values to be. `state` is defined as VARCHAR(2); that's all we need for entering states by their two-character abbreviations. The other string-valued columns need to be wider to accommodate longer values.

The other data type we've used is DATE. This type indicates, not surprisingly, that the column holds date values. However, what might surprise you is the format in which dates are represented. MySQL expects dates to be written in '*CCYY-MM-DD*' format, where *CC, YY, MM,* and *DD* represent the century, year within the century, month, and day of the month. This is the SQL standard for date representation (also known as "ISO 8601 format"). For example, to specify a date of "July 18, 2005" in MySQL, you use '2005-07-18', not '07-18-2005' or '18-07-2005'.

The only attributes we're using for the columns in the `president` table are NULL (values can be missing) and NOT NULL (values must be filled in). Most columns are NOT NULL, because we'll always require a value for them. The two columns that can have NULL values are `suffix` (most names don't have one), and `death` (for living presidents, there is no date of death).

For the `member` table, the CREATE TABLE statement looks like this:

```
CREATE TABLE member
(
  member_id   INT UNSIGNED NOT NULL AUTO_INCREMENT,
  PRIMARY KEY (member_id),
  last_name   VARCHAR(20) NOT NULL,
  first_name  VARCHAR(20) NOT NULL,
  suffix      VARCHAR(5) NULL,
  expiration  DATE NULL,
  email       VARCHAR(100) NULL,
  street      VARCHAR(50) NULL,
  city        VARCHAR(50) NULL,
  state       VARCHAR(2) NULL,
  zip         VARCHAR(10) NULL,
  phone       VARCHAR(20) NULL,
  interests   VARCHAR(255) NULL
);
```

As before, you can either type that statement manually into `mysql` or you can use a prewritten file. The file from the `sampdb` distribution that contains the CREATE TABLE statement for the `member` table is `create_member.sql`. To use it, execute this command:

```
% mysql sampdb < create_member.sql
```

In terms of data types, most columns of the `member` table except two are not very interesting because they are created as variable-length strings. The exceptions are `member_id` and `expiration`, which exist to hold sequence numbers and dates, respectively.

The main consideration for the `member_id` membership number column is that each of its values should be unique to avoid confusion between members. An AUTO_INCREMENT column is useful here because then we can let MySQL generate unique numbers for us automatically when we add new members. Even though it just contains numbers, the definition for `member_id` has several parts:

- INT signifies that the column holds integers (numeric values with no fractional part).

- UNSIGNED disallows negative values.

- NOT NULL requires that the column value must be filled in. This prevents members from being created without an ID number.

- AUTO_INCREMENT is a special attribute in MySQL. It indicates that the column holds sequence numbers. The AUTO_INCREMENT mechanism works like this: If you provide no value for the `member_id` column when you create a new `member` table row, MySQL automatically generates the next sequence number and assigns it to the column. This special behavior also occurs if you explicitly assign the value NULL to the column. The AUTO_INCREMENT feature makes it easy to assign a unique ID to each new member, because MySQL generates the values for us.

The PRIMARY KEY clause indicates that the `member_id` column is indexed to allow fast lookups. It also sets up the constraint that each value in the column must be unique. The latter property is desirable for member ID values, because it prevents us from using the same ID twice by mistake. Besides, MySQL requires every AUTO_INCREMENT column to have some kind of index, so the table definition would be illegal without one. (Any PRIMARY KEY column must also be NOT NULL, so if we omitted NOT NULL from the member_id definition, MySQL would add it automatically.)

If you don't understand that stuff about AUTO_INCREMENT and PRIMARY KEY, just think of them as giving us a magic way of generating indexed ID numbers. It doesn't particularly matter what the values are, as long as they're unique for each member. (When you're ready to learn more about how to use AUTO_INCREMENT columns, Chapter 3, "Data Types," covers them in detail.)

The expiration column is a DATE. It allows NULL values, so it has a default value of NULL as well. NULL which means no date has been entered. The reason for this is that, as mentioned earlier, we're using the convention that expiration can be NULL to indicate which members have a lifetime membership.

Now that you've told MySQL to create a couple of tables, check to make sure that it did so as you expect. In mysql, issue the following statement to see the structure of the president table:

```
mysql> DESCRIBE president;
+------------+-------------+------+-----+---------+-------+
| Field      | Type        | Null | Key | Default | Extra |
+------------+-------------+------+-----+---------+-------+
| last_name  | varchar(15) | NO   |     |         |       |
| first_name | varchar(15) | NO   |     |         |       |
| suffix     | varchar(5)  | YES  |     | NULL    |       |
| city       | varchar(20) | NO   |     |         |       |
| state      | varchar(2)  | NO   |     |         |       |
| birth      | date        | NO   |     |         |       |
| death      | date        | YES  |     | NULL    |       |
+------------+-------------+------+-----+---------+-------+
```

If you issue a DESCRIBE member statement, mysql will show you similar information for the member table.

DESCRIBE is useful when you forget the name of a column in a table, or need to know its data type or how wide it is, and so forth. It's also useful for finding out the order in which MySQL stores columns in table rows. That order is important when you issue INSERT or LOAD DATA statements that expect column values to be listed in the default column order.

The information produced by DESCRIBE can be obtained in different ways. It may be abbreviated as DESC, or written as an EXPLAIN or SHOW statement. The following statements all are synonymous:

```
DESCRIBE president;
DESC president;
EXPLAIN president;
SHOW COLUMNS FROM president;
SHOW FIELDS FROM president;
```

These statements also enable you to restrict the output to particular columns. For example, you can add a LIKE clause at the end of a SHOW statement to display information only for column names that match a given pattern:

```
mysql> SHOW COLUMNS FROM president LIKE '%name';
+------------+-------------+------+-----+---------+-------+
| Field      | Type        | Null | Key | Default | Extra |
+------------+-------------+------+-----+---------+-------+
| last_name  | varchar(15) | NO   |     |         |       |
| first_name | varchar(15) | NO   |     |         |       |
+------------+-------------+------+-----+---------+-------+
```

DESCRIBE president '%name' is equivalent. The '%' character used here is a special wildcard character that is described later in Section 1.4.9.7, "Pattern Matching."

SHOW FULL COLUMNS is like SHOW COLUMNS but displays additional column information. Try it now and see.

The SHOW statement has other forms that are useful for obtaining different types of information from MySQL. SHOW TABLES lists the tables in the default database, so with the two tables we've created so far in the sampdb database, the output looks like this:

```
mysql> SHOW TABLES;
+-------------------+
| Tables_in_sampdb  |
+-------------------+
| member            |
| president         |
+-------------------+
```

SHOW DATABASES lists the databases that are managed by the server to which you're connected:

```
mysql> SHOW DATABASES;
+--------------------+
| Database           |
+--------------------+
| information_schema |
| menagerie          |
| mysql              |
| sampdb             |
| test               |
+--------------------+
```

The list of databases varies from server to server, but you should see at least information_schema and sampdb. information_schema is a special database that always exists, and you created sampdb yourself. You'll likely also see a database named test, which is created during the MySQL installation procedure. Depending on your access rights, you might see the database named mysql, which holds the grant tables that control who can do what.

The `mysqlshow` client program provides a command-line interface to the same kinds of information that the `SHOW` statement displays. Remember that when you run `mysqlshow`, you might need to provide appropriate command-line options for username, password, and hostname. These options are the same as when you run `mysql`.

With no arguments, `mysqlshow` displays a list of databases:

```
% mysqlshow
+--------------------+
|     Databases      |
+--------------------+
| information_schema |
| menagerie          |
| mysql              |
| sampdb             |
| test               |
+--------------------+
```

With a database name, `mysqlshow` displays the tables in the given database:

```
% mysqlshow sampdb
Database: sampdb
+-----------+
|  Tables   |
+-----------+
| member    |
| president |
+-----------+
```

With a database and table name, `mysqlshow` displays information about the columns in the table, much like the `SHOW FULL COLUMNS` statement.

1.4.6.2 Tables for the Grade-Keeping Project

To determine what tables are required for the grade-keeping project, let's consider how you might write down scores when you use a paper-based gradebook. Figure 1.2 shows a page from your gradebook. The main body of this page is a matrix for recording scores. There is also other information needed for making sense of the scores. Student names and ID numbers are listed down the side of the matrix. (For simplicity, only four students are shown.) Along the top of the matrix, you put down the dates when you give quizzes and tests. The figure shows that you've given quizzes on September 3, 6, 16, and 23, and tests on September 9 and October 1.

To keep track of this kind of information using a database, we need a `score` table. What should rows in this table contain? That's easy. For each row, we need the student name, the date of the quiz or test, and the score. Figure 1.3 shows how some of the scores from the gradebook look when represented in a table like this. (Dates are written the way MySQL represents them, in `'CCYY-MM-DD'` format.)

students		scores						
		Q	Q	T	Q	Q	T	
ID	name	9/3	9/6	9/9	9/16	9/23	10/1	...
1	Billy	14	10	73	14	15	67	...
2	Missy	17	10	68	17	14	73	...
3	Johnny	15	10	78	12	17	82	...
4	Jenny	14	13	85	13	19	79	...
...	...	...	...	...	...	...	...	...

Figure 1.2   Example gradebook.

score table

name	date	score
Billy	2008-09-23	15
Missy	2008-09-23	14
Johnny	2008-09-23	17
Jenny	2008-09-23	19
Billy	2008-10-01	67
Missy	2008-10-01	73
Johnny	2008-10-01	82
Jenny	2008-10-01	79

Figure 1.3   Initial score table layout.

Unfortunately, there is a problem with setting up the table in this way, because it leaves out some information. For example, looking at the rows in Figure 1.3, we can't tell whether scores are for a quiz or a test. It could be important to know score categories when determining final grades if quizzes and tests are weighted differently. We might try to infer the category from the range of scores on a given date (quizzes usually are worth fewer points than a test), but that's problematic because it relies on inference and not something explicit in the data.

It's possible to distinguish scores by recording the category in each row by adding a column to the score table that contains 'T' or 'Q' for each row to indicate "test" or "quiz," as in Figure 1.4. This has the advantage of making the score category explicit in the data. The disadvantage is redundancy. Observe that for all rows with a given date, the score category column always has the same value. The scores for September 23 all have a category of 'Q', and those for October 1 all have a category of 'T'. This is unappealing. If we record a set of scores for a quiz or test this way, not only will we be putting in the same date for each new record in the set, we'll be putting in the same score category over and over again. Ugh. Who wants to enter all that redundant information?

Let's try an alternative representation. Instead of recording score categories in the score table, we'll figure them out from the dates. We can keep a list of dates and use it to keep track of what kind of "grade event" (quiz or test) occurred on each date. Then we can determine whether any given score was from a quiz or a test by combining it with the information in our event list: Match the date in the score table row with the date in the grade_event table to get the event category. Figure 1.5 shows this table layout and demonstrates how the association works for a score table row with a date of

score table

name	date	score	category
Billy	2008-09-23	15	Q
Missy	2008-09-23	14	Q
Johnny	2008-09-23	17	Q
Jenny	2008-09-23	19	Q
Billy	2008-10-01	67	T
Missy	2008-10-01	73	T
Johnny	2008-10-01	82	T
Jenny	2008-10-01	79	T

Figure 1.4   `score` table layout, revised to include score type.

September 23. By matching the row with the corresponding row in the `grade_event` table, we see that the score is from a quiz.

score table

name	date	score
Billy	2008-09-23	15
Missy	2008-09-23	14
Johnny	2008-09-23	17
Jenny	2008-09-23	19
Billy	2008-10-01	67
Missy	2008-10-01	73
Johnny	2008-10-01	82
Jenny	2008-10-01	79

grade_event table

date	category
2008-09-03	Q
2008-09-06	Q
2008-09-09	T
2008-09-16	Q
2008-09-23	Q
2008-10-01	T

Figure 1.5   `score` and `grade_event` tables, linked on date.

This is much better than trying to infer the score category based on some guess. Instead, we're deriving the category directly from data recorded explicitly in the database. It's also preferable to recording score categories in the `score` table; now we need record each category only one time, rather than once per score row.

However, now we're combining information from multiple tables. If you're like me, when you first hear about this kind of thing, you think, "Yeah, that's a cute idea, but isn't it a lot of work to do all that looking up all the time; doesn't it just make things more complicated?"

In a way, that's correct; it is more work. Keeping two lists of records is more complicated than keeping one list. But take another look at your gradebook (see Figure 1.2). Aren't you already keeping two sets of records? Consider these facts:

- You keep track of scores using the cells in the score matrix, where each cell is indexed by student name and date (down the side and along the top of the matrix). This represents one set of records; it's analogous to the contents of the `score` table.

- How do you know what kind of event each date represents? You've written a little 'T' or 'Q' above the date! Thus, you're also keeping track of the association between date and score category along the top of the matrix. This represents a second set of records; it's analogous to the grade_event table contents.

In other words, even though you may not think about it as such, you're really not doing anything with the gradebook different from what I'm proposing to do by keeping information in two tables. The only real difference is that the two kinds of information aren't so explicitly separated in the paper-based gradebook.

The page in the gradebook illustrates something about the way we think of information, and also something about the difficulty of figuring out how to put information in a database: Our minds tend to integrate different kinds of information and interpret them as a whole. Databases don't work like that, which is one reason they sometimes seem artificial and unnatural. Our natural tendency to unify information makes it quite difficult sometimes even to realize when we have multiple types of data instead of just one. Because of this, it can be a challenge to "think as a database system thinks" about how best to represent your data.

One requirement imposed on the grade_event table by the layout shown in Figure 1.5 is that the dates must be unique because each date is used to link together rows from the score and grade_event tables. In other words, you cannot give two quizzes on the same day, or a quiz and a test. If you do, you'll have two sets of records in the score table and two records in the grade_event table, all with the same date, and you won't be able to tell how to match score rows with grade_event rows.

That problem will never come up if there is never more than one grade event per day. But is it valid to assume that will never happen? It might seem so; after all, you don't consider yourself sadistic enough to give a quiz and a test on the same day. But I hope you'll pardon me if I'm skeptical. I've often heard people claim about their data, "That odd case will never occur." Then it turns out the odd case does occur on occasion, and usually you have to redesign your tables to fix problems that the odd case causes.

It's better to think about the possible problems in advance and anticipate how to handle them. So, let's suppose that you might need to record two sets of scores for the same day sometimes. How can we handle that? As it turns out, this problem isn't so difficult to solve. With a minor change to the way we lay out our data, multiple events on a given date won't cause trouble:

1. Add a column to the grade_event table and use it to assign a unique number to each row in the table. In effect, this gives each event its own ID number, so we'll call this the event_id column. (If this seems like an odd thing to do, consider that your gradebook in Figure 1.2 already has this property implicitly: The event ID is just like the column number in your gradebook score matrix. The number might not be written down explicitly there and labeled "event ID," but that's what it is.)

2. When you put scores in the score table, record the event ID rather than the date.

The result of these changes is shown in Figure 1.6. Now you link together the score and grade_event tables using the event ID rather than the date, and you use the `grade_event` table to determine not just the category of each score, but also the date on which it occurred. Also, it's no longer the date that must be unique in the `grade_event` table, it's the event ID. This means you can have a dozen tests and quizzes on the same day, and you'll be able to keep them straight in your records. (No doubt your students will be thrilled to hear this.)

score table

name	event_id	score
Billy	5	15
Missy	5	14
Johnny	5	17
Jenny	5	19
Billy	6	67
Missy	6	73
Johnny	6	82
Jenny	6	79

grade_event table

event_id	date	category
1	2008-09-03	Q
2	2008-09-06	Q
3	2008-09-09	T
4	2008-09-16	Q
5	2008-09-23	Q
6	2008-10-01	T

Figure 1.6　`score` and `grade_event` tables, linked on event ID.

Unfortunately, from a human standpoint, the table layout in Figure 1.6 seems less satisfactory than the previous ones. The `score` table is more abstract because it contains fewer columns that have a readily apparent meaning. The table layout shown earlier in Figure 1.4 was easy to look at and understand because the `score` table had columns for both dates and score categories. The current `score` table shown in Figure 1.6 has columns for neither. This seems highly removed from anything we can think about easily. Who wants to look at a `score` table that has "event IDs" in it? That just doesn't mean much to us.

At this point you reach a crossroads. You're intrigued by the possibility of being able to perform grade-keeping electronically and not having to do all kinds of tedious manual calculations when assigning grades. But after considering how you actually would represent score information in a database, you're put off by how abstract and disconnected the representation seems to make that information.

This leads naturally to a question: "Would it be better not to use a database at all? Maybe MySQL isn't for me." As you might guess, I will answer that question in the negative, because otherwise this book will come to a quick end. But when you're thinking about how to do a job, it's not a bad idea to consider various alternatives and to ask whether you're better off using a database system such as MySQL, or something else such as a spreadsheet program:

- The gradebook has rows and columns, and so does a spreadsheet. This makes the gradebook and a spreadsheet conceptually and visually very similar.
- A spreadsheet program can perform calculations, so you could total up each student's scores using a calculation field. It might be a little tricky to weight quizzes and tests differently, but you could do it.

On the other hand, if you want to look at just part of your data (quizzes only or tests only, for example), perform comparisons such as boys versus girls, or display summary information in a flexible way, it's a different story. A spreadsheet doesn't work so well, whereas relational database systems perform those operations easily.

Another point to consider is that the abstract and disconnected nature of your data as represented in a relational database is not really a big deal, anyway. It's necessary to think about that representation when setting up the database so that you don't lay out your data in a way that doesn't make sense for what you want to do with it. However, after you determine the representation, you're going to rely on the database engine to pull together and present your data in a way that is meaningful to you. You're not going to look at it as a bunch of disconnected pieces.

For example, when you retrieve scores from the `score` table, you don't want to see event IDs; you want to see dates. That's not a problem. The database can look up dates from the `grade_event` table based on the event ID and show them to you. You may also want to see whether the scores are for tests or quizzes. That's not a problem, either. The database can look up score categories the same way—using event ID. Remember, that's what a database system like MySQL is good at: relating one thing to another to pull out information from multiple sources to present you with what you really want to see. In the case of our grade-keeping data, MySQL does the thinking about pulling information together using event IDs so that you don't have to.

Now, just to provide a little advance preview of how you'd tell MySQL to do this relating of one thing to another, suppose that you want to see the scores for September 23, 2008. The query to pull out scores for an event given on a particular date looks like this:

```
SELECT score.name, grade_event.date, score.score, grade_event.category
FROM score INNER JOIN grade_event
ON score.event_id = grade_event.event_id
WHERE grade_event.date = '2008-09-23';
```

Pretty scary, huh? This query retrieves the student name, the date, score, and the score category by joining (relating) `score` table rows to `grade_event` table rows. The result looks like this:

```
+--------+------------+-------+----------+
| name   | date       | score | category |
+--------+------------+-------+----------+
| Billy  | 2008-09-23 |    15 | Q        |
| Missy  | 2008-09-23 |    14 | Q        |
| Johnny | 2008-09-23 |    17 | Q        |
| Jenny  | 2008-09-23 |    19 | Q        |
+--------+------------+-------+----------+
```

Notice anything familiar about the format of that information? You should; it's the same as the table layout shown in Figure 1.4! And you don't need to know the event ID to get this result. You specify the date you're interested in and let MySQL figure out which score rows go with that date. So, if you've been wondering whether all the abstraction and disconnectedness loses us anything when it comes to getting information out of the database in a form that's meaningful to us, it doesn't.

Of course, after looking at that query, you might be wondering something else, too. Namely, it looks long and complicated; isn't writing something like that a lot of work to go to just to find the scores for a given date? Yes, it is. However, there are ways to avoid typing several lines of SQL each time you want to issue a query. Generally, you figure out once how to perform a query such as that one and then you store it so that you can repeat it easily as necessary. We'll see how to do this in Section 1.5, "Tips for Interacting with mysql."

I've actually jumped the gun a little bit in showing you that query. It is, believe it or not, a little simpler than the one we're ultimately going to use to pull out scores. The reason for this is that we need to make one more change to our table layout. Instead of recording student name in the score table, we'll use a unique student ID. (That is, we'll use the value from the "ID" column of your gradebook rather than from the "Name" column.) Then we create another table called student that contains name and student_id columns (Figure 1.7).

student table

name	sex	student_id
Billy	M	1
Missy	F	2
Johnny	M	3
Jenny	F	4

score table

student_id	event_id	score
1	5	15
2	5	14
3	5	17
4	5	19
1	6	67
2	6	73
3	6	82
4	6	79

grade_event table

event_id	date	category
1	2008-09-03	Q
2	2008-09-06	Q
3	2008-09-09	T
4	2008-09-16	Q
5	2008-09-23	Q
6	2008-10-01	T

Figure 1.7   score, student, and grade_event tables, linked on student ID and event ID.

Why make this modification? For one thing, there might be two students with the same name. Using a unique student ID number helps you tell their scores apart. (This is exactly analogous to the way you can tell scores apart for a test and quiz given on the same day by using a unique event ID rather than the date.) After making this change to the table layout, the query we'll use to retrieve scores for a given date becomes a little more complex:

```
SELECT student.name, grade_event.date, score.score, grade_event.category
FROM grade_event INNER JOIN score INNER JOIN student
ON grade_event.event_id = score.event_id
AND score.student_id = student.student_id
WHERE grade_event.date = '2008-09-23';
```

If you're concerned because you don't find the meaning of that query immediately obvious, don't be. Most people wouldn't. We'll see the query again after we get further along into this tutorial, but the difference between now and later is that later it will make perfect sense to you. No, I'm not kidding.

You'll note from Figure 1.7 that I added something to the student table that wasn't in your gradebook: It contains a column for recording sex. This will allow for simple things such as counting the number of boys and girls in the class or more complex things like comparing scores for boys and girls.

We're almost done designing the tables for the grade-keeping project. We need just one more table to record absences for attendance purposes. Its contents are relatively straightforward: a student ID number and a date (see Figure 1.8). Each row in the table indicates that the given student was absent on the given date. At the end of the grading period, we'll call on MySQL's counting abilities to summarize the table's contents to tell us how many days each student was absent.

absence table

student_id	date
2	2008-09-02
4	2008-09-15
2	2008-09-20

Figure 1.8   absence table.

1.4.6.2.1 The student Table

Now that we know what our grade-keeping tables should look like, we're ready to create them. The CREATE TABLE statement for the student table looks like this:

```
CREATE TABLE student
(
  name       VARCHAR(20) NOT NULL,
  sex        ENUM('F','M') NOT NULL,
  student_id INT UNSIGNED NOT NULL AUTO_INCREMENT,
  PRIMARY KEY (student_id)
) ENGINE = InnoDB;
```

Observe that I've added something new to the CREATE TABLE statement (the ENGINE clause at the end). I'll explain its purpose shortly.

Type the CREATE TABLE statement into mysql or execute the following command:

```
% mysql sampdb < create_student.sql
```

The CREATE TABLE statement creates a table named student with three columns: name, sex, and student_id.

name is a variable-length string column that can hold up to 20 characters. This name representation is simpler than the one used for the Historical League tables; it uses a single column rather than separate first name and last name columns. That's because I know in advance that no grade-keeping query examples will need to do anything that would work better with separate columns. (Yes, that's cheating. I admit it. In practice, you would use multiple columns.)

sex indicates whether a student is a boy or a girl. It's an ENUM (enumeration) column, which means it can take only one of the values listed in the column specification: 'F' for female or 'M' for male. ENUM is useful when you have a restricted set of values that a column can hold. We could have used CHAR(1) instead, but ENUM makes it more explicit what the column values can be. If you forget what the possible values are, issue a DESCRIBE statement. For an ENUM column, MySQL displays the list of legal enumeration values:

```
mysql> DESCRIBE student 'sex';
+-------+---------------+------+-----+---------+-------+
| Field | Type          | Null | Key | Default | Extra |
+-------+---------------+------+-----+---------+-------+
| sex   | enum('F','M') | NO   |     |         |       |
+-------+---------------+------+-----+---------+-------+
```

Values in an ENUM column need not be just a single character. The sex column could have been defined as something like ENUM('female','male') instead.

student_id is an integer column that will contain unique student ID numbers. Normally, you'd probably get ID numbers for your students from a central source, such as the school office. We'll just make them up, using an AUTO_INCREMENT column that is defined in much the same way as the member_id column that is part of the member table created earlier.

If you really were going to get student ID numbers from the office rather than generating them automatically, you would define the student_id column without the AUTO_INCREMENT attribute, but leave in the PRIMARY KEY clause, to disallow duplicate or NULL ID values.

Now, what about the ENGINE clause at the end of the CREATE TABLE statement? This clause, if present, names the storage engine that MySQL should use for creating the table. A "storage engine" is a handler that manages a certain kind of table. MySQL has several storage engines, each with its own properties, as discussed in Section 2.6.1, "Storage Engine Characteristics."

If you omit the ENGINE clause, MySQL picks a default engine, which usually is MyISAM. "ISAM" stands for "indexed sequential access method," and the MyISAM engine is based on that access method with some MySQL-specific stuff added. Earlier, we provided no ENGINE clause when creating the Historical League tables (president and member), so they'll be MyISAM tables (unless you have reconfigured your server to use a different default engine). For the grade-keeping project, we're explicitly using the InnoDB storage engine instead. InnoDB offers something called "referential integrity" through the use of foreign keys. That means we can use MySQL to enforce certain constraints on the interrelationships *between* tables, something that is important for the grade-keeping project tables:

- Score rows are tied to grade events and to students: We don't want to allow entry of rows into the score table unless the student ID and grade event ID are known in the student and grade_event tables.

- Similarly, absence rows are tied to students: We don't want to allow entry of rows into the absence table unless the student ID is known in the student table.

To enforce these constraints, we'll set up foreign key relationships. "Foreign" means "in another table," and "foreign key" indicates a key value that must match a key value in that other table. These concepts will become clearer as we create the rest of the grade-keeping project tables.

1.4.6.2.2 The grade_event Table

The grade_event table has this definition:

```
CREATE TABLE grade_event
(
  date     DATE NOT NULL,
  category ENUM('T','Q') NOT NULL,
  event_id INT UNSIGNED NOT NULL AUTO_INCREMENT,
  PRIMARY KEY (event_id)
) ENGINE = InnoDB;
```

To create the grade_event table, type that CREATE TABLE statement into mysql or execute the following command:

```
% mysql sampdb < create_grade_event.sql
```

The date column holds a standard MySQL DATE value, in 'CCYY-MM-DD' (year-first) format.

category represents score category. Like sex in the student table, category is an enumeration column. The allowable values are 'T' and 'Q', representing "test" and "quiz."

event_id is an AUTO_INCREMENT column that is defined as a PRIMARY KEY, similar to student_id in the student table. Using AUTO_INCREMENT enables us to generate unique event ID values easily. As with the student_id column in the student table, the particular values are less important than that they be unique.

All the columns are defined as NOT NULL because none of them can be missing.

1.4.6.2.3 The score Table

The score table looks like this:

```
CREATE TABLE score
(
  student_id INT UNSIGNED NOT NULL,
  event_id   INT UNSIGNED NOT NULL,
  score      INT NOT NULL,
  PRIMARY KEY (event_id, student_id),
  INDEX (student_id),
  FOREIGN KEY (event_id) REFERENCES grade_event (event_id),
  FOREIGN KEY (student_id) REFERENCES student (student_id)
) ENGINE = InnoDB;
```

Here again the table definition contains something new: the FOREIGN KEY construct. We'll get to this in just a bit.

Create the table by typing the statement into mysql or by executing the following command:

```
% mysql sampdb < create_score.sql
```

The score column is an INT to hold integer score values. If you wanted to allow scores such as 58.5 that have a fractional part, you'd use one of the data types that can represent them, such as DECIMAL or FLOAT.

The student_id and event_id columns are integer columns that indicate the student and event to which each score applies. By using them to link to the corresponding ID value columns in the student and grade_event tables, we'll be able to look up the student name and event date. There are a couple important points to note about the student_id and event_id columns:

- We've made the combination of the two columns a PRIMARY KEY. This ensures that we won't have duplicate scores for a student for a given quiz or test. Note that it's the combination of event_id and student_id that is unique. In the score table, neither value is unique by itself. There will be multiple score rows for each event_id value (one per student), and multiple rows for each student_id value (one for each quiz and test) taken by the student.

- For each ID column, a FOREIGN KEY clause defines a constraint. The REFERENCES part of the clause indicates which table and column the score column refers to. The constraint on event_id is that each value in the column must match some event_id value in the grade_event table. Similarly, each student_id value in the score table must match some student_id value in the student table.

The PRIMARY KEY definition ensures that we won't create duplicate score rows. The FOREIGN KEY definitions ensure that we won't have rows with bogus ID values that don't exist in the grade_event or student tables.

Why is there an index on student_id? The reason is that, for any columns in a FOREIGN KEY definition, there should be an index on them, or they should be the columns that are listed first in a multiple-column index. For the FOREIGN KEY on event_id, that column is listed first in the PRIMARY KEY. For the FOREIGN KEY on student_id, the PRIMARY KEY cannot be used because student_id is not listed first. So, instead, we create a separate index on student_id.

InnoDB actually will create an index on columns in a foreign key definition, but it might not use the same index definition you would (as discussed further in Section 2.14.1, "Creating and Using Foreign Keys"). Defining the index explicitly avoids this issue.

1.4.6.2.4 The absence Table

The absence table for recording lapses in attendance looks like this:

```
CREATE TABLE absence
(
```

```
student_id INT UNSIGNED NOT NULL,
date        DATE NOT NULL,
PRIMARY KEY (student_id, date),
FOREIGN KEY (student_id) REFERENCES student (student_id)
) ENGINE = InnoDB;
```

Type that statement into `mysql` or execute the following command:

```
% mysql sampdb < create_absence.sql
```

The `student_id` and `date` columns both are defined as `NOT NULL` to disallow missing values. We make the combination of the two columns a primary key so that we don't accidentally create duplicate rows. It wouldn't be fair to count a student absent twice on the same day, would it?

The `absence` table also includes a foreign key relationship, defined to ensure that each `student_id` value matches a `student_id` value in the `student` table.

The inclusion of foreign key relationships in the grade-keeping tables is meant to enact constraints at data entry time: We want to insert only those rows that contain legal grade event and student ID values. However, the foreign key relationships have another effect as well. They set up dependencies that constrain the order in which you create and drop tables:

- The `score` table refers to the `grade_event` and `student` tables, so they must be created first before you can create the `score` table. Similarly, `absence` refers to `student`, so `student` must exist before you can create `absence`.

- If you drop (remove) tables, the reverse is true. You cannot drop the `grade_event` table if you have not dropped the `score` table first, and `student` cannot be dropped unless you have first dropped `score` and `absence`.

> **Note**
>
> If for some reason your MySQL server does not include InnoDB support, you can create the grade-keeping project tables as MyISAM tables instead. Substitute `MyISAM` for `InnoDB` in each `CREATE TABLE` statement or just omit the `ENGINE` clause. However, if you use MyISAM tables, the examples later in this book that use these tables to show the operation of foreign keys will not work.

1.4.7 Adding New Rows

At this point, our database and its tables have been created. Now we need to put some rows into the tables. However, it's useful to know how to check what's in a table after you put something into it, so although retrieval is not covered in any detail until later in Section 1.4.9, "Retrieving Information," you should know at least that the following statement will show you the complete contents of any table *tbl_name:*

```
SELECT * FROM tbl_name;
```

Example:

```
mysql> SELECT * FROM student;
Empty set (0.00 sec)
```

Right now, `mysql` indicates that the table is empty, but you'll see a different result after trying the examples in this section.

There are several ways to add data to a database. You can insert rows into a table manually by issuing `INSERT` statements. You can also add rows by reading them from a file, either in the form of prewritten `INSERT` statements that you feed to `mysql`, or as raw data values that you load using the `LOAD DATA` statement or the `mysqlimport` client program.

This section demonstrates each method of inserting rows into your tables. What you should do is play with all of them to familiarize yourself with them and to see how they work. After you've tried each of the methods, go to Section 1.4.8, "Resetting the `sampdb` Database to a Known State," and run the commands you find there. Those commands drop the tables, re-create them, and load them with a known set of data. By executing them, you'll make sure that the tables contain the same rows that I worked with while writing the sections that follow, and you'll get the same results shown in those sections. (If you already know how to insert rows and just want to populate the tables, you might want to skip directly to that section.)

1.4.7.1 Adding Rows with INSERT

Let's start adding rows by using `INSERT`, an SQL statement for which you specify the table into which you want to insert a row of data and the values to put in the row. The `INSERT` statement has several forms.

You can specify values for all the columns. The syntax looks like this:

```
INSERT INTO tbl_name VALUES(value1,value2,...);
```

Example:

```
mysql> INSERT INTO student VALUES('Kyle','M',NULL);
mysql> INSERT INTO grade_event VALUES('2008-09-03','Q',NULL);
```

With this syntax, the `VALUES` list must contain a value for each column in the table, in the order that the columns are stored in the table. (Normally, this is the order in which the columns are specified in the table's `CREATE TABLE` statement.) If you're not sure what the column order is, issue a `DESCRIBE tbl_name` statement to find out.

You can quote string and date values in MySQL using either single or double quotes, but single quotes are more standard. The `NULL` values are for the `AUTO_INCREMENT` columns in the `student` and `grade_event` tables. Inserting a "missing value" into an `AUTO_INCREMENT` column causes MySQL to generate the next sequence number for the column.

MySQL enables you to insert several rows into a table with a single `INSERT` statement by specifying multiple value lists:

```
INSERT INTO tbl_name VALUES(...),(...),... ;
```

Example:

```
mysql> INSERT INTO student VALUES('Avery','F',NULL),('Nathan','M',NULL);
```

This involves less typing than multiple INSERT statements, and also is more efficient for the server to execute. Note that parentheses enclose the set of column values for *each* row. The following statement is illegal because it does not contain the correct number of values within parentheses:

```
mysql> INSERT INTO student VALUES('Avery','F',NULL,'Nathan','M',NULL);
ERROR 1136 (21S01): Column count doesn't match value count at row 1
```

You can name the columns to which you want to assign values, and then list the values. This is useful when you want to create a record for which only a few columns need to be set up initially.

```
INSERT INTO tbl_name (col_name1,col_name2,...) VALUES(value1,value2,...);
```

Example:

```
mysql> INSERT INTO member (last_name,first_name) VALUES('Stein','Waldo');
```

This form of INSERT allows multiple value lists, too:

```
mysql> INSERT INTO student (name,sex) VALUES('Abby','F'),('Joseph','M');
```

For any column not named in the column list, MySQL assigns its default value. For example, the preceding statements contain no values for the member_id or student_id columns, so MySQL assigns the default value of NULL. member_id and student_id are AUTO_INCREMENT columns, so the net effect in each case is to generate and assign the next sequence number, just as if you had assigned NULL explicitly.

You can provide a list of column/value assignments. This syntax uses a SET clause containing col_name=value assignments rather than a VALUES() list:

```
INSERT INTO tbl_name SET col_name1=value1, col_name2=value2, ... ;
```

Example:

```
mysql> INSERT INTO member SET last_name='Stein',first_name='Waldo';
```

For any column not named in the SET clause, MySQL assigns its default value. This form of INSERT cannot be used to insert multiple rows with a single statement.

Now that you know how INSERT works, you can use it to see whether the foreign key relationships we set up really prevent entry of bad rows in the score and absence tables. Try inserting rows that contain ID values that are not present in the grade_event or student tables:

```
mysql> INSERT INTO score (event_id,student_id,score) VALUES(9999,9999,0);
ERROR 1452 (23000): Cannot add or update a child row: a foreign key
constraint fails (`sampdb`.`score`, CONSTRAINT `score_ibfk_1` FOREIGN
KEY (`event_id`) REFERENCES `grade_event` (`event_id`))
mysql> INSERT INTO absence SET student_id=9999, date='2008-09-16';
ERROR 1452 (23000): Cannot add or update a child row: a foreign key
```

```
constraint fails (`sampdb`.`absence`, CONSTRAINT `absence_ibfk_1`
FOREIGN KEY (`student_id`) REFERENCES `student` (`student_id`))
```

The error messages show that the constraints are working.

1.4.7.2 Adding New Rows from a File

Another method for loading rows into a table is to read them directly from a file. The file can contain INSERT statements or it can contain raw data. For example, the sampdb distribution contains a file named insert_president.sql that contains INSERT statements for adding new rows to the president table. Assuming that you are in the same directory where that file is located, you can execute those statements like this:

```
% mysql sampdb < insert_president.sql
```

If you're already running mysql, you can use a source command to read the file:

```
mysql> source insert_president.sql;
```

If you have the rows stored in a file as raw data values rather than as INSERT statements, you can load them with the LOAD DATA statement or with the mysqlimport client program.

The LOAD DATA statement acts as a bulk loader that reads data from a file. Use it from within mysql:

```
mysql> LOAD DATA LOCAL INFILE 'member.txt' INTO TABLE member;
```

Assuming that the member.txt data file is located in your current directory on the client host, this statement reads it and sends its contents to the server to be loaded into the member table. (The member.txt file can be found in the sampdb distribution.)

By default, the LOAD DATA statement assumes that column values are separated by tabs and that lines end with newlines (also known as "linefeeds"). It also assumes that the values are present in the order that columns are stored in the table. It's possible to read files in other formats or to specify a different column order. See the entry for LOAD DATA in Appendix E, "SQL Syntax Reference," for details.

The keyword LOCAL in the LOAD DATA statement causes the data file to be read by the client program (in this case mysql) and sent to the server to be loaded. It is possible to omit LOCAL, but then the file must be located on the server host and you need the FILE server access privilege, which most MySQL users don't have. You should also specify the full pathname to the file so that the server can find it.

If you get the following error with LOAD DATA LOCAL, the LOCAL capability might be disabled by default:

```
ERROR 1148 (42000): The used command is not allowed with this MySQL version
```

Try again after invoking mysql with the --local-infile option. For example:

```
% mysql --local-infile sampdb
mysql> LOAD DATA LOCAL INFILE 'member.txt' INTO TABLE member;
```

If that doesn't work, either, the server also needs to be told to allow LOCAL. See Chapter 12 for information on how to do this.

Another way to load a data file is to use the `mysqlimport` client program. You invoke `mysqlimport` from the command prompt, and it generates a LOAD DATA statement for you:

```
% mysqlimport --local sampdb member.txt
```

As with the `mysql` program, if you need to specify connection parameters, indicate them on the command line preceding the database name.

For the command just shown, `mysqlimport` generates a LOAD DATA statement to load `member.txt` into the `member` table. That's because `mysqlimport` determines the table name from the name of the data file, using everything up to the first period of the filename as the table name. For example, `mysqlimport` would load files named `member.txt` and `president.txt` into the `member` and `president` tables. This means you should choose your filenames carefully or `mysqlimport` won't use the correct table name. If you wanted to load files named `member1.txt` and `member2.txt`, `mysqlimport` would think it should load them into tables named `member1` and `member2`. If what you really want is to load both files into the `member` table, you could use names like `member.1.txt` and `member.2.txt`, or `member.txt1` and `member.txt2`.

1.4.8 Resetting the `sampdb` Database to a Known State

After you have tried the row-adding methods just described in the preceding discussion, you should re-create and load the `sampdb` database tables to reset the database so that its contents are the same as what the next sections assume. Using the `mysql` program in the directory containing the `sampdb` distribution files, issue these statements:

```
% mysql sampdb
mysql> source create_member.sql;
mysql> source create_president.sql;
mysql> source insert_member.sql;
mysql> source insert_president.sql;
mysql> DROP TABLE IF EXISTS absence, score, grade_event, student;
mysql> source create_student.sql;
mysql> source create_grade_event.sql;
mysql> source create_score.sql;
mysql> source create_absence.sql;
mysql> source insert_student.sql;
mysql> source insert_grade_event.sql;
mysql> source insert_score.sql;
mysql> source insert_absence.sql;
```

If you don't want to type those statements individually (which is likely), try this command on Unix:

```
% sh init_all_tables.sh sampdb
```

On Windows, use this command instead:

```
C:\> init_all_tables.bat sampdb
```

Whichever command you use, if you need to specify connection parameters, list them on the command line after the command name.

1.4.9 Retrieving Information

Our tables have been created and loaded with data now, so let's see what we can do with that data. To retrieve and display information from your tables, use the SELECT statement. It enables you to retrieve information in as general or specific a manner as you like. You can display the entire contents of a table:

```
SELECT * FROM president;
```

Or you can select as little as a single column of a single row:

```
SELECT birth FROM president WHERE last_name = 'Eisenhower';
```

The SELECT statement has several clauses that you combine as necessary to retrieve the information in which you're interested. Each of these clauses can be simple or complex, so SELECT statements as a whole can be simple or complex. However, rest assured that you won't find any page-long queries that take an hour to figure out in this book. (When I see arm-length queries in something that I'm reading, I generally skip right over them, and I'm guessing that you do the same.)

A simplified syntax of the SELECT statement is:

```
SELECT what to retrieve
FROM table or tables
WHERE conditions that data must satisfy;
```

To write a SELECT statement, specify what you want to retrieve and then some optional clauses. The clauses just shown (FROM and WHERE) are the most common ones, although others can be specified as well, such as GROUP BY, ORDER BY, and LIMIT. Remember that SQL is a free-format language, so when you write your own SELECT statements, you need not put line breaks in the same places I do.

The FROM clause is usually present, but it need not be if you don't need to name any tables. For example, the following query simply displays the values of some expressions. These can be calculated without referring to the contents of any table, so no FROM clause is necessary:

```
mysql> SELECT 2+2, 'Hello, world', VERSION();
+-----+--------------+-----------+
| 2+2 | Hello, world | VERSION() |
+-----+--------------+-----------+
|   4 | Hello, world | 5.0.60-log |
+-----+--------------+-----------+
```

When you do use a FROM clause to specify a table from which to retrieve data, you'll also indicate which columns you want to see. The most "generic" form of SELECT uses * as a column specifier, which is shorthand for "all columns." The following query retrieves all columns from the student table and displays them:

```
mysql> SELECT * FROM student;
+-----------+-----+------------+
| name      | sex | student_id |
+-----------+-----+------------+
| Megan     | F   |          1 |
| Joseph    | M   |          2 |
| Kyle      | M   |          3 |
| Katie     | F   |          4 |
...
```

The columns are displayed in the order that MySQL stores them in the table. This is the same order in which the columns are listed when you issue a DESCRIBE student statement. (The "..." shown at the end of the example indicates that the query returns more rows than are shown.)

You can explicitly name the column or columns you want to see. To select just student names, do this:

```
mysql> SELECT name FROM student;
+-----------+
| name      |
+-----------+
| Megan     |
| Joseph    |
| Kyle      |
| Katie     |
...
```

If you name more than one column, separate them by commas. The following statement is equivalent to SELECT * FROM student, but names each column explicitly:

```
mysql> SELECT name, sex, student_id FROM student;
+-----------+-----+------------+
| name      | sex | student_id |
+-----------+-----+------------+
| Megan     | F   |          1 |
| Joseph    | M   |          2 |
| Kyle      | M   |          3 |
| Katie     | F   |          4 |
...
```

You can name columns in any order:

```
SELECT name, student_id FROM student;
SELECT student_id, name FROM student;
```

You can even name a column more than once if you like, although generally that's kind of pointless.

It's also possible to select columns from more than one table at a time. This is called a "join" between tables. We'll get to joins in Section 1.4.9.10, "Retrieving Information from Multiple Tables."

Column names are not case sensitive in MySQL, so the following queries all retrieve the same information:

```
SELECT name, student_id FROM student;
SELECT NAME, STUDENT_ID FROM student;
SELECT nAmE, sTuDeNt_Id FROM student;
```

On the other hand, database and table names might be case sensitive. It depends on the filesystem used on the server host and on how MySQL is configured. Windows filenames are not case sensitive, so a server running on Windows does not treat database and table names as case sensitive. On Unix systems, filenames generally are case sensitive, so a server would treat database and table names as case sensitive. An exception to this occurs under Mac OS X, which offers both HFS+ and UFS filesystems: HFS+ is the default, and it uses case-insensitive filenames.

If you want to have MySQL treat database and table names as not case sensitive, you can configure the server that way. See Section 11.2.5, "How SQL Statements Map onto Table File Operations."

1.4.9.1 Specifying Retrieval Criteria

To restrict the set of rows retrieved by the SELECT statement, use a WHERE clause that specifies criteria for selecting rows. You can select rows by looking for column values that satisfy various criteria, and you can look for different types of values. For example, you can search for certain numeric values:

```
mysql> SELECT * FROM score WHERE score > 95;
+------------+----------+-------+
| student_id | event_id | score |
+------------+----------+-------+
|          5 |        3 |    97 |
|         18 |        3 |    96 |
|          1 |        6 |   100 |
|          5 |        6 |    97 |
|         11 |        6 |    98 |
|         16 |        6 |    98 |
+------------+----------+-------+
```

You can look for string values containing character data. For the default character set and collation (sort order), string comparisons are not case sensitive:

```
mysql> SELECT last_name, first_name FROM president
    -> WHERE last_name='ROOSEVELT';
+-----------+-------------+
| last_name | first_name  |
+-----------+-------------+
| Roosevelt | Theodore    |
| Roosevelt | Franklin D. |
+-----------+-------------+
```

```
mysql> SELECT last_name, first_name FROM president
    -> WHERE last_name='roosevelt';
+-----------+-------------+
| last_name | first_name  |
+-----------+-------------+
| Roosevelt | Theodore    |
| Roosevelt | Franklin D. |
+-----------+-------------+
```

You can look for dates:

```
mysql> SELECT last_name, first_name, birth FROM president
    -> WHERE birth < '1750-1-1';
+------------+------------+------------+
| last_name  | first_name | birth      |
+------------+------------+------------+
| Washington | George     | 1732-02-22 |
| Adams      | John       | 1735-10-30 |
| Jefferson  | Thomas     | 1743-04-13 |
+------------+------------+------------+
```

It's also possible to search for combinations of values:

```
mysql> SELECT last_name, first_name, birth, state FROM president
    -> WHERE birth < '1750-1-1' AND (state='VA' OR state='MA');
+------------+------------+------------+-------+
| last_name  | first_name | birth      | state |
+------------+------------+------------+-------+
| Washington | George     | 1732-02-22 | VA    |
| Adams      | John       | 1735-10-30 | MA    |
| Jefferson  | Thomas     | 1743-04-13 | VA    |
+------------+------------+------------+-------+
```

Expressions in WHERE clauses can use arithmetic operators (Table 1.1), comparison operators (Table 1.2), and logical operators (Table 1.3). You can also use parentheses to group parts of an expression. Operations can be performed using constants, table columns, and function calls. We will have occasion to use several of MySQL's functions in statements throughout this tutorial, but there are far too many to show here. See Appendix C, "Operator and Function Reference," for a complete list.

Table 1.1   **Arithmetic Operators**

Operator	Meaning
+	Addition
–	Subtraction

Table 1.1   **Arithmetic Operators**

Operator	Meaning
*	Multiplication
/	Division
DIV	Integer division
%	Modulo (remainder after division)

Table 1.2   **Comparison Operators**

Operator	Meaning
<	Less than
<=	Less than or equal to
=	Equal to
<=>	Equal to (works even for NULL values)
<> or !=	Not equal to
>=	Greater than or equal to
>	Greater than

Table 1.3   **Logical Operators**

Operator	Meaning
AND	Logical AND
OR	Logical OR
XOR	Logical exclusive-OR
NOT	Logical negation

When you're formulating a statement that requires logical operators, take care not to confuse the meaning of the logical AND operator with the way we use "and" in everyday speech. Suppose that you want to find "presidents born in Virginia and presidents born in Massachusetts." That condition is phrased using "and," which seems to imply that you'd write the statement as follows:

```
mysql> SELECT last_name, first_name, state FROM president
    -> WHERE state='VA' AND state='MA';
Empty set (0.36 sec)
```

It's clear from the empty result that the statement didn't work. Why not? Because what the statement really means is "Select presidents who were born both in Virginia and in Massachusetts," which makes no sense. In English, you might express the statement using "and," but in SQL, you connect the two conditions with OR:

```
mysql> SELECT last_name, first_name, state FROM president
    -> WHERE state='VA' OR state='MA';
+------------+-------------+-------+
| last_name  | first_name  | state |
+------------+-------------+-------+
| Washington | George      | VA    |
| Adams      | John        | MA    |
| Jefferson  | Thomas      | VA    |
| Madison    | James       | VA    |
| Monroe     | James       | VA    |
| Adams      | John Quincy | MA    |
| Harrison   | William H.  | VA    |
| Tyler      | John        | VA    |
| Taylor     | Zachary     | VA    |
| Wilson     | Woodrow     | VA    |
| Kennedy    | John F.     | MA    |
| Bush       | George H.W. | MA    |
+------------+-------------+-------+
```

This disjunction between natural language and SQL is something to be aware of, not just when formulating your own queries, but also when you write queries for other people. It's best to listen carefully as they describe what they want to retrieve, but you don't necessarily want to transcribe their descriptions into SQL using the same logical operators. For the example just described, the proper English equivalent for the query is "Select presidents who were born either in Virginia or in Massachusetts."

You might find it easier to use the IN() operator when formulating queries like this, where you're looking for any of several values. The preceding query can be rewritten using IN() like this:

```
SELECT last_name, first_name, state FROM president
WHERE state IN('VA','MA');
```

IN() is especially convenient when you're comparing a column to a large number of values.

1.4.9.2 The NULL Value

The NULL value is special. It means "no value" or "unknown value," so you can't compare it to known values the way you can compare two known values to each other. If you attempt to use NULL with the usual arithmetic comparison operators, the result is undefined:

```
mysql> SELECT NULL < 0, NULL = 0, NULL <> 0, NULL > 0;
```

```
+----------+----------+----------+----------+
| NULL < 0 | NULL = 0 | NULL <> 0 | NULL > 0 |
+----------+----------+----------+----------+
|     NULL |     NULL |      NULL |     NULL |
+----------+----------+----------+----------+
```

In fact, you can't even compare NULL to itself because the result of comparing two un-known values cannot be determined:

```
mysql> SELECT NULL = NULL, NULL <> NULL;
+-------------+--------------+
| NULL = NULL | NULL <> NULL |
+-------------+--------------+
|        NULL |         NULL |
+-------------+--------------+
```

To perform searches for NULL values, you must use a special syntax. Instead of using =, <>, or != to test for equality or inequality, use IS NULL or IS NOT NULL. For example, presidents who are still living have their death dates represented as NULL in the president table. To find them, use the following query:

```
mysql> SELECT last_name, first_name FROM president WHERE death IS NULL;
+-----------+-------------+
| last_name | first_name  |
+-----------+-------------+
| Carter    | James E.    |
| Bush      | George H.W. |
| Clinton   | William J.  |
| Bush      | George W.   |
+-----------+-------------+
```

To find non-NULL values, use IS NOT NULL. This query finds names that have a suffix part:

```
mysql> SELECT last_name, first_name, suffix
    -> FROM president WHERE suffix IS NOT NULL;
+-----------+------------+--------+
| last_name | first_name | suffix |
+-----------+------------+--------+
| Carter    | James E.   | Jr.    |
+-----------+------------+--------+
```

The MySQL-specific <=> comparison operator is true even for NULL-to-NULL compar-isons. The preceding two queries can be rewritten to use this operator as follows:

```
SELECT last_name, first_name FROM president WHERE death <=> NULL;
```

```
SELECT last_name, first_name, suffix
FROM president WHERE NOT (suffix <=> NULL);
```

1.4.9.3 Sorting Query Results

Every MySQL user notices sooner or later that if you create a table, load some rows into it, and then issue a SELECT * FROM *tbl_name* statement, the rows tend to be retrieved in the same order in which they were inserted. That makes a certain intuitive sense, so it's natural to assume that rows are retrieved in insertion order by default. But that is not the case. If you delete and insert rows after loading the table initially, those actions likely will change the order in which the server returns the table's rows. (Deleting rows puts "holes" in the table, which MySQL tries to fill later when you insert new rows.)

What you should remember about row retrieval order is this: There is *no guarantee* about the order in which the server returns rows, unless you specify that order yourself. To do so, add an ORDER BY clause to the statement that defines the sort order you want. The following query returns president names, sorted lexically (alphabetically) by last name:

```
mysql> SELECT last_name, first_name FROM president
    -> ORDER BY last_name;
+------------+---------------+
| last_name  | first_name    |
+------------+---------------+
| Adams      | John          |
| Adams      | John Quincy   |
| Arthur     | Chester A.    |
| Buchanan   | James         |
...
```

Ascending order is the default sort order in an ORDER BY clause. You can specify explicitly whether to sort a column in ascending or descending order by using the ASC or DESC keywords after column names in the ORDER BY clause. For example, to sort president names in reverse (descending) name order, use DESC like this:

```
mysql> SELECT last_name, first_name FROM president
    -> ORDER BY last_name DESC;
+------------+---------------+
| last_name  | first_name    |
+------------+---------------+
| Wilson     | Woodrow       |
| Washington | George        |
| Van Buren  | Martin        |
| Tyler      | John          |
...
```

You can sort using multiple columns, and each column can be sorted independently in ascending or descending order. The following query retrieves rows from the president table, sorts them by reverse state of birth, and by ascending last name within each state:

```
mysql> SELECT last_name, first_name, state FROM president
    -> ORDER BY state DESC, last_name ASC;
```

```
+------------+---------------+-------+
| last_name  | first_name    | state |
+------------+---------------+-------+
| Arthur     | Chester A.    | VT    |
| Coolidge   | Calvin        | VT    |
| Harrison   | William H.    | VA    |
| Jefferson  | Thomas        | VA    |
| Madison    | James         | VA    |
| Monroe     | James         | VA    |
| Taylor     | Zachary       | VA    |
| Tyler      | John          | VA    |
| Washington | George        | VA    |
| Wilson     | Woodrow       | VA    |
| Eisenhower | Dwight D.     | TX    |
| Johnson    | Lyndon B.     | TX    |
...
```

NULL values in a column sort at the beginning for ascending sorts and at the end for descending sorts. If you want to ensure that NULL values will appear at a given end of the sort order, add an extra sort column that distinguishes NULL from non-NULL values. For example, if you sort presidents by reverse death date, living presidents (those with NULL death dates) will appear at the end of the sort order. To put them at the beginning instead, use this query:

```
mysql> SELECT last_name, first_name, death FROM president
    -> ORDER BY IF(death IS NULL,0,1), death DESC;
+------------+---------------+------------+
| last_name  | first_name    | death      |
+------------+---------------+------------+
| Clinton    | William J.    | NULL       |
| Bush       | George H.W.   | NULL       |
| Carter     | James E.      | NULL       |
| Bush       | George W.     | NULL       |
| Ford       | Gerald R.     | 2006-12-26 |
| Reagan     | Ronald W.     | 2004-06-05 |
| Nixon      | Richard M.    | 1994-04-22 |
| Johnson    | Lyndon B.     | 1973-01-22 |
...
| Jefferson  | Thomas        | 1826-07-04 |
| Adams      | John          | 1826-07-04 |
| Washington | George        | 1799-12-14 |
+------------+---------------+------------+
```

The IF() function evaluates the expression given by its first argument and returns the value of its second or third argument, depending on whether the expression is true or false. For the query shown, IF() evaluates to 0 for NULL values and 1 for non-NULL values. This places all NULL values ahead of all non-NULL values.

1.4.9.4 Limiting Query Results

When a query returns many rows, but you want to see only a few of them, add a LIMIT clause. LIMIT is especially useful in conjunction with ORDER BY. MySQL enables you to limit the output of a query to the first *n* rows of the result that otherwise would be returned. The following query selects the five presidents who were born first:

```
mysql> SELECT last_name, first_name, birth FROM president
    -> ORDER BY birth LIMIT 5;
+------------+------------+------------+
| last_name  | first_name | birth      |
+------------+------------+------------+
| Washington | George     | 1732-02-22 |
| Adams      | John       | 1735-10-30 |
| Jefferson  | Thomas     | 1743-04-13 |
| Madison    | James      | 1751-03-16 |
| Monroe     | James      | 1758-04-28 |
+------------+------------+------------+
```

If you sort in reverse order, using ORDER BY birth DESC, you get the five most recently born presidents instead:

```
mysql> SELECT last_name, first_name, birth FROM president
    -> ORDER BY birth DESC LIMIT 5;
+------------+------------+------------+
| last_name  | first_name | birth      |
+------------+------------+------------+
| Clinton    | William J. | 1946-08-19 |
| Bush       | George W.  | 1946-07-06 |
| Carter     | James E.   | 1924-10-01 |
| Bush       | George H.W.| 1924-06-12 |
| Kennedy    | John F.    | 1917-05-29 |
+------------+------------+------------+
```

LIMIT also enables you to pull a section of rows out of the middle of a result set. To do this, you must specify two values. The first value is the number of rows to skip at the beginning of the result set, and the second is the number of rows to return. The following query is similar to the previous one but returns 5 rows after skipping the first 10:

```
mysql> SELECT last_name, first_name, birth FROM president
    -> ORDER BY birth DESC LIMIT 10, 5;
+------------+------------+------------+
| last_name  | first_name | birth      |
+------------+------------+------------+
| Truman     | Harry S    | 1884-05-08 |
| Roosevelt  | Franklin D.| 1882-01-30 |
| Hoover     | Herbert C. | 1874-08-10 |
| Coolidge   | Calvin     | 1872-07-04 |
| Harding    | Warren G.  | 1865-11-02 |
+------------+------------+------------+
```

To pull a randomly selected row or set of rows from a table, use ORDER BY RAND() in conjunction with LIMIT:

```
mysql> SELECT last_name, first_name FROM president
    -> ORDER BY RAND() LIMIT 1;
+-----------+------------+
| last_name | first_name |
+-----------+------------+
| Johnson   | Lyndon B.  |
+-----------+------------+
mysql> SELECT last_name, first_name FROM president
    -> ORDER BY RAND() LIMIT 3;
+-----------+-------------+
| last_name | first_name  |
+-----------+-------------+
| Harding   | Warren G.   |
| Bush      | George H.W. |
| Jefferson | Thomas      |
+-----------+-------------+
```

1.4.9.5 Calculating and Naming Output Column Values

Most of the queries shown so far produce output by retrieving values from tables. MySQL also enables you to calculate output values from the results of expressions, without reference to tables. Expressions can be simple or complex. The following query evaluates a simple expression (a constant) and a more complex expression involving several arithmetic operations and a couple of function calls that produce the square root of an expression and format the result to three decimal places:

```
mysql> SELECT 17, FORMAT(SQRT(25+13),3);
+----+-----------------------+
| 17 | FORMAT(SQRT(25+13),3) |
+----+-----------------------+
| 17 | 6.164                 |
+----+-----------------------+
```

Expressions can also refer to table columns:

```
mysql> SELECT CONCAT(first_name,' ',last_name),CONCAT(city,', ',state)
    -> FROM president;
+----------------------------------+-------------------------+
| CONCAT(first_name,' ',last_name) | CONCAT(city,', ',state) |
+----------------------------------+-------------------------+
| George Washington                | Wakefield, VA           |
| John Adams                       | Braintree, MA           |
| Thomas Jefferson                 | Albemarle County, VA    |
| James Madison                    | Port Conway, VA         |
...
```

That query formats president names as a single string by concatenating first and last names separated by a space. It also formats birthplaces as the birth cities and states separated by a comma and a space.

When you use an expression to calculate a column value, the expression becomes the column's name and is used for its heading. That can lead to a very wide column if the expression is long, as the preceding query illustrates. To deal with this, you can assign the column a different name using the AS *name* construct. Such names are called "column aliases." The output from the previous query can be made more meaningful like this:

```
mysql> SELECT CONCAT(first_name,' ',last_name) AS Name,
    -> CONCAT(city,', ',state) AS Birthplace
    -> FROM president;
+----------------------+-------------------------+
| Name                 | Birthplace              |
+----------------------+-------------------------+
| George Washington    | Wakefield, VA           |
| John Adams           | Braintree, MA           |
| Thomas Jefferson     | Albemarle County, VA    |
| James Madison        | Port Conway, VA         |
...
```

If the column alias contains spaces, put it in quotes:

```
mysql> SELECT CONCAT(first_name,' ',last_name) AS 'President Name',
    -> CONCAT(city,', ',state) AS 'Place of Birth'
    -> FROM president;
+----------------------+-------------------------+
| President Name       | Place of Birth          |
+----------------------+-------------------------+
| George Washington    | Wakefield, VA           |
| John Adams           | Braintree, MA           |
| Thomas Jefferson     | Albemarle County, VA    |
| James Madison        | Port Conway, VA         |
...
```

The keyword AS is optional when you provide a column alias:

```
mysql> SELECT 1, 2 AS two, 3 three;
+---+-----+-------+
| 1 | two | three |
+---+-----+-------+
| 1 |   2 |     3 |
+---+-----+-------+
```

I prefer to include the AS. Without it, it's easier to inadvertently write a query that is legal but does not produce the intended result. For example, you might write a query to select president names like this, forgetting the comma between the `first_name` and `last_name` columns:

```
mysql> SELECT first_name last_name FROM president;
+---------------+
| last_name     |
+---------------+
| George        |
| John          |
| Thomas        |
| James         |
+---------------+
...
```

As a result, the query does not display two columns. Instead, it displays only the `first_name` column and treats `last_name` as the column alias, which becomes its label. If a query does not retrieve the number of columns you expect and uses column names other than you expect, be on the lookout for a missing comma somewhere between columns.

1.4.9.6 Working with Dates

The principal thing to keep in mind when using dates in MySQL is that it always expects dates with the year first. To write July 27, 2008, use `'2008-07-27'`. Do not use `'07-27-2008'` or `'27-07-2008'`, as you might be more accustomed to writing.

You can perform many kinds of operations on dates:

- Sort by date. (We've seen this several times already.)
- Look for particular dates or a range of dates.
- Extract parts of a date value, such as the year, month, or day.
- Calculate the difference between dates.
- Compute a date by adding an interval to or subtracting an interval from another date.

Some examples of these operations follow.

To look for particular dates, either by exact value or in relation to another value, compare a DATE column to the value in which you're interested:

```
mysql> SELECT * FROM grade_event WHERE date = '2008-10-01';
+------------+----------+----------+
| date       | category | event_id |
+------------+----------+----------+
| 2008-10-01 | T        |        6 |
+------------+----------+----------+
mysql> SELECT last_name, first_name, death
    -> FROM president
    -> WHERE death >= '1970-01-01' AND death < '1980-01-01';
+-----------+------------+------------+
| last_name | first_name | death      |
+-----------+------------+------------+
```

```
| Truman    | Harry S    | 1972-12-26 |
| Johnson   | Lyndon B.  | 1973-01-22 |
+----------+-----------+------------+
```

To test or retrieve parts of dates, use functions such as YEAR(), MONTH(), or
DAYOFMONTH(). For example, to find presidents who were born in March, look for dates
with a month value of 3:

```
mysql> SELECT last_name, first_name, birth
    -> FROM president WHERE MONTH(birth) = 3;
+-----------+------------+------------+
| last_name | first_name | birth      |
+-----------+------------+------------+
| Madison   | James      | 1751-03-16 |
| Jackson   | Andrew     | 1767-03-15 |
| Tyler     | John       | 1790-03-29 |
| Cleveland | Grover     | 1837-03-18 |
+-----------+------------+------------+
```

The query also can be written in terms of the month name:

```
mysql> SELECT last_name, first_name, birth
    -> FROM president WHERE MONTHNAME(birth) = 'March';
+-----------+------------+------------+
| last_name | first_name | birth      |
+-----------+------------+------------+
| Madison   | James      | 1751-03-16 |
| Jackson   | Andrew     | 1767-03-15 |
| Tyler     | John       | 1790-03-29 |
| Cleveland | Grover     | 1837-03-18 |
+-----------+------------+------------+
```

To be more specific, you can combine tests for MONTH() and DAYOFMONTH() to find
presidents born on a particular day in March:

```
mysql> SELECT last_name, first_name, birth
    -> FROM president WHERE MONTH(birth) = 3 AND DAYOFMONTH(birth) = 29;
+-----------+------------+------------+
| last_name | first_name | birth      |
+-----------+------------+------------+
| Tyler     | John       | 1790-03-29 |
+-----------+------------+------------+
```

This is the kind of query you'd use for generating one of those list of "celebrities who
have birthdays today," such as you see in the Entertainment section of your newspaper.
However, if you want to select rows that match month and day for "the current date,"
you don't have to plug in literal values the way the previous query did. To check for presidents born today, no matter what day of the year today is, compare their birthdays to the
month and day parts of CURDATE(), which always returns the current date:

```
SELECT last_name, first_name, birth
FROM president WHERE MONTH(birth) = MONTH(CURDATE())
AND DAYOFMONTH(birth) = DAYOFMONTH(CURDATE());
```

You can subtract one date from another, which enables you to find the interval between dates. For example, to determine which presidents lived the longest, compute age at death by taking the difference from birth date. The TIMESTAMPDIFF() function is useful here because it takes an argument for specifying the unit in which to express the result (YEAR in this case):

```
mysql> SELECT last_name, first_name, birth, death,
    -> TIMESTAMPDIFF(YEAR, birth, death) AS age
    -> FROM president WHERE death IS NOT NULL
    -> ORDER BY age DESC LIMIT 5;
+-----------+------------+------------+------------+------+
| last_name | first_name | birth      | death      | age  |
+-----------+------------+------------+------------+------+
| Reagan    | Ronald W.  | 1911-02-06 | 2004-06-05 |   93 |
| Ford      | Gerald R.  | 1913-07-14 | 2006-12-26 |   93 |
| Adams     | John       | 1735-10-30 | 1826-07-04 |   90 |
| Hoover    | Herbert C. | 1874-08-10 | 1964-10-20 |   90 |
| Truman    | Harry S    | 1884-05-08 | 1972-12-26 |   88 |
+-----------+------------+------------+------------+------+
```

Another way to compute a difference between dates, when you want the difference in days, is to use the TO_DAYS() function that converts a date to days. Determining how far dates are from some reference date is one application for this function. For example, you can tell which Historical League members need to renew their memberships soon: Compute the difference between each member's expiration date and the current date, and if it's less than some threshold value, a renewal will soon be needed. The following query finds memberships that have already expired or that will be due for renewal within 60 days:

```
SELECT last_name, first_name, expiration FROM member
WHERE (TO_DAYS(expiration) - TO_DAYS(CURDATE())) < 60;
```

The equivalent statement using TIMESTAMPDIFF() looks like this:

```
SELECT last_name, first_name, expiration FROM member
WHERE TIMESTAMPDIFF(DAY, CURDATE(), expiration) < 60;
```

To calculate one date from another, you can use DATE_ADD() or DATE_SUB(). These functions take a date and an interval and produce a new date. For example:

```
mysql> SELECT DATE_ADD('1970-1-1', INTERVAL 10 YEAR);
+----------------------------------------+
| DATE_ADD('1970-1-1', INTERVAL 10 YEAR) |
+----------------------------------------+
| 1980-01-01                             |
+----------------------------------------+
mysql> SELECT DATE_SUB('1970-1-1', INTERVAL 10 YEAR);
+----------------------------------------+
```

```
| DATE_SUB('1970-1-1', INTERVAL 10 YEAR) |
+----------------------------------------+
| 1960-01-01                             |
+----------------------------------------+
```

A query shown earlier in this section selected presidents who died during the 1970s, using literal dates for the endpoints of the selection range. That query can be rewritten to use a literal starting date and an ending date calculated from the starting date and an interval:

```
mysql> SELECT last_name, first_name, death
    -> FROM president
    -> WHERE death >= '1970-1-1'
    -> AND death < DATE_ADD('1970-1-1', INTERVAL 10 YEAR);
+-----------+------------+------------+
| last_name | first_name | death      |
+-----------+------------+------------+
| Truman    | Harry S    | 1972-12-26 |
| Johnson   | Lyndon B.  | 1973-01-22 |
+-----------+------------+------------+
```

The membership-renewal query can be written in terms of DATE_ADD():

```
SELECT last_name, first_name, expiration FROM member
WHERE expiration < DATE_ADD(CURDATE(), INTERVAL 60 DAY);
```

If the expiration column is indexed, this will be more efficient than the original query, for reasons discussed in Chapter 5.

Near the beginning of this chapter, you saw the following query for determining which of a dentist's patients haven't come in for their checkup in a while:

```
SELECT last_name, first_name, last_visit FROM patient
WHERE last_visit < DATE_SUB(CURDATE(), INTERVAL 6 MONTH);
```

That query may not have meant much to you then. Is it more meaningful now?

1.4.9.7 Pattern Matching

MySQL supports pattern matching operations that enable you to select rows without supplying an exact comparison value. To perform a pattern match, you use special operators (LIKE and NOT LIKE), and you specify a string containing wildcard characters. The character '_' matches any single character, and '%' matches any sequence of characters (including an empty sequence).

This pattern matches last names that begin with a 'W' or 'w' character:

```
mysql> SELECT last_name, first_name FROM president
    -> WHERE last_name LIKE 'W%';
+------------+------------+
| last_name  | first_name |
+------------+------------+
| Washington | George     |
| Wilson     | Woodrow    |
+------------+------------+
```

The following query demonstrates a common error. The pattern match is erroneous because it does not use LIKE, it uses a pattern with an arithmetic comparison operator:

```
mysql> SELECT last_name, first_name FROM president
    -> WHERE last_name = 'W%';
Empty set (0.00 sec)
```

The only way for such a comparison to succeed is for the column to contain exactly the string 'W%' or 'w%'.

This pattern matches last names that contain 'W' or 'w' anywhere in the name, not just at the beginning:

```
mysql> SELECT last_name, first_name FROM president
    -> WHERE last_name LIKE '%W%';
+------------+------------+
| last_name  | first_name |
+------------+------------+
| Washington | George     |
| Wilson     | Woodrow    |
| Eisenhower | Dwight D.  |
+------------+------------+
```

This pattern matches last names that contain exactly four characters:

```
mysql> SELECT last_name, first_name FROM president
    -> WHERE last_name LIKE '____';
+-----------+-------------+
| last_name | first_name  |
+-----------+-------------+
| Polk      | James K.    |
| Taft      | William H.  |
| Ford      | Gerald R.   |
| Bush      | George H.W. |
| Bush      | George W.   |
+-----------+-------------+
```

MySQL also provides another form of pattern matching based on regular expressions and the REXEXP operator. LIKE and REGEXP are discussed further in Section 3.5.1.1, "Operator Types," and Appendix C.

1.4.9.8 Setting and Using User-Defined Variables

MySQL enables you to define your own variables. These can be set using query results, which provides a convenient way to save values for use in later queries. Suppose that you want to find out which presidents were born before Andrew Jackson. To determine that, you can retrieve his birth date into a variable and then select other presidents with a birth date earlier than the value of the variable:

```
mysql> SELECT @birth := birth FROM president
    -> WHERE last_name = 'Jackson' AND first_name = 'Andrew';
+-----------------+
| @birth := birth |
+-----------------+
| 1767-03-15      |
+-----------------+
mysql> SELECT last_name, first_name, birth FROM president
    -> WHERE birth < @birth ORDER BY birth;
+------------+------------+------------+
| last_name  | first_name | birth      |
+------------+------------+------------+
| Washington | George     | 1732-02-22 |
| Adams      | John       | 1735-10-30 |
| Jefferson  | Thomas     | 1743-04-13 |
| Madison    | James      | 1751-03-16 |
| Monroe     | James      | 1758-04-28 |
+------------+------------+------------+
```

User variables are named using @*var_name* syntax and assigned a value in a SELECT statement using an expression of the form @*var_name*: = *value*. The first query therefore looks up the birth date for Andrew Jackson and assigns it to the @birth variable. (The result of the SELECT still is displayed; assigning a query result to a variable doesn't suppress the query output.) The second query refers to the variable and uses its value to find other president rows with a lesser birth value.

The preceding problem actually could be solved in a single query using a join or a subquery, but we're not to the point of writing those yet. Besides, sometimes it's just easier to use a variable.

Variables also can be assigned using a SET statement. In this case, either = or := are allowable as the assignment operator:

```
mysql> SET @today = CURDATE();
mysql> SET @one_week_ago := DATE_SUB(@today, INTERVAL 7 DAY);
mysql> SELECT @today, @one_week_ago;
+------------+---------------+
| @today     | @one_week_ago |
+------------+---------------+
| 2008-03-21 | 2008-03-14    |
+------------+---------------+
```

1.4.9.9 Generating Summaries

One of the most useful things MySQL can do for you is to boil down lots of raw data and summarize it. MySQL becomes a powerful ally when you learn to use it to generate summaries because that is an especially tedious, time-consuming, error-prone activity when done manually.

One simple form of summarizing is to determine which unique values are present in a set of values. Use the DISTINCT keyword to remove duplicate rows from a result. For example, the different states in which presidents have been born can be found like this:

```
mysql> SELECT DISTINCT state FROM president ORDER BY state;
+-------+
| state |
+-------+
| AR    |
| CA    |
| CT    |
| GA    |
| IA    |
| IL    |
| KY    |
| MA    |
| MO    |
| NC    |
| NE    |
| NH    |
| NJ    |
| NY    |
| OH    |
| PA    |
| SC    |
| TX    |
| VA    |
| VT    |
+-------+
```

Another form of summarizing involves counting, using the COUNT() function. If you use COUNT(*), it tells you the number of rows selected by your query. If a query has no WHERE clause, it selects all rows, so COUNT(*) tells you the number of rows in your table. The following query shows how many membership rows the Historical League member table contains:

```
mysql> SELECT COUNT(*) FROM member;
+----------+
| COUNT(*) |
+----------+
|      102 |
+----------+
```

If a query does have a WHERE clause, COUNT(*) tells you how many rows the clause matches. This query shows how many quizzes you have given to your class so far:

```
mysql> SELECT COUNT(*) FROM grade_event WHERE category = 'Q';
+----------+
| COUNT(*) |
```

```
+----------+
|        4 |
+----------+
```

COUNT(*) counts every row selected. By contrast, COUNT(*col_name*) counts only non-NULL values. The following query demonstrates these differences:

```
mysql> SELECT COUNT(*), COUNT(email), COUNT(expiration) FROM member;
+----------+--------------+-------------------+
| COUNT(*) | COUNT(email) | COUNT(expiration) |
+----------+--------------+-------------------+
|      102 |           80 |                96 |
+----------+--------------+-------------------+
```

This shows that although the member table has 102 rows, only 80 of them have a value in the email column. It also shows that six members have a lifetime membership. (A NULL value in the expiration column indicates a lifetime membership, and since 96 out of 102 rows are not NULL, that leaves six.)

COUNT() combined with DISTINCT counts the number of distinct non-NULL values in a result. For example, to count the number of different states in which presidents have been born, do this:

```
mysql> SELECT COUNT(DISTINCT state) FROM president;
+-----------------------+
| COUNT(DISTINCT state) |
+-----------------------+
|                    20 |
+-----------------------+
```

You can produce an overall count of values in a column, or break down the counts by categories. For example, you may know the overall number of students in your class as a result of running this query:

```
mysql> SELECT COUNT(*) FROM student;
+----------+
| COUNT(*) |
+----------+
|       31 |
+----------+
```

But how many students are boys and how many are girls? One way to find out is by asking for a count for each sex separately:

```
mysql> SELECT COUNT(*) FROM student WHERE sex='f';
+----------+
| COUNT(*) |
+----------+
|       15 |
+----------+
mysql> SELECT COUNT(*) FROM student WHERE sex='m';
```

```
+----------+
| COUNT(*) |
+----------+
|       16 |
+----------+
```

However, although that approach works, it's tedious and not really very well suited for columns that might have several different values. Consider how you'd determine the number of presidents born in each state this way. You'd have to find out which states are represented so as not to miss any (SELECT DISTINCT state FROM president), and then run a SELECT COUNT(*) query for each state. That is clearly something you don't want to do.

Fortunately, it's possible to use a single query to count how many times each distinct value occurs in a column. For the student list, count boys and girls separately using a GROUP BY clause:

```
mysql> SELECT sex, COUNT(*) FROM student GROUP BY sex;
+-----+----------+
| sex | COUNT(*) |
+-----+----------+
| F   |       15 |
| M   |       16 |
+-----+----------+
```

The same form of query tells us how many presidents were born in each state:

```
mysql> SELECT state, COUNT(*) FROM president GROUP BY state;
+-------+----------+
| state | COUNT(*) |
+-------+----------+
| AR    |        1 |
| CA    |        1 |
| CT    |        1 |
| GA    |        1 |
| IA    |        1 |
| IL    |        1 |
| KY    |        1 |
| MA    |        4 |
| MO    |        1 |
| NC    |        2 |
| NE    |        1 |
| NH    |        1 |
| NJ    |        1 |
| NY    |        4 |
| OH    |        7 |
| PA    |        1 |
| SC    |        1 |
| TX    |        2 |
| VA    |        8 |
```

```
| VT    |        2 |
+-------+----------+
```

When you count values in groups this way, the GROUP BY clause is necessary; it tells MySQL how to cluster values before counting them. You'll just get an error if you omit it.

The use of COUNT(*) with GROUP BY to count values has a number of advantages over counting occurrences of each distinct column value individually:

- You don't have to know in advance what values are present in the column you're summarizing.
- You need only a single query, not several.
- You get all the results with a single query, so you can sort the output.

The first two advantages are important for expressing queries more easily. The third advantage is important because it affords more flexibility in displaying results. By default, MySQL uses the columns named in the GROUP BY clause to sort the results, but you can specify an ORDER BY clause to sort in a different order. For example, if you want number of presidents grouped by state of birth, but sorted with the most well-represented states first, you can use an ORDER BY clause as follows:

```
mysql> SELECT state, COUNT(*) AS count FROM president
    -> GROUP BY state ORDER BY count DESC;
+-------+-------+
| state | count |
+-------+-------+
| VA    |     8 |
| OH    |     7 |
| MA    |     4 |
| NY    |     4 |
| NC    |     2 |
| VT    |     2 |
| TX    |     2 |
| SC    |     1 |
| NH    |     1 |
| PA    |     1 |
| KY    |     1 |
| NJ    |     1 |
| IA    |     1 |
| MO    |     1 |
| CA    |     1 |
| NE    |     1 |
| GA    |     1 |
| IL    |     1 |
| AR    |     1 |
| CT    |     1 |
+-------+-------+
```

When the column you want to use for sorting is produced by a summary function, you cannot refer to the function directly in the ORDER BY clause. Instead, give the column an alias and refer to it that way. The preceding query demonstrates this, where the COUNT(*) column is aliased as count. Another way to refer to such a column in an ORDER BY clause is by its position in the output. The previous query could have been written as follows instead:

```
SELECT state, COUNT(*) FROM president
GROUP BY state ORDER BY 2 DESC;
```

Referring to columns by position is allowable in MySQL, but problematic:

- Use of column positions leads to less understandable queries because numbers are less meaningful than names.

- If you add, remove, or reorder output columns, you must remember to check the ORDER BY clause and fix the column number if it has changed.

- The syntax of referring to column positions in ORDER BY clauses is no longer part of standard SQL and should be considered deprecated.

Aliases have none of those problems.

If you want to group results using GROUP BY with a calculated column, you can refer to it using an alias or column position, just as with ORDER BY. The following query determines how many presidents were born in each month of the year:

```
mysql> SELECT MONTH(birth) AS Month, MONTHNAME(birth) AS Name,
    -> COUNT(*) AS count
    -> FROM president GROUP BY Name ORDER BY Month;
+-------+-----------+-------+
| Month | Name      | count |
+-------+-----------+-------+
|     1 | January   |     4 |
|     2 | February  |     4 |
|     3 | March     |     4 |
|     4 | April     |     4 |
|     5 | May       |     2 |
|     6 | June      |     1 |
|     7 | July      |     4 |
|     8 | August    |     4 |
|     9 | September |     1 |
|    10 | October   |     6 |
|    11 | November  |     5 |
|    12 | December  |     3 |
+-------+-----------+-------+
```

COUNT() can be combined with ORDER BY and LIMIT. For example, to find the four most well-represented states in the president table, use this statement:

```
mysql> SELECT state, COUNT(*) AS count FROM president
    -> GROUP BY state ORDER BY count DESC LIMIT 4;
+-------+-------+
| state | count |
+-------+-------+
| VA    |     8 |
| OH    |     7 |
| MA    |     4 |
| NY    |     4 |
+-------+-------+
```

If you don't want to limit query output with a LIMIT clause, but rather by looking for particular values of COUNT(), use a HAVING clause. HAVING is similar to WHERE in that it specifies conditions that must be satisfied by output rows. It differs from WHERE in that it can refer to the results of summary functions like COUNT(). The following query will tell you which states are represented by two or more presidents:

```
mysql> SELECT state, COUNT(*) AS count FROM president
    -> GROUP BY state HAVING count > 1 ORDER BY count DESC;
+-------+-------+
| state | count |
+-------+-------+
| VA    |     8 |
| OH    |     7 |
| MA    |     4 |
| NY    |     4 |
| NC    |     2 |
| VT    |     2 |
| TX    |     2 |
+-------+-------+
```

More generally, this is the type of query to run when you want to find duplicated values in a column. Or, to find nonduplicated values, use HAVING count = 1.

There are several summary functions other than COUNT(). The MIN(), MAX(), SUM(), and AVG() functions are useful for determining the minimum, maximum, total, and average values in a column. You can even use them all at the same time. The following query shows various numeric characteristics for each quiz and test you've given. It also shows how many scores go into computing each of the values. (Some students may have been absent and are not counted.)

```
mysql> SELECT
    -> event_id,
    -> MIN(score) AS minimum,
    -> MAX(score) AS maximum,
    -> MAX(score)-MIN(score)+1 AS span,
    -> SUM(score) AS total,
    -> AVG(score) AS average,
    -> COUNT(score) AS count
    -> FROM score
```

```
    -> GROUP BY event_id;
+----------+---------+---------+------+-------+---------+-------+
| event_id | minimum | maximum | span | total | average | count |
+----------+---------+---------+------+-------+---------+-------+
|        1 |       9 |      20 |   12 |   439 | 15.1379 |    29 |
|        2 |       8 |      19 |   12 |   425 | 14.1667 |    30 |
|        3 |      60 |      97 |   38 |  2425 | 78.2258 |    31 |
|        4 |       7 |      20 |   14 |   379 | 14.0370 |    27 |
|        5 |       8 |      20 |   13 |   383 | 14.1852 |    27 |
|        6 |      62 |     100 |   39 |  2325 | 80.1724 |    29 |
+----------+---------+---------+------+-------+---------+-------+
```

This information might be more meaningful if it was clear whether the event_id values represented quizzes or tests, of course. However, to produce that information, we need to consult the grade_event table as well; we'll revisit this query in Section 1.4.9.10, "Retrieving Information from Multiple Tables."

If you want to produce extra output lines that give you a "summary of summaries," add a WITH ROLLUP clause. This tells MySQL to calculate "super-aggregate" values for the grouped rows. Here's a simple example based on an earlier statement that counts the number of students of each sex. The WITH ROLLUP clause produces another line that summarizes the counts for both sexes:

```
mysql> SELECT sex, COUNT(*) FROM student GROUP BY sex WITH ROLLUP;
+-----+----------+
| sex | COUNT(*) |
+-----+----------+
| F   |       15 |
| M   |       16 |
| NULL|       31 |
+-----+----------+
```

The NULL in the grouped column indicates that corresponding count is the summary value for the preceding groups.

WITH ROLLUP can be used with the other aggregate functions as well. The following statement calculates grade summaries as just shown a few paragraphs earlier, but also produces an extra super-aggregate line:

```
mysql> SELECT
    -> event_id,
    -> MIN(score) AS minimum,
    -> MAX(score) AS maximum,
    -> MAX(score)-MIN(score)+1 AS span,
    -> SUM(score) AS total,
    -> AVG(score) AS average,
    -> COUNT(score) AS count
    -> FROM score
    -> GROUP BY event_id
    -> WITH ROLLUP;
```

```
+-----------+---------+---------+------+-------+---------+-------+
| event_id  | minimum | maximum | span | total | average | count |
+-----------+---------+---------+------+-------+---------+-------+
|         1 |       9 |      20 |   12 |   439 | 15.1379 |    29 |
|         2 |       8 |      19 |   12 |   425 | 14.1667 |    30 |
|         3 |      60 |      97 |   38 |  2425 | 78.2258 |    31 |
|         4 |       7 |      20 |   14 |   379 | 14.0370 |    27 |
|         5 |       8 |      20 |   13 |   383 | 14.1852 |    27 |
|         6 |      62 |     100 |   39 |  2325 | 80.1724 |    29 |
|      NULL |       7 |     100 |   94 |  6376 | 36.8555 |   173 |
+-----------+---------+---------+------+-------+---------+-------+
```

In this output, the final line displays aggregate values calculated based on all the preceding group summary values.

WITH ROLLUP is useful because it provides extra information that you otherwise would have to obtain by running another query. Using a single query is more efficient because the server need not examine the data twice. If the GROUP BY clause names more than one column, WITH ROLLUP produces additional super-aggregate lines that contain higher-level summary values.

Summary functions are fun to play with because they're so powerful, but it's easy to get carried away with them. Consider this query:

```
mysql> SELECT
    -> state AS State,
    -> AVG(TIMESTAMPDIFF(YEAR, birth, death)) AS Age
    -> FROM president WHERE death IS NOT NULL
    -> GROUP BY state ORDER BY Age;
+-------+---------+
| State | Age     |
+-------+---------+
| KY    | 56.0000 |
| VT    | 58.5000 |
| NC    | 59.5000 |
| OH    | 62.2857 |
| NH    | 64.0000 |
| NY    | 69.0000 |
| NJ    | 71.0000 |
| TX    | 71.0000 |
| MA    | 72.0000 |
| VA    | 72.3750 |
| PA    | 77.0000 |
| SC    | 78.0000 |
| CA    | 81.0000 |
| MO    | 88.0000 |
| IA    | 90.0000 |
| NE    | 93.0000 |
| IL    | 93.0000 |
+-------+---------+
```

The query selects presidents who have died, groups them by state of birth, determines their approximate age at time of death, computes the average age (per state), and then sorts the results by average age. In other words, the query determines, for nonliving presidents, the average age of death by state of birth.

And what does that demonstrate? It shows only that you can write the query. It certainly doesn't show that the query is worth writing. Not all things you can do with a database are equally meaningful. Nevertheless, people sometimes go query-happy when they find out what they can do with their database. This may account for the rise of increasingly esoteric and bizarre statistics on televised sporting events over the last few years. The sports statisticians can use their databases to figure out everything you'd ever want to know about a team, and also everything you'd *never* want to know. Do you really care which third-string quarterback holds the record for most interceptions on third down when his team is leading by more than 14 points with the ball inside the 15-yard line in the last two minutes of the second quarter?

1.4.9.10 Retrieving Information from Multiple Tables

The statements that we've written so far have pulled data from a single table. But MySQL is capable of working much harder for you. I've mentioned before that the power of a relational DBMS lies in its capability to combine information from multiple tables to answer questions that can't be answered from individual tables alone. This section describes how to write statements that do that.

One type of operation that selects information from multiple tables is called a "join" because you're producing a result by joining the information in one table to the information in another table. This is done by matching up common values in the tables. Another type of multiple-table operation uses one SELECT nested within another SELECT. The nested SELECT is called a "subquery." This section describes both types of operations.

Let's work through a join example. Earlier, in Section 1.4.6.2, "Tables for the Grade-Keeping Project," a query to retrieve quiz or test scores for a given date was presented without explanation. Now it's time for the explanation. The query actually involves a three-way join, so we'll build up to it in two steps. In the first step, we construct a query to select scores for a given date as follows:

```
mysql> SELECT student_id, date, score, category
    -> FROM grade_event INNER JOIN score
    -> ON grade_event.event_id = score.event_id
    -> WHERE date = '2008-09-23';
+------------+------------+-------+----------+
| student_id | date       | score | category |
+------------+------------+-------+----------+
|          1 | 2008-09-23 |    15 | Q        |
|          2 | 2008-09-23 |    12 | Q        |
|          3 | 2008-09-23 |    11 | Q        |
|          5 | 2008-09-23 |    13 | Q        |
|          6 | 2008-09-23 |    18 | Q        |
...
```

The query works by finding the `grade_event` row with the given date (`'2008-09-23'`), and using the event ID in that row to locate scores that have the same event ID. For each matching `grade_event` row and `score` row combination, it displays the student ID, score, date, and event category.

The query differs from others we have written in two important respects:

- The `FROM` clause names more than one table because we're retrieving data from more than one table:

  ```
  FROM grade_event INNER JOIN score
  ```

- The `ON` clause specifies that the `grade_event` and `score` tables are joined on the basis of matching up the `event_id` values in each table:

  ```
  ON grade_event.event_id = score.event_id
  ```

Notice how we refer to the `event_id` columns as `grade_event.event_id` and `score.event_id` using *tbl_name.col_name* syntax so that MySQL knows which tables we're referring to. This is because `event_id` occurs in both tables, so it's ambiguous if used without a table name to qualify it. The other columns in the query (`date`, `score`, and `category`) can be used without a table qualifier because they appear in only one of the tables and thus are unambiguous.

I generally prefer to qualify every column in a join to make it clearer (more explicit) which table each column is part of, and that's how I'll write joins from now on. In fully qualified form, the query looks like this:

```
SELECT score.student_id, grade_event.date, score.score, grade_event.category
FROM grade_event INNER JOIN score
ON grade_event.event_id = score.event_id
WHERE grade_event.date = '2008-09-23';
```

The first-stage query uses the `grade_event` table to map a date to an event ID, and uses the ID to find the matching scores in the `score` table. Output from the query contains `student_id` values, but names would be more meaningful. By using the `student` table, we can map student IDs onto names, which is the second step. To accomplish name display, use the fact that the `score` and `student` tables both have `student_id` columns enabling the rows in them to be linked. The resulting query is as follows:

```
mysql> SELECT
    -> student.name, grade_event.date, score.score, grade_event.category
    -> FROM grade_event INNER JOIN score INNER JOIN student
    -> ON grade_event.event_id = score.event_id
    -> AND score.student_id = student.student_id
    -> WHERE grade_event.date = '2008-09-23';
+-----------+------------+-------+----------+
| name      | date       | score | category |
+-----------+------------+-------+----------+
| Megan     | 2008-09-23 |    15 | Q        |
```

```
| Joseph     | 2008-09-23 |    12 | Q             |
| Kyle       | 2008-09-23 |    11 | Q             |
| Abby       | 2008-09-23 |    13 | Q             |
| Nathan     | 2008-09-23 |    18 | Q             |
...
```

This query has several differences from the previous one:

- The FROM clause now includes the student table because the statement uses it in addition to the grade_event and score tables.

- The student_id column was unambiguous before, so it was possible to refer to it in either unqualified (student_id) or qualified (score.student_id) form. Now it is ambiguous because it is present in both the score and student tables. Therefore, it *must* be qualified as score.student_id or student.student_id to make it clear which table to use.

- The ON clause has an additional term specifying that score table rows are matched against student table rows based on student ID:

  ```
  ON ... score.student_id = student.student_id
  ```

- The query displays the student name rather than the student ID. (You could display both if you wanted. Just add student.student_id to the list of output columns.)

With this query, you can plug in any date and get back the scores for that date, complete with student names and the score category. You don't have to know anything about student IDs or event IDs. MySQL takes care of figuring out the relevant ID values and using them to match up table rows.

Another task the grade-keeping project involves is summarizing student absences. Absences are recorded by student ID and date in the absence table. To get student names (not just IDs), we need to join the absence table to the student table, based on the student_id value. The following query lists student ID number and name along with a count of absences:

```
mysql> SELECT student.student_id, student.name,
    -> COUNT(absence.date) AS absences
    -> FROM student INNER JOIN absence
    -> ON student.student_id = absence.student_id
    -> GROUP BY student.student_id;
+------------+-------+----------+
| student_id | name  | absences |
+------------+-------+----------+
|          3 | Kyle  |        1 |
|          5 | Abby  |        1 |
|         10 | Peter |        2 |
|         17 | Will  |        1 |
|         20 | Avery |        1 |
+------------+-------+----------+
```

> **Note**
>
> Although the GROUP BY column has a qualifier, it isn't strictly necessary for this query.
> GROUP BY refers to output columns, and there is only one such column named
> student_id, so MySQL knows which one you mean.

The output produced by the query is fine if we want to know only which students had
absences. But if we turn in this list to the school office, they might say, "What about the
other students? We want a value for every student." That's a slightly different question. It
means we want to know the number of absences, even for students who had none. Because the question is different, the query that answers it is different as well.

To answer the question, we will use a LEFT JOIN rather than an inner join. LEFT JOIN
tells MySQL to produce a row of output for each row selected from the table named first
in the join (that is, the table named to the left of the LEFT JOIN keywords). By naming
the student table first, we'll get output for every student, even those who are not represented in the absence table. To write this query, use LEFT JOIN between the tables named
in the FROM clause (rather than separating them by a comma), and an ON clause that says
how to match up rows in the two tables. The query looks like this:

```
mysql> SELECT student.student_id, student.name,
    -> COUNT(absence.date) AS absences
    -> FROM student LEFT JOIN absence
    -> ON student.student_id = absence.student_id
    -> GROUP BY student.student_id;
+------------+----------+----------+
| student_id | name     | absences |
+------------+----------+----------+
|          1 | Megan    |        0 |
|          2 | Joseph   |        0 |
|          3 | Kyle     |        1 |
|          4 | Katie    |        0 |
|          5 | Abby     |        1 |
|          6 | Nathan   |        0 |
|          7 | Liesl    |        0 |
...
```

Earlier, in Section 1.4.9.9, "Generating Summaries," we ran a query that produced a
numeric characterization of the data in the score table. Output from that query listed
event ID but did not include event dates or categories, because we didn't know then how
to join the score table to the grade_event table to map the IDs onto dates and categories. Now we do. The following query is similar to one run earlier, but shows the dates
and categories rather than simply the numeric event IDs:

```
mysql> SELECT
    -> grade_event.date,grade_event.category,
    -> MIN(score.score) AS minimum,
```

```
    -> MAX(score.score) AS maximum,
    -> MAX(score.score)-MIN(score.score)+1 AS span,
    -> SUM(score.score) AS total,
    -> AVG(score.score) AS average,
    -> COUNT(score.score) AS count
    -> FROM score INNER JOIN grade_event
    -> ON score.event_id = grade_event.event_id
    -> GROUP BY grade_event.date;
```

date	category	minimum	maximum	span	total	average	count
2008-09-03	Q	9	20	12	439	15.1379	29
2008-09-06	Q	8	19	12	425	14.1667	30
2008-09-09	T	60	97	38	2425	78.2258	31
2008-09-16	Q	7	20	14	379	14.0370	27
2008-09-23	Q	8	20	13	383	14.1852	27
2008-10-01	T	62	100	39	2325	80.1724	29

You can use functions such as COUNT() and AVG() to produce a summary over multiple columns, even if the columns come from different tables. The following query determines the number of scores and the average score for each combination of event date and student sex:

```
mysql> SELECT grade_event.date, student.sex,
    -> COUNT(score.score) AS count, AVG(score.score) AS average
    -> FROM grade_event INNER JOIN score INNER JOIN student
    -> ON grade_event.event_id = score.event_id
    -> AND score.student_id = student.student_id
    -> GROUP BY grade_event.date, student.sex;
```

date	sex	count	average
2008-09-03	F	14	14.6429
2008-09-03	M	15	15.6000
2008-09-06	F	14	14.7143
2008-09-06	M	16	13.6875
2008-09-09	F	15	77.4000
2008-09-09	M	16	79.0000
2008-09-16	F	13	15.3077
2008-09-16	M	14	12.8571
2008-09-23	F	12	14.0833
2008-09-23	M	15	14.2667
2008-10-01	F	14	77.7857
2008-10-01	M	15	82.4000

We can use a similar query to perform one of the grade-keeping project tasks: computing the total score per student at the end of the semester. The query is as follows:

```
SELECT student.student_id, student.name,
SUM(score.score) AS total, COUNT(score.score) AS n
FROM grade_event INNER JOIN score INNER JOIN student
ON grade_event.event_id = score.event_id
AND score.student_id = student.student_id
GROUP BY score.student_id
ORDER BY total;
```

There is no requirement that a join be performed between different tables. It might seem odd at first, but you can join a table to itself. For example, you can determine whether any presidents were born in the same city by checking each president's birthplace against every other president's birthplace:

```
mysql> SELECT p1.last_name, p1.first_name, p1.city, p1.state
    -> FROM president AS p1 INNER JOIN president AS p2
    -> ON p1.city = p2.city AND p1.state = p2.state
    -> WHERE (p1.last_name <> p2.last_name OR p1.first_name <> p2.first_name)
    -> ORDER BY state, city, last_name;
+-----------+-------------+-----------+-------+
| last_name | first_name  | city      | state |
+-----------+-------------+-----------+-------+
| Adams     | John Quincy | Braintree | MA    |
| Adams     | John        | Braintree | MA    |
+-----------+-------------+-----------+-------+
```

There are two tricky things about this query:

- It's necessary to refer to two instances of the same table, so we create table aliases (p1, p2) and use them to disambiguate references to the table's columns. As with column aliases, the AS keyword is optional when naming table aliases.

- Each president's row matches itself, but we don't want to see that in the output. The WHERE clause disallows matches of a row to itself by making sure that the rows being compared are for different presidents.

A similar query finds presidents who were born on the same day. However, birth dates cannot be compared directly because that would miss presidents who were born in different years. Instead, use MONTH() and DAYOFMONTH() to compare month and day of the birth date:

```
mysql> SELECT p1.last_name, p1.first_name, p1.birth
    -> FROM president AS p1 INNER JOIN president AS p2
    -> WHERE MONTH(p1.birth) = MONTH(p2.birth)
    -> AND DAYOFMONTH(p1.birth) = DAYOFMONTH(p2.birth)
    -> AND (p1.last_name <> p2.last_name OR p1.first_name <> p2.first_name)
    -> ORDER BY p1.last_name;
+-----------+-------------+-------------+
```

```
| last_name | first_name | birth      |
+-----------+------------+------------+
| Harding   | Warren G.  | 1865-11-02 |
| Polk      | James K.   | 1795-11-02 |
+-----------+------------+------------+
```

Using DAYOFYEAR() rather than the combination of MONTH() and DAYOFMONTH() would result in a simpler query, but it would produce incorrect results when comparing dates from leap years to dates from nonleap years.

Another kind of multiple-table retrieval uses a "subquery," which is one SELECT nested within another. There are several types of subqueries, which are discussed further in Section 2.9, "Performing Multiple-Table Retrievals with Subqueries." For now, a couple of examples will do. Suppose that you want to identify those students who have perfect attendance. This is equivalent to determining which students are not represented in the absence table, which can be done like this:

```
mysql> SELECT * FROM student
    -> WHERE student_id NOT IN (SELECT student_id FROM absence);
+-----------+-----+------------+
| name      | sex | student_id |
+-----------+-----+------------+
| Megan     | F   |          1 |
| Joseph    | M   |          2 |
| Katie     | F   |          4 |
| Nathan    | M   |          6 |
| Liesl     | F   |          7 |
...
```

The nested SELECT determines the set of student_id values that are present in the absence table, and the outer SELECT retrieves student rows that don't match any of those IDs.

A subquery also provides a single-statement solution to the question asked in Section 1.4.9.8, "Setting and Using User-Defined Variables," about which presidents were born before Andrew Jackson. The original solution used two statements and a user variable, but it can be done with a subquery as follows:

```
mysql> SELECT last_name, first_name, birth FROM president
    -> WHERE birth < (SELECT birth FROM president
    -> WHERE last_name = 'Jackson' AND first_name = 'Andrew');
+------------+------------+------------+
| last_name  | first_name | birth      |
+------------+------------+------------+
| Washington | George     | 1732-02-22 |
| Adams      | John       | 1735-10-30 |
| Jefferson  | Thomas     | 1743-04-13 |
| Madison    | James      | 1751-03-16 |
| Monroe     | James      | 1758-04-28 |
+------------+------------+------------+
```

The inner SELECT determines Andrew Jackson's birth date, and the outer SELECT retrieves presidents with a birth date earlier than his.

1.4.10 Deleting or Updating Existing Rows

Sometimes you want to get rid of rows or change their contents. The DELETE and UPDATE statements let you do this. This section discusses how to use them.

The DELETE statement has this form:

```
DELETE FROM tbl_name
WHERE which rows to delete;
```

The WHERE clause that specifies which rows should be deleted is optional, but if you leave it out, all rows in the table are deleted. In other words, the simplest DELETE statement is also the most dangerous:

```
DELETE FROM tbl_name;
```

That statement wipes out the table's contents entirely, so be careful with it! To delete specific rows, use the WHERE clause to identify the rows in which you're interested. This is similar to using a WHERE clause in a SELECT statement to avoid selecting the entire table. For example, to specifically delete from the president table only those presidents born in Ohio, use this statement:

```
mysql> DELETE FROM president WHERE state='OH';
Query OK, 7 rows affected (0.00 sec)
```

If you're not really sure which rows a DELETE statement will remove, it's often a good idea to test the WHERE clause first by using it with a SELECT statement to find out which rows it matches. This can help you ensure that you'll actually delete the rows you intend, and only those rows. Suppose that you want to delete the row for Teddy Roosevelt. Would the following statement do the job?

```
DELETE FROM president WHERE last_name='Roosevelt';
```

Yes, in the sense that it would delete the row you have in mind. No, in the sense that it also would delete the row for Franklin Roosevelt. It's safer to check the WHERE clause with a SELECT statement first, like this:

```
mysql> SELECT last_name, first_name FROM president
    -> WHERE last_name='Roosevelt';
+-----------+-------------+
| last_name | first_name  |
+-----------+-------------+
| Roosevelt | Theodore    |
| Roosevelt | Franklin D. |
+-----------+-------------+
```

From that you can see the need to be more specific by adding a condition for the first name:

```
mysql> SELECT last_name, first_name FROM president
    -> WHERE last_name='Roosevelt' AND first_name='Theodore';
+-----------+------------+
| last_name | first_name |
+-----------+------------+
| Roosevelt | Theodore   |
+-----------+------------+
```

Now you know the WHERE clause that properly identifies only the desired row, and the DELETE statement can be constructed correctly:

```
mysql> DELETE FROM president
    -> WHERE last_name='Roosevelt' AND first_name='Theodore';
```

If that seems like a lot of work to delete a row, remember this: Better safe than sorry! But remember this, too: In some situations, you can minimize typing through the use of copy and paste or input line-editing techniques. See Section 1.5, "Tips for Interacting with mysql," for more information.

To modify existing rows, use UPDATE, which has this form:

```
UPDATE tbl_name
SET which columns to change
WHERE which rows to update;
```

The WHERE clause is just as for DELETE. It's optional, so if you don't specify one, every row in the table will be updated. For example, the following statement changes the name of each student to "George":

```
mysql> UPDATE student SET name='George';
```

Obviously, you must be careful with statements like that, so normally you add a WHERE clause to be more specific about which rows to update. Suppose that you recently added a new member to the Historical League but filled in only a few columns of his entry:

```
mysql> INSERT INTO member (last_name,first_name)
    -> VALUES('York','Jerome');
```

Then you realize you forgot to set his membership expiration date. You can fix that with an UPDATE statement that includes an appropriate WHERE clause to identify which row to change:

```
mysql> UPDATE member
    -> SET expiration='2009-7-20'
    -> WHERE last_name='York' AND first_name='Jerome';
```

You can update multiple columns with a single statement. The following UPDATE modifies Jerome's email and postal addresses:

```
mysql> UPDATE member
```

```
      -> SET email='jeromey@aol.com', street='123 Elm St',
      -> city='Anytown', state='NY', zip='01003'
      -> WHERE last_name='York' AND first_name='Jerome';
```

You can also "unset" a column by setting its value to NULL (assuming that the column allows NULL values). If at some point in the future Jerome later decides to pay the big membership renewal fee that enables him to become a lifetime member, you can mark his row as "never expires" by setting his expiration date to NULL:

```
mysql> UPDATE member
    -> SET expiration=NULL
    -> WHERE last_name='York' AND first_name='Jerome';
```

With UPDATE, just as for DELETE, it's not a bad idea to test a WHERE clause using a SELECT statement to make sure that you're choosing the right rows to update. Otherwise, if your selection criteria are too narrow or too broad, you'll update too few or too many rows.

If you've tried the statements in this section, you'll have deleted and modified rows in the sampdb tables. Before proceeding to the next section, you should undo those changes. Do that by reloading the tables using the instructions given earlier, in Section 1.4.8, "Resetting the sampdb Database to a Known State."

1.5 Tips for Interacting with `mysql`

This section discusses how to interact with the `mysql` client program more efficiently and with less typing. It also describes how to connect to the server more easily and how to enter statements without typing each one by hand.

1.5.1 Simplifying the Connection Process

When you invoke `mysql`, it's likely that you need to specify connection parameters such as hostname, username, or password. That's a lot of typing just to run a program, and it gets tiresome very quickly. There are several ways to minimize the amount of typing necessary to establish a connection to the MySQL server:

- Store connection parameters in an option file.
- Repeat commands by taking advantage of your shell's command history capabilities.
- Define a `mysql` command line shortcut using a shell alias or script.

1.5.1.1 Using an Option File

MySQL enables you to store connection parameters in an option file. Then you don't have to type the parameters each time you run `mysql`; they are used just as if you had entered them on the command line. A big advantage of this technique is that the parameters can also be used by other MySQL clients such as `mysqlimport` or `mysqlshow`. In other words, an option file makes it easier to use not just `mysql` but many other programs as well. This section briefly describes how to set up an option file for use by client programs. Additional details can be found in Section F.2.2, "Option Files."

Under Unix, you set up an option file by creating a file named ~/.my.cnf (that is, a file named .my.cnf in your home directory). Under Windows, create an option file named my.ini in your MySQL installation directory, or in the root directory of the C drive (that is, C:\my.ini). An option file is a plain text file; you can create it using any text editor. The file's contents should look something like this:

```
[client]
host=server_host
user=your_name
password=your_pass
```

The [client] line signals the beginning of the client option group. MySQL programs read the lines following it to obtain option values, until the end of the file or until a different option group begins. Replace server_host, your_name, and your_pass with the hostname, username, and password that you specify when you connect to the server. For example, if the server is running on the host cobra.snake.net and your MySQL username and password are sampadm and secret, put these lines in the .my.cnf file:

```
[client]
host=cobra.snake.net
user=sampadm
password=secret
```

The [client] line is required, to define where the option group begins, but the lines that define parameter values are optional; you can specify just the ones you need. For example, if you're using Unix and your MySQL username is the same as your Unix login name, there is no need to include a user line. The default host is localhost, so if you connect to a server running on the local host, no host line is necessary.

Under Unix, an additional precaution that you should take after creating the option file is to set its access mode to a restrictive value to make sure that no one else can read or modify it. Either of the following commands make the file accessible only to you:

```
% chmod 600 .my.cnf
% chmod u=rw,go-rwx .my.cnf
```

1.5.1.2 Using Your Shell's Command History

Shells such as tcsh and bash remember your commands in a history list and enable you to repeat commands from that list. If you use such a shell, your history list can help you avoid typing entire commands. For example, if you've recently invoked mysql, you can execute it again like this:

```
% !my
```

The '!' character tells your shell to search through your command history to find the most recent command that begins with "my" and reissue it as though you'd typed it again yourself. Some shells also enable you to move up and down through your history list using the Up arrow and Down arrow keys (or perhaps Control-P and Control-N). You can select the command you want this way and then press Enter to execute it. `tcsh` and `bash` have this facility, and other shells may as well. Check the documentation for your shell to find out more about using your history list.

1.5.1.3 Using Shell Aliases and Scripts

If your shell provides an alias facility, you can set up a short command name that maps to a long command. For example, in `csh` or `tcsh`, you can use the `alias` command to set up an alias named `sampdb` like this:

```
alias sampdb 'mysql -h cobra.snake.net -p -u sampadm sampdb'
```

The syntax for `bash` is slightly different:

```
alias sampdb='mysql -h cobra.snake.net -p -u sampadm sampdb'
```

Defining the alias makes the following two commands equivalent:

```
% sampdb
% mysql -h cobra.snake.net -p -u sampadm sampdb
```

Clearly, the first is easier to type than the second. To make the alias take effect each time you log in, put the `alias` command in one of your shell's startup files (for example, `.tcshrc` for `tcsh`, or `.bashrc` or `.bash_profile` for `bash`).

On Windows, a similar technique is to create a shortcut that points to the `mysql` program, and then edit the shortcut's properties to include the appropriate connection parameters.

Another way to invoke commands with less typing is to create a script that executes `mysql` for you with the proper options. On Unix, a shell script that is equivalent to the `sampdb` alias just shown looks like this:

```
#!/bin/sh
exec mysql -h cobra.snake.net -p -u sampadm sampdb
```

If you name the script `sampdb` and make it executable (with `chmod +x sampdb`), you can type `sampdb` at the command prompt to run `mysql` and connect to the `sampdb` database.

On Windows, a batch file can be used to do the same thing. Name the file `sampdb.bat` and put the following line in it:

```
mysql -h cobra.snake.net -p -u sampadm sampdb
```

This batch file can be run either by typing `sampdb` at the prompt in a console window or by double-clicking its Windows icon.

If you need to access several databases or connect to several hosts, you can define multiple aliases, shortcuts, or scripts, each of which invokes `mysql` with different options.

1.5.2 Issuing Statements with Less Typing

`mysql` is an extremely useful program for interacting with your database, but its interface is most suitable for short, single-line queries. Although `mysql` itself doesn't care whether a query spreads across multiple lines, long queries aren't much fun to type. And it's annoying to enter a query, only to discover that you must retype it because it has a syntax error. You can use several techniques to avoid needless retyping:

- Use `mysql`'s input line-editing facility.
- Use copy and paste.
- Run `mysql` in batch mode.

1.5.2.1 Using the `mysql` Input Line Editor

`mysql` has the GNU Readline library built in to enable input line editing. You can manipulate the line you're currently entering, or recall previous input lines and re-enter them, either as is or after further modification. This is convenient when you're entering a line and spot a typo; you can back up within the line to correct the problem before pressing Enter. If you enter a query that has a mistake in it, you can recall the query, edit it to fix the problem, and then resubmit it. (This is easiest if you type the entire query on one line.)

Some of the key sequences you will find useful are shown in Table 1.4, but there are many input editing commands available in addition to those shown in the table. You can read about them in the command editing chapter of the `bash` manual, available online from the GNU Project Web site at http://www.gnu.org/manual/.

Table 1.4   mysql Input Editing Commands

Key Sequence	Meaning
Up arrow or Control-P	Recall previous line
Down arrow or Control-N	Recall next line
Left arrow or Control-B	Move cursor left (backward)
Right arrow or Control-F	Move cursor right (forward)
Escape b	Move backward one word
Escape f	Move forward one word
Control-A	Move cursor to beginning of line
Control-E	Move cursor to end of line
Control-D	Delete character under cursor
Delete	Delete character to left of cursor
Escape D	Delete word
Escape Backspace	Delete word to left of cursor
Control-K	Erase everything from cursor to end of line

Table 1.4 mysql Input Editing Commands

Key Sequence	Meaning
Control-_	Undo last change; can be repeated

On Windows, the Readline editing capabilities are not available. However, Windows itself supports the commands shown in Table 1.5, so they become available to `mysql`.

Table 1.5 Windows Input Editing Commands

Key Sequence	Meaning
Up arrow	Recall previous line
Down arrow	Recall next line
Left arrow	Move cursor left (backward)
Right arrow	Move cursor right (forward)
Control-Left Arrow	Move backward one word
Control-Right Arrow	Move forward one word
Home	Move cursor to beginning of line
End	Move cursor to end of line
Delete	Delete character under cursor
Backspace	Delete character to left of cursor
Esc	Erase line
Page Up	Recall first command entered
Page Down	Recall last command entered
F3	Recall last command entered
F7	Display command pop-up; select with Up arrow/Down arrow
F9	Display command pop-up; select with command number
F8, F5	Cycle through command list

The following example describes a simple use for input editing. Suppose that you've entered this query while using `mysql`:

```
mysql> SHOW COLUMNS FROM persident;
```

If you notice that you've misspelled "president" as "persident" before pressing Enter, you can fix the query like this:

1. Press Left arrow a few times to move the cursor left until it's on the "s".
2. To erase the "er", press Delete or Backspace twice (whichever one erases the character to the left of the cursor on your system).
3. Type "re" to fix the error.
4. Press Enter to issue the query.

If you press Enter before you notice the misspelling, that's not a problem. After `mysql` displays its error message, press Up arrow to recall the line, and then edit it as just described.

1.5.2.2 Using Copy and Paste to Issue Statements

If you work in a windowing environment, the text of statements that you find useful can be saved in a file and recalled by copy and paste operations:

1. Invoke `mysql` in a terminal window.
2. Open the file containing your statements in a document window. (For example, I use vi on Unix and gvim on Windows.)
3. To execute a statement stored in your file, select it in the document and copy it. Then switch to your terminal window and paste the statement into `mysql`.

The procedure sounds cumbersome when written out like that, but when you're actually carrying it out, it provides a way to enter statements quickly and with no typing. With a little practice, it becomes second nature.

You can use copy and paste in the other direction, too (from your terminal window to your statement file). On Unix, when you enter statements in `mysql`, they are saved in a file named `.mysql_history` in your home directory. If you manually enter a statement that you want to save for further reference, quit `mysql`, open `.mysql_history` in an editor, and then copy and paste the statement from `.mysql_history` into your statement file.

1.5.2.3 Using `mysql` to Execute Script Files

It's not necessary to run `mysql` interactively. `mysql` can read input from a file in noninteractive (batch) mode. This is useful for statements that you run periodically because you certainly don't want to retype them every time you run them. It's easier to put the statements into a file once, and then have `mysql` execute the contents of the file as needed.

Suppose that you have a query to find Historical League members who have an interest in a particular area of U.S. history by looking in the `interests` column of the `member` table. For example, to find members with an interest in the Great Depression, you can write the query like this:

```
SELECT last_name, first_name, email, interests FROM member
WHERE interests LIKE '%depression%'
ORDER BY last_name, first_name;
```

Put the query in a file `interests.sql`, and then execute it by feeding it to `mysql` like this:

```
% mysql sampdb < interests.sql
```

By default, `mysql` produces output in tab-delimited format when run in batch mode. If you want the same kind of table-format output you get when you run `mysql` interactively, use the `-t` option:

```
% mysql -t sampdb < interests.sql
```

If you want to save the output, redirect it to a file:

```
% mysql -t sampdb < interests.sql > interests.out
```

If you are already running `mysql`, execute the contents of the file by using a `source` command:

```
mysql> source interests.sql
```

To use the query to find members with an interest in Thomas Jefferson, you could edit the query file to change `depression` to `Jefferson` and then run `mysql` again. That works okay as long as you don't use the query very often. If you do, a better method is needed. On Unix, one way to make the query more flexible is to put it in a shell script that takes an argument from the script command line and uses it to change the text of the query. That parameterizes the query so that you can specify the `interests` value when you run the script. To see how this works, write a little shell script, `interests.sh`:

```
#!/bin/sh
# interests.sh - find USHL members with particular interests
if [ $# -ne 1 ]; then echo 'Please specify one keyword'; exit; fi
mysql -t sampdb <<QUERY_INPUT
SELECT last_name, first_name, email, interests FROM member
WHERE interests LIKE '%$1%'
ORDER BY last_name, first_name;
QUERY_INPUT
```

The third line makes sure that there is one argument on the command line; it prints a short message and exits otherwise. Everything between `<<QUERY_INPUT` and the final `QUERY_INPUT` line becomes the input to `mysql`. Within the text of the query, the shell replaces the reference to `$1` with the argument from the command line. (In shell scripts, `$1`, `$2`, ... refer to the command arguments.) This causes the query to reflect whatever keyword you specify on the command line when you run the script.

Before you can run the script, you must make it executable:

```
% chmod +x interests.sh
```

Now you don't need to edit the script each time you run it. Just tell it what you're looking for on the command line:

```
% ./interests.sh depression
% ./interests.sh Jefferson
```

The `interests.sh` script is located in the `misc` directory of the `sampdb` distribution. An equivalent Windows batch file, `interests.bat`, is provided there as well.

> **Note**
>
> I suggest that you not install scripts like these publicly because they do not perform any safety checks on the arguments and thus are subject to SQL injection attacks. Suppose someone invokes the script like this:
>
> ```
> % ./interests.sh "Jefferson';DROP DATABASE sampdb;"
> ```
>
> The effect of this is to "inject" a DROP DATABASE statement into the statement to the `mysql` input in such a way that it actually executes.

1.6 Where to Now?

You know quite a bit about using MySQL now. You can set up a database and create tables. You can put rows into those tables, retrieve them in various ways, change them, or delete them. But the tutorial in this chapter only scratches the surface, and there's still a lot to know about MySQL. You can see this by considering the current state of our `sampdb` database. We've created it and its tables and populated them with some initial data. During the process we've seen how to write some of the queries needed for answering questions about the information in the database. But much remains to be done. For example, we have no convenient interactive way to enter new score rows for the grade-keeping project or new member entries for the Historical League directory. We have no convenient way to edit existing rows. And we still can't generate the printed or online forms of the League directory. These tasks and others are revisited in the upcoming chapters, particularly in Chapter 8, "Writing MySQL Programs Using Perl DBI," and Chapter 9, "Writing MySQL Programs Using PHP."

Where you go next in this book depends on what you're interested in. If you want to see how to finish the job we've started with our Historical League and grade-keeping projects, Part II covers how to write MySQL-based programs. If you're going to serve as the MySQL administrator for your site, Part III of this book deals with administrative tasks. However, I recommend acquiring additional general background in using MySQL first, by reading the remaining chapters in Part I. These chapters provide further information on the syntax and use of SQL statements, discuss how MySQL handles data, and show how to make your queries run faster. A good grounding in these topics will stand you in good stead no matter the context in which you use MySQL—whether you're running `mysql`, writing your own programs, or acting as a database administrator.

Using SQL to Manage Data

Structured Query Language (SQL) is the language that the MySQL server understands and is the means by which you tell the server how to perform data management operations. Therefore, fluency with SQL is necessary for effective communication with the server. When you use a program such as the `mysql` client, it functions primarily as a way for you to send SQL statements to the server to be executed. If you write programs in a language that has a MySQL interface, such as the Perl DBI module or PHP PDO extension, these interfaces enable you to communicate with the server by issuing SQL statements.

Chapter 1, "Getting Started with MySQL," presents a tutorial introduction to many of MySQL's capabilities, including some basic use of SQL. Now we'll build on that material to go into more detail about several areas of SQL implemented by MySQL:

- Changing the SQL mode to affect server behavior
- Naming rules for referring to elements of databases
- Using multiple character sets
- Creating and destroying databases, tables, and indexes
- Obtaining information about databases and their contents
- Retrieving data using joins, subqueries, and unions
- Creating views that provide alternative ways of looking at data in tables
- Using multiple-table deletes and updates
- Performing transactions that enable statements to be grouped or canceled
- Setting up foreign key relationships
- Using the FULLTEXT search engine

The items just listed cover a broad range of topics of what you can do with SQL. Other chapters provide additional SQL-related information:

- Chapter 4, "Stored Programs," discusses how to create and use stored functions and procedures, triggers, and events.

- Chapter 12, "General MySQL Administration," describes how administrative statements such as GRANT and REVOKE are used for managing user accounts. It also discusses the privilege system that controls what operations accounts are allowed to perform.

- Appendix E, "SQL Syntax Reference," shows the syntax for SQL statements implemented by MySQL. It also covers the syntax for using comments in your SQL statements.

You can also consult the MySQL Reference Manual, which is especially useful for changes made in the most recent versions of MySQL.

2.1 The Server SQL Mode

The MySQL server has a system variable named sql_mode that enables you to configure the SQL mode, which affects several aspects of SQL statement execution. This variable can be set globally and individual clients can change the mode to affect their own connection to the server. This means that any client can change how the server behaves in relation to itself without impact on other clients.

The SQL mode affects behaviors such as handling of invalid values during data entry and identifier quoting. The following list describes a few of the possible mode values:

- STRICT_ALL_TABLES and STRICT_TRANS_TABLES enable "strict" mode. In strict mode, the server is more restrictive about accepting bad data values. (Specifically, it rejects bad values rather than changing them to the closest legal value.)

- TRADITIONAL is another composite mode. It is like strict mode, but enables other modes that impose additional constraints for even stricter data checking. Traditional mode causes the server to behave like more traditional SQL servers with regard to how it handles bad data values.

- ANSI_QUOTES tells the server to recognize double quote as an identifier quoting character.

- PIPES_AS_CONCAT causes || to be treated as the standard SQL string concatenation operator rather than as a synonym for the OR operator.

- ANSI is a composite mode. It turns on ANSI_QUOTES, PIPES_AS_CONCAT, and several other mode values that result in server behavior more like standard SQL than how it operates by default.

Section 3.3, "How MySQL Handles Invalid Data Values," discusses the SQL mode values that affect handling of erroneous or missing values during data entry. Appendix D, "System, Status, and User Variable Reference," describes the full set of allowable mode values for the sql_mode variable.

When you set the SQL mode, specify a value consisting of one or more mode values separated by commas, or an empty string to clear the value. Mode values are not case sensitive.

To set the SQL mode when you start the server, use the `--sql-mode` option on the `mysqld` command line or in an option file. On the command line, you might use a setting like one of these:

```
--sql-mode="TRADITIONAL"
--sql-mode="ANSI_QUOTES,PIPES_AS_CONCAT"
```

To change the SQL mode at runtime, set the `sql_mode` system variable with a SET statement.

Any client can set its own session-specific SQL mode:

```
SET sql_mode = 'TRADITIONAL';
```

To set the SQL mode globally, add the GLOBAL keyword:

```
SET GLOBAL sql_mode = 'TRADITIONAL';
```

Setting the global variable requires the SUPER administrative privilege. The value becomes the default SQL mode for clients that connect afterward.

To determine the current value of the session or global SQL mode, use these statements:

```
SELECT @@SESSION.sql_mode;
SELECT @@GLOBAL.sql_mode;
```

The value returned consists of a comma-separated list of enabled modes, or an empty value if no modes are enabled.

For additional information on user privileges and setting or checking system variables, see Chapter 12.

2.2 MySQL Identifier Syntax and Naming Rules

Almost every SQL statement uses identifiers in some way to refer to a database or its constituent elements such as tables or views, columns, indexes, stored routines, triggers, or events. When you refer to elements of databases, identifiers must conform to the following rules.

Legal characters in identifiers. Unquoted identifiers may consist of alphanumeric characters in the system character set (`utf8`), plus the characters '_' and '$'. Identifiers can start with any character that is legal in an identifier, including a digit. However, an unquoted identifier cannot consist entirely of digits because that would make it indistinguishable from a number. MySQL's support for identifiers that begin with a number is somewhat unusual among database systems. If you use such an identifier, be particularly careful if it contains an 'E' or 'e' because those characters can lead to ambiguous expressions. For example, the expression `23e + 14` (with spaces surrounding the '+' sign) means column `23e` plus the number 14, but what about `23e+14`? Does it mean the same thing, or is it a number in scientific notation?

Identifiers can be quoted (delimited) within backtick characters ('`'), which allows use of any character except a byte with value 0 or 255:

```
CREATE TABLE `my table` (`my-int-column` INT);
```

Quoting is useful when an identifier is an SQL reserved word or contains spaces or other special characters. Quoting an identifier also enables it to be entirely numeric, something that is not true of unquoted identifiers. To include an identifier quote character within a quoted identifier, double it.

Prior to MySQL 5.1.6, there are two additional constraints for database and table identifiers, even for those that are quoted. First, you cannot use the '.' character, because it is used as the separator character in qualified names such as `db_name.tbl_name` or `db_name.tbl_name.col_name`. Second, you cannot use the Unix or Windows pathname separator characters ('/' or '\'). The pathname separator is disallowed in database and table identifiers because databases are represented on disk by directories, and tables are represented on disk by at least one file. Consequently, these types of identifiers must contain only characters that are legal in directory names and filenames. The Unix pathname separator is disallowed on Windows (and vice versa) to make it easier to transfer databases and tables between servers running on different platforms. (Suppose that you were allowed to use a slash in a table name on Windows. That would make it impossible to move the table to Unix, because filenames on that platform cannot contain slashes.)

As of MySQL 5.1.6, the mapping of identifiers as used in SQL statements onto directory names and filenames has been modified to enable use of characters that are illegal in earlier versions. In particular, the pathname characters ('/' or '\'), as well as '.' are legal, as long as the identifier is quoted.

Your operating system might impose additional constraints on database and table identifiers. See Section 11.2.6, "Operating System Constraints on Database Object Names."

Aliases for column and table names can be fairly arbitrary. You should quote an alias within identifier quoting characters if it is an SQL reserved word, is entirely numeric, or contains spaces or other special characters. Column aliases also can be quoted with single quotes or double quotes.

Server SQL mode. If the `ANSI_QUOTES` SQL mode is enabled, you can quote identifiers with double quotes (although backticks still are allowable).

```
CREATE TABLE "my table" ("my-int-column" INT);
```

> **Note**
>
> Enabling `ANSI_QUOTES` has the additional effect that string literals must be written using single quotes. If you use double quotes, the server will interpret the value as an identifier, not as a string.

Names of built-in functions normally are not reserved and can be used as identifiers without quotes. However, if the `IGNORE_SPACE` SQL mode is enabled, function names become reserved and must be quoted if used as identifiers.

For instructions on setting the SQL mode, see Section 2.1, "The Server SQL Mode."

Identifier length. Most identifiers have a maximum length of 64 characters. The maximum length for aliases is 256 characters.

Identifier qualifiers. Depending on context, an identifier might need to be qualified to make clear what it refers to. To refer to a database, just specify its name:

```
USE db_name;
SHOW TABLES FROM db_name;
```

To refer to a table, you have two choices:

- A fully qualified table name consists of a database identifier and a table identifier:
```
SHOW COLUMNS FROM db_name.tbl_name;
SELECT * FROM db_name.tbl_name;
```

- A table identifier by itself refers to a table in the default (current) database. If sampdb is the default database, the following statements are equivalent:
```
SELECT * FROM member;
SELECT * FROM sampdb.member;
```

If no database has been selected, you cannot refer to a table without specifying a database qualifier because it is unclear which database the table belongs to.

The same considerations about qualifying table names apply to names of views (which are "virtual" tables) and stored programs.

To refer to a table column, there are three choices:

- A name written as db_name.tbl_name.col_name is fully qualified.

- A partially qualified name written as tbl_name.col_name refers to a column in the named table in the default database.

- An unqualified name written simply as col_name refers to whatever table is indicated by the surrounding context. The following two queries use the same column names, but the context supplied by the FROM clause of each statement indicates the table from which to select the columns:
```
SELECT last_name, first_name FROM president;
SELECT last_name, first_name FROM member;
```

It's usually unnecessary to supply fully qualified names, although it's always legal to do so if you like. If you select a database with a USE statement, that database becomes the default database and is implicit in every unqualified table reference. If you're using a SELECT statement that refers to only one table, that table is implicit for every column reference in the statement. It's necessary to qualify identifiers only when a table or database cannot be determined from context. For example, if a statement refers to tables from multiple databases, any table not in the default database must be referenced using the db_name.tbl_name form to let MySQL know which database contains the table. Similarly, if a query uses multiple tables and refers to a column name that is used in more than one table, it's necessary to qualify the column identifier with a table identifier to make it clear which column you mean.

If you use quotes when referring to a qualified name, quote individual identifiers within the name separately. For example:

```
SELECT * FROM `sampdb`.`member` WHERE `sampdb`.`member`.`member_id` > 100;
```

Do not quote the name as a whole. This statement is incorrect:

```
SELECT * FROM `sampdb.member` WHERE `sampdb.member.member_id` > 100;
```

The requirement that a reserved word be quoted if used as an identifier is waived if the word follows a qualifier period because context then dictates that the reserved word is an identifier.

2.3 Case Sensitivity in SQL Statements

Case sensitivity rules in SQL statements vary for different statement elements, and also depend on what you are referring to and the operating system of the machine on which the server is running.

SQL keywords and function names. Keywords and function names are not case sensitive. They can be given in any lettercase. The following statements all retrieve the same information (although the column headings displayed for the result will differ in lettercase):

```
SELECT NOW();
select now();
sElEcT nOw();
```

Database, table, and view names. MySQL represents databases and tables using directories and files in the underlying filesystem on the server host. As a result, the default case sensitivity of database and table names depends on the way the operating system on that host treats filenames. Windows filenames are not case sensitive, so a MySQL server running on Windows does not treat database and table names as case sensitive. Servers running on Unix usually treat database and table names as case sensitive because Unix filenames are case sensitive. An exception is that names in HFS+ filesystems under Mac OS X are not case sensitive.

MySQL represents each view using a file, so the preceding remarks about tables also apply to views.

Stored program names. Stored function and procedure names and event names are not case sensitive. Trigger names are case sensitive, which differs from standard SQL.

Column and index names. Column and index names are not case sensitive in MySQL. The following statements all retrieve the same information:

```
SELECT name FROM student;
SELECT NAME FROM student;
SELECT nAmE FROM student;
```

Alias names. By default, table aliases are case sensitive. You can specify an alias in any lettercase (upper, lower, or mixed), but if you use it multiple times in a statement, you must use the same lettercase each time. If the `lower_case_table_names` variable is nonzero, table aliases are not case sensitive.

String values. Case sensitivity of a string value depends on whether it is a binary or non-binary string, and, for a non-binary string, on the collation of its character set. This is true for literal strings and the contents of string columns. For further information, see Section 3.1.2, "String Values."

You should consider lettercase issues when you create databases and tables on a machine with case sensitive filenames if it is possible that you will someday move them to a machine where filenames are not case sensitive. Suppose that you create two tables named abc and ABC on a Unix server where those names are treated differently. You would have problems moving the tables to a Windows machine, where abc and ABC would not be distinguishable because names are not case sensitive. You would also have trouble replicating the tables from a Unix master server to a Windows slave server.

One way to avoid having case sensitivity become an issue is to pick a given lettercase and always create databases and tables using names in that lettercase. Then case of names won't be a problem if you move a database to a different server. I recommend using lowercase. This will help also if you are using InnoDB tables, because InnoDB stores database and table names internally in lowercase.

To force creation of databases and tables with lowercase names even if not specified that way in CREATE statements, configure the server by setting the lower_case_table_names system variable. See Section 11.2.6, "Operating System Constraints on Database Object Names," for more information.

Regardless of whether a database or table name is case sensitive on your system, you must refer to it using the same lettercase throughout a given query. That is not true for SQL keywords, function names, or column and index names, all of which may be referred to in varying lettercase style throughout a query. However, the query will be more readable if you use a consistent lettercase rather than mixed lettercase (SelECt NamE FrOm ...).

2.4 Character Set Support

MySQL supports multiple character sets, and character sets can be specified independently at the server, database, table, column, or string constant level. For example, if you want a table's columns to use latin1 by default, but also to include a Hebrew column and a Greek column, you can do that. In addition, you can explicitly specify collations (sorting orders). It is possible to find out what character sets and collations are available, and to convert data from one character set to another.

This section provides general background on using MySQL's character set support. Chapter 3, "Data Types," provides more specific discussion of character sets, collations, binary versus non-binary strings, and how to define and work with character-based table columns. Chapter 12, discusses how to configure which character sets the server makes available.

MySQL character set support provides the following features:

- The server allows simultaneous use of multiple character sets.
- A given character set can have one or more collations. You can choose the collation most appropriate for your applications.

- Unicode support is provided by the `utf8` and `ucs2` character sets, with additional sets available as of MySQL 6.0.4.

- You can specify character sets at the server, database, table, column, and string constant level:

  - The server has a default character set.

  - `CREATE DATABASE` enables you to assign the database character set, and `ALTER DATABASE` enables you to change it.

  - `CREATE TABLE` and `ALTER TABLE` have clauses for table- and column-level character set assignment. (Details are given in Chapter 3.)

  - The character set for string constants is determined by context or can be specified explicitly.

- Functions and operators are available for converting individual values from one character set to another or for determining the character set of a value. Similarly, the `COLLATE` operator can be used to alter the collation of a string and the `COLLATION()` function returns the collation of a string.

- `SHOW` statements and `INFORMATION_SCHEMA` tables provide information about the available character sets and collations.

- The server automatically reorders indexes when you change the collation of an indexed character column.

You cannot mix character sets within a string, or use different character sets for different rows of a given column. However, by using a Unicode character set (which represents characters for many languages within a single encoding), you may be able to implement multi-lingual support of the type you desire.

2.4.1 Specifying Character Sets

Character set and collation assignments can be made at several levels, from the default used by the server to the character set used for individual strings.

The server's default character set and collation are built in at compile time. You can override them at server startup by using the `--character-set-server` and `--collation-server` options or at runtime by setting the `character_set_server` and `collation_server` system variables. If you specify only the character set, its default collation becomes the server's default collation. If you specify a collation, it must be compatible with the character set. (A collation is compatible with a character set if its name begins with the character set name. For example, `utf8_danish_ci` is compatible with `utf8` but not with `latin1`.)

In SQL statements that create databases and tables, two clauses are used for specifying database, table, and column character set and collation values:

```
CHARACTER SET charset
COLLATE collation
```

CHARSET can be used as a synonym for CHARACTER SET. *charset* is the name of a character set supported by the server, and *collation* is the name of one of that character set's collations. These clauses can be specified together or separately. If both are given, the collation name must be compatible with the character set. If only CHARACTER SET is given, its default collation is used. If only COLLATE is given, the character set is implicit in the first part of the character set name. These rules apply at several levels:

- To specify a default character set and collation for a database when you create it, use this statement:

  ```
  CREATE DATABASE db_name CHARACTER SET charset COLLATE collation;
  ```

  If no character set or collation is given, the server defaults are used for the database.

- To specify a default character set and collation for a table, use CHARACTER SET and COLLATE table options at table creation time:

  ```
  CREATE TABLE tbl_name (...) CHARACTER SET charset COLLATE collation;
  ```

  If no character set or collation is given, the database defaults are used for the table.

- Columns in a table can be assigned a character set and collation explicitly with CHARACTER SET and COLLATE attributes. For example:

  ```
  c CHAR(10) CHARACTER SET charset COLLATE collation
  ```

  If no character set or collation is given, the table defaults are used for the column. These attributes apply to the CHAR, VARCHAR, TEXT, ENUM, and SET data types.

It's also possible to sort string values according to a specific collation by using the COLLATE operator. For example, if c is a latin1 column that has a collation of latin1_swedish_ci, but you want to order it using Spanish sorting rules, do this:

```
SELECT c FROM t ORDER BY c COLLATE latin1_spanish_ci;
```

2.4.2 Determining Character Set Availability and Current Settings

To find out which character sets and collations are available, use these statements:

```
SHOW CHARACTER SET;
SHOW COLLATION;
```

Each statement supports a LIKE clause that narrows the results to those character set or collation names matching a pattern. For example, this statement lists the Latin-based character sets:

```
mysql> SHOW CHARACTER SET LIKE 'latin%';
```

Charset	Description	Default collation	Maxlen
latin1	cp1252 West European	latin1_swedish_ci	1
latin2	ISO 8859-2 Central European	latin2_general_ci	1

```
| latin5  | ISO 8859-9 Turkish         | latin5_turkish_ci |       1 |
| latin7  | ISO 8859-13 Baltic         | latin7_general_ci |       1 |
+---------+----------------------------+-------------------+---------+
```

This statement lists the collations available for the `utf8` character set (collation names always begin with the character set name):

```
mysql> SHOW COLLATION LIKE 'utf8%';
+--------------------+---------+-----+---------+----------+---------+
| Collation          | Charset | Id  | Default | Compiled | Sortlen |
+--------------------+---------+-----+---------+----------+---------+
| utf8_general_ci    | utf8    |  33 | Yes     | Yes      |       1 |
| utf8_bin           | utf8    |  83 |         | Yes      |       1 |
| utf8_unicode_ci    | utf8    | 192 |         | Yes      |       8 |
| utf8_icelandic_ci  | utf8    | 193 |         | Yes      |       8 |
| utf8_latvian_ci    | utf8    | 194 |         | Yes      |       8 |
| utf8_romanian_ci   | utf8    | 195 |         | Yes      |       8 |
| utf8_slovenian_ci  | utf8    | 196 |         | Yes      |       8 |
...
```

As can be seen in the output from these statements, each character set has at least one collation and one of them is its default collation.

Information about the available character sets and collations is also available in the `CHARACTER_SETS` and `COLLATIONS` tables in the `INFORMATION_SCHEMA` database (see Section 2.7, "Obtaining Database Metadata").

To display the server's current character set and collation settings, use `SHOW VARIABLES`:

```
mysql> SHOW VARIABLES LIKE 'character\_set\_%';
+--------------------------+--------+
| Variable_name            | Value  |
+--------------------------+--------+
| character_set_client     | latin1 |
| character_set_connection | latin1 |
| character_set_database   | latin1 |
| character_set_filesystem | binary |
| character_set_results    | latin1 |
| character_set_server     | latin1 |
| character_set_system     | utf8   |
+--------------------------+--------+
mysql> SHOW VARIABLES LIKE 'collation\_%';
+----------------------+-------------------+
| Variable_name        | Value             |
+----------------------+-------------------+
| collation_connection | latin1_swedish_ci |
| collation_database   | latin1_swedish_ci |
| collation_server     | latin1_swedish_ci |
+----------------------+-------------------+
```

Several of these system variables affect how a client communicates with the server after establishing a connection. For details, refer to Section 3.1.2.2, "Character Set-Related System Variables."

2.4.3 Unicode Support

One of the reasons there are so many character sets is that different character encodings have been developed for different languages. This presents several problems. For example, a given character that is common to several languages might be represented by different numeric values in different encodings. Also, different languages require different numbers of bytes to represent characters. The latin1 character set is small enough that every character fits in a single byte, but languages such as those used in Japan and China contain so many characters that they require multiple bytes per character.

The goal of Unicode is to provide a unified character-encoding system within which character sets for all languages can be represented in a consistent manner.

2.4.3.1 Unicode Support Prior to MySQL 6.0

Prior to MySQL 6.0.4, Unicode support includes only characters in the Basic Multilingual Plane (BMP), which is limited to 65,536 characters. There is no support for supplementary characters outside the BMP. Unicode capabilities are provided through two character sets:

- The ucs2 character set corresponds to the Unicode UCS-2 encoding. It represents each character using two bytes, most significant byte first. This character set does not represent characters that require more than two bytes. UCS is an abbreviation for Universal Character Set.

- The utf8 character set has a variable-length format in which characters are represented using from one to three bytes. It corresponds to the Unicode UTF-8 encoding. UTF is an abbreviation for Unicode Transformation Format.

2.4.3.2 Unicode Support in MySQL 6.0 and Up

As of MySQL 6.0.4, Unicode support includes supplementary characters that lie outside the Basic Multilingual Plane, which has the following implications:

- The ucs2 character set is not changed in MySQL 6.0. Each character still takes two bytes. However, there are new utf16 and utf32 character sets that are like ucs2 but with support for supplementary characters. For utf16, BMP characters take two bytes (as for ucs2) and supplementary characters take four bytes. For utf32, all characters take four bytes.

- Previously, utf8 characters required from one to three bytes each. With support for supplementary characters, utf8 characters require from one to four bytes each.

- For databases and tables created before MySQL 6.0 that used the utf8 character set, they will display as using the utf8mb3 character set in MySQL 6.0. (For example, you will see `utf8mb3` if you use `SHOW CREATE TABLE`.) Except for the name, `utf8mb3` in MySQL 6.0 is exactly the same as `utf8` before 6.0.

To convert tables from the old (three-byte) `utf8` to the new (four-byte) `utf8`, dump the tables with `mysqldump` before upgrading to MySQL 6.0 and reload the dump file after upgrading. Be sure to also run `mysql_upgrade` after upgrading to make sure that any additional required changes are made to the system tables in the `mysql` database.

2.5 Selecting, Creating, Dropping, and Altering Databases

MySQL provides several database-level statements: `USE` for selecting a default database, `CREATE DATABASE` for creating databases, `DROP DATABASE` for removing them, and `ALTER DATABASE` for modifying global database characteristics.

The keyword `SCHEMA` is a synonym for `DATABASE` in any statement where the latter occurs.

2.5.1 Selecting Databases

The `USE` statement selects a database to make it the default (current) database for a given connection to the server:

```
USE db_name;
```

You must have some access privilege for the database or you cannot select it.

It is not strictly necessary to select a database explicitly. If you have access to a database, you can use its tables without selecting it first if you use qualified names that identify both the database and the table. For example, to retrieve the contents of the `president` table in the `sampdb` database without selecting the database first, write the query like this:

```
SELECT * FROM sampdb.president;
```

However, it's usually more convenient to refer to tables without having to specify a database qualifier.

Selecting a database doesn't mean that it must be the default for the duration of the connection. You can issue `USE` statements as necessary to switch between databases. Nor does selecting a database limit you to using tables only from that database. While one database is the default, you can refer to tables in other databases by qualifying their names with the appropriate database identifier.

When you disconnect from the server, any notion by the server of which database was the default for the connection disappears. If you connect to the server again, it doesn't remember what database you had selected previously.

2.5.2 Creating Databases

To create a database, use a CREATE DATABASE statement:

```
CREATE DATABASE db_name;
```

The conditions on database creation are that the name must be a legal identifier, the database must not already exist, and you must have sufficient privileges to create it.

When you create a database, the MySQL server creates a directory under its data directory that has the same name as the database. The new directory is called the database directory. The server also creates a db.opt file in the database directory for storing database attributes.

CREATE DATABASE supports several optional clauses. The full syntax is as follows:

```
CREATE DATABASE [IF NOT EXISTS] db_name
  [CHARACTER SET charset] [COLLATE collation];
```

Normally, an error occurs if you try to create a database that already exists. To suppress this error and create a database only if it does not already exist, add an IF NOT EXISTS clause:

```
CREATE DATABASE IF NOT EXISTS db_name;
```

By default, the server character set and collation become the database default character set and collation. You can use the CHARACTER SET and COLLATE clauses to set these database attributes explicitly. For example:

```
CREATE DATABASE mydb CHARACTER SET utf8 COLLATE utf8_icelandic_ci;
```

If CHARACTER SET is given without COLLATE, the default collation for the character set is used. If COLLATE is given without CHARACTER SET, the first part of the collation name determines the character set.

The character set must be one of those supported by the server, such as latin1 or sjis. The collation should be a legal collation for the character set. For further discussion of character sets and collations, see Chapter 3.

MySQL stores the database character set and collation attributes in the db.opt file. When you create a new table, if the table definition does not specify its own default character set and collation, the database defaults become the table defaults.

To see the definition for an existing database, use a SHOW CREATE DATABASE statement:

```
mysql> SHOW CREATE DATABASE mydb\G
*************************** 1. row ***************************
       Database: mydb
Create Database: CREATE DATABASE `mydb`
                 /*!40100 DEFAULT CHARACTER SET utf8
                 COLLATE utf8_icelandic_ci */
```

2.5.3 Dropping Databases

Dropping a database is as easy as creating one, assuming that you have sufficient privileges:

```
DROP DATABASE db_name;
```

The DROP DATABASE statement is not something to use with wild abandon. It removes the database and all its contents (tables, stored routines, and so forth), which are therefore gone forever unless you have been making backups regularly.

A database is represented by a directory under the data directory, and the directory is intended for storage of objects such as tables, views, and triggers. If a DROP DATABASE statement fails, the reason most likely is that the database directory contains files not associated with database objects. DROP DATABASE will not delete such files, and as a result will not delete the directory, either. This means that the database directory continues to exist and will show up if you issue a SHOW DATABASES statement. To really drop the database if this occurs, manually remove any extraneous files and subdirectories from the database directory, and then issue the DROP DATABASE statement again.

2.5.4 Altering Databases

The ALTER DATABASE statement makes changes to a database's global attributes. Currently, the only such attributes are the default character set and collation:

```
ALTER DATABASE [db_name] [CHARACTER SET charset] [COLLATE collation];
```

The earlier discussion for CREATE DATABASE describes the effect of the CHARACTER SET and COLLATE clauses, at least one of which must be given.

If you omit the database name, ALTER DATABASE applies to the default database.

2.6 Creating, Dropping, Indexing, and Altering Tables

MySQL enables you to create tables, drop (remove) them, and change their structure with the CREATE TABLE, DROP TABLE, and ALTER TABLE statements. The CREATE INDEX and DROP INDEX statements enable you to add or remove indexes on existing tables. The following sections provide the details for these statements, but first it's necessary to discuss the storage engines that MySQL supports for managing different types of tables.

2.6.1 Storage Engine Characteristics

MySQL supports multiple storage engines (or "table handlers" as they used to be known). Each storage engine implements tables that have a specific set of properties or characteristics. Table 2.1 briefly describes the storage engines currently available in MySQL distributions, and later discussion provides more detail about individual engine features. In MySQL 5.0 and up, all of the engines shown are available except Falcon, which requires MySQL 6.0.

Table 2.1   **MySQL Storage Engines**

Storage Engine	Description
ARCHIVE	Archival storage (no modification of rows after insertion)
BLACKHOLE	Engine that discards writes and returns empty reads
CSV	Storage in comma-separated values format
EXAMPLE	Example ("stub") storage engine
Falcon	Transactional engine
FEDERATED	Engine for accessing remote tables
InnoDB	Transactional engine with foreign keys
MEMORY	In-memory tables
MERGE	Manages collections of MyISAM tables
MyISAM	The default storage engine
NDB	The engine for MySQL Cluster

Some of the engine names have synonyms. MRG_MyISAM and NDBCLUSTER are synonyms for MERGE and NDB, respectively. The MEMORY and InnoDB storage engines originally were known as HEAP and Innobase, respectively. The latter names are still recognized but deprecated.

For MySQL 5.1 and up, the server is based on a "pluggable" architecture that provides a standard interface and that enables engines to be loaded and unloaded at runtime. Consequently, storage engines from third-party developers can be integrated easily into the server.

2.6.1.1 Checking Which Storage Engines Are Available

The engines actually available to you for a given server depend on your version of MySQL, how the server was configured at build time, and the options with which it was started. For details on configuring and activating storage engines, see Section 12.7, "Storage Engine Configuration."

To see which storage engines the server knows about, use the SHOW ENGINES statement. It provides information that helps you determine the answers to questions such as which transactional storage engines are available. The output shown here uses the format from MySQL 5.0:

```
mysql> SHOW ENGINES\G
*************************** 1. row ***************************
  Engine: MyISAM
 Support: DEFAULT
 Comment: Default engine as of MySQL 3.23 with great performance
```

```
*************************** 2. row ***************************
  Engine: MEMORY
 Support: YES
 Comment: Hash based, stored in memory, useful for temporary tables
*************************** 3. row ***************************
  Engine: InnoDB
 Support: YES
 Comment: Supports transactions, row-level locking, and foreign keys
...
```

The value in the `Support` column is `YES` or `NO` to indicate that the engine is or is not available, `DISABLED` if the engine is present but turned off, or `DEFAULT` for the storage engine that the server uses by default. The engine designated as `DEFAULT` should be considered available.

`SHOW ENGINES` as of MySQL 5.1 displays the 5.0 columns plus columns related to transaction support:

```
mysql> SHOW ENGINES\G
*************************** 1. row ***************************
      Engine: InnoDB
     Support: YES
     Comment: Supports transactions, row-level locking, and foreign keys
Transactions: YES
          XA: YES
  Savepoints: YES
...
*************************** 8. row ***************************
      Engine: MyISAM
     Support: DEFAULT
     Comment: Default engine as of MySQL 3.23 with great performance
Transactions: NO
          XA: NO
  Savepoints: NO
...
```

The `Transactions` column indicates whether an engine supports transactions. `XA` and `Savepoints` indicate whether an engine supports distributed transactions (not covered in this book) and partial transaction rollback.

MySQL 5.1 and up has an `INFORMATION_SCHEMA` table named `ENGINES` that provides the same information as `SHOW ENGINES`. You can use this table as follows to check for available engines that support transactions (the output shown is from MySQL 6.0, which includes the Falcon storage engine):

```
mysql> SELECT ENGINE FROM INFORMATION_SCHEMA.ENGINES
    -> WHERE TRANSACTIONS = 'YES';
+--------+
| ENGINE |
+--------+
```

```
| Falcon |
| InnoDB |
+--------+
```

2.6.1.2 Table Representation on Disk

Each time you create a table, MySQL creates a disk file that contains the table's format (that is, its definition). The format file has a basename that is the same as the table name and an .frm extension. That is, for a table named t, the format file is named t.frm. The server creates the file in the database directory for the database that the table belongs to. The .frm file is an invariant because there is one for every table, no matter which storage engine manages the table. The name of a table as used in SQL statements might differ from the table-name part of the associated .frm file if the name contains characters that are problematic in filenames. See Section 11.2.6, "Operating System Constraints on Database Object Names," for a description of the rules for mapping from SQL names to filenames.

Individual storage engines may also create other files that are unique to the table, to be used for storing the table's content. For a given table, any files specific to it are located in the database directory for the database that contains the table. Table 2.2 shows the filename extensions for the table-specific files that some storage engines create.

Table 2.2   **Table Files Created by Storage Engines**

Storage Engine	Files on Disk
MyISAM	.MYD (data), .MYI (indexes)
MERGE	.MRG (list of constituent MyISAM table names)
InnoDB	.ibd (data and indexes)
ARCHIVE	.ARZ (data), .ARM (metadata)
CSV	.CSV (data), .CSM (metadata)

For some storage engines, the format file is the only file specifically associated with a particular table. Other engines may store table content elsewhere than on disk, or may use one or more tablespaces (storage areas shared by multiple tables):

- MEMORY table contents are stored in memory, not on disk.
- By default, InnoDB stores table data and indexes in its shared tablespace. That is, all InnoDB table contents are managed within a shared storage area, not within files specific to a particular table. InnoDB creates .ibd files only if you configure it to use individual per-table tablespaces.
- Falcon stores table data and indexes in tablespace files. There is a default Falcon tablespace, and you can create others on demand. Any of them can store the contents of multiple tables.

- The BLACKHOLE and EXAMPLE storage engines don't actually store any data, so they need not create any files.
- The FEDERATED engine provides access to tables located at remote MySQL servers. It doesn't create any data files itself.

The following sections characterize the features and behavior of selected MySQL storage engines. For additional information about how engines represent tables physically, see Section 11.2.3, "Representation of Tables in the Filesystem."

2.6.1.3 The MyISAM Storage Engine

The MyISAM storage engine is the default engine in MySQL, unless you have configured your server otherwise. The following list describes some of its features:

- MyISAM provides key compression. It uses compression when storing runs of successive similar string index values. MyISAM also can compress runs of similar numeric index values because numeric values are stored with the high byte first. (Index values tend to vary faster in the low-order bytes, so high-order bytes are more subject to compression.) To enable numeric compression, use the `PACK_KEYS=1` option when creating a MyISAM table.
- MyISAM provides more features for `AUTO_INCREMENT` columns than do other storage engines. For more information, see Section 3.4, "Working with Sequences."
- Each MyISAM table has a flag that is set when the table is checked by the server or by the `myisamchk` program. MyISAM tables also have a flag indicating whether a table was closed properly when last used. If the server shuts down abnormally or the machine crashes, the flags can be used to detect tables that need to be checked. To do this automatically, start the server with the `--myisam-recover` option. This causes the server to check the table flags whenever it opens a MyISAM table and perform a table repair if necessary.
- MyISAM supports full-text searching through the use of `FULLTEXT` indexes.
- MyISAM supports spatial data types and `SPATIAL` indexes.

2.6.1.4 The MERGE Storage Engine

MERGE tables provide a means for grouping a set of MyISAM tables into a single logical unit. Querying a MERGE table in effect queries all the constituent tables. One advantage of this is that you can exceed the maximum table size allowed by the filesystem for individual MyISAM tables.

The tables that make up a MERGE table must all have the same structure. This means the columns in each table must be defined with the same names and types in the same order, and the indexes must be defined in the same way and in the same order. It is allowable to mix compressed and uncompressed tables. (To produce compressed tables, use `myisampack`; see Appendix F, "MySQL Program Reference.")

For an example, see Section 2.6.2.5, "Using MERGE Tables." Partitioned tables provide an alternative to the use of MERGE tables, and are not limited to MyISAM tables. See Section 2.6.2.6, "Using Partitioned Tables."

2.6.1.5 The MEMORY Storage Engine

The MEMORY storage engine uses tables that are stored in memory and that have fixed-length rows, two properties that make them very fast.

MEMORY tables are temporary in the sense that their contents disappear when the server terminates. That is, a MEMORY table still exists when the server restarts, but will be empty. However, in contrast to temporary tables created with CREATE TEMPORARY TABLE, MEMORY tables are visible to other clients.

MEMORY tables have characteristics that enable them to be handled more simply, and thus more quickly:

- By default, MEMORY tables use hashed indexes, which are very fast for equality comparisons but slow for range comparisons. Consequently, hashed indexes are used only for comparisons performed with the = and <=> equality operators, but not for comparison operators such as < or >. Hashed indexes also are not used in ORDER BY clauses for this reason.

- Rows are stored in MEMORY tables using fixed-length format for easier processing. A consequence is that you cannot use the BLOB and TEXT variable-length data types. VARCHAR is a variable-length type, but is allowed because it is treated internally as CHAR, a fixed-length type.

If you want to use a MEMORY table for comparisons that look for a range of values using operators such as <, >, or BETWEEN, you can use BTREE indexes instead. (See Section 2.6.4.2, "Creating Indexes.")

2.6.1.6 The InnoDB Storage Engine

The InnoDB storage engine was originally developed by Innobase Oy, which subsequently was acquired by Oracle. InnoDB offers these features:

- Transaction-safe tables with commit and rollback. Savepoints can be created to enable partial rollback.

- Automatic recovery after a crash.

- Foreign key and referential integrity support, including cascaded delete and update.

- Row-level locking and multi-versioning for good concurrency performance under query mix conditions that include both retrievals and updates.

- By default, InnoDB manages tables within a single shared tablespace, rather than by using table-specific files like most other storage engines. The tablespace can consist of multiple files and can include raw partitions. The InnoDB storage engine, in effect, treats the tablespace as a virtual filesystem within which it manages the contents of all InnoDB tables. Tables thus can exceed the size allowed by the filesystem for individual files. You can also configure InnoDB to use individual tablespaces, one per table. In this case, each table has an `.ibd` file in its database directory.

2.6.1.7 The Falcon Storage Engine

The Falcon storage engine is available as of MySQL 6.0. Falcon offers these features:

- Transaction-safe tables with commit and rollback. Savepoints can be created to enable partial rollback.
- Automatic recovery after a crash.
- Flexible locking levels and multi-versioning for good concurrency performance under query mix conditions that include both retrievals and updates.
- Row compression during storage and decompression during retrieval to save space.
- Low overhead for administration.

2.6.1.8 The FEDERATED Storage Engine

The FEDERATED storage engine provides access to tables that are managed by other MySQL servers. In other words, the contents of a FEDERATED table really are located remotely. When you create a FEDERATED table, you specify the host where the other server is running and provide the username and password of an account on that server. When you access the FEDERATED table, the local server connects to the remote server using this account. For an example, see Section 2.6.2.7, "Using FEDERATED Tables."

2.6.1.9 The NDB Storage Engine

NDB is MySQL's cluster storage engine. For this storage engine, the MySQL server actually acts as a client to a cluster of other processes that provide access to the NDB tables. Cluster node processes communicate with each other to manage tables in memory. The tables are replicated among cluster processes for redundancy. Memory storage provides high performance, and the cluster provides high availability because it survives failure of any given node.

NDB configuration and use is beyond the scope of this book and is not covered further here. See the MySQL Reference Manual for current details.

2.6.1.10 Other Storage Engines

There are several other MySQL storage engines that I will group here under the "miscellaneous" category:

- The ARCHIVE engine provides archival storage. It's intended for storage of large numbers of rows that are written once and never modified thereafter. For this reason, it supports only a limited number of statements. INSERT and SELECT work, but

REPLACE always acts like INSERT, and you cannot use DELETE or UPDATE. Rows are compressed during storage and decompressed during retrieval to save space. The ARCHIVE engine does not support indexing until MySQL 5.1.6, at which point an ARCHIVE table can include an indexed AUTO_INCREMENT column; other columns still cannot be indexed.

- The BLACKHOLE engine creates tables for which writes are ignored and reads return nothing.

- The CSV engine stores data in comma-separated values format. For each table, it creates a .csv file in the database directory. This is a plain text file in which each table row appears as a single line. The CSV engine does not support indexing.

- The EXAMPLE engine is a minimal demonstration of how to get started writing a storage engine. It exists mainly for developers to examine its source code and study the basic concepts involved in hooking a storage engine into the server.

2.6.1.11 Storage Engine Portability Characteristics

Any table managed by a given MySQL server is portable to another server in the sense that you can dump it into a text file with mysqldump, move the dump file to the machine where the other server runs, and load the file to re-create the table. Another kind of portability is "binary portability," which means that you can directly copy the disk files that represent the table to another machine, install them into the corresponding locations under the data directory, and expect the MySQL server there to be able to use the table.

A general condition for binary portability of tables is that the source and destination servers must be feature compatible. For example, the destination server must support the storage engine that manages the tables. If the server does not have the appropriate engine, it cannot access tables created by that engine on the source server.

Some storage engines create tables that are binary portable and some do not. The following list summarizes binary portability for individual engines:

- MyISAM and InnoDB tables are stored in machine-independent format and are binary portable, assuming that your processor uses two's-complement integer arithmetic and IEEE floating-point format. Unless you have some kind of oddball machine, neither of these conditions should present any real issues. In practice, you're probably most likely to see portability-compromising variation in hardware if you're using an embedded server built for a special-purpose device, as these devices sometimes use processors that have nonstandard operating characteristics.

- MERGE tables are portable if their constituent MyISAM files are portable.

- MEMORY tables are not binary portable because their contents are stored in memory, not on disk.

- CSV tables are binary portable because their .csv data files are plain text.

- BLACKHOLE tables are binary portable because they contain no data.

- For the FEDERATED engine, the concept of portability does not apply because the contents of a FEDERATED table are stored by another server.
- Falcon log and tablespace files are stored in a machine-dependent format. They are binary portable only between machines that have identical hardware characteristics. For example, you cannot move the Falcon files from a little-endian machine to a big-endian machine.

The requirements described earlier for binary portability of MyISAM and InnoDB tables between two machines are that the tables either contain no floating-point columns, or that both machines use the same floating-point storage format. "Floating-point" means FLOAT and DOUBLE here. DECIMAL columns contain fixed-point values that use a portable storage format.

For InnoDB, an additional condition for binary portability is that database and table names should be lowercase. InnoDB stores these names in lowercase in its data dictionary, but the .frm file is created using the table name lettercase that you used in the CREATE TABLE statement. This can result in a case-sensitivity mismatch if you create databases or tables using names with uppercase characters and then try to move them to a platform with differing filename case sensitivity.

For InnoDB, binary portability must be assessed for all InnoDB tables taken as a whole, not at the individual table level. By default, the InnoDB storage engine stores the contents of all its tables within a shared tablespace rather than within table-specific files. Consequently, it's the InnoDB tablespace files that are or are not portable, not individual InnoDB tables. This means that the floating-point portability constraint applies if *any* InnoDB table uses floating-point columns. Even if you configure InnoDB to use individual (per-table) tablespaces, the data dictionary entries are stored in the shared tablespace.

Regardless of a storage engine's general portability characteristics, you should not attempt to copy table or tablespace files to another machine after you shut down the server unless the server shut down cleanly. If you perform a copy after an abnormal shutdown, you cannot assume the integrity of your tables. The tables may be in need of repair or there may be transaction information still stored in a storage engine's log files that needs to be applied or rolled back to bring tables up to date.

It is sometimes possible to tell a running server to leave tables alone while you copy their files. However, if the server is running and actively updating the tables or has changes still cached in memory, the table contents on disk will be in flux and the associated files will not yield usable table copies. For discussion of the conditions under which you can avoid stopping the server while copying tables, see Section 14.2, "Performing Database Maintenance with the Server Running."

2.6.2 Creating Tables

To create a table, use a CREATE TABLE statement. The full syntax for this statement is complex because there are so many optional clauses, but it's usually fairly simple to use in practice. For example, most of the CREATE TABLE statements that we used in Chapter 1 are reasonably uncomplicated. If you start with the more basic forms and work up, you shouldn't have much trouble.

A CREATE TABLE statement specifies, at a minimum, the table name and a list of the columns in it. For example:

```
CREATE TABLE mytbl
(
  name    CHAR(20),
  birth   DATE NOT NULL,
  weight  INT,
  sex     ENUM('F','M')
);
```

In addition to the column definitions, you can specify how the table should be indexed when you create it. Another option is to leave the table unindexed when you create it and add the indexes later. For MyISAM tables, that's a good strategy if you plan to populate the table with a lot of data before you begin using it for queries. Updating indexes as you insert each row is much slower than loading the data into an unindexed MyISAM table and creating the indexes afterward.

We have already covered the basic syntax for CREATE TABLE in Chapter 1. Details on how to write column definitions are given in Chapter 3. Here, we deal more generally with some important extensions to CREATE TABLE that give you a lot of flexibility in how you construct tables:

- Table options that modify storage characteristics
- Creating a table only if it doesn't already exist
- Temporary tables that the server drops automatically when the client session ends
- Creating a table from another table or from the result of a SELECT query
- Using MERGE, partitioned, and FEDERATED tables

2.6.2.1 Table Options

To modify a table's storage characteristics, add one or more table options following the closing parenthesis in the CREATE TABLE statement. A complete list of options is given in the description for CREATE TABLE in Appendix E.

One table option is ENGINE = *engine_name*, which specifies the storage engine to use for the table. For example, to create a MEMORY or InnoDB table, write the statement like this:

```
CREATE TABLE mytbl ( ... ) ENGINE = MEMORY;
CREATE TABLE mytbl ( ... ) ENGINE = InnoDB;
```

The engine name is not case sensitive. With no ENGINE option, the server creates the table using the default storage engine. The built-in default is MyISAM, but you can configure the server to use a different default by starting it with the `--default-storage-engine` option. At runtime, you can change the default storage engine by setting the `storage_engine` system variable.

In MySQL 5.0, a server is configured such that it knows about a fixed set of storage engines, some of which are always enabled and some of which might not be. If a CREATE TABLE statement names a storage engine that is known but unavailable, MySQL creates the table using the default engine and generates a warning. For example, if ARCHIVE is known to the server but not available, you would see something like this if you try to create an ARCHIVE table:

```
mysql> CREATE TABLE t (i INT) ENGINE = ARCHIVE;
Query OK, 0 rows affected, 1 warning (0.01 sec)
mysql> SHOW WARNINGS;
+---------+------+-----------------------------------------+
| Level   | Code | Message                                 |
+---------+------+-----------------------------------------+
| Warning | 1266 | Using storage engine MyISAM for table 't' |
+---------+------+-----------------------------------------+
```

If you name an unknown storage engine, an error occurs.

In MySQL 5.1 and up, the server uses a pluggable architecture that enables storage engines to be loaded at runtime. The concept of "known to the server" thus changes to mean "those engines that are currently loaded." If you create a table but name a storage engine that is not loaded, two warnings occur:

```
mysql> CREATE TABLE t (i INT) ENGINE = ARCHIVE;
Query OK, 0 rows affected, 2 warnings (0.01 sec)
mysql> SHOW WARNINGS;
+---------+------+-----------------------------------------+
| Level   | Code | Message                                 |
+---------+------+-----------------------------------------+
| Warning | 1286 | Unknown table engine 'ARCHIVE'          |
| Warning | 1266 | Using storage engine MyISAM for table 't' |
+---------+------+-----------------------------------------+
```

To make sure that a table uses a particular storage engine, be sure to include the ENGINE table option. The default engine can be changed, so you might not get the default that you expect if you omit ENGINE. In addition, verify that the CREATE TABLE statement produces no warnings, which typically indicate that the specified engine was not available and that the default engine was used instead.

To prevent MySQL from substituting the default storage engine if the engine you specify is not available, enable the NO_ENGINE_SUBSTITUTION SQL mode.

To determine which storage engine a table uses, issue a SHOW CREATE TABLE statement and look for the ENGINE option in the output:

```
mysql> SHOW CREATE TABLE t\G
*************************** 1. row ***************************
       Table: t
```

```
Create Table: CREATE TABLE `t` (
  `i` int(11) DEFAULT NULL
) ENGINE=MyISAM DEFAULT CHARSET=latin1
```

The storage engine is also available in the output from SHOW TABLE STATUS or the INFORMATION_SCHEMA.TABLES table.

Some table options apply only to particular storage engines. For example, a MIN_ROWS = n option can be useful for MEMORY tables to enable the MEMORY storage engine to optimize memory usage:

```
CREATE TABLE mytbl ( ... ) ENGINE = MEMORY MIN_ROWS = 10000;
```

If the MEMORY engine considers the value of MIN_ROWS to be large, it may allocate memory in larger hunks to avoid the overhead of making many allocation calls.

The MAX_ROWS and AVG_ROW_LENGTH options can help you size a MyISAM table. By default, MyISAM creates tables with an internal row pointer size that allows table files to grow up to 256TB. If you specify the MAX_ROWS and AVG_ROW_LENGTH options, that gives MyISAM information that it should use a pointer size for a table that can hold at least MAX_ROWS rows.

To modify the storage characteristics of an existing table, table options can be used with an ALTER TABLE statement. For example, to change mytbl from its current storage engine to InnoDB, do this:

```
ALTER TABLE mytbl ENGINE = InnoDB;
```

For more information about changing storage engines, see Section 2.6.5, "Altering Table Structure."

2.6.2.2 Provisional Table Creation

To create a table only if it doesn't already exist, use CREATE TABLE IF NOT EXISTS. You can use this statement for an application that makes no assumptions about whether a table that it needs has been set up in advance. The application can go ahead and attempt to create the table as a matter of course. The IF NOT EXISTS modifier is particularly useful for scripts that you run as batch jobs with mysql. In this context, a regular CREATE TABLE statement doesn't work very well. The first time the job runs, it creates the table, but the second time an error occurs because the table already exists. If you use IF NOT EXISTS, there is no problem. The first time the job runs, it creates the table, as before. For second and subsequent times, table creation attempts are silently ignored without error. This enables the job to continue processing as if the attempt had succeeded.

If you use IF NOT EXISTS, be aware that MySQL does not compare the table structure in the CREATE TABLE statement with that of the existing table. If a table exists with the given name but has a different structure, the statement does not fail. If that is a risk you do not want to take, it might be better instead to use DROP TABLE IF EXISTS followed by CREATE TABLE without IF NOT EXISTS.

2.6.2.3 Temporary Tables

If you add the TEMPORARY keyword to a table-creation statement, the server creates a temporary table that disappears automatically when your connection to the server terminates:

```
CREATE TEMPORARY TABLE tbl_name ... ;
```

This is handy because you don't have to bother issuing a DROP TABLE statement to get rid of the table, and the table doesn't hang around if your connection terminates abnormally. For example, if you have a complex query stored in a batch file that you run with mysql and you decide not to wait for it to finish, you can kill the script with impunity and the server will remove any TEMPORARY tables created by the script.

To create a temporary table using a particular storage engine, add an ENGINE table option to the CREATE TEMPORARY TABLE statement.

Although the server drops a TEMPORARY table automatically when your client session ends, you can drop it explicitly as soon as you're done with it to enable the server to free any resources associated with it. This is a good idea if your session with the server will not end for a while, particularly for temporary MEMORY tables.

A TEMPORARY table is visible only to the client that creates the table. Different clients can each create a TEMPORARY table with the same name and without conflict because each client sees only the table that it created.

The name of a TEMPORARY table can be the same as that of an existing permanent table. This is not an error, nor does the existing permanent table get clobbered. Instead, the permanent table becomes hidden (inaccessible) to the client that creates the TEMPORARY table while the TEMPORARY table exists. Suppose that you create a TEMPORARY table named member in the sampdb database. The original member table becomes hidden, and references to member refer to the TEMPORARY table. If you issue a DROP TABLE member statement, the TEMPORARY table is removed and the original member table "reappears." If you disconnect from the server without dropping the TEMPORARY table, the server automatically drops it for you. The next time you connect, the original member table is visible again. (The original table also reappears if you rename a TEMPORARY table that hides it to have a different name.)

The name-hiding mechanism works only to one level. That is, you cannot create two TEMPORARY tables with the same name.

Keep in mind the following caveats when considering whether to use a TEMPORARY table:

- If your client program automatically reconnects to the server if the connection is lost, any TEMPORARY tables will be gone when you reconnect. If you were using the TEMPORARY table to "hide" a permanent table with the same name, the permanent table now becomes the table that you use. For example, a DROP TABLE after an undetected reconnect will drop the permanent table. To avoid this problem, use DROP TEMPORARY TABLE instead.

- Because TEMPORARY tables are visible only to the connection that created them, they are not useful if you are using a connection pooling mechanism that does not guarantee the same connection for each statement that you issue.

- If you use connection pooling or persistent connections, your connection to the MySQL server will not necessarily close when your application terminates. Those mechanisms might hold the connection open for use by other clients, which means that you cannot assume that TEMPORARY tables will disappear automatically when your application terminates.

2.6.2.4 Creating Tables from Other Tables or Query Results

It's sometimes useful to create a copy of a table. For example, you might have a data file that you want to load into a table using LOAD DATA, but you're not quite sure about the options for specifying the data format. You can end up with malformed rows in the original table if you don't get the options right the first time. Using an empty copy of the original table enables you to experiment with the LOAD DATA options for specifying column and line delimiters until you're satisfied your input rows are being interpreted properly. Then you can load the file into the original table by rerunning the LOAD DATA statement with the original table name.

It's also sometimes desirable to save the result of a query into a table rather than watching it scroll off the top of your screen. By saving the result, you can refer to it later without rerunning the original query, perhaps to perform further analysis on it.

MySQL provides two statements for creating new tables from other tables or from query results. These statements have differing advantages and disadvantages:

- CREATE TABLE ... LIKE creates a new table as an empty copy of the original one. It copies the original table structure exactly so that each column is preserved with all of its attributes and the index structure also is copied. However, the new table is empty, so if you want to populate it, a second statement is needed (such as INSERT INTO ... SELECT). Also, CREATE TABLE ... LIKE cannot create a new table from a subset of the original table's columns, and it cannot use columns from any other table but the original one.

- CREATE TABLE ... SELECT creates a new table from the result of an arbitrary SELECT statement. By default, this statement does not copy all column attributes such as AUTO_INCREMENT. Nor does creating a table by selecting data into it automatically copy any indexes from the original table, because result sets are not themselves indexed. On the other hand, CREATE TABLE ... SELECT can both create and populate the new table in a single statement. It also can create a new table using a subset of the original table and include columns from other tables or columns created as the result of expressions.

To use CREATE TABLE ... LIKE for creating an empty copy of an existing table, write a statement like this:

```
CREATE TABLE new_tbl_name LIKE tbl_name;
```

To create an empty copy of a table and then populate it from the original table, use CREATE TABLE … LIKE followed by INSERT INTO … SELECT:

```
CREATE TABLE new_tbl_name LIKE tbl_name;
INSERT INTO new_tbl_name SELECT * FROM tbl_name;
```

To create a table as a temporary copy of itself, include the TEMPORARY keyword:

```
CREATE TEMPORARY TABLE new_tbl_name LIKE tbl_name;
INSERT INTO new_tbl_name SELECT * FROM tbl_name;
```

Using a TEMPORARY table with the same name as the original can be useful when you want to try some statements that modify the contents of the table, but you don't want to change the original table. To use prewritten scripts that use the original table name, you don't need to edit them to refer to a different table; just add the CREATE TEMPORARY TABLE and INSERT statements to the beginning of the script. The script will create a temporary copy and operate on the copy, which the server deletes when the script finishes. (However, bear in mind the auto-reconnect caveat noted in Section 2.6.2.3, "Temporary Tables.")

To insert into the new table only some of the rows from the original table, add a WHERE clause that identifies which rows to select. The following statements create a new table named student_f that contains only the rows for female students in the student table:

```
CREATE TABLE student_f LIKE student;
INSERT INTO student_f SELECT * FROM student WHERE sex = 'f';
```

If you don't care about retaining the exact column definitions from the original table, CREATE TABLE … SELECT sometimes is easier to use than CREATE TABLE … LIKE because it can create and populate the new table in a single statement:

```
CREATE TABLE student_f SELECT * FROM student WHERE sex = 'f';
```

CREATE TABLE … SELECT also can create new tables that don't contain exactly the same set of columns in an existing table. You can use it to cause a new table to spring into existence on the fly to hold the result of an arbitrary SELECT query. This makes it exceptionally easy to create a table fully populated with the data in which you're interested, ready to be used in further statements. However, the new table can contain strange column names if you're not careful. When you create a table by selecting data into it, the column names are taken from the columns that you are selecting. If a column is calculated as the result of an expression, the name of the column is the text of the expression, which creates a table with an unusual column name:

```
mysql> CREATE TABLE mytbl SELECT PI() * 2;
mysql> SELECT * FROM mytbl;
+----------+
| PI() * 2 |
+----------+
| 6.283185 |
+----------+
```

That's unfortunate, because the column name can be referred to directly only as a quoted identifier:

```
mysql> SELECT `PI() * 2` FROM mytbl;
+----------+
| PI() * 2 |
+----------+
| 6.283185 |
+----------+
```

To avoid this problem and provide a column name that is easier to work with, use an alias:

```
mysql> DROP TABLE mytbl;
mysql> CREATE TABLE mytbl SELECT PI() * 2 AS mycol;
mysql> SELECT mycol FROM mytbl;
+----------+
| mycol    |
+----------+
| 6.283185 |
+----------+
```

A related snag occurs if you select from different tables columns that have the same name. Suppose that tables t1 and t2 both have a column c and you want to create a table from all combinations of rows in both tables. The following statement fails because it attempts to create a table with two columns named c:

```
mysql> CREATE TABLE t3 SELECT * FROM t1 INNER JOIN t2;
ERROR 1060 (42S21): Duplicate column name 'c'
```

To solve this problem, provide aliases as necessary to give each column a unique name in the new table:

```
mysql> CREATE TABLE t3 SELECT t1.c, t2.c AS c2
    -> FROM t1 INNER JOIN t2;
```

As mentioned previously, a shortcoming of CREATE TABLE ... SELECT is that not all characteristics of the original data are incorporated into the structure of the new table. For example, creating a table by selecting data into it does not copy indexes from the original table, and it can lose column attributes. The retained attributes include whether the column is NULL or NOT NULL, the character set and collation, the default value, and the column comment.

In some cases, you can force specific attributes to be used in the new table by invoking the CAST() function in the SELECT part of the statement. The following CREATE TABLE ... SELECT statement forces the columns produced by the SELECT to be treated as INT UNSIGNED, TIME, and DECIMAL(10,5), as you can verify with DESCRIBE:

```
mysql> CREATE TABLE mytbl SELECT
    -> CAST(1 AS UNSIGNED) AS i,
    -> CAST(CURTIME() AS TIME) AS t,
    -> CAST(PI() AS DECIMAL(10,5)) AS d;
```

```
mysql> DESCRIBE mytbl;
+-------+-----------------+------+-----+---------+-------+
| Field | Type            | Null | Key | Default | Extra |
+-------+-----------------+------+-----+---------+-------+
| i     | int(1) unsigned | NO   |     | 0       |       |
| t     | time            | YES  |     | NULL    |       |
| d     | decimal(10,5)   | NO   |     | 0.00000 |       |
+-------+-----------------+------+-----+---------+-------+
```

The allowable cast types are BINARY (binary string), CHAR, DATE, DATETIME, TIME, SIGNED, SIGNED INTEGER, UNSIGNED, UNSIGNED INTEGER, and DECIMAL.

It is also possible to provide explicit column definitions in the CREATE TABLE part, to be used for the columns retrieved by the SELECT part. Columns in the two parts are matched by name, so provide aliases in the SELECT part as necessary to cause them to match properly:

```
mysql> CREATE TABLE mytbl (i INT UNSIGNED, t TIME, d DECIMAL(10,5))
    -> SELECT
    -> 1 AS i,
    -> CAST(CURTIME() AS TIME) AS t,
    -> CAST(PI() AS DECIMAL(10,5)) AS d;
mysql> DESCRIBE mytbl;
+-------+-----------------+------+-----+---------+-------+
| Field | Type            | Null | Key | Default | Extra |
+-------+-----------------+------+-----+---------+-------+
| i     | int(10) unsigned| YES  |     | NULL    |       |
| t     | time            | YES  |     | NULL    |       |
| d     | decimal(10,5)   | YES  |     | NULL    |       |
+-------+-----------------+------+-----+---------+-------+
```

The technique of providing explicit definitions enables you to create numeric columns with specified precision and scale, character columns that have a different width than that of the longest value in the result set, and so forth. Also note that the Null and Default attributes for some of the columns are different in this example from those in the previous one. You can provide explicit definitions for those attributes in the CREATE TABLE part if necessary.

2.6.2.5 Using MERGE Tables

The MERGE storage engine enables you to perform queries on a set of MyISAM tables simultaneously by treating them all as a single logical unit. As described earlier in Section 2.6.1, "Storage Engine Characteristics," MERGE can be applied to a collection of MyISAM tables that all have identical structure. The columns in each table must be defined with the same names and types in the same order, and the indexes must be defined in the same way and in the same order.

Suppose that you have a set of individual log tables that contain log entries on a year-by-year basis and that each is defined like this, where CC and YY represent the century and year:

```
CREATE TABLE log_CCYY
(
  dt    DATETIME NOT NULL,
  info  VARCHAR(100) NOT NULL,
  INDEX (dt)
) ENGINE = MyISAM;
```

If the current set of log tables includes log_2004, log_2005, log_2006, log_2007, and log_2008, you can set up a MERGE table that maps onto them like this:

```
CREATE TABLE log_merge
(
  dt    DATETIME NOT NULL,
  info  VARCHAR(100) NOT NULL,
  INDEX (dt)
) ENGINE = MERGE UNION = (log_2004, log_2005, log_2006, log_2007, log_2008);
```

The ENGINE value must be MERGE, and the UNION option lists the tables to be included in the MERGE table. After the table has been set up, you query it just like any other table, but the queries will refer to all the constituent tables at once. This query determines the total number of rows in all the log tables:

```
SELECT COUNT(*) FROM log_merge;
```

This query determines how many log entries there are per year:

```
SELECT YEAR(dt) AS y, COUNT(*) AS entries FROM log_merge GROUP BY y;
```

Besides the convenience of being able to refer to multiple tables without issuing multiple queries, MERGE tables offer some other nice features:

- A MERGE table can be used to create a logical entity that exceeds the allowable size of individual MyISAM tables.
- You can include compressed tables in the collection. For example, after a given year comes to an end, you wouldn't be adding any more entries to the corresponding log file, so you could compress it with myisampack to save space. The MERGE table will continue to function as before.

MERGE tables also support DELETE and UPDATE operations. INSERT is trickier because MySQL needs to know which table to insert new rows into. MERGE table definitions can include an INSERT_METHOD option with a value of NO, FIRST, or LAST to indicate that INSERT is forbidden or that rows should be inserted into the first or last table named in the UNION option. For example, the following definition would cause an INSERT into log_merge to be treated as an INSERT into log_2008, the last table named in the UNION option:

```
CREATE TABLE log_merge
(
  dt    DATETIME NOT NULL,
  info  VARCHAR(100) NOT NULL,
  INDEX (dt)
) ENGINE = MERGE UNION = (log_2004, log_2005, log_2006, log_2007, log_2008)
INSERT_METHOD = LAST;
```

When the year 2009 arrives, create a new underlying table, log_2009, that has the same structure as the other log_CCYY tables, and modify the log_merge table to include log_2009:

```
CREATE TABLE log_2009 LIKE log_2008;
ALTER TABLE log_merge
UNION = (log_2004, log_2005, log_2006, log_2007, log_2008, log_2009);
```

2.6.2.6 Using Partitioned Tables

MySQL 5.1 and up supports partitioned tables. Partitioning is similar in concept to the MERGE storage engine in the sense that it enables use of table contents that are stored in different locations. However, a partitioned table is a single table, not a logical construct that maps onto multiple underlying tables. Also, a partitioned table can use storage engines other than MyISAM, whereas MERGE tables require the use of MyISAM tables.

By sectioning table storage, partitioned tables offer benefits such as these:

- Table storage can be distributed over multiple devices, which may improve access time by virtue of I/O parallelism.

- The optimizer may be able to localize searches to specific partitions, or to search partitions in parallel.

To create a partitioned table, supply the list of columns and indexes in the CREATE TABLE statement, as usual. In addition, specify a PARTITION BY clause that defines a partitioning function to be used to assign rows to partitions, and possibly other partition-related options. The partitioning function is analogous to the INSERT_METHOD option for MERGE tables, but is more general because it distributes rows among all partitions, whereas INSERT_METHOD designates a single table for all inserts.

Partitioning functions assign rows based on ranges or lists of values or hash values:

- Use range partitioning when rows contain a domain of values such as dates, income level, or weight that can be divided into discrete ranges.

- Use list partitioning when it makes sense to specify an explicit list of values for each partition, such as sets of postal codes, phone number prefixes, or IDs for entities that you group by geographical region.

- Use hash partitioning to distribute the rows among partitions according to hash values computed from row keys. You can either supply the hash function yourself or tell MySQL which columns to use and it will compute values based on those columns using a built-in hash function.

The partitioning function must be deterministic so that the same input consistently results in row assignment to the same partition. This rules out the use of functions such as RAND() or NOW().

As a simple example, let's create a partitioned analog to the MERGE table developed in Section 2.6.2.5, "Using MERGE Tables." That MERGE table, log_merge, has several underlying log tables containing log entries for the years 2004 through 2008. The corresponding partitioned table will be a single table comprising several underlying partitions. For data consisting of log entries that each contain a date, the most natural partitioning is by range. To assign rows for each year to a given partition, use the year part of the date value:

```
CREATE TABLE log_partition
(
  dt    DATETIME NOT NULL,
  info  VARCHAR(100) NOT NULL,
  INDEX (dt)
)
PARTITION BY RANGE(YEAR(dt))
(
  PARTITION p0 VALUES LESS THAN (2005),
  PARTITION p1 VALUES LESS THAN (2006),
  PARTITION p2 VALUES LESS THAN (2007),
  PARTITION p3 VALUES LESS THAN (2008),
  PARTITION p4 VALUES LESS THAN MAXVALUE
);
```

The MAXVALUE partition is assigned all rows that have dates from the year 2008 or later. When the year 2009 arrives, you can split this partition so that all year 2008 rows get their own partition and rows for 2009 and later go into the MAXVALUE partition:

```
ALTER TABLE log_partition REORGANIZE PARTITION p4
INTO (
  PARTITION p4 VALUES LESS THAN (2009),
  PARTITION p5 VALUES LESS THAN MAXVALUE
);
```

By default, partitions are stored under the directory for the database to which the partitioned table belongs. To distribute storage to other locations (for example, to place them on different physical devices), use the DATA_DIRECTORY and INDEX_DIRECTORY partition options. For more information about the syntax for these and other partitioning options, see the description for CREATE TABLE in Appendix E.

2.6.2.7 Using FEDERATED Tables

The FEDERATED storage engine enables you to access tables from one MySQL server that actually are managed by another server.

Suppose that there is no `sampdb` database on your local server, but there is one available from the MySQL server running on the host `corn.snake.net` and that you have an account for accessing that server. That account can be used by the local server through the FEDERATED storage engine to make the `sampdb` tables available on the local server. For each table that you want to access this way, create a FEDERATED table that has the same columns as the remote table, but include a connection string that indicates to the local server how to connect to the remote server.

Suppose that the `student` table on the remote server has this definition:

```
CREATE TABLE student
(
  name       VARCHAR(20) NOT NULL,
  sex        ENUM('F','M') NOT NULL,
  student_id INT UNSIGNED NOT NULL AUTO_INCREMENT,
  PRIMARY KEY (student_id)
) ENGINE = InnoDB;
```

To create a FEDERATED table on the local server, use the same definition, except that the `ENGINE` option should be `FEDERATED` and a `CONNECTION` table option should be given that provides connection information. (Prior to MySQL 5.0.13, use the `COMMENT` option instead of `CONNECTION`.) The following definition creates a table named `federated_student` that accesses the `student` table on `corn.snake.net`:

```
CREATE TABLE federated_student
(
  name       VARCHAR(20) NOT NULL,
  sex        ENUM('F','M') NOT NULL,
  student_id INT UNSIGNED NOT NULL AUTO_INCREMENT,
  PRIMARY KEY (student_id)
) ENGINE = FEDERATED
CONNECTION = 'mysql://sampadm:secret@corn.snake.net/sampdb/student';
```

The connection string in the `CONNECTION` value indicates that the username and password of the MySQL account on the remote server are `sampadm` and `secret`. The general connection string syntax is as follows, where square brackets indicate optional information:

```
mysql://user_name[:password]@host_name[:port_num]/db_name/tbl_name
```

After you create the `federated_student` table, you can select from it to access the remote `student` table. You can also use INSERT, UPDATE, and DELETE with `federated_student` to modify the contents of the `student` table.

Note that the entire `CONNECTION` string (including the username and password) is visible to anyone who can use SHOW CREATE TABLE or similar statements for the FEDERATED table. As of MySQL 5.1.15, you can avoid this problem: Create a stored server definition using the CREATE SERVER statement (this requires the SUPER privilege) and refer to the server name in the CONNECTION option. To name the server corn_sampdb_server, use this statement:

```
CREATE SERVER corn_sampdb_server
FOREIGN DATA WRAPPER mysql
OPTIONS (
  USER 'sampadm',
  PASSWORD 'secret',
  HOST 'corn.snake.net',
  DATABASE 'sampdb'
);
```

The MySQL server stores this definition as a row in the servers table in the mysql database. To create a table that refers to the server definition, name the server in the CONNECTION option using a statement like this:

```
CREATE TABLE federated_student2
(
  name       VARCHAR(20) NOT NULL,
  sex        ENUM('F','M') NOT NULL,
  student_id INT UNSIGNED NOT NULL AUTO_INCREMENT,
  PRIMARY KEY (student_id)
) ENGINE = FEDERATED
CONNECTION = 'corn_sampdb_server/student';
```

Using a server definition is more secure than listing connection parameters in the CONNECTION option because the definition is visible only to users who have access to the mysql database. Also, the server definition can make table setup easier because multiple FEDERATED tables that share the same connection parameters can use the same definition.

2.6.3 Dropping Tables

Dropping a table is much easier than creating it because you don't have to specify anything about the format of its contents. You just have to name it:

```
DROP TABLE tbl_name;
```

MySQL extends the DROP TABLE statement in several useful ways. To drop multiple tables, specify them all in the same statement:

```
DROP TABLE tbl_name1, tbl_name2, ... ;
```

If you're not sure whether a table exists, but you want to drop it if it does, include IF EXISTS in the statement:

```
DROP TABLE IF EXISTS tbl_name;
```

The IF EXISTS clause suppresses the error for nonexistent tables. (For each one, the server generates a warning that you can view with SHOW WARNINGS.)

IF EXISTS is particularly useful in scripts that you use with the mysql client. By default, mysql exits when an error occurs, and it is an error to try to remove a table that doesn't exist. For example, you might have a setup script that creates tables that you use as the basis for further processing in other scripts. In this situation, you want to make sure the setup script has a clean slate when it begins. If you use a regular DROP TABLE at the beginning of the script, it would fail the first time because the tables have never been created. If you use IF EXISTS, there is no problem. If the tables are there, they are dropped. If they are not there, no error occurs and the script continues to execute.

To drop a table only if it is a temporary table, include the TEMPORARY keyword:

```
DROP TEMPORARY TABLE tbl_name;
```

2.6.4 Indexing Tables

Indexes are the primary means of speeding up access to the contents of your tables, particularly for queries that involve joins on multiple tables. This is an important enough topic that an entire chapter discusses why you use indexes, how they work, and how best to take advantage of them to optimize your queries (Chapter 5, "Query Optimization"). This section covers the characteristics of indexes for the various table types and the syntax for creating and dropping indexes.

2.6.4.1 Storage Engine Index Characteristics

MySQL provides quite a bit of flexibility in the way you can construct indexes:

- You can index single columns or construct composite indexes that include multiple columns.

- An index can be constrained to contain only unique values or allowed to contain duplicate values.

- You can have more than one index on a table to help optimize different queries on the table that are based on different columns.

- For string data types other than ENUM or SET, you can elect to index a prefix of a column; that is, only the leftmost *n* characters, or *n* bytes for binary string types. (For BLOB and TEXT columns, you can set up an index only if you specify a prefix length.) If the column is mostly unique within the prefix length, you usually won't sacrifice performance, and may well improve it: Indexing a column prefix rather than the entire column can make an index much smaller and faster to access.

Not all storage engines offer all indexing features. Table 2.3 summarizes the index properties for some of MySQL's storage engines. The table does not include the MERGE storage engine, because MERGE tables are created from MyISAM tables and have similar index characteristics. Nor does it include the ARCHIVE, BLACKHOLE, CSV, or EXAMPLE engines, which support indexing either not at all or only in limited fashion.

Table 2.3   **Storage Engine Index Characteristics**

Index Characteristic	MyISAM	MEMORY	InnoDB	Falcon
NULL values allowed	Yes	Yes	Yes	Yes
Columns per index	16	16	16	16
Indexes per table	64	64	64	64
Maximum index row size (bytes)	1000	1024/3072	1024/3072	1100
Index column prefixes	Yes	Yes	Yes	Yes
Maximum prefix size (bytes)	1000	1024/3072	767	1100
BLOB/TEXT indexes	Yes	No	Yes	No
FULLTEXT indexes	Yes	No	No	No
SPATIAL indexes	Yes	No	No	No
HASH indexes	No	Yes	No	No

For the MEMORY and InnoDB storage engines, the index size limit is 1024 bytes before MySQL 5.0.17/5.1.4 and 3072 bytes from 5.0.17/5.1.4 on. The same is true for the
MEMORY index prefix size limit.

One implication of the differences in index characteristics for the various storage engines is that if you require an index to have certain properties, you may not be able to use
certain types of tables. For example, to use a FULLTEXT or SPATIAL index, you must use a
MyISAM table. To index a TEXT column, you must use MyISAM or InnoDB.

If you have an existing table that you would like to convert to use a different storage
engine that has more suitable index characteristics, use ALTER TABLE to change the engine.
Suppose that you are using a MyISAM table but need the transactional capabilities offered
by InnoDB or Falcon. Convert the table using one of these statements:

```
ALTER TABLE tbl_name ENGINE = InnoDB;
ALTER TABLE tbl_name ENGINE = Falcon;
```

2.6.4.2 Creating Indexes

MySQL can create several types of indexes:

- A unique index. This disallows duplicate values. For a single-column index, this ensures that the column contains no duplicate values. For a multiple-column (composite) index, it ensures that no combination of values in the columns is duplicated
  among the rows of the table.

- A regular (non-unique) index. This gives you indexing benefits but allows duplicates.

- A FULLTEXT index, used for performing full-text searches. This index type is supported only for MyISAM tables. For more information, see Section 2.15, "Using
  FULLTEXT Searches."

- A SPATIAL index. These can be used only with MyISAM tables for the spatial data types, which are described in Chapter 3. (For other storage engines that support spatial data types, you can create non-SPATIAL indexes.)

- A HASH index. This is the default index type for MEMORY tables, although you can override the default to create BTREE indexes instead.

You can create indexes for a new table when you use CREATE TABLE. Examples of this are shown in Section 1.4.6, "Creating Tables." To add indexes to existing tables, use ALTER TABLE or CREATE INDEX. (MySQL maps CREATE INDEX statements onto ALTER TABLE operations internally.)

ALTER TABLE is more versatile than CREATE INDEX because it can create any kind of index supported by MySQL. For example:

```
ALTER TABLE tbl_name ADD INDEX index_name (index_columns);
ALTER TABLE tbl_name ADD UNIQUE index_name (index_columns);
ALTER TABLE tbl_name ADD PRIMARY KEY (index_columns);
ALTER TABLE tbl_name ADD FULLTEXT index_name (index_columns);
ALTER TABLE tbl_name ADD SPATIAL index_name (index_columns);
```

tbl_name is the name of the table to which the index should be added, and index_columns indicates which column or columns to index. If the index consists of more than one column, separate the names by commas. The index name index_name is optional. If you leave it out, MySQL picks a name based on the name of the first indexed column.

Indexed columns must be NOT NULL if the index is a PRIMARY KEY or SPATIAL index. Otherwise, they can contain NULL values.

A single ALTER TABLE statement can include multiple table alterations if you separate them by commas. This enables you to create several indexes at the same time, which is faster than adding them one at a time with individual ALTER TABLE statements.

To place the constraint on an index that it contain only unique values, create the index as a PRIMARY KEY or as a UNIQUE index. The two types of index are very similar, but have two differences:

- A table can contain only one PRIMARY KEY. (This is because the name of a PRIMARY KEY is always PRIMARY and a table cannot have two indexes with the same name.) You can place multiple UNIQUE indexes on a table.

- A PRIMARY KEY cannot contain NULL values, whereas a UNIQUE index can. If a UNIQUE index can contain NULL values, it can contain multiple NULL values. The reason for this is that it is not possible to know whether one NULL represents the same value as another, so they cannot be considered equal.

CREATE INDEX can add most types of indexes, with the exception of a PRIMARY KEY:

```
CREATE INDEX index_name ON tbl_name (index_columns);
CREATE UNIQUE INDEX index_name ON tbl_name (index_columns);
```

```
CREATE FULLTEXT INDEX index_name ON tbl_name (index_columns);
CREATE SPATIAL INDEX index_name ON tbl_name (index_columns);
```

tbl_name, *index_name*, and *index_columns* have the same meaning as for ALTER TABLE. Unlike ALTER TABLE, the index name is not optional with CREATE INDEX, and you cannot create multiple indexes with a single statement.

To create indexes for a new table when you issue a CREATE TABLE statement, the syntax is similar to that used for ALTER TABLE, but you specify the index-creation clauses in addition to the column definitions:

```
CREATE TABLE tbl_name
(
  ... column definitions ...
  INDEX index_name (index_columns),
  UNIQUE index_name (index_columns),
  PRIMARY KEY (index_columns),
  FULLTEXT index_name (index_columns),
  SPATIAL index_name (index_columns),
  ...
);
```

As with ALTER TABLE, *index_name* is optional. MySQL picks an index name if you leave it out.

As a special case, you can create a single-column PRIMARY KEY or UNIQUE index by adding a PRIMARY KEY or UNIQUE clause to the end of a column definition. For example, the following CREATE TABLE statements are equivalent:

```
CREATE TABLE mytbl
(
  i INT NOT NULL PRIMARY KEY,
  j CHAR(10) NOT NULL UNIQUE
);
```

```
CREATE TABLE mytbl
(
  i INT NOT NULL,
  j CHAR(10) NOT NULL,
  PRIMARY KEY (i),
  UNIQUE (j)
);
```

The default index type for a MEMORY table is HASH. A hashed index is very fast for exact-value lookups, which is the typical way MEMORY tables are used. However, if you plan to use a MEMORY table for comparisons that can match a range of values (for example, id < 100), hashed indexes do not work well. In this case, you'll be better off creating a BTREE index instead. Do this by adding a USING BTREE clause to the index definition:

```
CREATE TABLE namelist
```

```
(
  id    INT NOT NULL,
  name CHAR(100),
  INDEX USING BTREE (id)
) ENGINE = MEMORY;
```

To index a prefix of a string column, the syntax for naming the column in the index definition is `col_name(n)` rather than simply `col_name`. The prefix value, *n*, indicates that the index should include the first *n* bytes of column values for binary string types, or the first *n* characters for non-binary string types. For example, the following statement creates a table with a CHAR column and a BINARY column. It indexes the first 10 characters of the CHAR column and the first 15 bytes of the BINARY column:

```
CREATE TABLE addresslist
(
  name    CHAR(30) NOT NULL,
  address BINARY(60) NOT NULL,
  INDEX (name(10)),
  INDEX (address(15))
);
```

When you index a prefix of a string column, the prefix length, just like the column length, is specified in the same units as the column data type—that is, bytes for binary strings and characters for non-binary strings. However, the maximum size of index entries are measured internally in bytes. The two measures are the same for single-byte character sets, but not for multi-byte character sets. For non-binary strings that have multi-byte character sets, MySQL stores into index values as many complete characters as fit within the allowed maximum byte length.

In some circumstances, you may find it not only desirable but necessary to index a column prefix rather than the entire column:

- Prefixes are required for indexing BLOB or TEXT columns.
- The length of index rows is equal to the sum of the length of the index parts of the columns that make up the index. If this length exceeds the maximum allowable number of bytes in index rows, you can make the index "narrower" by indexing a column prefix. Suppose that a MyISAM table that uses the latin1 single-byte character set contains four CHAR(255) columns named c1 through c4. An index value for each full column value takes 255 bytes, so an index on all four columns would require 1,020 bytes. However, the maximum length of a MyISAM index row is 1,000 bytes, so you cannot create a composite index that includes the entire contents of all four columns. However, you can create the index by indexing a shorter part of some or all of them. For example, you could index the first 250 characters from each column.

Columns in FULLTEXT indexes are indexed in full and do not have prefixes. If you specify a prefix length for a column in a FULLTEXT index, MySQL ignores it.

Columns with spatial data types such as POINT or GEOMETRY can be indexed as follows:

- SPATIAL indexes can be used only for MyISAM tables, and only for columns that are NOT NULL. The columns are indexed in full.
- Other index types (INDEX, UNIQUE, PRIMARY KEY) can be used with any storage engine other than ARCHIVE that supports spatial data types. Columns can be NULL unless part of a PRIMARY KEY. A prefix length in bytes must be specified for each spatial column in the index except POINT columns.

2.6.4.3 Dropping Indexes

To drop an index, use either a DROP INDEX or an ALTER TABLE statement. To use DROP INDEX, you must name the index to be dropped:

```
DROP INDEX index_name ON tbl_name;
```

To drop a PRIMARY KEY with DROP INDEX, specify the name PRIMARY as a quoted identifier:

```
DROP INDEX `PRIMARY` ON tbl_name;
```

That statement is unambiguous because a table may have only one PRIMARY KEY and its name is always PRIMARY.

Like the CREATE INDEX statement, DROP INDEX is handled internally as an ALTER TABLE statement. The preceding DROP INDEX statements correspond to the following ALTER TABLE statements:

```
ALTER TABLE tbl_name DROP INDEX index_name;
ALTER TABLE tbl_name DROP PRIMARY KEY;
```

If you don't know the names of a table's indexes, use SHOW CREATE TABLE or SHOW INDEX to find out.

When you drop columns from a table, indexes may be affected implicitly. If you drop a column that is a part of an index, MySQL removes the column from the index as well. If you drop all columns that make up an index, MySQL drops the entire index.

2.6.5 Altering Table Structure

ALTER TABLE is a versatile statement and has many uses. We've already seen a few of its capabilities earlier in this chapter (for changing storage engines and for creating and dropping indexes). You can also use ALTER TABLE to rename tables, add or drop columns, change column data types, and more. This section covers some of its features. Appendix E, describes the complete syntax for ALTER TABLE.

ALTER TABLE is useful when you find that the structure of a table no longer reflects what you want to do with it. You might want to use the table to record additional information. Perhaps the table contains information that has become superfluous. Maybe existing columns are too small, or it turns out that you've defined columns larger than you need and you'd like to make them smaller to save space and improve query performance. Here are some situations for which ALTER TABLE is valuable:

- You're running a research project. You assign case numbers to research records using an AUTO_INCREMENT column. You didn't expect your funding to last long enough to generate more than about 50,000 records, so you made the data type SMALLINT UNSIGNED, which holds a maximum of 65,535 unique values. However, the funding for the project was renewed, and it looks like you might generate another 50,000 records. You need to make the type bigger to accommodate more case numbers.

- Size changes can go the other way, too. Maybe you created a CHAR(255) column but now recognize that no value in the table is more than 100 characters long. You can shorten the column to save space.

- You want to convert a table to use a different storage engine to take advantage of features offered by that engine. For example, MyISAM tables are not transaction-safe, but you have an application that needs transactional capabilities. You can convert the affected tables to use InnoDB or Falcon, because those storage engines are transactional.

The syntax for ALTER TABLE looks like this:

```
ALTER TABLE tbl_name action [, action] ... ;
```

Each action specifies a modification that you want to make to the table. Some database systems allow only a single action in an ALTER TABLE statement, but MySQL allows multiple actions, separated by commas.

> **Tip**
>
> If you need to remind yourself about a table's current definition before using ALTER TABLE, issue a SHOW CREATE TABLE statement. This statement also can be useful after ALTER TABLE to verify that the alteration affected the table definition as you expect.

The following examples discuss some of the capabilities of ALTER TABLE.

Change a column's data type. To change a data type, you can use either a CHANGE or MODIFY clause. Suppose that the column in a table mytbl is SMALLINT UNSIGNED and you want to change it to MEDIUMINT UNSIGNED. Do so using either of the following commands:

```
ALTER TABLE mytbl MODIFY i MEDIUMINT UNSIGNED;
ALTER TABLE mytbl CHANGE i i MEDIUMINT UNSIGNED;
```

Why is the column named twice in the command that uses CHANGE? Because one thing that CHANGE can do that MODIFY cannot is to rename the column in addition to changing the type. If you had wanted to rename i to k at the same time you changed the type, you'd do so like this:

```
ALTER TABLE mytbl CHANGE i k MEDIUMINT UNSIGNED;
```

The important thing with CHANGE is that you name the column you want to change and then specify the column's new name and definition. Thus, you must specify the name twice if you don't want to rename the column.

To rename a column without changing its data type, use CHANGE *old_name new_name* followed by the column's current definition.

You can assign character sets to individual columns, so it's possible to use the CHARACTER SET attribute in a column's definition to change its character set:

```
ALTER TABLE t MODIFY c CHAR(20) CHARACTER SET ucs2;
```

An important reason for changing data types is to improve query efficiency for joins that compare columns from two tables. Indexes often can be used for comparisons in joins between similar column types, but comparisons are quicker when both columns are exactly the same type. Suppose that you're running a query like this:

```
SELECT ... FROM t1 INNER JOIN t2 WHERE t1.name = t2.name;
```

If t1.name is CHAR(10) and t2.name is CHAR(15), the query won't run as quickly as if they were both CHAR(15). You can make them the same by changing t1.name using either of these commands:

```
ALTER TABLE t1 MODIFY name CHAR(15);
ALTER TABLE t1 CHANGE name name CHAR(15);
```

Convert a table to use a different storage engine. To convert a table from one storage engine to another, use an ENGINE clause that specifies the new engine name:

```
ALTER TABLE tbl_name ENGINE = engine_name;
```

engine_name is a name such as MyISAM, MEMORY, or InnoDB. Lettercase does not matter.

One reason to change a storage engine is to make it transaction-safe. Suppose that you have a MyISAM table and discover that an application that uses it needs to perform transactional operations, including rollback in case failures occur. MyISAM tables do not support transactions, but you can make the table transaction-safe by converting it to an InnoDB or Falcon table:

```
ALTER TABLE tbl_name ENGINE = InnoDB;
ALTER TABLE tbl_name ENGINE = Falcon;
```

When you convert a table to use a different engine, the allowable or sensible conversions may depend on the feature compatibility of the old and new engines. For example, the following conversions are disallowed:

- If you have a table that includes a BLOB column, you cannot convert the table to use the MEMORY engine because MEMORY tables do not support BLOB columns.
- If you have a MyISAM table that includes FULLTEXT or SPATIAL indexes, you cannot convert it to another engine because only MyISAM supports those types of indexes.

There are circumstances under which you should not use ALTER TABLE to convert a table to use a different storage engine:

- MEMORY tables are held in memory and disappear when the server exits. It is not a good idea to convert a table to type MEMORY if you require the table contents to persist across server restarts.

- If you use a MERGE table to group a collection of MyISAM tables together, you should avoid using ALTER TABLE to modify any of the MyISAM tables unless you make the same change to all of them, and to the MERGE table as well. The proper functioning of a MERGE table depends on its having the same structure as all of its constituent MyISAM tables.

- An InnoDB table can be converted to use another storage engine. However, if the table has foreign key constraints, they will be lost because only InnoDB supports foreign keys.

Rename a table. Use a RENAME clause that specifies the new table name:

```
ALTER TABLE tbl_name RENAME TO new_tbl_name;
```

Another way to rename tables is with RENAME TABLE. The syntax looks like this:

```
RENAME TABLE old_name TO new_name;
```

One thing that RENAME TABLE can do that ALTER TABLE cannot is rename multiple tables in the same statement. For example, you can swap the names of two tables like this:

```
RENAME TABLE t1 TO tmp, t2 TO t1, tmp TO t2;
```

If you qualify a table name with a database name, you can move a table from one database to another by renaming it. Either of the following statements move the table t from the sampdb database to the test database:

```
ALTER TABLE sampdb.t RENAME TO test.t;
RENAME TABLE sampdb.t TO test.t;
```

You cannot rename a table to a name that already exists.

If you rename a MyISAM table that is part of a MERGE table, you must redefine the MERGE table to refer to the new name.

2.7 Obtaining Database Metadata

MySQL provides several ways to obtain information about databases and the objects in them (that is, database metadata):

- SHOW statements such as SHOW DATABASES or SHOW TABLES
- Tables in the INFORMATION_SCHEMA database
- Command-line programs such as mysqlshow or mysqldump

The following sections describe how to use each of these information sources to access metadata.

2.7.1 Obtaining Metadata with SHOW

MySQL provides a SHOW statement that displays database metadata in several forms. SHOW is helpful for keeping track of the contents of your databases and for reminding yourself about the structure of your tables. The following examples demonstrate a few uses for SHOW statements.

List the databases managed by the server:

```
SHOW DATABASES;
```

Display the CREATE DATABASE statement for a database:

```
SHOW CREATE DATABASE db_name;
```

List the tables in the default database or in a given database:

```
SHOW TABLES;
SHOW TABLES FROM db_name;
```

SHOW TABLES doesn't show TEMPORARY tables.

Display the CREATE TABLE statement for a table:

```
SHOW CREATE TABLE tbl_name;
```

Display information about columns or indexes in a table:

```
SHOW COLUMNS FROM tbl_name;
SHOW INDEX FROM tbl_name;
```

The DESCRIBE tbl_name and EXPLAIN tbl_name statements are synonymous with SHOW COLUMNS FROM tbl_name.

Display descriptive information about tables in the default database or in a given database:

```
SHOW TABLE STATUS;
SHOW TABLE STATUS FROM db_name;
```

Several forms of the SHOW statement take a LIKE 'pattern' clause allowing a pattern to be given that limits the scope of the output. MySQL interprets 'pattern' as an SQL pattern that may include the '%' and '_' wildcard characters. For example, this statement displays the names of columns in the student table that begin with 's':

```
mysql> SHOW COLUMNS FROM student LIKE 's%';
+------------+------------------+------+-----+---------+----------------+
| Field      | Type             | Null | Key | Default | Extra          |
+------------+------------------+------+-----+---------+----------------+
| sex        | enum('F','M')    | NO   |     |         |                |
| student_id | int(10) unsigned | NO   | PRI | NULL    | auto_increment |
+------------+------------------+------+-----+---------+----------------+
```

To match a literal instance of a wildcard character in a LIKE pattern, precede it with a backslash. Generally, this is done to match a literal '_', which occurs frequently in database, table, and column names.

Any SHOW statement that supports a LIKE clause can also be written to use a WHERE clause. The SHOW statement still displays a fixed set of columns, but WHERE provides more flexibility about specifying which rows to return. The WHERE clause should refer to the columns displayed by the SHOW statement. If the column name is a reserved word such as KEY, specify it as a quoted identifier. This statement determines which column in the student table is the primary key:

```
mysql> SHOW COLUMNS FROM student WHERE `Key` = 'PRI';
+------------+-----------------+------+-----+---------+----------------+
| Field      | Type            | Null | Key | Default | Extra          |
+------------+-----------------+------+-----+---------+----------------+
| student_id | int(10) unsigned | NO   | PRI | NULL    | auto_increment |
+------------+-----------------+------+-----+---------+----------------+
```

It's sometimes useful to be able to tell from within an application whether a given table exists. You can use SHOW TABLES to find out (but remember that SHOW TABLES does not list TEMPORARY tables):

```
SHOW TABLES LIKE 'tbl_name';
SHOW TABLES FROM db_name LIKE 'tbl_name';
```

If the SHOW TABLES statement lists information for the table, it exists. It's also possible to determine table existence, even for TEMPORARY tables, with either of the following statements:

```
SELECT COUNT(*) FROM tbl_name;
SELECT * FROM tbl_name WHERE FALSE;
```

Each statement succeeds if the table exists, and fails if it doesn't. The first statement is most appropriate for MyISAM tables, for which COUNT(*) with no WHERE clause is highly optimized. It's not so good for InnoDB tables, which require a full scan to count the rows. The second statement is more general because it runs quickly for any storage engine. These statements are most suitable for use within application programming languages such as Perl or PHP because you can test the success or failure of the query and take action accordingly. They're not especially useful in a batch script that you run from mysql because you can't do anything if an error occurs except terminate (or ignore the error, but then there's obviously no point in running the query at all).

To determine the storage engine for individual tables, you can use SHOW TABLE STATUS or SHOW CREATE TABLE. The output from either statement includes a storage engine indicator.

2.7.2 Obtaining Metadata with INFORMATION_SCHEMA

Another way to obtain information about databases is to access the INFORMATION_SCHEMA database. INFORMATION_SCHEMA is based on the SQL standard. That is, the access mechanism is standard, even though some of the content is MySQL-specific. This makes INFORMATION_SCHEMA more portable than the various SHOW statements, which are entirely MySQL-specific.

INFORMATION_SCHEMA is accessed through SELECT statements and can be used in a flexible manner. SHOW statements always display a fixed set of columns and you cannot capture the output in a table. With INFORMATION_SCHEMA, the SELECT statement can name specific output columns and a WHERE clause can specify any expression required to select the information that you want. Also, you can use joins or subqueries, and you can use CREATE TABLE ... SELECT or INSERT INTO ... SELECT to save the result of the retrieval in another table for further processing.

You can think of INFORMATION_SCHEMA as a virtual database in which the tables are views for different kinds of database metadata. To see what tables INFORMATION_SCHEMA contains, use SHOW TABLES. The output displayed here is from MySQL 5.1 (5.0 has fewer tables):

```
mysql> SHOW TABLES IN INFORMATION_SCHEMA;
+---------------------------------------+
| Tables_in_information_schema          |
+---------------------------------------+
| CHARACTER_SETS                        |
| COLLATIONS                            |
| COLLATION_CHARACTER_SET_APPLICABILITY |
| COLUMNS                               |
| COLUMN_PRIVILEGES                     |
| ENGINES                               |
| EVENTS                                |
| FILES                                 |
| GLOBAL_STATUS                         |
| GLOBAL_VARIABLES                      |
| KEY_COLUMN_USAGE                      |
| PARTITIONS                            |
| PLUGINS                               |
| PROCESSLIST                           |
| REFERENTIAL_CONSTRAINTS               |
| ROUTINES                              |
| SCHEMATA                              |
| SCHEMA_PRIVILEGES                     |
| SESSION_STATUS                        |
| SESSION_VARIABLES                     |
| STATISTICS                            |
| TABLES                                |
| TABLE_CONSTRAINTS                     |
```

```
| TABLE_PRIVILEGES                   |
| TRIGGERS                           |
| USER_PRIVILEGES                    |
| VIEWS                              |
+------------------------------------+
```

The following list briefly describes the INFORMATION_SCHEMA tables just shown:

- SCHEMATA, TABLES, VIEWS, ROUTINES, TRIGGERS, EVENTS, PARTITIONS, COLUMNS

  Information about databases; tables, views, stored routines, triggers, and events within databases; table partitions; and columns within tables

- FILES

  Information about NDB disk data files

- TABLE_CONSTRAINTS, KEY_COLUMN_USAGE

  Information about tables and columns that have constraints such as unique-valued indexes or foreign keys

- STATISTICS

  Information about table index characteristics

- REFERENTIAL_CONSTRAINTS

  Information about foreign keys

- CHARACTER_SETS, COLLATIONS, COLLATION_CHARACTER_SET_APPLICABILITY

  Information about supported character sets, collations for each character set, and mapping from each collation to its character set

- ENGINES, PLUGINS

  Information about storage engines and server plugins

- USER_PRIVILEGES, SCHEMA_PRIVILEGES, TABLE_PRIVILEGES, COLUMN_PRIVILEGES

  Global, database, table, and column privilege information from the user, db, tables_priv, columns_priv tables in the mysql database

- GLOBAL_VARIABLES, SESSION_VARIABLES, GLOBAL_STATUS, SESSION_STATUS

  Global and session values of system and status variables

- PROCESSLIST

  Information about the threads executing within the server

Individual storage engines may add their own tables to INFORMATION_SCHEMA. For example, Falcon does this if it is enabled.

To determine the columns contained in a given INFORMATION_SCHEMA table, use SHOW COLUMNS or DESCRIBE:

```
mysql> DESCRIBE INFORMATION_SCHEMA.CHARACTER_SETS;
+---------------------+-------------+------+-----+---------+-------+
| Field               | Type        | Null | Key | Default | Extra |
```

```
+----------------------+--------------+------+-----+---------+-------+
| CHARACTER_SET_NAME   | varchar(64)  | NO   |     |         |       |
| DEFAULT_COLLATE_NAME | varchar(64)  | NO   |     |         |       |
| DESCRIPTION          | varchar(60)  | NO   |     |         |       |
| MAXLEN               | bigint(3)    | NO   |     | 0       |       |
+----------------------+--------------+------+-----+---------+-------+
```

To display information from a table, use a SELECT statement. (Neither
INFORMATION_SCHEMA nor any of its table or column names are case sensitive.) The general
query to see all the columns in any given INFORMATION_SCHEMA table is as follows:

```
SELECT * FROM INFORMATION_SCHEMA.tbl_name;
```

Include a WHERE clause to be specific about what you want to see.

The preceding section described the use of SHOW statements to determine whether a
table exists or which storage engine it uses. INFORMATION_SCHEMA tables can provide the
same information. This query uses INFORMATION_SCHEMA to test for the existence of a particular table, returning 1 or 0 to indicate that the table does or does not exist, respectively:

```
mysql> SELECT COUNT(*) FROM INFORMATION_SCHEMA.TABLES
    -> WHERE TABLE_SCHEMA='sampdb' AND TABLE_NAME='member';
+----------+
| COUNT(*) |
+----------+
|        1 |
+----------+
```

Use this query to check which storage engine a table uses:

```
mysql> SELECT ENGINE FROM INFORMATION_SCHEMA.TABLES
    -> WHERE TABLE_SCHEMA='sampdb' AND TABLE_NAME='student';
+--------+
| ENGINE |
+--------+
| InnoDB |
+--------+
```

2.7.3 Obtaining Metadata from the Command Line

The mysqlshow command provides some of the same information as certain SHOW statements, which enables you to get database and table information at your command
prompt.

List databases managed by the server:

```
% mysqlshow
```

List tables in a database:

```
% mysqlshow db_name
```

Display information about columns in a table:

```
% mysqlshow db_name tbl_name
```

Display information about indexes in a table:

```
% mysqlshow --keys db_name tbl_name
```

Display descriptive information about tables in a database:

```
% mysqlshow --status db_name
```

The `mysqldump` client program enables you to see the structure of your tables in the form of a `CREATE TABLE` statement (much like `SHOW CREATE TABLE`). If you use `mysqldump` to review table structure, be sure to invoke it with the `--no-data` option so that you don't get swamped with your table's data!

```
% mysqldump --no-data db_name [tbl_name] ...
```

If you specify only the database name without any table names, `mysqldump` displays the structure for all tables in the database. Otherwise, it shows information only for the named tables.

For both `mysqlshow` and `mysqldump`, specify the usual connection parameter options as necessary, such as `--host`, `--user`, or `--password`.

2.8 Performing Multiple-Table Retrievals with Joins

It does no good to put records in a database unless you retrieve them eventually and do something with them. That's the purpose of the `SELECT` statement: to help you get at your data. `SELECT` probably is used more often than any other statement in the SQL language, but it can also be the trickiest; the conditions you use for choosing rows can be arbitrarily complex and can involve comparisons between columns in many tables.

The basic syntax of the `SELECT` statement looks like this:

```
SELECT select_list        # What columns to select
FROM table_list           # The tables from which to select rows
WHERE row_constraint      # What conditions rows must satisfy
GROUP BY grouping_columns # How to group results
ORDER BY sorting_columns  # How to sort results
HAVING group_constraint   # What conditions groups must satisfy
LIMIT count;              # Row count limit on results
```

Everything in this syntax is optional except the word `SELECT` and the *select_list* part that specifies what you want to produce as output. Some databases require the `FROM` clause as well. MySQL does not, which enables you to evaluate expressions without referring to any tables:

```
SELECT SQRT(POW(3,2)+POW(4,2));
```

In Chapter 1, we devoted quite a bit of attention to single-table SELECT statements, concentrating primarily on the output column list and the WHERE, GROUP BY, ORDER BY, HAVING, and LIMIT clauses. This section covers an aspect of SELECT that is often confusing: writing joins; that is, SELECT statements that retrieve rows from multiple tables. We'll discuss the types of join MySQL supports, what they mean, and how to specify them. This should help you employ MySQL more effectively, because in many cases, the real problem of figuring out how to write a query is determining the proper way to join tables together.

One problem with using SELECT is that when you first encounter a new type of problem, it's not always easy to see how to write a SELECT query to solve it. However, after you figure it out, you can use that experience when you run across similar problems in the future. SELECT is probably the statement for which past experience plays the largest role in being able to use it effectively, simply because of the sheer variety of problems to which it applies.

As you gain experience, you'll be able to adapt joins more easily to new problems, and you'll find yourself thinking things like, "Oh, yes, that's one of those LEFT JOIN things," or, "Aha, that's a three-way join restricted by the common pairs of key columns." (You may find it encouraging to hear that experience helps you. Or you may find it alarming to consider that you could wind up thinking in terms like that.)

Many of the examples that demonstrate how to use the forms of join operations that MySQL supports use the following two tables, t1 and t2:

```
Table t1:      Table t2:
+----+----+    +----+----+
| i1 | c1 |    | i2 | c2 |
+----+----+    +----+----+
|  1 | a  |    |  2 | c  |
|  2 | b  |    |  3 | b  |
|  3 | c  |    |  4 | a  |
+----+----+    +----+----+
```

The tables are deliberately chosen to be small so that the effect of each type of join can be readily seen.

Other types of multiple-table SELECT statement are subqueries (one SELECT nested within another) and UNION statements. These are covered in Section 2.9, "Performing Multiple-Table Retrievals with Subqueries," and Section 2.10, "Performing Multiple-Table Retrievals with UNION."

A related multiple-table feature that MySQL supports is the capability of deleting or updating rows in one table based on the contents of another. For example, you might want to remove rows in one table that aren't matched by any row in another, or copy values from columns in one table to columns in another. Section 2.12, "Multiple-Table Deletes and Updates," discusses these types of operations.

2.8.1 The Inner Join

If a SELECT statement names multiple tables in the FROM clause with the names separated by INNER JOIN, MySQL performs an inner join, which produces results by matching rows in one table with rows in another table. For example, if you join t1 and t2 as follows, each row in t1 is combined with each row in t2:

```
mysql> SELECT * FROM t1 INNER JOIN t2;
+----+----+----+----+
| i1 | c1 | i2 | c2 |
+----+----+----+----+
|  1 | a  |  2 | c  |
|  2 | b  |  2 | c  |
|  3 | c  |  2 | c  |
|  1 | a  |  3 | b  |
|  2 | b  |  3 | b  |
|  3 | c  |  3 | b  |
|  1 | a  |  4 | a  |
|  2 | b  |  4 | a  |
|  3 | c  |  4 | a  |
+----+----+----+----+
```

In this statement, SELECT * means "select every column from every table named in the FROM clause." You could also write this as SELECT t1.*, t2.*:

```
SELECT t1.*, t2.* FROM t1 INNER JOIN t2;
```

If you don't want to select all columns or you want to display them in a different left-to-right order, just name each column that you want to see, separated by commas.

A join where each row of each table is combined with each row in every other table to produce all possible combinations is known as the "cartesian product." Joining tables this way has the potential to produce a very large number of rows because the possible row count is the product of the number of rows in each table. A cross join between three tables that contain 100, 200, and 300 rows, respectively, could return $100 \times 200 \times 300 = 6$ million rows. That's a lot of rows, even though the individual tables are small. In cases like this, normally a WHERE clause is useful for reducing the result set to a more manageable size.

If you add a WHERE clause causing tables to be matched on the values of certain columns, the join selects only rows with equal values in those columns:

```
mysql> SELECT t1.*, t2.* FROM t1 INNER JOIN t2 WHERE t1.i1 = t2.i2;
+----+----+----+----+
| i1 | c1 | i2 | c2 |
+----+----+----+----+
|  2 | b  |  2 | c  |
|  3 | c  |  3 | b  |
+----+----+----+----+
```

The CROSS JOIN and JOIN join types are similar to INNER JOIN. For example, these statements are equivalent:

```
SELECT t1.*, t2.* FROM t1 INNER JOIN t2 WHERE t1.i1 = t2.i2;
SELECT t1.*, t2.* FROM t1 CROSS JOIN t2 WHERE t1.i1 = t2.i2;
SELECT t1.*, t2.* FROM t1 JOIN t2 WHERE t1.i1 = t2.i2;
```

The ',' (comma) join operator is similar as well:

```
SELECT t1.*, t2.* FROM t1, t2 WHERE t1.i1 = t2.i2;
```

However, the comma operator has a different precedence from the other join types, and it can sometimes produce syntax errors when the other types will not. I recommend that you avoid the comma operator.

INNER JOIN, CROSS JOIN, and JOIN (but not the comma operator) allow alternative syntaxes for specifying how to match table columns:

- One syntax uses an ON clause rather than a WHERE clause. The following example shows this using INNER JOIN:

  ```
  SELECT t1.*, t2.* FROM t1 INNER JOIN t2 ON t1.i1 = t2.i2;
  ```

  ON can be used regardless of whether the columns you're joining on have the same name.

- The other syntax involves a USING() clause; this is similar in concept to ON, but the name of the joined column or columns must be the same in each table. For example, the following query joins mytbl1.b to mytbl2.b:

  ```
  SELECT mytbl1.*, mytbl2.* FROM mytbl1 INNER JOIN mytbl2 USING (b);
  ```

2.8.2 Qualifying References to Columns from Joined Tables

References to table columns throughout a SELECT statement must resolve unambiguously to a single table named in the FROM clause. If only one table is named, there is no ambiguity; all columns must be columns of that table. If multiple tables are named, any column name that appears in only one table is similarly unambiguous. However, if a column name appears in multiple tables, references to the column must be qualified with a table identifier using tbl_name.col_name syntax to specify which table you mean. Suppose that a table mytbl1 contains columns a and b, and a table mytbl2 contains columns b and c. In this case, references to columns a or c are unambiguous, but references to b must be qualified as either mytbl1.b or mytbl2.b:

```
SELECT a, mytbl1.b, mytbl2.b, c FROM mytbl1 INNER JOIN mytbl2 ... ;
```

Sometimes a table name qualifier is not sufficient to resolve a column reference. For example, if you're performing a self-join (that is, joining a table to itself), you're using the table multiple times within the query and it doesn't help to qualify a column name with the table name. In this case, table aliases are useful for communicating your intent. You can assign an alias to any instance of the table and refer to columns from that instance as *alias_name.col_name*. The following query joins a table to itself, but assigns an alias to one instance of the table to enable column references to be specified unambiguously:

```
SELECT mytbl.col1, m.col2 FROM mytbl INNER JOIN mytbl AS m
WHERE mytbl.col1 > m.col1;
```

2.8.3 Left and Right (Outer) Joins

An inner join shows only rows where a match can be found in both tables. Outer joins show matches, too, but can also show rows in one table that have no match in the other table. Two kinds of outer joins are left and right joins. Most of the examples in this section use LEFT JOIN, which identifies rows in the left table that are not matched by the right table. RIGHT JOIN is the same except that the roles of the tables are reversed.

A LEFT JOIN works like this: You specify the columns to be used for matching rows in the two tables. When a row from the left table matches a row from the right table, the contents of the rows are selected as an output row. When a row in the left table has no match, it is still selected for output, but joined with a "fake" row from the right table that contains NULL in all the columns.

In other words, a LEFT JOIN forces the result set to contain a row for every row selected from the left table, whether or not there is a match for it in the right table. The left-table rows with no match can be identified by the fact that all columns from the right table are NULL. These result rows tell you which rows are missing from the right table. That is an interesting and important property, because this kind of problem comes up in many different contexts. Which customers have not been assigned an account representative? For which inventory items have no sales been recorded? Or, closer to home with our sampdb database: Which students have not taken a particular exam? Which students have no rows in the absence table (that is, which students have perfect attendance)?

Consider once again our two tables, t1 and t2:

```
Table t1:      Table t2:
+----+----+    +----+----+
| i1 | c1 |    | i2 | c2 |
+----+----+    +----+----+
|  1 | a  |    |  2 | c  |
|  2 | b  |    |  3 | b  |
|  3 | c  |    |  4 | a  |
+----+----+    +----+----+
```

If we use an inner join to match these tables on t1.i1 and t2.i2, we'll get output only for the values 2 and 3, because those are the values that appear in both tables:

```
mysql> SELECT t1.*, t2.* FROM t1 INNER JOIN t2 ON t1.i1 = t2.i2;
+----+----+----+----+
| i1 | c1 | i2 | c2 |
+----+----+----+----+
|  2 | b  |  2 | c  |
|  3 | c  |  3 | b  |
+----+----+----+----+
```

A left join produces output for every row in t1, whether or not t2 matches it. To write a left join, name the tables with LEFT JOIN in between rather than INNER JOIN:

```
mysql> SELECT t1.*, t2.* FROM t1 LEFT JOIN t2 ON t1.i1 = t2.i2;
+----+----+------+------+
| i1 | c1 | i2   | c2   |
+----+----+------+------+
|  1 | a  | NULL | NULL |
|  2 | b  |    2 | c    |
|  3 | c  |    3 | b    |
+----+----+------+------+
```

Now there is an output row even for the t1.i1 value of 1, which has no match in t2. All the columns in this row that correspond to t2 columns have a value of NULL.

One thing to watch out for with LEFT JOIN is that unless right-table columns are defined as NOT NULL, you may get problematic rows in the result. For example, if the right table contains columns with NULL values, you won't be able to distinguish those NULL values from NULL values that identify unmatched rows.

As mentioned earlier, a RIGHT JOIN is like a LEFT JOIN with the roles of the tables reversed. These two statements are equivalent:

```
SELECT t1.*, t2.* FROM t1 LEFT JOIN t2 ON t1.i1 = t2.i2;
SELECT t1.*, t2.* FROM t2 RIGHT JOIN t1 ON t1.i1 = t2.i2;
```

The following discussion in phrased in terms of LEFT JOIN only, but you can adjust it for RIGHT JOIN by reversing table roles.

LEFT JOIN is especially useful when you want to find *only* those left table rows that are unmatched by the right table. Do this by adding a WHERE clause that selects only the rows that have NULL values in a right table column—in other words, the rows in one table that are missing from the other:

```
mysql> SELECT t1.*, t2.* FROM t1 LEFT JOIN t2 ON t1.i1 = t2.i2
    -> WHERE t2.i2 IS NULL;
+----+----+------+------+
| i1 | c1 | i2   | c2   |
+----+----+------+------+
|  1 | a  | NULL | NULL |
+----+----+------+------+
```

Normally, when you write a query like this, your real interest is in the unmatched values in the left table. The NULL columns from the right table are of no interest for display purposes, so you would omit them from the output column list:

```
mysql> SELECT t1.* FROM t1 LEFT JOIN t2 ON t1.i1 = t2.i2
    -> WHERE t2.i2 IS NULL;
+----+----+
| i1 | c1 |
+----+----+
|  1 | a  |
+----+----+
```

Like INNER JOIN, a LEFT JOIN can be written using an ON clause or a USING() clause to specify the matching conditions. As with INNER JOIN, ON can be used whether or not the joined columns from each table have the same name, but USING() requires that they have the same names.

LEFT JOIN has a few synonyms and variants. LEFT OUTER JOIN is a synonym for LEFT JOIN. MySQL also supports an ODBC-style notation for LEFT OUTER JOIN that uses curly braces and OJ ("outer join"):

```
mysql> SELECT t1.* FROM { OJ t1 LEFT OUTER JOIN t2 ON t1.i1 = t2.i2 }
    -> WHERE t2.i2 IS NULL;
+----+----+
| i1 | c1 |
+----+----+
|  1 | a  |
+----+----+
```

NATURAL LEFT JOIN is similar to LEFT JOIN; it performs a LEFT JOIN, matching all columns that have the same name in the left and right tables. (Thus, no ON or USING clause is given.)

As already mentioned, LEFT JOIN is useful for answering "Which values are missing?" questions. Let's apply this principle to the tables in the sampdb database and consider a more complex example than those shown earlier using t1 and t2.

For the grade-keeping project, first mentioned in Chapter 1, we have a student table listing students, a grade_event table listing the grade events that have occurred, and a score table listing scores for each student for each grade event. However, if a student was ill on the day of some quiz or test, the score table wouldn't contain any score for the student for that event. A makeup quiz or test should be given in such cases, but how do we find these missing rows?

The problem is to determine which students have no score for a given grade event, and to do this for each grade event. Another way to say this is that we want to find out which combinations of student and grade event are not present in the score table. This "which values are not present" wording is a tip-off that we want a LEFT JOIN. The join isn't as simple as in the previous examples, though: We aren't just looking for values that are not present in a single column, we're looking for a two-column combination. The combinations we want are all the student/event combinations. These are produced by joining the student table to the grade_event table:

```
FROM student INNER JOIN grade_event
```

Then we take the result of that join and perform a LEFT JOIN with the score table to find the matches for student ID/event ID pairs:

```
FROM student INNER JOIN grade_event
    LEFT JOIN score ON student.student_id = score.student.id
                AND grade_event.event_id = score.event_id
```

Note that the ON clause allows the rows in the score table to be joined according to matches in different tables named earlier in the join. That's the key for solving this problem. The LEFT JOIN forces a row to be generated for each row produced by the cross join of the student and grade_event tables, even when there is no corresponding score table row. The result set rows for these missing score rows can be identified by the fact that the columns from the score table will all be NULL. We can identify these rows by adding a condition in the WHERE clause. Any column from the score table will do, but because we're looking for missing scores, it's probably conceptually clearest to test the score column:

```
WHERE score.score IS NULL
```

We can also sort the results using an ORDER BY clause. The two most logical orderings are by event per student and by student per event. I'll choose the first:

```
ORDER BY student.student_id, grade_event.event_id
```

Now all we need to do is name the columns we want to see in the output, and we're done. Here is the final statement:

```
SELECT
    student.name, student.student_id,
    grade_event.date, grade_event.event_id, grade_event.category
FROM
    student INNER JOIN grade_event
    LEFT JOIN score ON student.student_id = score.student_id
                AND grade_event.event_id = score.event_id
WHERE
    score.score IS NULL
ORDER BY
    student.student_id, grade_event.event_id;
```

Running the query produces these results:

```
+-----------+------------+------------+----------+----------+
| name      | student_id | date       | event_id | category |
+-----------+------------+------------+----------+----------+
| Megan     |          1 | 2008-09-16 |        4 | Q        |
| Joseph    |          2 | 2008-09-03 |        1 | Q        |
| Katie     |          4 | 2008-09-23 |        5 | Q        |
| Devri     |         13 | 2008-09-03 |        1 | Q        |
| Devri     |         13 | 2008-10-01 |        6 | T        |
| Will      |         17 | 2008-09-16 |        4 | Q        |
| Avery     |         20 | 2008-09-06 |        2 | Q        |
| Gregory   |         23 | 2008-10-01 |        6 | T        |
| Sarah     |         24 | 2008-09-23 |        5 | Q        |
| Carter    |         27 | 2008-09-16 |        4 | Q        |
```

```
| Carter    |        27 | 2008-09-23 |        5 | Q        |
| Gabrielle |        29 | 2008-09-16 |        4 | Q        |
| Grace     |        30 | 2008-09-23 |        5 | Q        |
+-----------+-----------+------------+----------+----------+
```

Here's a subtle point. The output displays the student IDs and the event IDs. The student_id column appears in both the student and score tables, so at first you might think that the output column list could name either student.student_id or score.student_id. That's not the case, because the entire basis for being able to find the rows we're interested in is that all the score table columns are returned by the LEFT JOIN as NULL. Selecting score.student_id would produce only a column of NULL values in the output. The same principle applies to deciding which event_id column to display. It appears in both the grade_event and score tables, but the query selects grade_event.event_id because the score.event_id values will always be NULL.

2.9 Performing Multiple-Table Retrievals with Subqueries

Subquery support is a capability that allows one SELECT statement to be written within parentheses and nested inside another. Here's an example that looks up the IDs for grade event rows that correspond to tests ('T') and uses them to select scores for those tests:

```
SELECT * FROM score
WHERE event_id IN (SELECT event_id FROM grade_event WHERE category = 'T');
```

Subqueries can return different types of information:

- A scalar subquery returns a single value.
- A column subquery returns a single column of one or more values.
- A row subquery returns a single row of one or more values.
- A table subquery returns a table of one or more rows of one or more columns.

Subquery results can be tested in different ways:

- Scalar subquery results can be evaluated using relative comparison operators such as = or <.
- IN and NOT IN test whether a value is present in a set of values returned by a subquery.
- ALL, ANY, and SOME compare a value to the set of values returned by a subquery.
- EXISTS and NOT EXISTS test whether a subquery result is empty.

A scalar subquery is the most restrictive because it produces only a single value. But as a consequence, scalar subqueries can be used in the widest variety of contexts. They are applicable essentially anywhere that you can use a scalar operand, such as a term of an expression, as a function argument, or in the output column list. Column, row, and table subqueries that return more information cannot be used in contexts that require a single value.

Subqueries can be correlated or uncorrelated. This is a function of whether a subquery refers to and is dependent on values in the outer query.

You can use subqueries with statements other than SELECT. However, for statements that modify tables (INSERT, REPLACE, DELETE, UPDATE, LOAD DATA) there is currently a restriction that the subquery cannot refer to the table being modified.

In some cases, subqueries can be rewritten as joins. You might find subquery rewriting techniques useful if you're writing queries that need to run on an older MySQL server, or if you want to see whether the MySQL optimizer does a better job with a join than a subquery.

The following sections discuss the kinds of operations you can use to test subquery results, how to write correlated subqueries, and how to rewrite subqueries as joins.

2.9.1 Subqueries with Relative Comparison Operators

The =, <>, >, >=, <, and <= operators perform relative-value comparisons. When used with a scalar subquery, they find all rows in the outer query that stand in particular relationship to the value returned by the subquery. For example, to identify the scores for the quiz that took place on '2008-09-23', use a scalar subquery to determine the quiz event ID and then match score rows against that ID in the outer SELECT:

```
SELECT * FROM score
WHERE event_id =
(SELECT event_id FROM grade_event
   WHERE date = '2008-09-23' AND category = 'Q');
```

With this form of statement, where the subquery is preceded by a value and a relative comparison operator, it is necessary that the subquery produce a single value. That is, it must be a scalar subquery; if it produces multiple values, the statement will fail. In some cases, it may be appropriate to satisfy the single-value requirement by limiting the subquery result with LIMIT 1.

Use of scalar subqueries with relative comparison operators is handy for solving problems where you'd be tempted to use an aggregate function in a WHERE clause. For example, to determine which of the presidents in the president table was born first, you might try this statement:

```
SELECT * FROM president WHERE birth = MIN(birth);
```

That doesn't work because you can't use aggregates in WHERE clauses. The WHERE clause determines which rows to select, but the value of MIN() isn't known until *after* the rows have already been selected. However, you can use a subquery to produce the minimum birth date like this:

```
SELECT * FROM president
WHERE birth = (SELECT MIN(birth) FROM president);
```

Other aggregate functions can be used to solve similar problems. The following statement uses a subquery to select the above-average scores from a given grade event:

```
SELECT * FROM score WHERE event_id = 5
AND score > (SELECT AVG(score) FROM score WHERE event_id = 5);
```

If a subquery returns a single row, you can use a row constructor to compare a set of values (that is, a tuple) to the subquery result. This statement returns rows for presidents who were born in the same city and state as John Adams:

```
mysql> SELECT last_name, first_name, city, state FROM president
    -> WHERE (city, state) =
    -> (SELECT city, state FROM president
    -> WHERE last_name = 'Adams' AND first_name = 'John');
+-----------+-------------+-----------+-------+
| last_name | first_name  | city      | state |
+-----------+-------------+-----------+-------+
| Adams     | John        | Braintree | MA    |
| Adams     | John Quincy | Braintree | MA    |
+-----------+-------------+-----------+-------+
```

You can also use ROW(city, state) notation, which is equivalent to (city, state). Both act as row constructors that represent tuples.

2.9.2 IN and NOT IN Subqueries

The IN and NOT IN operators can be used when a subquery returns multiple rows to be evaluated in comparison to the outer query. They test whether a comparison value is present in a set of values. IN is true for rows in the outer query that match any row returned by the subquery. NOT IN is true for rows in the outer query that match no rows returned by the subquery. The following statements use IN and NOT IN to find those students who have absences listed in the absence table, and those who have perfect attendance (no absences):

```
mysql> SELECT * FROM student
    -> WHERE student_id IN (SELECT student_id FROM absence);
+-------+-----+------------+
| name  | sex | student_id |
+-------+-----+------------+
| Kyle  | M   |          3 |
| Abby  | F   |          5 |
| Peter | M   |         10 |
| Will  | M   |         17 |
| Avery | F   |         20 |
+-------+-----+------------+
mysql> SELECT * FROM student
    -> WHERE student_id NOT IN (SELECT student_id FROM absence);
+-----------+-----+------------+
| name      | sex | student_id |
```

```
+-----------+-----+-----------+
| Megan     | F   |         1 |
| Joseph    | M   |         2 |
| Katie     | F   |         4 |
| Nathan    | M   |         6 |
| Liesl     | F   |         7 |
...
```

IN and NOT IN also work for subqueries that return multiple columns. In other words, you can use them with table subqueries. In this case, use a row constructor to specify the comparison values to test against each column:

```
mysql> SELECT last_name, first_name, city, state FROM president
    -> WHERE (city, state) IN
    -> (SELECT city, state FROM president
    -> WHERE last_name = 'Roosevelt');
+-----------+-------------+-----------+-------+
| last_name | first_name  | city      | state |
+-----------+-------------+-----------+-------+
| Roosevelt | Theodore    | New York  | NY    |
| Roosevelt | Franklin D. | Hyde Park | NY    |
+-----------+-------------+-----------+-------+
```

IN and NOT IN actually are synonyms for = ANY and <> ALL, which are covered in the next section.

2.9.3 ALL, ANY, and SOME Subqueries

The ALL and ANY operators are used in conjunction with a relative comparison operator to test the result of a column subquery. They test whether the comparison value stands in particular relationship to all or some of the values returned by the subquery. For example, <= ALL is true if the comparison value is less than or equal to every value that the subquery returns, whereas <= ANY is true if the comparison value is less than or equal to any value that the subquery returns. SOME is a synonym for ANY.

This statement determines which president was born first by selecting the row with a birth date less than or equal to all the birth dates in the president table (only the earliest date satisfies this condition):

```
mysql> SELECT last_name, first_name, birth FROM president
    -> WHERE birth <= ALL (SELECT birth FROM president);
+------------+-------------+------------+
| last_name  | first_name  | birth      |
+------------+-------------+------------+
| Washington | George      | 1732-02-22 |
+------------+-------------+------------+
```

Less usefully, the following statement returns all rows because every date is less than or equal to at least one other date (itself):

```
mysql> SELECT last_name, first_name, birth FROM president
    -> WHERE birth <= ANY (SELECT birth FROM president);
+------------+--------------+------------+
| last_name  | first_name   | birth      |
+------------+--------------+------------+
| Washington | George       | 1732-02-22 |
| Adams      | John         | 1735-10-30 |
| Jefferson  | Thomas       | 1743-04-13 |
| Madison    | James        | 1751-03-16 |
| Monroe     | James        | 1758-04-28 |
...
```

When ALL, ANY, or SOME are used with the = comparison operator, the subquery can be a table subquery. In this case, you test return rows using a row constructor to provide the comparison values.

```
mysql> SELECT last_name, first_name, city, state FROM president
    -> WHERE (city, state) = ANY
    -> (SELECT city, state FROM president
    -> WHERE last_name = 'Roosevelt');
+-----------+-------------+-----------+-------+
| last_name | first_name  | city      | state |
+-----------+-------------+-----------+-------+
| Roosevelt | Theodore    | New York  | NY    |
| Roosevelt | Franklin D. | Hyde Park | NY    |
+-----------+-------------+-----------+-------+
```

As mentioned in the previous section, IN and NOT IN are shorthand for = ANY and <> ALL. That is, IN means "equal to any of the rows returned by the subquery" and NOT IN means "unequal to all rows returned by the subquery."

2.9.4 EXISTS and NOT EXISTS Subqueries

The EXISTS and NOT EXISTS operators merely test whether a subquery returns any rows. If it does, EXISTS is true and NOT EXISTS is false. The following statements show some trivial examples of these subqueries. The first returns 0 if the absence table is empty, the second returns 1:

```
SELECT EXISTS (SELECT * FROM absence);
SELECT NOT EXISTS (SELECT * FROM absence);
```

EXISTS and NOT EXISTS actually are much more commonly used in correlated subqueries. For examples, see Section 2.9.5, "Correlated Subqueries."

With EXISTS and NOT EXISTS, the subquery uses * as the output column list. There's no need to name columns explicitly, because the subquery is assessed as true or false based on whether it returns any rows, not based on the particular values that the rows might contain. You can actually write pretty much anything for the subquery column selection list, but if you want to make it explicit that you're returning a true value when the subquery succeeds, you might write it with `SELECT 1` rather than with `SELECT *`.

2.9.5 Correlated Subqueries

Subqueries can be uncorrelated or correlated:

- An uncorrelated subquery contains no references to values from the outer query. An uncorrelated subquery can be executed by itself as a separate statement. For example, the subquery in the following statement is uncorrelated because it refers only to the table `t1` and not to `t2`:

```
SELECT j FROM t2 WHERE j IN (SELECT i FROM t1);
```

- A correlated subquery does contain references to values from the outer query, and thus is dependent on it. Due to this linkage, a correlated subquery cannot be executed by itself as a separate statement. For example, the subquery in the following statement is true for each value of column `j` in `t2` that matches a column `i` value in `t1`:

```
SELECT j FROM t2 WHERE (SELECT i FROM t1 WHERE i = j);
```

Correlated subqueries commonly are used for `EXISTS` and `NOT EXISTS` subqueries, which are useful for finding rows in one table that match or don't match rows in another. Correlated subqueries work by passing values from the outer query to the subquery to see whether they match the conditions specified in the subquery. For this reason, it's necessary to qualify column names with table names if they are ambiguous (appear in more than one table).

The following `EXISTS` subquery identifies matches between the tables—that is, values that are present in both. The statement selects students who have at least one absence listed in the `absence` table:

```
SELECT student_id, name FROM student WHERE EXISTS
(SELECT * FROM absence WHERE absence.student_id = student.student_id);
```

`NOT EXISTS` identifies non-matches—values in one table that are not present in the other. This statement selects students who have no absences:

```
SELECT student_id, name FROM student WHERE NOT EXISTS
(SELECT * FROM absence WHERE absence.student_id = student.student_id);
```

2.9.6 Subqueries in the FROM Clause

Subqueries can be used in the `FROM` clause to generate values. In this case, the result of the subquery acts like a table. A subquery in the `FROM` clause can participate in joins, its values can be tested in the `WHERE` clause, and so forth. When using this type of subquery, you must provide a table alias to give the subquery result a name:

```
mysql> SELECT * FROM (SELECT 1, 2) AS t1 INNER JOIN (SELECT 3, 4) AS t2;
+---+---+---+---+
```

```
| 1 | 2 | 3 | 4 |
+---+---+---+---+
| 1 | 2 | 3 | 4 |
+---+---+---+---+
```

2.9.7 Rewriting Subqueries as Joins

It's often possible to rephrase a query that uses a subquery in terms of a join, and it's not a bad idea to examine queries that you might be inclined to write in terms of subqueries. A join is sometimes more efficient than a subquery, so if a SELECT written as a subquery takes a long time to execute, try writing it as a join to see whether it performs better. This section shows how to do that.

2.9.7.1 Rewriting Subqueries That Select Matching Values

Here's an example statement containing a subquery; it selects scores from the score table only for tests (that is, it ignores quiz scores):

```
SELECT * FROM score
WHERE event_id IN (SELECT event_id FROM grade_event WHERE category = 'T');
```

The same statement can be written without a subquery by converting it to a simple join:

```
SELECT score.* FROM score INNER JOIN grade_event
ON score.event_id = grade_event.event_id WHERE grade_event.category = 'T';
```

As another example, the following query selects scores for female students:

```
SELECT * from score
WHERE student_id IN (SELECT student_id FROM student WHERE sex = 'F');
```

This can be converted to a join as follows:

```
SELECT score.* FROM score INNER JOIN student
ON score.student_id = student.student_id WHERE student.sex = 'F';
```

There is a pattern here. The subquery statements follow this form:

```
SELECT * FROM table1
WHERE column1 IN (SELECT column2a FROM table2 WHERE column2b = value);
```

Such queries can be converted to a join using this form:

```
SELECT table1.* FROM table1 INNER JOIN table2
ON table1.column1 = table2.column2a WHERE table2.column2b = value;
```

In some cases, the subquery and the join might return different results. This occurs when table2 contains multiple instances of column2a. The subquery form produces only one instance of each column2a value, but the join would produce them all and its output would include duplicate rows. To suppress these duplicates, begin the join with SELECT DISTINCT rather than SELECT.

2.9.7.2 Rewriting Subqueries That Select Non-Matching (Missing) Values

Another common type of subquery statement searches for values in one table that are not present in another table. As we've seen before, the "which values are not present" type of problem is a clue that a LEFT JOIN may be helpful. Here's the statement with a subquery seen earlier that tests for students who are *not* listed in the absence table (it finds those students with perfect attendance):

```
SELECT * FROM student
WHERE student_id NOT IN (SELECT student_id FROM absence);
```

This query can be rewritten using a LEFT JOIN as follows:

```
SELECT student.*
FROM student LEFT JOIN absence ON student.student_id = absence.student_id
WHERE absence.student_id IS NULL;
```

In general terms, the subquery statement form is as follows:

```
SELECT * FROM table1
WHERE column1 NOT IN (SELECT column2 FROM table2);
```

A query having that form can be rewritten like this:

```
SELECT table1.*
FROM table1 LEFT JOIN table2 ON table1.column1 = table2.column2
WHERE table2.column2 IS NULL;
```

This assumes that *table2.column2* is defined as NOT NULL.

The subquery does have the advantage of being more intuitive than the LEFT JOIN. "Not in" is a concept that most people understand without difficulty, because it occurs outside the context of database programming. The same cannot be said for the concept of "left join," for which there is no such basis for natural understanding.

2.10 Performing Multiple-Table Retrievals with UNION

If you want to create a result set that combines the results from several queries, you can do so by using a UNION statement. For the examples in this section, assume that you have three tables, t1, t2, and t3 that look like this:

```
mysql> SELECT * FROM t1;
+------+-------+
| i    | c     |
+------+-------+
|    1 | red   |
|    2 | blue  |
|    3 | green |
+------+-------+
mysql> SELECT * FROM t2;
```

```
+------+------+
| i    | c    |
+------+------+
|   -1 | tan  |
|    1 | red  |
+------+------+
mysql> SELECT * FROM t3;
+------------+------+
| d          | i    |
+------------+------+
| 1904-01-01 |  100 |
| 2004-01-01 |  200 |
| 2004-01-01 |  200 |
+------------+------+
```

Tables t1 and t2 have integer and character columns, and t3 has date and integer columns. To write a UNION statement that combines multiple retrievals, write several SELECT statements and put the keyword UNION between them (they must retrieve the same number of columns). For example, to select the integer column from each table, do this:

```
mysql> SELECT i FROM t1 UNION SELECT i FROM t2 UNION SELECT i FROM t3;
+------+
| i    |
+------+
|    1 |
|    2 |
|    3 |
|   -1 |
|  100 |
|  200 |
+------+
```

UNION has the following properties.

Column name and data types. The column names for the UNION result come from the names of the columns in the first SELECT. The second and subsequent SELECT statements in the UNION must select the same number of columns, but corresponding columns need not have the same names or data types. (Normally, you write UNION such that corresponding columns do have the same types, but MySQL performs type conversion as necessary if they do not.) Columns are matched by position rather than by name, which is why the following two statements return different results, even though they select the same values from the two tables:

```
mysql> SELECT i, c FROM t1 UNION SELECT i, d FROM t3;
+------+------------+
| i    | c          |
+------+------------+
|    1 | red        |
|    2 | blue       |
```

```
|     3 | green      |
|   100 | 1904-01-01 |
|   200 | 2004-01-01 |
+------+------------+
mysql> SELECT i, c FROM t1 UNION SELECT d, i FROM t3;
+------------+-------+
| i          | c     |
+------------+-------+
| 1          | red   |
| 2          | blue  |
| 3          | green |
| 1904-01-01 | 100   |
| 2004-01-01 | 200   |
+------------+-------+
```

In each statement, the data type for each column of the result is determined from the selected values. In the first statement, strings and dates are selected for the second column. The result is a string column. In the second statement, integers and dates are selected for the first column, strings and integers for the second column. In both cases, the result is a string column.

Duplicate-row handling. By default, UNION eliminates duplicate rows from the result set:

```
mysql> SELECT * FROM t1 UNION SELECT * FROM t2 UNION SELECT * FROM t3;
+------------+-------+
| i          | c     |
+------------+-------+
| 1          | red   |
| 2          | blue  |
| 3          | green |
| -1         | tan   |
| 1904-01-01 | 100   |
| 2004-01-01 | 200   |
+------------+-------+
```

t1 and t2 both have a row containing values of 1 and 'red', but only one such row appears in the output. Also, t3 has two rows containing '2004-01-01' and 200, one of which has been eliminated.

UNION DISTINCT is synonymous with UNION; both retain only distinct rows.

If you want to preserve duplicates, change each UNION to UNION ALL:

```
mysql> SELECT * FROM t1 UNION ALL SELECT * FROM t2 UNION ALL SELECT * FROM t3;
+------------+-------+
| i          | c     |
+------------+-------+
| 1          | red   |
| 2          | blue  |
| 3          | green |
```

```
| -1         | tan   |
| 1          | red   |
| 1904-01-01 | 100   |
| 2004-01-01 | 200   |
| 2004-01-01 | 200   |
+------------+-------+
```

If you mix UNION or UNION DISTINCT with UNION ALL, any distinct union operation takes precedence over any UNION ALL operations to its left.

ORDER BY and LIMIT handling. To sort a UNION result as a whole, place each SELECT within parentheses and add an ORDER BY clause following the last one. However, because the UNION uses column names from the first SELECT, the ORDER BY should refer to those names, not the column names from the last SELECT:

```
mysql> (SELECT i, c FROM t1) UNION (SELECT i, d FROM t3)
    -> ORDER BY c;
+------+------------+
| i    | c          |
+------+------------+
|  100 | 1904-01-01 |
|  200 | 2004-01-01 |
|    2 | blue       |
|    3 | green      |
|    1 | red        |
+------+------------+
```

If a sort column is aliased, an ORDER BY at the end of the UNION must refer to the alias. Also, the ORDER BY cannot refer to table names. If you need to sort by a column specified as tbl_name.col_name in the first SELECT, alias the column and refer to the alias in the ORDER BY clause.

Similarly, to limit the number of rows returned by a UNION, add LIMIT to the end of the statement:

```
mysql> (SELECT * FROM t1) UNION (SELECT * FROM t2) UNION (SELECT * FROM t3)
    -> LIMIT 2;
+------+------------+
| i    | c          |
+------+------------+
| 1    | red        |
| 2    | blue       |
+------+------------+
```

ORDER BY and LIMIT also can be used within a parenthesized individual SELECT of a UNION to apply only to that SELECT:

```
mysql> (SELECT * FROM t1 ORDER BY i LIMIT 2)
    -> UNION (SELECT * FROM t2 ORDER BY i LIMIT 1)
    -> UNION (SELECT * FROM t3 ORDER BY d LIMIT 2);
```

```
+------------+------------+
| i          | c          |
+------------+------------+
| 1          | red        |
| 2          | blue       |
| -1         | tan        |
| 1904-01-01 | 100        |
| 2004-01-01 | 200        |
+------------+------------+
```

ORDER BY within an individual SELECT is used only if LIMIT is also present, to determine which rows the LIMIT applies to. It does not affect the order in which rows appear in the final UNION result.

If you want to run a UNION-type query on MyISAM tables that have the same structure, you could set up a MERGE table and query that. One reason this is useful is that it is simpler to write a query on a MERGE table than the corresponding UNION statement. A query on the MERGE table is similar to a UNION that selects corresponding columns from the individual tables that make up the MERGE table. That is, SELECT on a MERGE table is like UNION ALL (duplicates are not removed), and SELECT DISTINCT is like UNION or UNION DISTINCT (duplicates are removed).

2.11 Using Views

A view is a virtual table. That is, it acts like a table but actually contains no data. Instead, it is defined in terms of base ("real") tables or other views and provides alternative ways to look at table data. Often this can simplify applications.

This section describes some applications for views. One thing it does not cover is the DEFINER clause that views have in common with stored programs and that can be used for security purposes to control access to view data. For information about DEFINER, see Section 4.5, "Security for Stored Programs and Views."

A simple view can be nothing more than a way to select a subset of a table's columns. Suppose that you often want to select only the last_name, first_name, city, and state columns from the president table, but you don't want to write out all the columns like this:

```
SELECT last_name, first_name, city, state FROM president;
```

Nor do you want to use SELECT *. That's easier to write, but * retrieves columns that you don't want. The solution is to define a view that retrieves only the desired columns:

```
CREATE VIEW vpres AS
SELECT last_name, first_name, city, state FROM president;
```

Now the view acts as a "window" into just those columns that you want to see. This means that you can use SELECT * with the view and get back only the columns named in the view definition:

```
mysql> SELECT * FROM vpres;
```

```
+-------------+---------------+---------------------+-------+
| last_name   | first_name    | city                | state |
+-------------+---------------+---------------------+-------+
| Washington  | George        | Wakefield           | VA    |
| Adams       | John          | Braintree           | MA    |
| Jefferson   | Thomas        | Albemarle County    | VA    |
| Madison     | James         | Port Conway         | VA    |
| Monroe      | James         | Westmoreland County | VA    |
...
```

If you include a WHERE clause, MySQL adds it to the view definition when executing the statement to further restrict the result:

```
mysql> SELECT * FROM vpres WHERE last_name = 'Adams';
+-----------+-------------+-----------+-------+
| last_name | first_name  | city      | state |
+-----------+-------------+-----------+-------+
| Adams     | John        | Braintree | MA    |
| Adams     | John Quincy | Braintree | MA    |
+-----------+-------------+-----------+-------+
```

The same is true if you add ORDER BY, LIMIT, and so forth.

When you use a view, you can refer only to those columns named in the view definition. That is, you cannot refer to a column that is not part of the view, even if the column is part of the base table:

```
mysql> SELECT * FROM vpres WHERE suffix <> '';
ERROR 1054 (42S22): Unknown column 'suffix' in 'where clause'
```

The column names for a view by default are those named in the output column list of its SELECT statement. To provide column names explicitly, add a list of names in parentheses following the view name in the view definition:

```
mysql> CREATE VIEW vpres2 (ln, fn) AS
    -> SELECT last_name, first_name FROM president;
```

Now when you refer to the view, you must use the given column names rather than the names in the SELECT:

```
mysql> SELECT last_name, first_name FROM vpres2;
ERROR 1054 (42S22) at line 1: Unknown column 'last_name' in 'field list'
mysql> SELECT ln, fn FROM vpres2;
+------------+---------------+
| ln         | fn            |
+------------+---------------+
| Washington | George        |
| Adams      | John          |
| Jefferson  | Thomas        |
| Madison    | James         |
| Monroe     | James         |
...
```

A view can be used to perform calculations automatically. In Section 1.4.9.6, "Working with Dates," we developed a statement that determines the age of presidents at death. The same calculation can be incorporated into a view definition:

```
mysql> CREATE VIEW pres_age AS
    -> SELECT last_name, first_name, birth, death,
    -> TIMESTAMPDIFF(YEAR, birth, death) AS age
    -> FROM president;
```

This view includes an `age` column that is defined as a calculation, and selecting that column from the view retrieves the results of the calculation:

```
mysql> SELECT * FROM pres_age;
+------------+------------+------------+------------+------+
| last_name  | first_name | birth      | death      | age  |
+------------+------------+------------+------------+------+
| Washington | George     | 1732-02-22 | 1799-12-14 |   67 |
| Adams      | John       | 1735-10-30 | 1826-07-04 |   90 |
| Jefferson  | Thomas     | 1743-04-13 | 1826-07-04 |   83 |
| Madison    | James      | 1751-03-16 | 1836-06-28 |   85 |
| Monroe     | James      | 1758-04-28 | 1831-07-04 |   73 |
...
```

By including the age calculation in the view definition, it's no longer necessary to write out the formula to see the age values. The view hides the details.

A view can refer to multiple tables, which makes it easier to run queries that involve joins. The following view looks up scores, joining them with student and grade event information:

```
mysql> CREATE VIEW vstudent AS
    -> SELECT student.student_id, name, date, score, category
    -> FROM grade_event INNER JOIN score INNER JOIN student
    -> ON grade_event.event_id = score.event_id
    -> AND score.student_id = student.student_id;
```

When you select from the view, MySQL executes the join and returns information from multiple tables:

```
mysql> SELECT * FROM vstudent;
+------------+------------+------------+-------+----------+
| student_id | name       | date       | score | category |
+------------+------------+------------+-------+----------+
|          1 | Megan      | 2008-09-03 |    20 | Q        |
|          3 | Kyle       | 2008-09-03 |    20 | Q        |
|          4 | Katie      | 2008-09-03 |    18 | Q        |
|          5 | Abby       | 2008-09-03 |    13 | Q        |
|          6 | Nathan     | 2008-09-03 |    18 | Q        |
|          7 | Liesl      | 2008-09-03 |    14 | Q        |
|          8 | Ian        | 2008-09-03 |    14 | Q        |
...
```

The view makes it trivial to retrieve the scores for a particular student by name:

```
mysql> SELECT * FROM vstudent WHERE name = 'emily';
+------------+-------+------------+-------+----------+
| student_id | name  | date       | score | category |
+------------+-------+------------+-------+----------+
|         31 | Emily | 2008-09-03 |    11 | Q        |
|         31 | Emily | 2008-09-06 |    19 | Q        |
|         31 | Emily | 2008-09-09 |    81 | T        |
|         31 | Emily | 2008-09-16 |    19 | Q        |
|         31 | Emily | 2008-09-23 |     9 | Q        |
|         31 | Emily | 2008-10-01 |    76 | T        |
+------------+-------+------------+-------+----------+
```

Some views are updatable, which means that you can insert, update, and delete rows in the underlying table by means of operations on the view. Here is a simple example:

```
mysql> CREATE TABLE t (i INT);
mysql> INSERT INTO t (i) VALUES(1),(2),(3);
mysql> CREATE VIEW v AS SELECT i FROM t;
mysql> SELECT i FROM v;
+------+
| i    |
+------+
|    1 |
|    2 |
|    3 |
+------+
mysql> INSERT INTO v (i) VALUES(4);
mysql> DELETE FROM v WHERE i < 3;
mysql> SELECT i FROM v;
+------+
| i    |
+------+
|    3 |
|    4 |
+------+
mysql> UPDATE v SET i = i + 1;
mysql> SELECT i FROM v;
+------+
| i    |
+------+
|    4 |
|    5 |
+------+
```

For a view to be updatable, it must map directly onto a single table, it must select only columns that are simple references to table columns (not arbitrary expressions), and any operation on a view row must correspond to an operation on a single row in the underlying table. For example, if a view involves a summary calculated using an aggregate function, each view row can be based on multiple underlying table rows. In this case, the view is not updatable because there is no way to tell which underlying table row should be updated.

2.12 Multiple-Table Deletes and Updates

Sometimes it's useful to delete rows based on whether they match or don't match rows in another table. Similarly, it's often useful to update rows in one table using the contents of rows in another table. This section describes how to perform multiple-table DELETE and UPDATE operations. These types of statements draw heavily on the concepts used for joins, so be sure you're familiar with the material discussed earlier in Section 2.8, "Performing Multiple-Table Retrievals with Joins."

To perform a single-table DELETE or UPDATE, you refer only to the columns of one table and thus need not qualify the column names with the table name. For example, to delete all rows in a table t that have id values greater than 100, you'd write a statement like this:

```
DELETE FROM t WHERE id > 100;
```

But what if you want to delete rows based not on properties inherent in the rows themselves, but rather on their relationship to rows in another table? Suppose that you want to delete from t those rows with id values that are found in another table t2?

To write a multiple-table DELETE, name all the tables in a FROM clause and specify the conditions used to match rows in the tables in the WHERE clause. The following statement deletes rows from table t1 where there is a matching id value in table t2:

```
DELETE t1 FROM t1 INNER JOIN t2 ON t1.id = t2.id;
```

Notice that if a column name appears in more than one of the tables, it becomes ambiguous and must be qualified with a table name.

The syntax also allows for deleting rows from multiple tables at once. To delete rows from *both* tables where there are matching id values, name them both after the DELETE keyword:

```
DELETE t1, t2 FROM t1 INNER JOIN t2 ON t1.id = t2.id;
```

What if you want to delete non-matching rows? A multiple-table DELETE can use any kind of join that you can write in a SELECT, so employ the same strategy that you'd use when writing a SELECT that identifies the non-matching rows. That is, use a LEFT JOIN or RIGHT JOIN. For example, to identify rows in t1 that have no match in t2, you'd write a SELECT like this:

```
SELECT t1.* FROM t1 LEFT JOIN t2 ON t1.id = t2.id WHERE t2.id IS NULL;
```

The analogous DELETE statement to find and remove those rows from t1 uses a LEFT
JOIN as well:

```
DELETE t1 FROM t1 LEFT JOIN t2 ON t1.id = t2.id WHERE t2.id IS NULL;
```

MySQL supports a second multiple-table DELETE syntax. With this syntax, use a FROM
clause to list the tables from which rows are to be deleted and a USING clause to join the
tables that determine which rows to delete. The preceding multiple-table DELETE statements can be rewritten using this syntax as follows:

```
DELETE FROM t1 USING t1 INNER JOIN t2 ON t1.id = t2.id;
DELETE FROM t1, t2 USING t1 INNER JOIN t2 ON t1.id = t2.id;
DELETE FROM t1 USING t1 LEFT JOIN t2 ON t1.id = t2.id WHERE t2.id IS NULL;
```

The principles involved in writing multiple-table UPDATE statements are quite similar
to those used for DELETE: Name all the tables that participate in the operation and qualify
column references as necessary. Suppose that the quiz you gave on September 23, 2008,
contained a question that everyone got wrong, and then you discover that the reason for
this is that your answer key was incorrect. As a result, you want to add a point to everyone's score. With a multiple-table UPDATE, you can do this as follows:

```
UPDATE score, grade_event SET score.score = score.score + 1
WHERE score.event_id = grade_event.event_id
AND grade_event.date ='2008-09-23' AND grade_event.category = 'Q';
```

In this case, you could accomplish the same objective using a single-table update and a
subquery:

```
UPDATE score SET score = score + 1
WHERE event_id = (SELECT event_id FROM grade_event
WHERE date = '2008-09-23' AND category = 'Q');
```

But other updates cannot be written using subqueries. For example, you might want
to not only identify rows to update based on the contents of another table, but to copy
column values from one table to another. The following statement copies t1.a to t2.a
for rows that have a matching id column value:

```
UPDATE t1, t2 SET t2.a = t1.a WHERE t2.id = t1.id;
```

To perform multiple-table deletes or updates for InnoDB tables, you need not use the
syntax just described. Instead set up a foreign key relationship between tables that includes
an ON DELETE CASCADE or ON UPDATE CASCADE constraint. For details, see Section 2.14,
"Foreign Keys and Referential Integrity."

2.13 Performing Transactions

A transaction is a set of SQL statements that execute as a unit and that can be canceled if
necessary. Either all the statements execute successfully, or none of them have any effect.
This is achieved through the use of commit and rollback capabilities. If all of the statements in the transaction succeed, you commit it to record their effects permanently in the

database. If an error occurs during the transaction, you roll it back to cancel it. Any statements executed up to that point within the transaction are undone, leaving the database in the state it was in prior to the point at which the transaction began.

Commit and rollback provide the means for ensuring that halfway-done operations don't make their way into your database and leave it in a partially updated (inconsistent) state. The canonical example of this involves a financial transfer where money from one account is placed into another account. Suppose that Bill writes a check to Bob for $100.00 and Bob cashes the check. Bill's account should be decremented by $100.00 and Bob's account incremented by the same amount:

```
UPDATE account SET balance = balance - 100 WHERE name = 'Bill';
UPDATE account SET balance = balance + 100 WHERE name = 'Bob';
```

If a crash occurs between the two statements, the operation is incomplete. Depending on which statement executes first, Bill is $100 short without Bob having been credited, or Bob is given $100 without Bill having been debited. Neither outcome is correct. If transactional capabilities are not available to you, you have to figure out the state of ongoing operations at crash time by examining your logs manually in order to determine how to undo them or complete them. The rollback capabilities of transaction support enable you to handle this situation properly by undoing the effect of the statements that executed before the error occurred. (You may still have to determine which transactions weren't entered and re-issue them, but at least you don't have to worry about half-transactions making your database inconsistent.)

Another use for transactions is to make sure that the rows involved in an operation are not modified by other clients while you're working with them. MySQL automatically performs locking for single SQL statements to keep clients from interfering with each other, but this is not always sufficient to guarantee that a database operation achieves its intended result, because some operations are performed over the course of several statements. In this case, different clients might interfere with each other. A transaction group statements into a single execution unit to prevent concurrency problems that could otherwise occur in a multiple-client environment.

Transactional systems typically are characterized as providing ACID properties. ACID is an acronym for Atomic, Consistent, Isolated, and Durable, referring to four properties that transactions should have:

- **Atomicity:** The statements a transaction consists of form a logical unit. You can't have just some of them execute.
- **Consistency:** The database is consistent before and after the transaction executes. In other words, the transaction doesn't make a mess of your database.
- **Isolation:** One transaction has no effect on another.
- **Durability:** When a transaction executes successfully to completion, its effects are recorded permanently in the database.

Transactional processing provides stronger guarantees about the outcome of database operations, but also requires more overhead in CPU cycles, memory, and disk space.

MySQL offers some storage engines that are transaction-safe (such as InnoDB and Falcon), and some that are not transaction-safe (such as MyISAM and MEMORY). Transactional properties are essential for some applications and not for others, and you can choose which ones make the most sense for your applications. Financial operations typically need transactions, and the guarantees of data integrity outweigh the cost of additional overhead. On the other hand, for an application that logs web page accesses to a database table, a loss of a few rows if the server host crashes might be tolerable. In this case, you can use a non-transactional storage engine to avoid the overhead required for transactional processing.

2.13.1 Using Transactions to Ensure Safe Statement Execution

To use transactions, you must use a transactional storage engine such as InnoDB or Falcon. Engines such as MyISAM and MEMORY will not work. If you're not sure whether your MySQL server supports any transactional storage engines, see Section 2.6.1.1, "Checking Which Storage Engines Are Available."

By default, MySQL runs in autocommit mode, which means that changes made by individual statements are committed to the database immediately to make them permanent. In effect, each statement is its own transaction implicitly. To perform transactions explicitly, disable autocommit mode and then tell MySQL when to commit or roll back changes.

One way to perform a transaction is to issue a START TRANSACTION (or BEGIN) statement to suspend autocommit mode, execute the statements that make up the transaction, and end the transaction with a COMMIT statement to make the changes permanent. If an error occurs during the transaction, cancel it by issuing a ROLLBACK statement instead to undo the changes. START TRANSACTION suspends the current autocommit mode, so after the transaction has been committed or rolled back, the mode reverts to its state prior to the START TRANSACTION. (If autocommit was enabled beforehand, ending the transaction puts you back in autocommit mode. If it was disabled, ending the current transaction causes you to begin the next one.)

The following example illustrates this approach. First, create a table to use:

```
mysql> CREATE TABLE t (name CHAR(20), UNIQUE (name)) ENGINE = InnoDB;
```

The statement creates an InnoDB table, but you can use a different transactional storage engine if you like. Next, initiate a transaction with START TRANSACTION, add a couple of rows to the table, commit the transaction, and then see what the table looks like:

```
mysql> START TRANSACTION;
mysql> INSERT INTO t SET name = 'William';
mysql> INSERT INTO t SET name = 'Wallace';
mysql> COMMIT;
mysql> SELECT * FROM t;
+---------+
| name    |
+---------+
| Wallace |
| William |
+---------+
```

You can see that the rows have been recorded in the table. If you had started up a second instance of mysql and selected the contents of t after the inserts but before the commit, the rows would not show up. They would not become visible to the second mysql process until the COMMIT statement had been issued by the first one.

If an error occurs during a transaction, you can cancel it with ROLLBACK. Using the t table again, you can see this by issuing the following statements:

```
mysql> START TRANSACTION;
mysql> INSERT INTO t SET name = 'Gromit';
mysql> INSERT INTO t SET name = 'Wallace';
ERROR 1062 (23000): Duplicate entry 'Wallace' for key 1
mysql> ROLLBACK;
mysql> SELECT * FROM t;
+---------+
| name    |
+---------+
| Wallace |
| William |
+---------+
```

The second INSERT attempts to place a row into the table that duplicates an existing name value. The statement fails because name has a UNIQUE index. After issuing the ROLLBACK, the table has only the two rows that it contained prior to the failed transaction. In particular, the INSERT that was performed just prior to the point of the error has been undone and its effect is not recorded in the table.

Issuing a START TRANSACTION statement while a transaction is in process commits the current transaction implicitly before beginning a new one.

Another way to perform transactions is to manipulate the autocommit mode directly using SET statements:

```
SET autocommit = 0;
SET autocommit = 1;
```

Setting the autocommit variable to zero disables autocommit mode. The effect of any statements that follow becomes part of the current transaction, which you end by issuing a COMMIT or ROLLBACK statement to commit or cancel it. With this method, autocommit mode remains off until you turn it back on, so ending one transaction also begins the next one. You can also commit a transaction by re-enabling autocommit mode.

To see how this approach works, begin with the same table as for the previous examples:

```
mysql> DROP TABLE t;
mysql> CREATE TABLE t (name CHAR(20), UNIQUE (name)) ENGINE = InnoDB;
```

Then disable autocommit mode, insert some rows, and commit the transaction:

```
mysql> SET autocommit = 0;
mysql> INSERT INTO t SET name = 'William';
```

```
mysql> INSERT INTO t SET name = 'Wallace';
mysql> COMMIT;
mysql> SELECT * FROM t;
+---------+
| name    |
+---------+
| Wallace |
| William |
+---------+
```

At this point, the two rows have been committed to the table, but autocommit mode remains disabled. If you issue further statements, they become part of a new transaction, which may be committed or rolled back independently of the first transaction. To verify that autocommit is still off and that ROLLBACK will cancel uncommitted statements, issue the following statements:

```
mysql> INSERT INTO t SET name = 'Gromit';
mysql> INSERT INTO t SET name = 'Wallace';
ERROR 1062 (23000): Duplicate entry 'Wallace' for key 1
mysql> ROLLBACK;
mysql> SELECT * FROM t;
+---------+
| name    |
+---------+
| Wallace |
| William |
+---------+
```

To re-enable autocommit mode, use this statement:

```
mysql> SET autocommit = 1;
```

As just described, a transaction ends when you issue a COMMIT or ROLLBACK statement, or when you re-enable autocommit while it is disabled. Transactions also end under other circumstances. In addition to the SET autocommit, START TRANSACTION, BEGIN, COMMIT, and ROLLBACK statements that affect transactions explicitly, certain other statements do so implicitly because they cannot be part of a transaction. In general, these tend to be DDL (data definition language) statements that create, alter, or drop databases or objects in them, or statements that are lock-related. For example, if you issue any of the following statements while a transaction is in progress, the server commits the transaction first before executing the statement:

```
ALTER TABLE
CREATE INDEX
DROP DATABASE
DROP INDEX
DROP TABLE
LOCK TABLES
RENAME TABLE
```

```
SET autocommit = 1 (if not already set to 1)
TRUNCATE TABLE
UNLOCK TABLES (if tables currently are locked)
```

For a complete list of statements that cause implicit commits in your version of MySQL, see the MySQL Reference Manual.

A transaction also ends if a client's connection ends or is broken before a commit occurs. In this case, the server automatically rolls back any transaction the client was performing.

If a client program automatically reconnects after its connection to the server is lost, the connection will be reset to its default state of having autocommit enabled.

Transactions are useful in all kinds of situations. Suppose that you're working with the score table that is part of the grade-keeping project and you discover that the grades for two students have gotten mixed up and need to be switched. The incorrectly entered grades are as follows:

```
mysql> SELECT * FROM score WHERE event_id = 5 AND student_id IN (8,9);
+------------+----------+-------+
| student_id | event_id | score |
+------------+----------+-------+
|          8 |        5 |    18 |
|          9 |        5 |    13 |
+------------+----------+-------+
```

To fix this, student 8 should be given a score of 13 and student 9 a score of 18. That can be done easily with two statements:

```
UPDATE score SET score = 13 WHERE event_id = 5 AND student_id = 8;
UPDATE score SET score = 18 WHERE event_id = 5 AND student_id = 9;
```

However, it's necessary to ensure that both statements succeed as a unit. This is a problem to which transactional methods may be applied. To use START TRANSACTION, do this:

```
mysql> START TRANSACTION;
mysql> UPDATE score SET score = 13 WHERE event_id = 5 AND student_id = 8;
mysql> UPDATE score SET score = 18 WHERE event_id = 5 AND student_id = 9;
mysql> COMMIT;
```

To accomplish the same thing by manipulating the autocommit mode explicitly instead, do this:

```
mysql> SET autocommit = 0;
mysql> UPDATE score SET score = 13 WHERE event_id = 5 AND student_id = 8;
mysql> UPDATE score SET score = 18 WHERE event_id = 5 AND student_id = 9;
mysql> COMMIT;
mysql> SET autocommit = 1;
```

Either way, the result is that the scores are swapped properly:

```
mysql> SELECT * FROM score WHERE event_id = 5 AND student_id IN (8,9);
```

```
+------------+----------+-------+
| student_id | event_id | score |
+------------+----------+-------+
|          8 |        5 |    13 |
|          9 |        5 |    18 |
+------------+----------+-------+
```

2.13.2 Using Transaction Savepoints

MySQL enables you to perform a partial rollback of a transaction. To do this, issue a SAVEPOINT statement within the transaction to set a marker. To roll back to just that point in the transaction later, use a ROLLBACK statement that names the savepoint. The following statements illustrate how this works:

```
mysql> CREATE TABLE t (i INT) ENGINE = InnoDB;
mysql> START TRANSACTION;
mysql> INSERT INTO t VALUES(1);
mysql> SAVEPOINT my_savepoint;
mysql> INSERT INTO t VALUES(2);
mysql> ROLLBACK TO SAVEPOINT my_savepoint;
mysql> INSERT INTO t VALUES(3);
mysql> COMMIT;
mysql> SELECT * FROM t;
+------+
| i    |
+------+
|    1 |
|    3 |
+------+
```

After executing these statements, the first and third rows have been inserted, but the second one has been canceled by the partial rollback to the my_savepoint savepoint.

2.13.3 Transaction Isolation

Because MySQL is a multiple-user database system, different clients can attempt to use any given table at the same time. Storage engines such as MyISAM use table locking to keep clients from modifying a table at the same time, but this does not provide good concurrency performance when there are many updates. The InnoDB storage engine takes a different approach. It uses row-level locking for finer-grained control over table access by clients. One client can modify a row at the same time that another client reads or modifies a different row in the same table. If both clients want to modify a row at the same time, whichever of them acquires a lock on the row gets to modify it first. This provides better concurrency than table locking. However, there is the question about whether one client's transaction should be able to see the changes made by another client's transaction.

InnoDB implements transaction isolation levels to give clients control over what kind of changes made by other transactions they want to see. Different isolation levels allow or prevent the various problems that can occur when different transactions run simultaneously:

- Dirty reads. A dirty read occurs when a change made by one transaction can be seen by other transactions before the transaction has been committed. Another transaction thus might think the row has been changed, even though that will not really be true if the transaction that changed the row later is rolled back.

- Nonrepeatable reads. A nonrepeatable read refers to the failure by a transaction to get the same result for a given SELECT statement each time it executes it. This might happen if one transaction performs a SELECT twice but another transaction changes some of the rows in between the two executions.

- Phantom rows. A phantom is a row that becomes visible to a transaction when it was not previously. Suppose that a transaction performs a SELECT and then another transaction inserts a row. If the first transaction runs the same SELECT again and sees the new row, that is a phantom.

To deal with these problems, InnoDB supports four transaction isolation levels. These levels determine which modifications made by one transaction can be seen by other transactions that execute at the same time:

- READ UNCOMMITTED

  A transaction can see row modifications made by other transactions even before they have been committed.

- READ COMMITTED

  A transaction can see row modifications made by other transactions only if they have been committed.

- REPEATABLE READ

  If a transaction performs a given SELECT twice, the result is repeatable. That is, it gets the same result each time, even if other transactions have changed or inserted rows in the meantime.

- SERIALIZABLE

  This isolation level is similar to REPEATABLE READ but isolates transactions more completely: Rows examined by one transaction cannot be modified by other transactions until the first transaction completes. This enables one transaction to read rows and at the same time prevent them from being modified by other transactions until it is done with them.

Table 2.4 shows for each isolation level whether it allows dirty reads, nonrepeatable reads, or phantom rows. The table is InnoDB-specific in that REPEATABLE READ does not allow phantom rows to occur. Some database systems do allow phantoms at the REPEATABLE READ isolation level.

Table 2.4   **Problems Allowed by Isolation Levels**

Isolation Level	Dirty Reads	Nonrepeatable Reads	Phantom Rows
READ UNCOMMITTED	Yes	Yes	Yes
READ COMMITTED	No	Yes	Yes
REPEATABLE READ	No	No	No
SERIALIZABLE	No	No	No

The default InnoDB isolation level is REPEATABLE READ. This can be changed at server startup with the `--transaction-isolation` option, or at runtime with the SET TRANSACTION statement. The statement has three forms:

```
SET GLOBAL TRANSACTION ISOLATION LEVEL level;
SET SESSION TRANSACTION ISOLATION LEVEL level;
SET TRANSACTION ISOLATION LEVEL level;
```

A client that has the SUPER privilege can use SET TRANSACTION to change the global isolation level, which then applies to any clients that connect thereafter. In addition, any client can change its own transaction isolation level, either for all subsequent transactions within its session with the server (if SESSION is specified) or for its next transaction only (if SESSION is omitted). No special privileges are required for the client-specific levels.

Most of the information in this section also applies to Falcon. Some differences from InnoDB are that Falcon does not support the READ UNCOMMITTED isolation level and currently does not support SERIALIZABLE (although work is in progress to add support for the latter level).

2.13.4 Non-Transactional Approaches to Transactional Problems

In a non-transactional environment, some transactional issues can be handled and some cannot. The following discussion covers what can and cannot be achieved without using transactions. You can use this information to determine whether an application can employ the techniques here and avoid the overhead of transaction-safe tables.

First, let's consider how concurrency problems can occur when multiple clients attempt to make changes to a database using operations that each require several statements. Suppose that you're in the garment sales business and your cash register software automatically updates your inventory levels whenever one of your salesmen processes a sale. The sequence of events shown here outlines the operations that take place when multiple sales occur. For the example, assume that the initial shirt inventory level is 47.

1. Salesman A sells three shirts and registers the sale. The register software begins to update the database by selecting the current shirt count (47):

   ```
   SELECT quantity FROM inventory WHERE item = 'shirt';
   ```

2. In the meantime, Salesman B has sold two shirts and registered the sale. The software at the second register also begins to update the database:

```
SELECT quantity FROM inventory WHERE item ='shirt';
```

3. The first register computes the new inventory level to be 47-3 = 44 and updates the shirt count accordingly:

```
UPDATE inventory SET quantity = 44 WHERE item = 'shirt';
```

4. The second register computes the new inventory level to be 47-2 = 45 and updates the count:

```
UPDATE inventory SET quantity = 45 WHERE item = 'shirt';
```

At the end of this sequence of events, you've sold five shirts. That's good. However, the inventory level says 45. That's bad, because it should be 42. The problem is that if you look up the inventory level in one statement and update the value in another statement, you have a multiple-statement operation. The action taken in the second statement is dependent on the value retrieved in the first. If separate multiple-statement operations occur during overlapping time frames, the statements from each operation intertwine and interfere with each other. To solve this problem, it's necessary that the statements for a given operation execute without interference from other operations.

To deal with the concurrency issues inherent in the situation just described, you can take a couple of approaches.

Lock the tables explicitly. You can group statements and execute them as a unit by surrounding them with LOCK TABLES and UNLOCK TABLES statements: Lock all the tables that you need to use, issue your statements, and release the locks. This prevents anyone else from changing the tables while you have them locked. Using table locking, the inventory update scenario might be handled like this:

1. Salesman A sells three shirts and registers the sale. The register software begins the inventory process by acquiring a table lock and retrieving the current shirt count (47):

```
LOCK TABLES inventory WRITE;
SELECT quantity FROM inventory WHERE item = 'shirt';
```

A WRITE lock is necessary here because the ultimate goal of the operation is to modify the inventory table, which involves writing to it.

2. In the meantime, Salesman B has sold two shirts and registered the sale. The software at the second register also begins to update the database by trying to acquire a lock:

```
LOCK TABLES inventory WRITE;
```

In this case, this statement blocks because Salesman A already holds a lock on the table.

3. The first register computes the new inventory level to be 47-3 = 44, updates the shirt count, and releases the lock:

```
UPDATE inventory SET quantity = 44 WHERE item = 'shirt';
UNLOCK TABLES;
```

4. When the first register releases the lock, the second register's lock request succeeds, and it can proceed to retrieve the current shirt count (44):

```
SELECT quantity FROM inventory WHERE item = 'shirt';
```

5. The second register computes the new inventory level to be 44-2 = 42, updates the shirt count, and releases the lock:

```
UPDATE inventory SET quantity = 42 WHERE item = 'shirt';
UNLOCK TABLES;
```

Now the statements from the two operations don't get mixed up and the inventory level is set properly.

If you're using multiple tables, you must lock all of them before you execute the grouped statements. If you only read from a particular table, however, you need only a read lock on it, not a write lock. (This lets other clients read the tables while you're using them, but prevents clients from writing to them.) Suppose that you have a set of queries in which you want to make some changes to the inventory table, and you also need to read some data from a customer table. In this case, you need a write lock on the inventory table and a read lock on the customer table:

```
LOCK TABLES inventory WRITE, customer READ;
... use the tables here ...
UNLOCK TABLES;
```

Use relative updates, not absolute updates. For the inventory updating method that uses explicit table locking, the operation involves looking up the current inventory level with one statement, computing the new value based on the number of shirts sold, and then updating the level to the new value with another statement. Another way to keep operations performed by multiple clients from interfering with each other is to reduce each operation to a single statement. This eliminates inter-statement dependencies that arise in multiple-statement operations. Not every operation can be handled by a single statement, but for the inventory update scenario, this strategy works well. It's possible to perform each inventory update in one step simply by modifying the shirt count relative to its current value:

1. Salesman A sells three shirts and the register software decrements the shirt count by three:

```
UPDATE inventory SET quantity = quantity - 3 WHERE item = 'shirt';
```

2. Salesman B sells two shirts and the register software decrements the shirt count by two:

```
UPDATE inventory SET quantity = quantity - 2 WHERE item = 'shirt';
```

With this method, each modification to the database no longer requires multiple statements. This eliminates concurrency issues, so there is no need to use explicit table locks. If an operation you want to perform is similar to this, there may be no need for transactions at all.

The non-transactional approaches just described can be applied successfully to many types of problems, but they have certain limitations:

- Not every operation can be written in terms of relative updates. Sometimes you *must* use multiple statements, in which case concurrency issues must be considered and dealt with.

- You may be able to keep clients from interfering with each other by locking tables for the duration of a multiple-statement operation, but what happens if an error occurs in the middle of the operation? In this case, you'd want the effects of the earlier statements to be undone so that the database isn't left in a half-modified and inconsistent state. Unfortunately, although table locking can help you address concurrency issues, non-transactional tables provide no assistance in recovering from errors.

- The locking strategy requires you to lock and unlock your tables yourself. If you revise an operation in such a way that changes the set of tables used, you must remember to modify the LOCK TABLES statement accordingly.

If any of these issues are significant for your applications, you should use transaction-safe tables instead, because transactional capabilities help you deal with each issue. A transaction handler executes a set of statements as a unit and manages concurrency issues by preventing clients from getting in the way of each other. It also enables rollback in the case of failure to keep half-executed operations from damaging your database, and it determines which locks are necessary and acquires them automatically.

Can You Mix Transactional and Non-Transactional Tables?

It is possible to use both transactional and non-transactional tables during the course of a transaction, but the result might not be what you expect. Statements for non-transactional tables always take effect immediately, even when `autocommit` is disabled. In effect, non-transactional tables are always in autocommit mode and each statement commits immediately. As a result, if you change a non-transactional table within a transaction and then attempt a rollback, the non-transactional table changes cannot be undone.

2.14 Foreign Keys and Referential Integrity

A foreign key relationship enables you to declare that an index in one table is related to an index in another. It also enables you to place constraints on what may be done to the tables in the relationship. The database enforces the rules of this relationship to maintain referential integrity. For example, the `score` table in the `sampdb` sample database contains a `student_id` column, which we use to relate score rows to students in the `student` table. When we created these tables in Chapter 1, we set up some explicit relationships between them. One of these was that we declared `score.student_id` to be a foreign key for the `student.student_id` column. That prevents a row from being entered into the `score` table unless its `student_id` value exists in the `student` table. In other words, the foreign key prevents entry of scores for non-existent students.

Foreign keys are not useful just for row entry, but for deletes and updates as well. For example, we could set up a constraint such that if a student is deleted from the `student` table, all corresponding rows for the student in the `score` table are deleted automatically as well. This is called "cascaded delete," because the effect of the delete cascades from one table to another. Cascaded update is possible as well. For example, with cascaded update, changing a student's `student_id` value in the `student` table also changes the value in the student's corresponding `score` table rows.

Foreign keys help maintain the consistency of your data, and they provide a certain measure of convenience. Without foreign keys, you are responsible for keeping track of inter-table dependencies and maintaining their consistency from within your applications. In some cases, doing this might not be much more work than issuing a few extra DELETE statements to make sure that when you delete a row from one table, you also delete the corresponding rows in any related tables. But it *is* extra work, and if the database engine will perform consistency checks for you, why not let it? Automatic checking capability becomes especially useful if your tables have particularly complex relationships. You likely will not want to be responsible for implementing these dependencies in your applications.

In MySQL, the InnoDB storage engine provides foreign key support. This section describes how to set up InnoDB tables to define foreign keys, and how foreign keys affect the way you use tables. First, it's necessary to define some terms:

- The parent is the table that contains the original key values.
- The child is the related table that refers to key values in the parent.

Parent table key values are used to associate the two tables. Specifically, an index in the child table refers to an index in the parent. The child index values must match those in the parent or else be set to NULL to indicate that there is no associated parent table row. The index in the child table is known as the "foreign key"—that is, the key that is foreign (external) to the parent table but contains values that point to the parent. A foreign key relationship can be set up to disallow NULL values, in which case all foreign key values must match a value in the parent table.

InnoDB enforces these rules to guarantee that the foreign key relationship stays intact with no mismatches. This is called "referential integrity."

2.14.1 Creating and Using Foreign Keys

The following syntax shows how to define a foreign key in a child table:

```
[CONSTRAINT constraint_name]
FOREIGN KEY [fk_name] (index_columns)
  REFERENCES tbl_name (index_columns)
  [ON DELETE action]
  [ON UPDATE action]
  [MATCH FULL | MATCH PARTIAL | MATCH SIMPLE]
```

Although all parts of this syntax are parsed, InnoDB does not implement the semantics for all the clauses: The MATCH clause is not supported and is ignored if you specify it. Also, some *action* values are recognized but have no effect. (For storage engines other than InnoDB, the entire FOREIGN KEY definition is parsed but ignored.)

InnoDB pays attention to the following parts of the definition:

- The CONSTRAINT clause, if given, supplies a name for the foreign key constraint. If you leave it out, InnoDB creates a name.

- FOREIGN KEY indicates the indexed columns in the child table that must match index values in the parent table. *fk_name* is the foreign key ID. If given, it is ignored unless InnoDB automatically creates an index for the foreign key; in that case, *fk_name* becomes the index name.

- REFERENCES names the parent table and the index columns in that table to which the foreign key in the child table refers. The *index_columns* part of the REFERENCES clause must have the same number of columns as the *index_columns* that follows the FOREIGN KEY keywords.

- ON DELETE enables you to specify what happens to the child table when parent table rows are deleted. The default if no ON DELETE clause is present is to reject any attempt to delete rows in the parent table that have child rows pointing to them. To specify an *action* value explicitly, use one of the following clauses:

  - ON DELETE NO ACTION and ON DELETE RESTRICT are the same as omitting the ON DELETE clause. (Some database systems have deferred checks, and NO ACTION is a deferred check. In MySQL, foreign key constraints are checked immediately, so NO ACTION and RESTRICT are the same.)

  - ON DELETE CASCADE causes matching child rows to be deleted when the corresponding parent row is deleted. In essence, the effect of the delete is cascaded from the parent to the child. This enables you to perform multiple-table deletes by deleting rows only from the parent table and letting InnoDB take care of deleting corresponding rows from the child table.

  - ON DELETE SET NULL causes index columns in matching child rows to be set to NULL when the parent row is deleted. If you use this option, all the indexed child table columns named in the foreign key definition must be defined to allow NULL values. (One implication of using this action is that you cannot

> define the foreign key to be a PRIMARY KEY because primary keys do not
> allow NULL values.)
>
> - ON DELETE SET DEFAULT is recognized but unimplemented and InnoDB
>   issues an error.

- ON UPDATE enables you to specify what happens to the child table when parent
  table rows are updated. The default if no ON UPDATE clause is present is to reject any
  inserts or updates in the child table that result in foreign key values that don't have
  any match in the parent table index, and to prevent updates to parent table index
  values to which child rows point. The possible *action* values are the same as for ON
  DELETE and have similar effects.

To set up a foreign key relationship, follow these guidelines:

- The child table must have an index where the foreign key columns are listed as its
  first columns. The parent table must also have an index in which the columns in the
  REFERENCES clause are listed as its first columns. (In other words, the columns in the
  key must be indexed in the tables on both ends of the foreign key relationship.) You
  must create the parent table index explicitly before defining the foreign key relationship. InnoDB automatically creates an index on foreign key columns (the refer-
  encing columns) in the child table if the CREATE TABLE statement does not include
  such an index. This makes it easier to write the CREATE TABLE statement in some
  cases. However, an automatically created index will be a non-unique index and will
  include only the foreign key columns. You should define the index in the child
  table explicitly if you want it to be a PRIMARY KEY or UNIQUE index, or if it should
  include other columns in addition to those in the foreign key.

- Corresponding columns in the parent and child indexes must have compatible
  types. For example, you cannot match an INT column with a CHAR column. Corresponding character columns must be the same length. Corresponding integer
  columns must have the same size and must both be signed or both be UNSIGNED.

- You cannot index prefixes of string columns in foreign key relationships. (That is,
  for string columns, you must index the entire column, not just a leading prefix of it.)

In Chapter 1, we created tables for the grade-keeping project that have simple foreign
key relationships. Now let's work through an example that is more complex. Begin by
creating tables named parent and child, such that the child table contains a foreign key
that references the par_id column in the parent table:

```
CREATE TABLE parent
(
  par_id    INT NOT NULL,
  PRIMARY KEY (par_id)
) ENGINE = INNODB;

CREATE TABLE child
(
```

```
par_id    INT NOT NULL,
child_id  INT NOT NULL,
PRIMARY KEY (par_id, child_id),
FOREIGN KEY (par_id) REFERENCES parent (par_id)
  ON DELETE CASCADE
  ON UPDATE CASCADE
) ENGINE = INNODB;
```

The foreign key in this case uses ON DELETE CASCADE to specify that when a row is deleted from the parent table, MySQL also should remove child rows with a matching par_id value automatically. ON UPDATE CASCADE indicates that if a parent row par_id value is changed, MySQL also should change any matching par_id values in the child table to the new value.

Now insert a few rows into the parent table, and then add some rows to the child table that have related key values:

```
mysql> INSERT INTO parent (par_id) VALUES(1),(2),(3);
mysql> INSERT INTO child (par_id,child_id) VALUES(1,1),(1,2);
mysql> INSERT INTO child (par_id,child_id) VALUES(2,1),(2,2),(2,3);
mysql> INSERT INTO child (par_id,child_id) VALUES(3,1);
```

These statements result in the following table contents, where each par_id value in the child table matches a par_id value in the parent table:

```
mysql> SELECT * FROM parent;
+--------+
| par_id |
+--------+
|      1 |
|      2 |
|      3 |
+--------+
mysql> SELECT * FROM child;
+--------+----------+
| par_id | child_id |
+--------+----------+
|      1 |        1 |
|      1 |        2 |
|      2 |        1 |
|      2 |        2 |
|      2 |        3 |
|      3 |        1 |
+--------+----------+
```

To verify that InnoDB enforces the key relationship for insertion, try adding a row to the child table that has a par_id value not found in the parent table:

```
mysql> INSERT INTO child (par_id,child_id) VALUES(4,1);
ERROR 1452 (23000): Cannot add or update a child row: a foreign key
```

```
constraint fails (`sampdb`.`child`, CONSTRAINT `child_ibfk_1` FOREIGN
KEY (`par_id`) REFERENCES `parent` (`par_id`) ON DELETE CASCADE
ON UPDATE CASCADE)
```

To test cascaded delete, see what happens when you delete a parent row:

```
mysql> DELETE FROM parent WHERE par_id = 1;
```

MySQL deletes the row from the parent table:

```
mysql> SELECT * FROM parent;
+--------+
| par_id |
+--------+
|      2 |
|      3 |
+--------+
```

In addition, it cascades the effect of the DELETE statement to the child table:

```
mysql> SELECT * FROM child;
+--------+----------+
| par_id | child_id |
+--------+----------+
|      2 |        1 |
|      2 |        2 |
|      2 |        3 |
|      3 |        1 |
+--------+----------+
```

To test cascaded update, see what happens when you update a parent row:

```
mysql> UPDATE parent SET par_id = 100 WHERE par_id =2;
mysql> SELECT * FROM parent;
+--------+
| par_id |
+--------+
|      3 |
|    100 |
+--------+
mysql> SELECT * FROM child;
+--------+----------+
| par_id | child_id |
+--------+----------+
|      3 |        1 |
|    100 |        1 |
|    100 |        2 |
|    100 |        3 |
+--------+----------+
```

The preceding example shows how to arrange for deletes or updates of a `parent` row to cause cascaded deletes or updates of any corresponding `child` rows. The `ON DELETE` and `ON UPDATE` clauses allow for other actions. For example, one possibility is to let the `child` rows remain in the table but have their foreign key columns set to `NULL`. To do this, it's necessary to make several changes to the definition of the `child` table:

- Use `ON DELETE SET NULL` rather than `ON DELETE CASCADE`. This tells InnoDB to set the foreign key column (`par_id`) to `NULL` instead of deleting the rows.
- Use `ON UPDATE SET NULL` rather than `ON UPDATE CASCADE`. This tells InnoDB to set the foreign key column (`par_id`) to `NULL` when matching parent rows are updated.
- The original definition of `child` defines `par_id` as `NOT NULL`. That won't work with `ON DELETE SET NULL` or `ON UPDATE SET NULL`, so the column definition must be changed to allow `NULL`.
- The original definition of `child` also defines `par_id` to be part of a `PRIMARY KEY`. However, a `PRIMARY KEY` cannot contain `NULL` values. Changing `par_id` to allow `NULL` therefore also requires that the `PRIMARY KEY` be changed to a `UNIQUE` index. `UNIQUE` indexes enforce uniqueness except for `NULL` values, which can occur multiple times in the index.

To see the effect of these changes, re-create the `parent` table using the original definition and load the same initial rows into it. Then create the `child` table using the new definition shown here:

```
CREATE TABLE child
(
  par_id    INT NULL,
  child_id  INT NOT NULL,
  UNIQUE (par_id, child_id),
  FOREIGN KEY (par_id) REFERENCES parent (par_id)
    ON DELETE SET NULL
    ON UPDATE SET NULL
) ENGINE = INNODB;
```

With respect to inserting new rows, the `child` table behaves similarly to the original definition. That is, it allows insertion of rows with `par_id` values found in the `parent` table, but disallows entry of values that aren't listed there:

```
mysql> INSERT INTO child (par_id,child_id) VALUES(1,1),(1,2);
mysql> INSERT INTO child (par_id,child_id) VALUES(2,1),(2,2),(2,3);
mysql> INSERT INTO child (par_id,child_id) VALUES(3,1);
mysql> INSERT INTO child (par_id,child_id) VALUES(4,1);
ERROR 1452 (23000): Cannot add or update a child row: a foreign key
constraint fails ('sampdb'.'child', CONSTRAINT 'child_ibfk_1' FOREIGN
KEY ('par_id') REFERENCES 'parent' ('par_id') ON DELETE SET NULL
ON UPDATE SET NULL)
```

There is one difference with respect to inserting rows. Because the par_id column now is defined as NULL, you can explicitly insert rows into the child table that contain NULL and no error will occur. A difference in behavior also occurs when you delete a parent row. Try removing a parent row and then check the contents of the child table to see what happens:

```
mysql> DELETE FROM parent WHERE par_id = 1;
mysql> SELECT * FROM child;
+--------+----------+
| par_id | child_id |
+--------+----------+
|   NULL |        1 |
|   NULL |        2 |
|      2 |        1 |
|      2 |        2 |
|      2 |        3 |
|      3 |        1 |
+--------+----------+
```

In this case, the child rows that had 1 in the par_id column are not deleted. Instead, the par_id column is set to NULL, as specified by the ON DELETE SET NULL constraint.

Updating a parent row has a similar effect:

```
mysql> UPDATE parent SET par_id = 100 WHERE par_id = 2;
mysql> SELECT * FROM child;
+--------+----------+
| par_id | child_id |
+--------+----------+
|   NULL |        1 |
|   NULL |        1 |
|   NULL |        2 |
|   NULL |        2 |
|   NULL |        3 |
|      3 |        1 |
+--------+----------+
```

To see what foreign key relationships an InnoDB table has, use the SHOW CREATE TABLE or SHOW TABLE STATUS statement.

If an error occurs when you attempt to create a table that has a foreign key, use the SHOW ENGINE INNODB STATUS statement to get the full error message.

2.14.2 Living Without Foreign Keys

If your MySQL server doesn't have InnoDB support, or you are using another storage engine because you need features that InnoDB does not support (such as FULLTEXT indexes or spatial data types), you cannot take advantage of foreign keys. What should you do to maintain the integrity of relationships between your tables?

The constraints that foreign keys enforce often are not difficult to implement through application logic. Sometimes, it's simply a matter of how you approach the data-entry process. Consider the `student` and `score` tables from the grade-keeping project. These are related by a foreign key relationship through the `student_id` values in each table. Suppose that we had created these as MyISAM tables rather than as InnoDB tables. MyISAM does not support foreign keys, so in this case the relationship between the tables would be implicit rather than explicit. When you administer a test or quiz and have a new set of scores to add to the database, you'd have to make sure that you don't add `score` rows containing `student_id` values that are not listed in the `student` table.

In some respects, this is just a matter of taking the proper approach to data entry. To avoid inserting scores for nonexistent students, the way you'd enter a set of scores probably would be to use an application that begins with a list of students from the `student` table. For each one, it would take the score and use the student's ID number to generate a new `score` table row. With this procedure, you would never enter a row for a student that doesn't exist. Nevertheless, it would still be *possible* to enter a bad row, for example, if you issued an INSERT statement manually. (With InnoDB tables and foreign keys, no such possibility exists.)

What about the case where you delete a student row? Suppose that you want to delete student number 13. This also implies you want to delete any score rows for that student. With a foreign key relationship in place that specifies cascading delete, you'd simply delete the `student` table row with the following statement and let MySQL take care of removing the corresponding `score` table rows automatically:

```
DELETE FROM student WHERE student_id = 13;
```

Without foreign key support, you must explicitly delete rows for all relevant tables to achieve the same effect as cascading on DELETE:

```
DELETE FROM student WHERE student_id = 13;
DELETE FROM score WHERE student_id = 13;
```

Another way to do this is to use a multiple-table delete that achieves the same effect as a cascaded delete with a single query. But watch out for a subtle trap. The following statement appears to do the trick, but it's actually not quite correct:

```
DELETE student, score FROM student INNER JOIN score
ON student.student_id = score.student_id WHERE student.student_id = 13;
```

The problem with this statement is that it will fail in the case where the student doesn't have any scores. The WHERE clause will find no matches and thus will not delete anything from the `student` table. In this case, a LEFT JOIN is more appropriate, because it will identify which `student` table row to delete even in the absence of any matching `score` table rows:

```
DELETE student, score FROM student LEFT JOIN score USING (student_id)
WHERE student.student_id = 13;
```

2.15 Using FULLTEXT Searches

MySQL includes the capability for performing full text searches. The full-text search engine enables you to look for words or phrases without using pattern-matching operations. There are three kinds of full-text search:

- Natural language searching. The search string is parsed into words and the search looks for rows containing these words.

- Boolean mode searching. The search string is parsed into words, but words can be modified by operator characters that indicate specific requirements such as that a given word should be present or absent in matching rows, or that rows must contain an exact phrase.

- Query expansion searching. This kind of search occurs in two phases. The first phase is a natural language search. Then a second search is done using the original search string concatenated with the most highly relevant matching rows from the first search. This expands the search on the basis of the assumption that words related to the original search string will match relevant rows that the original string did not.

Full-text search capability is enabled for a given table by creating a special kind of index and has the following characteristics:

- Full-text searches are based on FULLTEXT indexes, which can be created only for MyISAM tables. Only CHAR, VARCHAR, and TEXT columns can be included in a FULLTEXT index.

- Common words are ignored for FULLTEXT searches, where "common" means "present in at least half the rows." It's especially important to remember this when you're setting up a test table to experiment with the FULLTEXT capability. Be sure to insert at least three rows into your test table. If the table has just one or two rows, every word in it will occur at least 50% of the time and you'll never get any results!

- There is a built-in list of common words such as "the," "after," and "other" that are called "stopwords" and that are always ignored.

- Words that are too short also are ignored. By default, "too short" is defined as fewer than four characters, but you can reconfigure the server to set the minimum length to a different value.

- Words are defined as sequences of characters that include letters, digits, apostrophes, and underscores. This means that a string like "full-blooded" is considered to contain two words, "full" and "blooded." Normally, a full-text search matches whole words, not partial words, and the FULLTEXT engine considers a row to match a search string if it includes any of the words in the search string. If you use a boolean full-text search, you can impose the additional constraint that all the words must be present (either in any order, or, to perform a phrase search, in exactly the order listed in the search string). With a boolean search, it's also possible to match rows that do *not* include certain words, or to add a wildcard modifier to match all words that begin with a given prefix.

- A FULLTEXT index can be created for a single column or multiple columns. If it spans multiple columns, searches based on the index look through all the columns simultaneously. The flip side of this is that when you perform a search, you must specify a column list that corresponds exactly to the set of columns that matches some FULLTEXT index. For example, if you want to search col1 sometimes, col2 sometimes, and both col1 and col2 sometimes, you should have three indexes: one for each of the columns separately, and one that includes both columns.

The following examples show how to use full-text searching by creating FULLTEXT indexes and then performing queries on them using the MATCH operator. A script to create the table and some sample data to load into it are available in the fulltext directory of the sampdb distribution.

A FULLTEXT index is created much the same way as other indexes. That is, you can define it with CREATE TABLE when creating the table initially, or add it afterward with ALTER TABLE or CREATE INDEX. Because FULLTEXT indexes require you to use MyISAM tables, you can take advantage of one of the properties of the MyISAM storage engine if you're creating a new table to use for FULLTEXT searches: Table loading proceeds more quickly if you populate the table first and then add the indexes afterward, rather than loading data into an already indexed table. Suppose that you have a data file named apothegm.txt containing famous sayings and the people to whom they're attributed:

```
Aeschylus               Time as he grows old teaches many lessons
Alexander Graham Bell   Mr. Watson, come here. I want you!
Benjamin Franklin       It is hard for an empty bag to stand upright
Benjamin Franklin       Little strokes fell great oaks
Benjamin Franklin       Remember that time is money
Miguel de Cervantes     Bell, book, and candle
Proverbs 15:1           A soft answer turneth away wrath
Theodore Roosevelt      Speak softly and carry a big stick
William Shakespeare     But, soft! what light through yonder window breaks?
Robert Burton           I light my candle from their torches.
```

If you want to search by phrase and attribution separately or together, you need to index each column separately, and also create an index that includes both columns. You can create, populate, and index a table named apothegm as follows:

```
CREATE TABLE apothegm (attribution VARCHAR(40), phrase TEXT) ENGINE = MyISAM;
LOAD DATA LOCAL INFILE 'apothegm.txt' INTO TABLE apothegm;
ALTER TABLE apothegm
  ADD FULLTEXT (phrase),
  ADD FULLTEXT (attribution),
  ADD FULLTEXT (phrase, attribution);
```

2.15.1 Natural Language `FULLTEXT` Searches

After setting up the table, perform natural language full-text searches on it using `MATCH` to name the column or columns to search and `AGAINST()` to specify the search string. For example:

```
mysql> SELECT * FROM apothegm WHERE MATCH(attribution) AGAINST('roosevelt');
+--------------------+----------------------------------+
| attribution        | phrase                           |
+--------------------+----------------------------------+
| Theodore Roosevelt | Speak softly and carry a big stick |
+--------------------+----------------------------------+
mysql> SELECT * FROM apothegm WHERE MATCH(phrase) AGAINST('time');
+--------------------+-------------------------------------------+
| attribution        | phrase                                    |
+--------------------+-------------------------------------------+
| Benjamin Franklin  | Remember that time is money               |
| Aeschylus          | Time as he grows old teaches many lessons |
+--------------------+-------------------------------------------+
mysql> SELECT * FROM apothegm WHERE MATCH(attribution, phrase)
    -> AGAINST('bell');
+----------------------+----------------------------------+
| attribution          | phrase                           |
+----------------------+----------------------------------+
| Alexander Graham Bell | Mr. Watson, come here. I want you! |
| Miguel de Cervantes   | Bell, book, and candle           |
+----------------------+----------------------------------+
```

In the last example, note how the query finds rows that contain the search word in different columns, which demonstrates the `FULLTEXT` capability of searching multiple columns at once. Also note that the order of the columns as named in the query is `attribution, phrase`. That differs from the order in which they were named when the index was created (`phrase, attribution`), which illustrates that order does not matter. What matters is that there must be some `FULLTEXT` index that consists of exactly the columns named.

If you just want to see how many rows a search matches, use `COUNT(*)`:

```
mysql> SELECT COUNT(*) FROM apothegm WHERE MATCH(phrase) AGAINST('time');
+----------+
| COUNT(*) |
+----------+
|        2 |
+----------+
```

Output rows for natural language `FULLTEXT` searches are ordered by decreasing relevance when you use a `MATCH` expression in the `WHERE` clause. Relevance values are non-negative floating point values, with zero indicating "no relevance." To see these values, use a MATCH expression in the output column list:

```
mysql> SELECT phrase, MATCH(phrase) AGAINST('time') AS relevance
    -> FROM apothegm;
+------------------------------------------------+----------------+
| phrase                                         | relevance      |
+------------------------------------------------+----------------+
| Time as he grows old teaches many lessons      | 1.3253291845322 |
| Mr. Watson, come here. I want you!             |              0 |
| It is hard for an empty bag to stand upright   |              0 |
| Little strokes fell great oaks                 |              0 |
| Remember that time is money                    | 1.3400621414185 |
| Bell, book, and candle                         |              0 |
| A soft answer turneth away wrath               |              0 |
| Speak softly and carry a big stick             |              0 |
| But, soft! what light through yonder window breaks? |         0 |
| I light my candle from their torches.          |              0 |
+------------------------------------------------+----------------+
```

A natural language search finds rows that contain any of the search words, so a query such as the following returns rows that contain either "hard" or "soft":

```
mysql> SELECT * FROM apothegm WHERE MATCH(phrase)
    -> AGAINST('hard soft');
+--------------------+-------------------------------------------------+
| attribution        | phrase                                          |
+--------------------+-------------------------------------------------+
| Benjamin Franklin  | It is hard for an empty bag to stand upright    |
| Proverbs 15:1      | A soft answer turneth away wrath                |
| William Shakespeare| But, soft! what light through yonder window breaks? |
+--------------------+-------------------------------------------------+
```

Natural language mode is the default full-text search mode. In MySQL 5.1 and up, you can specify this mode explicitly by adding IN NATURAL LANGUAGE MODE after the search string. The following statement performs the same search as the preceding example:

```
SELECT * FROM apothegm WHERE MATCH(phrase)
AGAINST('hard soft' IN NATURAL LANGUAGE MODE);
```

2.15.2 Boolean Mode FULLTEXT Searches

Greater control over multiple-word matching can be obtained by using boolean mode FULLTEXT searches. This type of search is performed by adding IN BOOLEAN MODE after the search string in the AGAINST() function. Boolean searches have the following characteristics:

- The 50% rule is ignored; searches find words even if they occur in more than half of the rows.

- Results are not sorted by relevance.
- A phrase search can be performed to require all words to be present in a particular order. To match a phrase, specify the words of the phrase in double quotes. Matches occur for rows that contain the same words together in the same order as listed in the phrase:

```
mysql> SELECT * FROM apothegm
    -> WHERE MATCH(attribution, phrase)
    -> AGAINST('"bell book and candle"' IN BOOLEAN MODE);
+--------------------+------------------------+
| attribution        | phrase                 |
+--------------------+------------------------+
| Miguel de Cervantes | Bell, book, and candle |
+--------------------+------------------------+
```

- It's possible to perform a boolean mode full-text search on columns that are not part of a FULLTEXT index, although this is much slower than using indexed columns.

For boolean searches, modifiers may be applied to words in the search string. A leading plus or minus sign requires a word to be present or not present in matching rows. For example, a search string of `'bell'` matches rows that contain "bell," but a search string of `'+bell -candle'` in boolean mode matches only rows that contain "bell" and do not contain "candle."

```
mysql> SELECT * FROM apothegm
    -> WHERE MATCH(attribution, phrase)
    -> AGAINST('bell');
+----------------------+------------------------------------+
| attribution          | phrase                             |
+----------------------+------------------------------------+
| Alexander Graham Bell | Mr. Watson, come here. I want you! |
| Miguel de Cervantes   | Bell, book, and candle             |
+----------------------+------------------------------------+
mysql> SELECT * FROM apothegm
    -> WHERE MATCH(attribution, phrase)
    -> AGAINST('+bell -candle' IN BOOLEAN MODE);
+----------------------+------------------------------------+
| attribution          | phrase                             |
+----------------------+------------------------------------+
| Alexander Graham Bell | Mr. Watson, come here. I want you! |
+----------------------+------------------------------------+
```

A trailing asterisk acts as a wildcard so that any row containing words beginning with the search word match. For example `'soft*'` matches "soft," "softly," "softness," and so forth:

```
mysql> SELECT * FROM apothegm WHERE MATCH(phrase)
    -> AGAINST('soft*' IN BOOLEAN MODE);
+---------------------+----------------------------------------------------+
| attribution         | phrase                                             |
+---------------------+----------------------------------------------------+
| Proverbs 15:1       | A soft answer turneth away wrath                   |
| William Shakespeare | But, soft! what light through yonder window breaks?|
| Theodore Roosevelt  | Speak softly and carry a big stick                 |
+---------------------+----------------------------------------------------+
```

However, the wildcard feature cannot be used to match words shorter than the minimum index word length.

The entry for MATCH in Appendix C, "Operator and Function Reference," lists the full set of boolean mode modifiers.

Stopwords are ignored just as for natural language searches, even if marked as required. A search for `'+Alexander +the +great'` finds rows containing "Alexander" and "great," but ignores "the" as a stopword.

2.15.3 Query Expansion FULLTEXT Searches

A full-text search with query expansion performs a two-phase search. The initial search is like a regular natural language search. Then the most highly relevant rows from this search are used for the second phase. The words in these rows are used along with the original search terms to perform a second search. Because the set of search terms is larger, the result generally includes rows that are not found in the first phase but are related to them.

To perform this kind of search, add WITH QUERY EXPANSION following the search terms. The following example provides an illustration. The first query shows a natural language search. The second query shows a query expansion search. Its result includes an extra row that contains none of the original search terms. This row is found because it contains the word "candle" that is present in one of the rows found by the natural language search.

```
mysql> SELECT * FROM apothegm
    -> WHERE MATCH(attribution, phrase)
    -> AGAINST('bell book');
+----------------------+----------------------------------+
| attribution          | phrase                           |
+----------------------+----------------------------------+
| Miguel de Cervantes  | Bell, book, and candle           |
| Alexander Graham Bell| Mr. Watson, come here. I want you!|
+----------------------+----------------------------------+
```

```
mysql> SELECT * FROM apothegm
    -> WHERE MATCH(attribution, phrase)
    -> AGAINST('bell book' WITH QUERY EXPANSION);
+----------------------+-------------------------------------+
| attribution          | phrase                              |
+----------------------+-------------------------------------+
| Miguel de Cervantes  | Bell, book, and candle              |
| Alexander Graham Bell| Mr. Watson, come here. I want you!  |
| Robert Burton        | I light my candle from their torches. |
+----------------------+-------------------------------------+
```

2.15.4 Configuring the FULLTEXT Search Engine

Several full-text parameters are configurable and can be modified by setting system variables. The parameters that determine the shortest and longest words to index in FULLTEXT indexes are ft_min_word_len and ft_max_word_len. Words with lengths outside the range defined by these two variables are ignored when FULLTEXT indexes are built. The default minimum and maximum values are 4 and 84.

Suppose that you want to change the minimum word length from 4 to 3. Do so like this:

1. Start the server with the ft_min_word_len variable set to 3. To ensure that this happens whenever the server starts, it's best to place the setting in an option file such as /etc/my.cnf:

    ```
    [mysqld]
    ft_min_word_len=3
    ```

2. For any existing tables that already have FULLTEXT indexes, you must rebuild those indexes. You can drop and add the indexes, but it's easier and sufficient to perform a quick repair operation:

    ```
    REPAIR TABLE tbl_name QUICK;
    ```

3. Any new FULLTEXT indexes that you create after changing the parameter will use the new value automatically.

For more information on setting system variables, see Appendix D. For details on using option files, see Appendix F.

> **Note**
>
> If you use myisamchk to rebuild indexes for a table that contains any FULLTEXT indexes, see the FULLTEXT-related notes in the myisamchk description in Appendix F.

Data Types

Virtually everything you do in MySQL involves data in some way or another because, by definition, the purpose of a database management system is to manage data. Even a statement as simple as SELECT 1 involves evaluation of an expression to produce an integer data value.

Every data value in MySQL has a type. For example, 37.4 is a number and 'abc' is a string. Sometimes data types are explicit, such as when you issue a CREATE TABLE statement that specifies the type for each column you define as part of the table:

```
CREATE TABLE mytbl
(
  int_col   INT,        # integer-valued column
  str_col   CHAR(20),   # string-valued column
  date_col  DATE        # date-valued column
);
```

Other times data types are implicit, such as when you refer to literal values in an expression, pass values to a function, or use the value returned from a function. The following INSERT statement does all of those things:

```
INSERT INTO mytbl (int_col,str_col,date_col)
VALUES(14,CONCAT('a','b'),20090115);
```

The statement performs the following operations, all of which involve data types:

- It assigns the integer value 14 to the integer column int_col.
- It passes the string values 'a' and 'b' to the CONCAT() string-concatenation function. CONCAT() returns the string value 'ab', which is assigned to the string column str_col.
- It assigns the integer value 20090115 to the date column date_col. The assignment involves a type mismatch, but the integer value can reasonably be interpreted as a date value, so MySQL performs an automatic type conversion that converts the integer 20090115 to the date '2009-01-15'.

To use MySQL effectively, it's essential to understand how MySQL handles data. This chapter describes the types of data values that MySQL can handle, and discusses the issues involved in working with those types:

- The general categories of data values that MySQL can represent, including the NULL value.

- The specific data types MySQL provides for table columns, and the properties that characterize each data type. Some of MySQL's data types are fairly generic, such as the BLOB string type. Others behave in special ways that you should understand to avoid being surprised. These include the TIMESTAMP data type and integer types that have the AUTO_INCREMENT attribute.

- How the server's SQL mode affects treatment of bad data values, and the use of "strict" mode to reject bad values.

- How to generate and work with sequences.

- MySQL's rules for expression evaluation. You can use a wide range of operators and functions in expressions to retrieve, display, and manipulate data. Expression evaluation includes rules governing type conversion that come into play when a value of one type is used in a context requiring a value of another type. It's important to understand when type conversion happens and how it works; some conversions don't make sense and result in meaningless values. Assigning the string '13' to an integer column results in the value 13. However, assigning the string 'abc' to that column results in the value 0 (or an error in strict SQL mode) because 'abc' doesn't look like a number. Worse, if you perform a comparison without knowing the conversion rules, you can do considerable damage, such as updating or deleting every row in a table when you intend to affect only a few specific rows.

- How to choose data types appropriately for your table columns. It's important to know how to pick the best type for your purposes when you create a table, and when to choose one type over another when several related types might be applicable to the kind of values you want to store.

Two appendixes provide additional information that supplements the discussion in this chapter about MySQL's data types, operators, and functions. These are Appendix B, "Data Type Reference," and Appendix C, "Operator and Function Reference."

The examples shown throughout this chapter use the CREATE TABLE and ALTER TABLE statements extensively to create and alter tables. These statements should be reasonably familiar to you because we have used them in Chapter 1, "Getting Started with MySQL," and Chapter 2, "Using SQL to Manage Data." See also Appendix E, "SQL Syntax Reference."

MySQL supports several storage engines, which differ in their properties. In some cases, a column with a given data type behaves differently for different storage engines, so the way you intend to use a column might determine or influence which storage engine to choose when you create a table. This chapter refers to storage engines on occasion, but a more detailed description of the available engines and their characteristics can be found in Chapter 2.

Data handling depends in some cases on how default values are defined and on the current SQL mode. For general background on setting the SQL mode, see Section 2.1, "The Server SQL Mode." In the current chapter, Section 3.2.3, "Specifying Column Default Values," covers default value handing, and Section 3.3, "How MySQL Handles Invalid Data Values," covers strict mode and the rules for treatment of bad data.

3.1 Data Value Categories

MySQL knows about several general categories in which data values can be represented. These include numbers, string values, temporal values such as dates and times, spatial values, and the NULL value.

3.1.1 Numeric Values

Numbers are values such as 48, 193.62, or -2.378E12. MySQL understands numbers specified as integers (which have no fractional part), fixed-point or floating-point values (which may have a fractional part), and bit-field values.

3.1.1.1 Exact-Value and Approximate-Value Numbers

MySQL supports precision math for exact-value numbers, and approximate math for approximate-value numbers.

Exact-value numbers are used exactly as specified when possible. Exact values include integers (0, 14, -382) and numbers that have a decimal point (0.0, 38.5, -18.247).

Integers can be specified in decimal or hexadecimal format. In decimal format, an integer consists of a sequence of digits with no decimal point. Hexadecimal values are treated as strings by default, but in numeric contexts a hexadecimal constant is treated as a 64-bit integer. For example, 0x10 is 16 decimal. Section 3.1.2, "String Values," later in this chapter, describes hexadecimal value syntax.

An exact-value number with a fractional part consists of a sequence of digits, a decimal point, and another sequence of digits. The sequence of digits before or after the decimal point may be empty, but not both.

Approximate values are represented as floating-point numbers in scientific notation with a mantissa and exponent. This is indicated by immediately following an integer or number with a fractional part by 'e' or 'E', an optional sign character ('+' or '-'), and an integer exponent. The mantissa and exponent may be signed in any combination: 1.58E5, -1.58E5, 1.58E-5, -1.58E-5.

Hexadecimal numbers cannot be used in scientific notation; the 'e' that begins the exponent part is also a legal hex digit and thus would be ambiguous.

Any number can be preceded by a plus or minus sign character ('+' or '-') to indicate a positive or negative value.

Calculations with exact values are exact, with no loss of accuracy within the limits of the precision possible for such values. For example, you cannot insert 1.23456 as is into a column that allows only two digits after the decimal point. Calculations with approximate values are approximate and subject to rounding error.

MySQL evaluates an expression using exact or approximate math according to the following rules:

- If any approximate value is present in the expression, it is evaluated as a floating-point (approximate) expression.
- For expressions containing only exact values that are all integers, evaluation uses BIGINT (64-bit) precision.
- For expressions containing only exact values but where one or more values have a fractional part, DECIMAL arithmetic is used with 65 digits of precision.
- If any string must be converted to a number to evaluate an expression, it is converted to a double-precision floating-point value. Consequently, the expression is approximate by the preceding rules.

3.1.1.2 Bit-Field Values

Bit-field values can be written as b'val' or 0bval, where val consists of one or more binary digits (0 or 1). For example, b'1001' and 0b1001 represent 9 decimal. These bit-value notations coincide with the introduction of the BIT data type in MySQL 5.0.3, but bit-field values can be used more generally in other contexts.

A BIT value in a result set displays as a binary string, which may not print well. To convert it to an integer, add zero or use CAST():

```
mysql> SELECT b'1001' + 0, CAST(b'1001' AS UNSIGNED);
+-------------+---------------------------+
| b'1001' + 0 | CAST(b'1001' AS UNSIGNED) |
+-------------+---------------------------+
|           9 |                         9 |
+-------------+---------------------------+
```

3.1.2 String Values

Strings are values such as 'Madison, Wisconsin', 'patient shows improvement', or even '12345' (which looks like a number, but isn't). Usually, you can use either single or double quotes to surround a string value, but there are two reasons to prefer single quotes:

- The SQL standard specifies single quotes, so statements that use single-quoted strings are more portable to other database engines.
- If the ANSI_QUOTES SQL mode is enabled, MySQL treats the double quote as an identifier-quoting character, not as a string-quoting character. This means that a double-quoted value must refer to something like a database or table name. Consider the following statement:

```
SELECT "last_name" from president;
```

With ANSI_QUOTES disabled, the statement selects the literal string "last_name" once for each row in the president table. With ANSI_QUOTES enabled, the statement selects the values of the last_name column from the table.

For the examples following that use the double quote as a string quoting character, assume that ANSI_QUOTES mode is not enabled.

MySQL recognizes several escape sequences within strings that indicate special characters, as shown in Table 3.1. Each sequence begins with a backslash character ('\') to signify a temporary escape from the usual rules for character interpretation. Note that a NUL byte is not the same as the SQL NULL value; NUL is a zero-valued byte, whereas NULL in SQL signifies the absence of a value.

Table 3.1   **String Escape Sequences**

Sequence	Meaning
\0	NUL (zero-valued byte)
\'	Single quote
\"	Double quote
\b	Backspace
\n	Newline (linefeed)
\r	Carriage return
\t	Tab
\\	Single backslash
\z	Control-Z (Windows EOF character)

The escape sequences shown in the table are case sensitive, and any character not listed in the table is interpreted as itself if preceded by a backslash. For example, \t is a tab, but \T is an ordinary 'T' character.

Table 3.1 shows that you can escape single or double quotes using backslash sequences, but you actually have several options for including quote characters within string values:

- Double the quote character if the string itself is quoted using the same character:

```
'I can''t'
"He said, ""I told you so."""
```

- Quote the string with the other quote character. In this case, you do not double the quote characters within the string:

```
"I can't"
'He said, "I told you so."'
```

- Escape the quote character with a backslash; this works regardless of the quote characters used to quote the string:

```
'I can\'t'
"I can\'t"
"He said, \"I told you so.\""
'He said, \"I told you so.\"'
```

To turn off the special meaning of backslash and treat it as an ordinary character, enable the NO_BACKSLASH_ESCAPES SQL mode.

As an alternative to using quotes for writing string values, you can use two forms of hexadecimal notation. String values may be specified using the standard SQL notation X'*val*', where *val* consists of pairs of hexadecimal digits ('0' through '9' and 'a' through 'f'). For example, X'0a' is 10 decimal, and X'ffff' is 65535 decimal. The leading 'x' and the nondecimal hex digits ('a' through 'f') can be specified in uppercase or lowercase:

```
mysql> SELECT X'4A', x'4a';
+-------+-------+
| X'4A' | x'4a' |
+-------+-------+
| J     | J     |
+-------+-------+
```

In string contexts, pairs of hexadecimal digits are interpreted as 8-bit numeric byte values in the range from 0 to 255, and the result is used as a string. In numeric contexts, a hexadecimal constant is treated as a number. The following statement illustrates the interpretation of a hex constant in each type of context:

```
mysql> SELECT X'61626364', X'61626364'+0;
+-------------+---------------+
| X'61626364' | X'61626364'+0 |
+-------------+---------------+
| abcd        |    1633837924 |
+-------------+---------------+
```

Hexadecimal values also may be written using 0x followed by one or more hexadecimal digits. The leading 0x is case sensitive. 0x0a and 0x0A are legal hexadecimal values, but 0X0a and 0X0A are not.

As with X'*val*' notation, 0x values are interpreted as strings, but may be used as numbers in numeric contexts:

```
mysql> SELECT 0x61626364, 0x61626364+0;
+------------+--------------+
| 0x61626364 | 0x61626364+0 |
+------------+--------------+
| abcd       |   1633837924 |
+------------+--------------+
```

`X'val'` notation requires an even number of digits. A value such as `X'a'` is illegal. If a hexadecimal value written using `0x` notation has an odd number of hex digits, MySQL treats it as though the value has a leading zero. For example, `0xa` is treated as `0x0a`.

3.1.2.1 Types of Strings and Character Set Support

String values fall into two general categories, binary and non-binary:

- A binary string is a sequence of bytes. These bytes are interpreted without respect to any concept of character set. A binary string has no special comparison or sorting properties. Comparisons are done byte by byte based on numeric byte values; all bytes are significant, including trailing spaces.

- A non-binary string is a sequence of characters. It is associated with a character set, which determines the allowable characters that may be used and how MySQL interprets the string contents. Character sets have one or more collating (sorting) orders. The particular collation used for a string determines the ordering of characters in the character set, which affects comparison operations. The default character set and collation are `latin1` and `latin1_swedish_ci`.

  Trailing spaces in non-binary strings are not significant in comparisons, except that for the `TEXT` types, index-based comparisons are padded at the end with spaces and a duplicate-key error occurs if you attempt to insert into a unique-valued `TEXT` index a value that is different from an existing value only in the number of trailing spaces.

Character units vary in their storage requirements. A single-byte character set such as `latin1` uses one byte per character, but there also are multi-byte character sets in which some or all characters require more than one byte. For example, the Unicode character sets available in MySQL are multi-byte. `ucs2` is a double-byte character set in which each character requires two bytes. `utf8` is a variable-length multi-byte character set with characters that take from one to three bytes. (As of MySQL 6.0.4, `utf8` characters can require up to four bytes.)

To find out which character sets and collations are available in your server, use these two statements:

```
mysql> SHOW CHARACTER SET;
+----------+---------------------------+--------------------+--------+
| Charset  | Description               | Default collation  | Maxlen |
+----------+---------------------------+--------------------+--------+
| big5     | Big5 Traditional Chinese  | big5_chinese_ci    |      2 |
| dec8     | DEC West European         | dec8_swedish_ci    |      1 |
| cp850    | DOS West European         | cp850_general_ci   |      1 |
| hp8      | HP West European          | hp8_english_ci     |      1 |
| koi8r    | KOI8-R Relcom Russian     | koi8r_general_ci   |      1 |
| latin1   | cp1252 West European      | latin1_swedish_ci  |      1 |
...
| utf8     | UTF-8 Unicode             | utf8_general_ci    |      3 |
```

```
| ucs2     | UCS-2 Unicode                | ucs2_general_ci      |    2 |
...
mysql> SHOW COLLATION;
+--------------------+----------+-----+---------+----------+---------+
| Collation          | Charset  | Id  | Default | Compiled | Sortlen |
+--------------------+----------+-----+---------+----------+---------+
| big5_chinese_ci    | big5     |   1 | Yes     | Yes      |       1 |
| big5_bin           | big5     |  84 |         | Yes      |       1 |
...
| latin1_german1_ci  | latin1   |   5 |         | Yes      |       1 |
| latin1_swedish_ci  | latin1   |   8 | Yes     | Yes      |       1 |
| latin1_danish_ci   | latin1   |  15 |         | Yes      |       1 |
| latin1_german2_ci  | latin1   |  31 |         | Yes      |       2 |
| latin1_bin         | latin1   |  47 |         | Yes      |       1 |
| latin1_general_ci  | latin1   |  48 |         | Yes      |       1 |
| latin1_general_cs  | latin1   |  49 |         | Yes      |       1 |
| latin1_spanish_ci  | latin1   |  94 |         | Yes      |       1 |
...
```

As shown by the output from SHOW COLLATION, each collation is tied to a particular character set, and a given character set might have several collations. Collation names usually consist of a character set name, a language, and an additional suffix. For example, utf8_icelandic_ci is a collation for the utf8 Unicode character set in which comparisons follow Icelandic sorting rules and characters are compared in case-insensitive fashion. Collation suffixes have the following meanings:

- _ci indicates a case-insensitive collation.
- _cs indicates a case-sensitive collation.
- _bin indicates a binary collation. That is, comparisons are based on numeric character code values without reference to any language. For this reason, _bin collation names do not include any language name. Examples: latin1_bin and utf8_bin.

Binary and non-binary strings have different sorting properties:

- Binary strings are processed byte by byte in comparisons based solely on the numeric value of each byte. One implication of this property is that binary strings appear to be case sensitive ('abc' <> 'ABC'), but that is actually a side effect of the fact that uppercase and lowercase versions of a letter have different numeric byte values. There isn't really any notion of lettercase for binary strings. Lettercase is a function of collation, which applies only to character (non-binary) strings.
- Non-binary strings are processed character by character in comparisons, and the relative value of each character is determined by the collating sequence that is used for the character set. For many collations, uppercase and lowercase versions of a given letter have the same collating value, so non-binary string comparisons typically are not case sensitive. However, that is not true for case-sensitive or binary collations.

Because collations are used for comparison and sorting, they affect many operations:

- Comparisons operators: <, <=, =, <>, >=, >, and LIKE.
- Sorting: ORDER BY, MIN(), and MAX().
- Grouping: GROUP BY and DISTINCT.

To determine the character set or collation of a string, use the CHARSET() or COLLATION() function.

Quoted string literals are interpreted according to the current server settings. The default character set and collation are latin1 and latin1_swedish_ci:

```
mysql> SELECT CHARSET('abcd'), COLLATION('abcd');
+-----------------+-------------------+
| CHARSET('abcd') | COLLATION('abcd') |
+-----------------+-------------------+
| latin1          | latin1_swedish_ci |
+-----------------+-------------------+
```

MySQL treats hexadecimal constants as binary strings by default:

```
mysql> SELECT CHARSET(X'0123'), COLLATION(X'0123');
+------------------+--------------------+
| CHARSET(X'0123') | COLLATION(X'0123') |
+------------------+--------------------+
| binary           | binary             |
+------------------+--------------------+
```

Two notational conventions can be used to force a string literal to be interpreted with a given character set. First, a string constant can be designated for interpretation with a given character set using the following notation, where *charset* is the name of a supported character set:

```
_charset str
```

The _charset notation is called a "character set introducer." The string can be written as a quoted string or as a hexadecimal value. The following examples show how to cause strings to be interpreted in the latin2 or utf8 character set:

```
_latin2 'abc'
_latin2 X'616263'
_latin2 0x616263
_utf8 'def'
_utf8 X'646566'
_utf8 0x646566
```

For quoted strings, whitespace is optional between the introducer and the following string. For hexadecimal values, whitespace is required.

Second, the notation N'*str*' is equivalent to _utf8'*str*'. N (not case sensitive) and must be followed immediately by a quoted string literal with no intervening whitespace.

Introducer notation works for quoted string literals or hexadecimal constants, but not for string expressions or column values. However, any string value can be used to produce a string in a designated character set using the CONVERT() function:

```
CONVERT(str USING charset);
```

Introducers and CONVERT() are not the same. An introducer merely modifies how the string is interpreted. It does not change the string value (except that for multi-byte character sets, padding might be added if the string does not contain enough bytes). CONVERT() takes a string argument and produces a new string in the desired character set. To see the difference between introducers and CONVERT(), consider the following two statements that refer to the ucs2 double-byte character set:

```
mysql> SET @s1 = _ucs2 'ABCD';
mysql> SET @s2 = CONVERT('ABCD' USING ucs2);
```

Assume that the default character set is latin1 (a single-byte character set). The first statement interprets each pair of characters in the string 'ABCD' as a single double-byte ucs2 character, resulting in a two-character ucs2 string. The second statement converts each character of the string 'ABCD' to the corresponding ucs2 character, resulting in a four-character ucs2 string.

What is the "length" of a string? It depends. If you measure with CHAR_LENGTH(), you get the length in characters. If you measure with LENGTH(), you get the length in bytes. For strings that contain multi-byte characters the two values differ:

```
mysql> SELECT CHAR_LENGTH(@s1), LENGTH(@s1), CHAR_LENGTH(@s2), LENGTH(@s2);
+------------------+-------------+------------------+-------------+
| CHAR_LENGTH(@s1) | LENGTH(@s1) | CHAR_LENGTH(@s2) | LENGTH(@s2) |
+------------------+-------------+------------------+-------------+
|                2 |           4 |                4 |           8 |
+------------------+-------------+------------------+-------------+
```

Here is a somewhat subtle point. A binary string is not the same thing as a non-binary string that has a binary collation:

- The binary string has no character set. It is interpreted with byte semantics and comparisons use single-byte numeric codes.
- A non-binary string with a binary collation has character semantics and comparisons use numeric character values that might be based on multiple bytes per character.

Here's one way to see the difference between binary and non-binary strings with regard to lettercase. Create a binary string and a non-binary string that has a binary collation, and then pass each string to the UPPER() function:

```
mysql> SET @s1 = BINARY 'abcd';
mysql> SET @s2 = _latin1 'abcd' COLLATE latin1_bin;
mysql> SELECT UPPER(@s1), UPPER(@s2);
+------------+------------+
| UPPER(@s1) | UPPER(@s2) |
```

```
+------------+-----------+
| abcd       | ABCD      |
+------------+-----------+
```

Why doesn't UPPER() convert the binary string to uppercase? This happens because the string has no character set, so there is no way to know which byte values correspond to uppercase or lowercase characters. To use a binary string with functions such as UPPER() and LOWER(), you must first convert it to a non-binary string:

```
mysql> SELECT @s1, UPPER(CONVERT(@s1 USING latin1));
+------+---------------------------------+
| @s1  | UPPER(CONVERT(@s1 USING latin1)) |
+------+---------------------------------+
| abcd | ABCD                            |
+------+---------------------------------+
```

3.1.2.2 Character Set-Related System Variables

The server maintains several system variables that are involved in various aspects of character set support. Most of these variables refer to character sets and the rest refer to collations. Each of the collation variables is linked to a corresponding character set variable.

Some of the character set variables indicate properties of the server or the current database:

- character_set_system indicates the character set used for storing identifiers. This is always utf8.
- character_set_server and collation_server indicate the server's default character set and collation.
- character_set_database and collation_database indicate the character set and collation of the default database. These are read-only and set automatically by the server whenever you select a default database. If there is no default database, they're set to the server's default character set and collation. These variables come into play when you create a table but specify no explicit character set or collation. In this case, the table defaults are taken from the database defaults.

Other character set variables influence how communication occurs between the client and the server:

- character_set_client indicates the character set in which the client sends SQL statements to the server.
- character_set_results indicates the character set in which the server returns results to the client. "Results" include data values and also metadata such as column names.
- character_set_connection is used by the server. When it receives a statement string from the client, it converts the string from character_set_client to

`character_set_connection` and works with the statement in the latter character set. (There is an exception: Any literal string in the statement that is preceded by a character set introducer is interpreted using the character set indicated by the introducer.) `collation_connection` is used for comparisons between literal strings within statement strings.

- `character_set_filesystem` indicates the filesystem character set. It is used for interpreting literal strings known to refer to filenames in SQL statements such as LOAD DATA. These filename strings are converted from `character_set_client` to `character_set_filesystem` before opening the file. The default is `binary` (no conversion).

Very likely you'll find that most character set and collation variables are set to the same value by default. For example, the following output indicates that client/server communication takes place using the `latin1` character set:

```
mysql> SHOW VARIABLES LIKE 'character\_set\_%';
+------------------------+--------+
| Variable_name          | Value  |
+------------------------+--------+
| character_set_client   | latin1 |
| character_set_connection | latin1 |
| character_set_database | latin1 |
| character_set_filesystem | binary |
| character_set_results  | latin1 |
| character_set_server   | latin1 |
| character_set_system   | utf8   |
+------------------------+--------+
mysql> SHOW VARIABLES LIKE 'collation\_%';
+----------------------+-------------------+
| Variable_name        | Value             |
+----------------------+-------------------+
| collation_connection | latin1_swedish_ci |
| collation_database   | latin1_swedish_ci |
| collation_server     | latin1_swedish_ci |
+----------------------+-------------------+
```

A client that wants to talk to the server using another character set can change the communication-related variables. For example, if you want to use `utf8`, change three variables:

```
mysql> SET character_set_client = utf8;
mysql> SET character_set_results = utf8;
mysql> SET character_set_connection = utf8;
```

However, it's more convenient to use a SET NAMES statement for this purpose. The following statement is equivalent to the preceding three SET statements:

```
mysql> SET NAMES 'utf8';
```

One restriction on setting the communication character set is that you cannot use ucs2. (In MySQL 6.0 and up, this restriction also applies to utf16 and utf32.)

Many client programs support a --default-character-set option that produces the same effect as a SET NAMES statement by informing the server of the desired communication character set.

For variables that come in pairs (a character set variable and a collation variable), the members of the pair are linked in the following ways:

- Setting the character set variable also sets the associated collation variable to the default collation for the character set.

- Setting the collation variable also sets the associated character set variable to the character set implied by the first part of the collation name.

For example, setting character_set_connection to utf8 sets collation_connection to utf8_general_ci. Setting collation_connection to latin1_spanish_ci sets character_set_connection to latin1.

3.1.3 Date and Time (Temporal) Values

Dates and times are values such as '2011-06-17' or '12:30:43'. MySQL also understands combined date/time values, such as '2011-06-17 12:30:43'. Take special note of the fact that MySQL represents dates in year-month-day order. This syntax often surprises newcomers to MySQL, although it is standard SQL format (also known as "ISO 8601" format). You can display date values any way you like using the DATE_FORMAT() function, but the default display format lists the year first. Input values must be specified with the year first. For values in other formats, you might be able to convert them for input by using the STR_TO_DATE() function.

3.1.4 Spatial Values

MySQL supports spatial values, although only for MyISAM, and, as of MySQL 5.0.16, InnoDB, NDB, and ARCHIVE. This capability enables representation of values such as points, lines, and polygons. For example, the following statement uses the text representation of a point value with X and Y coordinates of (10, 20) to create a POINT and assigns the result to a user-defined variable:

```
SET @pt = POINTFROMTEXT('POINT(10 20)');
```

3.1.5 Boolean Values

In expressions, zero is considered false and any non-zero, non-NULL value is considered true.

The special constants TRUE and FALSE evaluate to 1 and 0, respectively. They are not case sensitive.

3.1.6 The NULL Value

NULL is something of a "typeless" value. Generally, it's used to mean "no value," "unknown value," "missing value," "out of range," "not applicable," "none of the above," and so forth. You can insert NULL values into tables, retrieve them from tables, and test whether a value is NULL. However, you cannot perform arithmetic on NULL values; if you try, the result is NULL. Also, many functions return NULL if you invoke them with a NULL or invalid argument.

The keyword NULL is written without quotes and is not case sensitive. MySQL also treats a standalone \N (case sensitive) as NULL:

```
mysql> SELECT \N, ISNULL(\N);
+------+------------+
| NULL | ISNULL(\N) |
+------+------------+
| NULL |          1 |
+------+------------+
```

3.2 MySQL Data Types

Each table in a database contains one or more columns. When you create a table using a CREATE TABLE statement, you specify a data type for each column. A data type is more specific than a general category such as "number" or "string." For a column, the data type is the means by which you precisely characterize the kind of values the column may contain, such as SMALLINT or VARCHAR(32). This in turn determines how MySQL treats those values. For example, if you have numeric values, you could store them using either a numeric or string column, but MySQL will treat the values somewhat differently depending on what type you use. Each data type has several characteristics:

- What kind of values it can represent.
- How much space values take up.
- Whether values are fixed-length (all values of the type take the same amount of space) or variable-length (the amount of space depends on the particular value being stored)
- How MySQL compares and sorts values of the type
- Whether the type can be indexed

The following discussion surveys MySQL's data types briefly, and then describes in more detail the syntax for defining them and the properties that characterize each type, such as their range and storage requirements. The type specifications are shown as you use them in CREATE TABLE statements. Optional information is indicated by square brackets ([]). For example, the syntax MEDIUMINT[(M)] indicates that the maximum display width, specified as (M), is optional. On the other hand, for VARCHAR(M), the lack of brackets indicates that (M) is required.

3.2.1 Overview of Data Types

MySQL has numeric data types for integer, fixed-point, floating-point, and bit values, as shown in Table 3.2. Numeric types other than BIT can be signed or unsigned. A special attribute enables sequential integer or floating-point column values to be generated automatically, which is useful in applications that require a series of unique identification numbers.

Table 3.2   **Numeric Data Types**

Type Name	Meaning
TINYINT	A very small integer
SMALLINT	A small integer
MEDIUMINT	A medium-sized integer
INT	A standard integer
BIGINT	A large integer
DECIMAL	A fixed-point number
FLOAT	A single-precision floating-point number
DOUBLE	A double-precision floating-point number
BIT	A bit field

Table 3.3 shows the MySQL string data types. Strings can hold anything, even arbitrary binary data such as images or sounds. Strings can be compared according to whether they are case sensitive. In addition, you can perform pattern matching on strings. (Actually, in MySQL, you can even perform pattern matching on numeric types, but it's more commonly done with string types.)

Table 3.3   **String Data Types**

Type Name	Meaning
CHAR	A fixed-length non-binary (character) string
VARCHAR	A variable-length non-binary string
BINARY	A fixed-length binary string
VARBINARY	A variable-length binary string
TINYBLOB	A very small BLOB (binary large object)
BLOB	A small BLOB
MEDIUMBLOB	A medium-sized BLOB
LONGBLOB	A large BLOB
TINYTEXT	A very small non-binary string

Table 3.3   **String Data Types**

Type Name	Meaning
TEXT	A small non-binary string
MEDIUMTEXT	A medium-sized non-binary string
LONGTEXT	A large non-binary string
ENUM	An enumeration; each column value may be assigned one enumeration member
SET	A set; each column value may be assigned zero or more set members

Table 3.4 shows the MySQL date and types, where CC, YY, MM, DD, hh, mm, and ss represent century, year, month, day of the month, hour, minute, and second, respectively. For temporal values, MySQL provides types for dates and times (either combined or separate) and timestamps (a special type that enables you to track when changes were last made to a row). There is also a type for efficiently representing year values when you don't need an entire date.

Table 3.4   **Date and Time Data Types**

Type Name	Meaning
DATE	A date value, in `'CCYY-MM-DD'` format
TIME	A time value, in `'hh:mm:ss'` format
DATETIME	A date and time value, in `'CCYY-MM-DD hh:mm:ss'` format
TIMESTAMP	A timestamp value, in `'CCYY-MM-DD hh:mm:ss'` format
YEAR	A year value, in `CCYY` or `YY` format

Table 3.5 shows the MySQL spatial data types. These represent various kinds of geometrical or geographical values.

Table 3.5   **Spatial Data Types**

Type Name	Meaning
GEOMETRY	A spatial value of any type
POINT	A point (a pair of X,Y coordinates)
LINESTRING	A curve (one or more POINT values)
POLYGON	A polygon
GEOMETRYCOLLECTION	A collection of GEOMETRY values
MULTILINESTRING	A collection of LINESTRING values
MULTIPOINT	A collection of POINT values
MULTIPOLYGON	A collection of POLYGON values

3.2.2 Specifying Column Types in Table Definitions

To create a table, issue a CREATE TABLE statement that includes a list of the columns in the table. Here's an example that creates a table named mytbl with three columns named f, c, and i:

```
CREATE TABLE mytbl
(
  f FLOAT(10,4),
  c CHAR(15) NOT NULL DEFAULT 'none',
  i TINYINT UNSIGNED NULL
);
```

Each column has a name and a type, and attributes can be associated with the type. The syntax for defining a column is as follows:

```
col_name col_type [type_attributes] [general_attributes]
```

The name of the column, col_name, is always first in the definition and must be a legal identifier. The precise rules for identifier syntax are given in Section 2.2, "MySQL Identifier Syntax and Naming Rules." Briefly summarized, column identifiers may be up to 64 characters long, and may consist of alphanumeric characters from the system character set, as well as the underscore and dollar sign characters ('_' and '$'). Keywords such as SELECT, DELETE, and CREATE normally are reserved and cannot be used. However, you can include other characters within an identifier or use a reserved word as an identifier if you are willing to put up with the bother of quoting it whenever you refer to it. To quote an identifier, enclose it within backtick (' ' ') characters. If the ANSI_QUOTES SQL mode is enabled, it is allowable to quote identifiers within double quote (' " ') characters instead.

col_type indicates the column data type; that is, the specific kind of values the column can hold. Some type specifiers indicate the maximum length of the values you store in the column. For others, the length is implied by the type name. For example, CHAR(10) specifies an explicit length of 10 characters, whereas TINYTEXT values have an implicit maximum length of 255 characters. Some of the type specifiers allow you to indicate a maximum display width (how many characters to use for displaying values). For fixed-point and floating-point types, you can specify the number of significant digits and number of decimal places.

Following the column's data type, you may specify optional type-specific attributes as well as more general attributes. These attributes function as type modifiers. They cause MySQL to change the way it treats column values in some way:

- The type-specific attributes that are allowable depend on the data type you choose. For example, UNSIGNED and ZEROFILL are allowable only for numeric types, and CHARACTER SET and COLLATE are allowable only for non-binary string types.

- The general attributes may be given for any data type, with a few exceptions. You may specify NULL or NOT NULL to indicate whether a column can hold NULL values. For most data types, you can specify a DEFAULT clause to define a default value for the column. Default value handling is described in Section 3.2.3, "Specifying Column Default Values."

If multiple column attributes are present, there are some constraints on the order in which they may appear. In general, you should be safe if you specify data type-specific attributes such as UNSIGNED or ZEROFILL before general attributes such as NULL or NOT NULL.

3.2.3 Specifying Column Default Values

For all but BLOB and TEXT types, spatial types, or columns with the AUTO_INCREMENT attribute, you can specify a DEFAULT *def_value* clause to indicate that a column should be assigned the value *def_value* when a new row is created that does not explicitly specify the column's value. With some limited exceptions for TIMESTAMP columns, *def_value* must be a constant. It cannot be an expression or refer to other columns.

If a column definition includes no explicit DEFAULT clause and the column can take NULL values, its default value is NULL. Otherwise, the handling of a missing DEFAULT clause is version dependent.

From MySQL 5.0.2 on, the column is created without any DEFAULT clause. That is, it has no default value. This affects how the server handles the column if a new row that does not specify a value for the column is inserted into the table:

- When strict SQL mode is not in effect, the column is set to the implicit default for its data type. (Implicit defaults are described shortly.)
- When strict SQL mode is in effect, an error occurs if the table is transactional. The statement aborts and rolls back. For non-transactional tables, an error occurs and the statement aborts if the row is the first row inserted by the statement. If it is not the first row, you can elect to have the statement abort or to have the column set to its implicit default with a warning. The choice depends on which strict mode setting is in effect. See Section 3.3, "How MySQL Handles Invalid Data Values," for details.

Before MySQL 5.0.2, MySQL defines the column with a DEFAULT clause that specifies the implicit default value.

The implicit default for a column depends on its data type:

- For numeric columns, the default is 0, except for columns that have the AUTO_INCREMENT attribute. For AUTO_INCREMENT, the default is the next number in the column sequence.
- For date and time types except TIMESTAMP, the default is the "zero" value for the type (for example, '0000-00-00' for DATE). For TIMESTAMP, the default is the current date and time for the first TIMESTAMP column in a table, and the "zero" value for any following TIMESTAMP columns. (TIMESTAMP defaults actually are more complex and are discussed in Section 3.2.6.2, "The TIMESTAMP Data Type.")

- For string types other than ENUM, the default is the empty string. For ENUM, the default is the first enumeration element. For SET, the default when the column cannot contain NULL actually is the empty set, but that is equivalent to the empty string.

You can use the SHOW CREATE TABLE statement to see which columns have a DEFAULT clause and what the default value is for those columns that have one.

3.2.4 Numeric Data Types

MySQL's numeric data types group into three groups:

- Exact-value types, which include the integer types and DECIMAL. Integer types are used for numbers that have no fractional part, such as 43, -3, 0, or -798432. You can use integer columns for data represented by whole numbers, such as weight to the nearest pound, height to the nearest inch, number of stars in a galaxy, number of people in a household, or number of bacteria in a petri dish. The DECIMAL type stores exact values that may have a fractional part, such as 3.14159, -.00273, or -4.78. This is a good data type for information such as monetary values. Integer and DECIMAL values are stored exactly as specified without rounding when possible, and calculations are exact.

- The floating-point types are available in single precision (FLOAT) and double precision (DOUBLE). These types, like DECIMAL, are used for numbers that may have a fractional part, but they hold approximate-value numbers such as 3.9E+4 or -0.1E-100 that are subject to rounding. They can be used when exact precision is not required or for values that are so large that DECIMAL cannot represent them. Some types of data you might represent as floating-point values are average crop yield, distances, or unemployment rates.

- The BIT type is used for storing bit-field values.

Values with a fractional part can be assigned to integer columns, but will be rounded using the "round half up" rule: If the fractional part is .5 or greater, the value is rounded away from zero to the next integer (up for positive values, down for negative values.) Conversely, integer values may be assigned to types that allow a fractional part. They are treated as having a fractional part of zero.

When you specify a number, you should not include commas as a separator. For example, 12345678.90 is legal, but 12,345,678.90 is not.

Table 3.6 shows the name and range of each numeric type, and Table 3.7 shows the amount of storage required for values of each type. M represents the maximum display width for integer types, the precision (number of significant digits) for floating-point and decimal types, and the number of bits for BIT. D represents the scale (number of digits following the decimal point) for types that have a fractional part; this is also known as the scale.

Storage for DECIMAL values depends on the number of digits on the left and right sides of the decimal point. For each side, 4 bytes are required for each multiple of nine digits,

Table 3.6   **Numeric Data Type Ranges**

Type Specification	Range
TINYINT[(*M*)]	Signed values: –128 to 127 (-2^7 to 2^7-1); Unsigned values: 0 to 255 (0 to 2^8-1)
SMALLINT[(*M*)]	Signed values: –32768 to 32767 (-2^{15} to 2^{15}-1); Unsigned values: 0 to 65535 (0 to 2^{16}-1)
MEDIUMINT[(*M*)]	Signed values: –8388608 to 8388607 (-2^{23} to 2^{23}-1); Unsigned values: 0 to 16777215 (0 to 2^{24}-1)
INT[(*M*)]	Signed values: –2147483648 to 2147483647 (-2^{31} to 2^{31}-1); Unsigned values: 0 to 4294967295 (0 to 2^{32}-1)
BIGINT[(*M*)]	Signed values: –9223372036854775808 to 9223372036854775807 (-2^{63} to 2^{63}-1); Unsigned values: 0 to 18446744073709551615 (0 to 2^{64}-1)
DECIMAL([*M*[,*D*]])	Varies depending on *M* and *D*
FLOAT[(*M,D*)]	Minimum non-zero values: ±1.175494351E-38; Maximum non-zero values: ±3.402823466E+38
DOUBLE[(*M*, *D*)]	Minimum non-zero values: ±2.2250738585072014E-308; Maximum non-zero values: ±1.7976931348623157E+308
BIT[(*M*)]	0 to 2^M-1

Table 3.7   **Numeric Data Type Storage Requirements**

Type Specification	Storage Required
TINYINT[(*M*)]	1 byte
SMALLINT[(*M*)]	2 bytes
MEDIUMINT[(*M*)]	3 bytes
INT[(*M*)]	4 bytes
BIGINT[(*M*)]	8 bytes
DECIMAL([*M*[,*D*]])	Varies depending on *M*, *D*
FLOAT[(*M*, *D*)]	4 bytes
DOUBLE[(*M*, *D*)]	8 bytes
BIT[(*M*)]	Varies depending on *M*

plus 1 to 4 bytes if there are any remaining digits. Storage per value is the sum of the left and right side storage.

A BIT(*M*) value requires approximately (*M*+7)/8 bytes.

3.2.4.1 Exact-Value Numeric Data Types

The exact-value data types include the integer types and the fixed-point DECIMAL type.

The integer types in MySQL are TINYINT, SMALLINT, MEDIUMINT, INT, and BIGINT. INTEGER is a synonym for INT. These types vary in the range of values they can represent and in the amount of storage space they require. (The larger the range, the more storage is required.) Integer columns can be defined as UNSIGNED to disallow negative values; this shifts the range for the column upward to begin at 0.

When you define an integer column, you can specify an optional display size M. If given, M should be an integer from 1 to 255. It represents the number of characters used to display values for the column. For example, MEDIUMINT(4) specifies a MEDIUMINT column with a display width of 4. If you define an integer column without an explicit width, a default width is assigned. The defaults are the lengths of the "longest" values for each type. Note that displayed values are not chopped to fit within M characters. If the printable representation of a particular value requires more than M characters, MySQL displays the full value.

The display size M for an integer column relates only to the number of characters used to display column values. It has *nothing* to do with the number of bytes of storage space required. For example, BIGINT values require 8 bytes of storage regardless of the display width. It is not possible to magically cut the required storage space for a BIGINT column in half by defining it as BIGINT(4). Nor does M have anything to do with the range of values allowed. If you define a column as INT(3), that doesn't restrict it to a maximum value of 999.

DECIMAL is a fixed-point type: Values have a fixed number of decimals. The significance of this fact is that DECIMAL values are not subject to roundoff error the way that floating-point values are—a property that makes DECIMAL especially applicable for storing currency values.

NUMERIC and FIXED are synonyms for DECIMAL.

DECIMAL columns can be defined as UNSIGNED. Unlike the integer types, defining a DECIMAL type as UNSIGNED doesn't shift the type's range upward, it merely eliminates the negative end.

For a DECIMAL column, you may specify a maximum number of significant digits M and the number of decimal places D. These correspond to the concepts of "precision" and "scale" with which you may be familiar. The value of M should be from 1 to 65. The value of D should be from 0 to 30 and no greater than M.

M and D are optional. If D is omitted, it defaults to 0. If M is omitted as well, it defaults to 10. In other words, the following equivalences hold:

```
DECIMAL = DECIMAL(10) = DECIMAL(10,0)
DECIMAL(n) = DECIMAL(n,0)
```

The maximum possible range for DECIMAL is determined by the values of M and D. *If you vary M and hold D fixed, the range becomes larger as M becomes larger* (Table 3.8). *If you hold M fixed and vary D, the range becomes smaller as D becomes larger* (Table 3.9).

Table 3.8   How *M* Affects the Range of DECIMAL *(M,D)*

Type Specification	Range
DECIMAL(4,1)	-999.9 to 999.9
DECIMAL(5,1)	-9999.9 to 9999.9
DECIMAL(6,1)	-99999.9 to 99999.9

Table 3.9   How *D* Affects the Range of DECIMAL(*M, D*)

Type Specification	Range
DECIMAL(4,0)	-9999 to 9999
DECIMAL(4,1)	-999.9 to 999.9
DECIMAL(4,2)	-99.99 to 99.99

> **Note**
>
> Before MySQL 5.0.3, DECIMAL values are stored as strings and have somewhat different properties from those of the current representation. See the MySQL Reference Manual for details. To convert DECIMAL columns in an old table to the current format, dump it with mysqldump and then reload the dump file:
>
> ```
> % mysqldump db_name tbl_name > file_name
> % mysql db_name < file_name
> ```

3.2.4.2 Approximate-Value Numeric Data Types

MySQL provides two floating-point types, FLOAT and DOUBLE, that hold approximate-value numbers. DOUBLE PRECISION is a synonym for DOUBLE. The REAL type is a synonym for DOUBLE by default. If the REAL_AS_DEFAULT SQL mode is enabled, REAL is a synonym for FLOAT.

Floating-point types can be defined as UNSIGNED, which eliminates the negative end of the type's range.

For each floating-point type (just as for DECIMAL), you may specify a maximum number of significant digits *M* and the number of decimal places *D*. The value of *M* should be from 1 to 255. The value of *D* should be from 0 to 30 and no greater than *M*.

For FLOAT and DOUBLE, *M* and *D* are optional. If you omit both from the column definition, values are stored to the full precision allowed by your hardware.

FLOAT(*p*) syntax also is allowed. However, whereas *p* stands for the required number of bits of precision in standard SQL, it is treated differently in MySQL. *p* may range from 0 to 53 and is used only to determine whether the column stores single-precision or double-precision values. For *p* values from 0 to 24, the column is treated as single precision. For values from 25 to 53, the column is treated as double precision. That is, the column is treated as a FLOAT or DOUBLE with no *M* or *D* values.

3.2.4.3 The BIT Data Type

The BIT data type was introduced in MySQL 5.0.3 as a type for holding bit-field values. When you define a BIT column, you can specify an optional maximum width *M* that indicates the "width" of the column in bits. *M* should be an integer from 1 to 64. If omitted, *M* defaults to 1.

Values retrieved from BIT columns are not displayed in printable form by default. To display a printable representation of bit-field values, add zero or use CAST():

```
mysql> CREATE TABLE t (b BIT(3));  # 3-bit column; holds values 0 to 7
mysql> INSERT INTO t (b) VALUES(0),(b'11'),(b'101'),(b'111');
mysql> SELECT b+0, CAST(b AS UNSIGNED) FROM t;
+------+---------------------+
| b+0  | CAST(b AS UNSIGNED) |
+------+---------------------+
|    0 |                   0 |
|    3 |                   3 |
|    5 |                   5 |
|    7 |                   7 |
+------+---------------------+
```

The BIN() function is useful for displaying bit-field values or the result of computations on them in binary notation:

```
mysql> SELECT BIN(b), BIN(b & b'101'), BIN(b | b'101') FROM t;
+--------+-----------------+-----------------+
| BIN(b) | BIN(b & b'101') | BIN(b | b'101') |
+--------+-----------------+-----------------+
| 0      | 0               | 101             |
| 11     | 1               | 111             |
| 101    | 101             | 101             |
| 111    | 101             | 111             |
+--------+-----------------+-----------------+
```

3.2.4.4 Numeric Data Type Attributes

The UNSIGNED attribute disallows negative values. It can be used with all numeric types except BIT, but is most commonly used with integer types. Making an integer column UNSIGNED doesn't change the "size" of the underlying data type's range; it just shifts the range upward. Consider this table definition:

```
CREATE TABLE mytbl
(
  itiny   TINYINT,
  itiny_u TINYINT UNSIGNED
);
```

`itiny` and `itiny_u` both are `TINYINT` columns with a range of 256 values, but differ in the set of allowable values. The range of `itiny` is –128 to 127, whereas the range of `itiny_u` is shifted up, resulting in a range of 0 to 255.

`UNSIGNED` is useful for columns into which you plan to store information that doesn't take on negative values, such as population counts or attendance figures. Were you to use a signed column for such values, you would use only half of the data type's range. By making the column `UNSIGNED`, you effectively double your usable range. For example, if you use the column for sequence numbers, it will take twice as long to run out of values if you make it `UNSIGNED`.

You can also specify `UNSIGNED` for `DECIMAL` or floating-point columns, although the effect is slightly different from that for integer columns. The range does not shift upward; instead, the upper end remains unchanged and the lower end becomes zero (effectively cutting the range in half).

The `SIGNED` attribute is allowed for all numeric types that allow `UNSIGNED`. However, it has no effect because such types are signed by default. `SIGNED` serves simply to indicate explicitly in a column definition that the column allows negative values.

The `ZEROFILL` attribute can be specified for all numeric types except `BIT`. It causes displayed values for the column to be padded with leading zeros to the display width. You can use `ZEROFILL` when you want to make sure column values always display using a given number of digits. Actually, it's more accurate to say "a given *minimum* number of digits" because values wider than the display width are displayed in full without being chopped. You can see this by issuing the following statements:

```
mysql> DROP TABLE IF EXISTS mytbl;
mysql> CREATE TABLE mytbl (my_zerofill INT(5) ZEROFILL);
mysql> INSERT INTO mytbl VALUES(1),(100),(10000),(1000000);
mysql> SELECT my_zerofill FROM mytbl;
+-------------+
| my_zerofill |
+-------------+
|       00001 |
|       00100 |
|       10000 |
|     1000000 |
+-------------+
```

Note that the final value is displayed in full, even though it is wider than the column's display width.

If you specify the `ZEROFILL` attribute for a column, it automatically becomes `UNSIGNED` as well.

One other attribute, `AUTO_INCREMENT`, is allowed for integer or floating-point data types. Specify the `AUTO_INCREMENT` attribute when you want to generate a series of unique identifier values. When you insert `NULL` into an `AUTO_INCREMENT` column, MySQL generates the next sequence value and stores it in the column. Normally, unless you take steps to cause otherwise, `AUTO_INCREMENT` values begin at 1 and increase by 1 for each new row. The sequence may be affected if you delete rows from the table. That is, sequence values might be reused; it is storage engine-dependent whether this occurs.

You can have at most one AUTO_INCREMENT column in a table. The column should have the NOT NULL constraint, and it must be indexed. Generally, an AUTO_INCREMENT column is indexed as a PRIMARY KEY or UNIQUE index. Also, because sequence values always are positive, you normally define the column UNSIGNED as well. For example, you can define an AUTO_INCREMENT column in any of the following ways:

```
CREATE TABLE ai (i INT UNSIGNED NOT NULL AUTO_INCREMENT PRIMARY KEY);
CREATE TABLE ai (i INT UNSIGNED NOT NULL AUTO_INCREMENT UNIQUE);
CREATE TABLE ai (i INT UNSIGNED NOT NULL AUTO_INCREMENT, PRIMARY KEY (i));
CREATE TABLE ai (i INT UNSIGNED NOT NULL AUTO_INCREMENT, UNIQUE (i));
```

The first two forms shown specify the index information as part of the column definition. The second two specify the index as a separate clause of the CREATE TABLE statement. Using a separate clause is optional if the index includes only the AUTO_INCREMENT column. If you want to create a multiple-column index that includes the AUTO_INCREMENT column, you must use a separate clause. (For an example of this, see Section 3.4.2.1, "AUTO_INCREMENT for MyISAM Tables."

It is always allowable to define an AUTO_INCREMENT column explicitly as NOT NULL, but if you omit NOT NULL, MySQL adds it automatically.

Section 3.4, "Working with Sequences," discusses the behavior of AUTO_INCREMENT columns further.

Following the attributes just described, which are specific to numeric columns, you may specify NULL or NOT NULL. If you do not specify NULL or NOT NULL for a numeric column, it allows NULL by default.

You also may specify a default value using the DEFAULT attribute. The following table contains three INT columns, having default values of -1, 1, and NULL:

```
CREATE TABLE t
(
  i1 INT DEFAULT -1,
  i2 INT DEFAULT 1,
  i3 INT DEFAULT NULL
);
```

Section 3.2.3, "Specifying Column Default Values," earlier in the chapter described the rules that MySQL uses for assigning a default value if a column definition includes no DEFAULT clause.

3.2.4.5 Choosing Numeric Data Types

When you choose a type for a numeric column, consider the range of values that you need to represent and choose the smallest type that will cover the range. Choosing a larger type wastes space, leading to tables that are unnecessarily large and that cannot be processed as efficiently as if you had chosen a smaller type. TINYINT is the best for integers if the range of values in your data is small, such as a person's age or number of siblings.

MEDIUMINT can represent millions of values and can be used for many more types of values, at some additional cost in storage space. BIGINT has the largest range of all but requires twice as much storage as the next smallest integer type (INT) and should be used only when really necessary. For floating-point values, DOUBLE takes twice as much space as FLOAT. Unless you need exceptionally high precision or an extremely large range of values, you can probably represent your data at half the storage cost by using FLOAT instead of DOUBLE.

Every numeric column's range of values is determined by its type. If you attempt to insert a value that lies outside the column's range, the result depends on whether strict SQL mode is enabled. If it is, an out of range value results in an error. If strict mode is not enabled, truncation occurs: MySQL clips the value to the appropriate endpoint of the range, uses the result, and generates a warning.

Value truncation occurs according to the range of the data type, not the display width. For example, a SMALLINT(3) column has a display width of 3 and a range from –32768 to 32767. The value 12345 is wider than the display width but within the range of the column, so it is inserted without clipping and retrieved as 12345. The value 99999 is outside the range, so it is clipped to 32767 when inserted. Subsequent retrievals return the value 32767.

For fixed-point or floating-point columns, if values are stored that have more digits in the fractional part than allowed by the column specification, rounding occurs. If you store 1.23456 in a FLOAT(8,1) column, the result is 1.2. If you store the same value in a FLOAT(8,4) column, the result is 1.2346. This means you should define such columns with a sufficient number of decimals to store values as precise as you require. If you need accuracy to thousandths, don't define a type with only two decimal places.

3.2.5 String Data Types

MySQL provides several data types for storing string values. Strings are often used for text values like these:

```
'N. Bertram, et al.'
'Pencils (no. 2 lead)'
'123 Elm St.'
'Monograph Series IX'
```

But strings are actually "generic" types in a sense because you can use them to represent any value. For example, you can use binary string types to hold binary data, such as images, sounds, or compressed gzip output.

Table 3.10 shows all the types provided by MySQL for defining string-valued columns, and the maximum size and storage requirements of each type. M represents the maximum length of column values (in bytes for binary strings and characters for non-binary strings), and L represents the actual length of a given value in bytes. w is the number of bytes required for the widest character in the character set. The BLOB and TEXT types each have several variants that are distinguished by the maximum size of values they can hold.

Table 3.10   **String Data Types**

Type Specification	Maximum Size	Storage Required
BINARY[(M)]	M bytes	M bytes
VARBINARY(M)	M bytes	L + 1 or 2 bytes
CHAR[(M)]	M characters	$M \times w$ bytes
VARCHAR(M)	M characters	L + 1 or 2 bytes
TINYBLOB	2^8-1 bytes	L + 1 bytes
BLOB	$2^{16}-1$ bytes	L + 2 bytes
MEDIUMBLOB	$2^{24}-1$ bytes	L + 3 bytes
LONGBLOB	$2^{32}-1$ bytes	L + 4 bytes
TINYTEXT	2^8-1 characters	L + 1 bytes
TEXT	$2^{16}-1$ characters	L + 2 bytes
MEDIUMTEXT	$2^{24}-1$ characters	L + 3 bytes
LONGTEXT	$2^{32}-1$ characters	L + 4 bytes
ENUM('value1','value2',...)	65,535 members	1 or 2 bytes
SET('value1','value2',...)	64 members	1, 2, 3, 4, or 8 bytes

Some types hold binary strings (byte strings) and others hold non-binary strings (character strings). Thus, maximum size as listed in Table 3.10 is given in number of bytes per value for binary string types and number of characters for non-binary string types. For example, BINARY(20) holds 20 bytes, whereas CHAR(20) holds 20 characters (which requires more than 20 bytes for multi-byte characters). The differences between byte and character semantics for binary and non-binary strings are characterized in Section 3.1.2, "String Values." Each of the binary string types for byte strings has a corresponding non-binary type for character strings, as shown in Table 3.11.

Table 3.11   **Corresponding Binary and Non-Binary String Types**

Binary String Type	Non-Binary String Type
BINARY	CHAR
VARBINARY	VARCHAR
BLOB	TEXT

Each of the non-binary string types, as well as ENUM and SET, can be assigned a character set and collation. Different columns can be assigned different character sets. Character set assignment is discussed in Section 3.2.5.5, "String Data Type Attributes."

BINARY and CHAR are fixed-length string types. For columns of these types, MySQL allocates the same amount of storage for every value and pads those that are shorter than the column length. Padding uses zero (0x00) bytes for BINARY and spaces for CHAR. Because CHAR(*M*) must be able to represent the largest possible string in the column's character set, each column requires $M \times w$ bytes, where w is the number of bytes required for the widest character in the character set. For example, ujis characters take from one to three bytes, so CHAR(20) must be allocated 60 bytes in case a value requires three bytes for all 20 characters.

Other string types are variable-length. The amount of storage taken by a value varies from row to row and depends on the length of the values actually stored in the column. This length is represented by L in the table for variable-length types. The extra bytes required in addition to L are the number of bytes needed to store the length of the value. MySQL handles variable-length values by storing both the content of the value and a prefix that records its length. These extra prefix "length bytes" are treated as an unsigned integer. There is a correspondence between a variable-length type's maximum length, the number of length bytes required for that type, and the range of the unsigned integer type that uses the same number of bytes. For example, a MEDIUMBLOB value may be up to $2^{24}-1$ bytes long and requires 3 bytes to record the length. The 3-byte integer type MEDIUMINT has a maximum unsigned value of $2^{24}-1$. That's not a coincidence.

The length prefix for VARBINARY and VARCHAR requires 1 byte if the maximum length of column values in bytes is less than 256. The requirement is 2 bytes otherwise.

Values for all string types except ENUM and SET are stored as a sequence of bytes and interpreted either as bytes or characters depending on whether the type holds binary or non-binary strings. Values that are too long to store are chopped to fit. (In strict mode, an error occurs instead unless the chopped characters are spaces.) But string types range from very small to very large, with the largest type able to hold nearly 4GB of data, so you should be able to find something long enough to avoid truncation of your information. (The effective maximum column size actually is imposed by the maximum packet size of the client/server communication protocol, which is 1MB by default.)

For ENUM and SET, the column definition includes a list of legal string values, but ENUM and SET values are stored internally as numbers, as detailed later in Section 3.2.5.4, "The ENUM and SET Data Types." Attempting to store a value other than those in the list causes the value to be converted to ' ' (the empty string) unless strict mode is enabled. In strict mode, an error occurs instead.

3.2.5.1 The CHAR and VARCHAR Data Types

The CHAR and VARCHAR string types hold non-binary strings, and thus are associated with a character set and collation.

The primary differences between CHAR and VARCHAR lie in whether they have a fixed or variable length, and in how trailing spaces are treated:

- CHAR is a fixed-length type, whereas VARCHAR is a variable-length type.
- Values retrieved from CHAR columns have trailing spaces removed. For a CHAR(*M*) column, values that are shorter than *M* characters are padded to a length of *M* when

stored, but trailing spaces are stripped when the values are retrieved. As of MySQL 5.1.20, you can enable the PAD_CHAR_TO_FULL_LENGTH SQL mode to cause retrieved CHAR column values to retain trailing spaces.

- For a VARCHAR(M) column, trailing spaces are retained both for storage and retrieval.

CHAR columns can be defined with a maximum length M from 0 to 255. M is optional for CHAR and defaults to 1 if missing. Note that CHAR(0) is legal. A CHAR(0) column can be used to represent on/off values if you allow it to be NULL. Values in such a column can have one of two values: NULL or the empty string. A CHAR(0) column takes very little storage space in the table—only a single bit.

The syntactically allowable range of M for VARCHAR(M) is 1 to 65,535, but the effective maximum number of characters is less than 65,535 because MySQL has a maximum row size of 65,535 bytes. That has certain implications:

- A long VARCHAR requires two length bytes, which count against the row size.
- Use of multi-byte characters reduces the number of characters that can fit within the maximum row size.
- Inclusion of other columns in the table reduces the amount of space for the VARCHAR column in the row.

Keep in mind two general principles when choosing between CHAR and VARCHAR data types:

- If your values all are M characters long, a VARCHAR(M) column actually will use more space than a CHAR(M) column due to the extra byte or bytes required to record the length of values. On the other hand, if your values vary in length, VARCHAR columns have the advantage of taking less space. A CHAR(M) column always takes M characters, even if it is empty or NULL.
- If you're using MyISAM tables and your values don't vary much in length, CHAR is a better choice than VARCHAR because the MyISAM storage engine can process fixed-length rows more efficiently than variable-length rows. See Section 5.3, "Choosing Data Types for Efficient Queries."

Note

Before MySQL 5.0.3, VARCHAR is handled somewhat differently:

- The maximum length for VARCHAR is 255.
- Trailing spaces are stripped from VARCHAR values when they are stored.

3.2.5.2 The BINARY and VARBINARY Data Types

The BINARY and VARBINARY types are similar to CHAR and VARCHAR, with the following differences:

- CHAR and VARCHAR are non-binary types that store characters and have a character set and collation. Comparisons are based on the collating sequence.

- BINARY and VARBINARY are binary types that store bytes and have no character set or collation. Comparisons are based on numeric byte values.

The rules for handling of padding for BINARY values are as follows:

- As of MySQL 5.0.15, short values are padded with 0x00 bytes. Nothing is stripped on retrieval.
- Before MySQL 5.0.15, short values are padded with spaces. Trailing spaces are stripped on retrieval.

For VARBINARY, no padding occurs when values are stored and no stripping occurs for retrieval.

3.2.5.3 The BLOB and TEXT Data Types

A "BLOB" is a binary large object—basically, a container that can hold anything you want to toss into it, and that you can make about as big as you want. In MySQL, the BLOB type is really a family of types (TINYBLOB, BLOB, MEDIUMBLOB, LONGBLOB). These types are identical except in the maximum amount of information they can hold (see Table 3.10). BLOB columns store binary strings. They are useful for storing data that may grow very large or that may vary widely in size from row to row. Some examples are compressed data, encrypted data, images, and sounds.

MySQL also has a family of TEXT types (TINYTEXT, TEXT, MEDIUMTEXT, LONGTEXT). These are similar to the corresponding BLOB types, except that TEXT types store non-binary strings rather than binary strings. That is, they store characters rather than bytes, and are associated with a character set and collation. This results in the general differences between binary and non-binary strings that were described earlier in Section 3.1.2, "String Values." For example, in comparison operations, BLOB values are compared in byte units and TEXT values are compared in character units using the column collation.

BLOB or TEXT columns sometimes can be indexed, depending on the storage engine you're using:

- The MyISAM and InnoDB storage engines support BLOB and TEXT indexing. However, you must specify a prefix size to be used for the index. This avoids creating index entries that might be huge and thereby defeat any benefits to be gained by that index. The exception is that prefixes are not used for FULLTEXT indexes on TEXT columns. FULLTEXT searches are based on the entire content of the indexed columns, so any prefix you specify is ignored.
- MEMORY tables do not support BLOB and TEXT indexes because the MEMORY engine does not support BLOB or TEXT columns at all.

BLOB or TEXT columns may require special care:

- Due to the typical large variation in the size of BLOB and TEXT values, tables containing them are subject to high rates of fragmentation if many deletes and updates are done. If you're using a MyISAM table to store BLOB or TEXT values, you can run

OPTIMIZE TABLE periodically to reduce fragmentation and maintain good performance. See Chapter 5, "Query Optimization," for more information.

- The max_sort_length system variable influences BLOB and TEXT comparison and sorting operations. Only the first max_sort_length bytes of each value are used. (For TEXT columns that use a multi-byte character set, this means that comparisons might involve fewer than max_sort_length characters.) If this causes a problem with the default max_sort_length value of 1024, you might want to increase the value before performing comparisons.

- If you're using very large values, you might need to configure the server to increase the value of the max_allowed_packet parameter. See Section 12.6.2, "General-Purpose System Variables," for more information. You will also need to increase the packet size for any client that wants to use very large values. The mysql and mysqldump clients support setting this value directly using a startup option.

3.2.5.4 The ENUM and SET Data Types

ENUM and SET are special string data types that allow only values chosen from a fixed (predefined) list of allowable strings. The primary difference between them is that ENUM column values must consist of exactly one member of the list of values, whereas SET column values may contain any or all members of the list. In other words, ENUM is used for values that are mutually exclusive, whereas SET allows multiple choices from the list.

The ENUM data type defines an enumeration. ENUM columns may be assigned values consisting of exactly one member chosen from a list of values specified at table-creation time. You can define an enumeration to have up to 65,535 members. Enumerations are commonly used to represent category values. For example, values in a column defined as ENUM('N', 'Y') can be either 'N' or 'Y'. Or you can use ENUM for such things as available sizes or colors for a product or for answers to multiple-choice questions in a survey or questionnaire where a single response must be selected:

```
employees ENUM('less than 100','100-500','501-1500','more than 1500')
color ENUM('red','green','blue','black')
size ENUM('S','M','L','XL','XXL')
vote ENUM('Yes','No','Undecided')
```

If you are processing selections from a Web page that includes mutually exclusive radio buttons, you can use an ENUM to represent the options from which a visitor to your site chooses. For example, if you run an online pizza-ordering service, ENUM columns can be used to represent the type of crust and size of pizza a customer orders:

```
crust ENUM('thin','regular','pan style','deep dish')
size ENUM('small','medium','large')
```

If enumeration categories represent counts, it's important to choose your categories properly when you create the enumeration. For example, when recording white blood cell counts from a laboratory test, you might group the counts into categories like this:

```
wbc ENUM('0-100','101-300','>300')
```

If any given test result is provided as an exact count, you can record the value in the wbc column using the category into which the count falls. But you cannot recover the original count if you decide you want to convert the column from a category-based ENUM to an integer column based on exact count. If you really need the exact count, use an integer column instead, and group integer values into categories when you retrieve them using the CASE construct. For example, if wbc is defined as an integer column, you can select it as a category like this:

```
SELECT CASE WHEN wbc <= 100 THEN '0-100'
            WHEN wbc <= 300 THEN '101-300'
            ELSE '>300' END AS 'wbc category'
FROM ...
```

The SET type is similar to ENUM in the sense that when you create a SET column, you specify a list of legal set members. But unlike ENUM, each column value may consist of any number of members from the set. The set may have up to 64 members. You can use a SET when you have a fixed set of values that are not mutually exclusive as they are in an ENUM column. For example, you might use a SET to represent options available for an automobile:

```
SET('luggage rack','cruise control','air conditioning','sun roof')
```

Then particular SET values would represent those options actually ordered by customers:

```
'cruise control,sun roof'
'luggage rack,air conditioning'
'luggage rack,cruise control,air conditioning'
'air conditioning'
''
```

The final value shown (the empty string) means that the customer ordered no options. This is a legal value for any SET column.

SET column definitions are written as a list of individual strings separated by commas to indicate what the set members are. A SET column value, on the other hand, is written as a single string. If the value consists of multiple set members, the members are separated within the string by commas. This means you shouldn't use a string containing a comma as a SET member.

Other uses for SET columns might be for representing information such as patient diagnoses or results from selections on Web pages. For a diagnosis, there may be a standard list of symptoms to ask a patient about, and the patient might exhibit any or all of them:

```
SET('dizziness','shortness of breath','cough')
```

For an online pizza service, the Web page for ordering could have a set of check boxes for ingredients that a customer wants as toppings on a pizza, several of which might be chosen:

```
SET('pepperoni','sausage','mushrooms','onions','ripe olives')
```

The way you define the legal value list for an ENUM or SET column is significant in several ways:

- The list determines the possible legal values for the column, as has already been discussed.

- If an ENUM or SET column has a collation that is not case sensitive, you can insert legal values in any lettercase and they will be recognized. However, the lettercase of the strings as specified in the column definition determines the lettercase of column values when they are retrieved later. For example, if you have an ENUM('Y','N') column and you store 'y' and 'n' in it, the values are displayed as 'Y' and 'N' when you retrieve them. If the column has a case sensitive or binary collation, you must insert values using exactly the lettercase used in the column definition or the values will not be recognized as legal. On the other hand, you can have distinct elements that differ only in lettercase, something that is not true when you use a collation that is not case sensitive.

- The order of values in an ENUM definition is the order used for sorting. The order of values in a SET definition also determines sort order, although the relationship is more complicated because column values may contain multiple set members.

- When MySQL displays a SET value that consists of multiple set members, the order in which it lists the members within the value is determined by the order in which they appear in the SET column definition.

ENUM and SET are classified as string types because enumeration and set members are specified as strings when you create columns of these types. However, the ENUM and SET types actually have a split personality: The members are stored internally as numbers and you can work with them as such. This means that ENUM and SET types are more efficient than other string types because they often can be handled using numeric operations rather than string operations. It also means that ENUM and SET values can be used in either string or numeric contexts. Finally, ENUM and SET columns can cause confusion if you use them in string context but expect them to behave as numbers, or vice versa.

MySQL sequentially numbers ENUM members in the column definition beginning with 1. (The value 0 is reserved for the error member, which is represented in string form by the empty string.) The number of enumeration values determines the storage size of an ENUM column. One byte can represent 256 values and two bytes can represent 65,536 values. (Compare this to the ranges of the one-byte and two-byte integer types TINYINT UNSIGNED and SMALLINT UNSIGNED.) Thus, counting the error member, the maximum number of enumeration members is 65,536 and the storage size depends on whether there are more than 256 members. You can specify a maximum of 65,535 (not 65,536) members in the ENUM definition because MySQL reserves a spot for the error member as an implicit member of every enumeration. When you assign an illegal value to an ENUM column, MySQL assigns the error member. (In strict mode, an error occurs instead.)

The following example demonstrates that you can retrieve ENUM values in either string or numeric form (which shows the numeric ordering of enumeration members and also that the NULL value has no number in the ordering):

```
mysql> CREATE TABLE e_table (e ENUM('jane','fred','will','marcia'));
mysql> INSERT INTO e_table
    -> VALUES('jane'),('fred'),('will'),('marcia'),(NULL);
mysql> SELECT e, e+0, e+1, e*3 FROM e_table;
+--------+------+------+------+
| e      | e+0  | e+1  | e*3  |
+--------+------+------+------+
| jane   |    1 |    2 |    3 |
| fred   |    2 |    3 |    6 |
| will   |    3 |    4 |    9 |
| marcia |    4 |    5 |   12 |
| NULL   | NULL | NULL | NULL |
+--------+------+------+------+
```

You can compare ENUM members either by name or number:

```
mysql> SELECT e FROM e_table WHERE e='will';
+------+
| e    |
+------+
| will |
+------+
mysql> SELECT e FROM e_table WHERE e=3;
+------+
| e    |
+------+
| will |
+------+
```

It is possible to define the empty string as a legal enumeration member, but this will only cause confusion. The string is assigned a non-zero numeric value, just as any other member listed in the definition. However, an empty string also is used for the error member that has a numeric value of 0, so it would correspond to two internal numeric element values. In the following example, assigning the illegal enumeration value 'x' to the ENUM column causes the error member to be assigned. This is distinguishable from the empty string member listed in the column definition only when retrieved in numeric form:

```
mysql> CREATE TABLE t (e ENUM('a','','b'));
mysql> INSERT INTO t VALUES('a'),(''),('b'),('x');
mysql> SELECT e, e+0 FROM t;
+------+------+
| e    | e+0  |
+------+------+
| a    |    1 |
```

```
|        |      2 |
| b      |      3 |
|        |      0 |
+--------+--------+
```

In strict mode, assigning the illegal value `'x'` causes an error and no value is stored.

The numeric representation of SET columns is a little different from that for ENUM columns. Set members are not numbered sequentially. Instead, members correspond to successive individual bits in the SET value. The first set member corresponds to bit 0, the second member corresponds to bit 1, and so on. In other words, the numeric values of SET members all are powers of two. The empty string corresponds to a numeric SET value of 0.

SET values are stored as bit values. Eight set members per byte can be stored this way, so the storage size for a SET column is determined by the number of set members, up to a maximum of 64 members. SET values take 1, 2, 3, 4, or 8 bytes for set sizes of 1 to 8, 9 to 16, 17 to 24, 25 to 32, and 33 to 64 members.

The representation of a SET as a set of bits is what allows a SET value to consist of multiple set members. Any combination of bits can be turned on in the value, so the value may consist of any combination of the strings in the SET definition that correspond to those bits.

The following example shows the relationship between the string and numeric forms of a SET column. It displays the numeric value in both decimal and binary form:

```
mysql> CREATE TABLE s_table (s SET('table','lamp','chair','stool'));
mysql> INSERT INTO s_table
    -> VALUES('table'),('lamp'),('chair'),('stool'),(''),(NULL);
mysql> SELECT s, s+0, BIN(s+0) FROM s_table;
+-------+------+----------+
| s     | s+0  | BIN(s+0) |
+-------+------+----------+
| table |    1 | 1        |
| lamp  |    2 | 10       |
| chair |    4 | 100      |
| stool |    8 | 1000     |
|       |    0 | 0        |
| NULL  | NULL | NULL     |
+-------+------+----------+
```

If you assign to the column s a value of `'lamp,stool'`, MySQL stores it internally as 10 (binary 1010) because `'lamp'` has a value of 2 (bit 1) and `'stool'` has a value of 8 (bit 3).

When you assign values to SET columns, the substrings don't need to be listed in the same order that you used when you defined the column. However, when you retrieve the value later, members are displayed within the value in definition order. Also, if you assign to a SET column a value containing substrings that are not listed as set members, those strings drop out and the column is assigned a value consisting of the remaining substrings. When you retrieve the value later, the illegal substrings will not be present.

If you assign a value of `'chair,couch,table'` to the column s in `s_table`, two things happen:

- `'couch'` drops out because it's not a member of the set. This occurs because MySQL determines which bits correspond to each substring of the value to be assigned and turns them on in the stored value. `'couch'` corresponds to no bit and is ignored.

- When you retrieve the value later, it appears as `'table,chair'`. On retrieval, MySQL constructs the string value from the numeric value by scanning the bits in order, which automatically reorders the substrings to the order used when the column was defined. This behavior also means that if you specify a set member more than once in a value, it will appear only once when you retrieve the value. If you assign `'lamp,lamp,lamp'` to a SET column, it will be simply `'lamp'` when retrieved.

In strict mode, use of an illegal SET member causes an error instead and the value is not stored. In the preceding example, assigning a value containing `'couch'` would cause an error and the assignment would fail.

The fact that MySQL reorders members in a SET value means that if you search for values using a string, you must list members in the proper order. If you insert `'chair,table'` and then search for `'chair,table'` you won't find the row; you must look for it as `'table,chair'`.

Sorting and indexing of ENUM and SET columns is done according to the internal (numeric) values of column values. The following example might appear to be incorrect because the values are not displayed in alphanumeric order:

```
mysql> SELECT e FROM e_table ORDER BY e;
+--------+
| e      |
+--------+
| NULL   |
|        |
| jane   |
| fred   |
| will   |
| marcia |
+--------+
```

You can better see what's going on by retrieving both the string and numeric forms of the ENUM values:

```
mysql> SELECT e, e+0 FROM e_table ORDER BY e;
+--------+------+
| e      | e+0  |
+--------+------+
| NULL   | NULL |
```

```
|        |    0 |
| jane   |    1 |
| fred   |    2 |
| will   |    3 |
| marcia |    4 |
+--------+------+
```

If you have a fixed set of values and you want them to sort in a particular order, you can exploit the ENUM sorting properties: Represent the values as an ENUM column in a table and list the enumeration values in the column definition in the order that you want them to be sorted. Suppose that you have a table representing personnel for a sports organization, such as a football team, and that you want to sort output by personnel position so that it comes out in a particular order, such as coaches, assistant coaches, quarterbacks, running backs, receivers, linemen, and so on. Define the column as an ENUM and list the enumeration elements in the order that you want to see them. Then column values automatically will come out in that order for sort operations.

For cases where you want an ENUM to sort in normal lexical order, you can convert the column to a non-ENUM string by using CAST() and sorting the result:

```
mysql> SELECT CAST(e AS CHAR) AS e_str FROM e_table ORDER BY e_str;
+--------+
| e_str  |
+--------+
| NULL   |
|        |
| fred   |
| jane   |
| marcia |
| will   |
+--------+
```

CAST() doesn't change the displayed values, but has the effect in this statement of performing an ENUM-to-string conversion that alters their sorting properties so they sort as strings.

3.2.5.5 String Data Type Attributes

The attributes unique to the string data types are CHARACTER SET (or CHARSET) and COLLATE for designating a character set and collating order. You can specify these as options for the table itself to set its defaults, or for individual columns to override the table defaults. (Actually, each database also has a default character set and collation, as does the server itself. These defaults sometimes come into play during table creation, as we'll see later.)

The CHARACTER SET and COLLATE attributes apply to the CHAR, VARCHAR, TEXT, ENUM, and SET data types. They do not apply to the binary string data types (BINARY, VARBINARY, and BLOB), because those types contain byte strings, not character strings.

When you specify the CHARACTER SET and COLLATE attributes, whether at the column, table, or database level, the following rules apply:

- The character set must be one that the server supports. To display the available character sets, use SHOW CHARACTER SET.

- For a definition that includes both CHARACTER SET and COLLATE, the character set and collation must be compatible. For example, with a character set of latin2, you could use a collation of latin2_croatian_ci, but not latin1_bin. To display the collations for each character set, use SHOW COLLATION.

- For a definition with CHARACTER SET but without COLLATE, the character set's default collation is used.

- For a definition with COLLATE but without CHARACTER SET, the character set is determined from the first part of the collation name.

To see how these rules apply, consider the following statement. It creates a table that uses several character sets:

```
CREATE TABLE mytbl
(
  c1   CHAR(10),
  c2   CHAR(40) CHARACTER SET latin2,
  c3   CHAR(10) COLLATE latin1_german1_ci,
  c4   BINARY(40)
) CHARACTER SET utf8;
```

The resulting table has utf8 as its default character set. No COLLATE table option is given, so the default table collation is the default utf8 collation (which is utf8_general_ci). The c1 column definition contains no CHARACTER SET or COLLATE attributes of its own, so the table defaults are used for it. The table-level character set and collation are not used for c2, c3, and c4: c2 and c3 have their own character set information, and c4 has a binary string type, so the character set attributes do not apply. For c2, the collation is latin2_general_ci, the default collation for latin2. For c3, the character set is latin1, as implied by the collation name latin1_german1_ci.

To see character set information for an existing table, use SHOW CREATE TABLE:

```
mysql> SHOW CREATE TABLE mytbl\G
*************************** 1. row ***************************
       Table: mytbl
Create Table: CREATE TABLE `mytbl` (
  `c1` char(10) default NULL,
  `c2` char(40) character set latin2 default NULL,
  `c3` char(10) character set latin1 collate latin1_german1_ci default NULL,
  `c4` binary(40) default NULL
) ENGINE=MyISAM DEFAULT CHARSET=utf8
```

If SHOW CREATE TABLE does not display a column character set, it is the same as the table default character set. If it does not display a column collation, it is the default collation for the character set.

You can also add the FULL keyword to SHOW COLUMNS to cause it to display collation information (from which character sets can be derived):

```
mysql> SHOW FULL COLUMNS FROM mytbl;
+-------+------------+-------------------+------+-----+---------+...
| Field | Type       | Collation         | Null | Key | Default |...
+-------+------------+-------------------+------+-----+---------+...
| c1    | char(10)   | utf8_general_ci   | YES  |     | NULL    |...
| c2    | char(40)   | latin2_general_ci | YES  |     | NULL    |...
| c3    | char(10)   | latin1_german1_ci | YES  |     | NULL    |...
| c4    | binary(40) | NULL              | YES  |     | NULL    |...
+-------+------------+-------------------+------+-----+---------+...
```

The preceding discussion mentions column and table character set assignments, but character sets actually can be designated at the column, table, database, or server level. When MySQL processes a character column definition, it determines which character set to use for it by trying the following rules in order:

1. If the column definition includes a character set, use that set. (This includes the case where only a COLLATE attribute is present, because that implies which character set to use.)

2. Otherwise, if the table definition includes a table character set option, use that set.

3. Otherwise, use the database character set as the table default character set, which also becomes the column character set. If the database was never assigned a character set explicitly (for example, if it was created prior to MySQL 4.1), the database character set is taken from the server character set.

In other words, MySQL searches up through the levels at which character sets may be specified until it finds a character set defined, and then uses that for the column. The database always has a default character set, so the search process is guaranteed to terminate at the database level even if no character set is specified explicitly at any of the lower levels.

The character set name binary is special. If you assign the binary character set to a non-binary string column, that is equivalent to defining the column using the corresponding binary string type. The following pairs of column definitions each show two equivalent definitions:

```
c1 CHAR(10) CHARACTER SET binary
c1 BINARY(10)

c2 VARCHAR(10) CHARACTER SET binary
c2 VARBINARY(10)

c3 TEXT CHARACTER SET binary
c3 BLOB
```

If you specify CHARACTER SET binary for a binary string column, it is ignored because the type already is binary. If you specify CHARACTER SET binary for an ENUM or SET, it is used as is.

If you assign the binary character set as a table option, it applies to each string column that does not have any character set information specified in its own definition.

MySQL provides some shortcut attributes for defining character columns:

- The ASCII attribute is shorthand for CHARACTER SET latin1.

- The UNICODE attribute is shorthand for CHARACTER SET ucs2.

- If you use the BINARY attribute for a non-binary string column, ENUM, or SET, it is shorthand for specifying the binary collation of the column's character set. For example, assuming a table default character set of latin1, these definitions are equivalent:

```
c1 CHAR(10) BINARY
c2 CHAR(10) CHARACTER SET latin1 BINARY
c3 CHAR(10) CHARACTER SET latin1 COLLATE latin1_bin
```

If you specify the BINARY attribute for a binary string column, it is ignored because the type already is binary.

The general attributes NULL or NOT NULL can be specified for any of the string types. If you don't specify either of them, NULL is the default. However, defining a string column as NOT NULL does not prevent you from storing an empty string (that is, ' ') in the column. In MySQL, an empty value is different from a missing value, so don't make the mistake of thinking that you can force a string column to contain non-empty values by defining it NOT NULL. If you require string values to be non-empty, that is a constraint you must enforce from within your own applications.

You can also specify a default value using a DEFAULT clause for all string data types except the BLOB and TEXT types. Section 3.2.3, "Specifying Column Default Values," earlier in this chapter, described the rules that MySQL uses for assigning a default value if a column definition includes no DEFAULT clause.

3.2.5.6 Choosing String Data Types

When you choose a data type for a string column, consider the following questions:

Are values represented as character or binary data? For character data, non-binary string types are most appropriate. For binary data, use a binary string type.

Do you want comparisons to be lettercase-aware? If so, use one of the non-binary string types, because those store characters and are associated with a character set and collation.

The case sensitivity of non-binary string values for comparison and sorting purposes is controlled by the collation that you assign to them. If you want string values to be regarded equal regardless of lettercase, use a case-insensitive collation. Otherwise, use either a binary or case-sensitive collation. A binary collation compares character units using the numeric character codes. A case-sensitive collation compares character units using a specific collating order, which need not correspond to character code order. In either case, the lowercase and uppercase versions of a given character are considered distinct for comparisons. Suppose that 'mysql', 'MySQL', and 'MYSQL' are strings in the latin1 character set. They are all considered the same if compared using a case-insensitive collation such as latin1_swedish_ci, but as three different strings if compared using the binary latin1_bin collation or case-sensitive latin1_general_cs collation.

If you want to use a string column both for case-sensitive and not case-sensitive comparisons, use a collation that corresponds to the type of comparison you will perform most often. For comparisons of the other type, apply the COLLATE operator to change the collation. For example, if mycol is a CHAR column that uses the latin1 character set, you can assign it the latin1_swedish_ci collation to perform case-insensitive comparisons by default. The following comparison is not case sensitive:

```
mycol = 'ABC'
```

For those times when you need case-sensitive comparisons, use the latin1_general_cs or latin1_bin collation. The following comparisons are case sensitive (it doesn't matter whether you apply the COLLATE operator to the left hand string or the right hand string):

```
mycol COLLATE latin1_general_cs = 'ABC'
mycol COLLATE latin1_bin = 'ABC'
mycol = 'ABC' COLLATE latin1_general_cs
mycol = 'ABC' COLLATE latin1_bin
```

Do you want to minimize storage requirements? If so, use a variable-length type, not a fixed-length type.

Will the allowable column values always be chosen from a fixed set of legal values? If so, ENUM or SET might be a good choice.

ENUM also can be useful if you have a limited set of string values that you want to sort in some non-lexical order. Sorting of ENUM values occurs according to the order in which you list the enumeration values in the column definition, so you can make the values sort in any order you want.

Are trailing pad values significant? If values must be retrieved exactly as they are stored without addition or removal of trailing spaces (or 0x00 bytes, for binary data types) during storage or retrieval, use a TEXT or VARCHAR column for non-binary strings and a BLOB or VARBINARY column for binary strings. This factor is important also if you are storing compressed, hashed, or encrypted values computed in such a way that the encoding method might result in trailing spaces. Table 3.12 shows how trailing padding is handled for storage and retrieval operations for various string data types.

As of MySQL 5.1.20, you can enable the PAD_CHAR_TO_FULL_LENGTH SQL mode to cause retrieved CHAR column values to retain trailing spaces. For BINARY columns prior to MySQL 5.0.15, short values are padded with spaces for storage and trailing spaces are stripped for retrieval.

Table 3.12   **String Data Type Pad-Value Handling**

Data Type	Storage	Retrieval	Result
CHAR	Padded	Stripped	Retrieved values have no trailing padding
BINARY	Padded	No action	Retrieved values have no trailing padding
VARCHAR, VARBINARY	No action	No action	Trailing padding is not changed
TEXT, BLOB	No action	No action	Trailing padding is not changed

3.2.6 Date and Time Data Types

MySQL provides several data types for storing temporal values: DATE, TIME, DATETIME, TIMESTAMP, and YEAR. Table 3.13 shows these types and the range of legal values for each type. The storage requirements for each type are shown in Table 3.14.

Table 3.13   **Date and Time Data Types**

Type Specification	Range
DATE	'1000-01-01' to '9999-12-31'
TIME	'-838:59:59' to '838:59:59'
DATETIME	'1000-01-01 00:00:00' to '9999-12-31 23:59:59'
TIMESTAMP	'1970-01-01 00:00:01' to '2038-01-19 03:14:07'
YEAR[(M)]	1901 to 2155 for YEAR(4), and 1970 to 2069 for YEAR(2)

Table 3.14   **Date and Time Data Type Storage Requirements**

Type Specification	Storage Required
DATE	3 bytes
TIME	3 bytes
DATETIME	8 bytes
TIMESTAMP	4 bytes
YEAR	1 byte

Each date and time type has a "zero" value that is stored when you insert a value that is illegal for the type, as shown in Table 3.15. The "zero" value also is the default value for date and time columns that are defined with the NOT NULL constraint. Depending on the SQL mode, illegal values might be treated as errors and rejected; see Section 3.3, "HowMySQL Handles Invalid Data Values."

Table 3.15   **Date and Time Type "Zero" Values**

Type Specification	Zero Value
DATE	'0000-00-00'
TIME	'00:00:00'
DATETIME	'0000-00-00 00:00:00'
TIMESTAMP	'0000-00-00 00:00:00'
YEAR	0000

MySQL always represents dates with the year first, in accordance with the standard SQL and ISO 8601 specifications. For example, December 3, 2008, is represented as '2008-12-03'. However, MySQL does allow some leeway in how you can specify input dates. For example, it will convert two-digit year values to four digits, and you need not supply a leading zero digit for month and day values that are less than 10. However, you must specify the year first and the day last. Formats that you may be more used to, such as '12/3/99' or '3/12/99', will not be interpreted as you might intend. In such cases, you might find the STR_TO_DATE() function useful for converting strings in non-ISO format to ISO-format dates. Section 3.2.6.5, "Working with Date and Time Values," further discusses the date interpretation rules that MySQL uses.

For combined date and time values, it is allowable to specify a 'T' character rather than a space between the date and time (for example, '2008-12-31T12:00:00').

Time or combined date and time values can include a microseconds part following the time, consisting of a decimal point and up to six digits. (For example, '12:30:15.5' or '2008-06-15 10:30:12.000045'.) However, current support in MySQL for microsecond values is only partial. Some temporal functions use them, but you cannot store a temporal value that includes a microseconds part in a table; the microseconds part is discarded.

For retrieval, you can display date and time values in a variety of formats by using the DATE_FORMAT() and TIME_FORMAT() functions.

3.2.6.1 The DATE, TIME, and DATETIME Data Types

The DATE and TIME types hold date and time values. The DATETIME type holds combined date and time values. The formats for the three types of values are 'CCYY-MM-DD', 'hh:mm:ss', and 'CCYY-MM-DD hh:mm:ss', where CC, YY, MM, DD hh, mm, and ss represent century, year, month, day, hour, minute, and second, respectively.

For the DATETIME type, the date and time parts are both required; if you assign a DATE value to a DATETIME column, MySQL automatically adds a time part of '00:00:00'. Conversions work in the other direction as well. If you assign a DATETIME value to a DATE or TIME column, MySQL discards the part that is irrelevant:

```
mysql> CREATE TABLE t (dt DATETIME, d DATE, t TIME);
mysql> INSERT INTO t (dt,d,t) VALUES(NOW(), NOW(), NOW());
mysql> SELECT * FROM t;
```

```
+---------------------+------------+----------+
| dt                  | d          | t        |
+---------------------+------------+----------+
| 2007-09-14 10:26:26 | 2007-09-14 | 10:26:26 |
+---------------------+------------+----------+
```

MySQL treats the time in DATETIME and TIME values slightly different. For DATETIME, the time part represents a time of day and must be in the range from '00:00:00' to '23:59:59'. A TIME value, on the other hand, represents elapsed time—that's why the range shown in Table 3.13 for TIME columns includes values larger than '23:59:59' and negative values.

One thing to watch out when inserting TIME values into a table is that if you use a "short" (not fully qualified) value, it may not be interpreted as you expect. For example, you'll probably find that if you insert '30' and '12:30', into a TIME column, one value will be interpreted from right to left and the other from left to right, resulting in stored values of '00:00:30' and '12:30:00'. If you consider '12:30' to represent a value of "12 minutes, 30 seconds," you should specify it in fully qualified form as '00:12:30'.

3.2.6.2 The TIMESTAMP Data Type

TIMESTAMP is a temporal data type that stores combined date and time values. (The word "timestamp" might appear to connote time only, but that is not the case.) The TIMESTAMP data type has the special properties noted in the following discussion.

TIMESTAMP columns have a range of values from '1970-01-01 00:00:01' to '2038-01-19 03:14:07'. The range is tied to Unix time, where the first day of 1970 is "day zero," also known as "the epoch." Values are stored as a four-byte number of seconds since the epoch. The beginning of 1970 determines the lower end of the TIMESTAMP range. The upper end of the range corresponds to the maximum four-byte value for Unix time.

Values are stored in Universal Coordinated Time (UTC). When you store a TIMESTAMP value, the server converts it from the connection's time zone to UTC. When you retrieve the value later, the server converts it back from UTC to the connection's time zone, so you see the same value that you stored. However, if another client connects to the server, uses a different time zone, and retrieves the value, it will see the value adjusted to its own time zone. In fact, you can see this effect within a single connection if you change your own time zone:

```
mysql> CREATE TABLE t (ts TIMESTAMP);
mysql> SET time_zone = '+00:00';   # set time zone to UTC
mysql> INSERT INTO t VALUES('2000-01-01 00:00:00');
mysql> SELECT ts FROM t;
+---------------------+
| ts                  |
+---------------------+
```

```
| 2000-01-01 00:00:00 |
+---------------------+
mysql> SET time_zone = '+03:00';    # advance time zone 3 hours
mysql> SELECT ts FROM t;
+---------------------+
| ts                  |
+---------------------+
| 2000-01-01 03:00:00 |
+---------------------+
```

These examples specify time zones using values given as a signed offset in hours and minutes relative to UTC. It is also possible to use named time zones such as 'Europe/Zurich' if the server time zone tables have been set up as described in Section 12.9.1, "Configuring Time Zone Support."

TIMESTAMP has automatic initialization and update properties. You can designate any single TIMESTAMP column in a table to have either or both of these properties:

- "Automatic initialization" means that for new rows the column is set to the current timestamp if you omit it from the INSERT statement or set it to NULL.

- "Automatic update" means that for existing rows the column is updated to the current timestamp when you change any other column. Setting a column to its current value does not count as a change. You must set it to a different value for automatic update to occur.

In addition, if you set any TIMESTAMP column to NULL, its value is set to the current timestamp. You can defeat this by defining the column with the NULL attribute to allow NULL values to be stored in the column.

Only one TIMESTAMP column in a table can be designated to have automatic properties. You cannot have automatic initialization for one TIMESTAMP column and automatic update for another. Nor can you have automatic initialization for multiple columns, or automatic update for multiple columns.

The syntax for specifying a TIMESTAMP column is as follows, assuming a column name of ts:

```
ts TIMESTAMP [DEFAULT constant_value] [ON UPDATE CURRENT_TIMESTAMP]
```

The DEFAULT and ON UPDATE attributes can be given in any order, if both are given. The default value can be CURRENT_TIMESTAMP or a constant value such as 0 or a value in 'CCYY-MM-DD hh:mm:ss' format. Synonyms for CURRENT_TIMESTAMP are CURRENT_TIMESTAMP() and NOW(); they're all interchangeable in a TIMESTAMP definition.

To have one or both of the automatic properties for the first TIMESTAMP column in a table, you can define it using various combinations of the DEFAULT and ON UPDATE attributes:

- With DEFAULT CURRENT_TIMESTAMP, the column has automatic initialization. It also has automatic update if ON UPDATE CURRENT_TIMESTAMP is given.
- With neither attribute, MySQL defines the column with both DEFAULT CURRENT_TIMESTAMP and ON UPDATE CURRENT_TIMESTAMP.
- With a DEFAULT *constant_value* attribute that specifies a constant value, the column does not have automatic initialization. It does have automatic update if ON UPDATE CURRENT_TIMESTAMP is given.
- Without DEFAULT but with ON UPDATE CURRENT_TIMESTAMP, the default value is 0 and the column has automatic update.

To use automatic initialization or update for a TIMESTAMP column other than the first one, you must explicitly define the first one with a DEFAULT *constant_value* attribute and without ON UPDATE CURRENT_TIMESTAMP. Then you can use DEFAULT CURRENT_TIMESTAMP or ON UPDATE CURRENT_TIMESTAMP (or both) with any other single TIMESTAMP column.

If you want to defeat automatic initialization or update for a TIMESTAMP column, set it explicitly to the desired value for insert or update operations. For example, you can prevent an update from changing the column by setting the column to its current value.

TIMESTAMP column definitions also can include NULL or NOT NULL. The default is NOT NULL. Its effect is that when you explicitly set the column to NULL, MySQL sets it to the current timestamp. (This is true both for inserts and updates.) If you specify NULL, setting the column to NULL stores NULL rather than the current timestamp.

If you want a table to contain a column that is set to the current timestamp for new rows and that remains unchanged thereafter, you can achieve that two ways:

- Use a TIMESTAMP column declared as follows without an ON UPDATE attribute:

```
ts TIMESTAMP DEFAULT CURRENT_TIMESTAMP
```

When you create a new row, initialize the column to the current timestamp by setting it to NULL or by omitting it from the INSERT statement. The column will retain its value for subsequent updates unless you change it explicitly.

- Use a DATETIME column. When you create a row, initialize the column to NOW(). Whenever you update the row thereafter, leave the column alone.

If you want a table to contain columns for both a time-created value and a last-modified value, use two TIMESTAMP columns:

```
CREATE TABLE t
(
  t_created  TIMESTAMP DEFAULT 0,
  t_modified TIMESTAMP DEFAULT CURRENT_TIMESTAMP
```

```
                    ON UPDATE CURRENT_TIMESTAMP
    ... other columns ...
);
```

When you insert a new row, set both TIMESTAMP columns to NULL to set them to the insertion timestamp. When you update an existing row, leave both columns alone; t_modified will be updated automatically to the modification timestamp if any other columns change value.

3.2.6.3 The YEAR Data Type

YEAR is a one-byte data type intended for efficient representation of year values. A YEAR column definition may include a specification for a display width M, which should be either 4 or 2. If you omit M from a YEAR definition, the default is 4. YEAR(4) has a range of 1901 to 2155. YEAR(2) has a range of 1970 to 2069, but only the last two digits are displayed. You can use the YEAR type when you want to store date information but only need the year part of the date, such as year of birth, year of election to office, and so forth. When you do not require a full date value, YEAR is much more space-efficient than other date types.

TINYINT has the same storage size as YEAR (one byte), but not the same range. To cover the same range of years as YEAR by using an integer type, you would need a SMALLINT, which takes twice as much space. If the range of years you need to represent coincides with the range of the YEAR type, YEAR is more space-efficient than SMALLINT. Another advantage of YEAR over an integer column is that MySQL converts two-digit values into four-digit values for you using MySQL's usual year-guessing rules. For example, 97 and 14 become 1997 and 2014. However, be aware that inserting the numeric value 00 into a four-digit YEAR column results in the value 0000 being stored, not 2000. If you want a value of 00 to convert to 2000, specify it in string form as '0' or '00'.

3.2.6.4 Date and Time Data Type Attributes

The following remarks apply to all temporal types except TIMESTAMP:

- The general attributes NULL or NOT NULL may be specified. If you don't specify either of them, NULL is the default.
- You can also specify a default value using a DEFAULT clause. Section 3.2.3, "Specifying Column Default Values," described the rules that MySQL uses for assigning a default value if a column definition includes no DEFAULT clause.

  Note that because default values must be constants, you cannot use a function such as NOW() to supply a value of "the current date and time" as the default for a DATETIME column. To achieve that result, set the column value explicitly to NOW() whenever you create a new row, or else consider using a TIMESTAMP column instead. Alternatively, set up a trigger that initializes the column to the appropriate value; see Section 4.3, "Triggers."

TIMESTAMP columns are special; the default for the first such column in a table is the current date and time, and the "zero" value for any others. However, the full set of rules governing default values is more complex. See Section 3.2.6.2, "The TIMESTAMP Data Type," for details.

3.2.6.5 Working with Date and Time Values

MySQL tries to interpret input values for date and time columns in a variety of formats, including both string and numeric forms. Table 3.16 shows the allowable formats for each of the date and time types.

Table 3.16   Date and Time Type Input Formats

Type	Allowable Formats
DATETIME,	`'CCYY-MM-DD hh:mm:ss'`
TIMESTAMP	`'YY-MM-DD hh:mm:ss'`
	`'CCYYMMDDhhmmss'`
	`'YYMMDDhhmmss'`
	`CCYYMMDDhhmmss`
	`YYMMDDhhmmss`
DATE	`'CCYY-MM-DD'`
	`'YY-MM-DD'`
	`'CCYYMMDD'`
	`'YYMMDD'`
	`CCYYMMDD`
	`YYMMDD`
TIME	`'hh:mm:ss'`
	`'hhmmss'`
	`hhmmss`
YEAR	`'CCYY'`
	`'YY'`
	`CCYY`
	`YY`

MySQL interprets formats that have no century part (*CC*) using the rules described in Section 3.2.6.6, "Interpretation of Ambiguous Year Values." For string formats that include delimiter characters, you don't have to use '-' for dates and ':' for times. Any punctuation character may be used as the delimiter. Interpretation of values depends on context, not on the delimiter. For example, although times are typically specified using a delimiter of ':', MySQL won't interpret a value containing ':' as a time in a context where a date is expected. In addition, for the string formats that include delimiters, you need not specify two digits for month, day, hour, minute, or second values that are less than 10. The following are all equivalent:

```
'2012-02-03 05:04:09'
'2012-2-03 05:04:09'
'2012-2-3 05:04:09'
'2012-2-3 5:04:09'
'2012-2-3 5:4:09'
'2012-2-3 5:4:9'
```

MySQL may interpret values with leading zeros in different ways depending on whether they are specified as strings or numbers. The string '001231' will be seen as a six-digit value and interpreted as '2000-12-31' for a DATE, and as '2000-12-31 00:00:00' for a DATETIME. On the other hand, the number 001231 will be seen as 1231 after the parser gets done with it and then the interpretation becomes problematic. This is a case where it's best to supply a string value '001231', or else use a fully qualified value if you are using numbers (that is, 20001231 for DATE and 200012310000 for DATETIME).

In general, you may freely assign values between the DATE, DATETIME, and TIMESTAMP types, although there are certain restrictions to keep in mind:

- If you assign a DATETIME or TIMESTAMP value to a DATE, the time part is discarded.
- If you assign a DATE value to a DATETIME or TIMESTAMP, the time part of the resulting value is set to zero ('00:00:00').
- The types have different ranges. In particular, TIMESTAMP has a more limited range (1970 to 2038); so, for example, you cannot assign a pre-1970 DATETIME value to a TIMESTAMP and expect reasonable results. Nor can you assign values that are far in the future to a TIMESTAMP.

MySQL provides many functions for working with date and time values. See Appendix C for more information.

3.2.6.6 Interpretation of Ambiguous Year Values

For all date and time types that include a year part (DATE, DATETIME, TIMESTAMP, YEAR), MySQL handles values that contain two-digit years by converting them to four-digit years:

- Year values from 00 to 69 become 2000 to 2069
- Year values from 70 to 99 become 1970 to 1999

You can see the effect of these rules most easily by storing different two-digit values into a YEAR column and then retrieving the results. This also demonstrates something you should take note of:

```
mysql> CREATE TABLE y_table (y YEAR);
mysql> INSERT INTO y_table VALUES(68),(69),(99),(00),('00');
```

```
mysql> SELECT * FROM y_table;
+------+
| y    |
+------+
| 2068 |
| 2069 |
| 1999 |
| 0000 |
| 2000 |
+------+
```

Observe that 00 is converted to 0000, not to 2000. That's because, as a number, 00 is the same as 0, and is a perfectly legal value for the YEAR type. If you insert a numeric zero, that's what you get. To get 2000 using a value that does not contain the century, insert the string '0' or '00'. You can make sure that MySQL sees a string and not a number by inserting YEAR values using CAST(*value* AS CHAR) to produce a string result uniformly regardless of whether *value* is a string or a number.

Keep in mind that the rules for converting two-digit to four-digit year values provide only a reasonable guess. There is no way for MySQL to be certain about the meaning of a two-digit year when the century is unspecified. MySQL's conversion rules are adequate for many situations, but if they don't produce the values that you want, it is necessary to provide unambiguous data with four-digit years. For example, to enter birth and death dates into the president table, which lists U.S. presidents back into the 1700s, four-digit year values are in order. Values in these columns span several centuries, so letting MySQL guess the century from a two-digit year is definitely the wrong thing to do.

3.2.7 Spatial Data Types

Spatial values enable representation of values such as points, lines, and polygons. These data types are implemented per the OpenGIS specification, which is available at the Open Geospatial Consortium Web site (http://www.opengeospatial.org/). Table 3.17 lists the spatial data types that MySQL supports.

Table 3.17 **Spatial Data Types**

Type Name	Meaning
GEOMETRY	A spatial value of any type
POINT	A point (a pair of X,Y coordinates)
LINESTRING	A curve (one or more POINT values)
POLYGON	A polygon
GEOMETRYCOLLECTION	A collection of GEOMETRY values
MULTILINESTRING	A collection of LINESTRING values
MULTIPOINT	A collection of POINT values
MULTIPOLYGON	A collection of POLYGON values

The level of support for spatial types varies by storage engine. The most complete support is implemented in MyISAM. Other engines such as InnoDB, NDB, and ARCHIVE offer more limited support. For example, in MyISAM tables, spatial values can be indexed using either SPATIAL or non-SPATIAL indexes (using INDEX, UNIQUE, or PRIMARY KEY). Other engines that support spatial data types can use only non-SPATIAL indexes (except ARCHIVE, which cannot index spatial columns at all). If a table is partitioned, it cannot contain spatial columns.

Spatial columns included in a SPATIAL index cannot use NULL to represent missing values within columns, because SPATIAL indexes do not allow NULL values. Depending on your application, it might be acceptable to use an empty (zero-dimensional) value instead.

MySQL works with spatial values in three formats. One is the internal format that MySQL uses for storing spatial values in tables. The other two are the Well-Known Text (WKT) and Well-Known Binary (WKB) formats; these are standards for representing spatial values as text strings or in binary format. The syntax for text strings and the binary representation are defined in the OpenGIS specification. For example, the WKT format for a POINT value with coordinates of x and y is written as a string:

```
'POINT(x y)'
```

Note the absence of a comma between the coordinate values. In lists of multiple coordinates, commas separate *pairs* of x and y values. The following string represents a LINESTRING value consisting of several points:

```
'LINESTRING(10 20, 0 0, 10 20, 0 0)'
```

More complex values have a more complex representation. This POLYGON has a rectangular outer boundary and a triangular inner boundary:

```
'POLYGON((0 0, 100 0, 100 100, 0 100, 0 0),(30 30, 30 60, 45 60, 30 30))'
```

Because spatial values can be complex, most operations on them are done by invoking functions. The set of spatial functions is extensive and includes functions for converting from one format to another (see Appendix C).

The following example shows how to use several aspects of spatial support:

```
mysql> CREATE TABLE pt_tbl (p POINT);
mysql> INSERT INTO pt_tbl (p) VALUES
    ->    (POINTFROMTEXT('POINT(0 0)')),
    ->    (POINTFROMTEXT('POINT(0 50)')),
    ->    (POINTFROMTEXT('POINT(100 100)'));
mysql> CREATE FUNCTION dist (p1 POINT, p2 POINT)
    ->    RETURNS FLOAT DETERMINISTIC
    ->    RETURN SQRT(POW(X(p2)-X(p1),2) + POW(Y(p2)-Y(p1),2));
mysql> SET @ref_pt = POINTFROMTEXT('POINT(0 0)');
mysql> SELECT ASTEXT(p), dist (p, @ref_pt) AS dist FROM pt_tbl;
+---------------+-----------------+
```

```
| ASTEXT(p)       | dist            |
+----------------+----------------+
| POINT(0 0)      |               0 |
| POINT(0 50)     |              50 |
| POINT(100 100)  | 141.42135620117 |
+----------------+----------------+
```

The example performs these operations:

1. It creates a table that includes a spatial column.

2. It populates the table with some POINT values, using the POINTFROMTEXT() function that produces an internal-format value from a WKT representation.

3. It creates a stored function that computes the distance between two points, using the X() and Y() functions to extract point coordinates.

4. It computes the distance of each point in the table from a given reference point.

3.3 How MySQL Handles Invalid Data Values

Historically, the dominant principle for data handling in MySQL has been, "Garbage in, garbage out." In other words, MySQL attempts to store any data value you give it, but if you don't verify the value first before storing it, you may not like what you get back out. However, as of MySQL 5.0.2, several SQL modes are available that enable you to reject bad values and cause an error to occur instead. The following discussion first discusses how MySQL handles improper data by default, and then covers the changes that occur when you enable the various SQL modes that affect data handling.

By default, MySQL handles out-of-range or otherwise improper values as follows:

- For numeric or TIME columns, values that are outside the legal range are clipped to the nearest endpoint of the range and the resulting value is stored.

- For string columns other than ENUM or SET, strings that are too long are truncated to fit the maximum length of the column.

- Assignments to an ENUM or SET column depend on the values that are listed as legal in the column definition. If you assign to an ENUM column a value that is not listed as an enumeration member, the error member is assigned instead (that is, the empty string that corresponds to the zero-valued member). If you assign to a SET column a value containing substrings that are not listed as set members, those strings drop out and the column is assigned a value consisting of the remaining members.

- For date or time columns, illegal values are converted to the appropriate "zero" value for the type (see Table 3.15).

These conversions are reported as warnings for statements such as INSERT, REPLACE, UPDATE, LOAD DATA, and ALTER TABLE. You can use SHOW WARNINGS after executing one of those statements to see the warning messages.

To turn on stricter checking of inserted or updated data values, enable one of the following SQL modes:

```
mysql> SET sql_mode = 'STRICT_ALL_TABLES';
mysql> SET sql_mode = 'STRICT_TRANS_TABLES';
```

For transactional tables, both modes are identical: If an invalid or missing value is found, an error occurs, the statement aborts and rolls back, and has no effect. For non-transactional tables, the modes have the following effects:

- For both modes, if an invalid or missing value is found in the first row of a statement that inserts or updates rows, an error occurs. The statement aborts and has no effect, which is similar to what happens for transactional tables.
- If an error occurs after the first row in a statement that inserts or updates multiple rows, some rows already will have been modified. The two strict modes control whether the statement aborts at that point or continues to execute:
  - With STRICT_ALL_TABLES, an error occurs and the statement aborts. Rows affected earlier by the statement will already have been modified, so the result is a partial update.
  - With STRICT_TRANS_TABLES, MySQL aborts the statement for non-transactional tables only if doing so would have the same effect as for a transactional table. That is true only if the error occurs in the first row; an error in a later row leaves the earlier rows already changed. Those changes cannot be undone for a non-transactional table, so MySQL continues to execute the statement to avoid a partial update. It converts each invalid value to the closest legal value, as defined earlier in this section. For a missing value, MySQL sets the column to the implicit default for its data type. Implicit defaults were described in Section 3.2.3, "Specifying Column Default Values."

Strict mode actually does not enable the strictest checking that MySQL can perform. You can enable any or all of the following modes to impose additional constraints on input data:

- ERROR_FOR_DIVISION_BY_ZERO prevents entry of values if division by zero occurs in strict mode. (Without strict mode, a warning occurs and NULL is inserted.)
- NO_ZERO_DATE prevents entry of the "zero" date value in strict mode.
- NO_ZERO_IN_DATE prevents entry of incomplete date values that have a month or day part of zero in strict mode.

For example, to enable strict mode for all storage engines and also check for divide-by-zero errors, set the SQL mode like this:

```
mysql> SET sql_mode = 'STRICT_ALL_TABLES,ERROR_FOR_DIVISION_BY_ZERO';
```

To turn on strict mode and all of the additional restrictions, you can simply enable TRADITIONAL mode:

```
mysql> SET sql_mode = 'TRADITIONAL';
```

TRADITIONAL is shorthand for "both strict modes, plus a bunch of other restrictions." This is more like the way that other "traditional" SQL DBMSs act with regard to data checking.

It is also possible to selectively weaken strict mode in some respects. If you enable the ALLOW_INVALID_DATES SQL mode, MySQL doesn't perform full checking of date parts. Instead, it requires only that months be in the range from 1 to 12 and days be in the range from 1 to 31 (which allows invalid values such as '2000-02-30' or '2000-06-31'). Another way to suppress errors is to use the IGNORE keyword with INSERT or UPDATE statements. With IGNORE, statements that would result in an error due to invalid values result only in a warning.

The various options available give you the flexibility to choose the level of validity checking that is appropriate for your applications.

3.4 Working with Sequences

Many applications need to generate unique numbers for identification purposes. The requirement for unique values occurs in a number of contexts: membership numbers, sample or lot numbering, customer IDs, bug report or trouble ticket tags, and so forth.

MySQL's mechanism for providing unique numbers is through the AUTO_INCREMENT column attribute, which enables you to generate sequential numbers automatically. However, AUTO_INCREMENT columns are handled somewhat differently by the various storage engines that MySQL supports, so it's important to understand not only the general concepts underlying the AUTO_INCREMENT mechanism, but also the differences between storage engines. This section describes how AUTO_INCREMENT columns work in general and for specific storage engines so that you can use them effectively without running into the traps that sometimes surprise people. It also describes how you can generate a sequence without using an AUTO_INCREMENT column.

3.4.1 General AUTO_INCREMENT Properties

AUTO_INCREMENT columns must be defined according to the following conditions:

- There can be only one column per table with the AUTO_INCREMENT attribute and it should have an integer data type. (AUTO_INCREMENT is also allowed for floating-point types, but is rarely used that way.)

- The column must be indexed. It is most common to use a PRIMARY KEY or UNIQUE index, but it is allowable to use a non-unique index.

- The column must have a NOT NULL constraint. MySQL makes the column NOT NULL even if you don't explicitly declare it that way.

Once created, an AUTO_INCREMENT column behaves like this:

- Inserting NULL into an AUTO_INCREMENT column causes MySQL to generate the next sequence number automatically and insert that value into the column.

AUTO_INCREMENT sequences normally begin at 1 and increase monotonically, so successive rows inserted into a table get sequence values of 1, 2, 3, and so forth. Under some circumstances and depending on the storage engine, it may be possible to set or reset the next sequence number explicitly or to reuse values deleted from the top end of the sequence.

- The value of the most recently generated sequence number can be obtained by calling the LAST_INSERT_ID() function. This enables you to reference the AUTO_INCREMENT value in subsequent statements even without knowing what the value is. LAST_INSERT_ID() returns 0 if no AUTO_INCREMENT value has been generated during the current connection.

  LAST_INSERT_ID() is tied *only* to AUTO_INCREMENT values generated during the current connection to the server. In particular, it is not affected by AUTO_INCREMENT activity associated with other clients. You can generate a sequence number, and then call LAST_INSERT_ID() to retrieve it later in the same connection, even if other clients have generated their own sequence values in the meantime.

  For a multiple-row INSERT that generates several AUTO_INCREMENT values, LAST_INSERT_ID() returns the first one.

  If you use INSERT DELAYED for storage engines that support delayed inserts, the AUTO_INCREMENT value is not generated until the row actually is inserted. In this case, LAST_INSERT_ID() cannot be relied on to return the sequence value.

- Inserting a row without specifying an explicit value for the AUTO_INCREMENT column is the same as inserting NULL into the column. If ai_col is an AUTO_INCREMENT column, these statements are equivalent:

```
INSERT INTO t (ai_col,name) VALUES(NULL,'abc');
INSERT INTO t (name) VALUES('abc');
```

- By default, inserting 0 into an AUTO_INCREMENT column has the same effect as inserting NULL. If you enable the NO_AUTO_VALUE_ON_ZERO SQL mode, inserting a 0 results in a 0 being stored, not the next sequence value.

- If you insert a row and specify a non-NULL, non-zero value for an AUTO_INCREMENT column that has a unique index, one of two things will happen. If a row already exists with that value, a duplicate-key error occurs. If a row does not exist with that value, the row is inserted with the AUTO_INCREMENT column set to the given value. If this value is larger than the current next sequence number, the sequence is reset to continue with the next value after that for subsequent rows. In other words, you can "bump up" the counter by inserting a row with a sequence value greater than the current counter value.

  Bumping up the counter can result in gaps in the sequence, but you also can exploit this behavior to generate a sequence that begins at a value higher than 1. Suppose that you create a table with an AUTO_INCREMENT column, but you want the sequence to begin at 1000 rather than at 1. To achieve this, insert a "fake" row with a value of

999 in the `AUTO_INCREMENT` column. Rows inserted subsequently are assigned sequence numbers beginning with 1000, after which you can delete the fake row.

Why might you want to begin a sequence with a value higher than 1? One reason is to make sequence numbers all have the same number of digits. If you're generating customer ID numbers, and you expect never to have more than a million customers, you could begin the series at 1,000,000. You'll be able to add well over a million customer records before the digit count for customer ID values changes.

- For some storage engines, values deleted from the top of a sequence are reused. In this case, if you delete the row containing the largest value in an `AUTO_INCREMENT` column, that value is reused the next time you generate a new value. An implication of this property is that if you delete all the rows in the table, all values are reused and the sequence starts over beginning at 1.

- If you use `UPDATE` to set an `AUTO_INCREMENT` column to a value that already exists in another row, a duplicate-key error occurs if the column has a unique index. If you update the column to a value larger than any existing column value, the sequence continues with the next number after that for subsequent rows. If you update the column by assigning 0 to it, it is set to 0 (regardless of whether `NO_AUTO_VALUE_ON_ZERO` is enabled).

- If you use `REPLACE` to update a row based on the value of the `AUTO_INCREMENT` column, the `AUTO_INCREMENT` value does not change. If you use `REPLACE` to update a row based on the value of some other `PRIMARY KEY` or `UNIQUE` index, the `AUTO_INCREMENT` column is updated with a new sequence number if you set it to `NULL`, or if you set it to 0 and `NO_AUTO_VALUE_ON_ZERO` is not enabled.

3.4.2 Storage Engine-Specific `AUTO_INCREMENT` Properties

The general `AUTO_INCREMENT` characteristics just described form the basis for understanding sequence behavior specific to other storage engines. Most engines implement behavior that for the most part is similar to that just described, so keep the preceding discussion in mind as you read on.

3.4.2.1 `AUTO_INCREMENT` for MyISAM Tables

MyISAM tables offer the most flexibility for sequence handling. The MyISAM storage engine has the following `AUTO_INCREMENT` characteristics:

- MyISAM sequences normally are monotonic. The values in an automatically generated series are strictly increasing and are not reused if you delete rows. If the maximum value is 143 and you delete the row containing that value, MySQL still generates the next value as 144. There are two exceptions to this behavior:

- If you empty a table with TRUNCATE TABLE, the counter is reset to begin at 1.
- Values deleted from the top of a sequence are reused if you use a composite index to generate multiple sequences within a table. (This technique is discussed shortly.)

- MyISAM sequences begin at 1 by default, but it is possible to start the sequence at a higher value. With MyISAM tables, you can specify the initial value explicitly by using an AUTO_INCREMENT = n option in the CREATE TABLE statement. The following example creates a MyISAM table with an AUTO_INCREMENT column named seq that begins at 1,000,000:

```
CREATE TABLE mytbl
(
    seq INT UNSIGNED NOT NULL AUTO_INCREMENT,
    PRIMARY KEY (seq)
) ENGINE = MYISAM AUTO_INCREMENT = 1000000;
```

A table can have only one AUTO_INCREMENT column, so there is never any ambiguity about the column to which the terminating AUTO_INCREMENT = n option applies, even if the table has multiple columns.

- You can change the current sequence counter for an existing MyISAM table with ALTER TABLE. If the sequence currently stands at 1000, the following statement causes the next number generated to be 2000:

```
ALTER TABLE mytbl AUTO_INCREMENT = 2000;
```

If you want to reuse values that have been deleted from the top of the sequence, you can do that, too. The following statement will set the counter down as far as possible, causing the next number to be one larger than the current maximum sequence value:

```
ALTER TABLE mytbl AUTO_INCREMENT = 1;
```

You cannot use the AUTO_INCREMENT option to set the current counter lower than the current maximum value in the table. If an AUTO_INCREMENT column contains the values 1 and 10, using AUTO_INCREMENT = 5 sets the counter so that the next automatic value is 11.

The MyISAM storage engine supports the use of composite (multiple-column) indexes for creating multiple independent sequences within the same table. To use this feature, create a multiple-column PRIMARY KEY or UNIQUE index that includes an AUTO_INCREMENT column as its final column. For each distinct key in the leftmost column or columns of the index, the AUTO_INCREMENT column will generate a separate sequence of values. For example, you might use a table named bugs for tracking bug reports of several software projects, where the table is defined as follows:

```
CREATE TABLE bugs
(
  proj_name    VARCHAR(20) NOT NULL,
  bug_id       INT UNSIGNED NOT NULL AUTO_INCREMENT,
  description VARCHAR(100),
  PRIMARY KEY (proj_name, bug_id)
) ENGINE = MYISAM;
```

Here, the `proj_name` column identifies the project name and the `description` column contains the bug description. The `bug_id` column is an `AUTO_INCREMENT` column; by creating an index that ties it to the `proj_name` column, you can generate an independent series of sequence numbers for each project. Suppose that you enter the following rows into the table to register three bugs for SuperBrowser and two for SpamSquisher:

```
mysql> INSERT INTO bugs (proj_name,description)
    -> VALUES('SuperBrowser','crashes when displaying complex tables');
mysql> INSERT INTO bugs (proj_name,description)
    -> VALUES('SuperBrowser','image scaling does not work');
mysql> INSERT INTO bugs (proj_name,description)
    -> VALUES('SpamSquisher','fails to block known blacklisted domains');
mysql> INSERT INTO bugs (proj_name,description)
    -> VALUES('SpamSquisher','fails to respect whitelist addresses');
mysql> INSERT INTO bugs (proj_name,description)
    -> VALUES('SuperBrowser','background patterns not displayed');
```

The resulting table contents are as follows:

```
mysql> SELECT * FROM bugs ORDER BY proj_name, bug_id;
+--------------+--------+-----------------------------------------+
| proj_name    | bug_id | description                             |
+--------------+--------+-----------------------------------------+
| SpamSquisher |      1 | fails to block known blacklisted domains |
| SpamSquisher |      2 | fails to respect whitelist addresses    |
| SuperBrowser |      1 | crashes when displaying complex tables  |
| SuperBrowser |      2 | image scaling does not work             |
| SuperBrowser |      3 | background patterns not displayed       |
+--------------+--------+-----------------------------------------+
```

The table numbers the `bug_id` values for each project separately, regardless of the order in which rows are entered for projects. You need not enter all rows for one project before you enter rows for another.

If you use a composite index to create multiple sequences, values deleted from the top of each individual sequence *are* reused. This differs from the usual MyISAM behavior of not reusing values.

3.4.2.2 `AUTO_INCREMENT` for MEMORY Tables

The MEMORY storage engine has the following `AUTO_INCREMENT` characteristics:

- The initial sequence value can be set with an `AUTO_INCREMENT` = n table option in the `CREATE TABLE` statement, and can be modified after table creation time using that option with `ALTER TABLE`.

- Values that are deleted from the top of the sequence normally are not reused. If you empty the table with `TRUNCATE TABLE`, the sequence is reset to begin at 1.

- Composite indexes cannot be used to generate multiple independent sequences within a table.

3.4.2.3 `AUTO_INCREMENT` for InnoDB Tables

The InnoDB storage engine has the following `AUTO_INCREMENT` characteristics:

- As of MySQL 5.0.3, the initial sequence value can be set with an `AUTO_INCREMENT` = n table option in the `CREATE TABLE` statement, and can be modified after table creation time using that option with `ALTER TABLE`.

- Values that are deleted from the top of the sequence normally are not reused. If you empty the table with `TRUNCATE TABLE`, the sequence is reset to begin at 1. Reuse can occur under the following conditions as well. The first time that you generate a sequence value for an `AUTO_INCREMENT` column, InnoDB uses one greater than the current maximum value in the column (or 1 if the table is empty). InnoDB maintains this counter in memory for use in generating subsequent values; it is not stored in the table itself. This means that if you delete values from the top of the sequence and then restart the server, the deleted values are reused. Restarting the server also cancels the effect of using an `AUTO_INCREMENT` table option in a `CREATE TABLE` or `ALTER TABLE` statement.

- Gaps in a sequence can occur if transactions that generate `AUTO_INCREMENT` values are rolled back.

- Composite indexes cannot be used to generate multiple independent sequences within a table.

3.4.3 Issues to Consider with `AUTO_INCREMENT` Columns

You should keep the following points in mind to avoid being surprised when you use `AUTO_INCREMENT` columns:

- Although it is common to use the term "`AUTO_INCREMENT` column," `AUTO_INCREMENT` is not a data type; it's a data type attribute. Furthermore, `AUTO_INCREMENT` is an attribute intended for use only with integer or floating-point types. Older versions of MySQL are lax in enforcing this constraint and will let you define a data type such as `CHAR` with the `AUTO_INCREMENT` attribute. However, only the integer or floating-point types work *correctly* as `AUTO_INCREMENT` columns.

- The primary purpose of the AUTO_INCREMENT mechanism is to enable you to generate a sequence of positive integers. The use of non-positive numbers in an AUTO_INCREMENT column is unsupported. Consequently, you may as well define AUTO_INCREMENT columns to be UNSIGNED. With integer columns, using UNSIGNED also has the advantage of giving you twice as many sequence numbers before you hit the upper end of the data type's range.

- Don't be fooled into thinking that adding AUTO_INCREMENT to a column definition is a magic way of getting an unlimited sequence of numbers. It's not; AUTO_INCREMENT sequences are always bound by the range of the underlying data type. For example, if you use a TINYINT column, the maximum sequence number is 127. When you reach that limit, your application begins to fail with duplicate-key errors. If you use TINYINT UNSIGNED instead, the limit is extended to 255, but there is still a limit.

- Clearing a table's contents entirely with TRUNCATE TABLE may reset a sequence to begin again at 1, even for storage engines that normally do not reuse AUTO_INCREMENT values. The sequence reset occurs due to the way that MySQL attempts to optimize a complete table erasure operation: When possible, it tosses the data rows and indexes and re-creates the table from scratch rather than deleting rows one at a time. This causes sequence number information to be lost. If you want to delete all rows but preserve the sequence information, you can suppress this optimization by using DELETE with a WHERE clause that is always true, to force MySQL to evaluate the condition for each row and thus to delete every row individually:

```
DELETE FROM tbl_name WHERE TRUE;
```

3.4.4 Tips for Working with AUTO_INCREMENT Columns

This section describes some useful techniques for working with AUTO_INCREMENT columns.

3.4.4.1 Adding a Sequence Number Column to a Table

Suppose that you create and populate a table:

```
mysql> CREATE TABLE t (c CHAR(10));
mysql> INSERT INTO t VALUES('a'),('b'),('c');
mysql> SELECT * FROM t;
+------+
| c    |
+------+
| a    |
| b    |
| c    |
+------+
```

Then you decide that you want to include a sequence number column in the table. To do this, issue an `ALTER TABLE` statement to add an `AUTO_INCREMENT` column, using the same kind of type definition that you'd use with `CREATE TABLE`:

```
mysql> ALTER TABLE t ADD i INT UNSIGNED NOT NULL AUTO_INCREMENT PRIMARY KEY;
mysql> SELECT * FROM t;
+------+---+
| c    | i |
+------+---+
| a    | 1 |
| b    | 2 |
| c    | 3 |
+------+---+
```

Note how MySQL assigns sequence values to the `AUTO_INCREMENT` column automatically. You need not do so yourself.

3.4.4.2 Resequencing an Existing Column

If a table already has an `AUTO_INCREMENT` column, but you want to renumber it to eliminate gaps in the sequence that may have resulted from row deletions, the easiest way to do it is to drop the column and then add it again. When MySQL adds the column, it assigns new sequence numbers automatically.

Suppose that a table t looks like this, where i is the `AUTO_INCREMENT` column:

```
mysql> CREATE TABLE t (c CHAR(10), i INT UNSIGNED AUTO_INCREMENT
    -> NOT NULL PRIMARY KEY);
mysql> INSERT INTO t (c)
    -> VALUES('a'),('b'),('c'),('d'),('e'),('f'),('g'),('h'),('i'),('j'),('k');
mysql> DELETE FROM t WHERE c IN('a','d','f','g','j');
mysql> SELECT * FROM t;
+------+----+
| c    | i  |
+------+----+
| b    | 2  |
| c    | 3  |
| e    | 5  |
| h    | 8  |
| i    | 9  |
| k    | 11 |
+------+----+
```

The following `ALTER TABLE` statement drops the column and then adds it again, renumbering the column in the process:

```
mysql> ALTER TABLE t
    -> DROP PRIMARY KEY,
    -> DROP i,
    -> ADD i INT UNSIGNED NOT NULL AUTO_INCREMENT PRIMARY KEY,
```

```
        -> AUTO_INCREMENT = 1;
mysql> SELECT * FROM t;
+------+---+
| c    | i |
+------+---+
| b    | 1 |
| c    | 2 |
| e    | 3 |
| h    | 4 |
| i    | 5 |
| k    | 6 |
+------+---+
```

The AUTO_INCREMENT = 1 clause resets the sequence to begin again at 1. For a MyISAM, MEMORY, or InnoDB table, you can use a value other than 1 to begin the sequence at a different value. For other storage engines, omit the AUTO_INCREMENT clause, because they do not allow the initial value to be specified this way. The sequence will begin at 1.

Note that although it's easy to resequence a column, and the question, "How do you do it?" is a common one, there is usually very little need to do so. MySQL doesn't care whether a sequence has holes in it, nor do you gain any performance efficiencies by resequencing. In addition, if you have rows in another table that refer to the values in the AUTO_INCREMENT column, resequencing the column destroys the correspondence between tables.

3.4.5 Generating Sequences Without AUTO_INCREMENT

MySQL supports a method for generating sequence numbers that doesn't use an AUTO_INCREMENT column at all. Instead, it uses an alternative form of the LAST_INSERT_ID() function that takes an argument. If you insert or update a column using LAST_INSERT_ID(expr), the next call to LAST_INSERT_ID() with no argument returns the value of expr. In other words, MySQL treats expr as though it was generated as an AUTO_INCREMENT value. This enables you to create a sequence number and then retrieve it later in your session, confident that the value will not have been affected by the activity of other clients.

One way to use this strategy is to create a single-row table containing a value that you update each time you want the next value in the sequence. For example, you can create and initialize the table like this:

```
CREATE TABLE seq_table (seq INT UNSIGNED NOT NULL);
INSERT INTO seq_table VALUES(0);
```

Those statements set up seq_table with a single row containing a seq value of 0. To use the table, generate the next sequence number and retrieve it like this:

```
UPDATE seq_table SET seq = LAST_INSERT_ID(seq+1);
SELECT LAST_INSERT_ID();
```

The UPDATE statement retrieves the current value of the seq column and increments it by 1 to produce the next value in the sequence. Generating the new value using LAST_INSERT_ID(seq+1) causes it to be treated like an AUTO_INCREMENT value, which allows it to be retrieved by calling LAST_INSERT_ID() without an argument. LAST_INSERT_ID() is client-specific, so you get the correct value even if other clients have generated other sequence numbers in the interval between the UPDATE and the SELECT.

Other uses for this method are to generate sequence values that increment by a value other than 1, or that are negative. For example, this statement can be executed repeatedly to generate a sequence of numbers that increase by 100 each time:

```
UPDATE seq_table SET seq = LAST_INSERT_ID(seq+100);
```

Repeating the following statement generates a sequence of decreasing numbers:

```
UPDATE seq_table SET seq = LAST_INSERT_ID(seq-1);
```

You can also use this technique to generate a sequence that begins at an arbitrary value, by setting the seq column to an appropriate initial value.

The preceding discussion describes how to set up a counter using a table with a single row. That's okay for a single counter. If you want several counters, add another column to the table to serve as a counter identifier, and use a different row in the table for each counter. Suppose that you have a Web site and you want to put some "this page has been accessed *n* times" counters in several pages. Create a table with two columns. One column holds a name that uniquely identifies each counter. The other holds the current counter value. You can still use the LAST_INSERT_ID() function, but you determine which row it applies to by using the counter name. For example, you can create such a table with the following statement:

```
CREATE TABLE counter
(
  name  VARCHAR(255) CHARACTER SET latin1 COLLATE latin1_general_cs NOT NULL,
  value INT UNSIGNED,
  PRIMARY KEY (name)
);
```

The name column is a string so that you can name a counter whatever you want, and it's defined as a PRIMARY KEY to prevent duplicate names. This assumes that applications using the table agree on the names they'll be using. For Web counters, uniqueness of counter names is ensured simply by using the pathname of each page within the document tree as its counter name. The name column has a case-sensitive collation to cause pathname values to be treated as case sensitive. (If your system has pathnames that are not case sensitive, use a collation that is not case sensitive.)

To use the counter table, the INSERT ... ON DUPLICATE KEY UPDATE statement is useful, because it can insert a new row for a page that has not yet been counted, or update the count for an existing page. Also, by using LAST_INSERT_ID(*expr*) to generate the counter value, you can easily retrieve the current counter after updating it. For example, to initialize or increment the counter for the site's home page, and then retrieve the counter for display, do this:

```
INSERT INTO counter (name, value)
  VALUES('index.html', LAST_INSERT_ID(1))
  ON DUPLICATE KEY UPDATE value = LAST_INSERT_ID(value+1);
SELECT LAST_INSERT_ID();
```

An alternative approach for incrementing counters of existing pages without using LAST_INSERT_ID() is to do this:

```
UPDATE counter SET value = value+1 WHERE name = 'index.html';
SELECT value FROM counter WHERE name = 'index.html';
```

However, that doesn't work correctly if another client increments the counter after you issue the UPDATE and before you issue the SELECT. You could solve that problem by putting LOCK TABLES and UNLOCK TABLES around the two statements. Or you could create the table using a transactional storage engine and update the table within a transaction. Either method blocks other clients while you're using the counter, but the LAST_INSERT_ID() method accomplishes the same thing more easily. Because its value is client-specific, you always get the value you inserted, not the one from some other client, and you don't have to complicate the code with locks or transactions to keep other clients out.

3.5 Expression Evaluation and Type Conversion

Expressions contain terms and operators and are evaluated to produce values. Terms can include values such as constants, function calls, references to table columns, and scalar subqueries. These values may be combined using different kinds of operators, such as arithmetic or comparison operators, and terms of an expression may be grouped with parentheses. Expressions occur most commonly in the output column list and WHERE clause of SELECT statements. For example, here is a query that is similar to one used for age calculations in Chapter 1:

```
SELECT
  CONCAT(last_name, ', ', first_name),
  TIMESTAMPDIFF(YEAR, birth, death)
FROM president
WHERE
  birth > '1900-1-1' AND DEATH IS NOT NULL;
```

Each selected value represents an expression, as does the content of the WHERE clause. Expressions also occur in the WHERE clause of DELETE and UPDATE statements, the VALUES() clause of INSERT statements, and so forth.

When MySQL encounters an expression, it evaluates the expression to produce a result. For example, (4*3) DIV (4-2) evaluates to the value 6. Expression evaluation may involve type conversion, such as when MySQL converts the number 960821 into a date '1996-08-21' if the number is used in a context requiring a DATE value.

This section discusses how you can write expressions in MySQL and the rules that govern the various kinds of type conversions that MySQL performs during the process of expression evaluation. Each of MySQL's operators is listed here, but MySQL has so many functions that only a few are touched on. For more information, see Appendix C.

3.5.1 Writing Expressions

An expression can be as simple as a single constant, such as the numeric value 0 or string value 'abc'.

Expressions can use function calls. Some functions take arguments (values inside the parentheses), and some do not. Multiple arguments should be separated by commas. When you invoke a built-in function, there can be spaces around arguments, but if there is a space between the function name and the opening parenthesis, the MySQL parser might misinterpret the function name. The usual result is a syntax error. You can tell MySQL to allow spaces after names of built-in functions by enabling the IGNORE_SPACE SQL mode. However, that also causes function names to be treated as reserved words.

Expressions can include references to table columns. In the simplest case, when the table to which a column belongs is clear from context, a column reference may be given simply as the column name. Only one table is named in each of the following SELECT statements, so the column references are unambiguous, even though the same column names are used in each statement:

```
SELECT last_name, first_name FROM president;
SELECT last_name, first_name FROM member;
```

If it's not clear which table should be used, a column name can be qualified by preceding it with the proper table name. If it's not even clear which database should be used, the table name can be preceded by the database name. You can also use these more-specific qualified forms in unambiguous contexts if you simply want to be more explicit:

```
SELECT
  president.last_name, president.first_name,
  member.last_name, member.first_name
FROM president INNER JOIN member
WHERE president.last_name = member.last_name;

SELECT sampdb.student.name FROM sampdb.student;
```

Scalar subqueries can be used to provide a single value in an expression. The subquery requires surrounding parentheses:

```
SELECT * FROM president WHERE birth = (SELECT MAX(birth) FROM president);
```

Finally, you can combine all these kinds of values (constants, function calls, column references, and subqueries) to form more complex expressions.

3.5.1.1 Operator Types

Terms of expressions can be combined using several kinds of operators. This section describes what they do, and Section 3.5.1.2, "Operator Precedence," discusses the order in which they are evaluated.

Arithmetic operators, listed in Table 3.18, include the usual addition, subtraction, multiplication, and division operators, as well as the modulo operator. Arithmetic is performed using BIGINT (64-bit) integer values for +, -, and * when both operands are integers. If both operands are integers, the result is unsigned if either operand is unsigned. For each operator other than DIV, if any operand is an approximate value, double-precision floating-point arithmetic is used. This is also true for strings converted to numbers, because strings are converted to double-precision numbers. Be aware that if an integer operation involves large values such that the result exceeds 64-bit range, you will get unpredictable results. (Actually, you should try to avoid exceeding 63-bit values; one bit is needed to represent the sign.)

Table 3.18 **Arithmetic Operators**

Operator	Syntax	Meaning
+	a + b	Addition; sum of operands
-	a - b	Subtraction; difference of operands
-	-a	Unary minus; negation of operand
*	a * b	Multiplication; product of operands
/	a / b	Division; quotient of operands
DIV	a DIV b	Division; integer quotient of operands
%	a % b	Modulo; remainder after division of operands

Logical operators, shown in Table 3.19, evaluate expressions to determine whether they are true (non-zero) or false (zero). It is also possible for a logical expression to evaluate to NULL if its value cannot be ascertained. For example, 1 AND NULL is of indeterminate value.

Table 3.19 **Logical Operators**

Operator	Syntax	Meaning
AND, &&	a AND b, a && b	Logical intersection; true if both operands are true
OR, ||	a OR b, a || b	Logical union; true if either operand is true
XOR	a XOR b	Logical exclusive-OR; true if exactly one operand is true
NOT, !	NOT a, !a	Logical negation; true if operand is false

As alternative forms of AND, OR, and NOT, MySQL supports the &&, ||, and ! operators, respectively, as used in the C programming language. Note in particular the || operator. Standard SQL specifies || as the string concatenation operator, but in MySQL it signifies a logical OR operation. If you use the following expression, expecting it to perform string concatenation, you may be surprised to discover that it returns the number 0:

```
'abc' || 'def'                              → 0
```

This happens because 'abc' and 'def' are converted to integers for the operation, and both turn into 0. In MySQL, you must use CONCAT('abc','def') or proximity to perform string concatenation:

```
CONCAT('abc','def')                         → 'abcdef'
'abc' 'def'                                 → 'abcdef'
```

If you want the standard SQL behavior for ||, enable the PIPES_AS_CONCAT SQL mode.

Bit operators, shown in Table 3.20, perform bitwise intersection, union, and exclusive-OR, where each bit of the result is evaluated as the logical AND, OR, or exclusive-OR of the corresponding bits of the operands. You can also perform bit shifts left or right. Bit operations are performed using BIGINT (64-bit) integer values.

Table 3.20   **Bit Operators**

Operator	Syntax	Meaning
&	a & b	Bitwise AND (intersection); each bit of result is set if corresponding bits of both operands are set
|	a | b	Bitwise OR (union); each bit of result is set if corresponding bit of either operand is set
^	a ^ b	Bitwise exclusive-OR; each bit of result is set only if exactly one corresponding bit of the operands is set
<<	a << b	Left shift of a by b bit positions
>>	a >> b	Right shift of a by b bit positions

Comparison operators, shown in Table 3.21, include operators for testing relative magnitude or lexical ordering of numbers and strings, as well as operators for performing pattern matching and for testing NULL values. The <=> operator is MySQL-specific.

For a discussion of the comparison properties of strings, see Section 3.1.2, "String Values."

Table 3.21 **Comparison Operators**

Operator	Syntax	Meaning
=	a = b	True if operands are equal
<=>	a <=> b	True if operands are equal (even if NULL)
<>, !=	a <> b, a != b	True if operands are not equal
<	a < b	True if a is less than b
<=	a <= b	True if a is less than or equal to b
>=	a >= b	True if a is greater than or equal to b
>	a > b	True if a is greater than b
IN	a IN (b1, b2, ...)	True if a is equal to any of b1, b2, ...
BETWEEN	a BETWEEN b AND c	True if a is between the values of b and c, inclusive
NOT BETWEEN	a NOT BETWEEN b AND c	True if a is not between the values of b and c, inclusive
LIKE	a LIKE b	SQL pattern match; true if a matches b
NOT LIKE	a NOT LIKE b	SQL pattern match; true if a does not match b
REGEXP	a REGEXP b	Regular expression match; true if a matches b
NOT REGEXP	a NOT REGEXP b	Regular expression match; true if a does not match b
IS NULL	a IS NULL	True if operand is NULL
IS NOT NULL	a IS NOT NULL	True if operand is not NULL

Pattern matching enables you to look for values without having to specify an exact literal value. MySQL provides SQL pattern matching using the LIKE operator and the wildcard characters '%' (match any sequence of characters) and '_' (match any single character). MySQL also provides pattern matching based on the REGEXP operator and regular expressions that are similar to those used in Unix programs such as grep, sed, and vi. You must use one of these pattern-matching operators to perform a pattern match; you cannot use the = operator. To reverse the sense of a pattern match, use NOT LIKE or NOT REGEXP.

The two types of pattern matching differ in important respects besides the use of different operators and pattern characters:

- LIKE is multi-byte safe. REGEXP works correctly only for single-byte character sets and does not take collation into account.
- LIKE SQL patterns match only if the entire string is matched. REGEXP regular expressions match if the pattern is found anywhere in the string.

Patterns used with the LIKE operator may include the '%' and '_' wildcard characters. For example, the pattern 'Frank%' matches any string that begins with 'Frank':

```
'Franklin' LIKE 'Frank%'                    → 1
'Frankfurter' LIKE 'Frank%'                 → 1
```

The wildcard character '%' matches any sequence of characters, including the empty sequence, so 'Frank%' matches 'Frank':

```
'Frank' LIKE 'Frank%'                       → 1
```

This also means the pattern '%' matches any string, including the empty string. However, '%' will not match NULL. In fact, any pattern match with a NULL operand fails:

```
'Frank' LIKE NULL                           → NULL
NULL LIKE '%'                               → NULL
```

MySQL's LIKE operator compares its operands as binary strings if either operand is a binary string. If the operands are non-binary strings, LIKE compares them according to their collation:

```
'Frankly' LIKE 'Frank%'                                    → 1
'frankly' LIKE 'Frank%'                                    → 1
BINARY 'Frankly' LIKE 'Frank%'                             → 1
BINARY 'frankly' LIKE 'Frank%'                             → 0
'Frankly' COLLATE latin1_general_cs LIKE 'Frank%'          → 1
'frankly' COLLATE latin1_general_cs LIKE 'Frank%'          → 0
'Frankly' COLLATE latin1_bin LIKE 'Frank%'                 → 1
'frankly' COLLATE latin1_bin LIKE 'Frank%'                 → 0
```

This behavior differs from that of the standard SQL LIKE operator, which is case sensitive.

The other wildcard character allowed with LIKE is '_', which matches any single character. The pattern '___' matches any string of exactly three characters. 'c_t' matches 'cat', 'cot', 'cut', and even 'c_t' (because '_' matches itself).

Wildcard characters may be specified anywhere in a pattern. '%bert' matches 'Englebert', 'Bert', and 'Albert'. '%bert%' matches all of those strings, and also strings like 'Berthold', 'Bertram', and 'Alberta'. 'b%t' matches 'Bert', 'bent', and 'burnt'.

To match literal instances of the '%' or '_' characters, turn off their special meaning by preceding them with a backslash ('\%' or '_'):

```
'abc' LIKE 'a%c'                            → 1
'abc' LIKE 'a\%c'                           → 0
'a%c' LIKE 'a\%c'                           → 1
'abc' LIKE 'a_c'                            → 1
'abc' LIKE 'a\_c'                           → 0
'a_c' LIKE 'a\_c'                           → 1
```

MySQL's other form of pattern matching uses regular expressions. The operator is REGEXP rather than LIKE. The following examples demonstrate several common regular expression pattern characters.

The '.' character is a wildcard that matches any single character:

```
'abc' REGEXP 'a.c'                              → 1
```

The [...] construction matches any character listed between the square brackets.

```
'e' REGEXP '[aeiou]'                            → 1
'f' REGEXP '[aeiou]'                            → 0
```

You can specify a range of characters by listing the endpoints of the range separated by a dash ('-'), or negate the sense of the class (to match any character not listed) by specifying '^' as the first character of the class:

```
'abc' REGEXP '[a-z]'                            → 1
'abc' REGEXP '[^a-z]'                           → 0
```

'*' means "match any number of the previous thing," so that, for example, the pattern 'x*' matches any number of 'x' characters:

```
'abcdef' REGEXP 'a.*f'                          → 1
'abc' REGEXP '[0-9]*abc'                        → 1
'abc' REGEXP '[0-9][0-9]*'                      → 0
```

"Any number" includes zero instances, which is why the second expression succeeds. To match one or more instances of the preceding thing rather than zero or more, use '+' instead of '*':

```
'abc' REGEXP 'cd*'                              → 1
'abc' REGEXP 'cd+'                              → 0
'abcd' REGEXP 'cd+'                             → 1
```

'^pattern' and 'pattern$' anchor a pattern match so that the pattern *pattern* matches only when it occurs at the beginning or end of a string, and '^pattern$' matches only if *pattern* matches the entire string:

```
'abc' REGEXP 'b'                                → 1
'abc' REGEXP '^b'                               → 0
'abc' REGEXP 'b$'                               → 0
'abc' REGEXP '^abc$'                            → 1
'abcd' REGEXP '^abc$'                           → 0
```

MySQL's regular expression matching has other special pattern elements as well. See Appendix C for more information.

A LIKE or REGEXP pattern can be taken from a table column, although this will be slower than a constant pattern if the column contains several different values. The pattern must be examined and converted to internal form each time the column value changes.

3.5.1.2 Operator Precedence

When MySQL evaluates an expression, it looks at the operators to determine the order in which it should group the terms of the expression. Some operators have higher precedence; that is, they are "stronger" than others in the sense that they are evaluated earlier than others. For example, multiplication and division have higher precedence than addition and subtraction. The following two expressions are equivalent because * and DIV are evaluated before + and -:

```
3 + 4 * 2 - 10 DIV 2                         → 6
3 + 8 - 5                                    → 6
```

Operator precedence is shown in the following list, from highest precedence to lowest. Operators listed on the same line have the same precedence. Operators at a higher precedence level are evaluated before operators at a lower precedence level. Operators at the same precedence level are evaluated left to right.

```
BINARY   COLLATE
!
- (unary minus)  ~ (unary bit negation)
^
*  /  DIV  %  MOD
+  -
<<  >>
&
|
<  <=  =  <=>  <>  !=  >=  >  IN  IS  LIKE  REGEXP  RLIKE
BETWEEN  CASE  WHEN  THEN  ELSE
NOT
AND  &&
XOR
OR  ||
:=
```

Some operators have a different precedence depending on the SQL mode or MySQL version. See Appendix C for details.

If you need to override the precedence of operators and change the order in which expression terms are evaluated, use parentheses to group terms:

```
1 + 2 * 3 - 4 / 5                            → 6.2000
(1 + 2) * (3 - 4) / 5                        → -0.6000
```

3.5.1.3 NULL Values in Expressions

Take care when using NULL values in expressions, because the result may not always be what you expect. The following guidelines will help you avoid surprises.

If you supply NULL as an operand to any arithmetic or bit operator, the result is NULL:

```
1 + NULL                                    → NULL
1 | NULL                                    → NULL
```

With logical operators, the result is NULL unless the result can be determined with certainty:

```
1 AND NULL                                  → NULL
1 OR NULL                                   → 1
0 AND NULL                                  → 0
0 OR NULL                                   → NULL
```

NULL as an operand to any comparison or pattern-matching operator produces a NULL result, except for the <=>, IS NULL, and IS NOT NULL operators, which are intended specifically for dealing with NULL values:

```
1 = NULL                                    → NULL
NULL = NULL                                 → NULL
1 <=> NULL                                  → 0
NULL LIKE '%'                               → NULL
NULL REGEXP '.*'                            → NULL
NULL <=> NULL                               → 1
1 IS NULL                                   → 0
NULL IS NULL                                → 1
```

Functions generally return NULL if given NULL arguments, except for those functions designed to deal with NULL arguments. For example, IFNULL() is able to handle NULL arguments and returns true or false appropriately. On the other hand, STRCMP() expects non-NULL arguments; if you pass it a NULL argument, it returns NULL rather than true or false.

In sorting operations, NULL values group together. They appear first in ascending sorts and last in descending sorts.

3.5.2 Type Conversion

Whenever a value of one type is used in a context that requires a value of another type, MySQL performs type conversion automatically according to the kind of operation you're performing. Conversion may occur for any of the following reasons:

- Conversion of operands to a type appropriate for evaluation of an operator
- Conversion of a function argument to a type expected by the function
- Conversion of a value for assignment into a table column that has a different type

You can also perform explicit type conversion using a cast operator or function.

The following expression involves implicit type conversion. It consists of the addition operator + and two operands, 1 and '2':

```
1 + '2'                                     → 3
```

The operands are of different types (number and string), so MySQL converts one of them to make them the same type. But which one should it change? In this case, + is a numeric operator, so MySQL wants the operands to be numbers thus and converts the string '2' to the number 2. Then it evaluates the expression to produce the result 3.

Here's another example. The CONCAT() function concatenates strings to produce a longer string as a result. To do this, it interprets its arguments as strings, no matter what type they are. If you pass it a bunch of numbers, CONCAT() converts them to strings, and then returns their concatenation:

```
CONCAT(1,23,456)                                    →  '123456'
```

If the call to CONCAT() is part of a larger expression, further type conversion may take place. Consider the following expression and its result:

```
REPEAT('X',CONCAT(1,2,3)/10)                        →  'XXXXXXXXXXXX'
```

CONCAT(1,2,3) produces the string '123'. The expression '123'/10 is converted to 123/10 because division is an arithmetic operator. The result of this expression is 12.3, but REPEAT() expects an integer repeat count, so the count is rounded to produce 12. Then REPEAT('X',12) produces a string result of 12 'x' characters.

If all arguments to CONCAT() are non-binary strings, the result is a non-binary string. If any argument is a binary string, the result is a binary string. The latter principle includes the case of numeric arguments, which are converted to binary strings. These examples both appear to produce the same result:

```
CONCAT('1','23')                                    →  '123'
CONCAT(1,'23')                                      →  '123'
```

But if you check the result with CHARSET(), you can see that the expressions return a non-binary and binary string, respectively:

```
CHARSET(CONCAT('1','23'))                           →  'latin1'
CHARSET(CONCAT(1,'23'))                             →  'binary'
```

A general principle to keep in mind is that, by default, MySQL attempts to convert values to the type required by an expression rather than generating an error. Depending on the context, it converts values of each of the three general categories (numbers, strings, or dates and times) to values in any of the other categories. However, values can't always be converted from one type to another. If a value to be converted to a given type doesn't look like a legal value for that type, the conversion fails. Conversion to numbers of things like 'abc' that don't look like numbers results in a value of 0. Conversion to date or time types of things that don't look like a date or time result in the "zero" value for the type. For example, converting the string 'abc' to a date results in the "zero" date '0000-00-00'. On the other hand, any value can be treated as a string, so generally it's not a problem to convert a value to a string.

If you want to prevent conversion of illegal values to the closest legal values during data input operations, you can enable strict mode to cause errors to occur instead. See Section 3.3, "How MySQL Handles Invalid Data Values."

MySQL also performs more minor type conversions. If you use a floating-point value in an integer context, the value is converted (with rounding). Conversion in the other direction works as well; an integer can be used without problem as a floating-point number.

Hexadecimal constants are treated as binary strings unless the context clearly indicates a number. In string contexts, each pair of hexadecimal digits is converted to a character and the result is used as a string. The following examples illustrate how this works:

```
0x61                                          → 'a'
0x61 + 0                                      → 97
X'61'                                         → 'a'
X'61' + 0                                     → 97
CONCAT(0x61)                                  → 'a'
CONCAT(0x61 + 0)                              → '97'
CONCAT(X'61')                                 → 'a'
CONCAT(X'61' + 0)                             → '97'
```

For comparisons, context determines whether to treat a hexadecimal constant as a binary string or a number:

- This expression treats the operands as binary strings and performs a byte-by-byte comparison.

  ```
  0x0d0a = '\r\n'                             → 1
  ```

- This expression compares a hexadecimal constant to a number, so it is converted to a number for the comparison.

  ```
  0x0a = 10                                   → 1
  ```

- This expression performs a binary string comparison. The first byte of the left operand has a lesser value than the first byte of the right operand, so the result is false.

  ```
  0xee00 > 0xff                               → 0
  ```

- In this expression, the right operand hex constant is converted to a number because of the arithmetic operator. Then for the comparison, the left operand is converted to a number. The result is false because 0xee00 (60928) is not numerically less than 0xff (255).

  ```
  0xee00 > 0xff+0                             → 1
  ```

It's possible to force a hexadecimal constant to be treated as a non-binary string by using a character set introducer or CONVERT():

```
0x61                                          → 'a'
0x61 = 'A'                                    → 0
```

```
_latin1 0x61 = 'A'                              → 1
CONVERT(0x61 USING latin1) = 'A'                → 1
```

Some operators force conversion of the operands to the type expected by the operator, no matter what the type of the operands is. Arithmetic operators are an example of this. They expect numbers, and the operands are converted accordingly:

```
3 + 4                                           → 7
'3' + 4                                         → 7
'3' + '4'                                       → 7
```

In a string-to-number conversion, it's not enough for a string simply to contain a number somewhere. MySQL doesn't look through the entire string hoping to find a number, it looks only at the beginning; if the string has no leading numeric part, the conversion result is 0.

```
'1973-2-4' + 0                                  → 1973
'12:14:01' + 0                                  → 12
'23-skidoo' + 0                                 → 23
'-23-skidoo' + 0                                → -23
'carbon-14' + 0                                 → 0
```

MySQL's string-to-number conversion rule converts numeric-looking strings to floating-point values:

```
'-428.9' + 0                                    → -428.9
'3E-4' + 0                                      → 0.0003
```

This conversion does not work for hexadecimal-looking constants, though. Only the leading zero is used:

```
'0xff' + 0                                      → 0
```

The bit operators are even stricter than the arithmetic operators. They want the operators to be not just numeric, but integers, and type conversion is performed accordingly. This means that a fractional number such as 0.3 is not considered true, even though it's non-zero; that's because when it's converted to an integer, the result is 0. In the following expressions, the operands are not considered true until they have a value of at least 1:

```
0.3 | .04                                       → 0
1.3 | .04                                       → 1
0.3 & .04                                       → 0
1.3 & .04                                       → 0
1.3 & 1.04                                      → 1
```

Pattern matching operators expect to operate on strings. This means you can use MySQL's pattern matching operators on numbers because it will convert them to strings in the attempt to find a match!

```
12345 LIKE '1%'                                 → 1
12345 REGEXP '1.*5'                             → 1
```

The magnitude comparison operators (<, <=, =, and so on) are context sensitive; that is, they are evaluated according to the types of their operands. The following expression compares the operands numerically because they both are numbers:

```
2 < 11                                        → 1
```

This expression involves string operands and thus results in a lexical comparison:

```
'2' < '11'                                    → 0
```

In the following comparisons, the types are mixed, so MySQL compares them as numbers. As a result, both expressions are true:

```
'2' < 11                                      → 1
2 < '11'                                      → 1
```

When evaluating comparisons, MySQL converts operands as necessary according to the following rules:

- Other than for the <=> operator, comparisons involving NULL values evaluate as NULL. (<=> is like =, except that NULL <=> NULL is true, whereas NULL = NULL is NULL.)
- If both operands are strings, they are compared lexically as strings. Binary strings are compared on a byte-by-byte basis using the numeric value of each byte. Comparisons for non-binary strings are performed character-by-character using the collating sequence of the character set in which the strings are expressed. If the strings have different character sets, the comparison may result in an error or fail to yield meaningful results. A comparison between a binary and a non-binary string is treated as a comparison of binary strings.
- If both operands are integers, they are compared numerically as integers.
- Hexadecimal constants that are not compared to a number are compared as binary strings.
- Other than for IN(), if either operand is a TIMESTAMP or DATETIME value and the other is a constant, the operands are compared as TIMESTAMP values. This is done to make comparisons work better for ODBC applications.
- Otherwise, the operands are compared numerically as double-precision floating-point values. Note that this includes the case of comparing a string and a number. The string is converted to a double-precision number, which results in a value of 0 if the string doesn't look like a number. For example, '14.3' converts to 14.3, but 'L4.3' converts to 0.

3.5.2.1 Date and Time Interpretation Rules

MySQL freely converts strings and numbers to date and time values as demanded by context in an expression, and vice versa. Date and time values are converted to numbers in numeric context; numbers are converted to dates or times in date or time contexts. This conversion to a date or time value happens when you assign a value to a date or time column or when a function requires a date or time value. In comparisons, the general rule is that date and time values are compared as strings.

If the table `mytbl` contains a DATE column `date_col`, the following statements are equivalent:

```
INSERT INTO mytbl SET date_col = '2025-04-13';
INSERT INTO mytbl SET date_col = '20250413';
INSERT INTO mytbl SET date_col = 20250413;
```

In the following examples, the argument to the TO_DAYS() function is interpreted as the same value for all three expressions:

```
TO_DAYS('2025-04-13')                        → 739719
TO_DAYS('20250413')                          → 739719
TO_DAYS(20250413)                            → 739719
```

3.5.2.2 Testing and Forcing Type Conversion

To see how type conversion will be handled in an expression, issue a SELECT query that evaluates the expression so that you can examine the result:

```
mysql> SELECT X'41', X'41' + 0;
+-------+-----------+
| X'41' | X'41' + 0 |
+-------+-----------+
| A     |        65 |
+-------+-----------+
```

If you cannot tell from inspection the type of an expression, select it into a new table and check the table definition:

```
mysql> CREATE TABLE t SELECT X'41' AS col1, X'41' + 0 AS col2;
mysql> DESCRIBE t;
+-------+--------------+------+-----+---------+-------+
| Field | Type         | Null | Key | Default | Extra |
+-------+--------------+------+-----+---------+-------+
| col1  | varbinary(1) | NO   |     |         |       |
| col2  | double(17,0) | NO   |     | 0       |       |
+-------+--------------+------+-----+---------+-------+
```

Testing expression evaluation is especially useful for statements such as DELETE or UPDATE that modify rows, because you want to be sure you're affecting only the intended rows. One way to check an expression is to run a preliminary SELECT statement with the same WHERE clause that you're going to use with the DELETE or UPDATE statement to verify that the clause selects the proper rows. Suppose that the table `mytbl` has a CHAR column `char_col` containing these values:

```
'abc'
'00'
'def'
```

```
'00'
'ghi'
```

Given these values, what is the effect of the following statement?

```
DELETE FROM mytbl WHERE char_col = 00;
```

The intended effect is probably to delete the two rows containing the value `'00'`. The actual effect would be to delete all the rows—an unpleasant surprise. This happens as a consequence of MySQL's comparison rules. `char_col` is a string column, but `00` in the statement is not quoted, so it is treated as a number. By MySQL's comparison rules, a comparison involving a string and a number evaluates as a comparison of two numbers. As MySQL executes the `DELETE` statement, it converts each value of `char_col` to a number and compares it to `0`. Unfortunately, although `'00'` converts to `0`, so do all the strings that don't look like numbers. As a result, the `WHERE` clause is true for every row, and the `DELETE` statement empties the table. This is a case where it would have been prudent to test the `WHERE` clause with a `SELECT` statement prior to executing the `DELETE`, because that would have shown you that too many rows are selected by the expression:

```
mysql> SELECT char_col FROM mytbl WHERE char_col = 00;
+----------+
| char_col |
+----------+
| abc      |
| 00       |
| def      |
| 00       |
| ghi      |
+----------+
```

When you're uncertain about the way a value will be used, you may want to exploit MySQL's type conversion to force an expression to a value of a particular type, or to call a function that performs the desired conversion. The following list demonstrates several useful conversion techniques.

Add `+0` or `+0.0` to a term to force conversion to a numeric value:

```
0x65                                        → 'e'
0x65 + 0                                    → 101
0x65 + 0.0                                  → 101.0
```

To chop off the fractional part of a number, use `FLOOR()` or `CAST()`. To add a fractional part to an integer, add an exact-value zero with the required number of decimal digits:

```
FLOOR(13.3)                                 → 13
CAST(13.3 AS SIGNED)                        → 13
13 + 0.0                                    → 13.0
13 + 0.0000                                 → 13.0000
```

If you want rounding instead, use `ROUND()` rather than `CAST()`.

Use CAST() or CONCAT() to turn a value into a string:

```
14                              → 14
CAST(14 AS CHAR)                → '14'
CONCAT(14)                      → '14'
```

CONCAT() returns a binary string if it must convert a numeric argument to string form, so the final two examples actually differ in their result. The CAST() expression returns a non-binary string, whereas the CONCAT() expression returns a binary string.

Use HEX() to convert a number to a hexadecimal string:

```
HEX(255)                        → 'FF'
HEX(65535)                      → 'FFFF'
```

You can also use HEX() with a string value to convert it to a string of hex digit pairs representing successive bytes in the string:

```
HEX('abcd');                    → '61626364'
```

Use ASCII() to convert a single-byte character to its ASCII value:

```
'A'                             → 'A'
ASCII('A')                      → 65
```

To go in the other direction from ASCII code to character, use CHAR():

```
CHAR(65)                        → 'A'
```

Use DATE_ADD() or INTERVAL arithmetic to force a string or number to be treated as a date:

```
DATE_ADD(20080101, INTERVAL 0 DAY)      → '2008-01-01'
20080101 + INTERVAL 0 DAY               → '2008-01-01'
DATE_ADD('20080101', INTERVAL 0 DAY)    → '2008-01-01'
'20080101' + INTERVAL 0 DAY             → '2008-01-01'
```

Generally, you can convert a date value to numeric form by adding zero:

```
CURDATE()                       → '2007-09-07'
CURDATE()+0                     → 20070907
```

Temporal values with a time part convert to a value with a microseconds part:

```
NOW()                           → '2007-09-07 16:15:29'
NOW()+0                         → 20070907161529.000000
CURTIME()                       → '16:15:29'
CURTIME()+0                     → 161529.000000
```

To chop off the fractional part, cast the value to an integer:

```
CAST(NOW() AS UNSIGNED)         → 20070907161529
CAST(CURTIME() AS UNSIGNED)     → 161529
```

To convert a string from one character set to another, use CONVERT(). To check whether the result has the desired character set, use the CHARSET() function:

```
'abcd'                                        →  'abcd'
CONVERT('abcd' USING ucs2)                    →  'abcd'
CHARSET('abcd')                               →  'latin1'
CHARSET(CONVERT('abcd' USING ucs2))           →  'ucs2'
```

Preceding a string with a character set introducer does not cause conversion of the string, but MySQL interprets it as though it has the character set indicated by the introducer:

```
CHARSET(_ucs2 'abcd')                         →  'ucs2'
```

To determine the hexadecimal value of the UTF-8 character that corresponds to a given hexadecimal UCS-2 character, combine CONVERT() with HEX(). The following expression determines the UTF-8 value of the trademark symbol:

```
HEX(CONVERT(_ucs2 0x2122 USING utf8))         →  'E284A2'
```

To change the collation of a string, use the COLLATE operator. To check whether the result has the desired collation, use the COLLATION() function:

```
COLLATION('abcd')                             →  'latin1_swedish_ci'
COLLATION('abcd' COLLATE latin1_bin)          →  'latin1_bin'
```

The character set and collation must be compatible. If they are not, use a combination of CONVERT() to convert the character set first and COLLATE to change the collation:

```
CONVERT('abcd' USING latin2) COLLATE latin2_bin
```

To convert a binary string to a non-binary string that has a given character set, use CONVERT():

```
0x61626364                                    →  'abcd'
0x61626364 = 'ABCD'                           →  0
CONVERT(0x61626364 USING latin1) = 'ABCD'     →  1
```

Alternatively, for binary quoted strings or hexadecimal values, use an introducer to change the interpretation of the binary string:

```
_latin1 0x61626364 = 'ABCD'                   →  1
```

To cast a non-binary string to a binary string, use the BINARY keyword:

```
'abcd' = 'ABCD'                               →  1
BINARY 'abcd' = 'ABCD'                         →  0
'abcd' = BINARY 'ABCD'                         →  0
```

3.6 Choosing Data Types

Section 3.2, "MySQL Data Types," described the various data types from which you can choose and the general properties of those types, such as the kind of values they may contain, how much storage space they take, and so on. But how do you actually decide which types to use when you create a table? This section discusses issues to consider that will help you choose.

The most "generic" data types are the string types. You can store anything in them because numbers and dates can be represented in string form. So should you just define all your columns as strings and be done with it? No. Let's consider a simple example. Suppose that you have values that look like numbers. You could represent these as strings, but should you? What happens if you do?

For one thing, you'll probably use more space, because numbers can be stored more efficiently using numeric columns than string columns. You'll also notice some differences in query results due to the different ways that numbers and strings are handled. For example, the sort order for numbers is not the same as for strings. The number 2 is less than the number 11, but the string '2' is lexically greater than the string '11'. You can work around this by using the column in a numeric context like this:

```
SELECT col_name + 0 as num ... ORDER BY num;
```

Adding zero to the column forces a numeric sort, but is that a reasonable thing to do? It's a useful technique sometimes, but you don't want to have to use it every time you want a numeric sort. Causing MySQL to treat a string column as a number has a couple of significant implications. It forces a string-to-number conversion for each column value, which is inefficient. Also, using the column in a calculation prevents MySQL from using any index on the column, which slows down the query further. Neither of these performance degradations occur if you store the values as numbers in the first place.

The preceding example illustrates that several issues come into play when you choose data types. The simple choice of using one representation rather than another has implications for storage requirements, query handling, and processing performance. The following list gives a quick rundown of factors to think about when picking a type for a column.

What kind of values will the column hold? Numbers? Strings? Dates? Spatial values? This is an obvious question, but you must ask it. You can represent any type of value as a string, but as we've just seen, it's likely that you'll get better performance if you use other more appropriate types for numeric values. (This is also true for temporal and spatial values.) However, assessing the kind of values you're working with isn't necessarily trivial, particularly for other people's data. It's especially important to ask what kind of values the column will hold if you're setting up a table for someone else, and you must be sure to ask enough questions to get sufficient information for making a good decision.

Do your values lie within some particular range? If they are integers, will they always be non-negative? If so, you can use UNSIGNED. If they are strings, will they always be chosen from among a fixed, limited set of values? If so, you may find ENUM or SET a useful type.

There is a tradeoff between the range of a type and the amount of storage it uses. How "big" a type do you need? For numbers, you can choose small types with a limited range of values, or large types with a much larger range. For strings, you can make them short or long, so you wouldn't choose CHAR(255) if all the values you want to store contain fewer than 10 characters.

What are the performance and efficiency issues? Some types can be processed more efficiently than others. Numeric operations generally can be performed more quickly than string operations. Short strings can be compared more quickly than long strings, and also involve less disk overhead. For MyISAM tables, performance is better for fixed-length rows than for variable-length rows.

The following sections consider these issues in more detail, except for the performance issues, which are covered in Section 5.3, "Choosing Data Types for Efficient Queries."

Before we proceed, I should point out that, although you want to make the best data type choices you can when you create a table, it's not the end of the world if you make a choice that turns out to be nonoptimal. You can use ALTER TABLE to change the type to a better one. This might be as simple as changing a SMALLINT to MEDIUMINT after finding out your data set contains values larger than you originally thought. Or it can be more complex, such as changing a CHAR to an ENUM with a specific set of allowed values. You can use PROCEDURE ANALYSE() to obtain information about your table's columns, such as the minimum and maximum values as well as a suggested optimal type to cover the range of values in a column:

```
SELECT * FROM tbl_name PROCEDURE ANALYSE();
```

The output from this query may help you determine that a smaller type can be used, which can improve the performance of queries that involve the table and reduce the amount of space required for table storage. For more information about PROCEDURE ANALYSE(), see Section 5.3, "Choosing Data Types for Efficient Queries."

3.6.1 What Kind of Values Will the Column Hold?

The first thing you think of when you're trying to decide on a data type is the kind of values the column will be used for because this has the most evident implications for the type you choose. In general, you do the obvious thing: You store numbers in numeric columns, strings in string columns, and dates and times in temporal columns. If your numbers have a fractional part, you use a DECIMAL or floating-point type rather than an integer type. But sometimes there are exceptions. The principle here is that you need to understand the nature of your data to be able to choose the type in an informed manner. If you're going to store your own data, you probably have a good idea of how to characterize it. On the other hand, if others ask you to set up a table for them, it's sometimes a different story. It may not be so easy to know just what you're working with. Be sure to ask enough questions to find out what kind of values the table really should contain.

Suppose that you're told that a table needs a column to record "amount of precipitation." Is that a number? Or is it "mostly" numeric—that is, typically but not always coded as a number? For example, when you watch the news on television, the weather report generally includes a measure of precipitation. Sometimes this is a number (as in "0.25 inches of rain"), but sometimes it's a "trace" of precipitation, meaning "not much at all." That's fine for the weather report, but what does it mean for storage in a database? You either need to quantify "trace" as a number so that you can use a numeric data type to record precipitation amounts, or you need to use a string so that you can record the word "trace." Or you could come up with some more complicated arrangement, using a number column and a string column where you fill in one column and leave the other one NULL. It should be obvious that you want to avoid that option, if possible; it makes the table harder to understand and it makes query-writing much more difficult.

I would probably try to store all rows in numeric form, and then convert them as necessary for display purposes. For example, if any non-zero amount of precipitation less than .01 inches is considered a trace amount, you could display values from the column like this:

```
SELECT IF(precip>0 AND precip<.01,'trace',precip) FROM ... ;
```

Some values are obviously numeric but you must determine whether to use an integer or non-integer type. You should ask what your units are and what accuracy you require. Is whole-unit accuracy sufficient or do you need to represent fractional units? This may help you distinguish between integer and fixed-point or floating-point data types. For example, if you're recording weights to the nearest pound, you can use an integer column. If you want to record fractional units, you'd use a fixed-point or floating-point column. In some cases, you might even use multiple columns—for example, to record weight in terms of pounds and ounces.

Height is a numeric type of information for which there are several representational possibilities:

- Use a string such as `'6-2'` for a value like "6 feet, 2 inches." This has the advantage of having a form that's easy to look at and understand (certainly more so than "74 inches"), but it's difficult to use this kind of value for mathematical operations such as summation or averaging.

- Use one numeric column for feet and another for inches. This would be a little easier to work with for numerical operations, but two columns are more difficult to use than one.

- Use one numeric column representing inches. This is easiest for a database to work with, and least meaningful for humans. But remember that you don't have to present values in the same format that you use to work with them. You can reformat values for meaningful display using MySQL's many functions. That means this might be the best way to represent height.

Another type of numeric information is currency, such as U.S. dollars. For monetary calculations, you're working with values that have dollars and cents parts. These look like floating-point values, but FLOAT and DOUBLE are subject to rounding error and may not be suitable except for rows in which you need only approximate accuracy. Because people tend to be touchy about their money, it's more likely you need a type that affords perfect accuracy. You have a couple of choices:

- You can represent money as a DECIMAL(M,2) type, choosing M as the maximum width appropriate for the range of values you need. This gives you values with two decimal places of accuracy. The advantage of DECIMAL is that values are not subject to roundoff error and calculations are exact.

- You can represent all monetary values internally as cents using an integer type. The advantage is that calculations are done internally using integers, which is very fast. The disadvantage is that you will need to convert values on input or output by multiplying or dividing by 100.

Some kinds of "numbers" aren't. Telephone numbers, credit card numbers, and Social Security numbers all can be written using non-digit characters such as spaces or dashes and cannot be stored directly in a numeric column unless you strip the non-digits. But even with non-digits stripped, you may want to store values as strings rather than as numbers to avoid loss of leading zeros.

If you need to store date information, do the values include a time? That is, will they *ever* need to include a time? MySQL doesn't provide a date type that has an optional time part: DATE never has a time, and DATETIME must have a time. If the time really is optional, use a DATE column to record the date, and a separate TIME column to record the time. Then allow the TIME column to be NULL and interpret that as "no time":

```
CREATE TABLE mytbl
(
   date DATE NOT NULL,    # date is required
   time TIME NULL         # time is optional (may be NULL)
);
```

One type of situation in which it's especially important to determine whether you need a time value occurs when you're joining two tables with a master-detail relationship that are "linked" based on date information. Suppose that you're conducting research involving test subjects. Following a standard initial battery of tests, you might run several additional tests, with the choice of tests varying according to the results of the initial tests. You can represent this information using a master-detail relationship, in which the subject identification information and the standard initial tests are stored in a master row and any additional tests are stored as rows in a secondary detail table. Then you link together the two tables based on subject ID and the date on which the tests are given.

The question you must answer in this situation is whether you can use just the date or whether you need both date and time. This depends on whether a subject might go through the testing procedure more than once during the same day. If so, record the time (for example, the time that the procedure begins), using either a DATETIME column or separate DATE and TIME columns that both must be filled in. Without the time value, you will not be able to associate a subject's detail rows with the proper master rows if the subject is tested twice in a day.

I've heard people claim "I don't need a time; I will never test a subject twice on the same day." Sometimes they're correct, but I have also seen some of these same people turn up later wondering how to prevent detail rows from being mixed up with the wrong master row after entering data for subjects who were tested multiple times in a day. Sorry, by then it's too late!

Sometimes you can deal with this problem by retrofitting a TIME column into the tables. Unfortunately, it's difficult to fix existing rows unless you have some independent data source, such as the original paper rows. Otherwise, you have no way to disambiguate detail rows to associate them with the proper master row. Even if you have an independent source of information, this is very messy and likely to cause problems for applications that you've already written to use the tables. It's best to explain the issues to the table owners and make sure that you've gotten a good characterization of the data values before creating their tables.

Sometimes you have incomplete data, and this will influence your choice of data types. You may be collecting birth and death dates for genealogical research, and sometimes all you can find out is the year or year and month someone was born or died, but not the exact date. If you use a DATE column, you can't enter a date unless you have the full date. If you want to be able to record whatever information you have, even if it's incomplete, you may have to keep separate year, month, and day columns. Then you can enter such parts of the date as you have and leave the rest NULL. Another possibility is to use DATE values in which the day or month and day parts are set to 0. Such "fuzzy" dates can be used to represent incomplete date values.

3.6.2 Do Your Values Lie Within Some Particular Range?

If you've decided on the general category from which to pick a data type for a column, thinking about the range of values you want to represent will help you narrow down your choices to a particular type within that category. Suppose that you want to store integer values. The range of your values determines the types you can use. If you need values in the range from 0 to 1000, you can use anything from a SMALLINT up to a BIGINT. If your values range up to 2 million, you can't use SMALLINT, so your choices range from MEDIUMINT to BIGINT.

You could, of course, simply use the largest type for the kind of value you want to store (BIGINT for the examples in the previous paragraph). Generally, however, you should use the smallest type that is large enough for your purposes. By doing so, you'll minimize the amount of storage used by your tables, and they will give you better performance because smaller columns usually can be processed more quickly than larger ones. (Reading smaller values requires less disk activity, and more key values fit into the key cache, allowing indexed searches to be performed faster.)

If you don't know the range of values you'll need to be able to represent, you either must guess or use BIGINT to accommodate the worst possible case. If you guess and the type you choose turns out later to be too small, all is not lost. Use ALTER TABLE later to make the column bigger.

Sometimes you even find out that you can make a column smaller. In Chapter 1, we created a score table for the grade-keeping project that had a score column for recording quiz and test scores. The column was created using INT in order to keep the discussion simpler, but you can see now that if scores are in the range from 0 to 100, a better choice would be TINYINT UNSIGNED, because that would use less storage.

The range of values in your data also affects the attributes you can use with your data type. If values never are negative, you can use UNSIGNED; otherwise, you can't.

String types don't have a "range" in the same way numeric columns do, but they have a length, and the maximum length you need affects the column types you can use. If you're storing character strings that are shorter than 256 characters, you can use CHAR, VARCHAR, or TINYTEXT. If you want longer strings, you can use VARCHAR or a longer TEXT type.

For a string column used to represent a fixed set of values, you might consider using an ENUM or SET data type. These can be good choices because they are represented internally as numbers. Operations on them are performed numerically, which makes them more efficient than other string types. They also can be more compact than other string types, which saves space. In addition, you can prevent entry of values not present in the list of legal values by enabling strict SQL mode. See Section 3.3, "How MySQL Handles Invalid Data Values."

When characterizing the range of values you have to deal with, the best terms are "always" and "never" (as in "always less than 1000" or "never negative"), because they enable you to constrain your data type choices more tightly. But be wary of using these terms when they're not really justified. Be especially wary if you're consulting with other people about their data and they start throwing around those two terms. When people say "always" or "never," be sure they really mean it. Sometimes people say their data always have a particular characteristic when they really mean "almost always."

Suppose that you're designing a table for a group of investigators who tell you, "Our test scores are always 0 to 100." Based on that statement, you choose TINYINT and you make it UNSIGNED because the values are always non-negative. Then you find out that the people who code the data for entry into the database sometimes use -1 to mean "student was absent due to illness." Oops. They didn't tell you that. It might be acceptable to use NULL to represent such values, but if not, you'll have to record a -1, and then you can't use an UNSIGNED column. (This is an instance where ALTER TABLE comes to your rescue.)

Sometimes decisions about these cases can be made more easily by asking a simple question: Are there ever exceptions? If an exceptional case ever occurs, even just once, you must allow for it. You will find that people who talk to you about designing a database invariably think that if exceptions don't occur very often, they don't matter. When you're creating a table, you can't think that way. The question you need to ask isn't "how often do exceptions occur?" It's "do exceptions *ever* occur?" If they do, you must take them into account.

3.6.3 Inter-Relatedness of Data Type Choice Issues

You can't always consider the issues involved in choosing data types as though they are independent of one another. For example, range is related to storage size for numeric types: As you increase the range, you require more storage, which affects performance. Or consider the implications of using AUTO_INCREMENT to create a column for holding unique sequence numbers. That single choice has several consequences involving the data type, indexing, and the use of NULL:

- AUTO_INCREMENT is a column attribute that is best used with integer types. That immediately limits your choices to TINYINT through BIGINT.

- An AUTO_INCREMENT column is intended only for generating sequences of positive values, so you should define it as UNSIGNED.

- AUTO_INCREMENT columns must be indexed. Furthermore, to prevent duplicates in the column, the index should be unique, so you should define the column as a PRIMARY KEY or as a UNIQUE index.

- AUTO_INCREMENT columns must be NOT NULL. (If you omit NOT NULL, MySQL adds it automatically.)

All of this means you do not just define an AUTO_INCREMENT column like this:

```
mycol arbitrary_type AUTO_INCREMENT
```

You define it like this:

```
mycol integer_type UNSIGNED NOT NULL AUTO_INCREMENT,
PRIMARY KEY (mycol)
```

Or like this:

```
mycol integer_type UNSIGNED NOT NULL AUTO_INCREMENT,
UNIQUE (mycol)
```

4

Stored Programs

MySQL supports several types of objects that are stored on the server side for later use. Some are invoked on demand; others execute automatically when table modifications occur or when a scheduled time is reached:

- Stored functions return a result from a calculation and can be used in expressions.
- Stored procedures do not return a result directly but can be used to perform general computations or produce result sets that are passed back to the client.
- Triggers are associated with a table and are defined to execute when the table is modified via INSERT, DELETE, or UPDATE statements.
- Events execute on a time-activated basis according to a schedule.

MySQL added support for stored functions and procedures in version 5.0.0, triggers in 5.0.2, and events in 5.1.6. Whether you use the MySQL 5.0 or 5.1 series, it is best to use recent versions to avoid problems in the early implementations of these object types.

Stored programs provide several benefits and capabilities:

- The executable part of the object can be written using compound statements that extend SQL syntax to include blocks, loops, and conditional statements. (Section E.1, "SQL Statement Syntax," shows the syntax for all such statements.)
- Stored programs are stored on the server side, so all the code needed to define them is sent over the network only once at program-creation time, not each time you want to execute them. This reduces overhead.
- They enable encapsulation of complex calculations into program units that can be easily invoked by name.
- They provide a means to standardize computational operations. If you provide a set of stored programs as a "library" that many applications can use, those applications all perform the operations in the same way.
- They provide a mechanism for handling errors.
- They improve database security because you can enable controlled access to sensitive data by appropriate selection of the privileges a program has when it executes.

This chapter uses the following terminology:

- "Stored programs" refers collectively to stored objects of all types (functions, procedures, triggers, and events).

- "Stored routines" is a more limited term that refers only to stored functions and procedures. Both types of objects are defined using very similar syntax, so it is often natural to discuss them together. In fact, the term "stored procedures" is frequently used to refer both to procedures and functions. However, I find this unhelpfully ambiguous and will not use the term that way.

Later sections in this chapter discuss how to write and use each type of stored program. However, before getting into the details of any particular type of stored program, we'll begin with a discussion of an issue common to all of them: how to write compound statements.

4.1 Compound Statements and Statement Delimiters

A simple stored program that has a body consisting of a single SQL statement can be written without any special treatment. The following procedure uses a SELECT statement that displays the names of the tables in the sampdb database:

```
CREATE PROCEDURE sampdb_tables ()
  SELECT TABLE_NAME FROM INFORMATION_SCHEMA.TABLES
  WHERE TABLE_SCHEMA = 'sampdb' ORDER BY TABLE_NAME;
```

However, a stored program need not be limited to a single simple statement. The code can contain multiple SQL statements, and it can use constructs such as local variables, conditional statements, loops, and nested blocks. To write a stored program that uses these features, use a compound statement, which consists of BEGIN and END to form a block within which an arbitrary number of statements can be written. The following procedure displays a greeting with your username, or "earthling" if you are an anonymous user:

```
CREATE PROCEDURE greetings ()
BEGIN
  # 77 = 16 for username + 60 for hostname + 1 for '@'
  DECLARE user CHAR(77) CHARACTER SET utf8;
  SET user = (SELECT CURRENT_USER());
  IF INSTR(user,'@') > 0 THEN
    SET user = SUBSTRING_INDEX(user,'@',1);
  END IF;
  IF user = '' THEN          # anonymous user
    SET user = 'earthling';
  END IF;
  SELECT CONCAT('Greetings, ',user, '!') AS greeting;
END;
```

An issue that arises in the use of compound statements is that the statements within a block must be separated semicolon ('; ') characters as delimiters. That also is the default statement delimiter for the mysql program, so there is a conflict if you try to define stored programs using mysql. To deal with this, use the delimiter command to redefine mysql's statement delimiter to a character or string that does not appear in the routine definition. That causes mysql not to interpret semicolons as terminators and to pass the entire object definition to the server as a single statement. You can redefine the terminator to semi-colon again after defining the stored program. The following example temporarily changes the mysql delimiter to $ while a stored procedure is being defined, and then executes the procedure after restoring the default delimiter:

```
mysql> delimiter $
mysql> CREATE PROCEDURE show_times()
    -> BEGIN
    ->   SELECT 'Local time is:', CURRENT_TIMESTAMP;
    ->   SELECT 'UTC time is:', UTC_TIMESTAMP;
    -> END$
mysql> delimiter ;
mysql> CALL show_times();
+----------------+---------------------+
| Local time is: | CURRENT_TIMESTAMP   |
+----------------+---------------------+
| Local time is: | 2008-05-15 18:20:13 |
+----------------+---------------------+
+--------------+---------------------+
| UTC time is: | UTC_TIMESTAMP       |
+--------------+---------------------+
| UTC time is: | 2008-05-15 23:20:13 |
+--------------+---------------------+
```

The delimiter need not be $, and it need not be a single character:

```
mysql> delimiter EOF
mysql> CREATE PROCEDURE show_times()
    -> BEGIN
    ->   SELECT 'Local time is:', CURRENT_TIMESTAMP;
    ->   SELECT 'UTC time is:', UTC_TIMESTAMP;
    -> END EOF
mysql> delimiter ;
```

The principle to keep in mind is this: If a stored program's body contains any internal semicolons, you should redefine the delimiter while defining the program.

A compound statement need not be used only for complex stored programs. You can use one even if a program body consists of a single statement, or even no statements:

```
CREATE PROCEDURE do_little ()
BEGIN
  DO SLEEP(1);
```

```
END;

CREATE PROCEDURE do_nothing ()
BEGIN
END;
```

For stylistic consistency, you might prefer to use BEGIN and END for all stored program definitions.

4.2 Stored Functions and Procedures

Stored functions calculate a value to be returned to the caller for use in expressions, just like built-in functions such as COS() or HEX(). Stored procedures are executed as stand-alone operations using the CALL statement rather than in expressions. Use a procedure if you need only to perform a computation to produce an effect or action without returning a value, or if the computation produces result sets (which a function is not allowed to do). These are guidelines, not hard and fast rules. For example, if you need to return more than one value, you cannot use a function. But you may be able to use a procedure, because procedures support parameter types that can have their values set when the procedure executes, such that those values can be accessed by the caller after the procedure finishes.

To create a stored function or procedure, use a CREATE FUNCTION or CREATE PROCEDURE statement. The following example creates a function that takes an integer-valued parameter representing a year. (I use p_ as a prefix to distinguish parameter names from other names such as those of tables or columns.) The function uses a subquery to determine how many presidents were born in that year and returns the count:

```
mysql> delimiter $
mysql> CREATE FUNCTION count_born_in_year(p_year INT)
    -> RETURNS INT
    -> READS SQL DATA
    -> BEGIN
    ->   RETURN (SELECT COUNT(*) FROM president WHERE YEAR(birth) = p_year);
    -> END$
mysql> delimiter ;
```

The function has a RETURNS clause to indicate the data type of its return value and a body that computes that value. The function body must include at least one RETURN statement to return a value to the caller. By defining a calculation as a function, you have a simple way to execute it without specifying all the logic each time, and it can be invoked just like a built-in function:

```
mysql> SELECT count_born_in_year(1908);
+--------------------------+
| count_born_in_year(1908) |
+--------------------------+
|                        1 |
+--------------------------+
```

```
mysql> SELECT count_born_in_year(1913);
+--------------------------+
| count_born_in_year(1913) |
+--------------------------+
|                        2 |
+--------------------------+
```

Here, the function is invoked by itself, but stored functions can be used within arbitrarily complex expressions.

You cannot return multiple values from a given function. You could write multiple functions and invoke them all from within a single statement, but another approach is to use a stored procedure that "returns" values via OUT parameters. The procedure should compute the desired values and assign them to the parameters, which then can be accessed by the caller after the procedure returns. For details, see Section 4.2.2, "Stored Procedure Parameter Types."

If you define a stored function with the same name as a built-in function, you should qualify the function name with the database name when you invoke it. For example, if you define a stored function named PI() in the sampdb database, invoke it as sampdb.PI() to make clear that you do not mean the built-in function. (To avoid this ambiguity, it's best not to use names of built-in functions.)

A stored procedure is similar to a stored function, but it doesn't return a value. Therefore, it does not have a RETURNS clause or any RETURN statements. The following simple stored procedure is similar to the count_born_in_year() function, but instead of calculating a count as a return value, it displays a result set containing a row of information for each president born in the given year.

```
mysql> delimiter $
mysql> CREATE PROCEDURE show_born_in_year(p_year INT)
    -> BEGIN
    ->     SELECT first_name, last_name, birth, death
    ->     FROM president
    ->     WHERE YEAR(birth) = p_year;
    -> END$
mysql> delimiter ;
```

Unlike stored functions, stored procedures are not used in expressions. They are invoked using the CALL statement:

```
mysql> CALL show_born_in_year(1908);
+------------+-----------+------------+------------+
| first_name | last_name | birth      | death      |
+------------+-----------+------------+------------+
| Lyndon B.  | Johnson   | 1908-08-27 | 1973-01-22 |
+------------+-----------+------------+------------+
mysql> CALL show_born_in_year(1913);
+------------+-----------+------------+------------+
| first_name | last_name | birth      | death      |
```

```
+------------+----------+------------+------------+
| Richard M. | Nixon    | 1913-01-09 | 1994-04-22 |
| Gerald R.  | Ford     | 1913-07-14 | 2006-12-26 |
+------------+----------+------------+------------+
```

The procedure body in this case executes a SELECT statement. As the example illustrates, the result set from this statement is not returned as the procedure value, but instead is sent to the client. A procedure can generate multiple result sets, each of which is sent in turn to the client.

The examples thus far have only selected information, but stored routines also can modify tables, as shown by the next example. update_expiration() is a stored routine that updates data. It takes the ID of a Historical League member and updates the appropriate membership row with the given expiration date:

```
CREATE PROCEDURE update_expiration (p_id INT UNSIGNED, p_date DATE)
BEGIN
  UPDATE member SET expiration = p_date WHERE member_id = p_id;
END;
```

The following calls of update_expiration() set member expirations to one year from the current date and to "lifetime membership" (NULL means "no expiration"):

```
mysql> CALL update_expiration(61, CURDATE() + INTERVAL 1 YEAR);
mysql> CALL update_expiration(87, NULL);
```

Stored functions are subject to the restriction that they cannot modify a table that is being read or written by the statement that invoked the function. Stored procedures normally do not have this restriction, but do become subject to it if they are invoked from within a stored function. For example, you cannot call update_expiration() from within a stored function that is used in a statement that selects from the member table.

4.2.1 Privileges for Stored Functions and Procedures

Stored functions and procedures belong to a database. To create a stored function or procedure, you must have the CREATE ROUTINE privilege for that database. By default, when you create a stored routine, the server automatically grants you the EXECUTE and ALTER ROUTINE privileges if you do not already have them, so that you can execute the routine or drop it. If you do drop the routine, the server also automatically revokes those privileges. You can set the automatic_sp_privileges system variable to 0 if you don't want automatic privilege granting and revocation to occur.

If the server has binary logging enabled, stored functions are subject to additional conditions that are intended to make the binary log safe for backups and replication by restricting creation of functions that are non–deterministic or modify data. (If a function produces different results for given input values, restoring data by re-executing the binary log can fail to restore the original data, and the function can replicate differently on master and slave servers.) These conditions are:

- If the `log_bin_trust_function_creators` system variable is not enabled, you must have the SUPER privilege to be able to create stored functions. Also, each function that you create should be deterministic and should not modify data. To signal this, declare it with one of the DETERMINISTIC, NO SQL, or READS SQL DATA characteristics. For example:

```
CREATE FUNCTION half (p_value DOUBLE)
RETURNS DOUBLE
DETERMINISTIC
BEGIN
  RETURN p_value / 2;
END;
```

- If the `log_bin_trust_function_creators` system variable is enabled, no restrictions are enforced. This is most appropriate in situations where you can trust all users of the MySQL server not to define unsafe stored functions.

The conditions relating to `log_bin_trust_function_creators` also apply to trigger creation. Before MySQL 5.1.6, you are not likely to notice this because you must have the SUPER privilege to create triggers, and SUPER overrides the `log_bin_trust_function_creators` restrictions.

4.2.2 Stored Procedure Parameter Types

Stored procedure parameters can have one of three types. For an IN parameter, the caller passes a value into the procedure. The value can be modified within the procedure, but any changes are not visible to the caller after the procedure returns. An OUT parameter is the opposite. The procedure assigns a value to the parameter, which can be accessed by the caller after the procedure returns. An INOUT parameter enables the caller to pass in a value, and to get back a value.

To specify a parameter type explicitly, use IN, OUT, or INOUT immediately preceding the parameter name in the parameter list. Parameters are IN by default if no type is given.

To use an OUT or INOUT parameter, specify a variable name when you call the procedure. The procedure can set the parameter value, and the corresponding variable will have that value when the procedure returns. The OUT and INOUT parameter types can be especially useful when you require a computation that produces multiple result values. (A stored function returns only a single value, so it is inapplicable to such situations.)

The following procedure demonstrates use of OUT parameters. It counts the number of male and female students in the student table and returns the counts via its parameters so that the caller can access them:

```
CREATE PROCEDURE count_students_by_sex (OUT p_male INT, OUT p_female INT)
BEGIN
```

```
    SELECT COUNT(*) FROM student WHERE sex = 'M' INTO p_male;
    SELECT COUNT(*) FROM student WHERE sex = 'F' INTO p_female;
END;
```

To invoke the procedure, supply user-defined variables for the parameters. The procedure puts the counts into these parameters, and after it returns, the variables contain the counts:

mysql> **CALL count_students_by_sex(@mcount, @fcount);**
mysql> **SELECT 'Number of male students: ', @mcount;**

```
+----------------------------+---------+
| Number of male students:   | @mcount |
+----------------------------+---------+
| Number of male students:   |      16 |
+----------------------------+---------+
```

mysql> **SELECT 'Number of female students:', @fcount;**

```
+----------------------------+---------+
| Number of female students: | @fcount |
+----------------------------+---------+
| Number of female students: |      15 |
+----------------------------+---------+
```

More involved examples might require additional parameters. For example, you might write a procedure that has an IN parameter that indicates the ID for a test or quiz in the score table. The procedure could compute descriptive statistics from the relevant scores (mean, standard deviation, range, and so forth), and then pass back all those values to the caller by means of OUT parameters.

The IN, OUT, and INOUT keywords do not apply to stored functions, triggers, or events. For stored functions, all parameters are like IN parameters. Triggers and events do not have parameters at all.

4.3 Triggers

A trigger is a stored program that is associated with a particular table and is defined to activate for INSERT, DELETE, or UPDATE statements for that table. A trigger can be set to activate either before or after each row processed by the statement. The trigger definition includes a statement that executes when the trigger activates.

The following list describes some of the benefits that triggers provide:

- A trigger can examine or change new data values to be inserted or used to update a row. This enables you to enforce data integrity constraints, such as verifying that a percentage is a value from 0 to 100. It also makes it possible to perform input data filtering.

- A trigger can supply default values for a column based on an expression. This enables you to work around the restriction that default values in column definitions must be constants.

- A trigger can examine the current contents of a row before it is deleted or updated. This capability can be exploited to perform logging of changes to existing rows, for example.

To create a trigger, use the CREATE TRIGGER statement. The definition indicates the particular type of statement for which the trigger activates (INSERT, UPDATE, or DELETE), and whether it activates before or after rows are modified. The basic syntax for trigger creation looks like this:

```
CREATE TRIGGER trigger_name      # the trigger name
  {BEFORE | AFTER}               # when the trigger activates
  {INSERT | UPDATE | DELETE}     # what statement activates it
  ON tbl_name                    # the associated table
  FOR EACH ROW trigger_stmt;     # what the trigger does
```

tbl_name is the table with which the trigger is associated; trigger_name is the name of the trigger itself. For trigger naming, I like to adopt a convention that helps make the trigger purpose and table association clear, such as bi_tbl_name or ai_tbl_name for a BEFORE INSERT or AFTER INSERT trigger on tbl_name.

trigger_stmt is the trigger body; that is, the statement that executes when the trigger activates. In a trigger body, the syntax NEW.col_name can be used to refer to columns in the new row to be inserted or updated in an INSERT or UPDATE trigger. Similarly, OLD.col_name can be used to refer to columns in the old row to be deleted or updated in a DELETE or UPDATE trigger. To change a column value within a BEFORE trigger before the value is stored in the table, use SET NEW.col_name = value.

The following example shows a trigger bi_t for INSERT statements for a table t that has an integer percent column for storing percentage values (0 to 100) and a DATETIME column. The trigger uses BEFORE so that it can examine data values before they are inserted into the table.

```
mysql> CREATE TABLE t (percent INT, dt DATETIME);
mysql> delimiter $
mysql> CREATE TRIGGER bi_t BEFORE INSERT ON t
    ->     FOR EACH ROW BEGIN
    ->         SET NEW.dt = CURRENT_TIMESTAMP;
    ->         IF NEW.percent < 0 THEN
    ->             SET NEW.percent = 0;
    ->         ELSEIF NEW.percent > 100 THEN
    ->             SET NEW.percent = 100;
    ->         END IF;
    ->     END$
mysql> delimiter ;
```

The trigger performs two actions:

- For attempts to insert a percentage value that lies outside the range from 0 to 100, the trigger converts the value to the nearest endpoint.

- The trigger automatically provides a value of CURRENT_TIMESTAMP for the DATETIME column. In effect, this works around the limitation that a column's default value must be a constant, and implements TIMESTAMP-like automatic initialization for a DATETIME column.

To see how the trigger works, insert some rows into the table, and then retrieve its contents:

```
mysql> INSERT INTO t (percent) VALUES(-2); DO SLEEP(2);
mysql> INSERT INTO t (percent) VALUES(30); DO SLEEP(2);
mysql> INSERT INTO t (percent) VALUES(120);
mysql> SELECT * FROM t;
+---------+---------------------+
| percent | dt                  |
+---------+---------------------+
|       0 | 2008-05-15 18:38:22 |
|      30 | 2008-05-15 18:38:24 |
|     100 | 2008-05-15 18:38:26 |
+---------+---------------------+
```

The privilege required to create and drop triggers is version-specific. Before MySQL 5.1.6, you must have the SUPER privilege. As of MySQL 5.1.6, access control is more correctly handled: Because a trigger is associated with a table, you must have the TRIGGER privilege for that table to be able to create and drop triggers for it.

4.4 Events

MySQL 5.1.6 and up has an event scheduler that enables you to perform time-activated database operations. An event is a stored program that is associated with a schedule. The schedule defines the time or times at which the event executes, and optionally when the event ceases to exist. Events are especially useful for performing unattended administrative operations such as periodic updates to summary reports, expiration of old data, or log table rotation. This section demonstrates row expiration. For an example that shows how to perform event-based log table rotation, see Section 12.5.7.4, "Expiring or Rotating Log Tables."

The event scheduler does not run by default, so you must turn it on if you want to use events. Put the following lines in an option file that the server reads at startup:

```
[mysqld]
event_scheduler=ON
```

To check the status of the event scheduler at runtime, use this statement:

```
SHOW VARIABLES LIKE 'event_scheduler';
```

To stop or start the scheduler at runtime, change the value of the event_scheduler system variable (it is a GLOBAL variable, so you must have the SUPER privilege):

```
SET GLOBAL event_scheduler = OFF;    # or 0
SET GLOBAL event_scheduler = ON;     # or 1
```

If you stop the scheduler, no events run. It is also possible to leave the scheduler running but disable individual events, as discussed later.

> **Note**
>
> If you set `event_scheduler` to `DISABLED` at startup, you can check but not change its status at runtime. Also, you can create events, but they will not execute.

The event scheduler writes to the server's error log, which you can check for information about what the scheduler is doing. It logs events as it runs them, as well as errors that occur during event execution. If the event scheduler is not running when you expect it to be, check the error log for a message that indicates the reason why.

The following example shows how to create a simple event that deletes old rows from a table. Suppose that you have a table named `web_session` that holds state information for sessions associated with users who visit your Web site, and that this table has a `DATETIME` column named `last_visit` that indicates the time of each user's most recent visit. To keep this table from accumulating stale rows, you can set up an event that periodically purges them. To execute the event every six hours and have it expire rows more than a day old, write the event definition like this:

```
CREATE EVENT expire_web_session
  ON SCHEDULE EVERY 4 HOUR
  DO
    DELETE FROM web_session
    WHERE last_visit < CURRENT_TIMESTAMP - INTERVAL 1 DAY;
```

The `EVERY n interval` clauses specifies periodic execution at fixed intervals. The `interval` values are like those used for the `DATE_ADD()` function, such as `HOUR`, `DAY`, or `MONTH`. Following `EVERY`, you can also include `STARTS datetime` and `ENDS datetime` options that specify the initial and final execution time. By default, an `EVERY` event runs for the first time immediately after it is created and has no final time.

The `DO` clause defines the event body, which is an SQL statement that executes when the event runs. As for other stored program types, this can be a simple statement or a compound statement written using `BEGIN` and `END`.

To create an event that runs only one time, use the `AT` scheduling type rather than `EVERY`. A definition such as the following creates an event that executes once, an hour in the future:

```
CREATE EVENT one_shot
  ON SCHEDULE AT CURRENT_TIMESTAMP + INTERVAL 1 HOUR
  DO ... ;
```

To disable an event to stop it from executing, or to re-enable a disabled event, use `ALTER EVENT`:

```
ALTER EVENT event_name DISABLE;
ALTER EVENT event_name ENABLE;
```

An event belongs to a database, so you must have the EVENT privilege for that database to create or drop events for it.

4.5 Security for Stored Programs and Views

When you create a stored program, you create an object that is to be executed later. The same is true when you define a view: It sets up a SELECT statement intended for later invocation. This "execute later" aspect of such objects means that the user who causes object execution might not be the user who originally created it, which raises an important question: What security context should the server use for checking access privileges at execution time? That is, which account's privileges should apply?

By default, the server uses the account of the user who defined the object. Suppose that I define a stored procedure p() that accesses tables belonging to me. If I give you the EXECUTE privilege for p(), you can say CALL p() to invoke the procedure and it will access my tables on your behalf because it runs with my privileges. This type of security context can be good or bad:

- It's good in the sense that it enables carefully written stored programs to be set up that provide controlled access to tables for users who are not able to access them directly.

- It's bad if a user creates a stored program that accesses sensitive data but forgets that other people who can invoke the object have the same access to that data as its definer.

The definer for a stored program or view can be specified explicitly by including a DEFINER = account clause in the CREATE statement for the object. This causes the named account to be treated as the definer for purposes of access checking at execution time. For example:

```
CREATE DEFINER = 'sampadm'@'localhost' PROCEDURE count_students()
  SELECT COUNT(*) FROM student;
```

In a DEFINER clause, the definer value can be an account name in 'user_name'@'host_name' format as used in account-management statements such as CREATE USER. (See Section 12.4.1.1, "Specifying Account Names.") For this format, user_name and host_name must both be given. Alternatively, the value can be CURRENT_USER or CURRENT_USER() to indicate the account of the user who executes the statement (the same account that is used by default if no DEFINER clause is present).

If you have the SUPER privilege, you can give any syntactically legal account name as the DEFINER value; a warning occurs if the account does not exist at the time. If you do not have the SUPER privilege, you can set the definer only to your own account, using either the literal account name or CURRENT_USER.

For views and stored functions and procedures, you can specify the SQL SECURITY characteristic, which gives you an additional means of control over execution time access-checking. SQL SECURITY takes a value of DEFINER (execute with the definer's privileges) or INVOKER (execute with the privileges of the user who invoked the object).

SQL SECURITY INVOKER is preferable for situations when you don't want a stored program or view to execute with any more privileges than a user already has. The following view accesses a table in the mysql database, but runs with invoker privileges. That way, if the invoker has no access to mysql.user, the view won't subvert that restriction.

```
CREATE SQL SECURITY INVOKER VIEW v
  AS SELECT CONCAT(User,'@',Host) AS Account, Password FROM mysql.user;
```

Triggers and events are invoked automatically by the server, so the concept of "invoking user" does not apply. Thus, they have no SQL SECURITY characteristic and always execute with definer privileges.

If a stored program or view runs with definer privileges at execution time and the definer account does not exist, an error occurs.

5

Query Optimization

The world of relational database theory is a world dominated by tables and sets, and operations on tables and sets. A database is a set of tables, and a table is a set of rows and columns. When you issue a SELECT statement to retrieve rows from a table, you get back another set of rows and columns—that is, another table. These are abstract notions that make no reference to the underlying representation a database system uses to operate on the data in your tables. Another abstraction in set theory is that operations on tables happen all at once; queries are conceptualized as set operations for which there is no concept of time.

The real world, of course, is quite different. Database management systems implement abstract concepts but do so on real hardware bound by real physical constraints. As a result, queries take time—sometimes an annoyingly long time. And we, being impatient creatures, don't like to wait, so we leave the abstract world of instantaneous mathematical operations on sets and look for ways to speed up our queries. Fortunately, there are several techniques for doing so:

- Create indexes on tables to enable the database server to look up rows more quickly.

- Consider how to write queries to take advantage of those indexes to the fullest extent, and use the EXPLAIN statement to check whether the MySQL server really is doing so.

- Write queries to affect the server's scheduling mechanism so that queries arriving from multiple clients cooperate better.

- Tune the server's configurable operating parameters to get it to perform more efficiently.

- Analyze what's going on with the underlying hardware and how to work around its physical constraints to improve performance.

This chapter focuses on those kinds of issues, with the goal of assisting you in optimizing the performance of your database system so that it processes your queries as quickly as possible. MySQL is already quite fast, but even the fastest database can run queries more quickly if you help it do so.

5.1 Using Indexing

Many techniques are available to you for speeding up queries, but indexing is the most important one. That is, in general, the one thing that makes the most difference is the proper use of indexes. It's often true that when a query runs slowly, adding indexes solves the problem immediately. But it doesn't always work like that, because optimization isn't always simple. Nevertheless, if you don't use indexes, in many cases you're just wasting your time trying to improve performance by other means. Use indexing first to get the biggest performance boost and then see what other techniques might be helpful.

This section describes what an index is and how indexing improves query performance. It also discusses the circumstances under which indexes might degrade performance and provides guidelines for choosing indexes for your table wisely. In the next section, we'll discuss MySQL's query optimizer that attempts to find the most efficient way to execute queries. It's good to have some understanding of the optimizer in addition to knowing how to create indexes because then you'll be better able to take advantage of the indexes you create. Certain ways of writing queries actually prevent your indexes from being useful, and you'll want to avoid having that happen.

5.1.1 Benefits of Indexing

Let's consider how an index works, beginning with a table that has no indexes. An unindexed table is simply an unordered collection of rows. Figure 5.1 shows the ad table that was discussed in Chapter 1, "Getting Started with MySQL." Because there are no indexes on this table, finding the rows for a particular company requires examination of each row in the table to see whether it matches the desired value. This involves a full table scan, which is slow, as well as tremendously inefficient if the table is large but contains only a few rows that match the search criteria.

ad table

company_num	ad_num	hit_fee
14	48	0.01
23	49	0.02
17	52	0.01
13	55	0.03
23	62	0.02
23	63	0.01
23	64	0.02
13	77	0.03
23	99	0.03
14	101	0.01
13	102	0.01
17	119	0.02

Figure 5.1   Unindexed ad table.

Figure 5.2 shows the same table, but with the addition of an index on the company_num column in the ad table. The index contains an entry for each row in the ad table, but the index entries are sorted by company_num value. Now, instead of searching through the table row by row looking for items that match, we can use the index. Suppose that we're looking for all rows for company 13. We begin scanning the index and find three values for that company. Then we reach the index value for company 14, which is higher than the one we're looking for. Index values are sorted, so when we read the index row containing 14, we know we won't find any more matches and can quit looking. Thus, one efficiency gained by using the index is that we can tell where the matching rows end and can skip the rest. Another efficiency comes about through the use of positioning algorithms for finding the first matching entry without doing a linear scan from the start of the index (for example, a binary search is much quicker than a scan). That way, we can quickly position to the first matching value and save a lot of time in the search. Databases use various techniques for positioning to index values quickly, but it's not so important here what those techniques are. What's important is that they work and that indexing is a good thing because it enables their use.

ad table

index		company_num	ad_num	hit_fee
13		14	48	0.01
13		23	49	0.02
13		17	52	0.01
14		13	55	0.03
14		23	62	0.02
17		23	63	0.01
17		23	64	0.02
23		13	77	0.03
23		23	99	0.03
23		14	101	0.01
23		13	102	0.01
23		17	119	0.02

Figure 5.2   Indexed ad table.

You might be asking why we don't just sort the data rows and dispense with the index. Wouldn't that produce the same type of improvement in search speed? Yes, it would—if the table had a single index. But you might want to add a second index, and you can't sort the data rows two different ways at once. For example, you might want one index on customer names and another on customer ID numbers or phone numbers. Using indexes as entities separate from the data rows solves the problem and enables multiple indexes to be created. In addition, rows in the index are generally shorter than data rows. When you insert or delete new values, it's easier to move around shorter index values to maintain the sort order than to move around the longer data rows.

The particular details of index implementations vary for different MySQL storage engines. For example, for a MyISAM table, the table's data rows are kept in a data file, and index values are kept in an index file. You can have more than one index on a table, but they're all stored in the same index file. Each index in the index file consists of a sorted array of key rows that are used for fast access into the data file.

By contrast, the InnoDB storage engine does not separate data rows and index values in the same way, although it does maintain indexes as sets of sorted values. By default, the InnoDB engine uses a single tablespace within which it manages data and index storage for all InnoDB tables. InnoDB can be configured to create each table with its own table-space, but even so, a given table's data and indexes are stored in the same tablespace file.

The preceding discussion describes the benefit of an index in the context of single-table queries, where the use of an index speeds searches significantly by eliminating the need for full table scans. Indexes are even more valuable when you're running queries involving joins on multiple tables. In a single-table query, the number of values you need to examine per column is the number of rows in the table. In a multiple-table query, the number of possible combinations skyrockets because it's the product of the number of rows in the tables.

Suppose that you have three unindexed tables, t1, t2, and t3, each containing a column i1, i2, and i3, respectively, and each consisting of 1,000 rows that contain the numbers 1 through 1000. A query to find all combinations of table rows in which the values are equal looks like this:

```
SELECT t1.i1, t2.i2, t3.i3
FROM t1 INNER JOIN t2 INNER JOIN t3
WHERE t1.i1 = t2.i2 AND t2.i2 = t3.i3;
```

The result of this query should be 1,000 rows, each containing three equal values. If we process the query in the absence of indexes, we have no idea which rows contain which values without scanning them all. Consequently, we must try all combinations to find the ones that match the WHERE clause. The number of possible combinations is 1,000 × 1,000 × 1,000 (one billion!), which is a million times more than the number of matches. That's a lot of wasted effort. To make things worse, as the tables grow, the time to process joins on those tables grows even more if no indexes are used, leading to very poor performance. We can speed things up considerably by indexing the tables, because the indexes enable the query to be processed like this:

1. Select the first row from table t1 and see what value the row contains.
2. Using the index on table t2, go directly to the row that matches the value from t1. Similarly, using the index on table t3, go directly to the row that matches the value from t2.
3. Proceed to the next row of table t1 and repeat the preceding procedure. Do this until all rows in t1 have been examined.

In this case, we still perform a full scan of table t1, but we can do indexed lookups on t2 and t3 to pull out rows from those tables directly. The query runs about a million times faster this way—literally. This example is contrived for the purpose of making a point, but the problems it illustrates are real, and adding indexes to tables that have none often results in dramatic performance gains.

MySQL uses indexes in several ways:

- As just described, indexes are used to speed up searches for rows matching terms of a WHERE clause or rows that match rows in other tables when performing joins.

- For queries that use the MIN() or MAX() functions, the smallest or largest value in an indexed column can be found quickly without examining every row.

- MySQL can often use indexes to perform sorting and grouping operations quickly for ORDER BY and GROUP BY clauses.

- Sometimes MySQL can use an index to read all the information required for a query. Suppose that you're selecting values from an indexed numeric column in a MyISAM table, and you're selecting no other columns from the table. In this case, when MySQL reads an index value from the index file, it obtains the same value that it would get by reading the data file. There's no reason to read values twice, so the data file need not even be consulted.

5.1.2 Costs of Indexing

In general, if MySQL can figure out how to use an index to process a query more quickly, it will. This means that, for the most part, if you don't index your tables, you're hurting yourself. You can see that I'm painting a rosy picture of the benefits of indexing. Are there disadvantages? Yes, there are. There are costs both in time and in space. In practice, these drawbacks tend to be outweighed by the advantages, but you should know what they are.

First, indexes speed up retrievals but slow down inserts and deletes, as well as updates of values in indexed columns. That is, indexes slow down most operations that involve writing. This occurs because writing a row requires writing not only the data row, it requires changes to any indexes as well. The more indexes a table has, the more changes need to be made, and the greater the average performance degradation. Most tables receive many reads and few writes, but for a table with a high percentage of writes, the cost of index updating might be significant. Section 5.4, "Loading Data Efficiently," discusses what you can do to reduce this cost.

Second, an index takes up disk space, and multiple indexes take up correspondingly more space. This might cause you to reach a table size limit more quickly than if there are no indexes:

- For a MyISAM table, indexing it heavily may cause the index file to reach its maximum size more quickly than the data file.

- All InnoDB tables that are located within the InnoDB shared tablespace compete for the same common pool of space, and adding indexes depletes storage within this tablespace more quickly. However, unlike the files used for MyISAM tables, the InnoDB shared tablespace is not bound by your operating system's file-size limit, because it can be configured to use multiple files. As long as you have additional disk space, you can expand the tablespace by adding new components to it.

InnoDB tables that use individual tablespaces store data and index values together in the same file, so adding indexes causes the table to reach the maximum file size more quickly.

The practical implication of both these factors is that if you don't need a particular index to help queries perform better, don't create it.

5.1.3 Choosing Indexes

The syntax for creating indexes is covered in Section 2.6.4.2, "Creating Indexes." I assume here that you've read that section. But knowing syntax doesn't in itself help you determine *how* your tables should be indexed. That requires some thought about the way you use your tables. This section gives some guidelines on how to identify candidate columns for indexing and how best to set up indexes.

Index columns that you use for searching, sorting, or grouping, not columns you select for output. In other words, the best candidate columns for indexing are the columns that appear in your WHERE clause, columns named in join clauses, or columns that appear in ORDER BY or GROUP BY clauses. Columns that appear only in the output column list following the SELECT keyword are not good candidates:

```
SELECT
    col_a                        ← not a candidate
FROM
    tbl1 LEFT JOIN tbl2
    ON tbl1.col_b = tbl2.col_c  ← candidates
WHERE
    col_d = expr;                ← a candidate
```

The columns that you display and the columns you use in the WHERE clause might be the same, of course. The point is that appearance of a column in the output column list is not in itself a good indicator that it should be indexed.

Columns that appear in join clauses or in expressions of the form `col1 = col2` in WHERE clauses are especially good candidates for indexing. `col_b` and `col_c` in the query just shown are examples of this. If MySQL can optimize a query using joined columns, it cuts down the potential table-row combinations quite a bit by eliminating full table scans.

Consider column cardinality. The cardinality of a column is the number of distinct values that it contains. For example, a column that contains the values 1, 3, 7, 4, 7, and 3 has a cardinality of four. Indexes work best for columns that have a high cardinality relative to the number of rows in the table (that is, columns that have many unique values and few duplicates). For a column that contains many different age values, an index readily differentiates rows. For a column that is used to record sex and contains only the two values 'M' and 'F', an index will not help. If the values occur about equally, you'll get about half of the rows whichever value you search for. Under these circumstances, the index might never be used at all, because the query optimizer generally skips an index in favor of a full table scan if it determines that a value occurs in a large percentage of a table's rows. The conventional wisdom for this percentage used to be 30%. Nowadays the optimizer is more complex and takes other factors into account, so the percentage is not the sole determinant of when MySQL prefers a scan over using an index.

Index short values. Use smaller data types when possible. For example, don't use a BIGINT column if a MEDIUMINT is large enough to hold the values you need to store, and don't use CHAR(100) if none of your values are longer than 25 characters. Smaller values improve index processing in several ways:

- Shorter values can be compared more quickly, so index lookups are faster.
- Smaller values result in smaller indexes that require less disk I/O.
- With shorter key values, index blocks in the key cache hold more key values. MySQL can hold more keys in memory at once, which improves the likelihood of locating key values without reading additional index blocks from disk.

For the InnoDB storage engine, which uses clustered indexes, it's especially beneficial to keep the primary key short. A clustered index is one where the data rows are stored together with (that is, clustered with) the primary key values. Other indexes are secondary indexes; these store the primary key value with the secondary index values. A lookup in a secondary index yields a primary key value, which then is used to locate the data row. The implication is that primary key values are duplicated into each secondary index, so if primary key values are longer, the extra storage is required for each secondary index as well.

Index prefixes of string values. If you're indexing a string column, specify a prefix length whenever it's reasonable to do so. For example, if you have a CHAR(200) column, don't index the entire column if most values are unique within the first 10 or 20 characters. Indexing the first 10 or 20 characters will save a lot of space in the index, and probably will make your queries faster as well. By indexing shorter values, you gain the advantages described in the previous item relating to comparison speed and disk I/O reduction. You want to use some common sense, of course. Indexing just the first character from a column isn't likely to be that helpful because the resulting index won't have very many distinct values.

You can index prefixes of CHAR, VARCHAR, BINARY, VARBINARY, TEXT, and BLOB columns, using the syntax described in Section 2.6.4.2, "Creating Indexes."

Take advantage of leftmost prefixes. When you create an *n*-column composite index, you actually create *n* indexes that MySQL can use. A composite index serves as several indexes because any leftmost set of columns in the index can be used to match rows. Such a set is called a "leftmost prefix." (This is different from indexing a prefix of a column, which creates an index using the first *n* characters or bytes of column values.)

Suppose that you have a table with a composite index on columns named state, city, and zip. Rows in the index are sorted in state/city/zip order, so they're automatically sorted in state/city order and in state order as well. This means that MySQL can take advantage of the index even if you specify only state values in a query, or only `state` and `city` values. Thus, the index can be used to search the following combinations of columns:

```
state, city, zip
state, city
state
```

MySQL cannot use the index for searches that don't involve a leftmost prefix. For example, if you search by `city` or by `zip`, the index isn't used. If you're searching for a given state and a particular ZIP code (columns 1 and 3 of the index), the index can't be used for the combination of values, although MySQL can narrow the search using the index to find rows that match the state.

Don't over-index. Don't index everything in sight based on the assumption "the more, the better." Every additional index takes extra disk space and hurts performance of write operations, as has already been mentioned. Indexes must be updated and possibly reorganized when you modify the contents of your tables, and the more indexes you have, the longer this takes. If you have an index that is rarely or never used, you'll slow down table modifications unnecessarily. In addition, MySQL considers indexes when generating an execution plan for retrievals. Creating extra indexes creates more work for the query optimizer. It's also possible (if unlikely) that MySQL will fail to choose the best index to use when you have too many indexes. Maintaining only the indexes you need helps the query optimizer avoid making such mistakes.

If you're thinking about adding an index to a table that is already indexed, consider whether the index you're considering adding is a leftmost prefix of an existing multiple-column index. If so, don't bother adding the index because, in effect, you already have it. For example, if you already have an index on `state`, `city`, and `zip`, there is no point in adding an index on `state`. The exception to this is that for FULLTEXT indexes, you must have a separate index for each distinct set of columns that you want to search.

Match index types to the type of comparisons you perform. When you create an index, most storage engines choose the index implementation they will use. For example, InnoDB always uses B-tree indexes. MyISAM also uses B-tree indexes, except that it uses R-tree indexes for spatial data types. The MEMORY storage engine uses hash indexes by default, but also supports B-tree indexes and enables you to select which one you want. To choose an index type, consider what kind of comparison operations you plan to perform on the indexed column:

- For a hash index, a hash function is applied to each column value. The resulting hash values are stored in the index and used to perform lookups. (A hash function implements an algorithm that is likely to produce distinct hash values for distinct input values. The advantage of using hash values is that they can be compared more efficiently than the original values.) Hash indexes are very fast for exact-match comparisons performed with the = or <=> operators. But they are poor for comparisons that look for a range of values, as in these expressions:

```
id < 30
weight BETWEEN 100 AND 150
```

- B-tree indexes can be used effectively for comparisons involving exact or range-based comparisons that use the `<`, `<=`, `=`, `>=`, `>`, `<>`, `!=`, and `BETWEEN` operators. B-tree indexes can also be used for `LIKE` pattern matches if the pattern begins with a literal string rather than a wildcard character.

If you use a MEMORY table only for exact-value lookups, a hash index is a good choice. This is the default index type for MEMORY tables, so you need do nothing special. If you need to perform range-based comparisons with a MEMORY table, you should use a B-tree index instead. To specify this type of index, add `USING BTREE` to your index definition. For example:

```
CREATE TABLE lookup
(
    id      INT NOT NULL,
    name    CHAR(20),
    PRIMARY KEY USING BTREE (id)
) ENGINE = MEMORY;
```

If the types of searches that you expect to use warrant it, a single MEMORY table can have both hash indexes and B-tree indexes, even on the same column.

Some types of comparisons cannot use indexes. If you perform comparisons only by passing column values to a function such as `STRCMP()`, there is no value in indexing the column. The server must evaluate the function value for each row, which precludes use of an index on the column.

Use the slow-query log to identify queries that may be performing badly. This log can help you find queries that might benefit from indexing. (See Section 12.5, "Maintaining Logs," for general discussion of MySQL's logs.) The slow-query log is written as text, so it is viewable with any file-display program, or you can use the `mysqldumpslow` utility to summarize its contents. If a given query shows up over and over in this log, that's a clue you've found a query that might not be written optimally. You may be able to rewrite it to make it run more quickly. Keep in mind when assessing your slow-query log that "slow" is measured in real time, so more queries will show up in the slow-query log on a heavily loaded server than on a lightly loaded one.

5.2 The MySQL Query Optimizer

When you issue a statement that selects rows, MySQL analyzes it to see whether any optimizations can be used to process the statement more quickly. In this section, we'll look at how the query optimizer works. For additional information about optimization measures that MySQL takes, consult the optimization chapter in the MySQL Reference Manual.

The MySQL query optimizer takes advantage of indexes, of course, but it also uses other information. For example, if you issue the following query, MySQL will execute it very quickly, no matter how large the table is:

```
SELECT * FROM tbl_name WHERE FALSE;
```

In this case, MySQL looks at the WHERE clause, realizes that no rows can possibly satisfy the query, and doesn't even bother to search the table. You can see this by issuing an EXPLAIN statement, which tells MySQL to display some information about how it would execute a SELECT query without actually executing it. To use EXPLAIN, just put the word EXPLAIN in front of the SELECT statement:

```
mysql> EXPLAIN SELECT * FROM tbl_name WHERE FALSE\G
*************************** 1. row ***************************
           id: 1
  select_type: SIMPLE
        table: NULL
         type: NULL
possible_keys: NULL
          key: NULL
      key_len: NULL
          ref: NULL
         rows: NULL
        Extra: Impossible WHERE
```

Normally, EXPLAIN returns more information than that, including values more informative than NULL about the indexes that will be used to scan tables, the types of joins that will be used, and estimates of the number of rows that will need to be examined from each table.

In some cases, EXPLAIN actually does execute part of a query, if it contains subqueries in the FROM clause: EXPLAIN must execute the subqueries to find out what they return before analyzing the main SELECT statement.

5.2.1 How the Optimizer Works

The MySQL query optimizer has several goals, but its primary aims are to use indexes whenever possible and to use the most restrictive index in order to eliminate from consideration as many rows as possible as soon as possible. That last part might sound backward and unintuitive. After all, your goal in issuing a SELECT statement is to find rows, not to reject them. The reason the optimizer tries to reject rows is that the faster it can eliminate rows, the more quickly the rows that do match your criteria can be found. Queries can be processed more quickly if the most restrictive tests can be done first. Suppose that you have a query that tests two columns, each of which has an index on it:

```
SELECT col3 FROM mytable
WHERE col1 = 'some value' AND col2 = 'some other value';
```

Suppose also that the test on `col1` matches 900 rows, the test on `col2` matches 300 rows, and that both tests together succeed on 30 rows. Testing `col1` first results in 900 rows that must be examined to find the 30 that also match the `col2` value. That's 870 failed tests. Testing `col2` first results in 300 rows that must be examined to find the 30 that also match the `col1` value. That's only 270 failed tests, so less computation and disk I/O is required. As a result, the optimizer will test `col2` first because doing so results in less work overall.

To help the optimizer take advantage of indexes, use the guidelines described here.

Analyze your tables. This generates index value distribution statistics that help the optimizer make better estimates about index effectiveness. By default, when you compare values in indexed columns to a constant, the optimizer assumes that key values are distributed evenly within the index. The optimizer will also do a quick check of the index to estimate how many entries will be used when determining whether the index should be used for constant comparisons. For MyISAM and InnoDB tables, you can tell the server to perform an analysis of key values by using `ANALYZE TABLE`.

A table that is populated only once and then remains static need be analyzed only once after being loaded. A table that undergoes updates should be reanalyzed occasionally (at a frequency corresponding to how often updates occur).

Use `EXPLAIN` to verify optimizer operation. The `EXPLAIN` statement can tell you whether indexes are being used. This information is helpful when you're trying different ways of writing a statement or checking whether adding indexes actually will make a difference in query execution efficiency. For examples, see Section 5.2.2, "Using `EXPLAIN` to Check Optimizer Operation."

Give the optimizer hints or override it when necessary. You can use `FORCE INDEX`, `USE INDEX`, or `IGNORE INDEX` after a table name in the table list of a join to give the server guidance about which indexes to prefer. See the description for `SELECT` in Appendix E, "SQL Syntax Reference."

You can also use `STRAIGHT_JOIN` to force the optimizer to use tables in a particular order. Normally, the MySQL optimizer considers itself free to determine the order in which to scan tables to retrieve rows most quickly. On occasion, the optimizer will make a nonoptimal choice. If you find this happening, you can override the optimizer's choice using the `STRAIGHT_JOIN` keyword. A join performed with `STRAIGHT_JOIN` is like a cross join but forces the tables to be joined in the order named in the `FROM` clause.

If you do this, you should order the tables so that the first table is the one from which the smallest number of rows will be chosen. If you are not sure which table this is, put the table with the greatest number of rows first. In other words, try to order the tables to cause the most restrictive selection to come first. Queries perform better the earlier you can narrow the possible candidate rows.

`STRAIGHT_JOIN` can be specified at two points in a `SELECT` statement. You can specify it between the `SELECT` keyword and the selection list to have a global effect on all cross joins in the statement, or you can specify it in the FROM clause. The following two state-ments are equivalent:

```
SELECT STRAIGHT_JOIN ... FROM t1 INNER JOIN t2 INNER JOIN t3 ... ;
SELECT ... FROM t1 STRAIGHT_JOIN t2 STRAIGHT_JOIN t3 ... ;
```

Be sure to try the query with and without STRAIGHT_JOIN. MySQL might have some good reason not to use indexes in the order you think is best, and STRAIGHT_JOIN may not actually help. (Check the execution plans with EXPLAIN to see how MySQL handles each statement.)

Compare columns that have the same data type. When you compare indexed columns, identical data types will give you better performance than dissimilar types. For example, INT is different from BIGINT, so an INT/INT or BIGINT/BIGINT comparison is faster than an INT/BIGINT comparison. CHAR(10) is considered the same as CHAR(10) or VARCHAR(10) but different from CHAR(12) or VARCHAR(12). If columns that you compare frequently have different types, you can use ALTER TABLE to modify one of them so that the types match.

Make indexed columns stand alone in comparison expressions. If you use a col-umn in a function call or as part of a more complex term in an arithmetic expression, MySQL can't use the index because it must compute the value of the expression for every row. Sometimes this is unavoidable, but many times you can rewrite a query to get the indexed column to appear by itself.

The following WHERE clauses illustrate how this works. They are equivalent arithmeti-cally, but quite different for optimization purposes:

```
WHERE mycol * 2 < 4
WHERE mycol < 4 / 2
```

For the first line, MySQL must retrieve the value of mycol for each row, multiply by 2, and then compare the result to 4. In this case, no index can be used. Each value in the column must be retrieved so that the expression on the left side of the comparison can be evaluated. For the second line, the optimizer simplifies the expression 4/2 to the value 2, and then uses an index on mycol to quickly find values less than 2. Therefore, the second line is better than the first.

Let's consider another example. Suppose that you have an indexed DATE column date_col. If you issue a query such as the one following, the index isn't used:

```
SELECT * FROM mytbl WHERE YEAR(date_col) < 1990;
```

The expression doesn't compare 1990 to an indexed column; it compares 1990 to a value calculated from the column, and that value must be computed for each row. As a re-sult, the index on date_col is not used and query execution requires a full table scan. What's the fix? Just use a literal date, and then the index on date_col can be used to find matching values in the columns:

```
WHERE date_col < '1990-01-01'
```

But suppose that you don't have a specific date. You might be interested instead in finding rows that have a date that lies within a certain number of days from today. There are several ways to express a comparison of this type—not all of which are equally efficient. Here are three possibilities:

```
WHERE TO_DAYS(date_col) - TO_DAYS(CURDATE()) < cutoff
WHERE TO_DAYS(date_col) < cutoff + TO_DAYS(CURDATE())
WHERE date_col < DATE_ADD(CURDATE(), INTERVAL cutoff DAY)
```

For the first line, no index is used because the column must be retrieved for each row so that the value of `TO_DAYS(date_col)` can be computed. The second line is better. Both *cutoff* and `TO_DAYS(CURDATE())` are constants, so the right-hand side of the comparison can be calculated by the optimizer once before processing the query, rather than once per row. But the `date_col` column still appears in a function call, preventing use of the index. The third line is best of all. Again, the right-hand side of the comparison can be computed once as a constant before executing the query, but now the value is a date. That value can be compared directly to `date_col` values, which no longer need to be converted to days. In this case, the index can be used.

Don't use wildcards at the beginning of a `LIKE` pattern. Some string searches use a `WHERE` clause of the following form:

```
WHERE col_name LIKE '%string%'
```

That's the correct thing to do if you want to find the string no matter where it occurs in the column. But don't put '%' on both sides of the string simply out of habit. If you're really looking for the string only when it occurs at the beginning of the column, leave out the first '%'. Suppose that you're looking in a column containing last names for names like MacGregor or MacDougall that begin with `'Mac'`. In that case, write the `WHERE` clause like this:

```
WHERE last_name LIKE 'Mac%'
```

The optimizer looks at the literal initial part of the pattern and uses the index to find rows that match as though you'd written the following expression, which is in a form that enables an index on `last_name` to be used:

```
WHERE last_name >= 'Mac' AND last_name < 'Mad'
```

This optimization does not apply to pattern matches that use the `REGEXP` operator. `REGEXP` expressions are never optimized.

Take advantage of areas in which the optimizer is more mature. MySQL can do joins and subqueries, but subquery support is more recent, having been added in MySQL 4.1. Consequently, the optimizer has been better tuned for joins than for subqueries in some cases. This has a practical implication when you have a subquery that runs slowly. As discussed in Section 2.9.7, "Rewriting Subqueries as Joins," some subqueries can be reformulated as logically equivalent joins. If your slow subquery is one of these, try writing it as a join to see whether it performs better.

Test alternative forms of queries, but run them more than once. When testing alternative forms of a query (for example, a subquery versus an equivalent join), run it several times each way. If you run a query only once each of two different ways, you'll often find that the second query is faster just because information from the first query is still cached and need not actually be read from the disk. You should also try to run queries when the system load is relatively stable to avoid effects due to other activities on your system.

Avoid overuse of MySQL's automatic type conversion. MySQL will perform automatic type conversion, but if you can avoid conversions, you may get better performance. For example, if `num_col` is an integer column, each of these queries will return the same result:

```
SELECT * FROM mytbl WHERE num_col = 4;
SELECT * FROM mytbl WHERE num_col = '4';
```

But the second query involves a type conversion. The conversion operation itself involves a small performance penalty for converting the integer and string to double to perform the comparison. A more serious problem is that if `num_col` is indexed, a comparison that involves type conversion may prevent the index from being used.

The opposite kind of comparison (comparing a string column to a numeric value) also can prevent use of an index. Suppose that you write a query like this:

```
SELECT * FROM mytbl WHERE str_col = 4;
```

In this case, an index on `str_col` cannot be used because there can be many different string values in `str_col` that are equal to 4 when converted to a number (for example, `'4'`, `'4.0'`, and `'4th'`). The only way to know which values qualify is to read each one, convert it, and perform the comparison. To avoid this problem if you are looking for a particular value such as `'4'`, specify it that way in the query:

```
SELECT * FROM mytbl WHERE str_col = '4';
```

5.2.2 Using EXPLAIN to Check Optimizer Operation

The EXPLAIN statement is useful for gaining insight into the execution plans that the optimizer generates for processing statements. In this section, I'll show two uses for EXPLAIN:

- To see whether writing a query different ways affects whether an index can be used.
- To see the effect that adding indexes to a table has on the optimizer's ability to generate efficient execution plans.

The discussion describes only those EXPLAIN output fields that are relevant for the examples. EXPLAIN output is discussed further in Appendix E. The output shown is what I see on my system. Depending on your server version and configuration, you might see somewhat different results.

In Section 5.2.1, "How the Optimizer Works," the point was made that the way you write an expression can determine whether the optimizer can use available indexes.

Specifically, the discussion there used the example that of the three following logically equivalent WHERE clauses, only the third enables use of an index:

```
WHERE TO_DAYS(date_col) - TO_DAYS(CURDATE()) < cutoff
WHERE TO_DAYS(date_col) < cutoff + TO_DAYS(CURDATE())
WHERE date_col < DATE_ADD(CURDATE(), INTERVAL cutoff DAY)
```

EXPLAIN enables you to check whether one way of writing an expression is better than another. To see this, let's try using each of the WHERE clauses to search for expiration column values in the member table, using a cutoff value of 30 days. However, as originally created, the member table has no index on the expiration column. To enable the relationship to be seen between index use and how an expression is written, first index the expiration column:

```
mysql> ALTER TABLE member ADD INDEX (expiration);
```

Then try EXPLAIN with each form of the expression to see what execution plans the optimizer comes up with:

```
mysql> EXPLAIN SELECT * FROM MEMBER
    -> WHERE TO_DAYS(expiration) - TO_DAYS(CURDATE()) < 30\G
*************************** 1. row ***************************
           id: 1
  select_type: SIMPLE
        table: MEMBER
         type: ALL
possible_keys: NULL
          key: NULL
      key_len: NULL
          ref: NULL
         rows: 102
        Extra: Using where
mysql> EXPLAIN SELECT * FROM MEMBER
    -> WHERE TO_DAYS(expiration) < 30 + TO_DAYS(CURDATE())\G
*************************** 1. row ***************************
           id: 1
  select_type: SIMPLE
        table: MEMBER
         type: ALL
possible_keys: NULL
          key: NULL
      key_len: NULL
          ref: NULL
         rows: 102
        Extra: Using where
mysql> EXPLAIN SELECT * FROM MEMBER
    -> WHERE expiration < DATE_ADD(CURDATE(), INTERVAL 30 DAY)\G
*************************** 1. row ***************************
```

```
             id: 1
     select_type: SIMPLE
           table: MEMBER
            type: range
   possible_keys: expiration
             key: expiration
         key_len: 4
             ref: NULL
            rows: 6
           Extra: Using where
```

The results for the first two statements show that the index is not used. The `type` value indicates how values will be read from a table. `ALL` means "all rows will be examined." That is, a full table scan will be performed, without benefit of an index. The `NULL` in each of the key-related columns also indicates that no index will be used.

By contrast, the result for the third statement shows that the `WHERE` clause has been written such that the optimizer can use the index on the `expiration` column:

- The `type` value indicates that it can use the index to search for a specific range of values (those less than the date given on the right side of the expression).

- The `possible_keys` and `key` values show that the index on `expiration` is considered a candidate index and also is the index that actually would be used.

- The `rows` value shows that the optimizer estimates that it would need to examine 6 rows to process the query. That's better than the value of 102 for the first two execution plans.

A second use for `EXPLAIN` is to find out whether adding indexes would help the optimizer execute a statement more efficiently. For this example, I will use just two tables that initially are unindexed. This suffices to show the effect of creating indexes. The same principles apply to more complex joins that involve many tables.

Suppose that we have two tables `t1` and `t2`, each with 1,000 rows containing the values 1 to 1000. The query that we'll examine looks for those rows where corresponding values from the two tables are the same:

```
mysql> SELECT t1.i1, t2.i2 FROM t1 INNER JOIN t2
    -> WHERE t1.i1 = t2.i2;
+------+------+
| i1   | i2   |
+------+------+
|    1 |    1 |
|    2 |    2 |
|    3 |    3 |
|    4 |    4 |
|    5 |    5 |
...
```

With no indexes on either of the tables, EXPLAIN produces this result:

```
mysql> EXPLAIN SELECT t1.i1, t2.i2 FROM t1 INNER JOIN t2
    -> WHERE t1.i1 = t2.i2\G
*************************** 1. row ***************************
           id: 1
  select_type: SIMPLE
        table: t1
         type: ALL
possible_keys: NULL
          key: NULL
      key_len: NULL
          ref: NULL
         rows: 1000
        Extra:
*************************** 2. row ***************************
           id: 1
  select_type: SIMPLE
        table: t2
         type: ALL
possible_keys: NULL
          key: NULL
      key_len: NULL
          ref: NULL
         rows: 1000
        Extra: Using where
```

Here, ALL in the type column indicates a full table scan that examines all rows. NULL in the possible_keys column indicates that no candidate indexes were found for speeding up the query. (The key, key_len, and ref columns all are NULL as well due to the lack of a suitable index.) Using where indicates that information in the WHERE clause is used to identify qualifying rows.

Those pieces of information tell us that the optimizer finds no useful information for executing the query more efficiently and will proceed as follows:

- It will perform a full scan of t1.
- For each row from t1, it will perform a full scan of t2, using the information in the WHERE clause to identify qualifying rows.

The rows values show the optimizer's estimates about how many rows it will need to examine at each stage of the query. The estimate is 1000 for t1 because a full scan will be done. Similarly, the estimate is 1000 for t2, but this is *for each row* in t1. In other words, the number of row combinations that the optimizer estimates it will examine to process the query is 1,000 × 1,000, or one million. That is highly wasteful of effort, because only 1,000 combinations actually satisfy the conditions in the WHERE clause.

To make this query more efficient, add an index on one of the joined columns and try the EXPLAIN statement again:

```
mysql> ALTER TABLE t2 ADD INDEX (i2);
mysql> EXPLAIN SELECT t1.i1, t2.i2 FROM t1 INNER JOIN t2
    -> WHERE t1.i1 = t2.i2\G
*************************** 1. row ***************************
           id: 1
  select_type: SIMPLE
        table: t1
         type: ALL
possible_keys: NULL
          key: NULL
      key_len: NULL
          ref: NULL
         rows: 1000
        Extra:
*************************** 2. row ***************************
           id: 1
  select_type: SIMPLE
        table: t2
         type: ref
possible_keys: i2
          key: i2
      key_len: 5
          ref: sampdb.t1.i1
         rows: 10
        Extra: Using where; Using index
```

This is an improvement. The output for t1 is unchanged (indicating that a full scan still will be done on the table), but the optimizer can process t2 differently:

- type has changed from ALL to ref, meaning that a reference value (the value from t1) can be used to perform an index lookup to locate qualifying rows in t2.
- The reference value is given in the ref field: sampdb.t1.i1.
- The rows value has dropped from 1000 to 10, which shows that the optimizer believes that it will need to examine only 10 rows in t2 for each row in t1. (That is a somewhat pessimistic estimate. In fact, only one row in t2 will match each row from t1. We'll see a bit later how to help the optimizer improve this estimate.) The total estimated number of row combinations is $1{,}000 \times 10 = 10{,}000$. That's much better than the previous estimate of one million in the absence of any indexing.

Is there any value in indexing t1? After all, for this particular join, it's necessary to scan one of the tables, and no index is needed to do that. To see whether there's any effect, index t1.i1 and run EXPLAIN again:

```
mysql> ALTER TABLE t1 ADD INDEX (i1);
mysql> EXPLAIN SELECT t1.i1, t2.i2 FROM t1 INNER JOIN t2
    -> WHERE t1.i1 = t2.i2\G
*************************** 1. row ***************************
           id: 1
  select_type: SIMPLE
        table: t1
         type: index
possible_keys: i1
          key: i1
      key_len: 5
          ref: NULL
         rows: 1000
        Extra: Using index
*************************** 2. row ***************************
           id: 1
  select_type: SIMPLE
        table: t2
         type: ref
possible_keys: i2
          key: i2
      key_len: 5
          ref: sampdb.t1.i1
         rows: 10
        Extra: Using where; Using index
```

This output is similar to that for the previous EXPLAIN, but adding the index did make some difference in the output for t1. type has changed from NULL to index and Extra has changed from blank to Using index. These changes indicate that, although a full scan of the indexed values still would be done, the optimizer now can read them directly from the index without touching the data file at all. You will see this kind of result for a MyISAM table when the optimizer knows that it can get all the information it needs by consulting only the index file. You'll also see it for InnoDB tables when the optimizer can use information solely from the index without another seek to get the data row.

One further step we can take to help the optimizer make better cost estimates is to run ANALYZE TABLE. This causes the server to generate statistics about the distribution of key values. Analyzing the tables and running EXPLAIN again yields a better rows estimate:

```
mysql> ANALYZE TABLE t1, t2;
mysql> EXPLAIN SELECT t1.i1, t2.i2 FROM t1 INNER JOIN t2
    -> WHERE t1.i1 = t2.i2\G
*************************** 1. row ***************************
           id: 1
  select_type: SIMPLE
        table: t1
         type: index
possible_keys: i1
```

```
          key: i1
      key_len: 5
          ref: NULL
         rows: 1000
        Extra: Using index
*************************** 2. row ***************************
           id: 1
  select_type: SIMPLE
        table: t2
         type: ref
possible_keys: i2
          key: i2
      key_len: 5
          ref: sampdb.t1.i1
         rows: 1
        Extra: Using where; Using index
```

In this case, the optimizer now estimates that each value from t1 will match only one row in t2.

5.3 Choosing Data Types for Efficient Queries

Your choice of data type can influence query performance in several ways. This section provides guidelines for choosing data types that can help queries run more quickly.

Use numeric rather than string operations. Calculations involving numbers generally are faster than those involving strings. Consider comparison operations. Numbers can be compared in a single operation. String comparisons may involve several byte-by-byte or character-by-character comparisons, more so as the strings become longer.

If a string column has a limited number of values, you can use an ENUM or SET type to get the advantages of numeric operations. These types are represented internally as numbers and can be processed more efficiently.

Consider alternative representations for strings. Sometimes you can improve performance by representing string values as numbers. For example, to represent IP numbers in dotted-quad notation, such as 192.168.0.4, you might use a string. Or you could instead convert the IP numbers to integer form by storing each part of the dotted-quad form in one byte of a four-byte INT UNSIGNED type. Storing integers would both save space and speed lookups. On the other hand, representing IP numbers as INT values might make it difficult to perform pattern matches such as you might do if you wanted to look for numbers in a given subnet. Perhaps you can do the same thing by using bitmask operations. These kinds of issues illustrate that you cannot consider only space issues; you must decide which representation is most appropriate based on what you want to do with the values. (Whatever choice you make, the INET_ATON() and INET_NTOA() functions can help convert between the two representations.)

Don't use larger types when smaller ones will do. Smaller types can be processed more quickly than larger types. For strings in particular, processing time is in direct relationship to string length. Also, with smaller types, your tables will be smaller and require less overhead for disk activity. If a column is indexed, using shorter values gives you even more of a performance boost. Not only will the index speed up queries, shorter index values can be processed more quickly than longer values.

For columns that use fixed-size data types, choose the smallest type that will hold the required range of values. Don't use BIGINT if MEDIUMINT will do. Don't use DOUBLE if you need only FLOAT precision. If you are using fixed-length CHAR columns, don't make them unnecessarily long. If the longest value you store in a column is 40 characters long, don't define it as CHAR(255); define it as CHAR(40).

For variable-size types, you may still be able to save space with smaller types. A BLOB uses 2 bytes to record the length of the value, a LONGBLOB uses 4 bytes. If you're storing values that are never as long as 64KB, using BLOB saves you 2 bytes per value. (Similar considerations apply for TEXT types.)

If you have a choice about row storage format, use one that is optimal for your storage engine. For MyISAM tables, use fixed-length columns rather than variable-length columns. For example, make all character columns CHAR rather than VARCHAR. The tradeoff is that your table will use more space, but if you can afford the extra space, fixed-length rows can be processed more quickly than variable-length rows. This is especially true for tables that are modified often and therefore more subject to fragmentation:

- With variable-length rows, you get more fragmentation of a table on which you perform many deletes or updates due to the differing sizes of the rows. You'll need to run OPTIMIZE TABLE periodically to maintain performance. This is not an issue with fixed-length rows.

- Tables with fixed-length rows are easier to reconstruct if you have a table crash. The beginning of each row can be determined because they all are at positions that are multiples of the fixed row size, something that is not true with variable-length rows. This is not a performance issue with respect to query processing, but it can certainly speed up the table repair process.

Although converting a MyISAM table to use fixed-length columns can improve performance, you should consider the following issues first:

- Fixed-length columns are faster but take more space. CHAR(n) columns always take n characters per value (even empty ones) because values are padded with trailing spaces when stored in the table. VARCHAR(n) columns take less space because only as many characters are allocated as necessary to store each value, plus one or two bytes per value to record the length. Thus, if you are choosing between CHAR and VARCHAR columns, the tradeoff is one of time versus space. If speed is your primary concern, use CHAR columns to get the performance benefits of fixed-length columns. If space is at a premium, use VARCHAR columns. As a rule of thumb, you can assume that fixed-length rows will improve performance even though more space is used. But for an especially critical application, you might want to implement a table both ways and run some tests to determine which alternative actually is better for your particular application.

- Sometimes you cannot use a fixed-length type, even if you want to. There is no fixed-length type for strings longer than 255 characters, for example.

MEMORY tables currently are stored using fixed-length rows, so it doesn't matter whether you use CHAR or VARCHAR columns. Both are treated implicitly as CHAR.

For InnoDB tables, the internal row storage format does not treat fixed-length and variable-length columns differently (all rows use a header containing pointers to the column values), so using fixed-length CHAR columns is not in itself intrinsically simpler than using variable-length VARCHAR columns. Consequently, the primary performance factor is the amount of storage used for rows. Because CHAR on average takes more space than VARCHAR, it's preferable to use VARCHAR to minimize the amount of storage and disk I/O needed to process rows.

Define columns to be NOT NULL. If a column is NOT NULL, it can be handled more quickly because MySQL doesn't have to check the column's values during query processing to see whether they are NULL. It also saves one bit per row in the table. Avoiding NULL in columns may make your queries simpler because you don't have to check for NULL as a special case, and simpler queries generally can be processed more quickly.

Consider using ENUM columns. If you have a string column that has low cardinality (contains only a limited number of distinct values), consider converting it to an ENUM column. ENUM values can be processed quickly because they are represented internally as numeric values.

Use PROCEDURE ANALYSE(). Run PROCEDURE ANALYSE() to see what it tells you about the columns in your table:

```
SELECT * FROM tbl_name PROCEDURE ANALYSE();
SELECT * FROM tbl_name PROCEDURE ANALYSE(16,256);
```

One column of the output will be a suggestion for the optimal data type for each of the columns in your table. The second example tells PROCEDURE ANALYSE() not to suggest ENUM types that contain more than 16 values or that take more than 256 bytes (you can change the values as you like). Without such restrictions, the output may be very long; ENUM definitions are often difficult to read.

Based on the output from PROCEDURE ANALYSE(), you may find that your table can be changed to take advantage of a more efficient type. If you decide to change a column's type, use ALTER TABLE.

Defragment tables that are subject to fragmentation. Tables that are modified a great deal, particularly those that contain variable-length columns, are subject to fragmentation. Fragmentation is bad because it leads to unused space in the disk blocks used to store your table. Over time, you must read more blocks to get the valid rows, and performance is reduced. This is true for any table with variable-length rows, but is particularly acute for BLOB or TEXT columns because they can vary so much in size.

Use of OPTIMIZE TABLE on a regular basis helps keep performance on the table from degrading. OPTIMIZE TABLE can be used to defragment MyISAM tables. A defragmentation method that works for any storage engine is to dump the table with mysqldump, and then drop and re-create it using the dump file:

```
% mysqldump db_name tbl_name > dump.sql
% mysql db_name < dump.sql
```

Pack data into a BLOB or TEXT column. Using a BLOB or TEXT column to store data that you pack and unpack in your application may enable you to get everything with a single retrieval operation rather than with several. This can also be helpful for data values that are not easy to represent in a standard table structure or that change over time. In the discussion of the ALTER TABLE statement in Chapter 2, "Using SQL to Manage Data," one of the examples dealt with a table being used to hold results from the fields in a Web-based questionnaire. That example discussed how you could use ALTER TABLE to add columns to the table whenever you add questions to the questionnaire.

Another way to approach this problem is to have the application program that processes the Web form pack the data into some kind of data structure, and then insert it into a single BLOB or TEXT column. For example, you could represent the questionnaire responses using XML and store the XML string in a TEXT column. This adds application overhead on the client side for encoding the data (and decoding it later when you retrieve rows from the table), but simplifies the table structure, and eliminates the need to change the table structure when you change your questionnaire.

On the other hand, BLOB and TEXT values can cause their own problems, especially if you do a lot of DELETE or UPDATE operations. Deleting such values can leave large holes in the table that will be filled in later with a row or rows of probably different sizes. (The preceding discussion of defragmentation suggests how you might deal with this.)

Use a synthetic index. Synthetic index columns can sometimes be helpful. One method is to create a hash value based on other columns and store it in a separate column. Then you can find rows by searching for hash values. However, note that this technique is good only for exact-match queries. (Hash values are useless for range searches with operators such as < or >=.) Hash values can be generated by using the MD5() function. Other options are to use SHA1() or CRC32(). Or you can compute your own hash values using logic within your application. Remember that a numeric hash value can be stored very efficiently. Also, if the hash algorithm might produce string values that have trailing spaces, do not store them using a data type that is subject to trailing-space removal.

A synthetic hash index can be particularly useful with BLOB and TEXT columns. It can be much quicker to find these kinds of values using a hash as an identifier value than by searching the BLOB or TEXT column itself.

Avoid retrieving large BLOB or TEXT values unless you must. For example, a SELECT * query that retrieves entire rows isn't a good idea unless you're sure the WHERE clause is going to restrict the results to just the rows you want. Otherwise, you may be pulling potentially very large values over the network for no purpose. This is another case where BLOB or TEXT identifier information stored in a synthetic index column can be useful. You can search that column to determine the row or rows you want and then retrieve the BLOB or TEXT values from the qualifying rows.

Segregate BLOB or TEXT columns into a separate table. Under some circumstances, it may make sense to move these columns out of a table into a secondary table, if that enables you to convert the table to fixed-length row format for the remaining columns. This will reduce fragmentation in the primary table and allow you to take advantage of the performance benefits of having fixed-length rows. It also enables you to run SELECT * queries on the primary table without pulling large BLOB or TEXT values over the network.

5.4 Loading Data Efficiently

Most of the time you'll probably be concerned about optimizing SELECT statements because they are the most common type of statement and because it's not always straightforward to figure out how to optimize them. By comparison, loading data into your database is straightforward. Nevertheless, there are strategies you can use to improve the efficiency of data-loading operations. The basic principles are these:

- Bulk loading is more efficient than single-row loading because the key cache need not be flushed after each input record is loaded. It can be flushed at the end of the batch of records. The more you can reduce key cache flushing, the faster data loading will be. (Index modifications are made in the key cache before being written to disk; flushing the cache once rather than many times significantly reduces disk I/O.)

- Loading is faster when a table has no indexes than when it is indexed. If there are indexes, not only must the row's contents be added to the table, each index must also be modified to reflect the addition of the new row.

- Shorter SQL statements are faster than longer statements because they involve less parsing on the part of the server and because they can be sent over the network from the client to the server more quickly.

Some of these factors may seem minor (the last one in particular), but if you're loading a lot of data, even small efficiencies make a difference. From the preceding general principles, several practical conclusions can be drawn about how to load data most quickly.

LOAD DATA (all forms) is more efficient than INSERT because it loads rows in bulk. The server must parse and interpret only one statement, not several. Also, the index needs flushing only after all rows have been processed, rather than after each row.

LOAD DATA is more efficient without LOCAL than with it. Without LOCAL, the file must be located on the server and you must have the FILE privilege, but the server can read the file directly from disk. With LOAD DATA LOCAL, the client reads the file and sends it over the network to the server, which is slower.

If you must use INSERT, try to use the syntax that specifies multiple rows to be inserted in a single statement:

```
INSERT INTO tbl_name VALUES(...),(...),... ;
```

The more rows you can specify in the statement, the better. This reduces the total number of statements required and minimizes the amount of index flushing. This principle might seem to contradict the earlier one that shorter statements can be processed faster than longer statements. But there is no contradiction. The issues here are that a single INSERT statement that inserts multiple rows is shorter overall than an equivalent set of individual single-row INSERT statements, and the multiple-row statement can be processed on the server with much less index flushing.

If you use mysqldump to generate database backup files, it generates multiple-row INSERT statements by default: The --opt (optimize) option is enabled, which turns on the --extended-insert option that produces multiple-row INSERT statements, as well as some other options that allow the dump file to be processed more efficiently when it is reloaded.

Avoid using the --complete-insert option with mysqldump; the resulting INSERT statements will be for single rows and will be longer and require more parsing than will multiple-row statements.

If you must use multiple INSERT statements, group them if possible to reduce index flushing. For transactional storage engines, do this by issuing the INSERT statements within a single transaction rather than in autocommit mode:

```
START TRANSACTION;
INSERT INTO tbl_name ... ;
INSERT INTO tbl_name ... ;
INSERT INTO tbl_name ... ;
COMMIT;
```

For non-transactional storage engines, obtain a write lock on the table and issue the INSERT statements while the table is locked:

```
LOCK TABLES tbl_name WRITE;
INSERT INTO tbl_name ... ;
INSERT INTO tbl_name ... ;
INSERT INTO tbl_name ... ;
UNLOCK TABLES;
```

Either way, you obtain the same benefit: The index is flushed once after all the statements have been executed rather than once per INSERT statement. The latter is what happens in autocommit mode or if the table has not been locked.

For MyISAM tables, another strategy for reducing index flushing is to use the DELAY_KEY_WRITE table option. With this option, data rows are written to the data file immediately as usual, but the key cache is flushed only occasionally rather than after each insert. To use delayed index flushing on a server-wide basis, start mysqld with the --delay-key-write=ALL option. In this case, index block writes for a table are delayed until blocks must be flushed to make room for other index values, until a FLUSH TABLES statement has been executed, or until the table is closed.

If you choose to use delayed key writes for MyISAM tables, abnormal server shut-downs can cause loss of index values. This is not a fatal problem because MyISAM in-dexes can be repaired based on the data rows. However, to make sure that the repairs do happen, start the server with the `--myisam-recover=FORCE` option. This option causes the server to check MyISAM tables when it opens them and repair them automatically as necessary.

For a replication slave server, you might want to use `--delay-key-write=ALL` to delay index flushing for all MyISAM tables, regardless of how they were created originally on the master server.

Use the compressed client/server protocol to reduce the amount of data going over the network. For most MySQL clients, this can be specified using the `--compress` command-line option. Generally, this should only be used on slow networks because compression requires quite a bit of processor time.

Let MySQL insert default values for you. That is, don't specify columns in INSERT statements that will be assigned the default value anyway. On average, your statements will be shorter, reducing the number of characters sent over the network to the server. In ad-dition, because the statements contain fewer values, the server does less parsing and value conversion.

For MyISAM tables, if you need to load a lot of data into a new table to populate it, it's faster to create the table without indexes, load the data, and then create the indexes. It's faster to create the indexes all at once rather than to modify them for each row. For a table that already has indexes, data loading may be faster if you drop or deactivate the in-dexes beforehand, and then rebuild or reactivate them afterward. These strategies do not apply to InnoDB tables; InnoDB has no optimizations for separate index creation.

If you're considering using the strategy of dropping or deactivating indexes for loading data into MyISAM tables, think about the overall circumstances of your situation in as-sessing whether any benefit is likely to be obtained. If you're loading a small amount of data into a large table, rebuilding the indexes probably will take longer than just loading the data without any special preparation.

To drop and rebuild indexes, use DROP INDEX and CREATE INDEX, or the index-related forms of ALTER TABLE. To deactivate and reactivate indexes, you have two choices:

- You can use the DISABLE KEYS and ENABLE KEYS forms of ALTER TABLE:

```
ALTER TABLE tbl_name DISABLE KEYS;
ALTER TABLE tbl_name ENABLE KEYS;
```

These statements turn off and on updating of any non-unique indexes in the table.

The DISABLE KEYS and ENABLE KEYS clauses for ALTER TABLE are the preferred method for index deactivation and activation, because the server does the work. (If you're using a LOAD DATA statement to load data into an empty MyISAM table, the server performs this optimization automatically.)

- The myisamchk utility can perform index manipulation. It operates directly on the table files, so to use it you must have write access to the table files. You should also observe the precautions described in Section 14.2, "Performing Database Maintenance with the Server Running," for keeping the server from accessing a table while you're using its files.

To deactivate a MyISAM table's indexes with `myisamchk`, first make sure you've told the server to leave the table alone, and then move into the appropriate database directory and run the following command:

```
% myisamchk --keys-used=0 tbl_name
```

After loading the table with data, reactivate the indexes:

```
% myisamchk --recover --quick --keys-used=n tbl_name
```

n is interpreted as a bitmask indicating which indexes to enable. Bit 0 (the first bit) corresponds to index 1. For example, if a table has three indexes, the value of n should be 7 (111 binary). You can determine index numbers with the `--description` option:

```
% myisamchk --description tbl_name
```

The preceding data-loading principles also apply to mixed-query environments involving clients performing different kinds of operations. For example, generally you should avoid long-running SELECT queries on tables that are changed (written to) frequently. That causes a lot of contention and poor performance for the writers. A possible way around this, if your writes are mostly INSERT operations, is to add new rows to an auxiliary table and then add those rows to the main table periodically. This is not a viable strategy if you need to be able to access new rows immediately, but if you can afford to leave them inaccessible for a short time, use of the auxiliary table will help you two ways. First, it reduces contention with SELECT queries that are taking place on the main table, so they execute more quickly. Second, it takes less time overall to load a batch of rows from the auxiliary table into the main table than it would to load the rows individually; the key cache need be flushed only at the end of each batch, rather than after each individual row.

One application for this strategy is when you're logging Web page accesses from your Web server into a MySQL database. In this case, it may not be a high priority to make sure that the entries get into the main table right away.

If you're using mixed INSERT and SELECT statements with a MyISAM table, you might be able to take advantage of concurrent inserts. This feature enables the inserts to take place at the same time as retrievals without the use of an auxiliary table. For details, see Section 5.5.3, "Using Concurrent Inserts."

5.5 Scheduling and Locking Issues

The previous sections focus primarily on making individual queries faster. MySQL also enables you to affect the scheduling priorities of statements, which may allow queries arriving from several clients to cooperate better so that individual clients aren't locked out for a long time. Changing the priorities can also ensure that particular kinds of queries are processed more quickly. This section looks at MySQL's default scheduling policy and the options that are available to you for influencing this policy. It also describes the use of concurrent inserts and the effect that storage engine locking levels have on concurrency among clients. For the purposes of this discussion, a client performing a retrieval (a SELECT) is a reader. A client performing an operation that modifies a table (DELETE, INSERT, REPLACE, or UPDATE) is a writer.

MySQL's default scheduling policy can be summarized like this:

- Writes have higher priority than reads.
- Writes to a table must occur one at a time, and write requests are processed in the order in which they arrive.
- Multiple reads from a table can be processed simultaneously.

The MyISAM, MERGE, and MEMORY storage engines implement this scheduling policy with the aid of table locks. Whenever a client accesses a table, a lock for it must be acquired first. When the client is finished with a table, the lock on it can be released. It's possible to acquire and release locks explicitly by issuing LOCK TABLES and UNLOCK TABLES statements, but normally the server's lock manager automatically acquires locks as necessary and releases them when they no longer are needed. The type of lock required depends on whether a client is writing or reading.

A client performing a write to a table must have a lock for exclusive table access. The table is in an inconsistent state while the operation is in progress because the data row is being deleted, added, or changed, and any indexes on the table may need to be updated to match. Allowing other clients to access the table while the table is in flux would cause problems. It's clearly a bad thing to allow two clients to write to the table at the same time because that would quickly corrupt the table into an unusable mess. But it's not good to allow a client to read from an in-flux table, either, because the table might be changing at the location being read, and the results would be inaccurate.

A client performing a read from a table must have a lock to prevent other clients from writing to the table and changing it during the read. The lock need not be for exclusive access, however. Reading doesn't change the table, so there is no reason one reader should prevent another from accessing the table. Therefore, a read lock enables other clients to read the table at the same time.

MySQL provides several statement modifiers that allow you to influence its scheduling policy:

- The LOW_PRIORITY keyword applies to DELETE, INSERT, LOAD DATA, REPLACE, and UPDATE statements.
- The HIGH_PRIORITY keyword applies to SELECT and INSERT statements.
- The DELAYED keyword applies to INSERT and REPLACE statements.

The LOW_PRIORITY and HIGH_PRIORITY modifiers have an effect only for storage engines that use table locks (MyISAM, MERGE, and MEMORY). The DELAYED modifier works for MyISAM, MEMORY, ARCHIVE, and (as of MySQL 5.1.19) BLACKHOLE tables.

5.5.1 Changing Statement Scheduling Priorities

The LOW_PRIORITY keyword affects execution scheduling for DELETE, INSERT, LOAD DATA, REPLACE, and UPDATE statements. Normally, if a write operation for a table arrives while the table is being read, the writer blocks until the reader is done. (Once a query has begun it will not be interrupted, so the reader is allowed to finish.) If another read request arrives while the writer is waiting, the reader blocks, too, because the default scheduling policy is that writers have higher priority than readers. When the first reader finishes, the writer proceeds, and when the writer finishes, the second reader proceeds.

If the write request is a LOW_PRIORITY request, the write is not considered to have a higher priority than reads. In this case, if a second read request arrives while the writer is waiting, the second reader is allowed to slip in ahead of the writer. Only when there are no more readers is the writer allowed to proceed. One implication of this scheduling modification is that, theoretically, it's possible for LOW_PRIORITY writes to be blocked forever: If additional read requests keep arriving while previous ones are still in progress, the new requests are allowed to get in ahead of the LOW_PRIORITY write.

The HIGH_PRIORITY keyword for SELECT queries is similar. It enables a SELECT to slip in ahead of a waiting write, even if the write normally has higher priority. Another effect is that a high-priority SELECT will execute ahead of normal SELECT statements, because those will block for the write.

If you want all statements that support the LOW_PRIORITY option to be treated as having low priority by default, start the server with the --low-priority-updates option. The effect of this option can be canceled for individual INSERT statements by using INSERT HIGH_PRIORITY to elevate them to the normal write priority.

5.5.2 Using Delayed Inserts

The DELAYED modifier applies to INSERT and REPLACE statements. When a DELAYED insert request arrives for a table, the server puts the rows in a queue and returns a status to the client immediately so that the client can proceed even before the rows have been inserted. If readers are reading from the table, the rows in the queue are held until there are no readers. Then the server begins inserting the rows in the delayed-row queue. The server checks periodically whether any new read requests have arrived and are waiting. If so, the delayed-row queue is suspended and the readers are allowed to proceed. When there are no readers left, the server begins inserting delayed rows again. This process continues until the queue is empty.

LOW_PRIORITY and DELAYED are similar in the sense that both allow row insertion to be deferred, but they are quite different in how they affect client operation.

LOW_PRIORITY forces the client to wait until the rows can be inserted. DELAYED enables the client to continue and the server buffers the rows in memory until it has time to process them.

INSERT DELAYED is useful if other clients may be running lengthy SELECT statements and you don't want to block waiting for completion of the insertion. The client issuing the INSERT DELAYED can proceed more quickly because the server simply queues the row to be inserted.

You should be aware of certain other differences between normal INSERT and INSERT DELAYED behavior, however. The client gets back an error if the INSERT DELAYED statement contains a syntax error, but other information that would normally be available is not. For example, you can't rely on getting the AUTO_INCREMENT value when the statement returns. Also, you won't get a count for the number of duplicates on unique indexes. This happens because the insert operation returns a status before the operation actually has been completed. Another implication is that because rows from INSERT DELAYED statements are queued in memory, the rows are lost if the server crashes or is killed with kill -9. (This doesn't happen with a normal kill -TERM kill; in that case, the server inserts the rows before exiting.)

5.5.3 Using Concurrent Inserts

The MyISAM storage engine allows an exception to the general principle that readers block writers. This occurs under the condition that a MyISAM table has no holes in the middle of the data file, such as can result from deleting or updating rows. When the table has no holes, any INSERT statements must necessarily add rows at the end rather than in the middle. Under such circumstances, MySQL allows clients to add rows to the table even while other clients are reading from it. These are known as "concurrent inserts" because they take place at the same time as retrievals without being blocked.

If you want to use concurrent inserts, note the following:

- Do not use the LOW_PRIORITY modifier with your INSERT statements. It causes INSERT always to block for readers and thus prevents concurrent inserts from being performed.

- Readers that need to lock the table explicitly but still want to allow concurrent inserts should use LOCK TABLES ... READ LOCAL rather than LOCK TABLES ... READ. The LOCAL keyword acquires a lock that enables concurrent inserts to proceed, because it applies only to existing rows in the table and does not block new rows from being added to the end.

- LOAD DATA operations should use the CONCURRENT modifier to allow SELECT statements for the table to take place at the same time.

- A MyISAM table that has holes in the middle cannot be used for concurrent inserts. However, you can defragment the table with the OPTIMIZE TABLE statement. That eliminates the holes, at least until further deletes or updates occur.

5.5.4 Locking Levels and Concurrency

The scheduling modifiers discussed in the preceding sections allow you to influence the default scheduling policy. For the most part, these modifiers were introduced to deal with issues that arise from the use of table-level locks, which is what the MyISAM, MERGE, and MEMORY storage engines use to manage table contention.

The InnoDB storage engine implements locking at a different level and thus has differing performance characteristics in terms of contention management. InnoDB uses row-level locks, but only as necessary. (In many cases, such as when only reads are done, InnoDB may use no locks at all.)

The locking level used by a storage engine has a significant effect on concurrency among clients. Suppose that two clients each want to update a row in a given table. To perform the update, each client requires a write lock. For a MyISAM table, the engine will acquire a table lock for the first client, which causes the second client to block until the first one has finished. With an InnoDB table, greater concurrency can be achieved: Both updates can proceed simultaneously as long as both clients aren't updating the same row.

The general principle is that table locking at a finer level enables better concurrency, because more clients can be using a table at the same time if they use different parts of it. The practical implication is that different storage engines will be better suited for different statement mixes:

- MyISAM is extremely fast for retrievals. However, the use of table-level locks can be a problem in environments with mixed retrievals and updates, especially if the retrievals tend to be long-running. Under these conditions, updates may need to wait a long time before they can proceed.
- InnoDB tables can provide better performance when there are many updates. Because locking is done at the row level rather than at the table level, the extent of the table that is locked is smaller. This reduces lock contention and improves concurrency.

Table locking does have an advantage over finer levels of locking in terms of deadlock prevention. With table locks, deadlock never occurs. The server can determine which tables are needed by looking at the statement and locking them all ahead of time. With InnoDB tables, deadlock can occur because the storage engine does not acquire all necessary locks at the beginning of a transaction. Instead, locks are acquired as they are determined to be necessary during the course of processing the transaction. It's possible that two statements will acquire locks and then try to acquire further locks that each depend on already-held locks being released. As a result, each client holds a lock that the other needs before it can continue. This results in deadlock, and the server must abort one of the transactions.

5.6 Administrative-Level Optimizations

The previous sections describe optimizations that can be performed by unprivileged MySQL users. Administrators who have control of the MySQL server or the machine on which it runs can perform additional optimizations. For example, some server parameters pertain to query processing and may be tuned, and certain hardware configuration factors have a direct effect on query processing speed. In many cases, these optimizations improve the performance of the server as a whole, and thus have a beneficial effect for all MySQL users.

In general, you should keep the following principles in mind when performing administrative optimizations:

- Accessing data in memory is faster than accessing data from disk.
- Keeping data in memory as long as possible reduces disk activity.
- Retaining information from an index is more important than retaining contents of data rows.

The most common way to apply these principles is to increase the size of the server's caches. The server has many parameters (system variables) that you can change to configure its operation. Several of these directly affect the speed of query processing. The most important parameters you can change are the sizes of the table cache and the caches used by the storage engines to buffer information for indexing operations. If you have memory available, allocating it to the server's caches enables information to be held in memory longer and reduces disk activity. This is good, because it's much faster to access information from memory than to read it from disk. You can configure the size of several caches:

- When the server opens table files, it tries to keep them open so as to minimize the number of file-opening operations. To do this, it maintains information about open files in the table cache. The `table_cache` system variable (`table_open_cache` in MySQL 5.1) controls the size of this cache. If the server accesses lots of tables, the table cache fills up and the server closes tables that haven't been used for a while to make room for opening new tables. To assess how effective the table cache is, check the `Opened_tables` status indicator:

  ```
  SHOW STATUS LIKE 'Opened_tables';
  ```

  `Opened_tables` indicates the number of times a table had to be opened because it wasn't already open. (This value is also displayed as the `Opens` value in the output of the `mysqladmin status` command.) If the number remains stable or increases slowly, it's probably set to about the right value. If the number grows quickly, it means the cache is too small and that tables often have to be closed to make room to open other tables. If you have file descriptors available, increasing the table cache size will reduce the number of table opening operations.

- The MyISAM key buffer is used to hold index blocks for index-related operations on MyISAM tables. Its size is controlled by the `key_buffer_size` system variable.

Larger values allow MySQL to hold more index blocks in memory at once, which increases the likelihood of finding key values in memory without having to read a new block from disk. The default size of the key buffer is 8MB. If you have lots of memory, that's a very conservative value and you should be able to increase it substantially and see a considerable improvement in performance for index-based retrievals and for index creation and modification operations.

You can create additional key caches for MyISAM tables and assign specific tables to them. This can help query processing for those tables, as explained in Section 5.6.1, "Using MyISAM Key Caches."

- The InnoDB storage engine has its own cache for buffering data and index values, and it also maintains a log buffer. The sizes for these resources are controlled by the `innodb_buffer_pool_size` and `innodb_log_buffer_size` system variables, respectively.

- Another special cache is the query cache, described later in Section 5.6.2, "Using the Query Cache."

Instructions for setting system variables can be found in Section 12.6.1, "Checking and Setting System Variable Values." When you change parameter values, follow these guidelines:

- Change one parameter at a time. Otherwise, you're varying multiple independent variables and it becomes more difficult to assess the effect of each change.

- Increase system variable values incrementally. If you increase a variable by a huge amount on the theory that more is always better, you may run your system out of resources, causing it to thrash or slow to a crawl because you've set the value too high.

- Rather than experimenting with parameter tuning on your production MySQL server, it might be prudent to set up a separate test server.

- To get an idea of the kinds of parameter variables that are likely to be appropriate for your system, take a look at the `my-small.cnf`, `my-medium.cnf`, `my-large.cnf`, and `my-huge.cnf` option files included with MySQL distributions. (On Unix, you can find them under the `share` directory in binary distributions and under the `support-files` directory in source distributions. On Windows, they are located in the base installation directory, and the filename suffix is `.ini`.) These files will give you some idea of which parameters are best to change for servers that receive different levels of use, and also some representative values to use for those parameters.

Other strategies you can adopt to help the server operate more efficiently include the following:

- Disable storage engines that you don't need. The server won't allocate any memory for disabled engines, allowing you to devote it to other uses. Most storage engines can be excluded from the server binary at configuration time if you build MySQL from source. For those engines that are included in the server, many can be disabled at runtime with the appropriate startup options. For details, see Section 12.7.1, "Selecting Which Storage Engines a Server Supports."

- Keep grant table permissions simple. Although the server caches grant table contents in memory, if you have any rows in the `tables_priv`, `columns_priv`, or `procs_priv` tables, the server must check their contents when it does privilege checking for SQL statements. If those tables are empty, the server can optimize its privilege checking to skip those privilege levels.

- If you build MySQL from source, configure it to use static libraries rather than shared libraries. Dynamic binaries that use shared libraries save on disk space, but static binaries are faster. However, some systems require dynamic linking if you use the user-defined function (UDF) mechanism. On such systems, static binaries will not work.

5.6.1 Using MyISAM Key Caches

When MySQL executes a statement that uses indexes from MyISAM tables, it uses a key cache to hold index values. The cache enables disk I/O to be reduced: If key values needed from a table are found in the cache, they need not be read from disk again. However, the key cache is a finite resource and it is shared among all MyISAM tables by default. If key values are not found in the cache and the cache is full, contention results: Some values currently in the cache must be discarded to make room for new values. The next time the discarded values are needed, they must be read from disk again.

If you have an especially heavily used MyISAM table, it would be beneficial to ensure that its keys remain in memory, but contention in the cache works against this. Contention can arise either when keys need to be read from the same table, or from other tables. You might avoid same-table contention by making the key cache large enough to hold all of a given table's indexes completely, but keys from other tables would still contend for space in the cache.

MySQL offers a solution to this problem because it supports setting up multiple key caches and enables a table's indexes to be assigned to and preloaded into a given cache. This can be useful if you have a table that sees especially heavy use and you have sufficient memory to load its indexes into the cache. This capability enables you to avoid both same-table and other-table contention: Create a cache that is large enough to hold a table's indexes completely and devote the cache exclusively to the use of that table. No disk I/O is necessary after the keys have been loaded into the cache. Also, key values will never need to be discarded from the cache and key lookups for the table can be done in memory.

The following example shows how to set up a key cache for the `member` table in the `sampdb` database, using a cache with a name of `member_cache` and a size of 1MB. You must have the SUPER privilege to carry out these instructions.

1. Set up a separate key cache large enough to hold the indexes from the table:

```
mysql> SET GLOBAL member_cache.key_buffer_size = 1024*1024;
```

2. Assign the table to the key cache:

```
mysql> CACHE INDEX member IN member_cache;
+---------------+--------------------+----------+----------+
| Table         | Op                 | Msg_type | Msg_text |
+---------------+--------------------+----------+----------+
| sampdb.member | assign_to_keycache | status   | OK       |
+---------------+--------------------+----------+----------+
```

3. Preload the table's indexes into its key cache:

```
mysql> LOAD INDEX INTO CACHE member;
+---------------+--------------+----------+----------+
| Table         | Op           | Msg_type | Msg_text |
+---------------+--------------+----------+----------+
| sampdb.member | preload_keys | status   | OK       |
+---------------+--------------+----------+----------+
```

If you want to load other tables into the same cache or create other key caches for other tables, that can be done as well. For more information about key caches, consult Section 12.7.2, "Configuring the MyISAM Storage Engine."

The effects of the statements that set up a separate key cache do not persist across server restarts. If you want the cache to be used each time the server runs, you must arrange to execute the statements at each restart. To do this, you can put them in a file and name the file with the --init-file server option.

5.6.2 Using the Query Cache

The MySQL server can use a query cache to speed up processing of SELECT statements that are executed repeatedly. The resulting performance improvement often is dramatic. The query cache has these characteristics:

- The first time a given SELECT statement is executed, the server remembers the text of the query and the results that it returns.

- The next time the server sees that statement, it doesn't bother to execute it again. Instead, the server pulls the result directly from the query cache and returns it to the client.

- Query caching is based on the literal text of query strings as they are received by the server. Queries are considered the same if the text of the queries is exactly the same. Queries are considered different if they differ in lettercase or come from clients that are using different character sets or communication protocols. They also are considered different if they are otherwise identical but do not actually refer to the same tables (for example, if they refer to identically named tables in different databases).

- A query is not cached if the query returns non-deterministic results. For example, a query that uses NOW() returns different results over time, so it cannot be cached.

- When a table is modified, any cached queries that refer to it become invalid and are discarded. This prevents the server from returning out-of-date results.

Support for the query cache is built in by default. If you don't want to use the cache, and want to avoid incurring even the minimal overhead that it involves, you can build the server without it by running the `configure` script with the `--without-query-cache` option.

To determine whether a server supports the query cache, check the value of the `have_query_cache` system variable:

```
mysql> SHOW VARIABLES LIKE 'have_query_cache';
+------------------+-------+
| Variable_name    | Value |
+------------------+-------+
| have_query_cache | YES   |
+------------------+-------+
```

Mode	Meaning
0	Don't cache query results or retrieve cached results
1	Cache queries except those that begin with SELECT SQL_NO_CACHE
2	Cache on demand only those queries that begin with SELECT SQL_CACHE

For servers that do include query cache support, cache operation is based on the values of three system variables:

- `query_cache_type` determines the operating mode of the query cache. The following table shows the possible mode values.
- `query_cache_size` determines the amount of memory to allocate for the cache, in bytes.
- `query_cache_limit` sets the maximum result set size that will be cached; query results larger than this value are never cached.

For example, to enable the query cache and allocate 16MB of memory for it, use the following settings in an option file:

```
[mysqld]
query_cache_type=1
query_cache_size=16M
```

The amount of memory indicated by `query_cache_size` is allocated even if `query_cache_type` is zero. To avoid wasting memory, set the size to zero unless you plan to enable the cache. Note that a size of zero effectively disables the cache even if `query_cache_type` is non-zero.

Individual clients begin with query caching behavior in the state indicated by the server's default caching mode. A client can change the default caching mode for its queries by using this statement:

```
SET query_cache_type = val;
```

val can be 0, 1, or 2, which have the same meanings as when setting the query_cache_type variable at server startup. In a SET statement, the symbolic values OFF, ON, and DEMAND are synonyms for 0, 1, and 2.

A client also can control caching of individual queries by adding a modifier following the SELECT keyword. SELECT SQL_CACHE for a cacheable query causes the result to be cached if the cache mode is ON or DEMAND. SELECT SQL_NO_CACHE causes the result not to be cached.

Suppression of caching can be useful for queries that retrieve information from a constantly changing table. In that case, the cache is unlikely to be of much use. Suppose that you're logging Web server requests to a table in MySQL, and also that you periodically run a set of summary queries on the table. For a reasonably busy Web server, new rows will be inserted into the table frequently and thus any query results cached for the table become invalidated quickly. The implication is that although you might issue the summary queries repeatedly, it's unlikely that the query cache will be of any value for them. Under such circumstances, it makes sense to issue the queries using the SQL_NO_CACHE modifier to tell the server not to bother caching their results.

5.6.3 Hardware Optimizations

The earlier part of this chapter discusses techniques that help improve your server's performance regardless of your hardware configuration. You can of course get better hardware to make your server run faster. But not all hardware-related changes are equally valuable. When assessing what kinds of hardware improvements you might make, the most important principles are the same as those that apply to server parameter tuning: Put as much information in fast storage as possible, and keep it there as long as possible.

The following items describe several aspects of hardware configuration that can be modified to improve server performance.

Install more memory into your machine. This enables you to configure larger values for the server's cache and buffer sizes, which enables it to keep data in memory longer and with less need to fetch information from disk.

Reconfigure your system to remove all disk swap devices. This may be possible if you have enough RAM to do all swapping into a memory filesystem. Otherwise, some systems will continue to swap to disk even if you have sufficient RAM for swapping.

Add faster disks to improve I/O latency. Seek time is typically the primary determinant of performance here. It's slow to move the heads laterally; after the heads have been positioned, reading blocks off the track is fast by comparison. However, if you have a choice between adding more memory and getting faster disks, add more memory. Memory is always faster than your disks, and adding memory enables you to use larger caches, which reduces disk activity.

Take advantage of parallelism by redistributing disk activity across physical devices. If you can split reading or writing across multiple physical devices, it will be quicker than reading and writing everything from the same device. For example, if you store databases on one device and logs on another, writing to both devices at once will be faster than if databases and logs share the same device. Note that using different partitions on the same physical device doesn't count as parallelism. That won't help because they'll still contend for the same physical resource (disk heads). The procedure for moving logs and databases is described in Section 11.3, "Relocating Data Directory Contents."

Before you relocate data to a different device, make sure that you understand your system's load characteristics. If there's some other major activity already taking place on a particular physical device, putting a database there may actually make performance worse. For example, you may not realize any overall benefit if you process a lot of Web traffic and move a database onto the device where your Web server document tree is located.

Use of RAID devices can give you some advantages of parallelism as well.

Use multi-processor hardware. For a multi-threaded application like the MySQL server, multi-processor hardware can execute multiple threads at the same time.

6

Introduction to MySQL Programming

This chapter describes some of the reasons for writing your own MySQL-based programs rather than using the standard client programs included in MySQL distributions. It also gives a conceptual overview of the interfaces we'll use for the three languages covered in the following chapters (C, Perl, and PHP), and discusses factors to consider when choosing a language for a program.

6.1 Why Write Your Own MySQL Programs?

MySQL distributions include a set of client programs. For example, `mysqldump` exports table definitions and contents, `mysqlimport` loads data files into tables, `mysqladmin` performs administrative operations, and `mysql` lets you interact with the server to execute arbitrary SQL statements.

The standard client programs handle many of the most common tasks that MySQL users need to perform, but applications sometimes have requirements that are outside the capabilities of those clients. To address this issue, the MySQL server has a client application programming interface (API) that gives you the flexibility to satisfy whatever specialized requirements your applications may have. The client API provides access to the MySQL server and opens up possibilities limited only by your own imagination.

In this part of the book, we'll discuss what you need to know to write MySQL-based programs for accessing your databases. To understand what you gain by writing your own programs, consider what you can accomplish that way in comparison to using the capabilities of the `mysql` client and its no-frills interface to the MySQL server:

- **You can customize input handling.** With `mysql`, you enter raw SQL statements. With your own programs, you can provide input methods for the user that are more intuitive and easier to use. Your program can eliminate the need for its users to know SQL, or even to be aware of the role of the database in the task being performed. Input collection can be something as rudimentary as a command-line interface that prompts the user and reads a value, or a more sophisticated screen-based entry form implemented using a screen management package such as `curses` or S-Lang, an X window using Tcl/Tk, or a form in a Web page.

For most people, it's a lot easier to specify search parameters by filling in a form than by issuing a `SELECT` statement. For example, a real estate agent looking for houses in a certain price range, style, or location just wants to enter search parameters into a form and get back the qualifying offerings with a minimum of fuss. Similar considerations apply for entering new rows or updating existing rows: A keyboard operator in a data entry department should need to know only the values to be entered into rows, not the SQL syntax for `INSERT`, `REPLACE`, or `UPDATE`.

- **You can validate input provided by the user.** For example, you can check dates to make sure they conform to the format that MySQL expects, or you can require certain fields to be filled in. This enhances the safety and security of your applications.

- **You can generate input automatically.** Some applications might not even involve a human user, such as when input for MySQL is generated by another program. You might configure your Web server to write log entries to MySQL rather than to a file, or set up a system-monitoring program that runs periodically and records status information to a database.

- **You can customize your output.** `mysql` output is essentially unformatted; you have a choice of tab-delimited or tabular style. If you want nicer-looking output, you must format it yourself. This might range from something as simple as printing "Missing" rather than `NULL` to more complex report-generation requirements. Consider the following report:

```
State  City        Sales
-------------------------------
AZ     Mesa         $94,384.24
       Phoenix      $17,328.28
       --------------------------
       Subtotal    $117,712.52
===============================
CA     Los Angeles $118,198.18
       Oakland      $38,838.36
       --------------------------
       Subtotal    $157,036.54
===============================
       TOTAL       $274,749.06
```

This report includes several specialized elements:

- Customized headers.

- Suppression of repeating values in the `state` column so that the values are printed only when they change.

- Subtotal and total calculations.

- Formatting of numbers, such as `94384.24`, to print as dollar amounts, such as `$94,384.24`.

  Another common task involving complex formatting is invoice production, where you need to associate each invoice header with information about the customer and about each item ordered. This kind of report can easily exceed `mysql`'s formatting capabilities.

  For some types of tasks, you may not want to produce any output at all. Perhaps you're simply retrieving information to calculate a result that you insert back into another database table. Or you want the output to go somewhere other than to the user running the query. For example, if you're extracting names and email addresses to feed automatically into a process that generates form letters for bulk email, your program does produce output, but it consists of messages that go to the mail recipients, not to the person running the program.

- **You can work around constraints imposed by the nature of SQL itself.** For the most part, SQL scripts consist of a set of statements executed one at a time from beginning to end, with minimal error checking. If you execute a file of SQL queries using `mysql` in batch mode, `mysql` either quits after the first error, or, if you specify the `--force` option, executes all the queries indiscriminately, no matter how many errors occur. By writing your own program, it's possible to selectively adapt to the success or failure of queries by providing flow control around statement-execution operations. You can make execution of one query contingent on the success or failure of another, or make decisions about what to do next based on the result of a previous query.

  It is true that MySQL supports stored programs, which provides additional flexibility at the SQL level by means of flow-control and error-handling constructs. However, these constructs are not as flexible as those provided by general-purpose programming languages.

  SQL has very limited persistence across statements. It's difficult to use the results from one query and apply them to another or to tie together the results of multiple queries. `LAST_INSERT_ID()` can be used to get the `AUTO_INCREMENT` value that was most recently generated by a prior statement, and user variables can be assigned values and referred to later. But that's about all. This limitation makes certain common operations difficult to perform using SQL alone, such as retrieving a set of rows and using each one as the basis for a complex series of subsequent operations. If you retrieve a list of customers and then look up a detailed credit history for each one, the process may involve several queries per customer.

  In general, a tool other than `mysql` is needed for tasks that involve master-detail relationships and have complex output-formatting requirements. A program provides the "glue" that links queries together and enables you to use the output from one query as the input to another.

- **You can integrate MySQL into any application.** Many programs stand to benefit by exploiting the capability of a database to provide information. The client-programming interface gives you the means to do this. An application that must verify a customer number or check whether an item is present in inventory can do so by issuing a quick query. A Web application that enables a client to ask for all books by a certain author can look them up in a database and send the results to the client's browser.

  It's possible to achieve a kind of rudimentary "integration" of MySQL into an application by using a shell script that invokes `mysql` with an input file containing SQL statements, and then postprocessing the output using other utilities. But that can become ugly, especially as your task becomes more involved. It may also produce a sense of "this works, but it feels wrong" as the application grows by accretion into a messy patchwork. In addition, the process-creation overhead of a shell script that runs other commands may be more than you want to incur. It can be more effective to use the client interface to interact with the MySQL server directly, extracting exactly the information you want as you need it at each phase of your application's execution.

Chapter 1, "Getting Started with MySQL," enumerated several goals with respect to our `sampdb` sample database that require us to write programs to interact with the MySQL server. Some of these goals are shown in the following list:

- Format the Historical League member directory for printing
- Enable online presentation and searching of the member directory
- Send membership renewal notices by email
- Easily enter student scores into the gradebook using a Web browser

One issue that we'll consider in some detail is the question of how to integrate MySQL's capabilities into a Web environment. MySQL provides no direct support for Web applications, but by combining MySQL with appropriate tools, you can issue queries from your Web server on behalf of a client user and report the results to the user's browser. This enables your databases to be accessed easily over the Web.

There are two complementary perspectives on the marriage of MySQL and the Web:

- **Use a Web server to provide enhanced access to MySQL.** In this case, your main interest is your database, and you want to use the Web as a tool to gain easier access to your data. This is the point of view that a MySQL administrator would take. The place of a database in such a scenario is explicit and obvious because it's the focus of your interest. For example, you can write Web pages that enable you to see a list of the tables in your database, and to examine the structure or contents of each one.

- **Use MySQL to enhance the capabilities of your Web server.** In this case, your primary interest is your Web site, and you may want to use MySQL as a tool for making your site's content more valuable to the people who visit it. This is the point of view a Web developer would take. For example, if you run a message board or discussion list at the site, you can use a database to keep track of the messages. The role of MySQL in this case is more subtle; users of the site might not even be aware that a database plays a part in the services the site offers.

These perspectives need not be mutually exclusive. For example, in the Historical League scenario, we'll use the Web as a means for members to gain easy access to the contents of the membership directory by making entries available online. That is a use of the Web to provide access to the database. At the same time, adding directory content to the League's Web site increases the site's value to members. That is a use of the database to enhance the services provided at the site.

No matter how you view the integration of MySQL with the Web, the implementation is similar. You connect your Web site front end to your MySQL back end, using the Web server as an intermediary. The Web server collects information from a client user, sends it to the MySQL server in the form of a query, and then retrieves the result and returns it to the client's browser for viewing.

You don't have to put your data online, of course, but often there are benefits to doing so, particularly in comparison with accessing your data via the standard MySQL client programs:

- People accessing your data through the Web can use whichever browser they prefer, on whatever platform they prefer. They're not limited to systems on which the standard MySQL client programs run. No matter how widespread the MySQL clients are, Web browsers are more so.

- The interface for a Web application can be made simpler to use than that of a standalone command-line MySQL client.

- A Web interface can be customized to the requirements of a particular application. The MySQL clients are general-purpose tools with a fixed interface.

- Dynamic Web pages extend MySQL's capabilities to do things that are difficult or impossible to do using only the standard MySQL clients. For example, you can't really use them to put together an application that incorporates a shopping cart.

Any programming language can be used to write Web-based applications, but some are more suitable than others. We'll consider this issue in Section 6.3, "Choosing an API."

6.2 APIs Available for MySQL

The MySQL server has a low-level "native" client-server protocol that defines how client programs establish connections to and communicate with it. Clients can use this protocol at various levels of abstraction:

- To facilitate application development, MySQL provides a client library written in the C programming language that enables you to access MySQL databases from within any C program. The client library implements an application programming interface (API) consisting of a set of data structures and functions that map onto native protocol operations. The C API provided by this library is much more convenient to work with than the native protocol.

- MySQL interfaces for other languages can link the C client library into the language processor. The client library thus provides the means whereby MySQL bindings for other languages can be built on top of the C API. This type of interface exists for Perl, PHP, Python, Ruby, C++, Tcl, and others.

- There are also interfaces for other languages that implement the native client-server protocol directly rather than using the C library to handle communication. These exist for Java, PHP, and Ruby, for example.

Each language binding defines its own interface that specifies the rules for accessing MySQL. There is insufficient space here to discuss all of the APIs available for MySQL. Instead, we'll concentrate on three of the most popular APIs:

- **The C client library API.** This is the primary programming interface to MySQL. It's used, for example, to implement the standard clients in the MySQL distribution, such as `mysql`, `mysqladmin`, and `mysqldump`.

- **The DBI (Database Interface) API for Perl.** DBI is implemented as a Perl module that interfaces with other modules at the DBD (Database Driver) level, each of which provides access to a specific database engine. The particular DBD module used here is the one that provides MySQL support. We'll use MySQL with DBI to create standalone scripts to be invoked from the command line and scripts to be invoked by a Web server to provide Web access to MySQL.

- **The PHP API.** PHP is a server-side scripting language that provides a convenient way of embedding programs in Web pages. Such a page is processed by PHP on the server host before being sent to the client, which enables the script to generate dynamic content, such as including the result of a MySQL query into the page. Like DBI, PHP includes support for accessing several database engines in addition to MySQL. It has engine-specific interfaces, and interfaces that are more engine-independent. This book uses one of the latter, known as PHP Data Objects (PDO).

The present chapter provides a comparative overview of these three APIs to describe their general characteristics and to give you an idea why you might choose one over another for particular applications. Each of the following three chapters discusses one of the APIs in detail.

There's no reason to consider yourself locked into a single API, of course. Get to know several APIs and arm yourself with the knowledge that enables you to choose between them wisely. If you have a large project with several components, you might use multiple APIs and write some parts in one language and other parts in another language, depending on which one is most appropriate for each piece of the job. You may also find it instructive to implement an application in several ways if you have time. This gives you direct experience with different APIs as they apply to your own applications.

If you do not have the software required for using any of the APIs, see Appendix A, "Obtaining and Installing Software."

Should you be interested in additional MySQL programming information beyond what the following chapters provide, other books are available. The two with which I am most familiar (because I wrote them) are *MySQL and Perl for the Web* (New Riders, 2001) and *MySQL Cookbook*, second edition (O'Reilly, 2006). The first provides extensive coverage of the use of MySQL and DBI in Web environments. The second discusses how to write MySQL programs using Perl DBI, the PHP PEAR DB module, Ruby DBI (similar to Perl DBI), Python's DB-API interface, and the Java JDBC interface. If you're interested specifically in Java, see *MySQL and Java Developer's Guide* (Matthews, Cole, and Gradecki; Wiley, 2003). One of the authors (Mark Matthews) is the creator of MySQL Connector/J, the official Java interface for MySQL.

6.2.1 The C API

The C API is used within the context of compiled C programs. It's a client library that provides an interface for talking to the MySQL server, giving you the capabilities you need for establishing a connection to and conversing with the server.

The C clients provided in the MySQL distribution are based on this API. The C client library also serves as the basis for most of the MySQL bindings for other languages. For example, the MySQL-specific driver for the Perl DBI module is made MySQL-aware by linking in the code for the MySQL C client library.

6.2.2 The Perl DBI API

The DBI API is used within the context of applications written for the Perl scripting language. This API tries to work with as many databases as possible, while at the same time hiding database-specific details from the script writer. DBI does this using Perl modules that work together in a two-level architecture (see Figure 6.1):

- The DBI (database interface) level provides the general-purpose interface for client scripts. This level provides an abstraction that does not refer to specific database engines.

- The DBD (database driver) level provides support for various database engines by means of drivers that are engine specific. The DBD-level module that implements DBI support for MySQL is named DBD::mysql.

The DBI architecture enables you to write applications in relatively generic fashion. When you write a DBI script, you use a standard set of database-access calls. The DBI layer invokes the proper driver at the DBD level to handle your requests, and the driver handles the specific issues involved in communicating with the particular database server you want to use. The DBD level passes data returned from the server back up to the DBI

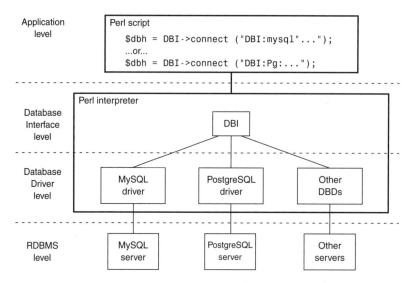

Figure 6.1   DBI architecture.

layer, which presents the data to your application. The form of the data is consistent no matter the database from which the data originated.

From the application writer's point of view, the result is an interface that hides differences between database engines, yet works with a wide variety of engines—as many as there are drivers for. DBI provides a consistent client interface that increases portability because you can access each database engine in a uniform fashion.

The one aspect of script writing that is necessarily engine-specific occurs when you connect to a database server, because you must indicate which driver to use to establish the connection. For example, to use a MySQL database, you connect like this:

```
$dbh = DBI->connect ("DBI:mysql:...");
```

To use PostgreSQL or Oracle instead, connect like this:

```
$dbh = DBI->connect ("DBI:Pg:...");
$dbh = DBI->connect ("DBI:Oracle:...");
```

After you've made the connection, you don't need to make any specific reference to the driver. DBI and the driver itself work out the database-specific details.

That's the theory, anyway. However, you should be aware of two factors that work against DBI script portability:

- SQL implementations differ between RDBMS engines, and it's perfectly possible to write SQL statements for one engine that another will not understand. If your SQL is reasonably generic, your scripts will be correspondingly portable between engines. But if your SQL is engine dependent, your scripts will be, too. For example, if you use the MySQL-specific `SHOW VARIABLES` statement, your script won't work with other database servers.

- DBD modules often provide engine-specific types of information to enable script writers to use particular features of particular database systems. For example, the DBD for MySQL provides a way to access properties of the columns in a query result such as the maximum length of values in each column, whether columns are numeric, and so forth. Other database servers don't necessarily make analogous types of information available. DBD-specific features are antithetical to portability; by using them, you make it more difficult to use a script written for MySQL with other database systems.

Despite the potential of these two factors for making your scripts database specific, the DBI mechanism for providing database access in an abstract fashion is a reasonable means of achieving portability. It's up to you to decide how much you want to take advantage of nonportable features. As you will discover in Chapter 8, "Writing MySQL Programs Using Perl DBI," I make little effort to avoid MySQL-specific constructs provided by the MySQL DBD. That's because you should know what those constructs are so that you can decide for yourself whether to use them. For further information, see Appendix H, "Perl DBI API Reference," which lists all the MySQL-specific constructs.

6.2.3 The PHP API

Like Perl, PHP is a scripting language. Unlike Perl, PHP is designed less as a general-purpose language than as a language for writing Web applications. The PHP API is used primarily as a means of embedding executable scripts into Web pages. This makes it easy for Web developers to write pages with dynamically generated content. When a client browser sends a request for a PHP page to a Web server, PHP executes any script it finds in the page and replaces it with the script's output. The result is sent to the browser. This enables the page that actually appears in the browser to change according to the circumstances under which the page is requested. For example, when the following short PHP script is embedded in a Web page, it displays the IP number of the client host that requested the page:

```
<?php echo $_SERVER["REMOTE_ADDR"]; ?>
```

As a less trivial and more interesting application, you can use a script to provide up-to-the-minute information to visitors based on the contents of your database. The following example shows a simple script such as might be used at the Historical League Web site. The script issues a query to determine the current League membership count and reports it to the person visiting the site:

```
<html>
<head>
<title>U.S. Historical League</title>
</head>
<body bgcolor="white">
```

```
<p>Welcome to the U.S. Historical League Web Site.</p>
<?php
# USHL home page

try
{
  $dbh = new PDO("mysql:host=localhost;dbname=sampdb", "sampadm", "secret");
  $dbh->setAttribute (PDO::ATTR_ERRMODE, PDO::ERRMODE_EXCEPTION);
  $sth = $dbh->query ("SELECT COUNT(*) FROM member");
  $count = $sth->fetchColumn (0);
  print ("<p>The League currently has $count members.</p>");
  $dbh = NULL;  # close connection
}
catch (PDOException $e) { } # empty handler (catch but ignore errors)
?>
</body>
</html>
```

PHP scripts typically look like HTML pages with executable code embedded inside `<?php` and `?>` tags. A page can contain any number of code fragments. This provides an extremely flexible approach to script development. For example, you can write a PHP script as a normal HTML page initially to set up the general page framework, and then add code later to generate the dynamic parts of the page.

PHP actually has multiple types of database interfaces. Among these is a set of low-level libraries, each of which works with a single database engine and which make no effort to unify the interface to different engines the way DBI does. Instead, the interface to each engine looks much like the interface for the corresponding C library that implements the low-level API for that engine. For example, the names of the PHP functions that you use to access MySQL from within PHP scripts are very similar to the names of the functions in the MySQL C client library.

A more DBI-like approach is available for PHP by using the PHP Data Objects (PDO) extension. This extension provides a more abstract interface to database engines using a two-level architecture similar to that used by DBI. The PHP scripts in Chapter 9, "Writing MySQL Programs Using PHP," employ the PDO extension for database access.

6.3 Choosing an API

This section provides general guidelines to help you choose an API for various types of applications. It compares the capabilities of the C, DBI, and PHP APIs to give you some idea of their relative strengths and weaknesses, and to indicate when you might choose one over another.

I am not advocating any one of these languages over the others, although I do have my preferences. You will have your own preferences, too, as have the technical reviewers for this book. One reviewer felt that I should emphasize the importance of C for MySQL programming to a much greater extent, whereas another thought I should come down much harder on C programming and discourage its use. The lesson from these varying viewpoints is that you should weigh the factors discussed in this section and come to your own conclusions.

A number of considerations enter into assessing which API is most suitable for a particular task:

- **Intended execution environment.** The context in which you expect the application to be used.

- **Performance.** How efficiently applications perform when written in the API language.

- **Ease of development.** How convenient the API and its language make application writing.

- **Portability.** Whether the application will be used for database systems other than MySQL.

The following discussion further examines each of these factors. Be aware that some of the factors interact. For example, you want an application that performs well, but it might be just as important to use a language that lets you develop the application quickly even if it doesn't perform quite as efficiently.

6.3.1 Execution Environment

When you write an application, you generally have some idea of the environment in which it will be used. For example, it might be a report generator program that you invoke from the shell, or an accounts payable summary program that runs as a cron job at the end of each month. Commands run from the shell or from cron generally stand on their own and require little information from the execution environment. On the other hand, you might be writing an application intended to be invoked by a Web server. Such a program might expect to be able to extract very specific types of information from its execution environment: What browser is the client using? What parameters were entered into a mailing list subscription request form? Did the client supply the correct password for accessing personnel information?

Each API language varies in its suitability for writing applications in these differing environments:

- C is a general-purpose language, so in principle you can use it for anything. In practice, C tends to be used more often for standalone programs rather than for Web programming. One reason might be that it's not as easy to perform text processing and memory management in C as it is in Perl or in PHP, and those capabilities tend to be heavily used in Web applications.

- Perl, like C, is suitable for writing standalone programs. However, it also happens that Perl is quite useful for Web site development—for example, by using the

CGI.pm module. This makes Perl a handy language for writing applications that link MySQL with the Web. Such an application can interface to the Web via the CGI.pm module and interface to MySQL using DBI.

- PHP is intended by design for writing Web applications, so that's obviously the environment to which it is best suited. Furthermore, database access is one of PHP's biggest strengths, so it's a natural choice for Web applications that perform MySQL-related tasks. It's possible to use PHP as a standalone interpreter (for example, to execute scripts from the shell), but it's not used that way very much.

Given these considerations, C and Perl are the most likely candidate languages if you're writing a standalone application. For Web applications, Perl and PHP are most suitable. If you need to write both types of applications, but don't know any of these languages and want to learn as few as possible, Perl might be your best option.

6.3.2 Performance

All other things being equal, we prefer to have applications run as quickly as possible. However, the actual importance of performance tends to be related to the frequency with which a program is used. For a program that you run once a month as a `cron` job during the night, performance might not matter that much. On the other hand, if you run a program many times a second on a heavily used Web site, every bit of efficiency you gain can make a big difference. In the latter case, performance plays a significant role in the usefulness and appeal of your site. A slow site is annoying for visitors, no matter what the site is about, and if you depend on the site as a source of income, decreased performance translates directly into reduced revenue. You cannot service as many connections at a time, and visitors who tire of waiting give up and go elsewhere.

Performance assessment is a complex issue. The best indicator of how well your application will perform when written for a particular API is to write it under that API and try it. And the best comparative test is to implement multiple versions under different APIs to see how they stack up against each other. Of course, that's not how development usually works. More often, you just want to get your program written. After it's working, you can think about tuning it to see whether it can run faster or use less memory, or whether it has some other aspect that you can improve. But there are at least two general factors that you can count on as affecting performance in a relatively consistent way:

- Compiled programs execute more quickly than interpreted scripts.
- For interpreted languages used in a Web context, performance is better when the interpreter is invoked as a module that is part of the Web server itself rather than as a separate process.

6.3.2.1 Compiled Versus Interpreted Languages

As a general principle, compiled applications are more efficient, use less memory, and execute more quickly than an equivalent version of the program written in a scripting language. This is due to the overhead involved with the language interpreter that executes the scripts. C is compiled and Perl and PHP are interpreted, so C programs generally will run faster than Perl or PHP scripts. Thus, C might be the best choice for a heavily used program.

Other factors tend to diminish the distinction between compiled and interpreted programs. For one thing, writing in C generally gives you a faster program, but it's quite possible to write inefficient C programs. Writing a program in a compiled language is no automatic passport to better performance; it's still necessary to think about what you're doing. In addition, the difference between compiled and interpreted programs is lessened if a scripted application spends most of its time executing code in compiled MySQL client library routines that are linked into the interpreter engine.

6.3.2.2 Standalone Versus Module Versions of Language Interpreters

For Web-based applications, script language interpreters are usually used in one of two forms—at least for Apache, the Web server used in this book for writing Web applications:

- You can arrange for Apache to invoke the script interpreter as a separate process. In this mode of operation, when Apache needs to run a Perl or PHP script, it starts the corresponding interpreter and tells it to execute the script. In this case, Apache uses the interpreters as CGI programs—that is, it communicates with them using the Common Gateway Interface (CGI) protocol.

- The interpreter can be used as a module that is linked in directly to the Apache binary and that runs as part of the Apache process itself. In Apache terms, the Perl and PHP interpreters take the form of the `mod_perl` and `mod_php` modules.

Perl and PHP advocates will argue the speed advantages of their favorite interpreter, but all agree that the form in which the interpreter runs is a much bigger factor than the languages themselves. Either interpreter runs much faster as a module than as a standalone CGI application. With a standalone application, it's necessary to start up the interpreter each time a script is to be executed, so you incur a significant penalty in process-creation overhead. When used as a module within an already running Apache process, an interpreter's capabilities can be accessed from your Web pages instantly. This dramatically improves performance by reducing overhead and translates directly into an increased capacity to handle incoming requests and to dispatch them quickly.

The startup penalty for a standalone interpreter typically results in at least an order of magnitude poorer performance than the module interpreter. Interpreter startup cost is particularly significant when you consider that Web page serving typically involves quick transactions with light processing rather than substantial ones with a lot of processing. If you spend a lot of time just starting up and not very much actually executing the script, you're wasting most of your resources. It's like spending most of the day getting ready for work, arriving at 4 o'clock in the afternoon, and then going home at 5.

You might wonder why there is any benefit with the module versions of the interpreters—after all, you must still start up Apache itself, right? The savings comes from the fact that a given Apache process handles multiple requests. When Apache starts, it immediately spawns a pool of child processes to be used to handle incoming requests. When a request arrives that involves execution of a script, there is already an Apache process ready and waiting to handle it. Also, each instance of Apache services multiple requests, so the process startup cost is incurred only once per set of requests, not once per request. (Apache 2 can use multiple threads rather than separate processes to reduce the overhead even more.)

One potentially significant difference between Perl and PHP is that Perl has a bigger memory footprint; Apache processes are larger with `mod_perl` linked in than with `mod_php`. PHP was designed under the assumptions that it must live cooperatively within another process and that it might be activated and deactivated multiple times within the life of that process. Perl was designed to be run from the command line as a standalone program, not as a language meant to be embedded in a Web server process. This probably contributes to its larger memory footprint; as a module, Perl simply isn't running in its natural environment. Other factors that contribute to the larger footprint are script caching and additional Perl modules that scripts use. In both cases, more code is brought into memory and remains there for the life of the Apache process. (To minimize this problem, there are techniques that allow you to designate only certain Apache processes as enabled for `mod_perl`. That way, you incur the extra memory overhead only for those processes that execute Perl scripts. The `mod_perl` area of the Apache Web site has a good discussion of various strategies from which to choose. Visit http://perl.apache.org/docs/ for more information.)

The standalone version of a language interpreter does have one advantage over its module counterpart, in that you can arrange for it to run scripts under a different user ID. The module versions run scripts under the same user ID as the Web server, which is typically an account with minimal privileges for security reasons. That doesn't work very well for scripts that require specific privileges (for example, if you need to read or write protected files). You can combine the module and standalone approaches if you like: Use the module version by default and the standalone version for situations in which scripts need to run with the privileges of a particular user.

What this adds up to is that, whether you choose Perl or PHP, you should try to use it as an Apache module rather than by invoking a separate interpreter process. Reserve use of the standalone interpreter only for those cases that cannot be handled by the module, such as scripts that require special privileges. For these instances, you can process your script by using Apache's suEXEC mechanism to start up the interpreter under a given user ID.

6.3.3 Development Time

The factors just described affect the performance of your applications, but raw execution efficiency may not be your only goal. Your own time is important, too, as is ease of programming, so another factor to consider in choosing an API for MySQL programming is how quickly you can develop your applications. If you can write a Perl or PHP script in half the time it takes to develop the equivalent C program, you might elect not to use the C API, even if the resulting application doesn't run quite as fast. It's often reasonable to be less concerned about a program's execution time than about the time you spend writing it, particularly for applications that aren't executed frequently. An hour of your time is worth a lot more than an hour of machine time!

Generally, scripting languages enable you to get a program going more quickly, especially for working out a prototype of the finished application. At least two factors contribute to this. First, scripting languages tend to provide higher-level constructs than compiled languages. This enables you to think at a higher level of abstraction, so you can think about what you want to do rather than about the details involved in doing it. For example, PHP associative arrays and Perl hashes are great time savers for maintaining data involving key/value relationships (such as student ID/student name pairs). C has no such construct. If you wanted to implement it in C, you would need to write code to handle many low-level details involving issues such as memory management and string manipulation, and you would need to debug it. This takes time.

Second, the development cycle has fewer steps for scripting languages than for compiled languages. With C, you engage in an edit-compile-test cycle during application development. Every time you modify a program, you must recompile it before testing. With Perl and PHP, the development cycle is simply edit-test because you can run a script immediately after each modification with no compiling. On the other hand, the C compiler enforces more constraints on your program in the form of stricter type checking. The greater discipline imposed by the compiler can help you avoid bugs that you would not catch as easily in looser languages, such as Perl and PHP. If you misspell a variable name in C, the compiler will warn you. PHP and Perl won't do so unless you ask them to. These tighter constraints can be especially valuable as your applications become larger and more difficult to maintain.

In general, the tradeoff is the usual one between compiled and interpreted languages for development time versus performance: Do you want to develop the program using a compiled language so that it will execute more quickly when it runs, but spend more time writing it? Or do you want to write the program as a script so that you can get it running in the least amount of time, even at the cost of some execution speed?

It's also possible to combine the two approaches. Write a script as a "first draft" to quickly develop an application prototype to test out your logic and make sure the algorithms are appropriate. If the program proves useful and is executed frequently enough that performance becomes a concern, you can recode it as a compiled application. This gives you the best of both worlds: quick prototyping for initial development of the application, and the best performance for the final product.

In a strict sense, the Perl DBI and PHP APIs give you no capabilities that are not already present in the C client library. However, the environment in which MySQL capabilities are embedded is very different for C than for Perl or PHP. Consider what tasks you'll need to perform as you interact with the MySQL server and ask how much each API language will help you carry them out. Here are some examples:

- **Memory management.** In C, you find yourself working with `malloc()` and `free()` for any tasks involving dynamically allocated data structures. Perl and PHP handle that for you. For example, they allow arrays to grow in size automatically, and dynamic-length strings can be used without ever thinking about memory management.

- **Text manipulation.** Perl has the most highly developed capabilities in this area, and PHP runs a close second. C is very rudimentary by comparison, coming in a distant third.

Of course, in C you can write your own libraries to encapsulate tasks such as memory management and text processing into functions that make the job easier. But then you still have to debug them, and you want your algorithms to be efficient, too. In these respects, it's a fair bet that the algorithms in Perl and PHP for these things have had the benefit of being examined by many pairs of eyes, so generally they should be both well debugged and reasonably efficient. You can save your own time by taking advantage of the time that others have already put into the job. (On the other hand, if an interpreter does happen to have a bug, you may simply have to live with it or try to find a workaround until the problem is fixed. When you write in C, you have a finer level of control over the behavior of your program.)

The languages differ in how "safe" they are. The C API provides the lowest-level interface to the server and enforces the least policy. In this sense, it provides the least amount of safety net. If you execute API functions out of order, you may be lucky and get an "out-of-sync" error, or you may be unlucky and have your program crash. Perl and PHP both protect you pretty well. A script will fail if you don't do things in the proper order, but the interpreter won't crash. Another fertile source of crashing bugs in C programs is the use of dynamically allocated memory and pointers associated with them. Perl and PHP handle memory management for you, so your scripts are much less likely to die from memory management bugs.

Development time is affected by the amount of external support that is available for a language. C external support is available in the form of wrapper libraries that encapsulate MySQL C API functions into routines that are easier to use. Libraries that do this are available for both C and C++. Perl undoubtedly has the largest number of add-ons, in the form of Perl modules (these are similar in concept to Apache modules). There is even an infrastructure in place designed to make it easy to locate and obtain these modules (the CPAN, or Comprehensive Perl Archive Network). Using Perl modules, you gain access to all kinds of functions without writing a line of code. Want to write a script that generates a report from a database, and then mail it to someone as an attachment? Just visit `cpan.perl.org`, get one of the MIME modules, and you have instant attachment-generation capability. PHP has archives known as PEAR (PHP Extension and Application Repository) and PECL (PHP Extension Community Library), available at `pear.php.net` and `pecl.php.net`.

6.3.4 Portability

The question of portability has to do with how easily a program written to use MySQL can be modified to use a different database engine. This may be something you don't care about. However, unless you can predict the future, it is a little risky to say, "I'll never use this program with any database other than MySQL." Suppose that you get a different job and want to use your old programs, but your new employer uses a different database system? What then? If portability is a priority, you should consider the clear differences between APIs:

- DBI provides the most portable API because database independence is an explicit DBI design goal.
- PHP script portability is similar to DBI if you use the PDO database-access extension mentioned earlier. If you use only the low-level database-access libraries, PHP is less portable because it doesn't provide the same sort of uniform interface to various database engines that DBI does. The PHP function calls for each supported database tend to resemble those in the corresponding underlying C API. To use a different engine, at a minimum you'll need to change the names of the database-related functions that you invoke. You may also have to revise your application's logic a bit as well because the interfaces for the various databases don't all work quite the same way.
- The C API provides the least portability between databases. By its very nature it is designed specifically for MySQL.

Portability in the form of database independence is especially important when you need to access multiple database systems within the same application. This can involve simple tasks such as moving data from one RDBMS to another, or more complex undertakings, such as generating a report based on information combined from a number of database systems.

Writing MySQL
Programs Using C

MySQL provides a client library written in the C programming language that you can use to write client programs that access MySQL databases. This library defines an application programming interface that includes the following facilities:

- Connection management routines that establish and terminate a session with a server
- Routines that construct SQL statements, send them to the server, and process the results
- Status-checking and error-reporting functions for determining the exact reason for an error when an API call fails
- Routines that help you process options given in option files or on the command line

This chapter shows how to use the C client library to write your own programs, using conventions that are reasonably consistent with those used by the client programs included in the MySQL distribution. I assume that you know something about programming in C, but I've tried not to assume that you're an expert.

The first part of this chapter develops a series of short programs. The series culminates in a simple program that serves as the framework for a client skeleton that does nothing but connect to and disconnect from the server. The reason for this is that although MySQL client programs are written for different purposes, one thing they all have in common is that they must establish a connection to the server.

The resulting skeleton program is generic, so it is usable as the basis for any number of other client programs. After developing it, we'll pause to consider how to execute various kinds of SQL statements. Initially, we'll discuss how to handle specific hardcoded statements, and then develop code that can be used to process arbitrary statements. After that, we'll add some statement-processing code to the skeleton to develop another program that's similar to the mysql client and that can be used to issue statements interactively.

The chapter then demonstrates several other activities that the client library enables you to perform:

- Writing client programs that communicate with the server over secure connections using the Secure Sockets Layer (SSL) protocol
- Writing applications that use `libmysqld`, the embedded server library
- Sending multiple statements to the server at once and processing the result sets that come back
- Using server-side prepared statements

This chapter discusses only those functions and data types from the client library that we need for the example programs. For a comprehensive listing of all functions and types, see Appendix G, "C API Reference" (online). You can use that appendix as a reference for further background on any part of the client library you're trying to use.

The example programs are available online so that you can try them directly without typing them in yourself. They are part of the `sampdb` distribution, located under the `capi` directory of the distribution. See Appendix A, "Obtaining and Installing Software," for downloading instructions.

Where to Find Example Programs

A common question on the MySQL mailing list is "Where can I find some examples of clients written in C?" The answer, of course, is "right here in this book." But something many people seem not to consider is that a MySQL source distribution includes several client programs that happen to be written in C (`mysql`, `mysqladmin`, and `mysqldump`, for example). Because the distribution is readily available, it provides you with quite a bit of example client code. Therefore, if you haven't already done so, grab a source distribution sometime and take a look at the programs in its `client` and `tests` directories.

7.1 Compiling and Linking Client Programs

This section describes the steps involved in compiling and linking a program that uses the MySQL client library. The commands to build clients vary somewhat from system to system, and you might need to modify the commands shown here a bit. However, the description is general and you should be able to apply it to most client programs you write.

When you write a MySQL client program in C, you'll need a C compiler, obviously. The examples shown here use `gcc`, which is probably the most common compiler used on Unix. You'll also need the MySQL header files and client library.

The header files and client library constitute the basis of MySQL client programming support. If MySQL was installed on your system from a source or binary distribution, client programming support should have been installed as part of that process. If RPM packages were used, this support won't be present unless you installed the developer RPM. Should you need to obtain the MySQL header files and library, see Appendix A.

To compile and link a client program, you might need to specify where the MySQL header files and client library are located, because often they are not installed in locations that the compiler and linker search by default. For the following examples, suppose that the header file and client library locations are `/usr/local/include/mysql` and `/usr/local/lib/mysql`. Modify the pathnames as appropriate for your own system.

To tell the compiler how to find the MySQL header files when you compile a source file into an object file, pass it an `-I` option that names the appropriate directory. For example, to compile `myclient.c` to produce `myclient.o`, you might use a command like this:

```
% gcc -c -I/usr/local/include/mysql myclient.c
```

To tell the linker where to find the client library and what its name is, pass `-L/usr/local/lib/mysql` and `-lmysqlclient` arguments when you link the object file to produce an executable binary, as follows:

```
% gcc -o myclient myclient.o -L/usr/local/lib/mysql -lmysqlclient
```

If your client consists of multiple files, name all the object files on the link command.

The link step may result in error messages having to do with functions that cannot be found. In such cases, you'll need to supply additional `-l` options to name the libraries containing the functions. If you see a message about `compress()` or `uncompress()`, try adding `-lz` or `-lgz` to tell the linker to search the `zlib` compression library:

```
% gcc -o myclient myclient.o -L/usr/local/lib/mysql -lmysqlclient -lz
```

If the message names the `floor()` function, add `-lm` to link in the math library. You might need to add other libraries as well. For example, you'll probably need `-lsocket` and `-lnsl` on Solaris.

As an alternative to figuring out the proper flags for compiling and linking MySQL programs yourself, you can use the `mysql_config` utility to do it for you. For example, the utility might indicate that the following options are needed:

```
% mysql_config --include
-I'/usr/local/mysql/include/mysql'
% mysql_config --libs
-L'/usr/local/mysql/lib/mysql' -lmysqlclient -lz -lcrypt -lnsl -lm
```

To use `mysql_config` directly within your compile or link commands, invoke it within backticks:

```
% gcc -c `mysql_config --include` myclient.c
% gcc -o myclient myclient.o `mysql_config --libs`
```

The shell will execute `mysql_config` and substitute its output into the surrounding command, which automatically provides the appropriate flags for `gcc`.

If you don't use `make` to build programs, I suggest you learn how so that you won't have to type a lot of program-building commands manually. Suppose that you have a client program, `myclient`, that comprises two source files, `main.c` and `lib.c`, and a header file, `myclient.h`. You might write a simple `Makefile` to build this program as follows. Note that indented lines are indented with tabs; if you use spaces, the `Makefile` will not work.

```
CC = gcc
INCLUDES = -I/usr/local/include/mysql
LIBS = -L/usr/local/lib/mysql -lmysqlclient

all: myclient

main.o: main.c myclient.h
        $(CC) -c $(INCLUDES) main.c
lib.o: lib.c myclient.h
        $(CC) -c $(INCLUDES) lib.c

myclient: main.o lib.o
        $(CC) -o myclient main.o lib.o $(LIBS)

clean:
        rm -f myclient main.o lib.o
```

Using the `Makefile`, you can rebuild your program whenever you modify any of the source files simply by running `make`, which displays and executes the necessary commands:

```
% make
gcc -c -I/usr/local/mysql/include/mysql myclient.c
gcc -o myclient myclient.o -L/usr/local/mysql/lib/mysql -lmysqlclient
```

That's easier and less error prone than typing long `gcc` commands. A `Makefile` also makes it easier to modify the build process. For example, if your system is one for which you need to link in additional libraries such as the math and compression libraries, edit the `LIBS` line in the `Makefile` to add `-lm` and `-lz`:

```
LIBS = -L/usr/local/lib/mysql -lmysqlclient -lm -lz
```

If you need other libraries, add them to the `LIBS` line as well. Thereafter when you run `make`, it will use the updated value of `LIBS` automatically.

Another way to change `make` variables other than editing the `Makefile` is to specify them on the command line. For example, if your C compiler is named `cc` rather than `gcc`, you can say so like this:

```
% make CC=cc
```

If `mysql_config` is available, you can use it to avoid writing literal include file and library directory pathnames in the `Makefile`. Write the `INCLUDES` and `LIBS` lines as follows instead:

```
INCLUDES = ${shell mysql_config --include}
LIBS = ${shell mysql_config --libs}
```

When `make` runs, it executes each `mysql_config` command and uses its output to set the corresponding variable value. The `${shell}` construct shown here is supported by GNU `make`; you might need to use a somewhat different syntax if your version of `make` isn't based on GNU `make`.

   If you're using an integrated development environment (IDE), you might not use a
`Makefile` at all. The details will depend on your particular IDE.

7.2 Connecting to the Server

Our first MySQL client program is about as simple as can be: It connects to a MySQL
server, disconnects, and exits. That's not very useful in itself, but you have to know how to
do it because you must be connected to a server before you can do anything with a
MySQL database. Connecting to a server is such a common operation that code you develop to establish the connection is code you'll use in every client program you write. Besides, this task gives us something simple to start with. The code can be fleshed out later to
do something more useful.

   Our first client program, `connect1`, consists of a single source file, `connect1.c`:

```
/*
 * connect1.c - connect to and disconnect from MySQL server
 */


#include <my_global.h>
#include <my_sys.h>
#include <mysql.h>

static char *opt_host_name = NULL;      /* server host (default=localhost) */
static char *opt_user_name = NULL;      /* username (default=login name) */
static char *opt_password = NULL;       /* password (default=none) */
static unsigned int opt_port_num = 0;   /* port number (use built-in value) */
static char *opt_socket_name = NULL;    /* socket name (use built-in value) */
static char *opt_db_name = NULL;        /* database name (default=none) */
static unsigned int opt_flags = 0;      /* connection flags (none) */

static MYSQL *conn;                     /* pointer to connection handler */

int
main (int argc, char *argv[])
{
  MY_INIT (argv[0]);
  /* initialize client library */
  if (mysql_library_init (0, NULL, NULL))
  {
    fprintf (stderr, "mysql_library_init() failed\n");
    exit (1);
  }
  /* initialize connection handler */
  conn = mysql_init (NULL);
  if (conn == NULL)
  {
    fprintf (stderr, "mysql_init() failed (probably out of memory)\n");
```

```
    exit (1);
  }
  /* connect to server */
  if (mysql_real_connect (conn, opt_host_name, opt_user_name, opt_password,
      opt_db_name, opt_port_num, opt_socket_name, opt_flags) == NULL)
  {
    fprintf (stderr, "mysql_real_connect() failed\n");
    mysql_close (conn);
    exit (1);
  }
  /* disconnect from server, terminate client library */
  mysql_close (conn);
  mysql_library_end ();
  exit (0);
}
```

The source file begins by including the header files `my_global.h`, `my_sys.h`, and `mysql.h`. Depending on what a MySQL client program does, it might need to include other header files as well, but these three usually are the bare minimum:

- `my_global.h` takes care of including several other header files that are likely to be generally useful, such as `stdio.h`. It also includes Windows compatibility information if you're compiling the program on Windows. (You might not intend to build the program under Windows yourself, but if you plan to distribute your code, using `my_global.h` will help anyone else who does compile under Windows.)

- `my_sys.h` contains various portability macros and definitions for structures and functions used by the client library.

- `mysql.h` defines the primary MySQL-related constants and data structures.

The order of inclusion is important; `my_global.h` is intended to be included before any other MySQL-specific header files.

Next, the program declares a set of variables corresponding to the parameters that need to be specified when connecting to the server. For this client, the parameters are hard-wired to have default values. Later, we'll develop a more flexible approach that enables the defaults to be overridden using values specified either in option files or on the command line. (That's why the names all begin with `opt_`; the intent is that eventually those variables will become settable through command options.) The program also declares a pointer to a `MYSQL` structure that will serve as a connection handler.

The `main()` function of the program establishes and terminates the connection to the server. Making a connection is a two-step process:

1. Call `mysql_init()` to obtain a connection handler.

2. Call `mysql_real_connect()` to establish a connection to the server.

When you pass `NULL` to `mysql_init()`, it automatically allocates a `MYSQL` structure, initializes it, and returns a pointer to it. The `MYSQL` data type is a structure containing information about a connection. Variables of this type are called "connection handlers."

Another approach is to pass a pointer to an existing MYSQL structure. In this case, mysql_init() initializes that structure and returns a pointer to it without allocating the structure itself.

mysql_real_connect() takes about a zillion parameters:

- A pointer to the connection handler. This should be the value returned by mysql_init().

- The server host. This value is interpreted in a platform-specific way. On Unix, if you specify a string containing a hostname or IP number, the client connects to the given host by using a TCP/IP connection. If you specify NULL or the host "localhost", the client connects to the server running on the local host by using a Unix socket file.

  On Windows, the behavior is similar, except that for "localhost", a shared-memory or TCP/IP connection is used rather than a Unix socket file connection. On Windows, the connection is attempted to the local server using a named pipe if the host is "." or NULL and the server supports named-pipe connections.

- The username and password for the MySQL account to be used. If the name is NULL, the client library sends your login name to the server (or ODBC, for Windows). If the password is NULL, no password is sent.

- The name of the database to select as the default database after the connection has been established. If this value is NULL, no database is selected.

- The port number. This is used for TCP/IP connections. A value of 0 tells the client library to use the default port number.

- The socket filename. On Unix, the name is used for Unix socket file connections. On Windows, the name is interpreted as the name to use for a pipe connection. A value of NULL tells the client library to use the default socket (or pipe) name.

- A flags value. The connect1 program passes a value of 0 because it isn't using any special connection options.

You can find more information about mysql_real_connect() in Appendix G (online). The description there discusses in more detail issues such as how the hostname parameter interacts with the port number and socket filename parameters, and lists the options that can be specified in the flags parameter. The appendix also describes mysql_options(), which you can use to specify other connection-related options prior to calling mysql_real_connect().

To terminate the connection, invoke mysql_close() and pass it a pointer to the connection handler. If you allocated the handler automatically by passing NULL to mysql_init(), mysql_close() automatically deallocates the handler when you terminate the connection. After calling mysql_close(), the handler cannot be used for further communication with the server.

In addition to the connection-establishment code, `connect1.c` uses three other calls:

- `MY_INIT()` is an initialization macro. It sets a global variable to point to the name of your program (which you pass as its argument), for use by MySQL libraries in error messages. It also calls `my_init()` to perform some setup operations.

- `mysql_library_init()` initializes the MySQL client library. You should call it before invoking any other `mysql_xxx()` functions.

- `mysql_library_end()` terminates use of the client library and performs any necessary cleanup. You should call it when you are done using the client library.

To try `connect1`, compile and link it using the instructions given earlier in the chapter for building client programs, and then run it. Under Unix, run the program like this:

```
% ./connect1
```

The leading ". /" might be necessary on Unix if your shell does not have the current directory (".") in its search path. If the current directory is in your search path, or you are using Windows, you can omit the ". /" from the command name:

```
% connect1
```

If `connect1` produces no output, it connected successfully. On the other hand, you might see something like this:

```
% ./connect1
mysql_real_connect() failed
```

This output indicates that no connection was established, but it doesn't tell you why. Very likely the reason for the failure is that the default connection parameters (hostname, username, and so on) are unsuitable. Assuming that is so, one way to fix the problem is to recompile the program after editing the initializers for the parameter variables and changing them to values that enable you to access your server. That might be beneficial in the sense that at least you'd be able to make a connection. But the program still would contain hardcoded values, which isn't very flexible if other people are to use it. It's also insecure because it exposes your password. You might think that the password becomes hidden when you compile your program into binary executable form, but it's not hidden at all if someone can run the `strings` utility on the binary. Also, anyone with read access to the source file can get the password with no work at all.

The preceding paragraph makes plain two significant shortcomings of the `connect1` program:

- The error output isn't very informative about specific causes of problems.

- There isn't a flexible way for the user who runs the program to specify connection parameters because they are hardwired into the source code. It would be better to give the user the ability to override the parameters by specifying them in an option file or on the command line.

The next section addresses these problems.

7.3 Handling Errors and Processing Command Options

Our next client, `connect2`, will be similar to `connect1` in the sense that it connects to the MySQL server, disconnects, and exits. However, `connect2` has two important differences:

- It provides more information when errors occur. `connect1` printed only a brief message if something went wrong, but we can do a better job of error reporting because the MySQL client library includes functions that return specific information about the causes of errors.

- It enables the user to specify connection parameters as options on the command line or in option files.

7.3.1 Checking for Errors

Let's consider the topic of error-handling first. To start off, I want to emphasize that it's important to check for errors whenever you invoke a MySQL function that can fail. It seems to be fairly common in programming texts to say "Error checking is left as an exercise for the reader." I suppose that this is because checking for errors is—let's face it—such a bore. Nevertheless, it is necessary for MySQL client programs to test for error conditions and respond to them appropriately. The client library functions that return status values do so for a reason, and you ignore them at your peril. For example, if a function returns a pointer to a data structure or NULL to indicate an error, you'd better check the return value. Attempts to use NULL later in the program when a pointer to a valid data structure is expected will lead to strange results or crash your program.

Failure to check return values is an unnecessary cause of programming difficulties and is a phenomenon that plays itself out frequently on the MySQL mailing lists. Typical questions are "Why does my program crash when it issues this statement?" or "How come my query doesn't return anything?" In many cases, the program in question didn't check whether the connection was established successfully before issuing the statement or didn't check to make sure the server successfully executed the statement before trying to retrieve the results.

Don't make the mistake of assuming that every client library call succeeds. If you don't check return values, you'll end up trying to track down obscure problems that occur in your programs, or users of your programs will wonder why those programs behave erratically, or both.

Routines in the MySQL client library that return a value generally indicate success or failure in one of two ways, depending on whether the return value is a pointer or an integer.

Pointer-valued functions return a non-NULL pointer for success and NULL for failure. (NULL in this context means "a C NULL pointer," not "a MySQL NULL column value.")

Of the client library routines we've used so far, `mysql_init()` and `mysql_real_connect()` both return a pointer to the connection handler to indicate success and NULL to indicate failure.

Integer-valued functions commonly return 0 for success and non-zero for failure. It's important not to test for specific non-zero values, such as -1. There is no guarantee that a client library function returns any particular value when it fails. On occasion, you may see code that tests a return value from a C API function mysql_*XXX*() incorrectly like this:

```
if (mysql_XXX () == -1)      /* this test is incorrect */
  fprintf (stderr, "something bad happened\n");
```

This test might work, and it might not. The MySQL API doesn't specify that any non-zero error return will be a particular value, other than that it (obviously) isn't zero. You should write the test like this:

```
if (mysql_XXX () != 0)       /* this test is correct */
  fprintf (stderr, "something bad happened\n");
```

Alternatively, write the test like this, which is equivalent and slightly simpler to write:

```
if (mysql_XXX ())            /* this test is correct */
  fprintf (stderr, "something bad happened\n");
```

If you look through the source code for MySQL itself, you'll find that generally it uses the second form of the test.

Not every API call returns a value. The other client routine we've used, mysql_close(), is one that does not. (How could it fail? And if it did, so what? You were done with the connection, anyway.)

When a client library call does fail, three calls in the API are useful for finding out why:

- mysql_error() returns a string containing an error message.
- mysql_errno() returns a MySQL-specific numeric error code.
- mysql_sqlstate() returns an SQLSTATE code. The SQLSTATE value is more vendor neutral because it is based on the ANSI SQL and ODBC standards.

The argument to each function is a pointer to the connection handler. You should call them immediately after an error occurs. If you issue another API call that returns a status, any error information you get from mysql_error(), mysql_errno(), or mysql_sqlstate() will apply to the later call instead.

Generally, the user of a program will find an error message more enlightening than either of the error codes, so if you report only one value, I suggest that it be the message. The examples in this chapter report all three values for completeness. However, it's a lot of work to write three function invocations every place an error might occur. Instead, let's write a utility function, print_error(), that prints an error message supplied by us as well as the error values provided by the MySQL client library routines. In other words, we won't write out the calls to the mysql_errno() mysql_error(), and mysql_sqlstate() functions like this each time an error test occurs:

```
if (...some MySQL function fails...)
{
  fprintf (stderr, "...some error message...:\nError %u (%s): %s\n",
          mysql_errno (conn), mysql_sqlstate (conn), mysql_error (conn));
```

```
}
```

It's easier to report errors by using a utility function that can be called like this instead:

```
if (...some MySQL function fails...)
{
  print_error (conn, "...some error message...");
}
```

`print_error()` prints the error message and calls the MySQL error functions. The `print_error()` call is simpler than the `fprintf()` call, so it's easier to write and it makes the program easier to read. Also, if `print_error()` is written to do something sensible even when `conn` is `NULL`, we can use it under circumstances such as when `mysql_init()` call fails. Then we won't have a mix of error-reporting calls—some to `fprintf()` and some to `print_error()`.

I can hear someone in the back row objecting: "Well, you don't really have to call every error function each time you want to report an error. You're deliberately overstating the tedium of reporting errors that way just so your utility function looks more useful. And you wouldn't really write out all that error-printing code a bunch of times anyway; you'd write it once, and then use copy and paste when you need it again." Those are reasonable objections, but I respond to them as follows:

- Even if you use copy and paste, it's easier to do so with shorter sections of code.
- If it's easy to report errors, you're more likely to be consistent about checking for them when you should.
- Whether or not you prefer to invoke all error functions each time you report an error, writing out all the error-reporting code the long way leads to the temptation to take shortcuts and be inconsistent when you do report errors. Wrapping the error-reporting code in a utility function that's easy to invoke lessens this temptation and improves coding consistency.
- If you ever do decide to modify the format of your error messages, it's a lot easier if you need to make the change only one place, rather than throughout your program. Or, if you decide to write error messages to a log file instead of (or in addition to) writing them to `stderr`, it's easier if you only have to change `print_error()`. This approach is less error prone and, again, lessens the temptation to do the job halfway and be inconsistent.
- If you use a debugger when testing your programs, putting a breakpoint in the error-reporting function is a convenient way to have the program break to the debugger when it detects an error condition.

For these reasons, programs in the rest of this chapter that need to check for MySQL-related errors use `print_error()` to report problems.

The following listing shows the definition of `print_error()`, which provides the benefits just discussed:

```
static void
print_error (MYSQL *conn, char *message)
{
  fprintf (stderr, "%s\n", message);
  if (conn != NULL)
  {
    fprintf (stderr, "Error %u (%s): %s\n",
             mysql_errno (conn), mysql_sqlstate (conn), mysql_error (conn));
  }
}
```

The part of connect2.c that will need to check for errors is similar to the correspon-ding code in connect1.c, and looks like this when we use print_error():

```
/* initialize connection handler */
conn = mysql_init (NULL);
if (conn == NULL)
{
  print_error (NULL, "mysql_init() failed (probably out of memory)");
  exit (1);
}

/* connect to server */
if (mysql_real_connect (conn, opt_host_name, opt_user_name, opt_password,
    opt_db_name, opt_port_num, opt_socket_name, opt_flags) == NULL)
{
  print_error (conn, "mysql_real_connect() failed");
  mysql_close (conn);
  exit (1);
}
```

The error-checking logic is based on the fact that both mysql_init() and mysql_real_connect() return NULL if they fail. Note that if mysql_init() fails, we pass NULL as the first argument to print_error(). That causes it not to invoke the MySQL error-reporting functions, because the connection handler passed to those functions can-not be assumed to contain any meaningful information. By contrast, if mysql_real_connect() fails, we do pass the connection handler to print_error(). The handler won't contain information that corresponds to a valid connection, but it *will* contain diagnostic information that can be extracted by the error-reporting functions. The handler also can be passed to mysql_close() to release any memory that may have been allocated auto-matically for it by mysql_init(). (Don't pass the handler to any other client routines, though! Because most of them assume a valid connection, your program may crash.)

The rest of the programs in this chapter perform error checking, and your own pro-grams should, too. It might seem like more work, but in the long run it's really less be-cause you spend less time tracking down subtle problems. I'll also take this approach of checking for errors in Chapter 8, "Writing MySQL Programs Using Perl DBI," and Chapter 9, "Writing MySQL Programs Using PHP."

7.3.2 Getting Connection Parameters at Runtime

Now we're ready to tackle the task of enabling users to specify connection parameters at runtime rather than using hardwired default parameters. The `connect1` client program had a significant shortcoming in that the connection parameters were written literally into the source code. To change any of those values, you'd have to edit the source file and recompile it. That's not very convenient, especially if you intend to make your program available for other people to use. One common way to specify connection parameters at runtime is by using command-line options. For example, the programs in the MySQL distribution accept parameters in either of two forms, as shown in the following table.

Parameter	Long Option Form	Short Option Form
Hostname	`--host=host_name`	`-h host_name`
Username	`--user=user_name`	`-u user_name`
Password	`--password or`	`-p or`
	`--password=your_pass`	`-pyour_pass`
Port number	`--port=port_num`	`-P port_num`
Socket name	`--socket=socket_name`	`-S socket_name`

For consistency with the standard MySQL clients, our `connect2` client program will accept those same formats. It's easy to do this because the client library includes support for option processing. In addition, `connect2` will have the capability to extract information from option files. This enables you to put connection parameters in `~/.my.cnf` (that is, the `.my.cnf` file in your home directory) or in any global option file. Then you don't have to specify the options on the command line each time you invoke the program. The client library makes it easy to check for MySQL option files and pull any relevant values from them. By adding only a few lines of code to your programs, you can make them option file-aware, and you don't have to reinvent the wheel by writing your own code to do it. (For a description of option file syntax, see Section F.2.2, "Option Files."

Before showing how option processing works in `connect2` itself, we'll develop a couple of programs that illustrate the general principles involved. These show how option handling works fairly simply and without the added complication of connecting to the MySQL server and processing statements.

> **Note**
>
> MySQL provides two other options that relate to connection establishment. `--protocol` specifies the connection protocol (TCP/IP, Unix socket file, and so on), and `--shared-memory-base-name` specifies the name of the shared memory to use for shared-memory connections on Windows. This chapter doesn't cover either of these options, but the `sampdb` distribution contains the source code for a program, `protocol`, that shows how to use them if you are interested.

7.3.2.1 Accessing Option File Contents

To read option files for connection parameter values, invoke the `load_defaults()` function. `load_defaults()` looks for option files, parses their contents for any option groups in which you're interested, and rewrites your program's argument vector (the `argv[]` array). It puts information from those option groups in the form of command line options at the beginning of `argv[]`. That way, the options appear to have been specified on the command line. When you parse the command options, you see the connection parameters in your normal option-processing code. The options are added to `argv[]` immediately after the command name and before any other arguments (rather than at the end), so that any connection parameters specified on the command line occur later than and thus override any options added by `load_defaults()`.

Here's a little program, `show_argv`, that demonstrates how to use `load_defaults()` and illustrates how it modifies your argument vector:

```
/*
 * show_argv.c - show effect of load_defaults() on argument vector
 */

#include <my_global.h>
#include <my_sys.h>
#include <mysql.h>

static const char *client_groups[] = { "client", NULL };

int
main (int argc, char *argv[])
{
int i;

  printf ("Original argument vector:\n");
  for (i = 0; i < argc; i++)
    printf ("arg %d: %s\n", i, argv[i]);

  MY_INIT (argv[0]);
  load_defaults ("my", client_groups, &argc, &argv);

  printf ("Modified argument vector:\n");
  for (i = 0; i < argc; i++)
    printf ("arg %d: %s\n", i, argv[i]);

  exit (0);
}
```

The option file-processing code involves several components:

- `client_groups[]` is an array of character strings indicating the names of the option file groups from which you want to obtain options. Client programs normally include at least `"client"` in the list (which represents the `[client]` group), but you can list as many groups as you like. The last element of the array must be NULL to indicate where the list ends.

- `MY_INIT()` is an initialization macro. We have used it before, but the important point here is that `MY_INIT()` calls `my_init()` to perform some setup operations required by `load_defaults()`.

- `load_defaults()` reads the option files. It takes four arguments: the prefix used in the names of your option files (this should always be `"my"`), the array listing the names of the option groups in which you're interested, and the addresses of your program's argument count and vector. Don't pass the values of the count and vector. Pass their addresses instead because `load_defaults()` needs to change their values. In particular, even though `argv` is already a pointer, you still pass `&argv`, that pointer's address.

`show_argv` prints its arguments twice to show the effect that `load_defaults()` has on the argument array. First it prints the arguments as they were specified on the command line. Then it calls `load_defaults()` and prints the argument array again.

To see how `load_defaults()` works, make sure that you have a `.my.cnf` file in your home directory with some settings specified for the `[client]` group. (On Windows, you can use the `C:\my.ini` file instead.) Suppose that the file looks like this:

```
[client]
user=sampadm
password=secret
host=some_host
```

If that is the case, executing `show_argv` should produce output like this:

```
% ./show_argv a b
Original argument vector:
arg 0: ./show_argv
arg 1: a
arg 2: b
Modified argument vector:
arg 0: ./show_argv
arg 1: --user=sampadm
arg 2: --password=secret
arg 3: --host=some_host
arg 4: a
arg 5: b
```

When `show_argv` prints the argument vector the second time, the values in the option file show up as part of the argument list. It's also possible that you'll see some options that were not specified on the command line or in your `~/.my.cnf` file. If this occurs, you will likely find that options for the `[client]` group are listed in a system-wide option file. This can happen because `load_defaults()` actually looks for option files in several locations. (For a list of these locations, see Section F.2.2, "Option Files.")

Client programs that use `load_defaults()` generally include `"client"` in the list of option group names (so that they get any general client settings from option files), but you can set up your option file-processing code to obtain options from other groups as well. Suppose that you want `show_argv` to read options in the `[client]` and `[show_argv]` groups. To accomplish this, find the following line in `show_argv.c`:

```
const char *client_groups[] = { "client", NULL };
```

Change the line to this:

```
const char *client_groups[] = { "show_argv", "client", NULL };
```

Then recompile `show_argv`, and the modified program will read options from both groups. To verify this, add a `[show_argv]` group to your `~/.my.cnf` file:

```
[client]
user=sampadm
password=secret
host=some_host

[show_argv]
host=other_host
```

With these changes, invoking `show_argv` again produces a result different from before:

```
% ./show_argv a b
Original argument vector:
arg 0: ./show_argv
arg 1: a
arg 2: b
Modified argument vector:
arg 0: ./show_argv
arg 1: --user=sampadm
arg 2: --password=secret
arg 3: --host=some_host
arg 4: --host=other_host
arg 5: a
arg 6: b
```

The order in which option values appear in the argument array is determined by the order in which they are listed in your option file, not the order in which option group names are listed in the `client_groups[]` array. This means you'll probably want to specify program-specific groups after the `[client]` group in your option file. That way, if you specify an option in both groups, the program-specific value takes precedence over the more general `[client]` group value. You can see this in the example just shown: The `host` option was specified in both the `[client]` and `[show_argv]` groups, but because the `[show_argv]` group appears last in the option file, its `host` setting appears later in the argument vector and takes precedence.

load_defaults() does not pick up values from your environment settings. If you want to use the values of environment variables such as MYSQL_TCP_PORT or MYSQL_UNIX_PORT, you must arrange for that yourself by using getenv(). I'm not going to add that capability to our clients, but here's a short code fragment that shows how to check the values of a couple of the standard MySQL–related environment variables:

```
extern char *getenv();
char *p;
int port_num = 0;
char *socket_name = NULL;

if ((p = getenv ("MYSQL_TCP_PORT")) != NULL)
  port_num = atoi (p);
if ((p = getenv ("MYSQL_UNIX_PORT")) != NULL)
  socket_name = p;
```

In the standard MySQL clients, environment variable values have lower precedence than values specified in option files or on the command line. If you want to check environment variables in your own programs and want to be consistent with that convention, check the environment before (not after) calling load_defaults() or processing command-line options.

load_defaults() and Security

On multiple-user systems, utilities such as the ps program can display argument lists from arbitrary processes, including those being run by other users. Because of this, you might be wondering if there are any process-snooping implications of load_defaults() taking passwords that it finds in option files and putting them in your argument list. This actually is not a problem because ps displays the original argv[] contents. Any password argument created by load_defaults() points to an area of memory that it allocates for itself. That area is not part of the original vector, so ps never sees it.

On the other hand, a password that is given on the command line *does* show up in ps. This is one reason why it's not a good idea to specify passwords that way. One precaution a program can take to help reduce the risk is to remove the password from the argument list as soon as it starts executing. Section 7.3.2.2, "Processing Command-Line Arguments," shows how to do that.

7.3.2.2 Processing Command-Line Arguments

Using load_defaults(), we can get all the connection parameters into the argument vector, but now we need a way to process the vector. The handle_options() function is designed for this. handle_options() is part of the MySQL client library, so you have access to it whenever you link in that library.

Some of the characteristics of the client library option-processing routines are as follows:

- Precise specification of the option type and range of legal values. For example, you can indicate not only that an option must have integer values, but that it must be positive and a multiple of 1024.

- Integration of help text to make it easy to print a help message by calling a standard library function. There is no need to write your own special code to produce a help message.

- Built-in support for the standard `--no-defaults`, `--print-defaults`, `--defaults-file`, and `--defaults-extra-file` options. (These options are described in Section F.2.2, "Option Files.")

- Support for a standard set of option prefixes, such as `--disable-`, `--enable-`, and `--loose-`, make it easier to implement boolean (on/off) and ignorable options. (This capability is not used in this chapter, but is described in Section F.2, "Specifying Program Options.")

To demonstrate how to use MySQL's option-handling facilities, this section describes a `show_opt` program that invokes `load_defaults()` to read option files and set up the argument vector, and then processes the result using `handle_options()`.

`show_opt` enables you to experiment with various ways of specifying connection parameters (whether in option files or on the command line), and to see the result by showing you what values would be used to make a connection to the MySQL server. `show_opt` is useful for getting a feel for what will happen in our next client program, `connect2`, which hooks up this option-processing code with code that actually does connect to the server.

To illustrate what happens at each phase of argument processing, `show_opt` performs the following actions:

1. Sets up default values for the hostname, username, password, and other connection parameters.

2. Prints the original connection parameter and argument vector values.

3. Calls `load_defaults()` to rewrite the argument vector to reflect option file contents, and then prints the resulting vector.

4. Calls the option processing routine `handle_options()` to process the argument vector, and then prints the resulting connection parameter values and whatever is left in the argument vector.

The following discussion explains how `show_opt` works, but first take a look at its source file, `show_opt.c`:

```
/*
 * show_opt.c - demonstrate option processing with load_defaults()
 * and handle_options()
 */

#include <my_global.h>
#include <my_sys.h>
#include <mysql.h>
#include <my_getopt.h>
```

```
static char *opt_host_name = NULL;      /* server host (default=localhost) */
static char *opt_user_name = NULL;      /* username (default=login name) */
static char *opt_password = NULL;       /* password (default=none) */
static unsigned int opt_port_num = 0;   /* port number (use built-in value) */
static char *opt_socket_name = NULL;    /* socket name (use built-in value) */

static const char *client_groups[] = { "client", NULL };

static struct my_option my_opts[] =    /* option information structures */
{
  {"help", '?', "Display this help and exit",
  NULL, NULL, NULL,
  GET_NO_ARG, NO_ARG, 0, 0, 0, 0, 0, 0},
  {"host", 'h', "Host to connect to",
  (uchar **) &opt_host_name, NULL, NULL,
  GET_STR, REQUIRED_ARG, 0, 0, 0, 0, 0, 0},
  {"password", 'p', "Password",
  (uchar **) &opt_password, NULL, NULL,
  GET_STR, OPT_ARG, 0, 0, 0, 0, 0, 0},
  {"port", 'P', "Port number",
  (uchar **) &opt_port_num, NULL, NULL,
  GET_UINT, REQUIRED_ARG, 0, 0, 0, 0, 0, 0},
  {"socket", 'S', "Socket path",
  (uchar **) &opt_socket_name, NULL, NULL,
  GET_STR, REQUIRED_ARG, 0, 0, 0, 0, 0, 0},
  {"user", 'u', "User name",
  (uchar **) &opt_user_name, NULL, NULL,
  GET_STR, REQUIRED_ARG, 0, 0, 0, 0, 0, 0},
  { NULL, 0, NULL, NULL, NULL, NULL, GET_NO_ARG, NO_ARG, 0, 0, 0, 0, 0, 0 }
};

static my_bool
get_one_option (int optid, const struct my_option *opt, char *argument)
{
  switch (optid)
  {
  case '?':
    my_print_help (my_opts);  /* print help message */
    exit (0);
  }
  return (0);
}

int
main (int argc, char *argv[])
{
```

```
int i;
int opt_err;

    printf ("Original connection parameters:\n");
    printf ("hostname: %s\n", opt_host_name ? opt_host_name : "(null)");
    printf ("username: %s\n", opt_user_name ? opt_user_name : "(null)");
    printf ("password: %s\n", opt_password ? opt_password : "(null)");
    printf ("port number: %u\n", opt_port_num);
    printf ("socket filename: %s\n",
            opt_socket_name ? opt_socket_name : "(null)");

    printf ("Original argument vector:\n");
    for (i = 0; i < argc; i++)
      printf ("arg %d: %s\n", i, argv[i]);

    MY_INIT (argv[0]);
    load_defaults ("my", client_groups, &argc, &argv);

    printf ("Argument vector after calling load_defaults():\n");
    for (i = 0; i < argc; i++)
      printf ("arg %d: %s\n", i, argv[i]);

    if ((opt_err = handle_options (&argc, &argv, my_opts, get_one_option)))
      exit (opt_err);

    printf ("Connection parameters after calling handle_options():\n");
    printf ("hostname: %s\n", opt_host_name ? opt_host_name : "(null)");
    printf ("username: %s\n", opt_user_name ? opt_user_name : "(null)");
    printf ("password: %s\n", opt_password ? opt_password : "(null)");
    printf ("port number: %u\n", opt_port_num);
    printf ("socket filename: %s\n",
            opt_socket_name ? opt_socket_name : "(null)");

    printf ("Argument vector after calling handle_options():\n");
    for (i = 0; i < argc; i++)
      printf ("arg %d: %s\n", i, argv[i]);

    exit (0);
}
```

Note

The source code for `show_opt.c` and several other programs later in this chapter uses the `uchar**` type in MySQL-related data structures. Before MySQL 5.1.20, you'll find that the MySQL header files use `gptr*`, which results in warnings when you compile the programs. You can ignore these warnings.

The option-processing approach illustrated by `show_opt.c` involves several aspects that are common to any program that uses the MySQL client library to handle command options. In your own programs, you should do the same things:

1. In addition to the other files that we already have been including, include `my_getopt.h` as well. `my_getopt.h` defines the interface to MySQL's option-processing facilities.

2. Define an array of `my_option` structures. In `show_opt.c`, this array is named `my_opts`. The array should have one structure per option that the program understands. Each structure provides information such as an option's short and long names, its default value, whether the value is a number or string, and so forth.

3. After invoking `load_defaults()` to read the option files and set up the argument vector, process the options by calling `handle_options()`. The first two arguments to `handle_options()` are the addresses of your program's argument count and vector. (Just as with `load_options()`, you pass the addresses of these variables, not their values.) The third argument points to the array of `my_option` structures. The fourth argument is a pointer to a helper function. The `handle_options()` routine and the `my_options` structures are designed to make it possible for most option-processing actions to be performed automatically for you by the client library. However, to allow for special actions that the library does not handle, your program should also define a helper function for `handle_options()` to call. In `show_opt.c`, this function is named `get_one_option()`.

The `my_option` structure defines the types of information that must be specified for each option that the program understands:

```
struct my_option
{
  const char *name;                      /* option's long name */
  int        id;                         /* option's short name or code */
  const char *comment;                   /* option description for help message */
  uchar      **value;                    /* pointer to variable to store value in */
  uchar      **u_max_value;              /* The user defined max variable value */
  struct st_typelib *typelib;            /* pointer to possible values (unused) */
  ulong      var_type;                   /* option value's type */
  enum get_opt_arg_type arg_type;        /* whether option value is required */
  longlong   def_value;                  /* option's default value */
  longlong   min_value;                  /* option's minimum allowable value */
  longlong   max_value;                  /* option's maximum allowable value */
  longlong   sub_size;                   /* amount to shift value by */
  long       block_size;                 /* option value multiplier */
  void       *app_type;                  /* reserved for application-specific use */
};
```

The members of the `my_option` structure are used as follows:

- `name` is the long option name. This is the `--name` form of the option, without the leading dashes. For example, if the long option is `--user`, list it as `"user"` in the `my_option` structure.

- `id` is the short (single-letter) option name, or a code value associated with the option if it has no single-letter name. For example, if the short option is `-u`, list it as `'u'` in the `my_option` structure. For options that have only a long name and no corresponding single-character name, you should make up a set of option code values to be used internally for the short names. The values must be unique and different from all the single-character names. (To satisfy the latter constraint, make the codes greater than 255, the largest possible single-character value. For an example of this technique, see Section 7.6, "Writing Clients That Include SSL Support.")

- `comment` is an explanatory string that describes the purpose of the option. This is the text that you want displayed in a help message.

- `value` is the address of a generic pointer, declared as a `uchar **` value. If the option takes an argument, `value` points to the variable where you want the argument to be stored. After the options have been processed, you can check that variable to see what the option has been set to. The data type of the variable that's pointed to must be consistent with the value of the `var_type` member. If the option takes no argument, `value` is `NULL`.

- `u_max_value` is another address of a generic pointer, but it's used only by the server. For client programs, set `u_max_value` to `NULL`.

- `typelib` currently is unused. In future MySQL releases, it may be used to allow a list of legal values to be specified, in which case any option value given will be required to match one of these values.

- `var_type` indicates what kind of value must follow the option name on the command line. The following table shows these types, their meanings, and the corresponding C type.

var_type Value	Meaning	C Type
GET_NO_ARG	No value	
GET_BOOL	Boolean value	my_bool
GET_INT	Integer value	int
GET_UINT	Unsigned integer value	unsigned int
GET_LONG	Long integer value	long
GET_ULONG	Unsigned long integer value	unsigned long
GET_LL	Long long integer value	long long

var_type Value	Meaning	C Type
GET_ULL	Unsigned long long integer value	`unsigned long long`
GET_STR	String value	`char *`
GET_STR_ALLOC	String value	`char *`
GET_DISABLED	Option is disabled	
GET_ENUM	Enumeration value (currently unused)	
GET_SET	Set value (currently unused)	
GET_DOUBLE	Double-precision (floating-point) value	`double`

GET_DOUBLE is available as of MySQL 5.1.21.

The difference between GET_STR and GET_STR_ALLOC is that for GET_STR, the client library sets the option variable to point directly at the value in the argument vector, whereas for GET_STR_ALLOC, it makes a copy of the argument and sets the option variable to point to the copy.

The GET_DISABLED type can be used to indicate that an option is no longer available, or that it is available only when the program is built a certain way (for example, with debugging support enabled). To see an example, take a look at the mysql.cc file in a MySQL source distribution.

- arg_type indicates whether a value follows the option name, and may be any of the values shown in the following table.

arg_type Value	Meaning
NO_ARG	Option takes no following argument
OPT_ARG	Option may take a following argument
REQUIRED_ARG	Option requires a following argument

If arg_type is NO_ARG, var_type should be set to GET_NO_ARG.

- def_value is for numeric-valued options. It is the default value to assign to the option if no explicit value is specified in the argument vector.

- min_value is for numeric-valued options. It is the smallest value that may be specified. Smaller values are bumped up to this value automatically. Use 0 to indicate "no minimum."

- max_value is for numeric-valued options. It is the largest value that may be specified. Larger values are bumped down to this value automatically. Use 0 to indicate "no maximum."

- `sub_size` is for numeric-valued options. It is an offset that is used to convert values from the range as given in the argument vector to the range that is used internally. For example, if values are given on the command line in the range from 1 to 256, but the program wants to use an internal range of 0 to 255, set `sub_size` to 1.

- `block_size` is for numeric-valued options. This value indicates a block size if it is non-zero. Option values given by the user are rounded down to the nearest multiple of this size if necessary. For example, if values must be even, set the block size to 2; `handle_options()` rounds odd values down to the nearest even number.

- `app_type` is reserved for application-specific use.

The `my_opts` array should have a `my_option` structure for each valid option, followed by a terminating structure that is set up as follows to indicate the end of the array:

```
{ NULL, 0, NULL, NULL, NULL, NULL, GET_NO_ARG, NO_ARG, 0, 0, 0, 0, 0, 0 }
```

When you invoke `handle_options()` to process the argument vector, it skips over the first argument (the program name), and then processes option arguments—that is, arguments that begin with a dash. This continues until it reaches the end of the vector or encounters the special two-dash "end of options" argument ('--'). As `handle_options()` moves through the argument vector, it calls the helper function once per option to enable that function to perform any special processing. `handle_options()` passes three arguments to the helper function: the short option value, a pointer to the option's `my_option` structure, and a pointer to the argument that follows the option in the argument vector (which will be NULL if the option is specified without a following value).

When `handle_options()` returns, the argument count and vector are reset appropriately to represent an argument list containing only the non-option arguments.

Here is a sample invocation of `show_opt` and the resulting output (assuming that `~/.my.cnf` still has the same contents as for the final `show_argv` example in Section 7.3.2.1, "Accessing Option File Contents"):

```
% ./show_opt -h yet_another_host --user=bill x
Original connection parameters:
hostname: (null)
username: (null)
password: (null)
port number: 0
socket filename: (null)
Original argument vector:
arg 0: ./show_opt
arg 1: -h
arg 3: yet_another_host
arg 3: --user=bill
arg 4: x
Argument vector after calling load_defaults():
arg 0: ./show_opt
arg 1: --user=sampadm
```

```
arg 2: --password=secret
arg 3: --host=some_host
arg 4: -h
arg 5: yet_another_host
arg 6: --user=bill
arg 7: x
Connection parameters after calling handle_options():
hostname: yet_another_host
username: bill
password: secret
port number: 0
socket filename: (null)
Argument vector after calling handle_options():
arg 0: x
```

The output shows that the hostname is picked up from the command line (overriding the value in the option file), and that the username and password come from the option file. `handle_options()` correctly parses options whether specified in short-option form (such as `-h yet_another_host`) or in long-option form (such as `--user=bill`).

The `get_one_option()` helper function is used in conjunction with `handle_options()`. For `show_opt`, it is fairly minimal and takes no action except for the `--help` or `-?` options (for which `handle_options()` passes an `optid` value of `'?'`):

```
static my_bool
get_one_option (int optid, const struct my_option *opt, char *argument)
{
  switch (optid)
  {
  case '?':
    my_print_help (my_opts);  /* print help message */
    exit (0);
  }
  return (0);
}
```

`my_print_help()` is a client library routine that automatically produces a help message for you, based on the option names and comment strings in the `my_opts` array. To see how it works, try the following command:

% ./show_opt --help

You can add other cases to the `switch()` statement in `get_one_option()` as necessary (and we'll do so in `connect2` shortly). For example, `get_one_option()` is useful for handling password options. When you specify such an option, the password value may or may not be given, as indicated by `OPT_ARG` in the option information structure. That is, you can specify the option as `--password` or `--password=your_pass` if you use the long-option form, or as `-p` or `-pyour_pass` if you use the short-option form. MySQL clients typically allow you to omit the password value on the command line, and then prompt you for it.

This enables you to avoid giving the password on the command line, which keeps people from seeing your password. In later programs, we'll use get_one_option() to check whether a password value was given. We'll save the value if so, and otherwise set a flag to indicate that the program should prompt the user for a password before attempting to connect to the server.

You might find it instructive to modify the option structures in show_opt.c to see how your changes affect the program's behavior. For example, if you set the minimum, maximum, and block size values for the --port option to 100, 1000, and 25, you'll find after recompiling the program that you cannot set the port number to a value outside the range from 100 to 1000, and that values get rounded down automatically to the nearest multiple of 25.

The option processing routines also handle the --no-defaults, --print-defaults, --defaults-file, and --defaults-extra-file options automatically. Try invoking show_opt with each of these options to see what happens.

7.3.3 Incorporating Option-Processing into a MySQL Client Program

Now we're ready to write connect2.c. It has the following characteristics:

- It connects to the MySQL server, disconnects, and exits. This is similar to what connect1.c does, but is modified to use the print_error() function developed earlier for reporting errors.

- It processes options from the command line or in option files. This is done using code similar to that from show_opt.c, but is modified to prompt the user for a password if necessary.

The resulting source file, connect2.c, looks like this:

```
/*
 * connect2.c - connect to MySQL server, using connection parameters
 * specified in an option file or on the command line
 */

#include <my_global.h>
#include <my_sys.h>
#include <m_string.h>   /* for strdup() */
#include <mysql.h>
#include <my_getopt.h>

static char *opt_host_name = NULL;    /* server host (default=localhost) */
static char *opt_user_name = NULL;    /* username (default=login name) */
static char *opt_password = NULL;     /* password (default=none) */
static unsigned int opt_port_num = 0; /* port number (use built-in value) */
static char *opt_socket_name = NULL;  /* socket name (use built-in value) */
static char *opt_db_name = NULL;      /* database name (default=none) */
static unsigned int opt_flags = 0;    /* connection flags (none) */
```

```
static int ask_password = 0;            /* whether to solicit password */

static MYSQL *conn;                     /* pointer to connection handler */

static const char *client_groups[] = { "client", NULL };

static struct my_option my_opts[] =   /* option information structures */
{
  {"help", '?', "Display this help and exit",
   NULL, NULL, NULL,
   GET_NO_ARG, NO_ARG, 0, 0, 0, 0, 0, 0},
  {"host", 'h', "Host to connect to",
   (uchar **) &opt_host_name, NULL, NULL,
   GET_STR, REQUIRED_ARG, 0, 0, 0, 0, 0, 0},
  {"password", 'p', "Password",
   (uchar **) &opt_password, NULL, NULL,
   GET_STR, OPT_ARG, 0, 0, 0, 0, 0, 0},
  {"port", 'P', "Port number",
   (uchar **) &opt_port_num, NULL, NULL,
   GET_UINT, REQUIRED_ARG, 0, 0, 0, 0, 0, 0},
  {"socket", 'S', "Socket path",
   (uchar **) &opt_socket_name, NULL, NULL,
   GET_STR, REQUIRED_ARG, 0, 0, 0, 0, 0, 0},
  {"user", 'u', "User name",
   (uchar **) &opt_user_name, NULL, NULL,
   GET_STR, REQUIRED_ARG, 0, 0, 0, 0, 0, 0},
  { NULL, 0, NULL, NULL, NULL, NULL, GET_NO_ARG, NO_ARG, 0, 0, 0, 0, 0, 0 }
};

static void
print_error (MYSQL *conn, char *message)
{
  fprintf (stderr, "%s\n", message);
  if (conn != NULL)
  {
    fprintf (stderr, "Error %u (%s): %s\n",
             mysql_errno (conn), mysql_sqlstate (conn), mysql_error (conn));
  }
}

static my_bool
get_one_option (int optid, const struct my_option *opt, char *argument)
{
  switch (optid)
  {
```

```
      case '?':
        my_print_help (my_opts);   /* print help message */
        exit (0);
      case 'p':                    /* password */
        if (!argument)             /* no value given; solicit it later */
          ask_password = 1;
        else                       /* copy password, overwrite original */
        {
          opt_password = strdup (argument);
          if (opt_password == NULL)
          {
            print_error (NULL, "could not allocate password buffer");
            exit (1);
          }
          while (*argument)
            *argument++ = 'x';
          ask_password = 0;
        }
        break;
    }
    return (0);
}

int
main (int argc, char *argv[])
{
int opt_err;

  MY_INIT (argv[0]);
  load_defaults ("my", client_groups, &argc, &argv);

  if ((opt_err = handle_options (&argc, &argv, my_opts, get_one_option)))
    exit (opt_err);

  /* solicit password if necessary */
  if (ask_password)
    opt_password = get_tty_password (NULL);

  /* get database name if present on command line */
  if (argc > 0)
  {
    opt_db_name = argv[0];
    --argc; ++argv;
  }

  /* initialize client library */
  if (mysql_library_init (0, NULL, NULL))
```

```
{
  print_error (NULL, "mysql_library_init() failed");
  exit (1);
}

/* initialize connection handler */
conn = mysql_init (NULL);
if (conn == NULL)
{
  print_error (NULL, "mysql_init() failed (probably out of memory)");
  exit (1);
}

/* connect to server */
if (mysql_real_connect (conn, opt_host_name, opt_user_name, opt_password,
    opt_db_name, opt_port_num, opt_socket_name, opt_flags) == NULL)
{
  print_error (conn, "mysql_real_connect() failed");
  mysql_close (conn);
  exit (1);
}

/* ... issue statements and process results here ... */

/* disconnect from server, terminate client library */
mysql_close (conn);
mysql_library_end ();
exit (0);
}
```

Compared to the `connect1` and `show_opt` programs that we developed earlier, `connect2` does a few new things:

- It enables a default database to be specified as a command-line argument. This is consistent with the behavior of the standard clients in MySQL distributions.

- If a password value is present in the argument vector, `get_one_option()` makes a copy of it and then overwrites the original. This minimizes the time window during which a password specified on the command line is visible to `ps` or to other system status programs. (The window is only *minimized*, not eliminated. Specifying passwords on the command line still is a security risk.)

- If a password option was given without a value, `get_one_option()` sets a flag to indicate that the program should prompt the user for a password. That's done in `main()` after all options have been processed, using the `get_tty_password()` function. This is a utility routine in the client library that prompts for a password without echoing it on the screen. You may ask, "Why not just call `getpass()`?" The answer is that not all systems have that function (for example, Windows does not).

`get_tty_password()` is portable across systems because it's configured to adjust to system idiosyncrasies.

Compile and link `connect2`, and then try running it:

```
% ./connect2
```

If `connect2` produces no output (as just shown), it connected successfully. On the other hand, you might see something like this:

```
% ./connect2
mysql_real_connect() failed:
Error 1045 (28000): Access denied for user 'sampadm'@'localhost'
(using password: NO)
```

This output indicates no connection was established, and it says why. In this case, `Access denied` means that you need to supply appropriate connection parameters. With `connect1`, there was no way to do so short of editing and recompiling. `connect2` connects to the MySQL server according to the options you specify on the command line or in an option file. Assume that there is no option file to complicate matters. If you invoke `connect2` with no arguments, it connects to `localhost` and passes your Unix login name and no password to the server. If instead you invoke `connect2` as shown in the following command, it prompts for a password (because there is no password value immediately following -p), connects to `some_host`, and passes the username `some_user` to the server as well as the password you type in:

```
% ./connect2 -h some_host -p -u some_user some_db
```

`connect2` also passes the database name `some_db` to `mysql_real_connect()` to make that the default database. If there is an option file, its contents are processed and used to modify the connection parameters accordingly.

Let's step back for a moment and consider what's been achieved so far. The work that has gone into producing `connect2` accomplishes something that's necessary for every MySQL client: connecting to the server using appropriate parameters. It also does a good job of reporting errors if the connection attempt fails. What we have now serves as a framework that can be used as the basis for many different client programs. To write a new client, do this:

1. Make a copy of `connect2.c`.

2. If the program accepts additional options other than the standard ones that `connect2.c` knows about, add them to the `my_opts` array and modify the option-processing loop.

3. Add your own application-specific code between the connect and disconnect calls.

And you're done.

All the real action for your application will take place between the `mysql_real_connect()` and `mysql_close()` calls, but having a reusable skeleton means that you can concentrate more on what you're really interested in—being able to access the content of your databases.

7.4 Processing SQL Statements

The purpose of connecting to the server is to conduct a conversation with it while the connection is open. This section shows how to communicate with the server to process statements. Each statement you execute involves the following steps:

1. Construct the statement. The way you do this depends on the contents of the statement—in particular, whether it contains binary data.

2. Issue the statement by sending it to the server. The server will execute the statement and generate a result.

3. Process the statement result. This depends on what type of statement you issued. For example, a SELECT statement returns rows of data for you to process. An INSERT statement does not.

The MySQL client library includes two sets of routines for statement execution. The first set is based on sending each statement as a string to the server and retrieving the results with all columns returned in string format. The second set is based on a binary protocol that enables non-string data values to be sent and returned in native format without conversion to and from string format.

This section discusses the original method for processing SQL statements. Section 7.9, "Using Server-Side Prepared Statements," covers the binary protocol.

One factor to consider in constructing statements is which function to use for sending them to the server. The more general statement-issuing routine is mysql_real_query(). With this routine, you provide the statement as a counted string (a string plus a length). You must keep track of the length of your statement string and pass that to mysql_real_query(), along with the string itself. Because the statement is treated as a counted string rather than as a null-terminated string, it may contain anything, including binary data or null bytes.

The other statement-issuing function, mysql_query(), is more restrictive in what it allows in the statement string but often is easier to use. Any statement passed to mysql_query() should be a null-terminated string. This means the statement text cannot contain null bytes because those would cause it to be interpreted erroneously as shorter than it really is. Generally speaking, if your statement can contain arbitrary binary data, it might contain null bytes, so you shouldn't use mysql_query(). On the other hand, when you are working with null-terminated strings, you have the luxury of constructing statements using standard C library string functions that you're probably already familiar with, such as strcpy() and sprintf().

Another factor to consider in constructing statements is whether you need to perform any character-escaping operations. This is necessary if you want to construct statements using values that contain binary data or other troublesome characters, such as quotes or backslashes. This is discussed in Section 7.4.7.1, "Working with Strings That Contain Special Characters."

A simple outline of statement handling looks like this:

```
if (mysql_query (conn, stmt_str) != 0)
{
  /* failure; report error */
}
else
{
  /* success; find out what effect the statement had */
}
```

`mysql_query()` and `mysql_real_query()` both return zero for statements that succeed and non-zero for failure. To say that a statement "succeeded" means the server accepted it as legal and was able to execute it. It does not indicate anything about the effect of the statement. For example, it does not indicate that a SELECT statement selected any rows or that a DELETE statement deleted any rows. Checking what effect the statement actually had involves additional processing.

A statement may fail for a variety of reasons. Common causes of failure include the following:

- It contains a syntax error.
- It's semantically illegal—for example, a statement that refers to a non-existent table.
- You don't have sufficient privileges to access a table referred to by the statement.

Statements may be grouped into two broad categories: those that modify rows and those that return a result set (a set of rows). Statements such as INSERT, DELETE, and UPDATE modify rows and return a count to indicate the number of affected rows.

Statements such as SELECT and SHOW return a result set. In the MySQL C API, the result set returned by such statements is represented by the MYSQL_RES data type. This is a structure that contains the data values for the rows, and also metadata about the values (such as the column names and data value lengths). Is it legal for a result set to be empty (that is, to contain zero rows).

7.4.1 Handling Statements That Modify Rows

To process a statement that modifies rows, issue it with `mysql_query()` or `mysql_real_query()`. If the statement succeeds, you can find out how many rows were inserted, deleted, or updated by calling `mysql_affected_rows()`.

The following example shows how to handle a statement that modifies rows:

```
if (mysql_query (conn, "INSERT INTO my_tbl SET name = 'My Name'") != 0)
{
  print_error (conn, "INSERT statement failed");
}
else
```

```
{
  printf ("INSERT statement succeeded; number of rows affected: %lu\n",
          (unsigned long) mysql_affected_rows (conn));
}
```

Note how the result of `mysql_affected_rows()` is cast to `unsigned long` for printing. This function returns a value of type `my_ulonglong`, but attempting to print a value of that type directly may not work on all systems. Casting the value to `unsigned long` and using a print format of `%lu` solves the problem. The same principle applies to any other functions that return `my_ulonglong` values, such as `mysql_num_rows()` and `mysql_insert_id()`. If you want your client programs to be portable across different systems, keep this in mind.

`mysql_affected_rows()` returns the number of rows affected by the statement, but the meaning of "rows affected" depends on the type of statement. For INSERT, REPLACE, or DELETE, it is the number of rows inserted, replaced, or deleted. For UPDATE, it is the number of rows updated, which means the number of rows that MySQL actually modified. MySQL does not update a row if its contents are the same as what you're updating it to. This means that although a row might be selected for updating (by the WHERE clause of the UPDATE statement), it might not actually be changed.

This meaning of "rows affected" for UPDATE actually is something of a controversial point because some people want it to mean "rows matched"—that is, the number of rows selected for updating, even if the update operation doesn't actually change their values. If your application requires such a meaning, you can request that behavior when you connect to the server by passing a value of CLIENT_FOUND_ROWS in the flags parameter to `mysql_real_connect()`.

7.4.2 Handling Statements That Return a Result Set

Statements that return data do so in the form of a result set that you retrieve after issuing the statement by calling `mysql_query()` or `mysql_real_query()`. It's important to realize that in MySQL, SELECT is not the only statement that returns rows. Statements such as SHOW, DESCRIBE, EXPLAIN, and CHECK TABLE do so as well. For all of these statements, you must perform additional row-handling processing after issuing the statement.

Handling a result set involves these steps:

1. Generate the result set by calling `mysql_store_result()` or `mysql_use_result()`. These functions return a MYSQL_RES pointer for success or NULL for failure. Later, we'll go over the differences between `mysql_store_result()` and `mysql_use_result()`, as well as the conditions under which you would choose one over the other. For now, our examples use `mysql_store_result()`, which retrieves the rows from the server immediately and buffers them in memory on the client side.

2. Call `mysql_fetch_row()` for each row of the result set. This function returns a MYSQL_ROW value, or NULL when there are no more rows. A MYSQL_ROW value is a pointer to an array of strings representing the values for each column in the row.

What you do with the row depends on your application. For example, you might print the column values or perform some statistical calculation on them.

3. When you are done with the result set, call `mysql_free_result()` to deallocate the memory it uses. If you neglect to do this, your application will leak memory. It's especially important to dispose of result sets properly for long-running applications. Otherwise, you will notice your system slowly being taken over by processes that consume ever-increasing amounts of system resources.

The following example outlines how to process a statement that returns a result set:

```
MYSQL_RES *res_set;

if (mysql_query (conn, "SHOW TABLES FROM sampdb") != 0)
  print_error (conn, "mysql_query() failed");
else
{
  res_set = mysql_store_result (conn);  /* generate result set */
  if (res_set == NULL)
    print_error (conn, "mysql_store_result() failed");
  else
  {
    /* process result set, and then deallocate it */
    process_result_set (conn, res_set);
    mysql_free_result (res_set);
  }
}
```

The example hides the details of result set processing within another function, `process_result_set()`, which we have not yet defined. Generally, operations that handle a result set are based on a loop that looks something like this:

```
MYSQL_ROW row;

while ((row = mysql_fetch_row (res_set)) != NULL)
{
  /* do something with row contents */
}
```

`mysql_fetch_row()` returns a `MYSQL_ROW` value, which is a pointer to an array of values. If the return value is assigned to a variable named `row`, each value within the row may be accessed as `row[i]`, where `i` ranges from 0 to one less than the number of columns in the row. There are several important points about the `MYSQL_ROW` data type to note:

- `MYSQL_ROW` is a pointer type, so you declare a variable of that type as `MYSQL_ROW row`, not as `MYSQL_ROW *row`.
- Values for all data types, even numeric types, are returned in the `MYSQL_ROW` array as strings. If you want to treat a value as a number, you must convert the string yourself.

- The strings in a MYSQL_ROW array are null-terminated. However, if a column can contain binary data, it might contain null bytes, so you should not treat the value as a null-terminated string. Get the column length to find out how long the column value is. (Section 7.4.6, "Using Result Set Metadata," discusses how to determine column lengths.)

- SQL NULL values are represented by C NULL pointers in the MYSQL_ROW array. Unless you know that a column is declared NOT NULL, you should always check whether values for the column are NULL, or your program may crash as a result of attempting to dereference a NULL pointer.

What you do with each row depends on the purpose of your application. For purposes of illustration, let's just print each row as a set of column values separated by tabs. To do that, it's necessary to know how many columns values rows contain. That information is returned by another client library function, mysql_num_fields().

Here's the code for process_result_set():

```
void
process_result_set (MYSQL *conn, MYSQL_RES *res_set)
{
MYSQL_ROW    row;
unsigned int i;

  while ((row = mysql_fetch_row (res_set)) != NULL)
  {
    for (i = 0; i < mysql_num_fields (res_set); i++)
    {
      if (i > 0)
        fputc ('\t', stdout);
      printf ("%s", row[i] != NULL ? row[i] : "NULL");
    }
    fputc ('\n', stdout);
  }
  if (mysql_errno (conn) != 0)
    print_error (conn, "mysql_fetch_row() failed");
  else
    printf ("Number of rows returned: %lu\n",
            (unsigned long) mysql_num_rows (res_set));
}
```

process_result_set() displays the contents of each row in tab-delimited format (displaying NULL values as the word "NULL"), and then prints a count of the number of rows retrieved. That count is available by calling mysql_num_rows(). Like mysql_affected_rows(), mysql_num_rows() returns a my_ulonglong value, so you should cast its value to unsigned long and use a %lu format to print it. But note that unlike mysql_affected_rows(), which takes a connection handler argument, mysql_num_rows() takes a result set pointer as its argument.

The code that follows the loop includes an error test as a precautionary measure. If you create the result set with `mysql_store_result()`, a NULL return value from `mysql_fetch_row()` always means "no more rows." However, if you create the result set with `mysql_use_result()`, a NULL return value from `mysql_fetch_row()` can mean "no more rows" or that an error occurred. Because `process_result_set()` has no idea whether its caller used `mysql_store_result()` or `mysql_use_result()` to generate the result set, the error test enables it to detect errors properly either way.

The version of `process_result_set()` just shown takes a rather minimalist approach to printing column values—one that has certain shortcomings. Suppose that you execute this query:

```
SELECT last_name, first_name, city, state FROM president
ORDER BY last_name, first_name
```

You will receive the following output, which is not so easy to read:

```
Adams    John       Braintree    MA
Adams    John Quincy Braintree    MA
Arthur   Chester A.  Fairfield    VT
Buchanan    James    Mercersburg PA
Bush     George H.W. Milton    MA
Bush     George W.   New Haven    CT
Carter   James E.    Plains  GA
...
```

We could make the output prettier by providing information such as column labels and making the values line up vertically. To do that, we need the labels, and we need to know the widest value in each column. That information is available, but not as part of the column data values—it's part of the result set's metadata (data about the data). After we generalize our statement handler a bit, we'll write a nicer display formatter in Section 7.4.6, "Using Result Set Metadata."

Printing Binary Data

Columns containing binary value that include null bytes will not print properly using the `%s` `printf()` format specifier. `printf()` expects a null-terminated string and prints the column value only up to the first null byte. For binary data, it's best to use a function that accepts a column length argument so that you can print the full value. For example, you could use `fwrite()`.

7.4.3 A General-Purpose Statement Handler

The preceding statement-handling examples were written using knowledge of whether the statement should return any data. That was possible because the statements were hardwired into the code: We used an INSERT statement, which does not return a result set, and a SHOW TABLES statement, which does.

However, you might not always know what kind of statement a given statement represents. For example, if you execute a statement that you read from the keyboard or from a file, it might be anything. You won't know ahead of time whether to expect it to return rows, or even whether it's legal. What then? You certainly don't want to try to parse the statement to determine what kind of statement it is. That's not as simple as it might seem. For example, it's not sufficient to check whether the first word is SELECT because the statement might begin with a comment, as follows:

```
/* comment */ SELECT ...
```

Fortunately, you don't have to know the statement type in advance to be able to handle it properly. The MySQL C API makes it possible to write a general-purpose statement handler that correctly processes any kind of statement, whether or not it returns a result set, and whether it executes successfully or fails. Before writing the code for this handler, let's outline the procedure that it implements:

1. Issue the statement. If it fails, we're done.

2. If the statement succeeds, call mysql_store_result() to retrieve the rows from the server and create a result set.

3. If mysql_store_result() succeeds, the statement returned a result set. Process the rows by calling mysql_fetch_row() until it returns NULL, and then free the result set.

4. If mysql_store_result() fails, it could be that the statement does not return a result set, or that it should have but an error occurred while trying to retrieve the set. You can distinguish between these outcomes by passing the connection handler to mysql_field_count() and checking its return value:

   - If mysql_field_count() returns 0, it means the statement returned no columns, and thus no result set. (This indicates that it was a statement such as INSERT, DELETE, or UPDATE.)

   - If mysql_field_count() returns a non-zero value, it means that an error occurred, because the statement should have returned a result set but didn't. This can happen for various reasons. For example, the result set may have been so large that memory allocation failed, or a network outage between the client and the server may have occurred while fetching rows.

The following listing shows a function that processes any statement, given a connection handler and a null-terminated statement string:

```
void
process_statement (MYSQL *conn, char *stmt_str)
{
MYSQL_RES *res_set;

  if (mysql_query (conn, stmt_str) != 0)  /* the statement failed */
  {
    print_error (conn, "Could not execute statement");
    return;
  }
```

```
  /* the statement succeeded; determine whether it returned data */
  res_set = mysql_store_result (conn);
  if (res_set)      /* a result set was returned */
  {
    /* process rows and then free the result set */
    process_result_set (conn, res_set);
    mysql_free_result (res_set);
  }
  else              /* no result set was returned */
  {
    /*
     * does the lack of a result set mean that the statement didn't
     * return one, or that it should have but an error occurred?
     */
    if (mysql_field_count (conn) == 0)
    {
      /*
       * statement generated no result set (it was not a SELECT,
       * SHOW, DESCRIBE, etc.); just report rows-affected value.
       */
      printf ("Number of rows affected: %lu\n",
              (unsigned long) mysql_affected_rows (conn));
    }
    else  /* an error occurred */
    {
      print_error (conn, "Could not retrieve result set");
    }
  }
}
```

7.4.4 Alternative Approaches to Statement Processing

The version of `process_statement()` just shown has these three properties:

- It uses `mysql_query()` to issue the statement.
- It uses `mysql_store_query()` to retrieve the result set.
- When no result set is obtained, it uses `mysql_field_count()` to distinguish occurrence of an error from a result set not being expected.

Alternative approaches are possible for all three of those aspects of statement handling:

- You can use a counted statement string and `mysql_real_query()` rather than a null-terminated statement string and `mysql_query()`.
- You can create the result set by calling `mysql_use_result()` rather than `mysql_store_result()`.

- You can call `mysql_error()` or `mysql_errno()` rather than `mysql_field_count()` to determine whether result set retrieval failed or whether there was simply no set to retrieve.

Any or all of these approaches can be used instead of those used in `process_statement()`. Here is a `process_real_statement()` function that is analogous to `process_statement()` but that uses all three alternatives:

```
void
process_real_statement (MYSQL *conn, char *stmt_str, unsigned int len)
{
MYSQL_RES *res_set;

  if (mysql_real_query (conn, stmt_str, len) != 0) /* the statement failed */
  {
    print_error (conn, "Could not execute statement");
    return;
  }

  /* the statement succeeded; determine whether it returned data */
  res_set = mysql_use_result (conn);
  if (res_set)       /* a result set was returned */
  {
    /* process rows and then free the result set */
    process_result_set (conn, res_set);
    mysql_free_result (res_set);
  }
  else               /* no result set was returned */
  {
    /*
     * does the lack of a result set mean that the statement didn't
     * return one, or that it should have but an error occurred?
     */
    if (mysql_errno (conn) == 0)
    {
      /*
       * statement generated no result set (it was not a SELECT,
       * SHOW, DESCRIBE, etc.); just report rows-affected value.
       */
      printf ("Number of rows affected: %lu\n",
              (unsigned long) mysql_affected_rows (conn));
    }
    else  /* an error occurred */
    {
      print_error (conn, "Could not retrieve result set");
    }
  }
}
```

7.4.5 `mysql_store_result()` Versus `mysql_use_result()`

The `mysql_store_result()` and `mysql_use_result()` functions are similar in that both take a connection handler argument and return a result set. However, the differences between them actually are quite extensive. The primary difference between the two functions lies in the way rows of the result set are retrieved from the server. `mysql_store_result()` retrieves all the rows immediately when you call it. `mysql_use_result()` initiates the retrieval but doesn't actually get any of the rows. These differing approaches to row retrieval give rise to all other differences between the two functions. This section compares them so that you'll know how to choose the one that's most appropriate for a given application.

When `mysql_store_result()` retrieves a result set from the server, it fetches the rows, allocates memory for them, and buffers them on the client side. Subsequent calls to `mysql_fetch_row()` never return an error because they simply pull a row out of a data structure that already holds the result set. Consequently, a NULL return from `mysql_fetch_row()` always means you've reached the end of the result set.

By contrast, `mysql_use_result()` doesn't retrieve any rows itself. Instead, it simply initiates a row-by-row retrieval, which you must complete yourself by calling `mysql_fetch_row()` for each row. In this case, although a NULL return from `mysql_fetch_row()` normally still means the end of the result set has been reached, it may mean instead that an error occurred while communicating with the server. You can distinguish the two outcomes by calling `mysql_errno()` or `mysql_error()`.

`mysql_store_result()` has higher memory and processing requirements than does `mysql_use_result()` because the entire result set is maintained in the client. The overhead for memory allocation and data structure setup is greater, and a client that retrieves large result sets runs the risk of running out of memory. If you're going to retrieve a lot of rows in a single result set, you might want to use `mysql_use_result()` instead.

`mysql_use_result()` has lower memory requirements because only enough space to handle a single row at a time need be allocated. This can be faster because you're not setting up as complex a data structure for the result set. On the other hand, `mysql_use_result()` places a greater burden on the server, which must hold rows of the result set until the client sees fit to retrieve all of them. This makes `mysql_use_result()` a poor choice for certain types of clients:

- Interactive clients that advance from row to row at the request of the user. (You don't want the server waiting to send the next row just because the user decides to take a coffee break.)
- Clients that do a lot of processing between row retrievals.

In both of these types of situations, the client fails to retrieve all rows in the result set quickly. This ties up the server and can have a negative impact on other clients, particularly if you are using a storage engine like MyISAM that uses table locks: Tables from which you retrieve data are read-locked for the duration of the query. Other clients that are trying to update those tables will be blocked.

Offsetting the additional memory requirements incurred by `mysql_store_result()` are certain benefits of having access to the entire result set at once. All rows of the set are available, so you have random access into them: The `mysql_data_seek()`, `mysql_row_seek()`, and `mysql_row_tell()` functions enable you to access rows in any order you want. With `mysql_use_result()`, you can access rows only in the order in which they are retrieved by `mysql_fetch_row()`. If you intend to process rows in any order other than sequentially as they are returned from the server, you must use `mysql_store_result()` instead. For example, if you have an application that enables the user to browse back and forth among the rows selected by a query, you'd be best served by using `mysql_store_result()`.

With `mysql_store_result()`, you have access to certain types of column information that are unavailable when you use `mysql_use_result()`. The number of rows in the result set is obtained by calling `mysql_num_rows()`. The maximum widths of the values in each column are stored in the `max_width` member of the `MYSQL_FIELD` column information structures. With `mysql_use_result()`, `mysql_num_rows()` doesn't return the correct value until you've fetched all the rows; similarly, `max_width` is unavailable because it can be calculated only after every row's data have been seen.

Because `mysql_use_result()` does less work than `mysql_store_result()`, it imposes a requirement that `mysql_store_result()` does not: The client must call `mysql_fetch_row()` for every row in the result set. If you fail to do this before issuing another statement, any remaining rows in the current result set become part of the next statement's result set and an "out of sync" error occurs. (You can avoid this by calling `mysql_free_result()` before issuing the second statement. `mysql_free_result()` will fetch and discard any pending rows for you.) One implication of this processing model is that with `mysql_use_result()` you can work only with a single result set at a time.

Sync errors do not happen with `mysql_store_result()` because when that function returns, there are no rows yet to be fetched from the server. In fact, with `mysql_store_result()`, you need not call `mysql_fetch_row()` explicitly at all. This can sometimes be useful if all that you're interested in is whether you got a non-empty result, rather than what the result contains. For example, to find out whether a table `mytbl` exists, you can execute this statement:

```
SHOW TABLES LIKE 'mytbl'
```

If, after calling `mysql_store_result()`, the value of `mysql_num_rows()` is non-zero, the table exists. `mysql_fetch_row()` need not be called.

Result sets generated with `mysql_store_result()` should be freed with `mysql_free_result()` at some point, but this need not necessarily be done before issuing another statement. This means that you can generate multiple result sets and work with them simultaneously, in contrast to the "one result set at a time" constraint imposed when you're working with `mysql_use_result()`.

If you want to provide maximum flexibility, give users the option of selecting either result set processing method. `mysql` and `mysqldump` are two programs that do this. They use
`mysql_store_result()` by default but switch to `mysql_use_result()` if the `--quick`
option is given.

7.4.6 Using Result Set Metadata

Result sets contain not only the column values for data rows but also information about
the data. This information is called the result set "metadata," which includes:

- The number of rows and columns in the result set, available by calling
  `mysql_num_rows()` and `mysql_num_fields()`.
- The length of each column value in the current row, available by calling
  `mysql_fetch_lengths()`.
- Information about each column, such as the column name and type, the maximum
  width of each column's values, and the table the column comes from. This information is stored in `MYSQL_FIELD` structures, which typically are obtained by calling
  `mysql_fetch_field()`. Appendix G (online) describes the `MYSQL_FIELD` structure
  in detail and lists all functions that provide access to column information.

Metadata availability is partially dependent on your result set processing method. As
indicated in Section 7.4.5, "`mysql_store_result()` Versus `mysql_use_result()`," if you
want to use the row count or maximum column length values, you must create the result
set with `mysql_store_result()`, not with `mysql_use_result()`.

Result set metadata is helpful for making decisions about how to process result set data:

- Column names and widths are useful for producing nicely formatted output that
  has column titles and that lines up vertically.
- The column count indicates how many times to iterate through a loop that
  processes successive column values for data rows.
- You can use the row or column counts if you need to allocate data structures that
  depend on knowing the dimensions of the result set.
- The data type of a column enables you to tell whether a column represents a number, whether it might contain binary data, and so forth.

Earlier, in Section 7.4.2, "Handling Statements That Return a Result Set," we wrote a
version of `process_result_set()` that printed columns from result set rows in tab-
delimited format. That's good for certain purposes (such as when you want to import the
data into a spreadsheet), but it's not a nice display format for visual inspection or for print-
outs. Recall that our earlier version of `process_result_set()` produced this output:

```
Adams    John     Braintree    MA
Adams    John Quincy Braintree    MA
Arthur   Chester A.  Fairfield    VT
```

```
Buchanan    James    Mercersburg PA
Bush    George H.W. Milton   MA
Bush    George W.   New Haven    CT
Carter  James E.    Plains  GA
...
```

Let's write a different version of `process_result_set()` that produces tabular output instead by titling and "boxing" each column. This version will display those same results in a format that's easier to interpret:

```
+------------+---------------+--------------------+-------+
| last_name  | first_name    | city               | state |
+------------+---------------+--------------------+-------+
| Adams      | John          | Braintree          | MA    |
| Adams      | John Quincy   | Braintree          | MA    |
| Arthur     | Chester A.    | Fairfield          | VT    |
| Buchanan   | James         | Mercersburg        | PA    |
| Bush       | George H.W.   | Milton             | MA    |
| Bush       | George W.     | New Haven          | CT    |
| Carter     | James E.      | Plains             | GA    |
...

+------------+---------------+--------------------+-------+
```

The display algorithm performs these steps:

1. Determines the display width of each column.

2. Prints a row of boxed column labels (delimited by vertical bars and preceded and followed by rows of dashes).

3. Prints the values in each row of the result set, with each column boxed (delimited by vertical bars) and lined up vertically. In addition, prints numbers right justified and prints the word "NULL" for NULL values.

4. At the end, prints a count of the number of rows retrieved.

This exercise provides a good demonstration showing how to use result set metadata because it requires knowledge of quite a number of things about the result set other than just the values of the data contained in its rows.

You may be thinking to yourself, "Hmm, that description sounds suspiciously similar to the way `mysql` displays its output." Yes, it does, and you're welcome to compare the source for `mysql` to the code we end up with for `process_result_set()`. They're not the same, and you might find it instructive to compare the two approaches to the same problem.

First, it's necessary to determine the display width of each column. The following listing shows how to do this. Observe that the calculations are based entirely on the result set metadata, and make no reference whatsoever to the row values:

```
MYSQL_FIELD   *field;
unsigned long col_len;
unsigned int  i;
```

```
/* determine column display widths -- requires result set to be */
/* generated with mysql_store_result(), not mysql_use_result() */
mysql_field_seek (res_set, 0);
for (i = 0; i < mysql_num_fields (res_set); i++)
{
  field = mysql_fetch_field (res_set);
  col_len = strlen (field->name);
  if (col_len < field->max_length)
    col_len = field->max_length;
  if (col_len < 4 && !IS_NOT_NULL (field->flags))
    col_len = 4;  /* 4 = length of the word "NULL" */
  field->max_length = col_len;  /* reset column info */
}
```

This code calculates column widths by iterating through the MYSQL_FIELD structures for the columns in the result set. We position to the first structure by calling mysql_field_seek(). Subsequent calls to mysql_fetch_field() return pointers to the structures for successive columns. The width of a column for display purposes is the maximum of three values, each of which depends on metadata in the column information structure:

- The length of field->name, the column title.
- field->max_length, the length of the longest data value in the column.
- The length of the string "NULL" if the column can contain NULL values. field->flags indicates whether the column can contain NULL.

Notice that after the display width for a column is known, we assign that value to max_length, which is a member of a structure that we obtain from the client library. Is that allowable, or should the contents of the MYSQL_FIELD structure be considered read-only? Normally, I would say "read-only," but some of the client programs in the MySQL distribution change the max_length value in a similar way, so I assume that it's okay. (If you prefer an alternative approach that doesn't modify max_length, allocate an array of unsigned long values and store the calculated widths in that array.)

The display width calculations involve one caveat. Recall that max_length has no meaning when you create a result set using mysql_use_result(). Because we need max_length to determine the display width of the column values, proper operation of the algorithm requires that the result set be generated using mysql_store_result(). In programs that use mysql_use_result() rather than mysql_store_result(), one possible workaround is to use the length member of the MYSQL_FIELD structure, which tells you the maximum length that column values can be.

When we know the column widths, we're ready to print. Titles are easy to handle. For a given column, we simply use the column information structure pointed to by field and print the name member, using the width calculated earlier:

```
printf (" %-*s |", (int) field->max_length, field->name);
```

For the data, we loop through the rows in the result set, printing column values for the current row during each iteration. Printing column values from the row is a bit tricky because a value might be NULL, or it might represent a number (in which case we print it right justified). Column values are printed as follows, where row[i] holds the data value and field points to the column information:

```
if (row[i] == NULL)        /* print the word "NULL" */
  printf (" %-*s |", (int) field->max_length, "NULL");
else if (IS_NUM (field->type))  /* print value right-justified */
  printf (" %*s |", (int) field->max_length, row[i]);
else                  /* print value left-justified */
  printf (" %-*s |", (int) field->max_length, row[i]);
```

The value of the IS_NUM() macro is true if the column data type indicated by field->type is one of the numeric types, such as INT, FLOAT, or DECIMAL.

The final code to display the result set is as follows. Because we're printing lines of dashes multiple times, it's easier to write a print_dashes() function to do so rather than to repeat the dash-generation code several places:

```
void
print_dashes (MYSQL_RES *res_set)
{
MYSQL_FIELD   *field;
unsigned int  i, j;

  mysql_field_seek (res_set, 0);
  fputc ('+', stdout);
  for (i = 0; i < mysql_num_fields (res_set); i++)
  {
    field = mysql_fetch_field (res_set);
    for (j = 0; j < field->max_length + 2; j++)
      fputc ('-', stdout);
    fputc ('+', stdout);
  }
  fputc ('\n', stdout);
}


void
process_result_set (MYSQL *conn, MYSQL_RES *res_set)
{
MYSQL_ROW     row;
MYSQL_FIELD   *field;
unsigned long col_len;
unsigned int  i;

  /* determine column display widths -- requires result set to be */
  /* generated with mysql_store_result(), not mysql_use_result() */
```

```
mysql_field_seek (res_set, 0);
for (i = 0; i < mysql_num_fields (res_set); i++)
{
  field = mysql_fetch_field (res_set);
  col_len = strlen (field->name);
  if (col_len < field->max_length)
    col_len = field->max_length;
  if (col_len < 4 && !IS_NOT_NULL (field->flags))
    col_len = 4;  /* 4 = length of the word "NULL" */
  field->max_length = col_len;  /* reset column info */
}

print_dashes (res_set);
fputc ('|', stdout);
mysql_field_seek (res_set, 0);
for (i = 0; i < mysql_num_fields (res_set); i++)
{
  field = mysql_fetch_field (res_set);
  printf (" %-*s |", (int) field->max_length, field->name);
}
fputc ('\n', stdout);
print_dashes (res_set);

while ((row = mysql_fetch_row (res_set)) != NULL)
{
  mysql_field_seek (res_set, 0);
  fputc ('|', stdout);
  for (i = 0; i < mysql_num_fields (res_set); i++)
  {
    field = mysql_fetch_field (res_set);
    if (row[i] == NULL)         /* print the word "NULL" */
      printf (" %-*s |", (int) field->max_length, "NULL");
    else if (IS_NUM (field->type))  /* print value right-justified */
      printf (" %*s |", (int) field->max_length, row[i]);
    else                 /* print value left-justified */
      printf (" %-*s |", (int) field->max_length, row[i]);
  }
  fputc ('\n', stdout);
}
print_dashes (res_set);
printf ("Number of rows returned: %lu\n",
        (unsigned long) mysql_num_rows (res_set));
}
```

The MySQL client library provides several ways of accessing the column information structures. For example, the code in the preceding example accesses these structures several times using loops of the following general form:

```
mysql_field_seek (res_set, 0);
for (i = 0; i < mysql_num_fields (res_set); i++)
{
  field = mysql_fetch_field (res_set);
  ...
}
```

However, the combination of `mysql_field_seek()` and `mysql_fetch_field()` is only one way of getting `MYSQL_FIELD` structures. See the descriptions of the `mysql_fetch_fields()` and `mysql_fetch_field_direct()` functions in Appendix G (online) for other ways of accessing column information structures.

> ### Use the `metadata` Program to Display Result Set Metadata
> The `sampdb` distribution contains the source for a program named `metadata` that you can compile and run to see what metadata various kinds of statements produce. It prompts for and executes SQL statements, but displays result set metadata rather than result set contents.

7.4.7 Encoding Special Characters and Binary Data

If a program executes statements entered by the user, it can assume either that those statements are legal or that the program can simply report an error to the user. For example, a user who wants to include a quote character within a quoted string must either double the quote or precede it by a backslash:

```
'O''Malley'
'O\'Malley'
```

Applications that construct their own statements must take the same precautions. This section describes how to handle quoting issues in string values and how to work with binary data.

7.4.7.1 Working with Strings That Contain Special Characters

If inserted literally into a statement, data values containing quotes, null bytes, or backslashes can cause problems when you try to execute the statement. The following discussion describes the nature of the difficulty and how to solve it.

Suppose that you want to construct a `SELECT` statement based on the contents of the null-terminated string pointed to by the `name_val` variable:

```
char stmt_buf[1024];

sprintf (stmt_buf, "SELECT * FROM mytbl WHERE name='%s'", name_val);
```

If the value of `name_val` is something like `O'Malley, Brian`, the resulting statement is illegal because a quote appears inside a quoted string:

```
SELECT * FROM mytbl WHERE name='O'Malley, Brian'
```

You need to treat the inner quote specially so that the server doesn't interpret it as the end of the name. The standard SQL convention for doing this is to double the quote within the string. MySQL understands that convention, and also allows the quote to be preceded by a backslash, so you can write the statement using either of the following formats:

```
SELECT * FROM mytbl WHERE name='O''Malley, Brian'
SELECT * FROM mytbl WHERE name='O\'Malley, Brian'
```

To deal with this problem, use `mysql_real_escape_string()`, which encodes special characters to make them usable in quoted strings. Characters that `mysql_real_escape_string()` considers special are the null byte, single quote, double quote, backslash, newline, carriage return, and Control-Z. (The last one is special on Windows, where it often signifies end-of-file.)

When should you use `mysql_real_escape_string()`? The safest answer is "always." However, if you're sure of the format of your data and know that it's okay—perhaps because you have performed some prior validation check on it—you need not encode it. For example, if you are working with strings that you know represent legal phone numbers consisting entirely of digits and dashes, you don't need to call `mysql_real_escape_string()`. Otherwise, you probably should.

`mysql_real_escape_string()` encodes problematic characters by turning them into two-character sequences that begin with a backslash. For example, a null byte becomes '\0', where the '0' is a printable ASCII zero, not a null. Backslash, single quote, and double quote become '\\', '\'', and '\"'.

To use `mysql_real_escape_string()`, invoke it like this:

```
to_len = mysql_real_escape_string (conn, to_str, from_str, from_len);
```

`mysql_real_escape_string()` encodes `from_str` and writes the result into `to_str`. It also adds a terminating null, which is convenient because you can use the resulting string with functions such as `strcpy()`, `strlen()`, or `printf()`.

`from_str` points to a `char` buffer containing the string to be encoded. This string may contain anything, including binary data. `to_str` points to an existing `char` buffer where you want the encoded string to be written; do not pass an uninitialized or NULL pointer, expecting `mysql_real_escape_string()` to allocate space for you. The length of the buffer pointed to by `to_str` must be at least `(from_len*2)+1` bytes long. (It's possible that every character in `from_str` will need encoding with two characters; the extra byte is for the terminating null.)

`from_len` and `to_len` are `unsigned long` values. `from_len` indicates the length of the data in `from_str`; it's necessary to provide the length because `from_str` may contain null bytes and cannot be treated as a null-terminated string. `to_len`, the return value from `mysql_real_escape_string()`, is the actual length of the resulting encoded string, not counting the terminating null.

When `mysql_real_escape_string()` returns, the encoded result in `to_str` can be treated as a null-terminated string because any null bytes in `from_str` are encoded as the printable '\0' sequence.

To rewrite the SELECT-constructing code so that it works even for name values that contain quotes, we could do something like this:

```
char stmt_buf[1024], *p;


p = strcpy (stmt_buf, "SELECT * FROM mytbl WHERE name='");
p += strlen (p);
p += mysql_real_escape_string (conn, p, name_val, strlen (name_val));
*p++ = '\'';
*p = '\0';
```

Yes, that's ugly. To simplify the code a bit, at the cost of using a second buffer, do this instead:

```
char stmt_buf[1024], buf[1024];


(void) mysql_real_escape_string (conn, buf, name_val, strlen (name_val));
sprintf (stmt_buf, "SELECT * FROM mytbl WHERE name='%s'", buf);
```

It's important to make sure that the buffers you pass to `mysql_real_escape_string()` really exist. Consider the following example, which violates that principle:

```
char *from_str = "some string";
char *to_str;
unsigned long len;


len = mysql_real_escape_string (conn, to_str, from_str, strlen (from_str));
```

What's the problem? `to_str` must point to an existing buffer, and it doesn't—it's not initialized and may point to some random location. Don't pass an uninitialized pointer as the `to_str` argument to `mysql_real_escape_string()` unless you want it to stomp merrily all over some random piece of memory.

7.4.7.2 Working with Binary Data

Another problematic situation involves the use of arbitrary binary data in a statement. This happens, for example, in applications that store images in a database. Because a binary value may contain any character (including null bytes, quotes, or backslashes), it cannot be considered safe to put into a statement as is.

`mysql_real_escape_string()` is essential for working with binary data. This section shows how to do so, using image data read from a file. The discussion applies to any other form of binary data as well.

Suppose that you want to read images from files and store them in a table named `picture`, along with a unique identifier. The MEDIUMBLOB type is a good choice for binary values less than 16MB in size, so you could use a table specification like this:

```
CREATE TABLE picture
(
  pict_id   INT NOT NULL PRIMARY KEY,
  pict_data MEDIUMBLOB
);
```

To actually get an image from a file into the `picture` table, the following function, `load_image()`, does the job, given an identifier number and a pointer to an open file containing the image data:

```
int
load_image (MYSQL *conn, int id, FILE *f)
{
char          stmt_buf[1024*1024], buf[1024*10], *p;
unsigned long from_len;
int           status;

  /* begin creating an INSERT statement, adding the id value */
  sprintf (stmt_buf,
           "INSERT INTO picture (pict_id,pict_data) VALUES (%d,'",
           id);
  p = stmt_buf + strlen (stmt_buf);
  /* read data from file in chunks, encode each */
  /* chunk, and add to end of statement */
  while ((from_len = fread (buf, 1, sizeof (buf), f)) > 0)
  {
    /* don't overrun end of statement buffer! */
    if (p + (2*from_len) + 3 > stmt_buf + sizeof (stmt_buf))
    {
      print_error (NULL, "image is too big");
      return (1);
    }
    p += mysql_real_escape_string (conn, p, buf, from_len);
  }
  *p++ = '\'';
  *p++ = ')';
  status = mysql_real_query (conn, stmt_buf, (unsigned long) (p - stmt_buf));
  return (status);
}
```

`load_image()` doesn't allocate a very large statement buffer (1MB), so it works only for relatively small images. In a real-world application, you might allocate the buffer dynamically based on the size of the image file.

Getting an image value (or any binary value) back out of a database isn't nearly as much of a problem as putting it in to begin with. The data value is available in raw form in the `MYSQL_ROW` variable, and the length is available by calling `mysql_fetch_lengths()`. Just be sure to treat the value as a counted string, not as a null-terminated string.

7.5 An Interactive Statement-Execution Program

We are now in a position to put together much of what we've developed so far and use it to write a simple interactive statement-execution client, `exec_stmt`. This program lets you enter statements, executes them using our general-purpose statement handler `process_statement()`, and displays the results using the `process_result_set()` display formatter developed in the preceding section.

`exec_stmt` is similar in some ways to `mysql`, although of course with not as many features. There are several restrictions on what `exec_stmt` will allow as input:

- Each input line must contain a single complete statement.

- Statements should not be terminated by a semicolon or by `\g`.

- The only non-SQL commands that are recognized are `quit` and `\q`, which terminate the program. You can also use Control-D to quit.

It turns out that `exec_stmt` is almost completely trivial to write (about a dozen lines of new code). Almost everything we need is provided by our client program skeleton (`connect2.c`) and by other functions that we have written already. The only thing we need to add is a loop that collects input lines and executes them.

To construct `exec_stmt`, begin by copying the client skeleton `connect2.c` to `exec_stmt.c`. Then add to that the code for the `process_statement()`, `process_result_set()`, and `print_dashes()` functions. Finally, in `exec_stmt.c`, look for the line in `main()` that says this:

```
/* ... issue statements and process results here ... */
```

Replace that line with this `while` loop:

```
while (1)
{
  char  buf[10000];

  fprintf (stderr, "query> ");                 /* print prompt */
  if (fgets (buf, sizeof (buf), stdin) == NULL) /* read statement */
    break;
  if (strcmp (buf, "quit\n") == 0 || strcmp (buf, "\\q\n") == 0)
    break;
  process_statement (conn, buf);               /* execute it */
}
```

Compile `exec_stmt.c` to produce `exec_stmt.o`, link `exec_stmt.o` with the client library to produce `exec_stmt`, and you're done. You have an interactive MySQL client

program that can execute any statement and display the results. The following example
shows how the program works, both for SELECT and non-SELECT statements, as well as for
statements that are erroneous:

```
% ./exec_stmt
query> USE sampdb
Number of rows affected: 0
query> SELECT DATABASE(), USER()
+------------+-------------------+
| DATABASE() | USER()            |
+------------+-------------------+
| sampdb     | sampadm@localhost |
+------------+-------------------+
Number of rows returned: 1
query> SELECT COUNT(*) FROM president
+----------+
| COUNT(*) |
+----------+
|       42 |
+----------+
Number of rows returned: 1
query> SELECT last_name, first_name FROM president ORDER BY last_name LIMIT 3
+-----------+-------------+
| last_name | first_name  |
+-----------+-------------+
| Adams     | John        |
| Adams     | John Quincy |
| Arthur    | Chester A.  |
+-----------+-------------+
Number of rows returned: 3
query> CREATE TABLE t (i INT)
Number of rows affected: 0
query> SELECT j FROM t
Could not execute statement
Error 1054 (42S22): Unknown column 'j' in 'field list'
query> USE mysql
Could not execute statement
Error 1044 (42000): Access denied for user 'sampadm'@'localhost' to
database 'mysql'
```

7.6 Writing Clients That Include SSL Support

MySQL includes SSL support, and you can use it to write your own programs that access
the server over secure connections. To show how this is done, this section describes the
process of modifying exec_stmt to produce a similar client named exec_stmt_ssl that
outwardly is much the same but enables encrypted connections to be established. For

exec_stmt_ssl to work properly, MySQL must have been built with SSL support, and the server must be started with the proper options that identify its certificate and key files. You'll also need certificate and key files on the client end. For more information, see Section 13.3, "Setting Up Secure Connections."

The sampdb distribution contains a source file, exec_stmt_ssl.c, from which the client program exec_stmt_ssl can be built. The following procedure describes how exec_stmt_ssl.c is created, beginning with exec_stmt.c:

1. Copy exec_stmt.c to exec_stmt_ssl.c. The remaining steps apply to exec_stmt_ssl.c.

2. To enable the compiler to detect whether SSL support is available, the MySQL header file my_config.h defines the symbol HAVE_OPENSSL appropriately. This means that when writing SSL-related code, you use the following construct so that the code will be ignored if SSL cannot be used:

```
#ifdef HAVE_OPENSSL
   ...SSL-related code here...
#endif
```

You need not include my_config.h explicitly because it is included by my_global.h, and exec_stmt_ssl.c already includes the latter file.

3. Modify the my_opts array that contains option information structures so that it includes entries for the standard SSL-related options (--ssl-ca, --ssl-key, and so forth). The easiest way to do this is to include the contents of the sslopt-longopts.h file into the my_opts array with an #include directive. After making the change, my_opts looks like this:

```
static struct my_option my_opts[] =   /* option information structures */
{
  {"help", '?', "Display this help and exit",
  NULL, NULL, NULL,
  GET_NO_ARG, NO_ARG, 0, 0, 0, 0, 0, 0},
  {"host", 'h', "Host to connect to",
  (uchar **) &opt_host_name, NULL, NULL,
  GET_STR, REQUIRED_ARG, 0, 0, 0, 0, 0, 0},
  {"password", 'p', "Password",
  (uchar **) &opt_password, NULL, NULL,
  GET_STR, OPT_ARG, 0, 0, 0, 0, 0, 0},
  {"port", 'P', "Port number",
  (uchar **) &opt_port_num, NULL, NULL,
  GET_UINT, REQUIRED_ARG, 0, 0, 0, 0, 0, 0},
  {"socket", 'S', "Socket path",
  (uchar **) &opt_socket_name, NULL, NULL,
  GET_STR, REQUIRED_ARG, 0, 0, 0, 0, 0, 0},
  {"user", 'u', "User name",
  (uchar **) &opt_user_name, NULL, NULL,
```

```
        GET_STR, REQUIRED_ARG, 0, 0, 0, 0, 0, 0},

#include <sslopt-longopts.h>

    { NULL, 0, NULL, NULL, NULL, NULL, GET_NO_ARG, NO_ARG, 0, 0, 0, 0, 0, 0 }
};
```

sslopt-longopts.h is a public MySQL header file. Its contents look like this (re-formatted slightly):

```
#ifdef HAVE_OPENSSL
  {"ssl", OPT_SSL_SSL,
  "Enable SSL for connection (automatically enabled with other flags).
  Disable with --skip-ssl.",
  (uchar **) &opt_use_ssl, (uchar **) &opt_use_ssl, 0,
  GET_BOOL, NO_ARG, 0, 0, 0, 0, 0, 0},
  {"ssl-ca", OPT_SSL_CA,
  "CA file in PEM format (check OpenSSL docs, implies --ssl).",
  (uchar **) &opt_ssl_ca, (uchar **) &opt_ssl_ca, 0,
  GET_STR, REQUIRED_ARG, 0, 0, 0, 0, 0, 0},
  {"ssl-capath", OPT_SSL_CAPATH,
  "CA directory (check OpenSSL docs, implies --ssl).",
  (uchar **) &opt_ssl_capath, (uchar **) &opt_ssl_capath, 0,
  GET_STR, REQUIRED_ARG, 0, 0, 0, 0, 0, 0},
  {"ssl-cert", OPT_SSL_CERT, "X509 cert in PEM format (implies --ssl).",
  (uchar **) &opt_ssl_cert, (uchar **) &opt_ssl_cert, 0,
  GET_STR, REQUIRED_ARG, 0, 0, 0, 0, 0, 0},
  {"ssl-cipher", OPT_SSL_CIPHER, "SSL cipher to use (implies --ssl).",
  (uchar **) &opt_ssl_cipher, (uchar **) &opt_ssl_cipher, 0,
  GET_STR, REQUIRED_ARG, 0, 0, 0, 0, 0, 0},
  {"ssl-key", OPT_SSL_KEY, "X509 key in PEM format (implies --ssl).",
  (uchar **) &opt_ssl_key, (uchar **) &opt_ssl_key, 0,
  GET_STR, REQUIRED_ARG, 0, 0, 0, 0, 0, 0},
#ifdef MYSQL_CLIENT
  {"ssl-verify-server-cert", OPT_SSL_VERIFY_SERVER_CERT,
   "Verify server's \"Common Name\" in its cert against hostname used
   when connecting. This option is disabled by default.",
   (uchar **) &opt_ssl_verify_server_cert,
   (uchar **) &opt_ssl_verify_server_cert, 0,
   GET_BOOL, NO_ARG, 0, 0, 0, 0, 0, 0},
#endif
#endif /* HAVE_OPENSSL */
```

4. The option structures defined by sslopt-longopts.h refer to the values
    OPT_SSL_SSL, OPT_SSL_KEY, and so forth. These are used for the short option codes

and must be defined by your program, which can be done by adding the following lines preceding the definition of the `my_opts` array:

```
#ifdef HAVE_OPENSSL
enum options_client
{
  OPT_SSL_SSL=256,
  OPT_SSL_KEY,
  OPT_SSL_CERT,
  OPT_SSL_CA,
  OPT_SSL_CAPATH,
  OPT_SSL_CIPHER,
  OPT_SSL_VERIFY_SERVER_CERT
};
#endif
```

When writing your own applications, if a given program also defines codes for other options, make sure that these OPT_SSL_*xxx* symbols have values different from those codes.

5. The SSL-related option structures in `sslopt-longopts.h` refer to a set of variables that are used to hold the option values. To declare these, use an `#include` directive to include the contents of the `sslopt-vars.h` file into your program preceding the definition of the `my_opts` array. `sslopt-vars.h` looks like this:

```
#ifdef HAVE_OPENSSL
static my_bool opt_use_ssl  = 0;
static char *opt_ssl_ca     = 0;
static char *opt_ssl_capath = 0;
static char *opt_ssl_cert   = 0;
static char *opt_ssl_cipher = 0;
static char *opt_ssl_key    = 0;
#ifdef MYSQL_CLIENT
static my_bool opt_ssl_verify_server_cert= 0;
#endif
#endif
```

6. In the `get_one_option()` routine, add a line near the end that includes the `sslopt-case.h` file:

```
static my_bool
get_one_option (int optid, const struct my_option *opt, char *argument)
{
  switch (optid)
  {
  case '?':
    my_print_help (my_opts);  /* print help message */
    exit (0);
```

```
      case 'p':                      /* password */
        if (!argument)               /* no value given; solicit it later */
          ask_password = 1;
        else                         /* copy password, overwrite original */
        {
          opt_password = strdup (argument);
          if (opt_password == NULL)
          {
            print_error (NULL, "could not allocate password buffer");
            exit (1);
          }
          while (*argument)
            *argument++ = 'x';
          ask_password = 0;
        }
        break;
#include <sslopt-case.h>
      }
    return (0);
}
```

sslopt-case.h includes additional cases for the switch() statement that detect
when any of the SSL options were given and sets the opt_use_ssl variable if so. It
looks like this:

```
#ifdef HAVE_OPENSSL
    case OPT_SSL_KEY:
    case OPT_SSL_CERT:
    case OPT_SSL_CA:
    case OPT_SSL_CAPATH:
    case OPT_SSL_CIPHER:
    /*
       Enable use of SSL if we are using any ssl option
       One can disable SSL later by using --skip-ssl or --ssl=0
    */
      opt_use_ssl= 1;
      break;
#endif
```

The effect of this is that after option processing has been done, it is possible to determine whether the user wants a secure connection by checking the value of opt_use_ssl.

If you use the preceding procedure, the usual load_defaults() and handle_
options() routines will take care of parsing the SSL-related options and setting their values for you automatically. The only other thing you need to do is pass SSL option information to the client library before connecting to the server if the options indicate that the

user wants an SSL connection. Do this by invoking `mysql_ssl_set()` after calling `mysql_init()` and before calling `mysql_real_connect()`. The sequence looks like this:

```
/* initialize connection handler */
conn = mysql_init (NULL);
if (conn == NULL)
{
  print_error (NULL, "mysql_init() failed (probably out of memory)");
  exit (1);
}


#ifdef HAVE_OPENSSL
  /* pass SSL information to client library */
  if (opt_use_ssl)
    mysql_ssl_set (conn, opt_ssl_key, opt_ssl_cert, opt_ssl_ca,
                   opt_ssl_capath, opt_ssl_cipher);
#if (MYSQL_VERSION_ID >= 50023 && MYSQL_VERSION_ID < 50100) \
    || MYSQL_VERSION_ID >= 50111
  mysql_options (conn,MYSQL_OPT_SSL_VERIFY_SERVER_CERT,
                 (char*)&opt_ssl_verify_server_cert);
#endif
#endif


  /* connect to server */
  if (mysql_real_connect (conn, opt_host_name, opt_user_name, opt_password,
     opt_db_name, opt_port_num, opt_socket_name, opt_flags) == NULL)
  {
    print_error (conn, "mysql_real_connect() failed");
    mysql_close (conn);
    exit (1);
  }
```

This code doesn't test `mysql_ssl_set()` to see whether it returns an error. Any problems with the information you supply to that function will result in an error when you call `mysql_real_connect()`. The complicated test to determine whether to invoke `mysql_options()` reflects that the addition of `MYSQL_OPT_SSL_VERIFY_SERVER_CERT` occurred in version 5.0.23 for MySQL 5.0 and 5.1.11 for MySQL 5.1.

Compile `exec_stmt_ssl.c` to produce the `exec_stmt_ssl` program and then run it. Assuming that the `mysql_real_connect()` call succeeds, you can proceed to issue statements. If you invoke `exec_stmt_ssl` with the appropriate SSL options, communication with the server should occur over an encrypted connection. To determine whether that is so, issue the following statement:

```
SHOW STATUS LIKE 'Ssl_cipher'
```

The value of `Ssl_cipher` will be non-blank if an encryption cipher is in use. (To make this easier, the version of `exec_stmt_ssl` included in the `sampdb` distribution actually issues the statement for you and reports the result.)

7.7 Using the Embedded Server Library

MySQL includes an embedded server library, `libmysqld`, that contains the MySQL server in a form that can be linked (embedded) into applications. This enables you to produce MySQL-based standalone applications, as opposed to applications that connect as a client over a network to a separate server program.

To write an embedded server application, two requirements must be satisfied. First, the embedded server library must be installed:

- If you're building from source, enable the library by using the `--with-embedded-server` option when you run `configure`. This applies equally to MySQL 5.0 and 5.1.

- If you want to use a binary distribution, you must use MySQL 5.1 because 5.0 binary distributions do not include `libmysqld`. Current versions of 5.1 do include `libmysqld`. However, if you use RPM packages, be aware that there is a separate "embedded" RPM that you must install for `libmysqld` support.

Second, you'll need to include a small amount of code in your application to start up and shut down the server.

After making sure that both requirements are met, it's necessary only to compile the application and link in the embedded server library (`-lmysqld`) rather than the regular client library (`-lmysqlclient`). The design of the server library is such that if you write an application to use it, you can easily produce either an embedded or a client/server version of the application simply by linking in the appropriate library. This works because the regular client library contains interface functions that perform initialization and finalization appropriate to client/server communication rather than to communication with an embedded server.

7.7.1 Writing an Embedded Server Application

Writing an application that uses the embedded server is little different from writing one that operates in a client/server context. In fact, if you begin with a program that is written as a client/server application, you can easily convert it to use the embedded server instead. The following procedure describes how to produce an embedded application named `embapp`, beginning with `exec_stmt.c`:

1. Copy `exec_stmt.c` to `embapp.c`. The remaining steps apply to `embapp.c`. (The reason we begin with `exec_stmt.c` rather than `exec_stmt_ssl.c` is that there is no need to use SSL for connections that are set up internally within a single application.)

2. Add `mysql_embed.h` to the set of MySQL header files used by the program:

```
#include <my_global.h>
#include <my_sys.h>
```

```
#include <m_string.h>   /* for strdup() */
#include <mysql.h>
#include <mysql_embed.h>
#include <my_getopt.h>
```

3. An embedded application includes both a client side and a server side, so it can process one group of options for the client, and another group for the server. For example, an application named embapp might read the [client] and [embapp] groups from option files for the client part. To set that up, modify the definition of the client_groups array to look like this:

```
static const char *client_groups[] =
{
  "client", "embapp", NULL
};
```

Options in these groups can be processed by load_defaults() and handle_options() in the usual fashion. Then define another list of option groups for the server side to use. By convention, this list should include the [server] and [embedded] groups, and also the [appname_server] group, where appname is the name of your application. For a program named embapp, the application-specific group will be [embapp_server], so you declare the list of group names as follows:

```
static const char *server_groups[] =
{
  "server", "embedded", "embapp_server", NULL
};
```

4. Call mysql_library_init() before initiating communication with the server, modifying the call so that it passes any options to be processed by the server. A good place to do this is before you call mysql_init().

5. Call mysql_library_end() after you're done using the server. A good place to do this is after you call mysql_close().

After making these changes, the main() function in embapp.c looks like this:

```
int
main (int argc, char *argv[])
{
int opt_err;

  MY_INIT (argv[0]);
  load_defaults ("my", client_groups, &argc, &argv);

  if ((opt_err = handle_options (&argc, &argv, my_opts, get_one_option)))
    exit (opt_err);

  /* solicit password if necessary */
```

```
if (ask_password)
  opt_password = get_tty_password (NULL);

/* get database name if present on command line */
if (argc > 0)
{
  opt_db_name = argv[0];
  --argc; ++argv;
}

/* initialize embedded server library */
if (mysql_library_init (0, NULL, (char **) server_groups))
{
  print_error (NULL, "mysql_library_init() failed");
  exit (1);
}

/* initialize connection handler */
conn = mysql_init (NULL);
if (conn == NULL)
{
  print_error (NULL, "mysql_init() failed (probably out of memory)");
  exit (1);
}

/* connect to server */
if (mysql_real_connect (conn, opt_host_name, opt_user_name, opt_password,
    opt_db_name, opt_port_num, opt_socket_name, opt_flags) == NULL)
{
  print_error (conn, "mysql_real_connect() failed");
  mysql_close (conn);
  exit (1);
}

while (1)
{
  char  buf[10000];

  fprintf (stderr, "query> ");                     /* print prompt */
  if (fgets (buf, sizeof (buf), stdin) == NULL) /* read statement */
    break;
  if (strcmp (buf, "quit\n") == 0 || strcmp (buf, "\\q\n") == 0)
    break;
  process_statement (conn, buf);                   /* execute it */
}

/* disconnect from server */
```

```
  mysql_close (conn);
  /* shut down embedded server library */
  mysql_library_end ();
  exit (0);
}
```

7.7.2 Producing the Application Executable Binary

To produce the embedded-server executable binary for `embapp`, link in the `-lmysqld` library rather than the `-lmysqlclient` library. The `mysql_config` utility is useful here. Just as it can show you the flags to use for linking in the regular client library, it also can display the flags necessary for the embedded server:

```
% mysql_config --libmysqld-libs
 -L'/usr/local/mysql/lib/mysql' -lmysqld -lz -lm
```

Thus, to produce an embedded version of `embapp`, use commands like these:

```
% gcc -c `mysql_config --include` embapp.c
% gcc -o embapp embapp.o `mysql_config --libmysqld-libs`
```

> **Note**
>
> In these commands, you might find it necessary to use a C++ compiler such as `g++` rather than a C compiler.

At this point, you have an embedded application that contains everything you need to access your MySQL databases. However, be sure when you execute `embapp` that it does not attempt to use the same data directory as any standalone servers that may already be running on the same machine.

Also, under Unix, the application must run with privileges that give it access to the data directory. You can either run `embapp` while logged in as the user that owns the data directory, or you can make it a setuid program that changes its user ID to that user when it starts. For example, to set `embapp` to run with the privileges of a user named `mysql`, issue the following commands as `root`:

```
# chown mysql embapp
# chmod 4755 embapp
```

Alternatively, have the embedded application use a different data directory. You can specify the location by placing a `datadir` option in the `[embapp_server]` group of an option file. (The option group for the server half of the application.)

Should you decide that you want to produce a non-embedded version of the application that operates in a client/server context, link it against the regular client library. You can do so by building it like this:

```
% gcc -c `mysql_config --include` embapp.c
% gcc -o embapp embapp.o `mysql_config --libs`
```

The regular client library includes versions of `mysql_library_init()` and `mysql_library_end()` that perform initialization and finalization appropriate to client/server communication rather than to communication with an embedded server.

7.8 Using Multiple-Statement Execution

The MySQL client library supports multiple-statement execution capability. This enables you to send a string to the server consisting of multiple statements separated by semicolons, and then retrieve the result sets one after the other.

Multiple-statement execution is not enabled by default, so you must tell the server that you want to use it. There are two ways to do this. The first is to add the `CLIENT_MULTI_STATEMENTS` option in the flags argument to `mysql_real_connect()` at connect time:

```
opt_flags |= CLIENT_MULTI_STATEMENTS;
if (mysql_real_connect (conn, opt_host_name, opt_user_name, opt_password,
    opt_db_name, opt_port_num, opt_socket_name, opt_flags) == NULL)
{
  print_error (conn, "mysql_real_connect() failed");
  mysql_close (conn);
  exit (1);
}
```

The other is to use `mysql_set_server_option()` to enable the capability for an existing connection. For example:

```
if (mysql_set_server_option (conn, MYSQL_OPTION_MULTI_STATEMENTS_ON) != 0)
  print_error (conn, "Could not enable multiple-statement execution");
```

Which method is preferable? If the program does not use stored procedures, either one is suitable. If the program does use stored procedures and invokes a CALL statement that returns a result set, the first method is better. That's because `CLIENT_MULTI_STATEMENTS` also turns on the `CLIENT_MULTI_RESULTS` option, which must be enabled or an error occurs if a stored procedure attempts to return a result. (More preferable yet might be to add `CLIENT_MULTI_RESULTS` to the flags argument to `mysql_real_connect()`, because that makes it explicit that you're enabling the option.)

Two functions form the basis for checking the current status of result retrieval when you're processing multiple result sets:

- `mysql_more_results()` returns non-zero if more results are available and zero otherwise.

- `mysql_next_result()` returns a status and also initiates retrieval of the next set if more results are available. The status is zero if more results are available, -1 if not, and a value greater than zero if an error occurred.

You can use these functions by putting your result-retrieval code inside a loop. After retrieving a result with your usual code, check whether there are any results yet to be retrieved. If so, perform another iteration of the loop. If not, exit the loop. Depending on how you structure your loop, you may not need to call `mysql_more_results()` at all. That's because you can also tell from the return value of `mysql_next_result()` whether more results are available.

In Section 7.4.3, "A General-Purpose Statement Handler," we wrote a function, `process_statement()`, that executes a statement and retrieves the result or displays the number of rows affected. By placing the result-retrieval code into a loop and incorporating `mysql_next_result()`, we can write a similar function, `process_multi_statement()`, that can retrieve multiple results:

```
void
process_multi_statement (MYSQL *conn, char *stmt_str)
{
MYSQL_RES *res_set;
int        status;
int        keep_going = 1;

  if (mysql_query (conn, stmt_str) != 0)  /* the statement(s) failed */
  {
    print_error (conn, "Could not execute statement(s)");
    return;
  }

  /* the statement(s) succeeded; enter result-retrieval loop */
  do {
    /* determine whether current statement returned data */
    res_set = mysql_store_result (conn);
    if (res_set)      /* a result set was returned */
    {
      /* process rows and then free the result set */
      process_result_set (conn, res_set);
      mysql_free_result (res_set);
    }
    else              /* no result set was returned */
    {
      /*
       * does the lack of a result set mean that the statement didn't
       * return one, or that it should have but an error occurred?
       */
      if (mysql_field_count (conn) == 0)
      {
        /*
         * statement generated no result set (it was not a SELECT,
         * SHOW, DESCRIBE, etc.); just report rows-affected value.
         */
        printf ("Number of rows affected: %lu\n",
```

```
                        (unsigned long) mysql_affected_rows (conn));
    }
    else  /* an error occurred */
    {
      print_error (conn, "Could not retrieve result set");
      keep_going = 0;
    }
  }
  /* determine whether more results exist */
  /* 0 = yes, -1 = no, >0 = error */
  status = mysql_next_result (conn);
  if (status != 0)    /* no more results, or an error occurred */
  {
    keep_going = 0;
    if (status > 0)   /* error */
      print_error (conn, "Could not execute statement");
  }
} while (keep_going);
}
```

If you like, you can just test whether the result of `mysql_next_result()` is zero, and exit the loop if not. The disadvantage of this simpler strategy is that if there are no more results, you don't know whether you've reached the end normally or an error occurred. In other words, you don't know whether to print an error message.

7.9 Using Server-Side Prepared Statements

In the earlier parts of this chapter, the code for SQL statement processing is based on the set of functions provided by the MySQL client library that send and retrieve all information in string form. This section discusses how to use the binary client/server protocol. The binary protocol supports server-side prepared statements and enables transmission of data values in native format.

Not all statements can be prepared. The prepared-statement API applies to these statements: CREATE TABLE, DELETE, DO, INSERT, REPLACE, SELECT, SET, UPDATE, and most variations of SHOW. The list of supported statements was considerably expanded in MySQL 5.1. See the MySQL Reference Manual for 5.1 for the exact current list.

To use the binary protocol, you must create a statement handler. With this handler, send a statement to the server to be "prepared," or preprocessed. The server analyzes the statement, remembers it, and sends back information about it that the client library stores in the statement handler. Further processing for the statement uses this handler.

A statement to be prepared can be parameterized by including '?' characters to indicate where data values appear that you will supply later when you execute the statement. For example, you might prepare a statement that looks like this:

```
INSERT INTO score (event_id,student_id,score) VALUES(?,?,?)
```

This statement includes three '?' characters that act as parameter markers or place-holders. Later, you can supply data values to be bound to the placeholders. These complete the statement when you execute it. By parameterizing a statement, you make it reusable: The same statement can be executed multiple times, each time with a new set of data values. What this means is that you send the text of the statement only once. Each time you execute the statement, you need send only the data values. For repeated statement execution, this provides a performance boost:

- The server needs to analyze the statement only once, not each time it is executed.
- Network overhead is reduced, because you send only the data values for each execution, not an entire statement.
- Data values are sent without conversion to string form, which reduces execution overhead. For example, the three columns named in the preceding INSERT statement all are INT columns. Were you to use mysql_query() or mysql_real_query() to execute a similar INSERT statement, it would be necessary to convert the data values to strings for inclusion in the text of the statement. With the prepared statement interface, you send the data values separately in binary format.
- No conversion is needed for retrieving results, either. In result sets returned by prepared statements, non-string values are returned in binary format without conversion to string form.

The binary protocol does have some disadvantages, compared to the original non-binary protocol:

- It is more difficult to use because more setup is necessary for transmitting and receiving data values.
- The binary protocol does not support all statements. For example, USE statements don't work.
- For interactive programs, you may as well use the original protocol. In that case, each statement received from the user is executed only once. There is little benefit to using prepared statements, which provide the greatest efficiency gain for statements that you execute repeatedly.

The general procedure for using a prepared statement involves several steps:

1. Allocate a statement handler by calling mysql_stmt_init(). This function returns a pointer to the handler, which you use for the following steps.

2. Call mysql_stmt_prepare() to send a statement to the server to be prepared and associated with the statement handler. The server determines certain characteristics of the statement, such as what kind of statement it is, how many parameter markers it contains, and whether it will produce a result set when executed.

3. If the statement contains any placeholders, you must provide data for each of them before you can execute it. To do this, set up a MYSQL_BIND structure for each parameter. Each structure indicates one parameter's data type, its value, whether it is NULL,

and so on. Then bind these structures to the statement by calling
`mysql_stmt_bind_param()`.

4. Invoke `mysql_stmt_execute()` to execute the statement.

5. If the statement modifies data rather than producing a result set (for example, if it is
   an `INSERT` or `UPDATE`), call `mysql_stmt_affected_rows()` to determine the number of rows affected by the statement.

6. If the statement produces a result set, call `mysql_stmt_result_metadata()` if you
   want to obtain metadata about the result set. To fetch the rows, you use `MYSQL_BIND`
   structures again, but this time they serve as receptacles for data returned from the
   server rather than a source of data to send to the server. You must set up one
   `MYSQL_BIND` structure for each column in the result set. They contain information
   about the values you expect to receive from the server in each row. Bind the structures to the statement handler by calling `mysql_stmt_bind_result()`, and then invoke `mysql_stmt_fetch()` repeatedly to get each row. After each fetch, you can
   access the column values for the current row.

   An optional action you can take before calling `mysql_stmt_fetch()` is to call
   `mysql_stmt_store_result()`. If you do this, the result set rows are fetched all at
   once from the server and buffered in memory on the client side. Also, the number
   of rows in the result set can be determined by calling `mysql_stmt_num_rows()`,
   which otherwise returns zero.

   After fetching the result set, call `mysql_stmt_free_result()` to release memory
   associated with it.

7. If you want to re-execute the statement, return to step 4.

8. If you want to prepare a different statement using the handler, return to step 2.

9. When you're done with the statement handler, dispose of it by calling
   `mysql_stmt_close()`. If the client connection closes while the server still has
   prepared statements associated with the connection, the server disposes of them
   automatically.

   A client application can prepare multiple statements, and then execute each in the
order appropriate to the application.
   The following discussion describes how to write a simple program that inserts some
rows into a table and then retrieves them. The part of the program that processes `INSERT`
statement illustrates how to use placeholders in a statement and transmit data values to the
server to be bound to the prepared statement when it is executed. The part that processes
a `SELECT` statement shows how to retrieve a result set produced by executing a prepared
statement. You can find the source for this program in the `prepared.c` and

process_prepared_statement.c files in the capi directory of the sampdb distribution. I won't show the code for setting up the connection because it is similar to that for earlier programs.

The main part of the program that sets up to use prepared statements looks like this:

```
void
process_prepared_statements (MYSQL *conn)
{
MYSQL_STMT *stmt;
char       *use_stmt = "USE sampdb";
char       *drop_stmt = "DROP TABLE IF EXISTS t";
char       *create_stmt =
  "CREATE TABLE t (i INT, f FLOAT, c CHAR(24), dt DATETIME)";

  /* select database and create test table */

  if (mysql_query (conn, use_stmt) != 0
    || mysql_query (conn, drop_stmt) != 0
    || mysql_query (conn, create_stmt) != 0)
  {
    print_error (conn, "Could not set up test table");
    return;
  }

  stmt = mysql_stmt_init (conn);  /* allocate statement handler */
  if (stmt == NULL)
  {
    print_error (conn, "Could not initialize statement handler");
    return;
  }

  /* insert and retrieve some records */
  insert_rows (stmt);
  select_rows (stmt);

  mysql_stmt_close (stmt);        /* deallocate statement handler */
}
```

First, we select a database and create a test table. The table contains four columns of varying data types: an INT, a FLOAT, a CHAR, and a DATETIME. These different data types need to be handled in slightly different ways, as will become evident.

After the table has been created, we invoke mysql_stmt_init() to allocate a prepared statement handler, insert and retrieve some rows, and deallocate the handler. All the real work takes place in the insert_rows() and select_rows() functions, which we will get to shortly. For error handling, the program also uses a function, print_stmt_error(),

that is similar to the `print_error()` function used in earlier programs but invokes the
error functions that are specific to prepared statements:

```
static void
print_stmt_error (MYSQL_STMT *stmt, char *message)
{
  fprintf (stderr, "%s\n", message);
  if (stmt != NULL)
  {
    fprintf (stderr, "Error %u (%s): %s\n",
             mysql_stmt_errno (stmt),
             mysql_stmt_sqlstate (stmt),
             mysql_stmt_error (stmt));
  }
}
```

The `insert_rows()` function takes care of adding new rows to the test table:

```
static void
insert_rows (MYSQL_STMT *stmt)
{
char           *stmt_str = "INSERT INTO t (i,f,c,dt) VALUES(?,?,?,?)";
MYSQL_BIND     param[4];
int            my_int;
float          my_float;
char           my_str[26]; /* ctime() returns 26-character string */
MYSQL_TIME     my_datetime;
unsigned long  my_str_length;
time_t         clock;
struct tm      *cur_time;
int            i;

  printf ("Inserting records...\n");

  if (mysql_stmt_prepare (stmt, stmt_str, strlen (stmt_str)) != 0)
  {
    print_stmt_error (stmt, "Could not prepare INSERT statement");
    return;
  }

  /*
   * zero the parameter structures, and then perform all parameter
   * initialization that is constant and does not change for each row
   */

  memset ((void *) param, 0, sizeof (param));

  /* set up INT parameter */
```

```
param[0].buffer_type = MYSQL_TYPE_LONG;
param[0].buffer = (void *) &my_int;
param[0].is_unsigned = 0;
param[0].is_null = 0;
/* buffer_length, length need not be set */

/* set up FLOAT parameter */

param[1].buffer_type = MYSQL_TYPE_FLOAT;
param[1].buffer = (void *) &my_float;
param[1].is_null = 0;
/* is_unsigned, buffer_length, length need not be set */

/* set up CHAR parameter */

param[2].buffer_type = MYSQL_TYPE_STRING;
param[2].buffer = (void *) my_str;
param[2].buffer_length = sizeof (my_str);
param[2].is_null = 0;
/* is_unsigned need not be set, length is set later */

/* set up DATETIME parameter */

param[3].buffer_type = MYSQL_TYPE_DATETIME;
param[3].buffer = (void *) &my_datetime;
param[3].is_null = 0;
/* is_unsigned, buffer_length, length need not be set */

if (mysql_stmt_bind_param (stmt, param) != 0)
{
  print_stmt_error (stmt, "Could not bind parameters for INSERT");
  return;
}

for (i = 1; i <= 5; i++)
{
  printf ("Inserting record %d...\n", i);

  (void) time (&clock); /* get current time */

  /* set the variables that are associated with each parameter */

  /* param[0]: set my_int value */
  my_int = i;
```

```
    /* param[1]: set my_float value */
    my_float = (float) i;

    /* param[2]: set my_str to current ctime() string value */
    /* and set length to point to var that indicates my_str length */
    (void) strcpy (my_str, ctime (&clock));
    my_str[24] = '\0';  /* chop off trailing newline */
    my_str_length = strlen (my_str);
    param[2].length = &my_str_length;

    /* param[3]: set my_datetime to current date and time components */
    cur_time = localtime (&clock);
    my_datetime.year = cur_time->tm_year + 1900;
    my_datetime.month = cur_time->tm_mon + 1;
    my_datetime.day = cur_time->tm_mday;
    my_datetime.hour = cur_time->tm_hour;
    my_datetime.minute = cur_time->tm_min;
    my_datetime.second = cur_time->tm_sec;
    my_datetime.second_part = 0;
    my_datetime.neg = 0;

    if (mysql_stmt_execute (stmt) != 0)
    {
      print_stmt_error (stmt, "Could not execute statement");
      return;
    }

    sleep (1);  /* pause briefly (to let the time change) */
  }
}
```

The overall purpose of insert_rows() is to insert five rows into the test table, each of which will contain these values:

- An INT value from 1 to 5.
- A FLOAT value from 1.0 to 5.0.
- A CHAR value. To generate these values, we'll call the ctime() system function to get the value of "now" as a string. ctime() returns values that have this format:

  Sun Sep 19 16:47:23 CDT 2004

- A DATETIME value. This also will be the value of "now," but stored in a MYSQL_TIME structure. The binary protocol uses MYSQL_TIME structures to transmit DATETIME, TIMESTAMP, DATE, and TIME values.

The first thing we do in `insert_rows()` is prepare an `INSERT` statement by passing it to `mysql_stmt_prepare()`. The statement looks like this:

```
INSERT INTO t (i,f,c,dt) VALUES(?,?,?,?)
```

The statement contains four placeholders, so it's necessary to supply four data values each time the statement is executed. Placeholders typically represent data values in `VALUES()` lists or in `WHERE` clauses. But there are places in which they cannot be used:

- As identifiers such as table or column names. This statement is illegal:

```
SELECT * FROM ?
```

- You can use placeholders on one side of an operator, but not on both sides. This statement is legal:

```
SELECT * FROM student WHERE student_id = ?
```

However, this statement is illegal:

```
SELECT * FROM student WHERE ? = ?
```

This restriction is necessary so that the server can determine the data type of parameters.

The next step is to set up an array of `MYSQL_BIND` structures, one for each placeholder. As demonstrated in `insert_rows()`, setting these up involves two stages:

1. Initialize all parts of the structures that will be the same for each row inserted.
2. Perform a row-insertion loop that, for each row, initializes the parts of the structures that vary for each row.

You could actually perform all initialization within the loop, but that would be less efficient.

The first initialization stage begins by zeroing the contents of the `param` array containing the `MYSQL_BIND` structures. The program uses `memset()`, but you could use `bzero()` if your system doesn't have `memset()`. These two statements are equivalent:

```
memset ((void *) param, 0, sizeof (param));
bzero ((void *) param, sizeof (param));
```

Clearing the `param` array implicitly sets all structure members to zero. Code that follows sets some members to zero to make it explicit what's going on, but that is not strictly necessary. In practice, you need not assign zero to any structure members after clearing the structures.

The next step is to assign the proper information to each parameter in the
MYSQL_BIND array. For each parameter, the structure members that need to be set depend
on the type of value you're transmitting:

- The buffer_type member always must be set; it indicates the data type of the value.
  Appendix G (online) contains a table that lists each of the allowable type codes and
  shows the SQL and C types that correspond to each code.

- The buffer member should be set to the address of the variable that contains the
  data value. insert_rows() declares four variables to hold row values: my_int,
  my_float, my_str, and my_datetime. Each param[i].buffer value is set to point
  to the appropriate variable. When it comes time to insert a row, we'll set these four
  variables to the table column values and they will be used to create the new row.

- The is_unsigned member applies only to integer data types. It should be set to true
  (non-zero) or false (zero) to indicate whether the parameter corresponds to an
  UNSIGNED integer type. Our table contains a signed INT column, so we set
  is_unsigned to zero. Were the column an INT UNSIGNED, we would set is_unsigned
  to 1, and would also declare my_int as unsigned int rather than as int.

- The is_null member indicates whether you're transmitting a NULL value. In the
  general case, you set this member to the address of a my_bool variable. Then, before
  inserting any given row, you set the variable true or false to specify whether the
  value to be inserted is NULL. If no NULL values are to be sent (as is the case here),
  you can set is_null to zero and no my_bool variable is needed.

- For character string values or binary data (BLOB values), two more MYSQL_BIND
  members come into play. These indicate the size of the buffer in which the value is
  stored and the actual size of the current value being transmitted. In many cases
  these might be the same, but they will be different if you're using a fixed-size buffer
  and sending values that vary in length from row to row. buffer_length indicates
  the size of the buffer. length is a pointer; it should be set to the address of an
  unsigned long variable that contains the actual length of the value to be sent.

  For numeric and temporal data types, buffer_length and length need not be set.
  The size of each of these types is fixed and can be determined from the
  buffer_type value. For example, MYSQL_TYPE_LONG and MYSQL_TYPE_FLOAT indicate four-byte and eight-byte values.

After the initial setup of the MYSQL_BIND array has been done, we bind the array to the
prepared statement by passing the array to mysql_stmt_bind_param(). Then it's time to
assign values to the variables that the MYSQL_BIND structures point to and execute the
statement. This takes place in a loop that executes five times. Each iteration of the loop
assigns values to the statement parameters:

- For the integer and floating-point parameters, it's necessary only to assign values to
  the associated int and float variables.

- For the string parameter, we assign the current time in string format to the associated char buffer. This value is obtained by calling `ctime()`, and then chopping off the newline character.

- The datetime parameter also is assigned the current time, but this is done by assigning the component parts of the time to the individual members of the associated `MYSQL_TIME` structure.

With the parameter values set, we execute the statement by invoking `mysql_stmt_execute()`. This function transmits the current values to the server, which incorporates them into the prepared statement and executes it.

When `insert_rows()` returns, the test table has been populated and `select_rows()` can be called to retrieve them:

```
static void
select_rows (MYSQL_STMT *stmt)
{
char          *stmt_str = "SELECT i, f, c, dt FROM t";
MYSQL_BIND    param[4];
int           my_int;
float         my_float;
char          my_str[24];
unsigned long my_str_length;
MYSQL_TIME    my_datetime;
my_bool       is_null[4];

  printf ("Retrieving records...\n");

  if (mysql_stmt_prepare (stmt, stmt_str, strlen (stmt_str)) != 0)
  {
    print_stmt_error (stmt, "Could not prepare SELECT statement");
    return;
  }

  if (mysql_stmt_field_count (stmt) != 4)
  {
    print_stmt_error (stmt, "Unexpected column count from SELECT");
    return;
  }

  /*
   * initialize the result column structures
   */

  memset ((void *) param, 0, sizeof (param)); /* zero the structures */

  /* set up INT parameter */
```

```
param[0].buffer_type = MYSQL_TYPE_LONG;
param[0].buffer = (void *) &my_int;
param[0].is_unsigned = 0;
param[0].is_null = &is_null[0];
/* buffer_length, length need not be set */

/* set up FLOAT parameter */

param[1].buffer_type = MYSQL_TYPE_FLOAT;
param[1].buffer = (void *) &my_float;
param[1].is_null = &is_null[1];
/* is_unsigned, buffer_length, length need not be set */

/* set up CHAR parameter */

param[2].buffer_type = MYSQL_TYPE_STRING;
param[2].buffer = (void *) my_str;
param[2].buffer_length = sizeof (my_str);
param[2].length = &my_str_length;
param[2].is_null = &is_null[2];
/* is_unsigned need not be set */

/* set up DATETIME parameter */

param[3].buffer_type = MYSQL_TYPE_DATETIME;
param[3].buffer = (void *) &my_datetime;
param[3].is_null = &is_null[3];
/* is_unsigned, buffer_length, length need not be set */

if (mysql_stmt_bind_result (stmt, param) != 0)
{
  print_stmt_error (stmt, "Could not bind parameters for SELECT");
  return;
}

if (mysql_stmt_execute (stmt) != 0)
{
  print_stmt_error (stmt, "Could not execute SELECT");
  return;
}

/*
 * fetch result set into client memory; this is optional, but it
 * allows mysql_stmt_num_rows() to be called to determine the
 * number of rows in the result set.
 */
```

```
if (mysql_stmt_store_result (stmt) != 0)
{
  print_stmt_error (stmt, "Could not buffer result set");
  return;
}
else
{
  /* mysql_stmt_store_result() makes row count available */
  printf ("Number of rows retrieved: %lu\n",
          (unsigned long) mysql_stmt_num_rows (stmt));
}

while (mysql_stmt_fetch (stmt) == 0)  /* fetch each row */
{
  /* display row values */
  printf ("%d  ", my_int);
  printf ("%.2f  ", my_float);
  printf ("%*.*s  ", my_str_length, my_str_length, my_str);
  printf ("%04d-%02d-%02d %02d:%02d:%02d\n",
          my_datetime.year,
          my_datetime.month,
          my_datetime.day,
          my_datetime.hour,
          my_datetime.minute,
          my_datetime.second);
}

mysql_stmt_free_result (stmt);      /* deallocate result set */
}
```

select_rows() prepares a SELECT statement, executes it, and retrieves the result. In this case, the statement contains no placeholders:

```
SELECT i, f, c, dt FROM t
```

That means we don't need to set up any MYSQL_BIND structures before executing the statement. But we're not off the hook. The bulk of the work in select_rows(), just as in insert_rows(), is setting up an array of MYSQL_BIND structures. The difference is that they're used to receive data values from the server *after* executing the statement rather than to set up data values to be sent to the server *before* executing the statement.

Nevertheless, the procedure for setting up the MYSQL_BIND array is somewhat similar to the corresponding code in insert_rows():

1. Zero the array.

2. Set the buffer_type member of each parameter to the appropriate type code.

3. Point the `buffer` member of each parameter to the variable where the corresponding column value should be stored when rows are fetched.

4. Set the `is_unsigned` member for the integer parameter to zero.

5. For the string parameter, set the `buffer_length` value to the maximum number of bytes that should be fetched, and set `length` to the address of an `unsigned long` variable. At fetch time, this variable will be set to the actual number of bytes fetched.

6. For every parameter, set the `is_null` member to the address of a `my_bool` variable. At fetch time, these variables will be set to indicate whether the fetched values are NULL. (Our program ignores these variables after fetching rows because we know that the test table contains no NULL values. In the general case, you should check them.)

After setting up the parameters, we bind the array to the statement by calling `mysql_stmt_bind_result()`, and then execute the statement.

At this point, you can immediately begin fetching rows by calling `mysql_stmt_fetch()`. Our program demonstrates an optional step that you can do first: It calls `mysql_stmt_store_result()`, which fetches the entire result set and buffers it in client memory. The advantage of doing this is that you can call `mysql_stmt_num_rows()` to find out how many rows are in the result set. The disadvantage is that it uses more memory on the client side.

The row-fetching loop involves calling `mysql_stmt_fetch()` until it returns a nonzero value. After each fetch, the variables associated with the parameter structures contain the column values for the current row.

Once all the rows have been fetched, a call to `mysql_stmt_free_result()` releases any memory associated with the result set.

At this point, `select_rows()` returns to the caller, which invokes `mysql_stmt_close()` to dispose of the prepared statement handler.

The preceding discussion provides a broad overview of the prepared statement interface and some of its key functions. The client library includes several other related functions; for more information, consult Appendix G (online).

Writing MySQL Programs
Using Perl DBI

This chapter describes how to use the Perl DBI interface for MySQL. It does not discuss DBI philosophy or architecture. For information about those aspects of DBI (particularly in comparison with the C and PHP APIs), see Chapter 6, "Introduction to MySQL Programming."

The examples discussed here draw on our sample database, sampdb, using the tables created for the grade-keeping project and for the Historical League in Chapter 1, "Getting Started with MySQL." To get the most from this chapter, it's best if you know something about Perl. If you don't, you may be able to get along and write your own scripts simply by copying the sample code you see here, but you will probably find a good Perl book a worthwhile investment. One such book is *Programming Perl, Third Edition* by Wall, Christiansen, and Orwant (O'Reilly, 2000).

DBI is currently at version 1.601, although most of the discussion here applies to earlier versions as well. DBI requires at least Perl 5.6.0 (and 5.6.1 is preferred to 5.6.0). You must also have the DBD::mysql Perl module installed, as well as the MySQL C client library and header files. If you plan to write Web-based DBI scripts in the manner discussed here, you should also obtain the CGI.pm module. In this chapter, CGI.pm is used in conjunction with the Apache Web server. If you need to obtain any of these packages, see Appendix A, "Obtaining and Installing Software." Instructions for obtaining the example scripts developed in this chapter are also given in that appendix. They are part of the sampdb distribution, which you can download to avoid retyping the scripts yourself. The scripts used in this chapter are located under the perlapi directory of the distribution.

For the most part, this chapter describes Perl DBI methods and variables only as they are needed for the discussion here. For a more comprehensive listing of methods and variables, see Appendix H, "Perl DBI API Reference" (online). You can use that appendix as a reference for further background on any part of DBI that you're trying to use. Online documentation is available by running the following commands:

```
% perldoc DBI
```

```
% perldoc DBI::FAQ
% perldoc DBD::mysql
```

At the database driver (DBD) level, the driver for MySQL is built on top of the MySQL C client library, and therefore shares some of its characteristics. See Chapter 7, "Writing MySQL Programs Using C," for more information about the client library.

8.1 Perl Script Characteristics

Perl scripts are text files, so you can create them using any text editor. All Perl scripts in this chapter follow the Unix convention that they begin with a `#!` (shebang) line that specifies the pathname of the program to use for executing the script. The line I use is as follows:

```
#!/usr/bin/perl
```

On Unix, you'll need to modify the `#!` line if the pathname to Perl is different on your system, such as `/usr/local/bin/perl5` or `/opt/bin/perl`. Otherwise, Perl scripts won't run properly on your system.

You can invoke a Perl script `myscript.pl` as follows on any system to run it:

```
% perl myscript.pl
```

However, you may also be able to execute the script without naming the `perl` program explicitly. On Unix, do this by changing the file mode with `chmod` to make the script executable:

```
% chmod +x myscript.pl
```

Then you can run the script just by typing its name:

```
% ./myscript.pl
```

That is the script invocation style that will be used for examples shown in this chapter. The leading "`./`" should be used if the script is located in your current directory ("`.`") and your shell does not have the current directory in its search path. Otherwise, you can omit the "`./`" from the command name:

```
% myscript.pl
```

Under Windows, you can set up a filename association between Perl and filenames ending in `.pl`. For example, if you install ActiveState Perl, its installation program enables you to set up an association so that filenames ending with `.pl` are run by Perl. In that case, you can run a Perl script just by naming it on the command line:

```
C:\> myscript.pl
```

8.2 Perl DBI Overview

This section provides background information for DBI that you'll need for writing your own scripts and for understanding scripts written by others. If you're already familiar with DBI, you may want to skip directly to Section 8.3, "Putting DBI to Work."

8.2.1 DBI Data Types

In some ways, using the Perl DBI API is similar to using the C client library described in Chapter 7. When you use the C client library, you call functions and access MySQL-related data primarily by means of pointers to structures or to arrays. When you use the DBI API, you also call functions and use pointers to structures, except that functions are called "methods," pointers are called "references," pointer variables are called "handles," and the structures that handles point to are called "objects."

DBI uses several kinds of handles. These tend to be referred to in DBI documentation by the conventional names shown in Table 8.1. The way you use these handles will become clear as we go along. Several conventional names for non-handle variables are used as well (see Table 8.2). This chapter doesn't actually use every one of these variable names, but it's useful to know them when you read DBI scripts written by other people.

Table 8.1   **Conventional Perl DBI Handle Variable Names**

Name	Meaning
$dbh	A handle to a database object
$sth	A handle to a statement (query) object
$fh	A handle to an open file
$h	A "generic" handle; the meaning depends on context

Table 8.2   **Conventional Perl DBI Non-Handle Variable Names**

Name	Meaning
$rc	The return code from operations that return true or false
$rv	The return value from operations that return an integer
$rows	The return value from operations that return a row count
@ary	An array (list) representing a row of values returned by a query

8.2.2 A Simple DBI Script

Let's start with a simple script, dump_members.pl, that illustrates several standard concepts in DBI programming, such as connecting to and disconnecting from the MySQL server, issuing SQL statements, and retrieving data. This script produces output consisting of the

Historical League's member list in tab-delimited format. The format is not so interesting in itself. At this point, it's more important see how to use DBI than to produce pretty output. dump_members.pl looks like this:

```perl
#!/usr/bin/perl
# dump_members.pl - dump Historical League's membership list

use strict;
use warnings;
use DBI;

# data source name, username, password, connection attributes
my $dsn = "DBI:mysql:sampdb:localhost";
my $user_name = "sampadm";
my $password = "secret";
my %conn_attrs = (RaiseError => 1, PrintError => 0, AutoCommit => 1);

# connect to database
my $dbh = DBI->connect ($dsn, $user_name, $password, \%conn_attrs);

# issue query
my $sth = $dbh->prepare ("SELECT last_name, first_name, suffix, email,"
        . " street, city, state, zip, phone FROM member ORDER BY last_name");
$sth->execute ();

# read and display query result
while (my @ary = $sth->fetchrow_array ())
{
  print join ("\t", @ary), "\n";
}
$sth->finish ();

$dbh->disconnect ();
```

To try the script for yourself, either use the copy that's included in the sampdb distribution or create it using a text editor. If you use a word processor, be sure to save the script as plain text. Don't save it in the word processor's native format. You'll probably need to change at least some of the connection parameters, such as the hostname, database name, username, or password. (That will be true for other scripts in this chapter that name the connection parameters as well.) Later, in Section 8.2.9, "Specifying Connection Parameters," we'll see how to get parameters from an option file instead of putting them directly in the script.

Now let's go through the script a piece at a time. The first line contains the standard where-to-find-Perl indicator:

```perl
#!/usr/bin/perl
```

This line is part of every script we'll discuss in this chapter; I won't mention it further.

It's a good idea to include in a script at least a minimal description of its purpose, so the next line is a comment to give anyone who looks at the script a clue about what it does:

```
# dump_members.pl - dump Historical League's membership list
```

Text from a '#' character to the end of a line is considered a comment. It's a useful practice to sprinkle comments throughout your scripts to explain how they work.

Next we have several `use` statements:

```
use strict;
use warnings;
use DBI;
```

`use strict` tells Perl to require you to declare variables before using them. You can write scripts without putting in a `use strict` line, but it's useful for catching mistakes, so I recommend you always include it. For example, if you declare a variable `$my_var` but then later erroneously refer to it as `$mv_var`, the following message will appear when you run the script in strict mode:

```
Global symbol "$mv_var" requires explicit package name at line n
```

When you see that, you think, "Huh? I never used any variable named `$mv_var`!" Then you look at line *n* of your script, see that you misspelled `$my_var` as `$mv_var`, and fix it. Without strict mode, Perl won't squawk about `$mv_var`; it simply creates a new variable by that name with a value of `undef` (undefined) and uses it without complaint. And you're left to wonder why your script doesn't work.

`use warnings` tells Perl to issue a warning if it finds that you use questionable language constructs or perform operations such as printing uninitialized variables. This is useful because it can alert you to code that should be rewritten.

`use DBI` tells the Perl interpreter that it needs to pull in the DBI module. Without this line, an error occurs as soon as you try to do anything DBI-related in the script. It's unnecessary to indicate which DBD-level driver module to use; DBI activates the right one for you when you connect to your database.

Because we're operating in strict mode, we must declare the variables the script uses, by means of the `my` keyword. Think of it as though the script is saying "I am explicitly indicating that these are my variables." The next section of the script sets up the variables that specify connection parameters, and then uses them to connect to the database:

```
# data source name, username, password, connection attributes
my $dsn = "DBI:mysql:sampdb:localhost";
my $user_name = "sampadm";
my $password = "secret";
my %conn_attrs = (RaiseError => 1, PrintError => 0, AutoCommit => 1);

# connect to database
my $dbh = DBI->connect ($dsn, $user_name, $password, \%conn_attrs);
```

The `connect()` call is invoked as `DBI->connect()` because it's a method of the DBI class. You don't really have to know what that means; it's just a little object-oriented jargon to make your head hurt. (If you do want to know, it means that `connect()` is a function that "belongs" to DBI.) `connect()` takes several arguments:

- The data source, also known as the "data source name," or "DSN." The DSN indicates which DBD module to use and possibly other parameters.
- The username and password for your MySQL account.
- An optional argument indicating additional connection attributes. If it is given, this argument should be passed as a reference to a hash that specifies connection attribute names and values.

Data source formats are determined by the requirements of the particular DBD module you want to use. For the MySQL driver, allowable DSN formats include either of the following:

```
DBI:mysql:db_name
DBI:mysql:db_name:host_name
```

The capitalization of `DBI` doesn't matter, but `mysql` must be lowercase. `db_name` represents the name of the database you want to use and `host_name` indicates the host where the server is running. If you omit the hostname, it defaults to `localhost`. (Section 8.2.9, "Specifying Connection Parameters," discusses other allowable data source formats.)

The connection-attribute hash that we've specified as the value for `%conn_attrs` enables the `RaiseError` attribute and disables `PrintError`. These settings cause DBI to check for database-related errors and exit with an error message if it detects one. (That's why you don't see error-checking code anywhere in the `dump_members.pl` script; DBI handles it all.) Section 8.2.3, "Handling Errors," covers alternative methods of responding to errors.

The attribute hash also enables the `AutoCommit` attribute. Currently, this is not strictly necessary, but it does make explicit that the script enables autocommit mode for transaction handling. The script doesn't include any explicit transactions, but there is some possibility that DBI will in the future require scripts to specify the `AutoCommit` attribute explicitly. Doing so in scripts now ensures that they are ready if such a change does occur.

To specify the connection attributes, you could instead provide the hash reference directly in the call to `connect()`:

```
my $dbh = DBI->connect ($dsn, $user_name, $password,
                        { RaiseError => 1, PrintError => 0, AutoCommit => 1 });
```

Different people find one style or the other easier to read or edit, but operationally both approaches are the same.

If the `connect()` call succeeds, it returns a database handle, which we assign to `$dbh`. By default, `connect()` returns `undef` if it fails. However, because the script enables `RaiseError`, DBI will exit after displaying an error message if something goes wrong in the `connect()` call. (This is true for other DBI methods, too. I'll describe what they return to indicate an error, but they won't return at all if `RaiseError` is enabled.)

After connecting to the database, `dump_members.pl` issues a `SELECT` statement to retrieve the membership list, and then executes a loop to process each of the rows returned. These rows constitute the result set. To perform a `SELECT`, prepare the statement first, and then execute it:

```
# issue query
my $sth = $dbh->prepare ("SELECT last_name, first_name, suffix, email,"
        . " street, city, state, zip, phone FROM member ORDER BY last_name");
$sth->execute ();
```

`prepare()` is invoked using the database handle; it passes the SQL statement to the driver for preprocessing before execution. Some drivers actually do something with the statement at this point. Others just remember it until you invoke `execute()` to cause the statement to be performed. The return value from `prepare()` is a statement handle, here assigned to `$sth`. The statement handle is used for all further processing related to the statement.

Notice that the statement string itself has no terminating semicolon. You no doubt have the habit of terminating SQL statements with a '`;`' character (developed through long hours of interaction with the `mysql` program). However, it's best to break yourself of that habit when using DBI, because semicolons often cause statements to fail with syntax errors. The same applies to adding `\g` or `\G` to statement strings—don't. Those statement terminators are conventions of `mysql` and are not used when issuing statements in DBI scripts. The end of the statement string implicitly terminates the statement and no explicit terminator is necessary.

When you invoke a method without passing it any arguments, you can leave off the parentheses. These two calls are equivalent:

```
$sth->execute ();
$sth->execute;
```

I prefer to include the parentheses because they make the call look less like a variable reference to me. Your preference may be different.

After you call `execute()`, the rows of the membership list are available for processing. In the `dump_members.pl` script, the row-fetching loop simply prints the contents of each row as a tab-delimited set of values:

```
# read and display query result
while (my @ary = $sth->fetchrow_array ())
{
  print join ("\t", @ary), "\n";
}
$sth->finish ();
```

`fetchrow_array()` returns an array containing the column values of the current row, or an empty array when there are no more rows. Thus, the loop fetches successive rows returned by the `SELECT` statement and prints each one with tabs between column values.

`NULL` values in the database are returned as `undef` values to the Perl script, but these print as empty strings, not as the word "NULL". `undef` column values also have another effect when you run the script; they result in warnings like this from the Perl interpreter:

```
Use of uninitialized value in join at dump_members.pl line n.
```

These warnings are triggered by the inclusion of the `use warnings` statement. If you remove the statement and run the script again, the warnings will go away. However, warnings mode is useful for discovering problems (such as printing uninitialized variables!), so a better way to eliminate the warnings is to detect and deal with `undef` values. Section 8.2.5, "Handling Statements That Return a Result Set," discusses some techniques for doing so.

In the `print` statement, note that the tab and newline characters (represented as the `\t` and `\n` sequences, respectively) are enclosed in double quotes. In Perl, escape sequences are interpreted only when they occur within double quotes, not within single quotes. If single quotes had been used, the output would be full of literal instances of `\t` and `\n`.

After the row-fetching loop terminates, the call to `finish()` indicates that the statement handle is no longer needed and that any temporary resources allocated to it can be freed. In this script, the call to `finish()` is for illustrative purposes only. It need not actually be invoked here, because the row-fetching call will do so automatically when it encounters the end of the result set. `finish()` is more useful in situations where you fetch only part of the result set and do not reach its end (for example, if you fetch only the first row). Examples from this point on do not use `finish()` unless it's necessary.

Having printed the membership list, we're done, so we can disconnect from the server before exiting:

```
$dbh->disconnect ();
```

`dump_members.pl` illustrates a number of concepts that are common to most DBI programs, and at this point you could probably start writing your own DBI programs without knowing anything more. For example, to write out the contents of some other table, all you'd need to do is change the text of the `SELECT` statement that is passed to the `prepare()` method. And in fact, if you want to see some applications of this technique, you can skip ahead immediately to the part of Section 8.3, "Putting DBI to Work," that discusses how to generate the member list for the Historical League's annual meeting program and the League's printed directory. However, DBI provides many other useful capabilities. The next sections cover some of these in more detail so that you can see how to do more than run simple `SELECT` statements in your Perl scripts.

8.2.3 Handling Errors

`dump_members.pl` turned on the `RaiseError` error-handling attribute when it invoked the `connect()` method so that errors would automatically terminate the script with an error message rather than just returning error codes. It's possible to handle errors in other ways. For example, you can check for errors yourself rather than having DBI do it.

To see how to control DBI's error-handling behavior, let's take a closer look at the connection attribute hash passed as the final argument to `connect()`:

```
# data source name, username, password, connection attributes
my $dsn = "DBI:mysql:sampdb:localhost";
my $user_name = "sampadm";
my $password = "secret";
my %conn_attrs = (RaiseError => 1, PrintError => 0, AutoCommit => 1);

# connect to database
my $dbh = DBI->connect ($dsn, $user_name, $password, \%conn_attrs);
```

The two attributes relevant for error handling are `RaiseError` and `PrintError`:

- If `RaiseError` is enabled (set to a non-zero value), DBI raises an exception when an error occurs in a DBI method. By default, this results in a call to `die()` to print a message and exit the script.

- If `PrintError` is enabled, DBI calls `warn()` to print a message when a DBI error occurs, but the script continues executing.

By default, `RaiseError` is disabled and `PrintError` is enabled. In this case, if the `connect()` call fails, DBI prints a message but continues executing. Thus, with the default error-handling behavior that you get if you omit the fourth argument to `connect()`, you might check for errors like this:

```
my $dbh = DBI->connect ($dsn, $user_name, $password)
            or exit (1);
```

In this case, if an error occurs, `connect()` returns `undef` to indicate failure, and that triggers the call to `exit()`. You need not print an error message because DBI already will have printed one.

If you were to explicitly specify the default values for the error-checking attributes, the settings passed to `connect()` would look like this:

```
my %conn_attrs = (RaiseError => 0, PrintError => 1, AutoCommit => 1);
my $dbh = DBI->connect ($dsn, $user_name, $password, \%conn_attrs)
            or exit (1);
```

That's more work to write out, but it's also more obvious to the casual reader what the error-handling behavior is.

To check for errors yourself and print your own messages, disable both `RaiseError` and `PrintError`:

```
my %conn_attrs = (RaiseError => 0, PrintError => 0, AutoCommit => 1);
my $dbh = DBI->connect ($dsn, $user_name, $password, \%conn_attrs)
            or die "Could not connect to server: $DBI::err ($DBI::errstr)\n";
```

The `$DBI::err` and `$DBI::errstr`, variables used in the code just shown are useful for constructing error messages. They contain the MySQL error code and error string, much like the `mysql_errno()` and `mysql_error()` C API functions. If no error occurred, `$DBI::err` will be 0 or `undef`, and `$DBI::errstr` will be the empty string or `undef`. (In other words, both variables will be false.)

If you want DBI to handle errors for you so that you don't have to check for them yourself, enable `RaiseError` and disable `PrintError`:

```
my %conn_attrs = (RaiseError => 1, PrintError => 0, AutoCommit => 1);
my $dbh = DBI->connect ($dsn, $user_name, $password, \%conn_attrs);
```

This is by far the easiest approach, and it is how almost all scripts presented in this chapter are written. The reason for disabling `PrintError` when enabling `RaiseError` is to prevent the possibility of having error messages being printed twice. (If both attributes are enabled, the DBI handlers for both might be called under some circumstances.)

Enabling `RaiseError` may not be appropriate if you want to execute some sort of cleanup code of your own when the script exits, although in this case you might be able to do what you want by redefining the `$SIG{__DIE__}` signal handler. Another reason you might want to avoid enabling the `RaiseError` attribute is that DBI prints technical information in its messages, like this:

```
disconnect(DBI::db=HASH(0x197aae4)) invalidates 1 active statement. Either
destroy statement handles or call finish on them before disconnecting.
```

That's useful information for a programmer, but it could be the kind of thing you want to avoid presenting to the everyday user. In that case, it can be better to check for errors yourself so that you can display messages that are more meaningful to the people you expect to be using the script. Or you might consider redefining the `$SIG{__DIE__}` handler here, too. That could be useful because you can enable `RaiseError` to simplify error handling, but replace the default error messages that DBI presents with your own messages. To provide your own `__DIE__` handler, do something like the following before executing any DBI calls:

```
$SIG{__DIE__} = sub { die "Sorry, an error occurred\n"; };
```

You can also define a subroutine in the usual fashion and set the signal handler value using a reference to the subroutine:

```
sub die_handler
{
  die "Sorry, an error occurred\n";
```

```
}

$SIG{__DIE__} = \&die_handler;
```

The following script, dump_members2.pl, illustrates how you might write a script when you want to check for errors yourself and print your own messages. dump_members2.pl processes the same statement as dump_members.pl, but explicitly disables PrintError and RaiseError and then tests the result of every DBI call. When an error occurs, the script invokes the subroutine bail_out() to print a message and the contents of $DBI::err and $DBI::errstr before exiting:

```perl
#!/usr/bin/perl
# dump_members2.pl - dump Historical League's membership list

use strict;
use warnings;
use DBI;

# data source name, username, password, connection attributes
my $dsn = "DBI:mysql:sampdb:localhost";
my $user_name = "sampadm";
my $password = "secret";
my %conn_attrs = (RaiseError => 0, PrintError => 0, AutoCommit => 1);

# connect to database
my $dbh = DBI->connect ($dsn, $user_name, $password, \%conn_attrs)
            or bail_out ("Cannot connect to database");

# issue query
my $sth = $dbh->prepare ("SELECT last_name, first_name, suffix, email,"
        . " street, city, state, zip, phone FROM member ORDER BY last_name")
          or bail_out ("Cannot prepare query");
$sth->execute ()
  or bail_out ("Cannot execute query");

# read and display query result
while (my @ary = $sth->fetchrow_array ())
{
  print join ("\t", @ary), "\n";
}
!$DBI::err
  or bail_out ("Error during retrieval");

$dbh->disconnect ()
  or bail_out ("Cannot disconnect from database");

# bail_out() subroutine - print error code and string, and then exit
```

```
sub bail_out
{
my $message = shift;

  die "$message\nError $DBI::err ($DBI::errstr)\n";
}
```

bail_out() is similar to the print_error() function that we used for writing C programs in Chapter 7, except that bail_out() exits rather than returning to the caller.
bail_out() saves you the trouble of writing out the values of $DBI::err and
$DBI::errstr every time you want to print an error message. Also, by encapsulating
error message printing into a subroutine, you can change the format of your error messages uniformly throughout your script simply by making a change to the subroutine.

The dump_members2.pl script has a test following the row-fetching loop. Because the
script doesn't automatically exit if an error occurs in fetchrow_array(), it's prudent to
determine whether the loop terminated because the result set was read completely (normal
termination) or because an error occurred. The loop terminates either way, of course, but
if an error occurs, output from the script will be truncated. Without an error check, the
person running the script wouldn't have any idea that anything was wrong! If you're
checking for errors yourself, be sure to test the result of your fetch loops.

8.2.4 Handling Statements That Modify Rows

Statements that modify rows, such as DELETE, INSERT, REPLACE, and UPDATE, are relatively
easy to process compared to statements that return rows, such as SELECT, DESCRIBE,
EXPLAIN, and SHOW. To process a non-SELECT statement, pass it to do() using the database
handle. The do() method prepares and executes the statement in one step. For example,
to create a new member entry for Marcia Brown with an expiration date of June 3, 2012,
you can do the following:

```
$rows = $dbh->do ("INSERT INTO member (last_name,first_name,expiration)"
                  . " VALUES('Brown','Marcia','2012-06-03')");
```

The do() method returns a count of the number of rows affected, undef if something
goes wrong, and –1 if the number of rows is unknown for some reason. Errors can occur
for various reasons. (For example, the statement might be malformed or you might not
have permission to access the table.) For a non-undef return value, watch out for the case
in which no rows are affected. When this happens, do() doesn't return the number 0;
instead, it returns the string "0E0" (Perl's scientific notation form of zero). "0E0" evaluates
to 0 in a numeric context but is considered true in conditional tests so that it can be distinguished easily from undef. If do() returned 0, it would be more difficult to distinguish
between the occurrence of an error (undef) and the "no rows affected" case. You can
check for an error using either of the following tests:

```
if (!defined ($rows))
{
  print "An error occurred\n";
}
if (!$rows)
{
  print "An error occurred\n";
}
```

In numeric contexts, `"0E0"` evaluates as `0`, so the following code will correctly print the number of rows for any non-undef value of `$rows`:

```
if (!$rows)
{
  print "An error occurred\n";
}
else
{
  $rows += 0; # force conversion to number if value is "0E0"
  print "Number of rows affected: $rows\n";
}
```

You could also print `$rows` using a `%d` format specifier with `printf()` to force an implicit conversion to a number:

```
if (!$rows)
{
  print "An error occurred\n";
}
else
{
  printf "Number of rows affected: %d\n", $rows;
}
```

The `do()` method is equivalent to using `prepare()` followed by `execute()`. This means that the preceding INSERT statement could be issued as follows rather than by invoking `do()`:

```
$sth = $dbh->prepare ("INSERT INTO member (last_name,first_name,expiration)"
                    . " VALUES('Brown','Marcia','2012-06-03')");
$rows = $sth->execute ();
```

8.2.5 Handling Statements That Return a Result Set

This section provides more information about several options that you have for executing row-fetching loops for SELECT statements (or for other SELECT-like statements that return rows, such as DESCRIBE, EXPLAIN, and SHOW). It also discusses how to get a count of the number of rows in a result, how to handle result sets for which no loop is necessary, and how to retrieve an entire result set all at once.

8.2.5.1 Writing Row-Fetching Loops

The `dump_members.pl` script retrieved data using a sequence of DBI methods: `prepare()` lets the driver preprocess the statement, `execute()` begins executing the statement, and `fetchrow_array()` fetches each row of the result set.

`prepare()` and `execute()` are fairly standard parts of processing any statement that returns rows. However, for fetching the rows, `fetchrow_array()` is actually only one choice from among several available methods (see Table 8.3).

Table 8.3   **DBI Row-Fetching Methods**

Method Name	Return Value
`fetchrow_array()`	Array of row values
`fetchrow_arrayref()`	Reference to array of row values
`fetch()`	Same as `fetchrow_arrayref()`
`fetchrow_hashref()`	Reference to hash of row values, keyed by column name

The following examples show how to use each row-fetching method. The examples loop through the rows of a result set, and for each row, print the column values separated by commas. There are more efficient ways to write the code in some cases, but the examples are written for illustrative purposes (to show the syntax for accessing individual column values), not for efficiency.

Use `fetchrow_array()` as follows:

```
while (my @ary = $sth->fetchrow_array ())
{
  my $delim = "";
  for (my $i = 0; $i < @ary; $i++)
  {
    $ary[$i] = "" if !defined ($ary[$i]); # NULL value?
    print $delim, $ary[$i];
    $delim = ",";
  }
  print "\n";
}
```

Each call to `fetchrow_array()` returns an array of row values, or an empty array when there are no more rows. The inner loop tests each column value to see whether it's defined, and sets it to the empty string if not. This converts NULL values (which are represented by DBI as `undef`) to empty strings. It might seem that this is an entirely superfluous action; after all, Perl prints nothing for both `undef` and the empty string. The reason for the test is that if the script is run with warnings enabled, Perl will issue a "Use of uninitialized value" warning message if you attempt to print an `undef` value. Converting undef to the empty string eliminates the warnings. You'll see a similar construct used elsewhere throughout this chapter.

If you prefer to print a different value for undef values, such as the string "NULL", just change the if-test a little:

```
while (my @ary = $sth->fetchrow_array ())
{
  my $delim = "";
  for (my $i = 0; $i < @ary; $i++)
  {
    $ary[$i] = "NULL" if !defined ($ary[$i]); # NULL value?
    print $delim, $ary[$i];
    $delim = ",";
  }
  print "\n";
}
```

When working with an array of values, you can shorten the code a bit by using map to convert all the undef array elements at once:

```
while (my @ary = $sth->fetchrow_array ())
{
  @ary = map { defined ($_) ? $_ : "NULL" } @ary;
  print join (",", @ary), "\n";
}
```

map processes each element of the array using the expression within the braces and returns an array containing the resulting values.

An alternative to assigning the return value of fetchrow_array() to an array variable is to fetch column values into a set of scalar variables. This enables you to work with variable names that are more meaningful than $ary[0], $ary[1], and so forth. Suppose that you want to retrieve member names and email values into variables. Using fetchrow_array(), you could select and fetch rows like this:

```
my $sth = $dbh->prepare ("SELECT last_name, first_name, suffix, email"
                    . " FROM member ORDER BY last_name");
$sth->execute ();
while (my ($last_name, $first_name, $suffix, $email)
                    = $sth->fetchrow_array ())
{
  # do something with variables
}
```

When you use a list of variables this way, you must make sure that the order of the columns selected by the statement matches the order of the variables into which you fetch the values. DBI has no idea of the order in which columns are named by your SELECT statement, so it's up to you to assign variables correctly. You can also cause column values to be assigned to individual variables automatically when you fetch a row, using a technique known as "parameter binding" (see Section 8.2.7, "Placeholders and Prepared Statements").

If you fetch a single value into a variable, be careful how you write the assignment. If you write the beginning of your loop like this, it will work correctly:

```
while (my ($val) = $sth->fetchrow->array ()) ...
```

The value is fetched in list context, so the test will fail only when there are no more rows. But if you write the test like this instead, it will fail in mysterious ways:

```
while (my $val = $sth->fetchrow->array ()) ...
```

The difference here is that the value is fetched in scalar context, so if $val happens to be zero, undef, or the empty string, the test evaluates as false and terminates the loop, even though you have not yet reached the end of the result set.

The second row-fetching method, fetchrow_arrayref(), is similar to fetchrow_array(), but instead of returning an array containing the column values for the current row, it returns a reference to the array, or undef when there are no more rows. Use it like this:

```
while (my $ary_ref = $sth->fetchrow_arrayref ())
{
  my $delim = "";
  for (my $i = 0; $i < @{$ary_ref}; $i++)
  {
    $ary_ref->[$i] = "" if !defined ($ary_ref->[$i]); # NULL value?
    print $delim, $ary_ref->[$i];
    $delim = ",";
  }
  print "\n";
}
```

You access array elements through the array reference, $ary_ref. This is something like dereferencing a pointer, so you use $ary_ref->[$i] rather than $ary[$i]. To convert the reference to an array, use the @{$ary_ref} construct.

fetchrow_arrayref() is unsuitable for fetching variables into a list. For example, the following loop does not work:

```
while (my ($var1, $var2, $var3, $var4) = @{$sth->fetchrow_arrayref ()})
{
  # do something with variables
}
```

As long as fetchrow_arrayref() actually fetches a row, the loop functions properly. But when there are no more rows, fetchrow_arrayref() returns undef, and @{undef} isn't legal. (It's like trying to de-reference a NULL pointer in a C program.)

The third row-fetching method, fetchrow_hashref(), is used like this:

```
while (my $hash_ref = $sth->fetchrow_hashref ())
```

```
{
  my $delim = "";
  foreach my $key (keys (%{$hash_ref}))
  {
    $hash_ref->{$key} = "" if !defined ($hash_ref->{$key}); # NULL value?
    print $delim, $hash_ref->{$key};
    $delim = ",";
  }
  print "\n";
}
```

Each call to `fetchrow_hashref()` returns a reference to a hash of row values keyed on column names, or `undef` when there are no more rows. In this case, column values don't come out in any particular order, because members of Perl hashes are unordered. However, DBI keys the hash elements using the column names, so `$hash_ref` gives you a single variable through which you can access any column value by name. This means you can pull out the values (or any subset of them) in any order you want, and you don't have to know the order in which the columns were retrieved by the SELECT statement. For example, to access the `name` and `email` columns, you can do this:

```
while (my $hash_ref = $sth->fetchrow_hashref ())
{
  my $delim = "";
  foreach my $key ("last_name", "first_name", "suffix", "email")
  {
    $hash_ref->{$key} = "" if !defined ($hash_ref->{$key}); # NULL value?
    print $delim, $hash_ref->{$key};
    $delim = ",";
  }
  print "\n";
}
```

`fetchrow_hashref()` is especially useful when you want to pass a row of values to a function without requiring the function to know the order in which columns are named in the SELECT statement. In this case, you would call `fetchrow_hashref()` to retrieve rows and write a function that accesses values from the row hash using column names.

Keep in mind the following caveats when you use `fetchrow_hashref()`:

- If you need every bit of performance, `fetchrow_hashref()` is not the best choice. It's less efficient than `fetchrow_array()` or `fetchrow_arrayref()`.
- By default, the column names are used as key values with the same lettercase as the column names written in the SELECT statement. In MySQL, column names are not case sensitive, so the statement will work the same way no matter what lettercase you use to write column names. But Perl hash key names *are* case sensitive, which may cause you problems. To avoid potential lettercase mismatch problems, you can

tell `fetchrow_hashref()` to force column names into a particular lettercase by passing it a `NAME_lc` or `NAME_uc` attribute:

```
$hash_ref = $sth->fetchrow_hashref ("NAME_lc"); # use lowercase names
$hash_ref = $sth->fetchrow_hashref ("NAME_uc"); # use uppercase names
```

- The hash contains one element per unique column name. If you're performing a join that returns columns from multiple tables with overlapping names, you won't be able to access all the column values. If you issue the following statement, `fetchrow_hashref()` will return a hash having only one element, `name`:

```
SELECT a.name, b.name FROM a INNER JOIN b WHERE a.name = b.name
```

To avoid this problem, use aliases to make sure that each column has a distinct name. For example, if you rewrite the statement as follows, `fetchrow_hashref()` will return a reference to a hash with two elements, `name` and `name2`:

```
SELECT a.name, b.name AS name2 FROM a INNER JOIN b WHERE a.name = b.name
```

8.2.5.2 Determining the Number of Rows Returned by a Statement

How can you tell the number of rows returned by a SELECT or SELECT-like statement? One way is to count the rows as you fetch them. In fact, this is the *only* portable way in DBI to know how many rows a SELECT statement returned. If you're using the MySQL driver, you can call the `rows()` method using the statement handle after invoking `execute()`. But this is not portable to other database systems, and the DBI documentation explicitly discourages using `rows()` for SELECT statements. Even for MySQL, if you've set the `mysql_use_result` attribute, `rows()` doesn't return the correct result until you've fetched all the rows. So you may as well just count the rows as you fetch them. (See Appendix H (online), for more information about `mysql_use_result`.)

8.2.5.3 Fetching Single-Row Results

It's not necessary to run a loop to get your results if the result set consists of a single row. Suppose that you want to write a script, `count_members.pl`, that tells you the current number of Historical League members. The code to perform the statement looks like this:

```
# issue query
my $sth = $dbh->prepare ("SELECT COUNT(*) FROM member");
$sth->execute ();

# read and display query result
my $count = $sth->fetchrow_array ();
$sth->finish ();
$count = "can't tell" if !defined ($count);
print "$count\n";
```

The SELECT statement will return only one row, so no loop is required; we call fetchrow_array() just once. In addition, because we're selecting only one column, it's not even necessary to assign the return value to an array. When fetchrow_array() is called in a scalar context (where a single value rather than a list is expected), it returns one column of the row, or undef if no row is available. DBI does not define which element of the row fetchrow_array() returns in scalar context, but that's all right for the statement just shown. It retrieves only a single value, so there is no ambiguity about what value is returned.

This code invokes finish() to free the result set, even though the set consists of just one row. (fetchrow_array() frees a result set implicitly when it notices that you have reached the end of the set, but that would happen here only if you called it a second time.)

Another type of query for which you expect at most a single row is one that contains LIMIT 1 to restrict the number of rows returned. A common use for this is to return the row that contains the maximum or minimum value for a particular column. For example, the following query prints the name and birth date of the president who was born most recently:

```
my $stmt = "SELECT last_name, first_name, birth FROM president"
        . " WHERE birth = (SELECT MAX(birth) FROM president)";
my $sth = $dbh->prepare ($stmt);
$sth->execute ();

my ($last_name, $first_name, $birth) = $sth->fetchrow_array ();
$sth->finish ();
if (!defined ($last_name))
{
  print "Query returned no result\n";
}
else
{
  print "Most recently born president: $first_name $last_name ($birth)\n";
}
```

Other types of statements for which no fetch loop is necessary are those that use MAX() or MIN() to select a single row. But in all these cases, an even easier way to get a single-row result is to use the database handle method selectrow_array(), which combines prepare(), execute() and row fetching into a single call. It returns an array (not a reference), or an empty array if the query returned no row or an error occurred. The previous example can be rewritten like this using selectrow_array():

```
my $stmt = "SELECT last_name, first_name, birth FROM president"
        . " WHERE birth = (SELECT MAX(birth) FROM president)";
my ($last_name, $first_name, $birth) = $dbh->selectrow_array ($stmt);
if (!defined ($last_name))
{
```

```
    print "Query returned no result\n";
}
else
{
  print "Most recently born president: $first_name $last_name ($birth)\n";
}
```

8.2.5.4 Working with Complete Result Sets

When you use a fetch loop, DBI provides no way to process the rows in any order other than that in which they are returned by the loop. Also, after you fetch a row, the previous row is lost unless you take steps to maintain it in memory. These behaviors aren't always desirable. For example, they're unsuitable if you need to make multiple passes through the rows to perform a statistical calculation. (Perhaps you want to go through the result set once to assess some general numeric characteristics of your data, and then step through the rows again performing a more specific analysis.)

It's possible to access your result set as a whole in a couple different ways. You can perform the usual fetch loop and save each row as you fetch it, or you can use a method that returns an entire result set all at once. Either way, you end up with a matrix containing one row per row in the result set, and as many columns as you selected. Then you can process elements of the matrix in any order you want, as many times as you want. The following discussion describes both approaches.

One way to use a fetch loop to capture the result set is to use `fetchrow_array()` and save an array of references to the rows. The following code does the same thing as the fetch-and-print loop in `dump_members.pl`, except that it saves all the rows, and then prints the matrix. It illustrates how to determine the number of rows and columns in the matrix and how to access individual members of the matrix:

```
my @matrix = (); # array of array references

while (my @ary = $sth->fetchrow_array ()) # fetch each row
{
  push (@matrix, [ @ary ]); # save reference to just-fetched row
}

# determine dimensions of matrix
my $rows = scalar (@matrix);
my $cols = ($rows == 0 ? 0 : scalar (@{$matrix[0]}));

for (my $i = 0; $i < $rows; $i++)      # print each row
{
  my $delim = "";
  for (my $j = 0; $j < $cols; $j++)
  {
    $matrix[$i][$j] = "" if !defined ($matrix[$i][$j]); # NULL value?
```

```
    print $delim, $matrix[$i][$j];
    $delim = ",";
  }
  print "\n";
}
```

When you check the dimensions of the matrix, the number of rows must be determined first because calculation of the number of columns is contingent on whether the matrix is empty. If $rows is 0, the matrix is empty and $cols becomes 0 as well. Otherwise, the number of columns can be calculated as the number of elements in the first row, using the syntax @{$matrix[0]} to access the row as a whole.

The preceding example fetches each row as an array, and then saves a reference to it. You might suppose that it would be more efficient to call fetchrow_arrayref() instead to retrieve row references directly:

```
my @matrix = (); # array of array references


while (my $ary_ref = $sth->fetchrow_arrayref ())
{
  push (@matrix, $ary_ref); # save reference to just-fetched row
}
```

That doesn't work, because fetchrow_arrayref() reuses the array to which the reference points. The resulting matrix is an array of references, each of which points to the same row—the final row retrieved. Therefore, if you want to construct a matrix by fetching a row at a time, use fetchrow_array() rather than fetchrow_arrayref().

As an alternative to using a fetch loop, invoke one of the DBI methods that return the entire result set. For example, fetchall_arrayref() returns a reference to an array of references, each of which points to the contents of one row of the result set. (That's a mouthful; it means that the return value is a reference to a matrix.) To use fetchall_arrayref(), call prepare() and execute(), and then retrieve the result like this:

```
# fetch all rows as a reference to an array of references
my $matrix_ref = $sth->fetchall_arrayref ();
```

You can determine the dimensions of the array and access its elements as follows:

```
# determine dimensions of matrix
my $rows = (!defined ($matrix_ref) ? 0 : scalar (@{$matrix_ref}));
my $cols = ($rows == 0 ? 0 : scalar (@{$matrix_ref->[0]}));

for (my $i = 0; $i < $rows; $i++)     # print each row
{
  my $delim = "";
  for (my $j = 0; $j < $cols; $j++)
  {
    $matrix_ref->[$i][$j] = "" if !defined ($matrix_ref->[$i][$j]); # NULL?
```

```
      print $delim, $matrix_ref->[$i][$j];
      $delim = ",";
  }
  print "\n";
}
```

`fetchall_arrayref()` returns a reference to an empty array if the result set is empty. The result is `undef` if an error occurs, so if you don't have `RaiseError` enabled, you must check the return value before you start using it.

The number of rows and columns is determined by whether the matrix is empty. If you want to access an entire row `$i` of the matrix as an array, use the syntax `@{$matrix_ref->[$i]}`.

It's certainly simpler to use `fetchall_arrayref()` to retrieve a result set than to write a row-fetching loop, although the syntax for accessing array elements is a little trickier. A method that's similar to `fetchall_arrayref()` but that does even more work is `selectall_arrayref()`. This method performs the entire `prepare()`, `execute()`, fetch loop sequence for you. To use `selectall_arrayref()`, pass your statement directly to it using the database handle:

```
# fetch all rows as a reference to an array of references
my $matrix_ref = $dbh->selectall_arrayref ($stmt);

# determine dimensions of matrix
my $rows = (!defined ($matrix_ref) ? 0 : scalar (@{$matrix_ref}));
my $cols = ($rows == 0 ? 0 : scalar (@{$matrix_ref->[0]}));

for (my $i = 0; $i < $rows; $i++)      # print each row
{
  my $delim = "";
  for (my $j = 0; $j < $cols; $j++)
  {
    $matrix_ref->[$i][$j] = "" if !defined ($matrix_ref->[$i][$j]); # NULL?
    print $delim, $matrix_ref->[$i][$j];
    $delim = ",";
  }
  print "\n";
}
```

8.2.5.5 Checking for NULL Values

When you retrieve information from a database, you might need to distinguish between column values that are NULL from those that are zero or the empty string. This is easy to do because DBI returns NULL column values as `undef`. However, you must be sure to use the correct test. If you try the following code fragment, it prints `"false!"` all three times:

```
$col_val = undef; if (!$col_val) { print "false!\n"; }
$col_val = 0;      if (!$col_val) { print "false!\n"; }
```

```
$col_val = "";    if (!$col_val) { print "false!\n"; }
```

What that demonstrates is that the form of the test is unable to distinguish between undef, 0, and the empty string. The next fragment prints "false!" for both tests, indicating that the test cannot distinguish undef from the empty string:

```
$col_val = undef; if ($col_val eq "") { print "false!\n"; }
$col_val = "";    if ($col_val eq "") { print "false!\n"; }
```

This fragment prints the same output, showing that the second test fails to distinguish 0 from the empty string:

```
$col_val = "";
if ($col_val eq "") { print "false!\n"; }
if ($col_val == 0)  { print "false!\n"; }
```

To distinguish between undef (NULL) column values and non-undef values, use defined(). After you know a value doesn't represent NULL, you can distinguish between other types of values using appropriate tests. For example:

```
if (!defined ($col_val)) { print "NULL\n"; }
elsif ($col_val eq "")   { print "empty string\n"; }
elsif ($col_val == 0)    { print "zero\n"; }
else                     { print "other\n"; }
```

It's important to perform the tests in the proper order because both the second and third comparisons are true if $col_val is an empty string. If you reverse the order of those comparisons, you'll incorrectly interpret empty strings as zero.

8.2.6 Quoting Special Characters in Statement Strings

Thus far, we have constructed statements in the most basic way possible, using simple quoted strings. That causes a problem at the Perl lexical level when your quoted strings contain quoted values. You can also have problems at the SQL level when you want to insert or select values that contain quotes, backslashes, or binary data. If you specify a statement as a Perl quoted string, you must escape any occurrences of the quoting character that occur within the statement string itself:

```
$stmt = 'INSERT INTO absence VALUES(14,\'2008-09-16\')';
$stmt = "INSERT INTO absence VALUES(14,\"2008-09-16\")";
```

Both Perl and MySQL allow you to quote strings using either single or double quotes, so you can sometimes avoid escaping by mixing quote characters:

```
$stmt = 'INSERT INTO absence VALUES(14,"2008-09-16")';
$stmt = "INSERT INTO absence VALUES(14,'2008-09-16')";
```

However, you must take care that the strings will be interpreted as you want. Consider these factors:

- The two types of quotes are not equivalent in Perl. Variable references are interpreted only within double quotes. Therefore, single quotes are not very useful when you want to construct statements by embedding variable references in the statement string. For example, if the value of $var is 14, the following two strings are not equivalent:

```
"SELECT * FROM member WHERE member_id = $var"
'SELECT * FROM member WHERE member_id = $var'
```

The resulting strings as Perl interprets them as follows:

```
"SELECT * FROM member WHERE member_id = 14"
'SELECT * FROM member WHERE member_id = $var'
```

Clearly, the first string is more like something you'd want to pass to the MySQL server. For the second, the server will interpret $var as the literal name of a column in the member table.

- Single quotes and double quotes are not always equivalent in MySQL. If the server is running with the ANSI_QUOTES SQL mode disabled, you can indeed use either type of quote to quote a string. But if ANSI_QUOTES is enabled, strings must be quoted with single quotes; double quotes can be used only for quoting identifiers such as database or table names. Consequently, it's safest to quote strings with single quotes, because that works regardless of whether ANSI_QUOTES is on or off.

At the Perl level, an alternative to quoting strings with double quotes is to use the qq{} construct, which tells Perl to treat everything between qq{ and } as a double-quoted string. (Think of double-q as meaning "double-quote.") For example, these two lines are equivalent:

```
$date = "2008-09-16";
$date = qq{2008-09-16};
```

When you use qq{}, you can construct statements without thinking so much about quoting issues because you can use quote characters (single or double) freely within the statement string without having to escape them. In addition, variable references are interpreted. Both properties of qq{} are illustrated by the following INSERT statement:

```
$id = 14;
$date = "2008-09-16";
$stmt = qq{INSERT INTO absence VALUES($id,'$date')};
```

You don't have to use '{' and '}' as the qq delimiters. Other forms, such as qq() and qq//, will work, too, as long as the closing delimiter doesn't occur within the string. I prefer qq{} because the '}' character is less likely than ')' or '/' to occur within the text of the statement and be mistaken for the end of the statement string. For example, ')' occurs within the `INSERT` statement just shown, so `qq()` would not be a useful construct for quoting the statement string.

The `qq{}` construct can cross line boundaries, which is useful if you want to make the statement string stand out from the surrounding Perl code:

```
$id = 14;
$date = "2008-09-16";
$stmt = qq{
  INSERT INTO absence VALUES($id,'$date')
};
```

This is also useful if you simply want to format your statement on multiple lines to make it more readable. For example, the `SELECT` statement in the `dump_members.pl` script looks like this:

```
$sth = $dbh->prepare ("SELECT last_name, first_name, suffix, email,"
    . " street, city, state, zip, phone FROM member ORDER BY last_name");
```

With `qq{}`, it could be written like this instead:

```
$sth = $dbh->prepare (qq{
        SELECT
          last_name, first_name, suffix, email,
          street, city, state, zip, phone
        FROM member
        ORDER BY last_name
      });
```

It's true that double-quoted strings can cross line boundaries, too. But I find that `qq{` and `}` stand out better than two lone '"' characters and make the statement easier to read. This book uses both forms; see which you prefer.

The `qq{}` construct takes care of quoting issues at the Perl lexical level so that you can use quotes in a string easily without having Perl complain about them. However, you must also think about SQL-level syntax. Consider this attempt to insert a row into the `member` table:

```
$last = "O'Malley";
$first = "Brian";
$expiration = "2013-09-01";
$rows = $dbh->do (qq{
  INSERT INTO member (last_name,first_name,expiration)
  VALUES('$last','$first','$expiration')
});
```

The resulting string that `do()` sends to MySQL looks like this:

```
INSERT INTO member (last_name,first_name,expiration)
VALUES('O'Malley','Brian','2013-09-01')
```

That is not legal SQL because for `'O'Malley'` a single quote occurs within a single-quoted string. We encountered this quoting problem earlier in Chapter 7. There we dealt with the issue by using the `mysql_real_escape_string()` function. DBI provides a similar mechanism: For each quoted value that you want to use literally in a statement, call the `quote()` method and use its return value instead. The preceding example is more properly written as follows:

```
$last = $dbh->quote ("O'Malley");
$first = $dbh->quote ("Brian");
$expiration = $dbh->quote ("2013-09-01");
$rows = $dbh->do (qq{
  INSERT INTO member (last_name,first_name,expiration)
  VALUES($last,$first,$expiration)
});
```

Now the string that `do()` sends to MySQL looks like this, with the quote that occurs within the quoted string properly escaped:

```
INSERT INTO member (last_name,first_name,expiration)
VALUES('O\'Malley','Brian','2013-09-01')
```

Note that when you refer to `$last` and `$first` in the statement string, you do not add any surrounding quotes; the `quote()` method supplies them for you. If you add quotes yourself, your statement will have too many of them, as shown by the following example:

```
$value = "paul";
$quoted_value = $dbh->quote ($value);

print "The quoted value is: $quoted_value\n";
print "The quoted value is: '$quoted_value'\n";
```

These statements produce the following output:

```
The quoted value is: 'paul'
The quoted value is: ''paul''
```

In the second case, the string contains too many quotes.

8.2.7 Placeholders and Prepared Statements

In the preceding sections, we constructed statements by putting data values to be inserted or used as selection criteria directly into the statement string. It's not necessary to do this. DBI allows you to use special markers called "placeholders" within a statement string, and then supply the values to be used in place of those markers when the statement is executed. This is called "binding the values to the statement." One reason for doing this is that you get the character-quoting benefits of the `quote()` method without having to invoke `quote()` explicitly. Another reason is improved performance: If you're executing a statement over and over within a loop, you can prepare it first and then execute it multiple times. This avoids the overhead of preparing the statement before each execution.

As an illustration of how placeholders work, suppose that you're beginning a new semester at school and you want to clear out the `student` table for your gradebook and then initialize it with the new students by using a list of student names contained in a file. Without placeholders, you can delete the existing table contents and load the new names like this:

```
$dbh->do (qq{ DELETE FROM student } );  # delete existing rows
while (<>)                              # read each input line,
{                                       # use it to add a new row
  chomp;
  $_ = $dbh->quote ($_);
  $dbh->do (qq{ INSERT INTO student SET name = $_ });
}
```

This approach requires that you handle special characters in the data values yourself by calling `quote()`. It's also inefficient, because the basic form of the `INSERT` statement is the same each time, and `do()` calls `prepare()` and `execute()` each time through the loop. It's more efficient to call `prepare()` a single time to set up the `INSERT` before entering the loop and invoke only `execute()` within the loop. That avoids all invocations of `prepare()` but one. DBI allows this to be done as follows:

```
$dbh->do (qq{ DELETE FROM student } );  # delete existing rows
my $sth = $dbh->prepare (qq{ INSERT INTO student SET name = ? });
while (<>)                              # read each input line,
{                                       # use it to add a new row
  chomp;
  $sth->execute ($_);
}
```

In general, if you find yourself calling `do()` inside a loop, it's better to invoke `prepare()` prior to the loop and `execute()` inside it. Note the '?' character in the `INSERT` statement. That's the placeholder. When `execute()` is invoked, you pass the value to be substituted for the placeholder when the statement is sent to the server. DBI automatically quotes special characters in the value, so there is no need to call `quote()`.

Some things to note about placeholders:

- Do not enclose the placeholder character in quotes within the statement string. If you do, it will not be recognized as a placeholder.
- Do not use the `quote()` method to specify placeholder values, or you will get extra quotes in the values you're inserting.
- You can have more than one placeholder in a statement string, but be sure to pass as many values to `execute()` as there are placeholder markers.

- Each placeholder must specify a single value, not a list of values. For example, when you want to specify multiple data values, you cannot prepare and execute a statement like this:

```
my $sth = $dbh->prepare (qq{
  INSERT INTO member last_name, first_name VALUES(?)
});
$sth->execute ("Adams,Bill,2014-07-19");
```

You must specify the values separately and provide one placeholder for each:

```
my $sth = $dbh->prepare (qq{
  INSERT INTO member last_name, first_name VALUES(?,?,?)
});
$sth->execute ("Adams","Bill","2014-07-19");
```

- To specify NULL as a placeholder value, use undef.
- Placeholders and quote() are intended only for data values. Do not try to use a placeholder for keywords such SELECT or for identifiers such database, table, or column names. It won't work because the keyword or identifier will be placed into the statement surrounded by quotes, and the statement will fail with a syntax error.

For some database engines, you get another performance benefit from using placeholders, in addition to improved efficiency in loops. Certain engines cache prepared statements and possibly the statement execution plan. That way, if the same statement is received by the server later, it can be reused and processed more quickly without the initial preparation overhead. Statement caching is especially helpful for complex SELECT statements because it may take some time to prepare the statement and generate a good execution plan. Placeholders give you a better chance at making the statement cacheable because they make statements more generic than statements constructed by embedding specific data values directly in the statement string.

MySQL does not cache execution plans. MySQL has a query cache, but it operates by caching result sets for query strings, not by caching execution plans. The query cache is discussed in Chapter 5, "Query Optimization."

By default, MySQL does not cache prepared statements, either. Parameter binding to placeholders takes place on the client side within the DBD::mysql module. However, the binary protocol implemented in the C client library does allow for statements to be prepared on the server side and for parameter binding to be handled by the server. DBD::mysql can take advantage of this capability.

To turn on server-side prepared statements and parameter binding, all you need to do is enable the mysql_server_prepare option. For example, given a database handle $dbh, this can be done as follows:

```
$dbh->{mysql_server_prepare} = 1;
```

To disable server-side prepared statements, set the option to 0.

For `mysql_server_prepare` support, it is best to use DBD::mysql 3.0009 or higher because there were some changes to the default value of this option in some of the preceding releases.

Even if you don't use MySQL's server-side capabilities for prepared statements, it still can be beneficial to write your statements using placeholders: When you port a script for use with a database engine that does cache execution plans, it will execute statements with placeholders more efficiently than those without.

The Mystery `undef`

Some DBI methods like `do()` and `selectrow_array()` that execute a statement string enable you to provide placeholder values to be bound to any '?' characters in the statement. For example, you can update a row like this:

```
my $rows = $dbh->do (
          "UPDATE member SET expiration = ? WHERE member_id = ?",
          undef, "2007-01-01", 14);
```

Or fetch a row like this:

```
my $ref = $dbh->selectrow_arrayref (
          "SELECT * FROM member WHERE member_id = ?",
          undef, 14);
```

Observe that, in both cases, the placeholder values are preceded by a mysterious `undef` argument that appears to do nothing. The reason it's there is that, for statement-execution methods that allow placeholder arguments, those arguments are preceded by another argument that can be used to specify statement-processing attributes. Such attributes are rarely (if ever) used, but the argument still must be present, so just specify it as `undef`.

8.2.8 Binding Query Results to Script Variables

Placeholders enable you to substitute values into a statement string at statement execution time. In other words, you can parameterize the "input" to the statement. DBI also provides a corresponding output operation called "parameter binding" that enables you to parameterize the "output" by retrieving column values into variables automatically when you fetch a row without having to assign values to the variables yourself.

Suppose that you have a query to retrieve names from the `member` table. You can tell DBI to assign the values of the selected columns to Perl variables. When you fetch a row, the variables are automatically updated with the corresponding column values, which makes the retrieval very efficient. Here's an example that shows how to bind the columns to variables and then access them in the fetch loop:

```
my ($last_name, $first_name, $suffix);
my $sth = $dbh->prepare (qq{
          SELECT last_name, first_name, suffix
          FROM member ORDER BY last_name, first_name
        });
$sth->execute ();
```

```
$sth->bind_col (1, \$last_name);
$sth->bind_col (2, \$first_name);
$sth->bind_col (3, \$suffix);
print "$last_name, $first_name, $suffix\n" while $sth->fetch ();
```

bind_col() should be called after execute() and before fetching rows. Each call should specify a column number and a reference to the variable you want to associate with the column. Column numbers begin with 1.

As an alternative to individual calls to bind_col(), you can pass all the variable references in a single call to bind_columns():

```
my ($last_name, $first_name, $suffix);
my $sth = $dbh->prepare (qq{
        SELECT last_name, first_name, suffix
        FROM member ORDER BY last_name, first_name
      });
$sth->execute ();
$sth->bind_columns (\$last_name, \$first_name, \$suffix);
print "$last_name, $first_name, $suffix\n" while $sth->fetch ();
```

bind_columns() should be called after execute() and before fetching rows.

8.2.9 Specifying Connection Parameters

The most direct way to establish a server connection is to specify all the connection parameters as arguments to the connect() method:

```
my $dsn = "DBI:mysql:db_name:host_name";
my $dbh = DBI->connect ($dsn, user_name, password);
```

If you leave out connection parameters, DBI attempts to determine what values to use as follows:

- The DBI_DSN environment variable is used if set and the data source name (DSN) is undefined or is the empty string. The DBI_USER and DBI_PASS environment variables are used if set and the username and password are undefined (but not if they are the empty string). Under Windows, the USER variable is used if the username is undefined.
- If you leave out the hostname, DBI attempts to connect to the local host.
- If you specify undef or an empty string for the username, it defaults to your Unix login name. Under Windows, the username defaults to ODBC.
- If you specify undef or an empty string for the password, no password is sent.

You can specify certain options in the DSN by appending them to the initial part of the string, each preceded by a semicolon. For example, you can use the mysql_read_default_file option to specify an option file pathname:

```
my $dsn = "DBI:mysql:sampdb;mysql_read_default_file=/home/paul/.my.cnf";
```

When the script executes, it will read the named file for connection parameters. Suppose that `/home/paul/.my.cnf` has the following contents:

```
[client]
host=localhost
user=sampadm
password=secret
```

In this case, the `connect()` call will attempt to connect to the MySQL server on `localhost` and will connect as user `sampadm` with password `secret`. Under Unix, you can tell your script to use the option file that belongs to the person who happens to be running it by parameterizing the filename like this:

```
my $dsn = "DBI:mysql:sampdb;mysql_read_default_file=$ENV{HOME}/.my.cnf";
```

`$ENV{HOME}` contains the pathname to the home directory of the user running the script, so the connection parameters that it uses will be pulled from that user's own option file. By writing a script in this way, you don't have to embed connection parameters literally in the script.

Using `mysql_read_default_file` causes the script to read only the named option file, which may be undesirable if you want it to look for parameters in system-wide option files as well (such as `/etc/my.cnf` under Unix or `C:\my.ini` under Windows). To have the script read all the standard option files for connection parameters, use `mysql_read_default_group` instead. This option causes parameters in the `[client]` group to be used, as well as in the group that you specify in the option's value. For example, if you have options that are specific to your `sampdb`-related scripts, you can list them in a `[sampdb]` group and then use a data source value like this:

```
my $dsn = "DBI:mysql:sampdb;mysql_read_default_group=sampdb";
```

If you want to read just the `[client]` group from the standard option files, specify the option like this:

```
my $dsn = "DBI:mysql:sampdb;mysql_read_default_group=client";
```

For more details on options for specifying the data source string, see Appendix H (online). For more information on the format of MySQL option files, see Appendix F, "MySQL Program Reference."

One difficulty with using `mysql_read_default_file` on Windows is that file pathnames typically begin with a drive letter and a colon. That's a problem, because DBI interprets colon as the character that separates parts of the DSN string. It's possible to work around this, although the method is ugly:

1. Use `chdir()` to change location to the root directory of the drive where the option file is located, so that pathnames specified without a drive letter will be interpreted relative to that drive.

2. Specify the filename as the value of the `mysql_read_default_file` option in the DSN, but without the leading drive letter or colon.

3. If it's necessary to leave the current directory undisturbed by the connect operation, save the current directory pathname before calling `connect()` and then `chdir()` back to it after connecting.

The following code fragment shows how to do this if you want to use the option file `C:\my.ini`. (Note that backslashes in Windows pathnames are specified as slashes in Perl strings.)

```
# save current directory pathname
use Cwd;
my $orig_dir = cwd ();
# change to root dir of drive where file is located
chdir ("C:/") or die "Cannot chdir: $!\n";
# connect using parameters in C:\my.ini
my $dsn = "DBI:mysql:sampdb:localhost;mysql_read_default_file=/my.ini";
my %conn_attrs = (RaiseError => 1, PrintError => 0, AutoCommit => 1);
my $dbh = DBI->connect ($dsn, undef, undef, \%conn_attrs);
# change back to original directory
chdir ($orig_dir) or die "Cannot chdir: $!\n";
```

Using an option file doesn't prevent you from specifying connection parameters in the `connect()` call (for example, if you want the script to connect as a particular user). Any explicit hostname, username, and password values specified in the `connect()` call override connection parameters found in the option file. For example, you might want your script to parse options such as `--host` and `--user` from the command line and use those values, if they are given, in preference to any found in an option file. That would be useful because it's the way the standard MySQL clients behave. Your DBI scripts would therefore be consistent with that behavior.

For the remaining command-line scripts that we develop in this chapter, I'll use some standard connection setup and teardown code. I'll just show it once here so that we can concentrate on the main body of each script as we write it:

```
#!/usr/bin/perl

use strict;
use warnings;
use DBI;

# parse connection parameters from command line if given

use Getopt::Long;
$Getopt::Long::ignorecase = 0; # options are case sensitive
$Getopt::Long::bundling = 1;   # -uname = -u name, not -u -n -a -m -e

# default parameters - all undefined initially
my ($host_name, $password, $port_num, $socket_name, $user_name);
```

```
GetOptions (
  # =i means an integer value is required after option
  # =s means a string value is required after option
  "host|h=s"        => \$host_name,
  "password|p=s"    => \$password,
  "port|P=i"        => \$port_num,
  "socket|S=s"      => \$socket_name,
  "user|u=s"        => \$user_name
) or exit (1);


# construct data source
my $dsn = "DBI:mysql:sampdb";
$dsn .= ";host=$host_name" if $host_name;
$dsn .= ";port=$port_num" if $port_num;
$dsn .= ";mysql_socket=$socket_name" if $socket_name;
$dsn .= ";mysql_read_default_group=client";


# connect to server
my %conn_attrs = (RaiseError => 1, PrintError => 0, AutoCommit => 1);
my $dbh = DBI->connect ($dsn, $user_name, $password, \%conn_attrs);
```

This code initializes DBI, looks for connection parameters on the command line, and then makes the connection to the MySQL server using parameters from the command line or found in the [client] group in the standard option files. If you have your connection parameters listed in your option file, you won't have to enter them when you run a script that uses this code.

The final part of each script will be similar, too; it simply terminates the connection before exiting:

```
$dbh->disconnect ();
```

When we get to Web programming, Section 8.4, "Using DBI in Web Applications," we'll modify the connection setup code a bit, but the basic idea will be similar.

There is one unfortunate difference between the way the standard MySQL clients and the Getopt module handle command-line options. The standard clients have special option-processing code that allows a password option (--password or -p) to be specified with or without an immediately following password value, and to prompt for a password if the value is not given.

With Getopt, if you try to make the password value optional for --password and -p, you cannot unambiguously specify the option without a value unless it is either the last argument on the command line or is immediately followed by another option. Suppose that you have a script that expects a table name argument to follow the options. If the script is invoked as follows, Getopt will interpret mytbl as the password value rather than prompting for a password:

```
% ./myscript.pl -u paul -p mytbl
```

To avoid this kind of problem, the code in the Perl framework just shown requires a password option, if given, to be specified with a value.

8.2.10 Debugging

To debug a malfunctioning DBI script, two techniques are commonly used, either alone or in tandem. First, you can sprinkle print statements throughout your script. This enables you to tailor your debugging output the way you want it, but you must add the statements manually. Second, you can use DBI's built-in tracing capabilities. This is more general and more systematic, and it occurs automatically after you turn it on. DBI tracing also shows you information about the operation of the driver that you cannot get otherwise.

8.2.10.1 Debugging Using Print Statements

Here's a common question: "I have a statement that works fine when I execute it using the mysql program, but it doesn't work from my DBI script. How come?" It's not unusual to find that the DBI script really is issuing a different statement than you think. If you print a statement before executing it, you might be surprised to see what you're actually sending to the server. Suppose that a statement as you type it into mysql looks like this:

```
mysql> INSERT INTO member (last_name,first_name,expiration)
    -> VALUES('Brown','Marcia','2012-06-03');
```

Then you try the same thing in a DBI script (leaving out the terminating semicolon, of course):

```
$last = "Brown";
$first = "Marcia";
$expiration = "2012-06-03";
$stmt = qq{
  INSERT INTO member (last_name,first_name,expiration)
  VALUES($last,$first,$expiration)
};
$rows = $dbh->do ($stmt);
```

That doesn't work, even though it's the same statement. Or is it? Try printing it:

```
print "$stmt\n";
```

Here is the result:

```
INSERT INTO member (last_name,first_name,expiration)
VALUES(Brown,Marcia,2012-06-03)
```

From this output, you can see that the statement is not the same at all. There are no quotes around the values in the VALUES() list. One way to specify the statement properly is like this, using quote():

```
$last = $dbh->quote ("Brown");
$first = $dbh->quote ("Marcia");
$expiration = $dbh->quote ("2012-06-03");
```

```
$stmt = qq{
  INSERT INTO member (last_name,first_name,expiration)
  VALUES($last,$first,$expiration)
};
$rows = $dbh->do ($stmt);
```

Alternatively, you can specify the statement using placeholders and pass the values to be inserted into it as arguments to the `do()` method:

```
$last = "Brown";
$first = "Marcia";
$expiration = "2012-06-03";
$stmt = qq{
  INSERT INTO member (last_name,first_name,expiration)
  VALUES(?,?,?)
};
$rows = $dbh->do ($stmt, undef, $last, $first, $expiration);
```

Unfortunately, when you use the latter approach, you cannot see what the complete statement looks like by printing it because the placeholder values aren't evaluated until you invoke `do()`. When you use placeholders, tracing may be a more helpful debugging method.

8.2.10.2 Debugging Using Tracing

DBI offers a tracing mechanism that generates debugging information to help you figure out why a script doesn't work properly. Trace levels range from 0 (off) to 15 (maximum information). Generally, trace levels 1 through 4 are the most useful. For example, a level 2 trace shows you the text of statements that you're executing (including the result of place-holder substitutions), the result of calls to `quote()`, and so forth. This can be of immense help in tracking down a problem.

You can control tracing from within individual scripts using the `trace()` method, or you can set the `DBI_TRACE` environment variable to affect tracing for all DBI scripts you run.

To use the `trace()` call, pass a trace level argument and optionally a filename. If you specify no filename, all trace output goes to `STDERR`; otherwise, it goes to the named file. The following call sets up a level 1 trace to `STDERR`:

```
DBI->trace (1);
```

This call sets up a level 2 trace to the `trace.out` file:

```
DBI->trace (2, "trace.out");
```

To disable tracing, specify a trace level of zero:

```
DBI->trace (0);
```

When invoked as `DBI->trace()`, all DBI operations are traced. For a more fine-grained approach, enable tracing at the individual handle level. This is useful when you have a good idea where a problem in your script lies and you don't want to wade through the trace output for everything that occurs up to that point. For example, if you're having problems with a particular SELECT query, you can trace the statement handle associated with the query:

```
$sth = $dbh->prepare (qq{ SELECT ... }); # create the statement handle
$sth->trace (1);                         # enable tracing on the statement
$sth->execute ();
```

If you specify a filename argument to any trace() call, whether for DBI as a whole or for an individual handle, all trace output goes to that file.

The TraceLevel attribute is an alternative to the trace() method. This attribute allows you to set or get the trace level for a given handle:

```
$dbh->{TraceLevel} = 3;                  # set database handle trace level
my $cur_level = $sth->{TraceLevel};      # get statement handle trace level
```

To turn on tracing globally so that it takes effect for all DBI scripts that you run, set the DBI_TRACE environment variable from your shell. The syntax for this depends on the shell you use:

- For csh or tcsh:
  ```
  % setenv DBI_TRACE value
  ```

- For sh, bash, or ksh:
  ```
  $ export DBI_TRACE=value
  ```

- For Windows:
  ```
  C:\> set DBI_TRACE=value
  ```

The format of value is the same for all shells: a number n to turn on tracing at level n to STDERR, a filename to turn on level 2 tracing to the named file, or n=file_name to turn on level n tracing to the named file. Here are some examples, using tcsh syntax:

- A level 1 trace to STDERR:
  ```
  % setenv DBI_TRACE 1
  ```

- A level 1 trace to the file trace.out:
  ```
  % setenv DBI_TRACE 1=trace.out
  ```

- A level 2 trace to the file trace.out:
  ```
  % setenv DBI_TRACE trace.out
  ```

Using DBI_TRACE is advantageous in that you can enable DBI script tracing without making any changes to your scripts. But if you turn on tracing to a file from your shell, be sure to turn it off after you resolve the problem. Debugging output is appended to the trace file without overwriting it, so the file can become quite large if you're not careful.

It's a particularly bad idea to define DBI_TRACE in a shell startup file such as .cshrc, .tcshrc, .login, or .profile!

To turn off DBI_TRACE for various command interpreters, use any of the commands shown:

- For csh or tcsh:

```
% setenv DBI_TRACE 0
% unsetenv DBI_TRACE
```

- For sh, bash, or ksh:

```
$ unset DBI_TRACE
$ export DBI_TRACE=0
```

- For Windows:

```
C:\> unset DBI_TRACE
C:\> set DBI_TRACE=0
```

8.2.11 Using Result Set Metadata

You can use DBI to gain access to result set metadata—that is, descriptive information about the rows selected by a query. To get this information, access the attributes of the statement handle associated with the query that generated the result set. Some of these are standard DBI attributes that are available across all database drivers (such as NUM_OF_FIELDS, the number of columns in the result set). Others, which are MySQL-specific, are provided by DBD::mysql, the MySQL driver for DBI. These attributes, such as mysql_max_length, which tells you the maximum width of the values in each column, are not applicable to other database systems. To the extent that you use any of the MySQL-specific attributes, you risk making your scripts nonportable to other databases. On the other hand, they can make it easier to get the information you want.

You must ask for metadata at the right time. Generally, result set attributes are not available for a SELECT statement until after you've invoked prepare() and execute(). In addition, attributes may become invalid after you reach the end of the result set with a row-fetching function or after you invoke finish().

The following example shows how to use one of the MySQL-specific metadata attributes, mysql_max_length, in conjunction with the more general attributes NUM_OF_FIELDS, which indicates the number of columns in the result set, and NAME, which holds their names. We can combine the information provided by these attributes to write a script, tabular.pl, that produces output from SELECT queries in the same tabular (boxed) style that you get when you run the mysql client program in interactive mode. The main body of tabular.pl follows. You can replace the SELECT statement with any other; the output-writing routines are independent of the particular statement.

```
my $sth = $dbh->prepare (qq{
        SELECT last_name, first_name, suffix, city, state
        FROM president ORDER BY last_name, first_name
```

```
            });
$sth->execute (); # attributes should be available after this call

# actual maximum widths of column values in result set
my @wid = @{$sth->{mysql_max_length}};
# number of columns in result set
my $ncols = $sth->{NUM_OF_FIELDS};

# adjust column widths if data values are narrower than column headings
# or than the word "NULL"
for (my $i = 0; $i < $ncols; $i++)
{
  my $name_wid = length ($sth->{NAME}->[$i]);
  $wid[$i] = $name_wid if $wid[$i] < $name_wid;
  $wid[$i] = 4 if $wid[$i] < 4;
}

# print tabular-format output
print_dashes (\@wid, $ncols);              # row of dashes
print_row ($sth->{NAME}, \@wid, $ncols);   #column headings
print_dashes (\@wid, $ncols);              #row of dashes
while (my $ary_ref = $sth->fetchrow_arrayref ())
{
  print_row ($ary_ref, \@wid, $ncols);     #row data values
}
print_dashes (\@wid, $ncols);              #row of dashes
```

After the statement has been initiated with `execute()`, we can grab the metadata we need. `$sth->{NUM_OF_FIELDS}` is a scalar value indicating how many columns are in the result set. `$sth->{NAME}` and `$sth->{mysql_max_length}` give us the column names and maximum width of each column's values. The value of each of these two attributes is a reference to an array that contains an element for each column of the result set, in the order that columns are named in the statement.

The remaining calculations are very much like those used for the `exec_stmt` program developed in Chapter 7. For example, to avoid misaligned output, we adjust the column width values upward if the name of a column is wider than any of the data values in the column.

The output functions, `print_dashes()` and `print_row()`, are written as follows. They too are similar to the corresponding code in `exec_stmt`:

```
sub print_dashes
{
my $wid_ary_ref = shift;  # reference to array of column widths
my $cols = shift;         # number of columns

  for (my $i = 0; $i < $cols; $i++)
  {
```

```
      print "+", "-" x ($wid_ary_ref->[$i]+2);
   }
   print "+\n";
}

# print row of data.  (doesn't right-align numeric columns)

sub print_row
{
my $val_ary_ref = shift;  # reference to array of column values
my $wid_ary_ref = shift;  # reference to array of column widths
my $cols = shift;         # number of columns

   for (my $i = 0; $i < $cols; $i++)
   {
     printf "| %-*s ", $wid_ary_ref->[$i],
            defined ($val_ary_ref->[$i]) ? $val_ary_ref->[$i] : "NULL";
   }
   print "|\n";
}
```

The output from `tabular.pl` looks like this:

```
+------------+---------------+--------+--------------------+-------+
| last_name  | first_name    | suffix | city               | state |
+------------+---------------+--------+--------------------+-------+
| Adams      | John          | NULL   | Braintree          | MA    |
| Adams      | John Quincy   | NULL   | Braintree          | MA    |
| Arthur     | Chester A.    | NULL   | Fairfield          | VT    |
| Buchanan   | James         | NULL   | Mercersburg        | PA    |
| Bush       | George H.W.   | NULL   | Milton             | MA    |
| Bush       | George W.     | NULL   | New Haven          | CT    |
| Carter     | James E.      | Jr.    | Plains             | GA    |
...
```

Our next script uses column metadata to produce output in a different format. This script, `show_member.pl`, enables you to take a quick look at Historical League member entries without entering any queries. Given a member's last name, it displays the selected entry like this:

```
% ./show_member.pl artel
last_name:  Artel
first_name: Mike
suffix:
expiration: 2011-04-16
email:      mike_artel@venus.org
street:     4264 Lovering Rd.
city:       Miami
```

```
state:      FL
zip:        12777
phone:      075-961-0712
interests:  Civil Rights,Education,Revolutionary War
member_id:  63
```

You can also invoke `show_member.pl` using a membership number, or using a SQL pattern to match several last names. The following commands show the entry for member 23 or the entries for members with last names that start with "C":

```
% ./show_member.pl 23
% ./show_member.pl C%
```

The main body of the `show_member.pl` script follows. It uses the NAME attribute to determine the labels to use for each row of output, and the NUM_OF_FIELDS attribute to find out how many columns the result set contains:

```
my $count = 0;  # number of entries printed so far
my @label = (); # column label array
my $label_wid = 0;

while (@ARGV)    # run query for each argument on command line
{
  my $arg = shift (@ARGV);

  # default is to do a pattern search by last name...
  my $clause = "last_name LIKE " . $dbh->quote ($arg);
  # ...but do ID search instead if argument is numeric
  $clause = "member_id = " . $dbh->quote ($arg) if $arg =~ /^\d+$/;

  # issue query
  my $sth = $dbh->prepare (qq{
              SELECT * FROM member
              WHERE $clause
              ORDER BY last_name, first_name
            });
  $sth->execute ();

  # get column names to use for labels and
  # determine max column name width for formatting
  # (but do this only the first time through the loop)
  if ($label_wid == 0)
  {
    @label = @{$sth->{NAME}};
    foreach my $label (@label)
    {
      $label_wid = length ($label) if $label_wid < length ($label);
    }
```

```
}

  # read and display query result
  my $matches = 0;
  while (my @ary = $sth->fetchrow_array ())
  {
    # print newline before 2nd and subsequent entries
    print "\n" if ++$count > 1;
    foreach (my $i = 0; $i < $sth->{NUM_OF_FIELDS}; $i++)
    {
      # print label
      printf "%-*s", $label_wid+1, $label[$i] . ":";
      # print value, if there is one
      print " ", $ary[$i] if defined ($ary[$i]);
      print "\n";
    }
    ++$matches;
  }
  print "\nNo match was found for \"$arg\"\n" if $matches == 0;
}
```

The purpose of show_member.pl is to show the entire contents of an entry, no matter what the fields are. By using SELECT * to retrieve all the columns and the NAME attribute to find out what they are, this script works without modification even if columns are added to or dropped from the member table.

If you just want to know what columns a table contains without retrieving any rows, you can issue this statement:

```
SELECT * FROM tbl_name WHERE FALSE
```

The WHERE FALSE clause is false for all rows, so executing the statement has the effect of generating column metadata but returning no rows. After invoking prepare() and execute() in the usual way for the statement, you can get the column names from @{$sth->{NAME}}. Be aware that although this little trick of using an "empty" query works for MySQL, it's not portable and may not work for other database systems.

For more information on the attributes provided by DBI and by DBD::mysql, see Appendix H (online). It's up to you to determine whether you want to strive for portability by avoiding MySQL-specific attributes, or take advantage of them at the cost of portability.

8.2.12 Performing Transactions

One way to perform transactions in a DBI script is to issue explicit SET autocommit, START TRANSACTION, COMMIT, and ROLLBACK statements. (Section 2.13, "Performing Trans-actions," describes these statements.) However, DBI provides its own abstraction for per-forming transactional operations. This abstraction is expressed in terms of DBI methods and attributes, and takes care of issuing the proper transaction-related SQL statements for you automatically. It's also portable to other database systems that support transactions, whereas the SQL statements may not be.

To use the DBI transaction mechanism, these requirements must be satisfied:

- Your MySQL server must support at least one transaction-safe storage engine such as InnoDB or Falcon. Section 2.6.1.1, "Checking Which Storage Engines Are Available," describes how to determine whether this is true.

- Your application must use tables that are of a transaction-safe type. If they are not, use ALTER TABLE to change their type. For example, to change a given table *tbl_name* to be an InnoDB table, use this statement:

```
ALTER TABLE tbl_name ENGINE = InnoDB;
```

Assuming that those requirements are satisfied, use this general procedure for transactional processing in DBI:

1. Disable (or temporarily suspend) autocommit mode so that SQL statements won't be committed until you commit them yourself.

2. Issue the statements that are part of a transaction, but do so within an eval block that executes with RaiseError enabled and PrintError disabled so that any errors will terminate the block without printing errors. If the block executes successfully, the last operation within it should be to invoke commit() to commit the transaction.

3. When the eval block finishes, check its termination status. If an error occurred, invoke rollback() to cancel the transaction and report the error if that's appropriate.

4. Restore the autocommit mode and error-handling attributes as necessary.

The following example shows how to implement this approach. It's based on a scenario from Chapter 2, "Using SQL to Manage Data," that showed how to issue transaction-related statements manually from the mysql client. The scenario is one in which you discover that you've mistakenly mixed up two scores for students in the score table and need to switch them: Student 8 has been given a score of 18, student 9 has been given a score of 13, and the scores should be the other way around. The two UPDATE statements needed to correct this problem are as follows:

```
UPDATE score SET score = 13 WHERE event_id = 5 AND student_id = 8;
UPDATE score SET score = 18 WHERE event_id = 5 AND student_id = 9;
```

You want to update both rows with the correct scores, but both updates must succeed as a unit. The example in the earlier chapter surrounded the updates by explicit SQL statements for setting the autocommit mode, committing, and rolling back. Within a Perl script that uses the DBI transaction mechanism, perform the updates as follows:

```
my $orig_re = $dbh->{RaiseError}; # save error-handling attributes
my $orig_pe = $dbh->{PrintError};
my $orig_ac = $dbh->{AutoCommit}; # save auto-commit mode

$dbh->{RaiseError} = 1;           # cause errors to raise exceptions
$dbh->{PrintError} = 0;           # but suppress error messages
```

```
$dbh->{AutoCommit} = 0;              # don't commit until we say so

eval
{
  # issue the statements that are part of the transaction
  my $sth = $dbh->prepare (qq{
            UPDATE score SET score = ?
            WHERE event_id = ? AND student_id = ?
         });
  $sth->execute (13, 5, 8);
  $sth->execute (18, 5, 9);
  $dbh->commit();                    # commit the transaction
};
if ($@)                              # did the transaction fail?
{
  print "A transaction error occurred: $@\n";
  # roll back, but use eval to trap rollback failure
  eval { $dbh->rollback (); }
}

$dbh->{AutoCommit} = $orig_ac;    # restore auto-commit mode
$dbh->{RaiseError} = $orig_re;    # restore error-handling attributes
$dbh->{PrintError} = $orig_pe;
```

The `eval` block does the work of performing the transaction, and its termination status is available in the `$@` variable. If the UPDATE statements and the `commit()` method execute without error, `$@` will be empty. If an error occurs, the `eval` block fails and `$@` holds the error message. In that case, the code prints the message, and then cancels the transaction by invoking `rollback()`. (The rollback operation is placed within its own `eval` block to prevent it from terminating the script if it fails.)

In this chapter, DBI scripts generally use an error-handling mode in which `RaiseError` is enabled and `PrintError` is disabled. This means that they already will have the values required for performing transactions, and thus it really wouldn't have been necessary to save, set, and restore those attributes as shown in the example. However, doing so is an approach that will work even for circumstances under which you're not sure in advance what the error-handling attributes might be.

8.3 Putting DBI to Work

At this point you've seen a number of the concepts involved in DBI programming, so let's move on to some of the things we wanted to be able to do with our sample database. Our goals were outlined initially in Chapter 1. Those that we'll tackle by writing DBI scripts in this chapter are listed here:

- For the grade-keeping project, we want to be able to retrieve scores for any given quiz or test.

- For the Historical League, we want to do the following:
  - Produce the member directory in different formats. We want a names-only list for use in the program distributed at the League's annual meeting, and in a format we can use for generating the printed directory.
  - Find League members that need to renew their memberships soon, and then send them email to let them know about it.
  - Edit member entries. (We'll need to update their expiration dates when they renew their memberships, after all.)
  - Find members that share a common interest.
  - Put the directory online.

For some of these tasks, we'll write scripts that run from the command line. For the others, we'll create scripts in Section 8.4, "Using DBI in Web Applications," that you can use in conjunction with your Web server. At the end of the chapter, we'll still have a number of goals left to accomplish. We'll finish up those that remain in Chapter 9, "Writing MySQL Programs Using PHP."

8.3.1 Generating the Historical League Directory

One of our goals is to be able to produce information from the Historical League directory in different formats. The simplest format to be generated is a list of member names for the printed program distributed to attendees at the League's annual meeting. The format can be a simple plain text listing. It will become part of the larger document used to create the meeting program, so all we need is something that can be pasted into that document.

For the printed member directory, a better representation than plain text is needed because we want something nicely formatted. A reasonable choice here is RTF (Rich Text Format), a format developed by Microsoft that is understood by many word processors. Word is one such program, of course, but many others such as OpenOffice understand it as well. Different word processors support RTF to varying degrees, but we'll use a basic subset of the full RTF specification that should be understandable by any program that is RTF-aware. For example, on Mac OS X, the TextEdit editor and the Safari Web browser can read the RTF output that we'll generate.

The procedures for generating the annual meeting list (plain text) and RTF directory formats are essentially the same: Issue a query to retrieve the entries, and then run a loop that fetches and formats each entry. Given that basic similarity, it would be nice to avoid writing separate scripts for each format. To that end, let's write a single script, gen_dir.pl, that can generate different types of output. We'll structure the script as follows:

1. Before writing out member entries, perform any initialization that might be necessary for the output format. No special initialization is necessary for the plain text member list, but we'll need to write out some initial control language for the RTF version.

2. Fetch and print each entry, formatted appropriately for the type of output we want.

3. After all the entries have been processed, perform any necessary cleanup and termination. Again, no special handling is needed for plain text format, but some closing control language is required for the RTF version.

It's possible that in the future we'll want to use this script to write output in other formats, so let's make it extensible by setting up a "switchbox," that is, a hash with an element for each output format. Each element specifies which functions to invoke to carry out each output generation phase for a given format: an initialization function, an entry-writing function, and a cleanup function:

```
# switchbox containing formatting functions for each output format
my %switchbox =
(
  "text" =>                    # functions for plain text format
  {
    "init"    => undef,     # no initialization needed
    "entry"   => \&text_format_entry,
    "cleanup" => undef      # no cleanup needed
  },
  "rtf" =>                     # functions for RTF format
  {
    "init"    => \&rtf_init,
    "entry"   => \&rtf_format_entry,
    "cleanup" => \&rtf_cleanup
  }
);
```

Each element of the switchbox is keyed by a format name ("text" or "rtf"). We'll write the script so that you specify the desired format on the command line when you run it:

```
% ./gen_dir.pl text
% ./gen_dir.pl rtf
```

By setting up a switchbox this way, we'll be able to add the capability for a new format easily, should we want to do so:

1. Write three formatting functions for the output generation phases.
2. Add a new element to the switchbox that defines a format name and that points to the output functions.
3. To produce output in the new format, invoke gen_dir.pl and specify the format name on the command line.

The code for selecting the proper switchbox entry according to the first argument on the command line follows. If no format name or an invalid name is specified on the command line, the script produces an error message and displays a list of the allowable names. Otherwise, $func_hashref will point to the appropriate switchbox entry:

```perl
my $formats = join (" ", sort (keys (%switchbox)));
# make sure one argument was specified on the command line
@ARGV == 1
    or die "Usage: gen_dir.pl format_type\nAllowable formats: $formats\n";

# determine proper switchbox entry from argument on command line;
# if no entry is found, the format type is invalid
my $func_hashref = $switchbox{$ARGV[0]};

defined ($func_hashref)
    or die "Unknown format: $ARGV[0]\nAllowable formats: $formats\n";
```

The format selection code is based on the fact that the output format names are the keys in the %switchbox hash. If a valid format name is given, the corresponding switchbox entry points to the output functions. If an invalid name is given, no entry will exist. This makes it unnecessary to hardwire any names into the format selection code. It also means that if you add a new entry to the switchbox, the code detects it automatically with no change.

If a valid format name is specified on the command line, the preceding code sets $func_hashref. Its value is a reference to the hash that points to the output-writing functions for the selected format. We can use it to invoke the initialization function, fetch and print the entries, and invoke the cleanup function:

```perl
# invoke the initialization function if there is one
&{$func_hashref->{init}} if defined ($func_hashref->{init});

# fetch and print entries if there is an entry formatting function
if (defined ($func_hashref->{entry}))
{
  my $sth = $dbh->prepare (qq{
            SELECT * FROM member ORDER BY last_name, first_name
          });
  $sth->execute ();
  while (my $entry_ref = $sth->fetchrow_hashref ("NAME_lc"))
  {
    # pass entry by reference to the formatting function
    &{$func_hashref->{entry}} ($entry_ref);
  }
}

# invoke the cleanup function if there is one
&{$func_hashref->{cleanup}} if defined ($func_hashref->{cleanup});
```

The entry-fetching loop uses fetchrow_hashref() for a reason. If the loop fetched an array, each formatting function would have to know the order of the columns. It's possible to figure that out by accessing the $sth->{NAME} attribute (which contains column names in the order in which they are returned), but why bother? By using a hash reference, formatting functions can just name the column values they want using $entry_ref->{col_name}. That technique is much easier than using the NAME attribute and it can be used for any format we want to generate, because we know that any fields we need will be in the hash.

All that remains is to write the functions named by the switchbox entries for each output format.

8.3.1.1 Generating the Plain Text Member List

For the text output format, no initialization or cleanup calls are necessary. We need only an entry-formatting function, text_format_entry(), that takes a reference to a member entry and prints the member's name. The tricky part of printing names is dealing with the suffix part. Suffixes such as "Jr." or "Sr." should be preceded by a comma and a space, whereas suffixes such as "II" or "III" should be preceded only by a space:

```
Michael Alvis IV
Clarence Elgar, Jr.
Bill Matthews, Sr.
Mark York II
```

The letters 'I', 'V', and 'X' are the only ones used in the roman numerals for the 1st to the 39th generation. It's unlikely that we'll need any numerals beyond that range, so we can determine whether to add a comma by checking whether the suffix value matches the following pattern:

```
/^[IVX]+$/
```

The code in text_format_entry() that puts the parts of the name together in the proper order is something we'll need for the RTF version of the directory as well. So instead of duplicating that code in rtf_format_entry(), let's stuff it into a helper function:

```
sub format_name
{
my $entry_ref = shift;

  my $name = $entry_ref->{first_name} . " " . $entry_ref->{last_name};
  if (defined ($entry_ref->{suffix}))     # there is a name suffix
  {
    # no comma for suffixes of I, II, III, etc.
    $name .= "," unless $entry_ref->{suffix} =~ /^[IVX]+$/;
    $name .= " " . $entry_ref->{suffix}
  }
  return ($name);
}
```

With `format_name()` in place, the implementation of the `text_format_entry()` function that prints an entry becomes almost completely trivial:

```
sub text_format_entry
{
  printf "%s\n", format_name ($_[0]);
}
```

8.3.1.2 Generating the Rich Text Format Directory

Generating the RTF version of the directory is a little more involved than generating the member list for the annual meeting program. For one thing, we need to print more information from each entry. For another, we need to put out some RTF control language with each entry to achieve the effects that we want, and some control language at the beginning and end of the document. A minimal RTF document framework looks like this:

```
{\rtf0
{\fonttbl {\f0 Times;}}
\plain \f0 \fs24
  ...document content goes here...
}
```

The document begins and ends with curly braces '{' and '}'. RTF keywords begin with a backslash, and the first keyword of the document must be \rtf*n*, where *n* is the version number of the RTF specification that the document uses. Version 0 is fine for our purposes.

Within the document, we specify a font table to indicate the font to use for the entries. Font table information is listed in a group consisting of curly braces containing a leading \fonttbl keyword and some font information. The font table in the framework just shown defines font number 0 to be in Times. (We need only one font, but you could use more if you wanted to be fancier.)

The next few directives set up the default formatting style: \plain selects plain format, \f0 selects font 0 (which is defined as Times in the font table), and \fs24 sets the font size to 12 points (the number following \fs indicates the size in half-points). It's unnecessary to set up margins because most word processors will supply reasonable defaults.

The initialization and cleanup functions produce the document framework. They look like this (note the doubled backslashes to get single backslashes in the output):

```
sub rtf_init
{
  print "{\\rtf0\n";
  print "{\\fonttbl {\\f0 Times;}}\n";
  print "\\plain \\f0 \\fs24\n";
}

sub rtf_cleanup
{
```

```
    print "}\n";
}
```

The entry-formatting function produces the document content. We take a very simple approach, printing each entry as a series of lines, with a label on each line. If the information corresponding to a particular output line is missing, the line is omitted. For example, the "Email:" line need not be printed for members that have no email address. Some lines, such as the "Address:" line, are composed from the information in multiple columns (`street`, `city`, `state`, `zip`), so the script must be able to deal with various combinations of missing values. Here's a sample of the output format we'll use:

Name: Mike Artel
Address: 4264 Lovering Rd., Miami, FL 12777
Telephone: 075-961-0712
Email: mike_artel@venus.org
Interests: Civil Rights,Education,Revolutionary War

For that entry, the RTF representation looks like this:

```
\b Name: Mike Artel\b0\par
Address: 4264 Lovering Rd., Miami, FL 12777\par
Telephone: 075-961-0712\par
Email: mike_artel@venus.org\par
Interests: Civil Rights,Education,Revolutionary War\par
```

To make the "Name:" line bold, it should begin with \b followed by a space to turn boldface on, and end with \b0 to turn boldface off. The member name is formatted by the `format_name()` function shown earlier in Section 8.3.1.1, "Generating the Plain Text Member List." Each line has a paragraph marker (\par) at the end to tell the word processor to move to the next line—nothing too complicated. The primary difficulties lie in formatting the address string and determining which output lines to print:

```
sub rtf_format_entry
{
my $entry_ref = shift;

    printf "\\b Name: %s\\b0\\par\n", format_name ($entry_ref);
    my $address = "";
    $address .= $entry_ref->{street}
                if defined ($entry_ref->{street});
    $address .= ", " . $entry_ref->{city}
                if defined ($entry_ref->{city});
    $address .= ", " . $entry_ref->{state}
                if defined ($entry_ref->{state});
    $address .= " " . $entry_ref->{zip}
                if defined ($entry_ref->{zip});
    print "Address: $address\\par\n"
                if $address ne "";
    print "Telephone: $entry_ref->{phone}\\par\n"
```

```
                        if defined ($entry_ref->{phone});
    print "Email: $entry_ref->{email}\\par\n"
                        if defined ($entry_ref->{email});
    print "Interests: $entry_ref->{interests}\\par\n"
                        if defined ($entry_ref->{interests});
    print "\\par\n";
}
```

You're not locked into this particular formatting style, of course. You can change how you print any of the fields, so you can change the style of your printed directory almost at will, simply by changing `rtf_format_entry()`. When the directory was in its original form (a word processing document), that was something not so easily done.

The `gen_dir.pl` script now is complete, and you can generate the directory in either plain text or RTF output format by running commands such as these:

```
% ./gen_dir.pl text > names.txt
% ./gen_dir.pl rtf > directory.rtf
```

At this point, it's a simple step to read the plain text name list and paste it into the annual meeting program document or to read the RTF file into any program that understands RTF.

DBI makes it easy to extract the information we want from MySQL, and Perl's text-processing capabilities make it easy to put that information into the format we want to see. MySQL doesn't provide any particularly fancy way of formatting output, but it doesn't matter because of the ease with which you can integrate MySQL's database handling abilities into a language such as Perl, which has excellent text manipulation capabilities.

8.3.2 Sending Membership Renewal Notices

With the Historical League directory maintained in its original form (as a word processing document), it's a time-consuming and error prone activity to determine which members need to be notified that their membership should be renewed. Now that we have the information in a database, it's possible to automate the renewal-notification process a bit. We can identify members who need to renew, and send them a message via email so that we don't have to contact them by phone or surface mail.

What we need to do is determine which memberships have expired already or are due for renewal within a certain number of days. The query for this involves a date calculation that's relatively simple:

```
SELECT ... FROM member
WHERE expiration < DATE_ADD(CURDATE(), INTERVAL cutoff DAY)
```

cutoff signifies the number of days of leeway we want to grant. The query selects member entries that are due for renewal in fewer than that many days (or that have already expired). To find only memberships that have expired, a cutoff value of 0 identifies rows with expiration dates in the past.

After identifying the rows that qualify for notification, what should we do with them? One option would be to send mail directly from the same script, but it might be useful to be able to review the list first before sending any messages. For this reason, we'll use a two-stage approach:

1. Run a `need_renewal.pl` script to produce a list of members that need to renew. You can examine this list to verify or edit it, and then use it as input to the second stage that sends the renewal notices.

2. Run a `renewal_notify.pl` script that sends members a "please renew" notice by email. The script should warn you about members that have no email address so that you can contact them by other means.

For the first part of this task, the `need_renewal.pl` script must identify which members need to renew. The main part of the script that does so looks like this:

```
# use default cutoff of 30 days...
my $cutoff = 30;
# ...but reset if a numeric argument is given on the command line
$cutoff = shift (@ARGV) if @ARGV && $ARGV[0] =~ /^\d+$/;

# inform user what cutoff the script is using
warn "Using cutoff of $cutoff days\n";

my $sth = $dbh->prepare (qq{
            SELECT
                member_id, email, last_name, first_name, expiration,
                TO_DAYS(expiration) - TO_DAYS(CURDATE()) AS days
            FROM member
            WHERE expiration < DATE_ADD(CURDATE(), INTERVAL ? DAY)
            ORDER BY expiration, last_name, first_name
          });
$sth->execute ($cutoff);  # pass cutoff as placeholder value

while (my $entry_ref = $sth->fetchrow_hashref ())
{
  # convert undef values to empty strings for printing
  foreach my $key (keys (%{$entry_ref}))
  {
    $entry_ref->{$key} = "" if !defined ($entry_ref->{$key});
  }
  print join ("\t",
                $entry_ref->{member_id},
                $entry_ref->{email},
                $entry_ref->{last_name},
                $entry_ref->{first_name},
                $entry_ref->{expiration},
```

```
                    $entry_ref->{days} . " days"),
          "\n";
}
```

The output from the need_renewal.pl script looks something like the following
(you'll get different output because the results are determined against the current date,
which will be different for you while reading this book than for me while writing it):

```
89  g.steve@pluto.com       Garner  Steve  2007-08-03  -38 days
18  york_mark@earth.com     York    Mark   2007-08-24  -17 days
82  john_edwards@venus.org  Edwards John   2007-09-12  2 days
```

Observe that some memberships need to be renewed in a negative number of days.
That means they've already expired! (This happens when you maintain rows manually;
people slip through the cracks. Now that we have the information in a database, we're
finding out that we missed a few people before.)

The second part of the renewal notification task involves a script renewal_notify.pl
that sends out the notices by email. To make renewal_notify.pl a little easier to use, we
can make it understand three kinds of command-line arguments: membership ID numbers, email addresses, and filenames. Numeric arguments signify membership ID values,
and arguments containing a '@' character signify email addresses. Anything else is interpreted as the name of a file that should be read to find ID numbers or email addresses.
This method enables you to specify members by their ID number or email address, and
you can do so either directly on the command line or by listing them in a file. (In particular, you can save the output of need_renewal.pl in a file, and then use the file as input to
renewal_notify.pl.)

For each member who is to be sent a notice, the script looks up the relevant member
table entry, extracts the email address, and sends a message to that address. If there is no
address in the entry, renewal_notify.pl generates a warning message that you need to
contact these members in some other way.

The main argument-processing loop follows. If no arguments were specified on the
command line, we read the standard input for input. Otherwise, we process each argument
by passing it to interpret_argument() for classification as an ID number, an email
address, or a filename:

```
if (@ARGV == 0)    # no arguments, read STDIN for values
{
  read_file (\*STDIN);
}
else
{
  while (my $arg = shift (@ARGV))
  {
    # interpret argument, with filename recursion
    interpret_argument ($arg, 1);
  }
}
```

The function `read_file()` reads the contents of a file (assumed to be open already) and looks at the first field of each line. (If we feed the output of `need_renewal.pl` to `renewal_notify.pl`, each line has several fields, but we want to look only at the first one, which will contain a member ID number.)

```
sub read_file
{
my $fh = shift;    # handle to already-opened file
my $arg;

  while (defined ($arg = <$fh>))
  {
    # strip off everything past column 1, including newline
    $arg =~ s/\s.*//s;
    # interpret argument, without filename recursion
    interpret_argument ($arg, 0);
  }
}
```

The `interpret_argument()` function classifies each argument to determine whether it's an ID number, an email address, or a filename. For ID numbers and email addresses, it looks up the appropriate member entry and passes it to `notify_member()`. We have to be careful with members specified by email address. It's possible that two members have the same address (for example, a husband and wife), and we don't want to send a message to someone to whom it doesn't apply. To avoid this, we look up the member ID corresponding to an email address to make sure that there is exactly one. If the address matches more than one ID number, it's ambiguous and we ignore it after printing a warning.

If an argument doesn't look like an ID number or email address, it's taken to be the name of a file to read for further input. We have to be careful here, too—we don't want to read a file if we're already reading a file, to avoid the possibility of an infinite loop:

```
sub interpret_argument
{
my ($arg, $recurse) = @_;

  if ($arg =~ /^\d+$/)     # numeric membership ID
  {
    notify_member ($arg);
  }
  elsif ($arg =~ /@/)      # email address
  {
    # get member_id associated with address
    # (there should be exactly one)
    my $stmt = qq{ SELECT member_id FROM member WHERE email = ? };
    my $ary_ref = $dbh->selectcol_arrayref ($stmt, undef, $arg);
    if (scalar (@{$ary_ref}) == 0)
    {
```

```
      warn "Email address $arg matches no entry: ignored\n";
    }
    elsif (scalar (@{$ary_ref}) > 1)
    {
      warn "Email address $arg matches multiple entries: ignored\n";
    }
    else
    {
      notify_member ($ary_ref->[0]);
    }
  }
  else                    # filename
  {
    if (!$recurse)
    {
      warn "filename $arg inside file: ignored\n";
    }
    else
    {
      open (IN, $arg) or die "Cannot open $arg: $!\n";
      read_file (\*IN);
      close (IN);
    }
  }
}
```

The `notify_member()` function is responsible for actually sending the renewal notice.
If it turns out that the member has no email address, `notify_member()` can't send any
message, but it prints a warning so that you know you need to contact the member in
some other way. You can invoke `show_member.pl` with the membership ID number
shown in the message to see the full entry—to find out what the member's phone number and address are, for example. `notify_member()` looks like this:

```
sub notify_member
{
my $member_id = shift;

  warn "Notifying $member_id...\n";
  my $stmt = qq{ SELECT * FROM member WHERE member_id = ? };
  my $sth = $dbh->prepare ($stmt);
  $sth->execute ($member_id);
  my @col_name = @{$sth->{NAME}};
  my $entry_ref = $sth->fetchrow_hashref ();
  $sth->finish ();
  if (!$entry_ref)                        # no member found!
  {
    warn "NO ENTRY found for member $member_id!\n";
```

```
    return;
  }
  if (!defined ($entry_ref->{email}))    # no email address in entry
  {
    warn "Member $member_id has no email address; no message was sent\n";
    return;
  }
  open (OUT, "| $sendmail") or die "Cannot open mailer\n";
  print OUT <<EOF;
To: $entry_ref->{email}
Subject: Your USHL membership is in need of renewal

Greetings.  Your membership in the U.S. Historical League is
due to expire soon.  We hope that you'll take a few minutes to
contact the League office to renew your membership.  The
contents of your member entry are shown below.  Please note
particularly the expiration date.

Thank you.

EOF
  foreach my $col_name (@col_name)
  {
    printf OUT "$col_name:";
    printf OUT " $entry_ref->{$col_name}"
          if defined ($entry_ref->{$col_name});
    printf OUT "\n";
  }
  close (OUT);
}
```

The `notify_member()` function sends mail by opening a pipe to the `sendmail` program and shoving the mail message into the pipe. The pathname to `sendmail` is set as a parameter near the beginning of the `renewal_notify.pl` script. You might need to change this path because the location of `sendmail` varies from system to system:

```
# change path to match your system
my $sendmail = "/usr/sbin/sendmail -t -oi";
```

If you don't have `sendmail`, the script will not work properly. (For example, Windows systems typically do not have `sendmail` installed.) To handle this case, the `sampdb` distribution contains a modified version of `renewal_notify.pl` named `renewal_notify2.pl` that uses the Mail::Sendmail module that works without the `sendmail` program. If you install that module, you can use `renewal_notify2.pl` instead.

You could get fancier with this script. For example, you could add a column to the `member` table to record when the most recent renewal reminder was sent out and then modify `renewal_notify.pl` to update that column when it sends mail. Doing so would help you to not send out notices too frequently. As it is, we'll just assume that you won't run this program more than once a month or so.

The two scripts are done now. You can use them as follows:

1. Run `need_renewal.pl` to generate a list of memberships that have expired or will soon do so:

    ```
    % ./need_renewal.pl > tmp
    ```

2. Take a look at `tmp` to see whether it looks reasonable.

3. If so, use it as input to `renewal_notify.pl` to send renewal messages:

    ```
    % ./renewal_notify.pl tmp
    ```

To notify individual members, you can specify them by ID number or email address. For example, the following command notifies member 18 and the member having the email address `g.steve@pluto.com`:

```
% ./renewal_notify.pl 18 g.steve@pluto.com
```

8.3.3 Historical League Member Entry Editing

After we start sending out renewal notices, it's safe to assume that some of the people we notify will renew their memberships. When that happens, we need a way to update their entries with new expiration dates. In the next chapter, we'll develop a way to edit member rows over the Web, but this section shows how to write a command-line script, `edit_member.pl`, that enables you to update entries using the simple approach of prompting for new values for each part of an entry. It works like this:

- If invoked with no argument on the command line, `edit_member.pl` assumes that you want to enter a new member. It prompts for the initial information to be placed in the member's entry, and creates a new entry.

- If invoked with a membership ID number on the command line, `edit_member.pl` looks up the existing contents of the entry, and then prompts for updates to each column. If you enter a value for a column, it replaces the current value. If you press Enter, the column is not changed. If you enter the word "none," it clears the column's current value. (If you don't know a member's ID number, you can run `show_member.pl` *last_name* to see which entries match the given last name and from that determine the proper ID.)

It's probably overkill to allow an entire entry to be edited this way if all you want to do is update a member's expiration date. On the other hand, a script like this also provides a simple general-purpose way for its user to update any part of an entry without knowing any SQL. (One special case is that `edit_member.pl` won't allow you to change the `member_id` field because that's automatically assigned when an entry is created and shouldn't change thereafter.)

The first thing `edit_member.pl` needs to know is the names of the columns in the `member` table and whether they can be assigned NULL values. The latter property will be used when a column value is cleared (we'll assign the column NULL if the column can take NULL values and the empty string otherwise). The required information is available in the COLUMNS table of the INFORMATION_SCHEMA database:

```
my @col_name = ();       # array of column names
my %nullable = ();       # column nullability, keyed on column name
# get member table column names
my $sth = $dbh->prepare (qq{
          SELECT COLUMN_NAME, UPPER(IS_NULLABLE)
          FROM INFORMATION_SCHEMA.COLUMNS
          WHERE TABLE_SCHEMA = ? AND TABLE_NAME = ?
       });
$sth->execute ("sampdb", "member");
while (my ($col_name, $is_nullable) = $sth->fetchrow_array ())
{
  push (@col_name, $col_name);
  $nullable{$col_name} = ($is_nullable eq "YES");
}
```

Using the column information, the script produces an array containing the column names in order, and a hash keyed by column name that indicates whether each column is nullable. Then `edit_member.pl` enters its main loop:

```
if (@ARGV == 0) # if no arguments were given, create a new entry
{
  # pass reference to array of column names
  new_member (\@col_name);
}
else            # otherwise edit entries using arguments as member IDs
{
  # save @ARGV, and then empty it so that when the script reads from
  # STDIN, it doesn't interpret @ARGV contents as input filenames
  my @id = @ARGV;
  @ARGV = ();
  # for each ID value, look up the entry, and then edit it
  while (my $id = shift (@id))
  {
    $sth = $dbh->prepare (qq{
            SELECT * FROM member WHERE member_id = ?
         });
    $sth->execute ($id);
    my $entry_ref = $sth->fetchrow_hashref ();
    $sth->finish ();
    if (!$entry_ref)
    {
      warn "No member exists with member ID = $id\n";
```

```
        next;
    }
    # pass reference to array of column names and reference to entry
    edit_member (\@col_name, $entry_ref);
  }
}
```

The code for creating a new member entry solicits values for each `member` table column, and then issues an `INSERT` statement to add a new row:

```perl
sub new_member
{
my $col_name_ref = shift; # reference to array of column names
my $entry_ref = { };    # create new entry as a hash

  return unless prompt ("Create new entry (y/n)? ") =~ /^y/i;
  # prompt for new values; user types in new value, or Enter
  # to leave value unchanged, "NONE" to clear the value, or
  # "EXIT" to exit without creating the record.
  foreach my $col_name (@{$col_name_ref})
  {
    next if $col_name eq "member_id";   # skip key field
    my $col_val = col_prompt ($col_name, undef);
    next if $col_val eq "";             # user pressed Enter
    return if uc ($col_val) eq "EXIT";  # early exit
    if (uc ($col_val) eq "NONE")
    {
      # enter NULL if column is nullable, empty string otherwise
      $col_val = ($nullable{$col_name} ? undef : "");
    }
    $entry_ref->{$col_name} = $col_val;
  }
  # show values, ask for confirmation before inserting
  show_member ($col_name_ref, $entry_ref);
  return unless prompt ("\nInsert this entry (y/n)? ") =~ /^y/i;

  # construct an INSERT query, and then issue it.
  my $stmt = "INSERT INTO member";
  my $delim = " SET "; # put "SET" before first column, "," before others
  foreach my $col_name (@{$col_name_ref})
  {
    # only specify values for columns that were given one
    next if !defined ($entry_ref->{$col_name});
    # quote() quotes undef as the word NULL (without quotes),
    # which is what we want.  Columns that are NOT NULL are
    # assigned their default values.
    $stmt .= sprintf ("%s %s=%s", $delim, $col_name,
                      $dbh->quote ($entry_ref->{$col_name}));
```

```
    $delim = ",";
  }
  $dbh->do ($stmt) or warn "Warning: new entry not created!\n"
}
```

edit_member.pl uses two routines to prompt the user for information. prompt() asks
a question and returns the answer:

```
sub prompt
{
my $str = shift;

  print STDERR $str;
  chomp ($str = <STDIN>);
  return ($str);
}
```

col_prompt() takes a column name argument. It prints the name as a prompt to solicit
a new column value, and returns the value entered by the user:

```
sub col_prompt
{
my ($col_name, $entry_ref) = @_;

  my $prompt = $col_name;
  if (defined ($entry_ref))
  {
    my $cur_val = $entry_ref->{$col_name};
    $cur_val = "NULL" if !defined ($cur_val);
    $prompt .= " [$cur_val]";
  }
  $prompt .= ": ";
  print STDERR $prompt;
  my $str = <STDIN>;
  chomp ($str);
  return ($str);
}
```

The second argument to col_prompt() is a reference to the hash that represents the
member entry. For creating a new entry, this value will be undef, but when editing existing rows, it will point to the current contents of the entry. In that case, col_prompt() includes the current value of the column that it's prompting for in the prompt string so that
the user can see what it is. The user can accept the value simply by pressing Enter.

The code for editing an existing member is similar to that for creating a new member.
However, we have an entry to work with, so the prompt routine displays the current entry
values, and the edit_member() function issues an UPDATE statement rather than an
INSERT:

```
sub edit_member
```

```
{
# references to an array of column names and to the entry hash
my ($col_name_ref, $entry_ref) = @_;

  # show initial values, ask for okay to go ahead and edit
  show_member ($col_name_ref, $entry_ref);
  return unless prompt ("\nEdit this entry (y/n)? ") =~ /^y/i;
  # prompt for new values; user types in new value, or Enter
  # to leave value unchanged, "NONE" to clear the value, or
  # "EXIT" to exit without changing the record.
  foreach my $col_name (@{$col_name_ref})
  {
    next if $col_name eq "member_id";   # skip key field
    my $col_val = col_prompt ($col_name, $entry_ref);
    next if $col_val eq "";                 # user pressed Enter
    return if uc ($col_val) eq "EXIT";   # early exit
    if (uc ($col_val) eq "NONE")
    {
      # enter NULL if column is nullable, empty string otherwise
      $col_val = ($nullable{$col_name} ? undef : "");
    }

    $entry_ref->{$col_name} = $col_val;
  }
  # show new values, ask for confirmation before updating
  show_member ($col_name_ref, $entry_ref);
  return unless prompt ("\nUpdate this entry (y/n)? ") =~ /^y/i;

  # construct an UPDATE query, and then issue it.
  my $stmt = "UPDATE member";
  my $delim = " SET "; # put "SET" before first column, "," before others
  foreach my $col_name (@{$col_name_ref})
  {
    next if $col_name eq "member_id"; # skip key field
    # quote() quotes undef as the word NULL (without quotes),
    # which is what we want.
    $stmt .= sprintf ("%s %s=%s", $delim, $col_name,
                      $dbh->quote ($entry_ref->{$col_name}));
    $delim = ",";
  }
  $stmt .= " WHERE member_id = " . $dbh->quote ($entry_ref->{member_id});
  $dbh->do ($stmt) or warn "Warning: entry not undated!\n"
}
```

A problem with edit_member.pl is that it doesn't do any input value validation. For most fields in the member table, there isn't much to validate—they're just string fields. But for the expiration column, input values really should be checked to make sure that they look like dates. In a general-purpose data entry application, you'd probably want to extract information about a table to determine the types of all its columns. Then you could base validation constraints on those types. That's more involved than I want to go into here, so I'm just going to add a quick hack to the col_prompt() function to check the format of the input if the column is expiration. A minimal date value check can be done like this:

```
sub col_prompt
{
my ($col_name, $entry_ref) = @_;

loop:
  my $prompt = $col_name;
  if (defined ($entry_ref))
  {
    my $cur_val = $entry_ref->{$col_name};
    $cur_val = "NULL" if !defined ($cur_val);
    $prompt .= " [$cur_val]";
  }
  $prompt .= ": ";
  print STDERR $prompt;
  my $str = <STDIN>;
  chomp ($str);
  # perform rudimentary check on the expiration date
  if ($str && $col_name eq "expiration")  # check expiration date format
  {
    if ($str !~ /^\d+\D\d+\D\d+$/)
    {
      warn "$str is not a legal date, try again\n";
      goto loop;
    }
  }
  return ($str);
}
```

The pattern tests for three sequences of digits separated by non-digit characters. This is only a partial check because it doesn't detect values such as "1999-14-92" as being illegal. To make the script better, you could give it more stringent date checks or add other checks such as requiring the first and last name fields to be given non-empty values.

Other improvements are possible:

- Skip the update operation for an existing entry if the user made no changes. You could do this by saving the original values of the member entry columns, and then writing the UPDATE statement to update only those columns that had changed. If there were none, the statement need not even be issued.

- Notify the user if the row was already changed by someone else while the user was editing it. To do this, write the WHERE clause to include AND col_name = col_val for each original column value. This will cause the UPDATE to fail if someone else had changed the row, which provides feedback that two people are trying to change the entry at the same time.

- Enable strict SQL mode and other input restrictions, which causes MySQL itself to reject bad values and return an error if the input cannot be used as given:

```
$dbh->do ("SET sql_mode = 'TRADITIONAL'");
```

Here's another shortcoming of the `edit_member.pl` script that you might consider how to address: As written, the script opens a connection to the database before executing the prompt loop and doesn't close the connection until after writing out the row within the loop. If the user takes a long time to enter or update the row, or just happens to do something else for a while, the connection can remain open for a long time. How would you modify `edit_member.pl` to hold the connection open only as long as necessary?

8.3.4 Finding Historical League Members with Common Interests

One of the duties of the Historical League secretary is to process requests from members for a list of other members who share a particular interest within the field of U.S. history, such as the Great Depression or the life of Abraham Lincoln. It's easy enough to find such members when the directory is maintained in a word processor document by using the word processor's "Find" function. However, producing a list consisting *only* of the qualifying member entries is more difficult because it involves a lot of copy and paste. With MySQL, the job becomes much easier because we can just run a query like this:

```
SELECT * FROM member WHERE interests LIKE '%lincoln%'
ORDER BY last_name, first_name
```

Unfortunately, the results don't look very nice if we run this query from the `mysql` client. Let's put together a little DBI script, `interests.pl`, that performs the search for us and produces better-looking output. `interests.pl` first checks to make sure that there is at least one argument named on the command line, because there is nothing to search for otherwise. Then, for each argument, the script runs a search on the `interests` column of the `member` table:

```
@ARGV or die "Usage: interests.pl keyword\n";
search_members (shift (@ARGV)) while @ARGV;
```

To search for the keyword string, we put '%' wildcard characters on each side and perform a pattern match so that the string can be found anywhere in the `interests` column. Then we print the matching entries:

```
sub search_members
{
my $interest = shift;

  print "Search results for keyword: $interest\n\n";
  my $sth = $dbh->prepare (qq{
            SELECT * FROM member WHERE interests LIKE ?
            ORDER BY last_name, first_name
```

```
            });
  # look for string anywhere in interest field
  $sth->execute ("%" . $interest . "%");
  my $count = 0;
  while (my $hash_ref = $sth->fetchrow_hashref ())
  {
    format_entry ($hash_ref);
    ++$count;
  }
  print "Number of matching entries: $count\n\n";
}
```

The `format_entry()` function turns an entry into its printable representation. I won't
show it here, because it's essentially the same as the `rtf_format_entry()` function from
the `gen_dir.pl` script, with the RTF control words stripped out. Take a look at the
`interests.pl` script in the `sampdb` distribution to see the implementation.

8.3.5 Putting the Historical League Directory Online

In Section 8.4, "Using DBI in Web Applications," we'll start writing scripts that connect to
the MySQL server to extract information and write that information in the form of Web
pages that appear in a client's Web browser. Those scripts generate HTML dynamically according to what the client requested. Before we reach that point, let's begin thinking
about HTML by writing a DBI script that generates a static HTML document that can
be loaded into a Web server's document tree. A good candidate for this task is to produce
the Historical League directory in HTML format (after all, one of our goals was to put
the directory online).

A simple HTML document has a structure something like the following:

```
<html>                          ← beginning of document
<head>                          ← beginning of document head
<title>My Page Title</title>    ← title of document
</head>                         ← end of document head
<body bgcolor="white">          ← beginning of document body
                                   (white background)
<h1>My Level 1 Heading</h1>     ← a level 1 heading

... content of document body ...

</body>                         ← end of document body
</html>                         ← end of document
```

It's not necessary to write a completely new script to generate the directory in HTML
format. Recall that when we wrote the `gen_dir.pl` script, we used an extensible framework so that we'd be able to plug in code for producing the directory in additional

formats. Let's take advantage of that extensibility now by adding code for generating HTML output. To do this, we need to make the following modifications to gen_dir.pl:

- Write document initialization and cleanup functions.
- Write a function to format individual member rows.
- Add a switchbox element that identifies the format name and associates it with the functions that produce output in that format.

The HTML document outline just shown breaks down pretty easily into prolog and epilog sections that can be handled by the initialization and cleanup functions, as well as a middle part that can be generated by the entry-formatting function. The HTML initialization function generates everything up through the heading, and the cleanup function generates the closing </body> and </html> tags:

```
sub html_init
{
  print "<html>\n";
  print "<head>\n";
  print "<title>U.S. Historical League Member Directory</title>\n";
  print "</head>\n";
  print "<body bgcolor=\"white\">\n";
  print "<h1>U.S. Historical League Member Directory</h1>\n";
}

sub html_cleanup
{
  print "</body>\n";
  print "</html>\n";
}
```

The real work, as usual, lies in formatting the entries. But even this isn't very difficult. We can make a copy of the rtf_format_entry() function named html_format_entry(), and modify it to make sure that any special characters in the entry are encoded and to replace the RTF control words with HTML markup tags:

```
sub html_format_entry
{
my $entry_ref = shift;

  # Convert <, >, ", and & to the corresponding HTML entities
  # (&lt;, &gt;, &quot, &)
  foreach my $key (keys (%{$entry_ref}))
  {
    next unless defined ($entry_ref->{$key});
    $entry_ref->{$key} =~ s/&/&/g;
    $entry_ref->{$key} =~ s/\"/&quot;/g;
    $entry_ref->{$key} =~ s/>/&gt;/g;
    $entry_ref->{$key} =~ s/</&lt;/g;
```

```
    }
    printf "<strong>Name: %s</strong><br />\n", format_name ($entry_ref);
    my $address = "";
    $address .= $entry_ref->{street}
                if defined ($entry_ref->{street});
    $address .= ", " . $entry_ref->{city}
                if defined ($entry_ref->{city});
    $address .= ", " . $entry_ref->{state}
                if defined ($entry_ref->{state});
    $address .= " " . $entry_ref->{zip}
                if defined ($entry_ref->{zip});
    print "Address: $address<br />\n"
                if $address ne "";
    print "Telephone: $entry_ref->{phone}<br />\n"
                if defined ($entry_ref->{phone});
    print "Email: $entry_ref->{email}<br />\n"
                if defined ($entry_ref->{email});
    print "Interests: $entry_ref->{interests}<br />\n"
                if defined ($entry_ref->{interests});
    print "<br />\n";
}
```

The function produces output that looks like this:

```
<strong>Name: Mike Artel</strong><br />
Address: 4264 Lovering Rd., Miami, FL 12777<br />
Telephone: 075-961-0712<br />
Email: mike_artel@venus.org<br />
Interests: Civil Rights,Education,Revolutionary War<br />
<br />
```

The reason for using `<br />` rather than `<br>` is to write the document as well-formed XHTML, which is more strict than HTML. Some distinctions between HTML and XHTML are discussed briefly in Section 8.4.2.2, "Producing Web Output."

The last modification needed for `gen_dir.pl` is to add to the switchbox another element that points to the HTML-writing functions. The modified switchbox looks like this, where the final element defines a format named `html` that points to the functions that produce the various parts of an HTML document:

```
# switchbox containing formatting functions for each output format
my %switchbox =
(
  "text" =>                  # functions for plain text format
  {
    "init"    => undef,      # no initialization needed
    "entry"   => \&text_format_entry,
    "cleanup" => undef       # no cleanup needed
  },
```

```
  "rtf" =>                    # functions for RTF format
  {
    "init"    => \&rtf_init,
    "entry"   => \&rtf_format_entry,
    "cleanup" => \&rtf_cleanup
  },
  "html" =>                   # functions for HTML format
  {
    "init"    => \&html_init,
    "entry"   => \&html_format_entry,
    "cleanup" => \&html_cleanup
  }
);
```

To make the directory available in HTML format, run the following command and install the resulting output file, `directory.html`, in your Web server's document tree:

```
% ./gen_dir.pl html > directory.html
```

Whenever you update the `member` table in the database, you can run the command again to update the online version. If you want to avoid running the command manually, another strategy is to set up a job that executes periodically to update the online directory automatically. On Unix, you can use `cron` for this. Suppose that the `gen_dir.pl` script is installed in `/usr/local/bin` and the Historical League directory in the Web server document tree is `/usr/local/apache/htdocs/ushl`. Then a `crontab` entry like this one can be used to update the directory every morning at 4 a.m. (enter the entire command on a single line):

```
0 4 * * * /usr/local/bin/gen_dir.pl
  > /usr/local/apache/htdocs/ushl/directory.html
```

The user who runs this `cron` job must have permission to write files into the document tree directory.

8.4 Using DBI in Web Applications

The DBI scripts developed thus far have been designed for use in a command-line environment. DBI is useful in other contexts as well, such as in the development of Web-based applications. When you write DBI scripts that can be invoked by your Web server in response to requests sent by Web browsers, you open up new and interesting possibilities for users to interact with your databases. For example, if you write a script that displays data in tabular form, it can easily turn each column heading into a link that can be selected to re-sort the data on that column. This enables users to view data in a different way with a single click, without entering any queries. Or you can provide a form into which a user can enter criteria for a database search, and then display a page containing the results of the search. Simple capabilities like this can dramatically alter the level of interactivity you provide for accessing the contents of your databases. In addition, Web browser display capabilities typically are better than what you get with a terminal window, so you can create nicer-looking output as well.

In this section, we'll create the following Web-based scripts:

- A general browser for the tables in the sampdb database. This isn't related to any specific task we want to accomplish with the database, but it illustrates several Web programming concepts and provides a convenient means of seeing what information the tables contain.

- A score browser that enables us to see the scores for any given quiz or test. This is handy as a quick means of reviewing grade event results for the grade-keeping project, and it's useful when we need to establish the grading curve for a test so that we can mark papers with letter grades.

- A script that finds Historical League members who share a common interest. This is done by allowing the user to enter a search phrase, and then searching the interests column of the member table for that phrase. We already wrote a command-line script, interests.pl, to do this earlier, in Section 8.3.4, "Finding Historical League Members with Common Interests." But the command-line version can be executed only by people who have login accounts on the machine where the script is installed. Providing a Web-based version opens up the directory to anyone who has a Web browser. Having another version also provides an instructive point of reference, allowing comparison of multiple approaches to the same task. (Actually, we'll develop two Web-based implementations. One is based on pattern matching, just like interests.pl. The other performs FULLTEXT searches.)

To write these scripts, we'll use the CGI.pm Perl module, which provides an easy way to link DBI to the Web. (For instructions on getting CGI.pm, see Appendix A.) The CGI.pm module is so called because it helps you write scripts that use the Common Gateway Interface protocol that defines how a Web server communicates with other programs. CGI.pm handles the details involved in a number of common housekeeping tasks, such as collecting the values of parameters passed as input to your script by the Web server. CGI.pm also provides convenient methods for generating HTML output, which reduces the chance of writing out malformed HTML compared to writing raw HTML tags yourself.

You'll learn enough about CGI.pm in this chapter to write your own Web applications, but not all of its capabilities are covered. To learn more about this module, see *Official Guide to Programming with CGI.pm*, by Lincoln Stein (John Wiley, 1998), or check http://stein.cshl.org/WWW/software/CGI/ to read the online documentation.

Another text covering CGI.pm that's specifically targeted to MySQL and DBI is my book *MySQL and Perl for the Web* (New Riders, 2000).

The Web-based scripts described in the remainder of this chapter are located under the perlapi/web directory of the sampdb distribution.

8.4.1 Setting Up Apache for CGI Scripts

In addition to DBI and CGI.pm, there's one more component we need for writing Web-based scripts: a Web server. The instructions here are geared toward using scripts with the Apache server, but you should be able to use a different server if you like by adapting the instructions a bit.

I assume here that the various parts of your Apache installation are located under `/usr/local/apache` for Unix and under `C:\Apache` for Windows. For our purposes, the most important subdirectories of the Apache top-level directory are `htdocs` (for the HTML document tree), `cgi-bin` (for executable scripts and programs to be invoked by the Web server), and `conf` (for configuration files). These directories might be located somewhere else on your system. If so, make the appropriate adjustments to the following notes.

You should verify that the `cgi-bin` directory is not located within the Apache document tree. This is a safety precaution that prevents clients from requesting the source code for your scripts as plain text. You don't want malicious clients to be able to examine your scripts for security holes by siphoning off the text of the scripts and studying them.

To install a CGI script for use with Apache, copy it to your `cgi-bin` directory. Under Unix, the script must begin with a `#!` line and have its mode set to be executable, just as for a command-line script. In addition, it's a good idea to set the script to be owned by the user that Apache runs as and to be accessible only to that user. For example, if Apache runs as a user named www, use the following commands to make a script named `myscript.pl` owned by and executable and readable only by that user:

```
# chown www myscript.pl
# chmod u=rx,go-rwx myscript.pl
```

You might need to run these commands as `root`. If you don't have permission to install scripts in the `cgi-bin` directory, ask your system administrator to do so on your behalf.

Under Windows, the `chown` and `chmod` commands are unnecessary, but the script should still begin with a `#!` line. The line can list the full pathname to your Perl program. For example, if Perl is installed as `C:\Perl\bin\perl.exe`, the `#!` line can be written like this:

```
#!C:/Perl/bin/perl
```

Alternatively, on Windows, you can write the line more simply as follows if your PATH environment variable is set to include the directory in which Perl is installed:

```
#!perl
```

The Perl scripts in the `sampdb` distribution all specify the pathname of Perl on the `#!` line as `/usr/bin/perl`. Modify each script if necessary to provide a pathname that is appropriate for your own system.

After a script has been installed in the `cgi-bin` directory, you can request it from your browser by sending the appropriate URL to your Web server. For example, for a Web server running on the local host, you would request `myscript.pl` from it using a URL like this:

```
http://localhost/cgi-bin/myscript.pl
```

Remember to change the example URLs throughout this chapter to point to your own Web server host rather than to `localhost`.

Requesting a script with your browser causes it to be executed by the Web server. The script's output is sent back to you, and the result appears as a page in your browser.

When you run DBI scripts from the command line, warnings and error messages go to your terminal. In a Web environment, there is no terminal, so these messages go to the Apache error log. You should determine where this log is located because it can provide useful information to help debug your scripts. On my system, it's the `error_log` file in the `logs` directory under the Apache root, `/usr/local/apache`. It may be somewhere else on your system. The location of the log is determined by the `ErrorLog` directive in the `httpd.conf` configuration file, which is located in Apache's `conf` directory.

8.4.2 A Brief CGI.pm Primer

To write a Perl script that uses the CGI.pm module, put a `use CGI` statement near the beginning of the script that imports the module's function names. The standard set of the most commonly used functions can be imported like this:

```
use CGI qw(:standard);
```

Then you can invoke CGI.pm functions to produce various kinds of HTML structures. In general, the functions are named after the corresponding HTML elements. For example, to produce a level 1 header and a paragraph, invoke the `h1()` and `p()` functions:

```
print h1 ("This is a header");
print p ("This is a paragraph");
```

CGI.pm also supports an object-oriented style of use that allows you to invoke its functions without importing the names. To do this, include a `use` statement and create a CGI object:

```
use CGI;
my $cgi = new CGI;
```

The object gives you access to CGI.pm functions, which you invoke as methods of the object:

```
print $cgi->h1 ("This is a header");
print $cgi->p ("This is a paragraph");
```

The object-oriented interface requires that you write the `$cgi->` prefix all the time; in this book I'll use the simpler function call interface. However, one disadvantage of the function call interface is that if a CGI.pm function has the same name as a Perl built-in function, you must invoke it in a non-conflicting way. For example, CGI.pm has a function named `tr()` that produces the `<tr>` and `</tr>` tags that surround the cells in a row of an HTML table. That function's name conflicts with the name of the built-in Perl `tr` transliteration function. To work around this problem when using the CGI.pm function call interface, invoke `tr()` either as `Tr()` or as `TR()`. When you use the object-oriented interface, this problem does not occur, because you invoke `tr()` as a method of your `$cgi` object (that is, as `$cgi->tr()`), which makes it clear that you're not referring to the built-in Perl function.

8.4.2.1 Checking for Web Input Parameters

One of the things that CGI.pm does for you is to take care of all the ugly details involved in collecting input information provided by the Web server to your script. All you need to do to get that information is invoke the `param()` function. You can get the names of all available parameters like this:

```
my @param = param ();
```

To retrieve the value of a particular parameter, pass its name to `param()`. If the parameter is set, `param()` returns its value, or `undef` if it isn't set:

```
my $my_param = param ("my_param");
print "my_param value: ", (defined ($my_param) ? $my_param : "not set"), "\n";
```

8.4.2.2 Producing Web Output

Many of CGI.pm's functions generate output to be sent to the client browser. Consider the following HTML document:

```
<html>
<head>
<title>My Simple Page</title>
</head>
<body bgcolor="white">
<h1>Page Heading</h1>
<p>Paragraph 1.</p>
<p>Paragraph 2.</p>
</body>
</html>
```

The following script uses CGI.pm output functions to produce the equivalent document:

```
#!/usr/bin/perl
# simple_doc.pl - produce simple HTML page

use strict;
use warnings;
use CGI qw(:standard);

print header ();
print start_html (-title => "My Simple Page", -bgcolor => "white");
print h1 ("Page Heading");
print p ("Paragraph 1.");
print p ("Paragraph 2.");
print end_html ();
```

The `header()` function generates a `Content-Type:` header that precedes the page content. It's necessary to write this header when producing Web pages from scripts, to let the browser know what kind of document to expect. (This differs from the way you write static HTML pages. For those, it's not necessary to produce a header because the Web server sends one to the browser automatically.) By default, `header()` writes a header that looks like this:

```
Content-Type: text/html
```

Following the `header()` invocation are calls to functions that generate the page content. `start_html()` produces the tags from the opening `<html>` tag through the opening `<body>` tag, `h1()` and `p()` write the heading and paragraph elements, and `end_html()` adds the closing document tags.

As illustrated by the `start_html()` call, many CGI.pm functions allow you to specify named parameters, with each parameter given in `-name=>value` format. This is advantageous for functions that take many parameters that are optional, because you can specify just those parameters you need, and you can list them in any order.

Using CGI.pm output-generating functions doesn't preclude you from writing out raw HTML yourself if you want. You can mix the two approaches, combining calls to CGI.pm functions with print statements that generate literal tags. However, one of the advantages of using CGI.pm to generate output instead of writing HTML yourself are that you can think in logical units rather than in terms of individual markup tags, and your HTML is less likely to contain errors. (The reason I say "less likely" is that CGI.pm won't prevent you from doing bizarre things, such as including a list inside of a heading.)

CGI.pm also provides some portability advantages that you don't get by writing your own HTML. For example, as of version 2.69, CGI.pm automatically writes XHTML output. If you're using an older version of CGI.pm that writes plain HTML, all you need to do to upgrade your scripts to start writing XHTML instead is update CGI.pm itself.

XHTML is similar to HTML but has a more well-defined format. HTML is easy to learn and use, but one of its problems is that browser implementations tend to differ in how they interpret it. For example, they are forgiving of malformed HTML in different ways. This means that a not-quite-correct page may display properly in one browser but incorrectly in another. XHTML's requirements are stricter, to help ensure that documents are well formed. Some of the differences between HTML and XHTML follow:

- Unlike HTML, every opening tag in XHTML must have a closing tag. For example, paragraphs are written using `<p>` and `</p>` tags, but the closing `</p>` tag often is omitted in HTML documents. In XHTML, the `</p>` tag is required. For HTML tags that don't have any body, such as `<br>` and `<hr>`, the XHTML requirement that all tags be closed in leads to ungainly constructs like `<br></br>` and `<hr></hr>`. To deal with this, XHTML allows single-tag shortcut forms (`<br/>`, `<hr/>`) that serve for both the opening and closing tags. However, older browsers that see tags like these will sometimes mistake the tag names as `br/` and `hr/`. Inserting a space before the slash and writing the tags as `<br />` and `<hr />` helps to minimize the occurrence of such problems.

- In HTML, tag and attribute names are not case sensitive. For example, `<BODY BGCOLOR="white">` and `<body bgcolor="white">` are the same. In XHTML, tag and attribute names should be lowercase, so only `<body bgcolor="white">` is allowable.

- HTML attribute values can be unquoted or even missing. For example, this table data cell construct is legal in HTML:

```
<td width=40 nowrap>Some text</td>
```

In XHTML, attributes must have values, and they must be quoted. A common convention for HTML attributes that normally are used without a value is to use the attribute name as its value. The XHTML equivalent of the preceding `<tr>` element looks like this:

```
<td width="40" nowrap="nowrap">Some text</td>
```

All the Web scripts in this book generate output that conforms to XHTML rules. In this chapter, we'll rely on CGI.pm to generate properly formatted XHTML markup. The scripts discussed in Chapter 9 also produce XHTML but generate the markup tags for themselves because PHP doesn't provide tag-generating functions the way CGI.pm does.

8.4.2.3 Escaping HTML and URL Text

If text that you write to a Web page may contain special characters, you should make sure that they are escaped properly by processing the text with `escapeHTML()`. This is also true when you construct URLs that may contain special characters, although in that case you should use the `escape()` function instead. It's important to use the appropriate encoding function because each one recognizes a different set of special characters and encodes them differently. `escapeHTML()` escapes special characters as their equivalent HTML entities. For example, '<' becomes the `&lt;` entity. `escape()` escapes each special character as `%` followed by two hexadecimal digits representing the numeric character code, so '<' becomes `%3C`. Consider the following short Perl script, `escape_demo.pl`, which demonstrates both forms of escaping:

```perl
#!/usr/bin/perl
# escape_demo.pl - demonstrate CGI.pm output-encoding functions

use strict;
use warnings;
use CGI qw(escapeHTML escape);  # import escapeHTML() and escape()

# Assign default string value, but use command-line argument if present
my $s = "1<=2, right?";
$s = shift (@ARGV) if @ARGV;
print "Unencoded string:            ", $s, "\n";
print "Encoded for use as HTML text: ", escapeHTML ($s), "\n";
print "Encoded for use in a URL:     ", escape ($s), "\n";
```

The script encodes the string $s using each function and prints the result. When you run it, the script produces the following output, from which you can see that encoding conventions for HTML text are not the same as encoding for URLs:

```
unencoded string:          1<=2, right?
encoded for use as HTML text: 1&lt;=2, right?
encoded for use in a URL:    1%3C%3D2%2C%20right%3F
```

If you provide a command-line argument to escape_demo.pl, the script encodes that argument rather than the default string. This enables you to see the encoding for a string of your own choosing.

The escape_demo.pl script imports the names of the encoding functions in the use CGI statement. Depending on how current your version of CGI.pm is, they might not be included in the standard set of functions, so you'll need to import them even if you also import the standard set, like this:

```
use CGI qw (:standard escapeHTML escape);
```

8.4.2.4 Writing Multiple-Purpose Pages

One of the primary reasons to write Web-based scripts that generate HTML instead of writing static HTML documents is that a script can produce different kinds of pages depending on the way it's invoked. All the CGI scripts we're going to write have that property. Each one operates as follows:

- When you first request the script from your browser, it generates an initial page that enables you to select what kind of information you want.

- When you make a selection, your browser sends a request back to the Web server that causes the script to be re-invoked. The script then retrieves and displays in a second page the specific information you requested.

An issue that must be addressed here is that you want the selection that you make from the first page to determine the contents of the second page, but Web pages normally are independent of one another unless you make some sort of special arrangements. The solution is to have the script generate pages that set a parameter to a value that tells the next invocation of the script what you want. When you first invoke the script, the parameter will have no value; this tells the script to present its initial page. When you indicate what information you'd like to see, the script is invoked again, but this time the parameter will be set to a value that instructs the script what to do.

There are different ways for Web pages to pass instructions to a script. One way is for the page to include a form that the user fills in. When the user submits the form, its contents are submitted to the Web server. The server passes the information along to the script, which can find out what was submitted by invoking the param() function. This is what we'll do to implement keyword searches of the Historical League directory: The search page includes a form in which the user enters the keyword to search for.

Another way of specifying instructions for a script is to add parameter values to the end of the URL that you send to the Web server when you request the script. This is the approach we'll use for our sampdb table browser and score browser scripts. The way this works is that the script generates a page containing hyperlinks. When you select a link, it invokes the script again, but the link includes a parameter value that instructs the script what to do. In effect, the script invokes itself in different ways to provide different kinds of results, depending on which link you select.

A script can allow itself to be invoked by sending to the browser a page containing a self-referential hyperlink—that is, a link to its own URL. For example, if a script myscript.pl is installed in the Web server's cgi-bin directory, it can produce a page that contains this link:

```
<a href="/cgi-bin/myscript.pl">Click Me!</a>
```

When the user clicks on the text "Click Me!" in the page, the user's browser sends a request for myscript.pl back to the Web server. Of course, in and of itself, all that will do is cause the script to send out the same page again because no other information is supplied in the URL. However, if you add a parameter to it, that parameter is sent back to the Web server when the user selects the link. The server invokes the script and the script can call param() to detect that the parameter was set and take action according to its value.

To attach a parameter to the end of the URL, add a '?' character followed by a *name=value* pair indicating the parameter name and its value. For example, to add a size parameter with a value of large, write the URL like this:

```
/cgi-bin/myscript.pl?size=large
```

To attach multiple parameters, separate them by ';' or '&' characters:

```
/cgi-bin/myscript.pl?size=large;color=blue
```

CGI.pm understands either ';' or '&' as a parameter separator character. Other language APIs for Web programming vary in their conventions, so you'll need to know whether they expect ';' or '&' and construct URLs accordingly. We'll use ';' here.

To construct a self-referencing URL with attached parameters, a script should begin by calling the CGI.pm url() function to obtain its own URL, and then append parameters to it like this:

```
$url = url ();          # get URL for script
$url .= "?size=large";  # add first parameter
$url .= ";color=blue";  # add second parameter
```

Using url() to get the script path enables you to avoid hardwiring the path into the code.

To generate a hyperlink, pass the URL to CGI.pm's a() function:

```
print a ({-href => $url}, "Click Me!");
```

The print statement produces a hyperlink that looks like this:

```
<a href="/cgi-bin/url.pl?size=large;color=blue">Click Me!</a>
```

The preceding example constructs the value of $url in somewhat cavalier fashion, because it doesn't take into account the possibility that the parameter values or the link label might contain special characters. Unless you're certain that the values and the label don't require any encoding, it's best to use the CGI.pm encoding functions. The escape() function encodes values to be appended to a URL, and escapeHTML() encodes regular HTML text. For example, if the value of the hyperlink label is stored in $label, and the values for the size and color parameters are stored in the variables $size and $color, you can perform the proper encoding like this:

```
$url = sprintf ("%s?size=%s;color=%s",
                url (), escape ($size), escape ($color));
print a ({-href => $url}, escapeHTML ($label));
```

To see how self-referential URL construction works in the context of an application, consider the following short CGI script, flip_flop.pl. When first invoked, it presents a page called Page A that contains a single hyperlink. Selecting the link invokes the script again, but the link also includes a pageb parameter to tell flip_flop.pl to display Page B. (In this case, we don't care about the parameter's value, just whether it's set.) Page B will also contain a link to the script, but without a pageb parameter. This means that selecting the link in Page B causes the original page to be redisplayed. In other words, subsequent invocations of the script flip the page back and forth between Page A and Page B:

```perl
#!/usr/bin/perl
# flip_flop.pl - simple multiple-output-page CGI.pm script

use strict;
use warnings;
use CGI qw(:standard);

my $url;
my $this_page;
my $next_page;

# determine which page to display based on absence or presence
# of the pageb parameter

if (!defined (param ("pageb"))) # display page A w/link to page B
{
  $this_page = "A";
  $next_page = "B";
  $url = url () . "?pageb=1";
}
else                           # display page B w/link to page A
{
  $this_page = "B";
  $next_page = "A";
  $url = url ();
```

```
}

print header ();
print start_html (-title => "Flip-Flop: Page $this_page",
                  -bgcolor => "white");
print p ("This is Page $this_page. To select Page $next_page, "
        . a ({-href => $url}, "click here"));
print end_html ();
```

Install the script in your `cgi-bin` directory, and then request it from your browser using a URL like this one, but substituting the name of your own Web server for `localhost`:

```
http://localhost/cgi-bin/flip_flop.pl
```

Select the link in the page several times to see how the script alternates the pages that it generates.

Now, suppose that another client comes along and starts requesting `flip_flop.pl`. What happens? Will the two of you interfere with each other? No, because the initial request from each of you will include no `pageb` parameter, and the script will respond with its initial page. Thereafter, the requests sent by each of you will include or omit the parameter according to which page you currently happen to be viewing. `flip_flop.pl` generates an alternating series of pages properly for each client, independent of the actions of any other client.

8.4.3 Connecting to the MySQL Server from Web Scripts

The command-line scripts developed earlier in Section 8.3, "Putting DBI to Work," shared a common preamble for establishing a connection to the MySQL server. Most of our CGI scripts share some preamble code, too, but it's a little different:

```perl
#!/usr/bin/perl

use strict;
use warnings;
use DBI;
use CGI qw(:standard);

use Cwd;
# option file that should contain connection parameters for UNIX
my $option_file = "/usr/local/apache/conf/sampdb.cnf";
my $option_drive_root;
# override file location for Windows
if ($^O =~ /^MSWin/i || $^O =~ /^dos/)
{
  $option_drive_root = "C:/";
  $option_file = "/Apache/conf/sampdb.cnf";
}
```

```
# construct data source and connect to server (under Windows, save
# current working directory first, change location to option file
# drive, connect, and then restore current directory)
my $orig_dir;
if (defined ($option_drive_root))
{
  $orig_dir = cwd ();
  chdir ($option_drive_root)
    or die "Cannot chdir to $option_drive_root: $!\n";
}
my $dsn = "DBI:mysql:sampdb;mysql_read_default_file=$option_file";
my %conn_attrs = (RaiseError => 1, PrintError => 0, AutoCommit => 1);
my $dbh = DBI->connect ($dsn, undef, undef, \%conn_attrs);
if (defined ($option_drive_root))
{
  chdir ($orig_dir)
    or die "Cannot chdir to $orig_dir: $!\n";
}
```

This preamble differs from the one we used for command-line scripts in the following respects:

- The first section now contains use CGI and use Cwd statements. The first is for the CGI.pm module. The second is for the module that returns the pathname of the current working directory; it's used in case the script is running under Windows, as described later.

- No connection parameters are parsed from the command-line arguments. Instead, the code assumes that they'll be listed in an option file.

- Instead of using mysql_read_default_group to read the standard option files, we use mysql_read_default_file to read a single file intended specifically for options to be used by Web scripts that access the sampdb database. As shown, the code looks for options stored in /usr/local/apache/conf/sampdb.cnf under Unix, or in C:\Apache\conf\sampdb.cnf under Windows. Note that, under Windows, the code changes location to the root directory of the drive where the option file is located before connecting, and back to the original directory afterward. The rationale for this ugly hack is described in Section 8.2.9, "Specifying Connection Parameters."

The sampdb distribution contains a sampdb.cnf file that you can install for use by your DBI-based Web scripts. It looks like this:

```
[client]
host=localhost
user=sampadm
password=secret
```

To use the Web-based scripts developed in this chapter on your own system, you should change the option file location in the preamble if you use a different location. You should also install the `sampdb.cnf` option file in the appropriate location and list in it option values for the MySQL server host and the MySQL account name and password that you want to use.

Under Unix, you should set the option file to be owned by the account used to run Apache and set the file's mode to 400 or 600 so that no other user can read it. This prevents one form of security exploit because it keeps other users who have login accounts on the Web server host from reading the option file directly.

Unfortunately, the option file still can be read by other users who can install a script for the Web server to execute. Scripts invoked by the Web server execute with the privileges of the login account used for running the Web server. This means that another user who can install a Web script can write the script so that it opens the option file and displays its contents in a Web page. Because that script runs as the Web server user, it will have full permission to read the file, which exposes the connection parameters necessary to connect to MySQL and access the `sampdb` database. If you are the only person with login access on your Web server host, this doesn't matter. But if other users that you don't trust have login access on the machine, you might find it prudent to create a MySQL account that has read-only (`SELECT`) privileges on the `sampdb` database, and then list that account's name and password in the `sampdb.cnf` file, rather than your own name and password. That way you don't risk allowing scripts to connect to your database through a MySQL account that has permission to modify its tables. Chapter 12, "General MySQL Administration," discusses how to create a MySQL user account with restricted privileges. The downside of this strategy is that with a read-only MySQL account, you can write scripts only for data retrieval, not for data entry.

Alternatively, you can arrange to execute scripts under Apache's suEXEC mechanism. This enables you to execute a script as a specific trusted login user, and then write the script to get the connection parameters from an option file that is readable only to that user.

Still another option for writing a script is to have it solicit a MySQL account username and password from the client, and then use those values to establish a connection to the MySQL server. This is more suitable for scripts that you create for administrative purposes than for scripts that you provide for general use. In any case, you should be aware that some methods of name and password solicitation are subject to attack by anyone who can put a sniffer on the network between the Web server and your browser, so you may want to set up a secure connection. That is beyond the scope of this book.

As you may gather from the preceding paragraphs, Web script security can be a tricky thing. It's definitely a topic about which you should read more for yourself, because it's a big subject which I really cannot do justice to here. The book *MySQL and Perl for the Web* mentioned earlier includes a chapter devoted specifically to Web security, including instructions for setting up secure connections using SSL. Other good sources of information are the security material in the Apache manual, and the WWW security FAQ is available at http://www.w3.org/Security/Faq/.

8.4.4 A Web-Based Database Browser

Our first Web-based MySQL application is a simple script, db_browse.pl, that enables you to see what tables exist in the sampdb database and to examine the contents of any of these tables interactively from your Web browser. The script works like this:

- When you first request db_browse.pl from your browser, it connects to the MySQL server, retrieves a list of tables in the sampdb database, and sends your browser a page that presents each table as a hyperlink. When you select a table name link from this page, your browser sends a request to the Web server asking db_browse.pl to display the contents of that table.

- If db_browse.pl finds when it's invoked that you've selected a table name, it retrieves the contents of the table and presents the information to your Web browser. The heading for each column of data is the name of the column in the table. Headings are presented as hyperlinks; if you select one of them, your browser sends a request to the Web server to redisplay the same table, but this time sorted by the column you selected.

Warning

Before we go any further, you should be aware that although db_browse.pl is instructive in terms of illustrating several useful Web programming concepts, it also represents a security hole. The script will display any table in the sampdb, which can be a problem: In Chapter 9, we'll write a script that Historical League members can use to edit their membership entries over the Web. Access to the entries is controlled through passwords that are stored in a member_pass table. Having db_browse.pl enabled at that point would enable anyone to look through the password table, and thus gain access to the information necessary to edit any member table entry! Thus, it's a good idea to remove the script from your cgi-bin directory after you've tried it and understand how it works. (Alternatively, install it on a private Web server that is not accessible to untrusted users.)

Okay, assuming that you haven't been spooked by the preceding dire warnings, let's see how db_browse.pl works. The main body of the script puts out the initial part of the Web page and then checks the tbl_name parameter to see whether it's supposed to display some particular table:

```perl
#!/usr/bin/perl
# db_browse.pl - Allow sampdb database browsing over the Web

use strict;
use warnings;
use DBI;
use CGI qw (:standard escapeHTML escape);

# ... set up connection to database (not shown) ...

my $db_name = "sampdb";
```

```
# put out initial part of page
my $title = "$db_name Database Browser";
print header ();
print start_html (-title => $title, -bgcolor => "white");
print h1 ($title);

# parameters to look for in URL
my $tbl_name = param ("tbl_name");
my $sort_col = param ("sort_col");

# If $tbl_name has no value, display a clickable list of tables.
# Otherwise, display contents of the given table.  $sort_col, if
# set, indicates which column to sort by.

if (!defined ($tbl_name))
{
  display_table_names ($dbh, $db_name)
}
else
{
  display_table_contents ($dbh, $db_name, $tbl_name, $sort_col);
}

print end_html ();
```

It's easy to find out what value a parameter has because CGI.pm does all the work of finding out what information the Web server passes to the script. We need only call param() with the name of the parameter in which we're interested. In the main body of db_browse.pl, that parameter is named tbl_name. If it's not set, this is the initial invocation of the script and it displays the table list. Otherwise, it displays the contents of the table named by the tbl_name parameter, sorted by the column named in the sort_col parameter.

The display_table_names() function generates the initial page. display_table_names() retrieves the table list and writes out a bullet list in which each item is the name of a table in the sampdb database:

```
sub display_table_names
{
my ($dbh, $db_name) = @_;

  print p ("Select a table by clicking on its name:");

  # retrieve reference to single-column array of table names
  my $sth = $dbh->prepare (qq{
            SELECT TABLE_NAME FROM INFORMATION_SCHEMA.TABLES
            WHERE TABLE_SCHEMA = ? ORDER BY TABLE_NAME
```

```
            });
  $sth->execute ($db_name);

  # Construct a bullet list using the ul() (unordered list) and
  # li() (list item) functions.  Each item is a hyperlink that
  # re-invokes the script to display a particular table.
  my @item;
  while (my ($tbl_name) = $sth->fetchrow_array ())
  {
    my $url = sprintf ("%s?tbl_name=%s", url (), escape ($tbl_name));
    my $link = a ({-href => $url}, escapeHTML ($tbl_name));
    push (@item, li ($link));
  }
  print ul (@item);
}
```

The li() function adds <li> and </li> tags around each list item and ul() adds the <ul> and </ul> tags around the set of items. Each table name in the list is presented as a hyperlink that reinvokes the script to display the contents of the named table. The resulting list generated by display_table_names() looks like this:

```
<ul>
<li><a href="/cgi-bin/db_browse.pl?tbl_name=absence">absence</a></li>
<li><a href="/cgi-bin/db_browse.pl?tbl_name=grade_event">grade_event</a></li>
<li><a href="/cgi-bin/db_browse.pl?tbl_name=member">member</a></li>
...
</ul>
```

If the tbl_name parameter has a value when db_browse.pl is invoked, the script passes that value to display_table_contents(), along with the name of the column by which to sort the results if one was given:

```
sub display_table_contents
{
my ($dbh, $db_name, $tbl_name, $sort_col) = @_;
my $sort_clause = "";
my @rows;
my @cells;

  # if sort column is specified, use it to sort the results
  if (defined ($sort_col))
  {
    $sort_clause = " ORDER BY " . $dbh->quote_identifier ($sort_col);
  }

  # present a link that returns user to table list page
  print p (a ({-href => url ()}, "Show Table List"));
```

```perl
print p (strong ("Contents of $tbl_name table:"));

my $sth = $dbh->prepare (
            "SELECT * FROM "
            . $dbh->quote_identifier ($db_name, $tbl_name)
            . "$sort_clause LIMIT 200"
            );
$sth->execute ();

# Use the names of the columns in the database table as the
# headings in an HTML table.  Make each name a hyperlink that
# causes the script to be reinvoked to redisplay the table,
# sorted by the named column.

foreach my $col_name (@{$sth->{NAME}})
{
  my $url = sprintf ("%s?tbl_name=%s;sort_col=%s",
                     url (),
                     escape ($tbl_name),
                     escape ($col_name));
  my $link = a ({-href => $url}, escapeHTML ($col_name));
  push (@cells, th ($link));
}
push (@rows, Tr (@cells));

# display table rows
while (my @ary = $sth->fetchrow_array ())
{
  @cells = ();
  foreach my $val (@ary)
  {
    # display value if non-empty, else display non-breaking space
    if (defined ($val) && $val ne "")
    {
      $val = escapeHTML ($val);
    }
    else
    {
      $val = " ";
    }
    push (@cells, td ($val));
  }
  push (@rows, Tr (@cells));
}

# display table with a border
```

```
    print table ({-border => "1"}, @rows);
}
```

The query also includes a LIMIT 200 clause, as a simple precaution against the script sending huge amounts of data to your browser. (That's not likely to happen for the tables in the sampdb database, but it might occur if you adapt the script to display the contents of tables in other databases.) display_table_contents() shows the rows from the table as an HTML table, using the th() and td() functions to produce table header and data cells, Tr() to group cells into rows, and table() to produce the <table> tags that surround the rows.

The HTML table presents column headings as hyperlinks that redisplay the database table. These links include a sort_col parameter that explicitly specifies the column to use for sorting. For example, for a page that displays the contents of the grade_event table, the column heading links look like this:

```
<a href="/cgi-bin/db_browse.pl?tbl_name=grade_event&sort_col=date">
date</a>
<a href="/cgi-bin/db_browse.pl?tbl_name=grade_event&sort_col=category">
category</a>
<a href="/cgi-bin/db_browse.pl?tbl_name=grade_event&sort_col=event_id">
event_id</a>
```

display_table_contents() uses a little trick of turning empty values into a non-breaking space ( ). In a bordered table, some browsers don't display borders for empty cells properly; putting a non-breaking space in the cell fixes that problem.

If you want to write a more general script, you could alter db_browse.pl to browse multiple databases. For example, you could have the script begin by displaying a list of databases on the server, rather than a list of tables within a particular database. Then you could pick a database to get a list of its tables and go from there.

8.4.5 A Grade-Keeping Project Score Browser

Our next Web script, score_browse.pl, is designed to display scores that have been recorded for the grade-keeping project. Strictly speaking, we should have a way of entering the scores before we create a way of retrieving them, but I'm saving the score entry script until the next chapter. In the meantime, we do have several sets of scores in the database already from the early part of the grading period. We can use the script to display those scores, even in the absence of a convenient score entry method. The script displays an ordered list of scores for any test or quiz, which is useful for determining the grading curve and assigning letter grades.

score_browse.pl has some similarities to db_browse.pl (both serve as information browsers), but is intended for the more specific purpose of looking at scores for a given quiz or test. The initial page presents a list of the possible grade events from which to choose, and enables the user to select any of them to see the scores associated with the event. Scores for a given event are sorted by score with the highest scores first, so you can use the result to determine the grading curve.

The `score_browse.pl` script needs to examine only one parameter, `event_id`, to see whether a grade event was specified. If not, `score_browse.pl` displays the rows of the `grade_event` table so that the user can select one. Otherwise, it displays the scores associated with the chosen event:

```
# ... set up connection to database (not shown) ...


# put out initial part of page
my $title = "Grade-Keeping Project -- Score Browser";
print header ();
print start_html (-title => $title, -bgcolor => "white");
print h1 ($title);

# parameter that tells us which grade event to display scores for
my $event_id = param ("event_id");

# if $event_id has no value, display the event list.
# otherwise display the scores for the given event.
if (!defined ($event_id))
{
  display_events ($dbh)
}
else
{
  display_scores ($dbh, $event_id);
}

print end_html ();
```

The `display_events()` function pulls out information from the `grade_event` table and displays it as a table, using column names from the query for the table column headings. Within each row, the `event_id` value is displayed as a hyperlink that can be selected to trigger a query that retrieves the scores for the event. The URL for each event is simply the path to `score_browse.pl` with a parameter attached that specifies the event number:

```
/cgi-bin/score_browse.pl?event_id=n
```

`display_events()` looks like this:

```
sub display_events
{
my $dbh = shift;
my @rows;
my @cells;

  print p ("Select an event by clicking on its number:");
```

```
  # get list of events
  my $sth = $dbh->prepare (qq{
               SELECT event_id, date, category
               FROM grade_event
               ORDER BY event_id
           });
  $sth->execute ();

  # use column names for table column headings
  for (my $i = 0; $i < $sth->{NUM_OF_FIELDS}; $i++)
  {
    push (@cells, th (escapeHTML ($sth->{NAME}->[$i])));
  }
  push (@rows, Tr (@cells));

  # display information for each event as a row in a table
  while (my ($event_id, $date, $category) = $sth->fetchrow_array ())
  {
    @cells = ();
    # display event ID as a hyperlink that reinvokes the script
    # to show the event's scores
    my $url = sprintf ("%s?event_id=%d", url (), event_id;
    my $link = a ({-href => $url}, escapeHTML ($event_id));
    push (@cells, td ($link));
    # display event date and category
    push (@cells, td (escapeHTML ($date)));
    push (@cells, td (escapeHTML ($category)));
    push (@rows, Tr (@cells));
  }

  # display table with a border
  print table ({-border => "1"}, @rows);
}
```

When the user selects an event, the browser sends a request for score_browse.pl that has an event ID at the end. score_browse.pl finds the event_id parameter set and calls the display_scores() function to list all the scores for the specified event. This function also displays the text "Show Event List" as a hyperlink back to the initial page so that the user can easily return to the event list page and select a different event:

```
sub display_scores
{
my ($dbh, $event_id) = @_;
my @rows;
my @cells;

  # Generate a link to the script that does not include any event_id
```

```perl
# parameter.  If the user selects this link, the script will display
# the event list.
print p (a ({-href => url ()}, "Show Event List"));

# select scores for the given event
my $sth = $dbh->prepare (qq{
            SELECT
              student.name,
              grade_event.date,
              score.score,
              grade_event.category
            FROM
              student INNER JOIN score INNER JOIN grade_event
            ON
              student.student_id = score.student_id
              AND score.event_id = grade_event.event_id
            WHERE
              grade_event.event_id = ?
            ORDER BY
              grade_event.date ASC,
              grade_event.category ASC,
              score.score DESC
});
$sth->execute ($event_id);  # bind event ID to placeholder in query

print p (strong ("Scores for grade event $event_id"));

# use column names for table column headings
for (my $i = 0; $i < $sth->{NUM_OF_FIELDS}; $i++)
{
  push (@cells, th (escapeHTML ($sth->{NAME}->[$i])));
}
push (@rows, Tr (@cells));

while (my @ary = $sth->fetchrow_array ())
{
  @cells = ();
  foreach my $val (@ary)
  {
    # display value if non-empty, else display non-breaking space
    if (defined ($val) && $val ne "")
    {
      $val = escapeHTML ($val);
    }
    else
    {
```

```
          $val = " ";
        }
        push (@cells, td ($val));
      }
    push (@rows, Tr (@cells));
  }

  # display table with a border
  print table ({-border => "1"}, @rows);
}
```

The statement that `display_scores()` executes is quite similar to one that we developed way back in Section 1.4.9.10, "Retrieving Information from Multiple Tables," which describes how to write joins. In that section, we asked for scores for a given date because dates are more meaningful than event ID values. In contrast, when we use `score_browse.pl`, we know the exact event ID. That's not because we think in terms of event IDs (we don't), but because the script presents a list of them from which to choose, along with their dates and categories. You can see that this type of interface reduces the need to know particular details. You don't need to know an event ID; it's necessary only to be able to recognize the date of the event you want. The script associates it with the proper ID for you.

8.4.6 Historical League Common-Interest Searching

The `db_browse.pl` and `score_browse.pl` scripts enable the user to make a selection from a list of choices in an initial page, where the choices are presented as hyperlinks that re-invoke the script with particular parameter values. Another way to enable users to provide information is to present a form that the user fills in. This is more appropriate when the range of possible choices isn't constrained to some easily determined set of values. Our next script demonstrates this method of soliciting user input.

In Section 8.3, "Putting DBI to Work," we constructed a command-line script, `interests.pl`, for finding Historical League members who share a particular interest. However, that script isn't something that League members have access to; the League secretary must run the script from the command prompt and then mail the result to the member who requested the list. It'd be nice to make this search capability more widely available so that members could use it for themselves. Writing a Web-based script is one way to do that. The rest of this section discusses two approaches to table searching. The first is based on pattern matching, and the second uses MySQL FULLTEXT search capabilities.

8.4.6.1 Performing Searches Using Pattern Matching

The first search script, `ushl_browse.pl`, displays a form into which the user can enter a keyword. When the user submits the form, the script is re-invoked to search the `member` table for qualifying members and display the results. The search is done by adding the '%' wildcard character to both ends of the keyword and performing a LIKE pattern match, which finds rows that have the keyword anywhere in the `interests` column value.

The main part of the script displays the keyword form. It also checks to see if a keyword was just submitted and performs a search if so:

```
my $title = "U.S. Historical League Interest Search";
print header ();
print start_html (-title => $title, -bgcolor => "white");
print h1 ($title);

# parameter to look for
my $keyword = param ("keyword");

# Display a keyword entry form.  In addition, if $keyword is defined,
# search for and display a list of members who have that interest.

print start_form (-method => "post");
print p ("Enter a keyword to search for:");
print textfield (-name => "keyword", -value => "", -size => 40);
print submit (-name => "button", -value => "Search");
print end_form ();

# connect to server and run a search if a keyword was specified
if (defined ($keyword) && $keyword !~ /^\s*$/)
{
  # ... set up connection to database (not shown) ...
  search_members ($dbh, $keyword);
  # ... disconnect (not shown) ...
}
```

The script communicates information to itself a little differently than db_browse.pl or score_browse.pl. It does not add a parameter to the end of a URL. Instead, the browser encodes the information in the form and sends it as part of a post request. However, CGI.pm makes it irrelevant how the information is sent, because param() returns the parameter value no matter how it was sent—just one more thing that CGI.pm does to make Web programming easier.

Keyword searches are performed by the search_members() function. It takes a database handle and the keyword as arguments, and then runs the search query and displays the list of matching member rows:

```
sub search_members
{
my ($dbh, $interest) = @_;

  print p ("Search results for keyword: " . escapeHTML ($interest));
  my $sth = $dbh->prepare (qq{
            SELECT * FROM member WHERE interests LIKE ?
            ORDER BY last_name, first_name
          });
```

```
  # look for string anywhere in interest field
  $sth->execute ("%" . $interest . "%");
  my $count = 0;
  while (my $ref = $sth->fetchrow_hashref ())
  {
    html_format_entry ($ref);
    ++$count;
  }
  print p ("Number of matching entries: $count");
}
```

When you run the ushl_browse.pl script, you'll notice that each time you submit a keyword value, it's redisplayed in the form on the next page. This happens even though the script specifies an empty string as the value of the keyword field when it generates the form. The reason is that CGI.pm automatically fills in form fields with values from the script execution environment if they are present. If you want to defeat this behavior and make the field blank every time, include an override parameter in the textfield() call:

```
print textfield (-name => "keyword",
                 -value => "",
                 -override => 1,
                 -size => 40);
```

search_members() uses a helper function html_format_entry() to display individual entries. That function is much like the one of the same name that we wrote earlier for the gen_dir.pl script. (See Section 8.3.1, "Generating the Historical League Directory.") However, whereas the earlier version of the function generated HTML by printing markup tags directly, the version used by ushl_browse.pl uses CGI.pm functions to produce the tags:

```
sub html_format_entry
{
my $entry_ref = shift;

  # encode characters that are special in HTML
  foreach my $key (keys (%{$entry_ref}))
  {
    next unless defined ($entry_ref->{$key});
    $entry_ref->{$key} = escapeHTML ($entry_ref->{$key});
  }
  print strong ("Name: " . format_name ($entry_ref)), br ();
  my $address = "";
  $address .= $entry_ref->{street}
              if defined ($entry_ref->{street});
  $address .= ", " . $entry_ref->{city}
              if defined ($entry_ref->{city});
  $address .= ", " . $entry_ref->{state}
```

```
                    if defined ($entry_ref->{state});
    $address .= " " . $entry_ref->{zip}
                    if defined ($entry_ref->{zip});
    print "Address: $address", br ()
                    if $address ne "";
    print "Telephone: $entry_ref->{phone}", br ()
                    if defined ($entry_ref->{phone});
    print "Email: $entry_ref->{email}", br ()
                    if defined ($entry_ref->{email});
    print "Interests: $entry_ref->{interests}", br ()
                    if defined ($entry_ref->{interests});
    print br ();
}
```

html_format_entry() uses the format_name() function to glue the first_name,
last_name, and suffix column values together. It's identical to the function of the same
name in the gen_dir.pl script.

8.4.6.2 Performing Searches Using a FULLTEXT Index

Historical League members may have multiple interests. If so, they are separated by commas in the interests column of the member table. For example:

```
Revolutionary War,Spanish-American War,Colonial period,Gold rush,Lincoln
```

Can you use ushl_browse.pl, to search for rows that match any of several keywords?
Sort of, but not really. You can enter several words into the search form, but rows won't
match unless you construct a more complicated query that looks for a match on each
word. A more flexible way to approach the interest-searching task is to use a FULLTEXT index. This section describes a script ushl_ft_browse.pl that does so. For more information about MySQL's FULLTEXT capabilities, see Section 2.15, "Using FULLTEXT Searches."

Before you can use the member table for FULLTEXT searching, it must be a MyISAM
table. If you created member using some other storage engine, convert it to a MyISAM
table with ALTER TABLE:

```
ALTER TABLE member ENGINE = MyISAM;
```

Next, it's necessary to index the member table properly. To do that, use the following
statement:

```
ALTER TABLE member ADD FULLTEXT (interests);
```

That allows the interests column to be used for FULLTEXT searches. The
ushl_ft_browse.pl script in the sampdb distribution is based on ushl_browse.pl, and
differs from it only in the search_members() function that constructs the search query.
The modified version of the function looks like this:

```
sub search_members
{
my ($dbh, $interest) = @_;
```

```
  print p ("Search results for keyword: " . escapeHTML ($interest));
  my $sth = $dbh->prepare (qq{
            SELECT * FROM member WHERE MATCH(interests) AGAINST(?)
            ORDER BY last_name, first_name
         });
  # look for string anywhere in interest field
  $sth->execute ($interest);
  my $count = 0;
  while (my $ref = $sth->fetchrow_hashref ())
  {
    html_format_entry ($ref);
    ++$count;
  }
  print p ("Number of matching entries: $count");
}
```

This version of `search_members()` has the following changes relative to the earlier one:

- The query uses MATCH() ... AGAINST() rather than LIKE.
- No '%' wildcard characters are added to the keyword string to convert it to a pattern.

With these changes, you can invoke `ush1_ft_browse.pl` from your Web browser and enter multiple keywords into the search form (with or without commas). The script will find member entries that match any of them.

You could get a lot fancier with this script. One possibility is to take advantage of the fact that FULLTEXT searches can search multiple columns at once by setting up the index to span several columns and then modifying `ush1_ft_browse.pl` to search them all. For example, you could drop the original FULLTEXT index and add another that uses the `last_name` and `full_name` columns in addition to the `interests` column:

```
ALTER TABLE member DROP INDEX interests;
ALTER TABLE member ADD FULLTEXT (interests,last_name,first_name);
```

To use the new index, modify the SELECT statement in the `search_members()` function to change MATCH(interests) to MATCH(interests,last_name,first_name).

Another change you might make to `ush1_ft_browse.pl` would be to add a couple of radio buttons to the form to enable the user to choose between "match any keyword" and "match all keywords" modes. The "match any" mode is the one that the script uses currently. To implement a "match all" mode, change the statement to use an IN BOOLEAN MODE type of FULLTEXT search, and precede each keyword by a '+' character to require that it be present in matching rows. For information about boolean mode searching, see Section 2.15.2, "Boolean Mode FULLTEXT Searches."

Writing MySQL Programs Using PHP

PHP is a scripting language for writing Web pages containing embedded code that is executed whenever a page is accessed and that can generate dynamic content to be included as part of the output sent to a client's Web browser. This chapter describes how to write PHP-based Web applications that use MySQL. For a comparison of PHP with the C and Perl DBI APIs for MySQL programming, see Chapter 6, "Introduction to MySQL Programming."

The examples in this chapter draw on our sampdb sample database, using the tables created for the grade-keeping project and for the Historical League in Chapter 1, "Getting Started with MySQL." The applications described here should run under PHP 5 or higher.

This chapter refers to PDO constants using the class-constant notation for PHP 5.1 and up (for example, PDO::FETCH_NUM). For PHP 5.0, use global-constant notation instead (for example, PDO_FETCH_NUM).

This chapter was written under the assumption that you'll use PHP in conjunction with the Apache Web server, although you can probably substitute a different server. In addition, PHP currently must be built with the MySQL C client library linked in, or it will not know how to access MySQL databases. (This requirement will be lifted when mysqlnd becomes available, as described shortly.) If you need to obtain any of this software, see Appendix A, "Obtaining and Installing Software." That appendix also provides instructions for obtaining the sampdb distribution that contains the example scripts developed in this chapter. You can download the scripts to avoid typing them in yourself. You'll find the scripts for the chapter under the phpapi directory of that distribution.

Under Unix, PHP may be used as an Apache module or as a standalone interpreter used as a traditional CGI program. Under Windows, PHP can run only as a standalone program unless you use Apache 2.x. In that case, you have the option of running PHP as an Apache module. On either platform, running PHP as a module is preferable for performance reasons.

PHP offers several ways to interface with MySQL:

- In PHP 5 and up, you can use the "MySQL improved" extension, `mysqli`. This extension provides two calling styles. You can use it as a set of functions with names of the form `mysqli_xxx()`, or through an object-oriented interface.

- The `mysql` extension is the original interface to MySQL. It consists of functions with names of the form `mysql_xxx()`. For the most part, these map directly onto the C API functions with the same names. There is no object-oriented interface for this extension. `mysql` is less capable than `mysqli`, not only because it has less flexibility in calling style, but also because it provides no access to features developed in MySQL 4.1 and up. `mysql` was developed before MySQL 4.1 and probably should be treated as deprecated.

- Other interfaces are less tied to specific database engines. This chapter uses PHP Data Objects (PDO), an extension that provides an object-oriented database-independent interface similar in design to the Perl DBI module. It uses a two-level architecture in which the top level presents a uniform interface and the lower level consists of drivers for various database engines. To switch from one driver to another, you modify the arguments passed to the connection call so that they are appropriate for the driver that you want to use.

  PDO requires PHP 5.0 or higher because it uses object-oriented features not available in older versions of PHP.

The `mysql` and `mysqli` extensions and the PDO driver for MySQL were originally designed to be linked against the MySQL C client library (the `libmysqlclient` library described in Appendix G, "C API Reference" [online]). One effect of this design is that it introduces a dependency of PHP on a part of the MySQL distribution if you want to install PHP for purposes of accessing MySQL databases. A newer library, `mysqlnd`, is under development that can be used as a `libmysqlclient` replacement. `mysqlnd` is a native driver that implements the same communication protocol but requires no part of a MySQL distribution. `mysqlnd` will be included in PHP as of version 5.3, which means that it will be possible to access MySQL databases from PHP without having the MySQL client library installed.

For the most part, this chapter describes only those PDO objects and methods that are needed for the discussion here. It also covers only the MySQL driver for PDO. Drivers for other database engines are available as well, but are not discussed here. For a more comprehensive listing of the PDO interface, see Appendix I, "PHP API Reference" (online). You'll likely also want to consult the PHP manual, which describes all PHP capabilities. The manual is available from the PHP Web site, http://www.php.net/.

Filenames for PHP scripts generally end with a suffix that enables your Web server to recognize that they should be executed by invoking the PHP interpreter. If you use a suffix that the server doesn't recognize, it will serve your PHP scripts as plain text. Scripts in this chapter use the `.php` suffix. For instructions on configuring Apache to recognize the suffix you want to use, see Appendix A. (If you are not in control of the Apache installation on your machine, check with the system administrator to find out the proper suffix

to use.) The appendix also describes how to set up Apache to treat any script named
`index.php` as the default page for the directory in which it is located, similar to the way
Apache treats files named `index.html`.

To use the scripts developed in this chapter, you'll need to install them where your
Web server can access them. The convention used here is that the U.S. Historical League
and grade-keeping projects have their own directories called `ushl` and `gp` at the top level
of the Apache document tree. To set up your Web server that way, you should create those
directories now. For a server running on the local host, pages in those two directories will
have URLs that begin like this:

```
http://localhost/ushl/...
http://localhost/gp/...
```

For example, the home pages in each directory can be called `index.php` and would be
accessed as follows:

```
http://localhost/ushl/index.php
http://localhost/gp/index.php
```

If you have Apache configured to use `index.php` as the default page for a directory,
the following URLs are equivalent in practice to the preceding ones:

```
http://localhost/ushl/
http://localhost/gp/
```

Remember to change the example URLs throughout this chapter to point to your
own Web server host rather than to `localhost`.

9.1 PHP Overview

The basic operation of PHP is to interpret a script to produce a Web page that is sent to a
client. A PHP script typically contains a mix of HTML and executable code. The HTML
is sent literally to the client without modification, whereas the PHP code is executed and
replaced by whatever output it produces. Consequently, the client never sees the code; it
sees only the resulting HTML page. (The PHP scripts developed in this chapter generate
pages that are well formed as XHTML, not just as HTML. For a brief description of
XHTML, see Section 8.4.2.2, "Writing Web Output.")

When PHP begins reading a file, it simply copies whatever it finds there to the output,
under the assumption that the contents of the file represent literal text, such as HTML
content. When the PHP interpreter encounters a special opening tag, it switches from
text copy mode to PHP code mode and starts interpreting the file as PHP code to be executed. The interpreter switches from code mode back to text mode when it sees another
special tag that signals the end of the code. This enables you to mix static text (the HTML
part) with dynamically generated results (output from the PHP code part) to produce a
page that varies depending on the circumstances under which it is called. For example,
you might use a PHP script to process the result of a form into which a user has entered
parameters for a database search. Depending on what the user types, the search parameters

might be different each time the form is submitted, so when the script searches for and displays the information the user requested, each resulting page will be different.

Let's see how PHP works beginning with an extremely simple script:

```
<html>
<body>
<p>hello, world</p>
</body>
</html>
```

This script is in fact *so* simple that it contains no PHP code! "What good is that?," you ask. That's a reasonable question. The answer is that it's sometimes useful to set up a script containing just the HTML framework for the page you want to produce and then add the PHP code later. This is perfectly legal, and the PHP interpreter has no problem with it.

To include PHP code in a script, distinguish it from the surrounding text with the special opening and closing tags: `<?php` and `?>`. When the PHP interpreter encounters the opening `<?php` tag, it switches from text mode to PHP code mode and treats whatever it finds as executable code until it sees the closing `?>` tag. The code between the tags is interpreted and replaced by its output. The previous example could be rewritten to include a small section of PHP code like this:

```
<html>
<body>
<p><?php print ("hello, world"); ?></p>
</body>
</html>
```

In this case, the code part is minimal, consisting of a single line. When the code executes, it produces the output `hello, world`, which becomes part of the output sent to the client's browser. Thus, the Web page produced by this script is equivalent to the one produced by the preceding example, where the script consisted entirely of HTML.

You can use PHP code to generate any part of a Web page. We've already seen one extreme, in which the entire script consists of literal HTML and contains no PHP code. The other extreme is to produce the HTML completely from within code mode:

```
<?php
print ("<html>\n");
print ("<body>\n");
print ("<p>hello, world</p>\n");
print ("</body>\n");
print ("</html>\n");
?>
```

These three examples demonstrate that PHP gives you a lot of flexibility in how you produce output. PHP leaves it up to you to decide whatever combination of HTML and PHP code is appropriate. PHP is also flexible in that you don't need to put all your code in one place. You can switch between text mode and PHP code mode throughout the script however you please, as often as you want.

PHP allows tag styles other than the `<?php` and `?>` style that is used for examples in this chapter. See Appendix I (online) for a description of the tag styles that are available and instructions on enabling them.

Standalone PHP Scripts

The example scripts in this chapter are written with the expectation that they will be invoked by a Web server to generate a Web page. However, if you have a standalone version of PHP, you can use it to execute PHP scripts from the command line. Suppose that you have a script named hello.php that looks like this:

```
<?php print ("hello, world\n"); ?>
```

To execute the script from the command line yourself, use this command:

```
% php hello.php
hello, world
```

This is sometimes useful when you're working on a script, because you can see right away whether it has syntax errors or other problems without having to request the script from a browser each time you make a change. For this reason, you may want to build a standalone version of PHP even if normally you use it as a module from within Apache.

9.1.1 A Simple PHP Script

If PHP provided only the capability of producing what is essentially static HTML by means of print statements, it wouldn't be very useful. PHP's power is that it generates dynamic pages: output that can vary from one invocation of a script to the next. The script described in this section shows a simple example of this capability. It's still relatively short, but a bit more substantial than the previous examples. It shows how easily you can access a MySQL database from PHP and use the results of a query in a Web page. The script forms a simple basis for a home page for the Historical League Web site. As we go on, we'll make the script a bit more elaborate, but for now all it does is display a short welcome message and a count of the current League membership:

```
<html>
<head>
<title>U.S. Historical League</title>
</head>
<body bgcolor="white">
<p>Welcome to the U.S. Historical League Web Site.</p>
<?php
# USHL home page

try
{
  $dbh = new PDO("mysql:host=localhost;dbname=sampdb", "sampadm", "secret");
```

```
$dbh->setAttribute (PDO::ATTR_ERRMODE, PDO::ERRMODE_EXCEPTION);
$sth = $dbh->query ("SELECT COUNT(*) FROM member");
$count = $sth->fetchColumn (0);
print ("<p>The League currently has $count members.</p>");
$dbh = NULL;  # close connection
}
catch (PDOException $e) { } # empty handler (catch but ignore errors)
?>
</body>
</html>
```

The welcome message is just static text, so it's easiest to write it as literal HTML. The membership count, on the other hand, is dynamic and changes over time, so it must be determined at execution time by querying the member table in the sampdb database. To perform that task, the code within the opening and closing script tags follows these steps:

1. Opens a connection to the MySQL server and makes the sampdb database the default database.

2. Enables exceptions for subsequent PDO calls so that errors can be caught easily without testing for them explicitly.

3. Sends a query to the server to determine how many members the Historical League has at the moment (assessed as the number of rows in the member table).

4. Uses the query result to construct a message containing the membership count.

5. Closes the connection to the MySQL server.

The script just shown can be found as the file named index.php in the phpapi/ushl directory of the sampdb distribution. Change the connection parameters as necessary, install a copy of the script as index.php in the ushl directory of your Web server's document tree, and request it from your browser using either of these URLs (changing the hostname and pathname as appropriate for your own Web server):

```
http://localhost/ushl/
http://localhost/ushl/index.php
```

Let's break down the script into pieces to see how it works. The first step is to connect to the server:

```
$dbh = new PDO("mysql:host=localhost;dbname=sampdb", "sampadm", "secret");
```

new PDO() invokes the constructor for the PDO class. The constructor attempts to connect to the database server and raises an exception if it fails. Otherwise, it returns a PDO object that serves as a database handle.

The first argument to new PDO() is a string called a "data source name." The second and third arguments are the username and password to use for connecting to the server, sampadm and secret. The DSN string tells PDO which driver to use, followed by driver-specific parameters. For MySQL, the driver name is mysql, and the parameters are the host where the server is running and the database to select as the default database. The DSN shown indicates that the MySQL server host and default database are localhost and sampdb. Both parameters following the colon are optional. The default value for host is localhost, so this parameter actually could have been omitted. If you omit dbname, no default database is selected. (The DSN can take other forms, and other parameters are allowed. For details, see Appendix I [online].)

Perhaps it makes you nervous that the username and password are embedded in the script for all to see. And, indeed, it should. It's true that the name and password don't appear in the resulting Web page that is sent to the client, because the script's contents are replaced by its output. Nevertheless, if the Web server becomes misconfigured somehow and fails to recognize that your script needs to be processed by PHP, it will send the script as plain text, which exposes the connection parameters. We'll deal with this problem in Section 9.1.2, "Using PHP Library Files for Code Encapsulation."

The database handle returned by new PDO() becomes the means for further interaction with the MySQL server, such as issuing SQL statements to be executed. After a successful connection, the default error mode for PDO calls is to fail silently, which requires that you check for errors explicitly. To make it easier to handle problems, the script enables exceptions for PDO errors:

```
$dbh->setAttribute (PDO::ATTR_ERRMODE, PDO::ERRMODE_EXCEPTION);
```

With exceptions enabled, a try/catch construct can be used to "route" errors to an exception handler without explicit tests. If you don't use try/catch, exceptions terminate your script.

The script next sends the member-counting query to the server by invoking the database handle's query() method, and then extracts and displays the result:

```
$sth = $dbh->query ("SELECT COUNT(*) FROM member");
$count = $sth->fetchColumn (0);
print ("<p>The League currently has $count members.</p>");
```

The query() method sends the query to the server to be executed. Note that the query string contains no terminating semicolon character or \g or \G sequence, in contrast to the way you issue statements from within the mysql program. query() is used for statements that return rows. (Use a different method, exec(), for statements that modify rows.) query() returns a PDOStatement object that is a statement handle for manipulating the result set.

For the query shown, the result set consists of a single row with a single column value representing the membership count. The script invokes the $sth object's fetchColumn() method to fetch the row and extract the first column (column 0).

After printing the count, the script closes the connection to the server by setting the database handle to NULL. This is optional. If you don't close the connection, PHP closes it when the script terminates.

The code for interacting with MySQL occurs within a try block so that any exception raised for an error can be caught and handled by the corresponding catch block.

The connection attempt raises an exception automatically if it fails, and the
`setAttribute()` call enables exceptions for any subsequent PDO calls that fail. The
`catch` block in the example is empty, so its effect is to trap and ignore errors. The script
writes no message for an error because printing the membership count is ancillary to the
greeting presented by the home page. (An error message in this context is likely simply to
be confusing to people visiting the Web site.) Section 9.1.8, "Handling Errors," discusses
other ways to deal with errors.

Variables in PHP

In PHP, you can make variables spring into existence simply by using them. Our home page
script uses three such variables, $dbh, $sth, and $count, none of which are declared any-
where. (There are contexts for which you do declare a variable, such as in an exception handler or when you reference a global variable inside a function.)

Variables are signified by an identifier preceded by a dollar sign ('$'). This is true no matter
what kind of value the variable represents, although for arrays and objects you tack on
some extra stuff to access individual elements of the value. If a variable $x represents a
single scalar value, such as a number or a string, you access it as just $x. If $x represents
an array with numeric indices, you access its elements as $x[0], $x[1], and so on. If $x rep-
resents an array with associative indices such as "yellow" or "large," you access its elements as $x["yellow"] or $x["large"]. PHP arrays can even have both numeric and
associative elements. For example, $x[1] and $x["large"] both can be elements of the same
array. If $x represents an object, it has properties that you access as $x->*property_name*.
For example, $x->yellow and $x->large may be properties of $x. Numbers are not legal as
property names unless you use curly braces, so $x->{1} is a valid construct in PHP, but
$x->1 is not. Curly braces can also be used if you need to refer to property names that con-
tain spaces or other illegal characters.

9.1.2　Using PHP Library Files for Code Encapsulation

PHP scripts differ from DBI scripts in that PHP scripts are located within your Web
server document tree, whereas DBI scripts typically are located in a `cgi-bin` directory
that's located outside of the document tree. This brings up a security issue: A server configuration error can cause pages located within the document tree to be served as plain
text to clients. This means that usernames and passwords for establishing connections to
the MySQL server are at a higher risk of being exposed to the outside world in a PHP
script than in a DBI script.

Our initial Historical League home page script is subject to this problem because it
contains the literal values of the MySQL username and password. Let's move these connection parameters out of the script using two of PHP's capabilities: functions and include
files. We'll write a function `sampdb_connect()` that establishes a connection and returns a
database handle, and put that function in an include file—a library file that is not part of
our main script but that can be referenced from it. This approach has several benefits:

- **It's easier to write connection establishment code.** We can write out the connection parameters once in the `sampdb_connect()` helper function, not in every

individual script that needs to connect. Moving details like this into a library and out of our scripts tends to make them more understandable because you can concentrate on the unique aspects of each script without being distracted by common connection setup code.

- **The include file can be used by multiple scripts.** This promotes code reusability and makes code more maintainable. It also enables global changes to be made easily to every script that accesses the file. For example, if we move the sampdb database from localhost to boa.snake.net, we don't need to change a bunch of individual scripts. Instead, we just change the hostname parameter in the include file where the sampdb_connect() function is defined.

- **The include file can be moved outside of the Apache document tree.** This means that clients cannot request the include file directly from their browsers, so its contents cannot be exposed to them even if the Web server becomes misconfigured. Using an include file is a good strategy for hiding any kind of sensitive information that you don't want to be sent offsite by your Web server. However, although this is a security improvement, don't be lulled into thinking that it makes the username and password secure in all senses. Other users who have login accounts on the Web server host (and thus have access to its filesystem) might be able to read the include file directly unless you take certain precautions. Section 8.4.3, "Connecting to the MySQL Server from Web Scripts," has some notes that pertain to installing DBI configuration files so as to protect them from other users. Similar precautions apply to the use of PHP include files.

To use include files, you need to have a place to put them, and you need to tell PHP to look for them. If your system already has such a location, you can use that. If not, use the following procedure to establish an include file location:

1. Create a directory outside of the Web server document tree in which to store PHP include files. I use /usr/local/apache/lib/php, which is outside the location of my document tree, /usr/local/apache/htdocs.

2. Include files can be accessed from scripts by full pathname or, if you set up PHP's search path, by just their basename (the last component of the pathname). The latter approach is more convenient because PHP will find the file for us. The search path used by PHP when searching for include files is controlled by the value of the include_path configuration setting in the PHP initialization file, php.ini. Find this file on your system (mine is installed in /usr/local/lib), and locate the include_path line. If it has no value, set it to the full pathname of your new include directory:

```
include_path = "/usr/local/apache/lib/php"
```

If include_path already has a value, add the new directory to that value:

```
include_path = "/usr/local/apache/lib/php:current_value"
```

For Unix, use colon characters as shown to separate directories listed in
include_path. For Windows, use semicolons instead.

After modifying php.ini, restart Apache so that your changes take effect.

Use of PHP include files is analogous to the use of C header files. For example, the
way that PHP can look for include files in several directories is similar to the way
the C preprocessor looks in multiple directories for C header files.

3. Create the include file that you want to use and put it into the include directory.
   The file should have some distinctive name; we'll use sampdb_pdo.php. This file
   eventually will contain several functions, but to start with, it need contain only the
   sampdb_connect() function:

```php
<?php
# sampdb_pdo.php - common functions for sampdb PDO-based PHP scripts

# Function that uses our top-secret username and password to connect
# to the MySQL server to use the sampdb database. It also enables
# exceptions for errors that occur for subsequent PDO calls.
# Return value is the database handle produced by new PDO().

function sampdb_connect ()
{
  $dbh = new PDO("mysql:host=localhost;dbname=sampdb",
                 "sampadm", "secret");
  $dbh->setAttribute (PDO::ATTR_ERRMODE, PDO::ERRMODE_EXCEPTION);
  return ($dbh);
}
?>
```

The sampdb_connect() function connects to the database server by constructing a
data source name and passing it to new PDO() along with the MySQL account username and password. Then it sets the error-handling mode to cause exceptions to be
raised for PDO errors and returns the database handle to use for further interaction
with the server. Use the function like this:

```php
$dbh = sampdb_connect ();
```

The reason for enabling exceptions in sampdb_connect() is that it's more convenient to turn them on in the library file rather than individually in each script that
uses the library file.

Observe that the PHP code in the sampdb_pdo.php file is bracketed within
<?php and ?> script tags. That's because PHP begins reading include files in text
copy mode. If you omit the tags, PHP will send out the file as plain text rather than
interpreting it as PHP code. That's just fine if you intend the file to produce literal

HTML, but if you want its contents to be executed, you must enclose the PHP code within script tags.

4. To reference the include file from a script, use one of the following statements:

```
include "sampdb_pdo.php";
require "sampdb_pdo.php";
include_once "sampdb_pdo.php";
require_once "sampdb_pdo.php";
```

PHP handles the four statements as follows:

- `include` and `require` include and evaluate the contents of the named file. They differ in that if the file is missing, `include` produces a warning and execution continues, whereas `require` produces an error and execution terminates.

- The `include_once` and `require_once` statements are similar to `include` and `require`, except that if PHP already has read the named file, it will not read it again. This can be useful when include files include other files, to avoid the possibility of including a file multiple times and perhaps triggering function redefinition errors.

The scripts in this chapter use `require_once`. When PHP sees the file-inclusion statement, it searches for the file and reads its contents. Anything in the file becomes accessible to the following parts of the script.

The `sampdb` distribution includes the `sampdb_pdo.php` file in its `phpapi` directory. Modify the connection parameters as necessary to reflect those that you use for connecting to MySQL. Then copy the file to the include directory that you want to use, and set the file's mode and ownership so that it's readable by your Web server (and not by other users).

Now we can modify the Historical League home page to reference the `sampdb_pdo.php` include file and connect to the MySQL server by invoking `sampdb_connect()`:

```
<html>
<head>
<title>U.S. Historical League</title>
</head>
<body bgcolor="white">
<p>Welcome to the U.S. Historical League Web Site.</p>
<?php
# USHL home page - version 2

require_once "sampdb_pdo.php";

try
```

```
{
  $dbh = sampdb_connect ();
  $sth = $dbh->query ("SELECT COUNT(*) FROM member");
  $count = $sth->fetchColumn (0);
  print ("<p>The League currently has $count members.</p>");
  $dbh = NULL;  # close connection
}
catch (PDOException $e) { } # empty handler (catch but ignore errors)
?>
</body>
</html>
```

The script just shown can be found as `index2.php` in the `phpapi/ush1` directory of the `sampdb` distribution. Copy it to the `ush1` directory in your Web server's document tree, naming it `index.php` to replace the file of that name that is there now. This action replaces the less secure version with a more secure one because the new file contains no literal MySQL username or password.

You may be thinking that we haven't really saved all that much coding in the home page by using an include file. But just wait. The `sampdb_pdo.php` file can be used for other functions as well, and thus serves as a convenient repository for any routine that we expect to be useful in multiple scripts. In fact, we can create two more such functions to put in that file right now. Every Web script we write in the remainder of the chapter will generate a fairly stereotypical set of HTML tags at the beginning of a page and another set at the end. Rather than writing out those tags in each script, we can write functions `html_begin()` and `html_end()` to generate them for us. The `html_begin()` function can take a couple of arguments that specify a page title and header. The code for the two functions looks like this:

```
function html_begin ($title, $header)
{
  print ("<html>\n");
  print ("<head>\n");
  if ($title != "")
    print ("<title>$title</title>\n");
  print ("</head>\n");
  print ("<body bgcolor=\"white\">\n");
  if ($header != "")
    print ("<h2>$header</h2>\n");
}

function html_end ()
{
  print ("</body>\n");
  print ("</html>\n");
}
```

After putting `html_begin()` and `html_end()` in `sampdb_pdo.php`, the Historical League home page can be modified to use them. The resulting script (`index3.php`) looks like this:

```php
<?php
# USHL home page - version 3

require_once "sampdb_pdo.php";

$title = "U.S. Historical League";
html_begin ($title, $title);
?>

<p>Welcome to the U.S. Historical League Web Site.</p>

<?php
try
{
  $dbh = sampdb_connect ();
  $sth = $dbh->query ("SELECT COUNT(*) FROM member");
  $count = $sth->fetchColumn (0);
  print ("<p>The League currently has $count members.</p>");
  $dbh = NULL;  # close connection
}
catch (PDOException $e) { } # empty handler (catch but ignore errors)

html_end ();
?>
```

Notice that the PHP code has been split into two pieces, with the literal HTML text of the welcome message appearing between the pieces. Copy `index3.php` to the `ushl` directory in your Web server's document tree, naming it `index.php` to replace the file of that name that is there now.

The use of functions for generating the initial and final part of the page provides an important capability. If you want to change the look of your page headers or footers, just modify the functions appropriately, and every script that uses them will be affected automatically. For instance, you might want to put a message "Copyright USHL" at the bottom of each Historical League page. Adding the message to a page-trailer function such as `html_end()` is an easy way to do that.

9.1.3 A Simple Data-Retrieval Page

The script that we've embedded in the Historical League home page runs a query that returns just a single row (the membership count). Our next script shows how to process a multiple-row result set (the full contents of the `member` table). This is the PHP equivalent of the DBI script `dump_members.pl` developed in Section 8.2.2, "A Simple DBI Script," so we'll call it `dump_members.php`. The PHP version differs from the DBI version in that it's intended to be used in a Web environment rather than from the command line. For this reason, it needs to produce HTML output rather than tab-delimited text. To make rows and columns line up nicely, dump_members.php writes the member rows as an HTML table. The script looks like this:

```php
<?php
# dump_members.php - dump U.S. Historical League membership as HTML table

require_once "sampdb_pdo.php";

$title = "U.S. Historical League Member List";
html_begin ($title, $title);

$dbh = sampdb_connect ();

# issue statement
$stmt = "SELECT last_name, first_name, suffix, email,"
      . " street, city, state, zip, phone FROM member ORDER BY last_name";
$sth = $dbh->query ($stmt);

print ("<table>\n");          # begin table
# read results of statement, and then clean up
while ($row = $sth->fetch (PDO::FETCH_NUM))
{
  print ("<tr>\n");           # begin table row
  for ($i = 0; $i < $sth->columnCount (); $i++)
  {
    # escape any special characters and print table cell
    print ("<td>" . htmlspecialchars ($row[$i]) . "</td>\n");
  }
  print ("</tr>\n");          # end table row
}
print ("</table>\n");         # end table

$dbh = NULL;  # close connection

html_end ();
?>
```

sampdb_connect() enables exceptions for PDO errors, but dump_members.php contains no try/catch construct to handle exceptions. What happens if an error occurs? In this case, PHP's default behavior is to terminate the script and print a message that describes the problem. This contrasts with the Historical League home page, where we used an empty exception handler to cause errors to be ignored. For the home page, displaying the membership count was just a little addition to the script's main purpose of presenting a greeting to the visitor, so printing a message if the count could not be retrieved would have just been a distraction. For dump_members.php, displaying database content is the entire reason for the script's existence, so if a problem occurs that prevents the result from being displayed, it's reasonable to print an error message indicating what the problem was.

After issuing the query to select the member table rows, the script uses the fetch() method, which returns the next row of the result set, or FALSE if there are no more. The PDO::FETCH_NUM argument tells fetch() to return a row with numerically indexed columns.

To encode values for display in the Web page, dump_members.php uses the htmlspecialchars() function to take care of escaping characters that are special in HTML, such as '<', '>', or '&'. (To encode values for inclusion with URLs, use urlencode() instead.) These two PHP encoding functions are similar to the CGI.pm escapeHTML() and escape() methods for Perl that are discussed in Section 8.4.2.3, "Escaping HTML and URL Text."

To try the dump_members.php script, install it in the ushl directory of your Web server document tree and access it from your Web browser using this URL:

```
http://localhost/ushl/dump_members.php
```

To let people know about dump_members.php, place a link to it in the Historical League home page script. The modified script (index4.php) looks like this:

```php
<?php
# USHL home page - version 4

require_once "sampdb_pdo.php";

$title = "U.S. Historical League";
html_begin ($title, $title);
?>

<p>Welcome to the U.S. Historical League Web Site.</p>

<?php
try
{
  $dbh = sampdb_connect ();
  $sth = $dbh->query ("SELECT COUNT(*) FROM member");
  $count = $sth->fetchColumn (0);
  print ("<p>The League currently has $count members.</p>");
  $dbh = NULL;  # close connection
}
catch (PDOException $e) { } # empty handler (catch but ignore errors)
?>

<p>
You can view the directory of members <a href="dump_members.php">here</a>.
</p>
```

```
<?php
html_end ();
?>
```

As for earlier home page revisions, copy `index4.php` to the `ush1` directory in your Web server's document tree, naming it `index.php` to replace the file of that name that is there now.

The `dump_members.php` script demonstrates how a PHP script can retrieve information from MySQL and convert it into Web page content. If you like, you can modify the script to produce more elaborate results. One such modification is to display the values from the `email` column as live hyperlinks rather than as static text, to make it easier for site visitors to send mail to League members. The `sampdb` distribution contains a `dump_members2.php` script that does this. It differs from `dump_members.php` only slightly, in the loop that fetches and displays member entries. The original loop looks like this:

```
while ($row = $sth->fetch (PDO::FETCH_NUM))
{
  print ("<tr>\n");            # begin table row
  for ($i = 0; $i < $sth->columnCount (); $i++)
  {
    # escape any special characters and print table cell
    print ("<td>" . htmlspecialchars ($row[$i]) . "</td>\n");
  }
  print ("</tr>\n");           # end table row
}
```

The email addresses are in the fourth column of the query result, so `dump_members2.php` treats that column differently from the rest, printing a hyperlink if the value is not empty:

```
while ($row = $sth->fetch (PDO::FETCH_NUM))
{
  print ("<tr>\n");            # begin table row
  for ($i = 0; $i < $sth->columnCount (); $i++)
  {
    print ("<td>");
    # escape any special characters and print table cell;
    # email is in column 4 (index 3) of result
    if ($i == 3 && $row[$i] != "")
    {
      printf ("<a href=\"mailto:%s\">%s</a>",
              $row[$i],
              htmlspecialchars ($row[$i]));
    }
    else
    {
      print (htmlspecialchars ($row[$i]));
    }
```

```
    print ("</td>\n");
  }
  print ("</tr>\n");            # end table row
}
```

9.1.4 Processing Statement Results

PDO provides several ways to execute SQL statements:

- A PDO object has exec() and query() methods that take an SQL statement argument, execute the statement immediately, and return the result:

  - For statements such as DELETE, INSERT, REPLACE, and UPDATE that modify rows, invoke exec(), which returns a count to indicate how many rows were changed (deleted, inserted, replaced, or updated, as the case may be).

  - For statements such as SELECT that produce a result set, invoke query(), which returns a PDOStatement statement-handle object. You can use this object to obtain further information about the result set. For example, you can find out how many columns the result set has by calling its columnCount() method, or access the rows in the result by invoking fetch().

- PDO also supports two-stage statement execution via prepared statements. The PDO object has a prepare() method that takes an SQL statement argument, but instead of executing the statement immediately, prepare() performs some initial processing and returns a PDOStatement statement-handle object. The statement handle has an execute() method for executing the statement and other methods for processing the result.

  prepare() and execute() can be used for all statements. They are not specific to statements that modify rows or statements that return rows.

  Prepared statements also offer the important capabilities of statement re-execution for improved performance and handling of special characters in data values. See Section 9.1.6, "Using Prepared Statements."

The following sections examine PDO statement-execution capabilities in more detail. *The examples assume that exceptions are enabled for errors.*

9.1.4.1 Handling Statements That Modify Rows

Use the database handle exec() method for statements that modify rows. exec() returns a row count that indicates how many rows were affected. Suppose that you want to delete the row for member 149 in the member table and report the result. The following example shows how to determine whether the statement actually deleted any rows:

```
$count = $dbh->exec ("DELETE FROM member WHERE member_id = 149");
if ($count > 0)
```

```
    print ("Member 149 was deleted\n");
else
  print ("No record for member 149 was found\n");
```

9.1.4.2 Handling Statements That Return a Result Set

Use the database handle `query()` method for statements that produce a result set. `query()` returns a `PDOStatement` statement-handle object that gives you access to the result set. The statement handle has a number of useful methods, such as these:

- `fetch()` returns successive rows of the result, or `FALSE` when there are no more.
- `fetchColumn()` is similar but returns a single column of each row.
- `columnCount()` returns the number of columns in the result set. (The row count is not available from a method call. You must fetch the rows and count them.)

The earlier examples that discuss the USHL home page showed how to fetch a single-value result using a single call to `fetchColumn()`. For cases when you expect to get back multiple rows containing multiple columns, it's common to invoke the `fetch()` method in a loop to fetch the results. The following example illustrates one way to do this. It also counts the rows while fetching them to determine how many there are.

```
$sth = $dbh->query ("SELECT * FROM member");
# fetch each row in result set
$count = 0;
while ($row = $sth->fetch (PDO::FETCH_NUM))
{
  # print values in row, separated by commas
  for ($i = 0; $i < $sth->columnCount (); $i++)
    print ($row[$i] . ($i < $sth->columnCount () - 1 ? "," : "\n"));
  $count++;
}
printf ("Number of rows returned: %d\n", $count);
```

`fetch()` takes an argument that specifies what kind of value to return. Table 9.1 lists some of the common fetch modes.

Table 9.1   Row-Fetching Mode Values

Argument	Return Value
PDO::FETCH_ASSOC	An array; access the elements by associative index.
PDO::FETCH_NUM	An array; access the elements by numeric index.
PDO::FETCH_BOTH	An array; access the elements by associative or numeric index.
PDO::FETCH_OBJ	An object; access the elements as properties.

The `fetch()` argument is optional; without it, the default mode is used. Unless you reset the default, it is `PDO::FETCH_BOTH`, so `fetch()` returns each row as an array with elements that can be accessed by column name or numeric index.

To set the default fetch mode prior to fetching rows, pass an extra argument to `query()` or invoke the statement handle `setFetchMode()` method. Each of the following examples sets the fetch mode to `PDO::FETCH_NUM` to affect subsequent retrieval of the result set:

```
$sth = $dbh->query ($stmt, PDO::FETCH_NUM);
```

```
$sth = $dbh->query ($stmt);
$sth->setFetchMode (PDO::FETCH_NUM);
```

With a fetch mode of `PDO::FETCH_ASSOC`, `fetch()` returns the next row of the result set as an associative array. Element names are the names of the columns selected by the query. For example, if you retrieve the `last_name` and `first_name` values from the `president` table, access the columns as follows:

```
$stmt = "SELECT last_name, first_name FROM president";
$sth = $dbh->query ($stmt);
while ($row = $sth->fetch (PDO::FETCH_ASSOC))
  printf ("%s %s\n", $row["first_name"], $row["last_name"]);
```

With a fetch mode of `PDO::FETCH_NUM`, `fetch()` returns the next row of the result set as an array, with elements that are accessed by numeric index beginning with 0. To determine the number of columns in the result set, invoke the statement handle's `columnCount()` method. The following simple loop fetches and prints row values in tab-delimited format:

```
$stmt = "SELECT * FROM president";
$sth = $dbh->query ($stmt);
while ($row = $sth->fetch (PDO::FETCH_NUM))
{
  for ($i = 0; $i < $sth->columnCount (); $i++)
    print ($row[$i] . ($i < $sth->columnCount () - 1 ? "\t" : "\n"));
}
```

A fetch mode of `PDO::FETCH_BOTH` causes `fetch()` to return an array with elements that can be accessed either by numeric index or column name. This is like a combination of `PDO::FETCH_NUM` and `PDO::FETCH_ASSOC`.

With a fetch mode of `PDO::FETCH_OBJ`, `fetch()` returns the next row of the result set as an object with properties that you access using `$row->`*`col_name`* syntax:

```
while ($row = $sth->fetch (PDO::FETCH_OBJ))
  printf ("%s %s\n", $row->first_name, $row->last_name);
```

What if your query contains calculated columns? For example, you might issue a query that returns values that are calculated as the result of an expression:

```
SELECT CONCAT(first_name, ' ', last_name) FROM president
```

A query that is written like that is unsuitable when fetching rows as objects. The name of the selected column is the expression itself, which isn't a legal property name. However, you can supply a legal name by giving the column an alias. The following query aliases the column as `full_name`:

```
SELECT CONCAT(first_name, ' ', last_name) AS full_name FROM president
```

If you fetch each row from that query as an object, the alias allows the column to be accessed as `$row->full_name`.

The preceding examples use a row-fetching loop of this form that assigns each row to the `$row` variable:

```
while ($row = $sth->fetch ([fetch_mode]))
    ... handle row ...
```

However, there are other ways to fetch rows. One is to fetch an array and assign the result to a list of variables. For example, to assign the `last_name` and `first_name` columns to variables named `$ln` and `$fn` and print the names in first name, last name order, do this:

```
$stmt = "SELECT last_name, first_name FROM president";
$sth = $dbh->query ($stmt);
while (list ($ln, $fn) = $sth->fetch (PDO::FETCH_NUM))
  printf ("%s %s\n", $fn, $ln);
```

The variables can have any legal names you like, but their order in the `list()` must correspond to the order of the columns selected by the query.

It's also possible to retrieve individual column values directly into PHP variables. To do this, bind columns of the result set to variables using `bindColumn()`, and fetch rows using the `PDO::FETCH_BOUND` fetch mode. That causes `fetch()` to return TRUE while rows remain, and to assign column values to the bound variables for each row fetched:

```
$stmt = "SELECT last_name, first_name FROM president";
$sth = $dbh->query ($stmt);
$sth->bindColumn (1, $ln);
$sth->bindColumn (2, $fn);
while ($sth->fetch (PDO::FETCH_BOUND))
  printf ("%s %s\n", $fn, $ln);
```

To fetch all rows at once into an array, use `fetchAll()`:

```
$rows = $sth->fetchAll ();
```

Like `fetch()`, `fetchAll()` uses the default fetch mode, or accepts an explicit fetch-mode argument.

A statement handle can be used as an iterator without invoking `fetch()` explicitly:

```
foreach ($sth as $row)
  printf ("%s %s\n", $row["first_name"], $row["last_name"]);
```

The default fetch mode determines how the rows are returned.

9.1.5 Testing for NULL Values in Query Results

PHP represents the SQL NULL value in result sets using the PHP NULL value. One way to check for NULL in a column value returned from a SELECT query is to use the is_null() function. The following example selects and prints names and email addresses from the member table, printing "No email address available" if the address is NULL:

```
$stmt = "SELECT last_name, first_name, email FROM member";
$sth = $dbh->query ($stmt);
while (list ($last_name, $first_name, $email) = $sth->fetch (PDO::FETCH_NUM))
{
  printf ("Name: %s %s, Email: ", $first_name, $last_name);
  if (is_null ($email))
    print ("No email address available");
  else
    print ($email);
  print ("\n");
}
```

You can also test for SQL NULL values by comparing a value to the PHP NULL constant using the === identically-equal-to operator:

```
if ($email === NULL)
  print ("No email address available");
else
  print ($email);
```

PHP NULL is the same as an unset value, so isset() provides another way to test for NULL values:

```
if (!isset ($email))
  print ("No email address available");
else
  print ($email);
```

9.1.6 Using Prepared Statements

The exec() and query() methods described earlier execute SQL statements and return their results immediately. PDO can also prepare and execute statements in separate steps. Use the database handle with prepare() to obtain a statement handle, and use the statement handle to execute the statement:

```
$sth = $dbh->prepare ($stmt);
$sth->execute ();
```

After executing the statement, if it modifies rows, you can get the rows-affected count by invoking `rowCount()`:

```
$count = $sth->rowCount ();
```

If the statement returns rows, methods such as `fetch()` and `columnCount()` apply. To determine the number of rows, count them as you fetch them. (`rowCount()` applies only to statements that modify rows.)

Prepared statements provide some important capabilities:

- Statement strings can contain placeholders rather than literal data values. After preparing a statement, bind specific data values to the placeholders prior to each execution, and PDO takes care of any handling needed to escape or quote special characters or `NULL` values. There are several ways to bind values to placeholders, as described in Section 9.1.7, "Using Placeholders to Handle Data Quoting Issues."

- A prepared statement can be executed repeatedly. This avoids the preparation overhead for each execution, which is very useful for statements that you plan to execute multiple times because it can provide enhanced performance. For example, to insert multiple rows, you can `prepare()` an `INSERT` statement once. Then `execute()` it within a loop that supplies data values for individual rows each time through the loop, using placeholders to bind the values to the statement.

9.1.7 Using Placeholders to Handle Data Quoting Issues

It's necessary to be aware of quoting issues when you're constructing SQL statement strings in PHP, just as it is in other languages such as C and Perl. Suppose that you're constructing a statement to insert a new row into a table. In the statement string, you might put quotes around each value to be inserted into a string column:

```
$last = "O'Malley";
$first = "Brian";
$expiration = "2013-09-01";
$stmt = "INSERT INTO member (last_name,first_name,expiration)"
      . " VALUES('$last','$first','$expiration')";
```

The problem here is that one of the quoted values itself contains a quote (`O'Malley`), which results in a syntax error if you send the statement to the MySQL server. To deal with this in C, we could call `mysql_real_escape_string()` or `mysql_escape_string()`. In a Perl DBI script, we could use `quote()`. PDO has a database handle `quote()` method that accomplishes much the same objective. For example, a call to `quote("O'Malley")` returns the value `'O\'Malley'`. To use `quote()` for statement construction, insert the value that it returns directly into the statement string, without adding any extra quotes yourself:

```
$last = $dbh->quote ("O'Malley");
$first = $dbh->quote ("Brian");
$expiration = $dbh->quote ("2013-09-01");
$stmt = "INSERT INTO member (last_name,first_name,expiration)"
      . " VALUES($last,$first,$expiration)";
```

Unfortunately, `quote()` has some shortcomings that reduce its usefulness in comparison to its DBI counterpart of the same name:

- It is not implemented for all drivers, in which case it returns FALSE rather than a quoted string.
- For a value of NULL, you'd want to insert the word "NULL" into the statement string without any surrounding quotes. But if you pass NULL to `quote()`, it returns the empty string (`''`). To deal with this, you must either know somehow what a value is, or test it and handle it differentially depending on whether it represents a NULL value. This gets messy quickly.

Because of these deficiencies, I recommend avoiding `quote()` except perhaps when you know you'll be working only with non-NULL string-valued data. A better approach is to use prepared statements. Then you can specify placeholders in SQL statements and let PDO do all the quoting for you. To indicate where data values should go when you prepare an SQL statement, use '?' characters as placeholder markers. Then supply the data values as an array of parameters to the statement when you execute it:

```
$stmt = "INSERT INTO member (last_name,first_name,expiration) VALUES(?,?,?)";
$sth = $dbh->prepare ($stmt);
$sth->execute (array ("O'Malley", "Brian", "2013-09-01"));
```

PDO takes care of any handling required for special characters in strings, and correctly processes non-string values such as numbers and NULL.

A different way to supply the data values is to bind them to the placeholders individually with `bindValue()` before calling `execute()`:

```
$stmt = "INSERT INTO member (last_name,first_name,expiration) VALUES(?,?,?)";
$sth = $dbh->prepare ($stmt);
$sth->bindValue (1, "O'Malley");
$sth->bindValue (2, "Brian");
$sth->bindValue (3, "2013-09-01");
$sth->execute ();
```

The preceding examples use positional placeholders: '?' markers that are all the same and distinguished only by their position within the statement string. PDO also supports named-placeholder style in which a placeholder consists of a name preceded by a colon. Prepare the statement to be executed, and then pass to `execute()` an associative array of values that ties each value to the appropriate name:

```
$stmt = "INSERT INTO member (last_name,first_name,expiration)
         VALUES(:last_name,:first_name,:expiration)";
$sth = $dbh->prepare ($stmt);
$sth->execute (array (
                ":last_name" => "O'Malley",
                ":first_name" => "Brian",
                ":expiration" =>"2013-09-01"
              ));
```

Alternatively, bind each value to its placeholder name before calling `execute()`:

```
$stmt = "INSERT INTO member (last_name,first_name,expiration)
        VALUES(:last_name,:first_name,:expiration)";
$sth = $dbh->prepare ($stmt);
$sth->bindValue (":last_name", "O'Malley");
$sth->bindValue (":first_name", "Brian");
$sth->bindValue (":expiration", "2013-09-01");
$sth->execute ();
```

One advantage of named placeholders is that it is easier to keep track of the association between placeholders and data values when there are large numbers of parameters.

9.1.8 Handling Errors

It's essential to arrange to handle errors when you interact with MySQL. If you assume that every call will succeed, you'll have a much more difficult time figuring out why your script doesn't work when an error does occur.

When you attempt to connect to the database server by invoking `new PDO()`, an exception occurs if the attempt fails. Assuming that the attempt succeeds and you get back a valid database handle, PDO processes errors for subsequent operations that are based on that handle according to the PDO error mode. You can set the error mode as follows:

```
$dbh->setAttribute (PDO::ATTR_ERRMODE, mode_value);
```

PDO supports three error mode values:

- `PDO::ERRMODE_SILENT`: PDO does nothing other than set error information for the object that caused the error. This is the default error mode.
- `PDO::ERRMODE_WARNING`: This is similar to silent mode, but PDO emits a warning message in addition to setting the error information.
- `PDO::ERRMODE_EXCEPTION`: PDO raises an exception after setting the error information.

In all cases, if you know the object for which the error occurred, you can invoke its `errorCode()` or `errorInfo()` methods to obtain error information:

- `errorCode()` returns a five-character SQLSTATE value. A return value equal to `PDO::ERR_NONE` (`"00000"`) means "no error."
- `errorInfo()` returns a three-element array containing the SQLSTATE value and a driver-specific code and message. For MySQL, the latter two values are a numeric error code and descriptive error message.

In silent or warning mode, error handling involves checking the result of each PDO operation that might fail. For example:

```
if (!($sth = $dbh->prepare ("SELECT * FROM non_existent_table")))
  die ("Cannot prepare statement: " . $dbh->errorCode () . "\n");
```

```
else if (!$sth->execute ())
  die ("Cannot execute statement: " . $sth->errorCode () . "\n");
```

Note that errorCode() is invoked using the handle for which the error occurred. The same is true for errorInfo().

If you enable exceptions, PHP throws a PDOException when an error occurs for a PDO operation. If no error occurs, the operation succeeded. Otherwise, the exception causes PHP to terminate your script unless you catch the error. To do so, put the code that might fail into a try block and the error-processing code in the corresponding catch block:

```
try
{
  # ... perform a database operation ...
}
catch (PDOException $e)
{
  # ... handle the error ...
}
```

The exception object ($e in the example) has its own methods that provide error information:

- getCode() returns an error code.
- getMessage() returns a string containing an error message.

The following example enables exceptions and shows how to display error information when a statement fails to execute:

```
$dbh->setAttribute (PDO::ATTR_ERRMODE, PDO::ERRMODE_EXCEPTION);
try
{
  $dbh->exec ("DELETE FROM non_existent_table");
}
catch (PDOException $e)
{
  # Print error information from exception object
  print ("getCode value: " . $e->getCode () . "\n");
  print ("getMessage value: " . $e->getMessage () . "\n");
  # Print error information from database handle
  print ("errorCode value: " . $dbh->errorCode () . "\n");
  print ("errorInfo value: " . join (",", $dbh->errorInfo ()) . "\n");
}
```

The example displays information from the exception object ($e), and also from the database-handle object ($dbh). That's possible here because the only PDO handle used in the try block is $dbh. Were you using multiple handles in the try block, you wouldn't know in the catch block which of them caused the error, so you'd need to rely only on the exception methods. Alternatively, you could restructure the code to isolate use of each PDO handle into its own `try/catch` construct.

Some PHP functions or operations produce an error message if an error occurs, in addition to returning a status value. In Web contexts, this message appears in the page sent to the client browser, which may not be what you want. To suppress the (possibly cryptic) error message that a function normally would produce, precede the function name by the @ operator: For example, to suppress the error message from a function named `some_func()` so that you can report failure in a more suitable manner, you might do something like this:

```
$status = @some_func ();
```

9.2 Putting PHP to Work

The remaining part of this chapter tackles the goals set out in Chapter 1 that we have yet to accomplish:

- For the grade-keeping project, we need to write a script that enables us to enter and edit test and quiz scores.
- For visitors to the Historical League Web site, we want to develop an online quiz about U.S. presidents, and to make it interactive so that the questions can be generated on the fly.
- We also want to make it possible for Historical League members to edit their directory entries online. This will keep the information up to date and reduce the amount of entry editing that must be done by the League secretary.

Each of these scripts generates multiple Web pages and communicates from one invocation of the script to the next by means of information embedded in the pages it creates. If you're not familiar with the concept of inter-page communication, you might want to read Section 8.4.2.4, "Writing Multiple-Purpose Pages."

9.2.1 An Online Score-Entry Application

In this section, we'll turn our attention to the grade-keeping project and write a `score_entry.php` script for managing test and quiz scores. The Web directory for the project is named `gp` under the Apache document tree root, which corresponds to this URL for our site:

```
http://localhost/gp/
```

The directory is thus far unpopulated, so visitors requesting that URL may receive only a "page not found" error or an empty directory listing page. To rectify that problem, create a short script named `index.php` and place it in the `gp` directory to serve as the project's home page. The following script suffices for now. It contains two links. One link is to the `score_browse.pl` script that we wrote in Section 8.4.5, "A Grade-Keeping Project

Score Browser," because that script pertains to the grade-keeping project. The other link is to the `score_entry.php` script that we're about to write:

```php
<?php
# Grade-Keeping Project home page

require_once "sampdb_pdo.php";

$title = "Grade-Keeping Project";
html_begin ($title, $title);
?>

<p>
<a href="/cgi-bin/score_browse.pl">View</a> test and quiz scores
</p>
<p>
<a href="score_entry.php">Enter or edit</a> test and quiz scores
</p>

<?php
html_end ();
?>
```

You can find this `index.php` script in the `phpapi/gp` directory of the `sampdb` distribution. Copy it to the `gp` directory of your Web server document tree.

Let's consider how to design and implement the `score_entry.php` script that will let us enter a set of test or quiz scores or edit existing sets of scores. Entry capability will be useful whenever we have a new set of scores to add to the database. Editing capability is necessary for changing scores later; for example, to handle scores of students who take a test or quiz later than the rest of the class due to absence for illness or other reason (or, perish the thought, to correct errors should we happen to enter a score incorrectly). Conceptually, the score entry script operates like this:

- The initial page presents a list of known grade events and enables you to choose one, or to indicate that you want to create a new event.

- If you choose to create a new event, the script presents a page that enables you to specify the date and event category (test or quiz). After it adds the event to the database, the script redisplays the event list page, which at that point will include the new event.

- If you choose an existing event from the list, the script presents a score-entry page showing the event ID, date, and category, a table that lists each student in the class, and a Submit button. Each row in the table shows one student's name and current score for the event. For new events, all scores will be blank. For existing events, the scores will be those you entered at some earlier time. You can fill in or change the scores, and then select the Submit button. At that point, the script will enter the scores into the `score` table or revise existing scores. This operation needs to be done as a transaction to make sure that all score modifications succeed as a unit or all are canceled if an error occurs.

9.2.1.1 Collecting Web Input in PHP

Before implementing the `score_entry.php` script, we must take a slight detour to discuss how input parameters work in PHP. The script needs to perform several different actions, which means that it must pass a status value from page to page so that the script can tell what it's supposed to do each time it's invoked. One way to do this is to pass parameters at the end of the URL. For example, we can add a parameter named `action` to the script URL like this:

```
http://localhost/gp/score_entry.php?action=value
```

Parameter values may also come from the contents of a form submitted by the user. Each field in the form that is returned by the user's browser as part of a form submission will have a name and a value.

PHP makes input parameters available to scripts through special arrays. Parameters encoded at the end of a URL and sent as part of a `get` request are placed in the `$HTTP_GET_VARS` global array and `$_GET` superglobal array. For parameters received in a `post` request (such as the contents of a form that has a `method` attribute value of `post`), the parameters are placed in the `$HTTP_POST_VARS` global array and `$_PUT` superglobal array.

The global arrays must be declared explicitly if you use them in contexts other than at the top level of your PHP scripts, such as within function definitions. The superglobal arrays are accessible in any scope without any special declaration. For simplicity, we'll use the `$_GET` and `$_PUT` superglobal arrays. (`$HTTP_GET_VARS` and `$HTTP_POST_VARS` are deprecated now, anyway.)

`$_GET` and `$_PUT` are associative arrays, with elements keyed to the parameter names. For example, an `action` parameter sent in the URL becomes available to a PHP script as the value of `$_GET["action"]`. Suppose that a form contains fields called `name` and `address`. When a user submits the form, the Web server invokes a script to process the form's contents. If the form is submitted as a `get` request, the script can find out what values were entered into the form by checking the values of the `$_GET["name"]` and `$_GET["address"]` variables. If the form is submitted as a `post` request, the variables will be in `$_POST["name"]` and `$_POST["address"]`.

For forms that contain a lot of fields, it can be inconvenient to give them all unique names. PHP makes it easy to pass arrays in and out of forms. If you use field names such as `x[0]`, `x[1]`, and so forth, PHP will store them in `$_GET["x"]` or `$_POST["x"]`, the value of which will itself be an array. If you assign the array value to a variable `$x`, the array elements are available as `$x[0]`, `$x[1]`, and so on.

In most cases, we won't care whether a parameter was submitted via `get` or `post`, so we can write a utility routine, `script_param()`, that takes a parameter name and checks both arrays to find the parameter value. If the parameter is not present, the routine returns NULL:

```
function script_param ($name)
{
```

```
  $val = NULL;
  if (isset ($_GET[$name]))
    $val = $_GET[$name];
  else if (isset ($_POST[$name]))
    $val = $_POST[$name];
  if (get_magic_quotes_gpc ())
    $val = remove_backslashes ($val);
  return ($val);
}
```

script_param() enables a script to easily access the values of input parameters by name, without being concerned which array they might be stored in. It also processes the parameter value after extracting it by passing the value to remove_backslashes(). The purpose of doing this is to adapt to configurations that have the magic_quotes_gpc setting enabled with a line like this in the PHP initialization file:

```
magic_quotes_gpc = On;
```

If that setting is turned on, PHP adds backslashes to parameter values to quote special characters such as quotes or backslashes. The extra backslashes make it more difficult to check parameter values to see whether they're valid, so remove_backslashes() strips them out. It's implemented using a recursive algorithm because in PHP it's possible to create parameters that take the form of nested arrays:

```
function remove_backslashes ($val)
{
  if (is_array ($val))
  {
    foreach ($val as $k => $v)
      $val[$k] = remove_backslashes ($v);
  }
  else if (!is_null ($val))
    $val = stripslashes ($val);
  return ($val);
}
```

Web Input Parameters and register_globals

You may be familiar with PHP's register_globals configuration setting that causes Web input parameters to be registered directly into script variables. For example, a form field or URL parameter named x would be stored directly into a variable named $x in your script. Unfortunately, enabling this capability means that clients can set variables in your scripts in ways you may not intend. This is a security risk, for which reason the PHP development team recommends that register_globals be disabled. The script_param() routine deliberately uses only the arrays provided specifically for input parameters, which is more secure and also works regardless of the register_globals setting.

9.2.1.2 Displaying and Entering Scores

Now that we have support in place for extracting Web input parameters conveniently, we can use that support for writing `score_entry.php`. That script needs to be able to communicate information from one invocation of itself to the next. We'll use a parameter called `action` for this, which can be obtained as follows when the script executes:

```
$action = script_param ("action");
```

If the parameter isn't set, that means the script is being invoked for the first time. Otherwise, it can test the value of $action to find out what to do. The general framework for `script_entry.php` looks like this:

```php
<?php
# score_entry.php - Score Entry script for grade-keeping project

require_once "sampdb_pdo.php";

# define action constants
define ("SHOW_INITIAL_PAGE", 0);
define ("SOLICIT_EVENT", 1);
define ("ADD_EVENT", 2);
define ("DISPLAY_SCORES", 3);
define ("ENTER_SCORES", 4);

# ... put input-handling functions here ...

$title = "Grade-Keeping Project -- Score Entry";
html_begin ($title, $title);

$dbh = sampdb_connect ();

# determine what action to perform (the default is to
# present the initial page if no action is specified)

$action = script_param ("action");
if (is_null ($action))
  $action = SHOW_INITIAL_PAGE;

switch ($action)
{
case SHOW_INITIAL_PAGE:   # present initial page
  display_events ($dbh);
  break;
case SOLICIT_EVENT:       # ask for new event information
  solicit_event_info ();
  break;
case ADD_EVENT:           # add new event to database
  add_new_event ($dbh);
```

```
    display_events ($dbh);
    break;
case DISPLAY_SCORES:        # display scores for selected event
    display_scores ($dbh);
    break;
case ENTER_SCORES:          # enter new or edited scores
    enter_scores ($dbh);
    display_events ($dbh);
    break;
default:
    die ("Unknown action code ($action)\n");
}

$dbh = NULL;   # close connection

html_end ();
?>
```

The $action variable can take on several values, which we test in the `switch` state-
ment. In PHP, `switch` is much like its C counterpart; it's used here to determine which
action to take and to call the functions that implement the action. To avoid having to use
literal action values, the `switch` statement refers to symbolic action names that are set up
earlier in the script using PHP's `define()` construct.

Let's examine the functions that handle these actions one at a time. The first one,
`display_events()`, presents a list of allowable events by retrieving rows of the
`grade_event` table from MySQL and displaying them. Each row of the table lists the
event ID, date, and event category (test or quiz). The event ID appears in the page as a hyperlink that you can select to edit the scores for that event. Following the event rows, the
function adds one more row containing a link that enables a new event to be created:

```
function display_events ($dbh)
{
    print ("Select an event by clicking on its number, or select\n");
    print ("New Event to create a new grade event:<br /><br />\n");
    print ("<table border=\"1\">\n");

    # Print a row of table column headers

    print ("<tr>\n");
    display_cell ("th", "Event ID");
    display_cell ("th", "Date");
    display_cell ("th", "Category");
    print ("</tr>\n");

    # Present list of existing events.  Associate each event id with a
    # link that will show the scores for the event.
```

```
$stmt = "SELECT event_id, date, category
         FROM grade_event ORDER BY event_id";
$sth = $dbh->query ($stmt);

while ($row = $sth->fetch ())
{
  print ("<tr>\n");
  $url = sprintf ("%s?action=%d&event_id=%d",
                  script_name (),
                  DISPLAY_SCORES,
                  $row["event_id"]);
  display_cell ("td",
                "<a href=\"$url\">"
                . $row["event_id"]
                . "</a>",
                FALSE);
  display_cell ("td", $row["date"]);
  display_cell ("td", $row["category"]);
  print ("</tr>\n");
}

# Add one more link for creating a new event

print ("<tr align=\"center\">\n");
$url = sprintf ("%s?action=%d",
                script_name (),
                SOLICIT_EVENT);
display_cell ("td colspan=\"3\"",
              "<a href=\"$url\">Create New Event</a>",
              FALSE);
print ("</tr>\n");

print ("</table>\n");
}
```

The URLs for the hyperlinks that re-invoke `score_entry.php` are constructed using `script_name()`, a function that figures out the script's own pathname. `script_name()` is useful because it enables you to avoid hardwiring the name of the script into the code. (If you write the name literally, the script will break if you rename it.) `script_name()` can be found in the `sampdb_pdo.php` file.

`script_name()` is somewhat similar to `script_param()` in that it accesses a PHP superglobal array. However, it uses a different array because the script name is part of the information supplied by the Web server, not as part of the input parameters:

```
function script_name ()
{
  return ($_SERVER["SCRIPT_NAME"]);
}
```

The `display_cell()` function used by `display_events()` generates cells in the event table:

```
# Display a cell of an HTML table.  $tag is the tag name ("th" or "td"
# for a header or data cell), $value is the value to display, and
# $encode should be true or false, indicating whether or not to perform
# HTML-encoding of the value before displaying it.  $encode is optional,
# and is true by default.

function display_cell ($tag, $value, $encode = TRUE)
{
  if (strlen ($value) == 0) # is the value empty/unset?
    $value = " ";
  else if ($encode) # perform HTML-encoding if requested
    $value = htmlspecialchars ($value);
  print ("<$tag>$value</$tag>\n");
}
```

If you select the "Create New Event" link in the table that `display_events()` presents, `score_entry.php` is re-invoked with an action of SOLICIT_EVENT. That triggers a call to `solicit_event_info()`, which displays a form that enables you to enter the date and category for the new event:

```
function solicit_event_info ()
{
  printf ("<form method=\"post\" action=\"%s?action=%d\">\n",
          script_name (),
          ADD_EVENT);
  print ("Enter information for new grade event:<br /><br />\n");
  print ("Date: ");
  print ("<input type=\"text\" name=\"date\" value=\"\" size=\"10\" />\n");
  print ("<br />\n");
  print ("Category: ");
  print ("<input type=\"radio\" name=\"category\" value=\"T\"");
  print (" checked=\"checked\" />Test\n");
  print ("<input type=\"radio\" name=\"category\" value=\"Q\" />Quiz\n");
  print ("<br /><br />\n");
  print ("<input type=\"submit\" name=\"submit\" value=\"Submit\" />\n");
  print ("</form>\n");
}
```

The form generated by `solicit_event_info()` contains an edit field for entering the date, a pair of radio buttons for specifying whether the new event is a test or a quiz, and a Submit button. The default event category is 'T' (test). (The script writes out literal HTML to construct the form here. For later scripts in this chapter, we'll develop a set of helper functions that generate form elements.)

When you fill in this form and submit it, `score_entry.php` is invoked again, this time with an `action` value equal to `ADD_EVENT`. The `add_new_event()` function then is called to enter a new row into the `grade_event` table:

```
function add_new_event ($dbh)
{
  $date = script_param ("date");          # get date and event category
  $category = script_param ("category");  # entered by user

  if (empty ($date))  # make sure a date was entered, and in ISO 8601 format
    die ("No date specified\n");
  if (!preg_match ('/^\d{4}\D\d{1,2}\D\d{1,2}$/', $date))
    die ("Please enter the date in ISO 8601 format (CCYY-MM-DD)\n");
  if ($category != "T" && $category != "Q")
    die ("Bad event category\n");

  $stmt = "INSERT INTO grade_event (date,category) VALUES(?,?)";
  $sth = $dbh->prepare ($stmt);
  $sth->execute (array ($date, $category));
}
```

`add_new_event()` uses the `script_param()` library routine to access the parameter values that correspond to the `date` and `category` fields in the new-event entry form. Then it performs some minimal safety checks:

- The date should not be empty, and it should have been entered in ISO 8601 format. The `preg_match()` function performs a pattern match for ISO 8601 format:

  ```
  preg_match ('/^\d{4}\D\d{1,2}\D\d{1,2}$/', $date)
  ```

  Single quotes are used here to prevent interpretation of the dollar sign and the backslash as special characters. The test is true if the date consists of three sequences of digits separated by non-digit characters. That's not bullet-proof, but it's easy to add to the script, and it catches many common errors.

  For additional safety, you might want to enable input data restrictions by setting the SQL mode before inserting the data. For example:

  ```
  $dbh->exec ("SET sql_mode = 'TRADITIONAL'");
  ```

- The event category must be one of the values allowed in the `category` column of the `grade_event` table (`'T'` or `'Q'`).

If the parameter values look okay, `add_new_event()` enters a new row into the `grade_event` table. The statement-execution code uses placeholders to make sure the data values are quoted properly for insertion into the query string. After executing the statement, `add_new_event()` returns to the main part of the script (the `switch` statement), which displays the event list again so that you can select the new event and begin entering scores for it.

When you select an item from the event list shown by the `display_events()` function, the `score_entry.php` script invokes the `display_scores()` function. Each event link contains an event number encoded as an `event_id` parameter, so `display_scores()` gets the parameter value, checks it to make sure it's an integer, and uses it in a query to retrieve a row for each student and any current scores the students may have for the event:

```php
function display_scores ($dbh)
{
  # Get event ID number, which must look like an integer
  $event_id = script_param ("event_id");
  if (!ctype_digit ($event_id))
    die ("Bad event ID\n");

  # Select scores for the given event
  $stmt = "
    SELECT
      student.student_id, student.name, grade_event.date,
      score.score AS score, grade_event.category
    FROM student
      INNER JOIN grade_event
      LEFT JOIN score ON student.student_id = score.student_id
                      AND grade_event.event_id = score.event_id
    WHERE grade_event.event_id = ?
    ORDER BY student.name";
  $sth = $dbh->prepare ($stmt);
  $sth->execute (array ($event_id));

  # fetch the rows into an array so we know how many there are
  $rows = $sth->fetchAll ();
  if (count ($rows) == 0)
    die ("No information was found for the selected event\n");

  printf ("<form method=\"post\" action=\"%s?action=%d&event_id=%d\">\n",
          script_name (),
          ENTER_SCORES,
          $event_id);

  # print scores as an HTML table

  for ($row_num = 0; $row_num < count ($rows); $row_num++)
  {
    $row = $rows[$row_num];
    # Print event info and table heading preceding the first row
    if ($row_num == 0)
    {
      printf ("Event ID: %d, Event date: %s, Event category: %s\n",
              $event_id,
```

```
              $row["date"],
              $row["category"]);
    print ("<br /><br />\n");
    print ("<table border=\"1\">\n");
    print ("<tr>\n");
    display_cell ("th", "Name");
    display_cell ("th", "Score");
    print "</tr>\n";
  }
  print ("<tr>\n");
  display_cell ("td", $row["name"]);
  $col_val = sprintf ("<input type=\"text\" name=\"score[%d]\"",
                      $row["student_id"]);
  $col_val .= sprintf (" value=\"%d\" size=\"5\" /><br />\n",
                       $row["score"]);
  display_cell ("td", $col_val, FALSE);
  print ("</tr>\n");
  }

  print ("</table>\n");
  print ("<br />\n");
  print ("<input type=\"submit\" name=\"submit\" value=\"Submit\" />\n");
  print "</form>\n";
}
```

The query that `display_scores()` uses to retrieve score information for the selected event is not just a simple join between tables, because that wouldn't select a row for any student who has no score for the event. In particular, for a new event, the join would select no rows, and we'd have an empty entry form! We need to use a LEFT JOIN to force a row to be retrieved for each student, regardless of whether the student already has a score in the `score` table. If the student has no score for the given event, the value retrieved by the query is NULL. (Background for a query similar to the one that `display_scores()` uses to retrieve score rows from MySQL is given in Section 2.7.3, "Left and Right Joins.")

The script places scores retrieved by the query into the form as input fields having names like `score[n]`, where n is a `student_id` value. You can enter or edit the scores and then submit the form to have them stored in the database. When your browser sends the form back to the Web server, PHP converts these fields into elements of an array associated with the name `score` that can be retrieved as follows:

```
$score = script_param ("score");
```

Elements of the array are keyed by student ID, so we can easily associate each student with the corresponding score submitted in the form. Form processing might involve execution of several statements (one per student) and we don't want the update to succeed only partially. In Chapter 1, we created the `score` table as an InnoDB table. That enables us to take advantage of InnoDB's transactional capabilities. In particular, we can make sure that the entire data-entry operation takes place as an atomic unit by performing it as a transaction. That way, the changes either all succeed together, or no changes are all are made to the database. Transaction processing in PDO has this general structure (assuming that exceptions are enabled for PDO errors):

```
try
{
  $dbh->beginTransaction ();              # start the transaction
  # ... perform database operation ...
  $dbh->commit ();                        # transaction succeeded
}
catch (PDOException $e)
{
  $dbh->rollback ();                      # transaction failed
}
```

score_entry.php uses that structure ensure integrity of the data-entry operation. (The rollback operation is placed within its own try/catch construct to prevent it from terminating the script if it fails.)

The enter_scores() function processes the form contents to determine which scores need to be updated or deleted:

```
function enter_scores ($dbh)
{
  # Get event ID number and array of scores for the event

  $event_id = script_param ("event_id");
  $score = script_param ("score");

  if (!ctype_digit ($event_id)) # must look like integer
    die ("Bad event ID\n");

  # Prepare the statements that are executed repeatedly
  $sth_del = $dbh->prepare ("DELETE FROM score
                            WHERE event_id = ? AND student_id = ?");
  $sth_repl = $dbh->prepare ("REPLACE INTO score
                             (event_id, student_id, score)
                             VALUES(?,?,?)");

  # enter scores within a transaction
  try
  {
    $dbh->beginTransaction ();

    $blank_count = 0;
    $nonblank_count = 0;
    foreach ($score as $student_id => $new_score)
    {
      $new_score = trim ($new_score);
```

```
      if (empty ($new_score))
      {
        # if no score is provided for student in the form, delete any
        # score the student may have had in the database previously
        ++$blank_count;
        $sth = $sth_del;
        $params = array ($event_id, $student_id);
      }
      else if (ctype_digit ($new_score)) # must look like integer
      {
        # if a score is provided, replace any score that
        # might already be present in the database
        ++$nonblank_count;
        $sth = $sth_repl;
        $params = array ($event_id, $student_id, $new_score);
      }
      else
      {
        throw new PDOException ("invalid score: $new_score");
      }
      $sth->execute ($params);
    }
    # transaction succeeded, commit it
    $dbh->commit ();
    printf ("Number of scores entered: %d<br />\n", $nonblank_count);
    printf ("Number of scores missing: %d<br />\n", $blank_count);
  }
  catch (PDOException $e)
  {
    printf ("Score entry failed: %s<br />\n",
            htmlspecialchars ($e->getMessage ()));
    # roll back, but use empty exception handler to catch rollback failure
    try
    {
      $dbh->rollback ();
    }
    catch (PDOException $e) { }
  }
  print ("<br />\n");
}
```

Student ID values and the scores associated with them are obtained by iterating through the $score array. The loop processes each score as follows:

- If the score is blank after any whitespace is trimmed from its ends, there is nothing to be entered. But just in case there was a score previously, the script tries to delete it. (Perhaps we mistakenly entered a score earlier for a student who actually was absent, and now we need to remove it.) If the student had no score, the DELETE finds no row to remove, but that's harmless.

- If the score is not blank, the function performs some rudimentary validation of the value and accepts it if it looks like an integer. Note that integer testing is done using a pattern match rather than PHP's is_int() function. The latter is for testing whether a variable's type is integer, but form values are encoded as strings. is_int() returns FALSE for any string, even if it contains only digit characters. What we need here is a content check to verify the string. The following function returns TRUE if every character from the beginning to the end of the string $str is a digit:

```
ctype_digit ($str)
```

If the score looks okay, we add it to the score table. The statement is REPLACE rather than INSERT because we may be replacing an existing score rather than entering a new one. If the student had no score for the grade event, REPLACE adds a new row, just like INSERT. Otherwise, REPLACE replaces the old score with the new one.

Prior to the loop, the script invokes beginTransaction(), which disables autocommit mode. Following the loop, the script commits the transaction if no errors occurred. If something goes wrong, the script rolls back the transaction.

That takes care of the score_entry.php script. All score entry and editing can be done from your Web browser now. One obvious shortcoming is that the script provides no security; anyone who can connect to the Web server can edit scores. The script that we'll write later for Historical League member entry editing shows a simple authentication scheme that could be adapted for this script.

9.2.2 Creating an Interactive Online Quiz

One of the goals for the Historical League Web site was to provide an online version of a quiz, similar to some of the quizzes that the League publishes in the children's section of its newsletter, "Chronicles of U.S. Past." We created the president table, in fact, precisely so that we could use it as a source of questions for a history-based quiz. Let's do this now, using a script called pres_quiz.php.

The basic idea is to pick and ask a question about a president at random, and then solicit an answer from the user and check whether the answer is correct. The types of questions the script might present could be based on any part of the president table rows, but for simplicity, we'll constrain it to asking only where presidents were born. Another simplifying measure is to present the questions in multiple-choice format. That's easier for the user, who need only pick from among a set of choices, rather than typing in a response. It's also easier for us because we don't have to do any pattern matching to check whatever the user might have typed in. We need only a simple comparison of the user's choice and the value that we're looking for.

The pres_quiz.php script must perform two functions:

- When initially invoked, it should generate and display a new question by looking up information from the president table.

- If the user has just submitted a response, the script must check it and provide feedback to indicate whether it was correct. If the response was incorrect, the script should redisplay the same question. Otherwise, it should generate and display a new question.

The outline for the script is quite simple. It presents the initial question page if the user isn't submitting a response, and checks the answer otherwise:

```php
<?php
# pres_quiz.php - script to quiz user on presidential birthplaces

require_once "sampdb_pdo.php";

# ... put quiz-handling functions here ...

$title = "U.S. President Quiz";
html_begin ($title, $title);

$dbh = sampdb_connect ();

$response = script_param ("response");
if (is_null ($response))   # invoked for first time
  present_question ($dbh);
else                       # user submitted response to form
  check_response ($dbh);

$dbh = NULL;  # close connection

html_end ();
?>
```

To create the questions, we'll use ORDER BY RAND(). Using the RAND() function, we can select rows at random from the president table. For example, to pick a president name and birthplace randomly, this query does the job:

```
SELECT CONCAT(first_name, ' ', last_name) AS name,
CONCAT(city, ', ', state) AS place
FROM president ORDER BY RAND() LIMIT 1;
```

The name is the president about whom we ask the question, and the birthplace is the correct answer to the question, "Where was this president born?" We'll also need to present some incorrect choices, which we can select using a similar query:

```
SELECT DISTINCT CONCAT(city, ', ', state) AS place
FROM president ORDER BY RAND();
```

From the result of that query, we'll select the first four values that differ from the correct response. The reason for using DISTINCT in this query is to avoid the possibility of selecting the same birthplace for the choice list more than once. DISTINCT would be unnecessary if birthplaces were unique, but they are not, as you can discover by issuing the following statement:

```
mysql> SELECT city, state, COUNT(*) AS count FROM president
    -> GROUP BY city, state HAVING count > 1;
+-----------+-------+-------+
| city      | state | count |
+-----------+-------+-------+
| Braintree | MA    |     2 |
+-----------+-------+-------+
```

The function that generates the question and the set of possible responses looks like this:

```
function present_question ($dbh)
{
  # issue statement to pick a president and get birthplace
  $stmt = "SELECT CONCAT(first_name, ' ', last_name) AS name,
          CONCAT(city, ', ', state) AS place
          FROM president ORDER BY RAND() LIMIT 1";
  $sth = $dbh->query ($stmt);
  $row = $sth->fetch ();
  $name = $row["name"];
  $place = $row["place"];

  # Construct the set of birthplace choices to present.
  # Set up the $choices array containing five birthplaces, one
  # of which is the correct response.
  $stmt = "SELECT DISTINCT CONCAT(city, ', ', state) AS place
          FROM president ORDER BY RAND()";
  $sth = $dbh->query ($stmt);
  $choices[] = $place;  # initialize array with correct choice
  while (count ($choices) < 5 && $row = $sth->fetch ())
  {
    if ($row["place"] != $place)
      $choices[] = $row["place"]; # add another incorrect choice
  }
  # randomize choices, display form
  shuffle ($choices);
  display_form ($name, $place, $choices);
}
```

The `display_form()` function called by `present_question()` generates the quiz question using a form that displays the name of the president, a set of radio buttons that lists the possible choices, and a Submit button. This form serves the obvious purpose of presenting quiz information to the user, but it also needs to do something else: It must present the quiz information to the client, and it must arrange that when the user submits a response, the information sent back to the Web server enables the script to check whether the response is correct and redisplay the question if not.

Presenting the quiz question is a matter of displaying the president's name and the possible birthplace choices, which is straightforward enough. Arranging to check the response and possibly redisplay the question is a little trickier. It requires that we have access to the correct answer and also to all the information needed to regenerate the question. One way to do this is to use a set of hidden fields to include all the necessary information in the form. These fields become part of the form and will be returned when the user submits a response, but are not displayed for the user to see.

We'll call the hidden fields `name`, `place`, and `choices` to represent the president's name, correct birthplace, and the set of possible choices, respectively. The choices can be encoded as a single string easily by using `implode()` to concatenate the values with a special delimiter character in between. (The delimiter enables us to properly break apart the string later with `explode()` if it becomes necessary to redisplay the question.) The `display_form()` function takes care of producing the form:

```
function display_form ($name, $place, $choices)
{
  printf ("<form method=\"post\" action=\"%s\">\n", script_name ());
  hidden_field ("name", $name);
  hidden_field ("place", $place);
  hidden_field ("choices", implode ("#", $choices));
  printf ("Where was %s born?<br /><br />\n", htmlspecialchars ($name));
  for ($i = 0; $i < 5; $i++)
  {
    radio_button ("response", $choices[$i], $choices[$i], FALSE);
    print ("<br />\n");
  }
  print ("<br />\n");
  submit_button ("submit", "Submit");
  print ("</form>\n");
}
```

`display_form()` uses several helper functions to generate the form fields. The first is `hidden_field()`, which generates the `<input>` tag for a hidden field:

```
function hidden_field ($name, $value)
{
  printf ("<input type=\"%s\" name=\"%s\" value=\"%s\" />\n",
          "hidden",
          htmlspecialchars ($name),
          htmlspecialchars ($value));
}
```

Because `hidden_field()` is a general-purpose routine likely to be useful in many scripts, the logical place to put it is in our library file, `sampdb_pdo.php`. Note that it uses `htmlspecialchars()` to encode both the name and value attributes of the `<input>` tag, in case the `$name` or `$value` variable contains special characters such as quotes.

Two other helper functions, `radio_button()` and `submit_button()`, are implemented as follows:

```
function radio_button ($name, $value, $label, $checked)
{
  printf ("<input type=\"%s\" name=\"%s\" value=\"%s\"%s />%s\n",
          "radio",
          htmlspecialchars ($name),
          htmlspecialchars ($value),
          ($checked ? " checked=\"checked\"" : ""),
          htmlspecialchars ($label));
}

function submit_button ($name, $value)
{
  printf ("<input type=\"%s\" name=\"%s\" value=\"%s\" />\n",
          "submit",
          htmlspecialchars ($name),
          htmlspecialchars ($value));
}
```

When the user chooses a birthplace from among the available options and submits the form, the response is returned to the Web server as the value of the `response` parameter. We can discover the value of `response` by calling `script_param()`, which also gives us a way to figure out whether the script is being called for the first time or whether the user is submitting a response to a previously displayed form. The parameter will not be present if this is a first-time invocation, so the main body of the script can determine what it should do based on the parameter's presence or absence:

```
$response = script_param ("response");
if (is_null ($response))   # invoked for first time
  present_question ($dbh);
else                       # user submitted response to form
  check_response ($dbh);
```

We still need to write the `check_response()` function that compares the user's response to the correct answer. For this, the values present in the `name`, `place`, and `choices` hidden fields are needed. We encoded the correct answer in the `place` field of the form, and the user's response will be in the `response` field, so to check the answer all we need to do is compare the two. Based on the result of the comparison, `check_response()` provides some feedback and then either generates and displays a new question, or else redisplays the same question:

```
function check_response ($dbh)
{
  $name = script_param ("name");
  $place = script_param ("place");
  $choices = script_param ("choices");
```

```
$response = script_param ("response");

# Is the user's response the correct birthplace?

if ($response == $place)
{
  print ("That is correct!<br />\n");
  printf ("%s was born in %s.<br />\n",
          htmlspecialchars ($name),
          htmlspecialchars ($place));
  print ("Try the next question:<br /><br />\n");
  present_question($dbh);
}
else
{
  printf ("\"%s\" is not correct.  Please try again.<br /><br />\n",
          htmlspecialchars ($response));
  $choices = explode ("#", $choices);
  display_form ($name, $place, $choices);
}
}
```

We're done. Add a link for `pres_quiz.php` to the Historical League home page, and
visitors can try the quiz to test their knowledge. (You can copy `index5.php` from the
`phpapi/ush1` directory of the `sampdb` distribution to the `ush1` directory in your Web
server's document tree, naming it `index.php` to replace the file of that name that is there
now.)

> **Hidden Fields Are Insecure**
>
> `pres_quiz.php` relies on hidden fields as a means of transmitting information that is
> needed for the next invocation of the script but that the user should not see. That's fine for
> a script like this, which is intended only for fun. But hidden fields should *not* be used for any
> information that the user must not ever be allowed to examine directly, because they are
> not secure in any sense. To see why not, install `pres_quiz.php` in the `ush1` directory of
> your Web server document tree and request it from your browser. Then use the browser's
> View Source command to see the raw HTML for the quiz page. There you'll find the contents
> of the `place` hidden field that contains the correct answer for the current quiz question, ex-
> posed for anyone to see. This means it's very easy to cheat on the quiz. That's no big deal
> for this particular application, but the example does illustrate that hidden fields are not se-
> cure in the least. For information that really must be kept secure from the user, use some
> other method such as a session where information is stored on the server side.

9.2.3 Historical League Online Member Entry Editing

Our final PHP script, `edit_member.php`, is intended to enable the Historical League
members to edit their own directory entries online. Using this script, members will be
able to correct or update their membership information whenever they want without

having to contact the League office to submit the changes. Providing this capability should help keep the member directory more up to date, and, not incidentally, reduce the workload of the League secretary.

One precaution we need to take is to make sure each entry can be modified only by the member the entry is for, or by the League secretary. This means we need some form of security. As a demonstration of a simple form of authentication, we'll use MySQL to store passwords for each member and require that a member supply the correct password to gain access to the editing form that our script presents. The script works as follows:

- When initially invoked, `edit_script.php` presents a login form containing fields for the member ID and a password.
- When the login form is submitted, the script looks in a password table that associates member IDs and passwords. If the password matches, the script looks up the member entry from the `member` table and displays it for editing.
- When the edited form is submitted, we update the entry in the database using the contents of the form.

For any of this to work, we'll need to assign passwords. An easy way to do this is to generate them randomly. The following statements set up a table named `member_pass`, and then create a password for each member by generating an MD5 checksum from a random number and using the first eight characters of the result. In a real situation, you might let members pick their own passwords, but this technique provides a quick and easy way to set something up initially:

```
mysql> CREATE TABLE member_pass (
    -> member_id INT UNSIGNED NOT NULL PRIMARY KEY,
    -> password CHAR(8));
mysql> INSERT INTO member_pass (member_id, password)
    -> SELECT member_id, LEFT(MD5(RAND()), 8) AS password FROM member;
```

In addition to a password for each person listed in the `member` table, we'll add a special entry to the `member_pass` table for member 0, with a password of `bigshot` that will serve as the administrative (superuser) password. The League secretary can use this password to gain access to any entry:

```
mysql> INSERT INTO member_pass (member_id, password) VALUES(0, 'bigshot');
```

> **Note**
>
> Before creating the `member_pass` table, you might want to remove the `db_browse.pl` script from your Web server's script directory. That script, written in Section 8.4.4, "A Web-Based Database Browser," allows anyone to browse the contents of any table in the `sampdb` database—including the `member_pass` table. Thus, it could be used to see any League member's password or the administrative password.

After the `member_pass` table has been set up, we're ready to begin building `edit_member.php`. The framework for the script is as follows:

```php
<?php
# edit_member.php - Edit U.S. Historical League member entries via the Web

require_once "sampdb_pdo.php";

# define action constants
define ("SHOW_INITIAL_PAGE", 0);
define ("DISPLAY_ENTRY", 1);
define ("UPDATE_ENTRY", 2);

# ... put input-handling functions here ...

$title = "U.S. Historical League -- Member Editing Form";
html_begin ($title, $title);

$dbh = sampdb_connect ();

# determine what action to perform (the default if
# none is specified is to present the initial page)

$action = script_param ("action");
if (is_null ($action))
  $action = SHOW_INITIAL_PAGE;

switch ($action)
{
case SHOW_INITIAL_PAGE:    # present initial page
  display_login_page ();
  break;
case DISPLAY_ENTRY:        # display entry for editing
  display_entry ($dbh);
  break;
case UPDATE_ENTRY:         # store updated entry in database
  update_entry ($dbh);
  break;
default:
  die ("Unknown action code ($action)\n");
}

$dbh = NULL;  # close connection

html_end ();
?>
```

The `display_login_page()` function presents the initial page containing a form that asks for a member ID and password:

```
function display_login_page ()
{
  printf ("<form method=\"post\" action=\"%s?action=%d\">\n",
          script_name (),
          DISPLAY_ENTRY);
  print ("Enter your membership ID number and password,\n");
  print ("then select Submit.\n<br /><br />\n");
  print ("<table>\n");
  print ("<tr>");
  print ("<td>Member ID</td><td>");
  text_field ("member_id", "", 10);
  print ("</td></tr>");
  print ("<tr>");
  print ("<td>Password</td><td>");
  password_field ("password", "", 10);
  print ("</td></tr>");
  print ("</table>\n");
  submit_button ("button", "Submit");
  print "</form>\n";
}
```

The form presents the captions and the value entry fields within an HTML table so that they line up nicely. With only two fields, this is a minor touch, but it's a generally useful technique, especially when you create forms with captions of very dissimilar lengths, because it eliminates vertical raggedness. Lining up the form components can make the form easier for the user to read and understand.

`display_login_form()` uses two more helper functions that can be found in the `sampdb_pdo.php` library file. `text_field()` presents an editable text input field:

```
function text_field ($name, $value, $size)
{
  printf ("<input type=\"%s\" name=\"%s\" value=\"%s\" size=\"%s\" />\n",
          "text",
          htmlspecialchars ($name),
          htmlspecialchars ($value),
          htmlspecialchars ($size));
}
```

`password_field()` is similar, except that the `type` attribute is `password`.

When the user enters a member ID and password and submits the form, the `action` parameter will be equal to `DISPLAY_ENTRY`, and the `switch` statement in the next invocation of `edit_member.php` invokes the `display_entry()` function to check the password and display the member entry if the password matches:

```
function display_entry ($dbh)
```

```
{
  # Get script parameters; trim whitespace from the ID, but not
  # from the password, because the password must match exactly.

  $member_id = trim (script_param ("member_id"));
  $password = script_param ("password");

  if (empty ($member_id))
    die ("No member ID was specified\n");
  if (!ctype_digit ($member_id))                # must look like integer
    die ("Invalid member ID was specified (must be an integer)\n");
  if (empty ($password))
    die ("No password was specified\n");
  if (check_pass ($dbh, $member_id, $password)) # regular member
    $admin = FALSE;
  else if (check_pass ($dbh, 0, $password))     # administrator
    $admin = TRUE;
  else
    die ("Invalid password\n");

  $stmt = "SELECT
             last_name, first_name, suffix, email, street, city,
             state, zip, phone, interests, member_id, expiration
           FROM member WHERE member_id = ?
           ORDER BY last_name";
  $sth = $dbh->prepare ($stmt);
  $sth->execute (array ($member_id));

  if (!($row = $sth->fetch ()))
    die ("No user with member_id = $member_id was found\n");

  printf ("<form method=\"post\" action=\"%s?action=%d\">\n",
          script_name (),
          UPDATE_ENTRY);

  # Add member ID and password as hidden values so that next invocation
  # of script can tell which record the form corresponds to and so that
  # the user need not re-enter the password.

  hidden_field ("member_id", $member_id);
  hidden_field ("password", $password);

  # Format results of statement for editing

  print ("<table>\n");
```

```
# Display member ID as static text

display_column ("Member ID", $row, "member_id", FALSE);

# $admin is true if the user provided the administrative password,
# false otherwise. Administrative users can edit the expiration
# date, regular users cannot.

display_column ("Expiration", $row, "expiration", $admin);

# Display other values as editable text

display_column ("Last name", $row, "last_name");
display_column ("First name", $row, "first_name");
display_column ("Suffix", $row, "suffix");
display_column ("Email", $row, "email");
display_column ("Street", $row, "street");
display_column ("City", $row, "city");
display_column ("State", $row, "state");
display_column ("Zip", $row, "zip");
display_column ("Phone", $row, "phone");
display_column ("Interests", $row, "interests");

print ("</table>\n");

submit_button ("button", "Submit");
print "</form>\n";
}
```

The first thing that display_entry() does is to verify the password. If the password supplied by the user matches the password stored in the member_pass table for the given member ID, or if it matches the administrative password (that is, the password for the special member ID 0), edit_member.php displays the entry in a form so that its contents can be edited. The password-checking function check_pass() runs a simple query to yank a row from the member_pass table and compare its password column value to the password supplied by the user in the login form:

```
function check_pass ($dbh, $id, $pass)
{
  $stmt = "SELECT password FROM member_pass WHERE member_id = ?";
  $sth = $dbh->prepare ($stmt);
  $sth->execute (array ($id));
  # TRUE if a password was found and it matches
  return (($row = $sth->fetch ()) && $row["password"] == $pass);
}
```

Assuming that the password matches, `display_entry()` looks up the row from the `member` table corresponding to the given member ID, and then goes on to generate an editing form initialized with the values from the row. Most of the fields are presented as editable text fields so that the user can change them, but there are two exceptions. First, the `member_id` value is displayed as static text. This is the key value that uniquely identifies the row, so it should not be changed. Second, the expiration date is not something that we want League members to be able to change. (They'd be able to push the date farther into the future, in effect renewing their memberships without paying their dues.) On the other hand, if the administrative password was given at login time, the script does present the expiration date in an editable field. Assuming that the League secretary knows this password, this enables the secretary to update the expiration date for members who renew their memberships.

The `display_column()` function handles display of field labels and values. Its arguments are the label to display next to the field value, the array that contains the row to be edited, the name of the column within the row that contains the field value, and a boolean value that indicates whether to present the value in editable or static form. The last value is optional, with a default value of TRUE:

```
function display_column ($label, $row, $col_name, $editable = TRUE)
{
  print ("<tr>\n");
  print ("<td>" . htmlspecialchars ($label) . "</td>\n");
  print ("<td>");
  if ($editable)  # display as editable field
    text_field ("row[$col_name]", $row[$col_name], 80);
  else            # display as read-only text
    print (htmlspecialchars ($row[$col_name]));
  print ("</td>\n");
  print ("</tr>\n");
}
```

For editable values, `display_column()` generates text fields using names that have the format `row[col_name]`. That way, when the user submits the form, PHP will place all the field values into an array variable, with elements keyed by column name. This makes it easy to extract the form contents and to associate each field value with its corresponding `member` table column when we update the row in the database. For example, by fetching the array into a `$row` variable, we can access the telephone number as `$row["phone"]`.

The `display_entry()` function also embeds the `member_id` and `password` values as hidden fields in the form so that they will carry over to the next invocation of `edit_script.php` when the user submits the edited entry. The ID enables the script to determine which `member` table row to update, and the password enables it to verify that the user logged in before. (Notice that this simple authentication method involves passing the password back and forth in clear text, which isn't generally such a great idea. But the Historical League is not a high-security organization, so this method suffices for our purposes. Were you performing operations such as financial transactions, you'd certainly use a more secure form of authentication.)

The function that updates the membership entry when the form is submitted looks like this:

```
function update_entry ($dbh)
{
  # Get script parameters; trim whitespace from the ID, but not
  # from the password, because the password must match exactly,
  # or from the row, because it is an array.

  $member_id = trim (script_param ("member_id"));
  $password = script_param ("password");
  $row = script_param ("row");

  $member_id = trim ($member_id);
  if (empty ($member_id))
    die ("No member ID was specified\n");
  if (!ctype_digit ($member_id))              # must look like integer
    die ("Invalid member ID was specified (must be an integer)\n");
  if (!check_pass ($dbh, $member_id, $password)
      && !check_pass ($dbh, 0, $password))
    die ("Invalid password\n");

  # Examine the metadata for the member table to determine whether
  # each column allows NULL values. (Make sure nullability is
  # retrieved in uppercase.)

  $stmt = "SELECT COLUMN_NAME, UPPER(IS_NULLABLE)
           FROM INFORMATION_SCHEMA.COLUMNS
           WHERE TABLE_SCHEMA = ? AND TABLE_NAME = ?";
  $sth = $dbh->prepare ($stmt);
  $sth->execute (array ("sampdb", "member"));
  $nullable = array ();
  while ($info = $sth->fetch ())
    $nullable[$info[0]] = ($info[1] == "YES");

  # Iterate through each field in the form, using the values to
  # construct an UPDATE statement that contains placeholders, and
  # the array of data values to bind to the placeholders.

  $stmt = "UPDATE member ";
  $delim = "SET";
  $params = array ();
  foreach ($row as $col_name => $val)
  {
    $stmt .= "$delim $col_name=?";
```

```
    $delim = ",";
    # if a form value is empty, update the corresponding column value
    # with NULL if the column is nullable.  This prevents trying to
    # put an empty string into the expiration date column when it
    # should be NULL, for example.
    $val = trim ($val);
    if (empty ($val))
    {
      if ($nullable[$col_name])
        $params[] = NULL; # enter NULL
      else
        $params[] = "";   # enter empty string
    }
    else
      $params[] = $val;
  }
  $stmt .= " WHERE member_id = ?";
  $params[] = $member_id;

  $sth = $dbh->prepare ($stmt);
  $sth->execute ($params);
  printf ("<br /><a href=\"%s\">Edit another member record</a>\n",
          script_name ());
}
```

First we re-verify the password to make sure someone isn't attempting to hoax us by sending a faked form, and then we update the entry. The update requires some care because if a field in the form is blank, it may need to be entered as NULL rather than as an empty string. The expiration column is an example of this. Suppose that the League secretary logs in with the administrative password (so that the expiration field is editable) and clears the field to indicate "lifetime membership." This should correspond to a NULL membership expiration date in the database, not an empty string (which isn't a legal date). Therefore, it's necessary to be able to tell which columns can take NULL values and insert NULL (rather than an empty string) when such a column is left blank in the form.

To handle this problem, update_entry() looks up the metadata for the member table and constructs an associative array keyed on column name that indicates which columns can have NULL values and which cannot. This information is available in the COLUMNS table of the INFORMATION_SCHEMA database. The values that we need from the table are the column name and whether it allows NULL values (that is, the COLUMN_NAME and IS_NULLABLE values).

At this point, the edit_member.php script is finished. Install it in the ushl directory of the web document tree, let the members know their passwords, and they'll be able to update their own membership information over the Web.

10

Introduction to MySQL Administration

MySQL has grown in complexity somewhat over time as it has become more capable. But as database systems go, MySQL is relatively simple to use, and the effort required to bring up a MySQL installation and use it is modest as well. This simplicity accounts for much of MySQL's popularity, especially among people who aren't, and don't want to be, system administrators. It helps to be a trained computer professional, but that's certainly not a requirement for running MySQL successfully.

Nevertheless, a MySQL installation doesn't run itself, regardless of your level of expertise. Someone must watch over it to make sure it operates smoothly and efficiently, and someone must know what to do when problems occur. If the job falls on you to make sure MySQL is happy at your site, keep reading.

Part III of this book, "MySQL Administration," examines the various duties of MySQL administrators. This chapter provides a brief overview of the responsibilities involved in administering a MySQL installation. The following chapters provide detailed instructions for carrying them out.

If you are a new or inexperienced MySQL administrator, don't let the long list of responsibilities presented in this chapter scare you. Each task listed in the following sections is important, but you need not learn them all at once. If you like, you can use the chapters in this part of the book as a reference, looking up topics as you discover that you need to know about them.

If you have experience administering other database systems, you will find that running a MySQL installation is similar in some ways and that your experience is a valuable resource. But MySQL administration also has its own unique requirements. This part of the book will help you become familiar with them.

10.1 MySQL Components

The MySQL database system consists of several components. You should be familiar with what these components are and the purpose of each, so that you understand both the nature of the system you're administering and the tools available to help you do your job. If you take the time to understand what you're overseeing, your work will be much easier. To that end, you should acquaint yourself with the following aspects of MySQL.

The MySQL server. The server, `mysqld`, is the hub of a MySQL installation; it performs all manipulation of databases and tables. On Unix, several related scripts are available to assist in server startup. `mysqld_safe` is a related program used to start the server, monitor it, and restart it in case it goes down. The `mysql.server` script is useful on versions of Unix that use run-level directories for starting system services. If you run multiple servers on a single host, `mysqld_multi` can help you manage them more easily. On Windows, you have the choice of running the server from the command line or as a Windows service.

The MySQL clients and utilities. Several MySQL programs are available to help you communicate with the server. For administrative tasks, some of the most important ones are listed here:

- `mysql`—An interactive program that enables you to send SQL statements to the server and to view the results. You can also use `mysql` to execute batch scripts (text files containing SQL statements).

- `mysqladmin`—An administrative program for performing tasks such as shutting down the server, checking its configuration, or monitoring its status if it appears not to be functioning properly.

- `mysqldump` and `mysqlhotcopy`—Tools for backing up your databases or copying databases to another server.

- `mysqlcheck` and `myisamchk`—Programs that help you perform table checking, analysis, and optimization, as well as repairs if tables become damaged. `mysqlcheck` works with MyISAM tables and to some extent with tables for other storage engines. `myisamchk` is for use only with MyISAM tables.

The server's language, SQL. You should be able to talk to the server in its own language. As a simple example, you might need to find out why a user's privileges aren't working the way you expect them to work. There is no substitute for being able to go in and communicate with the server directly, which you can do by using the `mysql` client program to issue SQL statements that let you examine the grant tables.

If you don't know any SQL, be sure to acquire at least a basic understanding of it. A lack of SQL fluency will only hinder you in your administrative tasks, whereas the time you take to learn will be repaid many times over. A real mastery of SQL takes some time, but the basic skills can be attained quickly. For instruction in SQL and the use of the `mysql` command-line client, see Chapter 1, "Getting Started with MySQL."

The MySQL data directory. The data directory is where the server stores its databases and status files. It's important to understand the structure and contents of the data directory so that you know how the server uses the filesystem to represent databases and tables, as well as where the server logs are located and what they contain. You should also know your options for managing allocation of disk space across filesystems should you find that the filesystem on which the data directory is located is becoming too full.

10.2 General MySQL Administration

General administration deals primarily with the operation of `mysqld`, the MySQL server, and with providing your users with access to the server. The following duties are most important in carrying out this responsibility.

Server startup and shutdown. You should know how to start and stop the server manually from the command line and how to arrange for automatic startup and shutdown when your system starts and stops. It's also important to know what to do to get the server going again if it crashes or will not start properly.

User account maintenance. You should understand the difference between MySQL user accounts and Unix or Windows login accounts. You should know how to set up MySQL accounts by specifying which users can connect to the server, where they can connect from, and what they are allowed to do. You'll also need to know how to reset forgotten passwords.

Log maintenance. You should understand what types of logs are available and which ones will be useful to you, as well as when and how to perform log maintenance. Log rotation and expiration are essential for preventing the logs from filling up your filesystem.

Server configuration and tuning. The MySQL server is highly configurable. Some of the operational characteristics that you can control include which storage engines the server supports, the default character set, and its default time zone.

Another configuration issue involves server tuning. Your users want the server to perform at its best. The quick-and-dirty method for improving how well your server runs is to buy more memory or to get faster disks. But those brute-force techniques are no substitute for understanding how the server works. You should know what parameters are available for tuning the server's operation and how they apply to your situation. At some sites, queries tend to be mostly retrievals. At others, inserts and updates dominate. The choice of which parameters to change will be influenced by the query mix that you observe at your own site.

Multiple server management. It's useful to run multiple servers on the same machine under some circumstances. You can test a new MySQL release while leaving your current production server in place, or provide better privacy for different groups of users by giving each group its own server. (The latter scenario is particularly relevant to Internet service providers.) For such situations, you should know how to set up multiple simultaneous installations.

Updating MySQL software. New MySQL releases appear from time to time. You should know how to keep up to date with these releases to take advantage of bug fixes and new features. Understand the circumstances under which it's more reasonable to hold off on upgrading, and know how to choose between the stable and development releases.

10.3 Access Control and Security

When you maintain a MySQL installation, it's important to make sure that the information your users entrust to their databases is kept secure. The MySQL administrator is responsible for controlling access to the data directory and the server, and should understand the following issues.

Filesystem security. A Unix machine may host several user accounts that have no MySQL-related administrative duties. It's important to ensure that these accounts have no access to the data directory. This prevents them from compromising data on a filesystem level by copying database tables or removing them, or by being able to read logs that may contain sensitive information. You should know how to set up a Unix user account to be used for running the MySQL server, how to set up the data directory so that it is owned by that user, and how to start up the server to run with that user's privileges.

MySQL server security. You must understand how the MySQL security system works so that when you set up user accounts, you grant them the proper privileges for accessing the MySQL server. Users connecting to the server over the network should have permission to do only what they are supposed to be able to do. You don't want to inadvertently grant overly permissive access to accounts due to faulty understanding of the security system!

10.4 Database Maintenance, Backups, and Replication

Every MySQL administrator hopes to avoid having to deal with corrupted or destroyed database tables. But hope alone won't keep problems from occurring. You should take steps to minimize your risks and learn what to do if bad things do happen.

Preventive maintenance. A regular program of preventive maintenance should be put in place to minimize the likelihood of database corruption or damage. You should also be making backups, of course, but preventive maintenance reduces the chance that you'll need to use them.

Database backups. In the event of a severe system crash, database backups are of crucial importance. You want to be able to restore your databases to the state they were in at the time of the crash with as little data loss as possible. Note that backing up your databases is not the same thing as performing general system backups (as is done, for example, by using the Unix `dump` program). The files corresponding to your database tables might be in flux due to server activity when system backups take place, so restoring those files will not give you internally consistent tables. The `mysqldump` program generates backup files that are more useful for database restoration, and it enables you to create backups without taking down the server. You might also need the backup files for moving databases to a different location in the event of a full disk.

Crash recovery. Should disaster strike in spite of your best efforts, you should know how to repair or restore your tables. Crash recovery should be necessary only rarely, but when it is, it's an unpleasant, high-stress business (especially with the phone ringing and people knocking on the door while you're scrambling to fix things). Nevertheless, you must know how to do it because your users will be quite unhappy otherwise! Be familiar with MySQL's table-checking and repair programs. Know how to recover data using your backup files and how to use the binary log to recover changes that were made after your most recent backup.

Database migration. If you decide to run MySQL on a faster host, you'll need to copy your databases to a different machine. You should understand the procedure for doing this, should the need arise. Database file contents might be machine dependent; if so, you can't just copy them from one system to another.

Database replication. Making a backup or a copy of a database takes a snapshot of its state at one point in time. Another option available to you is to use replication, which involves setting up two servers in cooperative fashion such that changes to databases managed by one server are propagated on a continuing basis to the corresponding databases managed by the other server.

To use replication, you should know how to set up a server as a master replication server, and how to set up slave servers that replicate the master. If trouble occurs and replication stops, you must know where to look to identify the problem and how to get replication started again.

The preceding outline summarizes the responsibilities you undertake by becoming a MySQL administrator. The next few chapters discuss them in more detail and describe procedures to follow so that you can carry out these responsibilities effectively. We'll discuss the MySQL data directory first; that's the primary resource you're maintaining and you should understand its layout and contents. From there, we move on to general administrative duties, a discussion of MySQL's security system, and maintenance and backups.

The MySQL Data Directory

Conceptually, most relational database systems are broadly similar: They manage a set of databases, and each database includes a set of tables. But every system has its own way of organizing the data it manages, and MySQL is no exception. By default, all information managed by the MySQL server mysqld is stored under a location called the MySQL data directory. All databases are stored here, and so are the status files and logs that provide information about the server's operation. If you have any administrative responsibilities for a MySQL installation, familiarity with the layout and use of the data directory is fundamental to carrying out your duties. Even if you don't perform any MySQL administration, you can benefit from reading this chapter because it never hurts to have a better idea of how the server operates.

This chapter covers the following topics:

- **How to determine the location of the data directory.** Because the data directory is so central to the operation of the MySQL server, you should know how to determine where it is located so that you can administer its contents effectively.

- **How the server organizes and provides access to the databases and tables it manages.** This is important for setting up preventive maintenance schedules, and for performing crash recovery should table corruption ever occur.

- **What status files and logs the server generates and what they contain.** Their contents provide useful information about how the server is running, which is useful if you encounter problems.

- **How to change the default location or organization of the data directory.** This can be important for managing the allocation of disk resources on your system—for example, by balancing disk activity across drives or by relocating data to filesystems with more free space. You can also use this knowledge in planning placement of new databases.

For Unix systems, the chapter assumes the existence of a login account that is used for performing MySQL administrative tasks and for running the server. In this book, the user and group names for that account both are mysql. Section 12.2.1.1, "Running the Server

Using an Unprivileged Login Account," discusses the reasons for using a designated login account for MySQL administration.

11.1 Location of the Data Directory

A default data directory location is compiled into the server. Under Unix, typical defaults are `/usr/local/mysql/var` if you install MySQL from a source distribution, `/usr/local/mysql/data` if you install from a binary distribution, or `/var/lib/mysql` if you install from an RPM package. Under Windows, the default data directory location often is `C:\Program Files\MySQL\MySQL Server 5.0\data` or `C:\mysql\data`.

If you compile MySQL from source, you can designate the default data directory location by using the `--localstatedir=dir_name` command-line option when you run `configure`.

At server startup, you can specify the data directory location by using a `--datadir=dir_name` option. This is useful for naming a location different from the compiled-in default. Another way to name the location is to list it in an option file that the server reads at startup time. Then you need not specify it on the command line each time you start the server.

As a MySQL administrator, you should know where your server's data directory is located, but if you don't know (perhaps you are taking over for a previous administrator who left poor notes), there are several ways to find out. The following notes describe a method that you can use when the server is not running, and another that you can use when it is.

Look in an option file that the server reads when it starts. For example, if you look in `/etc/my.cnf` under Unix or `C:\my.ini` under Windows, you may find a `datadir` line in the `[mysqld]` option group of the file:

```
[mysqld]
datadir=/path/to/data/directory
```

The pathname indicates the location of the data directory.

If you are not sure where the server looks for option files, invoke it as follows and check the help message, which lists option file locations near the beginning:

```
% mysqld --verbose --help
```

If the server is running, connect to it and ask it for the data directory location. The server maintains a number of system variables pertaining to its operation, and it can report any of their values. The data directory location is indicated by the `datadir` variable, which you can obtain using a `SHOW VARIABLES` statement or a `mysqladmin variables` command. To determine the value using `SHOW VARIABLES`, issue this statement:

```
mysql> SHOW VARIABLES LIKE 'datadir';
+---------------+-----------------------+
| Variable_name | Value                 |
+---------------+-----------------------+
| datadir       | /usr/local/mysql/var/ |
+---------------+-----------------------+
```

From the command line, use `mysqladmin`. On Unix, the output might look like this:

```
% mysqladmin variables
+---------------+-----------------------+
| Variable_name | Value                 |
+---------------+-----------------------+
...
| datadir       | /usr/local/mysql/var/ |
...
```

On Windows, the output might look like this instead:

```
C:\> mysqladmin variables
+---------------+---------------------------------------------+
| Variable_name | Value                                       |
+---------------+---------------------------------------------+
...
| datadir       | c:\Program Files\MySQL\MySQL Server 5.0\data\ |
...
```

If you have multiple servers running, they will be listening on different network interfaces (TCP/IP ports, Unix socket files, or Windows named pipes or shared memory). You can get data directory information by connecting to each server in turn using appropriate connection parameter options.

If the data directory already has been created at one location and you want to move it somewhere else, see Section 11.3, "Relocating Data Directory Contents."

11.2 Structure of the Data Directory

The MySQL data directory contains all the databases managed by the server. In general, these are organized into a tree structure implemented in straightforward fashion by taking advantage of the hierarchical structure of the Unix or Windows filesystem:

- Each database has a database directory located under the data directory.
- Tables, views, and triggers within a database correspond to files in the database directory.

A given storage engine might use a storage structure that varies from the general hierarchical implementation of databases using directories and files. For example, the InnoDB storage engine can store all InnoDB tables from all databases within a single common tablespace. This tablespace is implemented using one or more large files that are treated as a single unified data structure within which tables and indexes are represented. InnoDB stores tablespace files in the data directory by default.

The data directory also may contain other files:

- The server's process ID (PID) file. When it starts, the server writes its process ID to this file so that other programs can discover the value if they need to send signals to it. (This file is not used by the embedded server.)

- Status and log files that are generated by the server. These files provide important information about the server's operation and are valuable for administrators, especially when something goes wrong and you're trying to determine the cause of the problem. If some particular statement crashes the server, for example, you may be able to identify the offending statement by examining the logs. (If you configure the server to log to database tables rather than to files, the log tables are in the mysql database.)

- Server-related files, such as the DES key file or the server's SSL certificate and key files. It's common for administrators to use the data directory as the location for these files.

11.2.1 How the MySQL Server Provides Access to Data

When MySQL is used in the usual client/server setup, all databases under the data directory are managed by a single entity, the MySQL server mysqld. Client programs never manipulate data directly. Instead, the server provides the sole point of contact through which databases are accessed, acting as the intermediary between client programs and the data they want to use. Figure 11.1 illustrates this architecture.

When the server starts, it opens any logs that you request it to maintain, and then presents a network interface to the data directory by listening for various types of network connections. (Section 12.3, "Controlling How the Server Listens for Connections" presents the details of selecting which network interfaces to use.) To access data, a client program establishes a connection to the server, and then communicates requests as SQL statements to perform the desired operations such as creating a table, selecting rows, or updating rows. The server performs each operation and sends back the result to the client. The server is multi-threaded and can service multiple simultaneous client connections. However, because update operations are performed one at a time, the server in effect serializes requests so that two clients can never change a given row at exactly the same time.

If you're running an application that uses the embedded server, a slightly different architecture applies, because there is only one "client"; that is, the application into which the server is linked. In this case, the server listens to an internal communication channel rather than to network interfaces. However, it's still the embedded server part of the application that manages access to the data directory, and it's still necessary to coordinate SQL statement activity arriving over multiple connections if the application happens to open several connections to its embedded server.

Under normal conditions, having the server act as the sole arbiter of database access provides assurance against the kinds of corruption that can result from multiple processes accessing the database tables at the same time. Nevertheless, administrators should be aware that there are times when the server does not have exclusive control of the data directory:

- **When you run multiple servers on a single data directory.** Normally a single server manages all databases on a host, but you can run multiple servers if you like. If each server manages its own data directory, there is no problem of interaction. It's *possible* to start multiple servers and point them at the same data directory, but this is not a good idea and it is not recommended. If you try it, you'd better make sure that your system provides good file locking or the servers will not cooperate properly. You also risk having your logs become a source of confusion (rather than a source of helpful information) if you have multiple servers writing to them at the same time.

- **When you use direct-access maintenance utilities.** Programs such as `myisamchk` and `myisampack` are used for MyISAM table maintenance, troubleshooting, repair, and compression operations. These programs operate directly on the files that correspond to the tables. Because these utilities can change table contents, using them to operate on tables at the same time the server is doing so can cause table damage. The best way to avoid problems of this sort is to stop the server before running these table utilities. If that is not possible, it's very important to understand how to tell the server not to access a table while you're using a utility that operates directly on the table files. See Section 14.2, "Performing Database Maintenance with the Server Running," for instructions on how to cooperate with the server when using these programs. An alternative to `myisamchk` is to use statements such as CHECK TABLE and REPAIR TABLE (or the `mysqlcheck` program, which issues the statements for you). Those statements eliminate the problem of interaction with the server by instructing the server itself to perform the table maintenance operations.

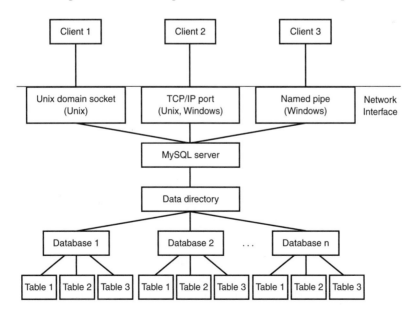

Figure 11.1   How the MySQL server controls access to the data directory.

11.2.2 Representation of Databases in the Filesystem

Each database managed by the MySQL server has its own database directory. Database directories exist as subdirectories of the data directory, each with the same name as the database it represents. For example, if *DATADIR* represents the location of the data directory for the server on your machine, a database named mydb corresponds to the database directory *DATADIR*/mydb on Unix, or *DATADIR*\mydb on Windows.

SHOW DATABASES produces essentially nothing more than a list of the names of the directories located within the data directory.

CREATE DATABASE *db_name* creates a directory named *db_name* under the data directory to act as the database directory. It also creates a db.opt file in the database directory that lists the database default character set and collation. Under Unix, the database directory is owned by and accessible only to the login account that is used for running the server.

The DROP DATABASE statement is implemented nearly as simply. DROP DATABASE *db_name* removes the *db_name* directory in the data directory, along with any files contained within it for tables and other database objects such as views or triggers. This is almost the same as manually removing the database directory with a filesystem-level command such as rm on Unix or del on Windows. The differences between a DROP DATABASE statement and a filesystem command are as follows:

- For DROP DATABASE, the server removes only files with extensions known to be used for tables and other database objects. If you've created other files or directories in the database directory, the server leaves them intact. In this case, the database directory cannot be removed and the DROP DATABASE statement returns an error. One implication of this is that the database name continues to be displayed by SHOW DATABASES. To deal with this, remove any extraneous files and subdirectories manually, and then issue the DROP DATABASE statement again.

- You cannot safely remove InnoDB tables in a database by removing the database directory. For each InnoDB table, InnoDB maintains a data dictionary entry in its shared tablespace, and it might also store the table's contents there as well. If a database contains InnoDB tables, you must use DROP DATABASE so that the InnoDB storage engine can update its data dictionary and delete any table contents from the tablespace.

11.2.3 Representation of Tables in the Filesystem

MySQL supports several storage engines, such as MyISAM, MERGE, MEMORY, InnoDB, Falcon, CSV, and FEDERATED. MySQL represents every table on disk by at least one file, which is the .frm format file that contains a description of the table's structure. The server creates the .frm file. Individual storage engines may create additional files that contain the data rows and index information. The names and structure of these files vary according to the storage engine.

The following discussion outlines the characteristics of some representative storage engines in terms of how they store files on disk. For additional information about how these engines differ in features and behavior, see Section 2.6.1, "Storage Engine Characteristics."

MyISAM is the default storage engine. MySQL represents each MyISAM table by three files in the database directory of the database that contains the table. Each file has a basename that is the same as the table name, and an extension that indicates the purpose of the file. For example, a MyISAM table named `mytbl` has these three files:

- `mytbl.frm` is the format file that contains a description of the table structure.
- `mytbl.MYD` is the data file that stores the contents of the table's rows.
- `mytbl.MYI` contains index information for any indexes the table has.

A MERGE table is a logical construct. It represents a collection of identically structured MyISAM tables that are treated as a single larger table. Within a database directory, a MERGE table named `mytbl` is represented by two files:

- `mytbl.frm` is the format file.
- `mytbl.MRG` is a text file that contains a list of the names of the table's constituent MyISAM tables, one name per line.

MEMORY tables are in-memory tables. A MEMORY table has only an `.frm` file that describes its format in the database directory. The table is not otherwise represented in the filesystem at all because the server stores a MEMORY table's data and indexes in memory rather than on disk. When the server shuts down, the contents of a MEMORY table are lost. When the server restarts, the table still exists (because the `.frm` file still exists), but it is empty.

An InnoDB table has an `.frm` format file containing the table structure in the database directory. For table contents, InnoDB has two representations, both based on tablespaces:

- The shared tablespace. This tablespace consists of one or more large files in the data directory. These component files of the tablespace form a logically contiguous storage area equal in size to the sum of the sizes of the individual files. By default, InnoDB stores its tables in the shared tablespace. For such tables, the only table-specific file is the `.frm` file.

- Individual tablespaces. You can configure InnoDB to use one tablespace file per table. In this case, each InnoDB table has two table-specific files in the database directory: The `.frm` file and an `.ibd` file that contains the table's data and indexes.

The shared tablespace is used for another purpose, too. InnoDB maintains an internal data dictionary that contains information about each of its tables. This dictionary is stored in the shared tablespace, which therefore is necessary even if you are using individual tablespaces to store table contents.

A Falcon table has an `.frm` format file containing the table structure in the database directory. Falcon stores table contents in tablespace files. There are three standard tablespace files, one of which is used for user tables:

- `falcon_master.fts` is for internal tables.
- `falcon_temporary.fts` is for temporary tables.
- `falcon_user.fts` is the default tablespace file for user tables.

Falcon creates the standard tablespace files in the data directory. Additional tablespace files can be created by user request. These need not be located in the data directory.

The CSV storage engine stores table rows as plain text using comma-separated values format. Each table has two files in the database directory: The `.frm` file contains the table structure and a `.csv` file contains the table rows.

A FEDERATED table is a table that points to a remote table on another MySQL server. That is, rows are not stored locally, but retrieved from the remote table as necessary. Because of this, no data or indexes are stored locally. The only local file is the `.frm` file in the database directory that describes the table format.

11.2.4 Representation of Views and Triggers in the Filesystem

Each view and trigger object is associated with a single file in the database directory of the database containing the object.

A view consists of an `.frm` file that contains the view definition and other related attributes. The file basename corresponds to the view name, so a view named `myview` is represented by `myview.frm`.

A trigger is stored in a `.TRG` file that contains the trigger definition and other related attributes. The trigger file has a basename corresponding to the table to which the trigger belongs. For example, a trigger named `mytrig` associated with a table named `mytbl` will be stored in `mytbl.TRG`, not `mytrig.TRG`. There might in fact be more than one trigger stored in this file: A table can have multiple triggers; if so, the server stores the definitions for all of them in the same `.TRG` file.

11.2.5 How SQL Statements Map onto Table File Operations

Every storage engine uses an `.frm` file to store the table format (definition), so the output from SHOW TABLES FROM *db_name* is the same as a listing of the basenames of the `.frm` files in the database directory for *db_name*.

To create a table of any of the types supported by MySQL, you issue a CREATE TABLE statement that defines the table's structure, and that includes an ENGINE = *engine_name* clause to indicate which storage engine you want to use. If you omit the ENGINE clause, MySQL uses the default storage engine (MyISAM, unless you change it). The server creates an `.frm` file for the new table that contains the internal encoding of its definition, and then tells the appropriate storage engine to create any other files that are associated with the table. For example, MyISAM creates `.MYD` and `.MYI` data and index files, and CSV creates a `.CSV` data file. For InnoDB tables, the storage engine creates a data dictionary entry and initializes data and index information for the table within the appropriate InnoDB tablespace. Under Unix, the ownership and mode of any files created to represent the table are set to enable access only to the account that is used to run the server.

When you issue an `ALTER TABLE` statement, the server re-encodes the table's `.frm` file to reflect the structural change indicated by the statement and modifies the contents of the data and index files likewise. This happens for `CREATE INDEX` and `DROP INDEX` as well because they are handled by the server as equivalent `ALTER TABLE` statements. If the `ALTER TABLE` statement changes the table's storage engine, the table constants are transferred to the new engine, which rewrites the contents using the appropriate type of files used by the engine to represent tables.

MySQL implements `DROP TABLE` by removing the files that represent the table. If you drop an InnoDB table, the InnoDB storage engine also updates its data dictionary and marks as free any space associated with the table within the InnoDB shared tablespace. Falcon similarly frees the table contents within the appropriate tablespace file.

For some storage engines, such as MyISAM, MERGE, or CSV, you can remove a table manually by removing the files in the database directory to which the table corresponds. For other storage engines, such as InnoDB, Falcon, or MEMORY, parts of the table might not be represented within the filesystem in table-specific files, so `DROP TABLE` does not have a filesystem command equivalent. For example, an InnoDB table that is stored in the shared tablespace is always uniquely associated with an `.frm` file, but removing that file does not properly drop the table. The InnoDB data dictionary must be updated by InnoDB itself, and removing the `.frm` file leaves the table data and indexes "stranded" within the shared tablespace.

If the InnoDB table has an individual tablespace, it is represented in the database directory by the `.frm` file and its own `.ibd` file. However, it is still not correct to "drop" the table by removing those files because that does not give InnoDB a change to update the data dictionary. It is necessary to use `DROP TABLE` so that InnoDB can remove the files *and* update the data dictionary.

11.2.6 Operating System Constraints on Database Object Names

MySQL has general rules for identifiers that name databases and other objects such as tables. The rules are detailed in Section 2.2, "MySQL Identifier Syntax and Naming Rules," but may be summarized briefly as follows:

- Unquoted identifiers may be constructed from the alphanumeric characters in the system character set (`utf8`), as well as the underscore and dollar characters ('_' and '$').
- Quoting an identifier within backticks enables it to contain other characters (for example, `` `odd?name!` ``). Quoting is also often necessary if you use an SQL reserved

word as an identifier. If the ANSI_QUOTES SQL mode is enabled, identifiers can be quoted within either backticks or double quotes.

- Identifiers may be up to 64 characters long.

In addition, the operating system on which a MySQL server runs may impose other constraints on identifiers. These stem from filesystem naming conventions because database and table names correspond to names of directories and files: Every database is represented in the filesystem by its database directory, and every table, no matter what storage engine is used, is represented in the filesystem by at least an .frm file. Therefore, these restrictions apply:

- MySQL allows database and table names to be up to 64 characters long, but the length of names is also bound by the length allowed by your operating system.
- Case sensitivity of the underlying filesystem affects how you name and refer to databases and tables. If the filesystem is case sensitive (as is typical for Unix), the two filenames abc and ABC refer to different files. If the filesystem is not case sensitive (as for Windows, or for HFS+ filesystems under Mac OS X), abc and ABC refer to the same file. You should keep this issue in mind if you develop a database on a server that uses case-sensitive filenames and there is a possibility you might move or replicate the database to a server where filenames are not case sensitive.

Before MySQL 5.1.6, additional filesystem-related naming constraints are enforced:

- Database and table names cannot contain characters that are illegal in filenames. However, the rules for legal characters vary per operating system, which means there are characters that MySQL might allow in a name but that you would be well advised to avoid. For example, by using a quoted identifier, you can include a '*' character in a table name on Unix. But Windows does not allow '*' characters in filenames, so you would not be able to replicate or move the table to Windows without renaming it first. It's best to stick with plain characters and avoid exotic ones.
- A database or table name cannot include the pathname separator character, even if quoted. On Unix and Windows, pathname components are separated by '/' and '\', respectively, and neither character may be used. Both are disallowed regardless of platform to make it easier to move databases and tables from one platform to another. (For example, if you were allowed to use '/' in the name of a table on Windows, you could not move or replicate the table to Unix.)

The problems just described that are caused by illegal or nonportable characters in filenames go away as of MySQL 5.1.6, because the server encodes special characters in identifiers that may be problematic in filenames. This encoding enables the restriction in names against '/', '\', and other characters to be lifted. In a name as used in SQL statements, any character outside the set of digits and Latin letters is mapped in the corresponding filename to '@' followed by an encoded character value. For example, '?' and '!' have encodings of `003f` and `0021`, so a table named `odd?name!` has an `.frm` file named `odd@003fname@0021.frm`. Other files associated with the table are named similarly.

If you upgrade to MySQL 5.1.6 or later from an older version, be sure to tell the server to re-encode any database and table names as necessary by using this command:

```
% mysqlcheck --all-databases --check-upgrade --fix-db-names --fix-table-names
```

As mentioned earlier, filesystem case sensitivity affects database and table naming. One way to deal with this issue is to always use names that have a given lettercase. Another is to run the server with the `lower_case_table_names` system variable set to 1, which has two effects:

- The server converts a table's name to lowercase before creating the corresponding disk files.
- When the table is referenced later in a statement, the server converts its name to lowercase before attempting to find the table on disk.

The result of these actions is that names uniformly are treated as not case sensitive, regardless of the filesystem case sensitivity. This makes it easier to move databases and tables between systems. However, if you plan to use this strategy, you should configure the server to set the `lower_case_table_names` variable *before* you start creating databases or tables, not after. If you set the variable after having already created databases or tables that have names that include uppercase characters, the setting will not have the desired effect because you will already have names stored on disk that are not entirely lowercase. To avoid this problem, rename any tables that have names containing uppercase characters to names that are entirely lowercase before setting `lower_case_table_names`. (To rename a table, use ALTER TABLE or RENAME TABLE.) If you have a lot of tables that need to be renamed, or databases that have names containing uppercase characters, it is easier to dump the databases and then re-create them after setting `lower_case_table_names`:

1. Dump each database using `mysqldump`:

   ```
   % mysqldump --databases db_name > db_name.sql
   ```

2. Drop each database with DROP DATABASE.
3. Stop the server, reconfigure it to set `lower_case_table_names`, and restart the server.
4. Reload each dump file using `mysql`:

   ```
   % mysql < db_name.sql
   ```

With `lower_case_table_names` set, each database and table will be re-created with a lowercase name on disk.

`lower_case_table_names` actually has several possible values. For more information, see Appendix D, "System, Status, and User Variable Reference."

Falcon handles database and table names in case-insensitive fashion, regardless of the actual `lower_case_table_names` setting.

11.2.7 Factors That Affect Maximum Table Size

Table sizes in MySQL are bounded, but sizes are limited by a combination of factors, so it is not always a simple matter to determine precisely what the bounds are.

The operating system imposes a maximum file-size limit. Limits as low as 2GB used to be common, but this is no longer true because the trend has been for operating systems to relax file size constraints over time. The operating system size limit applies to files used to represent tables, such as the `.MYD` and `.MYI` files for a MyISAM table. It also applies to the files that make up any InnoDB tablespace. However, the overall InnoDB shared table-space size can easily exceed the maximum file size: Just configure it to consist of multiple files, each of which can be the maximum file size. Another way to circumvent the file-size limit is to use raw partitions in the InnoDB tablespace. Tablespace components that are on raw partitions can be as large as the partition itself. Instructions for configuring InnoDB are given in Section 12.7.3.1, "Configuring the InnoDB Tablespace."

In addition to operating-system limits, MySQL has its own internal limits on table sizes. These vary by storage engine:

- For MyISAM tables, the `.MYD` and `.MYI` files are limited to 256TB apiece by default. However, by using the `AVG_ROW_LENGTH` and `MAX_ROWS` options when you create the table, the files can be up to 65,536TB each. (See the description of `CREATE TABLE` in Appendix E, "SQL Syntax Reference.") These options affect internal row pointer width, which determines the maximum number of rows the table can hold. If a MyISAM table has grown to its maximum size and you are getting error 135 or 136, you can use `ALTER TABLE` to increase the option values. To change the default MyISAM pointer width directly, set the `myisam_data_pointer_size` system variable; the new setting applies to tables created thereafter.

- The maximum size of a MERGE table is the sum of the maximum sizes of its constituent MyISAM tables.

- For InnoDB, the maximum size of the InnoDB shared tablespace is 4 billion pages, where the default page size is 16KB. (MySQL can be recompiled from source to use an InnoDB page size ranging from 8KB to 64KB.) The maximum tablespace size also is the bound on the size of any individual InnoDB table stored in the tablespace. If InnoDB is configured to use individual tablespaces, each table's contents are stored in its `.ibd` file. In this case, InnoDB table size is bound by operating system file-size limits.

- Falcon tablespace files have a maximum size of 128TB, and Falcon tables are limited to 2^{32} rows.

For storage engines that represent data and indexes in separate files, a table's size limit is reached when any of its individual files hits the file-size limit. For a MyISAM table, the table's indexing characteristics affect which file this will be. For a table with no or few indexes, it is likely that the data file will reach its size limit first. For a heavily indexed table, the index file may reach the limit first.

The presence of an AUTO_INCREMENT column implicitly limits the number of rows a table may have. For example, if the column is TINYINT UNSIGNED, the maximum value it may hold is 255, so that also becomes the maximum number of rows the table may hold. Larger integer types allow more rows. More generally, including any PRIMARY KEY or UNIQUE index in a table limits its row count to the maximum number of unique values in the index.

To determine the actual table size you can achieve, you must consider all applicable factors. The effective maximum table size likely will be determined by the smallest of those factors. Suppose that you want to create a MyISAM table. MySQL will allow the data and index files to reach 256TB each, using the default data pointer size. But if your operating system imposes a size limit on files of 2GB, that will be the effective limit for the table files. On the other hand, if your system supports files that can be larger than 256TB, the determining factor on table size then will be a MySQL factor, namely the internal data pointer size. This is a factor that you can control.

With respect to InnoDB tables that are stored in the shared tablespace, a single InnoDB table can grow as large as that tablespace and the tablespace can span multiple files to become quite large. But if, as is more likely, you have many InnoDB tables, they all share the same space and thus each is constrained in size not only by the size of the tablespace, but also by how much of the tablespace is allocated to other tables. Any individual InnoDB table can grow as long as the tablespace is not full. Conversely, when the tablespace fills up, no InnoDB table can grow any larger until you add another component to the tablespace to make it bigger. Alternatively, you can make the last tablespace component auto-extending, so that it will grow as long as it does not exceed the file-size limit of your system and disk space is available. See Section 12.7.3.1, "Configuring the InnoDB Tablespace," for details on tablespace configuration.

Falcon tablespace files grow automatically from their initial size but are limited to 128TB. You can create additional tablespaces and move tables from one tablespace to another should a given tablespace become too "crowded." Section 12.7.4, "Configuring the Falcon Storage Engine," discusses Falcon tablespace creation.

11.2.8 Implications of Data Directory Structure for System Performance

The structure of the MySQL data directory is easy to understand because it uses the hierarchical structure of the filesystem in such a natural way. At the same time, this structure has certain performance implications, particularly regarding operations that open the files that represent database tables.

One consequence of the data directory structure is that, for storage engines that represent individual tables each with their own files, each open table can require a file descriptor. If a table is represented by multiple files, opening the table requires multiple file descriptors, not just one. The server caches descriptors intelligently, but a busy server can easily use up lots of them while servicing many simultaneous client connections or executing complex statements that reference several tables. This can be a problem, because file descriptors are a scarce resource on many systems, particularly those that set the default per-process descriptor limit fairly low. An operating system that imposes a low limit and makes no provision for increasing it would not make a good choice for running a high-activity MySQL server.

Another effect of representing each table by its own files is that table-opening time increases with the number of tables. Operations that open tables map onto the file-opening operations provided by the operating system, and as such are bound by the efficiency of the system's directory-lookup routines. Normally this isn't much of an issue, but it is something to consider if you'll need large numbers of tables in a database. For example, a MyISAM table is represented by three files. If you want to have 10,000 MyISAM tables, your database directory will contain 30,000 files. With that many files, you may notice a slowdown due to the time taken by file-opening operations. If this is cause for concern, you might want to think about using a type of filesystem that is highly efficient at dealing with large numbers of files. For example, XFS or JFS exhibit good performance even with large numbers of small files. If it is not possible to choose a different filesystem, it may be necessary to re-evaluate the structure of your tables in relation to the needs of your applications and reorganize your tables accordingly. Consider whether you really require so many tables; sometimes applications multiply tables needlessly. An application that creates a separate table per user results in many tables, all of which have identical structures. If you wanted to combine the tables into a single table, you might be able to do so by adding another column identifying the user to which each row applies. If this significantly reduces the number of tables, the application's performance improves.

As always in database design, you must consider whether this particular strategy is worthwhile for a given application. Reasons not to combine tables in the manner just described are as follows:

- Increased disk space requirements. Combining tables reduces the number of tables required (decreasing table-opening times), but adds another column (increasing disk space requirements). This is a typical time versus space tradeoff and you'd need to decide which factor is most important. If speed is paramount, you'd probably be willing to sacrifice a little extra disk space. If space is tight, it might be more acceptable to use multiple tables and live with a slight delay.

- Security considerations. These may constrain your ability or desire to combine tables. One reason to use a separate table per user is to enable access to each table for only a single MySQL account by means of table-level privileges. If you combine tables, data for all users will be in the same table.

    MySQL has no provision for restricting access to particular rows to a given user; thus, you might not be able to combine tables without compromising access control. One possibility is to use views that select rows only for the current user, and grant access through the views. Alternatively, if all access to the data is controlled by your application (users never connect directly to the database), you can combine the tables and use application logic to enforce row-level access to the combined result.

Another way to create many tables without requiring so many individual files is to use InnoDB tables and store them in the InnoDB shared tablespace. In this case, the InnoDB storage engine associates only an .frm file uniquely with each table, and stores the data and index information for all InnoDB tables together. This minimizes the number of disk files needed to represent the tables, and it also substantially reduces the number of file descriptors required for open tables. InnoDB needs only one descriptor per component file of the tablespace (which is constant during the life of the server process), and briefly a descriptor for any table that it opens while it reads the table's .frm file.

A similar strategy can be used with Falcon, which enables the data and indexes of multiple tables to be stored in a single tablespace file.

11.2.9 MySQL Status and Log Files

In addition to database directories, the MySQL data directory contains a number of status and log files, as summarized in Table 11.1. The default location for each file is the server's data directory, and the default name for many of them is derived using the server host name, denoted as *HOSTNAME* in the table. The binary and relay logs are created as a numbered sequence of files, denoted by *nnnnnn*. The table lists only the server-level status and log files. Individual storage engines may create their own logs or other files. For example, InnoDB and Falcon do this.

Table 11.1   **MySQL Status and Log Files**

File Type	Default Name	File Contents
Process ID file	*HOSTNAME*.pid	The server process ID
Error log	*HOSTNAME*.err	Startup and shutdown events and error conditions
General query log	*HOSTNAME*.log	Connect/disconnect events and statement information
Binary log	*HOSTNAME*-bin.*nnnnnn*	Binary representation of statements that modify data
Binary log index	*HOSTNAME*-bin.index	List of current binary log files
Relay log	*HOSTNAME*-relay-bin.*nnnnnn*	Data modifications received by slave server from master
Relay log index	*HOSTNAME*-relay-bin.index	List of current relay log files
Master info file	master.info	Parameters for connecting to master server
Relay info file	relay-log.info	Status of relay log processing
Slow-query log	*HOSTNAME*-slow.log	Text of statements that take a long time to process

For the general query log and the slow-query log, you can select whether the server writes to a log file, to a log table in the `mysql` database, or both. Section 12.5.6, "Using Log Tables," describes logging to tables in more detail.

11.2.9.1 The Process ID File

The MySQL server writes its process ID (PID) into the PID file when it starts, and removes the file when it shuts down. Other processes can use this file to determine whether the server is running and what its process ID is if so. For example, if the operating system runs the `mysql.server` script at system shutdown time to stop the MySQL server, that script examines the PID file to determine which process it needs to send a termination signal to.

If the server cannot create the PID file (for example, if you run it on read-only media such as a CD-ROM), it writes a message to the error log and continues.

The PID file is not used by the embedded server, which needs no PID file because it is started and stopped by the application within which it is embedded.

11.2.9.2 The MySQL Logs

MySQL can maintain several types of log files. Most logging is optional; you use server startup options to enable just the logs you need and also to specify their names if you don't like the default names. Be aware that logs can grow quite large, so it's important to make sure they don't fill up your filesystem. You can expire the logs periodically to keep the amount of space that they use within bounds.

This section briefly describes a few of the log files. For more information about the logs, the options that control the server's logging behavior, and log expiration, see Section 12.5, "Maintaining Logs."

The error log contains a record of diagnostic information produced by the server when exceptional conditions occur. If the server fails to start up or exits unexpectedly, this log is useful because it will often contain the reason why.

The general query log provides general information about server operation: who is connecting from where and what statements they are issuing. The binary log contains statement information, too, but only for statements that modify database contents. It also contains information such as timestamps needed to keep slave servers synchronized when the server is a master server in a replication setup. The contents of the binary log are written in binary format as "events" that can be executed by providing them as input to the `mysql` client. The accompanying binary log index file lists which binary log files the server currently is maintaining.

The binary log is useful if you have a crash and must revert to backup files, because you can repeat the updates performed after the backup was made by feeding the log files to the server. This enables you to bring your databases up to the state they were in when the crash occurred. The binary log is also used if you set up replication servers, because it serves as a record of the updates that must be transmitted from a master server to slave servers. Backup procedures and replication are discussed in more detail in Chapter 14, "Database Maintenance, Backups, and Replication."

Here is a sample of the kind of information that appears in the general query log as the result of a short client session that creates a table in the test database, inserts a row into the table, and then drops the table:

```
080412 11:38:34      31 Connect      sampadm@localhost on sampdb
080412 11:38:42      31 Query        CREATE TABLE mytbl (val INT)
080412 11:38:47      31 Query        INSERT INTO mytbl VALUES(1)
080412 11:38:52      31 Query        DROP TABLE mytbl
080412 11:38:56      31 Quit
```

The general log contains columns for date and time, server thread ID (connection ID), event category, and event-specific information. For any line that is missing the date and time fields, the values are the same as for the previous line that does have them. (In other words, the server logs the date and time only when they change from the previously logged date and time.)

The same session appears in the binary log as follows when viewed by displaying its contents with the mysqlbinlog program. (The output is slightly reformatted to accommodate long lines.) The statements include terminating semicolons, allowing them to be given as input to the mysql program should the updates need to be repeated for a database recovery operation. Comment lines begin with '#' characters.

```
# at 1222
#080412 11:38:42 server id 1  log_pos 1222      Query   thread_id=31
exec_time=0      error_code=0
use sampdb;
SET TIMESTAMP=1092328722;
CREATE TABLE mytbl (val INT);
# at 1287
#080412 11:38:47 server id 1  log_pos 1287      Query   thread_id=31
exec_time=0      error_code=0
SET TIMESTAMP=1092328727;
INSERT INTO mytbl VALUES(1);
# at 1351
#080412 11:38:52 server id 1  log_pos 1351      Query   thread_id=31
exec_time=0      error_code=0
SET TIMESTAMP=1092328732;
DROP TABLE mytbl;
```

It's a good idea to make sure that your log files are secure and not readable by arbitrary users, because they may contain the text of statements that include sensitive information such as passwords. For example, the following log entry displays the password for the root user; it's certainly not the kind of information you want just anyone to have access to:

```
080412 16:47:24      44 Query      SET PASSWORD FOR
                                    'root'@'localhost'=PASSWORD('secret')
```

The server writes log files to the data directory by default, so a good precaution for securing your logs is to secure the data directory against being accessed on the server host by login accounts other than the one used by the MySQL administrator. For details of this procedure, see Section 13.1.2, "Securing Your MySQL Installation."

11.3 Relocating Data Directory Contents

Earlier parts of this chapter discuss the data directory structure in its default configuration, which is that all databases, status files, and log files are located within it. However, you have some latitude in determining the placement of the data directory's contents. MySQL enables you to relocate the data directory itself or certain elements within it. There are several reasons why you might want to do this:

- The filesystem that contains the data directory has become full and you need to move it to a filesystem with more capacity.

- If your data directory is on a busy disk drive, you can put it on a less active drive to balance disk activity across physical devices. You can put databases and log files on different drives or distribute databases across drives for the same reasons. Similarly, the InnoDB shared tablespace is conceptually a single large block of storage, but you can put its individual component files on different drives to improve performance. If you use partitioned tables, you can do the same with individual table partitions.

- Putting databases on one disk and logs on another disk helps minimize the damage that can be caused by a failure of a single disk.

- You might want to run multiple servers, each with its own data directory. This is one way to work around problems with per-process file descriptor limits, especially if you cannot reconfigure the kernel for your system to enable higher limits.

The rest of this section discusses which parts of the data directory can be moved and how you go about making such changes.

11.3.1 Relocation Methods

There are two ways to relocate the data directory or elements within it.

First, on any platform, you can specify an option at server startup, either on the command line or in an option file. For example, to specify the data directory location, start the server with a `--datadir=dir_name` option on the command line or put the following lines in an option file:

```
[mysqld]
datadir=dir_name
```

Typically, the option file group name for server options is `[mysqld]`, as shown in the example. However, depending on your circumstances, other option group names may be more appropriate. For example, the `[embedded]` group applies to the embedded server. If you're running multiple servers using `mysqld_multi`, the group names will be of the form [mysqld*n*], where *n* is some integer associated with a particular server instance. Section 12.2.3, "Specifying Server Startup Options," discusses which option groups apply to different server startup methods, and also provides instructions for running multiple servers.

Second, on Unix, you can move the file or directory to be relocated, and then make a symlink (symbolic link) in the original location that points to the new location.

Neither of these methods works universally for everything that you can relocate. Table 11.2 summarizes what can be relocated and which relocation methods can be used. If you use an option file, it is possible to specify options in a global option file such as /etc/my.cnf under Unix or C:\my.ini on Windows.

Table 11.2   **Relocation Method Summary**

Entity to Relocate	Applicable Relocation Methods
Entire data directory	Startup option or symlink
Individual database directories	Symlink
Individual database tables	Symlink
InnoDB tablespace files	Startup option
Server PID file	Startup option
Log files	Startup option

11.3.2 Relocation Precautions

Before you attempt to relocate anything, it is prudent to make a backup of your data so that you can restore it if you mess up the relocation operation. Also, you should stop the MySQL server before relocating, and then restart it afterward. For certain types of relocations, such as moving a database directory, it is sometimes *possible* to keep the server running, but not recommended. If you do that, you must make sure that the server is not accessing the database you're moving. You should also be sure to issue a FLUSH TABLES statement before moving the database to make sure that the server closes all open table files. Failure to observe these precautions can result in damaged tables.

11.3.3 Assessing the Effect of Relocation

Before attempting to relocate anything, it's a good idea to verify that the operation will have the desired effect. For example, on Unix, you can use the du, df, and ls -l commands for obtaining disk space information. However, you must correctly understand the layout of your filesystem for any of these to be useful.

The following example illustrates a subtle trap to watch out for when assessing a data directory relocation. Suppose that your data directory is /usr/local/mysql/data and you want to move it to `/var/mysql` because `df` indicates the `/var` filesystem has more free space:

```
% df -k /usr /var
Filesystem          1K-blocks       Used Available Use% Mounted on
/dev/sda5           28834716K 24078024K  3291968K  88% /usr
/dev/sda6           28834716K  9175456K 18194536K  34% /var
```

To find out how much space relocating the data directory should free up on the `/usr` filesystem, use `du -s`:

```
% du -s /usr/local/mysql/data
3264308K /usr/local/mysql/data
```

This result indicates that moving the `data` directory from `/usr` to `var` should free about 3GB on `/usr`. But would it really? To find out, try `df` in the data directory. Suppose that you get output like this:

```
% df -k /usr/local/mysql/data
Filesystem          1K-blocks       Used Available Use% Mounted on
/dev/sda6           28834716K  9175456K 18194536K  34% /var
```

That's odd. Why does `df` report the space on the `/var` filesystem? The following `ls -l` command provides the answer:

```
% ls -l /usr/local/mysql/data
lrwxrwxr-x  1 mysql  mysql  10 Dec 11 23:46 data -> /var/mysql
```

This output shows that `/usr/local/mysql/data` is a symlink to `/var/mysql`. In other words, the data directory *already* has been relocated to the `/var` filesystem and replaced with a symlink that points there. So much for freeing up a lot of space on `/usr` by moving the data directory to `/var`!

The lesson here is that a few moments spent assessing the effect of relocation can keep you from wasting a lot of time moving things around, only to find that you've failed to achieve your objective.

11.3.4 Relocating the Entire Data Directory

To relocate the data directory, stop the MySQL server, and then move the data directory to its new location. After the move, you should restart the server with a `--datadir` option that explicitly indicates the new location. On Unix, an alternative to using `--datadir` is to create a symbolic link in the original data directory location that points to the new location.

11.3.5 Relocating Individual Databases

The server always looks for database directories in the data directory, so the only way to relocate a database is by the symlink method. The procedure for this differs for Unix and Windows.

Under Unix, relocate a database as follows:

1. Stop the server if it is running.

2. Move the database directory to its new location, or copy it and remove the original.

3. Create a symlink in the data directory that has the name of the original database and that points to the new database location.

4. Restart the server.

The following example shows how to relocate a database `bigdb` from the `/usr/local/mysql/data` directory to `/var/db`:

```
% mysqladmin -p -u root shutdown
Enter password: ******
% cd /usr/local/mysql/data
% tar cf - bigdb | (cd /var/db; tar xf -)
% rm -rf bigdb
% ln -s /var/db/bigdb bigdb
% mysqld_safe &
```

You should execute these commands while logged in as the MySQL administrator. Under Windows, database relocation is handled somewhat differently:

1. Stop the server if it is running.

2. Move the database directory to its new location, or copy it and remove the original.

3. Create a file in the MySQL data directory that acts as a symbolic link to let the MySQL server know where to find the relocated database directory. The file should have a `.sym` extension and a basename that is the database name. For example, if you move the `sampdb` database from `C:\mysql\data\sampdb` to `E:\mysql-book\sampdb`, you should create a file named `C:\mysql\data\sampdb.sym` that contains this line:

   ```
   E:\mysql-book\sampdb\
   ```

4. Make sure that symbolic link support is enabled when you restart the server. Windows servers should have this enabled by default, but you can enable it explicitly by using the `--symbolic-links` option on the command line or by placing these lines in an option file:

   ```
   [mysqld]
   symbolic-links
   ```

If you're moving a database to another filesystem as an attempt to redistribute database storage, remember that if you are using InnoDB tables that are stored in the InnoDB shared tablespace, the contents of those tables are *not* located in the database directory. For a database composed primarily of such InnoDB tables, relocating the database directory will relocate only their `.frm` files, not their contents. This will have little effect on storage distribution.

Similarly, Falcon table contents are stored in Falcon tablespace files, not in database directories.

11.3.6 Relocating Individual Tables

Relocation of an individual table is supported only under certain limited circumstances:

- You must be using Unix and the table to be relocated must be a MyISAM table.

- Your operating system must have a working `realpath()` system call. If you do, the result of the following query will be YES:

```
mysql> SHOW VARIABLES LIKE 'have_symlink';
+---------------+-------+
| Variable_name | Value |
+---------------+-------+
| have_symlink  | YES   |
+---------------+-------+
```

If both of those conditions are true, you can move the table's `.MYD` data and `.MYI` index files to their new locations and then create symlinks to them in the database directory under the original data and index filenames. (Leave the `.frm` file in the database directory.) Before doing this, either stop the server while you move the files, or lock the table to prevent the server from using it, as described in Section 14.2, "Performing Database Maintenance with the Server Running."

11.3.7 Relocating the InnoDB Shared Tablespace

You configure the InnoDB shared tablespace initially by listing the locations of its component files in an option file, using the `innodb_data_home_dir` and `innodb_data_file_path` options. (For details on configuring the shared tablespace, see Section 12.7.3.1, "Configuring the InnoDB Tablespace.") If you have already created the tablespace, it's possible to relocate regular files that are part of it; for example, to distribute them across different filesystems. Because you list the file locations using startup options, the way to relocate some or all of the tablespace files is as follows:

1. Stop the server if it is running.

2. Move the tablespace file or files that you want to relocate.

3. Update the option file where the InnoDB configuration is defined, to reflect the new locations of any files that you moved.

4. Restart the server.

11.3.8 Relocating Status and Log Files

To relocate the PID file or a log file, stop the server, and then restart it with the appropriate option to specify the file's new location. For example, to create the PID file as `/tmp/mysql.pid`, use `--pid-file=/tmp/mysql.pid` on the command line or include these lines in an option file:

```
[mysqld]
pid-file=/tmp/mysql.pid
```

If you specify the filename as an absolute pathname, the server creates the file using that pathname. If you use a relative name, the server creates the file under the data directory. For example, if you specify `--pid-file=mysqld.pid`, the PID file will be `mysqld.pid` in the data directory.

Some systems keep server PID files in a specific directory, such as `/var/run`. You might want to put the MySQL PID file there, too, for consistency of system operation. In similar fashion, if your system uses `/var/log` for log files, you can put the MySQL logs there, too. However, many systems allow only `root` to write to these directories. That means you'd need to run the server as `root`, which for security reasons is not a good idea. What you can do instead is create subdirectories `/var/run/mysql` and `/var/log/mysql` and set them to be owned by the account you use for running the server. For example, if that account has user and group names of `mysql`, you can execute the following commands as `root`:

```
# mkdir /var/run/mysql
# chown mysql /var/run/mysql
# chgrp mysql /var/run/mysql
# chmod u=rwx,go-rwx /var/run/mysql
# mkdir /var/log/mysql
# chown mysql /var/log/mysql
# chgrp mysql /var/log/mysql
# chmod u=rwx,go-rwx /var/log/mysql
```

Then the server won't have any problems writing files in those directories and you can start it with options that specify files there. For example:

```
[mysqld]
pid-file = /var/run/mysql/mysql.pid
log-error = /var/log/mysql/log.err
log = /var/log/mysql/querylog
log-bin = /var/log/mysql/binlog
```

For more information about log file options and how to use them, see Section 12.5, "Maintaining Logs."

12

General MySQL Administration

This chapter discusses the responsibilities that you must carry out to keep MySQL running smoothly if you administer MySQL at your site:

- Securing your MySQL setup after installing it
- Making sure that the server is up and running as much of the time as possible
- Setting up user accounts so that clients can access the server
- Maintaining server logs
- Modifying and monitoring the server's operating parameters for better performance
- Running multiple servers
- Determining whether and when to upgrade MySQL to a newer version

Other significant administrative concerns are covered in Chapter 13, "Access Control and Security," and Chapter 14, "Database Maintenance, Backups, and Replication."

This chapter covers several programs that are essential for MySQL administrators to know about:

- `mysqld` is the MySQL server.
- `mysqld_safe`, `mysql.server`, and `mysqld_multi` are used for starting the server.
- `mysqladmin` performs miscellaneous administrative operations.

Much of the information in this chapter can be better appreciated if you have an understanding of MySQL's data directory, which is where the server stores databases, log files, and other information. For details, see Chapter 11, "The MySQL Data Directory." For additional information specific to the SQL statements and programs discussed here, see Appendix E, "SQL Syntax Reference," and Appendix F, "MySQL Program Reference."

> **Note**
>
> For simplicity (and to keep pathnames shorter), most of the Windows-related material in this chapter assumes that MySQL is installed at `C:\mysql`. However, the MySQL installation wizard for Windows likes to install the distribution under `C:\Program Files\MySQL\MySQL`

Server *X.Y*, where *X.Y* is a number like 5.0 or 5.1. If you use that installation location, be sure to adjust Windows pathnames shown in this chapter accordingly.

12.1 Securing a New MySQL Installation

Let's begin by covering an administrative task that you should perform immediately after installing MySQL: Making sure that the server can be accessed only by authorized users. This is a matter of understanding which MySQL user accounts are created during installation, setting up passwords for those that are needed, and removing the rest.

The MySQL installation procedure sets up the server's data directory and populates it with two databases:

- A mysql database containing the grant tables that control access by clients to the server
- A test database that can be used for testing purposes

If you've just installed MySQL for the first time (for example, using the instructions in Appendix A, "Obtaining and Installing Software."), the grant tables in the mysql database contain accounts in their initial state that enables anyone to connect to the server without a password. This is insecure, so you should assign passwords to these accounts. If you're upgrading MySQL by installing a newer version on top of an existing installation for which the grant tables are already set up, passwords probably have already been assigned. If you're setting up a second installation on a machine that already has MySQL installed in another location, you'll need to set up passwords for the new server. However, in this case, you might run into the complication that passwords might be picked up from option files created for the existing installation, as discussed in Section 12.1.3, "Setting Up Passwords for a Second Server."

For concreteness, the examples in the following discussion assume that you are running the MySQL server on a machine with a hostname of cobra.snake.net and that you will be connecting to the server from that same machine. Whenever you see that hostname in the instructions, substitute the name of your own server host. The examples also assume that your MySQL server has already been started, because you'll need to connect to it.

> **Note**
>
> Some MySQL installers give you the option of creating passwords during the installation procedure, but even if you use one of those installers, the information here will help you better understand the initial MySQL user accounts. The following discussion assumes that you have not yet established any passwords. An installer may also give you the option of creating only some of the initial accounts described here, in which case you need not deal with those not created.

12.1.1 Establishing Passwords for the Initial MySQL Accounts

This section describes how to check which accounts are present in your grant tables and how to set their passwords.

The grant tables in the mysql database are set up during the MySQL installation procedure with two kinds of accounts:

- Accounts that have a username of root. These are superuser accounts intended for administrative purposes. The root accounts have all privileges and can do anything, including deleting all your databases and shutting down the server. (The fact that the MySQL and Unix superuser accounts both have the name root is coincidental. Each has exceptional privileges, but they have nothing to do with each other.)

- Accounts that have a blank username. These are "anonymous" accounts; they enable people to connect to the server without having accounts explicitly set up for them in advance. Anonymous users usually are given very few privileges, to limit the scope of what they can do. (On Windows, versions of MySQL prior to 5.0.36/5.1.16 may include an anonymous account that has superuser privileges, which you should handle as described later in this section.)

Every account known to a MySQL server is listed in the user table of its mysql database, so that's where you'll find the initial accounts. None of these accounts have passwords by default, because it's expected that you'll supply your own. Therefore, one of your first acts in administering a MySQL installation should be to establish passwords. Otherwise, unauthorized users can gain superuser access to your server by connecting as root. After you secure the initial accounts, you can proceed to set up other accounts to enable the members of your user community to connect to the server under names that you specify and with privileges appropriate for what those users should be allowed to do. Section 12.4, "Managing MySQL User Accounts," provides instructions for setting up new accounts and modifying existing ones.

Each entry (row) in the user table contains a Host value that indicates the host from which a user can connect, and User and Password values that indicate the name and password the user must give when connecting from that host. The user table also has a number of columns that indicate what superuser privileges each account has.

To see what accounts are present and whether they have passwords, connect to the server as root and query the mysql.user table. This should be possible without specifying a password because even root has no password initially:

```
% mysql -u root
mysql> SELECT Host, User, Password FROM mysql.user;
+-----------------+------+----------+
| Host            | User | Password |
+-----------------+------+----------+
| localhost       | root |          |
| cobra.snake.net | root |          |
| 127.0.0.1       | root |          |
| localhost       |      |          |
| cobra.snake.net |      |          |
+-----------------+------+----------+
```

The output that you see on your own server may not be exactly the same as shown here, but each account that you see with a blank Password value is one to which you should assign a password.

Under Unix, the data directory is initialized during the installation procedure by the mysql_install_db script. If you install MySQL on Linux from RPM packages on or Mac OS X using a DMG package, mysql_install_db is run for you automatically. Otherwise, you run it yourself. See Appendix A for details.

One purpose of mysql_install_db is to set up the grant tables in the mysql database. On a server host named cobra.snake.net, mysql_install_db initializes the user table with the accounts shown in the following table.

Host	User	Password	Superuser Privileges
localhost	root		All
127.0.0.1	root		All
cobra.snake.net	root		All
localhost			None
cobra.snake.net			None

These user table account entries enable connections by client programs as follows:

- The root entries enable you to connect to the local MySQL server, using a hostname of localhost, 127.0.0.1, or cobra.snake.net. For example, if you invoke the mysql program while logged in on cobra.snake.net, you can connect as root using either of these commands:

```
% mysql -h localhost -u root
% mysql -h cobra.snake.net -u root
```

As root, you have all privileges and can perform any operation.

- The entries with blank User values are the anonymous accounts. They enable connections to the local MySQL server, using a hostname of localhost or cobra.snake.net, and without specifying any username:

```
% mysql -h localhost
% mysql -h cobra.snake.net
```

Anonymous users have no superuser privileges.

Under Windows, the data directory and the mysql database are included pre-initialized with the MySQL distribution, with accounts that are somewhat different from those on Unix systems. The Windows user table entries look like those in the following table.

Host	User	Password	Superuser Privileges
localhost	root		All
127.0.0.1	root		All
localhost			Depends on version

These `user` table account entries enable connections by client programs as follows:

- You can connect as `root` from the local host. As `root`, you have all privileges and can perform any operation.
- You can connect anonymously with no username from the local host. For current versions of MySQL, this account has no superuser privileges. Before MySQL 5.0.36/5.1.16, the account has the same superuser privileges as `root` and can do anything. In this case, you may want to revoke those privileges in addition to assigning a password to the account, or perhaps just delete the account entirely.

Another grant table (the `db` table, not shown) contains privilege information that enables anonymous users to use the `test` database or any database having a name that begins with `test_`.

The rest of this section describes how to set the `root` and anonymous-user passwords. The examples use a representative set of accounts, but the particular set of SQL statements that you'll need to use depends on which accounts actually are present on your system.

Depending on how you assign passwords, you may also need to tell the server to reload the grant tables so that it notices the change. The server performs access control using in-memory copies of the grant tables. For some methods of changing passwords in the `user` table, the server may not recognize that you've changed anything, so you must explicitly tell it to re-read the tables.

One password-assignment method is to connect to the server as `root`, determine which accounts have no password, and use a SET PASSWORD statement for each one. Suppose that you connect to the server and find that the following accounts have no password:

```
% mysql -u root
mysql> SELECT Host, User FROM mysql.user WHERE Password = '';
+-----------------+------+
| Host            | User |
+-----------------+------+
| localhost       | root |
| cobra.snake.net | root |
| 127.0.0.1       | root |
| localhost       |      |
| cobra.snake.net |      |
+-----------------+------+
```

These accounts can be assigned passwords with SET PASSWORD statements. Each statement should specify an account name in `'user_name'@'host_name'` format, using the

User and Host values of the user table row that you want to modify. (If the User value is blank, the *user_name* value is `''`, the empty string.) To set the root and anonymous-user passwords for the accounts just shown, use the following statements:

```
mysql> SET PASSWORD FOR 'root'@'localhost' = PASSWORD('rootpass');
mysql> SET PASSWORD FOR 'root'@'cobra.snake.net' = PASSWORD('rootpass');
mysql> SET PASSWORD FOR 'root'@'127.0.0.1' = PASSWORD('rootpass');
mysql> SET PASSWORD FOR ''@'localhost' = PASSWORD('anonpass');
mysql> SET PASSWORD FOR ''@'cobra.snake.net' = PASSWORD('anonpass');
```

An alternative to SET PASSWORD is to modify the user table directly with UPDATE. This method can be used to specify a password for all accounts with a given User value, regardless of their Host value, and thus modify multiple accounts simultaneously. To set the password for all root accounts and all anonymous-user accounts, use these statements:

```
mysql> UPDATE mysql.user SET Password=PASSWORD('rootpass') WHERE User='root';
mysql> UPDATE mysql.user SET Password=PASSWORD('anonpass') WHERE User='';
mysql> FLUSH PRIVILEGES;
```

When you use SET PASSWORD to change passwords, the server notices that you've made a change to the grant tables and automatically re-reads them to refresh its in-memory copy of the tables. If you use UPDATE to modify the user table directly, it's necessary to explicitly tell the server to reload the tables. That's the purpose of the FLUSH PRIVILEGES statement following the UPDATE statements.

On Windows, if an anonymous-user account with the same superuser privileges as root is present, that is likely more power than you want the account to have. If you want to retain the account but with no superuser privileges, you can revoke them. Check which privileges the account has with this statement:

```
mysql> SHOW GRANTS for ''@'localhost';
```

If the account has no superuser privileges, the output will look like this and you need take no further action:

```
+------------------------------------+
| Grants for @localhost              |
+------------------------------------+
| GRANT USAGE ON *.* TO ''@'localhost' |
+------------------------------------+
```

If the account has superuser privileges, you'll see this instead:

```
+-----------------------------------------------------------------+
| Grants for @localhost                                           |
+-----------------------------------------------------------------+
| GRANT ALL PRIVILEGES ON *.* TO ''@'localhost' WITH GRANT OPTION |
+-----------------------------------------------------------------+
```

To revoke the account's privileges, use these REVOKE statements:

```
mysql> REVOKE ALL ON *.* FROM ''@'localhost';
mysql> REVOKE GRANT OPTION ON *.* FROM ''@'localhost';
```

Another option for dealing with anonymous-user accounts is to remove them entirely. I recommend this if you have no need for them. To remove the accounts, use DROP USER:

```
mysql> DROP USER ''@'localhost';
mysql> DROP USER ''@'cobra.snake.net';
```

The main benefit of removing the anonymous-user accounts is that it significantly simplifies the task of setting up non-anonymous accounts. Otherwise, you may have to deal with the curious phenomenon described in Section 13.2.3, "A Privilege Puzzle." You can read that section for the details behind this phenomenon.

For REVOKE and DROP USER, the server automatically re-reads the grant tables and no FLUSH PRIVILEGES statement is needed.

Now that you have established the account passwords (and reloaded the grant tables if necessary), the appropriate password is needed for each attempt to connect to the server. In particular, no one can connect as root without knowing the password:

```
% mysql -u root
ERROR 1045 (28000): Access denied for user 'root'@'localhost'
(using password: NO)
% mysql -p -u root
Enter password: rootpass
mysql>
```

The need to specify a password when connecting to the server from this point on will be true not just for mysql, but also for other programs such as mysqladmin and mysqldump. For brevity, many of the examples in later sections of this chapter do not show the -u or -p options. I assume that you'll add them as necessary whenever you connect to the server.

12.1.2 Setting Up Passwords for a Second Server

The preceding instructions assume that you're establishing passwords on a system that hasn't had MySQL installed on it before. However, if MySQL is already installed in one location and you're setting the passwords for a new server installed in a second location on the same machine, you may find when you attempt to connect to the new server without a password that it rejects the attempt with the following error:

```
% mysql -u root
ERROR 1045 (28000): Access denied for user 'root'@'localhost'
(using password: YES)
```

Hm! Why did the server say it received a password, when you didn't specify one? This usually indicates that you have an option file set up that contains the password for accessing the previously installed server. mysql finds the option file and automatically uses the password listed there. To override that and explicitly specify "no password," use a -p option and press Enter when mysql prompts for the password:

```
% mysql -p -u root
Enter password:              ← just press Enter
```

You can use this strategy when you invoke `mysqladmin` or other MySQL client programs as well.

Additional discussion on using several servers can be found in Section 12.10, "Running Multiple Servers."

12.2 Arranging for MySQL Server Startup and Shutdown

One general goal that you have as a MySQL administrator is to make sure that the server, `mysqld`, is running as much of the time as possible so that your users can access it. Occasionally, however, it's necessary to stop the server. For example, if you're relocating a database, you can't have the server updating tables in that database at the same time, so you must shut it down. The tension between the desire to keep the server running and the need to stop it occasionally is something this book can't resolve for you. But we can at least discuss how to get the server started and stopped so that you have the ability to perform either operation as you see fit. Many aspects of the procedures for this are different for Unix and Windows, so the following discussion covers them separately.

12.2.1 Running the MySQL Server On Unix

On Unix, the MySQL server can be started manually from the command line. It's also possible to arrange for the server to run automatically at system boot time as part of the standard startup procedure. (This is in fact probably how you'll start the server under normal operating conditions after you get everything set up the way you want.) But before discussing how to start the server, let's consider which login account should be used to start it. On a multi-user operating system such as Unix, you have a choice about which login account to use for running the server. If you start the server manually, it runs as the Unix user you happen to be logged in as. For example, if I log in as `paul` and start the server, it runs as `paul`. If instead I use the `su` command to switch user to `root` and then start the server, it runs as `root`.

Keep in mind two goals for your MySQL server startup procedures under Unix:

The server should run as some user other than `root`. To say the server runs "as" a given user means that the server process is associated with the user ID of that user's Unix login account, and that it has that user's privileges for reading and writing files in the filesystem. This has certain security implications, particularly for processes that run as the `root` user, because `root` is enabled to do anything, however dangerous. One way to avoid these dangers is to have the server relinquish its special privileges. Processes that start as `root` have the capability to change their user ID to that of another account and thus give up `root`'s privileges in exchange for those of a regular unprivileged user. This makes the process less dangerous. In general, you should limit the power of any process unless it really needs `root` access, and `mysqld` in particular does not. The server needs to access and manage the contents of the MySQL data directory, but little else. This means that if the server starts as `root`, you should tell it to change its user ID during startup to run as an unprivileged user.

The server should run as the same user every time it executes. It's inconsistent for the server to run with one user's privileges sometimes and with another user's privileges other times. That leads to files and directories being created under the data directory with varying ownerships, and results in the server not being able to access certain databases or tables depending on who it runs as. By consistently running the server as the same user, you avoid this problem.

12.2.1.1 Running the Server Using an Unprivileged Login Account

Using a separate, unprivileged account rather than `root` for MySQL-related activity has several benefits:

- If you do not run the server as `root`, no one can exploit it as a security hole to gain `root` access.

- As it runs, the server will create files owned by the `mysql` account rather than by `root`. For example, MySQL users who have the `FILE` privilege cannot cause the server to write `root`-owned files. The fewer such files on your system, the better.

- It's safer to perform MySQL administrative tasks while you are logged in as an unprivileged user than as `root`. If you make a mistake while performing a filesystem operation as `root`, the consequences can be devastating.

- It's cleaner conceptually and administratively to create a separate account that is devoted exclusively to MySQL activity. It's also easier to see what things on your system are MySQL related. For example, in the directory where `crontab` files are kept, you'll have a separate file for the MySQL user, `mysql`. Otherwise, the MySQL cron jobs will be listed in `root`'s `crontab` file, along with everything else done as `root` on a periodic basis.

To set up `mysqld` to run as an unprivileged non-`root` user, follow this procedure:

1. Stop the server if it's running:

   ```
   % mysqladmin -p -u root shutdown
   ```

2. Choose which login account to use for running `mysqld`. You can also designate a group name specifically for use with MySQL. Here, we'll use `mysql` for both the user and group names. If you use different names, substitute them anywhere you see `mysql` used as a user or group name elsewhere in this book. For example, if you install MySQL under your own account because you have no special administrative privileges on your system, you'll probably also run the server as yourself. In this case, substitute your own login name and group name for `mysql`.

3. If necessary, create the login account for the username you've chosen, using your system's usual account-creation procedure. You'll need to do this as `root`.

   Should you elect to use the account named `mysql` for running the server, you might not need to create it yourself. If you install MySQL on Linux using an RPM package, the installation procedure creates the account automatically. Current versions of

Mac OS X come with a `mysql` account already set up. Other systems might do the same.

4. Modify the user and group ownership of the MySQL data directory and any subdirectories and files under it so that the `mysql` user owns them. For example, if the data directory is `/usr/local/mysql/data`, you can set up ownership for that directory and its contents as follows:

```
# chown -R mysql /usr/local/mysql/data
# chgrp -R mysql /usr/local/mysql/data
```

Run those commands as `root`.

5. It's a good security precaution to set the access mode of the data directory to keep other people out of it. To do this, modify its permissions so that it can be accessed only by the `mysql` user. If the data directory is `/usr/local/mysql/data`, you can set up everything in and under it to be accessible only to `mysql` by turning off all the "group" and "other" permissions as follows:

```
# chmod -R go-rwx /usr/local/mysql/data
```

The last couple of steps actually are part of a more comprehensive lockdown procedure that is detailed in Section 13.1.2, "Securing Your MySQL Installation." Be sure to check that section for additional instructions on making ownership and mode assignments, particularly if your MySQL installation has a nonstandard layout.

After completing the preceding procedure, you should make sure always to start the server with an option of `--user=mysql` so that it will switch its user ID to `mysql` if it's invoked by `root`. This is true both for when you run the server manually as `root`, and for setting up the server to be invoked during your system's startup procedure. Unix systems perform startup operations as the Unix `root` user, so any processes initiated as part of that procedure execute by default with `root` privileges.

The best way to ensure that the user is specified consistently is to list it in an option file that the server reads. For example, put the following lines in `/etc/my.cnf`:

```
[mysqld]
user=mysql
```

For more information on option files, see Section 12.2.3, "Specifying Server Startup Options."

If you happen to start the server while logged in as `mysql`, the presence of the `user` line in your option file will result in a warning to the effect that the option can be used only by `root`. This means that the server does not have the capability to change its user ID and will run as `mysql`. That's what you want anyway, so just ignore the warning.

12.2.1.2 Starting the Server on Unix

After deciding which login account to use for running the server, you have several choices about how to start it. It's possible to run the server manually from the command line or automatically during the system startup procedure. Methods for doing this include the following:

- **Invoke** `mysqld` **directly.** This is probably the least common method. I won't discuss it further, except to say that the following command is useful for finding out what startup options the server supports:

    % **mysqld --verbose --help**

- **Invoke the** `mysqld_safe` **script.** `mysqld_safe` invokes the server for you and then monitors it and restarts it if it terminates abnormally. `mysqld_safe` commonly is used on BSD-style versions of Unix, and it also is invoked by `mysql.server` on non-BSD systems and on Mac OS X.

    `mysqld_safe` redirects error messages and other diagnostic output from the server to `syslog` or to a file in the data directory to produce an error log. If you send error output to a file, `mysqld_safe` sets the ownership of the file so that it is owned by the login account named by the `--user` option. This can lead to trouble if you to use different `--user` values at different times. The symptom is that `mysqld_safe`'s attempt to write to the error log file will fail with a "permission denied" error. This can be especially problematic because if you examine the error log to see what the difficulty is, it will contain no useful information related to the cause! If this problem occurs, remove the error log file and invoke `mysqld_safe` again.

- **Invoke the** `mysqld.server` **script.** `mysql.server` starts the server by executing `mysqld_safe`. This script can be invoked with an argument of `start` or `stop` to indicate whether you want the server to start or stop. It serves as a wrapper around `mysqld_safe` and commonly is used on systems that employ the System V method of arranging startup and shutdown scripts into several directories. Each directory corresponds to a particular run level and contains scripts to be invoked when the machine enters or exits that run level.

- **To coordinate several servers, use the** `mysqld_multi` **script.** This script reads an option file in which you list startup parameters for multiple servers. It enables you to start or stop each one, or check whether it is running. This startup script is more complicated than the others, so I'll defer discussion to Section 12.10, "Running Multiple Servers."

The `mysqld_safe` and `mysqld_multi` scripts are installed in the `bin` directory under the MySQL installation directory or can be found in the `scripts` directory of MySQL source distributions. The `mysql.server` script is installed under the `share/mysql` directory under the MySQL installation directory or can be found in the `support-files` directory of MySQL source distributions. If you want to use `mysql.server`, you might need to copy it to the proper run-level directory and make it executable. (Some installation methods install `mysql.server` for you. Linux RPM and Mac OS X DMG packages do so, for example.) If you use a MySQL RPM obtained from another vendor, a similar startup script might be installed under a different name, such as `mysqld`.

The type of system you have determines the arrangements that you'll need to make to have a startup script execute at system boot time. Read through the following examples and use or adapt the instructions that most closely match the startup procedures for your system.

For BSD-style systems, it's common to have a few files in the /etc directory that initiate services at boot time. These files often have names that begin with rc, and it's likely that there will be a file named rc.local (or something similar) intended specifically for starting locally installed services. On an rc-based system, you might add lines such as the following to rc.local to start the server:

```
if [ -x /usr/local/bin/mysqld_safe ]; then
  /usr/local/bin/mysqld_safe &
fi
```

Modify the lines appropriately if the pathname to mysqld_safe is different on your system.

For System V-style systems, you can install mysql.server. Copy it to the appropriate run-level directory under /etc. This may have been done for you already if you run Linux and installed MySQL from an RPM package. Otherwise, install the script in the main startup script directory with the name you want to use, make sure the script is executable, and place links to it in the appropriate run-level directory.

> **Note**
>
> Normally, you install mysql.server into the run-level directory under the name mysql, but I'll generally continue to discuss it as mysql.server to make it clear what I'm referring to.

The layout for run-level directories varies from system to system, so you'll need to check to see how your system organizes them. For example, under Solaris, the general multi-user run level is 2. The main script directory is /etc/init.d, and the run-level directory is /etc/rc2.d, so the commands would look like this:

```
# cp mysql.server /etc/init.d/mysql
# cd /etc/init.d
# chmod +x mysql
# cd /etc/rc2.d
# ln -s ../init.d/mysql S99mysql
```

At system startup time, the boot procedure automatically invokes the S99mysql script with an argument of start.

Many Linux variants have a similar set of directories, but organized under /etc/init.d and /etc/rc.d. Such Linux systems typically have a chkconfig command that is intended for startup script management. You can use it to help you install the mysql.server script instead of manually running commands like those just shown. The following instructions show how to install mysql.server into the startup directories using a name of mysql:

1. Copy the `mysql.server` script from wherever it's located into the `init.d` directory and make it executable:

```
# cp mysql.server /etc/init.d/mysql
# chmod +x /etc/init.d/mysql
```

2. Register the script and enable it:

```
# chkconfig --add mysql
# chkconfig mysql on
```

3. To verify that the script has been properly enabled, run `chkconfig` with the `--list` option:

```
# chkconfig --list mysql
mysql            0:off   1:off   2:on    3:on    4:on    5:on    6:off
```

That output indicates that the script will execute automatically for run levels 3, 4, and 5.

If you don't have `chkconfig`, you can use a procedure similar to that used for Solaris, although the pathnames are slightly different. To enable the script for run level 3, use these commands:

```
# cp mysql.server /etc/init.d/mysql
# cd /etc/init.d
# chmod +x mysql
# cd /etc/rc.d/rc3.d
# ln -s /etc/init.d/mysql S99mysql
```

Under Mac OS X, the startup procedure is different yet. The `/Library/StartupItems` and `/System/Library/StartupItems` directories contain subdirectories for the services that are initiated at system boot time. The DMG package provided for Mac OS X at the MySQL Web site contains an installer that places a startup item for the MySQL server into one of these directories.

12.2.2 Running the MySQL Server On Windows

On Windows, you can start the MySQL server manually from the command line. It's also possible to install the server as a Windows service. You can set the service to run automatically when Windows starts and control it from the command line or by using the Windows Services Manager.

MySQL distributions for Windows include several servers, each of which is built with different options. You can find a summary of the different servers in Appendix A. For this discussion, I'll use the name `mysqld` for examples, but your distribution might contain servers with different names such as `mysqld-nt` or `mysqld-debug`.

Windows servers provide two types of connections that Unix servers do not:

- Connections via named pipes, if the server is started with the `--enable-named-pipe` option.

- Connections via shared memory, if the server is started with the `--shared-memory` option.

Prior to MySQL 5.1.21, only the servers named `mysqld-nt` and `mysqld-debug` support named pipes. (The "nt" derives from the fact that named pipes are a feature first available in Windows NT, the predecessor to Windows 2000. `mysqld-debug` is like `mysqld-nt` with the addition of debugging support.) As of 5.1.21, all Windows servers are built with named-pipe support, and there are no longer any servers with -nt in the name.

12.2.2.1 Running the Server Manually on Windows

To start a server manually, invoke it from the command line in a console window:

```
C:\> mysqld
```

If you want error messages to go to the console window rather than to the error log (the *host_name*.`err` file in the data directory), use the `--console` option:

```
C:\> mysqld --console
```

When you run a MySQL server from the command line, you will not necessarily see another command prompt until the server exits. That's okay. It just means that you need to open another console window to use for running client programs.

If you add the `--shared-memory` option to the startup command, the server enables local clients to connect using shared memory. Similarly, if your server was built with named-pipe support, start it with the `--enable-named-pipe` option to enable local clients to connect via named pipes.

To stop the server, use `mysqladmin`:

```
C:\> mysqladmin -p -u root shutdown
```

12.2.2.2 Running the Server as a Windows Service

On Windows, any MySQL server can be installed as a Windows service using this command:

```
C:\> C:\mysql\bin\mysqld --install
```

The command uses the full pathname to the server. If the server is installed in a different location, modify the pathname accordingly.

The service-installation command does not actually start `mysqld`. Instead, it causes `mysqld` to run automatically whenever Windows starts. If you prefer to use a service that does not run automatically, install the server as a "manual" service:

```
C:\> C:\mysql\bin\mysqld --install-manual
```

As a general rule, when you install a server as a Windows service, you give no other options on the command line and list them in an option file instead. (See Section 12.2.3, "Specifying Server Startup Options.") However, it is possible to specify a service name and option file as arguments, as described in the following discussion. This is especially useful when you install several Windows servers as services. (See Section 12.10, "Running Multiple Servers.")

When you install a MySQL server as a Windows service, the default service name is
MySQL. (Service names are not case sensitive.) It's possible to specify a service name explicitly following the `--install` option:

```
C:\> C:\mysql\bin\mysqld --install service_name
```

Windows services each must have a unique name, so one reason for choosing a service
name other than MySQL is that it enables you to run multiple MySQL servers as services.
The service name affects which option groups the server reads from option files when it
starts:

- With no `service_name` argument or a service name of MySQL, the server uses the
  default service name (MySQL) and reads the `[mysqld]` group from the standard
  option files.
- With a `service_name` argument different from MySQL, the server uses that name as
  the service name and reads the `[mysqld]` and `[service_name]` groups from the
  standard option files.

If you specify a service name, you can also specify a `--defaults-file` option as the
final option on the command line when you install a server:

```
C:\> C:\mysql\bin\mysqld --install service_name --defaults-file=file_name
```

This gives you an alternative means of providing server-specific options. The name of
the file is remembered and used by the server whenever it starts, and it reads options only
from the `[mysqld]` group of that file. This syntax requires a service name to be given, so
to use the default service name, specify a `service_name` value of MySQL.

A single option other than `--defaults-file` is allowed following the service name,
but `--defaults-file` is more flexible because you can put as many options as you need
in the file.

After the server has been installed as a service, you control it using the service name.
This can be done from the command line, or from the Windows Services Manager if you
prefer a graphical interface. Depending on your version of Windows, the Services Manager can be found as a Services item in the Windows Control Panel or in the Administrative Tools item in the Control Panel.

To start or stop the service from the command line, use the following commands:

```
C:\> net start MySQL
C:\> net stop MySQL
```

If you use the Services Manager, it presents a window that displays a list of the services
it knows about, along with additional information such as whether each service is running
and whether it is automatic or manual. To start or stop the MySQL server, select its entry
in the services list and then choose the appropriate button or menu item.

You can also stop the server from the command line with `mysqladmin shutdown`.

> **Note**
>
> Although you can control services using either the Services Manager or commands at the command prompt, you should avoid interactions between the two approaches. Make sure to close the Services Manager whenever you invoke service-related commands from the prompt.

To remove the MySQL server from the list of services, first stop it if it is running, and then issue this command:

```
C:\> mysqld --remove
```

The command removes the MySQL service having the default service name of MySQL. To indicate explicitly which service to remove, specify its name following the --remove option:

```
C:\> mysqld --remove service_name
```

12.2.3 Specifying Server Startup Options

On any platform, there are two primary methods for specifying startup options when you invoke the server:

- List the options on the command line. In this case, it's possible to use either the long or short forms of any option for which both forms are available. For example, you can use either --user=mysql or -u mysql.

- List the options in an option file. Options specified this way are given one per line. Only the long option form can be used, and it's written without the leading dashes:

  ```
  [mysqld]
  user=mysql
  ```

See Section F.1.3, "Option Files," for a general discussion of the format and syntax of option files, and the locations in which the server looks for them.

The two option-specification methods are not mutually exclusive. The server looks for options both in option files and on the command line, with options on the command line taking precedence.

It's generally easiest to use an option file because options specified that way take effect each time the server starts, whatever startup method you use. Listing options on the command line works only if you start the server manually or by using mysqld_safe. It does not work for mysql.server, which is intended to support only the start and stop arguments on the command line. Also, with limited exceptions, you cannot specify startup options on the command line if you use --install, --install-manual, or --remove to install or remove a Windows server as a service. (Section 12.2.2.2, "Running the Server as a Windows Service," discusses the exceptions.)

The locations in which the server looks for option files depends on your version of MySQL (see Section F.1.3, "Option Files"). However, /etc/my.cnf on Unix and

C:\my.ini on Windows work for any version from MySQL 5.0 and up. If the file you want to use doesn't exist, create it as a plain text file.

Server startup options typically are placed in the [mysqld] option group. For example, to indicate that you want the server to run as mysql and to use a base directory location of /usr/local/mysql, you can put the following group of lines in the option file:

```
[mysqld]
user=mysql
basedir=/usr/local/mysql
```

That is equivalent to launching the server as follows with the options on the command line:

```
% mysqld --user=mysql --basedir=/usr/local/mysql
```

Table 12.1 shows the standard list of option groups used by servers and the server startup programs. The line for mysqld also applies to servers with variant names such as mysqld-debug on Windows.

Table 12.1   **Option Groups Used by Server Programs**

Program	Option Groups Used By Program
mysqld	[mysqld], [server], [mysqld-X.Y]
mysqld_safe	[mysqld], [server], [mysqld_safe], [safe_mysqld]
mysql.server	[mysqld], [server], [mysql_server], [mysql.server]
libmysqld	[server], [embedded], [appname_server]

The [mysqld-X.Y] notation for mysqld indicates that servers read the release series-specific group. MySQL 5.0 servers read [mysqld-5.0], MySQL 5.1 servers read [mysqld-5.1], and so on.

mysqld_safe reads the [safe_mysqld] group for compatibility reasons; mysqld_safe was known as safe_mysqld before MySQL 4.0.

mysql.server reads option files only to look for basedir, datadir, and pid-file option values.

The line for libmysqld refers to the embedded server library that can be linked into programs to produce MySQL-based applications that do not require a separate standalone server. (Chapter 7, "Writing MySQL Programs Using C," describes how to write applications that use the embedded server.) The [appname_server] notation indicates the application-specific option group to be read by an application named appname that includes the embedded server. (This is only a suggested convention. It must be implemented by the application itself.)

On Windows, if you install a MySQL server as a Windows service and do not use the default service name, that affects the option groups that the server reads. For details, see Section 12.2.2.2, "Running the Server as a Windows Service."

When you place options in a group, choose the group that will be used in the context or contexts that you want. The [server] group can be used for options that apply to any server, whether standalone or embedded. The [mysqld] or [embedded] groups can be used for options that apply only to standalone servers or to embedded servers. Similarly, the [mysqld_safe] or [mysql.server] groups enable you to specify options that apply only to one startup script or the other.

If you launch the server by using the mysqld_safe or mysql.server script, another way to specify options is to edit the script to pass those options directly to the server. This is a last resort because it has a significant disadvantage: Each time you upgrade MySQL, your modified script gets wiped out with the new version and you must redo your changes.

12.2.4 Stopping the Server

To stop the server manually, use mysqladmin:

```
% mysqladmin -p -u root shutdown
```

This works for both Unix and Windows. If you installed the server as a service under Windows, it's also possible to use the graphical interface offered by the Services Manager to select and stop the server, or to stop the server manually from the command line like this:

```
C:\> net stop MySQL
```

If you have set up the server to start automatically when your system boots, you shouldn't need to do anything special to stop it automatically at system shutdown time. BSD Unix systems normally shut down processes by sending a TERM signal; they respond to the signal appropriately (or are killed unceremoniously if they fail to do so). mysqld responds by terminating when it receives this signal.

For System V-style Unix systems that start the server with mysql.server, the shutdown process invokes that script with an argument of stop to tell the server to shut down. You can also invoke the script yourself to stop the server manually. For example, if you've installed the mysql.server script as /etc/init.d/mysql, you can invoke it as follows (you'll need to be root to do this):

```
# /etc/init.d/mysql stop
```

If you run the MySQL server as a Windows service, the service manager automatically tells the server to stop when Windows shuts down. If you do not run the server as a service, you should stop the server manually with mysqladmin shutdown or net stop MySQL at the command line before shutting down Windows.

12.2.5 Regaining Control of the Server When You Cannot Connect to It

Under certain circumstances you might need to restart the server manually if you find that you no longer can connect to it. This presents something of a conundrum, because typically you stop the server by connecting to it so that you can tell it to shut down (for example, by executing a mysqladmin shutdown command). How can this situation arise?

First, the MySQL `root` password might have gotten set to a value that you don't know. This can happen when you change the password—for example, if you accidentally type an invisible control character when you enter the new password value. Or you may simply have forgotten the password.

Second, under Unix, connections to `localhost` by default are made through a Unix domain socket file such as `/tmp/mysql.sock`. If the socket file gets removed, local clients won't be able to use it to connect. This might happen if your system runs a `cron` job that removes temporary files in the `/tmp` directory now and then.

If the reason you can't connect to the server is that the Unix socket file has been removed, you can get it back simply by restarting the server. (The server will re-create the socket file when it comes back up.) The trick here is that because the socket file is gone, you can't use it to establish a connection for telling the server to stop. You must establish a TCP/IP connection instead. To do this, connect to the local server by using the `--protocol=tcp` option or by specifying a host value of `127.0.0.1` rather than `localhost`:

```
% mysqladmin -p -u root --protocol=tcp shutdown
% mysqladmin -p -u root -h 127.0.0.1 shutdown
```

`127.0.0.1` is an IP number (it refers to the local host's loopback interface), so it explicitly forces a TCP/IP connection to be used rather than a socket connection.

If it is the case that the Unix socket file is being removed by a `cron` job, the missing-socket problem will recur until you change the `cron` job or use a socket file located somewhere else. You can specify a different socket by naming it in a global option file. For example, if the MySQL base directory is `/usr/local/mysql`, you can use a socket file in that directory by adding these lines to `/etc/my.cnf`:

```
[mysqld]
socket=/usr/local/mysql/mysql.sock

[client]
socket=/usr/local/mysql/mysql.sock
```

Restart the server after making the change so that it creates the socket file in the new location. It's necessary to specify the Unix socket file pathname both for the server and for client programs so that they all use the same file. If you set the pathname only for the server, client programs still will expect to find the file at the old location. A limitation of this method is that it works only for clients that read the option file; some third-party programs might not. If you recompile MySQL from source, you can reconfigure the distribution to use a different pathname by default both for the server and clients. This automatically affects third-party programs that use the client library, unless they have been statically linked with the old library. In that case, you must recompile them to use the new library.

If you can't connect because you can't remember or don't know the `root` password, you need to regain control of the server so that you can set the password again. To do this, use the following procedure:

1. Stop the server. Under Unix, if you can log in as `root` on the server host, you can terminate the server using the `kill` command. Find out the server's process ID by looking in the server's PID file (which is usually located in the data directory), or by using the `ps` command. Then try telling the server process to shut down normally by sending it a `TERM` signal:

```
# kill -TERM PID
```

That way, tables and logs will be flushed properly. If the server is jammed and unresponsive to a normal termination signal, you can use `kill -9` to forcibly terminate it.

```
# kill -9 PID
```

`kill -9` is a last resort because there might be unflushed modifications in memory, and you risk leaving tables in an inconsistent state.

Under Linux, `ps` might show several `mysqld` "processes." These are really threads of the same process, so you can kill any of them to kill them all.

If you start the server using `mysqld_safe`, it will be monitoring the server for abnormal termination. If you kill the server with `kill -9`, `mysqld_safe` will immediately restart it. To avoid this, determine the PID of the `mysqld_safe` process and kill it first before killing `mysqld`.

If you run the server as a service under Windows, you can stop it normally without knowing any passwords by using the Services Manager or by issuing this command:

```
C:\> net stop MySQL
```

To forcibly terminate the server on Windows, use the Task Manager (Alt-Control-Del). Like `kill -9` on Unix, this is a last resort.

2. Restart the server with the `--skip-grant-tables` option to disable use of the grant tables for verifying connections. That enables you to connect with no password and with all privileges. However, it also leaves your server wide open so that other people can connect the same way, so issue a `FLUSH PRIVILEGES` statement as soon as you connect:

```
% mysql
mysql> FLUSH PRIVILEGES;
```

The `FLUSH` statement tells the server to reread the grant tables, causing it to start using them again for access control. You will remain connected, but the server will require any subsequent connection attempts by other clients to be validated with the grant tables as usual. The `FLUSH` statement also re-enables the `SET PASSWORD` statement, which is disabled when the server is not using the grant tables. After reloading the tables, you can change the `root` password with `SET PASSWORD` or `UPDATE`, as shown in Section 12.1, "Securing a New MySQL Installation." For example:

```
mysql> SET PASSWORD FOR 'root'@'localhost' = PASSWORD('rootpass');
```

Be sure to change the password for all `root` accounts if there is more than one.

3. After changing the `root` password, shut down the server and restart it using your normal startup procedure. You now should be able to connect to it as `root` using the new password.

Should you be forced to terminate the server with `kill -9` under Unix or with the Task Manager under Windows, the abrupt nature of the shutdown gives the server no chance to flush any unsaved changes to disk. To help deal with problems that may occur due to this kind of shutdown, it's a good idea to enable auto-recovery in the server. For details, see Section 14.2.1, "Using the Server's Auto-Recovery Capabilities."

12.3 Controlling How the Server Listens for Connections

The MySQL server listens for connections on several network interfaces, which you can control as follows:

- On all platforms, the server listens on a network port for TCP/IP connections, unless started with the `--skip-networking` option. The default port number is 3306; to specify a different number, use the `--port` option. If the server host has more than one IP number, you can specify which one the server should use when listening for connections by starting it with a `--bind-address` option.

- Under Unix, the server listens on a Unix domain socket file for connections from local clients that connect to the special hostname `localhost` or that specify the `--protocol=socket` option. Use of the socket file by the server cannot be turned off. The default socket file usually is `/tmp/mysql.sock`, although operating system distributions that include MySQL often use a different location. To specify a socket file pathname explicitly, use the `--socket` option.

- For Windows servers that include support for named pipes, named-pipe connections are disabled by default. To enable this capability, start the server with the `--enable-named-pipe` option. This enables local clients to connect through the named pipe by specifying the `--protocol=pipe` option or by connecting to the special hostname "." (period). By default, the pipe name is `MySQL` (not case sensitive). To specify a different name, use the `--socket` option.

- MySQL supports shared-memory connections on Windows, but this capability is disabled by default. To enable it, start the server with the `--shared-memory` option. When enabled, it becomes the default connection protocol for local clients. Local clients also can use the `--protocol=memory` option to specify use of shared memory explicitly. By default, the shared-memory name is MYSQL (case sensitive). To specify a different name, use the --shared-memory-base-name option.

A client that wants to connect to a local server using TCP/IP even when some other protocol might be used by default should specify 127.0.0.1 as the server hostname. That's the address of the TCP/IP loopback interface. Another way to force a TCP/IP connection is to use the --protocol=tcp option.

If you run a single server, it's typical to let the server use its default network settings. If you run more than one server, it's necessary to make sure each one uses unique networking parameters. See Section 12.10, "Running Multiple Servers," for more information.

The preceding discussion applies only to standalone servers that operate in a client/server environment. It does not apply to the embedded server, which communicates with the application program that it's linked into by means of an internal channel and does not listen to any external network interfaces at all.

12.4 Managing MySQL User Accounts

A MySQL administrator should know how to set up MySQL user accounts by specifying which users can connect to the server, where they can connect from, and what they can do while connected. This information is stored in the grant tables in the mysql database, which are manipulated primarily by means of these account-management SQL statements:

- CREATE USER, DROP USER, and RENAME USER create, remove, and rename MySQL accounts.
- GRANT specifies account privileges (and creates accounts if they do not exist).
- REVOKE removes privileges from existing MySQL accounts.
- SET PASSWORD assigns passwords to existing accounts.
- SHOW GRANTS displays the privileges held by existing accounts.

The account-management statements affect several grant tables in the mysql database (Table 12.2).

Table 12.2 **MySQL Grant Tables**

Grant Table	Contents
user	Users who can connect to the server and their global privileges
db	Database privileges
tables_priv	Table privileges
columns_priv	Column privileges
procs_priv	Stored-routine privileges

There is a another grant table named `host`, but it is not affected by account-management statements, is obsolete, and is not discussed here.

When you issue a CREATE USER statement, you specify an account name consisting of a username and hostname, and optionally assign a password to the account. The server creates a row for the account in the `user` table. This is also true for GRANT if the account does not already exist. For GRANT, if the statement specifies any global privileges (administrative privileges or privileges that apply to all databases), those are recorded in the `user` table, too. If GRANT specifies privileges that are specific to a given database, table, table column, or stored routine, they are recorded in the `db`, `tables_priv`, `columns_priv`, or `procs_priv` tables. REVOKE removes privileges from the grant tables, and DROP USER removes all rows associated with the account from the tables.

It is also possible to manipulate the contents of the grant tables directly by issuing SQL statements like INSERT and UPDATE. However, account-management statements such as GRANT and REVOKE make it easier to manage user accounts by acting as a front end to the grant tables. They are generally more convenient to work with conceptually because you describe the access modifications that you want to perform and the server maps your requests onto the proper grant table changes automatically. Nevertheless, although it's easier to use GRANT and REVOKE than to modify the grant tables directly, I advise that you supplement the material in this chapter by reading Chapter 13. That chapter discusses the grant tables in more detail, to help you understand how they work "underneath" the level of the account-management statements.

The following sections describe how to set up and remove MySQL user accounts, how to grant and revoke privileges, and how to change passwords or reset lost passwords.

> **Note**
>
> Some versions of MySQL introduce new privileges, which changes the structure of the grant tables. The first time you install MySQL on a machine, the installation procedure creates the grant tables with the structure that is current for the version that you install. If you upgrade MySQL to a newer version, you should run `mysql_upgrade` to update the grant tables with any modifications that have been made since your current version.
>
> `mysql_upgrade` needs to connect to the local server as the MySQL `root` user, so invoke it with the appropriate password:
>
> ```
> % mysql_upgrade --password=rootpass
> ```

12.4.1 High-Level MySQL Account Management

Three statements perform high-level operations on MySQL accounts:

- CREATE USER creates a new account and optionally assigns a password:

  ```
  CREATE USER account [IDENTIFIED BY 'password'];
  ```

  CREATE USER grants no privileges; that is done with GRANT.

- DROP USER removes an existing account and any privileges associated with it:

  ```
  DROP USER account;
  ```

DROP USER does not drop any databases or objects within databases that were accessible to the dropped account.

- RENAME USER changes the name of an existing account:

```
RENAME USER from_account TO to_account;
```

All three statements can be used if you have the global CREATE USER privilege. Otherwise, you must have the INSERT, DELETE, or UPDATE privilege for the mysql database to use CREATE USER, DROP USER, or RENAME USER, respectively.

To set up a new account, it's generally possible to figure out the kind of CREATE USER statement to issue by asking these questions:

- What is the user's name?
- From which host or hosts should the user be able to connect?
- What is the user's password?

The first two questions determine the *account* value to use in the statement, and the third determines the password for the IDENTIFIED BY clause. The rules for the *account* value are given in Section 12.4.1.1, "Specifying Account Names." For IDENTIFIED BY, the *password* value should be the literal text of the password. CREATE USER will encode the password for you; don't use the PASSWORD() function as you do with the SET PASSWORD statement. If you specify no IDENTIFIED BY clause, the account is created with no password, which is insecure and should be avoided.

12.4.1.1 Specifying Account Names

The *account* value in account-management statements such as CREATE USER consists of a username and hostname in `'user_name'@'host_name'` format: In MySQL, you specify not only who can connect but from where. This enables you to set up separate accounts for two users who have the same name but that connect from different locations. MySQL lets you distinguish between them and assign privileges to each one independent of the other. The server stores the *user_name* and *host_name* values in the User and Host columns of the user table row for the account, and in any other grant table rows associated with the account.

Your username in MySQL is just a name that you use to identify yourself when you connect to the server. The name has no necessary connection to your Unix or Windows login name. By default, the MySQL username that client programs use on Unix is your login name if you don't specify a name explicitly, but that's just a convention. There also is nothing special about the name root that is used for the MySQL superuser that can do anything. You could just as well change this name to superduper in the grant tables and then connect as superduper to perform operations that require superuser privileges.

By choosing an *account* value appropriately, you can enable a user to connect from as specific or broad a set of hosts as you like. At one extreme, you can limit access to a single host if you know users will be connecting only from that host:

```
CREATE USER 'boris'@'localhost' IDENTIFIED BY 'frost';
CREATE USER 'fred'@'ares.mars.net' IDENTIFIED BY 'steam';
```

Keep in mind that the hostname part is the host *from* which the client will be connecting. It is not the server host *to* which the client will connect (unless they are the same).

Enabling a user to connect only from a single host is the strictest form of access you can allow. At the other extreme, you might have a user who travels a lot and needs to be able to connect from hosts all over the world. If the user's name is max, you can enable him to connect from anywhere like this:

```
CREATE USER 'max'@'%' IDENTIFIED BY 'mist';
```

The '%' character functions as a wildcard with the same meaning as in a LIKE pattern match. Thus, as a hostname specifier, % means "any host." This is the easiest way to set up a user, but it's also the least secure. (Using it also may result in occasional head scratching on your part, for reasons described in Section 13.2.3, "A Privilege Puzzle.")

The other LIKE wildcard character ('_') can be used in host values to match any single character.

To specify a literal '%' or '_' wildcard character, precede it by a backslash.

To take a middle ground, you can enable a user to connect from a limited set of hosts. For example, to enable mary to connect from any host in the snake.net domain, use a host specifier of %.snake.net:

```
CREATE USER 'mary'@'%.snake.net' IDENTIFIED BY 'fog';
```

The host part of the *account* value can be given using an IP number rather than a hostname if you like. You can specify a literal IP number, a number that contains pattern characters, or an IP number with a netmask that indicates which bits to use for the network number:

```
CREATE USER 'joe'@'192.168.128.3' IDENTIFIED BY 'water';
CREATE USER 'ardis'@'192.168.128.%' IDENTIFIED BY 'snow';
CREATE USER 'rex'@'192.168.128.0/255.255.255.0' IDENTIFIED BY 'ice';
```

The first of these statements indicates a specific single address, 192.168.128.3, from which the user can connect. The second specifies an IP pattern for the 192.168.128 Class C subnet. In the third statement, 192.168.128.0/255.255.255.0 specifies a netmask that has the first 24 bits turned on. It matches any host with 192.168.128 in the first 24 bits of its IP number. Netmask values must be 255.0.0.0, 255.255.0.0, 255.255.255.0, or 255.255.255.255.

Using a hostname of localhost in an account name enables a user to connect to the server from the local host in a number of ways:

- On Unix, the user can connect by specifying a host value of localhost or 127.0.0.1. The localhost connection is made using the Unix socket file. 127.0.0.1 causes a TCP/IP connection to be made using the local host's loopback IP interface.

- On Windows, the user can connect by specifying a host value of `localhost` or `127.0.0.1`. Both of these connections are made using TCP/IP, except that if the server supports shared-memory connections, a connection to `localhost` is made using shared memory by default. If the server supports named-pipe connections, the user can connect through the pipe by specifying a hostname of "`.`" (period).

If the username or hostname part of an *account* value can be used as an unquoted identifier, you need not quote it. If it contains any special characters such as '`-`' or '`%`', you must quote it. For example, in `boris@localhost`, both parts are legal without quotes. However, it is always safe to use quotes, and the examples in this book do so as a rule. Usernames and hostnames can be quoted either with string quoting characters or identifier quoting characters. Quote the username and hostname separately: Use `'boris'@'localhost'`, not `'boris@localhost'`.

If you give no hostname part at all in an account specifier, it's the same as using a host part of `%`. Thus, `'max'` and `'max'@'%'` are equivalent *account* values. This means that if you intend to specify an account of `'boris'@'localhost'` but mistakenly write `'boris@localhost'` instead, MySQL will accept it as legal. What happens is that MySQL interprets `'boris@localhost'` as containing only a user part and adds the default host part of `%` to it, resulting in an effective account name of `'boris@localhost'@'%'`. To avoid this, remember to quote the user and host parts of account names separately.

12.4.1.2 Specifying the Local Hostname in Account Names

It's common to have problems connecting from the server host if you use the server's hostname rather than `localhost`. This can occur due to a mismatch between the way the name is specified in the grant tables and the way your DNS name resolver reports the name to programs. Suppose that the server host's fully qualified name is `cobra.snake.net`. If the resolver reports an unqualified name, such as `cobra`, but the grant tables contain rows with the fully qualified name (or vice versa), this mismatch will occur.

To determine if this is happening on your system, try connecting to the local server using a `-h` option that specifies the name of your host:

```
% mysql -h cobra.snake.net
```

Then look in the server's general log file. How does the server write the hostname there when it reports the connection attempt? Is the name in unqualified or fully qualified form? That tells you how you'll need to specify the hostname part when you use it in account names.

12.4.2 Granting Privileges

To give access privileges to an account, use the GRANT statement, which looks like this:

```
GRANT privileges (columns)
  ON what
  TO account [IDENTIFIED BY 'password']
```

```
[REQUIRE encryption requirements]
[WITH grant or resource management options];
```

If the named account exists, GRANT modifies its privileges. If the account does not exist, GRANT creates it with the given privileges. To avoid the possibility of GRANT creating a new account that has no password (and thus is insecure), enable the NO_AUTO_CREATE_USER SQL mode. This mode is available as of MySQL 5.0.2 and prevents GRANT from creating the account unless an IDENTIFIED BY clause is present.

Several of these clauses are optional and need not be specified at all. In general, you'll most commonly use the following parts:

- *privileges* indicates the privileges to assign to the account. For example, the SELECT privilege enables a user to issue SELECT statements and the SHUTDOWN privilege enables the user to shut down the server. Multiple privileges can be named, separated by commas.

- *columns* indicates the columns to which a privilege applies, separated by commas and listed within parentheses. This is optional, and you use it only to set up column-specific privileges. The column list must follow the name of *each* privilege to which it applies.

- *what* indicates the level at which the privileges apply. The most powerful level is the global level, for which any given privilege applies to all databases and all tables. Global privileges can be thought of as superuser privileges. Privileges also can be made database-specific, table-specific, column-specific (if you specify a *columns* clause), or routine-specific.

- *account* indicates which account is being granted the privileges. The *account* format is '*user_name*'@'*host_name*', as described in Section 12.4.1.1, "Specifying Account Names."

- *password* indicates the password to assign to the account. This is optional and is unnecessary if the account already exists and has a password. If you include the IDENTIFIED BY clause for an existing account, the new password replaces the current one. As with CREATE USER, when you do use IDENTIFIED BY, the *password* value should be the literal text of the password. GRANT will encode the password for you; don't use the PASSWORD() function.

The REQUIRE and WITH clauses are optional. REQUIRE is used for setting up accounts that must connect over secure connections using SSL. WITH is used to grant the GRANT OPTION privilege that enables the account to give its own privileges to other users. WITH also is used to specify resource management options that enable you to place limits on how many connections or statements an account can use per hour. These options help you prevent the account from hogging the server.

To specify what an account can do, it's generally possible to figure out the kind of GRANT statement to issue by asking these questions:

- What type of access should the account be given? That is, what level of privileges should the user have, and what should they apply to?
- Are secure connections required?
- Should the user be allowed to administer privileges?
- Should the user's resource consumption be limited?

The following sections show how to answer these questions and provide examples that illustrate how to use the various clauses of the GRANT statement.

12.4.2.1 Defining the Privileges an Account Has

You can grant several types of privileges. These are summarized in Table 12.3, Table 12.4, and Table 12.5, and are described in more detail in Chapter 13, "Access Control and Security." That chapter discusses the privileges in terms of both their purpose and their relationship to the underlying grant tables.

Table 12.3   **Administrative Privileges**

Privilege Name	Operation Enabled by Privilege
CREATE USER	Use high-level account-management statements
FILE	Read and write files on the server host
GRANT OPTION	Grant the account's privileges to other accounts
PROCESS	View information about the threads executing within the server
RELOAD	Reload the grant tables or flush the logs or caches
REPLICATION CLIENT	Ask about master and slave server locations
REPLICATION SLAVE	Act as a replication slave server
SHOW DATABASES	See all database names with SHOW DATABASES
SHUTDOWN	Shut down the server
SUPER	Kill threads and perform other supervisory operations

Table 12.4   **Object Privileges**

Privilege Name	Operation Enabled by Privilege
ALTER	Alter tables and indexes
ALTER ROUTINE	Alter or drop stored functions and procedures
CREATE	Create databases and tables
CREATE ROUTINE	Create stored functions and procedures

Table 12.4   **Object Privileges**

Privilege Name	Operation Enabled by Privilege
CREATE TEMPORARY TABLES	Create temporary tables using the TEMPORARY keyword
CREATE VIEW	Create views
DELETE	Delete rows from tables
DROP	Remove databases, tables, and other objects
EVENT	Create, drop, or alter events for the event scheduler
EXECUTE	Execute stored functions and procedures
INDEX	Create or drop indexes
INSERT	Insert new rows into tables
LOCK TABLES	Explicitly lock tables with LOCK TABLES statements
REFERENCES	Unused (reserved for future use)
SELECT	Retrieve rows from tables
SHOW VIEW	See view definitions with SHOW CREATE VIEW
TRIGGER	Create or drop triggers
UPDATE	Modify table rows

Table 12.5   **Miscellaneous Privileges**

Privilege Name	Operation Enabled by Privilege
ALL [PRIVILEGES]	All operations (except GRANT)
USAGE	A special "no privileges" privilege

The privileges shown in Table 12.3 are administrative privileges. Normally, you grant them relatively sparingly because they enable users to affect the operation of the server. (The SHUTDOWN privilege is not one you should hand out on an everyday basis, for example.) The privileges in Table 12.4 apply to databases, tables, columns, and stored routines. They control access to data managed by the server. The privilege specifiers in Table 12.5 are special. ALL means "all privileges" (except that it does not include the GRANT OPTION privilege). USAGE means "no privileges." That is, "create the account, but don't grant it any privileges." USAGE also can be used to modify non-privilege-related aspects of an existing account without changing its current privileges. (See Section 12.4.2.2, "Using the 'No Privileges' USAGE Privilege.)

CREATE VIEW and SHOW VIEW were introduced in MySQL 5.0.1. ALTER ROUTINE, CREATE ROUTINE, and CREATE USER were introduced in MySQL 5.0.3, which is also the version in which the EXECUTE privilege became operational. EVENT and TRIGGER were introduced in MySQL 5.1.6. (Before 5.1.6, SUPER rather than TRIGGER is required to manipulate triggers.)

To grant a privilege, you must have that privilege yourself, and you must have the GRANT OPTION privilege.

You can grant privileges at different levels, from global to very specific. This is controlled by the ON clause specifier, as shown in Table 12.6.

Table 12.6   **Privilege-Level Specifiers**

Privilege Specifier	Level at Which Privileges Apply
ON *.*	Global privileges: all databases, all objects in databases
ON *	Global privileges if no default database has been selected; database privileges for the default database otherwise
ON db_name.*	Database privileges: all objects in the named database
ON db_name.tbl_name	Table privileges: all columns in the named table
ON tbl_name	Table privileges: all columns in the named table in the default database
ON db_name.routine_name	Privileges for the named routine in the named database

As of MySQL 5.0.6, to specify explicitly the type of object to which the privileges apply if there is an ambiguity, you can include a TABLE, FUNCTION, or PROCEDURE keyword (for example, ON TABLE mydb.mytbl or ON FUNCTION mydb.myfunc).

The USAGE privilege should be specified only at the global level (that is, with ON *.*).

For the table-level specifiers, you can specify a (columns) clause following a privilege name to grant that privilege at the column level. The syntax for this is shown in a later example.

The ALL privilege specifier grants all privileges that are available at a given level. For example, at the global level, it grants all privileges. At the table level, it grants only privileges that apply to tables. ALL can be used only when granting global, database, table, or routine privileges. For column privileges, you must name each privilege that you want to grant.

Global privileges are the most powerful because they apply to any database. To create a superuser account that can do anything, including being able to grant privileges to other users, issue these statements:

```
CREATE USER 'ethel'@'localhost' IDENTIFIED BY 'coffee';
GRANT ALL ON *.* TO 'ethel'@'localhost' WITH GRANT OPTION;
```

The ON *.* clause means "all databases and all objects in them." As a safety precaution, the account created in the example is allowed to connect only from the local host. Limiting the hosts from which a superuser can connect is a good idea because it restricts the set of hosts from which password-cracking attempts can be mounted.

The privileges in Table 12.3 are administrative in nature and, except for GRANT, can be granted only using the ON *.* global-privilege specifier. For example, the RELOAD privilege enables use of FLUSH, so the following statements set up a user named flush that can do nothing but issue FLUSH statements:

```
CREATE USER 'flush'@'localhost' IDENTIFIED BY 'flushpass';
GRANT RELOAD ON *.* TO 'flush'@'localhost';
```

This type of MySQL account can be useful for writing administrative scripts that perform operations such as flushing the logs during log file maintenance (see Section 12.5.7, "Log Management").

Database-level privileges apply to a particular database and all objects in it. To grant privileges at this level, use an ON *db_name*.* clause:

```
CREATE USER 'bill'@'racer.snake.net' IDENTIFIED BY 'rock';
GRANT ALL ON sampdb.* TO 'bill'@'racer.snake.net';

CREATE USER 'reader'@'%' IDENTIFIED BY 'dirt';
GRANT SELECT ON menagerie.* TO 'reader'@'%';
```

The first set of statements grants bill full privileges for any table in the sampdb database when he connects from racer.snake.net. The second creates a restricted-access user named reader that can connect from any host to access any table in the menagerie database, but only with SELECT statements. That is, reader is a "read-only" user.

You can list multiple privileges to be granted, separated by commas. For example, to give a user the ability to read and modify the contents of existing tables in the sampdb database, but not to create new tables or drop tables, do not grant the ALL privilege for the database. Instead, name only the specific privileges to be enabled:

```
CREATE USER 'jennie'@'%' IDENTIFIED BY 'boron';
GRANT SELECT,INSERT,DELETE,UPDATE ON sampdb.* TO 'jennie'@'%';
```

For more fine-grained access control below the database level, you can grant privileges for individual tables, or even for individual columns in tables. Column-specific privileges are useful when there are parts of a table you want to hide from a user, or when you want a user to be able to modify only particular columns. Suppose that someone volunteers to help you out at the Historical League as an office assistant. That's good news, but you decide to begin by granting your new assistant read-only access to the member table that contains membership information, plus a column-specific UPDATE privilege on the expiration and address-related columns of that table. That way, your assistant will have write access only for the rather modest tasks of updating expiration dates as people renew their memberships and making address changes. The statements needed to set up this MySQL account are as follows:

```
CREATE USER 'assistant'@'localhost' IDENTIFIED BY 'officehelp';
GRANT SELECT, UPDATE (expiration,street,city,state,zip)
  ON sampdb.member TO 'assistant'@'localhost';
```

The GRANT statement grants read access to the entire member table (because no column list follows SELECT), and grants update access only for the columns named in parentheses following the UPDATE privilege keyword.

To grant privileges at the column level for multiple privileges in a GRANT statement, the column list in parentheses must follow each privilege name.

If you quote database, table, or column names in a GRANT statement, quote them as identifiers, not as strings. For example:

```
GRANT SELECT, UPDATE (`expiration`,`street`,`city`,`state`,`zip`)
  ON `sampdb`.`member` TO 'assistant'@'localhost';
```

Rows in the grant tables do not "follow" database object renaming operations. For example, privileges for a given table or column no longer apply if you rename the table or column.

12.4.2.2 Using the "No Privileges" USAGE Privilege

The special USAGE privilege specifier means "no privileges." This may not seem very useful at first glance, but it is. It enables you to change characteristics of an account other than those that pertain to privileges, while leaving the existing privileges alone. To use it, "grant" the USAGE privilege at the global level, specify the account name, and provide the new non-privilege characteristics of the account. For example, if you want to change an account password, require that the user connect using SSL, or impose a connection limit on an account without affecting the privileges held by the account, use statements like these:

```
GRANT USAGE ON *.* TO account IDENTIFIED BY 'new_password';
GRANT USAGE ON *.* TO account REQUIRE SSL;
GRANT USAGE ON *.* TO account WITH MAX_CONNECTIONS_PER_HOUR 10;
```

12.4.2.3 Requiring an Account to Use Secure Connections

MySQL enables clients to establish secure connections using the SSL (Secure Sockets Layer) protocol, which encrypts the data stream between the client and the server so that it is not sent in the clear. In addition, X509 can be used as a means for the client to provide identification information over SSL connections. Secure connections provide an extra measure of protection, at the price of the extra CPU cycles required to perform encryption and decryption.

To specify requirements for secure connections, use a REQUIRE clause. To require only that a user connect via SSL without being more specific about the type of secure connection the user must make, use REQUIRE SSL:

```
CREATE USER 'eladio'@'%.snake.net' IDENTIFIED BY 'flint';
GRANT ALL ON sampdb.* TO 'eladio'@'%.snake.net' REQUIRE SSL;
```

To be more strict, you can require that the client present a valid X509 certificate:

```
GRANT ALL ON sampdb.* TO 'eladio'@'%.snake.net' REQUIRE X509;
```

REQUIRE X509 imposes no constraints on the certificate's contents other than that it be valid. To be even more strict, REQUIRE enables you to indicate that the client's X509 certificate must have certain characteristics. These characteristics are given with ISSUER or SUBJECT options in the REQUIRE clause. ISSUER and SUBJECT refer to the certificate issuer and recipient. For example, the ssl directory of the sampdb distribution includes a client certificate file, client-cert.pem, that you can use for testing SSL connections. The issuer and subject values in the certificate can be displayed using the openssl command:

```
% openssl x509 -issuer -subject -noout -in client-cert.pem
issuer= /C=US/ST=WI/L=Madison/O=sampdb/OU=CA/CN=sampdb
subject= /C=US/ST=WI/L=Madison/O=sampdb/OU=client/CN=sampdb
```

The following GRANT statement indicates an account for which the client must present a certificate that matches both of those values:

```
GRANT ALL ON sampdb.* TO 'eladio'@'%.snake.net'
  REQUIRE ISSUER '/C=US/ST=WI/L=Madison/O=sampdb/OU=CA/CN=sampdb'
  AND SUBJECT '/C=US/ST=WI/L=Madison/O=sampdb/OU=client/CN=sampdb';
```

You can also use REQUIRE to indicate that the connection must be encrypted using a particular cipher type:

```
GRANT ALL ON sampdb.* TO 'eladio'@'%.snake.net'
  REQUIRE CIPHER 'DHE-RSA-AES256-SHA';
```

To indicate explicitly that secure connections are not required, use REQUIRE NONE. This is the default when you create a new account, but it can be useful for removing a requirement for SSL from an account that currently has it.

Some additional points to be aware of when using a REQUIRE clause:

- Issuing a GRANT statement that requires an account to use secure connections only sets up a constraint on the account. It doesn't actually provide the means for a client program to connect securely with that account. For that to happen, MySQL must be configured to include SSL support, and you must start the server and clients in a particular way. Section 13.3, "Setting Up Secure Connections," describes how to do this.

- If you specify that connections for an account must use SSL, but SSL is not supported by either the server or client programs, the account is effectively unusable.

- REQUIRE is used only to indicate whether an account *must* connect using secure connections. If the server and client programs are configured with SSL support, any user is still *able* to use secure connections, even if not required to do so.

- There is little point in using a REQUIRE clause for accounts that don't connect to the server over an external network. Such connections can't be snooped, so making them encrypted gains you nothing and incurs increased computational load without benefit. Accounts like this include those that connect to the server only through a Unix socket file, a named pipe, shared memory, or to the IP number

127.0.0.1 (the host's loopback interface). These connections use interfaces that are handled internally to the host and for which no traffic crosses an external network.

12.4.2.4 Enabling an Account to Administer Privileges

You can enable an account to grant its own privileges to other accounts by specifying the WITH GRANT OPTION clause. To use this clause, you must have the GRANT OPTION privilege yourself.

One reason to give an account the GRANT OPTION privilege is to enable the owner of a database to control access to the database: Grant the owner all privileges on the database, including the GRANT OPTION privilege. For example, if you want alicia to be able to connect from any host in the big-corp.com domain and administer privileges for all tables in the sales database, set up the account this way:

```
CREATE USER 'alicia'@'%.big-corp.com' IDENTIFIED BY 'shale';
GRANT ALL ON sales.* TO 'alicia'@'%.big-corp.com' WITH GRANT OPTION;
```

In effect, the WITH GRANT OPTION clause enables you to delegate access-granting rights to another user. But be aware that two users with the GRANT OPTION privilege can grant each other their own privileges. If you've given one user only the SELECT privilege but another user has GRANT OPTION plus other privileges in addition to SELECT, the second user can make the first one "stronger."

Another way to grant the GRANT OPTION privilege is simply to list it in the beginning part of the GRANT statement:

```
GRANT GRANT OPTION ON sales.* TO 'alicia'@'%.big-corp.com';
```

However, a statement such as this one will not work:

```
GRANT ALL,GRANT OPTION ON sales.* TO 'alicia'@'%.big-corp.com';
```

In a GRANT statement, ALL can be used only by itself, not in a list that names other privilege specifiers.

GRANT OPTION applies to all privileges at or below the level at which it is granted, not to individual privileges. If you give an account the GRANT OPTION privilege at a given level, the account can grant any privilege that it holds at that level. You cannot specify that the account can grant some of the privileges that it holds at that level but not others.

12.4.2.5 Limiting an Account's Resource Consumption

The MySQL grant system enables you to place limits on the number of times per hour that an account can connect to the server, and the number of statements or updates per hour the account can issue. To specify these limits, use a WITH clause. The following statement sets up an account 'spike'@'localhost' that has full access to the sampdb database, but can connect only ten times per hour and issue 200 statements per hour (of which at most 50 can be updates):

```
CREATE USER 'spike'@'localhost' IDENTIFIED BY 'pyrite';
GRANT ALL ON sampdb.* TO 'spike'@'localhost'
```

```
WITH MAX_CONNECTIONS_PER_HOUR 10 MAX_QUERIES_PER_HOUR 200
MAX_UPDATES_PER_HOUR 50;
```

The default value for each option is zero, which means "no limit." This means that if you have placed a resource limit on an account, you can remove the limit by changing the limit value to zero. For example, to remove the limit on the number of times per hour that spike can connect, use this statement:

```
GRANT USAGE ON *.* TO 'spike'@'localhost'
  WITH MAX_CONNECTIONS_PER_HOUR 0;
```

A user cannot subvert these limits by using multiple connections to the server, because all connections for a given account are counted together.

As of MySQL 5.0.3, a fourth resource limit, MAX_USER_CONNECTIONS, is available to control the maximum number of simultaneous connections that the account can have. If the limit is zero (the default), the limit is controlled by the value of the max_user_connections system variable. A non-zero value limits the account to that many simultaneous connections.

The order of the resource management options within the WITH clause does not matter.

Any administrative user who has the RELOAD privilege can reset the current counter values by issuing a FLUSH USER_RESOURCES statement. FLUSH PRIVILEGES does this as well. After the counters have been reset, accounts that have reached their hourly limits once again can connect and issue statements. A reset also occurs for an individual account if you issue a GRANT statement that sets that account's limits.

12.4.3 Displaying Account Privileges

To see what privileges an account has, use the SHOW GRANTS statement:

```
SHOW GRANTS FOR 'sampadm'@'localhost';
```

To see your own privileges, use either of these statements:

```
SHOW GRANTS;
SHOW GRANTS FOR CURRENT_USER();
```

12.4.4 Revoking Privileges and Removing Users

To take away some or all of an account's privileges, use the REVOKE statement. The syntax for REVOKE is somewhat similar to that for the GRANT statement, except that TO is replaced by FROM, and there are no IDENTIFIED BY, REQUIRE, or WITH clauses:

```
REVOKE privileges [(columns)] ON what FROM account;
```

For example, the following GRANT statement grants all privileges on the sampdb database, and the REVOKE statement removes the account's privileges for making changes to existing rows:

```
GRANT ALL ON sampdb.* TO 'boris'@'localhost';
REVOKE DELETE,UPDATE ON sampdb.* FROM 'boris'@'localhost';
```

The GRANT OPTION privilege is not included in ALL. If you have granted it, revoke it by naming it explicitly in the *privileges* part of a REVOKE statement:

```
REVOKE GRANT OPTION ON sales.* FROM 'alicia'@'%.big-corp.com';
```

To revoke a privilege, you must have that privilege yourself, and you must have the GRANT OPTION privilege.

To revoke all privileges held by an account at all levels, use this statement:

```
REVOKE ALL PRIVILEGES,GRANT OPTION FROM account;
```

Notice that there is no ON clause in this syntax. It requires the global CREATE USER privilege or the UPDATE privilege for the mysql database.

If you revoke all of an account's privileges at the database, table, column, or routine level, MySQL removes the corresponding account row from the db, tables_priv, columns_priv, or procs_priv table. Revoking all of an account's global privileges sets the privilege columns to 'N' in its user table row, but does not delete the row. That is, REVOKE does not delete the account entirely, which means that the user can still connect to the server. To remove an account completely, use DROP USER instead of REVOKE (see Section 12.4.1, "High-Level MySQL Account Management").

Somewhat paradoxically, there are a few revocation operations that are done with GRANT. For example, if you specify that an account must connect using SSL, there is no REVOKE syntax for rescinding that requirement. Instead, issue a GRANT statement that grants the USAGE privilege at the global level (to leave existing privileges unchanged) and include a REQUIRE NONE clause to indicate that SSL is not required:

```
GRANT USAGE ON *.* TO account REQUIRE NONE;
```

Similarly, if you set up resource limits on a user, you don't remove those limits with REVOKE. Instead, use GRANT with USAGE to set the limit values to zero ("no limit"):

```
GRANT USAGE ON *.* TO account
  WITH MAX_CONNECTIONS_PER_HOUR 0 MAX_QUERIES_PER_HOUR 0
  MAX_UPDATES_PER_HOUR 0;
```

12.4.5 Changing Passwords or Resetting Lost Passwords

One way to change or reset an account's password is to use an UPDATE statement that identifies the User and Host values for the account's user table row, and then flush the privileges:

```
mysql> USE mysql;
mysql> UPDATE user SET Password=PASSWORD('silicon')
    -> WHERE User='boris' AND Host='localhost';
mysql> FLUSH PRIVILEGES;
```

However, it's easier to use SET PASSWORD because you name the account using the same format as for other account-management statements, and it's unnecessary to flush the privileges explicitly:

```
mysql> SET PASSWORD FOR 'boris'@'localhost' = PASSWORD('silicon');
```

You can always change your own password with SET PASSWORD, unless you have connected as an anonymous user. To change the password for another account, you must have the UPDATE privilege for the mysql database.

Another, less common, way to change a password is to use GRANT USAGE with an IDENTIFIED BY clause, in which case you specify the password literally rather than by using the PASSWORD() function:

```
mysql> GRANT USAGE ON *.* TO 'boris'@'localhost' IDENTIFIED BY 'silicon';
```

If you need to reset the root password because you've forgotten it and can't connect to the server, you have something of a problem, because normally you must connect as root to change the root password. If you don't know the password, you'll need to force the server to stop and restart it without grant table validation. The procedure is described in Section 12.2.5, "Regaining Control of the Server When You Cannot Connect to It."

12.5 Maintaining Logs

The MySQL server has the capability of producing several kinds of logs. These are useful for diagnosing problems, improving server performance, enabling replication, and crash recovery. When the server begins executing, it examines its startup options to see whether it should perform logging and opens the appropriate logs if so. There are several types of logs you can tell the server to produce. The following list describes each one briefly, and the next several sections provide more detail.

- **The error log.** This log contains a record of server startups and shutdowns, as well as messages about problems or exceptional conditions. This is the place to look if the server fails to start. When that happens, the server writes a message to the error log before it terminates to indicate what problem occurred.

- **The general query log.** This log contains a record of client connections, SQL statements received from clients, and various other miscellaneous events. It is useful for monitoring server activity: who is connecting, from where, and what they are doing. It's the most convenient log to use when you want to find out what statements clients are sending to the server, which can be very useful for troubleshooting or debugging.

- **The slow-query log.** This log's purpose is to help you identify statements that may be in need of being rewritten for better performance. The server maintains a long_query_time system variable that defines "slow" queries (10 seconds by default). If a query takes more than that many seconds of real time, it is considered slow and is recorded in the slow-query log. The slow-query log also can be used to log queries for which no indexes were used.

- **The binary log and the binary log index file.** This log consists of one or more files that contain a record of modifications performed by UPDATE, DELETE, INSERT,

CREATE TABLE, DROP TABLE, GRANT, and so forth. Binary log contents are written as data modification "events" encoded in binary format. The binary log files are accompanied by an index file that lists which binary log files exist on the server.

The binary log has two purposes:

- It can be used in conjunction with your backups to restore tables after a crash. You can restore databases from your backup files, and then use mysqlbinlog to convert the binary log contents to text statements. Any statements that modified the databases subsequent to the backup can be used as input to mysql to bring databases to the state they were in at the time of the crash.
- The data modification events stored in the binary log are transmitted to replication slave servers.

- **The relay log and the relay log index file.** If the server acts as a replication slave, it maintains a relay log that contains a record of data-modification events received from the master that need to be executed. Relay log files have the same format as binary log files, and there is an index file that lists which relay log files exist on the slave.

Of all the logs, the general query log is most useful for monitoring the server, so when you first start using MySQL, I recommend that you enable the general log in addition to whatever other logs you want. After you have gained some experience with MySQL, you may want to turn off the general log to reduce your disk space requirements.

By default, each enabled log is written as a file (or sequence of files) in the data directory. In MySQL 5.1, you have a choice of writing some logs to alternative destinations: The error log can be sent to syslog, and the general and slow-query logs can be written to tables in the mysql database.

The server doesn't create any log unless you ask for it, with these exceptions:

- On Unix, if you start the server with the mysqld_safe script, that script sets up the error log and tells the server to use it.
- On Windows, the server creates the error log *unless* you specify the --console option to send diagnostic information to the console window rather than to a file.

Logs are controlled by specifying startup options for mysqld. Other than the binary and relay logs, these logs are written in text format and can be viewed directly. To display the contents of a binary or relay log file, use the mysqlbinlog utility.

To enable server logging, use the options shown in the following table. If the log filename is optional (as indicated by square brackets) and you don't provide a name, the server uses a default name and writes the log file in the data directory. The server derives the default name for each of the log files from the name of your server host, represented by HOSTNAME in the following discussion. If you specify a log name as a relative pathname, the server interprets it relative to the data directory. A full pathname can be specified to place the log in some other directory. The server will create any log file that does not exist. However, it will not create the directory in which the file is to be written, so create that directory if necessary before starting the server.

Logging Option	Log Enabled by Option
`--log-error[=file_name]`	Error log file
`--log[=file_name]`	General log file
`--log-slow-queries[=file_name]`	Slow-query log file
`--log-output[=destination]`	General/slow-query log destination
`--log-bin[=file_name]`	Binary log file
`--log-bin-index=file_name`	Binary log index file
`--relay-log[=file_name]`	Relay log file
`--relay-log-index=file_name`	Relay log index file

You can specify options for server logs on the command line for `mysqld` or `mysqld_safe`. However, because you usually specify log options the same way each time you start the server, it's most common to list them in an appropriate group of an option file. Typically, options are listed in the `[mysqld]` or `[mysqld_safe]` group, but they need not always be. Section 12.2.3, "Specifying Server Startup Options," details the option groups applicable to the server and to the server startup programs.

There also are some special-purpose logs that are managed by individual storage engines. The ISAM log is used for debugging purposes to record changes to MyISAM tables; I won't mention it further. The InnoDB and Falcon engines, if they are enabled, create logs to be used for auto-recovery after a crash. You cannot control whether these engines generate their logs, but you can specify where they write them by using the options in the following table. The default location is the data directory.

Logging Option	Purpose
`--innodb_log_group_home_dir=dir_name`	InnoDB log file directory
`--falcon-serial-log-dir=dir_name`	Falcon log file directory

Flushing the Logs

Flushing the logs causes the server to close and reopen log files. This can be done by executing a `mysqladmin flush-logs` command or a `FLUSH LOGS` statement. On Unix, sending a `SIGHUP` signal to the server also flushes the logs. `mysqladmin refresh` flushes the logs, but it does other things as well, such as flushing the table cache, so it's overkill if you just want to flush the logs.

> The binary and relay log files are created in numbered sequence. Flushing the logs causes
> the server to close the current log file and open a new one with the next number in the se-
> quence.
>
> Log flushing can be useful for log expiration or rotation purposes, as discussed in Section
> 12.5.7, "Log Management."
>
> Log flushing does not apply to storage engine-specific logs.

12.5.1 The Error Log

The error log is used for recording when the server starts and stops, and for diagnostic and
error information. The amount of information logged can be influenced by using the
`--log-warnings` option, which takes values from 0 to 2 to select increasing levels of
logging.

If the server is logging errors to a file, `FLUSH LOGS` causes server to rename the file with
an extension of `-old` and begin logging to a new file with the original name.

Other error log properties are handled differently on Unix and Windows, as described
in the following discussion.

12.5.1.1 The Error Log on Unix

On Unix, `mysqld` does not create an error log by default, but instead sends diagnostic output to the console. If you invoke `mysqld` directly, you can send error output to a file rather
than to the console by specifying a `--log-error` option, either on the command line or
in the `[mysqld]` group of an option file.

If you start the server by invoking `mysqld_safe`, an error log is created by default because `mysqld_safe` invokes `mysqld` with the server's output redirected to the error log.
The default error log filename is `HOSTNAME.err`. You can indicate a different error log
name by specifying a `--log-error` option, either on the command line or in the
`[mysqld_safe]` or `[mysqld]` group of an option file. (`mysqld_safe` looks in `[mysqld]`
option groups and uses the `--log-error` option there if it finds one.)

`mysqld_safe` and `mysqld` treat the `--log-error` option somewhat differently, so you
probably should specify the option only to one of them if you use it explicitly:

- For `mysqld`, you can specify the option without a filename. In this case, it creates the
  file using the name `HOSTNAME.err` in the data directory. For `mysqld_safe`, you must
  specify a filename if you use the option.

- If you specify a relative filename for the `--log-error` option, `mysqld` and
  `mysqld_safe` interpret it in different ways. `mysqld` interprets the name relative to
  the data directory, as does `mysqld_safe` from MySQL 5.1.11 and up. Prior to
  5.1.11, `mysqld_safe` interprets the name relative to the directory from which it is
  invoked. Consequently, if you use `mysqld_safe` but don't always invoke it from the
  same directory (for example, if you execute it manually from different locations on
  different occasions), it's best to specify the error log name as an absolute pathname
  to ensure that it is created in the same location.

- `mysqld` adds an extension of `.err`, as does `mysqld_safe` from MySQL 5.1.11 and up. Prior to 5.1.11, `mysqld_safe` uses the filename as given even if it has no extension.

If the error log file already exists but is not writable to the login account used for running the server, startup will fail with no output being written to the error log. This can happen if you start the server with different `--user` values at different times. It's best to use the same account consistently, as discussed in Section 12.2.1.1, "Running the Server Using an Unprivileged Login Account."

As of MySQL 5.1.20, you can send error output to `syslog` rather than to a log file if you start the server with `mysqld_safe`. (It is best to use 5.1.21 or higher to avoid problems in the early implementation of this feature.) To use `syslog` for diagnostic output, start `mysqld_safe` with the `--syslog` option rather than `--log-error`. With logging to `syslog`, messages from `mysqld` and `mysqld_safe` are written with a tag (prefix) of `mysqld` and `mysqld_safe`, respectively. If you specify a `--syslog-tag=str` option, the tags are `mysqld-str` and `mysqld_safe-str` instead.

If you start the server using the `mysql.server` script, an error log is always created because `mysql.server` invokes `mysqld_safe`. However, `mysql.server` doesn't recognize any error-logging options on the command line or in its `[mysql.server]` option group. You can specify any required options to `mysqld_safe` or `mysqld` as described earlier in this section.

12.5.1.2 The Error Log on Windows

On Windows, the server writes diagnostic information to a file named *HOSTNAME*`.err` in the data directory by default. If you start the server manually with the `--console` option, it writes diagnostic output to the console window and does not create an error log. (If the server runs as a Windows service, the `--console` option has no effect because there is no console to write to in that case.)

12.5.2 The General Query Log

This log contains a record of when clients connect to the server, each statement that is sent to it by clients, and various other events such as server startup and shutdown. The server writes statements to this log in the order that it receives them. This may well be different from the order in which they finish executing, particularly for a mix of simple and complex statements.

To enable the general log, specify the `--log` option. If you give the option without a filename, the default name is *HOSTNAME*`.log` in the data directory.

As of MySQL 5.1.6, you can write the general log to a file, a database table, or both. For details, see Section 12.5.6, "Using Log Tables."

12.5.3 The Slow-Query Log

The slow-query log provides a record of which queries took a long time to execute:

- "Long" is defined as the value of the `long_query_time` system variable in seconds (10 seconds by default). The minimum and default values are 1 and 10 before

MySQL 5.1.21. As of 5.1.21, the value can have a fractional part in microseconds and the minimum value is 0.

- As of MySQL 5.1.21, queries must also examine at least `min_examined_row_limit` rows or they are not logged. The default value is 0.

Because the time a query takes is not known until it finishes, queries are written to the slow-query log after they execute, not when they are received. Slow queries also cause the server to increment its `Slow_queries` status variable.

The slow-query log is written as text, so it is viewable with any file-display program, or you can use the `mysqldumpslow` utility to summarize its contents.

The slow-query log can be useful for identifying queries that you might be able to improve if you rewrite them. However, when interpreting its contents, you'll need to take general system load into account. "Slowness" is measured in real time (not CPU time), so if your server is bogged down, it's more likely that a query will be assessed as slow, even if at some other time it runs under the limit.

To enable the slow-query log, specify the `--log-slow-queries` option. If you give the option without a filename, the default name is *HOSTNAME*-slow.log in the data directory.

As of MySQL 5.1.6, you can write the slow-query log to a file, a database table, or both. For details, see Section 12.5.6, "Using Log Tables." For logging to a table, the fractional part of query execution time is discarded.

Several related options affect what is written to the slow-query log: With `--log-short-format`, the server writes less information to the log. With `--log-queries-not-using-indexes`, the server also logs queries that execute without benefit of any index. `--log-slow-admin-statements` causes the server to log slow administrative statements such as `ANALYZE TABLE` or `ALTER TABLE`.

12.5.4 The Binary Log and the Binary Log Index File

The server uses the binary log to record data-modification "events" such as those resulting from `INSERT`, `DELETE`, or `UPDATE` statements. It does not write `SELECT` operations to this log. An `UPDATE` statement such as the following one does not appear in the binary log, either, because it doesn't actually change any values:

```
UPDATE t SET i = i;
```

MySQL must execute a statement first to determine whether it modifies data, so it writes information to the binary log after statements finish executing rather than when it receives them.

The binary log also contains information that is useful for replication purposes, such as statement execution timestamps.

Unlike other logs, information is not written to the binary log as text, but in a more efficient binary format. This takes less space than text, but the binary nature of this log means that it is not directly viewable. You can use the `mysqlbinlog` utility to display the contents of binary log files in readable text form.

The binary log can be used for database backup and recovery. Also, if you want to set up a server as a master server that is replicated to a slave server, you *must* enable the binary log.

The server writes events to the binary log in order of execution. That is, they're logged in the order they finish, not the order in which they are received, which is an important property for making replication work properly. For statements that are part of a transaction, the server caches them until the transaction is committed. Then the server logs all events in the transaction. If the transaction is rolled back, the transaction is not written to the binary log, because it results in no changes to the database.

Actually, it is more correct to say that rolled-back transactions *usually* are not written to the binary log. If a transaction makes changes to non-transactional tables such as MyISAM tables, those changes cannot be rolled back. In this case, even a rolled-back transaction is logged to the binary log, to ensure that in a replication setup the changes to the non-transactional tables replicate properly.

To enable the binary log, specify the `--log-bin` option. If you give the option without a filename, the server generates binary log files in numbered sequence, using *HOSTNAME*-bin as the basename: *HOSTNAME*-bin.000001, *HOSTNAME*-bin.000002, and so forth. Otherwise, the server uses the name that you specify as the sequence basename (if the name includes an extension, the extension is ignored). The server generates the next file in the sequence each time you start it or flush the logs, or when the current log reaches its maximum size. This size is determined by the value of the `max_binlog_size` system variable.

If you enable binary logging, the server also creates an accompanying binary log index file that lists the names of the existing binary log files. The default index filename is the same as the basename of the binary log files, with an `.index` extension. To specify a name explicitly, use the `--log-bin-index` option. If the name includes no extension, `.index` is added to the name automatically. For example, if you specify `--log-bin-index=binlog`, the index filename becomes `binlog.index`.

If you use the `--log-short-format` option in conjunction with `--log-bin`, MySQL writes less information to the binary log.

Before MySQL 5.1, events written to the binary log are statement-based. As of 5.1, logging can be done using either statement-based or row-based format. For example, with statement-based logging, an `UPDATE` is logged as an `UPDATE` statement, whereas with row-based logging the `UPDATE` is logged in terms of the changes to be made to individual rows that are updated. (See Section 14.7.3, "Binary Logging Formats.") The `--binlog-format=format` option specifies which type of logging to use. The allowable option values are `STATEMENT`, `ROW`, and `MIXED`. As of MySQL 5.1.12, the default is `MIXED`, which uses row-based logging except in cases where statement-based logging must be used instead.

If you are using the binary log for replication purposes, be sure not to delete any given binary log file until you are sure that its contents have been replicated to all applicable slave servers and it is no longer needed. Section 12.5.7.2, "Expiring Binary Log and Relay Log Files," describes how to check this.

> **Binary Log Files and System Backups**
>
> Your binary (and relay) logs won't be any good for database recovery or replication if a disk crash causes you to lose them. Make sure you're performing regular filesystem backups. It's also a good idea to write these logs to a different disk from the one on which your databases are stored, which requires that you relocate them from the data directory where the server writes them by default. To do this, use the logging options to specify different log locations.

12.5.5 The Relay Log and the Relay Log Index File

A server that is a replication slave writes data modifications ("events") from the master server to its relay log as it receives them. The relay log acts as a holding area for these modifications where they are held pending execution on the slave server.

Two separate slave server threads handle event reading and execution. The I/O thread reads events from the master and logs them to the relay logs. The SQL thead reads the relay log files, executes the events, and deletes each file when it has been completely processed. This decoupling of function enables the threads to run independently.

The relay log shares several characteristics with the binary log:

- The server creates relay log files in numbered sequence.
- There is an index file that lists the current set of relay log files.
- Relay log files have the same format as binary log files, so you can display their contents with the `mysqlbinlog` program.

To enable the relay log, specify the `--relay-log` option. If you give the option without a filename, the server generates relay log files in numbered sequence, using *HOSTNAME*-relay-bin as the basename: *HOSTNAME*-relay-bin.000001, *HOSTNAME*-relay-bin.000002, and so forth. Otherwise, the server uses the name that you specify as the sequence basename (if the name includes an extension, the extension is ignored). The server generates the next file in the sequence each time you start it or flush the logs, or when the current log reaches its maximum size. This size is determined by the value of the `max_relay_log_size` system variable.

If you enable relay logging, the server also creates an accompanying relay log index file that lists the names of the existing relay log files. The default index filename is the same as the basename of the relay log files, with an `.index` extension. To specify a name explicitly, use the `--relay-log-index` option. If the name includes no extension, `.index` is added to the name automatically. For example, if you specify `--relay-log-index=relay-log`, the index filename becomes `relay-log.index`.

12.5.6 Using Log Tables

Before MySQL 5.1.6, the server writes entries for the general query log and slow-query log to files if they are enabled. As of 5.1.6, when these logs are enabled, you can write log output to a log file, a log table in the `mysql` database, or both. (It is best to use 5.1.21 or higher to avoid problems in the early implementation of this feature. The following discussion assumes a version at least that recent.)

To select the log output destinations, use the `--log-output=destinations` option when you start the server. The `destinations` value is a list of one or more comma-separated values: `FILE` (log to files), `TABLE` (log to tables), or `NONE` (do not log). `NONE`, if present, overrides any other destinations. The default is `FILE` if `--log-output` is not given or given without a value.

`--log-output` determines only which log destinations to use but does not enable logging. To enable the general query log or slow-query log, use the `--log` or `--log-slow-queries` option, just as before log table tables are available. (See Section 12.5.2, "The General Query Log," and Section 12.5.3, "The Slow-Query Log.")

Logging destinations can be changed at runtime by setting the global `log_output` system variable. For example, to temporarily disable logging, use this statement:

```
SET GLOBAL log_output='NONE';
```

To re-enable logging and use files as well as tables, do this:

```
SET GLOBAL log_output='FILE,TABLE';
```

If a log is enabled, the server writes startup messages to its log file, but writes no queries to the file thereafter unless the `FILE` destination has been selected.

The server implements `TABLE` logging using the `general_log` and `slow_log` tables in the `mysql` database. (Be sure to run `mysql_upgrade` to ensure that these tables exist if you upgrade to MySQL 5.1.6 or higher from an older version.)

The global `general_log_file` and `slow_query_log_file` system variables are set to the names of the log files. If logging to files is enabled, changing the value of either variable changes the name of the file to which the server writes the corresponding log.

The contents of the log tables are intended for viewing but cannot be modified except as done by the server itself. Consequently, you can use them with `SELECT`, but not `INSERT`, `DELETE`, or `UPDATE`. (You can empty a log table with `TRUNCATE TABLE`, however.)

12.5.7 Log Management

Logging is important, but one danger of enabling logging is that it has the potential to generate huge amounts of information, possibly filling up your disks. This is especially true if you have a busy server that processes lots of statements. You can use log file expiration techniques to keep the last few logs available online while preventing logs from growing without bound. Several methods are available for keeping logs manageable:

- **Log rotation.** This applies to log files that have a fixed name, such as the general and slow-query log files.

- **Age-based expiration.** This method removes log files that are older than a certain age. It can be applied to numbered log files that are created in numbered sequence, such as the binary log. However, you should not use this technique if you use the binary log for replication.

- **Replication-related expiration.** If you use the binary log files for replication, it's better not to expire them based on age. You should expire them only after you know they have been sent completely to each slave. This form of expiration therefore is based on determining which binary log files are still in use.

A replication slave server creates the relay log files in numbered sequence and removes them automatically as it finishes processing them. To reduce the amount of relay log information stored on disk, you can lower the maximum allowable size by setting the `max_relay_log_size` system variable.

- **Log table truncation or rotation.** If you are logging to tables in the `mysql` database, you can truncate them or rename and replace them with empty tables.

Log rotation often is used in conjunction with log flushing, to make sure that any buffered log information has been written to disk. Logs can be flushed by executing a `mysqladmin flush-logs` command or by issuing a `FLUSH LOGS` statement.

The following sections describe how to use these expiration methods. The example log-expiration scripts discussed here are located in the `admin` directory of the `sampdb` distribution.

For any techniques that you put into practice, you should also consider how the log files fit into your database backup methods. It's a good idea to back up any log files that may be needed for recovery operations, so you shouldn't expire them before backing them up.

12.5.7.1 Rotating Fixed-Name Log Files

The MySQL server writes some types of log information to files that have fixed names, such as the general query log file and the slow-query log file. To expire fixed-name log files, use log rotation. This enables you to maintain the last few logs online but limit the number to as many as you choose, to prevent them from overrunning your disk.

Log file rotation works as follows. Suppose that your general query log file is named `qlog`. At the first rotation, rename `qlog` to `qlog.1` and tell the server to begin writing a new log file named `qlog`. At the second rotation, rename `qlog.1` to `qlog.2`, `qlog` to `qlog.1`, and tell the server to begin writing another new `qlog` file. In this way, each file rotates through the names `qlog.1`, `qlog.2`, and so forth. When the file reaches a certain point in the rotation, expire it by letting the previous file overwrite it. For example, if you rotate the logs daily and you want to keep a week's work of logs, you would keep `qlog.1` through `qlog.7`. At each rotation, you expire `qlog.7` by letting `qlog.6` overwrite it to become the new `qlog.7`.

The frequency of log rotation and the number of old logs you keep will depend on how busy your server is (active servers generate more log information) and how much disk space you're willing to allocate to old logs.

On Unix, you can rename the current log file while the server has it open. After doing so, flushing the logs causes the server to close that file and open a new one, thereby creating a new log file with the original name. The following shell script, `rotate_fixed_logs.sh`, performs rotation of fixed-name log files:

```
#!/bin/sh
# rotate_fixed_logs.sh - rotate MySQL log file that has a fixed name
```

```
# Argument 1: log filename

if [ $# -ne 1 ]; then
  echo "Usage: $0 logname" 1>&2
  exit 1
fi

logfile=$1

mv $logfile.6 $logfile.7
mv $logfile.5 $logfile.6
mv $logfile.4 $logfile.5
mv $logfile.3 $logfile.4
mv $logfile.2 $logfile.3
mv $logfile.1 $logfile.2
mv $logfile $logfile.1
mysqladmin flush-logs
```

The script takes the log filename as its argument. You can either specify the full pathname of the file or change directory into the log directory and specify the file's name in
that directory. For example, to rotate a log file named qlog in /usr/mysql/data, execute
the script like this:

% **rotate_fixed_logs.sh /usr/mysql/data/qlog**

Or like this:

% **cd /usr/mysql/data**
% **rotate_fixed_logs.sh qlog**

> **Note**
>
> The first few times the log rotation script executes, you won't have a full set of log files in the
> rotation, so the script complains that it can't find all the files to be rotated. That's normal.

To make sure that you have permission to rename the log files, run the script while
logged in under the same account that you use for running the server (that's the mysql
account in this book). Note that the mysqladmin command in the script includes no connection parameter arguments such as -u or -p. If the relevant parameters for invoking
mysqladmin are stored in the .my.cnf option file in the mysql account home directory,
you don't need to specify them on the mysqladmin command in the script. If you don't
use an option file, the mysqladmin command needs to know how to connect to the server
using a MySQL account that has sufficient privileges to flush the logs. To handle this, you
might want to set up a limited-privilege account that can't do anything but issue flush
commands. Then you can put that account's password in the script with minimal risk if
you make the script accessible only to mysql. If you want to do this, the MySQL account

should have only the RELOAD privilege. For example, to call the user flush and assign a password of flushpass, use the following statements:

```
CREATE USER 'flush'@'localhost' IDENTIFIED BY 'flushpass';
GRANT RELOAD ON *.* TO 'flush'@'localhost';
```

After creating this account, change the mysqladmin command in the rotate_fixed_logs.sh script to look like this:

```
mysqladmin -u flush -pflushpass flush-logs
```

To protect the script against being read by other login accounts, you can make the script readable only to mysql. Execute the following command while logged in as mysql:

```
% chmod go-rwx rotate_fixed_logs.sh
```

To see how to use the rotate_fixed_logs.sh script to rotate and flush the logs periodically, consult Section 12.5.7.3, "Automating the Log Expiration Procedure."

Under Linux, you may prefer to use the logrotate utility to install the mysql-log-rotate script that comes with the MySQL distribution, rather than using rotate_fixed_logs.sh or writing your own script. Look for mysql-log-rotate in /usr/share/mysql for RPM distributions, or in the support-files directory of your MySQL installation for binary distributions, or under the share/mysql directory of MySQL source distributions.

On Windows, log file renaming can be performed using the following batch script, rotate_fixed_logs.bat:

```
@echo off
REM rotate_fixed_logs.bat - rotate MySQL log file that has a fixed name

REM Argument 1: log filename

if not "%1" == "" goto ROTATE
@echo Usage: rotate_fixed_logs logname
goto DONE

:ROTATE
set logfile=%1
erase %logfile%.7
rename %logfile%.6 %logfile%.7
rename %logfile%.5 %logfile%.6
rename %logfile%.4 %logfile%.5
rename %logfile%.3 %logfile%.4
rename %logfile%.2 %logfile%.3
rename %logfile%.1 %logfile%.2
rename %logfile% %logfile%.1
:DONE
```

Invoke `rotate_fixed_logs.bat` much like the `rotate_fixed_logs.sh` shell script, with a single argument that names the log file to be rotated. For example, to rotate a log file named `qlog` in `C:\mysql\data`, execute the script like this:

```
C:\> rotate_fixed_logs C:\mysql\data\qlog
```

Or like this:

```
C:\> cd \mysql\data
C:\> rotate_fixed_logs qlog
```

> **Note**
>
> Until MySQL 5.0.17/5.1.3, you cannot rename the general query log or slow-query log file on Windows while the server has it open; a "file in use" error occurs. Therefore, for older servers, to ensure that a log file is not open so that you can rotate it, first stop the server, and then perform the file renaming and restart the server.

12.5.7.2 Expiring Binary Log and Relay Log Files

Fixed-name log files can be expired using filename rotation, as just discussed. For numbered logs such as the binary log and the relay log, the server generates logs in numbered sequence, and expiration needs to be handled a bit differently.

For the binary log, there are two approaches that you can take:

- Expire log files based on age (assessed as time of last modification). You can do this if you are not using the binary log for replication.
- Expire log files based on whether they are still in use. This is more applicable if you are using the binary log for replication.

If you are not using the binary log for replication, the easiest way to expire the log files is to set the `expire_logs_days` system variable. When this variable has a value n greater than zero, the server automatically expires binary log files that are older than n days old and updates the binary log index file. For example, to set this variable to expire binary log files that have not been changed for a week, put these lines in an option file:

```
[mysqld]
expire_logs_days=7
```

The server checks whether to expire binary log files when it starts and when it opens a new log file.

If you use the binary log for replication, do not use age-based replication. In this case, age is not an indicator of whether a log file can be removed. Suppose that a slave server is down and has not been sent the contents of a given binary log file. If the slave does not come back up by the time the file reaches its expiration age, the file would be discarded and replication would fail. To avoid this problem, you should consider a binary log file eligible for expiration only after its contents have been replicated to all slave servers.

A difficulty here is that, due to the asynchronous nature of MySQL replication, the master server itself doesn't know how many slaves there are or which files have been propagated to them. The master won't purge binary log files that have not yet been sent to connected slaves, but there is no guarantee that a given slave is connected at any particular time. You must know which servers are acting as slaves, and then connect to each one and issue a SHOW SLAVE STATUS statement to determine which of the master's binary log files the slave currently is processing. (The file's name is the value in the Master_Log_File column.) Any binary log that is no longer used by any of the slaves can be removed.

To understand how this works, suppose that you have the following scenario:

- The local server is the master and it has two slaves, S1 and S2.
- The binary log files that exist on the master have names of binlog.000038 through binlog.000042.
- SHOW SLAVE STATUS produces the following result on S1:

```
mysql> SHOW SLAVE STATUS\G
...
Master_Log_File: binlog.000041
...
```

And this result on S2:

```
mysql> SHOW SLAVE STATUS\G
...
Master_Log_File: binlog.000040
...
```

In this case, the lowest-numbered binary log still required by the set of slave servers is binlog.000040, so any log with a lower number can be removed. To do that, connect to the master server and issue the following statement:

```
mysql> PURGE MASTER LOGS TO 'binlog.000040';
```

That causes the server to delete all binary log files with numbers lower than the named file, which for the situation just described includes binlog.000038 and binlog.000039.

The SHOW SLAVE STATUS and PURGE MASTER LOGS statements each require the SUPER privilege.

To expire relay log files, you need take no special action. A replication slave server creates the relay log files in numbered sequence. It generates a new relay log file when the current one reaches the maximum allowable size (or when the logs are flushed), and removes old files automatically as it finishes processing them. However, if the maximum relay log size is large, the current file also grows large. To reduce the amount of relay log information stored on disk, you can lower the maximum allowable size by setting the max_relay_log_size system variable.

12.5.7.3 Automating the Log Expiration Procedure

It's possible to invoke log expiration scripts manually, but you need not remember to execute them yourself if you have a way to schedule the commands to run automatically. On Unix, one way to do this is to use the cron utility and set up a crontab file that defines the expiration schedule. If you're not familiar with `cron`, check the relevant Unix manual pages using these commands:

```
% man cron
% man crontab
```

You might need to use another command to read about the `crontab` file format:

```
% man 5 crontab
```

Suppose that you want to rotate a general query log named `qlog` by using the `rotate_fixed_logs.sh` script, that this script is installed in `/home/mysql/bin`, and that the log files are located in the `/var/mysql/data` directory. Log in as `mysql`, and then edit the `mysql` user's `crontab` file using this command:

```
% crontab -e
```

This command enables you to edit a copy of your current `crontab` file (which might be empty if no `cron` jobs have yet been set up). Add a line to the file that looks like this:

```
30 4 * * * /home/mysql/bin/rotate_fixed_logs.sh /var/mysql/data/qlog
```

This entry tells `cron` to run the script at 04:30 each day. You can vary the time or scheduling as desired; check the `crontab` manual page for the format of the entries. You'll probably want to rotate the logs more frequently for a busy server that generates lots of log information than for one that is less active.

To make sure that the logs are flushed regularly (for example, to generate the next numbered binary log), you can schedule a `mysqladmin flush-logs` command to execute periodically by adding another `crontab` entry. You might need to list the full pathname to `mysqladmin` to make sure that `cron` can find it.

Automatic log file expiration is more problematic on Windows before MySQL 5.0.17/5.1.3, because you cannot rename the general query log or slow-query log file while the server has it open (see Section 12.5.7.1, "Rotating Fixed-Name Log Files"). This means that you cannot rotate any current log file without stopping and restarting the server, and there might be no time of day when you can guarantee that the server will not be in use.

12.5.7.4 Expiring or Rotating Log Tables

If the server is writing the general query log or slow-query log to tables in the `mysql` database, you can either truncate the tables or use a form of table rotation.

To truncate the tables, use these statements:

```
USE mysql;
TRUNCATE TABLE general_log;
TRUNCATE TABLE slow_log;
```

To rotate a log table, first create an empty copy. Then perform an atomic rename that "swaps out" the current table and replaces it with the empty one in a single statement:

```
USE mysql;
```

```
CREATE TABLE general_log_tmp LIKE general_log;
RENAME TABLE general_log TO general_log_old, general_log_tmp TO general_log;
CREATE TABLE slow_log_tmp LIKE slow_log;
RENAME TABLE slow_log TO slow_log_old, slow_log_tmp TO slow_log;
```

RENAME TABLE for log tables requires MySQL 5.1.13 or higher.

If you have the event scheduler running, log table rotation can be done automatically by creating an event such as the one following. The event rotates the log tables each day. Change the ON SCHEDULE clause to vary the frequency.

```
CREATE EVENT mysql.rotate_log_tables
ON SCHEDULE EVERY 1 DAY
DO BEGIN
  DROP TABLE IF EXISTS general_log_old, general_log_tmp;
  CREATE TABLE general_log_tmp LIKE general_log;
  RENAME TABLE
    general_log TO general_log_old,
    general_log_tmp TO general_log;
  DROP TABLE IF EXISTS slow_log_old, slow_log_tmp;
  CREATE TABLE slow_log_tmp LIKE slow_log;
  RENAME TABLE
    slow_log TO slow_log_old,
    slow_log_tmp TO slow_log;
END;
```

12.6 Tuning the Server

The MySQL server has several system variables (parameters) that affect how it operates. You can display these variables with the SHOW VARIABLES statement. If the default variable values are not appropriate, you can change them to configure the server with values that are better for the environment in which it runs. Some of these variables are used for performance tuning, such as those that control the size of memory buffers. For example, if you have plenty of memory, you can tell the server to use larger buffers for disk and index operations. This will hold more information in memory and decrease the number of disk accesses that need to be made. If your system is more modest, you can tell the server to use smaller buffers. This will likely make the server run more slowly but may improve overall system performance by preventing the MySQL server from hogging system resources to the detriment of other processes.

Other variables affect how the server interacts with clients, such as the variables that control the SQL mode, the default storage engine, and the current time zone.

The server also has a set of status variables that provide information about how it is actually performing as it runs. You can display these variables with the SHOW STATUS statement. These status variables help you monitor the server and check the effect of configuration changes that you make by modifying the system variables.

The following sections discuss the general syntax for setting or examining system variables and describe some of the variables that have application to the operation of the server as a whole. For tuning parameters specific to individual storage engines, see Section 12.7, "Storage Engine Configuration." You can also find additional discussion of server tuning in the optimization chapter of the MySQL Reference Manual.

12.6.1 Checking and Setting System Variable Values

Most system variables can be set at server startup time using options on the command line or in option files. The general syntax is described in Section F.1, "Specifying Program Options." System variables can be displayed at runtime with SHOW VARIABLES, and many of them can be modified while the server is running. The ability to set variables at runtime gives you better control over server operation, and can help you avoid stopping the server to reconfigure it under circumstances when that might otherwise be necessary. (For example, you can experiment with buffer sizes to see how that affects server performance, without having to stop and restart the server for each change.) Changes made at runtime do not last beyond termination of the server process, but if you determine a value for a variable that is better than its current default, you can set the variable in an option file to cause the value to be used whenever the server starts in the future.

Several system variables pertain to the manner in which the server interacts with clients. The ability to change these variables affords clients a measure of control over how the server operates and enables applications to customize the behavior they require.

System variables can exist at two levels: global and session-specific. Global variables affect the operation of the server as a whole. Session-specific variables affect only how the server treats a given client connection. For variables that exist at both levels, the global values are used to initialize the corresponding session variables. This happens only when a new client connection begins; changing a global variable during a connection does not affect the current value of the client's corresponding session variable.

It is possible for a system variable to have both global and session forms, only a global form, or only a session form:

- The sql_mode system variable that indicates the default SQL mode is an example of a variable that exists at both the global and session levels. The SQL mode affects several aspects of SQL statement processing by the server. When each client connects, it gets its own session-specific sql_mode variable, which initially has the same value as the global variable. Any client can modify the value of its session variable to change the server's behavior for its own connection without affecting how the server treats other clients. A client that has the SUPER privilege also can change the global sql_mode variable. The new global value is used to initialize the session variable for clients that connect after the change.

- The key_buffer_size system variable is an example of a global-only variable. It controls the size of the default key cache that buffers the contents of MyISAM table indexes. This key cache is shared among all clients, so there is no reason to have a session value for each client.

- Some variables exist only at the session level. The `autocommit` variable is one of these. Each client begins with its autocommit mode enabled by default, but can disable it as necessary.

Appendix D, "System, Status, and User Variable Reference," lists all system variables and indicates which of them can be set at startup time and runtime. The following discussion indicates the syntax for checking system variables and for setting their values.

12.6.1.1 Checking System Variable Values

To see the current values of system variables, use `SHOW VARIABLES`:

```
mysql> SHOW VARIABLES;
+---------------------------------+------------------+
| Variable_name                   | Value            |
+---------------------------------+------------------+
| auto_increment_increment        | 1                |
| auto_increment_offset           | 1                |
| autocommit                      | ON               |
| automatic_sp_privileges         | ON               |
| back_log                        | 50               |
| basedir                         | /usr/local/mysql |
| big_tables                      | OFF              |
...
```

With a `LIKE` clause, you can restrict output to rows for variables with names that match a given SQL pattern:

```
mysql> SHOW VARIABLES LIKE 'key%';
+-------------------------+---------+
| Variable_name           | Value   |
+-------------------------+---------+
| key_buffer_size         | 8388572 |
| key_cache_age_threshold | 300     |
| key_cache_block_size    | 1024    |
| key_cache_division_limit| 100     |
+-------------------------+---------+
```

As of MySQL 5.0.2, a `WHERE` clause can be used to specify general conditions for selecting rows. The following statement finds timeouts that are set to less than 60 seconds:

```
mysql> SHOW VARIABLES
    -> WHERE Variable_name LIKE '%timeout%' AND Value < 60;
+---------------------------+-------+
| Variable_name             | Value |
+---------------------------+-------+
| connect_timeout           | 10    |
| innodb_lock_wait_timeout  | 50    |
| innodb_rollback_on_timeout| OFF   |
```

```
| net_read_timeout         | 30    |
| table_lock_wait_timeout  | 50    |
+--------------------------+-------+
```

SHOW VARIABLES returns each variable's session value if one exists at that level and the global value if not. To specifically request the values of global or session variables, add GLOBAL or SESSION to the statement:

```
SHOW GLOBAL VARIABLES;
SHOW SESSION VARIABLES;
```

LOCAL is a synonym for SESSION.

The mysqladmin variables command displays the current values of the server's global system variables.

Individual variable values can be selected using @@GLOBAL.*var_name* syntax for a global variable, or @@SESSION.*var_name* or @@LOCAL.*var_name* for a session variable. If you use @@*var_name* syntax without a level qualifier, the session variable is used if it exists and the global value if not.

The @@- syntax is general purpose and can be used in SET, SELECT, or other SQL statements:

```
SELECT 'Default storage engine:', @@storage_engine;
```

Most of the session-only variables are not displayed at all by SHOW VARIABLES, but you can access their values by name:

```
SELECT @@autocommit, @@warning_count;
```

As of MySQL 5.1.12, you can also query the INFORMATION_SCHEMA tables named GLOBAL_VARIABLES and SESSION_VARIABLES to obtain system variable information.

12.6.1.2 Setting System Variables at Server Startup Time

Many global system variables can be set when the server starts. There are two syntaxes for doing this:

- You can treat a variable name as an option name and set it directly. For example, the max_connections variable controls the maximum number of simultaneous client connections. To set this variable to 200, you can do so using this option on the mysqld command line:

  ```
  % mysqld --max_connections=200
  ```

  You can also set the variable in an option file using this syntax:

  ```
  [mysqld]
  max_connections=200
  ```

Another feature of the variable-as-option syntax is that underscores can be given as dashes so that the variable reference looks more like other options. On the command line, set the variable like this:

```
% mysqld --max-connections=200
```

In an option file, set it like this:

```
[mysqld]
max-connections=200
```

- You can set a variable at server startup with the `--set-variable` or `-O` option. This syntax is older and is deprecated but still supported for now. On the command line, set a variable like this:

```
% mysqld --set-variable=max_connections=200
% mysqld -O max_connections=200
```

In option files, only the long-option form is allowable:

```
[mysqld]
set-variable=max_connections=200
```

It's usually more convenient to set system variables in an option file than on the command line because you don't have to remember to set them each time you start the server.

For variables that represent buffer sizes or lengths, values are in bytes if specified as a number with no suffix, or may be specified with a suffix of 'K', 'M', or 'G', to indicate kilobytes, megabytes, or gigabytes, respectively. Suffixes are not case sensitive, so you can also use 'k', 'm', or 'g'.

Some system variables cannot be set directly using a startup option. In such cases, there often is a related option. For example, you cannot directly set the `storage_engine` variable at startup, but the `--default-storage-engine` option can be used instead. Appendix D indicates which global system variables can be set directly. For those that cannot, the appendix lists the related option for setting the variable if there is one.

12.6.1.3 Setting System Variables at Runtime

The syntax for setting system variables at runtime depends on whether you want to set a global variable or a session variable. To set a global variable named *var_name*, use a SET statement having one of these formats:

```
SET GLOBAL var_name = value;
SET @@GLOBAL.var_name = value;
```

To set a session variable, similar syntax applies:

```
SET SESSION var_name = value;
SET @@SESSION.var_name = value;
```

LOCAL is a synonym for SESSION.

If no level indicator is present, the SET statement modifies the session variable:

```
SET var_name = value;
SET @@var_name = value;
```

You can set several variables in a single SET statement by separating the assignments with commas:

```
SET SESSION sql_warnings = 0, GLOBAL storage_engine = InnoDB;
```

In a statement that sets multiple variables, an explicit GLOBAL or SESSION level indicator applies to following variable settings that do not include a level of their own. The following statement sets the global *v1* and *v2* variables, and the session *v3* and *v4* variables:

```
SET GLOBAL v1 = val1, v2 = val2, SESSION v3 = val3, v4 = val4;
```

You must have the SUPER privilege to set a global variable. The setting persists until changed again or the server exits. No special privileges are needed to set a session variable. The setting persists until changed again or the current connection terminates.

Unlike variables that are set at startup time, you cannot specify runtime values using suffix letters of 'K', 'M', or 'G'. However, you can use expressions, and expressions can refer to the values of other variables. The following statements set the global read_buffer_size value to 2MB, and the session value to twice that:

```
SET GLOBAL read_buffer_size = 2*1024*1024;
SET SESSION read_buffer_size = 2*@@GLOBAL.read_buffer_size;
```

Many system variables can be set to the special value DEFAULT. For those variables that understand this syntax, assigning DEFAULT to a global variable sets it to the compiled-in default (even if a different value was given with a startup option). Assigning DEFAULT to a session variable sets it to the current value of the corresponding global variable.

MySQL supports the concept of a structured system variable, which consists of a set of related system variables that are grouped and accessed as components of the structured variable. Currently, the only structured variables that exist are used for configuring MyISAM key caches, so their syntax is discussed in Section 12.7.2, "Configuring the MyISAM Storage Engine."

12.6.2 General-Purpose System Variables

The following list describes several system variables that are useful for general performance tuning:

- delayed_queue_size determines the number of rows from INSERT DELAYED statements that can be queued per table (for those storage engines that support DELAYED inserts) before clients issuing additional INSERT DELAYED statements get blocked. If you have many clients that use INSERT DELAYED to avoid being blocked but find that they are being blocked anyway because too many rows are being queued, increasing the value of this variable can be useful. That enables a larger queue and reduces the amount of client blocking that occurs. (Section 5.5, "Scheduling and Locking Issues," discusses INSERT DELAYED in detail.)

- `max_allowed_packet` is the maximum size to which the buffer used for client communications can grow. The largest value to which this variable can be set is 1GB.

  The default buffer size for the server is 1MB. Some clients also have their own `max_allowed_packet` variable. If you have clients that send very long statements to the server (for example, statements that include large BLOB or TEXT values), this variable may need to be increased both on the server end and on the client end. For example, to start the server with a 64MB packet limit, you could add these lines to the server option file:

```
[mysqld]
max_allowed_packet=64M
```

  For occasions when you need to invoke mysql or mysqldump with a 64MB packet limit, do so like this:

```
% mysql --max_allowed_packet=64M ...other options...
% mysqldump --max_allowed_packet=64M ...other options...
```

  To use these settings all the time, add these lines to your option file:

```
[mysql]
max_allowed_packet=64M

[mysqldump]
max_allowed_packet=64M
```

- `max_connections` is the maximum number of simultaneous client connections the server allows. If your server is busy, you might need to increase this value. For example, if your MySQL server is used by an active Web server to process lots of statements generated by DBI or PHP scripts, visitors to your site might find requests being refused if this variable is set too low.

- `table_cache` (`table_open_cache` as of MySQL 5.1.3.)

  The size of the table cache. Increasing this value enables mysqld to keep more tables open simultaneously by reducing the number of file open and close operations that must be done.

If you increase the values of max_connections or table_cache/table_open_cache, the server will require a larger number of file descriptors. That may cause problems with operating system limits on the per-process number of file descriptors, in which case you'll need to increase the limit or work around it. Procedures vary for increasing the limit on the number of file descriptors. You can try setting the open_files_limit variable for mysqld. If you cannot set the open files limit high enough using one of those methods, you might need to configure your system to allow more file descriptors. Some systems can be configured simply by editing a system description file and restarting. For others, you must edit a kernel description file and rebuild the kernel. Consult the documentation for your system to see how to proceed.

One way to work around per-process file descriptor limits is to split your data directory into multiple data directories and run multiple servers. This effectively multiplies the number of file descriptors available by the number of servers you run. On the other hand, this strategy can result in complications. For example, you cannot access databases in different data directories from a single server, and you need to set up privileges in the grant tables of multiple servers for users that need access to more than one server.

Another possibility for reducing file-descriptor requirements is to set up replication of your main MySQL server to one or more slave servers. All updates should be directed to the main server, but requests from clients that perform only retrievals can be distributed among all the servers. This lessens the client load of the main server and reduces its file descriptor requirements.

Some variables control resources that are allocated on a per-client basis. Increasing these variables has the potential to increase the server's resource requirements dramatically if many clients connect to it simultaneously. Two values that you might increase in hopes of improving performance are those of the `read_buffer_size` and `sort_buffer_size` variables, which determine the size of the buffers that are used during read and sort operations. Be careful, though: These buffers are allocated for each connection, so if you make the values of the corresponding variables quite large, performance may actually suffer due to exorbitant system resource consumption.

It's best to change the sizes of per-connection buffers incrementally and then test your changes rather than bump them up by a large amount all at once. Doing so enables you to assess the effect of each change with less likelihood of serious performance degradation. Be sure to use realistic test conditions as well. These buffers are allocated only as needed rather than as soon as a client connects. For example, the sort buffer is not allocated for a client unless it performs a query that requires a sort operation. The `join_buffer_size` variable controls the size of the buffer used for non-indexed joins between tables, but a client that runs no joins needs no join buffer. (Conversely, a client that runs complex many-table joins might need multiple join buffers simultaneously.) Your test conditions should use clients that connect at the same time and run complex statements so that you can see the real effect on the server's memory requirements.

12.6.3 Checking Status Variable Values

The server maintains status variables that enable you to monitor its runtime operation. You can display these variables with the `SHOW STATUS` statement:

```
mysql> SHOW STATUS;
+---------------------------------+----------+
| Variable_name                   | Value    |
+---------------------------------+----------+
| Aborted_clients                 | 0        |
| Aborted_connects                | 1        |
| Binlog_cache_disk_use           | 0        |
```

```
| Binlog_cache_use              | 3      |
| Bytes_received                | 125    |
| Bytes_sent                    | 151    |
| Com_admin_commands            | 0      |
...
```

As of MySQL 5.0.2, the status variables (like system variables) have global and session-specific values, so the statement can take GLOBAL or SESSION modifiers:

```
SHOW GLOBAL STATUS;
SHOW SESSION STATUS;
```

GLOBAL shows the status for the server as a whole (all connections together). SESSION shows the status for the current connection. The default is SESSION. LOCAL is a synonym for SESSION.

To write a SHOW STATUS statement that uses a modifier but is portable to MySQL versions older than 5.0.2, put the modifier in a version-specific comment. For example:

```
SHOW /*!50002 GLOBAL */ STATUS;
```

If a variable has only a global value, you get the same value for GLOBAL and SESSION. Appendix D indicates which values each status variable has.

Similar to SHOW VARIABLES, a LIKE clause restricts output to those variables with names that match a given SQL pattern. For example, to check the values of the MyISAM key cache variables, use this statement:

```
mysql> SHOW GLOBAL STATUS LIKE 'Key%';
+-----------------------+-------+
| Variable_name         | Value |
+-----------------------+-------+
| Key_blocks_not_flushed | 0    |
| Key_blocks_unused     | 7247  |
| Key_blocks_used       | 13    |
| Key_read_requests     | 41    |
| Key_reads             | 14    |
| Key_write_requests    | 40    |
| Key_writes            | 2     |
+-----------------------+-------+
```

As of MySQL 5.0.2, a WHERE clause can be used to specify general conditions for selecting rows.

As of MySQL 5.1.12, you can also query the INFORMATION_SCHEMA tables named GLOBAL_STATUS and SESSION_STATUS to obtain status variable information. For example:

```
SELECT * FROM INFORMATION_SCHEMA.GLOBAL_STATUS
WHERE VARIABLE_NAME LIKE 'Qcache%' OR VARIABLE_NAME LIKE 'Key%';
```

Status variables are set only by the server, so they are read only to users and cannot be modified with SET the way that system variables can.

12.7 Storage Engine Configuration

The MySQL server supports multiple storage engines and is highly configurable in terms of which engines to make available. General storage engine characteristics are discussed in Chapter 2, "Using SQL to Manage Data." The following discussion describes how to configure which engines your server uses. It also provides specific configuration information for the MyISAM, InnoDB, and Falcon storage engines.

12.7.1 Selecting Which Storage Engines a Server Supports

The MySQL server provides flexible control over which storage engines are available:

- If you build MySQL from source, you can determine which of the optional storage engines to build.
- For any server, whether or not you compile it yourself, you can selectively enable or disable at startup some of the optional storage engines that are built. You might disable engines that you don't need so as to reduce server memory requirements. (Keep in mind that if you disable an engine, you cannot access any tables that might already have been created by it.)
- You can find out at runtime which engines are available, and which one is the default engine.

Table 12.7 shows the options to use with `configure` to include or exclude each engine when building MySQL from source. Some engines, if built, can be disabled with an option to `mysqld` at startup time if you do not want to use them. Falcon requires MySQL 6.0 or higher. The `--skip-archive` option requires MySQL 5.1 or higher.

Table 12.7 **Storage Engine Configuration and Runtime Options**

Engine	Configuration Options	Runtime Options
ARCHIVE	`--with-archive-storage-engine,` `--without-archive-storage-engine`	`--skip-archive`
BLACKHOLE	`--with-blackhole-storage-engine,` `--without-blackhole-storage-engine`	
CSV	`--with-csv-storage-engine,` `--without-csv-storage-engine`	
EXAMPLE	`--with-example-storage-engine,` `--without-example-storage-engine`	
Falcon	`--with-falcon-storage-engine,` `--without-falcon-storage-engine`	`--skip-falcon`
FEDERATED	`--with-federated-storage-engine,` `--without-federated-storage-engine`	
InnoDB	`--with-innodb,`	`--skip-innodb`

Table 12.7   **Storage Engine Configuration and Runtime Options**

Engine	Configuration Options	Runtime Options
	`--without-innodb`	
MyISAM	Always built	Always enabled
MEMORY	Always built	Always enabled
MERGE	Always built	Always enabled

The MyISAM storage engine is always available. It can be neither excluded at configuration time nor disabled at server startup time. (The grant tables are MyISAM tables, so it is necessary that the MyISAM engine be available to read them.) The MERGE and MEMORY engines are always available as well.

In a given MySQL source distribution, there may be other storage engines that you can use other than those shown in the preceding table. In the top directory of the distribution, use this command to see which engines can be built:

```
% ./configure --help
```

To see which options enable or disable engines for a given server at runtime, invoke it like this:

```
% mysqld --verbose --help
```

As the server runs, it designates one storage engine as the default, which it uses for tables that are created without an explicit ENGINE = engine_name option. MyISAM is compiled in as the default engine, but you can select a different default at server startup or at runtime.

To select a default engine at startup, use the --default-storage-engine=engine_name option. For example, to make InnoDB the default engine, put the following lines in your server option file:

```
[mysqld]
default-storage-engine = innodb
```

To change the default storage engine at runtime, use one of the following statements:

```
SET GLOBAL storage_engine = engine_name;
SET SESSION storage_engine = engine_name;
```

The first statement requires the SUPER privilege and sets the default engine for all clients that connect thereafter. The second requires no special privilege and affects only the current client session. It can be used by any client to change its own default engine.

To check which storage engines are the global and session defaults, use this statement:

```
SELECT @@GLOBAL.storage_engine, @@SESSION.storage_engine;
```

To determine which storage engines are available, use the SHOW ENGINES statement or query the ENGINES table of the INFORMATION_SCHEMA database. For examples, see Section 2.6.1.1, "Checking Which Storage Engines Are Available."

12.7.2 Configuring the MyISAM Storage Engine

MyISAM tables have separate data and index files, which are handled differently:

- For caching data rows read from or written to a MyISAM table, the server relies on the operating system to use its own filesystem caching mechanism.

- For index processing, MyISAM manages its own key cache, which is the most important configurable resource for the MyISAM storage engine. The key cache is used for index-based retrievals and sorts, and for index creation and modification operations.

This section describes the general operation of the key cache and the system variables that you use to configure it.

The MyISAM key cache operates as follows:

- Initially, the key cache is empty.

- When the server needs to examine index values from a table during statement execution, it checks whether they have already been read into the key cache. If so, it consults the in-memory values. Otherwise, it reads the index file for the table to read the index values from disk into a buffer block in the cache.

- If the cache is full when new index values need to be read in, the server must discard values from one of the buffer blocks. By default, it determines which values to discard on the basis of a least recently used (LRU) algorithm. That is, the server chooses the cache buffer that has been unused for the longest time. Blocks are maintained as a chain ordered by last access time, so the server simply picks the one at the end of the chain.

- If the chosen buffer has not been modified, its contents are overwritten with newly read index values. Otherwise, the buffer first must be flushed to the index file before being overwritten.

Values not found in the cache when requested are "misses" and must be read from disk. Values that are found are "hits." The purpose of the key cache is to reduce disk accesses (that is, to minimize the ratio of misses to requests). It boosts performance greatly because memory access is much faster than disk access.

Index buffers containing frequently used values tend to stay in the key cache, but a larger cache increases the chance of a hit. This in turn decreases the need to discard buffers to make room for new ones and minimizes the number of disk accesses needed for index processing. If your server's key cache currently is small and you have memory available, making the cache larger generally is one of the single easiest and best configuration changes you can make.

To configure the key cache size, set the `key_buffer_size` system variable. Its default value is 8MB, but can be increased up to 4GB if you have the memory available. For example, to set the key cache to 512MB, you can put these lines in an option file:

```
[mysqld]
key_buffer_size = 512M
```

Be careful not to set the key cache size so large that you use all available memory. That can cause the key cache itself to get paged out, which defeats the purpose of using a cache to hold information in memory. Remember too that other storage engines use their own buffers for which memory must be allocated, and that generally there are other processes running on the server host that require memory.

The preceding discussion is written as though there is a single key cache. However, MySQL actually supports multiple key caches, which provides more control over cache operation through the following features:

- You can use the default single key cache or create multiple caches.
- You have control over total cache size, cache block size, and the buffer discard algorithm.
- You can assign tables to specific caches.
- You can preload table indexes into a cache.

Multiple key caches can serve to reduce cache contention. If you have a table or set of tables that are heavily used, you can assign them to a separate key cache so that index caching for them does not have to compete with all the other tables that are processed through the default cache.

Each key cache is associated with a set of system variables. Because these variables are related, they are grouped as components that form a structured system variable. Structured variables are an extension of simple system variables, so they are accessed using a syntax that combines a cache name and a variable name:

cache_name.var_name

Each key cache structured variable has these components:

- `key_buffer_size` is the total size of the key cache, in bytes.
- `key_cache_block_size` is the size of blocks in the key cache, in bytes. By default, blocks are 1024 bytes.
- `key_cache_limit` influences the cache buffer reuse algorithm. If set to its default value of 100, the key cache uses a least recently used strategy for determining which cache buffers to reuse. If set lower than 100, the key cache uses a midpoint insertion strategy that splits the cache into warm and hot sub-chains. The value of `key_cache_limit` is the percentage of the key cache to use for the warm buffer sub-chain. The value should be from 1 to 100.

With the midpoint insertion strategy that uses warm and hot sub-chains, an attempt is made to keep the most frequently accessed buffer blocks in the hot sub-chain. Buffers can move between the hot or warm sub-chains as access to them increases or decreases. Buffers to reuse and overwrite always are chosen from the warm sub-chain.

- `key_cache_age_threshold` indicates how long buffers stay unused in the hot sub-chain of the key cache before being moved to the warm sub-chain. Higher values enable blocks to remain in the hot sub-chain longer. The default is 300. The minimum value is 100.

One key cache is the default and has a name of `default`. If you refer to a key cache component variable without using a cache name, MySQL uses the default cache. Thus, `key_buffer_size` and `default.key_buffer_size` refer to the same variable. Key cache names must be legal identifiers and are not case sensitive. They can be quoted like any other identifier (see Section 2.2, "MySQL Identifier Syntax and Naming Rules").

To create a new key cache, simply assign a value to one of the components of the associated variable. For example, to create a cache named `my_cache` with a size of 24MB, at server startup, add these lines to the server option file:

```
[mysqld]
my_cache.key_buffer_size = 24M
```

To create the cache at runtime, use this statement:

```
SET GLOBAL my_cache.key_buffer_size = 24*1024*1024;
```

The `GLOBAL` keyword is necessary because key caches are global. No special privileges are required to access component values, but you must have the `SUPER` privilege to set them.

After you create a key cache, you can assign MyISAM tables to it with `CACHE INDEX`. This statement names a key cache and one or more tables to be assigned to it. The following statement assigns the `member` and `president` tables from the `sampdb` database to the cache named `my_cache`:

```
CACHE INDEX member, president IN my_cache;
```

You can also preload table indexes into their assigned cache with `LOAD INDEX INTO CACHE` if you choose:

```
LOAD INDEX INTO CACHE member, president;
```

It is not necessary to preload the indexes, but the server reads index blocks sequentially if you do. This is more efficient than waiting for them to be fetched as needed.

The `CACHE INDEX` and `LOAD INDEX INTO CACHE` statements require that you have the `INDEX` privilege for the tables that are to be assigned to or preloaded into a cache.

To destroy a key cache, set its size to zero. Any tables assigned to the cache are reassigned to the default cache. If you set the size of the default key cache to zero, indexes of tables assigned to it are processed using filesystem caching the same way as for MyISAM data files.

Key cache assignments last only until the server shuts down. To make assignments each time the server starts, place the appropriate `CACHE INDEX` and `LOAD INDEX INTO CACHE` statements in a file and start the server with an `--init-file` option that names the file.

12.7.3 Configuring the InnoDB Storage Engine

The InnoDB storage engine manages a shared tablespace for storing table contents and its data dictionary. You also have the option of configuring InnoDB to use one tablespace per table. InnoDB has its own log files and memory buffers as well.

12.7.3.1 Configuring the InnoDB Tablespace

By default, the InnoDB storage engine does not use separate files for each table the way that other storage engines such as MyISAM do. Instead, it manages all InnoDB tables within a single shared tablespace, which is a logically unified block of storage that the engine treats as a giant data structure. (In a sense, the tablespace is something like a virtual filesystem.) For an InnoDB table stored in the shared tablespace, the only file uniquely associated with the table is the .frm format file that is stored in the database directory of the database that the table belongs to. The shared tablespace also contains the InnoDB data dictionary that stores information about table structure.

It is also possible to configure InnoDB to represent each table using its own tablespace file. In other words, tables are created using individual tablespaces. To use individual tablespaces, start the server with the ---innodb-file-per-table option. The shared tablespace still is needed even in this case because it contains the InnoDB data dictionary, although it need not be as large.

12.7.3.1.1 Shared InnoDB Tablespace Configuration Parameters

The InnoDB shared tablespace, although logically a single storage area, comprises one or more files on disk. Each component can be a regular file or a raw partition. This section describes the configuration options that you use to set up and manage the shared tablespace. It's possible to specify these options on the server command line, but in practice this is rarely done. Instead, you should configure the tablespace using an appropriate server group in an option file (for example, the [mysqld] or [server] group), so that the server uses the same configuration consistently each time it starts. Two options are the most important:

- innodb_data_home_dir specifies the parent directory of all the component files that make up the tablespace. If you don't specify this option, its default value is the data directory.

- innodb_data_file_path indicates the specifications for the component files of the tablespace under the InnoDB home directory. The value of this option is a list of one or more file specifications, separated by semicolons. Each specification consists of a filename, a size, and possibly other options, separated by colons. The combined size of the tablespace components must be at least 10MB.

If you provide no values for either option, the InnoDB storage engine creates a default tablespace consisting of a single 10MB auto-extending file named ibdata1 in the server's data directory. By using these options, you can explicitly control the number, size, and placement of the files in the shared tablespace.

As a simple example, suppose that you want to create a tablespace consisting of two 50MB files named `innodata1` and `innodata2` in the data directory. Configure the files as follows:

```
[mysqld]
innodb_data_file_path = innodata1:50M;innodata2:50M
```

No `innodb_data_home_dir` setting is required in this case because its default value is the server's data directory, the desired location for the files.

The following rules describe how the InnoDB storage engine combines the values of `innodb_data_home_dir` and `innodb_data_file_path` to determine the pathnames of the tablespace files:

- If `innodb_data_home_dir` is empty, InnoDB treats all file specifications in `innodb_data_file_path` as absolute pathnames. "Empty" means that you specify the option with no value after the equal sign; it does not mean the option is unspecified.

- If `innodb_data_home_dir` is not empty, it should name the directory under which all the file specifications in `innodb_data_file_path` are located. In this case, InnoDB interprets those filenames relative to the `innodb_data_home_dir` value.

- If `innodb_data_home_dir` is not specified, its default value is the pathname to the MySQL data directory, and InnoDB interprets the filenames in `innodb_data_file_path` relative to the data directory.

Based on the preceding rules, the following three configurations each specify the same set of tablespace files, assuming that the data directory is `/var/mysql/data`:

```
[mysqld]
innodb_data_home_dir=
innodb_data_file_path=/var/mysql/data/ibdata1:50M;/var/mysql/data/ibdata2:50M
```

```
[mysqld]
innodb_data_home_dir=/var/mysql/data
innodb_data_file_path=ibdata1:50M;ibdata2:50M
```

```
[mysqld]
innodb_data_file_path=ibdata1:50M;ibdata2:50M
```

The `innodb_data_file_path` value consists of file specifications that are separated by semicolons. The parts of each specification are separated by colons. The simplest file specification syntax consists of a filename and a size, but other syntaxes are legal:

```
path:size
path:size:autoextend
path:size:autoextend:max:maxsize
```

The first format specifies a file with a fixed size of *size*. A *size* value should be a positive integer followed by M or G to indicate units of megabytes or gigabytes, respectively. The second format specifies an auto-extending file; if the file fills up, InnoDB extends it incrementally. The third format is similar, but includes a value indicating the maximum size to which the auto-extending file is allowed to grow. Only the final component of the tablespace may be listed as auto-extending.

The default auto-extend increment is 8MB. To specify a different increment, set the `innodb_autoextend_increment` system variable.

12.7.3.1.2 Configuring the Shared InnoDB Tablespace

In the usual case, the shared tablespace consists only of regular files and does not include any raw partitions (device files). To perform the initial setup for a shared tablespace that contains only regular files, use this procedure:

1. Add the appropriate lines to the option file.

2. Make sure that the directories exist in which the tablespace component files are to be created. InnoDB creates files, but it will not create directories.

3. Make sure that none of the component files already exist.

4. Start the server. InnoDB will notice that the files do not exist, and will create and initialize them.

If you've already started the server without configuring InnoDB explicitly, InnoDB will have created a shared tablespace using the default configuration. To configure the tablespace explicitly, first stop the server and remove the InnoDB-related files (tablespace and log files). Then specify the configuration options you want to use and restart the server. (Do this *before* creating any InnoDB tables. Otherwise, you must dump the tables with `mysqldump` before reconfiguring and reload them afterward.)

It is a little more complex to use raw partitions as components of the InnoDB shared tablespace, but there are several reasons to consider doing so:

- You can easily create very large tablespaces. A partition component can span the entire extent of the partition, whereas regular file components are limited in size to the maximum file size allowed by your operating system.

- Raw partition files are guaranteed to be composed of entirely contiguous space on disk, whereas regular files are subject to filesystem fragmentation. When it initializes the tablespace, InnoDB tries to minimize fragmentation of regular files by writing enough zeros to the files to force space for them to be allocated all at once rather than incrementally. But this can only reduce fragmentation; it cannot guarantee that it will not occur.

- Raw partitions reduce overhead by eliminating the filesystem management layer. On some systems, this overhead may not be significant, but on others the difference might be enough to justify using partitions.

A factor that counts against using raw partitions in the InnoDB tablespace is that your system backup software might be oriented toward use with filesystems rather than partitions. In this case, using partitions would make it more difficult to perform system backups.

Including a raw partition in the tablespace is a two-step procedure. Suppose that you want to use a 20GB partition on a Unix system that has a pathname of /dev/rdsk8. In this case, it's necessary to specify a value for innodb_data_home_dir because the partition doesn't lie under the data directory. For example, if you set innodb_data_home_dir to an empty value, you can list the full pathname of the device file in innodb_data_file_path to configure the partition as follows:

1. Configure the partition initially with a size value that has a newraw suffix. This suffix tells InnoDB that the file is a raw partition that needs to be initialized:

```
[mysqld]
innodb_data_home_dir =
innodb_data_file_path = /dev/rdsk8:20Gnewraw
```

2. Start the server. InnoDB sees the newraw suffix and initializes the partition. It also treats the tablespace as read-only, because it knows that you have not completed the second step.

3. After the partition has been initialized, stop the server.

4. Modify the configuration information to change the suffix from newraw to raw:

```
[mysqld]
innodb_data_home_dir =
innodb_data_file_path = /dev/rdsk8:20Graw
```

5. Start the server again. InnoDB sees that the suffix is raw rather than newraw and assumes that the partition has been initialized and that it can use the tablespace in read/write fashion.

If you specify a raw partition as part of the InnoDB tablespace, make sure its permissions are set so that the server has read/write access to it. Also, make sure the partition is being used for no other purpose. Otherwise you will have competing processes each thinking that they own the partition and can use it as they please, with the result that they'll stomp all over each other's data. For example, if you mistakenly specify a swap partition for use by InnoDB, your system will behave quite erratically!

When configuring the InnoDB shared tablespace on Windows systems, backslashes in pathnames can be specified using either single forward slashes ('/') or doubled backslashes ('\\'). Also, you should still separate the parts of each file specification with colons, even though colons may also appear in filenames (full Windows pathnames begin with a drive letter and a colon). When it encounters a colon, InnoDB resolves this ambiguity by looking at the following character. If it is a digit, the next part of the specification is taken to be a size. Otherwise, it's taken as part of a pathname. For example, the following configuration sets up a tablespace consisting of files on the C and D drives with sizes of 50MB and 60MB:

```
[mysqld]
innodb_data_home_dir =
innodb_data_file_path = C:/ibdata1:50M;D:/ibdata2:60M
```

When you're setting up the initial tablespace, if startup fails because InnoDB cannot create some necessary file, check the error log to see what the problem was. Then remove all the files that InnoDB created (excluding any raw partitions you may be using), correct the configuration error, and start the server again. If you have raw partitions, remember to change the specification to say `newraw` when initializing the partitions and back to `raw` after starting and stopping the server.

12.7.3.1.3 Reconfiguring the Shared InnoDB Tablespace

After the shared tablespace has been initialized and you have begun to use it, you cannot change the size of its component files. However, you can add another file at the end of the list of existing files, which may be helpful if the tablespace fills up. One symptom of a full tablespace is that InnoDB transactions consistently fail and roll back when they should succeed. You can determine the amount of free space with the following statement, where `tbl_name` is the name of any InnoDB table that is located in the shared tablespace:

```
mysql> SHOW TABLE STATUS LIKE 'tbl_name';
```

To make the shared tablespace larger by adding another component, use this procedure:

1. Stop the server if it is running.
2. If the final component of the tablespace is an auto-extending file, you must change its specification to that of a fixed-size file before adding another file after it. To do this, determine the current actual size of the file. Then round the size down to the nearest multiple of 1 megabyte (measured as 1,048,576 bytes, not 1,000,000 bytes) and use that size in the file's specification. Suppose that you have a file currently listed like this:

   ```
   [mysqld]
   innodb_data_file_path = ibdata1:100M:autoextend
   ```

   If the file's actual size now is 121,634,816 bytes, that is 121,634,816 / 1,048,576 = 116 megabytes. Change the specification as follows:

   ```
   [mysqld]
   innodb_data_file_path = ibdata1:116M
   ```

3. Add the specification for the new component to the end of the current file list. If the new component is a regular file, make sure that it does not already exist. If the component is a raw partition, add it using the two-step procedure described earlier for specifying a partition as part of the tablespace. (That is, first with `newraw`, and then with `raw` after starting and stopping the server.)
4. Restart the server.

If you want to reconfigure the shared tablespace in some way other than adding a new file to the end, you should dump it and then reconstruct it using the new configuration:

1. Use `mysqldump` to dump all your InnoDB tables that are stored in the shared table-space.

2. Stop the server and delete your existing InnoDB shared tablespace files (other than raw partitions), the InnoDB log files, and the `.frm` files that correspond to the dumped InnoDB tables. (An alternative to deleting `.frm` files is to use `DROP TABLE` for every InnoDB table while the server is running.)

3. Reinitialize the tablespace according to the new configuration you want to use.

4. Reload the dump file into the server to re-create the InnoDB tables.

12.7.3.1.4 Using Individual (Per-Table) InnoDB Tablespaces

To use one tablespace per InnoDB table, start the server with the `--innodb-file-per-table` option. In this case, each InnoDB table has an `.frm` format file and an `.ibd` data file, both stored in the database directory for the database that contains the table.

The choice of whether to use individual tablespaces affects only how InnoDB creates new tables. InnoDB can always access tables already created in the shared tablespace or with individual tablespaces, regardless of whether the `--innodb-file-per-table` option is used.

12.7.3.2 InnoDB Storage Engine Variables

The preceding section discusses how to configure InnoDB's tablespace. InnoDB also has its own log files and memory buffers, and several other configuration parameters. The following list describes a few parameters that commonly are used to affect the operation of the InnoDB storage engine.

- `innodb_buffer_pool_size`

  If you have the memory available, making the InnoDB buffer pool larger can reduce disk usage for accessing table data and indexes.

- `innodb_log_buffer_size`

  InnoDB tries to buffer information about each transaction in memory and flush it to disk in a single operation when the transaction finishes. If a transaction is large and exceeds the size of the buffer, more disk activity is required to flush the buffer multiple times before the transaction finishes. Increasing the size of the buffer enables larger transactions to be buffered in memory without early flushing. The default value is 1MB. The maximum useful value is 8MB.

- `innodb_log_group_home_dir`

  InnoDB has its own log files, which it creates during server startup if they do not exist. By default, these logs are created in the data directory and have names that be-gin with `ib_`. `innodb_log_group_home_dir` can be used to set the pathname to the directory where InnoDB should write its log files. InnoDB will create only files, not directories, so make sure that the log file directory exists prior to starting the server.

- `innodb_log_file_size`, `innodb_log_files_in_group`

    When its logs fill up, InnoDB checkpoints the buffer pool by flushing it to disk. Using larger InnoDB log files reduces the frequency with which the logs fill up, and thus reduces the number of times this flushing occurs. (The tradeoff is that with larger logs, the time for recovery after a crash increases.) You can modify `innodb_log_file_size` to change the size of the log files or `innodb_log_files_in_group` to change the number of files. The important characteristic is the total size of the logs, which is the product of the two values. The total size of the logs must not exceed 4GB.

12.7.4 Configuring the Falcon Storage Engine

The Falcon storage engine is designed with the goal of being self-tuning and relatively maintenance free so as to simplify administration. For example, Falcon log and tablespace files grow automatically as necessary and free space is reclaimed as it becomes available.

The following list describes some of the Falcon parameters that you might want to change when configuring your server:

- `falcon_page_size`

    Falcon writes tablespaces using a fixed page size (4KB by default). You can assign `falcon_page_size` a value in bytes to select a page size. The allowable values are 1KB, 2KB, 4KB, 8KB, 16KB or 32KB. You must configure the page size before Falcon creates any tablespace files. To change the page size if Falcon has already created tablespaces, you must back up and drop your Falcon tables, stop the server and remove the Falcon files, and then restart the server with the new page size and reload the dump file.

- `falcon_serial_log_dir`

    The directory in which Falcon creates its log files. The default location is the data directory.

Falcon enables you to create additional tablespaces for table storage. You might do this to distribute storage across multiple physical devices for better I/O efficiency, for example. To create a new tablespace for Falcon tables, use CREATE TABLESPACE:

```
CREATE TABLESPACE myts
  ADD DATAFILE '/usr/local/mysql/data/falcon_myts.fts'
  ENGINE = FALCON;
```

By default, Falcon tables are assigned to the default tablespace when they are created. To put a table in your new tablespace, use a TABLESPACE option in the CREATE TABLE statement:

```
CREATE TABLE mytbl (i INT) ENGINE = Falcon TABLESPACE myts;
```

12.8 Enabling or Disabling `LOCAL` Capability for `LOAD DATA`

The `LOCAL` capability for the `LOAD DATA` statement need not be enabled. It can be controlled at build time and at runtime as follows:

- At build time, `LOCAL` capability for the client library can be enabled or disabled by default by using the `--enable-local-infile` or `--disable-local-infile` option when you run `configure`.

- At runtime, the server can be started with the `--local-infile` or `--skip-local-infile` options to enable or disable `LOCAL` capability on the server side.

If `LOCAL` is disabled on the server side, clients cannot use this capability at all. If `LOCAL` is enabled on the server side, the client library might still have `LOCAL` disabled by default on the client side, but certain programs may allow it to be enabled on demand. For example, `mysql` has a `--local-infile` option to enable `LOCAL`, and `mysqlimport` has a `--local` option.

For programs that have no explicit option for enabling or disabling `LOCAL`, you might still be able to control this capability if the program reads option files implicitly. This depends on whether the program invokes the `mysql_options()` C API function with the `MYSQL_READ_DEFAULT_FILE` or `MYSQL_READ_DEFAULT_GROUP` option that causes option files to be read when the connection to the server is made. If the program does use `mysql_options()` in this way, you can list a `local-infile` or `disable-local-infile` option in an appropriate option file to enable or disable `LOCAL`. The `mysql_options()` function is described in Appendix G, "C API Reference" (online).

Programming interfaces for MySQL in other languages also may be able to control `LOCAL` this way if they are based on the C API and invoke `mysql_options()`. For example, in a Perl DBI script, you can use the `mysql_read_default_file` and `mysql_read_default_group` options in the data source name string that controls how the script connects to the MySQL server.

12.9 Internationalization and Localization Issues

"Internationalization" refers to the capability of software to be used according to local convention, for any of a variety of locations. "Localization" refers to selecting a particular set of local conventions from among those sets that are supported. The following aspects of MySQL configuration relate to internationalization and localization:

- The server default time zone
- The language used for displaying diagnostic and error messages
- The available character sets and the default character set

12.9.1 Configuring Time Zone Support

In MySQL the server sets its default time zone by examining its environment. Most often, this will be the local time zone of the server host, but you can specify the time zone explicitly at server startup. In addition, the server enables each client that connects to override the default setting and set its own time zone. This enables applications to use time settings that depend on where the client program is running rather than where the server is running. The following discussion describes MySQL's capabilities for supporting multiple time zones.

Two system variables hold time zone information:

- `system_time_zone` represents the time zone that the server determines to be the server host time zone at startup time. This variable exists only as a global system variable and cannot be reset at runtime. You can influence how the server sets `system_time_zone` at startup time by setting the `TZ` environment variable to the desired time zone before starting the server. However, it may not be easy to guarantee that `TZ` will be set in some contexts, such as when the server is started during the system boot sequence. On Unix, another way to set the time zone is by specifying a `--timezone` option to the `mysqld_safe` startup script (not to `mysqld`, which does not understand the option). It's probably best to list this option in the `[mysqld_safe]` group of an option file, especially if you invoke `mysqld_safe` indirectly through `mysql.server`, which does not support command-line options. For example, to specify the U.S. Central time zone for `mysqld_safe`, add the following to your server option file:

  ```
  [mysqld_safe]
  timezone=US/Central
  ```

  The example shows one widely used syntax (it works on Solaris, Linux, and Mac OS X, for example). Another common syntax is as follows:

  ```
  [mysqld_safe]
  timezone=CST6CDT
  ```

  Use whatever syntax is indicated in your system documentation.

- `time_zone` represents the MySQL server's default time zone. By default, this variable is set to `SYSTEM`, which means "use the `system_time_zone` setting." You can set `time_zone` at startup time by using the `--default-time-zone` option for `mysqld`. As the server runs, it uses the global value of `time_zone` to set the session `time_zone` value for each client that connects, which becomes the client's default time zone. Any client can reset the time zone for its own connection by setting the session `time_zone` variable. An administrative client that has the `SUPER` privilege can set the global `time_zone` variable to change the default for clients that connect thereafter.

To determine the current values of the global and session time zone variables, use this statement:

```
SELECT @@GLOBAL.time_zone, @@SESSION.time_zone;
```

You can set the `time_zone` variable using three kinds of values, although one of them requires additional administrative action. The statements shown here set the session value. If you have the SUPER privilege, you can substitute GLOBAL to set the global value.

- You can use the value SYSTEM to set `time_zone` to the value of `system_time_zone`:

  ```
  SET SESSION time_zone = 'SYSTEM';
  ```

- You can use values that specify a signed hour and minute offset from UTC:

  ```
  SET SESSION time_zone = '+00:00';     # UTC
  SET SESSION time_zone = '+03:00';     # 3 hours ahead of UTC
  SET SESSION time_zone = '-11:00';     # 11 hours behind UTC
  ```

- You can use named time zones that refer to a locale:

  ```
  SET SESSION time_zone = 'US/Central';
  SET SESSION time_zone = 'CST6CDT';
  SET SESSION time_zone = 'Asia/Jakarta';
  ```

To use the last method (setting the time zone by name), you must enable the server to understand time zone names by loading information from the operating system's time zone files into a set of tables in the `mysql` database. This does not happen automatically during MySQL installation. You must populate the tables manually by using the `mysql_tzinfo_to_sql` program, which reads time zone files and constructs SQL statements from their contents. Feed these statements to the `mysql` program to execute them.

To set up the time zone tables on a system that has time zone files, determine where they are installed. If this location is `/usr/share/zoneinfo`, the command to load the files into the `mysql` database looks like this:

```
% mysql_tzinfo_to_sql /usr/share/zoneinfo | mysql -p -u root mysql
```

Then restart the server. That should suffice for most versions of Unix. For Windows and for Unix systems that do not have a set of time zone files, you can obtain a package containing a set of pre-built MyISAM tables containing time zone information from this location:

```
http://dev.mysql.com/downloads/timezones.html
```

Download the package and unpack it. With the MySQL server stopped, copy the `.frm`, `.MYD`, and `.MYI` files into the `mysql` database directory under your data directory. Then restart the server.

12.9.2 Selecting the Language for Error Messages

The MySQL server can produce diagnostic and error messages in any of several languages. The default is `english`, but you can specify others. To see which are available, look under the `share/mysql` directory of your MySQL installation. The directories that have language names correspond to the available languages. To change the message language, use the `--language` startup option. The argument can be either the language name or the pathname to the language directory. For example, to use French if your installation is located under `/usr/local/mysql`, use either `--language=french` or `--language=/usr/local/mysql/share/mysql/french`.

12.9.3 Configuring Character Set Support

A character set determines which characters are allowed in string values. MySQL supports multiple character sets and you can select character sets at the server, database, table, column, and string constant levels. MySQL also supports multiple collating sequences per character set. Collations affect string comparison and sorting operations.

This section describes how to configure MySQL's character set support. For general background on the server's character set capabilities, see Chapter 2. For details on creating character columns and using them, see Chapter 3, "Data Types."

When you configure the server at build time, you can specify which character sets the server should support, as well as the default character set and collation. Use the following options to the `configure` script:

- To specify which of the available character sets the server should support, use the `--with-extra-charsets` option. Its argument is a comma-separated list of character set names. For example, you can include support for the `latin1`, `big5`, and `hebrew` character sets like this:

  ```
  % ./configure --with-extra-charsets=latin1,big5,hebrew
  ```

  Two special character set names select groups of character sets: `all` includes all available character sets, and `complex` includes all complex character sets. A set is complex if it is either a multi-byte character set or it requires special rules for sorting.

  To determine which character sets can be selected, use the following command and look for the description of the `--with-charset` option in the output:

  ```
  % ./configure --help
  ```

- The default character set is `latin1`. To configure a different default, use the `--with-charset` option.

- The default collation is `latin1_swedish_ci`. To configure a different default, use the `--with-collation` option. The collation must be compatible with the default character set. (That is, the beginning part of the collation name must be the same as the character set name.)

Here is a sample configuration command that uses all three options:

```
% ./configure --with-charset=utf8 \
  --with-collation=utf8_icelandic_ci \
  --with-extra-charsets=all
```

At runtime, the server sets its default character set and collation to the built-in defaults unless you specify otherwise. To select different default values, use the `--character-set-server` and `--collation-server` startup options. The collation must be compatible with the character set.

When you run a client program, you can specify the character set that you want the program to use by giving the `--default-character-set` option. If the character set you want isn't available as part of your MySQL installation, but you do have the necessary character set files installed under another directory, you can tell the client program their location by specifying the `--character-sets-dir` option.

12.10 Running Multiple Servers

Most people run a single MySQL server on a given machine, but there are circumstances under which multiple servers can be useful:

- You want to test a new version of the server while leaving your production server undisturbed. In this case, you'll be running different server binaries.

- You want to try replication to familiarize yourself with it, but you have only a single server host and must run the master and slave on the same machine.

- Operating systems typically impose per-process limits on the number of open file descriptors. If your system makes it difficult to raise the limit, running multiple instances of the server binary is one way to work around that limitation. (For example, raising the limit might require recompiling the kernel, and you cannot to do that if you're not in charge of administering the machine.)

- Internet service providers often provide individual customers with their own MySQL installation, which necessarily requires multiple servers. This may involve running multiple instances of the same binary if all customers run the same version of MySQL, or different binaries if some customers run different versions than others.

Those are some of the more common reasons to run multiple servers, but there are others. For example, if you write MySQL documentation, it's often necessary to test various server versions empirically to see how their behavior differs. I fall into this category, for which reason I have several dozen servers installed. However, I run very few of them all the time. The others I run only on occasion for testing purposes, so I must be able to start and stop them easily on demand.

12.10.1 General Multiple Server Issues

Running multiple servers is more complicated than running just one because you need to keep them from interfering with each other. Some of the issues that arise occur when you install MySQL. If you want to have several different versions installed simultaneously, they must each be placed into a different location. For precompiled binary distributions, you can accomplish this by unpacking them into different directories. For source distributions that you compile yourself, you can use the `--prefix` option for `configure` to specify a different installation location for each distribution.

Other issues occur at runtime when you start the servers. Every server process must have unique values for several parameters. For example, each server must listen to a different TCP/IP port for incoming connections or they will collide with each other. This is true whether you run different server binaries or multiple instances of a single binary. The same principle applies to other connection interfaces: Unix socket files, Windows named pipes, or shared memory. If you enable logging, each server must write to its own set of log files, because having different servers write to the same files is sure to cause problems.

You can specify a server's options at runtime when you start it, typically in an option file. Alternatively, if you run several server binaries that you compile from source yourself, you can specify during the build process a different set of parameter values for each server to use. These become its built-in defaults, and you need not specify them explicitly at runtime.

When you run multiple servers, be sure to keep good notes on the parameters you're using so that you don't lose track of what's going on. One way to do this is to use option files to specify the parameters. The option files serve as a form of explicit documentation, which can be useful even for servers that have unique default parameter values compiled in.

The following discussion enumerates several types of runtime options that have the potential for causing conflicts if they're not set on a per-server basis. Note that some options influence others, so you may not need to set each one explicitly for every server. For example, each server must use a unique set of log files when it runs. But the data directory is the default location for all of them, so if each server uses a different data directory, that implicitly results in different sets of log files.

- If you're running different server versions, it's typical for each distribution to be installed under a different base directory. Each server also should have a separate data directory. (Use of separate data directories is mandatory on Windows and strongly recommended on Unix.) To specify these values explicitly, use the options in the following table.

Option	Purpose
`--basedir=dir_name`	Pathname to root directory of MySQL installation
`--datadir=dir_name`	Pathname to data directory

In many cases, the data directory will be a subdirectory of the base directory, but not always. For example, an Internet service provider might provide a common set of MySQL server and client programs for its customers, but run for each customer an instance of the server that uses a customer-specific data directory. In this case, the base directory would be the same for all servers, but individual data directories would be located in different places, perhaps under customer home directories.

- The network interface options in the following table must have different values for each server, to prevent multiple servers from listening on the same interfaces.

Option	Purpose
`--port=port_num`	Port number for TCP/IP connections
`--socket=file_name`	Unix domain socket-file pathname or Windows named-pipe name
`--pid-file=file_name`	Pathname to file in which server writes its process ID
`--shared-memory-base-name=name`	Name of shared memory to use for shared-memory connections (Windows only)

On Windows, the `--socket` or `--shared-memory-base-name` options need be given only for those servers that are run with the `--enable-named-pipe` or `--shared-memory` options to enable named-pipe or shared-memory connections. In this case, one server can use the default named-pipe and shared-memory names (MySQL and MYSQL, respectively), but any others must specify different names.

- If you enable logging, any log filenames that you use must be different for each server. Otherwise, you'll have multiple servers contending to write to the same log files. That is at best confusing, and at worst prevents things like replication from working correctly. Log files named by the options in the following table are created under the server's data directory if you specify relative filenames. If each server uses a different data directory, you need not specify absolute pathnames to get each one to log to a distinct set of files. (See Section 12.5, "Maintaining Logs," for more information about naming log files.)

Logging Option	Log Enabled by Option
`--log-error[=file_name]`	Error log file
`--log[=file_name]`	General log file
`--log-slow-queries[=file_name]`	Slow-query log file
`--log-output[=destination]`	General/slow-query log destination
`--log-bin[=file_name]`	Binary log file
`--log-bin-index=file_name`	Binary log index file

Logging Option	Log Enabled by Option
`--relay-log[=file_name]`	Relay log file
`--relay-log-index=file_name`	Relay log index file

 of master
and relay log information files. These are created in the data directory by default and
are set explicitly with the `--master-info-file` and `--relay-log-info-file`
options.

■ Under Unix, if you use `mysqld_safe` to start your servers, it creates an error log file
(in the data directory by default). You can specify the error log name explicitly with
`--log-error=file_name`. However, before MySQL 5.1.11, if you specify a relative
pathname, `mysqld_safe` interprets it as relative to the directory from which it is invoked, not relative to the data directory. Specify an absolute pathname to make sure
you always create the error log in the proper location. Alternatively, as of MySQL
5.1.20, you can send error output to `syslog`. For details, see Section 12.5.1, "The
Error Log."

■ If the InnoDB or Falcon storage engine is enabled, the directory in which it writes
its logs must be unique per server. By default, these engines write their logs to the
data directory. To change the location, use the options in this table.

Logging Option	Purpose
`--innodb_log_group_home_dir=dir_name`	InnoDB log file directory
`--falcon-serial-log-dir=dir_name`	Falcon log file directory

Each server that uses InnoDB must be configured to use its own shared tablespace.
The options for this are described in Section 12.7.3.1, "Configuring the InnoDB
Tablespace."

■ Under Unix, it may be necessary to specify a `--user` option on a per-server basis to
indicate the login account to use for running each server. This is very likely if you're
providing individual MySQL server instances for different users, each of whom
"owns" a separate data directory.

■ Under Windows, different servers that are installed as services each must use a
unique service name.

12.10.2 Configuring and Compiling Different Servers

If you're going to build different versions of the server, you should install them in different
locations. The easiest way to keep different distributions separate is to indicate a different
installation base directory for each one by using the `--prefix` option when you run
`configure`. If you incorporate the version number into the base directory name, it's easy
to tell which directory corresponds to which version of MySQL. This section illustrates

one way to accomplish that goal. It describes the particular configuration conventions that I use to keep my own MySQL installations separate.

My layout places all MySQL installations under a common directory, `/var/mysql`. To install a given distribution, I put it in a subdirectory of `/var/mysql` named using the distribution's version number. For example, I use `/var/mysql/50124` as the installation base directory for MySQL 5.1.24, which can be accomplished by running `configure` with a `--prefix=/var/mysql/50124` option. I also use other options for additional server-specific values, such as the TCP/IP port number and socket pathname. The configuration I use makes the TCP/IP port number equal to the version number, puts the socket file directly in the base directory, and names the data directory as `data` there.

To set up these configuration options, I use a shell script named `config-ver` that looks like this (note that the data directory option for `configure` is `--localstatedir`, not `--datadir`):

```
VERSION=50124
BASEDIR=/var/mysql/$VERSION
TCP_PORT=$VERSION
HANDLERS="
  --with-archive-storage-engine
  --with-csv-storage-engine
  --with-federated-storage-engine
  --with-innodb
"
OTHER="
  --enable-local-infile
  --with-embedded-server
  --with-extra-charsets=all
  --with-partition
  --with-row-based-replication
  --with-ssl
"
rm -f config.cache
CXX=gcc \
./configure \
  --prefix=$BASEDIR \
  --localstatedir=$BASEDIR/data \
  --with-unix-socket-path=$BASEDIR/mysql.sock \
  --with-tcp-port=$TCP_PORT \
  $HANDLERS $OTHER
```

I make sure the first line is set to the proper version number and modify the other values as necessary according to which of the optional storage engines I want to compile in, whether to enable LOCAL support for LOAD DATA, and so forth. That done, the following commands configure, build, and install the distribution:

```
% sh config-ver
% make
% make install
```

These commands work for a source distribution that has been packaged as a release. If you are working with a source tree obtained as a clone of the latest development sources, the `configure` script must be created as described in the MySQL Reference Manual before you can use `config-ver`.

After installing a given version of MySQL, it's necessary to change location into its installation base directory and initialize the data directory and grant tables:

```
# cd /var/mysql/50124
# ./bin/mysql_install_db --user=user_name
```

`user_name` is the name of the login account to be used for running the server (for example, the `mysql` account). You should run these commands while logged in as `root` or as `user_name`.

At this point, I perform the lockdown procedure for the MySQL installation directory that is described briefly in Section 12.2.1.1, "Running the Server Using an Unprivileged Login Account," and in more detail in Section 13.1.2, "Securing Your MySQL Installation".

After that, all that remains is to set up any options that I want to use in option files and to arrange for starting the server. Section 12.10.4, "Using `mysqld_multi` for Server Management," discusses one way to do this.

12.10.3 Strategies for Specifying Startup Options

After you have your servers installed, how do you get them started up with the proper set of runtime options that each one needs? You have several choices:

- If you run different servers that you build yourself, you can compile in a different set of defaults for each one and no options need to be given at runtime. This has the disadvantage that it's not necessarily obvious what parameters any given server is using.
- To specify options at runtime, you can list them on the command line or in option files. If you need to specify lots of options, writing them on the command line is likely to be impractical. Putting them in option files is more convenient, although then the trick is to get each server to read the proper set of options. Strategies for accomplishing this include the following:
  - Use a `--defaults-file` option to specify the file that the server should read to find all of its options, and specify a different file for each server. This way, you can put all the options needed by a given server into one file to fully specify its setup in a single place. (Note that when you use this option, none of the usual option files, such as `/etc/my.cnf`, will be read.)
  - Put any options that are common to all servers in a global option file such as `/etc/my.cnf` and use a `--defaults-extra-file` option on the command line to specify a file that contains additional options that are specific to a given server. For example, use the `[mysqld]` group in `/etc/my.cnf` for options that

should apply to all servers. These need not be replicated in individual per-server option files.

Be sure that any options placed into a common option group are understood by all servers that you run. For example, you can't use `event_manager=1` to enable the event scheduler if any of your servers are older than version 5.1.6, because that is when events were introduced. Its presence in a common option group will cause startup failure for older servers.

If all of your servers are from MySQL 4.0.2 or newer, you can use the `loose-`*opt_name* syntax to specify options that are not understood by all servers. Servers that do not understand an option given this way will ignore the option and continue to execute after logging a warning. For more information about "loose" options, see Section F.1, "Specifying Program Options."

- Use the `mysqld_multi` script to manage startup for multiple servers. This script enables you to list the options for all servers in a single file but associate each server with its own particular option group in the file.

- Under Windows, you can run multiple services, using the special option file group naming conventions specific to this style of server setup. See Section 12.2.2.2, "Running the Server as a Windows Service."

The following sections show some ways to apply these strategies by demonstrating how to use `mysqld_multi` and how to run multiple servers under Windows.

12.10.4 Using `mysqld_multi` for Server Management

On Unix, the `mysqld_safe` and `mysql.server` scripts that are commonly used to start the server both work best in a single-server setting. To make it easier to handle several servers, the `mysqld_multi` script can be used instead.

`mysqld_multi` works on the basis that you assign a specific number to each server setup you want to create, and then list that server's options in an option file `[mysqld`*n*`]` group, where *n* is the number. The option file can also contain a `[mysqld_multi]` group that lists options specifically for `mysqld_multi` itself. For example, if I have servers installed for MySQL 5.0.56, 5.1.24, and 6.0.5, I might designate their option groups as `[mysqld50056]`, `[mysqld50124]`, and `[mysqld60005]` and set up the options in the `/etc/my.cnf` file like this:

```
[mysqld50056]
basedir=/var/mysql/50056
datadir=/var/mysql/50056/data
mysqld=/var/mysql/50056/bin/safe_mysqld
socket=/var/mysql/50056/mysql.sock
port=50056
user=mysql
log=qlog
log-bin=binlog
innodb_data_file_path = ibdata1:100M
```

```
[mysqld50124]
basedir=/var/mysql/50124
datadir=/var/mysql/50124/data
mysqld=/var/mysql/50124/bin/mysqld_safe
socket=/var/mysql/50124/mysql.sock
port=50124
user=mysql
log=qlog
log-bin=binlog
innodb_data_file_path = ibdata1:50M:autoextend
event_scheduler=ON

[mysqld60005]
basedir=/var/mysql/60005
datadir=/var/mysql/60005/data
mysqld=/var/mysql/60005/bin/mysqld_safe
socket=/var/mysql/60005/mysql.sock
port=60005
user=mysql
log=qlog
log-bin=binlog
skip-innodb
language=french
character-set-server=utf8
```

The layout parameters that I've set up here for each server correspond to the directory configuration described in Section 12.10.2, "Configuring and Compiling Different Servers." I've also specified additional server-specific parameters that correspond to variations in types of logs, storage engines, and so forth.

To start a given server, invoke `mysqld_multi` with a command word of `start` and the server's option group number on the command line:

```
% mysqld_multi --no-log start 50124
```

The `--no-log` option causes status messages to be sent to the terminal rather than to a log file. This enables you to see what's going on more easily. You can specify more than one server by giving the group numbers as a comma-separated list. A range of server numbers can be specified by separating the numbers with a dash. However, there must be no whitespace in the server list. For example:

```
% mysqld_multi --no-log start 50056,50124-60005
```

To stop servers or obtain a status report indicating whether they are running, use a command word of `stop` or `report` followed by the server list. For these commands, `mysqld_multi` invokes `mysqladmin` to communicate with the servers, so you'll also need to specify a username and password for an administrative account:

```
% mysqld_multi --nolog --user=root --password=rootpass stop 50056
% mysqld_multi --nolog --user=root --password=rootpass report 50056,60005
```

The user and password must be applicable to all servers that you want to control with a given command. `mysqld_multi` attempts to determine the location of `mysqladmin` automatically, or you can specify the path explicitly in the `[mysqld_multi]` group of an option file. You can also list a default administrative username and password in that option group to be used for the `stop` and `report` commands. For example:

```
[mysqld_multi]
mysqladmin=/usr/local/mysql/bin/mysqladmin
user=leeloo
password=multipass
```

From a security standpoint, it is preferable to list the administrative password in an option file rather than to expose it on the command line. If you put the password in a file, make sure that the file isn't publicly readable! For instructions on making the file private, see Section 13.1.2.2, "Securing Option Files."

12.10.5 Running Multiple Servers on Windows

There are a couple ways to run multiple servers on Windows. One method is based on starting the servers manually, and the other is to use multiple Windows services. You can mix the two approaches if you like.

To start multiple servers manually, create an option file for each one that lists its parameters. For example, to run two servers that use the same program binaries but different data directories, you might create two option files that look like this:

`C:\my.ini1` file:

```
[mysqld]
basedir=C:/mysql
datadir=C:/mysql/data
port=3306
```

`C:\my.ini2` file:

```
[mysqld]
basedir=C:/mysql
datadir=C:/mysql/data2
port=3307
```

The data directory must exist before you can start a server, because there is no `mysql_install_db` equivalent for Windows. `C:\mysql\data` should already have been created for you if you installed MySQL into `C:\mysql`. The easiest way to set up `C:\mysql\data2` is to create it as a copy of `C:\mysql\data`. Use the following command (while no server is running):

```
C:\> xcopy C:\mysql\data C:\mysql\data2 /E
```

Then start the servers from the command line, using `--defaults-file` to tell each one to read a specific option file:

```
C:\> mysqld --defaults-file=C:\my.ini1
C:\> mysqld --defaults-file=C:\my.ini2
```

Clients should connect by specifying the port number appropriate for the server they want to access. This includes the use of `mysqladmin` for shutting down the servers. The first of the following commands uses the default port (3306) and the second specifies port 3307 explicitly:

```
C:\> mysqladmin -p -u root shutdown
C:\> mysqladmin -p -u root -P 3307 shutdown
```

To install a MySQL server as a Windows service, use the `--install` option. For example, to install `mysqld` as a service, you might use one of these commands:

```
C:\> C:\mysql\bin\mysqld --install
C:\> C:\mysql\bin\mysqld --install service_name
```

The `--install` command uses the full pathname to the server. With no `service_name` argument or a name of `MySQL`, the default service name (`MySQL`) is used; otherwise, the given name is used. (The rules about which option groups are read in the two cases are given in Section 12.2.2.2, "Running the Server as a Windows Service.")

Suppose that you want to run two instances of `mysqld`, using service names of `MySQL` and `mysqlsvc2`, shared-memory names of `MYSQL` and `mysqlsvc2`, and the same data directories shown in the previous example. Set up the options for each server in one of the standard option files (such as `C:\my.ini`) as follows:

```
# group for default ("MySQL") service
[mysqld]
basedir=C:/mysql
datadir=C:/mysql/data
port=3306
shared-memory
shared-memory-base-name=MYSQL

# group for "mysqlsvc2" service
[mysqlsvc2]
basedir=C:/mysql
datadir=C:/mysql/data2
port=3307
shared-memory
shared-memory-base-name=mysqlsvc2
```

The order of the groups is significant. The server installed under the default service name of `MySQL` reads only the `[mysqld]` option group. However, the server installed under the non-default service name of `mysqlsvc2` reads both the `[mysqld]` and `[mysqlsvc2]` groups. By placing the `[mysqlsvc2]` group second in the option file, it can be used to override all the options in the `[mysqld]` group with values that are appropriate for the server running as the `mysqlsvc2` service.

To install and start the services, use these commands:

```
C:\> C:\mysql\bin\mysqld --install
C:\> net start MySQL
```

```
C:\> C:\mysql\bin\mysqld --install mysqlsvc2
C:\> net start mysqlsvc2
```

If you provide a service name, you can also specify a `--defaults-file` option as the final option on the command line when you install a server:

```
C:\> C:\mysql\bin\mysqld --install service_name --defaults-file=file_name
```

This gives you an alternative means of providing server-specific options. The name of the file is remembered and used by the server whenever it starts, and it reads options only from the `[mysqld]` group of that file.

When there are multiple servers running, clients can connect to the default server using the default TCP/IP port or shared-memory name. To connect to the second server, specify its TCP/IP or shared-memory parameters explicitly:

```
C:\> mysql --protocol=tcp --port=3307
C:\> mysql --protocol=memory --shared-memory-base-name=mysqlsvc2
```

To shut down the servers, use `mysqladmin shutdown`, `net stop`, or the Services Manager. To uninstall the services, shut down the servers if they are running, and then remove each service by specifying `--remove` and the same service name that you used at server installation time. You can omit the service name if it is the default name (`MySQL`):

```
C:\> mysql --remove
C:\> mysql --remove mysqlsvc2
```

12.11 Updating MySQL

Because MySQL is under active development, updates appear regularly. This raises the question for the administrator as to whether to upgrade an MySQL installation when new releases appear. The following guidelines should help you make this decision.

The first thing you should do when a new release appears is to determine how it differs from previous releases. To make sure you're aware of new releases, subscribe to the `announce@lists.mysql.com` mailing list. (Visit http://lists.mysql.com/ to find out how to subscribe.) Each announcement includes the new change notes, so this is a good way to remain apprised of new developments. (Alternatively, check the "Release Notes" or "Change Notes" appendix in the MySQL Reference Manual to familiarize yourself with what's new.) Also, you should read the section on upgrading in the MySQL Reference Manual for the relevant release series. That section indicates any important issues you should consider and points out any special steps you must take when upgrading. This information is particularly important if the new release introduces behaviors that are incompatible with earlier releases.

After checking the change notes and upgrading sections in the manual, ask yourself these questions:

- Are you experiencing problems with your current version that the new version fixes?
- Does the new version have additional features that you want or need?
- Is performance improved for certain types of operations that you use?

If the answer to all these questions is no, you have no compelling reason to upgrade. If the answer to any question is yes, you might want to go ahead. However, at this point, it's often useful to wait a few days and watch the MySQL mailing list to see what other people report about the release. Was the upgrade helpful? Were bugs or other problems found?

Some other factors to consider that may help you make your decision are as follows:

- Releases in a stable series are most often for bug fixes, not new features. There is generally less risk for upgrades within a stable series than within a development series.

- If you upgrade MySQL, you might need to upgrade other programs that are built with the MySQL C client library linked in. For example, after a MySQL upgrade, other libraries or applications that depend on the MySQL C client library might need to be rebuilt to link the new client library. (Examples include the Perl DBD::mysql module and PHP. An obvious symptom that you need to rebuild them is that all your MySQL-related DBI and PHP scripts start dumping core after you upgrade MySQL.) If you prefer to avoid these rebuilds, you might be better off not upgrading MySQL. If you use statically linked rather than dynamically linked programs, the likelihood of this problem is much reduced, but then your system memory requirements increase.

If you're still not sure whether to upgrade, you can test the new server independently of your current server. You can do this either by running it in parallel with your production server, or by installing it on a different machine. It's easier to maintain independence between servers if you use a different machine because you have greater freedom to configure it as you choose. If you elect to run the new server in parallel with an existing server on the same host, be sure to configure it with unique values for parameters such as the installation location, the data directory, and the network interfaces on which the server listens for connections. For details, see Section 12.10, "Running Multiple Servers."

In either case, you'll probably want to test the new server using a copy of the data in your existing databases. See Section 14.3, "Making Database Backups," for instructions on copying databases.

If you upgrade to a version that it not backward compatible with older versions and then decide to revert to the earlier version, it may not be so easy to downgrade. For example, several changes were made in the early releases of MySQL 5.0 (storage format for the VARCHAR and DECIMAL data types being notable examples). If you upgrade from MySQL 4.1 to 5.0 or higher and convert your tables to 5.0 format, they'll be incompatible with your older server. If you decide to downgrade back to 4.1, one useful strategy is to dump your databases using the `--compatible` option of `mysqldump` to generate dump files for loading into the older server.

Don't Be Afraid to Try Development Releases

It's not a wise idea to use a development release for production purposes, such as managing your business assets. On the other hand, I do encourage you to test new releases, perhaps with a copy of your production data. The greater the number of people that try new releases, the more thoroughly they are exercised. This improves the likelihood of finding any bugs that may exist, which is a good thing. Bug reports are a significant factor in helping MySQL development move forward, because the developers do fix problems that the user community reports.

If you want an ongoing source of statements to be executed by a test server, consider using a production server as a replication master and setting up the test server as a replication slave. That way, updates executed by the master server will be sent to the slave server, providing it with a continual stream of input. The master will not send any retrievals to the slave, but you can point client programs at the slave and issue SELECT statements to see how it processes them.

Access Control and Security

As a MySQL administrator, you are responsible for keeping the contents of databases secure so that data can be accessed by only those who have the proper authorization. To accomplish this goal, you must maintain the security and integrity of your MySQL installation. Chapter 12, "General MySQL Administration," already touched on a few security-related topics, such as the importance of assigning passwords to the initial MySQL root accounts and how to set up additional user accounts. Those topics were dealt with as part of the process of getting your installation up and running. In this chapter, we'll look more closely at security-related issues:

- Why security is important and what kind of attacks you should guard against
- Internal security risks you face from other users with login accounts on the server host and what you can do about them
- External security risks you face from clients connecting to the server over the network and what you can do about them

Internal security concerns the issues that arise in relation to other users who have direct access to the MySQL server host—that is, other users who have login accounts on that host. Generally, internal security exploits involve filesystem access. To counter this, you need to protect the contents of your MySQL installation from being attacked by people who have accounts on the machine on which the server runs. In particular, the server's data directory should be owned and controlled by the login account used for running the MySQL server. If you don't do this, your other security-related efforts may be compromised. For example, you'll want to make sure you've properly set up the MySQL accounts listed in the grant tables that control client connections over the network, but the integrity of those tables depends on adequate filesystem protection. If the access mode for the data directory contents is too permissive, someone might be able to put in place an entirely different client access policy by replacing the files that correspond to the grant tables.

External security concerns the issues involved with clients connecting from outside. It's necessary to protect the MySQL server from being attacked through connections coming in over the network asking for access to database contents. You should set up the

MySQL grant tables so that they don't allow access to the databases managed by the server unless a valid name and password are supplied. Another danger is that it may be possible for a third party to monitor the network and capture traffic between the server and a client. To deal with such concerns, you can configure your MySQL installation to support connections that use the Secure Sockets Layer (SSL) protocol.

This chapter provides a guide to the security issues you should be aware of and gives instructions that show how to prevent unauthorized access at both the internal and external levels. The chapter often refers to the login account used for running the MySQL server and for performing other MySQL-related administrative tasks. The user and group names used here for this account both are `mysql`. Change the names in the examples if you use other user and group names (for example, if you run the MySQL server using your own login account).

13.1 Internal Security: Preventing Unauthorized Filesystem Access

This section shows how to lock down your MySQL installation to keep it from being tampered with by unauthorized users on the server host. The section applies only to Unix systems; I assume that if you're running a server on Windows, you have complete control of the machine and that there are no other local users.

The MySQL installation procedure creates several directories, some of which require protection different from others. For example, there is no need for the server program to be accessible to anyone other than the MySQL administrative login account. By contrast, the client programs normally should be publicly accessible so that other users can run them—but not so accessible that they can be modified or replaced.

Other files to be protected are created after the initial installation, either by yourself as part of your post-installation configuration procedure, or by the server as it runs. Files created by you include option files or SSL-related files. Directories and files that the server creates for itself as it runs include database directories, the files under those directories that correspond to tables in the databases, log files, and the Unix socket file.

Clearly you want to maintain the privacy of the databases maintained by the server. Database owners usually, and rightly, consider database contents private. Even if they don't, it should be their choice to make the contents of a database public rather than having its contents exposed due to insufficient protection of the database directory.

Log files must be kept secure because they contain the text of statements sent by clients to the server. This is a general concern in that anyone with log file access can monitor changes to the contents of databases. A more specific security issue relating to log files is that they might contain the text of sensitive statements, including passwords. MySQL uses password encryption, but this applies to connection establishment after passwords already have been set up. The process of setting up a password involves a statement such as CREATE USER, GRANT, or SET PASSWORD, and these statements are logged in plain text form in some of the logs. An attacker who has read access to the logs may be able to discover sensitive information through an act as simple as running `grep` on the log files to look for words such as `GRANT` or `PASSWORD`.

Certain other files must be accessible to client programs, such as the Unix socket file. Normally you'll want to allow access to the file, but not full control of it. For example, users should be able to connect to the server through the socket file, but they should not be able to delete the file; that would compromise the ability of other users to connect to the server.

13.1.1 How to Steal Data

The following description provides a brief example that illustrates why security is important. It underscores the fact that you don't want other users to have direct access to the MySQL data directory.

The MySQL server provides a flexible privilege system implemented by means of the grant tables in the `mysql` database. You can set up the contents of these tables to allow or deny database access to clients. This provides you with security against unauthorized network access to your data. However, setting up good security for network access to your databases is an exercise in futility if other users on the server host have direct access to the contents of the data directory. Unless you know that you are the only person who ever logs in on the machine where the MySQL server is running, you need to be concerned about the possibility of other people on that machine gaining access to the data directory.

Obviously you don't want other users on the server host to have direct write access to data directory files, because then they can stomp all over your status files or database tables. But direct read access is just as dangerous. If a table's files can be read, it is trivial to steal the files and to get MySQL itself to show you the contents of the table. How? Like this:

1. Install your own rogue MySQL server on the server host, but with a port, socket file, and data directory that are different from those used by the official server.

2. Run `mysql_install_db` to initialize your data directory. This action gives you full access to your server as the MySQL `root` user, and sets up a `test` database that can serve as a convenient repository for stolen tables.

3. Access the data directory of the server you want to attack, copying the files corresponding to the table or tables that you want to steal into the `test` directory under your own server's data directory. This action requires only read access to the targeted data directory.

4. Start your rogue server. Presto! Its `test` database now contains copies of the stolen tables, which you can access at will. `SHOW TABLES FROM test` shows which tables you have a copy of, and `SELECT *` shows the entire contents of any of them.

5. To be really nasty, open up the permissions on the anonymous user accounts for your server so that anyone can connect to the server from any host to access your `test` database. That effectively publishes the stolen tables to the world.

Think about this scenario for a moment, and then reverse the perspective. Do you want someone to do that to you? Of course not. So protect yourself using the instructions in the following discussion.

13.1.2 Securing Your MySQL Installation

The procedure described here shows how to set up ownerships and access modes for the directories and files that make up your MySQL installation. The instructions here use `mysql` for both the user and group names that are to be given ownership of the installation. (Whatever the user is, it should be something other than `root`, for reasons discussed in Section 12.2.1.1, "Running the Server Using an Unprivileged Login Account.") The instructions also assume a layout such that all parts of your MySQL installation are located under a single base directory, rather than scattered in various places throughout your filesystem. In the examples, the installation base directory is `/usr/local/mysql` and the data directory is located under that with a pathname of `/usr/local/mysql/data`.

After going through the procedure, I'll describe how to handle some non-standard types of installation layouts. Your system layout may vary from any of those described here, but you should be able to adapt the general principles appropriately. Change the names and pathnames as necessary for your own system. If you run multiple servers, you should perform the procedure for each one.

You can determine whether your data directory contains insecure files or directories by executing `ls -la`. Look for files or directories that have the "group" or "other" permissions turned on. Here's a listing of a data directory that is insecure, as are some of the database directories within it:

```
% ls -la /usr/local/mysql/data
total 10148
drwxrwxr-x   11 mysql   wheel      1024 May  8 12:20 .
drwxr-xr-x   22 root    wheel       512 May  8 13:31 ..
drwx------    2 mysql   mysql       512 Apr 16 15:57 menagerie
drwxrwxr-x    2 mysql   wheel       512 Jun 25  1998 mysql
drwx------    7 mysql   mysql      1024 May  7 10:45 sampdb
drwxrwxr-x    2 mysql   wheel      1536 Jun 25  1998 test
drwx------    2 mysql   mysql      1024 May  8 18:43 tmp
```

'.' represents the directory being listed, that is, `/usr/local/mysql/data`. '..' represents the parent directory, `/usr/local/mysql`. Some of the database directories have the proper permissions: `drwx------` enables read, write, and execute access to the owner, but no access to anyone else. But other directories have an overly permissive access mode: `drwxrwxr-x` enables read and execute access to all other users, even those outside of the `mysql` group. The situation shown in this example is one that resulted over time, starting with a (very) old MySQL installation that was progressively upgraded to successive newer versions. The less-restrictive permissions were created by older MySQL servers that were less stringent than more recent servers about setting permissions. (You can see that the more restrictive database directories, `menagerie`, `sampdb`, and `tmp`, all have more recent dates.) Current MySQL servers set the permissions on database directories that they create to be accessible only to the account they run as.

You can also use `ls -la` to check the base directory of the MySQL installation, `/usr/local/mysql`. For example, you might get a result something like this:

```
% ls -la /usr/local/mysql
total 44
drwxrwxr-x  13 mysql  mysql     1024 May  7 10:45 .
drwxr-xr-x  24 root   wheel     1024 May  1 12:54 ..
drwxr-xr-x   2 mysql  mysql     1024 Jul 16 20:58 bin
drwxrwxr-x  12 mysql  wheel     1024 May  8 12:20 data
drwxr-xr-x   3 mysql  mysql      512 May  7 10:45 include
drwxr-xr-x   2 mysql  mysql      512 May  7 10:45 info
drwxr-xr-x   3 mysql  mysql      512 May  7 10:45 lib
drwxr--r-x   2 mysql  mysql      512 Jul 16 20:58 libexec
drwxr-xr-x   3 mysql  mysql      512 May  7 10:45 man
drwxr-xr-x   6 mysql  mysql     1024 May  7 10:45 mysql-test
drwxr-xr-x   3 mysql  mysql      512 May  7 10:45 share
drwxr-xr-x   7 mysql  mysql     1024 May  7 10:45 sql-bench
```

The `data` directory permissions and ownership need to be changed, as already indicated. One other change you might make is to restrict access to the `libexec` directory, which is where the `mysqld` server lives. Nobody but the MySQL administrator needs access to the server, so you can make that directory private to the `mysql` login account.

To correct the problems just described, use the following procedure. The general idea is to lock down everything to be accessible only to the `mysql` account, except for those parts of the installation that other users have a legitimate need to access.

Note that some parts of this procedure *do not apply* if your installation is such that the MySQL server and client programs are installed in general system directories along with other non-MySQL programs. (This is typical if you install MySQL using RPM packages.) For example, the server might be located in `/usr/sbin` and the clients in `/usr/bin`. In that case, the ownership and mode of the MySQL programs should be set the same as other programs in those directories.

1. If the MySQL server is running, tell it to stop:

   ```
   % mysqladmin -p -u root shutdown
   ```

2. Set the owner and group name assignments of the entire MySQL installation to those of the MySQL administrative account using the following commands, which you must execute as `root`:

   ```
   # chown -R mysql /usr/local/mysql
   # chgrp -R mysql /usr/local/mysql
   ```

Another popular approach is to make everything owned by `root` except the data directory, which you can accomplish like this:

```
# chown -R root /usr/local/mysql
# chgrp -R mysql /usr/local/mysql
# chown -R mysql /usr/local/mysql/data
# chgrp -R mysql /usr/local/mysql/data
```

If you set the general ownership to `root`, you'll need to perform most of the following steps as `root`. Otherwise, you can perform them as `mysql`.

3. For the base directory and any of its subdirectories that clients should be able to access, change their mode so that `mysql` has full access and everyone else has only read and execute permission. That may be how they are set already, but if not, change them. For example, the base directory can be set using either of the following commands:

```
% chmod 755 /usr/local/mysql
% chmod u=rwx,go=rx /usr/local/mysql
```

Similarly, the `bin` directory that contains the client programs can be set with either of these commands:

```
% chmod 755 /usr/local/mysql/bin
% chmod u=rwx,go=rx /usr/local/mysql/bin
```

4. Directories that clients need not have access to can be made private to `mysql`. The `libexec` directory that contains the server is an example. Either of the following commands will set its mode appropriately:

```
% chmod 700 /usr/local/mysql/libexec
% chmod u=rwx,go-rwx /usr/local/mysql/libexec
```

5. Change the mode of your data directory and all files and directories under it so that they are private to `mysql`:

```
% chmod -R go-rwx /usr/local/mysql/data
```

That prevents login accounts other than the one used for running the server from directly accessing the contents of your data directory.

After using the preceding instructions, your MySQL installation base directory has ownerships and permissions that look something like this:

```
% ls -la /usr/local/mysql
total 44
drwxr-xr-x   13 mysql  mysql     1024 May  7 10:45 .
drwxr-xr-x   24 root   wheel     1024 May  1 12:54 ..
drwxr-xr-x    2 mysql  mysql     1024 Jul 16 20:58 bin
```

```
drwx------    12 mysql   mysql      1024 May  8 12:20 data
drwxr-xr-x     3 mysql   mysql       512 May  7 10:45 include
drwxr-xr-x     2 mysql   mysql       512 May  7 10:45 info
drwxr-xr-x     3 mysql   mysql       512 May  7 10:45 lib
drwx------     2 mysql   mysql       512 Jul 16 20:58 libexec
drwxr-xr-x     3 mysql   mysql       512 May  7 10:45 man
drwxr-xr-x     6 mysql   mysql      1024 May  7 10:45 mysql-test
drwxr-xr-x     3 mysql   mysql       512 May  7 10:45 share
drwxr-xr-x     7 mysql   mysql      1024 May  7 10:45 sql-bench
```

As shown, everything now is owned by `mysql`, with a group ownership of `mysql`. The exception is for '`. .`', which refers to the parent directory of `/usr/local/mysql`. That directory is owned by and modifiable only by `root`, which is good. You don't want unprivileged users to be able to mess with the directory containing your installation.

The data directory under the base directory has even more restrictive permissions:

```
% ls -la /usr/local/mysql/data
total 10148
drwx------    11 mysql   mysql      1024 May  8 12:20 .
drwxr-xr-x    22 mysql   mysql       512 May  8 13:31 ..
drwx------     2 mysql   mysql       512 Apr 16 15:57 menagerie
drwx------     2 mysql   mysql       512 Jun 25  1998 mysql
drwx------     7 mysql   mysql      1024 May  7 10:45 sampdb
drwx------     2 mysql   mysql      1536 Jun 25  1998 test
drwx------     2 mysql   mysql      1024 May  8 18:43 tmp
```

Here, the '`. .`' line refers to the parent of the data directory, that is, the MySQL base directory.

An exception to the `mysql`-only policy of access to the data directory may be necessary for particular files. For example, if you use the data directory as the location for the Unix socket file, it will be necessary to open up access to the directory a little. Otherwise, client programs won't be able to connect to the server through the socket. To allow client programs to access the socket file without providing full read access to the data directory, use this command:

```
% chmod go+x /usr/local/mysql/data
```

To avoid opening up the data directory this way, use a different location for the Unix socket file, such as the base directory. The same principle applies to other files that programs other than `mysqld` have a legitimate need to access, such as option files that contain global client parameters.

As stated earlier, the preceding procedure assumes that all MySQL-related files are located under a single base directory. If that's not true, you'll need to locate each MySQL-related directory and perform the appropriate operations on each of them. For example, if your data directory is located at `/var/mysql/data` rather than under

`/usr/local/mysql`, you'll need to issue these commands to change the ownership of your installation properly:

```
# chown -R mysql /usr/local/mysql
# chgrp -R mysql /usr/local/mysql
# chown -R mysql /var/mysql/data
# chgrp -R mysql /var/mysql/data
```

Or, suppose that you create an `innodb` directory under the MySQL installation directory in which to keep all InnoDB-related files. By default, these files are placed in the data directory. If you put them in your `innodb` directory instead, set that directory to have the same access mode as the data directory. This principle also applies if you relocate other files that normally would be placed in the data directory, such as log files.

Another complication occurs if some of the directories under the installation root are really symbolic links that point elsewhere. If your versions of `chown` and `chgrp` don't follow symlinks, you'll need to track down the links and apply the ownership changes in the locations to which the links point. One way to do this is to use `find`:

```
# find /usr/local/mysql -follow -print | xargs chown mysql
# find /usr/local/mysql -follow -print | xargs chgrp mysql
```

Similar considerations apply to changing access modes. For example, if there are symbolic links under your data directory and `chmod` doesn't follow them, use this command instead:

```
# find /usr/local/mysql/data -follow -print | xargs chmod go-rwx
```

Because the ownership and permissions of the data directory contents at this point are set to enable access only for the `mysql` login user, you should make sure the server always runs as `mysql` from now on. An easy way to ensure this is to specify the user in the `[mysqld]` section of the `/etc/my.cnf` file or other `my.cnf` file that the server reads when it starts:

```
[mysqld]
user=mysql
```

That way, the server will run as `mysql` whether you start it while logged in as `root` or as `mysql`. Additional information on running the server using a particular login account is given in Section 12.2.1.1, "Running the Server Using an Unprivileged Login Account."

After securing your MySQL installation, you can restart the server.

13.1.2.1 Securing the Unix Socket File

The server uses a Unix domain socket file for connections by clients to `localhost`. The socket file normally is publicly accessible so that client programs can use it. However, it should not be located in a directory where arbitrary clients have delete permission. For example, it's common for the socket file to be created in the `/tmp` directory, but on some Unix systems, that directory has permissions that enable users to delete files other than their own. That means any user can remove the socket file and as a result prevent client programs from establishing `localhost` connections to the server until the server is restarted to re-create the socket file. It's better if the `/tmp` directory has its "sticky bit" set, so that even if anyone can create files in the directory, users can remove only their own files. You can set the sticky bit for the directory by executing the following command as `root`:

```
# chmod +t /tmp
```

Some installations place the socket file in the data directory, which leads to a problem if you make the data directory private to `mysql`: No client program can access the socket file, unless it is run by `root` or `mysql`. In this case, one option is to open up the data directory slightly so that clients can see the socket file:

```
% chmod go+x /usr/local/mysql/data
```

Another approach is to change the location in which the server creates the socket file. For example, you might configure MySQL to create the file in the base directory by specifying a location of `/usr/local/mysql/mysql.sock`. Either specify the location in a global option file, or recompile from source to build in the location as the default. If you elect to use an option file, be sure to specify the location both for the server and for clients:

```
[mysqld]
socket=/usr/local/mysql/mysql.sock

[client]
socket=/usr/local/mysql/mysql.sock
```

Recompiling is more work, but is a more complete solution because using an option file will not work for client programs that do not check option files. (All the standard MySQL clients do, but third-party programs may not.) By recompiling, the new socket location will become the default known by the client library; any program that uses the client library thus gets the new location as its own default, whether or not it uses option files.

13.1.2.2 Securing Option Files

Option files represent a potential point of compromise to the extent that they contain options that should not be exposed:

- Don't make an option file publicly readable if it contains sensitive information such as MySQL account names or passwords.

- `/etc/my.cnf` normally is publicly readable because it's a common location in which to specify global client options. This means you should not use it for server options such as replication passwords.

- Each user-specific `.my.cnf` option file should be owned by and accessible only by the user in whose home directory the file appears. To do this for your own file, execute the following command in your home directory:

```
% chmod u=rw,go-rwx .my.cnf
```

- Other option files need to have their access mode set depending on what you use them for.

One way to ensure that user-specific option files have the proper mode and ownership is to run a program that looks for a `.my.cnf` file in each user's home directory and corrects any problems. The following Perl script, `chk_mysql_opt_files.pl`, will do this:

```perl
#!/usr/bin/perl
# chk_mysql_opt_files.pl - check user-specific .my.cnf files and make sure
# the ownership and mode is correct. Each file should be owned by the
# user in whose home directory the file is found. The mode should
# have the "group" and "other" permissions turned off.

# This script must be run as root.  Execute it with your password file as
# input.  If you have an /etc/passwd file, run it like this:
#   chk_mysql_opt_file.pl /etc/passwd
# For Mac OS X, use the netinfo database:
#   nidump passwd . | chk_mysql_opt_file.pl

use strict;
use warnings;

while (<>)
{
  my ($uid, $home) = (split (/:/, $_)) [2,5];
  my $cnf_file = "$home/.my.cnf";
  next unless -f $cnf_file;      # is there a .my.cnf file?
  if ((stat ($cnf_file))[4] != $uid)  # test ownership
  {
    warn "Changing ownership of $cnf_file to $uid\n";
    chown ($uid, (stat ($cnf_file))[5], $cnf_file);
  }
  my $mode = (stat ($cnf_file))[2];
  if ($mode & 077)               # test group/other access bits
  {
    warn sprintf ("Changing mode of %s from %o to %o\n",
               $cnf_file, $mode, $mode & ~077);
    chmod ($mode & ~077, $cnf_file);
  }
}
```

You can find `chk_mysql_opt_files.pl` in the `admin` directory of the `sampdb` distribution. You must run this script as `root` because it needs to be able to change mode and ownership of files owned by other users. To execute the script automatically, set it up as a nightly `cron` job run by `root`.

13.2 External Security: Preventing Unauthorized Network Access

The MySQL security system is flexible. It enables you to set up user access privileges in many different ways. Normally, you do this by using account-management statements such as CREATE USER, GRANT, and REVOKE, which modify on your behalf the grant tables that control client access. However, you might find that user privileges don't seem to be working the way you want. For such situations, it's helpful to understand the structure of the MySQL grant tables and how the server uses them to determine access permissions. Such an understanding enables you to add, remove, or modify user privileges by modifying the grant tables directly. It also enables you to diagnose privilege problems when you examine the tables.

I assume that you've read Section 12.4, "Managing MySQL User Accounts," and that you understand how the various account-management statements work. These statements provide a convenient way for you to set up MySQL user accounts and associate privileges with them, but they are just a front end. All the real action takes place in the MySQL grant tables.

13.2.1 Structure and Contents of the MySQL Grant Tables

Access to MySQL databases by clients that connect to the server over the network is controlled by the contents of the grant tables. These tables are located in the mysql database and are initialized during the process of installing MySQL on a machine for the first time (as described in Appendix A, "Obtaining and Installing Software," for example). These tables are named user, db, tables_priv, columns_priv, and procs_priv. The server uses these tables as follows:

- The user table lists accounts for users that can connect to the server, their passwords, and which global (superuser) privileges each user has, if any. It's important to recognize that any privileges that are enabled in the user table are global privileges that apply to *all databases*. For example, if you enable the DELETE privilege in a user table row, the account associated with the row will be able to delete rows from any table in any database. Consider carefully before you do this.

  Because of the superuser nature of privileges specified in the user table, it's generally best to leave all the privileges turned off for rows in this table and list more specific privileges in other tables that are more restrictive. There are two exceptions to this principle:

  First, superusers such as root and other administrative accounts need global privileges to operate the server. These accounts tend to be few.

  Second, a few specific global privileges usually can be granted safely. These pertain to creating temporary tables, locking tables, and (perhaps) being able to use the SHOW DATABASES statement. Many installations will grant these; others where tighter control is desired or necessary will not.

The `user` table also has columns for SSL options that pertain to the establishment of secure connections with SSL, and columns for resource management that can be used to prevent a given account from monopolizing the server.

- The `db` table lists which accounts have privileges for which databases. If you grant a privilege here, it applies to all objects in a database (tables, stored routines, and so forth).
- The `tables_priv` table lists table-level privileges. A privilege specified here applies to all columns in a table.
- The `columns_priv` table lists column-level privileges. A privilege specified here applies to a particular column in a table.
- The `procs_priv` table contains privileges for stored routines (functions and procedures). A privilege specified here applies to a particular routine in a database. This table was introduced in MySQL 5.0.3.

The `mysql` database also contains a grant table named `host`, which is used in combination with the `db` table. However, the `host` table is obsolete and is discussed no further here.

The structure of each grant table is shown in the next several tables, broken down by type of column. Each grant table contains two primary kinds of columns: scope-of-access columns that determine when a row applies, and privilege columns that determine which privileges a row grants. The privilege columns can be subdivided further into columns for administrative operations and those that are related to operations on particular kinds of objects. The `user` table has additional columns for SSL connections and resource management; these are present only in the `user` table because they apply globally. Some of the grant tables contain other miscellaneous columns, but they don't concern us here because they have no bearing on account management.

Table 13.1   **Grant Table Scope-of-Access Columns**

`user` Table	`db` Table	`tables_priv` Table	`columns_priv` Table	`procs_priv` Table
Host	Host	Host	Host	Host
User	User	User	User	User
Password	Db	Db	Db	Db
		Table_name	Table_name	Routine_name
			Column_name	Routine_type

Table 13.2   **Grant Table Administrative Privilege Columns**

user Table	db Table	host Table
Create_user_priv		
File_priv		
Grant_priv	Grant_priv	Grant_priv
Process_priv		
Reload_priv		
Repl_client_priv		
Repl_slave_priv		
Show_db_priv		
Shutdown_priv		
Super_priv		

Table 13.3   **Grant Table Object Privilege Columns**

user Table	db Table
Alter_priv	Alter_priv
Alter_routine_priv	Alter_routine_priv
Create_priv	Create_priv
Create_routine_priv	Create_routine_priv
Create_tmp_table_priv	Create_tmp_table_priv
Create_view_priv	Create_view_priv
Delete_priv	Delete_priv
Drop_priv	Drop_priv
Event_priv	Event_priv
Execute_priv	Execute_priv
Index_priv	Index_priv
Insert_priv	Insert_priv
Lock_tables_priv	Lock_tables_priv
References_priv	References_priv
Select_priv	Select_priv

Table 13.3   **Grant Table Object Privilege Columns**

user Table	db Table	
Show_view_priv	Show_view_priv	
Trigger_priv	Trigger_priv	
Update_priv	Update_priv	
tables_priv Table	**columns_priv Table**	**procs_priv Table**
Table_priv	Column_priv	Proc_priv
Column_priv		

Table 13.4   **Grant Table SSL and Resource Management Columns (user Table Only)**

SSL Columns	Resource Management Columns
ssl_type	max_connections
ssl_cipher	max_questions
x509_issuer	max_updates
x509_subject	max_user_connections

The grant table system includes `tables_priv`, `columns_priv`, and `procs_priv` tables for defining privileges for specific tables, columns, and stored functions and procedures. There is no `rows_priv` table because MySQL doesn't provide row-level privileges. For example, you cannot restrict a user's access to just those rows in a table that contain a particular value in some column. If you need this capability, you must implement it within your own applications. One way to implement cooperative row-level locking is to use advisory locking functions such as `GET_LOCK()` and `RELEASE_LOCK()`. The procedure for this is described in Section C.2.8, "Advisory Locking Functions."

New releases of MySQL sometimes add new privileges. For example, the `Event_priv` and `Trigger_priv` columns were implemented in MySQL 5.1.6. When you upgrade an existing MySQL installation to such a version, it's necessary to update the grant tables before you can use the new privileges. Section 12.3, "Managing MySQL User Accounts," describes the procedure for doing this.

13.2.1.1 Grant Table Scope-of-Access Columns

The grant table scope columns are used to determine which rows the server consults when an account attempts to perform a given operation. Each grant table row contains

`Host` and `User` columns to indicate that the row applies to connections from a given host by a particular user. For example, a `user` table row with `localhost` and `bill` in the `Host` and `User` columns would be used for connections from the local host by `bill`, but not for connections by `betty`. The other tables contain additional scope columns. The `db` table contains a `Db` column to indicate which database the row applies to. Similarly, rows in the `tables_priv` and `columns_priv` tables contain scope columns that further narrow their scope to a particular table in a database or column in a table. The `procs_priv` scope columns specify which stored function or procedure a row applies to.

13.2.1.2 Grant Table Privilege Columns

The grant tables also contain privilege columns. For each row, these indicate which privileges are held by the user who matches the values listed in the scope columns. The privileges supported by MySQL are shown in the following lists, which describe the administrative privileges and the privileges that control database and table access. Each list uses the privilege names that are used for the `GRANT` statement. For the most part, these privilege names bear an obvious resemblance to the names of privilege columns in the grant tables. For example, the `SELECT` privilege corresponds to the `Select_priv` column.

13.2.1.3 Administrative Privileges

The following privileges apply to administrative operations that control the operation of the server or a user's ability to grant privileges:

- `CREATE USER`

  Enables you to use the `CREATE USER`, `DROP USER`, `RENAME USER`, and `REVOKE ALL PRIVILEGES` statements. This privilege was introduced in MySQL 5.0.3.

- `FILE`

  Enables you to tell the server to read or write files on the server host. To keep the use of this privilege within certain bounds, the server takes certain precautions:

  - You can access only files that are world-readable, and thus likely not to be considered protected in any way.
  - Any file that you want to write must not already exist. This prevents you from coercing the server into overwriting important files, such as `/etc/passwd`, or database files in a database belonging to someone else. (If this constraint were not enforced, you could completely replace the contents of the grant tables in the `mysql` database, for example.)

Despite these precautions by the server, this privilege should not be granted without just cause; it can be extremely dangerous, as discussed in Section 13.2.4, "Grant Table Risks to Avoid." If you do grant the `FILE` privilege, be sure not to run the server as the root login user on Unix, because root can create new files anywhere in the filesystem. By running the server from an ordinary login account, you ensure that it can create files only in directories accessible to that account. See also Section 12.2.1.1, "Running the Server Using an Unprivileged Login Account."

- GRANT OPTION

  Enables you to grant other users the privileges you have yourself, including the GRANT OPTION privilege.

- PROCESS

  The MySQL server is multi-threaded, which enables it to service multiple client connections simultaneously. These threads may be thought of as processes running within the server. The PROCESS privilege enables you to use the SHOW PROCESSLIST statement or the mysqladmin processlist command to view information about activities that are currently executing. This privilege gives you the ability to see all activities, even those associated with other users. You can always see your own activities, even without the PROCESS privilege.

- RELOAD

  Enables you to perform a variety of administrative server operations. With the RELOAD privilege, you have the ability to issue statements such as FLUSH and RESET. You can also perform the following mysqladmin commands: reload, refresh, flush-hosts, flush-logs, flush-privileges, flush-status, flush-tables, and flush-threads.

- REPLICATION CLIENT

  Enables you to inquire about the location and status of master and slave servers using the SHOW MASTER STATUS and SHOW SLAVE STATUS statements.

- REPLICATION SLAVE

  Enables a client to connect to a master server and request slave server updates, and to use the SHOW SLAVE HOSTS and SHOW BINLOG EVENTS statements. This privilege must be granted to slave server accounts that are used to connect to the master.

- SHOW DATABASES

  Enables you to see all database names by issuing the SHOW DATABASES statement. If you don't have this privilege, you can see a given database name only if you have some privilege for it. However, this ability is conveyed by *any* global privilege that applies to databases, which includes the CREATE TEMPORARY TABLES and LOCK TABLES privileges that commonly are granted globally. To ensure that only users who have the SHOW DATABASES privilege can use the SHOW DATABASES statement, start the server with the --skip-show-database option.

- SHUTDOWN

  Enables you to shut down the server, for example, with the mysqladmin shutdown command.

- SUPER

  Enables you to kill server processes with the KILL statement or the mysqladmin kill command. This privilege gives you the ability to kill any process, even those associated with other users. You can always kill your own processes, even without the SUPER privilege.

Other statements enabled by this privilege are SET for modifying global system variables and the global transaction isolation level, CHANGE MASTER, PURGE MASTER LOGS, SHOW MASTER STATUS, SHOW SLAVE STATUS, START SLAVE, and STOP SLAVE. SUPER also enables you to perform DES decryption with the DES_DECRYPT() function based on the keys stored in the DES key file.

The SUPER privilege enables the use of mysqladmin debug, and it overrides any max_connections setting when connecting to the server, so that you can access the connection slot that the server reserves for administrative connections even when all the regular slots are taken. SUPER also enables adding and dropping triggers until MySQL 5.1.6, at which point the TRIGGER privilege is required instead.

13.2.1.4 Database and Table Privileges

The following privileges apply to operations on databases and tables:

- ALTER

  Enables you to use the ALTER TABLE statement, although you might also need additional privileges, depending on what you want to do with the table.

- ALTER ROUTINE

  Enables you to alter or drop stored functions and procedures. This privilege was introduced in MySQL 5.0.3.

- CREATE

  Enables you to create databases and tables. This privilege does not enable you to create indexes on a table, except those defined initially in its CREATE TABLE statement.

- CREATE ROUTINE

  Enables you to create stored functions and procedures. This privilege was introduced in MySQL 5.0.3.

- CREATE TEMPORARY TABLES

  Enables you to create temporary tables with the CREATE TEMPORARY TABLE statement.

- CREATE VIEW

  Enables you to create views. This privilege was introduced in MySQL 5.0.1.

- DELETE

  Enables you to remove existing rows from tables.

- DROP

  Enables you to drop databases and tables. This privilege does not enable you to drop indexes.

- EVENT

  Enables you to manipulate event scheduler events. This privilege was introduced in MySQL 5.1.6.

- EXECUTE

  Enables you to execute stored functions and procedures. This privilege was implemented in MySQL 5.0.3. (It existed before that but was not used for anything.)

- INDEX

  Enables you to create or drop indexes from tables, assign indexes to key caches, and preload indexes into key caches.

- INSERT

  Enables you to insert new rows in tables.

- LOCK TABLES

  Enables you to lock tables by issuing explicit LOCK TABLES statements. This privilege applies only to tables for which you also have the SELECT privilege, but enables you to place read or write locks, not just read locks. The privilege does not apply to locks that are acquired implicitly on your behalf by the server during the process of statement execution. Such locks are set and released automatically regardless of your LOCK TABLES privilege setting.

- REFERENCES

  This privilege currently is unused. Eventually it may be used to define who can set up foreign key constraints.

- SELECT

  Enables you to retrieve data from tables using SELECT statements. This privilege is unnecessary for SELECT statements such as SELECT NOW() or SELECT 4/2, which do nothing more than evaluate expressions and involve no tables.

- SHOW VIEW

  Enables use of the SHOW CREATE VIEW statement to see view definitions. This privilege was introduced in MySQL 5.0.1.

- TRIGGER

  Enables you to add and drop triggers. This privilege was introduced in MySQL 5.1.6. Before that, trigger manipulation requires the SUPER privilege.

- UPDATE

  Enables you to modify existing rows in tables.

Some operations require a combination of privileges. For example, REPLACE may implicitly cause a DELETE followed by an INSERT, so it requires both the DELETE and INSERT privileges.

13.2.1.5 How the Grant Tables Represent Privileges

In the `user` and `db` tables, each privilege is specified as a separate column. These columns are all defined to have a type of `ENUM('N','Y')`, with a default value of `'N'` (off). For example, the `Select_priv` column is defined like this:

```
Select_priv ENUM('N','Y') CHARACTER SET utf8 NOT NULL DEFAULT 'N'
```

Privileges in the `tables_priv` and `columns_priv` tables are represented by a `SET`, which allows any combination of privileges to be stored in a single column. The `Table_priv` column in the `tables_priv` table is defined like this (`Trigger` is absent before MySQL 5.1.6):

```
SET('Select','Insert','Update','Delete','Create','Drop','Grant',
    'References','Index','Alter','Create_view','Show_view','Trigger')
CHARACTER SET utf8 NOT NULL DEFAULT ''
```

The `Column_priv` column in the `columns_priv` table is defined like this:

```
SET('Select','Insert','Update','References')
CHARACTER SET utf8 NOT NULL DEFAULT ''
```

The reason there are fewer column privileges than table privileges is that fewer operations make sense at the column level. For example, you can delete a row from a table to remove it, but you can't delete individual columns of a row.

Note that `INSERT` exists at the column level. If you have the `INSERT` privilege only for some columns in a table, you can specify values only for those columns when inserting new rows; the other columns will be set to their default values.

The `tables_priv`, `columns_priv`, and `procs_priv` tables are newer than the `user` and `db` tables, which is why they use the more efficient `SET` representation to list multiple privileges in a single column.

The `user` table contains several administrative privilege columns that are not present in any of the other grant tables, such as `File_priv`, `Process_priv`, `Reload_priv`, and `Shutdown_priv`. These privileges are present only in the `user` table because they are global privileges that are not associated with any particular database or table. It doesn't make sense to allow or not allow a user to shut down the server based on what the default database is, for example.

13.2.1.6 Grant Table SSL-Related Columns

Several columns in the `user` table apply to authentication of secure connections over SSL. The primary column is `ssl_type`, which indicates whether and what type of secure connection is required for an account. `ssl_type` is represented as an `ENUM` with four possible values:

```
ENUM('','ANY','X509','SPECIFIED') CHARACTER SET utf8 NOT NULL DEFAULT ''
```

The `ssl_type` enumeration values have the following meanings:

- `''` (the empty string) indicates that the account is not required to use secure connections. This is the default value; it's used when you set up an account but do not specify any `REQUIRE` clause or when you specify `REQUIRE NONE` explicitly.

- `'ANY'` indicates that the account must use a secure connection, but that it can be any kind of secure connection; it's a kind of "generic" requirement. The column is set to this value when you specify `REQUIRE SSL` in a `GRANT` statement.

- `'X509'` indicates that the account must use a secure connection and that the client must supply a valid X509 certificate. The contents of the certificate are not otherwise relevant. The column is set to this value when you specify `REQUIRE X509`.

- `'SPECIFIED'` indicates that the client must use a secure connection that meets specific requirements. The column is set to this value when you specify any combination of `ISSUER`, `SUBJECT`, or `CIPHER` values in the `REQUIRE` clause.

For all `ssl_type` values except `'SPECIFIED'`, the server ignores the values in the other SSL-related columns when validating client connection attempts. For `'SPECIFIED'`, the server checks the other columns, and for any that have non-empty values, the client must supply matching information:

- `ssl_cipher`, if non-empty, indicates the cipher method that the client must use when connecting. It can be used to prevent the client from using weak cipher methods.

- `x509_issuer`, if non-empty, indicates the issuer value that must be found in the X509 certificate presented by the client.

- `x509_subject`, if non-empty, indicates the subject value that must be found in the X509 certificate presented by the client.

`ssl_cipher`, `x509_issuer`, and `x509_subject` all are represented in the `user` table as `BLOB` columns.

More information about using SSL for secure connections is given later in the chapter, in Section 13.3, "Setting Up Secure Connections."

13.2.1.7 Grant Table Resource Management Columns

The following columns in the `user` table enable you to limit the extent to which any given MySQL account can consume server resources:

- `max_connections` indicates the number of times per hour the account can connect to the server. A value of zero means "no limit." This column has the same name as the `max_connections` system variable, but the two are unrelated.

- `max_questions` indicates the number of statements per hour the account can issue. A value of zero means "no limit."

- `max_updates` is like `max_questions`, but applies more specifically to statements that modify data. A value of zero means "no limit."

- `max_user_connections` indicates the maximum number of simultaneous client connections allowed to the account. If the value is zero, the server assesses the simultaneous-connection limit using the global value of the `max_user_connections` system variable. A value greater than zero takes precedence over the `max_user_connections` system variable. This column was introduced in MySQL 5.0.3.

If the server restarts, the current counters are reset to zero. A reset also occurs, except for the `max_user_connections` value, if you reload the grant tables or issue a FLUSH USER_RESOURCES statement.

More information about setting account limits is given in Section 12.3.1.5, "Limiting an Account's Resource Consumption."

13.2.2 How the Server Controls Client Access

The MySQL server enforces two stages of client access control. The first stage occurs when you attempt to connect to the server. The server looks at the `user` table to see whether it can find a row that matches the host you're connecting from, your name, and the password you supplied. If there is no match, you can't connect. If there is a match, the server also checks the `user` table SSL and resource management columns:

- If you've reached your connections-per-hour or simultaneous-connections limit, the server rejects the connection.

- If the `user` table row indicates that a secure connection is required, the server determines whether the credentials you supply match those required in the SSL-related columns. If not, the server rejects the connection.

If everything checks out okay, the server establishes the connection and you proceed to the second stage. If you are making a secure connection, your client program and the server encrypt the traffic between them.

In the second stage, the server checks two things for each statement you issue. First, it checks your statements-per-hour and updates-per-hour limits. Second, the server checks the grant tables to verify that you have sufficient access privileges to perform the statement. The limits are checked first because if you've reached them, there is little point in checking your privileges. The second stage continues until you disconnect from the server.

The following discussion describes in some detail the rules that the MySQL server uses to match grant table rows to incoming client connection requests and to statements. This includes the types of values that are legal in the grant table scope columns, how privilege values from different grant tables are combined, and the order in which the server searches rows from a given grant table.

13.2.2.1 Scope Column Contents

Each scope column is governed by rules that define what kinds of values are legal and how the server interprets those values. Some of the scope columns require literal values, but most of them allow wildcards or other special values.

- `Host`

  A `Host` column value can be a hostname or an IP number. The value `localhost` means the local host. It matches when a client connects from the local host to one of the server's local network interfaces, defined as follows:

  - The Unix socket file, on Unix systems.

  - A named pipe or shared memory, on Windows.

  - The TCP loopback interface, that is, the interface with an IP number of `127.0.0.1`. This works on any system.

  `localhost` does not match if the client connects using the host's actual name or IP number. Suppose that the name of the local host is `cobra.snake.net` and there are two rows for a user named `bob` in the user table, one with a `Host` value of `localhost` and the other with a value of `cobra.snake.net`. The row with `localhost` matches if `bob` connects from the local host using either of the following commands, on either Unix or Windows:

  ```
  % mysql -p -u bob -h localhost
  % mysql -p -u bob -h 127.0.0.1
  ```

  In addition, on Windows, the `localhost` row matches if `bob` connects like this:

  ```
  C:\> mysql -p -u bob -h .
  C:\> mysql -p -u bob --protocol=pipe
  C:\> mysql -p -u bob --protocol=memory
  ```

  The row with a `Host` value of `cobra.snake.net` matches if `bob` connects from the local host using the server's hostname (`cobra.snake.net`) or the IP number that corresponds to the hostname. The connection will use TCP/IP in both cases.

  You can specify `Host` values using wildcards. The '`%`' and '`_`' SQL pattern characters may be used and have the same meaning as when you use the `LIKE` operator in a query. (Regular expressions of the type used with `REGEXP` are not allowed.) The SQL pattern characters work both for names and for IP numbers. For example, `%.example.com` matches any host in the `example.com` domain, and `%.edu` matches any host at any educational institution. Similarly, `10.0.%` matches any host in the 10.0 class B subnet, whereas `192.168.3.%` matches any host in the 192.168.3 class C subnet.

  A `Host` value of `%` matches any host at all and may be used to enable a user to connect from anywhere. A blank `Host` value in a grant table is the same as `%`, with one exception: In the `db` table, a blank `Host` value means "check the `host` table for further information." However, the `host` table is obsolete, so you should not use a blank `Host` value.

You can also specify a network number with a netmask indicating which bits of the client IP number must match the network number. For example, `192.168.128.0/255.255.255.0` specifies a 24-bit network number and matches any client host for which the first 24 bits of its IP number have a value equal to `192.168.128`. You can think of this as another kind of wildcard. A netmask value must be `255.0.0.0`, `255.255.0.0`, `255.255.255.0`, or `255.255.255.255`. That is, it must begin with a multiple of eight bits set to 1, and have the remaining bits set to 0.

- `User`

Usernames must be either literal values or blank (empty). A blank value matches any name and thus means "anonymous." Otherwise, the value matches exactly the name specified. In particular, `%` as a `User` value does not mean blank. It matches a user with a literal name of `%`, which is probably not what you want.

When an incoming connection is verified against the `user` table, if the first matching row contains a blank `User` value, the client is considered to be an anonymous user.

- `Password`

`Password` values are either blank (empty) or non-blank, and wildcards are not allowed. A blank password doesn't mean that any password matches. It means that the user must specify no password.

Passwords are stored as encrypted values, not literal text. If you store a literal password in the `Password` column, the user will not be able to connect! The CREATE USER and GRANT statements and the `mysqladmin password` command encrypt the password for you automatically. If you use statements such as INSERT, REPLACE, UPDATE, or SET PASSWORD to modify the grant tables, you should specify the password as PASSWORD(`'new_password'`), not as `'new_password'`.

- `Db`

In the `db` table, `Db` values may be specified literally or by using the '`%`' or '`_`' SQL pattern characters to specify a wildcard. A value of `%` or blank matches any database. In the `columns_priv`, `tables_priv`, and `procs_priv` tables, `Db` values must be literal database names. They match exactly the name specified. Patterns and empty values are not allowed.

- `Table_name`, `Column_name`, `Routine_name`

A value in these columns must be a literal table name, column name, or stored routine name, respectively. The value matches exactly the name specified. Patterns and empty values are not allowed.

- `Routine_type`

A value in this column must be either `'FUNCTION'` or `'PROCEDURE'` and indicates whether the name in the row's `Routine_name` column applies to a stored function or procedure. The `Routine_name` and `Routine_type` values uniquely identify a stored routine in the database specified in the `Db` column.

Scope columns are treated by the server as case sensitive or not as indicated in Table 13.5. Note in particular that `Db` and `Table_name` values are always treated as case sensitive, even though treatment of database and table names in SQL statements depends on the filesystem case sensitivity of the host where the server runs (typically case sensitive under Unix, and not case sensitive under Windows).

Table 13.5   **Case Sensitivity in Grant Table Scope Columns**

Column	Case Sensitive
Host	No
User	Yes
Password	Yes
Db	Yes
Table_name	Yes
Column_name	No
Routine_name	No

How MySQL Encrypts Passwords in the `user` Table

The MySQL server encrypts passwords with the `PASSWORD()` function before storing them in the user table. This prevents passwords from being exposed as plain text even to users who have read access to the table. It seems to be a common assumption that `PASSWORD()` implements the same kind of encryption as is used for Unix passwords, but that is not true. The two kinds of encryption are similar in that both are one-way and not reversible, but MySQL doesn't use the same encryption algorithm that Unix does. This means that even if you use your Unix password as your MySQL password, you shouldn't expect the encrypted password strings to match. To perform Unix encryption for a MySQL application, use the `CRYPT()` function rather than `PASSWORD()`. If you're curious about other encryption options that are available for use in your applications, see Section C.2.7, "Security and Compression Functions."

13.2.2.2 Statement Access Verification

Each time you issue an SQL statement, the server determines whether you've reached your statement resource limits. These limits are given by the `max_questions` and `max_updates` values stored in the `user` table. If you have not reached your limits, the server also checks whether you have sufficient access privileges to execute the statement. It determines your privileges by checking the privileges from the `user`, `db`, `tables_priv`, `columns_priv`, and `procs_priv` tables, until the server either verifies that you have proper access or it has searched all the tables in vain. More specifically:

1. The server checks the `user` table row that matched when you connected initially, to see what global privileges you have. If you have any such privileges and they are sufficient for the statement, the server executes it.

2. If your global privileges are insufficient, the server looks for a row that matches you in the `db` table. If it finds one, it adds the privileges in that row to your global privileges. If the result is sufficient for the statement, the server executes it.

3. If the combination of your global and database-level privileges is insufficient, the server checks the `tables_priv`, `columns_priv`, and `procs_privs` tables to determine whether you have the necessary privileges to execute the statement.

4. If, after all the tables have been checked, you still don't have the privileges needed to execute the statement, the server rejects your attempt to do so.

In boolean terms, the server combines the privileges from the grant tables as follows:

```
user OR db OR tables_priv OR columns_priv or procs_priv
```

The preceding description no doubt makes access checking sound like a rather complicated process, especially when you consider that the server checks privileges for every single statement that each client issues. However, the process is quite fast because the server doesn't actually look up information from the grant tables for every statement. Instead, it reads the contents of the tables into memory when it starts, and then verifies statements using the in-memory copies. This gives a performance boost to access-checking operations. Furthermore, if you keep your privilege specifications simple, you can ensure that access checking is as fast as possible. When the server reads the grant tables into memory, it notices whether any accounts have resource limits, and whether any have table-level, column-level, or routine-level privileges. If not, it knows that it need not check any of those types of information when checking privileges for statements issued by clients. This means the server can omit certain steps from the full access-checking procedure.

The use of in-memory copies of the grant tables for access checking has an important side effect: If you change the contents of the grant tables directly, the server won't notice the privilege change. For example, if you add a new MySQL user by using an `INSERT` statement to add a new row to the `user` table, that in itself will not enable the user named in the row to connect to the server. This is something that often confuses new administrators (and sometimes more-experienced ones!), but the solution is quite simple: Tell the server to reload the contents of the grant tables after you modify them directly. You can do this by issuing a `FLUSH PRIVILEGES` statement or by executing `mysqladmin flush-privileges` or `mysqladmin reload`.

There is no need to tell the server to reload the grant tables when you use `CREATE USER`, `DROP USER`, `RENAME USER`, `GRANT`, `REVOKE`, or `SET PASSWORD` to set up or modify user accounts. The server maps those statements onto operations that modify the grant tables, and then refreshes its in-memory copies of the tables automatically.

13.2.2.3 Scope Column Matching Order

The MySQL server sorts rows from the grant tables in a particular way, and then tries to match incoming connections by looking through the rows in order. The first match found determines the row that is used. It's important to understand the sort order that MySQL uses, especially for the user table. This seems to trip up a lot of people in their attempts to understand MySQL security.

When the server reads the contents of the user table, it sorts rows according to the values in the Host and User columns. The Host column is dominant, so rows with the same Host value are sorted together, and then ordered according to the User value. However, sorting is not lexical, or rather, it's only partially so. The principle to keep in mind is that the server prefers literal values over patterns, and more-specific patterns over less-specific patterns. This means that if you're connecting from boa.snake.net and there are rows with Host values of boa.snake.net and %.snake.net, the server prefers the first row over the second. Similarly, %.snake.net is preferred over %.net, which in turn is preferred over %. Matching for IP numbers works that way, too. For a client connecting from a host with an IP number of 192.168.3.14, rows with the following Host values all match, but are preferred in the order shown:

```
192.168.3.14
192.168.3.%
192.168.%
192.%
%
```

Another principle to remember is that when the server tries to match user table rows, it looks for a Host value match first and a User value match second, not the other way around.

13.2.3 A Privilege Puzzle

This section describes a particular scenario that demonstrates why it's useful to understand the order in which the server searches user table rows when validating connection attempts. It also shows how to solve a problem that seems to be fairly common with new MySQL installations, at least judged by the frequency with which it comes up on the MySQL mailing lists: A MySQL administrator sets up a new installation, including the default root and anonymous-user rows in the user table. A good administrator will assign passwords for the root accounts, but it's common (if inadvisable) to leave the anonymous users as is, with no passwords. Now, suppose that the administrator wants to set up a new account for a user who will be connecting from several different hosts. The easiest way to enable this is by creating the account with % as the host part of the account name in the GRANT statement so that the user can connect from anywhere:

```
GRANT ALL ON sampdb.* TO 'fred'@'%' IDENTIFIED BY 'cocoa';
```

The intent here is to grant the user `fred` all privileges for the `sampdb` database and to enable him to connect from any host he likes. Unfortunately, the probable result is that `fred` will be able to connect from any host, *except* the server host itself! Suppose that the server host is named `cobra.snake.net`. If `fred` tries to connect remotely from the host `boa.snake.net`, the attempt succeeds:

```
% mysql -p -u fred -h cobra.snake.net sampdb
Enter password: cocoa
mysql>
```

But if `fred` tries to connect locally from the server host `cobra.snake.net`, the attempt fails, even though `fred` supplies his password correctly:

```
% mysql -p -u fred -h localhost sampdb
Enter password: cocoa
ERROR 1045 (28000): Access denied for user 'fred'@'localhost'
(using password: YES)
```

This problem occurs if your `user` table contains any default anonymous-user rows that have blank usernames. Such rows are created by the `mysql_install_db` initialization script under Unix and are present in the pre-initialized `user` table included with Windows distributions. (Section 12.1, "Securing a New MySQL Installation," has a detailed description of the initial `user` table rows.) The reason the second connection attempt fails is that when the server attempts to validate `fred`, one of the anonymous-user rows takes precedence over `fred`'s row in the matching order. The anonymous-user row requires the user to connect with no password (rather than with the password `cocoa`), so a password mismatch results.

Why does this happen? To understand what's going on, it's necessary to consider both how MySQL's grant tables are set up initially and how the server uses `user` table rows when it validates client connections. For example, under Unix, when you run the `mysql_install_db` script on `cobra.snake.net` to initialize the grant tables, the resulting `user` table contains rows with `Host` and `User` values that look like this:

```
+-----------------+------+
| Host            | User |
+-----------------+------+
| localhost       | root |
| cobra.snake.net | root |
| 127.0.0.1       | root |
| localhost       |      |
| cobra.snake.net |      |
+-----------------+------+
```

The first three rows enable users to connect as `root` from the local server. The last two rows enable users to connect anonymously from the local server. After the administrator sets up the account for `fred` with the GRANT statement shown earlier, the `user` table contains these rows:

```
+------------------+------+
| Host             | User |
+------------------+------+
| localhost        | root |
| cobra.snake.net  | root |
| 127.0.0.1        | root |
| localhost        |      |
| cobra.snake.net  |      |
| %                | fred |
+------------------+------+
```

But the order of the rows as shown is not the order that the server uses when validating connection requests. Instead, it sorts rows by host first and then by user within host, putting more-specific values first and less-specific values last:

```
+------------------+------+
| Host             | User |
+------------------+------+
| localhost        | root |
| localhost        |      |
| 127.0.0.1        | root |
| cobra.snake.net  | root |
| cobra.snake.net  |      |
| %                | fred |
+------------------+------+
```

The two rows with `localhost` in the `Host` column sort together, with the row for `root` first because that's a more specific username than the blank value. The rows with `cobra.snake.net` sort together in a similar way. Furthermore, all of these rows have a literal `Host` value without any wildcard characters, so they all sort ahead of the row for `fred`, which does use a wildcard character in its `Host` value. In particular, both of the anonymous-user rows take precedence over `fred`'s row in the sort order.

The result is that when `fred` attempts to connect from the local host, one of the rows with a blank username matches before the row containing `%` in the `Host` column. The blank password in the anonymous-user row doesn't match `fred`'s password of `cocoa`, so the connection fails. One implication of this phenomenon is that it is possible for `fred` to connect from the local host, *but only if he specifies no password.* Unfortunately, then he will be validated as an anonymous user and won't have the privileges associated with the `fred@%` account.

What all this means is that although it's very convenient to use wildcards when you set up an account for a user who will connect from multiple hosts, the user may have problems connecting from the local host due to the anonymous rows in the `user` table.

What is the solution to this problem? Actually, you can solve it two ways. First, you can set up a second account for `fred` that explicitly lists `localhost` as the host value:

```
GRANT ALL ON sampdb.* TO 'fred'@'localhost' IDENTIFIED BY 'cocoa';
```

If you do that, the server will sort the rows from the `user` table as follows:

```
+-----------------+------+
| Host            | User |
+-----------------+------+
| localhost       | fred |
| localhost       | root |
| localhost       |      |
| 127.0.0.1       | root |
| cobra.snake.net | root |
| cobra.snake.net |      |
| %               | fred |
+-----------------+------+
```

Now when `fred` connects from the local host, the row with `localhost` and `fred` will match ahead of the anonymous-user rows. When he connects from any other host, the row with `%` and `fred` will match. The downside of having two accounts for `fred` is that whenever you want to change his privileges or password, you'll have to make the change twice.

The second solution is much easier: Remove the anonymous accounts from the `user` table with these `DROP USER` statements:

```
DROP USER ''@'localhost';
DROP USER ''@'cobra.snake.net';
```

The remaining `user` table rows sort into this order:

```
+-----------------+------+
| Host            | User |
+-----------------+------+
| localhost       | root |
| 127.0.0.1       | root |
| cobra.snake.net | root |
| %               | fred |
+-----------------+------+
```

Now when `fred` attempts to connect from the local host, he'll succeed, because there won't be any rows in the `user` table that will match ahead of his.

In general, I recommend that if you want to make your life easier as an administrator, you should delete any anonymous-user accounts that are present in the initial grant tables. In my view, these accounts are not very useful, and they tend to cause more problems than they're worth.

The puzzle presented in this section addresses a specific situation, but contains a more general lesson. If privileges for a given account don't work the way you expect, look in the grant tables to see whether there's some row containing `Host` values that are more specific than the row for the user in question and that will match connection attempts by that user. If so, that may explain the problem. You might need to make the user's row more specific, or add another row to cover the more specific case.

13.2.4 Grant Table Risks to Avoid

This section describes precautions to observe when you grant privileges, and the attendant risks of unwise choices.

Avoid creating anonymous-user accounts. Even if they don't have sufficient privileges to cause damage directly, allowing a user to connect still may provide access to that user to look around and gather information such as what databases and tables you have, or to monitor the server with SHOW STATUS and SHOW VARIABLES.

Find accounts that have no passwords and either remove them or assign passwords. To find such accounts, use this query:

```
mysql> SELECT Host, User FROM mysql.user WHERE Password = '';
```

Find accounts that have password hash values in the older pre-MySQL 4.1 format and change them to the more secure password hash format that is used as of MySQL 4.1. Values in the older format have a length of 16 and do not begin with the '*' character, so you can identify them using either of these statements:

```
mysql> SELECT Host, User FROM mysql.user WHERE LENGTH(Password) = 16;
mysql> SELECT Host, User FROM mysql.user WHERE Password NOT LIKE '*%';
```

However, that you cannot institute this security measure unless all client programs that connect to your server are from MySQL 4.1 or later and can authenticate using the newer password mechanism. Assuming that you can use newer passwords for all clients, you need only make sure that the server was not started with the --old-passwords option, and then use SET PASSWORD to set the password for each account that has an old-format password. The new password format will be used for each account. For additional security, start the server with the --secure-auth option. Otherwise, a client can reset its password to the old format with OLD_PASSWORD() and then connect using that password. --secure-auth prevents clients from connecting unless they have a new-format password.

Unless you really need to use patterns in hostname specifiers, avoid doing so when setting up accounts. Broadening the range of hosts from which a given user can connect also broadens the range from which an imposter claiming to be that user can try to break in.

Grant superuser privileges sparingly. That is, don't enable privileges in user table rows. Those privileges are global and enable the user to affect the operation of your server or to access any database. Grant privileges at a more specific level instead, to restrict user access to particular databases or database objects such as tables or stored routines.

Don't grant privileges for the mysql database that contains the grant tables. A user with privileges for that database may be able to modify its tables to acquire privileges on any other database as well. In effect, granting privileges that enable a user to modify the mysql database tables gives that user all global privileges: If the user can modify the tables directly, that's equivalent to being able to issue any account-management statement you can think of.

Be careful with the GRANT OPTION privilege. Two users with different privileges that both have the GRANT OPTION privilege can make each other's access rights more powerful.

The FILE privilege is particularly dangerous; don't grant it lightly. Here's an example of something a user with the FILE privilege can do:

```
CREATE TABLE etc_passwd (pwd_entry TEXT);
LOAD DATA INFILE '/etc/passwd' INTO TABLE etc_passwd;
```

After executing those statements, the user has access to the contents of your server host's password file just by issuing a SELECT:

```
SELECT * FROM etc_passwd;
```

The name of any publicly readable file on the server host may be substituted for /etc/passwd in the LOAD DATA statement. If a user has connected from a remote host, the effect is that granting the FILE privilege enables network access for that user to a potentially large portion of your server host's filesystem.

The FILE privilege also can be exploited to compromise databases on systems that aren't set up with sufficiently restrictive data directory permissions. This is one reason why you should set the data directory contents to be readable only by the server. If files corresponding to database tables are world-readable, not only can any user with an account on the server host read them, but any client user with the FILE privilege can connect over the network and read them, too! The following procedure demonstrates how:

1. Create a table containing a LONGBLOB column:

   ```
   USE test;
   CREATE TABLE tmp (b LONGBLOB);
   ```

2. Use the table to read in the contents of each of the files that correspond to the table you want to steal. For example, if a user has a MyISAM table named x in a database other_db, that table is represented by three files, x.frm, x.MYD, and x.MYI. You can read those files and copy them into corresponding files in the test database like this:

   ```
   LOAD DATA INFILE './other_db/x.frm' INTO TABLE tmp
      FIELDS ESCAPED BY '' LINES TERMINATED BY '';
   SELECT * FROM tmp INTO OUTFILE 'x.frm'
      FIELDS ESCAPED BY '' LINES TERMINATED BY '';
   DELETE FROM tmp;
   LOAD DATA INFILE './other_db/x.MYD' INTO TABLE tmp
      FIELDS ESCAPED BY '' LINES TERMINATED BY '';
   SELECT * FROM tmp INTO OUTFILE 'x.MYD'
      FIELDS ESCAPED BY '' LINES TERMINATED BY '';
   DELETE FROM tmp;
   LOAD DATA INFILE './other_db/x.MYI' INTO TABLE tmp
   ```

```
     FIELDS ESCAPED BY '' LINES TERMINATED BY '';
SELECT * FROM tmp INTO OUTFILE 'x.MYI'
     FIELDS ESCAPED BY '' LINES TERMINATED BY '';
```

3. After executing those statements, the `test` database directory also will contain files named `x.frm`, `x.MYD`, and `x.MYI`. In other words, the `test` database will contain a table x that is a stolen duplicate of the table in the `other_db` database.

To avoid having someone attack your users' tables in the same way, set the permissions on your data directory contents according to the instructions in given earlier in Section 13.1.2, "Securing Your MySQL Installation." As an additional measure, avoid granting the `SHOW DATABASE` privilege and run the server with the `--skip-show-database` option. This prevents users from using `SHOW DATABASES` and `SHOW TABLES` for databases to which they have no access, and helps to keep users from finding out about databases and tables they shouldn't be accessing.

The dangers of the `FILE` privilege are amplified if you run the MySQL server as `root`. That's inadvisable in the first place, and is particularly so when combined with `FILE`. Because `root` can create files anywhere in the filesystem, a user with the `FILE` privilege can do so as well, even a user who has connected from a remote host. The server won't create a file that already exists, but it's sometimes possible to create new files that will alter the operation of the server host or compromise its security. For example, if any of the files `/etc/resolv.conf`, `/etc/hosts.equiv`, `/etc/hosts.lpd`, or `/etc/sudoers` do not already exist, a user who is able to cause the MySQL server to create them can drastically change the way your server host behaves. To avoid these problems, don't run `mysqld` as `root`. (See Section 12.2.1.1, "Running the Server Using an Unprivileged Login Account.")

The `PROCESS` and `SUPER` privileges should be granted only to trusted MySQL accounts. With `PROCESS`, a user can use `SHOW PROCESSLIST` to see the text of statements being executed by the server. This enables a user to snoop on other users and possibly see information that should remain private. With `SUPER`, the user can kill statements being executed by other users, disrupting their activities. `SUPER` also enables a user to purge log files and perform other actions that can compromise server operation.

Don't give the `RELOAD` privilege to people who don't need it. `RELOAD` enables a user to issue `FLUSH` and `RESET` statements, which can be abused in several ways:

- Binary and relay log files are created with names that form a numbered sequence. If you have configured the server to perform binary or relay logging, each `FLUSH LOGS` statement creates the next log in the sequence. A user with the `RELOAD` privilege who performs many log flushing operations can cause the server to create large numbers of files.

- A user with the `RELOAD` privilege can defeat the resource management mechanism by reloading the grant tables with `FLUSH PRIVILEGES` or with `FLUSH USER_RESOURCES`. Both statements reset resource management counters to zero.

- FLUSH TABLES can be used repeatedly to cause the server to flush its open-table cache, which degrades performance by preventing the server from taking advantage of the cache. Similarly, RESET QUERY CACHE can be used to negate the benefits of the query cache.

- RESET MASTER LOGS causes a replication master server to delete all of its binary log files even if they still are in use, which removes the information necessary to maintain replication integrity.

The ALTER privilege can be used in ways you may not intend. Suppose that you want one user to be able to access table1 but not table2. Another user with the ALTER privilege may be able to subvert your intent by using ALTER TABLE to rename table2 to table1.

13.3 Setting Up Secure Connections

MySQL provides support for secure, encrypted connections over SSL. By default, an SSL-enabled MySQL installation enables a client to ask for secure connections on an optional basis. It's also possible for administrators to use GRANT to indicate that a given account is *required* to connect securely. The tradeoff between connection types is that an unencrypted connection has higher performance, whereas an encrypted connection is secure but somewhat slower due to the additional computational burden that encryption imposes.

Note that there is little point in using SSL for connections to the local host that are made using a Unix socket file, a named pipe, shared memory, or to the IP number 127.0.0.1 (the network loopback interface). The traffic for such connections never leaves the local host. The real benefit of SSL comes when the information that you're transmitting goes over a network that may be susceptible to snooping.

To take advantage of SSL support for encrypted connections between the server and client programs, use the following general procedure:

1. Make sure the server and client programs have been compiled with SSL support.

2. Start the server with options that tell it where to find its certificate and key files; these are necessary to set up secure connections.

3. To connect securely with a client program, invoke it with options that tell it where to find your own certificate and key files.

The following discussion describes this process in more detail.

Your MySQL distribution must be built with SSL support included. Either get a binary distribution that has SSL compiled in, or build MySQL from source. Binary distributions for most platforms support SSL. If you compile MySQL yourself, be sure to supply the necessary options at configuration time (for example, one of the --with-*ssl options on Unix; see Section A.4.3.3, "Installing a Source Distribution"). After you start your SSL-capable server, verify that it supports SSL by connecting with mysql and issuing the following query:

```
mysql> SHOW VARIABLES LIKE 'have_ssl';
```

```
+---------------+----------+
| Variable_name | Value    |
+---------------+----------+
| have_ssl      | DISABLED |
+---------------+----------+
```

If you see `DISABLED` or `YES`, SSL support is available. `DISABLED` means that support is present but has not yet been enabled. That's okay; the files necessary to enable SSL are discussed next.

With a MySQL installation that includes SSL support, the server and its clients can communicate securely. Each end of a connection uses three files to set up secure communications:

- A Certificate Authority (CA) certificate. A CA is a trusted third party; its certificate is used to verify the authenticity of the client and server certificates. It's common to purchase a CA certificate from a commercial entity, but you can generate your own.
- A certificate file that authenticates one side of the connection to the other.
- A key file, used to encrypt and decrypt traffic over the connection.

The server's certificate and key files must be installed first. If you don't have files if your own, the `ssl` directory of the `sampdb` distribution contains some boilerplate files that you can use:

- `ca-cert.pem`, the Certificate Authority certificate
- `server-cert.pem`, the server's certificate
- `server-key.pem`, the server's public key

Copy these three files to your server's data directory, and then add some lines to the `[mysqld]` group of an option file that the server reads when it starts, such as `/etc/my.cnf` on Unix or `C:\my.ini` on Windows. The options should indicate the pathnames to the certificate and key files. For example, if the data directory is `/usr/local/mysql/data`, list the options like this:

```
[mysqld]
ssl-ca=/usr/local/mysql/data/ca-cert.pem
ssl-cert=/usr/local/mysql/data/server-cert.pem
ssl-key=/usr/local/mysql/data/server-key.pem
```

You can put the certificate and key files elsewhere if you like, but the location should be one to which only the server has access. After you install the SSL files and modify the option file, restart the server.

At this point, you have enabled the server to allow encrypted connections, and `have_ssl` should have a value of `YES`. However, client programs still can connect to the server only over unencrypted connections. To enable a client to use secure connections, specify certificate and key files for the client side as well. The `ssl` directory of the `sampdb` distribution contains files for this. You can use the same CA certificate file (`ca-cert.pem`).

The client certificate and key files are named `client-cert.pem` and `client-key.pem`. Copy these three files to some directory under your own account. Then let the client program know where they are by adding some lines to an option file that the client reads when you execute it, such as the `.my.cnf` file in your home directory on Unix.

Suppose that I want to use encrypted connections for the `mysql` program. I can copy the SSL files to my home directory, `/home/paul`, and then put the following lines in my `.my.cnf` file:

```
[mysql]
ssl-ca=/home/paul/ca-cert.pem
ssl-cert=/home/paul/client-cert.pem
ssl-key=/home/paul/client-key.pem
```

You can set up your own account similarly. It's also a good precaution to make sure your certificate and key files are accessible only to yourself. After modifying `.my.cnf` to indicate where the SSL files are located, invoke `mysql` and issue a `\s` or `status` command. The SSL line in the output should indicate that the connection is encrypted:

```
mysql> status;
--------------

mysql  Ver 14.14 Distrib 5.1.25-rc, for pc-linux-gnu (i686)

Connection id:          5
Current database:
Current user:           sampadm@localhost
SSL:                    Cipher in use is DHE-RSA-AES256-SHA
...
```

You can also issue the following query to see what values the SSL-related server status variables have:

```
SHOW STATUS LIKE 'Ssl%';
```

The presence of the SSL-related options in the `[mysql]` option file group causes `mysql` to use SSL connections by default. If you comment out those lines or remove them from your option file, `mysql` uses a regular non-encrypted connection. It's also possible to ignore the SSL options by invoking `mysql` like this:

```
% mysql --skip-ssl
```

The SSL options in the `[mysql]` group can be copied to other program-specific groups to enable use of SSL for other programs. However, it may not be a good idea to put the options in the general `[client]` group. That will cause any client program to fail that doesn't understand how to use SSL. (If you want to put the options there anyway, use the `loose-` prefix so that non-SSL-aware programs will ignore them.)

As an alternative to listing SSL options in the option file, you can specify them on the command line. For example, in the directory where the SSL files are located, I might invoke `mysql` like this (enter the command all on one line):

```
% mysql --ssl-ca=ca-cert.pem --ssl-cert=client-cert.pem
   --ssl-key=client-key.pem
```

However, all that typing is burdensome to do often.

The certificate and key files in the `sampdb` distribution suffice to enable you to establish encrypted connections. However, they're publicly available (anyone can get the distribution), so connections thus established cannot truly be said to be secure. After you use these files to verify that SSL is working properly, you should replace them with ones that you generate yourself. For instructions on making your own certificate and key files, see the `ssl/README.txt` file in the `sampdb` distribution. You may also want to consider purchasing a commercial certificate.

The discussion thus far describes how any account can use SSL on an optional basis. You can also set up an account to disallow unencrypted connections and require it to use SSL. This can be done for a new or existing account.

If you use `GRANT` to create a new account, add a `REQUIRE` clause that specifies the constraints that connections must satisfy. Suppose that you want to set up a user named `laura` who will be connecting to the server on `cobra.snake.net` from the host `rat.snake.net` to access the `finance` database. To require only that connections be encrypted, use this statement:

```
GRANT ALL ON finance.* TO 'laura'@'rat.snake.net'
   IDENTIFIED BY 'moneymoneymoney'
   REQUIRE SSL;
```

For more security, use `REQUIRE X509` instead. In that case, `laura` must supply a valid X509 client certificate when connecting. (This will be the file named by the `--ssl-cert` option.) As long as the certificate is valid, its contents don't otherwise matter. To require specific certificate contents, use some combination of `CIPHER`, `ISSUER`, and `SUBJECT` in the `REQUIRE` clause. `CIPHER` indicates the type of encryption method you want the connection to use. `ISSUER` or `SUBJECT` indicate that the client certificate must have been issued by a particular source or for a particular recipient. These clauses narrow the scope of otherwise-valid certificates to include only those with specific content. The following `GRANT` statement requires a particular issuer in the client certificate and specifies the use of EXP1024-RC4-SHA encryption:

```
GRANT ALL ON finance.* TO 'laura'@'rat.snake.net'
   IDENTIFIED BY 'moneymoneymoney'
   REQUIRE ISSUER '/C=US/ST=WI/L=Madison/O=sampdb/OU=CA/CN=sampdb'
   CIPHER 'EXP1024-RC4-SHA';
```

To modify an existing account to require SSL connections, use a `GRANT USAGE` statement of the following form, where `require_options` specifies the SSL characteristics that you want to enforce:

```
GRANT USAGE ON *.* TO 'user_name'@'host_name' REQUIRE require_options;
```

`GRANT USAGE ON *.*` leaves the account's privileges unchanged and modifies only SSL-related account attributes.

If an account currently is set to require SSL and you want to rescind that requirement, use `GRANT USAGE` in conjunction with `REQUIRE NONE`:

```
GRANT USAGE ON *.* TO 'user_name'@'host_name' REQUIRE NONE;
```

If you are using a MySQL API for a language such as Perl or PHP, SSL capabilities depend not only on the language API but on the MySQL client library that is linked into it. The client library must have been compiled with SSL support so that it can support SSL connections to the server. Also, the language API must be recent enough to use the SSL capabilities of the client library. For example, the PHP `mysqli` extension supports SSL connections, but the older `mysql` extension does not.

Database Maintenance, Backups, and Replication

Ideally, MySQL runs smoothly from the time that you first install it. But problems sometimes do occur for a variety of reasons, ranging from power outages to hardware failure to improper shutdown of the MySQL server (such as when you force-terminate it with `kill -9` or when the server host crashes). Events such as these, many of which are beyond your control, can result in damage to database tables, typically caused by incomplete writes in the middle of table changes.

This chapter describes what you can do to minimize your risks and to be ready if disaster strikes anyway. The techniques covered here include making database backups, performing table checking and repair operations, and how to use recovery procedures in case you do lose data. The chapter also discusses database copying procedures for transferring a database from one server to another because these are often are quite similar to backup techniques. Another "copy" technique covered here is replication, in which a slave server is initialized with a duplicate of a master server's data, and then when changes occur thereafter on the master, they are propagated to the slave as well. The slave thus serves as a "continuous copy" of the master. Replication can be used to achieve other purposes as well. To name two, client load can be split between servers to lessen the load on the master, and the slave can be more easily paused or stopped than the master for making backups.

14.1 Principles of Preventive Maintenance

This section summarizes general principles of preventive maintenance. Later sections provide details on implementing these principles.

To prepare in advance against database problems, take the following actions:

- Enable the auto-recovery capabilities that the MySQL server provides.

- Set up scheduled preventive maintenance to perform table checking periodically. Routine table-checking procedures can help you detect and correct minor problems before they become worse.

- Set up a database backup schedule. Should the worst occur and you be faced with catastrophic system failure, you'll need the backups to perform recovery operations. Enable your binary log, too, so that you have a record of updates that took place after the backup was made. (See Section 12.5.4, "The Binary Log and the Binary Log Index File.") Binary logging provides significant advantages for backup and replication and has negligible performance overhead (about 1%), so there is little reason not to enable it.

If table damage or data loss does occur despite your efforts, exercise your options for dealing with such problems:

- Check your tables, and then fix any that are found to be corrupt if possible. Minor damage often can be corrected by using MySQL's table repair capabilities.

- For circumstances under which table checking and repair isn't sufficient to get you up and running, perform data recovery using your backups and your binary log. Begin by using the backups to restore your tables to their state at the time of the backup. After that, use the log files to re-apply any updates that were made after the backup, to bring your tables to their state when the crash occurred.

The tools at your disposal for carrying out these tasks include the capabilities of the MySQL server itself and also several other utilities included in the MySQL distribution:

- When the server starts, transactional storage engines can perform auto-recovery. You can also enable automatic table repair for the MyISAM storage engine. These capabilities are useful when the server restart follows a crash.

- Use the `mysqldump` or `mysqlhotcopy` program to make backups of your databases, should you need to recover them later.

- To tell the server to perform table maintenance operations on demand, use SQL statements such as CHECK TABLE and REPAIR TABLE. For a command-line interface to these statements, use the `mysqlcheck` program. The `myisamchk` utility also can check tables for problems and perform various corrective actions.

Some of these programs, such as `mysqlcheck` and `mysqldump`, work in cooperation with the server. They connect as clients to the server and issue SQL statements that instruct the server what kind of table maintenance operation to perform. By contrast, `myisamchk` is an independent standalone program that operates directly on the files used to represent tables. Because the server also accesses those files while it runs, `myisamchk` acts in effect as a competitor to the server. This means that you must take steps to prevent `myisamchk` and the server from interfering with each other. For example, if you're repairing a table with `myisamchk`, it's necessary to keep the server from trying to write to the table at the same time. Failure to do so can result in much worse problems than those you're trying to correct!

The need to cooperate with the server arises in connection with several of the administrative tasks discussed in this chapter, from making backups to performing table repairs. Therefore, the next section begins by describing how to keep the server at bay when necessary, and sections following discuss how to prepare for problems, how to make backups, and how to use repair and recovery techniques if necessary.

Under Unix, operations that require you to directly work with table files or other files under the data directory should be performed while you're logged in as the MySQL administrator so that you have permission to access the files. In this book, the name of that login account is `mysql`. It's also possible to access the files as `root`, but in that case, make sure when you're done that any files you work with have the same mode and ownership as when you began.

For a full listing of the options supported by the SQL statements and programs discussed in this chapter, see Appendix E, "SQL Syntax Reference," and Appendix F, "MySQL Program Reference."

14.2 Performing Database Maintenance with the Server Running

Some maintenance operations are performed by connecting to the server and telling it what to do. To perform consistency checks or table repairs on a MyISAM table, one way to do so is to issue a `CHECK TABLE` or `REPAIR TABLE` statement (or invoke the `mysqlcheck` program) and let the server do the work. In this case, the server will access the `.frm`, `.MYD`, and `.MYI` files that represent the table. In general, this is the best approach to take if possible: When the server performs the requested maintenance operations, it handles any issues involved in coordinating access to the table so that you need not think about them.

Other maintenance operations are performed by a program external to the server, in which case, you *must* think about issues of table access coordination. For example, another way to check or repair a MyISAM table is to invoke the `myisamchk` utility, which opens the table files directly without going through the server. While `myisamchk` accesses the table files, it's necessary to prevent the server from changing the table at the same time. If you don't do that, the competing efforts to access the table can damage it and make it unusable. It's obviously a bad thing for the server and `myisamchk` both to be writing to the table at the same time, but even having one of them reading while the other program is writing isn't good, either. The program doing the reading can become confused if the table is being changed by the other program at the same time.

The need to prevent the server from accessing tables comes up in other contexts as well:

- Compressing a MyISAM table with `myisampack`.
- Relocating a MyISAM table's data file or index file.
- Relocating a database.

- Some backup techniques involve copying table files. To ensure consistent backup files, it's necessary to keep the server from changing the tables during the backup procedure.

- Some recovery methods are based on replacing damaged tables with good backup copies. While you are replacing the table, you must not allow the server to access it at all.

The most effective way to prevent the server from interfering with you is to shut it down. Clearly, if the server is not running, it can't access the tables you're working with. But administrators are understandably reluctant to take the server completely offline because that makes all databases and tables unavailable, not just those that you want to check or repair.

To avoid stopping the server while at the same time preventing problems of interaction between a running server and operations that you're performing externally to it, coordinate with the server by using a locking protocol. The server has two kinds of locking:

- The server uses internal locking to keep requests from different clients from getting mixed up with each other—for example, to keep one client's SELECT query from being interrupted by another client's UPDATE statement. But you can also exploit internal locking to prevent clients from accessing a table while you are working with the table externally to the server.

- The server can use external locking to prevent other programs from modifying table files while it's using them. This is based on the locking capabilities available for your operating system at the filesystem level. Normally, the reason the server uses external locking is for cooperation with programs like myisamchk during table checking operations. However, external locking doesn't work reliably on some systems. Another limitation is that external locking is useful only for operations that require read-only access to table files, such as table checking. External locking cannot be used for operations that require read/write access, such as table repair. External locking is based on file locking, but repair operations performed by myisamchk copy table files to new files as they work, and then use the new files to replace the originals. The server knows nothing of the new files, which renders useless any attempt at coordinating access by means of file locks.

The following discussion covers only the use of internal locking to coordinate with the server for table access. Because external locking is problematic, I discuss it no further.

14.2.1 Locking Individual Tables for Read-Only or Read/Write Access

To use the server's internal locking mechanism to prevent it from accessing a table while you work on it, the general idea is that you connect to the server with mysql and issue a LOCK TABLE statement for the table you want to use. Then, with mysql idle (that is, sitting there not doing anything with the table except keeping it locked), you do whatever you need to do with the table files. When you're done, switch back to your mysql session and release the lock to tell the server it's okay to use the table again.

The locking protocol to use depends on whether you need read-only access or read/write access to the table's files:

- For operations that just check or copy the files, read-only access is sufficient.

- For operations that modify the files, such as table repair or replacing damaged files with good ones, you need read/write access.

The locking protocols use the LOCK TABLE and UNLOCK TABLE statements to acquire and release locks. They also use FLUSH TABLE to tell the server to flush any pending changes to disk and as a means of informing the server that it will need to reopen the table when next it accesses it. The examples use the FLUSH TABLE syntax that takes a table-name argument and flushes only that specific table.

You *must* perform all the LOCK, FLUSH, and UNLOCK statements from within a single session with the server. For example, you cannot connect to the server with the mysql program, lock a table, and then quit, intending to connect again later to unlock the table. That doesn't work because when you quit mysql, the server releases the lock automatically. At that point, the server considers itself free to use the table again, with the result that it is no longer safe for you to work with the table files.

One easy way to perform the locking procedures is to keep two windows open. This enables you to leave mysql running in one window while you work with the table files in the other. If you're not using a windowing environment, you can suspend and resume mysql using your shell's job control facilities while you work with the table.

The internal-locking techniques described here for locking individual tables apply only when working with table files for storage engines such as MyISAM that represent each table with its own unique files. They *do not apply* to storage engines such as InnoDB or Falcon that store information about multiple tables in a given file. For example, InnoDB by default represents all InnoDB tables together within the files that make up its shared tablespace. (Even when configured to use individual per-table tablespaces, InnoDB still stores some information about each table in its data dictionary, which is stored in the shared tablespace.)

14.2.1.1 Locking a Table for Read-Only Access

The read-only locking protocol is appropriate for operations that need only to read a table's files, such as making copies of the files or checking them for inconsistencies. It's sufficient to acquire a read lock in this case; the server will prevent other clients from modifying the table, but will allow them to read from it. This protocol should *not* be used when you need to modify a table.

1. In window A, invoke mysql and issue the following statements to obtain a read lock and flush the table:

```
% mysql db_name
mysql> LOCK TABLE tbl_name READ;
mysql> FLUSH TABLE tbl_name;
```

LOCK TABLE acquires a lock that prevents other clients from writing to the table and modifying it while you're checking it. The FLUSH statement causes the server to close the table files, which flushes any unwritten changes that might still be cached in memory.

2. With `mysql` sitting idle, switch to window B so that you can work with the table files. For example, you can check a MyISAM table like this:

```
% myisamchk tbl_name
```

If your current directory is the table's database directory, you can use the command as shown. Otherwise, you'll need to precede the table name with the path to that directory. For example:

```
% myisamchk /usr/local/mysql/data/tbl_name
```

This example is for illustration only. The particular commands you issue will depend on what maintenance operation you're performing.

3. When you're done working with the table, switch back to the `mysql` session in window A and release the table lock:

```
mysql> UNLOCK TABLE;
```

It's possible that your work with the table will indicate that further action is necessary. For example, if you check a table with `myisamchk`, it may find problems that need correction. The corrective procedure will require read/write access, which you can obtain safely using the protocol described in the next section.

14.2.1.2 Locking a Table for Read/Write Access

The read/write locking protocol is appropriate for operations such as table repair that need to modify a table's files. To do this, you must acquire a write lock to completely prevent all server access to the table while you're working on it.

The locking procedure for repairing a table is similar to the procedure for checking it, with two differences. First, you must obtain a write lock rather than a read lock. Because you'll be modifying the table, you can't let the server access it at all, not even to read it. Second, you should issue a second FLUSH TABLE statement after working with the table. Some operations involve building a new index file, such as repairing a table with `myisamchk`, and the server won't notice the new index unless you flush the table cache again. To lock a table for read/write access, use this procedure:

1. Invoke `mysql` in window A and issue the following statements to obtain a write lock and flush the table:

```
% mysql db_name
mysql> LOCK TABLE tbl_name WRITE;
mysql> FLUSH TABLE tbl_name;
```

2. With `mysql` sitting idle, switch to window B so that you can work directly with the table files. For example, you can repair a MyISAM table like this:

```
% myisamchk --recover tbl_name
```

This example is for illustration only. The particular commands you issue will depend on what maintenance operation you're performing. (It might be prudent to make copies of the table files first, in case something goes wrong.)

3. When you're done working with the table, switch back to the `mysql` session in window A, flush the table again, and release the table lock:

```
mysql> FLUSH TABLE tbl_name;
mysql> UNLOCK TABLE;
```

14.2.2 Locking All Databases for Read-Only Access

A convenient way to prevent clients from making any changes to any table is to place a read lock on all tables in all databases at once. To do this, issue the following statements:

```
mysql> FLUSH TABLES WITH READ LOCK;
mysql> SET GLOBAL read_only = ON;
```

The FLUSH statement acquires a global read lock, and the SET statement blocks until all other clients release any table locks they have and finish any outstanding transactions. When the statement returns, other clients can read but not change tables.

To allow changes to be made once again, use these statements:

```
mysql> SET GLOBAL read_only = OFF;
mysql> UNLOCK TABLES;
```

While the tables are locked this way, other clients can read from them but cannot make changes. This is a good way to make the server quiescent for operations such as making copies of all your database directories. On the other hand, it's unfriendly to all clients that need to make updates, so you should hold the server lock no longer than necessary. It is also insufficient for operations such as making a binary backup of all tables managed by a transactional storage engine because the engine might have outstanding transactions pending and only partly flushed to its log files. Operations like that require that you stop the server to make sure everything is flushed and all files are closed.

14.3 General Preventative Maintenance

This section outlines some general strategies to help you maintain the integrity of your databases:

- Enable the auto-recovery capabilities that the MySQL server provides.
- Schedule regular preventive maintenance to check your tables.

- Have a policy of making regular database backups, so that you have something to fall back on if your databases are damaged or lost.

The first two items are discussed here. Section 14.4, "Making Database Backups," covers several backup techniques.

14.3.1 Using the Server's Auto-Recovery Capabilities

One of your first lines of defense in maintaining database integrity is the MySQL server's crash recovery capabilities. One of these (transactional storage engine recovery) is automatic and happens at server startup. Another (MyISAM recovery) is optional and must be enabled explicitly.

When the server starts, it can perform certain types of table checking to help deal with problems resulting from an earlier server or machine crash. MySQL is designed to recover from a variety of problems, so if you do nothing more than restart the server normally, it will make the necessary corrections for you in many cases:

- If the InnoDB storage engine is enabled, it checks for a variety of problems automatically. Committed transactions that are present in its redo log but not yet flushed to tables are rolled forward (redone). Uncommitted transactions in progress at the time of the crash are rolled back (discarded) using the undo log. The result is to leave your InnoDB tables in a consistent state, so that their contents reflect all transactions that had been committed up to the point of the crash.

- The Falcon storage engine, if enabled, has a similar capability. It attempts auto-recovery based on the contents of its serial log.

If InnoDB auto-recovery fails due to a non-recoverable problem, the server exits after writing a message to the error log. To force the server to start up anyway so that you can attempt a manual recovery procedure, see Section 14.7.4, "Coping with InnoDB Auto-Recovery Problems."

For MyISAM tables, the server supports an optional form of table recovery that you must enable explicitly. When you do so, the server performs a check each time it opens a MyISAM table. If the table was not closed properly after its most recent use or is marked as crashed, the server checks and repairs it. To enable MyISAM table recovery, start the server with the `--myisam-recover=level` option. The value of `level` is a comma-separated list of one or more of the following values: `BACKUP` (create a backup of the table if the repair will change it), `FORCE` (force recovery even if more than a row of data will be lost), `QUICK` (quick recovery), or `DEFAULT` (recover without any of the other special handling; this is the same as specifying the option with no value at all). For example, to force recovery if problems are found, but create a backup first, start the server with `--myisam-recover=BACKUP,FORCE`.

Enabling MyISAM auto-recovery is useful as a general maintenance strategy because otherwise a MyISAM table that is found to have problems becomes unavailable until you notice the problem and initiate repair manually. MyISAM recovery is especially important if you run the server with the `--delay-key-write` option or have individual MyISAM tables configured to use delayed key writes. Under those conditions, index changes are not flushed until tables close, which increases performance as the server runs, but also means that indexes will need repair for any delayed-key tables that are open at the time of a crash.

14.3.2 Scheduling Preventive Maintenance

In addition to enabling auto-recovery, you should consider setting up a schedule of preventive maintenance. This helps detect problems automatically so that you can take steps to correct them. By arranging to check your tables on a regular basis, you'll reduce the likelihood of having to resort to your backups. On Unix, this is most easily accomplished by using a cron job, typically invoked from the `crontab` file of the account used to run the server. (See Section 12.5.7.3, "Automating the Log Expiration Procedure," for information about setting up `cron` jobs.)

The `mysqlcheck` program is useful for checking MyISAM and InnoDB tables while the server is online. Suppose that you want to set up a maintenance job that invokes `mysqlcheck`. If you run the server as the `mysql` user, you can set up periodic check from that user's `crontab` file. Add an entry to the file that looks something like this. Enter everything on a single line and use the path for `mysqlcheck` that is correct for your system:

```
45 3 * * 0 /usr/local/mysql/bin/mysqlcheck
    --all-databases --check-only-changed --silent
```

The entry tells `cron` to run `mysqlcheck` at 03:45 every Sunday. You can vary the time or scheduling as desired.

The `--all-databases` option causes `mysqlcheck` to check all tables in all databases. This gives you an easy way to use it for maximum effect. For the proper options to use to have `mysqlcheck` check only certain databases or tables, see the program description in Appendix F.

The `--check-only-changed` option tells `mysqlcheck` to skip any table that hasn't been modified since it was last checked successfully, and the `--silent` option suppresses output unless there are errors in the tables. `cron` jobs typically generate a mail message if a job produces any output at all, and there's little reason to receive mail for table-checking jobs that find no problems. Note that even with `--silent`, you may get some diagnostic output if your databases have tables for storage engines that `mysqlcheck` doesn't know how to check.

Note

While a table is being checked, it cannot be updated. Automatic-maintenance strategies might not be appropriate for large tables that need to be updated frequently if you cannot afford to block updates for the duration of the check operation.

14.4 Making Database Backups

It's important to back up your databases in case tables are lost or damaged. If a serious system crash occurs, you want to be able to restore your tables to the state they were in at the time of the crash with as little data loss as possible. Likewise, a user who issues an unwise DROP DATABASE, DROP TABLE, or DELETE statement may show up at your door requesting that you perform data recovery.

Database backups also are useful for copying databases to another server. Most commonly, a database is transferred to a server running on another host, but you can also transfer data to a different server running on the same host. You might do this if you're testing a server for a new release of MySQL and want to use it with real data from your production server.

Another use for a backup is to set up a replication server, because one of the first steps in setting up a slave server is to take a snapshot of the master server at a specific point in time. The backup serves as this snapshot, and loading it into the slave server brings it up to date with respect to the master server. Thereafter, updates made on the master server are replicated to the slave server through the standard replication protocol. Section 14.8.2, "Establishing a Master-Slave Replication Relationship," discusses the procedure for setting up replication.

Let's begin with some general principles that govern backup practices and that will help you decide which techniques to use. Then we'll get to the details of specific backup methods.

There are two general categories of database backups:

- Text-format backups made by using mysqldump to write table contents into dump files. These files consist of CREATE TABLE and INSERT SQL statements that can be reloaded into the server later to restore the tables.
- Binary backups made by directly copying the files containing table contents. This type of backup can be made in various ways. For example, you can use a program such as mysqlhotcopy, cp, tar, or rsync.

Each method has its own advantages and disadvantages. Some of the factors to consider are whether you can leave the server running, the time needed to make the backup, portability of the backup, and the scope of what is backed up.

- mysqldump operates in cooperation with the MySQL server, so you can use it while the server is running. Binary-backup methods involve file copy operations that are done external to the server. Some of these methods require that you stop the server. For those that do not, you still must take steps to ensure that the server does not modify the tables while you copy them.
- mysqldump is slower than binary-backup techniques because the dump operation involves transferring the information over the network connection between mysqldump and the server. Binary-backup methods operate by copying files at the filesystem level and require no network traffic.

- `mysqldump` generates text files containing SQL statements. These files are portable to other machines, even those with a different hardware architecture. They are therefore usable for copying databases from one server to another. Files generated by direct-copy binary backup methods may or may not be portable to other machines. It depends on whether your tables use a machine-independent storage format. MyISAM and InnoDB tables normally are machine independent. For those storage engines, directly copied files can be moved to a server running on a machine with a different hardware architecture. Falcon log and tablespace files are stored in a machine-dependent format. They are binary portable only between machines that have identical hardware characteristics. For further discussion of the portability of various storage engines, see Section 2.6.1.11, "Storage Engine Portability Characteristics."

- `mysqldump` dumps output consisting of database contents (tables, views, stored routines, and so forth). It does not back up information not stored within a database, such as configuration files, log files, or replication status files. Binary backups can include any or all of these because you can copy any files you like as part of the backup.

Whichever backup method you choose, adherence to the following principles ensures the best results if you ever need to restore database contents:

- Perform backups regularly. Set a schedule and stick to it.
- Configure the server to perform binary logging (see Section 12.5, "Maintaining Logs"). The binary log can help when you need to restore databases after a crash: After you use your backup files to restore the databases to the state they were in at the time of the backup, you can re-apply the changes that occurred after the backup was made by re-executing the contents of the log files. This restores the tables in the databases to their state at the time the crash occurred.
- Use a consistent and meaningful naming scheme for your backup files. Names like `backup1`, `backup2`, and so forth are not particularly helpful. When it comes time to perform a restore operation, you'll waste time figuring out what's in the files. You may find it useful to construct backup filenames using database names and dates. For example, if you dump the `sampdb` database on January 2, 2008, you might name the backup file `sampdb-2008-01-02`. If you run multiple servers, incorporate a server identifier into the name.
- Put your backup files on a filesystem different from the one you use for your databases. This reduces the likelihood of filling up the filesystem containing the data directory as a result of generating backups. If the filesystem where you store the backups is on a different physical drive, you further reduce the extent of damage that can be caused by drive failure, because loss of any one drive cannot destroy both your data directory and your backups.

- Include your database backup files in your regular filesystem backups. If you have a complete crash that wipes out not only your data directory but also the disk drive containing your database backups, you'll be in real trouble. Back up your log files, too.

- Expire your backup files periodically to keep them from filling your disk. One way to do this is to use file rotation techniques. Section 12.5.7, "Log Management," discusses these techniques in relation to log files, but the same principles apply to backup file expiration as well.

The sections immediately following describe several specific backup methods. If you are using replication, Section 14.8.4, "Using a Replication Slave for Making Backups," describes a method that leaves your master server completely undisturbed.

14.4.1 Making Text Backups with `mysqldump`

The `mysqldump` program creates text dump files. By default, it writes a dump file in SQL format consisting of CREATE TABLE statements that create the tables being dumped and INSERT statements containing the data for the rows in the tables. To re-create the dumped tables later, reload the dump file into MySQL by using it as input to `mysql`. For example, to dump and reload a single table (`sampdb.member`), use these commands:

```
% mysqldump sampdb member > member.sql
% mysql sampdb < member.sql
```

Don't use `mysqlimport` to reload SQL-format `mysqldump` output. `mysqlimport` expects to read rows of data, not SQL statements.

To back up all tables from all databases into a single file, you can use a command like this:

```
% mysqldump --all-databases > /archive/mysql/dump-all.2008-01-02
```

However, the result is a rather large dump file if you have a lot of data. You can dump each single database into its own file as follows:

```
% mysqldump mysql > /archive/mysql/mysql.2008-01-02
% mysqldump sampdb > /archive/mysql/sampdb.2008-01-02
% ...
```

The beginning of a `mysqldump` output file looks something like this:

```
-- MySQL dump 10.11
--
-- Host: localhost    Database: sampdb
-- ------------------------------------------------------
-- Server version       5.0.54-log

 ... several SET statements ...


--
-- Table structure for table `absence`
--
```

```
DROP TABLE IF EXISTS `absence`;
CREATE TABLE `absence` (
  `student_id` int(10) unsigned NOT NULL,
  `date` date NOT NULL,
  PRIMARY KEY  (`student_id`,`date`),
  CONSTRAINT `absence_ibfk_1` FOREIGN KEY (`student_id`)
  REFERENCES `student` (`student_id`)
) ENGINE=InnoDB DEFAULT CHARSET=latin1;
--
-- Dumping data for table `absence`
--
LOCK TABLES `absence` WRITE;
/*!40000 ALTER TABLE `absence` DISABLE KEYS */;
INSERT INTO `absence` VALUES (3,'2008-09-03'),(5,'2008-09-03'),
(10,'2008-09-06'),(10,'2008-09-09'),(17,'2008-09-07'),(20,'2008-09-07');
/*!40000 ALTER TABLE `absence` ENABLE KEYS */;
UNLOCK TABLES;
...
```

The rest of the file consists of more SQL statements such as CREATE TABLE and INSERT.

Dump files often are large, so you'll likely want to do what you can to make them smaller. mysqldump has an --opt option, which enables several other options that have the effect of optimizing the dump process to generate smaller output. These options also optimize the restore process because the output can be processed more quickly when you reload the dump file later. For example, one effect of --opt is to cause mysqldump to write multiple-row INSERT statements. These take less space and can be reloaded more quickly than the equivalent set of single-row INSERT statements.

The --opt option is enabled by default (this has been true since MySQL 4.1), so it need not be specified explicitly. If you want to disable it, use --skip-opt.

Another way to reduce the size of a dump file is to compress it. On Windows, you can use WinZip or similar program to compress the dump and produce a file in Zip format. On Unix, you might use gzip or bzip2 instead. You can even compress the backup as you generate it by using a command pipeline:

```
% mysqldump sampdb | gzip > /archive/mysql/sampdb.2008-01-02.gz
% mysqldump sampdb | bzip2 > /archive/mysql/sampdb.2008-01-02.bz2
```

If large dump files are difficult to manage, it's possible to dump the contents of individual tables by naming them following the database name on the mysqldump command line. mysqldump will dump just the named tables rather than all the tables in the database, resulting in smaller, more manageable files. The following example shows how to dump subsets of the sampdb tables into separate files:

```
% mysqldump sampdb member president > hist-league.sql
% mysqldump sampdb student score grade_event absence > gradebook.sql
```

`mysqldump` has many options. Some of those that you may find useful include the following:

- Typically, you name a database on the `mysqldump` command line, optionally followed by specific table names. To dump several databases at once, use the `--databases` option. `mysqldump` will interpret all names as database names and dump all the tables in each of them. To dump all of a server's databases, use `--all-databases`. In this case, you supply no database or table name arguments. Both `--databases` and `--all-databases` cause the output for each database to be preceded by CREATE DATABASE IF NOT EXISTS and USE statements.

  Be careful with the `--all-databases` option if you intend to load the dump output into another server: The dump will include the grant tables in the `mysql` database, and you may not really want to replace the other server's grant tables.

- By default, `mysqldump` dumps both table structure (the CREATE TABLE statements) and table contents (the INSERT statements). To dump just one or the other, use the `--no-create-info` or `--no-data` options.

- As already mentioned, the `--opt` option optimizes the dump process. It turns on other options that speed up dumping the data. In addition, the dump file is written in such a way that it can be processed more quickly later when loaded back into the server.

  The `--opt` option is on by default, so you need not specify it explicitly. If you really want an unoptimized dump, use the `--skip-opt` option.

  Making backups using `--opt` is probably the most common method because of the benefits for backup speed. Be warned, however, that the `--opt` option does have a price; what `--opt` optimizes is your backup procedure, not access by other clients to the database. The `--opt` option prevents anyone from updating any of the tables that you're dumping because it locks all the tables at once. You can easily see for yourself the effect of this on general database access. Just try making a backup at the time of day when your database is normally most heavily used. It won't take long for your phone to start ringing with people calling to find out what's going on. (I'd appreciate it if you would refrain from asking how I happen to know this.)

  `--opt` is useful for generating backup files that you intend to use for periodically refreshing the contents of another database (for example, a database on another server). That's because it automatically enables the `--add-drop-table` option, which tells `mysqldump` to precede each CREATE TABLE statement in the file with a DROP TABLE IF NOT EXISTS statement for the same table. When you take the backup file and load it into the second database later, you won't get an error if the tables already exist. If you're running a second test server that's not a replication slave, you can use this technique to reload it periodically with a copy of the data from the databases on your production server.

- One effect of `--opt` is that it enables the `--extended-insert` option that causes `mysqldump` to write multiple-row INSERT statements. This is a disadvantage if you want a more readable dump file. To produce single-row INSERT statements, use the `--skip-extended-insert` option.

- The combination of `--flush-logs` and `--lock-all-tables` is helpful for check-pointing your database. `--lock-all-tables` acquires a global read lock, and `--flush-logs` closes and reopens the log files. If binary logging is enabled, flushing the logs creates a new binary log file that will contain only those data modifications that occur subsequent to the checkpoint. This synchronizes your log to the time of the backup. (The downside is that locking all the tables is detrimental to client access during the backups if you have clients that need to perform updates.)

  If you use `--flush-logs` to checkpoint the logs to the time of the backup, it's probably best to dump entire databases at a time. During restore operations, it's common to extract log contents on a per-database basis. If you dump individual tables, it's much more difficult to synchronize log checkpoints against your backup files. (There is no option for extracting updates for individual tables from the logs, so you'll have to extract them yourself.)

- If you're dumping InnoDB or Falcon tables, the `--single-transaction` option dumps the tables within a transaction so that you get a consistent backup.

- If your databases contain stored routines, triggers, and events, you can explicitly include them in dump output with the `--routines`, `--triggers`, and `--events` options, which are available as of MySQL 5.0.13, 5.0.11, and 5.1.8, respectively. Each of these options has a `--skip` form as well (for example, `--skip-triggers`) to disable dumping of the corresponding objects. By default, triggers are included, but stored routines and events are not.

`mysqldump` has several other options; see Appendix F.

14.4.2 Making Binary Database Backups

A method for backing up databases or tables that doesn't involve `mysqldump` is to copy table files directly. Typically this is done using regular filesystem utilities (such as `cp`, `tar`, or `rsync`), or a special program developed for the task (such as `mysqlhotcopy` or InnoDB Hot Backup). There are two key points to observe when you use a direct-copy backup method:

- You must make sure the tables aren't being used. If the server is changing a table while you're copying it, the copy will be worthless. The best way to ensure the integrity of your backups is to stop the server, copy the files, and restart the server. Some binary backup methods in fact require that you stop the server. If you don't want to stop the server (and the backup method doesn't require that you do so), use a read-only locking protocol to prevent the server from changing the tables while you're copying them. See Section 14.2, "Performing Database Maintenance with the Server Running."

- You must copy all files that are required to restore the tables that you're backing up. Direct-copy methods are easiest to use for storage engines such as MyISAM that represent a given table using a unique set of files in the database directory. To back up a MyISAM table, you need to copy only its `.frm`, `.MYD`, and `.MYI` files. For a storage engine such as InnoDB, it's more complicated: You must copy the `.frm` files, plus all the tablespace files and the InnoDB log files.

If you make a binary backup, beware of symbolic links, such as symlinks in the data directory to database directories or symlinks to MyISAM data or index files. These present a problem because your file-copying technique might copy only the symlinks and not the data that they point to.

14.4.2.1 Making a Complete Binary Backup

A complete binary backup includes all files in which table contents are stored and any log files that are used by specific storage engines. For good measure, you should also copy the binary log files. If the server is a replication slave, copy the relay log files and the `master.info` and `relay-log.info` files. Also, the slave may have created files with names of the form `SQL_LOAD-xxx` in its temporary file directory. You should back these up, too; they're needed for `LOAD DATA` statements. These files will be in the directory named by the `--slave-load-tmpdir` option; if not given, it defaults to the value of the `tmpdir` system variable. To make it easier to identify these files for backup, create a directory to be devoted to use by the slave server, and start the slave with the `--slave-load-tmpdir` option set to that value.

To properly copy all the files just discussed, you must stop the server and it must shut down cleanly, so that storage engines close their log files and the server closes any other logs that it is writing.

All of that sounds like a lot of stuff to back up, but it is not necessarily complicated to do so. For example, all of your database directories are under the data directory, and logs and information files are created there by default as well. In this case, you can make a backup by stopping the server and copying the entire data directory. For example, to create a backup as a compressed `tar` file under the `/archive/mysql` directory, change location into the data directory and back up the whole thing. For example:

```
% cd /usr/local/mysql/data
% tar czf /archive/mysql/backup-all-2008-04-11.tar.gz .
```

14.4.2.2 Making a Partial Binary Backup

Making a partial binary backup by copying files is similar to making a complete backup, except that you copy only a subset of the full set of files. Suppose that you want to back up the `mydb` database located under the data directory `/usr/local/mysql/data` and store the backup under the archive directory `/archive/mysql`. Stop the server and then execute these commands:

```
% cd /usr/local/mysql/data
```

```
% cp -r mydb /archive/mysql
```

After executing these commands, the `/archive/mysql/mydb` directory contains a copy of the `mydb` database. Individual MyISAM tables can be backed up like this (create `/archive/mysql/mydb` first if it does not exist):

```
% cd /usr/local/mysql/data/mydb
% cp tbl1.* /archive/mysql/mydb
% cp tbl2.* /archive/mysql/mydb
...
```

When you're done making the backup, restart the server.

In some cases, a partial backup can be made without stopping the server if you use a read-locking protocol to lock the tables that you want to copy. This is true if a database contains only MyISAM tables, for example. If the `mydb` database used in the preceding examples is such a database, you can read-lock and flush the tables prior to executing the backup commands, and then release the table locks after the backup is complete.

14.4.2.3 Making Backups with `mysqlhotcopy`

`mysqlhotcopy` is a Perl DBI script that helps you make database backups. The "hot" in the name refers to the fact that the backups are made while the server is running.

`mysqlhotcopy` has the following principal benefits:

- It's faster than `mysqldump` because it directly copies table files rather than requesting the tables from the server the way `mysqldump` does. (This means that you must run `mysqlhotcopy` on the server host; it does not work with remote servers.)

- It's convenient, because it automatically manages for you the locking protocol necessary to keep the server from changing the tables while they're being copied. `mysqlhotcopy` does this by using internal locking as described in Section 14.2.1.1, "Locking a Table for Read-Only Access."

- It can flush the binary log, which synchronizes the checkpoints for the backup files and the log files. This makes the backups easier to use for recovery, should that be necessary later.

`mysqlhotcopy` also has certain limitations:

- It must be used while the server is running because it tells the server to read-lock the tables that it wants to copy, and it must be run on the server host because it directly accesses the table files.

- It can be used only for MyISAM and ARCHIVE tables.

- It works only on Unix and NetWare, not on Windows.

The following examples assume that databases to be backed up contain only MyISAM or ARCHIVE tables.

There are several ways to invoke `mysqlhotcopy`. Suppose that you want to copy a database named `mydb`. The following command creates a directory `mydb_copy` in the server's data directory and copies the files in the `mydb` database directory into it:

```
% mysqlhotcopy mydb
```

However, I recommend that you *not* back up a database into the data directory because the new database directory will also appear to the server to be a database that it can access. You can see this by issuing a SHOW DATABASES statement after executing the preceding command. The output will show both `mydb` and `mydb_copy`. Because of this, the tables in the backup directory could be modified by clients that connect to the server.

To make a copy of the `mydb` database under a specific directory, give the directory pathname following the database name. For example, to copy the `mydb` database to a directory named `/archive/mysql/mydb`, use this command:

```
% mysqlhotcopy mydb /archive/mysql
```

To determine what actions `mysqlhotcopy` would perform for any given command, include the `--dryrun` or `-n` option in your invocation syntax. This runs `mysqlhotcopy` in "no execution" mode, so that it just prints commands rather than executing them.

14.4.3 Backing Up InnoDB or Falcon Tables

Tables for transactional storage engines such as InnoDB or Falcon can be dumped using `mysqldump`, just like any other kind of tables. One option that is useful for transactional engines is `--single-transaction`, which causes `mysqldump` to dump the tables as part of a transaction. For InnoDB and Falcon, this ensures that the tables are not modified during the dump so that you get a consistent backup. (This option does not provide consistent backup for MySQL Cluster.)

You can also make a binary backup of InnoDB tables by using InnoDB Hot Backup, which is available from Innobase. InnoDB Hot Backup is a commercial tool that enables you to make InnoDB backups with the server running. Visit http://innodb.com for details.

To make a binary InnoDB backup yourself, take care to observe the following special requirements:

- InnoDB has its own log files for transaction management that are active while the server is running. Therefore, to make a binary backup, you *must* stop the server. Furthermore, the server must shut down cleanly, not abnormally, so that InnoDB has a chance to finish outstanding transactions and close its logs properly.
- To make a binary backup of your InnoDB tables, you must copy the these files:
  - The shared tablespace files.
  - The `.frm` file for each table.
  - The `.ibd` file for each table, if you have configured InnoDB to use individual tablespace files.

- The InnoDB log files.
- The option file in which the shared tablespace configuration is specified. (Make a copy of the option file because you'll want it for reinitializing the shared tablespace should you suffer loss of the current option file.)

To make a binary Falcon backup, the procedure is similar except that you copy the Falcon tablespace and log files (the files with .fts, .f11, and .f12 extensions).

14.5 Copying Databases to Another Server

Database backups can be used to copy a database from one MySQL server to another. This section describes some methods for performing database transfers. For purpose of this discussion, I assume that the objective is to transfer a database from the server on the local host to a server on the remote host boa.snake.net. However, the two servers could just as well be running on the same host. Also, although the following discussion describes how to copy entire databases, you can adapt the techniques to copying individual tables.

The following discussion shows how to use two methods for copying a database to another server. The first makes a backup of the database that results in a file or set of files. You can copy the files to the second server host and load them into the second MySQL server. The second method dumps the database over the network from one server and loads it directly into the other server. This avoids the need for any intermediate files.

14.5.1 Copying Databases Using a Backup File

To copy a database using a text backup file, create the file using mysqldump, copy it to the second server host, and load it into the MySQL server there. The following example illustrates how to copy the sampdb database with this procedure:

1. Create a dump file:

```
% mysqldump --databases sampdb > sampdb.sql
```

The --databases option causes mysqldump to add CREATE DATABASE IF EXISTS and USE statements for the sampdb database. That way, when you load the dump file on the remote host, it automatically creates and selects the database so the dumped tables are loaded into that database.

2. Copy the dump file to the remote host. The following command uses scp to copy the file to the /tmp directory on boa.snake.net:

```
% scp sampdb.sql boa.snake.net:/tmp
```

3. Log in on the remote host and load the dump file into the MySQL server there:

```
% mysql < /tmp/sampdb.sql
```

Another approach is to use binary-backup techniques: Copy database files (rather than a dump file) from one host to the other. Suppose that the `mydb` database has only My-ISAM tables. In this case, table information is contained entirely in the files in the `mydb` database directory. If the local data directory is `/usr/local/mysql/data` and the remote data directory on `boa.snake.net` is `/var/mysql/data`, the following commands copy the `mydb` database directory to that host:

```
% cd /usr/local/mysql/data
% scp -r mydb boa.snake.net:/var/mysql/data
```

To copy database files to another host this way, certain requirements must be satisfied:

- Both machines must have the same hardware architecture, or the tables you're copying must all be for a binary-portable storage engine. The resulting tables on the second host may appear to have very strange contents otherwise.

- You must prevent the servers on *both* hosts from attempting to change the tables while you're copying them. The safest approach is to stop both servers while you're working with the tables.

14.5.2 Copying Databases from One Server to Another

The `mysqldump` technique shown in the previous section creates a dump file to be copied to the destination server host. Alternatively, you can write the output of `mysqldump` over the network directly to the other server so that no intermediate file is needed. For example, to copy the `sampdb` database from the local host to the server on `boa.snake.net`, do so like this:

```
% mysqldump --databases sampdb | mysql -h boa.snake.net
```

`mysql` reads the dump output, connects to the server on `boa.snake.net`, and loads the dump into that server.

If you cannot access the remote MySQL server from the local host, but you can access it by logging in there, use `ssh` to invoke `mysql` remotely:

```
% mysqldump --databases sampdb | ssh boa.snake.net mysql
```

On a slow network, the `--compress` option can improve performance when copying a database to another machine because it reduces the number of bytes traveling over the network:

```
% mysqldump --databases sampdb | mysql --compress -h boa.snake.net sampdb
```

The `--compress` option is given for the program that communicates with the server on the remote host, not the one that communicates with the local server. Compression applies only to network traffic; it does not cause compressed tables to be created in the destination database.

14.6 Checking and Repairing Database Tables

Database damage occurs for a number of reasons and varies in extent. If you're lucky, you may simply have minor damage to a table or two (for example, if your machine goes down briefly due to a power outage). In this case, it's likely that the server can repair the damage when it comes back up. If you're not so lucky, you may have to replace your entire data directory (for example, if a disk dies and takes your data directory with it). Recovery also is needed under other circumstances, such as when users mistakenly drop databases or tables or delete a table's contents. Whatever the reason for these unfortunate events, you'll need to perform some sort of recovery.

This section describes table checking and repair procedures you can use to deal with more minor forms of damage. If you suspect that a table has become corrupted, check it for errors. If the table checks okay, you're done. If not, try to repair it using these guidelines:

- Begin with a faster but less thorough repair method to see whether it will correct the damage.
- If you find that it is not sufficient, escalate to more thorough (but slower) repair methods, until either the damage has been repaired or you cannot escalate further.

In practice, most problems can be fixed without going to more extensive and slower repair methods.

In the event that tables or databases are lost or irreparably damaged, you'll need to restore them from your database backups and binary log. For instructions, see Section 14.7, "Using Backups for Data Recovery."

A general outline of the alternatives available to you for checking and repairing MyISAM and InnoDB tables follows. Specific details are given after that.

To check and repair MyISAM tables, you have a choice of approaches:

- Use the CHECK TABLE and REPAIR TABLE statements, or use the mysqlcheck program, which connects to the server and issues those statements for you.
- Use the myisamchk program, which operates on the table files directly.

As mentioned earlier in the chapter, if you have a choice when performing table maintenance between letting the server do the work or running an external utility, it's easier to let the server do the work. Then you need not be concerned about using any locking protocols to coordinate table access. That advantage applies when using CHECK TABLE and REPAIR TABLE (or mysqlcheck). If you use myisamchk, you must ensure that the server does not use the tables while you're working on them. Nevertheless, you might decide to use myisamchk for the following reasons:

- You can use myisamchk when the server is stopped. CREATE TABLE and REPAIR TABLE require that the server be running.

- You can tell `myisamchk` to use larger buffers to make checking and repair operations run faster. This can be helpful if you have very large tables.

To check an InnoDB table, use `CHECK TABLE` or `mysqlcheck`. If the table is found to have problems, dump it with `mysqldump`. Then drop the table and reload the dump file to re-create it. The following sequence of commands shows how you might check, dump, and reload the `absence` table in the `sampdb` database:

```
% mysqlcheck sampdb absence
% mysqldump sampdb absence > absence.sql
% mysql sampdb < absence.sql
```

14.6.1 Using the Server to Check and Repair Tables

To have the server do the work of checking or repairing tables, you can use the `CHECK TABLE` or `REPAIR TABLE` statements or the `mysqlcheck` program.

14.6.1.1 Checking Tables with `CHECK TABLE`

The `CHECK TABLE` statement provides an interface to the server's table checking capabilities. It works for MyISAM and InnoDB tables. It also works for views as of MySQL 5.0.2, for ARCHIVE tables as of 5.0.16, and CSV tables as of 5.1.9.

To use `CHECK TABLE`, provide a list of one or more table names, optionally followed by modifiers that indicate what type of check to do. For example, the following statement performs a medium-level check on three tables, but only if they have not been properly closed:

```
CHECK TABLE tbl1, tbl2, tbl3 FAST MEDIUM;
```

The full list of check options is detailed in Appendix E. The options apply to MyISAM tables, but may not be used by other storage engines.

It's possible that `CHECK TABLE` will actually modify a table in some cases. For example, if a table is marked as corrupt or as not having been closed properly, but the check finds no problems, `CHECK TABLE` marks the table as okay. This change involves only modifying an internal flag.

14.6.1.2 Repairing Tables with `REPAIR TABLE`

The `REPAIR TABLE` statement provides an interface to the server's table repair capabilities. It works with MyISAM and ARCHIVE tables, and with CSV tables as of MySQL 5.1.19.

To use `REPAIR TABLE`, provide a list of one or more table names, optionally followed by modifiers that indicate what type of repair to do. For example, the following statement tries to repair three tables in quick repair mode:

```
REPAIR TABLE tbl1, tbl2, tbl3 QUICK;
```

The full list of repair options is detailed in Appendix E. The options apply to MyISAM tables, but may not be used by other storage engines.

14.6.2 Using `mysqlcheck` to Check and Repair Tables

The `mysqlcheck` program provides a command-line interface to the CHECK TABLE and REPAIR TABLE statements. It connects to the server and issues the appropriate statements for you based on the options you specify. Therefore, `mysqlcheck` can check or repair tables for the same storage engines as CHECK TABLE and REPAIR TABLE.

Typically, you invoke `mysqlcheck` with a database name, optionally followed by one or more table names. With just a database name, `mysqlcheck` checks all the tables in the database:

```
% mysqlcheck sampdb
```

With table names following the database name, `mysqlcheck` checks only those tables:

```
% mysqlcheck sampdb president member
```

If you specify the `--databases` option, all following arguments are interpreted as database names and `mysqlcheck` checks all the tables in each database:

```
% mysqlcheck --databases sampdb test
```

If you specify `--all-databases`, `mysqlcheck` checks all tables in all databases. No database or table name arguments are needed:

```
% mysqlcheck --all-databases
```

`mysqlcheck` is more convenient than issuing the CHECK TABLE and REPAIR TABLE statements directly, because those statements require that you explicitly name each table to be checked or repaired. With `mysqlcheck`, it's much easier to check all tables in a database: It looks up the names of the tables in the database for you and constructs statements that name the appropriate tables.

By default, `mysqlcheck` checks tables using a medium check, but supports options that enable explicit selection of the type of operation to perform. The following table shows some `mysqlcheck` options and the CHECK TABLE options to which they correspond. (As with CHECK TABLE, these options apply to MyISAM tables but may not be used by other storage engines.)

`mysqlcheck` Option	CHECK TABLE Option
`--check-only-changed`	CHANGED
`--extended`	EXTENDED
`--fast`	FAST
`--medium-check`	MEDIUM
`--quick`	QUICK

mysqlcheck can also perform table repair operations, but only for MyISAM tables. The following table shows some mysqlcheck options and the REPAIR TABLE options to which they correspond. (As with REPAIR TABLE, these options apply to MyISAM tables but may not be used by other storage engines.)

mysqlcheck Option	REPAIR TABLE Option
--repair	no options (performs a standard repair operation)
--repair --extended	EXTENDED
--repair --quick	QUICK
--repair --use-frm	USE_FRM

14.6.3 Using myisamchk to Check and Repair Tables

The myisamchk utility can check and repair MyISAM tables. myisamchk does its work by accessing table files directly, so before invoking it, it is advisable to stop the server to prevent the server from accessing the table files at the same time as myisamchk. If you leave the server running, make sure you read Section 14.2.1, "Locking Individual Tables for Read-Only or Read/Write Access." That section discusses the proper locking protocols for preventing the server from using a table at the same time that you're performing checking or repair procedures on it with myisamchk. The following discussion assumes that you have either stopped the server or are using the appropriate locking protocol.

myisamchk makes no assumptions about where tables are located. To run it, specify the pathnames to the table files you want to use. It's most convenient to do this if you're in the directory that contains the tables. Typically, you change location into the relevant database directory first before invoking myisamchk, and then tell it which tables you want to check or repair, along with the options that indicate what type of operation to perform:

```
% myisamchk options tbl_name ...
```

A tbl_name argument can be either a table name or the name of the table's index file. These commands are equivalent:

```
% myisamchk member
% myisamchk member.MYI
```

To name all the relevant index files in the database directory, you can use a filename pattern (assuming that your command interpreter understands and expands wildcards):

```
% myisamchk options *.MYI
```

If you don't want to perform a myisamchk maintenance operation on the original table files, copy them to another directory and then work with the copies in that directory.

14.6.3.1 Checking Tables with `myisamchk`

`myisamchk` provides table-checking methods that vary in how thoroughly they examine a table. To perform a normal table check, use either of the following commands:

```
% myisamchk tbl_name
% myisamchk --check tbl_name
```

`myisamchk`'s default action with no options is `--check`, so those commands are equivalent.

The normal check method usually is sufficient to identify problems. If it reports no errors but you still suspect damage (perhaps because queries do not seem to return the correct results), perform an intermediate-level check by specifying the `--medium-check` option. This is somewhat slower but more thorough. Finally, you can perform the most extensive check by specifying the `--extend-check` option. This can be very slow, but it is extremely thorough. For each row in the table's data file, the associated key for every index in the index file is checked to make sure it really points to the correct row.

If no errors are reported for a check with `--extend-check`, you can be sure your table is okay. If you still have problems with the table, the cause must lie elsewhere. Re-examine any statements that seem to yield problematic results to verify that they are written correctly. If you believe the problem might be with the MySQL server, consider filing a bug report or upgrading to a newer version.

If `myisamchk` reports that a table has errors, you should try to repair it.

14.6.3.2 Repairing Tables with `myisamchk`

To perform a repair operation on a table with `myisamchk`, use the following procedure. It first tries the repair types that are faster but less thorough, and then escalates to slower but more thorough methods if faster methods fail to correct the problems. Before using the repair procedure, make copies of the table files in case something goes wrong. That is unlikely, but if it happens, you can make a new copy of the table from the copied files and try a different recovery method.

> **Note**
>
> If the table contains any `FULLTEXT` indexes, it might be necessary to use additional `myisamchk` options during repairs. For details, see the `FULLTEXT`-related notes in the `myisamchk` description in Appendix F.

1. Try to fix the table using the `--recover` option. Use the `--quick` option as well to attempt recovery based only on the contents of the index file without touching the data file:

   ```
   % myisamchk --recover --quick tbl_name
   ```

2. If problems remain, rerun the command without the `--quick` option to enable `myisamchk` to modify the data file, too:

   ```
   % myisamchk --recover tbl_name
   ```

3. If that doesn't work, try the `--safe-recover` repair mode. This is slower than regular recovery mode, but is capable of fixing a few problems that `--recover` mode will not:

```
% myisamchk --safe-recover tbl_name
```

It's possible when you run these commands that `myisamchk` will stop with an error message of the form `Can't create new temp file: file_name`. Typically, this indicates the presence of a temporary file that was left around from a previous failed repair attempt. To force removal of the temporary file, repeat the command but add the `--force` option.

If the preceding repair procedure fails to repair the table, your index file may be missing or damaged beyond repair. It's also possible, although unlikely, that the table's `.frm` format file is missing. In either of these cases, you'll need to replace the affected files, and then try the repair procedure again.

To regenerate the index file for a table `t`, use this procedure if you have the table's format file, `t.frm`:

1. Change location into the database directory that contains the crashed table.

2. Move the table's data file, `t.MYD`, to a safe place.

3. Invoke `mysql` and re-create a new empty table by executing the following statement:

```
mysql> TRUNCATE TABLE t;
```

`TRUNCATE TABLE` uses the table format file, `t.frm`, to regenerate new data and index files from scratch.

4. Exit `mysql` and move the original data file back into the database directory, replacing the new empty data file you just created. That creates a mismatch between the data file and the index file, but the index file has a legal internal structure that the server can interpret and rebuild based on the contents of the data file and table format file.

5. Attempt a table repair again using the procedure at the beginning of this section.

If you don't have the table's `.frm` format file, you'll need to recover it from your backup files first. Then use the procedure at the beginning of this section. If you are missing the `.frm` file and also have no backup, but you know the `CREATE TABLE` statement that must be issued to create the table, you still might be able to repair it as follows:

1. Change location into the database directory that contains the crashed table.

2. Move the table's data file, `t.MYD`, to a safe place. If you want to try to use the index file, `t.MYI`, move that, too.

3. Invoke `mysql` and issue the `CREATE TABLE` statement that creates the table. This creates new `.frm`, `.MYD`, and `.MYI` files.

4. Exit `mysql` and move the original data file back into the database directory, replacing the new data file you just created. If you moved the index file in step 2, move it back into the database directory, too.

5. Attempt a table repair again using the procedure at the beginning of this section.

14.6.3.3 Getting `myisamchk` to Run Faster

`myisamchk` can take a long time to run, especially if you're working with a large table or using one of the more-extensive checking or repair methods. You can speed up this process by telling `myisamchk` to use more memory when it runs. `myisamchk` has several variables that can be set, the most important of which control the sizes of the buffers that it uses (see following table).

Variable	Meaning
`key_buffer_size`	Size of buffer used to hold index blocks
`read_buffer_size`	Size of buffer used for read operations
`sort_buffer_size`	Size of buffer used for sorting
`write_buffer_size`	Size of buffer used for write operations

To find out what values `myisamchk` uses for these variables by default, run it with the `--help` option. To specify a different value, use `--`*var_name*`=`*value* on the command line. For example, if you have sufficient memory to spare, you can tell `myisamchk` to use a 16MB sort buffer and 1MB read and write buffers by invoking it like this:

```
% myisamchk --sort_buffer_size=16M --read_buffer_size=1M \
   --write_buffer_size=1M other-options tbl_name
```

For repair operations, `--sort_buffer_size` applies when the `--recover` option is given, but not with `--safe-recover`. A `--key_buffer_size` setting applies when `--safe-recover` is given or when you check the table with `--extend-check`.

14.7 Using Backups for Data Recovery

Recovery procedures involve two sources of information: your backup files and your binary log. Backup files can be either dump files generated with `mysqldump` or files copied using one of the binary backup methods.

The backup files restore tables to the state they were in at the time the backup was performed. The binary log files that were written after the backup contain the statements that have modified the tables since then. `mysqlbinlog` converts these log files back into text SQL statements so that you can execute them with `mysql`. This enables you to re-apply the changes made between the time of the backup and the time at which problems occurred.

The recovery procedure varies depending on how much information you must restore. In fact, it may be easier to restore an entire database than a single table, because it's easier to apply the binary log files for a database than for a table.

The discussion here assumes that you've been performing database backups and have binary logging enabled. If that's not true, you're living dangerously. You should enable the binary log right now and generate a new backup before reading further. You don't ever want to be in the position of having irretrievably lost a table because you were lax about saving the information necessary to restore it. To find out how to enable the binary log, see Section 12.5.4, "The Binary Log and the Binary Log Index File." To make a backup, see the instructions in Section 14.3, "Making Database Backups."

14.7.1 Recovering Entire Databases

The general procedure for recovering one or more databases involves the following steps:

1. Make a copy of the contents of the database directory or directories. You may want this later if you make a mistake or something goes wrong during recovery.

2. Reload the databases using your most recent backup files:

    - If your backups are dump files generated by `mysqldump`, reload each file by using it as input to `mysql`.

      If the database or databases that you need to recover include the `mysql` database that contains the grant tables and you are using dump files to recover the tables, you'll need to reload them while running the server using the `--skip-grant-tables` option. Otherwise, it may complain about not being able to find the grant tables. It's also a good idea to use `--skip-networking` to cause the server to reject all remote connection attempts while you're performing the restoration. After you've restored the tables, stop the server and restart it normally so that it uses the grant tables and listens to its network interfaces as usual.

    - If you're using files from a binary backup (for example, a backup made with `mysqlhotcopy`, `tar`, or `cp`), stop the server so that it doesn't try to access the databases while they are being restored. Then copy the backup files back to their original locations (probably under the data directory), and restart the server.

3. Use the binary log to re-execute the data modifications that occurred subsequent to the time at which the backup was made. The procedure for this is given in Section 14.6.3, "Re-Executing Statements in Binary Log Files."

14.7.2 Recovering Individual Tables

Recovering an individual table can be more difficult than recovering a database. If you have a dump file generated by `mysqldump` that contains only that table, just reload the file. If you have a dump file that contains data for many tables, you can recover one of them by editing the file to delete the data for the other tables and then reloading the remainder. That's the easy part.

The more difficult part of recovery is extracting the parts of the binary logs that apply to the table. `mysqlbinlog` supports a `--database` option to limit its output to the statements for a single database, but there is no corresponding single-table option. A strategy that you might find useful in this situation is to restore more than you need, and then discard what you don't want. This procedure can actually be easier than trying to restore a single table by extracting the relevant parts from the binary log.

1. Restore the entire contents of the database that contains the table you want, but do so into a second, empty database. You can do this with your backups and by re-applying the binary log. However, there are two complications:

   - A dump file from `mysqldump` might contain a USE statement for the original database. You'll need to either change it or remove it before using the dump file as input to `mysql`.

   - Output from `mysqlbinlog` will contain one or more USE statements for the original database. Save the output in a file so that you can edit these statements to name the second database before using the file as input to `mysql`.

2. From the second database, use `mysqldump` to dump the table in which you are interested.

3. Drop the original table and load the dump file into the original database to re-create the table. If you run `mysqldump` with the `--opt` or `--add-drop-table` option, the dump file itself will contain a DROP TABLE statement that removes the table before re-creating it.

For MyISAM tables, an alternative to using `mysqldump` is to directly copy the table files from the second database directory to the original database directory. Make sure that no server is working with either copy of the table when you perform the copy operation.

14.7.3 Re-Executing Statements in Binary Log Files

After you restore databases or tables from your backup files, re-apply the portions of your binary log files that contain the statements executed after the backup was made. This brings your tables up to date.

The `mysqlbinlog` program converts binary log files to statements in text form, making them easy to execute: Use the output from `mysqlbinlog` as input to `mysql`.

Depending on what you restored from backup, you might need to apply all statements in the binary log files, or just those for a particular database. You might also need to select only those statements that were executed within a particular time interval. `mysqlbinlog` can do these things. It can process multiple binary log files, and it can limit its output to statements for a given database or time interval.

The following instructions for applying the binary log files assume that the logs all have names of the form `binlog.`*nnnnnn*, where *nnnnnn* is the six-digit extension indicating the log sequence number. Adjust the instructions if your logs have a basename different from `binlog`. Also, I focus here on the use of local binary log files that exist on the same host where you execute `mysqlbinlog`. The program is capable of reading remote binary log files, but that is not covered here. For details on `mysqlbinlog` remote log processing options, see Appendix F.

If the backup from which you restored your databases was made before all of your current binary log files were written, you'll need to apply the contents of each file. To do so, use this command in the directory where the files are located:

```
% mysqlbinlog binlog.[0-9]* | mysql
```

If you need to edit the logs before re-executing them, convert them to text format and save the result in a file. Then edit the file and feed the result to `mysql`. Here is an example:

```
% mysqlbinlog binlog.[0-9]* > text_file
% vi text_file
% mysql < text_file
```

This strategy is necessary if the reason that you're performing recovery and using the logs to restore information is because someone issued an ill-advised DROP DATABASE, DROP TABLE, or DELETE statement. You'll need to remove that statement from the logs before executing their contents.

The `binlog.[0-9]*` pattern in the preceding `mysqlbinlog` commands expands to the list of binary log files, normally in the same order in which they were generated by the server.

Do not use `mysqlbinlog` and `mysql` to process binary log files one by one. There might be inter-file dependencies that will be broken unless you process the files as a group. For example, a TEMPORARY table created in one log file might be used in a later log file. If you process each log file separately, all TEMPORARY tables created by each log are dropped as the corresponding `mysql` invocation finishes and become unavailable to statements in the following logs.

To extract only those statements that pertain to a particular database, use the `--database` option to `mysqlbinlog`:

```
% mysqlbinlog --database=db_name binlog.[0-9]* | mysql
```

`mysqlbinlog` also supports several options for extracting statements that occur within a particular time window (for example, statements written after a given backup was made). You may need to examine what's in the log files to see what option values to supply. Here is a sample of `mysqlbinlog` output (with some of the comment lines shortened to fit the page):

```
...
# at 1077
#071030 16:50:36 server id 1  end_log_pos 106   Query....
```

```
SET TIMESTAMP=1193781036;
INSERT INTO absence VALUES (3,'2008-09-03');
# at 1183
#071030 16:50:36 server id 1  end_log_pos 1210  Xid = 386
COMMIT;
# at 1210
#071030 16:50:36 server id 1  end_log_pos 106   Query....
SET TIMESTAMP=1193781036;
INSERT INTO absence VALUES (5,'2008-09-03');
# at 1316
#071030 16:50:36 server id 1  end_log_pos 1343  Xid = 387
COMMIT;
# at 1343
#071030 16:50:36 server id 1  end_log_pos 107   Query....
SET TIMESTAMP=1193781036;
INSERT INTO absence VALUES (10,'2008-09-06');
# at 1450
#071030 16:50:36 server id 1  end_log_pos 1477  Xid = 388
COMMIT;
...
```

Suppose that you want to re-execute the modifications in the binary log that were made beginning at `2007-10-30 16:50:36`. That value can be given to the `--start-datetime` option in either of these formats:

```
% mysqlbinlog --start-datetime=20071030165036 binlog.[0-9]* | mysql
% mysqlbinlog --start-datetime="2007-10-30 16:50:36" binlog.[0-9]* | mysql
```

There is a corresponding `--stop-datetime` option for giving the ending time. There are also position-based options that take `log_pos` values shown in the log. For information, see the description of `mysqlbinlog` in Appendix F.

14.7.4 Coping with InnoDB Auto-Recovery Problems

If the MySQL server or the server host crashes, the InnoDB storage engine attempts to perform auto-recovery when the MySQL server restarts. In rare instances, auto-recovery might fail. This section describes what to do if that happens.

In the event that InnoDB detects a non-recoverable problem during server startup, its auto-recovery process fails. In this case, set the `innodb_force_recovery` system variable to a non-zero value between 1 and 6 to cause the server to start up even if InnoDB recovery after a crash otherwise fails. To set the variable, put a line in the `[mysqld]` group of your server's option file:

```
[mysqld]
innodb_force_recovery=level
```

The InnoDB storage engine uses more conservative strategies for lower values of *level*. A typical recommended starting value is 4. After the server starts, dump your InnoDB tables with `mysqldump` to get back as much information as possible, drop the tables, and restore them from the `mysqldump` output file. This procedure re-creates the tables in a form that is internally consistent, and may be sufficient to achieve a satisfactory recovery. After performing the recovery, remove the line that sets `innodb_force_recovery` from the option file.

If you need to restore all of your InnoDB tables, you'll need to use your backups. The approach to take depends on what kind of backup you made:

- If you made a binary backup, you should have copies of the shared and individual tablespace files, the InnoDB log files, the `.frm` file for each table, and the option file that defines your InnoDB configuration. After making sure the server is stopped, delete any existing InnoDB files and replace them with your backup copies. Then make sure your current server option file lists the InnoDB configuration the same way as your saved option file and restart the server.

- If you backed up your InnoDB tables by running `mysqldump` to generate a dump file, you should reinitialize the shared tablespace and InnoDB logs and reload the dump file into InnoDB:

   1. Stop the server and remove any existing InnoDB-related files: the shared and individual tablespace files (other than raw partitions), the InnoDB log files, and the `.frm` files for all InnoDB tables.

   2. Configure the shared tablespace the same way you did initially and restart the server. InnoDB then will re-create its shared tablespace and log files. For instructions, see Section 12.7.3.1, "Configuring the InnoDB Tablespace." Remember that initializing the tablespace is a two-step process if you're using any raw partitions.

   3. Reload your dump file or files by using them as input to `mysql`. This re-creates the InnoDB tables.

After restoring the InnoDB tables from the backups, re-apply any updates from your binary log that occurred after the backup was made. (See Section 14.7.3, "Re-Executing Statements in Binary Log Files.") This is easiest if you're restoring your InnoDB tables as part of restoring your entire set of databases, because in that case you can apply all the updates made subsequent to the backup. If you're restoring only your InnoDB tables, applying the logs will be trickier because you should use the updates only for those tables.

14.8 Setting Up Replication Servers

One form of database "replication" involves simply copying a database to another server. But if the original database changes and you want to keep the copy up to date, you must repeat the operation later. To achieve continual updating of a secondary database as changes are made to the contents of a master database, use MySQL's live replication capabilities. This gives you a means of keeping a copy of a database and making sure that changes to the original database propagate on a timely basis to the copy automatically.

14.8.1 How Replication Works

Database replication in MySQL is based on the following principles:

- In a replication relationship, one server acts as the master and another server acts as the slave. Each server must be assigned a unique replication ID.

- There can be multiple slaves per master. A slave can serve as a master to another slave, thus creating a chain of replication servers. Multiple-master replication to a slave is also possible, but is trickier to set up and is not covered here.

- Each slave must begin with its databases synchronized to those of its master. That is, any database to be replicated on the slave must be an identical copy of the master database when replication begins. After that, updates that are made on the master server propagate to the slave. Updates should not be made directly to the replicated databases on the slave.

- Communication of updates is based on the master server's binary logs, which is where updates are recorded that are to be sent to the slaves. Binary logging therefore must be enabled on the master server. Stored updates in the binary log are called "events."

- Each slave server must have permission to connect to the master and request updates. When a slave connects to its master, it tells the master how far into the master's binary log it had progressed when it last connected. This progress is measured in terms of replication coordinates: A binary log filename and position within that file. The master then begins sending to the slave those events in the binary log that occurred after the given coordinates. When the slave has read all available events, it pauses and waits for more.

- As new updates occur on the master server, it writes them to its binary log for later transmission to its slaves.

- The master server handles connected slaves much as it handles regular clients, and connected slaves count against the limit set by the `max_connections` system variable.

- On the slave side, the server uses two threads to handle replication duties. The I/O thread receives events to be processed from the master server and writes them to the slave's relay log. The SQL thread reads events from the relay log and executes them. The relay log serves as the means by which the I/O thread communicates changes to the SQL thread. As each relay log file is processed completely, the slave removes it automatically. The I/O and SQL threads operate independently, so each can be stopped or started separately from the other. This decoupling of function into different threads has important benefits. For example, the I/O thread can continue to read events from the master server while you stop the SQL thread so that no updates occur in the slave's databases while you make a backup.

Replication support is an area of active development, so it's sometimes difficult to keep track of just which replication-related feature was added when. You should consider compatibility constraints between different server versions. Replication compatibility is based on the binary log format, of which there have been several versions. The original format was developed in MySQL 3.23 when replication support was added, and others were developed in MySQL 4.0, 5.0, and 5.1.

In general, I recommend that you follow these guidelines:

- Within a given MySQL series (5.0, 5.1, and so forth), try to use the most recent version possible. This gives you the benefit of the richest feature set and the greatest number of restrictions removed and problems eliminated.
- Try to match binary log formats for your master and slave servers. For example, try to match 5.1 masters with 5.1 slaves, not 5.1 masters with 5.0 slaves or vice versa. If your master and slave versions must differ, replicate from older masters to newer slaves, not the other way around.

Assuming that your servers have compatible binary log formats, they must also be feature-compatible. For example, if the master server replicates InnoDB tables that require the use of transactions or foreign keys, the slave server must include the InnoDB storage engine.

14.8.2 Establishing a Master-Slave Replication Relationship

The following procedure describes how to set up a master-slave replication relationship between two servers:

1. Determine what ID value you want to assign to each server and record it in an option file that the server reads when it starts. These IDs must be different and each should be a positive integer from 1 to $2^{32}-1$. The ID values will be needed for the `server-id` startup option used with each server. In addition, enable binary logging on the master if it is not already enabled. To accomplish this on the master and slave, respectively, use option groups with the following lines:

```
[mysqld]
server-id=master_server_id
log-bin=binlog_name

[mysqld]
server-id=slave_server_id
```

Restart both servers so that the changes take effect.

2. On the master server, set up an account that the slave server can use to connect to the master server and request updates:

```
CREATE USER 'slave_user'@'slave_host' IDENTIFIED BY 'slave_pass';
GRANT REPLICATION SLAVE ON *.* TO 'slave_user'@'slave_host';
```

Remember the *slave_user* and *slave_pass* values for later when you tell the slave server how to connect to the master. No other privileges are needed if the account is used only for the single, limited purpose of replication. However, you may want to grant additional privileges to the account if you plan to use it connect to the master from the slave host "manually" with the mysql program for testing. Then you won't be so limited in what you can do. (For example, if REPLICATION SLAVE is the only privilege granted to the account, you might not even be able to see database names on the master server with SHOW DATABASES.)

3. Connect to the master server and determine its current replication coordinates by executing SHOW MASTER STATUS:

```
mysql> FLUSH TABLES; SHOW MASTER STATUS;
+----------------+----------+--------------+------------------+
| File           | Position | Binlog_Do_DB | Binlog_Ignore_DB |
+----------------+----------+--------------+------------------+
| binlog.000093  |     1707 |              |                  |
+----------------+----------+--------------+------------------+
```

Remember the File and Position values. You will need them later so that you can tell the slave the point from which to start reading binary log events from the master.

Important: You must make sure that no updates occur on the master from the time that you determine its replication coordinates until after you make a snapshot of its data to be transferred to the slave.

4. The slave server must begin with an exact copy of the databases to be replicated. Perform the initial synchronization of the slave to the master server by copying the master's databases to the slave. One way to do this is to make a backup on the master host, and then move it to the slave host and load it into the slave server. Another method is to copy all the databases over the network from the master to the slave. Database backup and copying techniques are discussed elsewhere in this chapter.

If you haven't created any databases or tables on the master, you can skip this step because there is nothing to take a snapshot of.

5. Connect to the slave and use CHANGE MASTER to configure it with the parameters for connecting to the master server and the initial replication coordinates:

```
CHANGE MASTER TO
  MASTER_HOST = 'master_host',
  MASTER_USER = 'slave_user',
  MASTER_PASSWORD = 'slave_pass',
  MASTER_LOG_FILE = 'log_file_name',
  MASTER_LOG_POS = log_file_pos;
```

'*master_host*' is the name of the host where the master server is running. The '*slave_user*' and '*slave_pass*' values should be the name and password of the account that you set up on the master server earlier for the slave server to use when it connects to the master to request updates. '*log_file_name*' and *log_file_pos* are the values you obtained from SHOW MASTER STATUS.

On Unix, a socket file is used for connections to localhost, but replication through a socket file is not supported. Therefore, if the master host is the same as the slave host, use 127.0.0.1 rather than localhost to make sure that the slave uses a TCP/IP connection.

If the master isn't listening on the default port, you can include a MASTER_PORT option in the CHANGE statement to indicate a port number.

6. Tell the slave to start replicating:

    ```
    START SLAVE;
    ```

    The slave should connect to the master and start replicating. You can check this with the SHOW SLAVE STATUS statement on the slave.

The slave stores the CHANGE MASTER parameters in a file named master.info in its data directory to record the initial replication status, and updates the file as replication proceeds. If you need to change replication parameters later, connect to the slave and use CHANGE MASTER again. The slave automatically updates the master.info file with these changes.

The information stored in the master.info file includes the username and password for connecting to the master server. This information should be confidential, so make sure that the file is accessible only to the MySQL administrator's login account on the slave server. For example, lock down the data directory contents as described in Section 13.1.2, "Securing Your MySQL Installation."

The procedure just described is based on the assumption that you want to replicate all databases from the master to the slave. However, it's very likely that you don't want to use the same user accounts on both servers. (For example, you might want to set up a private replication slave that people cannot connect to even if they have an account on the master.) To maintain accounts on the slave separately from those on the master, do two things:

1. When you transfer the initial data snapshot from the master to the slave, don't include the mysql database, or else back up the slave's mysql database before the transfer and restore it after.

2. Tell the slave to ignore any updates from the master for the mysql database. Do this as follows in the slave's option file:

    ```
    [mysqld]
    replicate-ignore-db=mysql
    ```

The replicate-ignore-db option can be given multiple times, once per database, if you want the slave to ignore several databases.

It's possible to exclude databases on the master side rather than on the slave side by using the `binlog-ignore-db` option in the master's option file. This reduces traffic between the master and slave, but also unfortunately causes the binary log to contain no information for the ignored databases. That information is useful for performing recovery on the master after a crash, so database exclusion on the slave side is usually preferable.

After you have replication set up and running, there are several statements that you may find useful for monitoring or controlling the master and the slave. Details about these statements are available in Appendix E. A brief summary follows:

- `SHOW SLAVE STATUS` on a slave shows whether replication is running and the current replication coordinates. The coordinates can be used to determine which binary log files from the master are no longer needed.

- `PURGE MASTER` on the master expires binary log files. You can use this after issuing a `SHOW SLAVE STATUS` statement on each of the slaves to determine which log files no longer are needed.

- The `STOP SLAVE` and `START SLAVE` statements suspend and resume a slave server's replication-related activity. These statements can be useful for telling the slave to be quiescent while you're making a backup, for example. (See Section 14.8.4, "Using a Replication Slave for Making Backups.")

As mentioned earlier, a slave server uses two threads internally to manage replication. The I/O thread talks to the master server, receives updates from it, and writes updates to its relay log. The SQL thread reads the relay log and executes the updates it finds there. You can use `STOP SLAVE` and `START SLAVE` to suspend or resume each thread individually by adding `IO_THREAD` or `SQL_THREAD` to the end of the statement. For example, `STOP SLAVE SQL_THREAD` stops execution by the slave of the updates in the relay log, but enables the slave to continue to read updates from the master and record them in the relay log.

Relay log files are generated in numbered sequence, much like the binary log files. There also is a relay log index file analogous to the binary log index. The default relay log and index files are *HOSTNAME*-relay-bin.*nnnnnn* and *HOSTNAME*-relay-bin.index in the data directory. The defaults can be changed with the `--relay-log` and `--relay-log-index` server startup options.

14.8.3 Binary Logging Formats

Before MySQL 5.1, the server writes data-modification events to the binary log as SQL statements. This is known as statement-based binary logging, and replication based on it is statement-based replication. Beginning with MySQL 5.1.5, an alternative format is available in which the server logs changes to individual data rows. This is row-based logging and replication. Mixed-format logging was added in 5.1.8, for which the server switches between statement-based and row-based logging as it deems best.

In general, statement-based logging produces smaller log files with contents that are easier to understand. Row-based logging provides finer specification of updates to be made, which is advantageous for replication when the original statements might be non-deterministic and produce different effects on master and slave.

As of MySQL 5.1, the logging format is selected by using the `--binlog-format` option at startup or (as of 5.1.8) by setting the global `binlog_format` system variable at runtime. The default format as of 5.1.12 is MIXED. Other values are STATEMENT or ROW to force a given format.

14.8.4 Using a Replication Slave for Making Backups

If you have a replication slave server set up, it can help you resolve a conflict of interest that arises from your duties as a MySQL administrator:

- On the one hand, it's important to maximize the availability of your server to the members of your user community, which includes allowing them to make database updates.

- On the other hand, it's important to make backups, which is best done while you prevent anyone from making database changes. Also, for recovery purposes, backups are most useful if you make sure your backup file and log file checkpoints are synchronized, either by stopping the server or by locking all the tables at once.

The goal of maintaining accessibility conflicts with enforcing complete or partial loss of database access to clients while making backups. A replication slave provides a way out of this dilemma. Rather than making backups of the master server, use the slave server instead. Stop the slave or suspend replication on it before you make the backup. Then restart the slave or resume replication afterward, and the slave will catch up on any updates made by the master server during the backup period. This way you need not stop the master or otherwise make it unavailable to clients during the backup.

The following list describes some possible strategies for backing up the slave:

- For a binary backup of all slave data, stop the slave server, follow the instructions in Section 14.4.2.1, "Making a Complete Binary Backup," and restart the server.

- For a backup using a method such as `mysqldump` that does not require the slave to be stopped, you can back up the slave while the SQL thread is stopped, and then restart the thread after making the backup: Suspend replication on the slave with STOP SLAVE SQL_THREAD and flush its logs. Then make the backup and resume replication with START SLAVE. This way the slave won't make changes to databases while you're backing them up. The I/O thread can be left running; it will continue to write events to the relay log that it receives from the master. When you restart the SQL thread after making the backup, it catches up with any accumulated updates.

This approach assumes that clients do not make updates on the slave server. You should also not use this method if you intend to use a binary backup method that copies database files directly. Even though the SQL thread is stopped, there might be information cached in memory that has not been flushed to disk.

- Some backup methods do not require even that you suspend replication. For example, if you're backing up a single database containing only MyISAM tables, you can use `mysqlhotcopy` or `mysqldump` with the appropriate options to lock all the tables at once. In these cases, the slave server can continue to run, but it won't attempt any updates to the locked tables during the backup. When the backup program finishes and releases the locks, the slave resumes update processing automatically.

A

Obtaining and Installing Software

This appendix describes how to obtain the `sampdb` distribution that is used for setting up the sample database that serves for examples throughout this book. To use the distribution, you'll also need to have MySQL running. To that end, the appendix also discusses how to obtain and install MySQL and related software such as the Perl DBI and CGI.pm modules, PHP, and Apache. It provides information for both Unix and Windows.

The purpose of this appendix is to bring together in one place summary installation instructions for each of the packages that are discussed here, not to replace the instructions that come with the packages. In fact, I encourage you to read the package instructions. This appendix provides general information that should suffice for many situations, but each package also contains instructions to help you troubleshoot problems when a standard installation procedure fails. For example, the MySQL manual contains a chapter that deals extensively with installation procedures and includes solutions for many operating system-specific problems.

A.1 Obtaining the `sampdb` Sample Database Distribution

The `sampdb` distribution is available at http://www.kitebird.com/mysql-book/ and contains the files that are used to set up and access the `sampdb` sample database. The distribution is available in compressed `tar` file and Zip archive formats. To unpack a distribution in `tar` format, use one of these commands (use the second command if your version of `tar` doesn't understand the `z` option):

```
% tar zxf sampdb.tar.gz
% gunzip < sampdb.tar.gz | tar xf -
```

To unpack a Zip-format distribution, use a utility such as WinZip, `pkunzip`, or `unzip`.

When you unpack the distribution, it will create a directory named sampdb containing several files and subdirectories:

- A README.txt file containing additional general instructions for using the distribution. This is the first file you should look at. Individual subdirectories of the distribution may also contain a README.txt file with more information.

- Files for creating and loading the sampdb database. These are used in Chapter 1, "Getting Started with MySQL."

- A capi directory containing the C programs used in Chapter 7, "Writing MySQL Programs Using C."

- A perlapi directory containing the Perl DBI scripts used in Chapter 8, "Writing MySQL Programs Using Perl DBI."

- A phpapi directory containing the PHP scripts used in Chapter 9, "Writing MySQL Programs Using PHP."

- An ssl directory containing certificate and key files for setting up SSL connections between MySQL client programs and the server.

The sampdb directory also includes a few other directories containing files that are referenced at various other points in this book. Check the README.txt file for further information.

A.2 Obtaining MySQL and Related Software

To use this book, you must install MySQL if you haven't already done so. For third-party tools, you need install only those that you plan to use:

- To write Perl scripts that access MySQL databases, you must install the DBI and DBD::mysql modules. If you plan to write Web-based DBI scripts, you'll probably want to install the CGI.pm module as well, and you'll need a Web server. The Apache server is used in this book, but others may work, too.

- If you want to write PHP scripts as described in this book, you must install PHP and also the PHP Data Objects (PDO) database-access extension. Normally, PHP is used for Web scripting, which means you also need a Web server. The Apache server is used in this book for PHP scripts.

Precompiled binaries are available for many of the installation packages. For example, RPM packages are available for Linux. If you prefer to compile software from source, or if a binary distribution isn't available for your platform, you'll need a C compiler (C++ for MySQL).

If you have an account with an Internet service provider that offers MySQL services, it's very likely that all these packages have been installed already. In that case, you can go ahead and use them and skip the rest of this appendix. Otherwise, the primary distribution points for each of the packages you'll need are shown in the following table. Several of these sites offer mirror sites that provide the same software but that may be closer to you and result in better download times.

Package	Location
MySQL	`http://dev.mysql.com/`
Perl modules	`http://cpan.perl.org/`
PHP	`http://www.php.net/`
Apache	`http://httpd.apache.org/`

The version and distribution format of a package that you install depends on your needs:

- If you need maximum stability, you should be conservative and use the most recent stable version of a package. That gives you the benefit of the newest features and the greatest number of bug fixes without exposing you to experimental code in development versions.

- If you're interested in being on the cutting edge, or you require a feature that's available only in the newest version, you should use the latest development release.

- For MySQL, pre-built binary distributions often are built using optimization flags that are better than what the configuration script in the source distribution might figure out by itself. The MySQL developers recommend that you use a binary distribution of MySQL obtained from `dev.mysql.com` if possible. They build some distributions using commercial optimizing compilers to make MySQL even faster. Consequently, programs in a binary distribution may run faster than those you'd compile yourself. In addition, the developers have extensive experience in avoiding or working around compiler and system library bugs that prevent MySQL from working properly.

The Web sites for each package indicate which versions are the latest stable releases and which are development releases. They also provide per-version feature change lists to help you decide which release is best for you.

Binary distributions are available in the native packaging format for some platforms, such as RPM packages for Linux or DMG packages for Mac OS X. Other more generic formats also are available, such as compressed `tar` files for Unix systems and Zip archives for Windows.

If you are working with a binary distribution, unpacking it is equivalent to installing it because the files are unpacked into the directories where you want them to end up. On Unix, you might need to be `root` to unpack a distribution if it installs files in protected directories.

Source distributions generally take the form of compressed `tar` files or Zip archives. You can unpack a source distribution into the area that you want to use for compiling, and then install the software into the desired installation location. On Unix, you might need to be `root` to perform the install step, but that should not be necessary for any configuration or compilation steps.

If you are installing from source on Unix, several of the packages discussed here are configured with the `configure` utility, which makes it easy to set up and build software on a variety of systems. If a build fails, you might need to rerun `configure` with options different from those you originally specified. Before doing so, you should prevent `configure` from picking up information that it saved from the previous time you ran it. Clean out the stored configuration like this:

```
% make distclean
```

Or like this:

```
% rm config.cache
% make clean
```

Subscribing to Mailing Lists for Help

When you install a package, it's a good idea to subscribe to the general discussion list for that package so that you can ask questions and receive helpful answers. If you install development releases, you definitely should join and read the mailing list associated with the software to stay abreast of bug reports and fixes. If you don't want all the traffic from a general discussion list, you can subscribe to the announcement list so that you receive notices of new releases. Instructions for subscribing to mailing lists and using them are provided in the Introduction. The Web sites for each package also provide subscription information.

A.3 Choosing a Version of MySQL

Distributions are available for several MySQL release series. Generally, you should use the highest-numbered version available in the series you want to use. Currently, stable releases are being produced in the 5.0 series and development releases come from 5.1 and up. This book uses MySQL 5.0 as its baseline but covers features available in the 5.1 and early 6.0 releases.

Normally, I recommend that you use a stable release and not a development release, so my recommendation for most readers is to use MySQL 5.0. If you want to experiment with newer features such as the event scheduler, use MySQL 5.1 or later. (As I write, stable releases will soon be available for 5.1, at which point you can choose either 5.0 or 5.1 without using a development release.)

A.4 Installing MySQL on Unix

MySQL distributions for Unix are available in binary (pre-built) and source formats. Binary distributions are easier to install, but you must accept the installation layout and configuration defaults that are built into the distribution. Source distributions are more difficult to install because you must compile the software, but you also get more control over configuration parameters. For example, you can compile the distribution to include only the storage engines and character sets that you want, and you can install the software wherever you like.

In the instructions here, I cover how to install MySQL on Unix for the following distribution types:

- `tar` file binary distributions
- RPM packages on Linux
- `tar` file source distributions

However, you should be aware that there are other installation methods for MySQL, such as by using a DMG disk image on Mac OS X, a FreeBSD port, a Gentoo Linux ebuild, or `apt-get` on Debian Linux. If you're using a Unix or Unix-like system that has its own packaging system, you might want to use that for installing MySQL instead of the instructions here. (If so, you should still take a look at the instructions in Section A.4.3, "Post-Installation Steps," after performing the initial installation.)

MySQL distributions contain one or more of the following components:

- The `mysqld` server
- Client programs (`mysql`, `mysqladmin`, and so forth)
- Client programming support (C libraries and header files)
- Language support
- Documentation
- The benchmark database

Source and binary distributions contain all of these components. Individual RPM packages contain only some of them, so you might need to install multiple RPMs to get everything you need.

If you plan to connect to a server that's running on another machine, you don't need to install a server. But you should always install client software so that you can connect to whichever server you use. Also, the C client library is required for writing programs using any API that incorporates that library. For example, you'll need it for DBI if you plan to write MySQL-based Perl scripts.

Installing MySQL on Unix involves the following steps:

1. If you are going to install a server, create a login account for the user and group that you'll use for running it. (This is for a first-time installation only, not for an upgrade to a newer version.) On Linux, installing a server RPM automatically causes the login account to be created if necessary.

2. Obtain and unpack any distributions you want to install. If you are using a source distribution, compile it and install it.

3. Run the `mysql_install_db` script to initialize the data directory and grant tables. (This is for a first-time installation only, not for an upgrade to a newer version.) Some distribution types run `mysql_install_db` for you when you install them. This includes server RPM packages on Linux and DMG packages on Mac OS X.

4. Start the server.

5. Read Chapter 12, "General MySQL Administration," to become familiar with general administrative procedures. In particular, you should read the sections on server startup and shutdown and on running the server using an unprivileged user account.

A.4.1 Creating a Login Account for the MySQL User

This step is necessary only for a first-time installation, and only if you're going to run a MySQL server. You can skip it for an upgrade or if you're installing MySQL client software only.

The MySQL server can be run as any Unix user on your system, but for security and administrative reasons, you should not run the server as `root`. I recommend that you create a separate account to use for MySQL administration and that you run the server as that user. That way, you can log in as that user and have full privileges in the data directory for performing maintenance and troubleshooting. For additional discussion on the benefits of using an account other than `root` for MySQL, see Section 12.2.1.1, "Running the Server Using an Unprivileged Login Account."

Procedures for creating user accounts vary from system to system. Consult your local documentation for specific details. (If you use RPM packages, the server RPM installation procedure creates a login account for a user named `mysql` automatically for you.)

This book uses `mysql` for both the Unix user and group names of the MySQL administrative account. If you plan to install MySQL only for your own use, you can run it from your own account, in which case you'll use your own login and group names wherever you see `mysql` for a user or group name in this book.

Before you create an account to use for running MySQL, check first to see whether your system already has one. Many Unix systems include a `mysql` user and group among the set of standard accounts. For example, current versions of Mac OS X include a `mysql` account (which satisfies the assumption made by Mac OS X DMG packages that a login account named `mysql` already exists).

A.4.2 Obtaining and Installing a MySQL Distribution on Unix

The following sections describe how to install MySQL using different types of distributions. The instructions use *version* to stand for the MySQL version number, *platform* to stand for the type of system on which you're installing it, and *cpu* to indicate the processor type or types for which the distribution was built. These values are used in distribution filenames so that distributions can be identified easily and distinguished from one another. A version number is something like 5.0.56, 5.1.24-rc, or 6.0.5-alpha. Platform/CPU names look like `solaris10-sparc` for a system running Solaris 10 on SPARC hardware or `linux-i686` for a system running Linux on Intel hardware.

A.4.2.1 Installing a `tar` File Binary Distribution

`tar` file binary distribution files have names such as `mysql-`*version-platform-cpu*`.tar.gz`. Obtain the distribution file for the version and platform you want and put it in the directory under which you want to install MySQL (for example, `/usr/local`).

Unpack the distribution using one of the following commands (use the second command if your version of `tar` doesn't understand the `z` option):

```
% tar zxf mysql-version-platform-cpu.tar.gz
% gunzip < mysql-version-platform-cpu.tar.gz | tar xf -
```

Unpacking a distribution file creates a directory named `mysql-`*version-platform-cpu* that contains the distribution's contents. To make it easier to refer to this directory, create a symbolic link to it named `mysql`:

```
% ln -s mysql-version-platform-cpu mysql
```

After creating the link, you can refer to the installation directory as `/usr/local/mysql` (assuming that you installed MySQL under `/usr/local`).

Now proceed to Section A.4.3, "Post-Installation Steps."

A.4.2.2 Installing an RPM Distribution

RPM packages are available for installing MySQL on RPM-based Linux systems. The following list describes some of the more commonly used packages. In the package file-names, *version* stands for the MySQL version number, *platform* stands for the target system type (or `glibc23` for generic packages that should work on any Linux distribution that supports `glibc` 2.3), and *cpu* indicates the processor type or types for which the distribution was built.

- `MySQL-server-`*version-platform-cpu*`.rpm`

  The server software.

- `MySQL-client-`*version-platform-cpu*`.rpm`

  The client programs. If you install MySQL from RPM packages, you should always install the client package.

- `MySQL-embedded-`*version-platform-cpu*`.rpm`

  The embedded server, `libmysqld`. (Available for MySQL 5.1 and up.)

- `MySQL-devel-`*version-platform-cpu*`.rpm`

  Development support (client libraries and header files) for writing client programs. You'll need this RPM if you want to write your own C programs or Perl DBI scripts for accessing MySQL databases. MySQL APIs for other languages might depend on these client libraries and header files as well.

- `MySQL-shared-`*version-platform-cpu*`.rpm`

Shared client libraries.

- `MySQL-bench-`*version-platform-cpu*`.rpm`

  Benchmarks and tests. These require Perl DBI support. (See Section A.4.4, "Installing Perl DBI Support on Unix.")

- `MySQL-`*version*`.src.rpm`

  The source for the server, clients, benchmarks, and tests.

You don't need to be in any particular directory when you install an RPM package, because RPMs include information indicating where their contents should be placed. For any RPM package *rpm_file*, you can find out where its contents will be installed with the following command:

```
% rpm -qpl rpm_file
```

To install an RPM package, use this command (you'll need to do this as `root`):

```
# rpm -i rpm_file
```

Various parts of MySQL are divided into different RPM packages, so you may need to install more than one RPM. For a typical installation, you should install both the server and client RPMs. If you install only the server RPM, you won't be able to do much with it, because it doesn't include the client programs.

For server support, use this command:

```
# rpm -i MySQL-version-platform-cpu.rpm
```

To install the client programs, use this command:

```
# rpm -i MySQL-client-version-platform-cpu.rpm
```

If you plan to write your own programs using the client programming support, make sure to install the development RPM package:

```
# rpm -i MySQL-devel-version-platform-cpu.rpm
```

If you want to install MySQL from the source RPM package, the following command should be sufficient:

```
# rpmbuild --recompile --clean MySQL-version.src.rpm
```

Now proceed to Section A.4.3, "Post-Installation Steps."

A.4.2.3 Installing a Source Distribution

MySQL source distributions have names such as `mysql-`*version*`.tar.gz`, where *version* is the MySQL version number. (Unlike binary distributions, source distributions apply to all systems, so there are no *platform* or *cpu* values in the filename.) Pick the directory under which you want to unpack the distribution and move into it. Obtain the distribution file and unpack it using one of the following commands (use the second command if your version of `tar` doesn't understand the `z` option):

```
% tar zxf mysql-version.tar.gz
% gunzip < mysql-version.tar.gz | tar xf -
```

Unpacking the distribution file creates a directory named `mysql-version` that contains the distribution's contents. Change location into that directory:

```
% cd mysql-version
```

Now you need to configure and compile the distribution before you can install it. If the following steps fail, check the installation chapter in the MySQL Reference Manual, particularly any platform-specific notes it contains about your type of system.

Use the `configure` command to configure the distribution:

```
% ./configure
```

You may want to specify options for `configure`. To obtain a list of available options, run this command:

```
% ./configure --help
```

The following list shows some common configuration options:

- `--with-innodb`, `--without-innodb`

  Include or exclude support for the InnoDB storage engine. Excluding InnoDB makes the server smaller and causes it to use less memory. However, you should include this engine if you plan to use InnoDB tables.

- `--without-server`

  Configure the distribution to build client support only (client programs or client libraries). You might do this if you're planning to access a server that's running on another machine.

- `--with-embedded-server`

  Build the embedded server library, `libmysqld`.

- `--with-yassl`, `--with-openssl`, `--with-ssl`

  Configure the distribution to include SSL support. This is necessary if you want to use encrypted SSL connections between clients and the server. Before MySQL 5.1.11, use `--with-yassl` or `--with-openssl` to select yaSSL or OpenSSL. As of 5.1.11, use `--with-ssl` to select yaSSL, or `--with-ssl=path_name` to select OpenSSL; the pathname indicates where the OpenSSL header files and libraries can be found.

- `--prefix=dir_name`

  By default, the installation base directory is `/usr/local`. The data directory, server, clients, client libraries, header files, manual pages, and language files are installed in the `var`, `libexec`, `bin`, `lib`, `include`, `man`, and `share` directories under the base directory. If you want to change the installation base, use the `--prefix` option. `dir_name` should be a full pathname. For example, to install everything under the `/usr/local/mysql` directory, use `--prefix=/usr/local/mysql`.

- `--localstatedir=dir_name`

  This option changes the location of the data directory. You can use this if you don't want to put your databases under the installation base directory. `dir_name` should be a full pathname.

After you run `configure`, compile the distribution and install it:

```
% make
% make install
```

You might need to be `root` to run the install command if you didn't run `configure` with a `--prefix` option that specifies an installation directory in which you have write permission.

Now proceed to Section A.4.3, "Post-Installation Steps."

A.4.3 Post-Installation Steps

For a first-time installation, there are certain steps that you should take after you install MySQL:

1. Set your PATH environment variable to include the directory where the MySQL client programs are installed. If you installed only the client programs and are not running a server, this is the only step that applies here and you can skip the others.

2. Initialize the MySQL data directory and grant tables.

3. Start the MySQL server.

4. Set up the time zone tables to enable named time zones to be used.

5. Set up the server-side help tables.

If you are upgrading an existing MySQL installation to a newer version, you probably have taken care of a number of those items already, such as setting your PATH and initializing the data directory. However, it's possible that you'll need to do one or more of these things:

- Update your grant tables to make sure that they have the current structure.
- Set up the time zone tables, if your previous installation was from a version older than 4.1.3 that does not understand multiple time zones. These tables enable support for named time zones.
- Update the server-side help tables to use the current help text.

The following sections describe how to perform these actions. Use those sections that apply to your situation.

A.4.3.1 Setting Your PATH Environment Variable

If you want to be able to invoke MySQL client programs from the command line without typing their full pathnames, set your PATH environment variable to include the `bin` directory located under the MySQL installation directory. Your shell uses this variable to determine where to look for commands. `PATH` usually is set in one of your shell's startup files, such as `.tcshrc` for `tcsh`, or `.bashrc` or `.bash_profile` for `bash`. For example, if you use `tcsh`, there might be a line in your `.tcshrc` file that looks like this:

```
setenv PATH /bin:/usr/bin:/usr/local/bin
```

If the MySQL client programs are installed in `/usr/local/mysql/bin`, change the value of `PATH` as follows:

```
setenv PATH /usr/local/mysql/bin:/bin:/usr/bin:/usr/local/bin
```

If you use `bash`, one or more of your shell startup files might contain a line like this:

```
PATH=/bin:/usr/bin:/usr/local/bin
```

Change the setting to this:

```
PATH=/usr/local/mysql/bin:/bin:/usr/bin:/usr/local/bin
```

After you modify the shell startup file or files, the new setting takes effect each time you log in thereafter.

A.4.3.2 Initializing the Data Directory and Grant Tables

Before you can use your MySQL installation, you must initialize the `mysql` database that contains the grant tables controlling network access to your server. This step is needed only for a first-time installation and only if you will run a server. It is not needed for an upgrade to an existing installation or for a client-only installation.

In the following instructions, *DATADIR* represents the pathname to your data directory. It is typically located under your MySQL installation base directory and named `data` or `var`. Normally, you run the commands shown here as `root`. If you're logged in as the MySQL user (for example, `mysql`) or you've installed MySQL under your own account because you intend to run it for yourself, you can execute the commands without being `root` and should omit the `--user` option. You can also skip the `chown` and `chgrp` commands.

To initialize the data directory, the `mysql` database, and the default grant tables, change location into the MySQL installation directory and run the `mysql_install_db` script. (You need not do this if you are installing from RPM packages or a Mac OS X package because they run `mysql_install_db` for you.) For example, if you installed MySQL into `/usr/local/mysql`, the commands look like this:

```
# cd /usr/local/mysql
# bin/mysql_install_db --user=mysql
```

If `mysql_install_db` fails, consult the installation chapter in the MySQL Reference Manual to see what it says about the problem you're encountering. If `mysql_install_db` doesn't run to completion successfully, any grant tables it may have created are likely incomplete. You should remove them because `mysql_install_db` does not try to re-create any tables that it finds already created. You can remove the entire `mysql` database like this:

```
# rm -rf DATADIR/mysql
```

After running `mysql_install_db`, change the user and group ownership and the access mode of all files under the data directory. Assuming that the user and group names both should be `mysql`, the commands look like this:

```
# chown -R mysql DATADIR
# chgrp -R mysql DATADIR
# chmod -R go-rwx DATADIR
```

The `chown` and `chgrp` commands change the ownership to the MySQL login account user and group, and `chmod` changes the access mode to keep everybody out of the data directory except that user.

A.4.3.3 Starting the Server

This step is needed only if you plan to run a server. Skip it for a client-only installation. Run the commands in this section from the MySQL installation directory (just as for the commands in the previous section). Normally, you run the commands as `root`. If you're logged in as the MySQL user (for example, `mysql`) or you've installed MySQL under your own account, you can execute the commands without being `root` and should omit the `--user` option.

Change location into the MySQL installation base directory (for example, `/usr/local/mysql`), and then use the following command to start the server:

```
# cd /usr/local/mysql
# bin/mysqld_safe --user=mysql &
```

The `--user` option tells the server to run as `mysql`.

If you are installing MySQL for the first time on this machine, there are other actions that you'll probably want to perform at this point:

- The default installation enables anyone to use the MySQL `root` accounts without a password. For security reasons, it's a good idea to assign passwords to them.

- You can arrange for the server to start and stop automatically as part of your system's normal startup and shutdown procedures.

- You can put the `--user` option in an option file to avoid having to specify it each time you start the server.

- Various kinds of logging can be enabled. These are useful for monitoring the server, for replication, and for data recovery procedures.

- You can enable or disable storage engines, or specify tuning parameters for them.

Instructions for performing these actions are given in Chapter 12.

A.4.3.4 Installing or Upgrading Additional System Tables

If you are upgrading a MySQL installation, it is possible that the grant table structure has changed since your original installation. To update the tables to the current structure, use the instructions in Section 12.4, "Managing MySQL User Accounts."

To set up the time zone tables that are needed for named time zone support, use the instructions in Section 12.9.1, "Configuring Time Zone Support."

The `mysql` command-line client can access server-side help via the `help` command. For this to work, the help tables in the `mysql` database must be set up. Most installation methods do this automatically for a first-time install, but if you use a method for which this does not occur, you can load the help tables manually. To do this, make sure that the server is running. Then locate the `fill_help_tables.sql` file, which contains SQL statements that create and load the tables. Likely locations are in `/usr/share/mysql`, the `share` directory under the MySQL base installation directory, or the `scripts` directory of a source distribution. After you find the file, execute the following command in the directory where the file is located:

```
% mysql -p -u root mysql < fill_help_tables.sql
```

The command will prompt you for the `root` account password. Omit the `-p` option if you have not yet set up a password.

A.4.4 Installing Perl DBI Support on Unix

Install the DBI software if you want to write Perl scripts that access MySQL databases:

- You must install the DBI module that provides the general DBI driver, and the DBD::mysql module that provides the MySQL-specific driver. DBI requires Perl 5.6.0 or later. (If you don't have Perl installed, visit http://www.perl.com/, download a Perl distribution, and install it before you install DBI support.)

- The MySQL C client libraries and header files must be available as well, because DBD::mysql uses them. They should already have been installed as part of the MySQL installation procedure.

- If you want to write Web-based DBI scripts, install the CGI.pm module.

To find out whether a given Perl module already is installed, use the `perldoc` command. If the module is installed, `perldoc` will display its documentation:

```
% perldoc DBI
% perldoc DBD::mysql
% perldoc CGI
```

The easiest way to install Perl modules under Unix is to use the CPAN shell. Issue the following commands as `root`:

```
# perl -MCPAN -e shell
cpan> install DBI
cpan> force install DBD::mysql
cpan> install CGI
```

The installation command for DBD::mysql uses `force install` to cause installation to proceed even if the test phase fails. The tests assume that they can connect to a server running on the local host using an anonymous-user MySQL account with no password. That means the tests fail unless you happen to have an insecure account. (If you do have such an account, the tests should succeed and you can omit force, but you really should assign passwords to all your MySQL accounts.)

Another way to install Perl modules is to download source distributions from cpan.perl.org as compressed tar files. Unpack a distribution file *dist_file*.tar.gz using one of the following commands (use the second command if your version of tar doesn't understand the z option):

```
% tar zxf dist_file.tar.gz
% gunzip < dist_file.tar.gz | tar xf -
```

Then change location into the distribution directory created by the tar command and run these commands (you might need to be root to run the installation step):

```
% perl Makefile.PL
% make
% make test
# make install
```

The make test command will fail unless you have an insecure anonymous-user MySQL account, as described earlier in this section. If you want to use a different account, run perl Makefile.PL --help to see how. Otherwise, just ignore failed tests and proceed to the installation command.

If you have problems installing the Perl modules, consult the README file for the relevant distribution, as well as the mail archives for the DBI mailing list. The answers for most installation problems can be found there.

A.4.5 Installing Apache and PHP on Unix

The PDO database-access extension for PHP requires PHP 5.0 or higher. For PHP 5.1 or higher, PDO is included with PHP. For PHP 5.0, PDO must be installed separately. This can be done using the pecl command-line program. See http://www.php.net/pdo for more information.

The following instructions assume that you'll run PHP as a dynamic shared object (DSO) module using the Apache httpd server. This means that Apache should be installed first, and then you can build and install PHP. If Apache is not installed on your system already, you can either install a binary distribution that has DSO support enabled, or else compile a source distribution to include DSO support.

After Apache has been installed, configure your PHP distribution using a command such as the one following (enter it on a single line). The command assumes that Apache and MySQL are installed under /usr/local. Adjust the pathnames as necessary for your system.

```
% ./configure
    --with-apxs=/usr/local/apache/bin/apxs
    --enable-pdo
    --with-pdo-mysql=/usr/local/mysql
```

```
--with-mysqli=/usr/local/mysql/bin/mysql_config
--with-mysql=/usr/local/mysql
--with-zlib
```

The options are used as follows. For each option that includes a pathname value, if `configure` can determine the location of the required information for itself, you can give the option without the pathname.

- `--with-axps[=/path/to/apxs]`

  Tells `configure` where to find `apxs`, the Apache Extension Tool helper script that provides other modules with information about your Apache configuration.

- `--enable-pdo`

  Includes support for the PDO extension.

- `--with-pdo-mysql[=/path/to/mysql]`

  Includes MySQL support for PDO. The pathname indicates where MySQL is installed so that `configure` can determine where the MySQL header files and libraries are located.

- `--with-mysqli[=/path/to/mysql_config]`

  Includes support for the `mysqli` "MySQL improved" extension. *This option is not needed for PDO.* You might use this option to enable people who aren't using PDO to run scripts based on the `mysqli` extension. */path/to/mysql_config* is the pathname to the `mysql_config` script. `configure` invokes the script to obtain MySQL configuration information.

- `--with-mysql[=/path/to/mysql]`

  Includes support for `mysql`, the original MySQL extension. *This option is not needed for PDO.* You might use this option to build in `mysql`, to enable people who aren't using PDO to run scripts based on the original extension. The pathname indicates where MySQL is installed so that `configure` can determine where the MySQL header files and libraries are located.

- `--with-zlib`

  This option is needed because the MySQL client library accesses compression functions.

After configuring PHP, build and install it as follows (you might need to be `root` to perform the installation commands):

```
% make
# make install
# cp php.ini-dist /usr/local/lib/php.ini
```

The `cp` command installs a baseline PHP initialization file where PHP can find it. You can substitute `php.ini-recommended` for `php.ini-dist` if you like. Take a look at both and choose the one you prefer.

After PHP and PDO have been installed, edit the Apache configuration file, `httpd.conf`. You'll need to instruct Apache to load the PHP module when it starts, and also how to recognize PHP scripts. (`httpd.conf` might include other files via `Include` directives. If you don't see the information described in the following paragraphs, check any included files as well.)

To tell Apache to load the PHP module, `httpd.conf` will need to include `LoadModule` and `AddModule` directives in the appropriate sections (look for other similar directives). The directives might already have been added for you during the installation step. If not, you must add them yourself. They should look something like this, although the pathname in the `LoadModule` directive might need adjustment for your system:

```
LoadModule php5_module libexec/libphp5.so
AddModule mod_php5.c
```

Next, edit `httpd.conf` to tell Apache how to recognize PHP scripts. PHP recognition is based on the filename extension that you use for PHP scripts. The most common extension is `.php`, which is the extension used for examples in this book. To enable `.php` as the PHP script extension, include the following line in the `httpd.conf` file:

```
AddType application/x-httpd-php .php
```

You can also tell Apache to recognize `index.php` as an allowable default file for a directory when no filename is specified at the end of a URL. You'll probably find a line in `httpd.conf` that looks like this:

```
DirectoryIndex index.html
```

Change it to this:

```
DirectoryIndex index.php index.html
```

After editing the Apache configuration file, stop the `httpd` server if it was already running, and then restart it. On many systems, commands such as those following accomplish this (executed as `root`):

```
# /usr/local/apache/bin/apachectl stop
# /usr/local/apache/bin/apachectl start
```

You can also set up Apache to start and stop at system startup and shutdown time. See the Apache documentation for instructions. Normally, this involves running `apachectl start` at boot time and `apachectl stop` at shutdown time.

If you encounter problems setting up PHP, check the "VERBOSE INSTALL" section of the `INSTALL` file included with the PHP distribution. (It's a good idea to read that file anyway. It contains lots of useful information.)

A.5 Installing MySQL on Windows

I assume that you have a relatively recently version such as Windows 2000, XP, 2003, or Vista. Some features covered in this book such as named pipes and Windows services are not available in older versions (Windows 95, 98, or Me).

There are three distribution types to choose from on Windows:

- A Noinstall package is a Zip archive containing all components needed for a MySQL installation. A Noinstall package has a filename that begins with `mysql-noinstall`. You simply unpack the archive to produce a folder, and then move the folder to where you want MySQL to be installed. For example, unpacking a distribution named `mysql-noinstall-5.0.51-win32.zip` produces a folder named `mysql-noinstall-5.0.51-win32`. If you want to install MySQL at `C:\mysql`, rename the folder to `mysql` and move it to the root directory on the `C:` drive.

- A Complete package contains a Configuration Wizard and all components needed for a MySQL installation. A Complete package has a filename of the form `mysql-version-win32.zip`. To install a Complete package, download it, launch the `Setup.exe` program that it contains, and then follow the instructions in the dialogs that it presents.

- An Essentials package is similar to the Complete package, but contains only a minimal set of files needed for a MySQL installation. For example, it omits the debugging version of the MySQL server. An Essentials package is a self-contained installer and has a filename that begins with `mysql-essential` and a suffix of `.msi`. To install an Essentials package, download it, launch it, and then follow the instructions in the dialogs that it presents.

The Complete and Essentials package installers like to put MySQL under `C:\Program Files\MySQL` rather than at `C:\mysql`. They also create a Start Menu entry and a key in the Windows registry, which the Noinstall package does not.

For additional information about installing MySQL on Windows, see the installation chapter in the MySQL Reference Manual.

To be able to invoke MySQL programs from the command line without typing their full pathnames, set your `PATH` environment variable to include the `bin` directory under the location where MySQL is installed. For example, if you install MySQL in `C:\mysql`, add `C:\mysql\bin` to your path. You can set your path by using the System item in the Control Panel. You might need to restart Windows for the change to take effect.

The following instructions assume that you have set your `PATH` variable, so they omit the leading path to command names (except for `mysqld --install` commands, which use the full pathname to `mysqld`).

After installing MySQL on Windows, it is not necessary to initialize the data directory or the grant tables because they are included pre-initialized in the distribution. However, if you install MySQL in any place other than the default location selected by the installer, you *must* place a `[mysqld]` option group in an option file that the server reads when it starts, so that it can determine where the installation base directory and the data directory are located. Typical option files are the `my.ini` file in the MySQL installation directory or `C:\my.ini`. For example, if you install MySQL in `C:\mysql`, the option group should look like this (note the use of forward slashes in the pathnames rather than backslashes):

```
[mysqld]
basedir=C:/mysql
datadir=C:/mysql/data
```

If you select a different installation directory, you'll need to change the pathnames in the option file.

MySQL distributions for Windows include several servers, each of which is built with different options:

- Prior to MySQL 5.1.21, `mysqld-nt` and `mysqld` are separate servers with and without support for named pipes, respectively.

- As of MySQL 5.1.21, `mysqld` includes support for named pipes and there is no separate `mysqld-nt` server.

- `mysql-debug` in all versions has support for named pipes, debugging, and automatic memory allocation checking.

In general, unless you need the debugging support provided by the `mysqld-debug` server, you are better off choosing another server. `mysqld-debug` uses much more memory and runs more slowly than the other Windows servers.

For servers that support connections using named pipes, this connection type is disabled by default. All servers support shared-memory connections, but these too are disabled by default. To enable these capabilities, you must add the appropriate lines to the `[mysqld]` group in your option file:

```
[mysqld]
enable-named-pipe
shared-memory
```

On Windows, any MySQL server can be installed to run as a service that starts automatically whenever Windows starts. For example, to install the `mysqld` server as a Windows service, use this command:

```
C:\> C:\mysql\bin\mysqld --install
```

The install command uses the full pathname to the server. If the server is installed in a different location, modify the pathname accordingly.

If you use `--install-manual` rather than `--install`, the server is installed as a Windows service, but does not run automatically when Windows starts. You must use the Windows Services Manager or the `net start` command.

If you install a MySQL server as a Windows service, you can specify other options by putting them in the `[mysqld]` group of an option file.

For a server that is installed as a service, you can start it manually using the Windows Services Manager. You should be able to find this as a Services item in the Windows Control Panel or in the Administrative Tools item in the Control Panel. The service also can be started using the following command:

```
C:\> net start MySQL
```

To stop the server, use the Services Manager or one of the following commands:

```
C:\> net stop MySQL
C:\> mysqladmin -u root shutdown
```

To remove MySQL as a service, shut down the server if it is running, and then invoke this command:

```
C:\> mysqld --remove
```

To avoid interactions between the Services Manager and commands issued from the command prompt, it is best to close the Services Manager whenever you invoke service-related commands from the prompt.

If you do not install the server as a service, you can start and stop the server manually from the command line. For example, to run mysqld, start it as follows:

```
C:\> mysqld
```

You can specify other options on the command line if you want. To shut down the server, use mysqladmin:

```
C:\> mysqladmin -u root shutdown
```

To run a server in console mode so that it displays error messages in a console window, invoke it with the --console option. For example, to run mysqld this way, use the following command:

```
C:\> mysqld --console
```

When you run a MySQL server in console mode, you can specify other options on the command line after the --console option or in an option file. To shut down the server, use mysqladmin.

> **Note**
>
> When you run a MySQL server from the command line, you will not necessarily see another command prompt until the server exits. If this occurs, just open another console window in which to run MySQL client programs.

If you have problems getting the server to run, check the Windows notes in the installation chapter in the MySQL Reference Manual.

If you are installing MySQL for the first time on this machine, there are other actions that you'll probably want to perform at this point:

- The default installation enables anyone to use the MySQL root accounts without a password. For security reasons, it's a good idea to assign passwords to them.
- You can arrange for the server to start and stop automatically as part of your system's normal startup and shutdown procedures.
- You can put the --user option in an option file to avoid having to specify it each time you start the server.

- Various kinds of logging can be enabled. These are useful for monitoring the server, for replication, and for data recovery procedures.
- You can enable or disable storage engines, or specify tuning parameters for them.

Instructions for performing these actions are given in Chapter 12.

If you are upgrading a MySQL installation, it is possible that the grant table structure has changed since your original installation. To update the tables to the current structure, use the instructions in Section 12.4, "Managing MySQL User Accounts."

Current distributions of MySQL for Windows include the server-side help tables used for the `help` command of the `mysql` client. It should not be necessary to set up the help tables manually. However, the time zone tables that are needed for named time zone support may be missing or empty. To set up these tables, use the instructions in Section 12.9.1, "Configuring Time Zone Support."

A.5.1 Installing Perl DBI Support on Windows

The easiest way to install Perl modules under Windows is to get the ActiveState Perl distribution from `www.activestate.com` and install it. Then fetch and install the additional Perl modules that you need. The `ppm` (Perl Package Manager) program is used for this.

```
C:\> ppm
ppm> install DBI
ppm> install DBD-mysql
ppm> install CGI
```

A.5.2 Installing Apache and PHP on Windows

Apache and PHP are available as Windows binaries from the Apache and PHP Web sites listed in Section A.2, "Obtaining MySQL and Related Software." Under Apache 2.x, you can run PHP either as a standalone program or as an Apache module.

The PDO database-access extension for PHP requires PHP 5.0 or higher. PHP binary distributions for Windows are available in Zip archive and `.msi` installer formats. If you use a Zip archive, unpack it at the location where you want PHP installed. The `.msi` package is more convenient because it will walk you through configuring Apache for PHP support and set your `PATH` to include the PHP installation location. However, if you use the installer, be sure to select extension installation or PDO and MySQL support will not be installed.

B

Data Type Reference

This appendix describes the data types provided by MySQL. More information on the use of each type is given in Chapter 3, "Data Types." Changes in behavior since 5.0.0 are indicated in the descriptions for individual types.

Type name specifications are written using the following conventions:

- Square brackets ([]) in syntax descriptions indicate optional information.
- M represents the maximum display width for integer types, the precision (number of significant digits) for floating-point and decimal types, the number of bits for BIT, and the maximum length for string types. In string column definitions, the length is specified in bytes for binary string types and in characters for non-binary string types.
- D represents the scale (number of digits following the decimal point) for types that have a fractional part; this is also known as the scale. D should be no greater than M. As of MySQL 5.0.10, M cannot be less than D or an error occurs. Before MySQL 5.0.10, the value of M is adjusted to be $D+1$ if it is smaller than that.

Each type description includes one or more of the following kinds of information:

Meaning. A short description of the type.

Allowable attributes. Optional attribute keywords that may be associated with the data type in CREATE TABLE or ALTER TABLE statements. Attributes are listed in alphabetical order, but this does not necessarily correspond to the order imposed by the syntax of CREATE TABLE or ALTER TABLE (described in Appendix E, "SQL Syntax Reference"). The attributes listed for individual data type descriptions are in addition to global attributes that apply to all or almost all data types. The global attributes are listed here rather than in each type description:

- NULL or NOT NULL may be specified for any type.
- DEFAULT default_value may be specified in all column definitions except for integer columns that have the AUTO_INCREMENT attribute, BLOB and TEXT columns, and spatial columns. With the exception of the TIMESTAMP type, default values must be constants. For example, you cannot specify DEFAULT CURDATE() for a DATE column.

Allowable length. For columns with string data types, this is the maximum allowable length of values that can be stored in the column.

Range. For numeric or temporal (date and time) types, the range of values that the type can represent. For integer numeric types, two ranges are given because integer columns can be signed or unsigned, and the ranges are different for each case.

Zero value. For temporal types, the "zero" value that is stored if an illegal value is inserted into the column. (The SQL mode must be set to allow this or an error occurs for illegal values.)

Default value. The default value if no explicit DEFAULT attribute is present in the type specification. This applies only when strict SQL mode is not enabled. If no DEFAULT clause is given in strict mode, the column is defined with a default of NULL if it can take NULL values, and with no default value otherwise. For further information, see Section 3.2.3, "Specifying Column Default Values."

Storage required. The number of bytes or characters required to store values of the type. For some types, this value is fixed. For other types, the number varies depending on the length of the value stored in the column.

Comparisons. For string types, this value specifies how comparisons are performed. It applies to grouping, sorting, and indexing as well, because those operations are based on comparisons. Binary string types are compared byte by byte using the numeric value of each byte. Non-binary string types are compared character by character based on the character set collating sequence.

Synonyms. Synonyms for the type name.

Note. Miscellaneous observations about the type.

Here's a general tip that's useful if you're not sure how your version of MySQL will treat a given column definition. Create a table that contains a column defined the way you're wondering about, and then use SHOW CREATE TABLE or DESCRIBE to see how MySQL reports the definition. For example, if you can't remember the effect of the UNICODE character type attribute or SERIAL shorthand data type, create a table that uses them and then tell MySQL to display the resulting table definition:

```
mysql> CREATE TABLE t (c CHAR(10) UNICODE, s SERIAL);
mysql> SHOW CREATE TABLE t\G
*************************** 1. row ***************************
       Table: t
Create Table: CREATE TABLE `t` (
  `c` char(10) character set ucs2 default NULL,
  `s` bigint(20) unsigned NOT NULL auto_increment,
  UNIQUE KEY `s` (`s`)
) ENGINE=MyISAM DEFAULT CHARSET=latin1
```

B.1 Numeric Types

MySQL provides exact-value and approximate-value numeric data types. Numeric types have different ranges, so choose them according to the range of values you need to represent. There is also a BIT type for representing bit-field values.

The integer and fixed-point (DECIMAL) types are exact-value data types. FLOAT and DOUBLE types are approximate-value data types. For the exact-value types, values are stored exactly as given and calculations are performed exactly with no rounding error if the values and calculations are within range of the types. Exact-value types are platform-independent, so results obtained using them are the same on all systems. For approximate-value types, calculations are subject to rounding error and variations due to differences in hardware implementations of floating-point operations.

For integer types, a column must be indexed if the AUTO_INCREMENT attribute is specified. Inserting NULL into an AUTO_INCREMENT column causes the next sequence value to be inserted into the column. Typically, this is a value that is one greater than the column's current maximum value. Chapter 3 details the precise behavior of AUTO_INCREMENT columns. (Actually, AUTO_INCREMENT can be used with floating-point data types as well, but use with integer columns is much more common.)

The ZEROFILL and UNSIGNED attributes can be given for numeric types other than BIT:

- Values are padded with leading zeros to the column's display width if the ZEROFILL attribute is specified.

- If the UNSIGNED attribute is specified, negative values are disallowed. (SIGNED is also an allowable attribute, but has no effect because numeric types are signed by default.)

SERIAL DEFAULT VALUE as an attribute for integer or floating-point data types is shorthand for NOT NULL AUTO_INCREMENT UNIQUE.

In some cases, specifying one attribute causes another to be enabled as well. Specifying ZEROFILL for a numeric type automatically causes the column to be UNSIGNED. Specifying AUTO_INCREMENT automatically causes the column to be NOT NULL.

Note that the DESCRIBE and SHOW COLUMNS statements report the default value for an AUTO_INCREMENT column as NULL, although you cannot store a literal NULL into such a column. This indicates that you produce the default column value (the next sequence number) by setting the column to NULL when you create a new row.

B.1.1 Integer Types

- TINYINT[(M)]

    Meaning. A very small integer. M is the maximum display width, from 1 to 255. If omitted, M defaults to 4 (or 3 if the column is UNSIGNED).

    Allowable attributes. AUTO_INCREMENT, SERIAL DEFAULT VALUE, UNSIGNED, ZEROFILL

    Range. –128 to 127 (-2^7 to 2^7-1), or 0 to 255 (0 to 2^8-1) if UNSIGNED

    Default value. NULL if the column can be NULL, 0 if NOT NULL

Storage required. 1 byte

Synonyms. INT1[(*M*)].BOOL and BOOLEAN are synonyms for TINYINT(1). Before MySQL 5.0.3, BIT is a synonym for TINYINT(1); as of 5.0.3, BIT is a separate data type.

- SMALLINT[(*M*)]

  Meaning. A small integer. *M* is the maximum display width, from 1 to 255. If omitted, *M* defaults to 6 (or 5 if the column is UNSIGNED).

  Allowable attributes. AUTO_INCREMENT, SERIAL DEFAULT VALUE, UNSIGNED, ZEROFILL

  Range. -32768 to 32767 (-2^{15} to $2^{15}-1$), or 0 to 65535 (0 to $2^{16}-1$) if UNSIGNED

  Default value. NULL if the column can be NULL, 0 if NOT NULL

  Storage required. 2 bytes

  Synonyms. INT2[(*M*)]

- MEDIUMINT[(*M*)]

  Meaning. A medium-sized integer. *M* is the maximum display width, from 1 to 255. If omitted, *M* defaults to 9 (or 8 if the column is UNSIGNED).

  Allowable attributes. AUTO_INCREMENT, SERIAL DEFAULT VALUE, UNSIGNED, ZEROFILL

  Range. -8388608 to 8388607 (-2^{23} to $2^{23}-1$), or 0 to 16777215 (0 to $2^{24}-1$) if UNSIGNED

  Default value. NULL if the column can be NULL, 0 if NOT NULL

  Storage required. 3 bytes

  Synonyms. INT3[(*M*)] and MIDDLEINT[(*M*)]

- INT[(*M*)]

  Meaning. A normal-sized integer. *M* is the maximum display width, from 1 to 255. If omitted, *M* defaults to 11 (or 10 if the column is UNSIGNED).

  Allowable attributes. AUTO_INCREMENT, SERIAL DEFAULT VALUE, UNSIGNED, ZEROFILL

  Range. -2147483648 to 2147483647 (-2^{31} to $2^{31}-1$), or 0 to 4294967295 (0 to $2^{32}-1$) if UNSIGNED

  Default value. NULL if the column can be NULL, 0 if NOT NULL

  Storage required. 4 bytes

  Synonyms. INTEGER[(*M*)] and INT4[(*M*)]

- BIGINT[(*M*)]

  Meaning. A large integer. *M* is the maximum display width, from 1 to 255. If omitted, *M* defaults to 20.

Allowable attributes. AUTO_INCREMENT, SERIAL DEFAULT VALUE, UNSIGNED, ZEROFILL

Range. -9223372036854775808 to 9223372036854775807 (-2^{63} to $2^{63}-1$), or 0 to 18446744073709551615 (0 to $2^{64}-1$) if UNSIGNED

Default value. NULL if the column can be NULL, 0 if NOT NULL

Storage required. 8 bytes

Synonyms. INT8[(M)]

Note. SERIAL as a data type name is shorthand for BIGINT UNSIGNED NOT NULL AUTO_INCREMENT UNIQUE.

B.1.2 Fixed-Point Types

- DECIMAL[(M,[D])]

  Meaning. A fixed-point number. M is the number of significant digits that values can have, from 1 to 65. D is the number of decimal places, from 0 to 30. If D is 0, column values have no decimal point or fractional part. If omitted, M and D default to 10 and 0, respectively.

  Allowable attributes. UNSIGNED, ZEROFILL

  Range. The range for a given DECIMAL column is determined by M and D and whether the UNSIGNED attribute is given.

  Default value. NULL if the column can be NULL, 0 if NOT NULL

  Storage required. Storage depends on the number of digits on the left and right sides of the decimal point. For each side, 4 bytes are required for each multiple of nine digits, plus 1 to 4 bytes if there are any remaining digits. Storage per value is the sum of the left and right side storage.

  Synonyms. NUMERIC[(M,[D])], DEC[(M,[D])], and FIXED[(M,[D])]

  Note. Before MySQL 5.0.3, DECIMAL values are stored as strings and have somewhat different properties than those of the current representation. See the MySQL Reference Manual for details.

B.1.3 Floating-Point Types

- FLOAT(p)

  Meaning. A floating-point number. In standard SQL, the precision p represents the minimum required bits of precision. In MySQL, p is used only to determine whether the data type is single-precision or double-precision:

  - For values of p from 0 to 24, the type is single-precision, equivalent to FLOAT with no M or D specifiers.
  - For values of p from 25 to 53, the type is double-precision, equivalent to DOUBLE with no M or D specifiers.

Values of p outside the range from 0 to 53 are illegal.

Allowable attributes. UNSIGNED, ZEROFILL

Range. See the FLOAT and DOUBLE type descriptions later in this section.

Default value. NULL if the column can be NULL, 0 if NOT NULL

Storage required. 4 bytes for single-precision, 8 bytes for double-precision.

- FLOAT[(M,D)]

  Meaning. A small floating-point number; single-precision (less precise than DOUBLE). M is the number of significant digits that values can have, from 1 to 255. D is the number of decimal places, from 0 to 30. If D is 0, column values have no decimal point or fractional part. If M and D are omitted, the display size and number of decimals are undefined; values are stored to the full precision allowed by your hardware.

  Allowable attributes. UNSIGNED, ZEROFILL

  Range. Minimum non-zero values are $\pm1.175494351\text{E}{-}38$; maximum non-zero values are $\pm3.402823466\text{E}{+}38$. Negative values are disallowed if the column is UNSIGNED.

  Default value. NULL if the column can be NULL, 0 if NOT NULL

  Storage required. 4 bytes

  Synonyms. FLOAT4 is a synonym for FLOAT with no M or D specifiers. If the REAL_AS_FLOAT SQL mode is enabled, REAL[(M,D)] is a synonym for FLOAT[(M,D)].

- DOUBLE[(M,D)]

  Meaning. A large floating-point number; double-precision (more precise than FLOAT). M and D have the same meaning as for FLOAT.

  Allowable attributes. UNSIGNED, ZEROFILL

  Range. Minimum non-zero values are $\pm2.2250738585072014\text{E}{-}308$, maximum non-zero values are $\pm1.7976931348623157\text{E}{+}308$. Negative values are disallowed if the column is UNSIGNED.

  Default value. NULL if the column can be NULL, 0 if NOT NULL

  Storage required. 8 bytes

  Synonyms. DOUBLE PRECISION[(M,D)] is a synonym for DOUBLE[(M,D)], as is REAL[(M,D)] if the REAL_AS_FLOAT SQL mode is not enabled. FLOAT8 is a synonym for DOUBLE with no M or D specifiers.

B.1.4 `BIT` Type

- `BIT[(M)]]`

    Meaning. A bit-field value. *M* should be an integer from 1 to 64 indicating the number of bits per value. If omitted, *M* defaults to 1.

    Allowable attributes. None, other than the global attributes

    Default value. `NULL` if the column can be `NULL`, 0 if `NOT NULL`

    Storage required. Approximately (*M*+7)/8 bytes.

    Note. The `BIT` type was introduced as a separate data type in MySQL 5.0.3. Initial `BIT` support was limited to MyISAM; this was extended to InnoDB, MEMORY, and ARCHIVE in 5.0.5, and to Falcon in MySQL 6.0. Prior to 5.0.3, `BIT` is a synonym for `TINYINT(1)`.

B.2 String Types

The MySQL string types are general-purpose types and commonly are used to store binary or character (text) data. Types are available to hold values of varying maximum lengths and can be chosen according to whether you want values to be treated as binary or non-binary strings.

`BINARY`, `VARBINARY`, and the `BLOB` types are binary string types. A binary string is a sequence of bytes, and its length is measured in bytes. Binary strings have no character set and values are compared based on their numeric byte values.

`CHAR`, `VARCHAR`, and the `TEXT` types are non-binary string types. A non-binary string is a sequence of characters. It has a character set and collation. The character set defines the allowable characters for the data type and the collation defines the character sort order. A length as specified in a non-binary string column definition indicates how many characters you want the column to be able to hold.

Lengths of non-binary string values normally are measured in characters but can be measured in bytes instead. To obtain the length of a non-binary string in characters or bytes, use the `CHAR_LENGTH()` or `LENGTH()` function, respectively. A non-binary string that is *n* characters long is also *n* bytes long if it contains single-byte characters, but more than *n* bytes long if it contains multi-byte characters. This affects the storage requirements for non-binary string columns:

- Fixed-length columns such as `CHAR(M)` require enough space to store *M* instances of the widest character in the character set. For example, characters in the `utf8` character set vary from one to three bytes each, so `CHAR(M)` requires *M* × 3 bytes. (In MySQL 6.0.4 and up, `utf8` characters can require up to four bytes.)

- Variable-length columns such as `VARCHAR(M)` require only enough space to store the actual characters in a given value, plus the prefix that store the value's length in bytes. A `VARCHAR(10)` column with the double-byte `ucs2` character set requires one byte for the length prefix, plus anywhere from 0 bytes for an empty string to 20 bytes for a 10-character string.

You can specify a character set and collation for the non-binary string types (CHAR, VARCHAR, TEXT), as well as for the ENUM and SET types:

- The syntax for specifying a character set is CHARACTER SET *charset*, where *charset* is a character set name such as latin1, greek, or utf8. CHARSET is a synonym for CHARACTER SET.

- The syntax for specifying a collation is COLLATE *collation*, where *collation* names one of the allowable collations for the character set.

- If no character set or collation are given, they are determined from the table defaults. If a character set is given without a collation, the collation is the default collation for the character set. If a collation is given without a character set, the character set is implied by the collation name. If a character set and collation both are given, the collation must be compatible with the character set. For example, the latin1_bin collation is compatible with latin1 but not with utf8.

- The binary character set and the BINARY column attribute are treated specially:

  - If you specify CHARACTER SET binary for a non-binary string type, it causes conversion to the corresponding binary string type. That is, CHAR becomes BINARY, VARCHAR becomes VARBINARY, and the TEXT types become BLOB types. ENUM and SET have no corresponding binary types, so CHARACTER SET binary simply becomes a column attribute as is.

  - The BINARY attribute is equivalent to specifying the binary collation for the character set (the collation name that ends with _bin). For example, a column defined as CHAR(10) CHARACTER SET utf8 BINARY becomes CHAR(10) CHARACTER SET utf8 COLLATE utf8_bin.

- For non-binary string types, the ASCII and UNICODE attributes are shorthand for CHARACTER SET latin1 and CHARACTER SET ucs2, respectively.

The allowable character sets and collations supported by the server can be determined by issuing the SHOW CHARACTER SET and SHOW COLLATION statements. These statements show which collation is the default for each character set. You can also examine the CHARACTER_SETS and COLLATIONS tables in the INFORMATION_SCHEMA database, which contain equivalent information.

Handling of values that are too long to be stored in a string column is dependent on the SQL mode value. If strict mode is not enabled, values are chopped to fit. Also, a warning is generated unless the chopped characters are spaces. In strict mode, an error occurs and no value is inserted if non-space characters must be chopped.

Handling of trailing pad values varies for different string types:

- For CHAR, values are padded with spaces if necessary to the column length when stored. Trailing spaces are removed when values are retrieved.

- For BINARY, values are padded with 0x00 bytes if necessary to the column length when stored. Nothing is removed when values are retrieved. (Before MySQL

5.0.15, BINARY values are padded with spaces when stored, and trailing spaces are removed on retrieval.)

- For VARBINARY and VARCHAR, no padding is added or removed when values are stored or retrieved. (Before MySQL 5.0.3, trailing spaces are removed when values are stored.)

- For the BLOB and TEXT types, no pad values are added or removed for storage or retrieval.

- For ENUM and SET, any trailing spaces in member values listed in the column definition are ignored. Consequently, any trailing spaces are stripped from values stored in the column because MySQL converts each value to the corresponding internal numeric value of the column member. This affects comparisons as well, in that trailing spaces are not significant in values compared to ENUM or SET columns.

B.2.1 Binary String Types

- BINARY[(M)]

    Meaning. A fixed-length binary string 0 to M bytes long. M should be an integer from 0 to 255. If omitted, M defaults to 1.

    Allowable attributes. None, other than the global attributes

    Allowable length. 0 to M bytes

    Default value. NULL if the column can be NULL, ' ' (empty string) if NOT NULL

    Storage required. M bytes

    Comparisons. Byte by byte, based on numeric byte values

- VARBINARY(M)

    Meaning. A variable-length binary string 0 to M bytes long. M should be an integer from 0 to 65535 (0 to 255 prior to MySQL 5.0.3).

    Allowable attributes. None, other than the global attributes

    Allowable length. 0 to M bytes

    Default value. NULL if the column can be NULL, ' ' (empty string) if NOT NULL

    Storage required. Length of value (in bytes), plus a 1-byte or 2-byte prefix to record the length. The prefix requires 1 byte if the maximum length of column values in bytes is less than 256, 2 bytes otherwise.

    Comparisons. Byte by byte, based on numeric byte values

    Note. In practice, the maximum length of a VARBINARY column may be less than 65535 bytes, depending on storage engine internal row-size limits and the space required by other columns in the table.

- TINYBLOB

    Meaning. A small BLOB (binary string) value

Allowable attributes. None, other than the global attributes

Allowable length. 0 to 255 (0 to 2^8-1) bytes

Default value. NULL if the column can be NULL, ' ' (empty string) if NOT NULL

Storage required. Length of value (in bytes), plus 1 byte to record the length

Comparisons. Byte by byte, based on numeric byte values

- BLOB[(M)]

Meaning. A normal-sized BLOB (binary string) value

Allowable attributes. None, other than the global attributes

Allowable length. 0 to 65535 (0 to 2^{16}-1) bytes. If a length M is given, it is used to choose the appropriate data type and then discarded. For lengths of 1 to 65535, the data type becomes BLOB. For lengths of 65536 or greater, the data types becomes whichever of MEDIUMBLOB or LONGBLOB is required to accommodate values of the given length.

Default value. NULL if the column can be NULL, ' ' (empty string) if NOT NULL

Storage required. Length of value (in bytes), plus 2 bytes to record the length

Comparisons. Byte by byte, based on numeric byte values

- MEDIUMBLOB

Meaning. A medium-sized BLOB (binary string) value

Allowable attributes. None, other than the global attributes

Allowable length. 0 to 16777215 (0 to 2^{24}-1) bytes

Default value. NULL if the column can be NULL, ' ' (empty string) if NOT NULL

Storage required. Length of value (in bytes), plus 3 bytes to record the length

Comparisons. Byte by byte, based on numeric byte values

Synonyms. LONG VARBINARY

- LONGBLOB

Meaning. A large BLOB (binary string) value

Allowable attributes. None, other than the global attributes

Allowable length. 0 to 4294967295 (0 to 2^{32}-1) bytes

Default value. NULL if the column can be NULL, ' ' (empty string) if NOT NULL

Storage required. Length of value (in bytes), plus 4 bytes to record the length

Comparisons. Byte by byte, based on numeric byte values

B.2.2 Non-Binary String Types

- CHAR[(*M*)]

  Meaning. A fixed-length non-binary string 0 to *M* characters long. *M* should be an integer from 0 to 255. If omitted, *M* defaults to 1.

  Allowable attributes. BINARY, CHARACTER SET, COLLATE

  Allowable length. 0 to *M* characters

  Default value. NULL if the column can be NULL, ' ' (empty string) if NOT NULL

  Storage required. *M* characters, which is *M* × *w* bytes, where *w* is the number of bytes required for the widest character in the column character set

  Comparisons. Character by character, based on the column collation

  Synonyms. NCHAR(*M*) and NATIONAL CHAR(*M*) are synonyms for CHAR(*M*) CHARACTER SET utf8.

- VARCHAR(*M*)

  Meaning. A variable-length non-binary string 0 to *M* characters long. *M* should be an integer from 0 to 65535 (0 to 255 prior to MySQL 5.0.3).

  Allowable attributes. BINARY, CHARACTER SET, COLLATE

  Allowable length. 0 to *M* characters, possibly less as indicated in the Note

  Default value. NULL if the column can be NULL, ' ' (empty string) if NOT NULL

  Storage required. Length of value (in bytes), plus a 1-byte or 2-byte prefix to record the length. The prefix requires 1 byte if the maximum length of column values in bytes is less than 256, 2 bytes otherwise.

  Comparisons. Character by character, based on the column collation

  Synonyms. CHAR VARYING(*M*). NVARCHAR(*M*), NCHAR VARYING(*M*) and NATIONAL CHAR VARYING(*M*) are synonyms for VARCHAR(*M*) CHARACTER SET utf8.

  Note. In practice, the maximum length of a VARCHAR column is limited to 65535 bytes, and possibly less depending on storage engine internal row-size limits, whether the column character set is single-byte or multi-byte, and the space required by other columns in the table.

- TINYTEXT

  Meaning. A small TEXT (non-binary string) value

  Allowable attributes. BINARY, CHARACTER SET, COLLATE

  Allowable length. 0 to 255 (0 to 2^8-1) characters, possibly less as indicated in the Note

  Default value. NULL if the column can be NULL, ' ' (empty string) if NOT NULL

  Storage required. Length of value (in bytes), plus 1 byte to record the length

  Comparisons. Character by character, based on the column collation

Note. The value can contain up to 255 bytes; the number of characters allowed is less than 255 if the value contains multi-byte characters.

- TEXT[(*M*)]

Meaning. A normal-sized TEXT (non-binary string) value

Allowable attributes. BINARY, CHARACTER SET, COLLATE

Allowable length. 0 to 65535 (0 to 2^{16}-1) characters, possibly less as indicated in the Note. If a length *M* is given, it is used to choose the appropriate data type and then discarded. For lengths of 1 to 65535, the data type becomes TEXT. For lengths of 65536 or greater, the data types becomes whichever of MEDIUMTEXT or LONGTEXT is required to accommodate values of the given length.

Default value. NULL if the column can be NULL, ' ' (empty string) if NOT NULL

Storage required. Length of value (in bytes), plus 2 bytes to record the length

Comparisons. Character by character, based on the data type collation

Note. The value can contain up to 65535 bytes; the number of characters allowed is less than 65535 if the value contains multi-byte characters.

- MEDIUMTEXT

Meaning. A medium-sized TEXT (non-binary string) value

Allowable attributes. BINARY, CHARACTER SET, COLLATE

Allowable length. 0 to 16777215 (0 to 2^{24}-1) characters, possibly less as indicated in the Note

Default value. NULL if the column can be NULL, ' ' (empty string) if NOT NULL

Storage required. Length of value (in bytes), plus 3 bytes to record the length

Comparisons. Character by character, based on the data type collation

Note. The value can contain up to 16777215 bytes; the number of characters allowed is less than 16777215 if the value contains multi-byte characters.

Synonyms. LONG VARCHAR

- LONGTEXT

Meaning. A large TEXT (non-binary string) value

Allowable attributes. BINARY, CHARACTER SET, COLLATE

Allowable length. 0 to 4294967295 (0 to 2^{32}-1) characters, possibly less as indicated in the Note

Default value. NULL if the column can be NULL, ' ' (empty string) if NOT NULL

Storage required. Length of value (in bytes), plus 4 bytes to record the length

Comparisons. Character by character, based on the data type collation

Note. The value can contain up to 4294967295 bytes; the number of characters allowed is less than 4294967295 if the value contains multi-byte characters.

B.2.3 ENUM and SET Types

- ENUM('*value1*','*value2*',...)

  Meaning. An enumeration; column values can be assigned exactly one member of the value list

  Allowable attributes. CHARACTER SET, COLLATE

  Default value. NULL if the column can be NULL, first enumeration value if NOT NULL

  Storage required. 1 byte for enumerations with 1 to 255 members, 2 bytes for enumerations with 256 to 65535 members

  Comparisons. Based on the numeric value of column values

  Note. In the data type definition, any trailing spaces present in member values are ignored.

- SET('*value1*','*value2*',...)

  Meaning. A set; column values can be assigned zero or more members of the value list

  Allowable attributes. CHARACTER SET, COLLATE

  Default value. NULL if the column can be NULL, ' ' (empty set) if NOT NULL

  Storage required. 1 byte (for sets with 1 to 8 members), 2 bytes (9 to 16 members), 3 bytes (17 to 24 members), 4 bytes (25 to 32 members), or 8 bytes (33 to 64 members)

  Comparisons. Based on the numeric value of column values

  Note. In the data type definition, any trailing spaces present in member values are ignored.

B.3 Date and Time Types

MySQL provides several types to represent temporal data. Types are available for dates and times, either separate or in combination. There is a special timestamp type that is updated automatically when a row changes, and a type for storing years when you don't need a complete date.

The terms *CC*, *YY*, *MM*, and *DD* in date formats represent century, year, month, and day of month, respectively. The terms *hh*, *mm*, and *ss* in time formats represent hour, minute, and second, respectively.

- DATE

  Meaning. A date, in '*CCYY-MM-DD*' format

  Allowable attributes. None, other than the global attributes

  Range. '1000-01-01' to '9999-12-31'

  Zero value. '0000-00-00'

  Default value. NULL if the column can be NULL, '0000-00-00' if NOT NULL

Storage required. 3 bytes

- DATETIME

  Meaning. A date and time value, in `'CCYY-MM-DD hh:mm:ss'` format

  Allowable attributes. None, other than the global attributes

  Range. `'1000-01-01 00:00:00'` to `'9999-12-31 23:59:59'`

  Zero value. `'0000-00-00 00:00:00'`

  Default value. NULL if the column can be NULL, `'0000-00-00 00:00:00'` if NOT NULL

  Storage required. 8 bytes

- TIME

  Meaning. A time, in `'hh:mm:ss'` format (or `'-hh:mm:ss'` for negative values).

  Allowable attributes. None, other than the global attributes

  Range. `'-838:59:59'` to `'838:59:59'`

  Zero value. `'00:00:00'`

  Default value. NULL if the column can be NULL, `'00:00:00'` if NOT NULL

  Storage required. 3 bytes

  Note. Although `'00:00:00'` is used as the zero value when illegal values are inserted into a TIME column, it is also a legal value that lies within the normal column range.

- TIMESTAMP

  Meaning. A timestamp (date and time), in `'CCYY-MM-DD hh:mm:ss'` format. The TIMESTAMP type has several special behaviors:

    - Inserting a NULL into any TIMESTAMP column of a table inserts the current date and time, unless the column has been declared to allow NULL.

    - One TIMESTAMP column per table can have two auto-modification properties:

        - Automatic initialization: When a row is created, the default value for the column is the current timestamp.

        - Automatic updating: When a row is updated, changing the value of any other column in the row causes the TIMESTAMP column to be updated to the date and time at which the modification occurs.

    You can designate which TIMESTAMP should be treated this way, and you can suppress automatic initialization, updating, or both. See Chapter 3 for additional details.

  Allowable attributes. One TIMESTAMP column in a table can have attributes of DEFAULT CURRENT_TIMESTAMP or ON UPDATE CURRENT_TIMESTAMP, or both. (You cannot use one attribute with one TIMESTAMP column and the other attribute with another TIMESTAMP column, nor can you use either attribute with more than one TIMESTAMP column.) DEFAULT CURRENT_TIMESTAMP causes the column to be set to the current date and time at row creation time if no value is given for the column. ON UPDATE CURRENT_TIMESTAMP causes the column to be updated the current date and time when any other column in the row is changed from its current value. CURRENT_TIMESTAMP() and NOW() are understood as synonyms for CURRENT_TIMESTAMP.

A constant DEFAULT value can be specified to assign a TIMESTAMP column a fixed date and time value or zero.

The NULL attribute can be given to allow a TIMESTAMP column to store NULL values. Without this attribute, storing a NULL into a TIMESTAMP column sets it to the current date and time.

Range. '1970-01-01 00:00:01' UTC to '2038-01-19 03:14:07' UTC

Zero value. '0000-00-00 00:00:00'

Default value. DESCRIBE and SHOW COLUMNS display the default value as CURRENT_TIMESTAMP if the column is set automatically to the current date and time when rows are created. Otherwise the constant date and time default value is displayed. See the discussion of the allowable attributes.

Storage required. 4 bytes

Note. During table creation, TIMESTAMP columns are subject to the setting of the SQL mode. If the MAXDB SQL mode is enabled, any TIMESTAMP column is created as a DATETIME column instead, for compatibility with the MaxDB DBMS.

- YEAR[(M)]

  Meaning. A year value. If given, M must be 2 or 4 for formats of YY or CCYY. If omitted, M defaults to 4.

  Allowable attributes. None, other than the global attributes

  Range. 1901 to 2155, and 0000 for YEAR(4). 1970 to 2069 for YEAR(2), but only the last two digits are displayed.

  Zero value. 0000 for YEAR(4), 00 for YEAR(2)

  Default value. NULL if the column can be NULL, 0000 or 00 if NOT NULL

  Storage required. 1 byte

B.4 Spatial Types

These types are used to represent spatial or geometric values. In MySQL, spatial values can be represented in Well-Known Text, Well-Known Binary, or internal spatial format. The spatial data types are used for storing internal-format values.

Spatial data types are available only if the server has been compiled with support for them, as indicated by the value of the have_geometry system variable.

Support for spatial types and the types of indexes that may be created for them varies by storage engine. MyISAM tables support spatial types as well as SPATIAL and non-SPATIAL indexes on them. Other engines such as InnoDB and ARCHIVE support spatial types but only allow non-SPATIAL indexes on them. See Section 3.2.7, "Spatial Data Types," for more information.

For all spatial types, the allowable attributes are NULL and NOT NULL.

- GEOMETRY

  Meaning. A geometry object. This type can hold a single value of any spatial type.

- GEOMETRYCOLLECTION

  Meaning. A collection of one or more geometry objects (values of any spatial type).

- LINESTRING

  Meaning. A curve, represented as a set of one or more POINT values.

- MULTILINESTRING

  Meaning. A collection of one or more LINESTRING values.

- MULTIPOINT

  Meaning. A collection of one or more POINT values.

- MULTIPOLYGON

  Meaning. A collection of one or more POLYGON values.

- POINT

  Meaning. A point (a pair of X/Y coordinates).

- POLYGON

  Meaning. A polygon, represented as a set of one or more simple, closed LINESTRING values.

C

Operator and Function Reference

This appendix lists the operators and functions you can use to construct expressions in SQL statements. Changes in behavior since 5.0.0 are indicated in the descriptions for individual operators and functions.

Operator and function examples are written in the following format:

```
expr                                        → result
```

The expression `expr` demonstrates how to use an operator or function, and `result` shows the value that results from evaluating the expression. For example:

```
RIGHT('my cat',3)                           → 'cat'
```

This means that the function call `RIGHT('my cat',3)` produces the string result `'cat'`. You can try the examples shown in this appendix for yourself using the `mysql` program. To try the preceding example, invoke the `mysql` program, type in the example expression with `SELECT` in front of it and a semicolon after it, and press Enter:

```
mysql> SELECT RIGHT('my cat',3);
+-------------------+
| RIGHT('my cat',3) |
+-------------------+
| cat               |
+-------------------+
```

MySQL does not require a `SELECT` statement to have a `FROM` clause, which makes it easy to experiment with operators and functions by entering expressions in this way.

Examples in this appendix include complete `SELECT` statements for functions that cannot be demonstrated otherwise. Section C.2.6, "Summary Functions," is written that way because those functions make no sense except in reference to a particular table.

Function names, as well as operators that are words, such as `BETWEEN`, may be specified in any lettercase.

Certain types of function arguments occur repeatedly and are represented by names with the following conventional meanings:

- `expr` represents an expression; depending on the context, this may be a numeric, string, or date or time expression, and may incorporate constants, references to table columns, or other expressions.
- `str` represents a string; it can be a literal string, a reference to a table column that has a string data type, or an expression that produces a string.
- `n` represents an integer (as do letters near to `n` in the alphabet).
- `x` represents a floating-point number (as do letters near to `x` in the alphabet).

Other argument names are used less often and are defined where used. Square brackets (`[]`) in syntax descriptions indicate optional parts of operator or function call sequences.

Evaluation of an expression often involves type conversion of the values in that expression. See Section 3.5.2, "Type Conversion," for details on the circumstances under which conversions occur and the rules that MySQL uses to convert values from one type to another.

C.1 Operators

Operators are used to combine terms in expressions to perform arithmetic, compare values, perform bitwise or logical operations, and match patterns.

C.1.1 Operator Precedence

Operators have differing precedence levels. The levels are shown in the following list, from highest to lowest. Operators on the same line have the same precedence. Operators at a given precedence level are evaluated left to right. Operators at a higher precedence level are evaluated before operators at a lower precedence level.

```
BINARY  COLLATE
!
- (unary minus)   ~ (unary bit negation)
^
*  /  DIV  %  MOD
+  -
<<  >>
&
|
<  <=  =  <=>  <>  !=  >=  >  IN  IS  LIKE  REGEXP  RLIKE
BETWEEN  CASE  WHEN  THEN  ELSE
NOT
AND  &&
XOR
OR  ||
:=
```

The unary operators (unary minus, unary bit negation, NOT, BINARY, and COLLATE) bind more tightly than the binary operators. That is, they group with the immediately following term in an expression, not with the rest of the expression as a whole.

```
-2+3                                              → 1
-(2+3)                                            → -5
```

Some operator precedences vary depending on the server SQL mode or MySQL version:

- If the PIPES_AS_CONCAT SQL mode is enabled, || becomes a string concatenation operator rather than logical OR, and its precedence is elevated to a level between ^ and the unary operators.

- NOT has a lower precedence than the ! operator. To make NOT have the same precedence as ! (which was the behavior before MySQL 5.0.2), enable the HIGH_NOT_PRECEDENCE SQL mode.

C.1.2 Grouping Operators

These operators enable you to group expression terms to control order of evaluation or to group values into tuples.

- (...)

   Parentheses can be used to group parts of an expression. They override the default operator precedence that otherwise determines the order in which terms of an expression are evaluated. (See Section C.1.1, "Operator Precedence.") Parentheses also may be used simply for visual clarity to make an expression more readable. Nested parenthesized expressions are evaluated from innermost to outermost.

```
1 + 2 * 3 / 4                                     → 2.5000
(((1 + 2) * 3) / 4)                               → 2.2500
```

- (expr[,expr]...)
   ROW(expr[,expr]...)

   These row constructors can be used to express a comparison between two tuples (sets) of values. The tuples to be compared must contain the same number of values. The two syntaxes (with and without the ROW keyword) are equivalent. For example, if a subquery returns a row containing three values, you can compare the result to a given three-value tuple using either of the following constructs:

```
SELECT ... FROM t2 WHERE (0,1,2) = (SELECT col1, col2, col3 FROM ...);
SELECT ... FROM t2 WHERE ROW(0,1,2) = (SELECT col1, col2, col3 FROM ...);
```

   Row constructors can be used in non-subquery contexts as well. The following statement is legal:

```
SELECT * FROM president WHERE (first_name,last_name) = ('John','Adams');
```

C.1.3 Arithmetic Operators

These operators perform standard arithmetic. The arithmetic operators work on numbers, not strings (although MySQL automatically converts strings that look like numbers to the corresponding numeric value).

Arithmetic operators follow these rules:

- Strings are converted to double-precision numbers when used in numeric context.
- Calculations use 64-bit integer arithmetic for +, -, and * if both operands are integers. This means that expressions involving large values might exceed the range of 64-bit integer calculations, with unpredictable results.

```
999999999999999999 * 999999999999999999      → -7527149226598858751
99999999999 * 99999999999 * 99999999999       → -1504485813132150785
18014398509481984 * 18014398509481984         → 0
```

- If both operands are integers and at least one is unsigned, the result is unsigned.
- The operand with the greatest precision determines the precision of the result for +, -, /, *, and % if either operand is real.
- Division performed with / uses 64-bit integer arithmetic in contexts where the result is used as an integer.
- Division of two exact-value numbers performed with / has a scale equal to the scale of the dividend plus the value of the div_precision_increment system variable, which is 4 by default.
- Arithmetic involving NULL values produces a NULL result.

The following arithmetic operators are available:

- +

    Addition; evaluates to the sum of the operands.

    ```
    2 + 2                                    → 4
    3.2 + 4.7                                → 7.9
    '43bc' + '21d'                           → 64
    'abc' + 'def'                            → 0
    ```

    The final example in this listing shows that + does not serve as the string concatenation operator the way it does in some languages. Instead, the strings are converted to numbers before the arithmetic operation takes place. Strings that don't look like numbers are converted to 0. To concatenate strings, use the CONCAT() function.

- -

    Subtraction or unary minus; evaluates to the difference of the operands when used between two terms of an expression, or to the negative of the operand when used in front of a single term (that is, it flips the sign of the term).

    ```
    10 - 7                                   → 3
    -(10 - 7)                                → -3
    ```

- `*`

  Multiplication; evaluates to the product of the operands.

  ```
  2 * 3                                        → 6
  2.3 * -4.5                                   → -10.35
  ```

- `/`

  Division; evaluates to the quotient of the operands. Division by zero produces a NULL result.

  ```
  3 / 1                                        → 3.0000
  1 / 3                                        → 0.3333
  1 / 0                                        → NULL
  ```

- `DIV`

  Integer division; evaluates to the quotient of the operands with no fractional part. Division by zero produces a NULL result.

  ```
  3 DIV 1                                      → 3
  1 DIV 3                                      → 0
  1 DIV 0                                      → NULL
  ```

- `%, MOD`

  The modulo operator; evaluates to the remainder of m divided by n. The m % n or m MOD n operator syntax is the same as the MOD(m, n) function syntax. As with division, the modulo operator with a divisor of zero returns NULL.

  ```
  12 % 4                                       → 0
  12 % 5                                       → 2
  12 % 0                                       → NULL
  ```

  For values with a fractional part, modulo returns the exact remainder after division.

  ```
  14.4 % 3.2                                   → 1.6
  ```

C.1.4 Comparison Operators

Comparison operators return 1 if the comparison is true and 0 if the comparison is false. You can compare numbers or strings. Operands are converted as necessary according to the following rules:

- Other than for the <=> operator, comparisons involving NULL values evaluate as NULL. (<=> is like =, except that NULL <=> NULL is true, whereas NULL = NULL is NULL.)
- If both operands are strings, they are compared lexically as strings. Binary strings are compared on a byte-by-byte basis using the numeric value of each byte. Comparisons for non-binary strings are performed character-by-character using the

collating sequence of the character set in which the strings are expressed. If the strings have different character sets, the comparison may result in an error or fail to yield meaningful results. A comparison between a binary and a non-binary string is treated as a comparison of binary strings.

- If both operands are integers, they are compared numerically as integers.
- Hexadecimal constants that are not compared to a number are compared as binary strings.
- Other than for IN(), if either operand is a TIMESTAMP or DATETIME value and the other is a constant, the operands are compared as TIMESTAMP values. This is done to make comparisons work better for ODBC applications.
- Otherwise, the operands are compared numerically as double-precision floating-point values. Note that this includes the case of comparing a string and a number. The string is converted to a double-precision number, which results in a value of 0 if the string doesn't look like a number. For example, '14.3' converts to 14.3, but 'L4.3' converts to 0.

The following comparisons illustrate these rules:

```
2 < 12                                      → 1
'2' < '12'                                  → 0
'2' < 12                                    → 1
```

The first comparison involves two integers, which are compared numerically. The second comparison involves two strings, which are compared lexically. The third comparison involves a string and a number, so the string is converted to double precision and the operands are compared as double-precision values.

MySQL performs string comparisons as follows: Binary strings are compared on a byte-by-byte basis using the numeric value of each byte. Comparisons for non-binary strings are performed character by character using the collating sequence of the character set in which the strings are expressed. If the strings have different character sets, the comparison may result in an error or fail to yield meaningful results. A comparison between a binary and a non-binary string is treated as a comparison of binary strings.

- =

Evaluates to 1 if the operands are equal, 0 otherwise.

```
1 = 1                                       → 1
1 = 2                                       → 0
'abc' = 'abc'                               → 1
'abc' = 'ABC'                               → 1
'abc' = 'def'                               → 0
'abc' = 0                                   → 1
```

'abc' is equal to both 'abc' and 'ABC' because string comparisons are not case sensitive for non-binary strings. 'abc' is equal to 0 because it's converted to a number in accordance to the comparison rules. Because `'abc'` doesn't look like a number, it's converted to `0` for purposes of the comparison.

For non-binary strings, the character set collation of the operands determines the comparison value of characters that are similar but differ in lettercase or in accent or diacritical marks.

String comparisons are not case sensitive unless the comparison involves a binary string or a non-binary string with a binary or case-sensitive collation. For example, a case-sensitive comparison is performed if you use the BINARY keyword or are comparing values from BINARY, VARBINARY, or BLOB columns.

```
'abc' = 'ABC'                                    → 1
BINARY 'abc' = 'ABC'                             → 0
BINARY 'abc' = 'abc'                             → 1
_latin1 'abc' COLLATE latin1_bin = 'ABC'         → 0
_latin1 'abc' COLLATE latin1_general_cs = 'ABC'  → 0
```

Trailing spaces are significant for binary string comparisons, but not for non-binary string comparisons.

```
BINARY 'a' = 'a '                                → 0
'a' = 'a '                                       → 1
```

- `<=>`

  NULL-safe equality; this operator is similar to `=`, except that it evaluates to 1 when the operands are equal, even when they are NULL.

```
1 <=> 1                                          → 1
1 <=> 2                                          → 0
NULL <=> NULL                                    → 1
NULL = NULL                                      → NULL
```

  The final two examples show how `<=>` and `=` handle NULL comparisons differently.

- `<>`, `!=`

  Evaluates to 1 if the operands are unequal, 0 otherwise.

```
3.4 != 3.4                                       → 0
'abc' <> 'ABC'                                   → 0
BINARY 'abc' <> 'ABC'                            → 1
'abc' != 'def'                                   → 1
```

- `<`

  Evaluates to 1 if the left operand is less than the right operand, 0 otherwise.

```
3 < 10                                           → 1
105.4 < 10e+1                                    → 0
'abc' < 'ABC'                                    → 0
'abc' < 'def'                                    → 1
```

- `<=`

  Evaluates to 1 if the left operand is less than or equal to the right operand, 0 otherwise.

  ```
  'abc' <= 'a'                              → 0
  'a' <= 'abc'                              → 1
  13.5 <= 14                                → 1
  (3 * 4) - (6 * 2) <= 0                    → 1
  ```

- `>`

  Evaluates to 1 if the left operand is greater than the right operand, 0 otherwise.

  ```
  PI() > 3                                  → 1
  'abc' > 'a'                               → 1
  SIN(0) > COS(0)                           → 0
  ```

- `>=`

  Evaluates to 1 if the left operand is greater than or equal to the right operand, 0 otherwise.

  ```
  'abc' >= 'a'                              → 1
  'a' >= 'abc'                              → 0
  13.5 >= 14                                → 0
  (3 * 4) - (6 * 2) >= 0                    → 1
  ```

- `expr BETWEEN min AND max`
  `expr NOT BETWEEN min AND max`

  BETWEEN evaluates to 1 if *expr* lies within the range of values spanned by *min* and *max* (inclusive), 0 otherwise. For NOT BETWEEN, the opposite is true. If the operands *expr*, *min*, and *max* are all of the same type, these expressions are equivalent:

  ```
  expr BETWEEN min AND max
  (min <= expr AND expr <= max)
  ```

  If the operands are not of the same type, type conversion occurs and the two expressions may not be equivalent. BETWEEN is evaluated using comparisons determined according to the type of *expr*:

  - If *expr* is a string, the operands are compared lexically as strings, using the rules given at the beginning of this section.
  - If *expr* is an integer, the operands are compared numerically as integers.
  - If neither of the preceding rules is true, the operands are compared numerically as floating-point numbers.

  ```
  'def' BETWEEN 'abc' AND 'ghi'             → 1
  'def' BETWEEN 'abc' AND 'def'             → 1
  13.3 BETWEEN 10 AND 20                    → 1
  ```

```
13.3 BETWEEN 10 AND 13                          → 0
2 BETWEEN 2 AND 2                               → 1
'B' BETWEEN 'A' AND 'a'                         → 0
BINARY 'B' BETWEEN 'A' AND 'a'                  → 1
```

For BETWEEN expressions that use mixed temporal types or mixed temporal types and strings, it is best to use CAST() to ensure that all operands have the same type.

- CASE [*expr*] WHEN *expr1* THEN *result1* ... [ELSE *default*] END

When the initial expression, *expr*, is present, CASE compares it to the expression following each WHEN. For the first one that is equal, the corresponding THEN value becomes the result. This is useful for comparing a given value to a set of values.

```
CASE 0 WHEN 1 THEN 'T' WHEN 0 THEN 'F' END      → 'F'
CASE 'F' WHEN 'T' THEN 1 WHEN 'F' THEN 0 END    → 0
```

When the initial expression, *expr*, is not present, CASE evaluates WHEN expressions. For the first one that is true (non-zero, non-NULL), the corresponding THEN value becomes the result. This is useful for performing non-equality tests or testing arbitrary conditions.

```
CASE WHEN 1=0 THEN 'absurd' WHEN 1=1 THEN 'obvious' END
                                                → 'obvious'
```

If no WHEN expression matches, the ELSE value is the result. If there is no ELSE clause, CASE evaluates to NULL.

```
CASE 0 WHEN 1 THEN 'true' ELSE 'false' END      → 'false'
CASE 0 WHEN 1 THEN 'true' END                   → NULL
CASE WHEN 1=0 THEN 'true' ELSE 'false' END      → 'false'
CASE WHEN 1/0 THEN 'true' END                   → NULL
```

The return type for a CASE expression is determined from the aggregated types of the return values by default.

```
CASE 1 WHEN 0 THEN 0 ELSE 1 END                 → 1
CASE 1 WHEN 0 THEN '0' ELSE '1' END             → '1'
```

However, the default return type is also affected by surrounding context, which may cause conversion to string, number, and so forth.

Note that the CASE expression differs from the CASE statement described in Section E.2.1, "Control Structure Statements."

- *expr* IN (*value1*,*value2*,...)
  expr NOT IN (*value1*,*value2*,...)

IN() evaluates to 1 if *expr* is one of the values in the list, 0 otherwise. For NOT IN(), the opposite is true. The following expressions are equivalent:

```
expr NOT IN (value1,value2,...)
NOT (expr IN (value1,value2,...))
```

If all values in the list are constants, MySQL sorts them and evaluates the `IN()` test using a binary search, which is very fast.

```
3 IN (1,2,3,4,5)                          → 1
'd' IN ('a','b','c','d','e')              → 1
'f' IN ('a','b','c','d','e')              → 0
3 NOT IN (1,2,3,4,5)                      → 0
'd' NOT IN ('a','b','c','d','e')          → 0
'f' NOT IN ('a','b','c','d','e')          → 1
```

■ *expr* IS {FALSE | TRUE | UNKNOWN}

These constructs test *expr* against logical false, true, or unknown, and return 0 (false) or 1 (true). A value of 0 is considered false, non-zero, non-NULL values are considered true, and NULL is unknown.

```
2 IS FALSE            → 0
2 IS TRUE             → 1
2 IS UNKNOWN          → 0
NULL IS FALSE         → 0
NULL IS TRUE          → 0
NULL IS UNKNOWN       → 1
```

■ *expr* IS NULL
    expr IS NOT NULL

`IS NULL` evaluates to 1 if the value of expr is NULL, 0 otherwise. `IS NOT NULL` is the opposite. The following expressions are equivalent:

```
expr IS NOT NULL
NOT (expr IS NULL)
```

`IS NULL` and `IS NOT NULL` should be used to determine whether the value of *expr* is NULL. You cannot use the regular equality and inequality comparison operators (=, <>, !=) for this purpose. (However, you can use <=> to test for equality with NULL.)

```
NULL IS NULL          → 1
0 IS NULL             → 0
NULL IS NOT NULL      → 0
0 IS NOT NULL         → 1
NOT (0 IS NULL)       → 1
NOT (NULL IS NULL)    → 0
```

C.1.5 Bit Operators

This section describes operators that perform bitwise calculations. Bit operations are performed using BIGINT values (64-bit integers), which limits the maximum range of the operations. Bit operations produce 64-bit unsigned values, or NULL if any operand is NULL.

- &

  Evaluates to the bitwise AND (intersection) of the operands.

  ```
  1 & 1                                      → 1
  1 & 2                                      → 0
  7 & 5                                      → 5
  ```

- |

  Evaluates to the bitwise OR (union) of the operands.

  ```
  1 | 1                                      → 1
  1 | 2                                      → 3
  1 | 2 | 4 | 8                              → 15
  1 | 2 | 4 | 8 | 15                         → 15
  ```

- ^

  Evaluates to the bitwise XOR (exclusive-OR) of the operands.

  ```
  1 ^ 1                                      → 0
  1 ^ 0                                      → 1
  255 ^ 127                                  → 128
  ```

- <<

  Shifts the leftmost operand left the number of bit positions indicated by the right operand. Shifting by a negative amount results in a value of zero.

  ```
  1 << 2                                     → 4
  2 << 2                                     → 8
  1 << 63                                    → 9223372036854775808
  1 << 64                                    → 0
  ```

  The last two examples demonstrate the limits of 64-bit calculations.

- >>

  Shifts the leftmost operand right the number of bit positions indicated by the right operand. Shifting by a negative amount results in a value of zero.

  ```
  16 >> 3                                    → 2
  16 >> 4                                    → 1
  16 >> 5                                    → 0
  ```

- ~

  Performs bitwise negation (inversion) of the following operand. That is, all 0 bits become 1 and vice versa.

```
~0                                      → 18446744073709551615
~(-1)                                   → 0
~~(-1)                                  → 18446744073709551615
```

C.1.6 Logical Operators

Logical operators (also known as "boolean operators") test the truth or falsity of expressions. Logical operations return 1 for true, 0 for false, and NULL for unknown. Logical operators interpret non-zero, non-NULL operands as true, 0 as false, and NULL and unknown.

Logical operators expect operands to be numbers, so string operands are converted to numbers before the operator is evaluated.

In MySQL, !, ||, and && indicate logical operations, as they do in C. In particular, || does not perform string concatenation as it does in standard SQL. Use the CONCAT() function instead to concatenate strings. If you want || to be treated as the string concatenation operator, enable the PIPES_AS_CONCAT SQL mode.

- NOT, !

    Logical negation; evaluates to 1 if the following operand is false and 0 if the operand is true, except that NOT NULL is NULL.

```
NOT 0                                   → 1
NOT 1                                   → 0
NOT NULL                                → NULL
NOT 3                                   → 0
NOT NOT 1                               → 1
NOT '1'                                 → 0
NOT '0'                                 → 1
NOT 'abc'                               → 1
```

    The last several examples demonstrate conversion of a string operand to a number before operator evaluation.

    The precedence of NOT can be modified as described in Section C.1.1, "Operator Precedence."

- AND, &&

    Logical AND; evaluates to 1 if both operands are true (non-zero, non-NULL), 0 if either operand is false, and NULL otherwise (the result cannot be determined).

```
4 AND 2                                 → 1
0 AND 0                                 → 0
0 AND 3                                 → 0
1 AND NULL                              → NULL
0 AND NULL                              → 0
NULL AND NULL                           → NULL
```

- OR, ||

  Logical OR; evaluates to 1 if either operand is true (non-zero, non-NULL), 0 if both operands are false, and NULL otherwise (the result cannot be determined).

4 OR 2	→ 1
0 OR 3	→ 1
0 OR 0	→ 0
1 OR NULL	→ 1
0 OR NULL	→ NULL
NULL OR NULL	→ NULL

- XOR

  Logical exclusive-OR; evaluates to 1 if exactly one operand is true (non-zero, non-NULL), and 0 otherwise. Evaluates to NULL (unknown) if either operand is NULL.

0 XOR 0	→ 0
0 XOR 9	→ 1
7 XOR 0	→ 1
5 XOR 2	→ 0

C.1.7 Cast Operators

Cast operators convert values from one type to another.

- _charset str

  The _charset operator is called an "introducer." It causes the following string constant or column value to be interpreted using a given character set. charset must be the name of a character set supported by the server. For example, the following expressions interpret the string 'abcd' using a character set of latin2 or utf8.

  ```
  _latin2 'abcd'
  _utf8 'abcd'
  ```

  For introducers for multi-byte character sets, padding of the result may occur if the end of the operand does not have the proper number of bytes to create a complete character.

- BINARY str

  BINARY causes the following operand to be treated as a binary string. Comparisons involving the result will be performed byte by byte using the numeric value of each byte. If the following operand is a number, it is converted to string form.

'abc' = 'ABC'	→ 1
'abc' = BINARY 'ABC'	→ 0
BINARY 'abc' = 'ABC'	→ 0
'2' < 12	→ 1
'2' < BINARY 12	→ 0

In the last example, BINARY causes a number-to-string conversion. The operands then are compared as binary strings.

- *str* COLLATE *collation*

  The COLLATE operator causes the given string *str* to have the given collation (which must be one of the legal collations for the character set of *str*). COLLATE affects operations such as comparisons, sorting, grouping, and DISTINCT.

  ```
  SELECT ... WHERE utf8_str COLLATE utf8_icelandic_ci > 'M';
  SELECT MAX(greek_str COLLATE greek_general_ci) FROM ... ;
  SELECT ... GROUP BY latin1_str COLLATE latin1_german2_ci;
  SELECT ... ORDER BY sjis_str COLLATE sjis_bin;
  SELECT DISTINCT latin2_str COLLATE latin2_croatian_ci FROM ...;
  ```

C.1.8 Pattern-Matching Operators

MySQL provides SQL pattern matching using LIKE and regular expression pattern matching using REGEXP. SQL pattern matching succeeds only if the pattern matches the entire string to be matched. Regular expression pattern matching succeeds if the pattern is found anywhere in the string.

Section 3.5.1.1, "Operator Types," provides additional discussion and examples of pattern matching.

- *str* LIKE *pattern* [ESCAPE '*c*']
  str NOT LIKE *pattern* [ESCAPE '*c*']

  LIKE performs an SQL pattern match and evaluates to 1 if the pattern string *pattern* matches the entire string expression *str*. If the pattern does not match, LIKE evaluates to 0. For NOT LIKE, the opposite is true. These two expressions are equivalent:

  ```
  str NOT LIKE pattern [ESCAPE 'c']
  NOT (str LIKE pattern [ESCAPE 'c'])
  ```

  The result is NULL if either operand is NULL.

  Two characters have special meaning in SQL patterns and serve as wildcards:

  - '%' matches any sequence of characters (including an empty string) other than NULL.
  - '_' (underscore) matches any single character.

  Patterns may contain either or both wildcard characters.

  ```
  'catnip' LIKE 'cat%'                           → 1
  'dogwood' LIKE '%wood'                          → 1
  'bird' LIKE '____'                             → 1
  'bird' LIKE '___'                              → 0
  'dogwood' LIKE '%wo__'                          → 1
  ```

LIKE compares the strings as binary strings if either operand is a binary string, or using the operand collation if the operands are non-binary strings.

```
'abc' LIKE 'ABC'                                    → 1
BINARY 'abc' LIKE 'ABC'                             → 0
'abc' LIKE BINARY 'ABC'                             → 0
'abc' LIKE 'ABC' COLLATE latin1_general_ci          → 1
'abc' LIKE 'ABC' COLLATE latin1_general_cs          → 0
```

Because '%' matches any sequence of characters, it matches no characters.

```
'' LIKE '%'                                          → 1
'cat' LIKE 'cat%'                                    → 1
```

In MySQL, you can use LIKE with numeric expressions.

```
50 + 50 LIKE '1%'                                    → 1
200 LIKE '2__'                                       → 1
```

To match a wildcard character literally, turn off its special meaning in the pattern string by preceding it with the escape character, '\'.

```
'100% pure' LIKE '100%'                              → 1
'100% pure' LIKE '100\%'                             → 0
'100% pure' LIKE '100\% pure'                        → 1
```

To interpret '\' literally, enable the NO_BACKSLASH_ESCAPES SQL mode. Alternatively, to redefine the escape character, specify an ESCAPE clause.

```
'100% pure' LIKE '100^%' ESCAPE '^'                  → 0
'100% pure' LIKE '100^% pure' ESCAPE '^'             → 1
```

- *str* REGEXP *pattern*
  str NOT REGEXP *pattern*

  REGEXP performs a regular expression pattern match. It evaluates to 1 if the pattern string *pattern* matches the string expression *str*, 0 otherwise. For NOT REGEXP, the opposite is true. These two expressions are equivalent:

  ```
  str NOT REGEXP pattern
  NOT (str REGEXP pattern)
  ```

  The result of a regular expression match is NULL if either operand is NULL.

  REGEXP compares the strings as binary strings if either operand is a binary string, or using the operand collation if the operands are non-binary strings.

  ```
  'abc' REGEXP 'ABC'                                 → 1
  BINARY 'abc' REGEXP 'ABC'                          → 0
  'abc' REGEXP BINARY 'ABC'                          → 0
  'abc' REGEXP 'ABC' COLLATE latin1_bin              → 0
  'abc' COLLATE latin1_bin REGEXP 'ABC'              → 0
  ```

REGEXP is not multi-byte safe and works only for single-byte character sets.

Regular expressions are similar to the patterns used by the Unix utilities grep and sed. The following table shows the allowable pattern sequences.

Element	Meaning
^	Match the beginning of the string
$	Match the end of the string
.	Match any single character, including newline
[...]	Match any character appearing between the brackets
[^...]	Match any character not appearing between the brackets
e*	Match zero or more instances of pattern element e
e+	Match one or more instances of pattern element e
e?	Match zero or one instances of pattern element e
e1|e2	Match pattern element e1 or e2
e{m}	Match m instances of pattern element e
e{m,}	Match m or more instances of pattern element e
e{,n}	Match zero to n instances of pattern element e
e{m,n}	Match m to n instances of pattern element e
(...)	Group pattern elements into a single element
other	Non-special characters match themselves

A regular expression pattern need not match the entire string, it just needs to be found somewhere in the string.

```
'cats and dogs' REGEXP 'dogs'              → 1
'cats and dogs' REGEXP 'cats'              → 1
'cats and dogs' REGEXP 'c.*a.*d'           → 1
'cats and dogs' REGEXP 'o'                 → 1
'cats and dogs' REGEXP 'x'                 → 0
```

You can use ^ or $ to force a pattern to match only at the beginning or end of the string.

```
'abcde' REGEXP 'b'                         → 1
'abcde' REGEXP '^b'                        → 0
'abcde' REGEXP 'b$'                        → 0
```

```
'abcde' REGEXP '^a'                          → 1
'abcde' REGEXP 'e$'                          → 1
'abcde' REGEXP '^a.*e$'                      → 1
```

The [...] and [^...] constructs specify character classes. Within a class, a range of characters may be indicated using a dash between the first and last characters of the range. For example, [a-z] matches any lowercase letter from 'a' to 'z', and [0-9] matches any decimal digit.

```
'bin' REGEXP '^b[aeiou]n$'                   → 1
'bxn' REGEXP '^b[aeiou]n$'                   → 0
'oboeist' REGEXP '^ob[aeiou]+st$'            → 1
'wolf359' REGEXP '[a-z]+[0-9]+'              → 1
'wolf359' REGEXP '[0-9a-z]+'                 → 1
'wolf359' REGEXP '[0-9]+[a-z]+'              → 0
```

To include a literal ']' within a class, it must be the first character of the class. To include a literal '-', it must be the first or last character of the class. To include a literal '^', it must not be the first character after the '['.

Several special regular expression POSIX character class constructions having to do with collating sequences and equivalence classes are available as well, as shown in the following table. These class names include the '[' and ']' square bracket characters in their names, so when you write a character class expression that refers to any of them, be sure to include enough brackets.

Class	Meaning
[:alnum:]	Alphabetic and numeric characters
[:alpha:]	Alphabetic characters
[:blank:]	Whitespace (space or tab characters)
[:cntrl:]	Control characters
[:digit:]	Decimal digits (0-9)
[:graph:]	Graphic (non-blank) characters
[:lower:]	Lowercase alphabetic characters
[:print:]	Graphic or space characters
[:punct:]	Punctuation characters
[:space:]	Space, tab, newline, or carriage return
[:upper:]	Uppercase alphabetic characters
[:xdigit:]	Hexadecimal digits (0-9, a-f, A-F)

The POSIX constructors are used within a character class:

```
'abc' REGEXP '[[:space:]]'                          → 0
'a c' REGEXP '[[:space:]]'                          → 1
'abc' REGEXP '[[:digit:][:punct:]]'                 → 0
'a0c' REGEXP '[[:digit:][:punct:]]'                 → 1
'a,c' REGEXP '[[:digit:][:punct:]]'                 → 1
```

Within a character class, the special markers `[:<:]` and `[:>:]` match the beginning and end of word boundaries, respectively. A word character is considered to be any character in the `alnum` class or underscore. A word consists of one or more word characters not preceded by or followed by word characters.

```
'a few words' REGEXP '[[:<:]]few[[:>:]]'            → 1
'a few words' REGEXP '[[:<:]]fe[[:>:]]'             → 0
```

MySQL uses syntax similar to C for escape sequences within regular expression strings. For example, '\n', '\t', and '\\' are interpreted as newline, tab, and backslash. To specify such characters in a pattern, double the backslashes ('\\n', '\\t', and '\\\\'). One backslash is stripped off during query parsing; interpretation of the remaining escape sequence occurs during the pattern match operation.

- *str* RLIKE *pattern*
  str NOT RLIKE *pattern*

RLIKE and NOT RLIKE are synonyms for REGEXP and NOT REGEXP.

C.2 Functions

Functions are called to perform a calculation and return a value. By default, functions must be invoked with no space between the function name and the parenthesis following it or an error may occur:

```
mysql> SELECT NOW();
+---------------------+
| NOW()               |
+---------------------+
| 2008-04-30 22:39:26 |
+---------------------+
mysql> SELECT NOW ();
ERROR 1305 (42000): FUNCTION NOW does not exist
```

If the IGNORE_SPACE SQL mode is enabled, the server allows spaces after names of built-in functions, although a side effect is that all function names become reserved words. You also may be able to select this behavior on a connection-specific basis, depending on the client program. For example, you can start mysql with the

`--ignore-space` option; in C programs, you can call `mysql_real_connect()` with the `CLIENT_IGNORE_SPACE` option.

In most cases, multiple arguments to a function are separated by commas. Spaces are allowed around function arguments. Both of the following lines are legal:

```
CONCAT('abc','def')
CONCAT( 'abc' , 'def' )
```

There are a few exceptions to this syntax, such as `TRIM()` or `EXTRACT()`:

```
TRIM(' ' FROM ' x ')                              → 'x'
EXTRACT(YEAR FROM '2003-01-01')                   → 2003
```

Each function entry describes its allowable syntax.

C.2.1 Comparison Functions

These functions perform comparison of values.

- `ELT(n,str1,str2,...)`

  Returns the n-th string from the list of strings $str1$, $str2$, ... Returns `NULL` if n is `NULL`, the n-th string is `NULL`, or there is no n-th string. The index of the first string is 1. `ELT()` is complementary to `FIELD()`.

```
ELT(3,'a','b','c','d','e')                        → 'c'
ELT(0,'a','b','c','d','e')                        → NULL
ELT(6,'a','b','c','d','e')                        → NULL
ELT(FIELD('b','a','b','c'),'a','b','c')           → 'b'
```

- `FIELD(arg0,arg1,arg2,...)`

  Finds $arg0$ in the list of arguments $arg1$, $arg2$, ... and returns the index of the matching argument (beginning with 1). Returns 0 if there is no match or if $arg0$ is `NULL`. String comparison is used if all arguments are strings, numeric comparison if all arguments are numbers, and double-precision comparison otherwise. `FIELD()` is complementary to `ELT()`.

```
FIELD('b','a','b','c')                            → 2
FIELD('d','a','b','c')                            → 0
FIELD(NULL,'a','b','c')                           → 0
FIELD(ELT(2,'a','b','c'),'a','b','c')             → 2
```

- `GREATEST(expr1,expr2,...)`

  Returns the largest argument, where "largest" is defined according to the following rules:

    - If the function is called in an integer context or all its arguments are integers, the arguments are compared as integers.

- If the function is called in a floating-point context or all its arguments are floating-point values, the arguments are compared as floating-point values.

- If neither of the preceding two rules apply, the arguments are compared as strings. String comparison rules are as described at the beginning of Section C.1.4, "Comparison Operators."

```
GREATEST(2,3,1)                          → 3
GREATEST(38.5,94.2,-1)                    → 94.2
GREATEST('a','ab','abc')                  → 'abc'
GREATEST(1,3,5)                           → 5
GREATEST('A','b','C')                     → 'C'
GREATEST(BINARY 'A','b','C')              → 'b'
```

- IF(*expr1*,*expr2*,*expr3*)

If *expr1* is true (non-zero, non-NULL), returns *expr2*; otherwise, it returns *expr3*. The return type for IF() is determined using the following tests, in order: A string, if *expr2* or expr3 is a string; a floating-point value if either of them is a floating-point value; or an integer if either of them is an integer.

```
IF(1,'true','false')                      → 'true'
IF(0,'true','false')                      → 'false'
IF(NULL,'true','false')                   → 'false'
IF(1.3,'non-zero','zero')                 → 'non-zero'
IF(0.3 <> 0,'non-zero','zero')            → 'non-zero'
```

Note that the IF() function differs from the IF statement described in Section E.2.1, "Control Structure Statements."

- IFNULL(*expr1*,*expr2*)

Returns *expr2* if the value of the expression *expr1* is NULL; otherwise, it returns *expr1*. IFNULL() returns a number or string according to the context in which it is used.

```
IFNULL(NULL,'null')                       → 'null'
IFNULL('not null','null')                 → 'not null'
```

- INTERVAL(*n*,*n1*,*n2*,...)

Returns 0 if *n* < *n1*, 1 if *n* < *n2*, and so on, or –1 if *n* is NULL. That is, INTERVAL() finds the position of the first argument within the intervals defined by the remaining arguments. All arguments must be integers. The values *n1*, *n2*, ... must be in strictly increasing order (*n1* < *n2* < ...) because a fast binary search is used. INTERVAL() behaves unpredictably otherwise.

```
INTERVAL(2,0,1,3)                         → 2
INTERVAL(7,1,3,5,7,9)                     → 4
```

- ISNULL(*expr*)

  Returns 1 if the value of the expression *expr* is NULL; otherwise, it returns 0.

ISNULL(NULL)	→ 1
ISNULL(0)	→ 0
ISNULL(1)	→ 0

- LEAST(*expr1*, *expr2*, ...)

  Returns the smallest argument, where "smallest" is defined using the same comparison rules as for the GREATEST() function.

LEAST(2,3,1)	→ 1
LEAST(38.5,94.2,-1)	→ -1
LEAST('a','ab','abc')	→ 'a'

- NULLIF(*expr1*, *expr2*)

  Returns *expr1* if the two expression values differ, NULL if they are the same.

NULLIF(3,4)	→ 3
NULLIF(3,3)	→ NULL

- STRCMP(*str1*, *str2*)

  This function returns 1, 0, or -1, depending on whether the first argument is lexically greater than, equal to, or less than the second argument. If either argument is NULL, the function returns NULL. STRCMP() compares the strings as binary strings if either operand is a binary string, or uses the operand collation if the operands are non-binary strings.

STRCMP('a','a')	→ 0
STRCMP('a','A')	→ 0
STRCMP(BINARY 'a','A')	→ 1
STRCMP('A' COLLATE latin1_general_ci,'a')	→ 0
STRCMP('A' COLLATE latin1_general_cs,'a')	→ -1

C.2.2 Cast Functions

These functions convert values from one type to another.

- CAST(*expr* AS *type*)

  Cast an expression value *expr* to a given type. The *type* value may be BINARY(*n*) (binary string), CHAR(*n*) (non-binary string), DATE, DATETIME, TIME, SIGNED [INTEGER], UNSIGNED [INTEGER], or (as of MySQL 5.0.8) DECIMAL[(*M*[,*D*])].

CAST(304 AS BINARY)	→ '304'
CAST(-1 AS UNSIGNED)	→ 18446744073709551615
CAST(13 AS DECIMAL(5,2))	→ 13.00

An optional length *n* may be specified for BINARY and CHAR, which causes the result to have no more than *n* bytes or characters, respectively. For BINARY, values with less than *n* bytes are padded to a length of *n* with 0x00 bytes as of MySQL 5.0.17.

CAST() can be useful for forcing columns to have a particular type when creating a new table with CREATE TABLE ... SELECT.

```
mysql> CREATE TABLE t SELECT CAST(20080101 AS DATE) AS date_val;
mysql> SHOW COLUMNS FROM t;
+-----------+------+------+-----+---------+-------+
| Field     | Type | Null | Key | Default | Extra |
+-----------+------+------+-----+---------+-------+
| date_val  | date | YES  |     | NULL    |       |
+-----------+------+------+-----+---------+-------+
mysql> SELECT * FROM t;
+------------+
| date_val   |
+------------+
| 2008-01-01 |
+------------+
```

CONVERT() is similar to CAST(), but CONVERT() has ODBC syntax, whereas CAST() has standard SQL syntax.

- CONVERT(*expr*, *type*)
  CONVERT(*expr* USING *charset*)

  The first form of CONVERT() serves the same purpose as CAST(), but has slightly different syntax. The *expr* and *type* arguments have the same meaning. The second (USING) form converts the value to a string that has the given character set.

  ```
  CONVERT(304,BINARY)          → '304'
  CONVERT(-1,UNSIGNED)         → 18446744073709551615
  CONVERT('abc' USING utf8);   → 'abc'
  ```

C.2.3 Numeric Functions

Numeric functions return NULL if you pass arguments that are out of range or otherwise invalid.

- ABS(*x*)

  Returns the absolute value of *x*.

  ```
  ABS(13.5)       → 13.5
  ABS(-13.5)      → 13.5
  ```

- ACOS(*x*)

  Returns the arccosine of *x*, or NULL if *x* is not in the range from –1 to 1.

  ```
  ACOS(1)         → 0
  ```

```
ACOS(0)                                → 1.5707963267949
ACOS(-1)                               → 3.1415926535898
```

- ASIN(x)

Returns the arcsine of x, or NULL if x is not in the range from –1 to 1.

```
ASIN(1)                                → 1.5707963267949
ASIN(0)                                → 0
ASIN(-1)                               → -1.5707963267949
```

- ATAN(x)

ATAN(y, x)

The one-argument form of ATAN() returns the arctangent of x. The two-argument form is a synonym for ATAN2().

```
ATAN(1)                                → 0.78539816339745
ATAN(0)                                → 0
ATAN(-1)                               → -0.78539816339745
```

- ATAN2(y, x)

This is like ATAN(y/x) but it uses the signs of both arguments to determine the quadrant of the return value.

```
ATAN2(1,1)                             → 0.78539816339745
ATAN2(1,-1)                            → 2.3561944901923
ATAN2(-1,1)                            → -0.78539816339745
ATAN2(-1,-1)                           → -2.3561944901923
```

- CEILING(x)

CEIL(x)

Returns the smallest integer not less than x. If the argument has an exact-value numeric type, the return value does, too. Otherwise the return value has a floating-point (approximate-value) type. This is true even though the value has no fractional part.

```
CEILING(3.8)                           → 4
CEILING(-3.8)                          → -3
```

- COS(x)

Returns the cosine of x, where x is measured in radians.

```
COS(0)                                 → 1
COS(PI())                              → -1
```

- COT(x)

Returns the cotangent of x, where x is measured in radians.

```
COT(PI()/4)                            → 1
```

- CRC32(*str*)

  Computes a cyclic redundancy check value from the argument, which is treated as a string. The return value is a 32-bit unsigned value in the range from 0 to 2^{32}-1, or NULL if the argument is NULL.

  ```
  CRC32('xyz')                                → 3951999591
  CRC32('0')                                  → 4108050209
  CRC32(0)                                    → 4108050209
  CRC32(NULL)                                 → NULL
  ```

- DEGREES(*x*)

  Returns the value of *x*, converted from radians to degrees.

  ```
  DEGREES(PI())                               → 180
  DEGREES(PI()*2)                             → 360
  DEGREES(PI()/2)                             → 90
  DEGREES(-PI())                              → -180
  ```

- EXP(*x*)

  Returns e^x, where *e* is the base of natural logarithms.

  ```
  EXP(1)                                      → 2.718281828459
  EXP(2)                                      → 7.3890560989307
  EXP(-1)                                     → 0.36787944117144
  1/EXP(1)                                    → 0.36787944117144
  ```

- FLOOR(*x*)

  Returns the largest integer not greater than *x*. If the argument has an exact-value numeric type, the return value does, too. Otherwise the return value has a floating-point (approximate-value) type. This is true even though the value has no fractional part.

  ```
  FLOOR(3.8)                                  → 3
  FLOOR(-3.8)                                 → -4
  ```

- LN(*x*)

  This is a synonym for LOG().

- LOG(*x*)
  LOG(*b*, *x*)

  The one-argument form of LOG() returns the natural (base *e*) logarithm of *x*.

  ```
  LOG(0)                                      → NULL
  LOG(1)                                      → 0
  LOG(2)                                      → 0.69314718055995
  LOG(EXP(1))                                 → 1
  ```

The two-argument form returns the logarithm of x to the base b.

```
LOG(10,100)                                    → 2
LOG(2,256)                                     → 8
```

You can also compute the logarithm of x to the base b using `LOG(x)/LOG(b)`.

```
LOG(100)/LOG(10)                               → 2
LOG10(100)                                     → 2
```

- `LOG10(x)`

Returns the logarithm of x to the base 10.

```
LOG10(0)                                       → NULL
LOG10(10)                                      → 1
LOG10(100)                                     → 2
```

- `LOG2(x)`

Returns the logarithm of x to the base 2.

```
LOG2(0)                                        → NULL
LOG2(255)                                      → 7.9943534368589
LOG2(32767)                                    → 14.99995597177
```

`LOG2()` tells you the "width" of a value in bits. One use for this is to assess the amount of storage required for the value.

- `MOD(m,n)`

`MOD()` performs a modulo operation. `MOD(m, n)` function syntax is the same as `m % n` or `m MOD n` operator syntax (see Section C.1.3, "Arithmetic Operators").

- `PI()`

Returns the value of π.
```
PI()                                           → 3.141593
```

- `POW(x,y)`
  `POWER(x,y)`

Returns x^y, that is, x raised to the power y.

```
POW(2,3)                                       → 8
POW(2,-3)                                      → 0.125
POW(4,.5)                                      → 2
POW(16,.25)                                    → 2
```

- `RADIANS(x)`

Returns the value of x, converted from degrees to radians.

```
RADIANS(0)                                     → 0
RADIANS(360)                                   → 6.2831853071796
RADIANS(-360)                                  → -6.2831853071796
```

- RAND()
  RAND(n)

RAND() returns a random floating-point value in the range from 0.0 to 1.0. With a constant integer argument n, RAND(n) does the same thing, using n as the seed value for the randomizer. You can use a seed value when you need a repeatable sequence of numbers for the values in a column of a result set. (Non-constant arguments are disallowed as of MySQL 5.0.13; before that, their effect is undefined.)

RAND()	→ 0.1036697114852
RAND()	→ 0.5725383884949
RAND(10)	→ 0.65705152196535
RAND(10)	→ 0.65705152196535

Seeding operations are client-specific. If one client invokes RAND(n) to seed the random number generator, that does not affect the numbers returned for other clients.

If RAND() appears in the WHERE clause, it is invoked once for each execution of the clause.

- ROUND(x)
  ROUND(x, d)

ROUND() returns the value of x, rounded to a number with d decimal places. If d is 0 or missing, the result has no decimal point or fractional part. The return value has the same numeric type as the first argument, so the result has no decimals if that argument is an integer. Numbers specified as strings undergo the usual conversion to double-precision and are handled as such.

ROUND(15.3)	→ 15
ROUND(15.5)	→ 16
ROUND(-33.27834,2)	→ -33.28
ROUND(1,4)	→ 1
ROUND('1',4)	→ 1.0000

If d is negative, ROUND() trims any fractional part and zeros ABS(d) digits to the left of the decimal point.

ROUND(123456,-2)	→ 123500

Before MySQL 5.0.3, the precise behavior of ROUND() depends on the rounding behavior of your underlying math library. This means the results from ROUND() may vary from system to system. As of MySQL 5.0.3, ROUND() handles rounding for x as follows:

- For approximate-value numbers, rounding still depends on the underlying math library.

- Exact-value numbers with a fractional part of .5 or greater are rounded away from zero. Exact-value numbers with a fractional part less than .5 are rounded toward zero. For example, 1.5 and -1.5 round to 2 and -2, whereas 1.49 and -1.49 round to 1 and -1.

For information about what constitutes an exact or approximate number, see Section 3.1.1.1, "Exact-Value and Approximate-Value Numbers."

- SIGN(x)

Returns -1, 0, or 1, depending on whether the value of x is negative, zero, or positive.

```
SIGN(15.803)                              → 1
SIGN(0)                                   → 0
SIGN(-99)                                 → -1
```

- SIN(x)

Returns the sine of x, where x is measured in radians.

```
SIN(0)                                    → 0
SIN(PI()/2)                               → 1
```

- SQRT(x)

Returns the non-negative square root of x.

```
SQRT(625)                                 → 25
SQRT(2.25)                                → 1.5
SQRT(-1)                                  → NULL
```

- TAN(x)

Returns the tangent of x, where x is measured in radians.

```
TAN(0)                                    → 0
TAN(PI()/4)                               → 1
```

- TRUNCATE(x, d)

Returns the value x, with the fractional part truncated to d decimal places. If d is 0, the result has no decimal point or fractional part. If d is greater than the number of decimal places in x, the fractional part is right-padded with trailing zeros to the desired width.

```
TRUNCATE(1.23,1)                          → 1.2
TRUNCATE(1.23,0)                          → 1
TRUNCATE(1.23,4)                          → 1.2300
```

If d is negative, TRUNCATE() trims any fractional part and zeros ABS(d) digits to the left of the decimal point.

```
TRUNCATE(123456.789,-3)                   → 123000
```

C.2.4 String Functions

Most of the functions in this section return a string result. Some of them, such as
`LENGTH()`, take strings as arguments and return a number. For functions that operate on
strings based on string positions, the position of the first (leftmost) character is 1, not 0.

Several string functions are multi-byte safe: `CHAR_LENGTH()`, `INSERT()`, `INSTR()`,
`LCASE()`, `LEFT()`, `LOCATE()`, `LOWER()`, `LTRIM()`, `MID()`, `POSITION()`, `REPLACE()`,
`REVERSE()`, `RIGHT()`, `RPAD()`, `RTRIM()`, `SUBSTRING()`, `SUBSTRING_INDEX()`, `TRIM()`,
`UCASE()`, and `UPPER()`.

- `ASCII(str)`

    Returns the integer value of the leftmost byte of the string *str*, in the range from 0
    to 255. It returns 0 if *str* is empty or `NULL` if *str* is `NULL`. *str* should contain only
    8-bit characters.

    ```
    ASCII('abc')                          → 97
    ASCII('')                             → 0
    ASCII(NULL)                           → NULL
    ```

- `BIN(n)`

    Returns a string containing the binary-digit representation of the argument *n*. The
    following two expressions are equivalent:

    ```
    BIN(65)                               → '1000001'
    CONV(65,10,2)                         → '1000001'
    ```

    See the description of `CONV()` for more information.

- `CHAR(n1,n2,... [USING charset])`

    Before MySQL 5.0.15, interprets the *n1*, *n2*, ... arguments as numeric character
    codes and returns a string in the connection character set consisting of the concate-
    nation of the corresponding character values. The codes are interpreted modulo
    256 (only the lower 8 bits are used). As of MySQL 5.0.15, character codes larger
    than 255 produce multiple result bytes, and the `USING` option may be given. With-
    out `USING`, the return value is a binary string. With `USING`, the return value has the
    named character set. If the result is not legal for the character set, a warning occurs
    (and in strict SQL mode, the result is `NULL`). `NULL` arguments are ignored.

    ```
    CHAR(65)                              → 'A'
    CHAR(97)                              → 'a'
    CHAR(89,105,107,101,115,33)           → 'Yikes!'
    ```

- `CHAR_LENGTH(str)`
  `CHARACTER_LENGTH(str)`

These functions are similar to LENGTH(), except that the argument length is counted in characters, not bytes. (Multi-byte characters are each counted as having a length of 1.)

- CHARSET(*str*)

Returns the name of the character set of the given string, or NULL if the argument is NULL.

```
CHARSET('abc')                          → 'latin1'
CHARSET(CONVERT('abc' USING utf8))      → 'utf8'
CHARSET(123)                            → 'binary'
```

- COALESCE(*expr1,expr2,...*)

Returns the first non-NULL element in the list, or NULL if no argument is non-NULL.

```
COALESCE(NULL,1/0,2,'a',45+97)          → '2'
COALESCE(NULL,1/0)                      → NULL
```

- COERCIBILITY(*str*)

Returns the collation coercibility of a string, or NULL if the argument is illegal. Coercibility is the degree to which a string is subject to having its collation changed in expressions that involve other strings. The following table shows the return values, from lesser to greater coercibility.

Coercibility	Meaning
0	Collation is explicit, cannot be coerced
1	No collation specified
2	Collation is implicit
3	Collation of system values such as USER()
4	Collation is coercible
5	Collation is ignorable (as for NULL)

```
COERCIBILITY(_utf8 'abc' COLLATE utf8_bin)   → 0
COERCIBILITY('abc')                          → 4
```

- COLLATION(*str*)

Returns the name of the collation of the given string, or NULL if the argument is illegal.

```
COLLATION(_latin2 'abc')                         → 'latin2_general_ci'
COLLATION(CONVERT('abc' USING utf8) COLLATE utf8_bin)
                                                 → 'utf8_bin'
```

- CONCAT(*str1*,*str2*,...)

  Returns a string consisting of the concatenation of all of its arguments, or NULL if any argument is NULL. The result is a binary string if any argument is a binary string, or a non-binary string if each argument is a non-binary string. Any numeric argument is converted to a binary string unless you cast it to a non-binary string. CONCAT() may be called with a single argument.

CONCAT('abc','def')	→ 'abcdef'
CONCAT('abc')	→ 'abc'
CONCAT('abc',NULL)	→ NULL
CONCAT('Hello',', ','goodbye')	→ 'Hello, goodbye'

  Another way to concatenate strings is by proximity; specify them next to each other.

'three' 'blind' 'mice'	→ 'threeblindmice'
'abc' 'def' = 'abcdef'	→ 1

- CONCAT_WS(*delim*,*str1*,*str2*,...)

  Similar to CONCAT(), but returns a string consisting of the concatenation of its second and following arguments, with the *delim* string used as the separator between strings. Returns NULL if *delim* is NULL, but ignores any NULL values in the list of strings to be concatenated.

CONCAT_WS(',','a','b','','d')	→ 'a,b,,d'
CONCAT_WS('*-*','lemon','lime',NULL,'grape')	→ 'lemon*-*lime*-*grape'

- CONV(*n*,*from_base*,*to_base*)

  Given a number *n* represented in base *from_base*, returns a string representation of *n* in base *to_base*. The result is NULL if any argument is NULL. *from_base* and *to_base* should be integers in the range from 2 to 36. *n* is treated as a BIGINT value (64-bit integer) but may be specified as a string because numbers in bases higher than 10 may contain non-decimal digits. (This also is the reason that CONV() returns a string; the result may contain characters from 'A' to 'Z' for bases 11 to 36.) The result is 0 if *n* is not a legal number in base *from_base*. (For example, if *from_base* is 16 and *n* is 'abcdefg', the result is 0 because 'g' is not a legal hexadecimal digit.)

  Non-decimal characters in *n* may be specified in either uppercase or lowercase. Non-decimal characters in the result will be uppercase.

  Convert 14 specified as a hexadecimal number to binary:

CONV('e',16,2)	→ '1110'

  Convert 255 specified in binary to octal:

CONV(11111111,2,8)	→ '377'
CONV('11111111',2,8)	→ '377'

n is treated as an unsigned number by default. If you specify *to_base* as a negative number, *n* is treated as a signed number.

```
CONV(-10,10,16)                               → 'FFFFFFFFFFFFFFF6'
CONV(-10,10,-16)                              → '-A'
```

- EXPORT_SET(*n*, *on*, *off*[, *delim*[, *bit_count*]])

  Returns a string consisting of the strings *on* and *off*, separated by the delimiter string *delim*. The default delimiter is a comma. *on* is used to represent each bit that is set in the value *n*, and *off* is used to represent each bit that is not set. The left-most string in the result corresponds to the low-order bit in *n*. *bit_count* indicates the maximum number of bits in *n* to examine. The default *bit_count* value is 64, which also is its maximum value. Returns NULL if any argument is NULL.

```
EXPORT_SET(7,'+','-','',5)                    → '+++--'
EXPORT_SET(0xa,'1','0','',6)                  → '010100'
EXPORT_SET(97,'Y','N',',',8)                  → 'Y,N,N,N,N,Y,Y,N'
```

- FIND_IN_SET(*str*, *str_list*)

  str_list is a string consisting of substrings separated by commas (that is, it is like a SET value). FIND_IN_SET() returns the index of *str* within *str_list*. Returns 0 if *str* is not present in *str_list*, or NULL if either argument is NULL. The index of the first substring is 1.

```
FIND_IN_SET('cow','moose,cow,pig')            → 2
FIND_IN_SET('dog','moose,cow,pig')            → 0
```

- FORMAT(*x*, *d*)

  Formats the number *x* to *d* decimals using a format like 'nn,nnn.nnn' and returns the result as a string. If *d* is 0, the result has no decimal point or fractional part.

```
FORMAT(1234.56789,3)                          → '1,234.568'
FORMAT(999999.99,2)                           → '999,999.99'
FORMAT(999999.99,0)                           → '1,000,000'
```

Note the rounding behavior exhibited by the final example.

- HEX(*n*)
  HEX(*str*)

  With a numeric argument *n*, HEX() returns the hexadecimal-digit representation of the argument, as a string. The following two expressions are equivalent:

```
HEX(65)                                       → '41'
CONV(65,10,16)                                → '41'
```

See the description of CONV() for more information.

HEX() also can accept a string argument; in this case, it returns a string consisting of each character in the argument represented as two hex digits. This form of HEX() is the inverse of UNHEX().

HEX('255')	→ '323535'
HEX('abc')	→ '616263'
UNHEX(HEX('abc'))	→ 'abc'

- INSERT(*str*, *pos*, *len*, *ins_str*)

  Returns the string *str*, with the substring beginning at position *pos* and *len* characters long replaced by the string *ins_str*. Returns the original string if *pos* is out of range, or NULL if any argument is NULL.

INSERT('nighttime',6,4,'fall')	→ 'nightfall'
INSERT('sunshine',1,3,'rain or ')	→ 'rain or shine'
INSERT('sunshine',0,3,'rain or ')	→ 'sunshine'

- INSTR(*str*, *substr*)

  INSTR() is like the two-argument form of LOCATE(), but with the arguments reversed. The following two expressions are equivalent:

```
INSTR(str,substr)
LOCATE(substr,str)
```

- LCASE(*str*)

  This function is a synonym for LOWER().

- LEFT(*str*, *len*)

  Returns the leftmost *len* characters from the string *str*, or the entire string if there aren't that many characters. Returns NULL if either argument is NULL. Returns the empty string if *len* is NULL or less than 1.

LEFT('my left foot',2)	→ 'my'
LEFT(NULL,10)	→ NULL
LEFT('abc',NULL)	→ NULL
LEFT('abc',0)	→ ''

- LENGTH(*str*)

  Returns the length of the string *str*, in bytes. (Multi-byte characters are each counted as having a length greater than 1.) To measure the length in characters, use CHAR_LENGTH().

LENGTH('abc')	→ 3
LENGTH(CONVERT('abc' USING ucs2))	→ 6
LENGTH('')	→ 0
LENGTH(NULL)	→ NULL

- LOCATE(*substr*,*str*)
  LOCATE(*substr*,*str*,*pos*)

  The two-argument form of LOCATE() returns the position of the first occurrence of the string *substr* within the string *str*, or 0 if *substr* does not occur within *str*. Returns NULL if any argument is NULL. If the position argument *pos* is given, LOCATE() starts looking for *substr* at that position. LOCATE() compares the strings as binary strings if either operand is a binary string, or using the operand collation if the operands are non-binary strings.

  ```
  LOCATE('b','abc')                                 → 2
  LOCATE('b','ABC')                                 → 2
  LOCATE(BINARY 'b','ABC')                          → 0
  LOCATE('b' COLLATE latin1_general_ci,'ABC')       → 2
  LOCATE('b' COLLATE latin1_general_cs,'ABC')       → 0
  ```

- LOWER(*str*)

  Returns the string *str* with all the characters converted to lowercase, or NULL if *str* is NULL.

  ```
  LOWER('New York, NY')                             → 'new york, ny'
  LOWER(NULL)                                       → NULL
  ```

  Lettercase conversion is based on the collation of the argument's character set. If the argument is a binary string, there is no character set or collation and LOWER() returns the argument unchanged.

  ```
  LOWER(BINARY 'New York, NY')                      → 'New York, NY'
  LOWER(0x414243)                                   → 'ABC'
  ```

  To deal with this, convert or cast the argument to a non-binary string that has an appropriate collation.

  ```
  LOWER(CONVERT(BINARY 'New York, NY' USING latin1))
                                                    → 'new york, ny'
  LOWER(_latin1 0x414243)                           → 'abc'
  ```

- LPAD(*str*,*len*,*pad_str*)

  Returns a string consisting of the value of the string *str*, left-padded with the string *pad_str* to a length of *len* characters. Returns NULL if any argument is NULL.

  ```
  LPAD('abc',12,'def')                              → 'defdefdefabc'
  LPAD('abc',10,'.')                                → '.......abc'
  ```

  LPAD() shortens the result to *len* characters if *str* has a length greater than *len*.

  ```
  LPAD('abc',2,'.')                                 → 'ab'
  ```

- LTRIM(*str*)

  Returns the string *str* with leftmost (leading) spaces removed, or NULL if *str* is NULL.

  ```
  LTRIM('  abc  ')                                    → 'abc  '
  ```

- MAKE_SET(*n*, *bit0_str*, *bit1_str*, ...)

  Constructs a SET value (a string consisting of substrings separated by commas) based on the value of the integer *n* and the strings *bit0_str*, *bit1_str*, ... For each bit that is set in the value of *n*, the corresponding string is included in the result. (If bit 0 is set, the result includes *bit0_str*, and so on.) If *n* is 0, the result is the empty string. If *n* is NULL, the result is NULL. If any string in the list is NULL, it is ignored when constructing the result string.

  ```
  MAKE_SET(8,'a','b','c','d','e')                      → 'd'
  MAKE_SET(1|2|4,'a','b','c','d','e')                  → 'a,b,c'
  MAKE_SET(2+16,'a','b','c','d','e')                   → 'b,e'
  MAKE_SET(-1,'a','b','c','d','e')                     → 'a,b,c,d,e'
  ```

  The final example selects every string because the value -1 has all bits turned on.

- MATCH(*col_list*) AGAINST(*str* [*search_mode*])
  MATCH(*col_list*) AGAINST(*str* IN BOOLEAN MODE)
  MATCH(*col_list*) AGAINST(*str* WITH QUERY EXPANSION)

  MATCH performs a search operation using a FULLTEXT index. The MATCH list consists of one or more column names separated by commas. These must be the columns that make up a FULLTEXT index on the table you are searching. The *str* argument to AGAINST() indicates the word or words to search for in the given columns. Words are sequences of characters made up of letters, digits, apostrophes, or underscores. The parentheses are optional for MATCH, but not for AGAINST.

  By default, the search is performed in natural language mode. An explicit *search_mode* argument can have one of the following values:

  - IN NATURAL LANGUAGE MODE
  - IN BOOLEAN MODE
  - WITH QUERY EXPANSION
  - IN NATURAL LANGUAGE MODE WITH QUERY EXPANSION

  The modes that include IN NATURAL LANGUAGE MODE were introduced in MySQL 5.1.7.

  For a natural language search, MATCH() produces a relevance ranking for each row. Ranks are non-negative floating-point numbers, with a rank of zero indicating that the search words were not found. Positive values indicate that at least one search word was found. Words that are present in more than half the rows of the table are considered to have zero relevance because they are so common. In addition, MySQL has an internal list of stopwords that are never considered relevant (for example, "the" and "but").

If the search mode is IN BOOLEAN MODE, search results are based purely on absence or presence of the search words without regard to how often they occur in the table. For boolean searches, words in the search string can be modified with the following operators to affect how the search is done:

- A leading + or – indicates that the word must be present or absent.
- A leading < or > decreases or increases a word's contribution to the relevance value calculation.
- A leading ~ negates a word's contribution to the relevance value calculation, but does not exclude rows containing the word entirely as – would.
- A trailing * acts as a wildcard operator. For example, act* matches act, acts, action, and so forth.
- A phrase search may be performed by surrounding the phrase within double quotes ("phrase"). For a match to occur, each word must be present together in the order given in the phrase.
- Parentheses group words into expressions. Parenthesized expressions can be nested.

Words with no modifiers are treated as optional in a boolean search, just as for natural language searches.

It's possible to perform a boolean-mode search in the absence of a FULLTEXT index, but this can be quite slow.

If the search mode is WITH QUERY EXPANSION, a natural language search is done once using the search string, and then again using the search string and the information from the first few most highly relevant matches from the original search. This enables rows with content related to the original search string to be found.

For more information on FULLTEXT searching, see Section 2.15, "Using FULLTEXT Searches."

- MID(str,pos,len)
  MID(str,pos)

  The three-argument form of MID() returns a substring of the string str beginning at position pos and len characters long. The two-argument form returns the substring beginning at pos to the end of the string. Returns NULL if any argument is NULL.

```
MID('what a dull example',8,4)          → 'dull'
MID('what a dull example',8)            → 'dull example'
```

  MID() is actually a synonym for SUBSTRING() and can be used with any of the forms of syntax that SUBSTRING() allows.

- OCT(*n*)

  Returns a string containing the octal-digit representation of the argument *n*. The following two expressions are equivalent:

  ```
  OCT(65)                                        → '101'
  CONV(65,10,8)                                  → '101'
  ```

  See the description of CONV() for more information.

- OCTET_LENGTH(*str*)

  This function is a synonym for LENGTH().

- ORD(*str*)

  Returns the ordinal value of the first character of the string *str*, or NULL if *str* is NULL. If the first character is a single-byte character, ORD() is the same as ASCII().

  ```
  ORD('abc')                                     → 97
  ASCII('abc')                                   → 97
  ```

  For a multi-byte character, ORD() returns a value determined from the numeric values of the character's individual bytes *b1* through *bn* (from right to left):

  ```
  b1 + (b2 × 256) + (b3 × 256 × 256) + ...
  ```

- POSITION(*substr* IN *str*)

  This is like the two-argument form of LOCATE(). The following expressions are equivalent:

  ```
  POSITION(substr IN str)
  LOCATE(substr,str)
  ```

- QUOTE(*str*)

  Processes its argument to return a string that is properly quoted for use in an SQL statement. This is useful for writing queries that produce other queries as their result. For non-NULL values, the return value has each single quote, backslash, Control-Z character, and NUL (zero-valued byte) escaped with a leading backslash, and the result is surrounded by single quotes. If *str* is NULL, the return value is the word "NULL" without any surrounding single quotes.

  ```
  QUOTE("Let's go!")                             → 'Let\'s go!'
  QUOTE(NULL)                                     → 'NULL'
  ```

- REPEAT(*str*,*n*)

  Returns a string consisting of *n* repetitions of the string *str*. Returns the empty string if *n* is non-positive, or NULL if either argument is NULL.

  ```
  REPEAT('x',10)                                 → 'xxxxxxxxxx'
  REPEAT('abc',3)                                → 'abcabcabc'
  ```

- REPLACE(*str*, *from_str*, *to_str*)

  Returns a string consisting of the string *str* with all occurrences of the string *from_str* replaced by the string *to_str*. If *to_str* is empty, the effect is to delete occurrences of *from_str*. If *from_str* is empty, REPLACE() returns *str* unchanged. Returns NULL if any argument is NULL.

REPLACE('abracadabra','a','oh')	→ 'ohbrohcohdohbroh'
REPLACE('abracadabra','a','')	→ 'brcdbr'
REPLACE('abracadabra','','x')	→ 'abracadabra'

- REVERSE(*str*)

  Returns a string consisting of the string *str* with the characters reversed. Returns NULL if *str* is NULL.

REVERSE('abracadabra')	→ 'arbadacarba'
REVERSE('tararA ta tar a raT')	→ 'Tar a rat at Ararat'

- RIGHT(*str*, *len*)

  Returns the rightmost *len* characters from the string *str*, or the entire string if there aren't that many characters. Returns NULL if either argument is NULL. Returns the empty string if *len* is NULL or less than 1.

RIGHT('rightmost',4)	→ 'most'

- RPAD(*str*, *len*, *pad_str*)

  Returns a string consisting of the value of the string *str*, right-padded with the string *pad_str* to a length of *len* characters. Returns NULL if any argument is NULL.

RPAD('abc',12,'def')	→ 'abcdefdefdef'
RPAD('abc',10,'.')	→ 'abc.......'

  RPAD() shortens the result to *len* characters if *str* has a length greater than *len*.

RPAD('abc',2,'.')	→ 'ab'

- RTRIM(*str*)

  Returns the string *str* with rightmost (trailing) spaces removed, or NULL if *str* is NULL.

RTRIM(' abc ')	→ ' abc'

- SOUNDEX(*str*)

  expr1 SOUNDS LIKE *expr2*

  SOUNDEX() returns a soundex string calculated from the string *str*, or NULL if *str* is NULL. Non-alphanumeric characters in *str* are ignored. International non-alphabetic characters outside the range from 'A' to 'Z' are treated as vowels. SOUNDEX() results may not be meaningful for strings with multi-byte characters or for languages other than English.

```
SOUNDEX('Cow')                                    → 'C000'
SOUNDEX('Cowl')                                   → 'C400'
SOUNDEX('Howl')                                   → 'H400'
SOUNDEX('Hello')                                  → 'H400'
```

The SOUNDS LIKE operator is equivalent to the SOUNDEX() function.

- SPACE(*n*)

Returns a string consisting of *n* spaces, the empty string if *n* is non-positive, or NULL if *n* is NULL.

```
SPACE(6)                                          → '      '
SPACE(0)                                          → ''
SPACE(NULL)                                        → NULL
```

- SUBSTR(*arguments*)

SUBSTR() is a synonym for SUBSTRING(). The same argument formats are allowed.

- SUBSTRING(*str*,*pos*)
  SUBSTRING(*str*,*pos*,*len*)
  SUBSTRING(*str* FROM *pos*)
  SUBSTRING(*str* FROM *pos* FOR *len*)

Returns a substring from the string *str*, beginning at position *pos*, or NULL if any argument is NULL. If a *len* argument is given, returns a substring that many characters long; otherwise, it returns the entire rightmost part of *str*, beginning at position *pos*.

```
SUBSTRING('abcdef',3)                             → 'cdef'
SUBSTRING('abcdef',3,2)                           → 'cd'
```

The following expressions are equivalent:

```
SUBSTRING(str,pos,len)
SUBSTRING(str FROM pos FOR len)
MID(str,pos,len)
```

- SUBSTRING_INDEX(*str*,*delim*,*n*)

Returns a substring from the string *str*. If *n* is positive, SUBSTRING_INDEX() finds the *n*-th occurrence of the delimiter string *delim*, and then returns everything to the left of that delimiter. If *n* is negative, SUBSTRING_INDEX() finds the *n*-th occurrence of *delim*, counting back from the right end of *str*, and then returns everything to the right of that delimiter. If SUBSTRING_INDEX() does not find *delim* in *str*, it returns the entire string. It returns NULL if any argument is NULL.

```
SUBSTRING_INDEX('jar-jar','j',-2)                 → 'ar-jar'
SUBSTRING_INDEX('sampadm@localhost','@',1)        → 'sampadm'
SUBSTRING_INDEX('sampadm@localhost','@',-1)       → 'localhost'
```

- TRIM([*trim_str* FROM] *str*)
  TRIM([[|LEADING | TRAILING | BOTH} [*trim_str*] FROM] *str*)

  The first form returns the string *str* with leading and trailing instances of the string *trim_str* trimmed off. In the second form, if LEADING is specified, TRIM() strips leading occurrences of *trim_str*. If TRAILING is specified, TRIM() strips trailing occurrences of *trim_str*. If BOTH is specified, TRIM() strips leading and trailing occurrences of *trim_str*. The default is BOTH if none of LEADING, TRAILING, or BOTH is specified. Spaces are trimmed if *trim_str* is not specified.

  ```
  TRIM('^' FROM '^^^xyz^^')              → 'xyz'
  TRIM(LEADING '^' FROM '^^^xyz^^')      → 'xyz^^'
  TRIM(TRAILING '^' FROM '^^^xyz^^')     → '^^^xyz'
  TRIM(BOTH '^' FROM '^^^xyz^^')         → 'xyz'
  TRIM(BOTH FROM '  abc  ')              → 'abc'
  TRIM('  abc  ')                        → 'abc'
  ```

- UCASE(*str*)

  This function is a synonym for UPPER().

- UNHEX(*expr*)

  The argument is interpreted as a string containing pairs of hexadecimal digits. Each pair of digits is converted to a character and the return value is a binary string consisting of these characters. UNHEX() is the inverse of HEX().

  ```
  UNHEX('414243')              → 'ABC'
  HEX(UNHEX('414243'))         → '414243'
  UNHEX(HEX('ABC'))            → 'ABC'
  UNHEX(414243)                → 'ABC'
  CHARSET(UNHEX('414243'))     → 'binary'
  ```

- UPPER(*str*)

  Returns the string *str* with all the characters converted to uppercase, or NULL if *str* is NULL.

  ```
  UPPER('New York, NY')        → 'NEW YORK, NY'
  UPPER(NULL)                  → NULL
  ```

  See the description of the LOWER() function for notes regarding lettercase conversion of binary strings.

- WEIGHT_STRING(*str* [AS *type*(*n*)] [LEVEL *levels*] [*flags*])

  Returns the weight string for *str* as a binary string that indicates how *str* is handled for comparison and sorting operations. Two strings with equal weight strings compare as equal, otherwise they have the same relative ordering as their weight strings. The AS option causes *str* to have a given type and length, and the LEVEL option specifies which collation levels to return. No *flags* values are implemented currently.

If *str* is a binary string, the weight string is the same as *str*. If *str* is a non-binary string, it has a collation and the result string contains collation weights. If *str* is NULL, the result is NULL. The examples here use HEX() to present the weight strings in printable format:

```
HEX(WEIGHT_STRING(BINARY 'Hello'))              → '48656C6C6F'
HEX(WEIGHT_STRING('Hello'))                     → '48454C4C4F'
HEX(WEIGHT_STRING(_utf8'Hello'))                → '00480045004C004C004F'
```

str can be cast to a given type and length using an AS clause. To treat *str* as a CHAR string *n* characters long, use AS CHAR(*n*). The string will be padded at the end with spaces as necessary. AS BINARY(*n*) treats the string as a binary string *n* bytes long and padding uses 0x00 bytes. *n* must be 1 or greater. *str* is truncated rather than padded if its length is greater than *n*.

A collation might have levels. By default, the result includes weights for all levels. To return weights only for particular levels, use a LEVEL clause. The *levels* value can be a list of one or more comma-separated integers, or a range of two dash-separated integers. Levels in a list must be in increasing order. The second level in a range is treated as the first level if it is less than the first level. Individual level values are clipped to lie within 1 and the maximum level for the collation if they are outside that range.

Level values in a list can be followed by a modifier: ASC to return unmodified weights (the default), DESC to return bit-inverted weights, or REVERSE to return weights for the reversed value of *str*.

```
HEX(WEIGHT_STRING('abc' LEVEL 1 ASC))           → '414243'
HEX(WEIGHT_STRING('abc' LEVEL 1 DESC))          → 'BEBDBC'
HEX(WEIGHT_STRING('abc' LEVEL 1 REVERSE))       → '434241'
```

WEIGHT_STRING() was introduced in MySQL 5.2.4.

C.2.5 Date and Time Functions

The date and time functions take various types of arguments. In general, a function that expects a DATE argument also will accept a DATETIME or TIMESTAMP argument and will ignore the time part of the value. Some functions that expect a TIME value accept DATETIME or TIMESTAMP arguments and ignore the date part.

Many of the functions in this section are able to interpret numeric arguments as temporal values.

```
MONTH('2008-07-25')                             → 7
MONTH(20080725)                                 → 7
```

Similarly, for many functions that return a temporal value, the return value will be converted to a string or number, depending on context.

```
CURDATE()                               → '2008-05-01'
CONCAT('Today is ', CURDATE())          → 'Today is 2008-05-01'
CURDATE() + 0                           → 20080501
```

When conversion of a time or date and time value to number occurs, the numeric value will have a microseconds part of .000000. To chop this off, cast the result to an integer.

```
NOW()+0                                 → 20080501183210.000000
CURTIME()+0                             → 183210.000000
CAST(NOW() AS UNSIGNED)                 → 20080501183210
CAST(CURTIME() AS UNSIGNED)             → 183210
```

Several functions that extract part of a date return 0 for "incomplete" dates. For example, MONTH() and DAYOFMONTH() return 0 for an argument of '2013-00-00'. The same is true for date-part format specifiers as used with DATE_FORMAT().

If you don't supply legal date or time values to date and time functions, you can't expect a reasonable result. Verify your arguments first.

- ADDDATE(*date*, INTERVAL *expr interval*)
  ADDDATE(*date*, *expr*)

  For the first syntax, ADDDATE() takes a date or date and time value *date*, adds a temporal interval to it, and returns the result. This is a synonym for DATE_ADD().

  ```
  ADDDATE('2004-12-01', INTERVAL 1 YEAR)    → '2005-12-01'
  ```

  For the second syntax, ADDDATE() takes a date or date and time value *date*, adds a temporal value representing number of days to it, and returns the result.

  ```
  ADDDATE('2004-12-01', 365)                → '2005-12-01'
  ```

  The second syntax can be rewritten in terms of the first syntax like this:

  ```
  ADDDATE(date, expr) = ADDDATE(date, INTERVAL expr DAY)
  ```

- ADDTIME(*expr1*, *expr2*)

  Adds the two expressions and returns the result. *expr1* should be a time or date and time value, and *expr2* should be time value. Each value can contain a microseconds part.

  ```
  ADDTIME('06:30:00.5', '12:30:00.5')      → '19:00:01.000000'
  ADDTIME('2004-01-01 00:00:00', '12:30:00')  → '2004-01-01 12:30:00'
  ```

- CONVERT_TZ(*date*, *from_zone*, *to_zone*)

  Given the date or date and time value *date*, CONVERT_TZ() treats it as a value in the time zone *from_zone*, converts it to a value in the time zone *to_zone*, and returns the result. Returns NULL if any argument is invalid. Time zones can be specified as described in Section 12.9.1, "Configuring Time Zone Support." For CONVERT_TZ() to work properly, the resulting value must lie within the range of the TIMESTAMP data type.

```
CONVERT_TZ('2009-02-11 00:00:00','US/Central','US/Eastern')
                                      → '2009-02-11 01:00:00'
CONVERT_TZ('2009-02-11','+00:00','-03:00')    → '2009-02-10 21:00:00'
```

- CURDATE()

  Returns the current date in the connection time zone as a DATE value in 'CCYY-MM-DD' format.

  ```
  CURDATE()                             → '2008-05-01'
  ```

- CURRENT_DATE()

  This function is a synonym for CURDATE(). The parentheses are optional.

- CURRENT_TIME()

  This function is a synonym for CURTIME(). The parentheses are optional.

- CURRENT_TIMESTAMP()

  This function is a synonym for NOW(). The parentheses are optional.

- CURTIME()

  Returns the current time of day in the connection time zone as a TIME value in 'hh:mm:ss' format.

  ```
  CURTIME()                             → '18:32:58'
  ```

- DATE(expr)

  Returns the date part of expr, which should be a date or date and time expression.

  ```
  DATE('2008-03-12')                    → '2008-03-12'
  DATE('2008-03-12 16:15:00')           → '2008-03-12'
  ```

- DATE_ADD(date,INTERVAL expr interval)

  Takes a date or date and time value date, adds a temporal interval to it, and returns the result. expr specifies the time value to be added to date (or subtracted, if expr begins with '-'), and interval specifies how to interpret the interval. The result is a DATE value if date is a DATE value and no time-related values are involved in calculating the result. Otherwise, the result is a DATETIME value. The result is NULL if date is not a legal date.

  ```
  DATE_ADD('2009-12-01',INTERVAL 1 YEAR)         → '2010-12-01'
  DATE_ADD('2009-12-01',INTERVAL 60 DAY)         → '2010-01-30'
  DATE_ADD('2009-12-01',INTERVAL -3 MONTH)       → '2009-09-01'
  DATE_ADD('2009-12-01 08:30:00',INTERVAL 12 HOUR) → '2009-12-01 20:30:00'
  ```

  The following table shows the allowable interval values, their meanings, and the format in which values for each interval type should be specified. The keyword INTERVAL and the interval specifiers are not case sensitive.

Interval Type	Meaning	Value Format
MICROSECOND	Microseconds	*uuuuuu*
SECOND	Seconds	*ss*
SECOND_MICROSECOND	Seconds and microseconds	'*ss.uuuuuu*'
MINUTE	Minutes	*mm*
MINUTE_SECOND	Minutes and seconds	'*mm:ss*'
MINUTE_MICROSECOND	Minutes and microseconds	'*mm.uuuuuu*'
HOUR	Hours	*hh*
HOUR_MINUTE	Hours and minutes	'*hh:mm*'
HOUR_SECOND	Hours, minutes, and seconds	'*hh:mm:ss*'
HOUR_MICROSECOND	Hours and microseconds	'*hh.uuuuuu*'
DAY	Days	*DD*
DAY_HOUR	Days and hours	'*DD hh*'
DAY_MINUTE	Days, hours, and minutes	'*DD hh:mm*'
DAY_SECOND	Days, hours, minutes, and seconds	'*DD hh:mm:ss*'
DAY_MICROSECOND	Days and microseconds	'*DD.uuuuuu*'
WEEK	Weeks	*WW*
MONTH	Months	*MM*
QUARTER	Quarters	*QQ*
YEAR	Years	*YY*
YEAR_MONTH	Years and months	'*YY-MM*'

The expression *expr* that is added to the date may be specified as a number or as a string, unless it contains non-digit characters, in which case it must be a string. The delimiter characters may be any punctuation character.

```
DATE_ADD('2005-12-01',INTERVAL '2:3' YEAR_MONTH)  → '2008-03-01'
DATE_ADD('2005-12-01',INTERVAL '2-3' YEAR_MONTH)  → '2008-03-01'
```

The parts of the value of *expr* are matched from right to left against the parts to be expected based on the *interval* specifier. For example, the expected format for HOUR_SECOND is '*hh:mm:ss*'. An *expr* value of '15:21' is interpreted as '00:15:21', not as '15:21:00'.

```
DATE_ADD('2003-12-01 12:00:00',INTERVAL '15:21' HOUR_SECOND)
```
$\rightarrow$ `'2003-12-01 12:15:21'`

If *interval* is YEAR, MONTH, or YEAR_MONTH and the day part of the result is larger than the number of days in the result month, the day is set to the maximum number of days in that month.

```
DATE_ADD('2003-12-31',INTERVAL 2 MONTH)
```
$\rightarrow$ `'2004-02-29'`

An alternative syntax can be used for date addition.

```
'2003-12-31' + INTERVAL 2 MONTH
INTERVAL 2 MONTH + '2003-12-31'
```
$\rightarrow$ `'2004-02-29'`
$\rightarrow$ `'2004-02-29'`

- DATE_FORMAT(*date*, *format*)

  Formats a date or date and time value *date* according to the formatting string *format* and returns the resulting string. DATE_FORMAT() can be used to reformat date or date and time values from the form MySQL uses to provide any format you want.

```
DATE_FORMAT('2004-12-01','%M %e, %Y')
DATE_FORMAT('2004-12-01','The %D of %M')
```
$\rightarrow$ `'December 1, 2004'`
$\rightarrow$ `'The 1st of December'`

  The following table shows the specifiers that are allowed in the formatting string. The ranges shown for the numeric month and day specifiers begin with zero because zero may be produced for dates that are incomplete, such as `'2004-00-13'` or `'1998-12-00'`.

  The '%' character preceding each format code is required. Characters present in the formatting string that are not listed in the table are copied to the result string literally.

Specifier	Meaning
%f	Microseconds in six-digit form (000000, 000001, ...)
%S, %s	Second in two-digit form (00, 01, ..., 59)
%i	Minute in two-digit form (00, 01, ..., 59)
%H	Hour in two-digit form, 24-hour time (00, 01, ..., 23)
%h, %I	Hour in two-digit form, 12-hour time (01, 02, ..., 12)
%k	Hour in numeric form, 24-hour time (0, 1, ..., 23)
%l	Hour in numeric form, 12-hour time (1, 2, ..., 12)
%T	Time in 24-hour form (*hh:mm:ss*)
%r	Time in 12-hour form (*hh:mm:ss* AM or *hh:mm:ss* PM)

Specifier	Meaning
%p	AM or PM
%W	Weekday name (Sunday, Monday, ..., Saturday)
%a	Weekday name in abbreviated form (Sun, Mon, ..., Sat)
%d	Day of the month in two-digit form (00, 01, ..., 31)
%e	Day of the month in numeric form (0, 1, ..., 31)
%D	Day of the month with English suffix (0th, 1st, 2nd, 3rd, ...)
%w	Day of the week in numeric form (0=Sunday, 1=Monday, ..., 6=Saturday)
%j	Day of the year in three-digit form (001, 002, ..., 366)
%U	Week (00, ..., 53), where Sunday is the first day of the week
%u	Week (00, ..., 53), where Monday is the first day of the week
%V	Week (01, ..., 53), where Sunday is the first day of the week
%v	Week (01, ..., 53), where Monday is the first day of the week
%M	Month name (January, February, ..., December)
%b	Month name in abbreviated form (Jan, Feb, ..., Dec)
%m	Month in two-digit form (00, 01, ..., 12)
%c	Month in numeric form (0, 1, ..., 12)
%Y	Year in four-digit form
%y	Year in two-digit form
%X	Year for the week in which Sunday is the first day, four-digit form
%x	Year for the week in which Monday is the first day, four-digit form
%%	A literal '%' character

If you refer to time specifiers for a DATE value, the time part of the value is treated as '00:00:00'.

```
DATE_FORMAT('2004-12-01','%i')                    → '00'
```

- DATE_SUB(*date*,INTERVAL *expr interval*)

DATE_SUB() performs date arithmetic in the same manner as DATE_ADD(), except that *expr* is subtracted from the date or date and time value *date*. See DATE_ADD() for more information.

```
DATE_SUB('2009-12-01',INTERVAL 1 MONTH)              → '2009-11-01'
DATE_SUB('2009-12-01',INTERVAL '13-2' YEAR_MONTH)  → '1996-10-01'
DATE_SUB('2009-12-01 04:53:12',INTERVAL '13-2' MINUTE_SECOND)
                                                     → '2009-12-01 04:40:10'
DATE_SUB('2009-12-01 04:53:12',INTERVAL '13-2' HOUR_MINUTE)
                                                     → '2009-11-30 15:51:12'
```

An alternative syntax is supported for date subtraction.

```
'2009-12-01' - INTERVAL 1 MONTH                      → '2009-11-01'
```

Using this syntax, the INTERVAL clause must be on the right side of the subtraction operator, because you cannot subtract a date from an interval.

- DATEDIFF(*expr1*,*expr2*)

  Returns the difference in number of days between the two expressions, which should be date or date and time values. The result is positive if the first argument is later than the second. Any time part in the values is ignored.

  ```
  DATEDIFF('1987-01-01','1987-01-08')             → -7
  DATEDIFF('1987-01-08','1987-01-01')             → 7
  DATEDIFF('1987-01-01 12:00:00','1987-01-08')    → -7
  DATEDIFF('1987-01-08','1987-01-01 12:00:00')    → 7
  ```

- DAY(*date*)

  This function is a synonym for DAYOFMONTH().

- DAYNAME(*date*)

  Returns a string containing the weekday name for the date value *date*, or NULL if the name cannot be determined.

  ```
  DAYNAME('2004-12-01')                           → 'Wednesday'
  DAYNAME('1900-12-01')                           → 'Saturday'
  DAYNAME('1900-12-00')                           → NULL
  ```

- DAYOFMONTH(*date*)

  Returns the numeric value of the day of the month for the date value *date*, in the range from 0 to 31 (0 for partial dates with no day part).

  ```
  DAYOFMONTH('2002-12-01')                        → 1
  DAYOFMONTH('2002-12-25')                        → 25
  DAYOFMONTH('2002-12-00')                        → 0
  ```

- DAYOFWEEK(*date*)

  Returns the numeric value of the weekday for the date value *date*. Weekday values are in the range from 1 for Sunday to 7 for Saturday, per the ODBC standard. See also the WEEKDAY() function.

  ```
  DAYOFWEEK('2004-12-05')                         → 1
  DAYNAME('2004-12-05')                           → 'Sunday'
  DAYOFWEEK('2004-12-18')                         → 7
  DAYNAME('2004-12-18')                           → 'Saturday'
  ```

- DAYOFYEAR(*date*)

  Returns the numeric value of the day of the year for the date value *date*, in the range from 1 to 366.

  ```
  DAYOFYEAR('2002-12-01')                          → 335
  DAYOFYEAR('2004-12-31')                          → 366
  ```

- EXTRACT(*interval* FROM *datetime*)

  Returns the part of the date and time value *datetime* indicated by *interval*, which may be any of the interval specifiers that are allowed for DATE_ADD().

  ```
  EXTRACT(YEAR FROM '2002-12-01 13:42:19')         → 2002
  EXTRACT(MONTH FROM '2002-12-01 13:42:19')        → 12
  EXTRACT(DAY FROM '2002-12-01 13:42:19')          → 1
  EXTRACT(HOUR_MINUTE FROM '2002-12-01 13:42:19')  → 1342
  EXTRACT(SECOND FROM '2002-12-01 13:42:19')       → 19
  ```

  EXTRACT() can be used with dates that have "missing" parts.

  ```
  EXTRACT(YEAR FROM '2004-00-12')                  → 2004
  EXTRACT(MONTH FROM '2004-00-12')                 → 0
  EXTRACT(DAY FROM '2004-00-12')                   → 12
  ```

- FROM_DAYS(*n*)

  Given a numeric value *n* representing the number of days since the year 0 (typically obtained by calling TO_DAYS()), returns the corresponding date.

  ```
  TO_DAYS('2009-12-01')                            → 734107
  FROM_DAYS(734107 + 3)                            → '2009-12-04'
  ```

  FROM_DAYS() is intended only for dates covered by the Gregorian calendar (1582 on).

- FROM_UNIXTIME(*unix_timestamp*)

  FROM_UNIXTIME(*unix_timestamp*,*format*)

  Given a Unix timestamp value *unix_timestamp* such as is returned by UNIX_TIMESTAMP(), returns a date and time in the connection time zone as a DATETIME value in '*CCYY-MM-DD hh:mm:ss*' format. If the *format* argument is given, the return value is formatted as a string just as it would be by the DATE_FORMAT() function.

  ```
  UNIX_TIMESTAMP()                                 → 1209684883
  FROM_UNIXTIME(1209684883)                        → '2008-05-01 18:34:43'
  FROM_UNIXTIME(1209684883,'%Y')                   → '2008'
  ```

- GET_FORMAT(*val_type*,*format_type*)

  Returns a format string of the type that can be used with the DATE_FORMAT(), TIME_FORMAT(), and STR_TO_DATE() functions. The *val_type* argument indicates a data type and can be DATE, TIME, DATETIME, or TIMESTAMP. The *format_type* argument indicates which style of format string to return and can be 'EUR' (European), 'INTERNAL' (internal representation), 'ISO' (ISO 9075, not ISO 8601), 'JIS' (Japanese Industrial Standards), or 'USA' (United States).

GET_FORMAT() returns format strings for each combination of *val_type* and *format_type* as shown in the following table.

val_type	format_type	Format String
DATE	'EUR'	'%d.%m.%Y'
DATE	'INTERNAL'	'%Y%m%d'
DATE	'ISO'	'%Y-%m-%d'
DATE	'JIS'	'%Y-%m-%d'
DATE	'USA'	'%m.%d.%Y'
TIME	'EUR'	'%H.%i.%s'
TIME	'INTERNAL'	'%H%i%s'
TIME	'ISO'	'%H:%i:%s'
TIME	'JIS'	'%H:%i:%s'
TIME	'USA'	'%h:%i:%s %p'
DATETIME	'EUR'	'%Y-%m-%d %H.%i.%s'
DATETIME	'INTERNAL'	'%Y%m%d%H%i%s'
DATETIME	'ISO'	'%Y-%m-%d %H:%i:%s'
DATETIME	'JIS'	'%Y-%m-%d %H:%i:%s'
DATETIME	'USA'	'%Y-%m-%d %H.%i.%s'

Note that the date part of the 'EUR' and 'USA' format strings for DATETIME differs from the 'EUR' and 'USA' format strings for DATE.

- HOUR(*time*)

Returns the numeric value of the hour for the time value *time*, in the range from 0 to 23.

```
HOUR('12:31:58')                              → 12
HOUR(123158)                                  → 12
```

- LAST_DAY(*date*)

  Returns the date for the last day of the month in which the argument falls. *date* should be a date or date and time value.

  ```
  LAST_DAY('2003-07-01')                    → '2003-07-31'
  LAST_DAY('2003-07-01 12:30:00')           → '2003-07-31'
  ```

- LOCALTIME()
  LOCALTIMESTAMP()

  These functions are synonyms for NOW(). The parentheses are optional.

- MAKEDATE(*year*, *day_of_year*)

  Given a year and a day of the year, returns a date value. The result is NULL if *day_of_year* is less than 1.

  ```
  MAKEDATE(2010,365)                        → '2010-12-31'
  MAKEDATE(2010,367)                        → '2011-01-02'
  MAKEDATE(2010,0)                          → NULL
  ```

- MAKETIME(*hour*, *minute*, *second*)

  Returns a time value constructed from the given hour, minute, and second, or NULL if the arguments are out of range. The minute and second values should be in the range from 0 to 59. The hour can be outside that range. If the hour is negative, the result is negative.

  ```
  MAKETIME(0,0,0)                           → '00:00:00'
  MAKETIME(12,59,59)                        → '12:59:59'
  MAKETIME(12,59,60)                        → NULL
  MAKETIME(-12,59,59)                       → '-12:59:59'
  ```

- MICROSECOND(*expr*)

  Returns the microsecond part of the given time or date and time value. The return value has a range of 0 to 999999.

  ```
  MICROSECOND('00:00:00.000001');           → 1
  MICROSECOND('2004-06-30: 23:59:59.5');    → 500000
  ```

- MINUTE(*time*)

  Returns the numeric value of the minute for the time value *time*, in the range from 0 to 59.

  ```
  MINUTE('12:31:58')                        → 31
  MINUTE(123158)                            → 31
  ```

- MONTH(*date*)

  Returns the numeric value of the month of the year for the date value *date*, in the range from 0 to 12 (0 for partial dates with no month part).

```
MONTH('2002-12-01')                                  → 12
MONTH(20021201)                                      → 12
MONTH('2002-00-01')                                  → 0
```

- MONTHNAME(*date*)

  Returns a string containing the month name for the date value *date*, or NULL for partial dates with no month part.

```
MONTHNAME('2002-12-01')                              → 'December'
MONTHNAME(20021201)                                  → 'December'
MONTHNAME('2002-00-01')                              → NULL
```

- NOW()

  Returns the current date and time in the connection time zone as a DATETIME value in '*CCYY-MM-DD hh:mm:ss*' format.

```
NOW()                                                → '2008-05-01 18:36:09'
```

  NOW() returns the date and time when the statement in which it appears began to execute, regardless of how long the statement takes. If NOW() occurs within a stored routine or trigger, it returns the time when the routine or trigger began executing. (Compare this behavior with that of SYSDATE().)

- PERIOD_ADD(*period*,*n*)

  Adds *n* months to the period value *period* and returns the result. The return value format is *CCYYMM*. The *period* argument format may be *CCYYMM* or *YYMM* (neither is a date value).

```
PERIOD_ADD(201002,12)                                → 201102
PERIOD_ADD(0802,-3)                                  → 200711
```

- PERIOD_DIFF(*period1*,*period2*)

  Takes the difference of the period-valued arguments and returns the number of months between them. The arguments may be in the format *CCYYMM* or *YYMM* (neither is a date value).

```
PERIOD_DIFF(200302,200202)                           → 12
PERIOD_DIFF(200711,0802)                             → -3
```

- QUARTER(*date*)

  Returns the numeric value of the quarter of the year for the date value *date*, in the range from 1 to 4.

```
QUARTER('2008-12-01')                                → 4
QUARTER('2009-01-01')                                → 1
```

- SECOND(*time*)

  Returns the numeric value of the second for the time value *time*, in the range from 0 to 59.

  ```
  SECOND('12:31:58')                          → 58
  SECOND(123158)                              → 58
  ```

- SEC_TO_TIME(*seconds*)

  Given a number of seconds *seconds*, returns the corresponding time as a TIME value in '*hh:mm:ss*' format.

  ```
  SEC_TO_TIME(29834)                          → '08:17:14'
  ```

- STR_TO_DATE(*str*, *format_str*)

  Interprets the string argument *str* using the formatting argument *format_str* and returns a TIME, DATE, or DATETIME value, depending on the formatting specifiers present in *format_str*. You can use this function to interpret temporal values in non-ISO format. STR_TO_DATE() performs the inverse operation of DATE_FORMAT(), and the format specifiers listed in the description of DATE_FORMAT() also are legal for STR_TO_DATE(). If *str* is illegal or cannot be interpreted using the given format string, the result is NULL.

  ```
  STR_TO_DATE('3/16/1960','%m/%d/%Y')          → '1960-03-16'
  STR_TO_DATE('12.20.32','%H.%i.%s')           → '12:20:32'
  STR_TO_DATE('3/16/1960 12:20:32','%m/%d/%Y %H:%i:%s')
                                               → '1960-03-16 12:20:32'
  STR_TO_DATE('3/16/1960','%m-%d-%Y')          → NULL
  ```

- SUBDATE(*date*, INTERVAL *expr interval*)
  SUBDATE(*date*, *expr*)

  For the first syntax, SUBDATE() takes a date or date and time value *date*, subtracts a temporal interval from it, and returns the result. This is a synonym for DATE_SUB().

  ```
  SUBDATE('2009-12-01',INTERVAL 1 MONTH)       → '2009-11-01'
  ```

  For the second syntax, SUBDATE() takes a date or date and time value *date*, subtracts a temporal value representing number of days from it, and returns the result. This is similar to the corresponding syntax for ADDDATE().

  ```
  SUBDATE('2009-12-01',30)                     → '2009-11-01'
  ```

- SUBTIME(*expr1*, *expr2*)

  Subtracts the second expression from the first and returns the result. *expr1* should be a time or date and time value, and *expr2* should be a time value. The values can contain a microseconds part.

  ```
  SUBTIME('06:30:00.5','12:30:00.5')           → '-06:00:00.000000'
  SUBTIME('2009-01-01 00:00:00','12:30:00')    → '2008-12-31 11:30:00'
  ```

- SYSDATE()

Returns the current date and time in the connection time zone as a DATETIME value in `'CCYY-MM-DD hh:mm:ss'` format. This function is similar to NOW(), except that as of MySQL 5.0.13, SYSDATE() returns the date and time when it was invoked, whereas NOW() returns the beginning execution time of the statement within which it occurs. (See the description of NOW() for more detail.) To make SYSDATE() behave like NOW(), start the server with the --sysdate-is-now option (available as of 5.0.20).

- TIME(*expr*)

Returns the time part of *expr*, which should be a time or date and time expression.

```
TIME('16:15:00')                            → '16:15:00'
TIME('2005-03-12 16:15:00')                 → '16:15:00'
```

- TIME_FORMAT(*time*, *format*)

Formats the time value *time* according to the formatting string format and returns the resulting string. This function also accepts DATETIME or TIMESTAMP arguments. The formatting string is like that used by DATE_FORMAT(), but the only specifiers that may be used are those that are time-related. Other specifiers result in a NULL value or 0.

```
TIME_FORMAT('12:31:58','%H %i')             → '12 31'
TIME_FORMAT(123158,'%H %i')                 → '12 31'
```

- TIME_TO_SEC(*time*)

Given a value *time* representing elapsed time, returns a number representing the corresponding number of seconds. The return value may be passed to SEC_TO_TIME() to convert it back to a time.

```
TIME_TO_SEC('08:17:14')                     → 29834
SEC_TO_TIME(29834)                          → '08:17:14'
```

If given a DATETIME or TIMESTAMP value, TIME_TO_SEC() ignores the date part.

```
TIME_TO_SEC('2012-03-26 08:17:14')          → 29834
```

- TIMEDIFF(*expr1*, *expr2*)

Returns the time difference between the two expressions. The first and second expressions are the start and end times, respectively. They should both be time or date and time values; you cannot mix a time value and a date and time value.

```
TIMEDIFF('00:00:00','09:30:45')             → '-09:30:45'
TIMEDIFF('09:30:45','00:00:00')             → '09:30:45'
```

- TIMESTAMP(*expr1*[, *expr2*])

The single-argument form takes a date or date and time value *expr1* and returns a DATETIME value. The two-argument form adds the time value *expr2* to *expr1* and returns the result as a DATETIME value.

```
TIMESTAMP('1985-12-14');                           → '1985-12-14 00:00:00'
TIMESTAMP('1985-12-14 09:00:00');                  → '1985-12-14 09:00:00'
TIMESTAMP('1985-12-14','18:00:00');                → '1985-12-14 18:00:00'
TIMESTAMP('1985-12-14 09:00:00','18:00:00');       → '1985-12-15 03:00:00'
TIMESTAMP('1985-12-14 09:00:00','-18:00:00');      → '1985-12-13 15:00:00'
```

- TIMESTAMPADD(*interval*, *expr1*, *expr2*)

  Interprets *expr1* as an integer number of units given by the *interval* argument, adds it to the date or date and time value *expr2*, and returns the result. The allowable *interval* values are FRAC_SECOND, SECOND, MINUTE, HOUR, DAY, WEEK, MONTH, QUARTER, and YEAR. Any of these values also may be given with a prefix of SQL_TSI_. As of 5.0.60/5.1.24, FRAC_SECOND is deprecated; instead, MICROSECOND is preferred for specifying a unit of microseconds.

  ```
  TIMESTAMPADD(DAY,12,'1995-07-01')              → '1995-07-13'
  TIMESTAMPADD(MONTH,12,'1995-07-01')            → '1996-07-01'
  TIMESTAMPADD(SQL_TSI_MONTH,12,'1995-07-01')    → '1996-07-01'
  ```

- TIMESTAMPDIFF(*interval*, *expr1*, *expr2*)

  Calculates the difference between the date or date and time expressions *expr1* and *expr2*, and returns the result in the units given by the *interval* argument. Allowable *interval* values are the same as those given in the description for TIMESTAMPADD().

  ```
  TIMESTAMPDIFF(DAY,'1995-07-01','1995-08-01')     → 31
  TIMESTAMPDIFF(MONTH,'1995-07-01','1995-08-01')   → 1
  ```

- TO_DAYS(*date*)

  Returns a numeric value representing the date value *date* converted to the number of days since the year 0. The return value may be passed to FROM_DAYS() to convert it back to a date.

  ```
  TO_DAYS('2010-12-01')                → 734472
  FROM_DAYS(734472 - 365)              → '2009-12-01'
  ```

  If given a DATETIME or TIMESTAMP value, TO_DAYS() ignores the time part.

  ```
  TO_DAYS('2010-12-01 12:14:37')       → 734472
  ```

  TO_DAYS() is intended only for dates covered by the Gregorian calendar (1582 on).

- UNIX_TIMESTAMP()
  UNIX_TIMESTAMP(*date*)

  When called with no arguments, returns the number of seconds since the reference date '1970-01-01 00:00:00' UTC. When called with a date-valued argument *date*, returns the number of seconds between the reference date and the argument. *date* may be specified several ways: as a DATE, DATETIME, or TIMESTAMP value, or as a number in the format *CCYYMMDD* or *YYMMDD*. The server interprets *date* as a value in the connection time zone and converts it to UTC, unless the value comes from a TIMESTAMP column (for which the stored value is already in UTC).

```
UNIX_TIMESTAMP()                    → 1209685069
UNIX_TIMESTAMP('2007-12-01')        → 1196488800
UNIX_TIMESTAMP(20071201)            → 1196488800
```

- UTC_DATE()

Returns the current UTC date as a DATE value in 'CCYY:MM:DD' format. The parentheses are optional.

```
UTC_DATE()                          → '2008-05-01'
```

- UTC_TIME()

Returns the current UTC time as a TIME value in 'hh:mm:ss' format. The parentheses are optional.

```
UTC_TIME()                          → '23:37:56'
```

- UTC_TIMESTAMP()

Returns the current UTC date and time as a DATETIME value in 'CCYY-MM-DD hh:mm:ss' format. The parentheses are optional.

```
UTC_TIMESTAMP()                     → '2008-05-01 23:38:02'
```

- WEEK(date[,mode])

When called with a single argument, returns a number representing the week of the year for the date value date, in the range from 0 to 53. The week is assumed to start on Sunday. When called with two arguments, WEEK() returns the same kind of value, but the mode argument indicates the day on which the week starts and whether to return a value in the range from 0 to 53 or 1 to 53. The following table indicates the meaning of the possible mode values.

Mode	Starting Day	Return Range	Meaning
0	Sunday	0..53	Week 1 is first week containing a Sunday
1	Monday	0..53	Week 1 is first week with more than three days
2	Sunday	1..53	Week 1 is first week containing a Sunday
3	Monday	1..53	Week 1 is first week with more than three days
4	Sunday	0..53	Week 1 is first week with more than three days
5	Monday	0..53	Week 1 is first week containing a Monday
6	Sunday	1..53	Week 1 is first week with more than three days
7	Monday	1..53	Week 1 is first week containing a Monday

If *mode* is missing, the value of the `default_week_format` system variable is used.

WEEK('2003-12-08')	→ 49
WEEK('2003-12-08',0)	→ 49
WEEK('2003-12-08',1)	→ 50

A `WEEK()` value of 0 indicates that the date occurs prior to the first instance of the week starting day (Sunday or Monday, depending on the *mode* value).

WEEK('2005-01-01')	→ 0
DAYNAME('2005-01-01')	→ 'Saturday'
WEEK('2006-01-01',1)	→ 0
DAYNAME('2006-01-01')	→ 'Sunday'

- WEEKDAY(*date*)

  Returns the numeric value of the weekday for the date value *date*, or NULL if the name cannot be determined. Weekday values are in the range from 0 for Monday to 6 for Sunday; see also the DAYOFWEEK() function.

WEEKDAY('2002-12-08')	→ 6
DAYNAME('2002-12-08')	→ 'Sunday'
WEEKDAY('2002-12-16')	→ 0
DAYNAME('2002-12-16')	→ 'Monday'
WEEKDAY('2002-12-00')	→ NULL

- WEEKOFYEAR(*date*)

  This is the same as `WEEK(date,3)`.

- YEAR(*date*)

  Returns the numeric value of the year for the date value *date*.

YEAR('2002-12-01')	→ 2002
YEAR(20021201)	→ 2002

- YEARWEEK(*date*[,*mode*])

  Returns a number in the format *CCYYWW* representing the year and week of the year for the date value *date*. The *mode* argument, if given, is the same as for the WEEK() function.

YEARWEEK('2006-01-01')	→ 200601
YEARWEEK('2006-01-01',0)	→ 200601
YEARWEEK('2006-01-01',1)	→ 200552

  The year for the result may differ from the year in the argument for the first or last week of the year.

WEEK('2008-01-01')	→ 0
YEARWEEK('2008-01-01')	→ 200752

C.2.6 Summary Functions

Summary functions are also known as "aggregate" functions. They calculate a single value based on a group of values. However, the resulting value is based only on non-NULL values from the selected rows (with the exception that COUNT(*) counts all rows). Summary functions can be used to summarize an entire set of values, or to produce summaries for each subgroup of a set of values when the query includes a GROUP BY clause. See Section 1.4.9.9, "Generating Summaries."

For the examples in this section, assume the existence of a table mytbl with an integer column mycol that contains eight rows with the values 1, 3, 5, 5, 7, 9, 9, and NULL.

```
mysql> SELECT mycol FROM mytbl;
+-------+
| mycol |
+-------+
|     1 |
|     3 |
|     5 |
|     5 |
|     7 |
|     9 |
|     9 |
|  NULL |
+-------+
```

- AVG([DISTINCT] expr)

  Returns the average value of expr for all non-NULL values in the selected rows. Returns NULL if there are no non-NULL values.

  ```
  SELECT AVG(mycol) FROM mytbl              → 5.5714
  SELECT AVG(mycol)*2 FROM mytbl            → 11.1429
  SELECT AVG(mycol*2) FROM mytbl            → 11.1429
  ```

  DISTINCT is allowable as of MySQL 5.0.3. It causes AVG() to return the average of the distinct expr values.

- BIT_AND(expr)

  Returns the bitwise AND value of expr for all non-NULL values in the selected rows. Returns ~0 if there are no non-NULL values.

  ```
  SELECT BIT_AND(mycol) FROM mytbl          → 1
  ```

- BIT_OR(expr)

  Returns the bitwise OR value of expr for all non-NULL values in the selected rows. Returns 0 if there are no non-NULL values.

  ```
  SELECT BIT_OR(mycol) FROM mytbl           → 15
  ```

- BIT_XOR(expr)

Returns the bitwise exclusive-OR value of `expr` for all non-NULL values in the elected rows. Returns 0 if there are no non-NULL values.

```
SELECT BIT_XOR(mycol) FROM mytbl                    → 5
```

- `COUNT(expr)`
  `COUNT(*)`
  `COUNT(DISTINCT expr1,expr2,...)`

With an expression argument, returns a count of the number of non-NULL values in the result set. Returns 0 if there are no non-NULL values. With an argument of `*`, returns a count of all rows in the result set, regardless of their contents.

```
SELECT COUNT(mycol) FROM mytbl                      → 7
SELECT COUNT(*) FROM mytbl                          → 8
```

For MyISAM tables, COUNT(*) with no WHERE clause is optimized to return the number of rows in the table named in the FROM clause very quickly. When more than one table is named, COUNT(*) returns the product of the number of rows in the individual tables.

```
SELECT COUNT(*) FROM mytbl AS m1 INNER JOIN mytbl AS m2
                                                    → 64
```

COUNT(DISTINCT) can be used to count the number of distinct non-NULL values.

```
SELECT COUNT(DISTINCT mycol) FROM mytbl             → 5
SELECT COUNT(DISTINCT MOD(mycol,3)) FROM mytbl      → 3
```

If multiple expressions are given, COUNT(DISTINCT) counts the number of distinct combinations of non-NULL values.

- `GROUP_CONCAT([DISTINCT] var_list [ORDER BY ...] [SEPARATOR str])`

This function concatenates the non-NULL values in a group of strings and returns the result. It returns NULL if there are no non-NULL values. You can use DISTINCT to remove duplicates, ORDER BY to sort the results, and SEPARATOR to specify the delimiter between strings. By default, GROUP_CONCAT() does not perform duplicate removal or sorting, and separates values by commas.

Values returned by GROUP_CONCAT() are limited in length to the value of the `group_concat_max_len` system variable. You can change the value of this variable to enable longer values.

```
mysql> CREATE TABLE t (name CHAR(10));
mysql> INSERT INTO t VALUES('dog'),('cat'),('rat'),('dog'),('rat');
mysql> SELECT GROUP_CONCAT(name) FROM t;
+---------------------+
| GROUP_CONCAT(name)  |
+---------------------+
| dog,cat,rat,dog,rat |
```

```
+---------------------+
mysql> SELECT GROUP_CONCAT(name SEPARATOR ':') FROM t;
+--------------------------------+
| GROUP_CONCAT(name SEPARATOR ':') |
+--------------------------------+
| dog:cat:rat:dog:rat            |
+--------------------------------+
mysql> SELECT GROUP_CONCAT(name ORDER BY name DESC) FROM t;
+------------------------------------+
| GROUP_CONCAT(name ORDER BY name DESC) |
+------------------------------------+
| rat,rat,dog,dog,cat                |
+------------------------------------+
mysql> SELECT GROUP_CONCAT(DISTINCT name ORDER BY name) FROM t;
+-----------------------------------------+
| GROUP_CONCAT(DISTINCT name ORDER BY name) |
+-----------------------------------------+
| cat,dog,rat                             |
+-----------------------------------------+
```

- MAX([DISTINCT] *expr*)

  Returns the maximum value of *expr* for all non-NULL values in the selected rows. Returns NULL if there are no non-NULL values. MAX() also can be used with strings or temporal values, in which case it returns the lexically or temporally greatest value.

  ```
  SELECT MAX(mycol) FROM mytbl                          → 9
  ```

  DISTINCT causes MAX() to return the maximum of the distinct *expr* values (which does not change the result).

- MIN([DISTINCT] *expr*)

  Returns the minimum value of *expr* for all non-NULL values in the selected rows. Returns NULL if there are no non-NULL values. MIN() also may be used with strings or temporal values, in which case it returns the lexically or temporally least value.

  ```
  SELECT MIN(mycol) FROM mytbl                          → 1
  ```

  DISTINCT causes MIN() to return the minimum of the distinct *expr* values (which does not change the result).

- STD(*expr*)
  STDDEV(*expr*)
  STDDEV_POP(*expr*)

  Returns the population standard deviation of *expr* for all non-NULL values in the selected rows. Returns NULL if there are no non-NULL values.

  ```
  SELECT STDDEV_POP(mycol) FROM mytbl                   → 2.7701
  ```

STDDEV_POP() was introduced in MySQL 5.0.3.

- STDDEV_SAMP(*expr*)

  Returns the sample standard deviation of *expr* for all non-NULL values in the selected rows. Returns NULL if there are no non-NULL values.

  SELECT STDDEV_SAMP(mycol) FROM mytbl   → 2.9921

  STDDEV_SAMP() was introduced in MySQL 5.0.3.

- SUM([DISTINCT] *expr*)

  Returns the sum of *expr* for all non-NULL values in the selected rows. Returns NULL if there are no non-NULL values.

  SELECT SUM(mycol) FROM mytbl   → 39

  DISTINCT causes SUM() to return the sum of the distinct *expr* values.

- VARIANCE(*expr*)
  VAR_POP(*expr*)

  Returns the population variance of *expr* for all non-NULL values in the selected rows. Returns NULL if there are no non-NULL values.

  SELECT VAR_POP(mycol) FROM mytbl   → 7.6735

  VAR_POP() was introduced in MySQL 5.0.3.

- VAR_SAMP(*expr*)

  Returns the sample variance of *expr* for all non-NULL values in the selected rows. Returns NULL if there are no non-NULL values.

  SELECT VAR_SAMP(mycol) FROM mytbl   → 8.9524

  VAR_SAMP() was introduced in MySQL 5.0.3.

C.2.7 Security and Compression Functions

These functions perform various security-related operations such as encrypting or compressing strings. Several of these functions come in pairs, with one function producing an encrypted value and the other performing decryption. Such pairs of functions typically use a string as a key or password value. You must decrypt a value with the same key used to encrypt it if you want to get back the original value. The decrypted result will be meaningless otherwise.

If you want to save the result in a database when using encryption functions that return a binary string, it's common to use a column that is one of the BLOB types.

- AES_DECRYPT(*str*,*key_str*)

  Given an encrypted string *str* obtained as a result of a call to AES_ENCRYPT(), decrypts it using the key string *key_str* and returns the resulting string. Returns NULL if either argument is NULL.

```
AES_DECRYPT(AES_ENCRYPT('secret','scramble'),'scramble')
                                               → 'secret'
```

- AES_ENCRYPT(*str*, *key_str*)

Encrypts the string *str* with the key string *key_str* using the Advanced Encryption Standard (AES) and a 128-bit key length. Returns the result as a binary string, or NULL if either argument is NULL. The string may be decoded with AES_DECRYPT(), using the same key string.

- COMPRESS(*str*)

Returns a compressed version of the argument string as a binary string, or NULL if the server was not compiled with a compression library.

- DECODE(*str*, *key_str*)

Given an encrypted string *str* obtained as a result of a call to ENCODE(), decrypts it using the key string *key_str*. Returns the resulting string, or NULL if *str* is NULL.

```
DECODE(ENCODE('secret','scramble'),'scramble')    → 'secret'
```

- DES_DECRYPT(*str* [, *key_str*])

Decrypts a string *str*, which should be an encrypted value produced by DES_ENCRYPT(). If SSL support has not been enabled or decryption fails, DES_DECRYPT() returns NULL.

If a *key_str* argument is given, it is used as the decryption key. If no *key_str* argument is given, DES_DECRYPT() uses a key from the server's DES key file to decrypt the string. The key number is determined from bits 0-6 of the first byte of the encrypted string. The location of the key file is specified at server startup time by means of the --des-key-file option. If different keys are used to encrypt and decrypt the string, the result will not be meaningful.

If *str* does not look like an encrypted string, DES_DECRYPT() returns the string unchanged. (This will occur, for example, if the first byte does not have bit 7 set.)

Use of the single-argument form of DES_DECRYPT() requires the SUPER privilege.

- DES_ENCRYPT(*str* [, {*key_num*|*key_str*}])

Performs DES encryption on the string *str* and returns the encrypted result as a binary string. The encrypted string may be decrypted with DES_DECRYPT(). If SSL support has not been enabled or encryption fails, DES_ENCRYPT() returns NULL.

If a *key_str* argument is given, it is used as the encryption key. If a *key_num* argument is given, it should be a value from 0 to 9, indicating the key number of an entry in the server's DES key file. In this case, the encryption key is taken from that entry. If no *key_str* or *key_num* argument is given, the first key from the DES key file is used to perform encryption. (This is not necessarily the same as specifying a *key_num* value of 0.)

The first byte of the resulting string indicates how the string was encrypted. This byte will have bit 7 set, and bits 0-6 indicate the key number. The number is 0 to 9 to specify which key in the DES key file was used to encrypt the string, or 127 if a *key_str* argument was used. For example, if you encrypt a string using key 3, the first byte of the result will be 131 (that is, 128+3). If you encrypt a string with a *key_str* value, the first byte will be 255 (that is, 128+127).

For encryption performed on the basis of a key number, the server reads the DES key file to find the corresponding key string. The location of the key file is specified at server startup time by means of the `--des-key-file` option. The key file contains lines of the following format:

key_num key_str

Each *key_num* value should be a number from 0 to 9 and the *key_str* value is the corresponding encryption key. *key_num* and *key_str* should be separated by at least one whitespace character. Lines in the key file may be arranged in any order.

Unlike `DES_DECRYPT()`, `DES_ENCRYPT()` does not require the SUPER privilege to use keys from the DES key file. (Anyone can encrypt information based on the key file; only privileged users are allowed to use it for decryption.)

- `ENCODE(str, key_str)`

Encrypts the string *str* using the key string *key_str* and returns the result as a binary string. The string may be decoded with `DECODE()`, using the same key string.

- `ENCRYPT(str [,salt])`

Encrypts the string *str* and returns the resulting string, or NULL if either argument is NULL. This is a non-reversible encryption. The *salt* argument, if given, should be a string with two characters or more characters. By specifying a *salt* value, the encrypted result for *str* will be the same each time. With no *salt* argument, MySQL uses a random value, so identical calls to `ENCRYPT()` yield different results over time.

```
ENCRYPT('secret','AB')                      → 'ABS5SGh1EL6bk'
ENCRYPT('secret','AB')                      → 'ABS5SGh1EL6bk'
ENCRYPT('secret')                           → '9ai/2GobGFmXY'
ENCRYPT('secret')                           → 'Ea5Y.zUlAoUz.'
```

`ENCRYPT()` uses the Unix `crypt()` system call and is subject to the way `crypt()` operates for those systems on which it is present. In particular, on some systems, `crypt()` looks at only the first eight characters of the string to be encrypted. If `crypt()` is unavailable on your system, `ENCRYPT()` always returns NULL.

It is not recommended that *str* contain multi-byte characters unless it uses utf8 because `crypt()` expects the string to be null-terminated.

- MD5(*str*)

  Calculates a 128-bit checksum from the string *str* based on the RSA Data Security, Inc. MD5 Message-Digest algorithm. The return value is a binary string consisting of 32 hexadecimal digits, or NULL if the argument is NULL.

  MD5('secret')   → '5ebe2294ecd0e0f08eab7690d2a6ee69'

  See also the SHA1() function.

- OLD_PASSWORD(*str*)

  This function returns the encrypted password value that PASSWORD() returned prior to MySQL 4.1.

- PASSWORD(*str*)

  Given a string *str*, calculates and returns an encrypted password string of the form used in the MySQL grant tables. This is a non-reversible encryption.

  PASSWORD('secret')   → '*14E65567ABDB5135D0CFD9A70B3032C179A49EE7'

  PASSWORD() does *not* use the same algorithm as the one used on Unix to encrypt user account passwords. For that type of encryption, use ENCRYPT().

  If the old_passwords system variable is non-zero, PASSWORD() returns the password encrypted using the same hashing algorithm that was used prior to MySQL 4.1. In this case, PASSWORD() and OLD_PASSWORD() return the same value. old_passwords can be enabled by using a SET GLOBAL old_passwords = 1 statement or by starting the server with the --old-passwords option,

- SHA1(*str*)
  SHA(*str*)

  Calculates a 160-bit checksum from the string *str* using the Secure Hash Algorithm. The return value is a binary string consisting of 40 hexadecimal digits, or NULL if the argument is NULL.

  SHA1('secret')   → 'e5e9fa1ba31ecd1ae84f75caaa474f3a663f05f4'

- SHA2(*str*, *hash_length*)

  This function is similar to SHA1(), but is more secure. It hashes the first argument, producing a result with a bit length indicated by the second argument. The hash length must be 224, 256, 384, or 512. The result is a binary string of the specified number of bits, represented as hexadecimal digits. The result is NULL if either argument is NULL or the hash length is invalid.

  SHA2('secret',224)
          → '95c7fbca92ac5083afda62a564a3d014fc3b72c9140e3cb99ea6bf12'

  SHA2() was introduced in MySQL 6.0.5.

- UNCOMPRESS(*str*)

  Given a string that was compressed with the COMPRESS() function, UNCOMPRESS() returns the original string. Returns NULL if the argument is not a compressed string or if the server was not compiled with a compression library.

- UNCOMPRESSED_LENGTH(*str*)

  Given a string that was compressed with the COMPRESS() function, returns the length of the original uncompressed string. Returns NULL if the server was not compiled with a compression library.

C.2.8 Advisory Locking Functions

The functions in this section are used for advisory (cooperative) locking. You can use them to write applications that cooperate based on the status of an agreed-upon lock name. The primary functions for this purpose are GET_LOCK() and RELEASE_LOCK(), which are used to acquire and release locks. Two other functions, IS_FREE_LOCK() and IS_USED_LOCK(), can be used to query the status of a lock or determine which client holds a lock.

The basic for advisory locking is that you lock a name, which is nothing more than a string. An advisory lock is private in the sense that only the client that holds a lock on a name can release it, and global in the sense that any client can query the status of a lock name.

To acquire a lock, call GET_LOCK(*str*, *timeout*), where *str* indicates the lock name and *timeout* is a timeout value in seconds. GET_LOCK() returns 1 if the lock was obtained successfully within the timeout period, 0 if the lock attempt failed due to timing out, or NULL if an error occurred.

The *timeout* value determines how long to wait while attempting to obtain the lock, not the duration of the lock. After it is obtained, the lock remains in force until released.

The following call acquires a lock named 'Nellie', waiting up to 10 seconds for it:

```
GET_LOCK('Nellie',10)
```

The lock applies only to the string name itself. It does not lock a database, a table, or any rows or columns within a table. In other words, the lock does not prevent any other client from doing anything to database tables, which is why GET_LOCK() locking is advisory only—it simply enables other cooperating clients to determine whether the lock is in force.

A client that has a lock on a name blocks attempts by other clients to lock the name (or attempts by other threads within a multi-threaded client that maintains multiple connections to the server). Suppose that client 1 locks the string 'Nellie'. If client 2 attempts to lock the same string, it will block until client 1 releases the lock or until the timeout period expires. If client 1 releases the lock within the timeout period, client 2 will acquire the lock successfully. Otherwise, client 2 will fail.

Because two clients cannot lock a given string at the same time, applications that agree on a name can use the lock status of that name as an indicator of when it is safe to perform operations related to the name. For example, you can construct a lock name based on a unique key value for a row in a table to enable cooperative locking of that row.

To release a lock explicitly, call RELEASE_LOCK() with the lock name:

```
RELEASE_LOCK('Nellie')
```

RELEASE_LOCK() returns 1 if the lock was released successfully, 0 if the lock was held by another connection (you can release only your own locks), or NULL if no such lock exists.

Any lock held by a client is automatically released if the same client issues another GET_LOCK() call, because only one string at a time can be locked per client connection. In this case, the lock being held is released before the new lock is obtained, even if the lock name is the same. A lock also is released when the client's connection to the server terminates. Note that if you have a very long-running client and its connection times out due to inactivity, any lock held by the client is released.

To test the status of a lock name, you have two options:

- Invoke IS_FREE_LOCK(*str*), which returns 1 if the name is available (not currently being used as a lock), 0 if the name is in use, or NULL if an error occurred.

- Invoke IS_USED_LOCK(*str*), which returns NULL if there is no lock or the connection ID of the client that holds it if there is one.

You can also use GETLOCK(*str*, 0) as a simple poll to determine without waiting whether a lock on *str* is in force. However, this has the side effect of locking the string if it is not currently locked, so you must remember to call RELEASE_LOCK() as appropriate.

All advisory locking functions return NULL if the lock name argument is NULL.

- GET_LOCK(*str*, *timeout*)

  Attempt to acquire an advisory lock with the name indicated by the string *str* within a timeout value of *timeout* seconds. GET_LOCK() returns 1 if the lock was obtained successfully within the timeout period, 0 if the lock attempt failed due to timing out, or NULL if an error occurred.

- IS_FREE_LOCK(*str*)

  Checks the status of the advisory lock named by *str*. Returns 1 if the name is available (not currently being used as a lock), 0 if the name is in use, or NULL if an error occurred.

- IS_USED_LOCK(*str*)

  If there is a lock with the name given by *str*, IS_USED_LOCK() returns the connection ID of the client that created the lock. Returns NULL if there is no such lock.

- RELEASE_LOCK(*str*)

  Releases the advisory lock named by *str*. Returns 1 if the lock was released successfully, 0 if the lock was held by another connection, or NULL if no such lock exists.

C.2.9 Spatial Functions

The functions in this section operate on spatial values, also known here as "geometries."
For more information on spatial data types, see Chapter 3, "Data Types."

Spatial values can be represented in three formats:

- Well-Known Binary (WKB) format
- Well-Known Text (WKT) format
- Internal format

Functions that take spatial arguments expect them to be in the correct format. If you
pass a spatial value in a different format or pass a non-spatial value, the result is NULL.
There are functions for converting between spatial values in different formats.

Most functions that take spatial arguments expect them to be in internal format, and
MySQL uses only internal format when storing spatial values in columns that have a spatial data type. You can store values in WKT or WKB formats by using columns with other
data types, such as BLOB.

Spatial values can be associated with a spatial reference ID (SRID). Many of the spatial
functions take SRID as optional arguments.

> ### Note
> Because these spatial functions are implemented against the OpenGIS specification, the fol-
> lowing sections also point out when functions in the specification are not implemented, or
> are implemented in a different way from that described in the specification.

C.2.9.1 Spatial Value Format-Conversion Functions

The following functions accept a geometry value in Well-Known Binary format and return a geometry value in internal format. `wkb_expr` represents a WKB value for a geometry object of the type accepted by a given function. `srid` is an optional spatial reference
identifier.

- `GEOMCOLLFROMWKB(wkb_expr[,srid])`
  `GEOMETRYCOLLECTIONFROMWKB(wkb_expr[,srid])`

  Produces a GEOMETRYCOLLECTION value from its WKB value.

- `GEOMFROMWKB(wkb_expr[,srid])`
  `GEOMETRYFROMWKB(wkb_expr[,srid])`

  Produces a GEOMETRY value from its WKB value. This function can accept a WKB
  value for any spatial type.

- `LINEFROMWKB(wkb_expr[,srid])`
  `LINESTRINGFROMWKB(wkb_expr[,srid])`

  Produces a LINESTRING value from its WKB value.

- MLINEFROMWKB(*wkb_expr*[,*srid*])
  MULTILINESTRINGFROMWKB(*wkb_expr*[,*srid*])

  Produces a MULTILINESTRING value from its WKB value.

- MPOINTFROMWKB(*wkb_expr*[,*srid*])
  MULTIPOINTFROMWKB(*wkb_expr*[,*srid*])

  Produces a MULTIPOINT value from its WKB value.

- MPOLYFROMWKB(*wkb_expr*[,*srid*])
  MULTIPOLYGONFROMWKB(*wkb_expr*[,*srid*])

  Produces a MULTIPOLYGON value from its WKB value.

- POINTFROMWKB(*wkb_expr*[,*srid*])

  Produces a POINT value from its WKB value.

- POLYFROMWKB(*wkb_expr*[,*srid*])
  POLYGONFROMWKB(*wkb_expr*[,*srid*])

  Produces a POLYGON value from its WKB value.

Unimplemented functions. The OpenGIS specification describes optional functions BDPOLYFROMWKB() and BDMPOLYFROMWKB() for creating geometries from WKB values. MySQL does not implement these functions.

The following functions accept a geometry value in Well-Known Text format and return a geometry value in internal format. *wkt_expr* represents a WKT value for a geometry object of the type accepted by a given function. *srid* is an optional spatial reference identifier.

- GEOMCOLLFROMTEXT(*wkt_expr*[,*srid*])
  GEOMETRYCOLLECTIONFROMTEXT(*wkt_expr*[,*srid*])

  Produces a GEOMETRYCOLLECTION value from its WKT value.

- GEOMFROMTEXT(*wkt_expr*[,*srid*])
  GEOMETRYFROMTEXT(*wkt_expr*[,*srid*])

  Produces a GEOMETRY value from its WKT value. This function can accept a WKT value for any spatial type.

- LINEFROMTEXT(*wkt_expr*[,*srid*])
  LINESTRINGFROMTEXT(*wkt_expr*[,*srid*])

  Produces a LINESTRING value from its WKT value.

- MLINEFROMTEXT(*wkt_expr*[,*srid*])
  MULTILINESTRINGFROMTEXT(*wkt_expr*[,*srid*])

Produces a `MULTILINESTRING` value from its WKT value.

- `MPOINTFROMTEXT(wkt_expr[,srid])`
  `MULTIPOINTFROMTEXT(wkt_expr[,srid])`

  Produces a `MULTIPOINT` value from its WKT value.

- `MPOLYFROMTEXT(wkt_expr[,srid])`
  `MULTIPOLYGONFROMTEXT(wkt_expr[,srid])`

  Produces a `MULTIPOLYGON` value from its WKT value.

- `POINTFROMTEXT(wkt_expr[,srid])`

  Produces a `POINT` value from its WKT value.

- `POLYFROMTEXT(wkt_expr[,srid])`
  `POLYGONFROMTEXT(wkt_expr[,srid])`

  Produces a `POLYGON` value from its WKT value.

Unimplemented functions. The OpenGIS specification describes optional functions `BDPOLYFROMTEXT()` and `BDMPOLYFROMTEXT()` for creating geometries from WKT values. MySQL does not implement these functions.

The following functions take a geometry in internal format and return the corresponding value in Well-Known Binary format:

- `ASBINARY(geom)`
- `ASWKB(geom)`

The following functions take a geometry in internal format and return the corresponding value in Well-Known Text format:

- `ASTEXT(geom)`
- `ASWKT(geom)`

C.2.9.2 Spatial Property Functions

The following functions take a spatial value *geom* of any type in internal format and return a property of the value.

- `DIMENSION(geom)`

  Returns the dimension of the geometry. Dimension values have the meanings shown in the following table.

Dimension	Meaning
-1	Empty geometry
0	Geometry with no length or area
1	Geometry with a non-zero length and zero area
2	Geometry with a non-zero area

Examples: A POINT has a dimension of 0, a LINESTRING has a dimension of 1, and a POLYGON has a dimension of 2.

- ENVELOPE(*geom*)

Returns a POLYGON representing the minimum bounding rectangle of the geometry.

- GEOMETRYTYPE(*geom*)

Returns the spatial type of the geometry as a string.

```
GEOMETRYTYPE(GEOMFROMTEXT('LINESTRING(1 1,2 2)'))  →  'LINESTRING'
```

- SRID(*geom*)

Returns the spatial reference ID of the geometry as an integer.

Unimplemented functions. The OpenGIS specification also defines the following general spatial property functions, but MySQL does not implement them: BOUNDARY(), ISEMPTY(), and ISSIMPLE().

The following functions take a spatial POINT value *pt* in internal format and return a property of the value.

- X(*pt*)

Returns the X-coordinate of the point as a double-precision number.

- Y(*pt*)

Returns the Y-coordinate of the point as a double-precision number.

The following functions take a spatial LINESTRING value *ls* in internal format and return a property of the value.

- ENDPOINT(*ls*)

Returns the end point (final point) of *ls* as a POINT value.

- GLENGTH(*ls*)

Returns the length of *ls* as a double-precision value.

- ISCLOSED(*ls*)

Returns 1 if *ls* is closed, 0 if it is not, and –1 if it is NULL. A closed LINESTRING is one for which the starting point and end point are the same.

- NUMPOINTS(*ls*)

Returns the number of points in *ls*.

- POINTN(*ls*,*n*)

Returns the *n*-th point in *ls* as a POINT value. Points are numbered beginning with 1.

- STARTPOINT(*ls*)

Returns the starting point (first point) of *ls* as a POINT value.

Unimplemented function. The OpenGIS specification also defines the following `LINESTRING` property function, but MySQL does not implement it: `ISRING()`.

The following functions take a spatial `MULTILINESTRING` value `mls` in internal format and return a property of the value.

- `GLENGTH(mls)`

  Returns the length of `mls` as a double-precision value. The length of a `MULTILINESTRING` value is the sum of its constituent `LINESTRING` values.

- `ISCLOSED(mls)`

  Returns 1 if `ls` is closed, 0 if it is not, and –1 if it is `NULL`. A closed `MULTILINESTRING` is one for which the starting point and end point are the same for each of its constituent `LINESTRING` values.

The following functions take a spatial `POLYGON` value `poly` in internal format and return a property of the value.

- `AREA(poly)`

  Returns the area of `poly` as a double-precision number.

- `EXTERIORRING(poly)`

  Returns the exterior ring of `poly` as a `LINESTRING` value.

- `INTERIORRINGN(poly,n)`

  Returns the `n`-th interior ring of `poly` as a `LINESTRING` value. Rings are numbered beginning with 1.

- `NUMINTERIORRINGS(poly)`

  Returns the number of interior rings in `poly`.

The following function takes a spatial `MULTIPOLYGON` value `mpoly` in internal format and returns a property of the value.

- `AREA(mpoly)`

  Returns the area of `mpoly` as a double-precision number.

Unimplemented functions. The OpenGIS specification also defines the following `MULTIPOLYGON` property functions, but MySQL does not implement them: `CENTROID()`, `POINTONSURFACE()`.

The following functions take a spatial `GEOMETRYCOLLECTION` value `gc` in internal format and return a property of the value.

- `GEOMETRYN(gc,n)`

  Returns the `n`-th geometry of `gc`. The type of the return value depends on what the `n`-th geometry is. Geometries are numbered beginning with 1.

- `NUMGEOMETRIES(gc)`

  Returns the number of geometries in `gc`.

C.2.9.3 Spatial Relationship Functions

MySQL implements the following functions for testing spatial relationships between two geometries *geom1* and *geom2* in internal spatial format. These functions are based on the minimum bounding rectangle (MBR) of each geometry value.

- MBRCONTAINS(*geom1*, *geom2*)

  Returns 1 if the minimum bounding rectangle of *geom1* contains the minimum bounding rectangle of *geom2*, 0 if it does not.

- MBRDISJOINT(*geom1*, *geom2*)

  Returns 1 if the minimum bounding rectangles of *geom1* and *geom2* are disjoint, 0 if they are not. Geometries are disjoint if they do not intersect.

- MBREQUAL(*geom1*, *geom2*)

  Returns 1 if the minimum bounding rectangles of *geom1* and *geom2* are equal, 0 if they are not.

- MBRINTERSECTS(*geom1*, *geom2*)

  Returns 1 if the minimum bounding rectangles of *geom1* and *geom2* intersect, 0 if they do not.

- MBROVERLAPS(*geom1*, *geom2*)

  Returns 1 if the minimum bounding rectangles of *geom1* and *geom2* overlap, 0 if they do not.

- MBRTOUCHES(*geom1*, *geom2*)

  Returns 1 if the minimum bounding rectangles of *geom1* and *geom2* touch, 0 if they do not.

- MBRWITHIN(*geom1*, *geom2*)

  Returns 1 if the minimum bounding rectangle of *geom1* is within the minimum bounding rectangle of *geom2*, 0 if it does not.

The OpenGIS specification defines the following functions for testing spatial relationships. MySQL currently implements them the same way as the corresponding MBR-based functions.

- CONTAINS(*geom1*, *geom2*)
- DISJOINT(*geom1*, *geom2*)
- EQUALS(*geom1*, *geom2*)
- INTERSECTS(*geom1*, *geom2*)
- OVERLAPS(*geom1*, *geom2*)
- TOUCHES(*geom1*, *geom2*)
- WITHIN(*geom1*, *geom2*)

Unimplemented functions. The OpenGIS specification also defines these spatial-relationship functions, which are not implemented: CROSSES(), DISTANCE(), and RELATED().

C.2.10 XML Functions

The functions in this section enable a string representing an XML fragment to be processed with an XPath expression to extract text from the fragment or return the fragment with a matched element replaced by another string.

The XML string arguments to these functions must contain tags that are properly balanced and nested.

These functions use XPath 1.0. For general information about XPath, see the specification at http://www.w3.org/TR/xpath. There are some limitations on XPath support. See the MySQL Reference Manual for the current restrictions.

- EXTRACTVALUE(*xml_str*, *xpath_expr*)

  Applies the XPath expression to evaluate the XML string and returns the content of the first text node from the element matched by the expression. If the expression matches multiple elements, the result is the first text node from each of the matched elements concatenated with spaces between.

  ```
  EXTRACTVALUE('<a><b>B</b><c>C</c></a>','//b')       → 'B'
  EXTRACTVALUE('<a><b>B1</b><b>B2</b><b>B3</b></a>','//b')
                                                       → 'B1 B2 B3'
  ```

  If there is no match, the result is the empty string (the same as if there is a match for an element with no text content).

  EXTRACTVALUE() was introduced in MySQL 5.1.5.

- UPDATEXML(*xml_str*, *xpath_expr*, *xml_new*)

  Applies the XPath expression to evaluate the XML string, replaces the matched element with *xml_new*, and returns the result. If the expression matches nothing or matches multiple elements, the XML string is returned without modification.

  UPDATEXML() was introduced in MySQL 5.1.5.

C.2.11 Miscellaneous Functions

The functions in this section do not fall into any of the categories in the preceding sections.

- BENCHMARK(*n*, *expr*)

  Evaluates the expression *expr* repetitively *n* times. BENCHMARK() is something of an unusual function in that it is intended for use within the mysql client program. Its return value is always 0, and thus of no use. The value of interest is the elapsed time that mysql displays following the result of the query:

```
mysql> SELECT BENCHMARK(1000000,PASSWORD('secret'));
+---------------------------------------+
| BENCHMARK(1000000,PASSWORD('secret')) |
+---------------------------------------+
|                                     0 |
+---------------------------------------+
1 row in set (2.35 sec)
```

The time is only an approximate indicator of how quickly the server evaluates the expression because it represents wall-clock time on the client, not CPU time on the server. The time can be influenced by factors such as the load on the server, whether the server is in a runnable state or swapped out when the query arrives, and so forth. You may want to execute it several times to see what a representative value is.

- BIT_COUNT(n)

Returns the number of bits that are set in the argument, which is treated as a BIGINT value (a 64-bit integer).

```
BIT_COUNT(0)                                    → 0
BIT_COUNT(1)                                    → 1
BIT_COUNT(2)                                    → 1
BIT_COUNT(7)                                    → 3
BIT_COUNT(-1)                                   → 64
BIT_COUNT(NULL)                                 → NULL
```

- BIT_LENGTH(str)

Returns the length of the string str in bits, or NULL if the argument is NULL.

```
BIT_LENGTH('abc')                               → 24
BIT_LENGTH('a long string')                     → 104
BIT_LENGTH(CONVERT('abc' USING ucs2))           → 48
```

- CONNECTION_ID()

Returns the connection identifier that the server associates with the current client connection. Every client has an identifier that is unique among the set of currently connected clients.

```
CONNECTION_ID()                                 → 10146
```

- CURRENT_USER()

When you connect to the MySQL server, your connection is authenticated against some particular account row in the mysql.user table. The CURRENT_USER() function returns the values from the User and Host columns of that row, as a utf8 string in '$user\_name$@$host\_name$' format. The parentheses are optional.

```
CURRENT_USER()                                  → 'sampadm@localhost'
SUBSTRING_INDEX(CURRENT_USER(),'@',1)           → 'sampadm'
```

You can use CURRENT_USER() to determine who the server believes you to be. This might be different from the user that you specified when connecting if the server authenticates you as some other account. In particular, if the server authenticates you as an anonymous user, the username part of the return value is empty, whereas the username part of the value returned by USER() contains the username you specified when making the connection.

- DATABASE()

Returns a utf8 string containing the default database name, or NULL if there is no default database.

```
DATABASE()                                          → 'sampdb'
```

- FOUND_ROWS()

Returns the number of rows that a preceding SELECT statement would have returned without a LIMIT clause. For example, this statement would return a maximum of 10 rows:

```
mysql> SELECT * FROM mytbl LIMIT 10;
```

To determine how many rows the statement would have returned without the LIMIT clause, do this:

```
mysql> SELECT SQL_CALC_FOUND_ROWS * FROM mytbl LIMIT 10;
mysql> SELECT FOUND_ROWS();
```

- DEFAULT(col_name)

The INSERT statement allows you to specify the keyword DEFAULT to indicate explicitly that you want to insert a column's default value into a new row. However, that keyword is not allowable in arbitrary expressions or in other contexts. For example, you cannot use it if you want to reset a column to its default value in an UPDATE statement. The DEFAULT() function can be used for this. Given a column name, it returns the column's default value.

```
UPDATE counts SET counter = DEFAULT(counter)
WHERE max_time > expire_time;
```

- INET_ATON(str)

Given an IP number represented as a string in dotted-quad notation, returns the integer representation of the number, or NULL if the argument is not a valid IP number.

```
INET_ATON('64.28.67.70')              → 1075594054
INET_ATON('255.255.255.255')          → 4294967295
INET_ATON('256.255.255.255')          → NULL
INET_ATON('www.mysql.com')            → NULL
```

- INET_NTOA(*n*)

  Given the integer representation of an IP number, returns the corresponding dotted-quad representation as a string, or NULL if the value is illegal.

  ```
  INET_NTOA(1075594054)                              → '64.28.67.70'
  INET_NTOA(2130706433)                              → '127.0.0.1'
  ```

- LAST_INSERT_ID()
  LAST_INSERT_ID(*expr*)

  With no argument, returns the AUTO_INCREMENT value that was most recently generated during the current server session, or 0 if no such value has been generated. With an argument, the LAST_INSERT_ID() result is the argument value but is treated the same way as an automatically generated value, which is useful for generating sequences.

  More details can be found in Chapter 3. For both forms of LAST_INSERT_ID(), the value is maintained by the server on a per-connection basis and cannot be changed by other clients, even by those that cause their own new automatically generated values to be created.

- LOAD_FILE(*file_name*)

  Reads the file *file_name* and returns its contents as a string. The file must be located on the server, must be specified as an absolute (full) pathname, and must be world-readable to ensure that you're not trying to read a protected file. If the secure_file_priv system variable is non-empty, its value should be a directory and the file must be located in that directory. Because the file must be on the server, you must have the FILE privilege. If any of these conditions fail, LOAD_FILE() returns NULL.

- MASTER_POS_WAIT(*log_file*, *pos*[, *timeout*])

  This function is used when testing replication servers. When executed on a slave server, it blocks until the slave has read and processed events from the master server up to the given replication coordinates specified by the *log_file* and *pos* arguments. The optional *timeout* value can be given to tell MASTER_POS_WAIT() to place a limit on the number of seconds the function should wait. A value of 0 or less is equivalent to no timeout.

  MASTER_POS_WAIT() returns the number of log file events it had to wait for to get to the given replication coordinates. If the slave had already reached the coordinates, the function returns immediately with a value of 0. A return value of -1 indicates that the function timed out, an error occurred, or the master server information has not been initialized. A return value of NULL indicates that the slave SQL thread was not running or was stopped while the function was waiting.

- NAME_CONST(*name*, *value*)

  This function is used internally (for example, to write statements to the binary log). It returns *value*, with a column name of *name*. Both arguments must be constants. NAME_CONST() was introduced in MySQL 5.0.12.

- ROW_COUNT()

  This function operates as an SQL-level version of the mysql_affected_rows() C API function. It returns the number of rows affected by the previous statement. This is the number of rows inserted, deleted, or updated. A value of –1 indicates that the previous statement was a SELECT statement (or some other statement that returned a result set), or resulted in an error.

  ROW_COUNT() was introduced in MySQL 5.0.1.

- SCHEMA()

  This is a synonym for DATABASE(), introduced in MySQL 5.0.2.

- SESSION_USER()

  This function is a synonym for USER().

- SLEEP(*seconds*)

  Pauses for the given number of seconds and returns 0, or returns 1 if it is interrupted. The *seconds* argument may have a fractional part. SLEEP() was introduced in MySQL 5.0.12.

- SYSTEM_USER()

  This function is a synonym for USER().

- USER()

  Returns a utf8 string representing the username that the client specified when connecting to the MySQL server, and the host from which the client connected. The return value is a string in '*user_name*@*host_name*' format. The value is a utf8 string; take this into account when passing the value to functions that take multiple string arguments to avoid triggering a collation-mismatch error.

  ```
  USER()                              → 'paul@localhost'
  SUBSTRING_INDEX(USER(),'@',1)       → 'paul'
  SUBSTRING_INDEX(USER(),'@',-1)      → 'localhost'
  ```

- UUID()

  Returns a "universal unique identifier." The intent is that the return value from one call to UUID() should differ from the value from any other call. Uniqueness of the return value is not absolutely guaranteed, but duplicated values should be very unlikely.

  ```
  UUID()             → '4550868e-3c1f-1027-9cc8-78fa7f8d46b6'
  UUID()             → 'cbb9ad76-3d10-1027-8c06-349c71608da3'
  ```

The return value is a five-part `utf8` string of hexadecimal digits generated from a 128-bit number. The first four parts should be temporally unique, and the last part should be spatially unique. The first three parts of the value are derived from a time-stamp. The fourth part ensures uniqueness for situations in which the sequence of timestamp might not be monotonic, as happens when time changes for daylight saving time. The fifth part is an IEEE 802 node number. This might be generated from a value assumed to be unique to your server host, such as a network interface address. A 48-bit random number is used instead if no such unique value can be obtained.

- `VERSION()`

Returns a `utf8` string describing the server version.

`VERSION()`   → `'5.1.25-rc-log'`

The value consists of a version number, possibly followed by one or more suffixes. The suffixes may include the following:

- `-alpha`, `-beta`, or `-rc` indicate the stability of the MySQL release. If none of these is present, the release is General Availability (production quality).

- `-debug` means that the server is running in debug mode.

- `-embedded` indicates the embedded server, `libmysqld`.

- `-log` means logging is enabled.

System, Status, and User Variable Reference

This appendix describes several types of MySQL variables:

- System variables that provide information about server configuration
- System variables that exist in session-only form per client
- Status variables that provide information about the server's current operational state
- User variables that you can define, assign values to, and refer to in expressions

Values for variables that represent buffer sizes or lengths generally are given in bytes. Exceptions are noted as necessary.

Unless otherwise indicated, the variables listed here have been present in MySQL at least as early as MySQL 5.0.0. Variables that were introduced or that changed in meaning since then are noted.

D.1 System Variables

System variables provide information about the server's configuration and capabilities. Most system variables can be set at server startup time, and many can be modified dynamically while the server is running. This information is given in the description for each variable on the same line as the variable name:

- For variables that can be set at server startup time, you will see the word "startup" followed either by "set directly" or an option. The words "set directly" mean that you can set the variable directly on the command line or in an option file by using an option with the same name as the variable name. (Section F.1.2.2, "Setting Program Variables," describes the syntax for doing so.) Otherwise, "startup" is followed by the option that you use to set the variable. For example, you set the `storage_engine` variable by using the `--default-storage-engine` option. When an option is given, its meaning can be found in the description for the `mysqld` program in Appendix F, "MySQL Program Reference."

- For variables that can be modified while the server is running, you will see the word "runtime" followed by either or both of the words "global" or "session" to indicate whether the variable has a `GLOBAL` form or `SESSION` form, or both.

Some system variables exist only in session form. These are described in Section D.2, "Session-Only System Variables."

System variables can be displayed by the `SHOW VARIABLES` statement or by executing the `mysqladmin variables` command. You can also display the value of individual variables by using `SELECT @@GLOBAL.var_name` for global variables, or `SELECT @@SESSION.var_name` or `SELECT @@var_name` for session variables. As of MySQL 5.1.12, you can also examine the `INFORMATION_SCHEMA` tables named `GLOBAL_VARIABLES` and `SESSION_VARIABLES` to obtain system variable information.

For more information about setting system variables at runtime or examining their values, see Section 12.6.1, "Checking and Setting System Variable Values."

System variable names are not case sensitive.

Some of the variables described here are present only under certain configurations. For example, many of those that begin with `innodb_` are shown only if the InnoDB storage engine is available. There are several Falcon-related system variables, but I have not mentioned them because the implementation is still somewhat in flux.

- `auto_increment_increment` (startup: set directly; runtime: global, session)

  The amount by which to increment `AUTO_INCREMENT` values each time the server generates a new sequence value. The default value is 1; the range of values is 1 to 65,535. This variable was introduced in MySQL 5.0.2.

- `auto_increment_offset` (startup: set directly; runtime: global, session)

  The starting value for `AUTO_INCREMENT` sequences. The default value is 1; the range of values is 1 to 65,535. This variable was introduced in MySQL 5.0.2.

- `automatic_sp_privileges` (startup: set directly; runtime: global)

  When this variable is 1 (the default), the server automatically grants you the `EXECUTE` and `ALTER ROUTINE` privileges if necessary when you create a stored routine, so that you can execute, change, or drop the routine later. The server also revokes those privileges when you drop the routine. If `automatic_sp_privileges` is 0, automatic privilege granting and revocation does not occur. This variable was introduced in MySQL 5.0.3.

- `back_log` (startup: set directly)

  The maximum number of pending connection requests that can be queued while current connections are being processed.

- `basedir` (startup: set directly)

  The pathname to the root directory of the MySQL installation.

- `binlog_cache_size` (startup: set directly; runtime: global)

  The size of the cache that is used to store SQL statements that are part of a transaction before they are flushed to the binary log. (This occurs only if the transaction is committed or includes statements that update non-transactional tables. If the transaction updates only transactional tables and is rolled back, the statements are discarded.)

- `binlog_format` (startup: set directly; runtime: global)

  The binary logging format. Values can be STATEMENT, ROW, or (as of 5.1.8) MIXED, for statement-based, row-based, or mixed logging format. With mixed format, the server switches between statement- and row-based logging automatically. The default value as of 5.1.12 is MIXED. This variable was introduced in MySQL 5.1.5, and can be set at runtime as of 5.1.8.

- `bulk_insert_buffer_size` (startup: set directly; runtime: global, session)

  The size of the cache used to help optimize bulk inserts into MyISAM tables. This includes LOAD DATA statements, multiple-row INSERT statements, and INSERT INTO ... SELECT statements. Setting the value to zero disables the optimization.

- `character_set_client` (runtime: global, session)

  The character set of statements sent by the client to the server.

- `character_set_connection` (runtime: global, session)

  The character set of the client-server connection. This is used to interpret string literals (except those that begin with an introducer) and for the character set of strings that result from number-to-string conversions.

- `character_set_database`

  The character set of the default database, if there is one. If there is no default database (for example, if the client connects without selecting a database), this variable is set to the value of `character_set_server`. The value of `character_set_database` is set by the server each time you select a different database.

- `character_set_filesystem` (startup: set directly; runtime: global, session)

  The filesystem character set, used to evaluate string literals that indicate filenames, such as the data file in LOAD DATA statements. The server converts the filename from the character set named by `character_set_client` to that named by `character_set_filesystem` before accessing the file. The default value is `binary` (no conversion). This variable was introduced in MySQL 5.0.19/5.1.6.

- `character_set_results` (runtime: global, session)

  The character set of query results sent by the server to the client.

- `character_set_server` (startup: set directly; runtime: global, session)

  The server's default character set.

- `character_set_system`

  The system character set. Its value is always `utf8`. This is the character set used for metadata such as database, table, and column names. It is also used for functions such as `DATABASE()`, `CURRENT_USER()`, `USER()`, and `VERSION()`.

- `character_sets_dir` (startup: set directly)

  The directory where character set files are located.

- `collation_connection` (runtime: global, session)

  The connection character set collation.

- `collation_database`

  The database character set collation, if there is one. If there is no default database (for example, if the client connects without selecting one), this variable is set to the value of `collation_server`. The value of `collation_database` is set by the server each time you select a different database.

- `collation_server` (startup: set directly; runtime: global, session)

  The server character set collation.

- `completion_type` (startup: set directly; runtime: global, session)

  The completion type for transactions. A value of 0 (the default) leaves `COMMIT` and `ROLLBACK` unaffected. A value of 1 causes them to be equivalent to `COMMIT AND CHAIN` and `ROLLBACK AND CHAIN`. A value of 1 causes them to be equivalent to `COMMIT RELEASE` and `ROLLBACK RELEASE`. With `AND CHAIN`, when a transaction completes, the server starts a new one with the same isolation level. With `AND RELEASE`, when a transaction completes, the server terminates the connection. This variable was introduced in MySQL 5.0.3.

- `concurrent_insert` (startup: set directly; runtime: global)

  Whether the server allows `INSERT` statements on a MyISAM table that has no holes in the middle of the data file concurrently with active `SELECT` statements for the table. Values of 0 or 1 disable or enable this feature. A value of 2 (allowable as of MySQL 5.0.6) enables concurrent inserts for MyISAM tables regardless of whether they have with holes in the data file; if so, new rows are added to the end of the table if it is in use. This variable has a value of 1 by default, but can be disabled at startup by setting it directly or by using the `--skip-concurrent-insert` option.

- `connect_timeout` (startup: set directly; runtime: global)

  The number of seconds that `mysqld` waits for packets during the initial connection handshake. The default is 10 as of MySQL 5.0.52/5.1.23 and 5 for older versions.

- `datadir` (startup: set directly)

  The pathname to the MySQL data directory.

- `date_format`

  This variable is unused.

- `datetime_format`

  This variable is unused.

- `default_week_format` (startup: set directly; runtime: global, session)

  This variable indicates the default mode value to use when the `WEEK()` or `YEARWEEK()` function is invoked without the optional `mode` argument.

- `delay_key_write` (startup: set directly; runtime: global)

  Whether the server respects delayed key writes for MyISAM tables that are created with the `DELAY_KEY_WRITE` option. This variable can have three values:

  - `ON` (the default value) tells the server to honor the `DELAY_KEY_WRITE` option for tables defined with that option: Key writes are delayed for tables defined with `DELAY_KEY_WRITE=1`, but not for tables defined with `DELAY_KEY_WRITE=0`.

  - `OFF` means that key writes are never delayed for any table, no matter how it was defined.

  - `ALL` forces key writes always to be delayed for every table, no matter how it was defined.

- `delayed_insert_limit` (startup: set directly; runtime: global)

  The number of rows from `INSERT DELAYED` statements that the delayed-row handler for a table will insert before checking whether any new `SELECT` statements for the table have arrived. If any have arrived, the handler suspends the insert operation to enable retrievals to execute.

- `delayed_insert_timeout` (startup: set directly; runtime: global)

  When a handler for `INSERT DELAYED` operations finishes inserting queued rows, it waits this many seconds to see whether any new `INSERT DELAYED` rows arrive. If so, it handles them; otherwise, it terminates.

- `delayed_queue_size` (startup: set directly; runtime: global)

  The number of rows that may be queued per table for `INSERT DELAYED` statements. If the queue is full, further `INSERT DELAYED` statements for the table block until there is room in the queue.

- `div_precision_increment` (startup: set directly; runtime: global, session)

  For division of two exact-value numbers performed with the `/` operator, this variable indicates how many digits of scale to add. For example, `.1/.7` is `.14286` or `.1428571` when `div_precision_increment` has a value of 4 or 6, respectively. The value can range from 0 to 30 and has a default of 4. This variable was introduced in MySQL 5.0.6.

- `event_scheduler` (startup: set directly)

  The status of the event scheduler. Values can be `OFF`, `ON`, or `DISABLED`. If the event scheduler is set to `DISABLED` at startup, its status cannot be changed at runtime. If the scheduler is set to either OFF or ON at startup, its status can be changed between those two values at runtime. This variable was introduced in MySQL 5.1.6.

- expire_logs_days (startup: set directly; runtime: global)

If set to a value other than the default of 0, the server automatically removes binary log files older than this many days and updates the binary log index file. Expiration is checked when the server starts up and when it opens a new binary log file.

- flush (startup: use --flush; runtime: global)

A value of ON or OFF indicates whether the server flushes tables after each update. The default is OFF; use the --flush option on the command line to enable flushing after updates.

- flush_time (startup: set directly; runtime: global)

If this variable has a non-zero value, tables are closed to flush pending changes to disk every flush_time seconds. If your system is unreliable and tends to lock up or restart often, forcing out table changes this way degrades performance but can reduce the chance of table corruption or data loss. The default value is 0 for Unix and 1800 (30 minutes) for Windows.

- ft_boolean_syntax (startup: set directly; runtime: global)

The list of operators that are supported for FULLTEXT searches that use IN BOOLEAN MODE.

- ft_max_word_len (startup: set directly)

The maximum length of words that can be included in FULLTEXT indexes. Longer words are ignored. If you change the value of this variable, you should rebuild the FULLTEXT indexes for any tables that have them. The default value is 84.

- ft_min_word_len (startup: set directly)

The minimum length of words that can be included in FULLTEXT indexes. Shorter words are ignored. If you change the value of this variable, you should rebuild the FULLTEXT indexes for any tables that have them. The default value is 4.

- ft_query_expansion_limit (startup: set directly)

This variable is used for full-text searches that are done using the WITH QUERY EXPANSION clause. It determines the number of "top matches" to use for the second phase of each search.

- ft_stopword_file (startup: set directly)

The stopword file for FULLTEXT indexes. The default is to use the built-in list of stopwords. To disable stopwords, set the value to the empty string. If you change the value of this variable or the contents of the stopword list, you should rebuild the FULLTEXT indexes for any tables that have them.

- `general_log` (startup: set directly; runtime: global)

  Whether logging to the general query log is enabled. (If so, the log destinations are indicated by `log_output`.) This variable was introduced in MySQL 5.1.12 as a synonym for the `log` variable.

- `general_log_file` (runtime: global)

  The name of the general query log file, for use if the file logging destination is enabled. This variable was introduced in MySQL 5.1.12.

- `group_concat_max_len` (startup: set directly; runtime: global, session)

  The upper limit on the length of values that the `GROUP_CONCAT()` function should return (1024 by default).

- `have_compress`

  For the server to be able to implement the `COMPRESS()` and `UNCOMPRESS()` functions, it needs the `zlib` compression library. This variable indicates whether that library is available. If not, the functions cannot be used.

- `have_crypt`

  For the server to be able to implement the `CRYPT()` function, it needs the `crypt()` system call. This variable indicates whether that call is available. If not, the function cannot be used.

- `have_dynamic_loading`

  Whether the server supports dynamic plugin loading. This variable was introduced in MySQL 5.1.10.

- `have_engine_name`

  Each `have_engine_name` variable (for example, `have_innodb`) provides information about the server's support for a particular storage engine. Not every storage engine has such a variable. For those that do, a value of `YES` means that the engine is present and can be used and `NO` means that the engine is not present. Before MySQL 5.1.18, a value of `DISABLED` indicates that the engine is compiled in but was disabled at server startup.

- `have_geometry`

  `YES` if spatial data types can be used, `NO` if not.

- `have_openssl`

  `YES` or `NO` to indicate whether the server supports encrypted client connections using SSL. As of MySQL 5.0.38/5.1.17, `have_openssl` and `have_ssl` are synonymous.

- `have_query_cache`

  `YES` or `NO` to indicate whether the query cache is available.

- `have_raid`

  Always NO. RAID-table support is an older feature that was removed in MySQL 5.0.

- `have_rtree_keys`

  YES or NO to indicate whether RTREE indexes are available for SPATIAL indexes.

- `have_ssl`

  YES or NO to indicate whether the server supports encrypted client connections using SSL. This variable was introduced in MySQL 5.0.38/5.1.17 as a synonym for `have_openssl`.

- `have_symlink`

  This variable has a value of YES or NO, but the meaning is platform dependent. On Unix, it indicates whether table symbolic linking is supported for MyISAM tables. On Windows, it indicates whether database symlinking is supported.

- `hostname`

  The server hostname. The MySQL server determines the value when it starts. This variable was introduced in MySQL 5.0.38/5.1.17.

- `init_connect` (startup: set directly; runtime: global)

  A non-empty value indicates one or more SQL statements separated by semicolons to be executed for each client that connects to the server. This variable can be used to modify the initial session environment in which clients begin. `init_connect` is ignored for users who have the SUPER privilege, to prevent an incorrect or unwise statement in the variable value from causing administrative users to be unable to connect to the server to correct the problem.

- `init_file` (startup: set directly)

  A non-empty value indicates the name of a file containing SQL statements to be executed by the server when it starts. The file should contain one statement per line.

- `init_slave` (startup: set directly; runtime: global)

  A non-empty value indicates one or more SQL statements separated by semicolons to be executed by a slave server each time its SQL thread starts.

- `innodb_adaptive_hash_index` (startup: set directly)

  Enable or disable InnoDB adaptive hash indexes. This variable is enabled by default; it can be disabled by starting the server with `--skip-innodb_adaptive_hash_index`. This variable was introduced in MySQL 5.0.52/5.1.24.

- `innodb_additional_mem_pool_size` (startup: set directly)

  The size of the InnoDB memory pool for storing internal data structures.

- `innodb_autoextend_increment` (startup: set directly; runtime: global)

  The variable controls the amount in MB by which InnoDB increases the size of an auto-extending tablespace that has become full. The default is 8, with a maximum of 1000.

- `innodb_buffer_pool_awe_mem_mb` (startup: set directly)

  This variable is relevant only for 32-bit Windows systems that support Address Windowing Extensions. Its value should be the size in MB of the InnoDB buffer pool if it is placed in AWE memory. The maximum value is 63000. If you set this variable, `innodb_buffer_pool_size` is the window into the `mysqld` address space where InnoDB maps AWE memory. This variable was removed in MySQL 5.1.13.

- `innodb_buffer_pool_size` (startup: set directly)

  The size of the InnoDB cache for buffering table data and indexes.

- `innodb_checksums` (startup: set directly)

  A value of `ON` or `OFF` indicates whether InnoDB table checksum calculation is enabled. The default is `ON`. This variable was introduced in MySQL 5.0.3.

- `innodb_commit_concurrency` (startup: set directly; runtime: global)

  How may threads can commit simultaneously. A value of 0 (default) means "no limit." This variable was introduced in MySQL 5.0.12.

- `innodb_concurrency_tickets` (startup: set directly; runtime: global)

  When a thread wants to enter InnoDB, it can do so only if the number of threads is less than the limit set by `innodb_thread_concurrency`. Otherwise, the thread is queued until the number of threads drops below the limit. When the thread is allowed to enter, it can then leave and re-enter InnoDB without restriction as many times as the value of `innodb_concurrency_tickets`. This variable was introduced in MySQL 5.0.3.

- `innodb_data_file_path` (startup: set directly)

  The specification for the InnoDB tablespace component files.

- `innodb_data_home_dir` (startup: set directly)

  The pathname to the directory relative to which the InnoDB tablespace component files are located. If the value is empty, component filenames are interpreted as absolute pathnames.

- `innodb_doublewrite` (startup: set directly)

  A value of `ON` or `OFF` indicates whether the InnoDB doublewrite buffer is enabled. The default is `ON`. This variable was introduced in MySQL 5.0.3.

- `innodb_fast_shutdown` (startup: set directly; runtime: global)

  A value of 0 or 1 indicates whether InnoDB will use its quicker shutdown method that skips some of the operations that it performs normally.

- `innodb_file_io_threads` (startup: set directly)

  The number of threads used by InnoDB for file I/O. Changing this variable is effective only for Windows, where an increase from the default of 4 in some cases improves performance.

- `innodb_file_per_table` (startup: set directly)

  If this variable is set to 0 (the default), InnoDB creates each new table in its shared tablespace. If the value is set to 1, InnoDB uses individual tablespaces: Each new table gets its own `.ibd` file in the database directory where the table contents are stored. This variable affects only how new tables are created; InnoDB can access existing tables in the shared tablespace or individual tablespaces regardless of how `innodb_file_per_table` is set.

- `innodb_flush_log_at_trx_commit` (startup: set directly; runtime: global)

  This option controls how InnoDB log flushing occurs. The following table shows the allowable values.

Value	Meaning
0	Write to the log and flush to disk once per second
1	Write to the log and flush to disk at each commit
2	Write to the log at each commit, but flush to disk only once per second

  Note that if you do not set the value to 1, InnoDB does not guarantee ACID properties; up to about a second's worth of the most recent transactions may be lost if a crash occurs.

- `innodb_flush_method` (startup: set directly)

  This variable specifies the method that InnoDB uses for flushing files. It applies only on Unix. The allowable values are `fdatasync` (use `fsync()` to flush data and log files), `O_DSYNC` (use `fsync()` to flush data files and `O_SYNC` to open and flush log files), or `O_DIRECT` (use `fsync()` to flush data and log files and `O_DIRECT` or `directio()` as available to open data files). The default is `fdatasync`. On Windows, the value is always `async_unbuffered`.

- `innodb_force_recovery` (startup: set directly)

  Normally 0, but may be set to a value from 1 to 6 to cause the server to start up after a crash even if InnoDB recovery fails. For a description of how to use this variable, see Section 14.7.4, "Coping with InnoDB Auto-Recovery Problems."

- `innodb_lock_wait_timeout` (startup: set directly)

  The number of seconds InnoDB waits for a lock for a transaction. If the lock cannot be acquired, InnoDB rolls back the transaction.

- `innodb_locks_unsafe_for_binlog` (startup: set directly)

  A value of ON or OFF indicates whether InnoDB's use of next-key locking for index searching and scanning is disabled. The default is OFF (that is, next-key locking is enabled). An InnoDB row lock normally locks the row index record and also prevents other clients from inserting a new index record immediately before the locked one. This is called "next-key locking" and prevents phantom rows from appearing. Enabling `innodb_locks_unsafe_for_binlog` disables next-key locking so that a row lock locks only the index record and does not prevent insertion of a new index record before the locked one. This has the following implications:

  - Some inserts can proceed that otherwise would be blocked.

  - Phantom rows can appear.

  - InnoDB guarantees at most an isolation level of READ COMMITTED. Serializability is not guaranteed.

  - As of MySQL 5.0.2, enabling `innodb_locks_unsafe_for_binlog` causes InnoDB to lock rows that it examines (as usual), but for DELETE or UPDATE only retains the locks on rows that actually are to be changed. Locks for other rows are released after InnoDB determines that it can skip them. This reduces the likelihood of deadlock.

  `innodb_locks_unsafe_for_binlog` applies only to index searching and scanning, not to checking of foreign key constraints or duplicate keys.

- `innodb_log_arch_dir` (startup: set directly)

  This variable is unused. It was removed in MySQL 5.1.21.

- `innodb_log_archive` (startup: set directly)

  This variable is unused. It was removed in MySQL 5.1.18.

- `innodb_log_buffer_size` (startup: set directly)

  The size of the InnoDB transaction log buffer. The default is 1MB. Values usually range from 1MB to 8MB.

- `innodb_log_file_size` (startup: set directly)

  The size of each InnoDB log file. The product of `innodb_log_file_size` and `innodb_log_files_in_group` determines the total InnoDB log size.

- `innodb_log_files_in_group` (startup: set directly)

  The number of log files InnoDB maintains. The product of `innodb_log_file_size` and `innodb_log_files_in_group` determines the total InnoDB log size.

- `innodb_log_group_home_dir` (startup: set directly)

  The pathname to the directory where InnoDB should write its log files.

- `innodb_max_dirty_pages_pct` (startup: set directly; runtime: global)

  The percentage of dirty pages that InnoDB allows in its buffer pool before it considers it necessary to flush the log to disk. The value should be from 0 to 100. The default is 90.

- `innodb_max_purge_lag` (startup: set directly; runtime: global)

  InnoDB maintains a purge thread that purges rows to be deleted as a result of delete or update operations. In cases when small groups of rows are inserted and deleted at roughly the same rate, it is possible for the purge thread to fall behind in its operation, resulting in large numbers of to-be-deleted rows taking up space that otherwise would be freed. The `innodb_max_purge_lag` variable controls how much to delay INSERT, UPDATE, and DELETE statements, causing them to lag so that the purge thread can proceed more efficiently. The default value is 0 (that is, no delay). For non-zero values, the delay is proportional to ((n / `innodb_max_purge_lag`) × 10) - 5 milliseconds, where n is the number of transactions that have rows marked for deletion.

- `innodb_mirrored_log_groups` (startup: set directly)

  The number of InnoDB log file groups to maintain. The value should always be 1.

- `innodb_open_files` (startup: set directly)

  If `innodb_file_per_table` is set to 1 to enable individual tablespaces, this variable indicates how many file descriptors InnoDB can use to keep `.ibd` files open simultaneously. The minimum value is 10 and the default is 300. `innodb_file_per_table` controls allocation of file descriptors separate from those controlled by `open_files_limit`; descriptors used for `.ibd` files are not used by the table cache.

- `innodb_rollback_on_timeout` (startup: set directly)

  This variable controls what InnoDB does when a transaction times out. With a value of OFF (the default), InnoDB rolls back only the last statement. With a value of ON, InnoDB rolls back the entire transaction. This variable was introduced in MySQL 5.0.32/5.1.15. For older versions, InnoDB rolls back the entire transaction.

- `innodb_support_xa` (startup: set directly; runtime: global, session)

  ON or OFF to indicate whether InnoDB supports two-phase commit in XA transactions. The default is ON but can be set to OFF for better performance if you don't use XA transactions. This variable was introduced in MySQL 5.0.3.

- `innodb_sync_spin_loops` (startup: set directly; runtime: global)

  How many times a thread waits for InnoDB to free a mutex before being suspended. This variable was introduced in MySQL 5.0.3.

- `innodb_table_locks` (startup: set directly; runtime: global, session)

  This variable controls how InnoDB handles a LOCK TABLE statement to acquire a write lock for an InnoDB table when autocommit is disabled. A value of ON (the default) causes InnoDB to acquire an internal table lock. A value of OFF causes

InnoDB to wait until no other thread has a lock for the table. Disabling this variable can prevent some deadlocks for applications that use LOCK TABLES with autocommit mode disabled.

- innodb_thread_concurrency (startup: set directly; runtime: global)

  The limit on the number of threads that InnoDB tries to maintain. This variable can be set as a global runtime variable as of MySQL 5.0.3.

- innodb_thread_sleep_delay (startup: set directly; runtime: global)

  The time in microseconds that InnoDB threads sleep before being placed in the InnoDB queue. The default value is 10,000 (10 seconds); a value of 0 means "don't sleep." This variable was introduced in MySQL 5.0.3.

- interactive_timeout (startup: set directly; runtime: global, session)

  The number of seconds an interactive client connection can remain idle before the server considers itself free to close it. For non-interactive clients, the value of the wait_timeout variable is used instead.

- join_buffer_size (startup: set directly; runtime: global, session)

  The size of the buffer that is used for joins that are performed without use of indexes and require a table scan.

- keep_files_on_create (startup: set directly; runtime: global, session)

  If an explicit DATA DIRECTORY or INDEX DIRECTORY option is given for a CREATE TABLE statement for a MyISAM table and the server finds an existing data or index file, respectively, in the named directory, it returns an error. The keep_files_on_create variable controls how the server handles MyISAM table creation when no DATA DIRECTORY or INDEX DIRECTORY option specifies where to place the data or index file. If keep_files_on_create is OFF (the default), and the server finds an existing .MYD data file or .MYI index file, it overwrites it. If the variable is ON, the server returns an error. This variable was introduced in MySQL 5.0.48/5.1.21.

- key_buffer_size (startup: set directly; runtime: global)

  The size of the buffer used for caching index blocks for MyISAM tables. This buffer is shared among connection-handler threads.

  This variable and the other key cache variables (key_cache_age_threshold, key_cache_block_size, and key_cache_limit) exist as a group and can be accessed as components of a structured system variable. Multiple key caches can be created for finer control over key cache use. For more information, see Section 12.7.2, "Configuring the MyISAM Storage Engine."

- key_cache_age_threshold (startup: set directly; runtime: global)

  How long buffers stay unused in the hot sub-chain of the key cache before being moved to the warm sub-chain. Higher values enable blocks to remain in the hot sub-chain longer. The default is 300. The minimum value is 100.

- `key_cache_block_size` (runtime: global)

  The block size for the key cache. By default, a block is 1024 bytes.

- `key_cache_limit` (runtime: global)

  If set to the default value of 100, the key cache uses a least recently used strategy for cache buffer reuse. If set lower than 100, the key cache uses a midpoint insertion strategy and the variable value is the percentage of the key cache to use for the warm buffer sub-chain. The value should be from 1 to 100.

- `language` (startup: set directly)

  The language used to display error messages. The value may be either the language name or the pathname of the directory containing the language files.

- `large_files_support`

  Whether the server was built with support for handling large files.

- `large_page_size`

  The size of large memory pages, if large page support is enabled. Otherwise, the value is 0. This variable was introduced in MySQL 5.0.3.

- `large_pages` (startup: use `--large-pages`)

  Whether support for large memory pages is enabled. Large pages are supported only on Linux. This variable was introduced in MySQL 5.0.3.

- `lc_time_names` (startup: set directly; runtime: global, session)

  The locale for the language used for display of day and month names by the `DATE_FORMAT()`, `DAYNAME()`, and `MONTHNAME()` functions. The default locale value is `en_US` but can be set to other POSIX-style names such as `es_AR` (Spanish/Argentina) or `zh_HK` (Chinese/Hong Kong). This variable was introduced in MySQL 5.0.25/5.1.12.

- `license`

  The server license type; for example, `GPL` if the server is running under the terms of the GPL.

- `local_infile` (startup: set directly; runtime: global)

  Whether `LOCAL` is allowed for `LOAD DATA` statements.

- `locked_in_memory` (startup: use `--memlock`)

  Whether the server is locked in memory.

- `log` (runtime: global)

  Whether query logging is enabled. As of MySQL 5.1.12, this variable and `general_log` are synonyms, except that `log` cannot be set at runtime to enable or disable logging until MySQL 5.1.23.

- `log_bin`

  Whether the binary log is enabled.

- `log_bin_trust_function_creators` (startup: set directly; runtime: global)

  Creation or alteration of stored functions requires that you have the CREATE ROUTINE or ALTER ROUTINE privilege. However, if binary logging is enabled and `log_bin_trust_function_creators` is 0 (the default), you must also have the SUPER privilege and declare that the function is deterministic or does not modify data. To turn off these extra requirements, set `log_bin_trust_function_creators` to 1. This variable was introduced in MySQL 5.0.16. (From MySQL 5.0.6 through 5.0.15, the variable name is `log_bin_trust_routine_creators` and it also applies to stored procedures.)

- `log_error` (startup: set directly)

  The name of the error log file. If the value is empty, the server writes error output to the terminal.

- `log_output` (startup: use `--log-output`; runtime: global)

  The current set of output destinations for the general query log and slow-query log, if those logs are enabled. The value is a list of comma-separated destination names. Allowable destinations are TABLE, FILE and NONE. If present, NONE disables logging and takes precedence over any other values. This variable was introduced in MySQL 5.1.6.

  The `general_log` or `slow_query_log` system variable can be set at runtime to enable or disable the respective log. The `general_log_file` or `slow_query_log_file` system variable can be set at runtime to change the name of the respective log file.

- `log_queries_not_using_indexes` (startup: use `--log-queries-not-using-indexes`; runtime: global)

  Whether queries that do not use indexes should be logged to the slow-query log. This variable was introduced in MySQL 5.0.23/5.1.11.

- `log_slave_updates` (startup: set directly)

  For updates that a replication slave server receives from its master's binary log, this variable controls whether the slave logs the updates to its own binary log. By default, slave update logging is disabled but can be enabled to allow a slave to act as a master to another slave in a chained replication configuration.

- `log_slow_queries`

  Whether the slow-query log is enabled. This variable can be set at runtime to enable or disable logging as of MySQL 5.1.23.

- `log_warnings` (startup: set directly; runtime: global, session)

  The logging level for logging non-critical warnings to the error log. A value of 0 disables these warnings and 1 (the default) enables warnings. Values greater than 1 increase the logging level to include information about aborted connections and (as of MySQL 5.2.6) access-denied errors.

- `long_query_time` (startup: set directly; runtime: global, session)

  Any query taking longer than this value in seconds is considered "slow" and causes the `Slow_queries` counter to be incremented. In addition, if the slow-query log is enabled, the query is written to that log. (As of MySQL 5.1.21, slow-query logging also takes `min_examined_row_limit` into account.)

  The default value is 10. As of MySQL 5.1.21/6.0.4, the value can include a fractional part in microseconds and the minimum value is 0. (Any fractional part is logged only if the log destination is a file and not the `mysql.slow_log` table.) For older versions, the value must be an integer and the minimum is 1.

- `low_priority_updates` (startup: set directly; runtime: global, session)

  When this variable is set true, updates have a lower priority than retrievals, for storage engines that use table-level locking. Statements that modify table contents (`DELETE`, `INSERT`, `REPLACE`, `UPDATE`) wait until no `SELECT` is active or pending for the table. `SELECT` statements that arrive while another is active begin executing immediately rather than waiting for low-priority modification statements. It has the same effect as specifying the `LOW_PRIORITY` option for statements that support it, such as `INSERT` and `UPDATE`. For individual `INSERT` statements, the `HIGH_PRIORITY` modifier can be given to cancel the effect of this variable and elevate the insert to normal priority.

  `sql_low_priority_updates` is a deprecated synonym for `low_priority_updates`.

- `lower_case_file_system`

  This variable indicates the case sensitivity of filenames for the filesystem that contains the data directory. `ON` means that names are not case sensitive. (Think of `ON` as meaning that lowercase and uppercase versions of a filename are considered the same.) `OFF` means that names are case sensitive.

- `lower_case_table_names` (startup: set directly)

  This variable controls how the directory names and filenames corresponding to database and table names are treated when `CREATE DATABASE` and `CREATE TABLE` statements are issued. It also controls how name comparisons are performed when executing statements.

  - A value of 0 causes names to be created on disk as given in `CREATE DATABASE` and `CREATE TABLE` statements. Name comparisons are case sensitive. This is the default on systems that have case-sensitive filenames.

  - A value of 1 causes names to be forced to lowercase when databases and tables are created. Name comparisons are not case sensitive.

  - A value of 2 causes name lettercase to be preserved, but name comparisons to be not case sensitive. That is, names are created as given in `CREATE` statements, but not compared in case-sensitive fashion. You should use this value only for filesystems that do not have case-sensitive filenames.

If `lower_case_table_names` has not been set explicitly, the server sets `lower_case_table_names` to 2 automatically if filenames are not case sensitive on the filesystem that contains the data directory. Setting `lower_case_table_names` to a non-zero value also causes table aliases not to be case sensitive.

- `max_allowed_packet` (startup: set directly; runtime: global, session)

  The maximum size of the buffer used for communication between the server and the client. The buffer is initially allocated to be `net_buffer_length` bytes long but may grow up to `max_allowed_packet` bytes as necessary. The value also constrains the maximum size of strings handled within the server. The default and maximum values for `max_allowed_packet` are 1MB and 1GB, respectively.

- `max_binlog_cache_size` (startup: set directly; runtime: global)

  The maximum binary log cache size. Statements that make up a transaction are stored in the binary log cache and then written to the binary log at commit time. If the transaction exceeds this size, it must be flushed to a temporary disk file.

- `max_binlog_size` (startup: set directly; runtime: global)

  The maximum size of a binary log file. If the current binary log file reaches this size, the server closes it and begins the next one. The allowable range of values is 4KB to 1GB. The default is 1GB.

  `max_binlog_size` also controls the size of slave server relay log files if `max_relay_log_size` is set to 0.

- `max_connect_errors` (startup: set directly; runtime: global)

  The number of failed connections from a host that are allowed before the host is blocked from further connection attempts. This is done on the basis that someone may be attempting to break in from that host. The FLUSH HOSTS statement or `mysqladmin flush-hosts` command may be used to clear the host cache to re-enable blocked hosts.

- `max_connections` (startup: set directly; runtime: global)

  The maximum number of simultaneous client connections allowed. The default is 151 as of MySQL 5.1.15 and 100 for older versions.

- `max_delayed_threads` (startup: set directly; runtime: global, session)

  The maximum number of threads that will be created to handle INSERT DELAYED statements. Any such statements that are received while the maximum number of handlers is already in use will be treated as non-DELAYED statements. A client can set the session value to 0 to disable DELAYED inserts for its own connection.

- `max_error_count` (startup: set directly; runtime: global, session)

  The maximum number of error, warning, and note messages to be stored. (Such events are always counted; this variable controls only how many of the associated messages are stored and available to SHOW ERRORS and SHOW WARNINGS.)

- `max_heap_table_size` (startup: set directly; runtime: global, session)

  The maximum allowed size of new MEMORY tables. Existing tables are unaffected by changes to this variable unless they are modified with ALTER TABLE or TRUNCATE TABLE. This variable can be used to help prevent the server from using excessive amounts of memory. This variable also affects how the server treats internal memory tables; see the description for `tmp_table_size`.

- `max_insert_delayed_threads` (startup: use --max-delayed-threads; runtime: global, session)

  This variable is a synonym for `max_delayed_threads`.

- `max_join_size` (startup: set directly; runtime: global, session)

  When executing a join, the MySQL optimizer estimates how many row combinations it will need to examine. If the estimate exceeds `max_join_size` rows, an error is returned. This can be used if users tend to write indiscriminate SELECT statements that return an inordinate number of rows. The limit does not apply to query results stored in the query cache because cached results can be returned without executing the query again.

  This variable is used in combination with the `sql_big_selects` session-only variable, as discussed in the description for that variable. Setting `max_join_size` to a value other than DEFAULT automatically sets `sql_big_selects` to 0.

  `sql_max_join_size` is a deprecated synonym for `max_join_size`.

- `max_length_for_sort_data` (startup: set directly; runtime: global, session)

  This variable is used by the query optimizer to determine which type of `filesort` operation to perform for ORDER BY operations.

- `max_prepared_stmt_count` (startup: set directly; runtime: global)

  The maximum number of prepared statements that the server can maintain simultaneously. The value can be from 0 to 1,000,000; the default is 16,382. Lower values can be used to limit memory use by the server. This variable was introduced in MySQL 5.0.21/5.1.10.

- `max_relay_log_size` (startup: set directly; runtime: global)

  The maximum size of a slave server relay log file. If the current relay log file reaches this size, the server closes it and begins the next one. If the value is 0, the server uses the value of `max_binlog_size` to control relay log file sizes. The allowable range of non-zero values is 4KB to 1GB. The default is 0.

- `max_seeks_for_key` (startup: set directly; runtime: global, session)

  The query optimizer uses this variable when performing key-based lookups. If an index has low cardinality (few unique values), the optimizer may assume that key lookups will require many seeks and perform a table scan instead. Setting this variable to a low value tells the optimizer to assume that at most that many index seeks will be required, which causes it to favor use of the index over a table scan.

- `max_sort_length` (startup: set directly; runtime: global, session)

  BLOB or TEXT values are sorted using the first `max_sort_length` bytes of each value. The default value is 1024. Decreasing the variable value yields shorter comparison times without loss of accuracy if sorted values are unique within this many bytes. If sorted values are not unique within this many bytes, increasing this variable enables them to be better distinguished.

- `max_sp_recursion_depth` (startup: set directly; runtime: global, session)

  The maximum depth to which stored procedures may recurse. This is a limit per procedure, not across all procedures collectively. The default is 0 (no recursion allowed) and the maximum is 255. This variable was introduced in MySQL 5.0.17.

- `max_tmp_tables` (startup: set directly; runtime: global, session)

  The maximum number of temporary tables a client can have open simultaneously. This variable currently is unused.

- `max_user_connections` (startup: set directly; runtime: global, session)

  The maximum number of simultaneous client connections allowed to any single account. The default value is zero, which means "no limit." The number of per-account connections is bound in any case by the value of `max_connections`.

  The session value for this variable exists only as of MySQL 5.0.3 and is read-only. The session value is the same as the global value unless the account row in the user table has a non-zero MAX_USER_CONNECTIONS value. In that case, the session value is taken from the account record.

  To specify connection limits for specific accounts, use the GRANT statement.

- `max_write_lock_count` (startup: set directly; runtime: global)

  After this many write locks to a table, the server begins to elevate the priority of statements that are attempting to acquire a read lock for the table.

- `min_examined_row_limit` (startup: set directly; runtime: global, session)

  The minimum number of rows that a query must examine to qualify for logging to the slow-query log. The default is 0. This variable was introduced in MySQL 5.1.21.

- `myisam_block_size` (startup: set directly)

  The block size for MyISAM table index blocks.

- `myisam_data_pointer_size` (startup: set directly; runtime: global)

  The size in bytes to use for row pointers in MyISAM index files. The value may range from 2 to 7. The default is 6 as of MySQL 5.0.6 and 4 for older versions.

  The pointer size can be influenced for individual tables by specifying the MAX_ROWS table option.

- `myisam_max_sort_file_size` (startup: set directly; runtime: global)

  MyISAM table index rebuilding for statements such as REPAIR TABLE, ALTER TABLE, or LOAD DATA can use a temporary file or the key cache. The value of this variable determines which method is used; if the temporary file would be larger than this value, the key cache is used instead.

- `myisam_recover_options` (startup: use --myisam-recover)

  The value of the --myisam-recover option that the server was started with to specify the MyISAM auto-repair mode.

- `myisam_repair_threads` (startup: set directly; runtime: global, session)

  The number of threads to use for creating MyISAM table indexes during repair operations. (Flushing applies only to repairing by sorting, not to repairing using the key cache.) The default value is 1 for single-threaded repair. Setting the value higher than 1 for multi-threaded repair should be considered experimental.

- `myisam_sort_buffer_size` (startup: set directly; runtime: global, session)

  The size of the buffer that is allocated to sort an index for MyISAM tables during operations such as ALTER TABLE, CREATE INDEX, and REPAIR TABLE.

- `myisam_stats_method` (startup: set directly; runtime: global, session)

  Whether the server should consider NULL values equal or distinct when calculating index key value distribution statistics for MyISAM tables. The value can be nulls_equal (all NULL values are in the same group) or nulls_unequal (each NULL value forms a distinct group). This variable was introduced in MySQL 5.0.14. Before that, statistics calculation is the same as nulls_equal.

- `myisam_use_mmap` (startup: use --myisam_use_mmap; runtime: global)

  ON or OFF (the default) to indicate whether the server uses memory mapping to read and write MyISAM tables. This variable was introduced in MySQL 5.1.4.

- `named_pipe` (startup: use --enable-named-pipe)

  Whether support for named-pipe connections is enabled. Such connections are supported only on Windows.

- `net_buffer_length` (startup: set directly; runtime: global, session)

  The initial size of the connection and result buffers used for communication between the server and the client. This buffer may be expanded up to max_allowed_packet bytes long. The value may range from 1KB to 1MB; the default is 16KB.

- `net_read_timeout` (startup: set directly; runtime: global, session)

  The number of seconds to wait for data from a client connection before timing out. This timeout applies only to TCP/IP connections.

- `net_retry_count` (startup: set directly; runtime: global, session)

  The number of times to retry an interrupted read.

- `net_write_timeout` (startup: set directly; runtime: global, session)

  The number of seconds to wait while writing a block to a client connection before timing out. This timeout applies only to TCP/IP connections.

- `new` (startup: set directly; runtime: global, session)

  This variable was used in MySQL 4.0 to causes the server to use certain 4.1 behaviors. It is now unused.

- `old` (startup: set directly)

  A compatibility option that enables older behavior for some features. Currently this causes index hints not to apply to ORDER BY or GROUP BY execution. This variable was introduced in MySQL 5.1.18.

- `old_passwords` (startup: set directly; runtime: global, session)

  The password hashing algorithm used for user authentication changed in MySQL 4.1. `old_passwords` indicates whether the server should use the older pre-4.1 hashing algorithm.

- `open_files_limit` (startup: set directly)

  This variable is the number of file descriptors the server will attempt to reserve. If you set it to a non-zero value at startup time, but the actual value displayed by the server is smaller than specified, the value indicates the maximum number of file descriptors allowed by the operating system. (In the case that the server displays a value of zero, it means the operating system didn't allow `mysqld` to change the number of descriptors.) If you don't set the value at startup or set it to zero, the server uses the larger of `max_connections` × 5 and `max_connections` + `table_cache` × 2 as the number of descriptors to reserve. `open_files_limit` controls allocation of file descriptors separate from those controlled by `innodb_open_files`.

- `optimizer_prune_level` (startup: set directly; runtime: global, session)

  The query optimizer examines multiple execution plans to determine the best one. This variable determines how the optimizer handles intermediate plans. If `optimizer_prune_level` is 1 (the default), the optimizer discards intermediate plans based on estimates of the number of rows they will require to be examined. If the variable is set to 0, it performs an exhaustive search of all plans. This variable was introduced in MySQL 5.0.1.

- `optimizer_search_depth` (startup: set directly; runtime: global, session)

  Controls the depth to which the optimizer searches for execution plans. A value of 0 causes the optimizer to pick a reasonable value automatically. The default is to use the pre-MySQL 5.0 behavior, which is to do an exhaustive search. This variable was introduced in MySQL 5.0.1.

- `pid_file` (startup: set directly)

  The pathname of the file into which the server writes its process ID number.

- `plugin_dir` (startup: set directly)

  The pathname for the directory where plugins are located. This variable was introduced in MySQL 5.1.2.

- `port` (startup: set directly)

  The number of the TCP/IP port to which the server listens for client connections.

- `preload_buffer_size` (startup: set directly; runtime: global, session)

  This variable determines how large a buffer to allocate when preloading indexes with the `LOAD INDEX` statement.

- `protocol_version`

  The version number of the client/server protocol the server is using.

- `pseudo_thread_id`

  This variable is used internally by the server.

- `query_alloc_block_size` (startup: set directly; runtime: global, session)

  The block size for allocation of temporary memory while parsing and executing statements.

- `query_cache_limit` (startup: set directly; runtime: global)

  The maximum size of cached query results; larger results are not cached. The default value is 1MB.

- `query_cache_min_res_unit` (startup: set directly; runtime: global)

  The block size for allocation of memory for storing results in the query cache. The default value is 4KB.

- `query_cache_size` (startup: set directly; runtime: global)

  The amount of memory to use for query result caching. Setting this variable to zero disables the query cache, even if `query_cache_type` is not `OFF`. Conversely, setting this variable to a non-zero value causes that much memory to be allocated, even if `query_cache_type` is `OFF`. The value should be a multiple of 1024.

- `query_cache_type` (startup: set directly; runtime: global, session)

  The mode of operation of the query cache, if `query_cache_size` is greater than zero. The following table shows the allowable values.

Mode	Meaning
0	Don't cache query results or retrieve cached results
1	Cache cacheable queries except those that begin with `SELECT SQL_NO_CACHE`
2	Cache on demand only cacheable queries that begin with `SELECT SQL_CACHE`

If you set the `query_cache_type` variable in a `SET` statement, the symbolic values `OFF`, `ON`, and `DEMAND` can be used as synonyms for 0, 1, and 2.

sql_query_cache_type is a deprecated synonym for query_cache_type.

- query_cache_wlock_invalidate (startup: set directly; runtime: global, session)

  When this variable is 0 (the default), clients can retrieve cached query results for a table even if another client acquires a WRITE lock on the table. Setting this variable to 1 cause the cached results to be invalidated when a client acquires a WRITE lock, forcing other clients to wait for the lock to be released.

- query_prealloc_size (startup: set directly; runtime: global, session)

  The size of the buffer that is allocated for parsing and executing statements. This buffer is not freed between statements, unlike blocks allocated under the control of the query_alloc_block_size variable.

- range_alloc_block_size (startup: set directly; runtime: global, session)

  The block size for allocation of memory while performing range optimizations.

- read_buffer_size (startup: set directly; runtime: global, session)

  The size of the buffer used by threads that perform sequential table scans. A buffer is allocated as necessary per client.

- read_only (startup: set directly; runtime: global)

  This variable controls whether a slave server operates in read-only fashion for client connections. By default, read_only is OFF, updates by clients are accepted in the usual way (that is, they have privileges to do so). When set to ON, updates are allowed only for statements received from the master or issued by clients that have the SUPER privilege.

  As of MySQL 5.1.15, the server enforces additional constraints on use of read_only: You cannot enable the variable while you hold explicit table locks or have an outstanding transaction. If you attempt to enable read_only while other clients hold table locks or have outstanding transactions, your request blocks until those locks are released and transactions have terminated. While the request is blocked, other clients block if they attempt to acquire new table locks or begin transactions. These conditions for blocking do not apply to FLUSH TABLES WITH READ LOCK, which acquires a global read lock, not a table lock.

- read_rnd_buffer_size (startup: set directly; runtime: global, session)

  The size of the buffer used for reading rows in order after a sort. A buffer is allocated as necessary per client.

- relay_log_purge (startup: set directly; runtime: global)

  When set to 1 (the default), a slave server removes each relay log file as soon as it is no longer needed. If set to 0, the relay log files are not removed automatically.

- relay_log_space_limit (startup: set directly)

  The maximum allowable combined size of the relay log files.

- rpl_recovery_rank (runtime: global)

  This variable is unused.

- secure_auth (startup: set directly; runtime: global)

  When set to ON, the server allows connections only for accounts that have the newer password format introduced in MySQL 4.1. When set to OFF, the server also allows connections to accounts that have passwords in the older format. The default is OFF.

- secure_file_priv (startup: set directly)

  When set to a directory pathname, the server permits LOAD DATA and SELECT ... INTO OUTFILE statements and the LOAD_FILE() function only for operations in that directory. The value is empty by default (no such restriction). This variable was introduced in MySQL 5.0.38/5.1.17.

- server_id (startup: set directly; runtime: global)

  The server's replication ID number. If 0, the server is not participating in replication. Otherwise, the value should be an integer from 1 to 2^{32}-1. The value must be different from that of any other replication server that you are using.

- shared_memory (startup: set directly)

  If set to ON, the server allows shared-memory connections by clients. The default is OFF. Shared-memory connections are supported only on Windows.

- shared_memory_base_name (startup: set directly)

  The shared-memory name to use for shared-memory connections. The default name is MYSQL (case sensitive)

- skip_external_locking (startup: set directly)

  Whether use of external locking (filesystem locking) is suppressed.

- skip_networking (startup: use --skip-networking)

  OFF to enable TCP/IP connections, ON to disable them. In the latter case, clients can connect from the local host only, using Unix socket connections under Unix or named pipes or shared memory under Windows.

- skip_show_database (startup: set directly)

  When set to OFF (the default), the SHOW DATABASES statement can be used by any user. It displays all databases if the user has the SHOW DATABASES privilege, or those databases for which the user has some privilege otherwise. When set to ON, the SHOW DATABASES statement can be used only by users who have the SHOW DATABASES privilege, and it displays all databases.

- slave_allow_batching (startup: set directly; runtime: global)

  Enable a slave server to batch requests; applies only to MySQL Cluster. This variable was introduced in MySQL 5.2.5.

- slave_compressed_protocol (startup: set directly; runtime: global)

  Whether compression should be used to reduce the amount of traffic sent between a slave server and its master. This requires that both the master and slave support the compressed protocol.

- `slave_load_tmpdir` (startup: set directly)

  The pathname of the directory where the server creates temporary files for LOAD DATA statements if it is acting as a replication slave. The default value is the value of the `tmpdir` system variable.

- `slave_net_timeout` (startup: set directly; runtime: global)

  The number of seconds to wait for data from a master server before timing out. This timeout applies only to TCP/IP connections.

- `slave_skip_errors` (startup: use `--slave-skip-errors`)

  The list of errors that a slave server should ignore rather than suspending replication if they occur. (However, it's usually better to determine what is causing problems so that you can resolve them rather than using this option to ignore them.) A value of `all` means all errors should be ignored. Otherwise, the value should be a list of one or more error numbers separated by commas.

- `slave_transaction_retries` (startup: set directly; runtime: global)

  The number of times that a slave should retry a transaction that fails due to deadlock or because a storage engine's timeout has been reached. This variable was introduced in MySQL 5.0.3.

- `slow_launch_time` (startup: set directly; runtime: global)

  The number of seconds that defines "slow" thread creation. Any thread taking longer to create causes the `Slow_launch_threads` status counter to be incremented.

- `slow_query_log` (startup: set directly; runtime: global)

  Whether logging to the slow-query log is enabled. (If so, the log destinations are indicated by `log_output`.) This variable was introduced in MySQL 5.1.12. The value can be set at runtime to enable or disable logging as of 5.1.23.

- `slow_query_log_file` (runtime: global)

  The name of the slow-query log file, for use if the file logging destination is enabled. This variable was introduced in MySQL 5.1.12.

- `socket` (startup: set directly)

  The pathname to the Unix domain socket, or the name of the named pipe under Windows.

- `sort_buffer_size` (startup: set directly; runtime: global, session)

  The size of the buffer used by threads for performing sort operations (GROUP BY or ORDER BY). This buffer is allocated as necessary per client. Normally, if you may have many clients that do sorting at the same time, it is unwise to make this value very large (more than 1MB).

- `sql_mode` (startup: set directly; runtime: global, session)

  The server SQL mode. This variable modifies certain aspects of the server's behavior to cause it to act according to standard SQL, or to be compatible with other database servers or older MySQL servers. The value should be an empty string to clear the mode, or a comma-separated list of one or more of the mode values described following. Some mode values are simple and enable one behavior. Others are composite modes that serve as shorthand enabling a set of modes to be specified more easily. Mode values are not case sensitive.

  The term "strict mode" refers to a `sql_mode` setting that has `STRICT_TRANS_TABLES` or `STRICT_ALL_TABLES` enabled to cause the server to be strict about data checking. Section 3.3, "How MySQL Handles Invalid Data Values," further discusses strict mode and other modes that affect input data handling.

  The following list describes the simple SQL mode values:

  - `ALLOW_INVALID_DATES`

    In strict mode, suppresses full date validity checking for `DATE` and `DATETIME` values. The only requirements are that the month be in the range from 1 to 12 and the day in the range from 1 to 31. `TIMESTAMP` values must be valid regardless of whether this mode is enabled.

    `ALLOW_INVALID_DATES` was introduced in MySQL 5.0.2. Prior to 5.0.2, date handling is performed as though `ALLOW_INVALID_DATES` is enabled. That is, date checking is not strict.

  - `ANSI_QUOTES`

    Treats the double quote character as a quote character for identifiers such as database, table, and column names, and not as a string quote character. (Backticks are allowed for name quoting regardless of whether this mode is enabled.)

  - `ERROR_FOR_DIVISION_BY_ZERO`

    For inserts or updates, division (or modulo) operations with a divisor of zero normally produce a result of `NULL` and no warning, even in strict mode. Enabling `ERROR_FOR_DIVISION_BY_ZERO` changes this behavior. With strict mode not enabled, division by zero still produces a result of `NULL` but a warning occurs. With strict mode enabled, division by zero during `INSERT` and `UPDATE` statements causes an error and the statement fails. To suppress the error for inserts or updates and produce a result of `NULL` and a warning, use `INSERT IGNORE` or `UPDATE IGNORE`. This mode was introduced in MySQL 5.0.2.

  - `HIGH_NOT_PRECEDENCE`

    This mode was introduced in MySQL 5.0.2. It changes the precedence of the `NOT` operator to be the same as the `!` operator, which is the precedence that `NOT` had before MySQL 5.0.2.

- IGNORE_SPACE

  Causes the server to ignore spaces between names of built-in functions and the '(' character that introduces the argument list. Normally, function names should be followed immediately by the parenthesis with no intervening spaces. This mode causes function names to be treated as reserved words.

- NO_AUTO_CREATE_USER

  Prohibits GRANT statements from creating insecure new accounts. GRANT fails if it does not include an IDENTIFIED BY clause to provide an account password. This mode was introduced in MySQL 5.0.2.

- NO_AUTO_VALUE_ON_ZERO

  When this mode is not enabled, inserting 0 into an AUTO_INCREMENT column has the same result as inserting NULL: MySQL generates the next sequence number and stores it in the column. When this mode is enabled, inserting 0 into an AUTO_INCREMENT column causes 0 to be stored.

- NO_BACKSLASH_ESCAPES

  Causes backslash ('\') not to be treated as an escape character within strings, but rather as an ordinary character with no special meaning. This mode was introduced in MySQL 5.0.1.

- NO_DIR_IN_CREATE

  Ignores DATA DIRECTORY and INDEX DIRECTORY table options in CREATE TABLE and ALTER TABLE statements.

- NO_ENGINE_SUBSTITUTION

  This mode determines how the server handles CREATE TABLE or ALTER TABLE statements that include an ENGINE option for which the specified storage engine to use for the table is not available. (As of MySQL 5.1.12, "not available" means "not compiled in an not loaded at runtime." Before 5.1.12, it means "not compiled in, or compiled in but disabled at startup.")

  If NO_ENGINE_SUBSTITUTION is enabled, the table is not created (or altered) if the specified engine is not available and an error occurs. If NO_ENGINE_SUBSTITUTION is disabled, substitution of the default storage engine is allowed if the specified engine is not available. In this case, an error occurs only if the engine name is known to be illegal; this applies only before MySQL 5.1.2, when servers know a fixed set of engine names. (As of 5.1.12, engines can be loaded at runtime, so the set of all legal names cannot be known.) This mode was introduced in MySQL 5.0.8.

- NO_FIELD_OPTIONS

  Makes the output of SHOW CREATE TABLE statements more portable by suppressing inclusion of MySQL-specific column-related options.

- NO_KEY_OPTIONS

  Makes the output of SHOW CREATE TABLE statements more portable by suppressing inclusion of MySQL-specific index-related options.

- NO_TABLE_OPTIONS

  Makes the output of SHOW CREATE TABLE statements more portable by suppressing inclusion of MySQL-specific table-related options.

- NO_UNSIGNED_SUBTRACTION

  By default, subtraction between integer operands results in an unsigned result if either operand is unsigned. This mode allows signed results, which is compatible with the behavior of MySQL prior to version 4.0.

- NO_ZERO_DATE

  In strict mode, rejects '0000-00-00' as a valid date. Normally, MySQL allows "zero" date values to be stored. This mode can be overridden by using INSERT IGNORE rather than INSERT. This mode was introduced in MySQL 5.0.2.

- NO_ZERO_IN_DATE

  In strict mode, rejects dates that have a month or day part of zero. (A zero year is allowed.) Normally, MySQL allows such date values to be stored. In non-strict mode or if INSERT IGNORE is used, MySQL stores such dates as '0000-00-00'. This mode was introduced in MySQL 5.0.2.

- ONLY_FULL_GROUP_BY

  Normally, MySQL allows SELECT statements with non-aggregate columns in the output column list or the HAVING clause that are not named in the GROUP BY clause. For example:

  ```
  SELECT a, b, COUNT(*) FROM t GROUP BY a;
  ```

  The ONLY_FULL_GROUP_BY flag requires non-aggregate output columns (or HAVING columns) to be named in the GROUP BY:

  ```
  SELECT a, b, COUNT(*) FROM t GROUP BY a, b;
  ```

- PAD_CHAR_TO_FULL_LENGTH

  Normally, the server removes trailing spaces from CHAR column values when it retrieves them. This mode suppresses CHAR column trailing-space removal so that retrieved values have the full column length. This mode was introduced in MySQL 5.1.20.

- PIPES_AS_CONCAT

  Causes || to be treated as a string concatenation operator rather than as logical OR.

- REAL_AS_FLOAT

  The REAL data type becomes a synonym for FLOAT rather than for DOUBLE.

- STRICT_ALL_TABLES

  Enables strict checking of input data values for all storage engines to cause MySQL to reject most invalid values. This mode was introduced in MySQL 5.0.2. Use TRADITIONAL to be even more strict.

- STRICT_TRANS_TABLES

  Enables strict checking of input data values for transactional storage engines to cause MySQL to reject most invalid values. In addition, enable strict checking for non-transactional storage engines when that is possible (such as for single-row INSERT statements). This mode was introduced in MySQL 5.0.2. Use TRADITIONAL to be even more strict.

The following table lists the composite SQL modes and shows the set of modes for which each one is shorthand.

Composite Mode	Constituent Modes
ANSI	ANSI_QUOTES, IGNORE_SPACE, PIPES_AS_CONCAT, REAL_AS_FLOAT
DB2	ANSI_QUOTES, IGNORE_SPACE, NO_FIELD_OPTIONS, NO_KEY_OPTIONS, NO_TABLE_OPTIONS, PIPES_AS_CONCAT
MAXDB	ANSI_QUOTES, IGNORE_SPACE, NO_AUTO_CREATE_USER, NO_FIELD_OPTIONS, NO_KEY_OPTIONS, NO_TABLE_OPTIONS, PIPES_AS_CONCAT
MSSQL	ANSI_QUOTES, IGNORE_SPACE, NO_FIELD_OPTIONS, NO_KEY_OPTIONS, NO_TABLE_OPTIONS, PIPES_AS_CONCAT
MYSQL323	HIGH_NOT_PRECEDENCE, NO_FIELD_OPTIONS
MYSQL40	HIGH_NOT_PRECEDENCE, NO_FIELD_OPTIONS
ORACLE	ANSI_QUOTES, IGNORE_SPACE, NO_AUTO_CREATE_USER, NO_FIELD_OPTIONS, NO_KEY_OPTIONS, NO_TABLE_OPTIONS, PIPES_AS_CONCAT
POSTGRESQL	ANSI_QUOTES, IGNORE_SPACE, NO_FIELD_OPTIONS, NO_KEY_OPTIONS, NO_TABLE_OPTIONS, PIPES_AS_CONCAT
TRADITIONAL	ERROR_FOR_DIVISION_BY_ZERO, NO_AUTO_CREATE_USER, NO_ZERO_DATE, NO_ZERO_IN_DATE, STRICT_ALL_TABLES, STRICT_TRANS_TABLES

Before MySQL 5.0.3, ANSI also includes ONLY_FULL_GROUP_BY.

TRADITIONAL mode is so called because it enables the modes that cause handling of input values to be like that of traditional databases that reject invalid data. It's like strict mode but includes several additional constraints for even stricter checking. TRADITIONAL mode was introduced in MySQL 5.0.2.

- sql_select_limit (runtime: global, session)

    Specifies the maximum number of rows to return from a SELECT statement. The presence of an explicit LIMIT clause in a statement takes precedence over this variable. The default value is the maximum number of rows allowed per table. A value of DEFAULT restores this default if you have changed it.

    This variable has no effect within stored routines, or for SELECT operations that do not return rows to the client (such as subqueries, INSERT INTO ... SELECT, and CREATE TABLE ... SELECT).

- sql_slave_skip_counter (runtime: global)

    If you have the SUPER privilege, you can set this as a GLOBAL variable to a value of n to tell a slave replication server to skip the next n events received from its master server.

- ssl_xxx (startup: use --ssl-xxx)

    The ssl_xxx variables indicate the values of the corresponding --ssl-xxx options given to the server at startup. (For example, ssl_ca indicates the value of the --ssl-ca option.) The value of each variable is the empty string if the corresponding option was not given. The values are NULL if SSL support is not available. These variables were introduced in MySQL 5.0.23/5.1.11.

- storage_engine (startup: use --default-storage-engine; runtime: global, session)

    The default storage engine to use for tables that are created without an ENGINE = engine_name option or with an unsupported engine_name value.

- sync_binlog (startup: set directly; runtime: global)

    When set to 0 (the default), the server does not flush the binary log to disk. When set to a positive value n, the server flushes the log after every n writes to the binary log. In this case, lower values provide greater safety in the event of a crash, but also affect performance more adversely.

- sync_frm (startup: set directly; runtime: global)

    When set to 0, the server does not flush the .frm file for non-temporary tables to disk when they are created. The default is 1, which does flush the file.

- system_time_zone

    The server's system time zone. The server tries to determine the variable value when it starts by consulting the system. You can set the TZ environment variable or specify the --timezone option to mysqld_safe to set the value explicitly.

- `table_cache`, `table_open_cache` (startup: set directly; runtime: global)

  The maximum number of tables that can be open. This cache is shared between threads. `table_cache` is the original variable name, which was changed to `table_open_cache` in MySQL 5.1.3.

- `table_definition_cache` (startup: set directly; runtime: global)

  The number of table definitions (from `.frm` files) that the server can store in its definition cache. This variable was introduced in MySQL 5.1.3.

- `table_lock_wait_timeout` (startup: set directly; runtime: global)

  How long in seconds to wait for table-level locks before timing out, for connections that have open cursors. The default value is 50. This variable was introduced in MySQL 5.0.10.

- `table_type` (startup: use `--default-storage-engine`; runtime: global, session)

  This variable is a deprecated synonym for `storage_engine`; it was removed in MySQL 5.2.5.

- `thread_cache_size` (startup: set directly; runtime: global)

  The maximum number of threads to maintain in the thread cache. Threads from clients that disconnect are put in the cache if it's not already full. This enables new connections to be serviced by reusing cached threads rather than creating new threads, as long as threads remain in the cache. The thread cache is used when the server uses one thread per currently connected client.

- `thread_concurrency` (startup: set directly)

  This variable applies only to Solaris. The value is passed to `thr_concurrency()` to provide a hint to the thread manager about how many threads to run simultaneously.

- `thread_handling` (startup: set directly)

  The thread model that the server uses for handling client connections. The value can be `one-thread` (a single connection thread), `one-pool-per-connection` (one thread per currently connected client), or (as of MySQL 6.0.4) `pool-of-threads` (a fixed size pool of threads that service all connected clients). This variable was introduced in MySQL 5.1.17.

- `thread_pool_size` (startup: set directly)

  The size of the pool of statement-processing threads to be used if the value of `thread_handling` is `pool-of-threads`. The default value is 20. This variable was introduced in MySQL 6.0.4.

- `thread_stack` (startup: set directly)

  The stack size for each thread.

- `time_format`

  This variable is unused.

- time_zone (startup: use --default-time-zone; runtime: global, session)

  The server's current time zone. A value of SYSTEM indicates that the server is using the value of the system_time_zone variable. A client can modify the session value of this variable to set the time zone for its own connection.

- timed_mutexes (startup: use --timed_mutexes; runtime: global)

  Whether to collect InnoDB mutex timing information. This variable was introduced in MySQL 5.0.3.

- tmp_table_size (startup: set directly; runtime: global, session)

  The maximum number of bytes allowed for internal temporary tables. (Tables that the server creates automatically while processing statements.) If a temporary table exceeds the smaller of max_heap_table_size and tmp_table_size, the server converts it from an internal in-memory table to a MyISAM table on disk. If you have memory to spare, higher values of this variable allow the server to maintain larger temporary tables in memory without converting them to on-disk format.

- tmpdir (startup: set directly)

  The pathname to the directory where the server creates temporary files. The option value can be given as a list of directories, to be used in round-robin fashion. Under Unix, separate directory names by colons; under Windows or NetWare, separate them by semicolons.

- transaction_alloc_block_size (startup: set directly; runtime: global, session)

  The block size for allocation of temporary memory needed for processing statements that are stored as part of a transaction prior to writing the transaction to the binary log at commit time.

- transaction_prealloc_size (startup: set directly; runtime: global, session)

  The size of the buffer that is allocated for processing statements that are part of a transaction. This buffer is not freed between statements, unlike blocks allocated under the control of the transaction_alloc_block_size variable.

- tx_isolation (startup: use --transaction-isolation; runtime: global, session)

  The default transaction isolation level.

- updatable_views_with_limit (startup: set directly; runtime: global, session)

  When set to 0 or NO, the server disallows updates (UPDATE or DELETE statements) to views that do not use a primary key in the underlying table, even if the update contains a LIMIT 1 clause to constrain the update to a single row. When set to 1 or YES (the default), the update is allowed and the server produces only a warning. This variable was introduced in MySQL 5.0.2.

- version

  The server version. The value consists of a version number, possibly followed by one or more suffixes. The suffix values are listed in the description of the VERSION() function in Appendix C, "Operator and Function Reference."

- `version_comment`

  The value of the `--with-comment` option specified to `configure` at the time the server was built. The default value is `"Source distribution"` if you don't specify any comment at configuration time.

- `version_compile_machine`

  The compilation machine (hardware type). The value is determined during the configuration process when MySQL is built.

- `version_compile_os`

  The compilation operating system. The value is determined during the configuration process when MySQL is built.

- `wait_timeout` (startup: set directly; runtime: global, session)

  The number of seconds a non-interactive client connection can remain idle before the server considers itself free to close it. For interactive clients, the value of the `interactive_timeout` variable is used instead. This applies only to TCP/IP and Unix socket file connections.

D.2 Session-Only System Variables

The following list describes system variables that exist in session-only form. That is, each client gets its own set of these variables when it connects to the server, but there are no corresponding global variables. A client that sets any of these variables affects server operation only for itself.

Most of the session-only system variables do not show up in the output from SHOW VARIABLES, but you can select the value for each with `SELECT @@SESSION.var_name` or `SELECT @@var_name`.

Session variable names are not case sensitive.

- `autocommit`

  The autocommit mode for transaction processing. This is 1 by default, so autocommit is enabled and statements take effect immediately; essentially, each statement is its own transaction. Setting the value to 0 disables autocommit so that subsequent statements do not take effect until a commit is performed (either with a COMMIT statement, or by setting `autocommit` to 1). Statements in the transaction may be canceled with ROLLBACK if a commit has not occurred. Setting `autocommit` to 1 re-enables autocommit (and implicitly commits any pending transaction).

- `big_tables`

  All internal temporary tables are stored on disk rather than in memory if this is variable is set to 1. Performance is slower, but SELECT statements that require large temporary tables will not generate "table full" errors. The default is 0 (hold temporary tables in memory). Normally you need not set this variable.

`sql_big_tables` is a deprecated synonym for `big_tables`.

- `error_count`

  This is a read-only variable that indicates the number of errors generated by the last statement that can generate errors.

- `foreign_key_checks`

  Setting this variable to 0 or 1 disables or enables foreign key checking for InnoDB tables. The default is to perform checking. Disabling key checks can be useful, for example, when restoring a dump file that creates and loads tables in an order different from that required by their foreign key relationships. You can re-enable key checking after loading the tables.

- `identity`

  This is a synonym for the `last_insert_id` session variable.

- `insert_id`

  Setting this variable specifies the value to be used by the next INSERT statement when inserting an AUTO_INCREMENT column. This is used for binary log processing.

- `last_insert_id`

  Setting this variable specifies the value to be returned by `LAST_INSERT_ID()`. This is used for binary log processing.

- `sql_auto_is_null`

  If this is set to 1 (the default), the most recently generated AUTO_INCREMENT value can be selected using a WHERE clause of the form WHERE *col_name* IS NULL, where *col_name* is the name of the AUTO_INCREMENT column. This feature is used by some ODBC programs. To disable it, set the variable to 0.

- `sql_big_selects`

  The server uses this variable in conjunction with the `max_join_size` system variable. If `sql_big_selects` is set to 1 (the default), the server allows queries that return result sets of any size. If `sql_big_selects` is set to 0, the server disallows queries that are likely to return a large number of rows. In this case, the value of `max_join_size` is used when executing a join: The server makes an estimate of the number of row combinations it will need to examine, and if that value exceeds the value of `max_join_size`, the server returns an error rather than executing the query.

  Setting `max_join_size` to a value other than DEFAULT automatically sets `sql_big_selects` to 0.

- `sql_buffer_result`

  Setting this variable to 1 causes the server to use internal temporary tables to hold results from SELECT statements. The effect is that the server can more quickly release locks held on the tables from which the results are produced. The default is 0.

- `sql_log_bin`

  Setting this variable to 0 or 1 disables or enables binary logging for the current client connection. The client must have the SUPER privilege for this statement to have any effect. This variable has no effect if the server's binary log is not enabled.

- `sql_log_off`

  Setting this variable to 0 or 1 enables or disables statement logging to the general query log for the current client connection. The client must have the SUPER privilege for this statement to have any effect. This variable has no effect if the server's general log is not enabled.

- `sql_log_update`

  This variable is obsolete as of MySQL 5.0 because the update log has been removed.

- `sql_notes`

  Setting this variable to 0 or 1 (the default) controls whether the server suppresses or records Note-level warnings. This variable was introduced in MySQL 5.0.3.

- `sql_quote_show_create`

  This variable controls whether to quote identifiers (database, table, column, and index names) in the output from SHOW CREATE TABLE and SHOW CREATE DATABASE statements. The default is 1 (use quoting). Turning quoting off by setting the variable to 0 may be useful when producing CREATE TABLE statements for use with other database servers, or very old MySQL servers that do not understand backtick quoting. If you turn quoting off, be sure that your tables do not use names that are reserved words or that contain special characters.

  Identifiers are quoted with backtick ('`') characters if the ANSI_QUOTES SQL mode is disabled, and with double quote ('"') characters if it is enabled.

- `sql_safe_updates`

  If this variable is set to 1, the server allows UPDATE and DELETE statements only if the rows to be modified are identified by key values or if a LIMIT clause is used. The default of 0 enforces no such restriction.

- `sql_warnings`

  If set to 1, MySQL reports warning counts even for single-row inserts. The default is 0: Warning counts are reported only for INSERT statements that insert multiple rows.

- `timestamp`

  Setting this variable specifies a TIMESTAMP value for the current connection. This is used for binary log processing. The timestamp value affects the value returned by NOW(), but not the value returned by SYSDATE().

- unique_checks

  Setting this variable to 0 or 1 disables or enables uniqueness checks for secondary indexes in InnoDB tables. Disabling these checks can increase performance when importing data into InnoDB tables, but this should not be done unless you know that data values do not violate uniqueness requirements.

- warning_count

  This is a read-only variable that indicates the number of errors, warnings, and notes generated by the last statement that can generate such messages.

D.3 Status Variables

Status variables provide information about the server's current operational state. These variables can be displayed by the SHOW STATUS statement or by executing the mysqladmin extended-status command. As of MySQL 5.0.2, the status variables (like system variables) have global and session-specific values. These represent the sum over all clients and the value for the current client, respectively. If a variable has only a global value, the same value is returned for the global and session variables. As of MySQL 5.1.12, you can also query the INFORMATION_SCHEMA tables named GLOBAL_STATUS and SESSION_STATUS to obtain status variable information.

For more information about examining status variables at runtime, see Section 12.6.3, "Checking Status Variable Values."

Status variable names are not case sensitive.

The more general variables are described in the following list. Separate sections after that describe sets of variables that are related to each other. These include variables for statement counters, the InnoDB storage engine, the query cache, and SSL.

- Aborted_clients

  The number of client connections aborted due to clients not closing the connection properly.

- Aborted_connects

  The number of attempts to connect to the server that failed.

- Binlog_cache_disk_use

  The number of transactions that had to use a temporary disk file because their size exceeded the value of the binlog_cache_size system variable.

- Binlog_cache_use

  The number of transactions that could be held in the binary log cache because their size did not exceed the value of the binlog_cache_size system variable.

- Bytes_received

  The total number of bytes received from all clients.

- `Bytes_sent`

  The total number of bytes sent to all clients.

- `Com_xxx`

  The server maintains a set of status variables that serve as counters to indicate the number of times particular types of statements (commands) have been executed. There are dozens of such variables, and they all have similar names, so they are not listed individually here. Each statement counter variable name begins with `Com_`, and has a suffix that indicates the type of statement to which the counter corresponds. For example, `Com_select` and `Com_drop_table` indicate, respectively, how many SELECT and DROP TABLE statements the server has executed.

- `Compression`

  Whether traffic sent via the client/server protocol uses compression. This variable was introduced in MySQL 5.0.16.

- `Connections`

  The number of attempts to connect to the server (both successful and unsuccessful).

- `Created_tmp_disk_tables`

  The number of on-disk temporary tables created by the server while processing statements.

- `Created_tmp_files`

  The number of temporary files created by the server.

- `Created_tmp_tables`

  The number of in-memory temporary tables created by the server while processing statements.

- `Delayed_errors`

  The number of errors that have occurred while processing INSERT DELAYED rows.

- `Delayed_insert_threads`

  The number of INSERT DELAYED handlers.

- `Delayed_writes`

  The number of INSERT DELAYED rows that have been written.

- `Flush_commands`

  The number of FLUSH statements that have been executed.

- `Handler_commit`

  The number of requests to commit a transaction.

- `Handler_delete`

  The number of requests to delete a row from a table.

- `Handler_discover`

  This is used with the NDBCLUSTER storage engine. It indicates how many times the server asked NDB about a table name and successfully found (discovered) the table.

- `Handler_prepare`

  The number of prepares for two-phase commits. This variable was introduced in MySQL 5.0.3.

- `Handler_read_first`

  The number of requests to read the first row from an index.

- `Handler_read_key`

  The number of requests to read a row based on an index value.

- `Handler_read_next`

  The number of requests to read the next row in index order.

- `Handler_read_prev`

  The number of requests to read the previous row in descending index order.

- `Handler_read_rnd`

  The number of requests to read a row based on its position.

- `Handler_read_rnd_next`

  The number of requests to read the next row. If this number is high, you are likely performing many statements that require full table scans or that are not using indexes properly.

- `Handler_rollback`

  The number of requests to roll back a transaction.

- `Handler_savepoint`

  The number of requests to create a transaction savepoint. This variable was introduced in MySQL 5.0.3.

- `Handler_savepoint_rollback`

  The number of requests to roll back to a transaction savepoint. This variable was introduced in MySQL 5.0.3.

- `Handler_update`

  The number of requests to update a row in a table.

- `Handler_write`

  The number of requests to insert a row in a table.

- `Innodb_xxx`

  See Section D.3.1, "InnoDB Status Variables."

- `Key_blocks_not_flushed`

  The number of blocks in the key cache that have been modified but not yet flushed to disk.

- `Key_blocks_unused`

  The number of unused blocks in the key cache.

- `Key_blocks_used`

  The maximum number of blocks in the key cache that have ever simultaneously been in use.

- `Key_read_requests`

  The number of requests to read a block from the key cache.

- `Key_reads`

  The number of reads of index blocks from disk.

- `Key_write_requests`

  The number of requests to write a block to the key cache.

- `Key_writes`

  The number of writes of index blocks to disk.

- `Last_query_cost`

  The query optimizer's most recent query cost calculation. The value is useful only for queries that do not use UNION or subqueries. The value if no query cost has yet been calculated is 0, or –1 before MySQL 5.0.7. As of 5.0.16, the value is set for queries served using the query cache. This variable was introduced in MySQL 5.0.1.

- `Max_used_connections`

  The maximum number of connections that have ever simultaneously been open.

- `Not_flushed_delayed_rows`

  The number of rows waiting to be written for INSERT DELAYED statements.

- `Open_files`

  The number of open files.

- `Open_streams`

  The number of open streams. A stream is a file opened with fopen(); this applies only to log files.

- `Open_table_definitions`

  The number of cached .frm files. This variable was introduced in MySQL 5.1.3.

- `Open_tables`

  The number of open tables. This does not count TEMPORARY tables.

- `Opened_files`

  The total number of files that the server has opened. (There may be some storage engines that do not increment this counter.) This variable was introduced in MySQL 5.1.21.

- `Opened_tables`

  The total number of tables that the server has opened. If this number is high, it may be a good idea to increase your table cache size.

- `Prepared_stmt_count`

  The number of prepared statements. This variable was introduced as the `prepared_stmt_count` system variable in MySQL 5.0.21/5.1.10 and converted to the `Prepared_stmt_count` status variable in 5.0.32/5.1.11.

- `Qcache_xxx`

  See Section D.3.2, "Query Cache Status Variables."

- `Questions`

  The number of statements that have been received by the server (this includes both successful and unsuccessful statements). The ratio of `Questions` to `Update` yields the number of statements per second.

- `Rpl_status`

  This variable is not used.

- `Select_full_join`

  The number of "full" joins; that is, joins performed without using indexes.

- `Select_full_range_join`

  The number of joins performed using a range search on a reference table.

- `Select_range`

  The number of joins performed using a range on the first table.

- `Select_range_check`

  The number of joins performed such that a range search must be used to fetch rows on a secondary table.

- `Select_scan`

  The number of joins performed that used a full scan of the first table.

- `Slave_open_temp_tables`

  The number of temporary tables the slave SQL thread has open.

- `Slave_retried_transactions`

  The number of times that the slave SQL thread has retried transactions. This variable was introduced in MySQL 5.0.4.

- `Slave_running`

  Whether the slave I/O and SQL threads both are running.

- `Slow_launch_threads`

  The number of threads that took longer than `slow_launch_time` seconds to create.

- `Slow_queries`

  The number of queries that look longer than `long_query_time` seconds to execute.

- `Sort_merge_passes`

  The number of merge passes performed by the sort algorithm.

- `Sort_range`

  The number of sort operations performed using a range.

- `Sort_rows`

  The number of rows sorted.

- `Sort_scan`

  The number of sort operations performed using a full table scan.

- `Ssl_xxx`

  See Section D.3.3, "SSL Status Variables."

- `Table_locks_immediate`

  The number of table lock requests that could be satisfied immediately with no waiting.

- `Table_locks_waited`

  The number of requests for a table lock that could be satisfied only after waiting. If this value is high, it indicates that you have a lot of contention for table locks.

- `Tc_log_max_pages_used`

  The maximum number of pages that have been used for the transaction coordinator recovery log file. This variable was introduced in MySQL 5.0.3.

- `Tc_log_page_size`

  The page size for the transaction coordinator recovery log file. This variable was introduced in MySQL 5.0.3.

- `Tc_log_page_waits`

  The number of times a two-phase commit had to wait for a free page in the transaction coordinator recovery log file. This variable was introduced in MySQL 5.0.3.

- `Threads_cached`

  The number of threads in the thread cache.

- `Threads_connected`

  The number of open connections.

- `Threads_created`

  The total number of threads that have been created to handle client connections.

- `Threads_running`

  The number of threads that are active (not sleeping).

- `Uptime`

  The number of seconds since the server started running.

- `Uptime_since_flush_status`

  The number of seconds since FLUSH STATUS was most recently executed. This variable was introduced in MySQL 5.0.35. This is a feature of MySQL Community Server only.

D.3.1 InnoDB Status Variables

The following variables display information about the operation of the InnoDB storage engine. Many of them are available in the output of SHOW ENGINE INNODB STATUS, but are more easily parsed in the output from SHOW STATUS. Most of these variables were introduced in MySQL 5.0.2; exceptions are so noted.

- `Innodb_buffer_pool_pages_data`

  The number of pages in the InnoDB buffer pool that contain data. This counts both clean pages that have not been modified and dirty pages that contain modified data.

- `Innodb_buffer_pool_pages_dirty`

  The number of pages in the InnoDB buffer pool that contain modified data.

- `Innodb_buffer_pool_pages_flushed`

  The number of InnoDB buffer pool pages for which flush requests have been issued.

- `Innodb_buffer_pool_pages_free`

  The number of free pages in the InnoDB buffer pool.

- `Innodb_buffer_pool_pages_latched`

  The number of pages in the InnoDB buffer pool that are in the process of being read or written or that for some other reason cannot be flushed and freed for reuse.

- `Innodb_buffer_pool_pages_misc`

  The number of pages in the InnoDB buffer pool that are allocated for internal operations.

- `Innodb_buffer_pool_pages_total`

  The total number of pages in the InnoDB buffer pool.

- `Innodb_buffer_pool_read_ahead_rnd`

  The number of random read-aheads initiated by InnoDB. These occur when InnoDB must read a large part of a table in non-sequential order.

- `Innodb_buffer_pool_read_ahead_seq`

  The number of sequential read-aheads initiated by InnoDB. These occur when InnoDB performs sequential full-table scans.

- `Innodb_buffer_pool_read_requests`

  The number of logical read requests issued by InnoDB.

- `Innodb_buffer_pool_reads`

  The number of single-page reads done due to not being able to perform a logical read from the InnoDB buffer pool.

- `Innodb_buffer_pool_wait_free`

  The number of times InnoDB had to wait for writes to the buffer pool to be flushed. Writes usually are done in the background, but InnoDB must perform a wait if no pages are available when it needs to read a page or create a new one.

- `Innodb_buffer_pool_write_requests`

  The number writes to the InnoDB buffer pool.

- `Innodb_data_fsyncs`

  The number of sync-to-disk operations performed by InnoDB.

- `Innodb_data_pending_fsyncs`

  The number of pending InnoDB data sync-to-disk operations.

- `Innodb_data_pending_reads`

  The number of pending InnoDB data-read operations.

- `Innodb_data_pending_writes`

  The number of pending InnoDB data-write operations.

- `Innodb_data_read`

  The number of bytes read by InnoDB.

- `Innodb_data_reads`

  The number of InnoDB data-read operations.

- `Innodb_data_writes`

  The number of InnoDB data-write operations.

- `Innodb_data_written`

  The number of bytes written by InnoDB.

- `Innodb_dblwr_pages_written`

  The number of pages written to the InnoDB doublewrite buffer.

- `Innodb_dblwr_writes`

  The number of writes to the InnoDB doublewrite buffer.

- `Innodb_log_waits`

  The number of times InnoDB had to wait for writes to the log buffer pool to be flushed.

- `Innodb_log_write_requests`

  The number of requests to write to the InnoDB log file.

- `Innodb_log_writes`

  The number of writes to the InnoDB log file.

- `Innodb_os_log_fsyncs`

  The number of sync-to-disk operations for the InnoDB log file.

- `Innodb_os_log_pending_fsyncs`

  The number of pending sync-to-disk operations for the InnoDB log file.

- `Innodb_os_log_pending_writes`

  The number of pending write operations for the InnoDB log file.

- `Innodb_os_log_written`

  The number of bytes written to the InnoDB log file.

- `Innodb_page_size`

  The compiled-in page size used by InnoDB. This can be used to convert measurements that are counted in page units to byte units. The default value is 16KB.

- `Innodb_pages_created`

  The number of pages created by InnoDB.

- `Innodb_pages_read`

  The number of pages read by InnoDB.

- `Innodb_pages_written`

  The number of pages written by InnoDB.

- `Innodb_row_lock_current_waits`

  The number of row locks that InnoDB is waiting to acquire. This variable was introduced in MySQL 5.0.3.

- `Innodb_row_lock_time`

  The total time in milliseconds spent acquiring InnoDB row locks. This variable was introduced in MySQL 5.0.3.

- `Innodb_row_lock_time_avg`

  The average time in milliseconds required to acquire an InnoDB row lock. This variable was introduced in MySQL 5.0.3.

- `Innodb_row_lock_time_max`

  The maximum time in milliseconds required to acquire an InnoDB row lock. This variable was introduced in MySQL 5.0.3.

- `Innodb_row_lock_waits`

  The number of times that InnoDB had to wait to acquire a row lock. This variable was introduced in MySQL 5.0.3.

- `Innodb_rows_deleted`

  The number of rows deleted from InnoDB tables.

- `Innodb_rows_inserted`

  The number of rows inserted into InnoDB tables.

- `Innodb_rows_read`

  The number of rows read from InnoDB tables.

- `Innodb_rows_updated`

  The number of rows updated in InnoDB tables.

D.3.2 Query Cache Status Variables

The following variables display information about the operation of the query cache.

- `Qcache_free_blocks`

  The number of free memory blocks in the query cache.

- `Qcache_free_memory`

  The amount of free memory in the query cache.

- `Qcache_hits`

  The number of query requests that were satisfied by queries held in the cache.

- `Qcache_inserts`

  The number of queries that have ever been registered in the query cache.

- `Qcache_lowmem_prunes`

  The number of cached query results that have been kicked out of the query cache to make room for newer results.

- `Qcache_not_cached`

  The number of queries that were uncacheable or for which caching was suppressed with the `SQL_NO_CACHE` keyword.

- `Qcache_queries_in_cache`

  The number of queries registered in the cache.

- `Qcache_total_blocks`

  The total number of memory blocks in the query cache.

D.3.3 SSL Status Variables

The following variables provide information about the SSL management code. Many of them reflect the state of the current connection, and will be blank unless the connection actually is secure. These variables are unavailable unless SSL support actually has been built into the server.

- `Ssl_accept_renegotiates`

  The number of start renegotiations in server mode.

- `Ssl_accepts`

  The number of started SSL/TLS handshakes in server mode.

- `Ssl_callback_cache_hits`

  The number of sessions successfully retrieved from the external session cache in server mode.

- `Ssl_cipher`

  The SSL cipher (protocol) for the connection (blank if no cipher is in effect). You can use this variable to determine whether the connection is encrypted.

- `Ssl_cipher_list`

  The list of available SSL ciphers.

- `Ssl_client_connects`

  The number of started SSL/TLS handshakes in client mode.

- `Ssl_connect_renegotiates`

  The number of start renegotiations in client mode.

- `Ssl_ctx_verify_depth`

  The SSL context verification depth.

- `Ssl_ctx_verify_mode`

  The SSL context verification mode.

- `Ssl_default_timeout`

  The default SSL session timeout.

- `Ssl_finished_accepts`

  The number of successfully established SSL/TLS sessions in server mode.

- `Ssl_finished_connects`

  The number of successfully established SSL/TLS sessions in client mode.

- `Ssl_session_cache_hits`

  The number of SSL sessions found in the session cache.

- `Ssl_session_cache_misses`

  The number of SSL sessions not found in the session cache.

- `Ssl_session_cache_mode`

  The type of SSL caching used by the server.

- `Ssl_session_cache_overflows`

  The number of sessions removed from the cache because it was full.

- `Ssl_session_cache_size`

  The number of sessions that can be stored in the SSL session cache.

- `Ssl_session_cache_timeouts`

  The number of sessions that have timed out.

- `Ssl_sessions_reused`

  Whether the session was reused from an earlier session.

- `Ssl_used_session_cache_entries`

  The number of sessions in the session cache.

- `Ssl_verify_depth`

  The SSL verification depth.

- `Ssl_verify_mode`

  The SSL verification mode.

- `Ssl_version`

  The SSL protocol version of the connection.

D.4 User-Defined Variables

User-defined variables (or, more simply, "user variables") can be assigned values, and you can refer to those variables in other statements later.

User-defined variable names consist of '@' followed by an identifier and follow rules similar to those for legal identifiers (see Section 2.2, "MySQL Identifier Syntax and Naming Rules"). However, a user variable name can contain '.' without needing to be quoted, unlike identifiers. User variable names are case sensitive before MySQL 5.0, and not case sensitive thereafter.

User variables can be assigned values with the `=` or `:=` operators in SET statements or with the `:=` operator in other statements such as SELECT. Multiple assignments can be performed in a single statement.

```
mysql> SET @x = 0, @y = 2;
mysql> SET @color := 'red', @size := 'large';
mysql> SELECT @x, @y, @color, @size;
+------+------+--------+-------+
| @x   | @y   | @color | @size |
+------+------+--------+-------+
| 0    | 2    | red    | large |
+------+------+--------+-------+
```

```
mysql> SELECT @count := COUNT(*) FROM member;
+--------------------+
| @count := COUNT(*) |
+--------------------+
|                102 |
+--------------------+
```

User variables can be assigned integer, decimal, floating-point, string, or NULL values, and can be assigned from arbitrary expressions, including those that refer to other variables. If you access a user variable that has not yet been assigned a value explicitly, its value is NULL.

User variable values do not persist across sessions with the server. That is, values are lost when a connection terminates.

In SELECT statements that return multiple rows, variable assignments are performed for each row. The final value is the value assigned for the last row.

String-valued user variables have the same character set and collation as those of the value they are assigned:

```
mysql> SET @s = CONVERT('abc' USING latin2) COLLATE latin2_czech_cs;
mysql> SELECT CHARSET(@s), COLLATION(@s);
+-------------+-----------------+
| CHARSET(@s) | COLLATION(@s)   |
+-------------+-----------------+
| latin2      | latin2_czech_cs |
+-------------+-----------------+
```

E

SQL Syntax Reference

This appendix describes the syntax for SQL statements provided by MySQL. It has three parts:

- SQL statements other than those for compound statements.
- SQL statements that are used for compound statements, which are written using BEGIN and END and can be used for writing stored programs that are stored on the server side (functions, procedures, triggers, and events).
- The syntax for writing comments in SQL code. Comments are used to write descriptive text that is ignored by the server, and to hide MySQL-specific keywords that will be executed by MySQL but ignored by other database servers.

Statement syntax descriptions use the following conventions:

- Square brackets ([]) indicate optional information.
- Vertical bars (|) separate alternative items in a list. If a list is enclosed in square brackets, one alternative may be chosen. If a list is enclosed in curly brackets ({}), one alternative must be chosen.
- Ellipsis notation (...) indicates that the term preceding the ellipsis may be repeated.
- *n* indicates an integer.
- '*str*' indicates a string value. A quoted value such as '*file_name*' or '*pattern*' indicates a more-specific kind of value such as a filename or a pattern.

Unless otherwise indicated, the statements listed in this appendix have been present in MySQL at least as early as MySQL 5.0.0. Statements that were introduced or that changed in meaning since then are noted.

Some statements have become deprecated, are scheduled to be removed, or (in my opinion) have extremely limited utility, so I have not included them here:

```
BACKUP TABLE
LOAD DATA FROM MASTER
LOAD TABLE tbl_name FROM MASTER
RESTORE TABLE
```

```
SHOW AUTHORS
SHOW CONTRIBUTORS
```

I have also not covered statements or statement clauses that relate to plugins, user-defined functions (UDFs), XA transactions, or that are specific to MySQL Cluster.

There are some general synonyms that always hold, so I list them here rather than every place in which they can be used:

To specify a character set, you can use any of the following formats:

```
CHARACTER SET charset
CHARSET = charset
CHARSET charset
```

These synonymous forms can be used in table and column definitions, and in the CREATE DATABASE and ALTER DATABASE statements.

As of MySQL 5.0.2, SCHEMA and SCHEMAS are synonyms for DATABASE and DATABASES, respectively, and can freely be substituted in statements anywhere you might use the latter two keywords. For example, you can create a database with either CREATE DATABASE or CREATE SCHEMA.

E.1 SQL Statement Syntax (Non-Compound Statements)

This section describes the syntax and meaning of each of MySQL's SQL statements, other than those for writing compound statements (see Section E.2, "Compound Statement Syntax," for the latter). A statement fails if you do not have the necessary privileges to perform it. For example, USE db_name fails if you have no permissions for accessing the database db_name.

ALTER DATABASE

```
ALTER DATABASE [db_name] db_attr ...
```

```
ALTER DATABASE db_name UPGRADE DATA DIRECTORY NAME
```

This statement changes database attributes or upgrades the database directory name encoding. It requires the ALTER privilege for the database.

For the first syntax, the allowable db_attr database attribute values are the same as those listed in the entry for CREATE DATABASE. The statement applies to the default database if the database name is omitted. If there is no default database, an error occurs.

The UPGRADE DATA DIRECTORY NAME syntax is for use when you upgrade to MySQL 5.1 or later from an older version. It re-encodes the name of the database directory if necessary to the filesystem encoding currently used by MySQL if the name contains special characters. This syntax was introduced in MySQL 5.1.23.

ALTER EVENT

```
ALTER
  [DEFINER = definer_name]
  EVENT event_name
  [ON SCHEDULE schedule]
  [ON COMPLETION [NOT] PRESERVE]
  [RENAME TO new_event_name]
  [ENABLE | DISABLE [ON SLAVE]]
  [COMMENT 'str']
  [DO event_stmt]
```

Alters an existing event to have the given definition. The RENAME TO clause renames the event. The other clauses are described in the entry for CREATE EVENT. You must have the EVENT privilege for the database to which the event belogs. (Prior to MySQL 5.1.12, you must have the SUPER privilege or be the event's definer.)

ALTER EVENT was introduced in MySQL 5.1.6.

ALTER FUNCTION, ALTER PROCEDURE

```
ALTER {FUNCTION | PROCEDURE} routine_name [characteristic] ...

characteristic:
    [NOT] DETERMINISTIC
  | LANGUAGE SQL
  | SQL SECURITY {DEFINER | INVOKER}
  | COMMENT 'str'
```

These statements alter the characteristics of stored routines. The characteristics are as described in the entry for the CREATE FUNCTION and CREATE PROCEDURE statements.

As of MySQL 5.0.3, these statements require the ALTER ROUTINE privilege for the given routine.

ALTER SERVER

```
ALTER SERVER server_name OPTIONS (option [, option] ...)
```

Modifies the definition for the FEDERATED table server named *server_name* and updates the corresponding row of the mysql.servers table. Omitted options retain their previous values. You must have the SUPER privilege.

See the description of CREATE SERVER for the OPTIONS clause allowable values. This statement was introduced in MySQL 5.1.15.

ALTER TABLE

```
ALTER [IGNORE] TABLE tbl_name action [, action] ...
```

ALTER TABLE enables you to rename tables or modify their structure. To use it, specify the table name along with one or more actions to be performed on the table. The IGNORE keyword comes into play if the action could produce duplicate key values in a unique index in the altered table. Without IGNORE, the effect of the ALTER TABLE statement is canceled. With IGNORE, the rows that duplicate values for unique key values are deleted.

Except for table renaming operations, ALTER TABLE works by creating from the original table a new one that incorporates the changes to be made. If an error occurs, the new table is discarded and the original remains unchanged. If the operation completes successfully, the original table is discarded and replaced by the new one. During the operation, other clients may read from the original table. Any clients that try to update the table are blocked until the ALTER TABLE statement completes, at which point the updates are applied to the new table.

action values specify alteration actions, each of which is performed in turn. Some actions cannot be combined with other actions, as indicated in the action descriptions.

For index-definition actions that include *index_type* or *index_option* clauses, some storage engines allow you to specify the indexing algorithm or other index definition modifiers. See the entry for CREATE INDEX for details about which indexing values are allowed in different versions of MySQL. For additional information about index creation, see Section 2.6.4, "Indexing Tables."

An *action* value may be any of the following:

- *table_option*

    Specifies a table option of the kind that may be given in the *table_option* part of a CREATE TABLE statement.

    ```
    ALTER TABLE score ENGINE = MyISAM CHECKSUM = 1;
    ALTER TABLE sayings CHARACTER SET utf8;
    ```

    Any version-specific or storage engine-specific constraints on the availability of a given table option are as described in the entry for CREATE TABLE. If you attempt to change a table to use a storage engine that is not available, the effect of the ALTER TABLE statement is subject to the setting of the NO_ENGINE_SUBSTITUTION SQL mode. It is not allowable to alter a table to use the MERGE or BLACKHOLE engines as of MySQL 5.0.23/5.1.11 because that might cause data loss.

    The [DEFAULT] CHARACTER SET table option changes the default table character set but does not convert existing the columns to that character set. To perform the latter operation, use a CONVERT TO CHARACTER SET action.

    ALTER TABLE ignores the DATA DIRECTORY and INDEX DIRECTORY table options.

- ADD [COLUMN] *col_name col_definition* [FIRST | AFTER *col_name*]

    Adds a column to the table. *col_name* is the column name. *col_definition* is the column definition; it has the same format as that used for the CREATE TABLE statement. The column becomes the first column in the table if the FIRST keyword is given or is placed after the named column if AFTER *col_name* is given. If the column placement is not specified, the column becomes the last column of the table.

```
ALTER TABLE t ADD id INT UNSIGNED NOT NULL AUTO_INCREMENT PRIMARY KEY;
ALTER TABLE t ADD id INT UNSIGNED NOT NULL AUTO_INCREMENT PRIMARY KEY FIRST;
ALTER TABLE t ADD id INT UNSIGNED NOT NULL AUTO_INCREMENT PRIMARY KEY
  AFTER suffix;
```

- ADD [COLUMN] (`create_definition,...`)

Adds columns or indexes to the table. Each `create_definition` is a column or index definition, in the same format as for CREATE TABLE.

- ADD [CONSTRAINT [`name`]] FOREIGN KEY [`fk_name`]
  (`index_columns`) `reference_definition`

Adds a foreign key definition to a table. This is supported only for InnoDB tables. The foreign key is based on the columns named in `index_columns`, which is a list of one or more columns in the table separated by commas. Any CONSTRAINT name, if given, is ignored. `fk_name` is the foreign key ID. If given, it is ignored unless InnoDB automatically creates an index for the foreign key; in that case, `fk_name` becomes the index name. `reference_definition` defines how the foreign key relates to the parent table. The syntax is as described in the entry for CREATE TABLE.

```
ALTER TABLE child
  ADD FOREIGN KEY (par_id) REFERENCES parent (par_id) ON DELETE CASCADE;
```

ADD FOREIGN KEY and DROP FOREIGN KEY actions cannot appear in the same ALTER TABLE statement.

- ADD FULLTEXT [INDEX | KEY] [`index_name`]
  (`index_columns`) [`index_option`] ...

Adds a FULLTEXT index to a MyISAM table. The index is based on the columns named in `index_columns`, which is a list of one or more non-binary string columns in the table separated by commas. `index_name` is specified as for the ADD INDEX action.

```
ALTER TABLE poetry ADD FULLTEXT (author,title,stanza);
```

- ADD {INDEX | KEY} [`index_name`] [`index_type`]
  (`index_columns`) [`index_option`] ...

Adds an index to the table. The index is based on the columns named in `index_columns`, which is a list of one or more columns in the table separated by commas. If the index name `index_name` is not specified, MySQL chooses a name automatically based on the name of the first indexed column.

- ADD [CONSTRAINT [*name*]] PRIMARY KEY [*index_type*]
    (*index_columns*) [*index_option*] ...

  Adds a primary key on the given columns. The key is given the name PRIMARY. *index_columns* is specified as for the ADD INDEX action. Each column must be defined as NOT NULL. An error occurs if a primary key already exists.

  ```
  ALTER TABLE president ADD PRIMARY KEY (last_name, first_name);
  ```

- ADD SPATIAL [INDEX | KEY] [*index_name*]
    (*index_columns*) [*index_option*] ...

  Adds a SPATIAL index to a MyISAM table. The index is based on the columns named in *index_columns*, which is a list of one or more spatial columns in the table separated by commas. Each column must be defined as NOT NULL. *index_name* is specified as for the ADD INDEX action.

  ```
  ALTER TABLE coordinates ADD SPATIAL (x,y);
  ```

- ADD [CONSTRAINT [*name*]] UNIQUE [INDEX | KEY]
    [*index_name*] [*index_type*]
    (*index_columns*) [*index_option*] ...

  Adds a unique-valued index to *tbl_name*. *index_name* and *index_columns* are specified as for the ADD INDEX action.

  ```
  ALTER TABLE absence ADD UNIQUE id_date (student_id, date);
  ```

- ALTER [COLUMN] *col_name* {SET DEFAULT *value* | DROP DEFAULT}

  Modifies the given column's default value, either to the specified value, or by dropping the current default value. In the latter case, a new implicit default value might be assigned, as described in Section 3.2.3, "Specifying Column Default Values."

  ```
  ALTER TABLE grade_event ALTER category SET DEFAULT 'Q';
  ALTER TABLE grade_event ALTER category DROP DEFAULT;
  ```

- CHANGE [COLUMN] *old_col_name* *new_col_name* *col_definition*
    [FIRST | AFTER *col_name*]

  Changes a column's name and definition. *old_col_name* and *new_col_name* are the column's current and new names, and *col_definition* is the definition to which the column should be changed. *col_definition* is in the same format as that used for the CREATE TABLE statement, including any column attributes such as NULL, NOT NULL, and DEFAULT. Note that if you want to change the definition but not the name, it's necessary to specify the same name twice. FIRST or AFTER have the same effect as for ADD COLUMN.

  ```
  ALTER TABLE student CHANGE name name VARCHAR(40);
  ALTER TABLE student CHANGE name student_name CHAR(30) NOT NULL;
  ```

- CONVERT TO CHARACTER SET *charset* [COLLATE *collation*]

  Converts the table default character set and all non-binary character columns in the table to the given character set. `binary` converts the columns to the corresponding binary string data types. DEFAULT converts the table to use the database character set. The COLLATE clause may be given to specify a collation as well. If COLLATE is omitted, the default collation for the character set is used.

- DISABLE KEYS

  For a MyISAM table, this action disables the updating of non-unique indexes that normally occurs when the table is changed. ENABLE KEYS can be used to re-enable index updating.

  ```
  ALTER TABLE score DISABLE KEYS;
  ```

- DISCARD TABLESPACE

  This action applies to InnoDB tables that use individual tablespaces. For such a table, it removes the *tbl_name*.ibd file that stores the table contents. This action cannot be used in conjunction with other actions.

- DROP [COLUMN] *col_name* [RESTRICT | CASCADE]

  Removes the given column from the table. If the column is part of any indexes, it is removed from those indexes. If all columns from an index are removed, the index is removed as well.

  ```
  ALTER TABLE president DROP suffix;
  ```

  The RESTRICT and CASCADE keywords are parsed but ignored and have no effect.

- DROP FOREIGN KEY *fk_name*

  Drops the foreign key definition that has the given name. ADD FOREIGN KEY and DROP FOREIGN KEY actions cannot appear in the same ALTER TABLE statement.

- DROP {INDEX | KEY} *index_name*

  Removes the given index from the table.

  ```
  ALTER TABLE member DROP INDEX name;
  ```

- DROP PRIMARY KEY

  Removes the primary key from the table. An error occurs if there is no primary key.

  ```
  ALTER TABLE president DROP PRIMARY KEY;
  ```

- ENABLE KEYS

  For a MyISAM table, re-enables updating for non-unique indexes that have been disabled with DISABLE KEYS.

  ```
  ALTER TABLE score ENABLE KEYS;
  ```

- IMPORT TABLESPACE

  This action applies to InnoDB tables that use individual tablespaces. For such a table, it associates the `tbl_name.ibd` file in the table's database directory with the table. (Presumably, the table's former `.ibd` file previously had been removed with DISCARD TABLESPACE.) This action cannot be used in conjunction with other actions.

- MODIFY [COLUMN] `col_name col_definition` [FIRST | AFTER `col_name`]

  Changes the definition of a column. `col_name` names the column to be modified. The column definition `col_definition` is given, using the same format for column definitions as is shown in the entry for the CREATE TABLE statement, including any column attributes such as NULL, NOT NULL, and DEFAULT. FIRST and AFTER have the same effect as for ADD COLUMN.

  ```
  ALTER TABLE student MODIFY name VARCHAR(40) DEFAULT '' NOT NULL;
  ```

- ORDER BY `col_list`

  Sorts the rows in the table according to the columns named in `col_list`, which should be a list of names or one or more columns in the table separated by commas. The default sort order is ascending. A column name may be followed by ASC or DESC to specify ascending or descending order explicitly. Sorting a table this way may improve performance of subsequent queries that retrieve rows in the same order. This is mostly useful for a table that will not be modified afterward, because rows will not remain in order if the table is modified after performing the ORDER BY operation.

  ```
  ALTER TABLE score ORDER BY event_id, student_id;
  ```

- RENAME [TO | AS] `new_tbl_name`

  Renames the table `tbl_name` to `new_tbl_name`. If you rename an InnoDB table on which other tables depend for foreign key relationships, InnoDB adjusts the dependencies to point to the renamed table.

  ```
  ALTER TABLE president RENAME TO prez;
  ```

Beginning with MySQL 5.1, ALTER TABLE supports partitioning modifications. The entry for CREATE TABLE defines the meaning of the `partition_scheme` and `partition_definition` terms used in the following action descriptions.

- *partition_scheme*

  Partitions the table according to the specified partitioning description. If the table is not partitioned, it becomes partitioned. Otherwise, the new partitioning replaces the old.

- ADD PARTITION (*partition_definition*)

  Adds a new partition to a partitioned table.

- COALESCE PARTITION *n*

  Causes a partitioned table to have *n* fewer partitions. This works only for HASH or KEY partitions. Data in the removed partitions is merged into those remaining. To remove LIST or RANGE partitions, use DROP PARTITION.

- [DROP | REBUILD] PARTITION *partition_name* [, *partition_name*] ...

  Causes the specified action to be performed on the named partitions. DROP works only for LIST or RANGE partitions; data in the dropped partitions is lost. To reduce the number of HASH or KEY partitions, use COALESCE PARTITION.

- REMOVE PARTITIONING

  Removes all partitioning, resulting in an unpartitioned table. This option was introduced in MySQL 5.1.8. (Before 5.1.8, using ALTER TABLE with the ENGINE table option on a partitioned table removes the partitioning.)

- REORGANIZE PARTITION *partition_name* [, *partition_name*] ...
    INTO (*partition_definition* [, *partition_definition*] ...)

  Repartitions the named partitions using the new partitioning definitions.

If any one of the following partitioning options appears in an ALTER TABLE statement, you cannot use any of the others: *partition_scheme*, ADD PARTITION, COALESCE PARTITION, DROP PARTITION, REORGANIZE PARTITION.

ALTER VIEW

```
ALTER
  [ALGORITHM = {MERGE | TEMPTABLE | UNDEFINED}]
  [DEFINER = definer_name]
  [SQL SECURITY = {DEFINER | INVOKER}]
  VIEW view_name [(col_list)] AS select_stmt
  [WITH [CASCADED | LOCAL] CHECK OPTION]
```

Alters an existing view to have the given definition. The various clauses have the same meanings as described in the entry for CREATE VIEW.

ALTER VIEW requires the CREATE VIEW and DROP privileges for the view and some privilege for each column used in the SELECT statement that defines the view. As of

MySQL 5.0.52/5.1.23, ALTER VIEW can be used only by the definer or a user that has the SUPER privilege.

ALTER VIEW as introduced in MySQL 5.0.1. The DEFINER and SQL SECURITY clauses were introduced in 5.0.16.

ANALYZE TABLE

```
ANALYZE
  [LOCAL | NO_WRITE_TO_BINLOG]
  {TABLE | TABLES} tbl_name [, tbl_name] ...
```

This statement causes MySQL to analyze each of the named tables, storing the distribution of key values present in each table's indexes. It works for MyISAM and InnoDB tables and requires SELECT and INSERT privileges on each table. After analysis, the Cardinality column of the output from SHOW INDEX indicates the approximate number of distinct values in the indexes. Information from the analysis can be used by the optimizer during subsequent queries to perform certain types of joins more quickly.

Analyzing a table requires a read lock, which prevents that table from being updated during the operation. If you run ANALYZE TABLE on a table that has already been analyzed and that has not been changed since, no analysis is performed.

ANALYZE TABLE produces output in the format described in the entry for CHECK TABLE.

If binary logging is enabled, MySQL writes the ANALYZE TABLE statement to the binary log unless the LOCAL or NO_WRITE_TO_BINLOG option is given.

BEGIN

```
BEGIN [WORK]
```

This statement is a synonym for START TRANSACTION; see the entry for that statement.

BEGIN can also be used with END in stored programs to create a compound statement; see Section E.2, "Compound Statement Syntax."

CACHE INDEX

```
CACHE INDEX
  tbl_name [[INDEX | KEY] (index_name [, index_name] ...)]
  [, tbl_name [[INDEX | KEY] (index_name [, index_name] ...)]] ...
  IN cache_name
```

Sets up an association between one or more MyISAM tables and the named key cache, which must already exist. You must have the INDEX privilege for each table named in the statement. The default key cache is named default. The table indexes can be loaded into the cache later with LOAD INDEX. Currently, the statement associates all indexes in each table with the cache, even though the syntax allows for designating only certain indexes. Individual-index cache association remains for future implementation.

The following statement caches indexes for the `member` statement in the key cache named `member_cache`:

```
CACHE INDEX member IN member_cache;
```

CACHE INDEX produces output in the format described in the entry for CHECK TABLE.

See Section 12.7.2, "Configuring the MyISAM Storage Engine," for more information about MyISAM key cache management.

CALL

```
CALL routine_name([proc_param [, proc_param] ...])
```

```
CALL routine_name[()]
```

Invokes the stored procedure that has the given name. The optional parameter list consists of one or more parameter values separated by commas. If any of these are OUT or INOUT parameters, the procedure can return values through them.

When the stored routine returns, you can get the rows-affected value for its most recent statement that modifies rows by invoking the ROW_COUNT() function. From C, the same value can be obtained by calling `mysql_affected_rows()`.

If the procedure takes no arguments, the () following the procedure name is optional as of MySQL 5.0.30/5.1.13.

CHANGE MASTER

```
CHANGE MASTER TO option [, option] ...
```

Changes replication parameters for a slave server, to indicate which master host to use, how to connect to it, or which logs to use. The parameters are saved in the slave's `master.info` and `relay-log.info` files, which are used for subsequent slave restarts.

Each *option* specifies a parameter definition in *param = value* format, chosen from the following list:

- `MASTER_CONNECT_RETRY = n`

  The number of seconds to wait between attempts to connect to the master.

- `MASTER_HOST = 'host_name'`

  The host where the master server is running.

- `MASTER_LOG_FILE = 'file_name'`

  The name of the master's binary log file to use for replication.

- `MASTER_LOG_POS = n`

  The position within the master log file from which to begin or resume replication.

- `MASTER_PASSWORD = 'pass_val'`

  The password to use for connecting to the master server.

- MASTER_PORT = *n*

  The TCP/IP port number to use for connecting to the master server.

- MASTER_SSL = {0 | 1}
  MASTER_SSL_CA = '*file_name*'
  MASTER_SSL_CAPATH = '*dir_name*'
  MASTER_SSL_CERT = '*file_name*'
  MASTER_SSL_CIPHER = '*str*'
  MASTER_SSL_KEY = '*file_name*'
  MASTER_SSL_VERIFY_SERVER_CERT = {0 | 1}

  These options specify parameters for establishing an SSL connection to the master.
  They have the same meaning as the corresponding --ssl-*xxx* options described in
  Section F.1.2.1, "Standard SSL Options." The values are saved to the master.info
  file but have no effect unless the slave has SSL support enabled.
  MASTER_SSL_VERIFY_SERVER_CERT was introduced in MySQL 5.1.18.

- MASTER_USER = '*user_name*'

  The username of the account to use for connecting to the master server.

- RELAY_LOG_FILE = '*file_name*'

  The slave relay log filename.

- RELAY_LOG_POS = *n*

  The current position within the slave relay log.

Parameters that are not specified in the statement maintain their current values, with
the following exception: Changes to MASTER_HOST or MASTER_PORT normally indicate
that you're switching to a different master server, so if you specify either of those options,
the MASTER_LOG_FILE and MASTER_LOG_POS values are set to the beginning of the master's first binary log file.

You should not mix the MASTER_LOG_FILE and MASTER_LOG_POS options with the
RELAY_LOG_FILE and RELAY_LOG_POS options in the same statement.

The CHANGE MASTER statement deletes any existing relay log files and begins a new
one unless the RELAY_LOG_FILE or RELAY_LOG_POS options are specified.

CHECK TABLE

CHECK {TABLE | TABLES} *tbl_name* [, *tbl_name*] ... [*option*] ...

This statement checks tables for errors. It works with MyISAM and InnoDB tables,
ARCHIVE tables as of MySQL 5.0.16, and CSV tables as of 5.1.19. As of 5.0.2, CHECK
TABLE can also check view definitions for problems such as references to tables that no
longer exist. CHECK TABLE requires the SELECT privilege for each table or view to be
checked.

For MyISAM tables, CHECK TABLE also updates index statistics. For InnoDB tables, the server terminates after writing a message to the error log if it finds a problem, to prevent further errors from occurring.

Each *option* value can be one of the following options. Unless otherwise specified, these options apply to MyISAM tables, are ignored for InnoDB tables and views, and may or may not be used by other storage engines.

- CHANGED skips table checking if the table was properly closed and has not been changed since the last time it was checked.

- EXTENDED performs an extended check that attempts to ensure that the table is fully consistent. This is the most thorough check available, and consequently the slowest. For example, it verifies that each key in each index points to a data row.

- FAST checks a table only if it was not properly closed.

- MEDIUM checks the index, scans the data rows for problems, and performs a checksum verification. This is the default if no options are given.

- QUICK scans only the indexes and not the data rows.

- FOR UPGRADE determines whether the checked table is compatible with your current version of MySQL, so this option is useful after an upgrade. If there is an incompatibility, the server runs a full check. If the full check fails, you should attempt to repair the table. The server updates the table's .frm file with the current MySQL version unless there was an incompatibility and the full check failed. This option is not specific to MyISAM tables. It was introduced in MySQL 5.0.19/5.1.7.

If you are not checking a table with FOR UPGRADE and you don't specify one of QUICK, MEDIUM, or EXTENDED when checking a MyISAM table, CHECK TABLE defaults to MEDIUM if the table has variable-length rows. If it has fixed-length rows, the default is QUICK if you specify CHANGED or FAST, and MEDIUM otherwise.

CHECK TABLE returns information about the result of the operation. For example:

```
mysql> CHECK TABLE t;
+--------+-------+----------+----------+
| Table  | Op    | Msg_type | Msg_text |
+--------+-------+----------+----------+
| test.t | check | status   | OK       |
+--------+-------+----------+----------+
```

ANALYZE TABLE, CACHE INDEX, LOAD INDEX INTO CACHE, OPTIMIZE TABLE, and REPAIR TABLE also return information in this format. Table indicates the table on which the operation was performed. Op indicates the type of operation carried out by the statement. The Msg_type and Msg_text columns provide information about the result of the operation; if this value does not indicate that the table is okay or already up to date, you should repair it.

CHECKSUM TABLE

```
CHECKSUM {TABLE | TABLES} tbl_name [, tbl_name] ...
  [QUICK | EXTENDED]
```

Reports a table checksum.

```
mysql> CHECKSUM TABLE president;
+------------------+------------+
| Table            | Checksum   |
+------------------+------------+
| sampdb.president | 3032762697 |
+------------------+------------+
```

If a table does not exist, the Checksum value is NULL, and (as of MySQL 5.0.3) a warning is generated.

By default, the statement reports the live checksum if the storage engine supports it. (A live checksum is one that is updated each time the table is modified.) For MyISAM tables, you can turn on live checksumming for a table by using the CHECKSUM = 1 option with CREATE TABLE or ALTER TABLE.

With the QUICK option, the statement reports the live checksum if there is one and NULL otherwise. With the EXTENDED option, a checksum is calculated by reading the entire table and then reported. This operation becomes slower as the table size increases.

COMMIT

```
COMMIT [WORK] [AND [NO] CHAIN] [[NO] RELEASE]
```

Commits changes made by statements in the current transaction, to record those changes permanently in the database. COMMIT works only for transaction-safe storage engines. (For non-transactional storage engines, statements are committed as they are executed.)

The optional keyword WORK has no effect. The CHAIN and RELEASE clauses affect how the server handles transaction completion. With AND CHAIN, when a transaction ends, another one begins with the same isolation level. With RELEASE, when a transaction ends, the server terminates the current connection. Adding NO to either CHAIN or RELEASE causes a new transaction not to begin or the connection not to terminate, respectively. The behavior of COMMIT in the absence of these clauses is affected by the setting of the completion_type system variable. By default, neither CHAIN nor RELEASE is applied.

COMMIT has no effect if autocommit has not been disabled with START TRANSACTION or by setting the autocommit variable to 0.

Some statements implicitly end any current transaction, as if a COMMIT had been performed, because they cannot be part of a transaction. In general, these tend to be DDL (data definition language) statements that create, alter, or drop databases or objects in them, or statements that are lock-related. For example, if you issue any of the following statements while a transaction is in progress, the server commits the transaction first before executing the statement:

```
ALTER TABLE
CREATE INDEX
DROP DATABASE
DROP INDEX
DROP TABLE
LOCK TABLES
RENAME TABLE
SET autocommit = 1 (if not already set to 1)
TRUNCATE TABLE
UNLOCK TABLES (if tables currently are locked)
```

For a complete list of statements that cause implicit commits in your version of MySQL, see the MySQL Reference Manual.

The WORK, CHAIN, and RELEASE clauses were introduced in MySQL 5.0.3.

CREATE DATABASE

```
CREATE DATABASE [IF NOT EXISTS] db_name [db_attr] ...

db_attr:
    [DEFAULT] CHARACTER SET [=] charset
  | [DEFAULT] COLLATE [=] collation
```

Creates a database with the given name. The statement fails if you don't have the CREATE privilege for the database. Attempts to create a database with a name that already exists normally result in an error; if the IF NOT EXISTS clause is specified, the database is not created but no error occurs.

The optional CHARACTER SET and COLLATE attributes may be given after the database name to specify a default character set and collation for the database. These attributes are used for tables for which no character set or collation is given explicitly. charset can be a character set name, or DEFAULT to use the current server character set. collation can be a collation name, or DEFAULT to use the current server collation.

If neither attribute is given, the server character set and collation are used. If CHARACTER SET is given without COLLATE, the default collation for the character set is used. If COLLATE is given without CHARACTER SET, the character set is determined from the collation. If both CHARACTER SET and COLLATE are used, the collation must be compatible with the character set.

MySQL stores database attributes in the db.opt file in the database directory.

CREATE EVENT

```
CREATE
  [DEFINER = definer_name]
  EVENT [IF NOT EXISTS] event_name
  ON SCHEDULE schedule
  [ON COMPLETION [NOT] PRESERVE]
  [ENABLE | DISABLE | DISABLE ON SLAVE]
```

```
[COMMENT 'str']
[DO event_stmt]
```

schedule:
   AT *datetime*
  | EVERY *expr interval* [STARTS *datetime*] [ENDS *datetime*]

Creates a new event named *event_name* for the event scheduler. You must have the EVENT privilege for the database to which the event belogs. By default, the event is created in the default database. To create the event in a specific database, give the name in *db_name.event_name* format.

The DEFINER clause determines the security context (the account to use for access checking) when the event executes, as described in Section 4.5, "Security for Stored Programs and Views." The default is to use the account for the user who executes the CREATE EVENT statement.

The ON SCHEDULE clause determines the execution schedule for the event (assuming that the event scheduler is running). In the various formats for this clause, *datetime* is a date and time value. The CURRENT_TIMESTAMP function (or its synonyms) can be used to represent the current date and time. *datetime* expressions can use INTERVAL *expr interval* arithmetic to add or subtract temporal intervals. This syntax is described in the entry for the DATE_ADD() function in Section C.2.5, "Date and Time Functions." The *interval* value should not use any specifier that involves microseconds.

For ON SCHEDULE, the AT scheduling type sets up an event that executes once at the specified time. The EVERY scheduling type sets up a repeating event that executes at regular intervals. The repeat time consists of a quantity and an *interval* modifier that specifies how to interpret the interval (for example, 5 HOUR or '1:30' MINUTE_SECOND). By default, the first execution occurs as soon as the event is created and execution occurs every interval thereafter. The STARTS clause can be used to specify the initial start time. An ENDS clause, if present, indicates the time at which the event no longer executes. In the ON SCHEDULE clause, do not use table references or references to stored functions or user-defined functions.

The DO clause specifies the statement to be executed when the event runs. It should be a single SQL statement. If you need to use multiple statements, enclose them within BEGIN and END to form a compound statement. (See Section E.2, "Compound Statement Syntax.")

An event that completes its final execution is dropped afterward by default. ON COMPLETION NOT PRESERVE specifies the same behavior explicitly. ON COMPLETION PRESERVE causes the event not to be dropped.

The ENABLE and DISABLE options specify that the event status when it is created should be enabled (run according to schedule) or disabled (do not run). As of MySQL 5.1.18, DISABLE ON SLAVE indicates an event that is enabled on the server where it is created but is disabled on any slave to which it replicates.

The value of the `sql_mode` system variable in effect at event creation time is saved and used when the event executes.

Events do not take input or produce output. That is, you cannot pass parameters to an event, and output is discarded for statements such as SELECT which produce a result set that normally is returned to the client.

CREATE EVENT was introduced in MySQL 5.1.6. The DEFINER clause was introduced in 5.1.17.

CREATE FUNCTION, CREATE PROCEDURE

```
CREATE
  [DEFINER = definer_name]
  FUNCTION routine_name ([func_param [, func_param] ...])
  RETURNS type
  [characteristic] ...
  routine_stmt

CREATE
  [DEFINER = definer_name]
  PROCEDURE routine_name ([proc_param [, proc_param] ...])
  [characteristic] ...
  routine_stmt

func_param:
  param_name type

proc_param:
  [IN | OUT | INOUT] param_name type

characteristic:
    [NOT] DETERMINISTIC
  | LANGUAGE SQL
  | SQL SECURITY {DEFINER | INVOKER}
  | COMMENT 'str'
```

These statements create new stored functions and stored procedures. As of MySQL 5.0.3, you must have the CREATE ROUTINE privilege for the given routine.

By default, the routine is created in the default database. To create the routine in a specific database, give the name in `db_name.routine_name` format. There cannot be two functions or two procedures with the same name in the same database. However, a function and a procedure can have the same name.

Parameters for functions are defined by giving the function name and its type. The type is any valid MySQL data type. Parameters supply values to a function when it is invoked, but changes to the parameters are not visible to the caller when the function returns. (That is, they are treated as IN parameters.)

For a function, a RETURNS statement must follow the parameter list to indicate the data type for the return value.

Parameters for procedures also are defined with a name and type, but the name can be preceded by IN, OUT, or INOUT to indicate that the parameter is for input only, output only, or both input and output:

- An IN parameter supplies a value to the procedure. The parameter can be modified inside the procedure, but remains unchanged in the calling program after the procedure terminates.

- An OUT parameter does not supply a value to the procedure. Its initial value inside the procedure is NULL and it can be modified inside the procedure. Its final value is visible to the calling program after the procedure terminates.

- An INOUT parameter supplies a value to the procedure and any changes to its value within the procedure become visible to the caller.

If none of these keywords is given, the default is IN.

One or more *characteristic* values can be given, separated by spaces:

- DETERMINISTIC, NOT DETERMINISTIC

    DETERMINISTIC indicates that a function always produces the same result when called with the same parameter values. NOT DETERMINISTIC indicates that it might not. DETERMINISTIC is used by the query optimizer as of MySQL 5.0.44/5.1.21. Before that, it is not.

- LANGUAGE SQL

    Indicates the language of the routine. Currently, this is parsed and ignored. In MySQL, SQL is the only supported stored routine language, so this directive is unneeded. However, if you're thinking about porting your stored routines to another database system that supports multiple languages, you might want to include a LANGUAGE directive to specify SQL explicitly.

- SQL SECURITY

    This characteristic, together with the DEFINER clause, determines the security context (the account to use for access checking) when the routine executes, as described in Section 4.5, "Security for Stored Programs and Views." If DEFINER is omitted, the default is to use the account for the user who executes the CREATE statement. (This is also the policy before MySQL 5.0.20/5.1.8 when DEFINER was introduced.) As of MySQL 5.0.3, the account against which privileges are checked must have the EXECUTE privilege for the routine to be able to invoke it. The EXECUTE and ALTER ROUTINE privileges are granted automatically to the routine creator. (This behavior can be turned off by disabling the automatic_sp_privileges system variable.)

- COMMENT

    A descriptive comment for the routine. The comment is displayed by the SHOW
    CREATE FUNCTION, SHOW CREATE PROCEDURE, SHOW FUNCTION STATUS, and SHOW
    PROCEDURE STATUS statements.

routine_stmt is the SQL statement that represents the body of the routine. It should
be a single SQL statement. If you need to use multiple statements, enclose them within
BEGIN and END to form a compound statement. (See Section E.2, "Compound Statement
Syntax.")

Functions return a value to the caller and thus must have at least one RETURN statement
in the body. However, functions cannot execute statements that produce a result set.

The value of the sql_mode system variable in effect at routine creation time is saved
and used when the routine executes.

CREATE INDEX

```
CREATE [UNIQUE | FULLTEXT | SPATIAL] INDEX
  index_name [index_type]
  ON tbl_name (index_columns) [index_option] ...

index_type: USING {BTREE | HASH | RTREE}

index_option:
    index_type
  | COMMENT 'str'
  | KEY_BLOCK_SIZE [=] n
  | WITH PARSER parser_name
```

Adds an index named *index_name* to the table *tbl_name*. The index is based on the
columns named in *index_columns*, which is a list of one or more columns in the table
separated by commas. This statement is handled internally as an ALTER TABLE statement.
See the entry for ALTER TABLE for details. (To create several indexes on a table, it's preferable to use ALTER TABLE; you can add all the indexes with a single statement, which is
faster than adding them individually.)

The UNIQUE, FULLTEXT, or SPATIAL keywords can be given to indicate a specific kind
of index. If none are given, a non-unique index is created. CREATE INDEX cannot be used
to create a PRIMARY KEY; use ALTER TABLE instead.

FULLTEXT and SPATIAL indexes are allowed only for MyISAM tables. FULLTEXT indexes are allowed only for non-binary string columns (CHAR, VARCHAR, TEXT), and
SPATIAL indexes only for NOT NULL spatial columns.

Some storage engines allow the indexing algorithm to be specified, as denoted by
index_type. The algorithm value can be BTREE for MyISAM and InnoDB tables, either
HASH or BTREE for MEMORY tables, and RTREE for SPATIAL indexes in MyISAM tables.

Before MySQL 5.0.60/5.1.10, the *index_type* clause, if given, must appear before ON *tbl_name*. After that, this position is deprecated and *index_type* should be given at the end of the index definition as an *index_option* value.

In MySQL 5.0 (as of 5.0.60), the only allowable *index_option* value at the end of an index definition is *index_type* (described previously). In MySQL 5.1 (as of 5.1.10), allowable *index_option* values are *index_type* or those following:

- COMMENT '*str*' provides a descriptive comment for the index (up to 1024 characters). This option can be used as of MySQL 5.2.4.
- KEY_BLOCK_SIZE [=] *n* suggests a size in bytes that the storage engine should use for key blocks in the index. A value of 0 means to use the default size.
- WITH PARSER *parser_name* is allowable only for FULLTEXT indexes. It names the parser plugin to use for the index. See the MySQL Reference Manual for details on parser plugins.

For additional information about index creation, see Section 2.6.4, "Indexing Tables."

CREATE SERVER

```
CREATE SERVER server_name
  FOREIGN DATA WRAPPER wrapper_name
  OPTIONS (option [, option] ...)

option:
    USER 'str'
  | PASSWORD 'str'
  | HOST 'str'
  | PORT n
  | DATABASE 'str'
  | SOCKET 'str'
  | OWNER 'str'
```

The definition of a FEDERATED table that accesses a remote MySQL table must specify how to connect to the remote server. One way to do this is with a table CONNECTION option that lists the connection parameters explicitly using this syntax:

```
CONNECTION =
  'mysql://user_name[:password]@host_name[:port_num]/db_name/tbl_name'
```

An alternative is to use the CREATE SERVER statement, which creates a server definition as a row that contains connection parameters in the mysql.servers table. CREATE SERVER requires the SUPER privilege. Once created, the definition can be named in the CONNECTION option for FEDERATED tables instead of using a connection string. If several FEDERATED tables share the same parameters, a server definition can simplify the table-creation process.

The *server_name* value is the name of the definition, which is what you refer to in the CONNECTION option for a FEDERATED table. The option should be given in one of these formats (in the second case, the remote table name is assumed to be the same as the local table name):

```
CONNECTION = 'server_name/remote_table_name'
CONNECTION = 'server_name'
```

The server name can be up to 64 characters long and is not case sensitive. The scope of the name is global to the local server and thus must be unique among server definitions named in the mysql.servers table.

The *wrapper_name* value should be mysql, either unquoted or quoted as a string.

The OPTIONS clause specifies connection parameters. Each option value must be either a literal string or number as indicated by the statement syntax description. The default for a missing string or numeric option is the empty string or 0, respectively. String options can be up to 64 characters long. Numeric options must be 0 or greater.

The wrapper name and most of the OPTIONS values in a server definition correspond to the parts of a 'mysql://...' string that specifies connection parameters explicitly. The OWNER option is stored in the mysql.servers table but currently is not used.

This statement was introduced in MySQL 5.1.15.

CREATE TABLE

```
CREATE [TEMPORARY] TABLE [IF NOT EXISTS] tbl_name
  {
      (create_definition,...) [table_option] ...
        [partition_scheme] [trailing_select]
    | [(create_definition,...) [table_option] ...
        [partition_scheme] trailing_select
    | LIKE tbl_name2
    | (LIKE tbl_name2)
  }

table_option: (see following discussion)

trailing_select:
  [IGNORE | REPLACE] [AS] select_stmt

create_definition:
    col_name col_definition [reference_definition]
  | [CONSTRAINT [name]] PRIMARY KEY
      [index_name] [index_type]
      (index_columns) [index_option] ...
  | [CONSTRAINT [name]] UNIQUE [INDEX | KEY]
      [index_name] [index_type]
      (index_columns) [index_option] ...
  | {INDEX | KEY} [index_name] [index_type]
```

```
        (index_columns) [index_option] ...
   | {FULLTEXT | SPATIAL} [INDEX | KEY]
        [index_name] (index_columns) [index_option] ...
   | [CONSTRAINT [name]] FOREIGN KEY [fk_name]
        (index_columns) [reference_definition]
   | CHECK (expr)

col_definition:
  data_type
    [NOT NULL | NULL] [DEFAULT default_value]
    [AUTO_INCREMENT] [PRIMARY KEY] [UNIQUE [KEY]]
    [COMMENT 'str']

index_type: (see following discussion)

index_option: (see following discussion)

reference_definition:
  REFERENCES tbl_name (index_columns)
    [ON DELETE reference_action]
    [ON UPDATE reference_action]
    [MATCH FULL | MATCH PARTIAL | MATCH SIMPLE]

reference_action:
  RESTRICT | CASCADE | SET NULL | NO ACTION | SET DEFAULT

partition_scheme:
  PARTITION BY
     {
         RANGE(expr)
       | LIST(expr)
       | [LINEAR] HASH(expr)
       | [LINEAR] KEY(col_list)
     }
     [PARTITIONS n]
     [SUBPARTITION BY
       {
           [LINEAR] HASH(expr)
         | [LINEAR] KEY(col_list)
       }
       [SUBPARTITIONS n]
     ]
     [(partition_definition [, partition_definition] ...)]

partition_definition:
  PARTITION partition_name
    [VALUES {LESS THAN {(expr) | MAXVALUE} | IN (value_list)}]
```

```
    [partition_option] ...
    [(subpartition_definition [, subpartition_definition] ...)]

subpartition_definition:
  SUBPARTITION subpartition_name
    [partition_option] ...

partition_option: (see following discussion)
```

The CREATE TABLE statement creates a new table named `tbl_name` in the default database. If the name is specified as `db_name.tbl_name`, the table is created in the named database. The statement requires the CREATE privilege for the table.

Normally, attempts to create a table with a name that already exists result in an error. No error occurs under two conditions. First, if the IF NOT EXISTS clause is specified, the table is not created and no error occurs. Second, if TEMPORARY is specified and the original table is not a temporary table, the new temporary table is created, and the original table named `tbl_name` becomes hidden to the client while the temporary table exists. The original table remains visible to other clients because a temporary table is visible only to the client that created it. The original table becomes visible again to the current client if an explicit DROP TABLE is issued for the temporary table, or if the temporary table is renamed to some other name. You must have the CREATE TEMPORARY TABLE privilege to create temporary tables.

If the TEMPORARY keyword is given, the table exists only until the current client connection ends (either normally or abnormally), or until a DROP TABLE statement is issued.

The `create_definition` list names the columns and indexes that you want to create. The list is optional if you create the table by means of a trailing SELECT statement. `table_option` values enable you to specify various properties for the table. `partition_scheme` defines partitioning characteristics if table storage is to be partitioned. If a trailing `select_stmt` is specified (in the form of an arbitrary SELECT statement), the table is created using the result set that it returns. A trailing LIKE clause creates the new table as an empty copy of an existing table. These clauses are described more fully in the following sections.

Column and index definitions. A `create_definition` may be a column or index definition, a FOREIGN KEY clause, or a CHECK clause. CHECK is parsed but ignored. FOREIGN KEY is treated similarly, except for InnoDB tables.

A column definition `col_definition` begins with a data type `data_type` and may be followed by several optional keywords. The type may be any of the data types listed in Appendix B, "Data Type Reference." See that appendix for type-specific attributes that apply to the columns you want to define. Other optional keywords that may follow the data type are as follows:

- NULL, NOT NULL

    Specifies that the column may or may not contain NULL values. If neither is specified, NULL is the default.

- DEFAULT *default_value*

  Specifies the default value for the column. This cannot be used for BLOB or TEXT types, spatial types, or columns with the AUTO_INCREMENT attribute. Except for TIMESTAMP, a default value must be a constant, specified as a number, a string, or NULL. For the rules that MySQL uses for assigning a default value if you include no DEFAULT clause, see Section 3.2.3, "Specifying Column Default Values."

- AUTO_INCREMENT

  This keyword applies only to integer and floating-point data types. An AUTO_INCREMENT column is special in that when you insert NULL into it, the value actually inserted is the next value in the column sequence. Typically, this is one greater than the current maximum value in the column. AUTO_INCREMENT values start at 1 by default. (Some storage engines allow the initial value to be specified with an AUTO_INCREMENT table option. See the discussion of table options that follows.) The column must also be indexed and should be NOT NULL. There can be at most one AUTO_INCREMENT column per table.

- [PRIMARY] KEY

  Specifies that the column is a PRIMARY KEY. A PRIMARY KEY must be NOT NULL. MySQL adds NOT NULL to the column definition if you omit it.

- UNIQUE [KEY]

  Specifies that the column is a UNIQUE index.

- COMMENT '*str*'

  A descriptive comment for the column. This attribute is displayed by SHOW CREATE TABLE and SHOW FULL COLUMNS. The comment can contain up to 1024 characters (255 characters before MySQL 5.2.4).

The PRIMARY KEY, UNIQUE, INDEX, KEY, FULLTEXT, and SPATIAL clauses specify indexes. PRIMARY KEY and UNIQUE specify indexes that must contain unique values. INDEX and KEY are synonymous; they specify indexes that may contain duplicate values. The index is based on the columns named in *index_columns*, which is a list of one or more columns in the table separated by commas. If the index name *index_name* is not specified, MySQL chooses a name automatically based on the name of the first indexed column.

FULLTEXT and SPATIAL indexes are allowed only for MyISAM tables. FULLTEXT indexes are allowed only for non-binary string columns (CHAR, VARCHAR, TEXT), and SPATIAL indexes only for NOT NULL spatial columns.

PRIMARY KEY columns must always be NOT NULL; MySQL adds NOT NULL to the definition of such columns if you omit it.

For index definitions that include *index_type* or *index_option* clauses, some storage engines allow you to specify the indexing algorithm or other index definition modifiers. See the entry for CREATE INDEX for details about which indexing values are allowed in

different versions of MySQL. For additional information about index creation, see
Section 2.6.4, "Indexing Tables."

Table options. Each `table_option` value specifies an additional characteristic of the
table, chosen from the following list. Each option setting applies to all storage engines unless otherwise noted. The = in each setting is optional and settings can be separated by
whitespace or commas.

- `AUTO_INCREMENT = n`

  The first `AUTO_INCREMENT` value to be generated for the table. This option is effective for MyISAM and MEMORY tables, and for InnoDB tables as of MySQL
  5.0.3. For InnoDB tables, the effect is canceled if you restart the server before generating any `AUTO_INCREMENT` values.

- `AVG_ROW_LENGTH = n`

  The approximate average row length of your table. For MyISAM tables, MySQL
  uses the product of the `AVG_ROW_LENGTH` and `MAX_ROWS` values to determine the
  maximum data file size. The MyISAM storage engine can use internal row pointers
  from 2 to 7 bytes wide. The default pointer width is wide enough to allow tables
  up to 256TB. If you require a larger table (and your operating system supports
  larger files), the `MAX_ROWS` and `AVG_ROW_LENGTH` table options provide information
  that allows the MyISAM storage engine to adjust the internal pointer width. A
  large product of these values causes the engine to use wider pointers, enabling file
  sizes up to 65,536TB. Conversely, a small product allows the engine to use smaller
  pointers. This won't save you much space for a single small table, but the cumulative
  savings may be significant if you have many of them.

  To size the data pointers directly, set the `myisam_data_pointer_size` system variable before creating the table.

- `[DEFAULT] CHARACTER SET = charset`

  The table's default character set. `charset` may be a character set name, or `DEFAULT`
  to use the database character set. This option determines which character set to use
  for character columns that are defined without an explicit character set. In the following example, `c1` will be assigned the `sjis` character set and `c2` the `ujis` character set:

```
CREATE TABLE t
(
  c1 CHAR(50) CHARACTER SET sjis,
  c2 CHAR(50)
) CHARACTER SET ujis;
```

  This table option also applies to subsequent table modifications made with `ALTER`
  `TABLE` for character column definition changes that do not name a character set
  explicitly.

- CHECKSUM = {0 | 1}

  If this option is set to 1, MySQL maintains a live checksum for the table that is updated whenever the table is modified. There is a slight penalty for updates to the table, but the presence of checksums improves the table checking process. (MyISAM tables only.)

- [DEFAULT] COLLATE = collation

  The table's default character set collation. collation may be a collation name, or DEFAULT to use the default collation of the table character set.

- COMMENT = 'str'

  A descriptive comment for the table. This comment is displayed by SHOW CREATE TABLE and SHOW TABLE STATUS. The comment can contain up to 2048 characters (60 characters before MySQL 5.2.4).

- CONNECTION = 'connect_str'

  The string that specifies how to connect to the remote server for a FEDERATED table. This option was introduced in MySQL 5.0.13. Older versions should use COMMENT to specify connect_str.

- DATA DIRECTORY = 'dir_name'

  This option is used only for MyISAM tables and only on Unix. It indicates the directory where the data (.MYD) file should be written. 'dir_name' must be a full pathname. This option works only if the server is started without the --skip-symbolic-links option. On some Unix variants, symlinks are not thread-safe and are disabled by default.

- DELAY_KEY_WRITE = {0 | 1}

  If this is set to 1, the key cache is flushed only occasionally for the table, rather than after each insert operation (MyISAM tables only). This improves performance but may require that the table be repaired if a crash occurs.

- ENGINE = engine_name

  The storage engine to use for the table. The various storage engines are described in the Section 2.6.1, "Storage Engine Characteristics." The default engine is MyISAM unless the server has been configured otherwise. You can start the server with a different default engine by using the --default-storage-engine option. The known engine names can be displayed with the SHOW ENGINES statement. If you attempt to create a table using a storage engine that is not available, the effect of the statement is subject to the setting of the NO_ENGINE_SUBSTITUTION SQL mode.

- INDEX DIRECTORY = 'dir_name'

  This option is like DATA DIRECTORY but indicates the directory where the index (.MYI) file should be written. It is subject to the same constraints as DATA DIRECTORY.

- `INSERT_METHOD = {NO | FIRST | LAST}`

This is used for MERGE tables to specify how to insert rows. A value of `NO` disallows inserts entirely. Values of `FIRST` or `LAST` indicate that rows should be inserted into the first or last of the MyISAM tables that make up the MERGE table.

- `KEY_BLOCK_SIZE = n`

A suggested size in bytes that the storage engine should use for key blocks in indexes. A value of 0 means to use the default size. This table default can be overridden by index definitions include their own `KEY_BLOCK_SIZE` option. This option was introduced in MySQL 5.1.10.

- `MAX_ROWS = n`

A hint to the storage engine about the maximum number of rows you plan to store in the table. The table will be created to allow at least this many rows. The description of the `AVG_ROW_LENGTH` option indicates how this value is used.

- `MIN_ROWS = n`

A hint to the storage engine about the minimum number of rows you plan to store in the table. This option can be used for MEMORY tables to give the MEMORY storage engine a hint about how to optimize memory usage.

- `PACK_KEYS = {0 | 1 | DEFAULT}`

This option controls index compression for MyISAM tables, which enables runs of similar index values to be compressed. The usual effect is an improvement in retrieval performance but an update penalty. A value of 0 specifies no index compression. A value of 1 specifies compression for string (`CHAR`, `VARCHAR`, `BINARY`, `VARBINARY`) and numeric index values. A value of `DEFAULT` can be used, which specifies compression only for long string columns.

- `PASSWORD = 'str'`

A password for encrypting the table's format file. This option normally has no effect; it is enabled only for certain support contract customers.

- `ROW_FORMAT =`
    `{DEFAULT | DYNAMIC | FIXED | COMPRESSED | REDUNDANT | COMPACT}`

The row storage type. For MyISAM tables, a value of `DYNAMIC` or `FIXED` specifies variable-length or fixed-length row format. A value of `COMPRESSED` can be set only by the `myisampack` program and indicates that the table is compressed and read-only.

The `REDUNDANT` and `COMPACT` formats apply to InnoDB tables. `COMPACT` format is used by default as of MySQL 5.0.3. The original format can be specified with `ROW_FORMAT = REDUNDANT`.

A storage engine may ignore this option if the specified row format cannot be used. For example, `FIXED` cannot be used if the table contains `BLOB` or `TEXT` columns. Use `SHOW TABLE STATUS` and check the `Row_format` value to see what format the storage engine actually chose.

- TYPE = *engine_name*

  This is a deprecated synonym for the ENGINE table option. MySQL recognizes it but generates a warning until MySQL 5.2.5, at which point it is unavailable.

- UNION = (*tbl_list*)

  This option is used for MERGE tables. It specifies a comma-separated list of the MyISAM tables that make up the MERGE table.

Trailing SELECT statement. If a *select_stmt* clause is specified (as a trailing SELECT statement), the table is created using the contents of the result set returned by the statement. Rows that duplicate values in a unique index are either ignored or replace existing rows according to whether IGNORE or REPLACE is specified. If neither is specified, the statement aborts with an error.

Trailing LIKE clause. If a trailing LIKE *tbl_name2* clause is given, the table is created as an empty copy of *tbl_name2*. You must have the SELECT privilege for *tbl_name2*. The copy will include the same column definitions, index definitions, and table options, with these exceptions: The DATA DIRECTORY and INDEX DIRECTORY table options are not copied, nor are foreign key definitions.

Foreign key support. The InnoDB storage engine provides foreign key support. A foreign key in a child table is indicated by FOREIGN KEY, an optional foreign key ID, a list of the columns that make up the foreign key, and a REFERENCES definition. The ID, if given, is ignored unless InnoDB automatically creates an index for the foreign key; in that case, *fk_name* becomes the index name. The REFERENCES definition names the parent table and columns to which the foreign key refers, and indicates what to do when a parent table row is deleted. The default actions are to prevent deletes or updates to the parent or child tables that would compromise referential integrity. The RESTRICT and NO ACTION actions are the same as specifying no action. The ON DEFAULT and ON UPDATE clauses may be given to specify explicit actions. The actions that InnoDB implements are CASCADE (delete or update the corresponding child table rows) and SET NULL (set the foreign key columns in the corresponding child table rows to NULL). The SET DEFAULT action is not implemented and InnoDB issues an error.

MATCH clauses in REFERENCE definitions are parsed but ignored. If you specify a foreign key definition for a storage engine other than InnoDB, the entire definition is ignored.

For further discussion of foreign keys, see Section 2.14, "Foreign Keys and Referential Integrity."

Partitioning options. MySQL 5.1 introduces support for table partitioning, a feature that enables you to define tables for which storage is divided into different sections. The following discussion provides a brief summary of the syntax for defining table partitions. See Section 2.6.2.6, "Using Partitioned Tables," for other discussion and examples, and the MySQL Reference Manual for additional information.

A partitioning description begins with PARTITION BY and a partitioning function that computes a value for each table row. This value determines which partition the row is stored in. The description optionally may also include these components:

- A PARTITIONS *n* clause to indicate how many partitions the table has. *n* should be a positive integer. If this clause is present and any *partition_definition* clauses are also present, there must be *n* such definitions. The maximum number of partitions is 1024, including subpartitions.

- A description of how to divide partitions into subpartitions.

- A list of *partition_definition* clauses for the partitions. Each *partition_definition* describes the characteristics of a single partition. It provides a name for the partition, and can include a VALUES clause describing which partitioning function values map into the partition, other partition options, and a list of subpartition definitions. Each *subpartition_definition* clause is similar but describes a subpartition and cannot contain a VALUES clause or subpartition definitions.

There are four types of partitioning functions that compute values for assigning table rows to partitions. In the following descriptions, *expr* is an expression that refers to one or more columns in the table, and *col_list* is a comma-separated list of one or more column names. Column names can refer only to the table being created, not to other tables.

- RANGE(*expr*) partitioning associates each partition with a subset of the range of possible values of *expr*. It must be used in conjunction with partition definitions that each include a VALUES LESS THAN clause specifying the integer upper limit on function values that map into the partition. (NULL values map into the first partition.) The VALUES clauses for successive partitions should list increasing upper limit values. The final partition can use MAXVALUES, which applies to all values not accounted for by the preceding partitions.

```
CREATE TABLE t (income BIGINT, ...)
PARTITION BY RANGE (income)
(
  PARTITION p0 VALUES LESS THAN (10000),
  PARTITION p1 VALUES LESS THAN (30000),
  PARTITION p2 VALUES LESS THAN (75000),
  PARTITION p3 VALUES LESS THAN (150000),
  PARTITION p4 VALUES LESS THAN MAXVALUE
);
```

- LIST(*expr*) partitioning associates each partition with a list of values. It must be used in conjunction with partition definitions that each include a VALUES IN clause enumerating a list of integer function values that map into the partition. If *expr* can evaluate to NULL, include NULL in one of the VALUES lists.

```
CREATE TABLE t (id INT NULL, ...)
PARTITION BY LIST(id)
(
  PARTITION p0 VALUES IN (1, 2, 3),
  PARTITION p1 VALUES IN (4, 5, 6, NULL)
);
```

- HASH(`expr`) partitioning associates rows with partitions based on `expr` values computed from row content. Typically, HASH() partitioning is used with a PARTITIONS `n` clause that specifies how many partitions to create. Row assignment is based on the remainder of dividing `expr` by `n`.

```
CREATE TABLE t (d DATE, ...)
PARTITION BY HASH(TO_DAYS(d))
PARTITIONS 5;
```

  The HASH() partitioning function can be preceded by LINEAR, which changes the hashing algorithm. One advantage of LINEAR is that certain partition management operations become more efficient, such as adding or dropping partitions with ALTER TABLE. However, it is also likely that rows will be less evenly distributed among partitions than if LINEAR is not used.

- KEY(`col_list`) partitioning is similar to HASH() partitioning, but you name the table columns from which to compute the hash value and the server supplies the hashing function. KEY() can be preceded by LINEAR.

If you include a list of partition definitions for HASH() or KEY() partitioning, the definitions should not have VALUES clauses. VALUES is used only with RANGE() and LIST().

`expr` must be deterministic, such that it always produces the same result for a given input. For example, `expr` can use ABS(), but not RAND(). CREATE TABLE returns an error if you use a function that is not allowed.

For RANGE() or LIST() partitioning, `expr` must evaluate to an integer value or NULL. For HASH(), `expr` must evaluate to a non-NULL, non-negative integer, so if the expression references any non-integer column, it must convert the column values to integer. For example, if d is a DATE column, you can use TO_DAYS(d) to convert dates to number of days so that HASH(TO_DAYS(d)) is a valid hash function.

For KEY(), the arguments are column names, but these columns need not have integer data types.

Each `partition_option` value specifies an additional characteristic for a partition, chosen from the following list. (The descriptions use the term "partition" but these options can also be used in subpartition definitions.) The = in each setting is optional.

- COMMENT = '`str`'

  A descriptive comment for the partition.

- DATA DIRECTORY = '`dir_name`', INDEX DIRECTORY = '`dir_name`'

  These options are similar to the previously described table options of the same names. They indicate where to store data or indexes for the partition. The default location is the database directory for the database that contains the table.

- MAX_ROWS = `n`, MIN_ROWS = `n`

  These options are hints that indicate the maximum and minimum number of rows you plan to store in the partition. `n` should be a positive integer.

- [STORAGE] ENGINE = *engine_name*

  The storage engine to use for the partition. Mixed engines are not supported, so if you use this clause, you must name the same engine for all partitions.

The following statements demonstrate some ways in which CREATE TABLE can be used:

- Create a table with three columns. The id column is a PRIMARY KEY, and the last_name and first_name columns are used in a multiple-column index:

```
CREATE TABLE customer
(
  id          SMALLINT UNSIGNED NOT NULL AUTO_INCREMENT,
  last_name   CHAR(30) NOT NULL,
  first_name  CHAR(20) NOT NULL,
  PRIMARY KEY (id),
  INDEX (last_name, first_name)
);
```

- Create a temporary table and make it a MEMORY table for greater speed:

```
CREATE TEMPORARY TABLE tmp_table
  (id MEDIUMINT NOT NULL UNIQUE, name CHAR(40))
  ENGINE = MEMORY;
```

- Create a table as an empty copy of another table:

```
CREATE TABLE prez_copy LIKE president;
```

- Create a table using the contents of another table:

```
CREATE TABLE prez_copy SELECT * FROM president;
```

- Create a table using only partial contents of another table:

```
CREATE TABLE prez_alive SELECT last_name, first_name, birth
  FROM president WHERE death IS NULL;
```

If column definitions are specified for a table that is created and populated by means of a trailing SELECT statement, the definitions are applied after the table contents have been inserted into the table. For example, you can define that a selected column should be indexed as a PRIMARY KEY:

```
CREATE TABLE new_tbl (PRIMARY KEY (a)) SELECT a, b, c FROM old_tbl;
```

You can specify definitions for the columns in the new table to override the definitions that would be used by default based on the characteristics of the result set:

```
CREATE TABLE new_tbl
(a INT UNSIGNED NOT NULL AUTO_INCREMENT, b DATE, PRIMARY KEY (a))
  SELECT a, b, c FROM old_tbl;
```

CREATE TRIGGER

```
CREATE
  [DEFINER = definer_name]
  TRIGGER trigger_name trigger_time trigger_event
  ON tbl_name
  FOR EACH ROW trigger_stmt
```

Associates a trigger with a table, such that when a given event occurs for the table, the trigger activates and executes the triggered statement. By default, `tbl_name` is assumed to be in the default database. To name a table in a specific database, give the name in `db_name.tbl_name` format.

As of MySQL 5.1.6, CREATE TRIGGER requires the TRIGGER privilege for the table with which the trigger is associated. Before 5.1.6, you must have the SUPER privilege.

When the trigger activates, the DEFINER clause determines the security context (the account to use for access checking), as described in Section 4.5, "Security for Stored Programs and Views." The default is to use the account for the user who executes the CREATE TRIGGER statement. Before MySQL 5.0.17 (when the DEFINER clause was introduced), activation-time privilege checks use the account for the user who executes the statement that causes trigger activation. The relevant account must have the TRIGGER privilege for the table (SUPER before MySQL 5.1.6), the SELECT privilege for `tbl_name` if the trigger definition refers to any of its columns via NEW or OLD, and the UPDATE privilege for `tbl_name` if the trigger definition modifies any of its columns via SET NEW.`col_name`. The account must also have any privileges normally required for the statements within the trigger definition.

The `trigger_time` value is either BEFORE or AFTER, indicating that the triggered statement should be executed before or after each row processed by the statement that caused the trigger to be activated.

The `trigger_event` value should be INSERT, UPDATE, or DELETE to indicate what kind of statement causes trigger activation.

`trigger_stmt` is the SQL statement that represents the body of the trigger. It should be a single SQL statement. If you need to use multiple statements, enclose them within BEGIN and END to form a compound statement. (See Section E.2, "Compound Statement Syntax.")

The syntax OLD.`col_name` can be used to refer to columns in the old row to be deleted or updated in a DELETE or UPDATE trigger. Similarly, NEW.`col_name` can be used to refer to columns in the new row to be inserted or updated in an INSERT or UPDATE trigger. OLD and NEW are not case sensitive.

In a BEFORE trigger, you can change the values in the new row by using a SET statement:

```
SET NEW.col_name = value
```

The value of the `sql_mode` system variable in effect at trigger creation time is saved and used when the trigger executes.

Triggers do not take parameters, and, like stored functions, cannot execute statements that produce a result set.

CREATE TRIGGER was introduced in MySQL 5.0.2.

CREATE USER

```
CREATE USER account [IDENTIFIED BY [PASSWORD] 'password']
  [, account [IDENTIFIED BY [PASSWORD] 'password'] ] ...
```

Creates one or more MySQL accounts. For each account, a row is created in the mysql.user table with no privileges. It is an error if the account already exists. Name each account in 'user_name'@'host_name' format, as described in Section 12.4.1.1, "Specifying Account Names."

The IDENTIFIED BY clause, if given, assigns a password to the account. Normally, you omit the PASSWORD keyword and specify the literal value of the password in plain text. Do not use the PASSWORD() function, in contrast to the way passwords are specified for the SET PASSWORD statement. In the special case that you want to specify the password hash value in the format returned by PASSWORD(), precede the value with the keyword PASSWORD. (This might be the case if you are using the output of SHOW GRANTS to re-create an account. SHOW GRANTS displays the hashed password value, not the literal password.)

This statement was introduced in MySQL 5.0.2. It requires the global CREATE USER privilege or the INSERT privilege for the mysql database.

CREATE VIEW

```
CREATE [OR REPLACE]
  [ALGORITHM = {MERGE | TEMPTABLE | UNDEFINED}]
  [DEFINER = definer_name]
  [SQL SECURITY = {DEFINER | INVOKER}]
  VIEW view_name [(col_list)] AS select_stmt
  [WITH [CASCADED | LOCAL] CHECK OPTION]
```

Creates a view. If a view with the same name already exists, an error occurs unless the OR REPLACE clause is given (in which case, the new view replaces the old one).

col_list, if present, provides names for the columns returned by the view, and there must be a name for each column. If no col_list is given, the view column names come from the SELECT statement in the view definition.

select_stmt is a SELECT statement that defines the view. It can refer to tables or other views.

To create the view, you must have the CREATE VIEW privilege for it, some privilege for every column selected by select_stmt, and the SELECT privilege for every column referred to elsewhere in select_stmt. You must also have the DROP privilege for the view if you use OR REPLACE.

When the view is invoked, the DEFINER and SQL SECURITY clauses determine the security context (the account to use for access checking), as described in Section 4.5, "Security for Stored Programs and Views." The default is to use the account for the user who executes the CREATE VIEW statement.

The ALGORITHM clause determines how the view is processed. For MERGE, when you issue a statement that references the view, the view definition is merged into the statement.
The resulting statement is executed. For TEMPTABLE, temporary tables are used during the
course of executing the view. For UNDEFINED, the server chooses which algorithm to use.
The default is UNDEFINED.

The WITH CHECK OPTION clause applies to updatable views (views that can be used
with UPDATE or other table-modifying statements to update the underlying table). It allows use of the view to insert or update only those rows in the underlying table for
which the WHERE clause in the SELECT statement is true. The CASCADED and LOCAL keywords apply in the case that the view definition refers to other views. With CASCADED,
checks cascade to underlying views. With LOCAL, checks are restricted to the current view.
The default is CASCADED if neither is given.

The CREATE VIEW statement was introduced in MySQL 5.0.1. The WITH CHECK
OPTION clause was introduced in MySQL 5.0.2. The DEFINER and SQL SECURITY clauses
were implemented in 5.0.16.

DEALLOCATE PREPARE

```
{DEALLOCATE | DROP} PREPARE stmt_name
```

Deallocates a prepared statement named *stmt_name* that previously was prepared with
PREPARE. After deallocation, the statement cannot be executed again.

DELETE

```
DELETE [LOW_PRIORITY] [QUICK] [IGNORE] FROM tbl_name
  [WHERE where_expr] [ORDER BY ...] [LIMIT n]

DELETE [LOW_PRIORITY] [QUICK] [IGNORE] tbl_name[.*] [, tbl_name[.*]] ...
  FROM tbl_refs
  [WHERE where_expr]

DELETE [LOW_PRIORITY] [QUICK] [IGNORE] FROM tbl_name[.*] [, tbl_name[.*]] ...
  USING tbl_refs
  [WHERE where_expr]
```

The first form of the DELETE statement deletes rows from the table *tbl_name*. The second and third forms can delete rows from multiple tables, or delete rows based on conditions that involve multiple tables. The syntax for *tbl_refs* is like that for SELECT, except
that you cannot specify a subquery as a table.

The rows deleted are those that match the conditions specified in the WHERE clause:

```
DELETE FROM score WHERE event_id = 14;
DELETE FROM member WHERE expiration < CURDATE();
```

If the WHERE clause is omitted, *all rows in the table are deleted*.

LOW_PRIORITY causes the statement to be deferred until no clients are reading from the table. This option is effective only for storage engines that use table-level locking, such as MyISAM, MEMORY, and MERGE.

For MyISAM tables, specifying QUICK may make the statement quicker; the MyISAM storage engine will not perform its usual index tree leaf merging.

With the IGNORE modifier, errors that occur while rows are being deleted are ignored. These errors generate warnings instead.

If the LIMIT clause is given, the value *n* specifies the maximum number of rows that will be deleted.

With ORDER BY, rows are deleted in the resulting sort order. Combined with LIMIT, this provides more precise control over which rows are deleted. ORDER BY has same syntax as for SELECT.

Normally, DELETE returns the number of rows deleted. DELETE with no WHERE clause will empty the table. This is extremely fast, but a row count of zero may be returned. To obtain a true count, specify a WHERE clause that matches all rows. For example:

```
DELETE FROM tbl_name WHERE TRUE;
```

There is a significant performance penalty for row-by-row deletion, however.

If you don't need a row count, another way to empty a table is to use TRUNCATE TABLE.

The second and third forms of DELETE allow rows to be deleted from multiple tables at once. They also enable you to identify the rows to delete based on joins between tables. Names in the list of tables from which rows are to be deleted may be given as *tbl_name* or *tbl_name.**; the latter form is supported for ODBC compatibility.

The *tbl_refs* clause specifies which tables to join for determination of the rows to delete. This clause may declare aliases for the tables named therein. Other parts of the statement may refer to but not declare table aliases.

To delete rows in t1 having id values that match those in t2, use the first multiple-table syntax like this:

```
DELETE t1 FROM t1 INNER JOIN t2 WHERE t1.id = t2.id;
```

Or the second syntax like this:

```
DELETE FROM t1 USING t1 INNER JOIN t2 WHERE t1.id = t2.id;
```

Multiple-table DELETE statements do not allow ORDER BY or LIMIT clauses. Also, the WHERE clause cannot include a subquery that selects rows from a table from which row are deleted.

DESCRIBE

```
{DESCRIBE | DESC} tbl_name [col_name | 'pattern']
```

```
{DESCRIBE | DESC} select_stmt
```

DESCRIBE with a table name (or view name, as of MySQL 5.0.1) produces the same kind of output as SHOW COLUMNS. See the SHOW entry for more information. With this syntax, a trailing column name restricts output to information for the given column. A trailing string is interpreted as a pattern, as for the LIKE operator, and restricts output to those columns having names that match the pattern.

- Display output for the last_name column of the president table:

  ```
  DESCRIBE president last_name;
  ```

- Display output for both the last_name and first_name columns of the president table:

  ```
  DESCRIBE president '%name';
  ```

DESCRIBE with a SELECT statement is a synonym for EXPLAIN. See the EXPLAIN entry for more information. (DESCRIBE and EXPLAIN actually are completely synonymous in MySQL, but DESCRIBE is more often used to obtain table descriptions and EXPLAIN to obtain SELECT statement execution information.)

DO

```
DO expr [, expr] ...
```

Evaluates the expressions without returning any results. This makes DO more convenient than SELECT for expression evaluation, because you need not deal with a result set. For example, DO can be used for setting variables or for invoking functions that you are interested in primarily for their side effects rather than for their return values.

```
DO @sidea := 3, @sideb := 4, @sidec := SQRT(@sidea*@sidea+@sideb*@sideb);
DO RELEASE_LOCK('mylock');
```

DROP DATABASE

```
DROP DATABASE [IF EXISTS] db_name
```

Removes the given database and its contents. The statement fails if the database does not exist (unless you specify IF EXISTS) or if you don't have the DROP privilege for it. The IF EXISTS clause may be specified to suppress the error that normally results if the database does not exist. In this case, a warning is generated instead.

A database is represented by a directory under the data directory. The server deletes only files and directories that it can identify as having been created by itself (for example, .frm files). It does not delete other files and directories. If you have put non-table files in that directory, those files are not deleted by the DROP DATABASE statement. This results in failure to remove the database directory and DROP DATABASE fails. In that case, the database will continue to be listed by SHOW DATABASES. To correct this problem, remove any extraneous files and subdirectories manually, and then issue the DROP DATABASE statement again.

A successful DROP DATABASE returns a row count that indicates the number of tables and views dropped. (This actually is the number of .frm files removed, which amounts to the same thing.)

DROP EVENT

```
DROP EVENT [IF EXISTS] event_name
```

Removes the given event. The IF EXISTS clause may be specified to suppress the error that normally results if an event does not exist. In this case, a warning is generated instead. You must have the EVENT privilege for the database to which the event belogs. (Prior to MySQL 5.1.12, you must have the SUPER privilege or be the event's definer.)

DROP EVENT was introduced in MySQL 5.1.6.

DROP FUNCTION, DROP PROCEDURE

```
DROP {FUNCTION | PROCEDURE} [IF EXISTS] routine_name
```

Removes the named stored function or stored procedure.

The IF EXISTS clause may be specified to suppress the error that normally results if the routine does not exist. In this case, a warning is generated instead.

As of MySQL 5.0.3, these statements require the ALTER ROUTINE privilege for the given routine.

DROP INDEX

```
DROP INDEX index_name ON tbl_name
```

Removes the index index_name from the table tbl_name. This statement is handled internally as an ALTER TABLE DROP INDEX statement. See the entry for ALTER TABLE for details. To use DROP INDEX to drop a PRIMARY KEY, the index name is PRIMARY, which must be quoted as an identifier:

```
DROP INDEX `PRIMARY` ON tbl_name;
```

DROP SERVER

```
DROP SERVER [IF EXISTS] server_name
```

Drops the definition for the FEDERATED table server named server_name by removing the corresponding row from the mysql.servers table. You must have the SUPER privilege. This statement was introduced in MySQL 5.1.15.

DROP TABLE

```
DROP [TEMPORARY] {TABLE | TABLES} [IF EXISTS] tbl_name [, tbl_name] ...
   [RESTRICT | CASCADE]
```

Removes each named table from the database to which it belongs. With the TEMPORARY keyword, drops only TEMPORARY tables.

The IF EXISTS clause may be specified to suppress the error that normally results if a table does not exist. In this case, a warning is generated instead.

The RESTRICT and CASCADE keywords are parsed but ignored and have no effect.

DROP TRIGGER

```
DROP TRIGGER [IF EXISTS] db_name.trigger_name
```

Removes a trigger from the named database. It is necessary to include the database name.

The IF EXISTS clause may be specified to suppress the error that normally results if the trigger does not exist. In this case, a warning is generated instead.

If a table has triggers, dropping the table also drops its triggers.

DROP TRIGGER was introduced in MySQL 5.0.2. As of MySQL 5.1.6, it requires the TRIGGER privilege for the table with which the trigger is associated. Before 5.1.6, you must have the SUPER privilege. The IF EXISTS clause was introduced in MySQL 5.0.32/5.1.14.

DROP USER

```
DROP USER account [, account] ...
```

From MySQL 5.0.2 on, DROP USER removes all grant table rows associated with the account. This drops the account and any privileges held by it.

Prior to MySQL 5.0.2, DROP USER drops only accounts that have no privileges and removes only the mysql.user table row associated with the account. To fully remove the account, first use SHOW GRANTS to see what privileges the account has and REVOKE to revoke those privileges. Then issue the DROP USER statement.

Name each account in 'user_name'@'host_name' format, as described in Section 12.4.1.1, "Specifying Account Names." It is an error if the account does not exist.

DROP USER requires the global CREATE USER privilege or the DELETE privilege for the mysql database.

DROP USER does not drop any databases or other objects created by the dropped account.

DROP VIEW

```
DROP VIEW [IF EXISTS] view_name [, view_name] ...
    [RESTRICT | CASCADE]
```

Removes each named view from the database to which it belongs. You must have the DROP privilege for the view.

The IF EXISTS clause may be specified to suppress the error that normally results if a view does not exist. In this case, a warning is generated instead.

The RESTRICT and CASCADE keywords are parsed but ignored and have no effect.

DROP VIEW was introduced in MySQL 5.0.1.

EXECUTE

```
EXECUTE stmt_name [USING @var_name [, @var_name] ...]
```

Executes a prepared statement named *stmt_name* that was previously prepared with
PREPARE. The USING clause must be given if the prepared statement contains any placeholder markers. The clause should provide a comma-separated list of user variables that
provides values for each successive placeholder in the statement.

EXPLAIN

```
EXPLAIN tbl_name [col_name | 'pattern']

EXPLAIN [EXTENDED | PARTITIONS] select_stmt
```

The first form of this statement is equivalent to DESCRIBE *tbl_name*. See the description of the DESCRIBE statement for more information.

The second form of the EXPLAIN statement provides information about the query execution plan that the MySQL optimizer would generate for processing the SELECT statement following the EXPLAIN keyword.

```
EXPLAIN SELECT score.* FROM score INNER JOIN grade_event
ON score.event_id = grade_event.event_id AND grade_event.event_id = 14;
```

The EXTENDED option causes EXPLAIN to produce additional execution plan information; use SHOW WARNINGS immediately after EXPLAIN to see this information. The
PARTITIONS option (introduced in MySQL 5.1.5) produces an extra output column containing information about partitions.

If *select_stmt* includes a subquery in the FROM clause, EXPLAIN must execute the
subquery. This occurs because the optimizer must know what the subquery returns so
that it can determine the execution plan for the outer query.

Output from EXPLAIN consists of one or more rows containing the following columns:

- id

  The ID number for the SELECT to which this output row applies. There can be
  more than one SELECT if the statement includes subqueries or is a UNION.

- select_type

  The type of the SELECT to which this output row applies, as shown in the following table.

Type	Meaning
SIMPLE	A SELECT with no UNION or subquery parts
PRIMARY	The outermost or leftmost SELECT
UNION	The second or later SELECT in a UNION
DEPENDENT UNION	Like UNION, but dependent on an outer query

Type	Meaning
UNION RESULT	The result of a UNION
SUBQUERY	The first SELECT in a subquery
DEPENDENT SUBQUERY	Like SUBQUERY, but dependent on an outer query
DERIVED	A subquery in the FROM clause

- table

    The table to which the output row refers.

- partitions

    The partitions that would be used. This column is displayed only if the PARTITIONS option is present. For non-partitioned tables, the value is NULL.

- type

    The type of join that MySQL will perform. The possible types are, from best to worst: system, const, eq_ref, ref, ref_or_null, index_merge, unique_subquery, index_subquery, range, index, and ALL. The better types are more restrictive, meaning that MySQL has to look at fewer rows from the table when performing the retrieval.

- possible_keys

    The indexes that MySQL considers candidates for finding rows in the table named in the table column. A value of NULL means that no indexes were found.

- key

    The index that MySQL actually will use for finding rows in the table. (There might be several keys listed here if MySQL uses an index_merge join type, because that optimization uses several indexes to process the query.) A value of NULL indicates that no index will be used.

- key_len

    How much of the index will be used. This will be less than the full index row length if MySQL will use a leftmost prefix of the index.

- ref

    The values to which MySQL will compare index values. The word const or '???' means the comparison is against a constant; a column name indicates a column-to-column comparison.

- rows

    An estimate of the number of rows from the table that MySQL must examine to perform the query. The product of the values in this column is an estimate of the total number of row combinations that must be examined from all tables.

- `Extra`

  Other information about the execution plan. The value can be blank or contain one or more values such as those following:

  - `Using filesort`: Index values need to be written to a file and sorted so that the associated rows can be retrieved in sorted order.

  - `Using index`: MySQL can retrieve information for the table using only information in the index without examining the data file.

  - `Using temporary`: A temporary table must be created.

  - `Using where`: Information in the `WHERE` clause of the `SELECT` statement is used for index processing.

  Other values might appear in this field that are not listed here; see the MySQL Reference Manual for the current set of `Extra` values.

FLUSH

```
FLUSH [LOCAL | NO_WRITE_TO_BINLOG] option [, option] ...
```

Flushes various internal caches used by the server. Each `option` value should be one of the following items:

- `DES_KEY_FILE`

  Reloads the DES key file used for encryption and decryption by the `DES_ENCRYPT()` and `DES_DECRYPT()` functions.

- `HOSTS`

  Flushes the host cache.

- `LOGS`

  Flushes the log files by closing and reopening them. If the binary log or relay log are enabled, this causes the next file in the sequence to be opened. For error logging to a file, the old file is renamed to have a suffix of `-old`.

- `MASTER`

  This has been renamed to `RESET MASTER`, which should be used instead.

- `PRIVILEGES`

  Reloads the grant tables. If you modify the tables with `GRANT` or `REVOKE`, the server reloads its in-memory copies of the tables automatically. If you modify the tables directly using statements such as `INSERT` or `UPDATE`, it's necessary to tell the server to reload them explicitly. Also, this option has the same effect as the `USER_RESOURCES` option on account resource management limits.

- QUERY CACHE

  Flushes the query cache to defragment it, without removing statements from the cache. (To clear the cache entirely, use RESET QUERY CACHE.)

- SLAVE

  This has been renamed to RESET SLAVE, which should be used instead.

- STATUS

  Reinitializes the server status variables.

- {TABLE | TABLES} [tbl_name [, tbl_name] ...]

  Without any table names, closes all open tables in the table cache. You can specify an optional comma-separated list of one or more table names to flush specific tables rather than the entire table cache.

  If the query cache is operational, FLUSH TABLES also flushes the query cache.

- TABLES WITH READ LOCK

  Flushes all tables in all databases and then places a global read lock on them, which is held until you issue an UNLOCK TABLES statement. This statement allows clients to read tables, but prohibits any changes from being made, which is useful for getting a backup for your entire server with the guarantee that no tables will change during the backup period. The disadvantage of doing this, from the client point of view, is that the period during which updates are disallowed is greater.

- USER_RESOURCES

  Resets the per-hour counters for account resource management limits (such as MAX_QUERIES_PER_HOUR). Accounts that have reached their limits can once again proceed in their activities. This option does not affect any MAX_USER_CONNECTIONS limit; it is not a per-hour restriction.

If binary logging is enabled, MySQL writes the FLUSH statement to the binary log unless the LOCAL or NO_WRITE_TO_BINLOG option is given.

The FLUSH statement requires the RELOAD privilege.

GRANT

```
GRANT priv_type [(col_list)] [, priv_type [(col_list)] ] ...
  ON [TABLE | FUNCTION | PROCEDURE]
  {*.* | * | db_name.* | db_name.tbl_name | tbl_name | db_name.routine_name}
  TO account [IDENTIFIED BY [PASSWORD] 'password']
  [, account [IDENTIFIED BY [PASSWORD] 'password'] ] ...
  [REQUIRE security_options]
  [WITH grant_or_resource_options]
```

The GRANT statement grants access privileges to one or more MySQL accounts. To use this statement, you must have the GRANT OPTION privilege and you must possess the privileges that you are trying to grant.

Each `priv_type` value specifies a privilege to be granted, chosen from the following table. `ALL` is used by itself. For the other privileges, you may specify one or more of them as a comma–separated list. `ALL` signifies the combination of all the other privileges, except for `GRANT OPTION`, which must be granted separately or by adding a `WITH GRANT OPTION` clause.

Privilege Name	Operation Enabled by Privilege
ALTER	Alter tables and indexes
ALTER ROUTINE	Alter or drop stored functions and procedures
CREATE	Create databases and tables
CREATE ROUTINE	Create stored functions and procedures
CREATE TEMPORARY TABLES	Create temporary tables using the `TEMPORARY` keyword
CREATE USER	Use high-level account-management statements
CREATE VIEW	Create views
DELETE	Delete rows from tables
DROP	Remove databases, tables, and other objects
EVENT	Create, drop, or alter events for the event scheduler
EXECUTE	Execute stored functions and procedures
FILE	Read and write files on the server host
GRANT OPTION	Grant the account's privileges to other accounts
INDEX	Create or drop indexes
INSERT	Insert new rows into tables
LOCK TABLES	Explicitly lock tables with `LOCK TABLES` statements
PROCESS	View information about the threads executing within the server
REFERENCES	Unused (reserved for future use)
RELOAD	Reload the grant tables or flush the logs or caches
REPLICATION CLIENT	Ask about master and slave server locations
REPLICATION SLAVE	Act as a replication slave server
SELECT	Retrieve rows from tables
SHOW DATABASES	See all database names with `SHOW DATABASES`

Privilege Name	Operation Enabled by Privilege
SHOW VIEW	See view definitions with SHOW CREATE VIEW
SHUTDOWN	Shut down the server
SUPER	Kill threads and perform other supervisory operations
TRIGGER	Create or drop triggers
UPDATE	Modify table rows
ALL [PRIVILEGES]	All operations (except GRANT)
USAGE	A special "no privileges" privilege

The LOCK TABLES privilege can be exercised only on tables for which you also have the SELECT privilege, but it enables you to place any kind of lock, not just read locks.

You can always view or kill your own threads. The PROCESS or SUPER privilege enables you to view or kill, respectively, threads that belong to any account, not just your own.

The CREATE VIEW and SHOW VIEW privileges were introduced in MySQL 5.0.1. ALTER ROUTINE and CREATE ROUTINE were introduced in MySQL 5.0.3; they apply only to stored routines, not to user-defined functions (UDFs). Also in MySQL 5.0.3, CREATE USER was introduced and the EXECUTE privilege became operational. EVENT and TRIGGER were introduced in MySQL 5.1.6. (Before 5.1.6, SUPER rather than TRIGGER is required to manipulate triggers.)

The ON clause specifies how widely privileges should be granted, as shown in the following table.

Privilege Specifier	Level at Which Privileges Apply
ON *.*	Global privileges; all databases, all tables
ON *	Global privileges if no default database has been selected; database-level privileges for the default database otherwise
ON db_name.*	Database-level privileges; all objects in the named database
ON db_name.tbl_name	Table-level privileges; all columns in the named table
ON tbl_name	Table-level privileges; all columns in the named table in the default database
ON db_name.routine_name	Privileges for the named routine in the named database

As of MySQL 5.0.6, to specify explicitly the type of object to which the privileges apply if there is an ambiguity, you can include a TABLE, FUNCTION, or PROCEDURE keyword (for example, ON TABLE mydb.mytbl or ON FUNCTION mydb.myfunc).

When you use ALL as a privilege name, it grants only those privileges that are available at the level for which you are granting privileges. For example, RELOAD is only available as a global privilege, so it would be granted by GRANT ALL if you specify ON *.*, but not if you specify ON db_name.*. In the latter case, only these privileges that apply to databases would be granted. ALL also can be used only when granting global, database, table, or routine privileges.

USAGE means "no privileges." It should be used only at the global level.

GRANT OPTION applies to all privileges granted at a given level. For example, you cannot grant SELECT and INSERT for a given database to an account, but make just one of them grantable by that account.

When a table is named in the ON clause, a privilege may be made column-specific by following it with a list of one or more comma-separated column names in a (col_list) clause. (This applies only for the INSERT, REFERENCES, SELECT, and UPDATE privileges, which are the only ones that may be granted on a column-specific basis.)

To grant table or column privileges, the table must already exist.

The TO clause specifies one or more accounts to which the privileges should be granted. Name each account in 'user_name'@'host_name' format, as described in Section 12.4.1.1, "Specifying Account Names." Each account name may be followed by an optional IDENTIFIED BY clause to specify a password.

Database, table, column, and routine names, if quoted, must be quoted using identifier quoting characters. Usernames and hostnames can be quoted using identifier or string quoting characters. For example:

```
GRANT INSERT (`mycol`) ON `test`.`t` TO 'myuser'@'localhost';
```

The IDENTIFIED BY clause, if given, assigns a password to the account, and has the same syntax as described in the entry for CREATE USER. If the account already exists and IDENTIFIED BY is specified, the new password replaces the old one. The existing password remains unchanged otherwise.

If the named account does not exist, GRANT creates it. To avoid the possibility of GRANT creating a new account that has no password (and thus is insecure), enable the NO_AUTO_CREATE_USER SQL mode. This mode is available as of MySQL 5.0.2 and prevents GRANT from creating the account unless an IDENTIFIED BY clause is present.

The REQUIRE clause, if given, enables you to specify that secure connections are to be used and what kinds of information the client is required to supply. The REQUIRE keyword may be followed by:

- NONE: Secure connections are not required.

- SSL: A generic connection type; it requires that connections for the account use SSL.

- X509: The user must supply a valid X509 certificate. In this case, the client can present any X509 certificate; it doesn't matter what its contents are other than that it is valid.

- One or more of the following options to require that the connection be established with certain characteristics:

  - CIPHER '*str*':The connection must be established with '*str*' as its encryption cipher.

  - ISSUER '*str*':The client certificate must have '*str*' as the certificate issuer value.

  - SUBJECT '*str*':The client certificate must have '*str*' as the certificate subject value.

  If you give more than one of these options, they may optionally be separated by AND. The order of the options doesn't matter.

The WITH clause, if given, is used to specify that the account is able to grant other accounts the privileges that it holds itself, and to place limits on the account's resource consumption. The allowable options are shown in the following list. You may specify more than one option; their order does not matter.

- GRANT OPTION: This account can grant its own privileges to other accounts, including the right to grant privileges.

- MAX_CONNECTIONS_PER_HOUR *n*: The account can make *n* connections to the server per hour.

- MAX_QUERIES_PER_HOUR *n*: The account can issue *n* statements per hour.

- MAX_UPDATES_PER_HOUR *n*: The account can issue *n* statements that modify data per hour.

- MAX_USER_CONNECTIONS *n*: The account can make a maximum of *n* simultaneous connections to the server. This option was introduced in MySQL 5.0.3.

For MAX_CONNECTIONS_PER_HOUR, MAX_QUERIES_PER_HOUR, and MAX_UPDATES_PER_HOUR, a value of 0 means "no limit." For MAX_USER_CONNECTIONS, a value of 0 means that the value of the max_user_connections system variable applies.

The following statements demonstrate some ways in which the GRANT statement can be used. See Section 12.4.2, "Granting Privileges," for other examples. See Section 13.3, "Setting Up Secure Connections," for information on enabling SSL. In each case, no IDENTIFIER clause is given because it is assumed that the account has already been created and assigned a password with CREATE USER.

- Enable paul to access all tables in the sampdb database from any host. The following two statements are equivalent because omitting the hostname part of an account identifier is equivalent to specifying % as the hostname:

```
GRANT ALL ON sampdb.* TO 'paul';
GRANT ALL ON sampdb.* TO 'paul'@'%';
```

- Grant an account read-only privileges for the tables in the `menagerie` database. The `lookonly` user can connect from any host in the `xyz.com` domain:

```
GRANT SELECT ON menagerie.* TO 'lookonly'@'%.xyz.com';
```

- Grant an account full privileges, but only for the `member` table in the `sampdb` database. The `member_mgr` user can connect from a single host:

```
GRANT ALL ON sampdb.member TO 'member_mgr'@'boa.snake.net';
```

- Grant an account superuser privileges, including the ability to grant privileges to other users. The user must connect from the local host:

```
GRANT ALL ON *.* TO 'superduper'@'localhost' WITH GRANT OPTION;
```

- Grant an anonymous user full access to the `menagerie` database:

```
GRANT ALL ON menagerie.* TO ''@'localhost';
```

- Grant an account full access to the `privatedb` database, but require that connections be made via SSL with a valid X509 certificate:

```
GRANT ALL ON privatedb.* TO 'paranoid'@'%.mydomain.com' REQUIRE X509;
```

- Grant an account limited access such that it can issue only 100 statements per hour, of which at most 10 may be updates:

```
GRANT ALL ON test.* TO 'caleb'@'localhost'
  WITH MAX_QUERIES_PER_HOUR 100 MAX_UPDATES_PER_HOUR 10;
```

HANDLER

```
HANDLER tbl_name OPEN [[AS] alias_name]

HANDLER tbl_name READ
  {FIRST | NEXT}
  [where_clause] [limit_clause]

HANDLER tbl_name READ index_name
  {FIRST | NEXT | PREV | LAST | < | <= | = | => | >} (expr_list)
  [where_clause] [limit_clause]

HANDLER tbl_name CLOSE
```

HANDLER provides a low-level interface to the MyISAM and InnoDB storage engines that bypasses the optimizer and accesses table contents directly. To access a table through the HANDLER interface, first use HANDLER ... OPEN to open it. The table remains available for use until you issue a HANDLER ... CLOSE statement to close it explicitly or until or the connection terminates. While the table is open, use HANDLER ... READ to access the table's contents.

HANDLER provides no protection against concurrent updates. It does not lock the table, so it's possible for the table to be modified while HANDLER has it open, and there is no guarantee that the modifications will be reflected in the rows that you read from the table.

INSERT

```
INSERT [DELAYED | LOW_PRIORITY | HIGH_PRIORITY] [IGNORE] [INTO]
  tbl_name [(col_list)]
  {VALUES|VALUE} (expr [, expr] ...) [, (...)] ...
  [ON DUPLICATE KEY UPDATE col_name=expr [, col_name=expr] ...]

INSERT [DELAYED | LOW_PRIORITY | HIGH_PRIORITY] [IGNORE] [INTO]
  tbl_name SET col_name=expr [, col_name=expr] ...
  [ON DUPLICATE KEY UPDATE col_name=expr [, col_name=expr] ...]

INSERT [LOW_PRIORITY | HIGH_PRIORITY] [IGNORE] [INTO]
  tbl_name [(col_list)]
  {SELECT ... | (SELECT ...)}
  [ON DUPLICATE KEY UPDATE col_name=expr [, col_name=expr] ...]
```

Inserts rows into an existing table *tbl_name* and returns the number of rows inserted. INSERT syntax has three forms.

The first form of INSERT requires a VALUES() list that specifies all values to be inserted. If no *col_list* is given, the VALUES() list must specify one value for each column in the table. If a *col_list* is given consisting of one or more comma-separated column names, one value per column must be specified in the VALUES() list. Columns not named in the column list are set to their default values. Multiple value lists may be specified, allowing multiple rows to be inserted using a single INSERT statement.

```
INSERT INTO absence (student_id, date) VALUES(14,'2008-11-03'),(34,NOW());
```

The *col_list* and VALUES() list may be empty, which can be used as follows to create a row for which all columns are set to their default values:

```
INSERT INTO t () VALUES();
```

The second form of INSERT inserts columns named in the SET clause to the values given by the corresponding expressions. Columns not named are set to their default values.

```
INSERT INTO absence SET student_id = 14, date = '2008-11-03';
INSERT INTO absence SET student_id = 34, date = NOW();
```

The word DEFAULT may be used in a VALUES() list or SET clause to set a column to its default value explicitly without knowing what the default value is. More generally, to refer to a column's default value in expressions, you can use DEFAULT(*col_name*). The following statement sets the column i to 0 if its default value is NULL and to 1 otherwise:

```
INSERT INTO t SET i = IF(DEFAULT(i) IS NULL,1,0);
```

The third form of INSERT inserts into *tbl_name* the rows retrieved by the SELECT statement. The rows must contain as many columns as are in *tbl_name*, or as many columns as are named in *col_list* if a column list is specified. When a column list is specified, any columns not named in the list are set to their default values.

```
INSERT INTO score (student_id, score, event_id)
  SELECT student_id, 100 AS score, 15 AS event_id FROM student;
```

You cannot select rows using a subquery from the same table into which you are inserting them.

If strict SQL mode is in effect when an INSERT executes, it is an error to omit a column that has no DEFAULT clause in its definition or to specify its value by using DEFAULT.

If inserting a row would result in a duplicate key value in a unique index, INSERT terminates in error and no more rows are inserted. Adding IGNORE causes such rows not to be inserted and no error occurs. In strict SQL mode, IGNORE also causes data conversion errors that otherwise would terminate the statement to be treated as non-fatal warnings. Columns are set to the nearest legal value in this case.

The ON DUPLICATE KEY UPDATE clause applies for rows that would result in a duplicate-key violation for a unique-valued index. With this clause, the INSERT is converted to an UPDATE that modifies the column of the existing row using the column assignments following the UPDATE keyword. If an update did occur, the rows-affected count returned by INSERT is 2 rather than 1.

The DELAYED, LOW_PRIORITY, and HIGH_PRIORITY options affect execution scheduling:

- DELAYED causes the rows to be placed into a queue for later insertion, and the statement returns immediately so that the client may continue on without waiting. However, in this case, LAST_INSERT_ID() will not return the AUTO_INCREMENT value for any AUTO_INCREMENT column in the table. DELAYED inserts work for MyISAM, MEMORY, ARCHIVE, and (as of MySQL 5.1.19) BLACKHOLE tables. DELAYED is ignored for INSERT INTO ... SELECT and INSERT INTO ... ON DUPLICATE KEY UPDATE. As of MySQL 5.0.42/5.1.19, DELAYED is ignored if mixed with stored functions or triggers such that an INSERT refers to stored functions that access tables or triggers or the INSERT is invoked within a stored function or trigger.

- LOW_PRIORITY causes the statement to be deferred until no clients are reading from the table.

- HIGH_PRIORITY causes the effect of the --low-priority-updates server option to be canceled for a single statement. (It the server is started with this option, it lowers the priority of INSERT and other update statements.) HIGH_PRIORITY also prevents the INSERT from being performed concurrently with SELECT statements if it otherwise would be.

The LOW_PRIORITY and HIGH_PRIORITY options are effective only for storage engines that use table-level locking, such as MyISAM, MEMORY, and MERGE.

KILL

```
KILL [CONNECTION | QUERY] thread_id
```

Kills the server thread with the given *thread_id*. You must have the SUPER privilege to kill the thread, unless it is one of your own. The KILL statement allows only a single ID. The mysqladmin kill command performs the same operation, but allows multiple thread ID values to be specified on the command line.

The CONNECTION option has the same effect as no option: The thread with the given ID is terminated. QUERY terminates any statement that the thread is executing, but not the thread itself.

LOAD DATA

```
LOAD DATA [LOW_PRIORITY | CONCURRENT ] [LOCAL] INFILE 'file_name'
  [IGNORE | REPLACE]
  INTO TABLE tbl_name
  [CHARACTER SET charset]
  [field_options] [line_options]
  [IGNORE n LINES]
  [(col_or_user_var_name, ...)]
  [SET col_name = expr, ...]
```

LOAD DATA reads input records from the file *file_name* and loads them in bulk into the table *tbl_name*. This is faster than using a set of INSERT statements.

LOAD DATA returns an information string that has the following format:

```
Records: n  Deleted: n  Skipped: n  Warnings: n
```

If the warning count is non-zero, the SHOW WARNINGS statement shows what the problems were.

LOW_PRIORITY causes the statement to be deferred until no clients are reading from the table. This option is effective only for storage engines that use table-level locking, such as MyISAM, MEMORY, and MERGE.

CONCURRENT applies only for MyISAM tables. If the table has no holes in the middle, new rows are loaded at the end of the table. In this case, other clients can retrieve from the table concurrently while rows are being loaded.

Without the LOCAL keyword, the file is read directly by the server on the server host. In this case, you must have the FILE privilege and the file must either be located in the database directory of the default database or be world-readable. If LOCAL is specified, the client reads the file on the client host and sends its contents over the network to the server. In this case, the FILE privilege is not required. LOCAL can be disabled or enabled selectively. If it is disabled on the server side, you cannot use it from the client side. If it is enabled on the server side, but disabled by default on the client side, you'll need to enable it explicitly. For example, with the mysql program, you can use the --local-infile flag to enable the LOCAL capability.

When LOCAL is not specified in the LOAD DATA statement, the server locates the file as follows:

- If 'file_name' is an absolute pathname, the server looks for the file starting from the root directory.
- If 'file_name' is a relative pathname, interpretation depends on whether the name contains a single component. If so, the server looks for the file in the database directory of the default database. If the filename contains multiple components, the server looks for the file beginning from the server's data directory.

If LOCAL is given, filename interpretation is as follows:

- If 'file_name' is an absolute pathname, the client looks for the file starting from the root directory.
- If 'file_name' is a relative pathname, the client looks for the file beginning from your current directory.

For Windows, backslashes in filenames may be written either as slashes ('/') or as doubled backslashes ('\\').

As of MySQL 5.0.19/5.1.6, the filename is evaluated using the character set named by the character_set_filesystem system variable.

By default, the contents of the file are interpreted using the character set named by the character_set_database system variable. As of MySQL 5.0.38/5.1.17, you can use the CHARACTER SET clause to indicate the file's character set explicitly. (However, it is not possible to load ucs2, utf18, or utf32 files.)

Rows that duplicate values in a unique index are either ignored or replace existing rows according to whether IGNORE or REPLACE is specified. If neither is specified, an error occurs, and any remaining records are ignored. If LOCAL is specified, transmission of the file cannot be interrupted, so the default behavior is like that of IGNORE if neither duplicate-handling option is given.

The field_options and line_options clauses indicate the format of the data. (The options available in these clauses also apply to the corresponding clauses of the SELECT ... INTO OUTFILE statement.) The two clauses have this syntax:

```
field_options:
  [FIELDS
    [TERMINATED BY 'str']
    [[OPTIONALLY] ENCLOSED BY 'char']
    [ESCAPED BY 'char' ] ]

line_options:
  [LINES
    [STARTING BY 'str']
    [TERMINATED BY 'str'] ]
```

The 'str' and 'char' values may include the escape sequences in the following table to indicate special characters. The sequences should be given in the lettercase shown.

Sequence	Meaning
\0	NUL (zero-valued byte)
\b	Backspace
\n	Newline (linefeed)
\r	Carriage return
\s	Space
\t	Tab
\'	Single quote
\"	Double quote
\\	Backslash
\Z	Control-Z (Windows EOF character)

You can also use hexadecimal constants to indicate arbitrary characters. For example, LINES TERMINATED BY 0x02 indicates that lines are terminated by Control-B (ASCII 2) characters.

If the FIELDS clause is given, at least one of the TERMINATED BY, ENCLOSED BY, or ESCAPED BY options must be given. If multiple options are present, they may appear in any order. Similarly, if the LINES clause is given, at least one of the STARTING BY or TERMINATED BY options must be given, but if both are present, they may appear in any order. FIELDS must precede LINES if both are given.

Options for the FIELDS clause are used as follows:

- TERMINATED BY specifies the character or characters that delimit values within a line.

- ENCLOSED BY specifies a quote character that is stripped from the ends of field values if it is present. This occurs regardless of whether OPTIONALLY is present. For output (SELECT ... INTO OUTFILE), the ENCLOSED BY character is used to enclose field values in output lines. If OPTIONALLY is given, values are quoted only for CHAR and VARCHAR columns.

  To include an instance of the ENCLOSED BY character within an input field value, it should either be doubled or preceded by the ESCAPED BY character. Otherwise, it will be interpreted as signifying the end of the field. For output, instances of the ENCLOSED BY character within field values are preceded by the ESCAPED BY character.

- The ESCAPED BY character specifies how to escape special characters. In the following examples, assume that the escape character is backslash ('\'). For input, the unquoted sequence \N (backslash-N) is interpreted as NULL. The \0 sequence (backslash-ASCII '0') is interpreted as a zero-valued byte. For other escaped characters, the escape character is stripped off, and the following character is used literally.

For example, \" is interpreted as a double quote, even if field values are enclosed within double quotes.

For output, the escape character is used to encode NULL as an unquoted \N sequence, and zero-valued bytes as \0. In addition, instances of the ESCAPED BY and ENCLOSED BY characters are preceded by the escape character, as are the first characters of the field and line termination strings. If the ESCAPED BY character is empty (ESCAPED BY ''), no escaping is done. (In this case, NULL is written as NULL, not \N.) To specify an escape character of '\', double it (ESCAPED BY '\\').

Options for the LINES clause are used as follows:

- The STARTING BY value specifies one or more characters that begin lines. (This value *and everything preceding it* on the line is taken as the line beginning.)
- The TERMINATED BY value specifies one or more characters that signify the ends of lines.

If neither FIELDS nor LINES is given, the defaults are as if you had specified them like this:

```
FIELDS
  TERMINATED BY '\t'
  ENCLOSED BY ''
  ESCAPED BY '\\'
LINES
  STARTING BY ''
  TERMINATED BY '\n'
```

In other words, fields within a line are tab-delimited without being quoted, backslash is treated as the escape character, and lines are terminated by newline characters.

If the TERMINATED BY and ENCLOSED BY values for the FIELDS clause are both empty, a fixed-width row format is used with no delimiters between fields. Column values are read (or written, for output) using a width large enough for all values in the column. For example, VARCHAR(15) and MEDIUMINT columns are read as 15-character and 8-character fields for input. For output, the columns are written using 15 characters and 8 characters. NULL values are written as strings of spaces. (Before MySQL 5.0.6, fixed-width interpretation was based on the display widths of the column data types.)

NULL values in an input data file are indicated by the unquoted sequence \N. If the FIELDS ENCLOSED BY character is not empty, all non-NULL input values must be quoted with the enclosed-by character and the unquoted word NULL also will be interpreted as a NULL value.

If the IGNORE n LINES clause is given, the first n lines of the input are discarded. For example, if your data file has a row of column headers that you don't want to read into the database table, use IGNORE 1 LINES:

```
LOAD DATA LOCAL INFILE 'mytbl.txt' INTO TABLE mytbl IGNORE 1 LINES;
```

By default, input lines are assumed to contain one value per column in the table. If a list consisting of one or more comma-separated column names is given, input lines should contain a value for each named column. Columns not named in the list are set to their default values. If an input line is short of the expected number of values, columns for which values are missing are set to their default values.

If strict SQL mode is in effect when LOAD DATA executes, it is an error for a value to be missing for a column that has no DEFAULT clause in its definition.

As of MySQL 5.0.3, the list can include column names or user variable names, and a SET clause can be given to perform additional processing of input values before they are loaded into the table. For example, the following statement loads the first input column into col1, ignores the second column, loads the sum of the third and fourth columns into col2, and uses UUID() to provide a generated value for col3:

```
LOAD DATA LOCAL INFILE 'mytbl.txt' INTO TABLE mytbl
  (col1,@skip,@addend1, @addend2)
  SET col2 = @addend1 + @addend2, col3 = UUID();
```

The SET clause can contain multiple assignment expressions separated by commas. The left hand side of each assignment must name a table column. User variables are not allowed for fixed-width input format because no column width can be determined. Scalar subqueries can be used to provide column values except that you cannot use a subquery to select values from the same table into which you are loading data.

If you have a tab-delimited text file that you created on Windows, you can use the default column separator, but the lines are probably terminated by carriage return/newline pairs. To load the file, specify a different line terminator ('\r' indicates a carriage return, and '\n' indicates a newline):

```
LOAD DATA LOCAL INFILE 'mytbl.txt' INTO TABLE mytbl
  LINES TERMINATED BY '\r\n';
```

You may end up with a malformed row in the database if you load a data file that was created on Windows by a program that uses the odd MS-DOS convention of putting the Control-Z character at the end of the file to indicate end-of-file. Either create the file using a program that doesn't do this, or delete the row after loading the file.

Files in comma-separated values (CSV) format have commas between fields, and fields may be quoted with double quotes. Assuming lines have newlines at the end, the LOAD DATA statement to load such a file looks like this:

```
LOAD DATA LOCAL INFILE 'mytbl.txt' INTO TABLE mytbl
  FIELDS TERMINATED BY ',' ENCLOSED BY '"';
```

Hexadecimal notation is useful for specifying arbitrary control characters. The following statement reads a file for which fields are separated by Control-A (ASCII 1) characters, and lines are terminated by Control-B (ASCII 2) characters:

```
LOAD DATA LOCAL INFILE 'mytbl.txt' INTO TABLE mytbl
  FIELDS TERMINATED BY 0x01 LINES TERMINATED BY 0x02;
```

LOAD INDEX INTO CACHE

```
LOAD INDEX INTO CACHE
    tbl_name [[INDEX | KEY] (index_name [, index_name] ...)
      [IGNORE LEAVES]]
    [, tbl_name [[INDEX | KEY] (index_name [, index_name] ...)]
      [IGNORE LEAVES]]...
```

Loads indexes from each named MyISAM table into the key cache to which the table is assigned. This is the default key cache unless the table has been assigned to another cache with the CACHE INDEX statement. By default, all index blocks are loaded. With the IGNORE LEAVES clause, only non-leaf blocks in the index tree are loaded.

As with the CACHE INDEX statement, the syntax for LOAD INDEX INTO CACHE allows individual indexes to be specified, but the current implementation is such that all indexes for a table are loaded.

You must have the INDEX privilege for each table named in the statement.

LOAD INDEX INTO CACHE produces output in the format described in the entry for CHECK TABLE.

See Section 12.7.2, "Configuring the MyISAM Storage Engine," for more information about MyISAM key cache management.

LOCK TABLE

```
LOCK {TABLE | TABLES}
    tbl_name [[AS] alias_name] lock_type
    [, tbl_name [[AS] alias_name] lock_type] ...
```

Obtains a lock on the named tables, waiting if necessary until all locks are acquired. Each lock_type value must be one of the following:

- READ [LOCAL]

  Acquires a read lock. This blocks other clients that want to write to the table, but allows other clients to read the table.

  READ LOCAL is a variation on a READ lock, designed for concurrent insert situations. It applies only to MyISAM tables that do not have any holes in the middle resulting from deleted or updated rows. READ LOCAL enables you to lock a table explicitly but still allow other clients to perform concurrent inserts. (If the table does have holes in it, the lock is treated as a regular READ lock.)

- [LOW_PRIORITY] WRITE

  Acquires a write lock. This blocks all other clients, whether they want to read from or write to the table.

  A LOW_PRIORITY WRITE lock allows other readers to read the table if the request is waiting for another client that is already reading the table. A request for this type of lock is not granted until there are no more readers.

LOCK TABLE releases any existing locks that you currently hold. Thus, to lock multiple tables, you must lock them all using a single LOCK TABLE statement. Any locks that are held by a client when it terminates are released automatically. While you have acquired locks with LOCK TABLE, you cannot refer to any not-locked tables.

LOCK TABLE allows an alias to be specified so that you can lock a table under an alias that you are going to use when referring to the table in a subsequent query. If you refer to a table multiple times in a query, you must obtain a lock for each instance of the table, locking aliases as necessary. You must request all the locks in the same statement.

```
LOCK TABLE student READ, score WRITE, grade_event READ;
LOCK TABLE member READ;
LOCK TABLE t AS t1 READ, t AS t2 READ;
```

If a transaction is in progress, LOCK TABLE causes an implicit commit. Table locks acquired with LOCK TABLE are released implicitly if you start a transaction with START TRANSACTION.

OPTIMIZE TABLE

```
OPTIMIZE [LOCAL | NO_WRITE_TO_BINLOG]
  {TABLE | TABLES} tbl_name [, tbl_name] ...
```

DELETE, REPLACE, and UPDATE statements may result in areas of unused space in a table, particularly for tables that have variable-length rows. To counter this, OPTIMIZE TABLE performs the following actions for a MyISAM table:

- Defragments the table to eliminate wasted space and reduce the table size.
- Coalesces the contents of variable-rows that have become fragmented into non-contiguous pieces, so that each row is stored contiguously.
- Sorts the index pages if necessary.
- Updates the internal table statistics.

Issuing an OPTIMIZE TABLE statement is like executing myisamchk with the --check-only-changed, --quick, --sort-index, and --analyze options. However, with myisamchk, you must arrange to prevent the server from accessing the table at the same time. With OPTIMIZE TABLE, the server does the work and takes care of making sure that other clients do not modify the table while it's being optimized.

For an InnoDB table, OPTIMIZE TABLE is mapped to ALTER TABLE to update the table index statistics and free unused space in the clustered index.

As of MySQL 5.0.16, for an ARCHIVE table, OPTIMIZE TABLE performs table analysis and recompresses the table to reduce the storage required.

OPTIMIZE TABLE requires SELECT and INSERT privileges on each table.

If binary logging is enabled, MySQL writes the OPTIMIZE TABLE statement to the binary log unless the LOCAL or NO_WRITE_TO_BINLOG option is given.

`OPTIMIZE TABLE` produces output in the format described in the entry for `CHECK TABLE`.

PREPARE

```
PREPARE stmt_name FROM {'str' | @var_name}
```

Prepares a statement and assigns it the name *stmt_name*. The statement can be executed later with `EXECUTE` and deallocated with `DEALLOCATE PREPARE`. If there was already a previously prepared statement that has the given name, the previous statement is deallocated before the new statement is prepared. Statement names are not case sensitive.

The statement to be prepared can be given either as a string literal or a user variable. The set of allowable statements that can be used with `PREPARE` has expanded over time. The initial set included `CREATE TABLE`, `DELETE`, `DO`, `INSERT`, `REPLACE`, `SELECT`, `SET`, `UPDATE`, and most variations of `SHOW`. Other statements have been added; consult the MySQL Reference Manual for your version of MySQL to see which statements qualify. `PREPARE`, `EXECUTE`, and `DEALLOCATE PREPARE` *cannot* be prepared.

The prepared statement can contain '?' characters that serve as placeholder markers. When you execute the statement later, supply data values to be bound to these placeholders. Placeholders enable you to parameterize the statement so that you can use the same prepared statement with different data values per execution.

`PREPARE`, `EXECUTE`, and `DEALLOCATE` provide an SQL-level interface to prepared statements. They are not the same as or as efficient as the binary API for prepared statements that is discussed in Chapter 7, "Writing MySQL Programs Using C," and Appendix G, "C API Reference (online)".

PURGE MASTER LOGS

```
PURGE {MASTER | BINARY} LOGS {TO 'log_name' | BEFORE 'date'}
```

Deletes all the binary log files on the server that were generated earlier than the named file or before the given date (in `'CCYY-MM-DD hh:mm:ss'` format), and resets the binary log index file to list only those log files that remain. Normally, you use this after running `SHOW SLAVE STATUS` on each of the master's slaves to determine which log files are still in use. This statement requires the `SUPER` privilege.

The following statement removes `binlog.000001` through `binlog.000009` (or whichever of them exist), and causes `binlog.000010` to become the first of the remaining log files:

```
PURGE MASTER LOGS TO 'binlog.000010';
```

RELEASE SAVEPOINT

```
RELEASE SAVEPOINT savepoint_name
```

Releases the savepoint with the given name from the savepoints for the current transaction, or returns an error if the savepoint does not exist. No commit or rollback occurs. This statement was introduced in MySQL 5.0.3.

RENAME TABLE

```
RENAME {TABLE | TABLES} tbl_name TO new_tbl_name
  [, tbl_name TO new_tbl_name] ...
```

Renames one or more tables. RENAME TABLE is similar to ALTER TABLE ... RENAME, except that it can rename multiple tables, and locks them all during the rename operation. This is advantageous if you need to perform an "atomic" rename that prevents any of the tables from being accessed during the operation.

If you rename an InnoDB table on which other tables depend for foreign key relationships, InnoDB adjusts the dependencies to point to the renamed table.

If you rename a MyISAM table that is part of a MERGE table, you must redefine the MERGE table accordingly.

RENAME TABLE cannot be used for TEMPORARY tables.

As of MySQL 5.0.2, an error occurs if you try to rename a table into another database if there are triggers for the table.

As of MySQL 5.0.14, RENAME TABLE applies to views unless you try to rename the view into another database.

RENAME USER

```
RENAME USER from_account TO to_account
  [, from_account TO to_account] ...
```

Renames one or more MySQL accounts. Each from_account is renamed to the corresponding to_account. An error occurs if from_account does not exist or if to_account already exists. Name each account in 'user_name'@'host_name' format, as described in Section 12.4.1.1, "Specifying Account Names."

This statement was introduced in MySQL 5.0.2. It requires the global CREATE USER privilege or the UPDATE privilege for the mysql database.

RENAME USER does not update privileges held by the original account to apply to the new account.

REPAIR TABLE

```
REPAIR [LOCAL | NO_WRITE_TO_BINLOG]
  {TABLE | TABLES} tbl_name [, tbl_name] ... [option] ...
```

This statement performs table repair operations. It works with MyISAM and ARCHIVE tables, and with CSV tables as of MySQL 5.1.19. REPAIR TABLE requires SELECT and INSERT privileges on each table.

REPAIR TABLE with no options performs a table repair option like that done by myisamchk --recover. The following list describes the allowable option values. These options apply to MyISAM tables; they may or may not be used by other storage engines.

- EXTENDED performs an extended repair that re-creates the indexes. This is similar to running myisamchk --safe-recover on the tables, except that the repair is performed by the server rather than by an external utility.

- QUICK attempts a quick repair of just the indexes; leaves the data file alone.
- USE_FRM uses the table's .frm file to reinitialize the index file and to determine how to interpret the contents of the data file so that the indexes can be rebuilt. This can be useful if the index has become lost or irrecoverably corrupted. However, it should be treated as a last resort and should be used *only* if your current version of MySQL is the same as that used to create the table; otherwise, you risk further damage to the table.

If binary logging is enabled, MySQL writes the REPAIR TABLE statement to the binary log unless the LOCAL or NO_WRITE_TO_BINLOG option is given.

REPAIR TABLE produces output in the format described in the entry for CHECK TABLE.

REPLACE

```
REPLACE [LOW_PRIORITY | DELAYED] [INTO]
  tbl_name [(col_list)]
  {VALUES|VALUE} (expr [, expr] ...) [, (...)] ...

REPLACE [LOW_PRIORITY | DELAYED] [INTO]
  tbl_name [(col_list)]
  {SELECT ... | (SELECT ...)}

REPLACE [LOW_PRIORITY | DELAYED] [INTO]
  tbl_name SET col_name=expr [, col_name=expr] ...
```

The basic action of REPLACE statement is like that of INSERT, with the exception that if a row to be inserted has a value for a unique index that duplicates the value in a row already present in the table, the old row is deleted before the new one is inserted. For this reason, there is no IGNORE clause option in the syntax of REPLACE. Also, REPLACE has no support for ON DUPLICATE KEY UPDATE. See the description of INSERT for more information.

It's possible for a REPLACE to delete more than one row if the table contains multiple unique indexes. This can happen if a new row matches values in several of the unique indexes, in which case all the matching rows are deleted before the new row is inserted.

REPLACE requires the INSERT and DELETE privileges for the table.

RESET

```
RESET option [, option] ...
```

The RESET statement is similar to FLUSH in that it affects log or cache information. option values should be chosen from the following list:

- MASTER deletes the existing binary log files for a replication master server, creates a new file with the numbering sequence set to 000001, and resets the binary log index to name just the new file.

- QUERY CACHE clears the query cache and removes any queries currently registered in it. To defragment the cache without clearing it, use the FLUSH QUERY CACHE statement instead.

- SLAVE tells the server, if it is acting as a replication slave, to remove any existing relay log files and begin a new relay log, and to forget its replication coordinates (that is, its current replication binary log filename and position within that file).

RESET requires the RELOAD privilege.

REVOKE

```
REVOKE priv_type [(col_list)] [, priv_type [(col_list)] ...]
  ON [TABLE | FUNCTION | PROCEDURE]
    {*.* | * | db_name.* | db_name.tbl_name | tbl_name | db_name.routine_name}
  FROM account [, account] ...

REVOKE ALL [PRIVILEGES], GRANT OPTION
  FROM account [, account] ...
```

The REVOKE statement revokes privileges from the named account or accounts. Name each account in 'user_name'@'host_name' format, as described in Section 12.4.1.1, "Specifying Account Names." An error occurs for non-existent accounts.

In the first syntax, the priv_type, col_list, and ON clauses are specified the same way as for the GRANT statement. To use this statement, you must have the GRANT OPTION privilege and you must possess the privileges that you are trying to revoke.

The second syntax has a fixed privilege list and no ON clause. It revokes all privileges held by each of the named accounts. The second syntax requires the global CREATE USER privilege or the UPDATE privilege for the mysql database.

REVOKE does not remove an account's row from the mysql.user grant table. This means that the account still can be used to connect to the MySQL server even when all its privileges have been revoked. To remove the account entirely, use the DROP USER statement (or manually delete the account row from the mysql.user table).

- Revoke privileges that allow the member_mgr user to modify the member table in the sampdb database:

```
REVOKE INSERT,DELETE,UPDATE ON sampdb.member
  FROM 'member_mgr'@'boa.snake.net';
```

- Revoke all privileges for a single table in the menagerie database from the anonymous user on the local host:

```
REVOKE ALL ON menagerie.pet FROM ''@'localhost';
```

- ALL revokes all but the GRANT OPTION privilege. To revoke that privilege as well, you must do so explicitly:

```
REVOKE GRANT OPTION ON menagerie.pet FROM ''@'localhost';
```

- Revoke all privileges held at all levels by `superduper@localhost`:

  ```
  REVOKE ALL PRIVILEGES, GRANT OPTION FROM 'superduper'@'localhost';
  ```

ROLLBACK

```
ROLLBACK [WORK] [AND [NO] CHAIN] [[NO] RELEASE]
```

```
ROLLBACK [WORK] TO [SAVEPOINT] savepoint_name
```

Rolls back changes made by statements that are part of the current transaction so that those changes are forgotten. This works only for transaction-safe storage engines. (For non-transactional storage engines, statements are committed as they are executed and thus cannot be rolled back.)

The optional keyword WORK has no effect. The CHAIN and RELEASE clauses have the same effect as described in the entry for COMMIT.

If the TO SAVEPOINT clause is given, the statement rolls back the current transaction only to the named savepoint. This clause works for InnoDB or Falcon transactions.

ROLLBACK does nothing if autocommit mode has not been disabled with START TRANSACTION or by setting the autocommit variable to 0.

The WORK, CHAIN, and RELEASE clauses were introduced in MySQL 5.0.3, and the SAVEPOINT keyword became optional.

SAVEPOINT

```
SAVEPOINT savepoint_name
```

Creates a transaction savepoint with the given name. Any existing savepoint with the given name is deleted. Statements executed later within the current transaction can be rolled back to the savepoint with the ROLLBACK TO SAVEPOINT statement.

SELECT

```
SELECT
  [select_option] ...
  select_expr [, select_expr] ...
  [FROM tbl_refs
  [WHERE where_expr]
  [GROUP BY {col_name | expr | position} [ASC | DESC], ...  [WITH ROLLUP]]
  [HAVING where_expr]
  [ORDER BY {col_name | expr | position} [ASC | DESC], ...]
  [LIMIT {[skip_count,] show_count | show_count OFFSET skip_count}]
  [PROCEDURE procedure_name([param_list])]
  [
      INTO OUTFILE 'file_name' [field_options] [line_options]
    | INTO DUMPFILE 'file_name'
    | INTO var_name [, var_name] ...
  ]
```

```
[FOR UPDATE | LOCK IN SHARE MODE] ]
```

SELECT normally is used to retrieve rows from one or more tables. However, because everything in the statement is optional except the SELECT keyword and at least one *select_expr*, it's also possible to write statements that simply evaluate expressions:

```
SELECT 'one plus one =', 1+1;
```

For compatibility with database systems that require a FROM clause, MySQL recognizes the DUAL pseudo-table:

```
SELECT 'one plus one =', 1+1 FROM DUAL;
```

A subquery is one SELECT nested within another; examples can be found in Section 2.9, "Performing Multiple-Table Retrievals with Subqueries." Subqueries also can be used in the WHERE clause of DELETE and UPDATE statements or with INSERT and REPLACE statements. However, you cannot use a subquery to select from a table that you are modifying.

Each *select_option* value can be one of the options in the following list:

- ALL, DISTINCT, DISTINCTROW

  These keywords control whether duplicate rows are returned. ALL causes all rows to be returned, which is the default. DISTINCT and DISTINCTROW specify that duplicate rows should be eliminated from the result set.

- HIGH_PRIORITY

  Specifying HIGH_PRIORITY gives the statement a higher priority if it normally would have to wait. If other statements, such as INSERT or UPDATE, are waiting to write to tables named in the SELECT because some other client is reading the tables, HIGH_PRIORITY causes a SELECT statement to be given priority over those write statements. This should be done only for SELECT statements that you know will execute quickly and that must be done immediately, because it slows down execution of the write statements. This option is effective only for storage engines that use table-level locking, such as MyISAM, MEMORY, and MERGE.

- SQL_BUFFER_RESULT

  Tells the server to buffer the query result in a separate temporary table rather than keeping the table or tables named in the SELECT locked while waiting for the entire query result to be sent to the client. This helps the server release the locks sooner, which gives other clients access to the tables more quickly. However, using this option also requires more disk space and memory.

- SQL_CACHE, SQL_NO_CACHE

  If the query result is cacheable and the query cache is operating in demand mode, SQL_CACHE causes the result to be cached. SQL_NO_CACHE suppresses any caching of the query result.

- SQL_CALC_FOUND_ROWS

Normally, the row count from a query that includes a `LIMIT` clause is the number of rows actually returned. `SQL_CALC_FOUND_ROWS` tells the server to determine how large the query result would be without the `LIMIT`. This row count can be obtained by issuing a `SELECT FOUND_ROWS()` statement following the initial `SELECT`.

- `SQL_BIG_RESULT`, `SQL_SMALL_RESULT`

  These keywords provide a hint that the result set will be large or small, which gives the optimizer information that it can use to process the query more effectively.

- `STRAIGHT_JOIN`

  Forces tables to be joined in the order named in the `FROM` clause. This option may be useful if you believe that the optimizer is not making the best choice.

The `select_expr` expressions list the output columns to be returned, separated by commas. Columns may be references to table columns or expressions (including scalar subqueries). Any column may be assigned a column alias using `AS alias_name` syntax (the `AS` keyword is optional). The alias then becomes the column name in the output and may also be referred to in `GROUP BY`, `ORDER BY`, and `HAVING` clauses. However, you cannot refer to column aliases in a `WHERE` clause.

The special notation `*` means "all columns from the tables named in the `FROM` clause," and `tbl_name.*` means "all columns from the named table."

The `FROM` clause names one or more tables from which rows should be selected. MySQL supports the following join syntax:

```
tbl_refs:
  tbl_ref [, tbl_ref] ...

tbl_ref:
    tbl_factor
  | join_tbl

tbl_factor:
    tbl_name
  | (subquery) [AS] alias_name
  | (tbl_refs)
  | { OJ tbl_ref LEFT OUTER JOIN tbl_ref ON conditional_expr }

join_tbl:
    tbl_ref [INNER | CROSS] JOIN tbl_factor [join_condition]
  | tbl_ref STRAIGHT_JOIN tbl_factor [ON conditional_expr]
  | tbl_ref {LEFT | RIGHT} [OUTER] JOIN tbl_ref join_condition
  | tbl_ref NATURAL [{LEFT | RIGHT} [OUTER]] JOIN tbl_factor

join_condition:
    ON conditional_expr
  | USING (col_list)
```

> **Note**
>
> This grammar describes the syntax that is allowable as of MySQL 5.0.12 when several changes wre made for better compliance with standard SQL. If you are interested in differences between this syntax that that allowed prior to 5.0.12, see the MySQL Reference Manual.

Each `tbl_name` may be accompanied by an alias or index hints. That is, the full syntax for referring to a table actually looks like this:

```
tbl_name
  [[AS] alias_name]
  [{USE | IGNORE | FORCE} {INDEX | KEY}
   [FOR {JOIN | ORDER BY | GROUP BY}]
   (index_list)]
```

Tables may be assigned aliases in the FROM clause using either `tbl_name alias_name` or `tbl_name AS alias_name` syntax. An alias provides an alternative name by which to refer to the table columns elsewhere in the query.

It is also allowable to specify a table in the FROM clause by means of a subquery within parentheses, as long as you provide an alias so that the table can be referred to elsewhere in the statement:

```
SELECT * FROM (SELECT 1) AS t;
```

The USE INDEX, IGNORE INDEX, and FORCE INDEX clauses provide index hints to the optimizer. They may be helpful in cases where the optimizer doesn't make the correct choice about which index to use in a join. USE INDEX tells the optimizer to select an index only from those named in `index_list`. IGNORE INDEX tells the optimizer which indexes not to use. FORCE INDEX is like USE INDEX but tells the optimizer to consider table scans very expensive compared to using the listed indexes.

`index_list` should name one or more indexes separated by commas (with one exception to be noted shortly). Each index should be the name of an index from the table, or the keyword PRIMARY to indicate the table's PRIMARY KEY.

Before MySQL 5.0.40, index hints apply only to selecting rows and joining tables, not to processing ORDER BY or GROUP BY clauses. In MySQL 5.0 as of 5.0.40, you can use FOR JOIN to make that same behavior explicit. In MySQL 5.1 as of 5.1.17, you can use FOR JOIN that way, and there are several other index hint changes:

- Hints with no FOR clause apply to row selection and joining tables (as before), but also to processing ORDER BY or GROUP BY clauses.
- The `index_list` for USE can be empty to indicate "use no indexes."
- Multiple index hints per `tbl_name` reference are allowed. However, you cannot use both USE INDEX and FORCE INDEX for the same reference.

Index hints have no effect for FULLTEXT indexes.

Joins select rows from the named tables as indicated in the following descriptions. The rows actually returned to the client may be limited by WHERE, HAVING, or LIMIT clauses.

- For a single table named by itself, SELECT retrieves rows from that table.

- If multiple tables are named and separated by commas, SELECT returns all possible combinations of rows from the tables. Using JOIN, CROSS JOIN, or INNER JOIN is similar to using a comma if there is no ON or USING clause. STRAIGHT_JOIN is similar, but forces the optimizer to join the tables in the order that the tables are named. It may be used if you believe that the optimizer is not making the best choice.

- Unlike the comma operator, joins performed with JOIN, CROSS JOIN, or INNER JOIN can be specified with an ON or USING() clause to constrain matches between tables. Matching rows are determined according to the condition specified in the ON *conditional_expr* clause or the USING (*col_list*) clause. *conditional_expr* is an expression of the form that may be used in the WHERE clause. *col_list* consists of one or more comma-separated column names, each of which must be a column that occurs in both of the joined tables.

- LEFT JOIN retrieves rows from the joined tables, but forces a row to be generated for every row in the left table, even if there is no matching row in the right table. When there is no match, columns from the right table are returned as NULL values. The ON or USING() clause following the table names is given as for JOIN, CROSS JOIN, or INNER JOIN. LEFT OUTER JOIN is equivalent to LEFT JOIN. So is the syntax that begins with OJ, which is included for ODBC compatibility. The curly braces shown for the OJ syntax are not metacharacters; they are literal characters that must be present in the statement.

- NATURAL LEFT JOIN is equivalent to LEFT JOIN USING (*col_list*), where *col_list* names all the columns that are common to both tables.

- The RIGHT JOIN types are like the corresponding LEFT JOIN types, but with the table roles reversed.

- The precedence of comma joins is less than that of other join types. Mixing comma joins with other types may result in "Unknown column" errors. Replacing comma with INNER JOIN often helps in such cases.

The WHERE clause specifies an expression that is applied to rows selected from the tables named in the FROM clause. Rows that do not satisfy the criteria given by the expression are rejected. The result set may be further limited by HAVING and LIMIT clauses. Column aliases may not be referred to in the WHERE clause.

The GROUP BY and ORDER BY clauses have similar syntax. GROUP BY *col_list* is used to group rows of the result set based on the columns named in the list. This clause is used when you specify summary functions such as COUNT() or MAX() in a *select_expr*. ORDER BY *col_list* indicates that the result set should be sorted based on the named columns. In either clause, columns may be referred to by column names or aliases, or by position within the list of *select_expr* expressions. Column positions are unsigned integers beginning with 1, but use of column positions is non-standard and deprecated. You can also use expressions to group or sort by expression results. For example, ORDER BY RAND() sorts rows in random order.

In a GROUP BY or ORDER BY clause, you can follow any column in the column list with ASC or DESC to indicate that the column should be sorted in ascending or descending order. The default for each column is ascending if neither keyword is present. Sort order indicators are allowed in GROUP BY clauses because, in MySQL, GROUP BY not only groups rows, it sorts the results. The output order resulting from GROUP BY is overridden by any ORDER BY clause that is present. To prevent the implicit ordering that results from GROUP BY (and thus not incur the sorting overhead), use ORDER BY NULL.

WITH ROLLUP can be used at the end of a GROUP BY clause. It causes the output to include summary rows for higher level combinations of the grouped columns, plus an overall summary at the end.

The HAVING clause specifies a secondary expression that is used to limit rows after they have satisfied the conditions named by the WHERE clause and after they have been grouped according to any GROUP BY clause. Rows that do not satisfy the HAVING condition are rejected. HAVING is useful for expressions involving summary functions that cannot be tested in the WHERE clause. However, if a condition is legal in either the WHERE clause or the HAVING clause, it is preferable to place it in the WHERE clause where it will be subject to analysis by the optimizer.

The LIMIT clause can be used to select a section of rows from the result set. It takes either one or two arguments, which must be integer constants. LIMIT *n* returns the first *n* rows. LIMIT *m, n* skips the first *m* rows and returns the next *n* rows.

PROCEDURE names a procedure to which the data in the result set will be sent before a result set is returned to the client. The optional parameter list, *param_list*, is a comma-separated list of values to pass to the procedure. You can use PROCEDURE ANALYSE() to obtain information about the characteristics of the data in the columns named in the column selection list.

The various INTO formats specify an alternative destination for the query result. If you use an INTO clause, the statement cannot be used as a nested SELECT. An alternative placement for INTO is to specify it earlier in the statement, following the *select_expr* list.

The result of a SELECT statement may be written into a file *file_name* using an INTO OUTFILE '*file_name*' clause. The syntax of the *field_options* and *line_options* clauses is the same as for the corresponding clauses of the LOAD DATA statement. See the LOAD DATA entry for more information.

INTO DUMPFILE '*file_name*' is similar to INTO OUTFILE but writes only a single row and writes the output entirely without interpretation. That is, it writes raw values without delimiters, quotes, or terminators. This can be useful if you want to write BLOB data such as an image or other binary data to a file.

For both INTO OUTFILE and INTO DUMPFILE, the location of the file is determined using the same rules that apply when reading non-LOCAL files with LOAD DATA. You must have the FILE privilege, the output file must not already exist, and the file is created by the server on the server host with a world-accessible mode. Its ownership will be set to the account used to run the server. As of MySQL 5.0.19/5.1.6, the filename is evaluated using the character set named by the character_set_filesystem system variable.

INTO followed by a comma-separated list of variable names stores the results of the SELECT into the variables. Each variable can be either a user-defined variable of the form @var_name, or, within a stored program, a parameter or local variable. The query must select a single row of values and must name one variable per output column.

The FOR UPDATE and LOCK IN SHARE MODE clauses place locks on the rows that are examined during query execution. The locks remain in force until the current transaction is committed or rolled back. These locking clauses can be useful in multiple-statement transactions. If you use FOR UPDATE with a table for which the storage engine uses row-level locks (InnoDB), the examined rows are write-locked for exclusive use. Using LOCK IN SHARE MODE sets read locks on the rows, enabling other clients to read but not modify them. Note that if the query optimizer finds no index to use for examining rows, it must scan (and thus lock) all rows in the table.

The following statements demonstrate some ways in which the SELECT statement can be used. See Chapter 1, "Getting Started with MySQL," and Chapter 2, "Using SQL to Manage Data," for many other examples.

- Select the entire contents of a table:

```
SELECT * FROM president;
```

- Select entire contents, but sort by name:

```
SELECT * FROM president ORDER BY last_name, first_name;
```

- Select rows for presidents born on or after '1900-01-01':

```
SELECT * FROM president WHERE birth >= '1900-01-01';
```

- Do the same, but sort in birth order:

```
SELECT * FROM president WHERE birth >= '1900-01-01' ORDER BY birth;
```

- Determine which states are represented by rows in the member table:

```
SELECT DISTINCT state FROM member;
```

- Select rows from member table and write columns as comma-separated values into a file:

```
SELECT * INTO OUTFILE '/tmp/member.txt'
  FIELDS TERMINATED BY ',' FROM member;
```

- Select the top five scores for a particular grade event:

```
SELECT * FROM score WHERE event_id = 9 ORDER BY score DESC LIMIT 5;
```

SET

```
SET [OPTION] assignment [, assignment ] ...

assignment: var_name = expr
```

The SET statement is used to assign values to system variables, user-defined variables, or stored program local variables. Appendix D, "System, Status, and User Variable Reference," provides information about system and user-defined variables. Section E.2.2, "Declaration Statements," describes declaration syntax for stored program local variables. SET also is used for a few miscellaneous settings that are described later in this entry.

Other statements that begin with SET (SET PASSWORD and SET TRANSACTION) are described in separate entries later in this appendix.

When SET is used to assign values to variables, var_name in each assignment is the variable to be assigned a value and expr is the expression that indicates the value to assign to the variable. The assignment operator in a SET statement can be either = or :=.

SET can be used to assign values to user-defined variables, which are named using @var_name syntax:

```
SET @day = CURDATE(), @time = CURTIME();
```

SET also can assign values to system variables, many of which are dynamic and can be changed while the server is running. Dynamic system variables exist at two levels. Global system variables are server-wide and affect all clients. Session system variables (also called local system variables) are specific to a given client connection only. For variables that exist at both levels, a given client's session variables are initialized from the values of the corresponding global variables when the client connects. It is necessary to have the SUPER privilege to modify a global variable, but any client can modify its own session variables.

The syntax for setting system variables has several forms. To set a global variable (for example, the global sql_mode value), use a statement having either of the following forms:

```
SET GLOBAL sql_mode = 'ANSI_QUOTES';
SET @@GLOBAL.sql_mode = 'ANSI_QUOTES';
```

To set a session variable, substitute the word SESSION for GLOBAL:

```
SET SESSION sql_mode = 'ANSI_QUOTES';
SET @@SESSION.sql_mode = 'ANSI_QUOTES';
```

You can also use LOCAL as a synonym for SESSION:

```
SET LOCAL sql_mode = 'ANSI_QUOTES';
SET @@LOCAL.sql_mode = 'ANSI_QUOTES';
```

If none of GLOBAL, SESSION, or LOCAL are present, the SET statement modifies the session-level variable:

```
SET sql_mode = 'ANSI_QUOTES';
SET @@sql_mode = 'ANSI_QUOTES';
```

To check the value of system variables, use the SHOW VARIABLES statement. You can also retrieve individual system variable values by using SELECT:

```
SELECT @@GLOBAL.sql_mode, @@SESSION.sql_mode, @@LOCAL.sql_mode;
```

Section 12.6.1, "Checking and Setting System Variable Values," further discusses the use of system variables.

The following list describes miscellaneous settings that can be controlled with SET.

- SET CHARACTER SET {charset | DEFAULT}

  Sets the character_set_client and character_set_results session variables to the named character set, and sets the character_set_connection session variable to the value of character_set_database. These variables affect conversion of character data sent to and from the server. A charset value of ucs2, utf18, or utf32 does not work.

  SET CHARACTER SET DEFAULT restores the default character set mapping.

- SET NAMES {charset | 'charset' | DEFAULT}

  Sets the character_set_client, character_set_connection, and character_set_results session variables to the named character set, and sets collation_connection to the default collation for character_set_connection. These variables affect conversion of character data sent to and from the server. A charset value of ucs2, utf18, or utf32 does not work.

  SET NAMES DEFAULT restores the default character set mapping.

SET PASSWORD

```
SET PASSWORD [FOR account] = PASSWORD('pass_val')
SET PASSWORD [FOR account] = OLD_PASSWORD('pass_val')
SET PASSWORD [FOR account] = 'encrypted_pass_val'
```

SET PASSWORD changes the password for a MySQL account. You can always change your own password, unless you have connected as an anonymous user. To change the password for another account, you must have the UPDATE privilege for the mysql database.

With no FOR clause, the statement sets the password for the current account. With a FOR clause, it sets the password for the named account, which should be given in 'user_name'@'host_name' format, as described in Section 12.4.1.1, "Specifying Account Names."

The password value, 'pass_val' should be encrypted using PASSWORD() for standard encryption or OLD_PASSWORD() for the older (pre-MySQL 4.1) encryption. If you use neither function, 'encrypted_pass_val' should be given as an already-encrypted password string.

```
SET PASSWORD = PASSWORD('secret');
SET PASSWORD FOR 'paul' = PASSWORD('secret');
SET PASSWORD FOR 'paul'@'localhost' = PASSWORD('secret');
SET PASSWORD FOR 'bill'@'%.bigcorp.com' = PASSWORD('old-sneep');
```

SET TRANSACTION

```
SET [GLOBAL | SESSION] TRANSACTION ISOLATION LEVEL level
```

This statement sets the isolation level for transaction processing:

- With the GLOBAL option, it sets the global (server-wide) isolation level, which becomes the default level for all clients that connect thereafter.
- With the SESSION option, it sets the session (client-specific) isolation level, which becomes the level for subsequent transactions within the current session.
- With neither option, it sets the isolation level only for the next transaction within the current session.

The SUPER privilege is required to set the global isolation level. Any client can change its own session or next-transaction isolation level.

The transaction level indicated by level should be one of the following values:

- READ UNCOMMITTED

  A transaction can see row modifications made by other transactions even if they have not been committed.

- READ COMMITTED

  A transaction can see row modifications made by other transactions only if they have been committed.

- REPEATABLE READ

  If a transaction performs a given SELECT twice, the result is repeatable. That is, it gets the same result each time, even if other transactions have changed or inserted rows in the meantime.

- SERIALIZABLE

  This isolation level is similar to REPEATABLE READ but isolates transactions more completely: Rows selected by one transaction cannot be modified by other transactions until the first transaction completes. This level is supported by InnoDB but not yet by Falcon.

The SET TRANSACTION statement applies to the InnoDB and Falcon storage engines. The default isolation level is REPEATABLE READ. Non-transactional storage engines do not have isolation levels.

Section 2.13.3, "Transaction Isolation," further discusses transaction isolation and isolation levels.

SHOW

```
SHOW BINLOG EVENTS
SHOW CHARACTER SET
SHOW COLLATION
```

```
SHOW COLUMNS
SHOW CREATE DATABASE
SHOW CREATE EVENT
SHOW CREATE {FUNCTION | PROCEDURE}
SHOW CREATE TABLE
SHOW CREATE TRIGGER
SHOW CREATE VIEW
SHOW DATABASES
SHOW ENGINE
SHOW ENGINES
SHOW ERRORS
SHOW EVENTS
SHOW {FUNCTION | PROCEDURE} STATUS
SHOW GRANTS
SHOW INDEX
SHOW INNODB STATUS
SHOW {MASTER | BINARY} LOGS
SHOW MASTER STATUS
SHOW MUTEX STATUS
SHOW OPEN TABLES
SHOW PRIVILEGES
SHOW PROCESSLIST
SHOW SLAVE HOSTS
SHOW SLAVE STATUS
SHOW STATUS
SHOW TABLE STATUS
SHOW TABLE TYPES
SHOW TABLES
SHOW TRIGGERS
SHOW VARIABLES
SHOW WARNINGS
```

The various SHOW statements provide information about databases and objects in them such as tables or stored programs, or information about server operation. Several of the statements take an optional FROM *db_name* clause, enabling you to specify the database for which information should be shown. If the clause is not present, the default database is used. In each of the statements that support FROM to specify a table or database name, IN can be used as a synonym.

Some forms allow an optional LIKE '*pattern*' clause to limit output to values that match the pattern. '*pattern*' is interpreted as an SQL pattern and may contain the '%' or '_' wildcard characters.

As of MySQL 5.0.2, INFORMATION_SCHEMA provides another way to obtain database metadata, and many INFORMATION_SCHEMA tables contain information similar to that displayed by SHOW statements. In addition, those SHOW statements that support LIKE '*pattern*' can be written with a WHERE clause instead to specify which rows to display. For more information, see Section 2.7, "Obtaining Database Metadata."

SHOW BINLOG EVENTS

```
SHOW BINLOG EVENTS [IN 'file_name'] [FROM position]
  [LIMIT [skip_count,] show_count]
```

This statement is used on replication master servers to display events in a binary log file. Events correspond roughly to SQL statements.

The output from this statement includes the following columns:

- Log_name

  The binary log filename.

- Pos

  The position of the event within the log file.

- Event_type

  The type of event, such as Query for a statement that is to be executed.

- Server_id

  The ID of the server that logged the event.

- End_log_pos

  The position of the next byte after the event in the log file.

- Info

  Event information, such as the statement text for a Query event.

This statement requires the REPLICATION SLAVE privilege.

SHOW CHARACTER SET

```
SHOW CHARACTER SET [LIKE 'pattern' | WHERE where_expr]
```

Displays a list of the character sets supported by the server. A LIKE clause may be included to display information only for character sets with names that match the given pattern. A WHERE clause restricts output to rows that satisfy the given expression.

The output from SHOW CHARACTER SET includes the following columns:

- Charset

  The short character set name. This is the name that can be used in SQL statements.

- Description

  A descriptive character set name.

- Default collation

  The name of the default collation for the character set.

- Maxlen

  The length of the "widest" character in the character set, in bytes. For multi-byte character sets, this value is greater than one. For non-multi-byte sets, all characters take a single byte, so the value is one.

SHOW COLLATION

```
SHOW COLLATION [LIKE 'pattern' | WHERE where_expr]
```

Displays a list of available collations for each character set. The LIKE clause may be included to display information only for collations with names that match the given pattern. A WHERE clause restricts output to rows that satisfy the given expression.

The output from SHOW COLLATION includes the following columns:

- Collation

  The collation name.

- Charset

  The name of the character set with which the collation is associated.

- Id

  The collation ID number.

- Default

  Yes if the collation is the default collation for its character set, blank otherwise.

- Compiled

  Yes if the collation is compiled into the server, blank otherwise.

- Sortlen

  A cost factor relating to the amount of memory that must be allocated for internal string conversion operations when the collation is used to sort values.

SHOW COLUMNS

```
SHOW [FULL] COLUMNS {FROM | IN} tbl_name
  [{FROM | IN} db_name] [LIKE 'pattern' | WHERE where_expr]
```

Displays the columns for the given table (or view, as of MySQL 5.0.1). The output includes only those columns for which you have some privilege. SHOW FIELDS is a synonym for SHOW COLUMNS. With the FULL keyword, the statement displays the Collation, Privilege, and Comment output fields. The LIKE clause may be included to display information only for columns with names that match the given pattern. A WHERE clause restricts output to rows that satisfy the given expression.

To specify the database that contains the table, use a FROM db_name clause or write the table name in db_name.tbl_name format:

```
SHOW COLUMNS FROM president;
SHOW COLUMNS FROM president FROM sampdb;
SHOW COLUMNS FROM sampdb.president;
```

The output from SHOW COLUMNS provides the following types of information about each column in the table:

- Field

  The column name.

- Type

  The column data type. This may include type attributes following the type name.

- Collation

  The collation name for non-binary string columns, NULL for other columns. The collation name implies the character set name. This information is displayed only if you specify the FULL keyword.

- Null

  YES if the column can contain NULL values. Otherwise, the value is NO as of MySQL 5.0.3 and blank before that.

- Key

  Whether the column is indexed.

- Default

  The column's default value.

- Extra

  Extra information about the column. auto_increment is shown here for columns that have the AUTO_INCREMENT attribute, otherwise the value is blank.

- Privileges

  The privileges that you hold for the column. This information is displayed only if you specify the FULL keyword.

- Comment

  The value of any COMMENT attribute in the column definition. This information is displayed only if you specify the FULL keyword.

SHOW CREATE

```
SHOW CREATE DATABASE [IF NOT EXISTS] db_name
SHOW CREATE EVENT event_name
SHOW CREATE FUNCTION func_name
SHOW CREATE PROCEDURE proc_name
SHOW CREATE TABLE tbl_name
SHOW CREATE TRIGGER trigger_name
SHOW CREATE VIEW view_name
```

The SHOW CREATE obj_type statements display the CREATE obj_type statement that creates the named object. Several of the statements also display other information about the object such as the sql_mode value in effect when it was created.

For SHOW CREATE DATABASE, if the statement includes an IF NOT EXISTS clause, the output CREATE DATABASE statement does as well.

SHOW CREATE VIEW was introduced in MySQL 5.0.1, SHOW CREATE EVENT in MySQL 5.1.6, and SHOW CREATE TRIGGER in MySQL 5.1.21.

SHOW DATABASES

```
SHOW DATABASES [LIKE 'pattern' | WHERE where_expr]
```

Displays the databases available on the server host. The LIKE clause may be included to display information only for databases with names that match the given pattern. A WHERE clause restricts output to rows that satisfy the given expression.

If you don't have the SHOW DATABASES privilege, you'll see only the databases for which you have some kind of access privilege. If the server was started with the --skip-show-database option, you'll see all databases if you have the SHOW DATABASES privilege and none otherwise.

SHOW ENGINE

```
SHOW ENGINE engine_name info_type
```

This statement displays information about storage engines. For InnoDB, these statement variants are supported:

- SHOW ENGINE INNODB STATUS

  Displays information about the internal operation of the InnoDB storage engine. This statement replaces SHOW INNODB STATUS. It requires the PROCESS privilege (SUPER prior to MySQL 5.1.24).

- SHOW ENGINE INNODB MUTEX

  Displays information about InnoDB mutexes. This statement was introduced in MySQL 5.1.2; it replaces SHOW MUTEX STATUS. It requires the PROCESS privilege (SUPER prior to MySQL 5.1.24).

SHOW ENGINES

```
SHOW [STORAGE] ENGINES
```

Displays the storage engines that the server knows about. For each engine, the output indicates the support level and provides a brief description of the engine characteristics.

The output from this statement includes the following columns:

- Engine

  The storage engine name (MyISAM, InnoDB, and so forth).

- Support

  The level of support for the engine: YES for supported, NO for not supported, DISABLED for supported but disabled at runtime, or DEFAULT to indicate that the storage engine is the default engine. The default engine is always enabled.

- Comment

  Descriptive text about the storage engine.

- Transactions

  Whether the engine supports transactions.

- XA

  Whether the engine supports distributed transactions.

- Savepoints

  Whether the engine supports partial transaction rollback.

The Transactions, XA, and Savepoints columns were added in MySQL 5.1.2.

SHOW ERRORS

```
SHOW ERRORS [LIMIT [skip_count,] show_count]
```

```
SHOW COUNT(*) ERRORS
```

SHOW ERRORS is like SHOW WARNINGS but displays only messages that have error severity. SHOW COUNT(*) ERRORS is like SHOW COUNT(*) WARNINGS but displays the value of the error_count variable rather than the value of warning_count. See the entry for SHOW WARNINGS for more information.

SHOW EVENTS

```
SHOW EVENTS [FROM db_name] [LIKE 'pattern' | WHERE where_expr]
```

This statement displays information about the events in the default database, or in the named database if the FROM clause is given. The LIKE clause may be included to display information only for events with names that match the given pattern. A WHERE clause restricts output to rows that satisfy the given expression.

SHOW EVENTS was introduced in MySQL 5.1.6.

SHOW FUNCTION STATUS, SHOW PROCEDURE STATUS

```
SHOW {FUNCTION | PROCEDURE} STATUS
  [LIKE 'pattern' | WHERE where_expr]
```

These statements display descriptive information about the stored functions or procedures in the default database. The LIKE clause may be included to display information only for routines with names that match the given pattern. A WHERE clause restricts output to rows that satisfy the given expression.

SHOW GRANTS

```
SHOW GRANTS [FOR account]
```

Displays grant information about the specified account, which should be given in `'user_name'@'host_name'` format, as described in Section 12.4.1.1, "Specifying Account Names."

```
SHOW GRANTS FOR 'root'@'localhost';
SHOW GRANTS FOR ''@'cobra.snake.net';
```

You can also use any of the following statements to display the privileges that are granted to the account that you are connected to the server as:

```
SHOW GRANTS FOR CURRENT_USER();
SHOW GRANTS FOR CURRENT_USER;
SHOW GRANTS;
```

As of MySQL 5.0.24/5.1.12, for the SHOW GRANTS formats that display current-user privileges, the output within a stored procedure that executes with SQL SECURITY DEFINER context corresponds to the procedure definer rather than its invoker.

SHOW INDEX

```
SHOW {INDEX | KEY} {FROM | IN} tbl_name [{FROM | IN} db_name]
```

Displays information about a table's indexes. To specify the database that contains the table, use a FROM db_name clause or write the table name in db_name.tbl_name format:

```
SHOW INDEX FROM score;
SHOW INDEX FROM score FROM sampdb;
SHOW INDEX FROM sampdb.score;
```

The output from SHOW INDEX includes the following columns:

- `Table`

  The name of the table that contains the index.

- `Non_unique`

  1 if the index can contain duplicate values, 0 if it cannot.

- `Key_name`

  The index name.

- `Seq_in_index`

  The number of the column within the index. Index columns are numbered beginning with 1.

- `Column_name`

  The name of the table column in the index to which the current output row applies.

- `Collation`

The column sort order within the index. The values may be A (ascending), D (descending), or NULL (not sorted). Currently, descending keys are not available.

- Cardinality

  The approximate number of unique values in the index. myisamchk updates this value for MyISAM tables when run with the --analyze option. The ANALYZE TABLE statement updates this value for MyISAM and InnoDB tables. OPTIMIZE TABLE does so for MyISAM tables.

- Sub_part

  The prefix length in bytes, if only a prefix of the column is indexed. This is NULL if the entire column is indexed.

- Packed

  How the key is packed, or NULL if it is not packed.

- Null

  YES if the column can contain NULL values, blank otherwise.

- Index_type

  The algorithm used to index the column, such as BTREE, FULLTEXT, or HASH.

- Comment

  Reserved for internal comments about the index.

SHOW INNODB STATUS

```
SHOW INNODB STATUS
```

Displays information about the internal operation of the InnoDB storage engine. It requires the SUPER privilege. This statement is deprecated in favor of SHOW ENGINE INNODB STATUS.

SHOW MASTER LOGS

```
SHOW {MASTER | BINARY} LOGS
```

This statement is used on replication master servers. It displays the names of the binary log files currently available on the master. It can be useful before issuing a PURGE MASTER LOGS statement after running SHOW SLAVE STATUS on each of the slaves to determine the binary log files to which they currently are positioned.

SHOW MASTER STATUS

```
SHOW MASTER STATUS
```

This statement is used on replication master servers. It displays information about the status of the master's binary log.

The output from SHOW MASTER STATUS includes the following columns:

- File

  The binary log filename.

- Position

  The current position at which the server is writing to the file.

- Binlog_Do_DB

  A comma-separated list of databases that are explicitly replicated to the binary log with `--binlog-do-db` options, blank if no such options were given.

- Binlog_Ignore_DB

  A comma-separated list of databases that are explicitly excluded from the binary log with `--binlog-ignore-db` options, blank if no such options were given.

SHOW MUTEX STATUS

```
SHOW MUTEX STATUS
```

This statement displays information about InnoDB mutexes. It was introduced in MySQL 5.0.3 and renamed to SHOW ENGINE INNODB MUTEX in MySQL 5.1.

SHOW OPEN TABLES

```
SHOW OPEN TABLES [{FROM | IN} db_name]
  [LIKE 'pattern' | WHERE where_expr]
```

Displays the list of open non-TEMPORARY tables that are registered in the table cache and for which you have some privilege. The LIKE clause may be included to display information only for tables with names that match the given pattern. A WHERE clause restricts output to rows that satisfy the given expression. These clauses were introduced in MySQL 5.0.12.

The output from SHOW OPEN TABLES includes the following columns:

- Database

  The database that contains the table.

- Table

  The name of the table.

- In_use

  The number of times the table currently is in use.

- Name_locked

  Indicates whether the table has a name lock such as is required to use the table without accessing its contents (for example, for RENAME TABLE).

SHOW PRIVILEGES

```
SHOW PRIVILEGES
```

Displays the privileges that can be granted and information about the purpose of each one.

The output from SHOW PRIVILEGES includes the following columns:

- Privilege

  The privilege name.

- Context

  The applicability of the privilege, such as Server Admin (server administration), Databases, or Tables.

- Comment

  A description of the purpose of the privilege.

SHOW PROCESSLIST

```
SHOW [FULL] PROCESSLIST
```

Displays information about the currently executing server activity. If you have the PROCESS privilege, the statement displays all information. Otherwise, it displays information only about your own activity.

The output includes the following columns:

- Id

  The process ID number for the client.

- User

  The username for the account associated with the process.

- Host

  The host from which the client is connected.

- db

  The default database for the process.

- Command

  The type of command being executed.

- Time

  The amount of time that the process has been in the current state, in seconds.

- State

  Information about what MySQL is doing while processing an SQL statement. The value may be useful for reporting a problem with MySQL or when asking a question on the MySQL mailing list about why a process stays in some state for a long time.

- `Info`

  The statement being executed. By default, the first 100 characters are displayed. If the FULL keyword is given, the entire statement is displayed.

SHOW SLAVE HOSTS

```
SHOW SLAVE HOSTS
```

This statement is used on replication master servers. It displays information about the slave servers that are currently registered with the master. A slave is not registered unless it is started with the `--report-host` option. Even for a registered slave, other conditions apply for display of certain columns. The `Port` column value is blank unless the slave is started with the `--report-port` option. The `User` and `Password` column values are blank unless the slave is started with the `--report-user` and `--report-password` options and the master is started with the `--show-slave-auth-info` option.

The output from `SHOW SLAVE HOSTS` includes the following columns:

- `Server_id`

  The slave server ID.

- `Host`

  The slave host.

- `User`

  The username for the account that the slave used to connect.

- `Password`

  The password for the account that the slave used to connect.

- `Port`

  The port to which the slave is connected.

- `Rpl_recovery_rank`

  The replication recovery rank.

- `Master_id`

  The master server ID.

SHOW SLAVE STATUS

```
SHOW SLAVE STATUS
```

This statement is used on slave servers and displays information about the replication status of the server. The output includes the following columns:

- `Slave_IO_State`

  The state of the slave I/O thread. This is the same value that SHOW PROCESSLIST will display for the thread.

- `Master_Host`

  The master hostname or IP number.

- `Master_User`

  The username of the account used for connecting to the master.

- `Master_Port`

  The port number for connecting to the master.

- `Connect_Retry`

  The number of seconds to wait between attempts to connect to the master.

- `Master_Log_File`

  The name of the current master binary log file.

- `Read_Master_Log_Pos`

  The current position within the master binary log file where the slave I/O thread is reading.

- `Relay_Log_File`

  The name of the current relay log file.

- `Relay_Log_Pos`

  The current position of the slave SQL thread within the relay log file.

- `Relay_Master_Log_File`

  The name of the master binary log file that contains the event most recently executed by the SQL thread.

- `Slave_IO_Running`

  Whether the slave I/O thread is running.

- `Slave_SQL_Running`

  Whether the slave SQL thread is running.

- `Replicate_Do_DB`

  A comma-separated list of databases that are explicitly replicated with `--replicate-do-db` options, blank if no such options were given.

- `Replicate_Ignore_DB`

  A comma-separated list of databases that are explicitly excluded from replication with `--replicate-ignore-db` options, blank if no such options were given.

- `Replicate_Do_Table`

  A comma-separated list of tables that are explicitly replicated with `--replicate-do-table` options, blank if no such options were given.

- `Replicate_Ignore_Table`

  A comma-separated list of tables that are explicitly excluded from replication with `--replicate-ignore-table` options, blank if no such options were given.

- `Replicate_Wild_Do_Table`

  A comma-separated list of table patterns that are explicitly replicated with `--replicate-wild-do-table` options, blank if no such options were given.

- `Replicate_Wild_Ignore_Table`

  A comma-separated list of table patterns that are explicitly excluded from replication with `--replicate-wild-ignore-table` options, blank if no such options were given.

- `Last_Errno`

  Before MySQL 5.1.20, this is the error number for the last executed statement. As of 5.1.20, this column is an alias for `Last_SQL_Errno`. The value is 0 if there was no error.

- `Last_Error`

  Before MySQL 5.1.20, this is the error msssage for the last executed statement. As of 5.1.20, this column is an alias for `Last_SQL_Error`. The value is blank if there was no error. The server also writes non-empty values to its error log.

- `Skip_Counter`

  The number of events from the master that the slave should skip. (You cause the slave to skip events by setting its global `sql_slave_skip_counter` system variable.)

- `Exec_Master_Log_Pos`

  The current position within the master binary log file where the slave SQL thread is executing.

- `Relay_Log_Space`

  The combined size of the relay log files.

- `Until_Condition`

  The condition specified in an `UNTIL` clause of a `START SLAVE` statement to indicate when the SQL thread should stop reading and executing events:

  - `None`: No `UNTIL` clause was specified.
  - `Master`: The slave is reading until its SQL thread reaches a specific position in the master binary log.
  - `Relay`: The slave is reading until its SQL thread reaches a specific position in its relay log.

  If the `Until_Condition` value is `Master` or `Relay`, the `Until_Log_File` and `Until_Log_Pos` column values indicate the filename and position at which the SQL thread will stop executing.

- `Until_Log_File`

  See the description of `Until_Condition`.

- Until_Log_Pos

  See the description of Until_Condition.

- Master_SSL_Allowed

  Whether SSL is used to connect to the master server: Yes if SSL connections can be used, No if they cannot, and Ignored if SSL connections are allowed, but the slave server was not built with SSL support enabled.

- Master_SSL_CA_File

  The pathname to the certificate authority file for SSL connections to the master, blank if none has been specified.

- Master_SSL_CA_Path

  The pathname to a directory of trusted certificates to be used for certificate verification for SSL connections to the master, blank if none has been specified.

- Master_SSL_Cert

  The pathname to the certificate file for SSL connections to the master, blank if none has been specified.

- Master_SSL_Cipher

  A string listing the SSL ciphers that may be used to encrypt traffic sent over SSL connections to the master, blank if none has been specified.

- Master_SSL_Key

  The pathname to the key file for SSL connections to the master, blank if none has been specified.

- Seconds_Behind_Master

  The difference in seconds between the current time and the timestamp recorded in the master event most recently executed by the slave SQL thread. This value is zero if the SQL thread has caught up with the I/O thread and is idle, and NULL if no event has been executed or the slave parameters have been changed with a CHANGE MASTER or RESET SLAVE statement.

- Last_IO_Errno

  The most recent error number for the IO thread. The value is 0 if there was no error. This column was introduced in MySQL 5.1.20.

- Last_IO_Error

  The most recent error message for the IO thread. The value is blank if there was no error. The server also writes non-empty values to its error log. This column was introduced in MySQL 5.1.20.

- Last_SQL_Errno

  Like Last_IO_Errno, but for the SQL thread. This column was introduced in MySQL 5.1.20.

- `Last_SQL_Error`

  Like `Last_IO_Error`, but for the SQL thread. This column was introduced in MySQL 5.1.20.

SHOW STATUS

```
SHOW [GLOBAL | SESSION] STATUS [LIKE 'pattern' | WHERE where_expr]
```

Displays the server's status variables and their values. These variables provide information about the server's operational state. Section 12.6.3, "Checking Status Variable Values," discusses the use of status variables. Appendix D describes each of the status variables.

The `LIKE` clause may be included to display information only for variables with names that match the given pattern. A `WHERE` clause restricts output to rows that satisfy the given expression.

As of MySQL 5.0.2, the server can display the values of status variables at the global (server-wide) or session (client-specific) level. These represent the sum over all clients and the value for the current client, respectively. By default, `SHOW` displays the session-level value for any given variable. To display global or session values explicitly, specify a level indicator:

```
SHOW GLOBAL VARIABLES;
SHOW SESSION VARIABLES;
```

If a variable has only a global value, you get the same value for `GLOBAL` and `SESSION`. `LOCAL` is a synonym for `SESSION`.

As of MySQL 5.1.12, you can also query the `INFORMATION_SCHEMA` tables named `GLOBAL_STATUS` and `SESSION_STATUS` to obtain status variable information.

SHOW TABLE STATUS

```
SHOW TABLE STATUS [{FROM | IN} db_name]
  [LIKE 'pattern' | WHERE where_expr]
```

Displays descriptive information about the tables in a database. The output includes only those tables for which you have some privilege. The `LIKE` clause may be included to display information only for tables with names that match the given pattern. A `WHERE` clause restricts output to rows that satisfy the given expression. As of MySQL 5.0.1, this statement also displays the views in a database, but all columns are `NULL` except that `Name` is the view name and `Comment` is view.

The output from `SHOW TABLE STATUS` includes the following columns:

- `Name`

  The table name.

- `Engine`

  The storage engine (MyISAM, InnoDB, and so forth).

- Version

  The version number of the `.frm` file for the table.

- Row_format

  The row storage format. For MyISAM tables, this can be `Fixed` (fixed-length rows), `Dynamic` (variable-length rows), or `Compressed` (compressed and read-only). As of MySQL 5.0.3, the format for InnoDB tables can be `Redundant` (the original format) or `Compact` (a newer format that requires less storage).

- Rows

  The number of rows in the table. For some storage engines such as InnoDB, this is an approximate count.

- Avg_row_length

  The average number of bytes used by table rows.

- Data_length

  The actual size in bytes of the table data file.

- Max_data_length

  The maximum size that the table data file can grow to.

- Index_length

  The actual size in bytes of the index file.

- Data_free

  The number of unused bytes in the data file. If this number is very high, it might be a good idea to issue an `OPTIMIZE TABLE` statement for the table to defragment it.

- Auto_increment

  The next value that will be generated for an `AUTO_INCREMENT` column.

- Create_time

  The time when the table was created.

- Update_time

  The time when the table was most recently modified.

- Check_time

  For MyISAM tables, the time at which the table was last checked or repaired by `myisamchk`, `CHECK TABLE`, or `REPAIR TABLE`. The value is `NULL` if the table has never been checked or repaired.

- Collation

  The table's collation. The collation name implies the character set name.

- Checksum

  The table checksum value, `NULL` if one has not been calculated.

- Create_options

  Extra options that were specified as *table_option* values in the CREATE TABLE statement that created the table or subsequent ALTER TABLE statements.

- Comment

  The text of any comment specified when the table was created. For an InnoDB table, the Comment value shows foreign key definitions, and prior to MySQL 5.1.24, it also displays the amount of free space in the InnoDB tablespace in which the table is stored. (The table might be in the shared tablespace or have its own tablespace.) As of 5.1.24, the free space is displayed as the Data_free value.

SHOW TABLE TYPES

```
SHOW TABLE TYPES
```

SHOW TABLE TYPES was the original syntax for the SHOW ENGINES statement. It is still recognized but is deprecated and its use produces a warning. See the entry for SHOW ENGINES for a description of the output.

SHOW TABLES

```
SHOW [FULL] TABLES [{FROM | IN} db_name]
  [LIKE 'pattern' | WHERE where_expr]
```

Displays the names of the non-TEMPORARY tables in a database. The output includes only those tables for which you have some privilege. The LIKE clause may be included to display information only for tables with names that match the given pattern. A WHERE clause restricts output to rows that satisfy the given expression.

Beginning with MySQL 5.0.1, this statement also displays view names. The FULL keyword may be given as of MySQL 5.0.2 to display for each row whether the name refers to a table or a view.

The output from this statement includes the following columns:

- Tables_in_*db_name*

  The table or view name.

- Table_type

  BASE_TABLE or VIEW to indicate whether the name refers to a table or a view. This column is displayed only if the FULL keyword is given.

SHOW TRIGGERS

```
SHOW TRIGGERS [FROM db_name] [LIKE 'pattern' | WHERE where_expr]
```

This statement displays information about the triggers in the default database, or in the named database if the FROM clause is given. The LIKE clause may be included to display information only for triggers from tables with names that match the given pattern. A WHERE clause restricts output to rows that satisfy the given expression.

SHOW TRIGGERS was introduced in MySQL 5.0.10. It requires the TRIGGER privilege as of 5.1.22, and the SUPER privilege before that.

SHOW VARIABLES

```
SHOW [GLOBAL | SESSION] VARIABLES [LIKE 'pattern' | WHERE where_expr]
```

Displays a list of system variables and their values. These variables provide information about the server's configuration and capabilities. Section 12.6.1, "Checking and Setting System Variable Values," discusses the use of system variables. Appendix D describes each of the system variables.

The LIKE clause may be included to display information only for variables with names that match the given pattern. A WHERE clause restricts output to rows that satisfy the given expression.

The server can display the values of system variables at the global (server-wide) or session (client-specific) level. By default, SHOW displays the session-level value for any given variable, or the global value if no session value exists. To display global or session values explicitly, specify a level indicator:

```
SHOW GLOBAL VARIABLES;
SHOW SESSION VARIABLES;
```

LOCAL is a synonym for SESSION. It is also possible to retrieve the values of individual dynamic variables with SELECT:

```
SELECT @@GLOBAL.sql_mode, @@SESSION.sql_mode, @@LOCAL.sql_mode;
```

Using SELECT has the advantage that you can more easily manipulate the query result in certain contexts.

As of MySQL 5.1.12, you can also examine the INFORMATION_SCHEMA tables named GLOBAL_VARIABLES and SESSION_VARIABLES to obtain system variable information.

SHOW WARNINGS

```
SHOW WARNINGS [LIMIT [skip_count,] show_count]
```

```
SHOW COUNT(*) WARNINGS
```

SHOW WARNINGS displays error, warnings, and notes generated by the most recent statement that generates such messages. If that statement executed successfully, SHOW WARNINGS returns an empty set.

SHOW COUNT(*) WARNINGS displays the value of the warning_count system variable that counts the number of messages. (A related variable, error_count, counts only errors.) It is possible for the value of warning_count to be larger than the number of messages displayed by SHOW WARNINGS. The max_error_count system variable limits the number of messages that can be stored for display by SHOW WARNINGS, but warning_count counts all messages regardless of whether they are stored.

The LIMIT clause can be used to restrict the number of rows returned by SHOW WARNINGS. Its syntax is the same as the LIMIT clause for SELECT.

START SLAVE

```
START SLAVE [slave_option [, slave_option] ...]

START SLAVE [SQL_THREAD] UNTIL
  MASTER_LOG_FILE = 'file_name', MASTER_LOG_POS = position

START SLAVE [SQL_THREAD] UNTIL
  RELAY_LOG_FILE = 'file_name', RELAY_LOG_POS = position
```

This statement, together with STOP SLAVE, controls the operation of replication threads on a slave server. With no options, START SLAVE initiates and STOP SLAVE terminates both the slave I/O and SQL threads. slave_option values may be specified to indicate which threads to start or stop:

- IO_THREAD

  Start or stop the I/O thread that reads events from the master server and stores them in the relay log.

- SQL_THREAD

  Start or stop the SQL thread that reads events from the relay log and executes them.

If no thread or SQL_THREAD is named, an UNTIL clause can be used. Depending on which pair of log file and position options are named in the clause, the slave runs until its SQL thread reaches the given position in the master binary log or slave relay log. If the SQL thread is already running, the server ignores the UNTIL clause and generates a warning. If the clause includes the SQL_THREAD option, the server starts only the SQL thread; otherwise, it starts both threads.

START TRANSACTION

```
START TRANSACTION [WITH CONSISTENT SNAPSHOT]
```

Begins a transaction by disabling autocommit mode until the next COMMIT or ROLLBACK statement. Statements executed while autocommit is disabled thus will be committed or rolled back as a unit.

After the transaction has been committed or rolled back, autocommit mode is restored to the state it was in prior to START TRANSACTION. To manipulate autocommit mode explicitly, use SET autocommit. The autocommit variable is described in Appendix D.

The WITH CONSISTENT SNAPSHOT clause can be used to cause the transaction to begin with a consistent read. For InnoDB, this clause does not change the current isolation level, so it is effective only if the level is REPEATABLE READ or SERIALIZABLE. For Falcon, WITH CONSISTENT SNAPSHOT provides a consistent read using the REPEATABLE READ isolation level, regardless of the current level.

START TRANSACTION implicitly releases any table locks that the client has acquired with LOCK TABLE but has not yet released. Executing START TRANSACTION while a transaction is in progress causes that transaction to be committed implicitly.

STOP SLAVE

```
STOP SLAVE [slave_option [, slave_option] ...]
```

This statement, together with START SLAVE, controls the operation of replication threads on a slave server. See the description of START SLAVE for details.

TRUNCATE

```
TRUNCATE [TABLE] tbl_name
```

TRUNCATE TABLE performs a fast truncation of table contents by dropping and re-creating the table. This is much faster than deleting each row individually. You must have the DROP privilege as of MySQL 5.1.16, and the DELETE privilege for older versions.

For InnoDB, this statement is implemented as DELETE FROM tbl_name before MySQL 5.0.3. As of 5.0.3, InnoDB implements fast truncation directly.

This statement is not transaction-safe. An error will occur should you issue a TRUNCATE TABLE statement within a transaction or while you are holding any explicit table locks.

UNION

```
select_stmt
  UNION [DISTINCT | ALL] select_stmt
  [UNION [DISTINCT | ALL] select_stmt] ...
  [ORDER BY col_list] [LIMIT [skip_count,] show_count]
```

UNION combines the results of multiple SELECT statements. Each SELECT statement must produce the same number of columns in its result set. The names of the columns in the final result are determined by the column names from the first SELECT. The data types of the columns are determined taking into account all values from the corresponding columns of the selected tables.

The UNION keyword can be followed by DISTINCT to eliminate duplicate rows or by ALL to preserve duplicates and return all selected rows. The implicit default is to eliminate duplicates if neither DISTINCT nor ALL is given. Any DISTINCT union operation (either explicit or implicit) takes precedence over any ALL union operations to its left:

```
mysql> SELECT 1 UNION ALL SELECT 2 UNION ALL SELECT 1;
+---+
| 1 |
+---+
| 1 |
| 2 |
| 1 |
+---+
```

```
mysql> SELECT 1 UNION ALL SELECT 2 UNION SELECT 1;
+---+
| 1 |
+---+
| 1 |
| 2 |
+---+
```

To use ORDER BY and LIMIT clauses with any individual SELECT, enclose each SELECT within parentheses. (ORDER BY within an individual SELECT is used only if LIMIT is also present, to determine which rows the LIMIT applies to. It does not affect the order in which rows appear in the final UNION result.) To apply ORDER BY or LIMIT to the UNION as a whole, enclose each SELECT within parentheses and add ORDER BY or LIMIT following the final closing parenthesis. In this case, any columns named in an ORDER BY should refer to the names of the columns in the first SELECT.

UNLOCK TABLE

```
UNLOCK {TABLE | TABLES}
```

This statement releases any table locks being held by the current client.

If a client connection terminates while the client holds table locks, the server releases them when it closes the connection.

If a client begins a transaction while holding table locks, the server implicitly releases those locks.

UPDATE

```
UPDATE [LOW_PRIORITY] [IGNORE] tbl_name
  SET col_name=expr [, col_name=expr] ...
  [WHERE where_expr] [ORDER BY ...] [LIMIT n]

UPDATE [LOW_PRIORITY] [IGNORE] tbl_refs
  SET col_name=expr [, col_name=expr] ...
  [WHERE where_expr] [ORDER BY ...] [LIMIT n]
```

For the first syntax, UPDATE modifies the contents of existing rows in the table tbl_name. The second UPDATE syntax is like the first, but enables multiple tables to be named to perform a multiple-table update. The syntax for tbl_refs is like that for SELECT, except that you cannot specify a subquery as a table.

The rows to be updated are those selected by the expression specified in the WHERE clause. For those rows that are selected, each column named in the SET clause is set to the value of the corresponding expression.

```
UPDATE member SET expiration = NULL, phone = '197-602-4832'
  WHERE member_id = 14;
```

The WHERE clause can include subqueries, but they cannot select from a table that is being updated.

If no WHERE clause is given, *all rows in the table are updated.*

By default, UPDATE returns the number of rows that were updated. However, a row is not considered as having been updated unless some column value actually changed. Setting a column to the value it already contains is not considered to affect the row. If your application really needs to have UPDATE return how many rows matched the WHERE clause regardless of whether the UPDATE actually changed any values, you should specify the CLIENT_FOUND_ROWS flag when you establish a connection to the server. See the entry for the mysql_real_connect() function in Appendix G (online).

LOW_PRIORITY causes the statement to be deferred until no clients are reading from the table. This option is effective only for storage engines that use table-level locking, such as MyISAM, MEMORY, and MERGE.

If updating a row would result in a duplicate key value in a unique index, UPDATE terminates in error and no more rows are updated. Adding IGNORE causes such rows not to be updated and no error occurs. In strict mode, IGNORE also causes data conversion errors that otherwise would terminate the statement to be treated as non-fatal warnings. Columns are updated to the nearest legal value in this case.

ORDER BY causes rows to be updated according to the resulting sort order. This clause has the same syntax as for SELECT.

If the LIMIT clause is given, the value *n* specifies the maximum number of rows to update.

For a multiple-table UPDATE, the WHERE clause can specify conditions based on a join between tables, and the SET clause can update columns in multiple tables. For example, the following statement updates rows in t1 having id values that match those in t2, copying the quantity values from t2 to t1:

```
UPDATE t INNER JOIN t2 SET t.quantity = t2.quantity WHERE t.id = t2.id;
```

USE

```
USE db_name
```

Selects *db_name* to make it the default database (the database for table, view, and stored program references that include no explicit database name). After a successful USE statement, the server sets the session character_set_database and collation_database system variables to the database character set and collation.

The USE statement fails if the database doesn't exist or if you have no privileges for accessing it.

E.2 Compound Statement Syntax

This section describes the syntax for statements that are used within compound statements, which are written using BEGIN and END and can be used for writing stored programs that are stored on the server side (functions, procedures, triggers, and events).

Each statement within a program body must be terminated by a semicolon ('; ') character. If you use the mysql program to create a stored routine that has a multiple-statement body, you should temporarily redefine the `mysql` statement delimiter so that `mysql` itself does not interpret ';' characters. You can do this with the `delimiter` command. Be sure to choose as your delimiter something that does not occur within the statements that define the routine. For example:

```
mysql> delimiter $
mysql> CREATE FUNCTION myfunc ()
    -> RETURNS INT DETERMINISTIC
    -> BEGIN
    -> DECLARE i INT;
    -> DECLARE j INT;
    -> SET i = 2;
    -> SET j = 4;
    -> RETURN i * j;
    -> END$
mysql> delimiter ;
mysql> SELECT myfunc();
+----------+
| myfunc() |
+----------+
|        8 |
+----------+
```

For more information about defining stored programs, see Section 4.1, "Compound Statements and Statement Delimiters."

E.2.1 Control Structure Statements

The statements in this section are used to group statements into blocks and provide flow-control constructs. Each occurrence of *stmt_list* in the syntax for these statements indicates a list of one or more statements, each terminated by a semicolon character (';').

Some of the constructs can be labeled (`BEGIN`, `LOOP`, `REPEAT`, and `WHILE`). Labels are not case sensitive but must follow these rules:

- If a label appears at the beginning of a construct, a label with the same name may also appear at the end.
- A label may not appear at the end without a matching label at the beginning.

BEGIN ... END

```
BEGIN [stmt_list] END
```

```
label: BEGIN [stmt_list] END [label]
```

The BEGIN ... END construct creates a block within which multiple statements can be grouped. If a stored program body needs to contain more than one statement, they must be grouped within a BEGIN block. Also, if the program contains any DECLARE statements, they can appear only at the beginning of a BEGIN block.

CASE

```
CASE [expr]
  WHEN expr1 THEN stmt_list1
  [WHEN expr2 THEN stmt_list2] ...
  [ELSE stmt_list]
END IF
```

The CASE statement provides a branching flow-control construct. When the initial expression, *expr*, is present, CASE compares it to the expression following each WHEN. For the first one that is equal, the statement list for the corresponding THEN value is executed. This is useful for comparing a given value to a set of values.

When the initial expression, *expr*, is not present, CASE evaluates WHEN expressions. For the first one that is true, the statement list for the corresponding THEN value is executed. This is useful for performing non-equality tests or testing arbitrary conditions.

If no WHEN expression matches, the statement list for the ELSE clause is executed, if there is one.

Note that the CASE statement differs from the CASE operator described in Section C.2.1, "Comparison Functions."

IF

```
IF expr1 THEN stmt_list1
  [ELSEIF expr2 THEN stmt_list2] ...
  [ELSE stmt_list]
END IF
```

The IF statement provides a branching flow-control construct. If the expression following the IF keyword is true, the statement list following the initial THEN is executed. Otherwise, expressions for any following ELSEIF clauses are evaluated. For the first one that is true, the corresponding statement list is executed. If no expression is true, the statement list for the ELSE clause is executed, if there is one.

Note that the IF statement differs from the IF() function described in Section C.2.1, "Comparison Functions."

ITERATE

```
ITERATE label
```

The ITERATE statement is used within looping constructs to begin the next iteration of the loop. It can appear within LOOP, REPEAT, and WHILE.

LEAVE

```
LEAVE label
```

The LEAVE statement is used to exit a labeled flow-control construct. The statement must appear within the construct that has the given label.

LOOP

```
LOOP stmt_list END LOOP
```

```
label: LOOP stmt_list END LOOP [label]
```

This statement sets up an execution loop. The statements within the loop execute repeatedly until control is transferred out of the loop.

REPEAT

```
REPEAT stmt_list UNTIL expr END REPEAT
```

```
label: REPEAT stmt_list UNTIL expr END REPEAT [label]
```

This statement sets up an execution loop. The statements within the loop execute repeatedly until the expression *expr* is true.

RETURN

```
RETURN expr
```

The RETURN statement is used only within stored functions (not stored procedures, triggers, or events). When executed, it terminates execution of the function, and the value of *expr* becomes the value returned to the statement that invoked the function. There can be multiple RETURN statements within a function, but there must be at least one.

WHILE

```
WHILE expr DO stmt_list END WHILE
```

```
label: WHILE expr DO stmt_list END WHILE [label]
```

This statement sets up an execution loop. The statements within the loop execute repeatedly as long as the expression *expr* is true.

E.2.2 Declaration Statements

The DECLARE statement is used for declaring local variables, conditions, cursors, and handlers.

DECLARE

```
DECLARE var_name [, var_name] ... type [DEFAULT value]
```

```
DECLARE condition_name CONDITION FOR named_condition

named_condition: {SQLSTATE [VALUE] sqlstate_value | mysql_errno}

DECLARE cursor_name CURSOR FOR select_stmt

DECLARE handler_type
  HANDLER FOR handler_condition [, handler_condition] ...
  statement

handler_type: {CONTINUE | EXIT}

handler_condition:
    SQLSTATE [VALUE] sqlstate_value
  | mysql_errno
  | condition_name
  | SQLWARNING
  | NOT FOUND
  | SQLEXCEPTION
```

Declares local variables, conditions, cursors, and handlers. DECLARE can appear only at the beginning of a BEGIN block. If multiple declarations occur, they must appear in this order:

1. Variable and condition declarations

2. Cursor declarations

3. Handler declarations

DECLARE followed by a list of comma-separated variables declares local variables for use within the routine. A local variable is accessible within the BEGIN block where it is declared and any nested blocks, but not in any outer blocks.

A local variable can be initialized in the DECLARE statement with a DEFAULT clause. If there is no DEFAULT clause, the initial value is NULL. To assign a value to a local variable later in the routine, use a SET statement or a SELECT ... INTO var_name statement.

DECLARE ... CONDITION creates a name for a condition. The name can be referred to in a DECLARE ... HANDLER statement. named_condition can be either an SQLSTATE value represented as a five-character quoted string or a numeric MySQL-specific error number.

DECLARE ... CURSOR declares a cursor to be associated with the given SELECT statement, which should not contain an INTO clause. The cursor can be opened with an OPEN statement, used with FETCH to retrieve rows, and closed with CLOSE.

DECLARE ... HANDLER associates one or more conditions with a statement to be executed when any of the conditions occur. The handler_type value indicates what happens after the condition statement executes. With CONTINUE, execution continues. With EXIT, the current BEGIN block terminates.

handler_condition can be any of the following types of values:

- An SQLSTATE value represented as a five-character string. The value should not be `'00000'` because that represents success, not an error.
- A numeric MySQL-specific error number. The value should not be zero because that represents success, not an error.
- A named condition previously declared with `DECLARE ... CONDITION`.
- `SQLWARNING`, which catches any SQLSTATE value that begins with `01`.
- `NOT FOUND`, which catches any SQLSTATE value that begins with `02`.
- `SQLEXCEPTION`, which catches any SQLSTATE value not caught by `SQLEXCEPTION` or `NOT FOUND`.

E.2.3 Cursor Statements

The statements in this section enable you to open and close cursors, and to use them for fetching rows while open. Cursors currently are read-only and can be used only to move forward a row at a time within a result set (that is, they are not scrollable).

CLOSE

```
CLOSE cursor_name
```

Closes the given cursor, which must be open. An open cursor is closed automatically when the `BEGIN` block within which the cursor was declared ends.

FETCH

```
FETCH [[NEXT] FROM] cursor_name INTO var_name [, var_name] ...
```

Fetches the next row from the given cursor into the named variable or variables. The cursor must be open. If no row is available, an error with an SQLSTATE value of `02000` (No Data) occurs.

OPEN

```
OPEN cursor_name
```

Opens the given cursor so that it can be used with `FETCH`.

E.3 Comment Syntax

MySQL allows you to intersperse comments with your SQL code. Comments can be useful for documenting statements that you store in files. This section describes how to write comments in your SQL statements.

The MySQL server understands three types of comments:

- Anything from '#' to the end of the line is treated as a comment. This syntax is the same as is used in most Unix shells and in many scripting languages, such as Perl, PHP, or Ruby.

```
# this is a single line comment
```

- Anything between '/*' and '*/' is treated as a comment. This form of comment may span multiple lines. The syntax is the same as is used in the C programming language.

```
/* this is a single line comment */
/* this
   is a multiple line
   comment
*/
```

- You can begin a comment with two dashes and a space ('-- '), or two dashes and a control character such as a newline. Everything from the dashes to the end of the line is treated as a comment.

```
--
-- This is a comment
--
```

The MySQL double-dash comment style is somewhat different from the comment style of standard SQL, which begins with just two dashes and does not require the space before any following text. MySQL requires a space after the dashes as an aid for disambiguation. Statements with expressions such as 5--7 might be taken as containing a comment starting sequence otherwise. It's not likely you'd write such an expression as 5-- 7, so this is a useful heuristic. Still, it is only a heuristic, and you should take care if you import SQL code that contains double-dash comments from other database systems into MySQL.

The server ignores comments when executing statements, with the exception that it gives C-style comments that begin with '/*!' special treatment. You can "hide" MySQL-specific keywords in C-style comments by beginning the comment with '/*!' rather than with '/*'. MySQL looks inside this special type of comment and uses the keywords, but other database servers will ignore them as part of the comment. This has a portability benefit, at least for other servers that understand C-style comments: It is possible to write code that takes advantage of MySQL-specific functions when executed by MySQL but that can be used with other database servers without modification. The following two statements are equivalent for database servers other than MySQL, but MySQL will perform an INSERT DELAYED operation for the second:

```
INSERT INTO mytbl (id,date) VALUES(13,'2008-09-28');
INSERT /*! DELAYED */ INTO mytbl (id,date) VALUES(13,'2008-09-28');
```

C-style comments can be version-specific. Follow the opening '/*!' sequence with a five-digit version number and the server will ignore the comment unless it is at least as recent as the version named. The comment in the following SHOW STATUS statement is ignored unless the server is version 5.0.2 or higher (the server understands the GLOBAL and SESSION modifiers only as of MySQL 5.0.2):

```
SHOW /*!50002 GLOBAL */ STATUS;
```

F

MySQL Program Reference

This appendix provides general information about invoking MySQL programs and describes in some detail the programs named in the following list. Each program's section includes a description of its purpose, its invocation syntax, the options it supports, and a description of any internal variables it has. Unless otherwise indicated, the program options and variables listed here are present in MySQL as least as early as MySQL 5.0.0. Changes made since then are so noted.

- myisamchk

  A utility for checking and repairing MyISAM tables, performing key distribution analysis, and disabling and enabling indexes.

- myisampack

  A utility for producing compressed, read-only MyISAM tables.

- mysql

  An interactive program with line-editing capabilities for sending SQL statements to the MySQL server. It can also be used in batch mode to execute statements stored in a file.

- mysql.server

  A script for starting and stopping the MySQL server.

- mysql_config

  A utility that displays the proper flags for compiling MySQL-based programs.

- mysql_install_db

  A script for initializing the server's data directory and grant tables.

- mysqladmin

  A client for performing administrative operations.

- mysqlbinlog

  A program for displaying binary and relay log files in text format.

- `mysqlcheck`

  A program for checking, repairing, optimizing, and analyzing tables.

- `mysqld`

  The MySQL server; this program must be running so that clients have access to the databases administered by the server.

- `mysqld_multi`

  A script for starting and stopping multiple servers.

- `mysqld_safe`

  A script for starting and monitoring the MySQL server.

- `mysqldump`

  A client for dumping the contents of database tables.

- `mysqlhotcopy`

  A database backup utility.

- `mysqlimport`

  A client for loading bulk data into tables.

- `mysqlshow`

  A client that provides information about databases or tables.

- `perror`

  A utility that displays error code meanings.

Square brackets (`[]`) in syntax descriptions indicate optional information.

F.1 Displaying a Program's Help Message

Each program description later in this appendix lists all options that the program currently understands. If a program doesn't seem to recognize an option listed in its description, you may have an older version of the program that precedes the addition of the option.

To get a list of supported options, check the program's help message, which provides a quick way to get information from the program itself. For the server (`mysqld`), invoke it with the `--version` and `--help` options; for other programs, use just `--help`. For example, if you're not sure how to use `mysqlimport`, invoke it like this for instructions:

```
% mysqlimport --help
```

The `-?` option is the same as `--help`, although your shell (command interpreter) might treat the '?' character as a filename wildcard character:

```
% mysqlimport -?
mysqlimport: No match.
```

If that happens to you, try this instead:

```
% mysqlimport -\?
```

Some options show up in help messages only under certain circumstances. For example, the SSL-related options appear only if MySQL has been compiled with SSL support, and Windows-only options such as `--pipe` appear only on Windows systems.

The help message from a MySQL program also displays the locations where the program looks by default for option files, and the variables that it supports.

F.2 Specifying Program Options

Most MySQL programs understand several options that affect their operation. Options may be specified on the command line or in option files. In addition, some options may be specified by setting environment variables. Options specified on the command line take precedence over options specified any other way, and options in option files take precedence over environment variable values.

Most options have both a long (full-word) form and a short (single-letter) form. The `--help` and `-?` options just described are an example of this. Long-form options that are followed by a value should be given in `--name=val` or `--name val` format, where `name` is the option name and `val` is its value. If a short-form option is followed by a value, in most cases the option and the value may be separated by whitespace. For example, when you specify a username, `-usampadm` is equivalent to `-u sampadm`. The `-p` (password) option is an exception; the password value is optional but if given *must* follow the `-p` with no intervening space.

Option names are case sensitive. For example, the `myisamchk` program supports both `--help` and `--HELP`, and the two options are slightly different.

Option values may or may not be case sensitive. For example, values such as usernames and passwords are case sensitive, but the value for the `--protocol` option is not case sensitive. To make a TCP/IP connection, `--protocol=tcp` and `--protocol=TCP` are equivalent.

Many options are "boolean" and have a value of on or off. Such options have a base form, and a standard set of related forms are recognized, as shown in the following table.

Option	Meaning
`--name`	Base option form; enables the option
`--enable-name`	`--enable-` prefix; enables the option
`--disable-name`	`--disable-` prefix; disables the option
`--skip-name`	`--skip-` prefix; disables the option
`--name=1`	`=1` suffix; enables the option
`--name=0`	`=0` suffix; disables the option

For example, many MySQL client programs enable you to specify that you want to turn on compression in the client/server protocol. For these programs, you can specify the `--compress` option to enable compression, or omit it to not use compression. However, there are other ways to indicate what you want: `--enable-compress` and `--compress=1` also enable compression, and `--disable-compress`, `--skip-compress`, and `--compress=0` cause compression not to be used.

The formats that explicitly disable an option are especially useful for options that are on by default. In the case of protocol compression, you can disable it simply by omitting the `--compress` option. But that does not work for options that are on by default. For example, the `--quote-names` option for `mysqldump` is enabled by default. You cannot disable name quoting by omitting the option, but you can do so by specifying any of `--skip-quote-names`, `--disable-quote-names`, or `--quote-names=0`.

The program descriptions in this appendix use the marker "(*boolean*)" to signify which options are subject to the preceding interpretation—that is, options for which the prefixes and suffixes shown in the table are supported.

When in doubt, check a program's help message to find out which option forms it supports (see Section F.1, "Displaying a Program's Help Message").

MySQL programs have other standard option-processing features:

- Long options can be shortened to unambiguous prefixes, which can make it easier to specify options that have very long names. If you specify a prefix that is not long enough to be unambiguous, the program you invoke will tell you so and list those options that match the prefix:

```
% mysql --h
mysql: ambiguous option '--h' (help, html)
```

- A `--loose-` prefix is supported to help make it easier to use differing versions of a program that may not all understand quite the same set of options. For example, servers from version 4.1 and up understand the `--old-passwords` option, but older servers do not. If you specify the option as `--loose-old-passwords`, any server from 4.0.2 on will use or ignore the option according to whether or not it understands `--old-passwords`. With `--loose`, an option that is not recognized results only in a warning, not program termination with an error.

- You can set program variables from the command line or in option files by treating variable names as option names. For more information, see Section F.2.1.2, "Setting Program Variables."

- The MySQL server, `mysqld`, supports a `--maximum-` prefix for specifying a maximum value to which user-modifiable variables may be set. For example, the server enables users to set their sort buffer size by changing the `sort_buffer_size` variable. If you want to place a maximum limit of 64MB on the value of this variable, start the server with a `--maximum-sort_buffer_size=64M` option.

F.2.1 Standard MySQL Program Options

Several options have a standard meaning and most or all MySQL programs interpret them the same way. Rather than writing out their meanings repeatedly in program descriptions, they are described here once, and the "Standard Options Supported" section for each program entry indicates which of these options a program understands. That section lists only long-format names, but programs understand the corresponding short-format options as well, unless otherwise specified.

The following list describes the standard options. The default values shown are those that apply unless MySQL has been reconfigured at compile time.

- `--character-sets-dir=`*dir_name*

  The directory where character set files are stored.

- `--compress`, `-C` (*boolean*)

  This option is used only by client programs. It requests the use of compression in the protocol used for communication between the client and the MySQL server, if both of them support it.

- `--debug=`*debug_options*, `-#` *debug_options*

  Turns on debugging output. This option has no effect unless MySQL was built with debugging support enabled. The *debug_options* string consists of colon-separated options. A typical value is `d:t:o,`*file_name*, which enables debugging, turns on function call entry and exit tracing, and sends output to the file *file_name*.

  If you expect to do much debugging, you should examine the DBUG library user manual for a description of all the options you can use. The manual is located in the `dbug` directory in MySQL source distributions.

- `--debug-check` (*boolean*)

  Checks the use of memory and open files when the program exits.

- `--debug-info` (*boolean*)

  This is like `--debug-check` but also displays information about memory and CPU use.

- `--default-character-set=`*charset*

  The character set to use as the default.

- `--help`, `-?`

  Prints a help message and exits. See also Section F.1, "Displaying a Program's Help Message."

- `--host=host_name, -h host_name`

  This option is used only by client programs. It indicates the host to connect to (that is, the host where the server is running). The default value is `localhost`.

- `--password[=pass_val], -p[pass_val]`

  This option is used only by client programs. It indicates the password to use when connecting to the server. If you specify no `pass_val` after the option name, the program asks you to enter a password. If you do specify `pass_val` after `-p`, it must immediately follow the option letter with no space in between. In other words, the short form must be given as `-ppass_val`, *not* as `-p pass_val`.

- `--pipe, -W`

  Specifies use of a named pipe to connect to the server. This option is used only for client programs running under Windows, and only for connecting to Windows servers that have named-pipe support enabled.

- `--port=port_num, -P port_num`

  For `mysqld`, this option specifies the port on which to listen for TCP/IP connections. The default port number is 3306. For client programs, this is the port number to use when connecting to the server via TCP/IP.

- `--protocol=protocol_type`

  This option is used only by client programs. It indicates what type of connection to make to the server. The `protocol_type` value can be `tcp` (use TCP/IP), `socket` (use a Unix socket file), `pipe` (use a Windows named pipe), or `memory` (use shared memory). The value is not case sensitive.

  Some connection types are platform specific or usable only for connecting to a local server running on the same host as the client program:

    - Socket, named-pipe, and shared-memory connections can be used only for connecting to a local server.
    - Socket connections can be used only on Unix.
    - Named-pipe and shared-memory connections can be used only on Windows.
    - TCP/IP connections can be used on any platform and can be used to connect to local or remote servers.

  The `--protocol` option can be used in conjunction with other options that provide information about how to connect to the server:

    - For TCP/IP connections, you can use the `--host` and `--port` options to specify the hostname and TCP/IP port number.
    - For socket and named-pipe connections, you can use the `--socket` option to specify the Unix socket filename on Unix or the named-pipe name on Windows.
    - For shared-memory connections, you can use the `--shared-memory-base-name` option to specify the shared-memory name.

- `--set-variable` *var=value*, `-O` *var=value*

  Assigns a value to a program operating parameter. *var* is the variable name, and *value* is the value to assign to it. `--set-variable` and `-O` are deprecated. See Section F.2.1.2, "Setting Program Variables," for more information.

- `--shared-memory-base-name=`*name*

  The name of the shared memory to use for shared-memory connections. The default value is `MYSQL`. The value is case sensitive.

- `--silent`, `-s`

  Tells the program to run in silent mode. This doesn't necessarily mean the program is completely silent, simply that it produces less output than usual. Some programs allow this option to be specified multiple times to cause the program to become increasingly silent.

- `--socket=`*file_name*, `-S` *file_name*

  For client programs on Unix, this is the full pathname of the Unix socket file to use when connecting to the server with a hostname of `localhost`. The default Unix socket filename is `/tmp/mysql.sock`. The pathname is case sensitive if filenames are case sensitive on the MySQL host. For client programs on Windows, this is the name of the named pipe to use when connecting to the server via a named pipe. The default pipe name is `MySQL`. Pipe names are not case sensitive.

- `--user=`*user_name*, `-u` *user_name*

  For `mysqld`, this option indicates the name or user ID of the Unix account to be used for running the server. For this option to be effective, the server must be started as `root` so that it can change its user ID to that of the account that you specify. For client programs, this is the MySQL username to use when connecting to the server. The default value is your login name under Unix and `ODBC` under Windows.

- `--verbose`, `-v`

  Tells the program to run in verbose mode; the program produces more output than usual. Some programs allow this option to be specified multiple times to cause the program to be increasingly verbose.

- `--version`, `-V`

  This option tells the program to print its version information string and exit.

F.2.1.1 Standard SSL Options

The following options are used for establishing secure connections. They are available only if MySQL is compiled with SSL support. See Section 13.3, "Setting Up Secure Connections," for information on enabling secure connections.

- `--ssl` (*boolean*)

  Enables SSL connections. `--ssl` is implied by each of the other SSL options; the more common use of this option is as `--skip-ssl` to disallow SSL connections.

- `--ssl-ca=file_name`

  The pathname to the certificate authority file.

- `--ssl-capath=dir_name`

  The pathname to a directory of trusted certificates to be used for certificate verification.

- `--ssl-cert=file_name`

  The pathname to the certificate file.

- `--ssl-cipher=str`

  A string listing the SSL ciphers that may be used to encrypt traffic sent over the connection. The value should name one or more cipher types separated by commas.

- `--ssl-key=file_name`

  The pathname to the key file.

- `--ssl-verify-server-cert` (*boolean*)

  This option applies only to client programs. It tells the client to check the Common Name value from the certificate received from the server. If this value differs from the host to which the client connected, the connection attempt is abandoned. This option was introduced in MySQL 5.0.23/5.1.11.

F.2.1.2 Setting Program Variables

Several MySQL programs have variables (operating parameters) that you can set. One way to set a variable is by treating its name as an option. For example, to invoke `mysql` with the `connect_timeout` variable set to 10, use this command:

```
% mysql --connect_timeout=10
```

This syntax also allows underscores in variable names to be given as dashes, which makes variable options look more like other options:

```
% mysql --connect-timeout=10
```

For variables that represent buffer sizes or lengths, values are in bytes if specified as a number with no suffix, or can be specified with a suffix of 'K', 'M', or 'G', to indicate kilobytes, megabytes, or gigabytes. Suffixes are not case sensitive; you can also use 'k', 'm', or 'g'.

An older method for setting program variables uses the `--set-variable` option to set variables (or its short-form equivalent, `-O`). The syntax for using these options to set the `connect_timeout` variable looks like this:

```
% mysql --set-variable=connect_timeout=10
% mysql -O connect_timeout=10
```

`--set-variable` and `-O` are deprecated.

Each program's variables are listed in the program's description in this appendix, and are also displayed in the program's help message (see Section F.1, "Displaying a Program's Help Message").

F.2.2 Option Files

Most MySQL programs support option files. These provide a means for storing program options so that you don't have to type them on the command line each time you invoke a program. For binary distributions, you can find sample option files under the MySQL installation directory. If you have a source distribution, look in the `support-files` directory for the sample files. They have names such as `my-huge.cnf`, `my-large.cnf`, and so forth. (The filename suffix is `.ini` on Windows.)

Any option specified in an option file can be overridden by explicitly specifying the option on the command line with a different value.

MySQL programs that support option files look for them in several locations. However, it is not an error for an option file to be missing. This means you normally must create option files yourself. Option files must be text files, so if you create an option file in a word processor, be sure to save it in plain text format, not in the word processor's native document format.

Under Unix, the option files shown in the following table are read in order if they exist.

Filename	Contents
`/etc/my.cnf`	Global options
`/etc/mysql/my.cnf`	Global options (as of MySQL 5.1.15)
`SYSCONFDIR/my.cnf`	Global options
`$MYSQL_HOST/my.cnf`	Server-specific options
`~/.my.cnf`	User-specific options

In addition, if a file is named with the `--defaults-extra-file` option, it is read just before `~/.my.cnf`. `~` represents the pathname to your home directory.

`SYSCONFDIR` comes from the `--sysconfdir` option given to `configure` at MySQL build time. Its default value is the `etc` directory under the installation directory compiled in to the distribution. This option file location is used as of MySQL 5.0.21/5.1.10, although until 5.0.53/5.1.22, the file named by this location is read last.

`$MYSQL_HOME` is an environment variable that can be set for use by `mysqld_safe` to a directory containing a server-specific option file. If it is not set, `mysqld_safe` tries to set it automatically to find a `my.cnf` file in the MySQL installation directory or data directory.

Under Windows, the option files shown in the following table are read in order if they exist.

Filename	Contents
WINDIR\my.ini, *WINDIR*\my.ini	Global options
C:\my.ini, C:\my.cnf	Global options
INSTALLDIR\my.ini, *INSTALLDIR*\my.ini	Global options

In addition, if a file named given with the `--defaults-extra-file` option, it is read after the others. *WINDIR* is the pathname to the Windows directory (usually something like `C:\Windows` or `C:\WinNT`). *INSTALLDIR* is the pathname to the MySQL installation directory.

Global option files are used by all MySQL programs that are option file-aware. User-specific files on Unix are read by programs run by that user. An option file in a server's data directory is used only by programs from a distribution that was built with that directory as the default data directory location. The data directory is now a deprecated option file location.

Windows users should be especially careful about the following issues when using option files:

- Windows pathnames often contain backslash ('\') characters, which are treated as escape characters by MySQL. For options that take pathname values, backslashes should be written as slashes ('/') or as doubled backslashes ('\\').

- On Windows, filenames may be displayed with extensions hidden. If you create an option file named `my.cnf`, the name may display as just `my`. Should you notice that and attempt to change the name to `my.cnf`, you may find that the option file no longer works. The reason is that you actually will have renamed the file from `my.cnf` to `my.cnf.cnf`!

Several options related to option-file processing are standard across most MySQL programs and have the following meanings; if you use any of them, it must be the first option on the command line.

- `--defaults-extra-file=`*file_name*

Specifies an option file to read in addition to the regular option files. The file is read after any global and server-specific option files and before the user-specific file. As of MySQL 5.0.6, the file must exist and be readable or an error occurs.

- `--defaults-file=`*file_name*

Specifies the sole file from which to read options. Normally, programs search for option files in several locations (as described earlier), but if `--defaults-file` is specified, only the named file is read. The file must exist and be readable or an error occurs.

- `--defaults-group-suffix=`*`suffix`*

  Reads the option groups with the usual names and also those with the concatenation of the usual names and the given suffix. This option was introduced in MySQL 5.0.10.

- `--no-defaults`

  Suppresses the use of any option files. In addition, this option causes other option-file-related options such as `--defaults-file` to be unrecognized.

- `--print-defaults`

  Prints the option values that will be used if you invoke the program with no options on the command line. This shows the values that will be read from option files (and environment variables). `--print-defaults` is useful for verifying proper setup of an option file. It's also useful if MySQL programs seem to be using options that you never specified; you can use `--print-defaults` to determine whether options are being read from some option file.

A program's help message lists the locations where the program looks by default for option files (see Section F.1, "Displaying a Program's Help Message"). The default set of files to read is affected by use of `--defaults-file`, `--defaults-extra-file`, or `--no-defaults`.

Options in option files are specified in groups (or sections). Here's an example:

```
[client]
user=sampadm
password=secret

[mysql]
skip-auto-rehash

[mysqlshow]
status
```

Group names are written inside square brackets and are not case sensitive. The special `[client]` group enables you to specify options that apply to all client programs. Otherwise, a group name usually corresponds to a specific program name. In the preceding example, `[mysql]` indicates the option group for the `mysql` client and `[mysqlshow]` indicates the option group for `mysqlshow`. The standard MySQL client programs look at both the `[client]` group and the group with the same name as the client name. For example, `mysql` looks at the `[client]` and `[mysql]` groups, and `mysqlshow` looks at the `[client]` and `[mysqlshow]` groups.

Be careful not to put options in the `[client]` group that really are understood only by a single client. For example, `skip-auto-rehash` is specific to `mysql`. If you put this option in the `[client]` group, you will suddenly find that other client programs such as `mysqlimport` no longer work. (They will display an error message followed by a help message.) Place `skip-auto-rehash` in a `[mysql]` group instead.

Any options following a group name are associated with that group. An option file may contain any number of groups, and groups listed later take precedence over groups listed earlier. If a given option is found multiple times in the groups a program looks at, the value listed last is used.

Each option should be specified on a separate line. The first word on the line is the option name, which must be specified in long-name format without the leading dashes. For example, to specify compression on the command line, you can use either `-c` or `--compress`, but in an option file, you can use only `compress`. Any long-format option supported by a program can be listed in an option file. If the option requires a value, list the name and value separated by an '=' character.

Consider the following command line:

```
% mysql --compress --user=sampadm --max_allowed_packet=16M
```

To specify the same information in an option file using the `[mysql]` group, do so as follows:

```
[mysql]
compress
user=sampadm
max_allowed_packet=16M
```

You can quote an option value with either single quotes or double quotes. This is useful if the value contains spaces.

Leading spaces in option file lines are ignored. Lines that are empty or that begin with '#' or ';' are treated as comments and ignored. You can also begin a comment in the middle of a line with a '#' character (but not with a ';' character).

The escape sequences shown in the following table can be used in option file values to specify special characters.

Sequence	Meaning
\b	Backspace
\n	Newline (linefeed)
\r	Carriage return
\s	Space
\t	Tab
\\	Backslash

As of MySQL 5.0.4, option files can include directives that cause other option files to be read:

- `!include file_name`

  Reads the named option file.

- `!includedir dir_name`

  Reads all option files in the named directory. Option files are identified as those having an extension of `.cnf` on Unix or either `.ini` or `.cnf` on Windows. The order in which the files are read is undefined.

Included files follow the usual option file syntax. Only options from the option group that is current at the point of inclusion will be used.

F.2.2.1 Keeping User-Specific Option Files Private

Under Unix, your user-specific option file, `~/.my.cnf`, should be owned by you and its mode should be set to 600 or 400 so that other users cannot read it. You don't want your MySQL username and password exposed to anyone other than yourself. To make your own option file private, issue either of the following commands in your home directory:

```
% chmod 600 .my.cnf
% chmod go-rwx .my.cnf
```

F.2.2.2 Using `my_print_defaults` to Check Options

The `my_print_defaults` utility is useful for determining what options a program will read from option files. It searches option files and shows which options are found there for one or more option groups. For example, the `mysql` program uses options from the `[client]` and `[mysql]` option groups. To find out which options in your option files apply to `mysql`, invoke `my_print_defaults` like this:

```
% my_print_defaults client mysql
```

Similarly, the server `mysqld` uses options in the `[mysqld]` and `[server]` groups. To determine what options are present in option files, use this command:

```
% my_print_defaults mysqld server
```

F.2.3 Environment Variables

MySQL programs look at the values of the several environment variables to obtain option settings. Environment variables have low precedence; option values specified using them can be overridden by options in an option file or on the command line.

MySQL programs check the following environment variables:

- `MYSQL_DEBUG`

  The options to use when debugging. This variable has no effect unless MySQL was built with debugging support enabled. Setting `MYSQL_DEBUG` is like using the `--debug` option.

- `MYSQL_PWD`

  The password to use when establishing connections to the MySQL server. Setting `MYSQL_PWD` is like using the `--password` option.

  Using the `MYSQL_PWD` variable to store a password constitutes a security risk because other users on your system can easily discover its value. For example, the `ps` utility shows environment variable settings for other users.

- `MYSQL_TCP_PORT`

  For `mysqld`, this is the port on which to listen for TCP/IP connections. For client programs, this is the port number to use when establishing a TCP/IP connection to the server. Setting `MYSQL_TCP_PORT` is like using the `--port` option.

- `MYSQL_UNIX_PORT`

  For `mysqld`, this is the socket file on which to listen for local connections. For client programs, this is the pathname of the Unix socket file to use when establishing socket file connections to the server running on `localhost`. Setting `MYSQL_UNIX_PORT` is like using the `--socket` option.

- `TMPDIR`

  The pathname of the directory in which to create temporary files. Setting this variable is like using the `--tmpdir` option. However, although `myisamchk` and `mysqld` understand a value containing a list of directories for `--tmpdir`, do not set `TMPDIR` that way: Other non-MySQL programs that do not understand the list-of-directories convention also use `TMPDIR`.

- `USER`

  This is the MySQL username to use when connecting to the server. This variable is used only by client programs running under Windows or NetWare; setting it is like using the `--user` option.

The `mysql` client checks the value of three additional environment variables:

- `MYSQL_HISTFILE`

  On Unix, the name of the file to use for storing command-line history during interactive use. The default value if this variable is not set is `$HOME/.mysql_history`, where `$HOME` is the location of your home directory.

- `MYSQL_HOST`

  The host to connect to when establishing a connection to the MySQL server. Setting this variable is like using the `--host` option.

- MYSQL_PS1

    The string to use instead of `mysql>` for the primary prompt. The string can contain the special sequences listed in the section of this appendix that describes the `mysql` program.

F.3 myisamchk

The `myisamchk` utility enables you to check and repair damaged tables, display table information, perform index key value distribution analysis, and disable or enable indexes. Chapter 5, "Query Optimization," provides more information on key analysis and index disabling. Chapter 14, "Database Maintenance, Backups, and Repair," provides more information on table checking and repair.

`myisamchk` is used for tables that are managed by the MyISAM storage engine. These tables have data and index filenames with `.MYD` and `.MYI` suffixes, respectively. If you tell `myisamchk` to operate on a table of the wrong type, it prints a warning message and ignores the table.

Invoke `myisamchk` with the names of the tables to be checked:

```
myisamchk [options] tbl_name[.MYI] ...
```

With no options, `myisamchk` checks the named tables for errors. Otherwise, it processes the tables according to the meaning of the specified options. If you perform an operation that might modify a table, it's a good idea to make a copy of it first.

A `tbl_name` argument can be either the name of a table or the name of its index file, `tbl_name.MYI`. Using index filenames is convenient if your command interpreter expands wildcards because you can use a wildcard to specify all index names in a single command. For example, you can check all the MyISAM tables in the current directory as follows:

```
% myisamchk *.MYI
```

`myisamchk` makes no assumptions about where table files are located. If the files that you want to use are not in the current directory, you must specify the pathname to them. Because table files are not assumed to be located under the server's data directory, you can copy table files into another directory and operate on the copies rather than the originals.

Many of the operations that `myisamchk` does can also be performed by issuing SQL statements to the server. These statements include ANALYZE TABLE, CHECK TABLE, OPTIMIZE TABLE, and REPAIR TABLE. You can issue these statements directly, or you can use the `mysqlcheck` program, which provides a command-line interface to several SQL table-maintenance statements. In general, it is easier and safer to use these statements or `mysqlcheck` rather than `myisamchk`.

One danger of using `myisamchk` to perform maintenance on a table is that you must prevent the server from accessing the table concurrently. This is necessary because the server and `myisamchk` both access table files directly. If they are allowed to do so at the same time, you can destroy the table. If you really want to use `myisamchk`, be sure to consult Section 14.1, "Performing Database Maintenance with the Server Running," which discusses how to prevent the server from using a table while myisamchk is working on it.

You must also take special care when using myisamchk for tables that contain FULLTEXT indexes if both of these conditions are true:

- You are using myisamchk to perform an operation that modifies indexes. These include analysis and repair operations.
- You are running the server using a non-default value for any of these FULLTEXT-related system variables: ft_max_word_len, ft_min_word_len, or ft_stopword_file.

When both of these conditions hold, you must use appropriate options to tell myisamchk what FULLTEXT parameters to use, because it does not know what values the server is using. If you do not do this, myisamchk will build FULLTEXT indexes using different parameter values than the server expects and FULLTEXT searches will return incorrect results. Suppose that you run your server using the following non-default option settings for the minimum word length and stopword file:

```
[mysqld]
ft_min_word_len=2
ft_stopword_file=/var/mysql/data/my-stopwords
```

In this case, you must indicate those same values to myisamchk for any index-changing operation that you perform on tables that contain FULLTEXT indexes. You can do this on the command line with --ft_min_word_len and --ft_stopword_list options, but it's better to record the values in an option file so that you don't forget to use them. Use an option group similar to the one used for the server:

```
[myisamchk]
ft_min_word_len=2
ft_stopword_file=/var/mysql/data/my-stopwords
```

You can avoid the problem of FULLTEXT parameter mismatch entirely by using SQL statements such as REPAIR TABLE or ANALYZE TABLE for table maintenance. Then the server does the index modification, and, because it knows what FULLTEXT parameters it is using, applies them for maintenance operations on tables that contain FULLTEXT indexes.

F.3.1 Standard Options Supported by myisamchk

```
--character-sets-dir    --set-variable          --version
--debug                 --silent
--help                  --verbose
```

The --silent option means that only error messages are printed. The --verbose option prints more information when given with the --check, --description, or --extend-check options. The --silent and --verbose options can be specified multiple times for increased effect.

The standard `--help` option prints the help message with options grouped by function. `myisamchk` also supports `--HELP` and `-H` options that display all options in a single alphabetical list.

F.3.2 Options Specific to `myisamchk`

Some of these options refer to index numbers. Indexes are numbered beginning with 1. You can issue a `SHOW INDEX` statement or use a `mysqlshow --keys` command to determine the index numbering for a particular table. The `Key_name` column in the output lists indexes in the same order that `myisamchk` sees them.

- `--analyze, -a`

  Performs key distribution analysis. This can help the server perform index-based lookups and joins more quickly. To obtain information about key distribution after the analysis, run `myisamchk` again with the `--description` and `--verbose` options.

- `--backup, -B`

  For options that modify the data (`.MYD`) file, makes a backup using a filename of the form `tbl_name-time.BAK`. `time` is a number representing a timestamp. `myisamchk` creates the backup file in the directory where the table files are located.

- `--block-search=n, -b n`

  Prints out the start of the table row that contains a block starting at block `n`. This is for debugging only.

- `--check, -c`

  Checks tables for errors. This is the default action if no options are specified.

- `--check-only-changed, -C`

  Checks tables only if they have not been changed since the last check.

- `--correct-checksum`

  For tables created with the `CHECKSUM = 1` option, ensures that the checksum information in the table is correct.

- `--data-file-length=n, -D n`

  The maximum length in bytes to which the data file should be allowed to grow when rebuilding a data file that has become full. (This occurs when a file reaches the size limit imposed by MySQL or by the file-size constraints of your operating system. It also occurs when the number of rows reaches the limit imposed by internal table data structures.) This option is effective only when used with `--recover` or `--safe-recover`.

- `--description, -d`

  Prints descriptive information about the table.

- `--extend-check, -e`

  Performs an extended table check. It should rarely be necessary to use this option because `myisamchk` normally finds any errors with one of the less extensive check modes.

- `--fast, -F`

  Checks tables only if they have not been closed properly. This can occur, for example, if the server host machine crashes while `mysqld` has the tables open, so that `mysqld` has no opportunity to close them.

- `--force, -f`

  Forces a table to be checked or repaired even if a temporary file for the table already exists. Normally, `myisamchk` simply exits after printing an error message if it finds a file named `tbl_name.TMD`, because that might indicate that another instance of the program is already running. However, the file might also exist because you killed a previous invocation of `myisamchk` while it was running, in which case the file safely can be removed. If you know that to be the case, use `--force` to tell `myisamchk` to run even if the temporary file exists. (Alternatively, remove the temporary file manually.)

  If you use `--force` when checking tables, `myisamchk` automatically restarts with `--recover` for any table found to have problems. In addition, `myisamchk` updates the table state in the same way that the `--update-state` option does.

- `--information, -i`

  Prints statistical information about table contents.

- `--keys-used=n, -k n`

  Used with `--recover`. The option value n is a bitmask that indicates which indexes to use. The first index is bit zero. (For example, a value of 6 is binary 110 and indicates that the second and third indexes should be used.) A value of 0 turns off all indexes, which can be used to improve the performance of INSERT, DELETE, and UPDATE operations. Turning the indexes back on restores normal indexing behavior (specify a bitmask that includes an enabled bit for each index).

- `--max-record-length=n`

  Ignores rows that are larger than n bytes if memory cannot be allocated for them.

- `--medium-check, -m`

  Checks a table using a method that is faster than `--extend-check`, but slightly less thorough. (The `myisamchk` help message says that this method finds "only" 99.99% of all errors.) This check mode should be sufficient for most circumstances. Medium check mode works by calculating CRC values for the keys in the index and comparing them with the CRC values calculated from the indexed columns in the data file.

- `--parallel-recover, -p`

Performs recovery the same way as for `--recover`, but rebuild the indexes in parallel using multiple threads. This can be faster than a non-parallel rebuild, but this option should be considered experimental.

- `--quick, -q` (*boolean*)

This option is used in conjunction with `--recover` for faster repair than when `--recover` is used alone. The data file is not touched when both options are given. To force the program to modify the data file if duplicate key values are found, specify the `--quick` option twice.

- `--read-only, -T`

Causes the table not to be marked as having been checked.

- `--recover, -r`

Performs a normal recovery operation. This can fix most problems except the occurrence of duplicate values in an index that should contain only unique values.

- `--safe-recover, -o`

Performs recovery using a method that is slower than one used for `--recover`, but that can fix a few problems that `--recover` cannot. `--safe-recover` also uses less disk space than `--recover`.

- `--set-auto-increment[=n], -A[n]`

Sets the AUTO_INCREMENT counter so that subsequent sequence values start at *n* (or at a higher value if the table already contains rows with AUTO_INCREMENT values as large as *n*). If no value *n* is specified, this option sets the next AUTO_INCREMENT value to one greater than the current maximum value stored in the table.

If *n* is specified after `-A`, there must be no intervening space or the value will not be interpreted correctly.

You can set the AUTO_INCREMENT value for a MyISAM table without using `myisamchk` by issuing a statement of the following form:

```
ALTER TABLE tbl_name AUTO_INCREMENT = n;
```

- `--set-character-set=charset`

The character set to use for rebuilding and sorting table index entries. This option was removed in MySQL 5.0.3 and replaced with `--set-collation`.

- `--set-collation=collation`

The collation to use for rebuilding and sorting table index entries. (The collation name implies the character set name.) This option was introduced in MySQL 5.0.3 and replaces `--set-character-set`.

- `--sort-index, -S`

Sorts the index blocks to speed up sequential block reads for subsequent retrievals.

- `--sort-records=n, -R n`

  Sorts data rows according to the order in which rows are listed in index *n*. Subsequent retrievals based on the given index should be faster. The first time you perform this operation on a table, it may be very slow because your rows will be unordered. `ALTER TABLE ... ORDER BY` accomplishes the same thing as `--sort-records`, and normally will be faster.

- `--sort-recover, -n`

  Forces sorted recovery even if the temporary file necessary to perform the operation would become quite large.

- `--start-check-pos=n`

  The position *n* at which to begin reading the data file. This option is used only for debugging.

- `--tmpdir=dir_name, -t dir_name`

  The pathname of the directory to use for temporary files. The default is the value of the `TMPDIR` environment variable, or `/tmp` if that variable is not set. The option value can be given as a list of directories, to be used in round-robin fashion. Under Unix, separate directory names by colons; under Windows or NetWare, separate them by semicolons.

- `--unpack, -u`

  Unpacks a packed table that was packed by `myisampack`. This option can be used to convert a compressed read-only table to modifiable form. It cannot be used with `--quick` or with `--sort-records`.

- `--update-state, -U`

  Updates the internal flag that is stored in the table to indicate its state. Tables that are okay are marked as such, and tables for which an error occurs are marked as in need of repair. Using this option makes subsequent invocations of `myisamchk` with the `--check-only-changed` option more efficient for tables that are okay.

- `--wait, -w`

  If a table is locked, waits until it is available. Without `--wait`, `myisamchk` waits 10 seconds for a lock and then prints an error message if no lock can be obtained.

F.3.3 Variables for `myisamchk`

The following `myisamchk` variables can be set using the instructions given in Section F.2.1.2, "Setting Program Variables."

For tables that contain `FULLTEXT` indexes, note the caution described in the introductory `myisamchk` program description.

- `decode_bits`

  The number of bits to use when decoding compressed tables. Larger values may result in faster operation but will require more memory. The default value of 9 generally is sufficient.

- `ft_max_word_len`

  The maximum length of words that can be included in FULLTEXT indexes. Longer words are ignored. The default value is 84.

- `ft_min_word_len`

  The minimum length of words that can be included in FULLTEXT indexes. Shorter words are ignored. The default value is 4.

- `ft_stopword_file`

  The stopword file for FULLTEXT indexes. There is no default, which means "use the built-in stopword list."

- `key_buffer_size`

  The size of the buffer used for index blocks. (This is used for `--safe-recover`, but not for `--recover` or `--sort-recover`.) The default value is 512KB.

- `key_cache_block_size`

  The size of blocks in the key buffer. The default value is 1MB.

- `myisam_block_size`

  The block size used for index blocks in the `.MYI` file. The default value is 1MB.

- `read_buffer_size`

  The read buffer size. The default value is 256KB.

- `sort_buffer_size`

  The size of the buffer used for key value sorting operations. (This is used for `--recover` or `--sort-recover`, but not for `--safe-recover`.) The default value is 2MB.

- `sort_key_blocks`

  This variable is related to the depth of the B-tree structure used for the index. The default value is 16; you should not need to change it.

- `stats_method`

  Whether NULL values should be considered equal or distinct for calculating index key value distribution statistics. The value can be `nulls_equal` (all NULL values are in the same group) or `nulls_unequal` (each NULL value forms a distinct group). This variable was introduced in MySQL 5.0.14. Before that, statistics calculation is the same as `nulls_equal`.

- `write_buffer_size`

  The write buffer size. The default value is 256KB.

F.4 myisampack

The myisampack utility produces compressed, read-only tables. It achieves typical storage requirement reductions of 40% to 70% while maintaining fast row access. myisampack packs MyISAM tables and works with all data types.

No special version of the MySQL server is needed to read tables that have been packed with myisampack. This makes them especially applicable for applications for which you want to distribute a table containing archival or encyclopedic information that is read-only and need not be updated. For example, if you are setting up a CD-ROM for an application that uses the embedded server, you'll be able to pack more data on the disk by using compressed MyISAM tables.

Invoke myisampack with the names of the tables to be packed:

```
myisampack [options] tbl_name ...
```

A tbl_name argument can be either the name of a table or the name of the index file for the table. (For MyISAM tables, index files have an extension of .MYI.) The name must include the pathname to the directory in which the table is located if that is not your current directory.

myisampack packs data files but does not touch index files, so after using it, you must update the indexes by running myisamchk --recover --quick.

To convert a packed file to unpacked and modifiable form, use myisamchk --unpack.

F.4.1 Standard Options Supported by myisampack

```
--character-sets-dir  --help        --verbose
--debug               --silent      --version
```

F.4.2 Options Specific to myisampack

- --backup, -b

  Makes a backup of the data file for each tbl_name argument as tbl_name.OLD before packing it.

- --force, -f

  Forces a table to be packed even if the resulting packed file is larger than the original or if a temporary file for the table already exists. Normally, myisampack simply exits after printing an error message if it finds a file named tbl_name.TMD, because that might indicate that another instance of the program is already running. However, the file might also exist because you killed a previous invocation of myisampack while it was running, in which case the file safely can be removed. If you know that to be the case, use `--force` to tell myisampack to pack the table even if the temporary file exists. (Alternatively, remove the temporary file manually.)

- `--join=join_tbl, -j join_tbl`

  Joins (merges) all the tables named on the command line into a single packed table named `join_tbl`. All the tables to be merged must have the same structure. (Column names, types, and indexes must be identical.) This option is unrelated to MERGE tables. The operation does not create the `.frm` file for the output table. You can create it by copying the `.frm` file from one of the source tables after myisampack completes.

- `--test, -t`

  Causes myisampack to run in test mode. A packing test is run, and information is printed about the results you would obtain if you actually packed the table.

- `--tmpdir=dir_name, -T dir_name`

  The pathname of the directory to use for temporary files.

- `--wait, -w` (*boolean*)

  Waits and retries if a table is in use. (You should not pack a table if it might be updated while you're packing it.)

F.5 mysql

The mysql client program enables you to connect to the server, issue SQL statements, and view the results.

```
mysql [options] [db_name]
```

If you specify a *db_name* argument, that database becomes the default database for your session. If you specify no *db_name* argument, mysql starts with no default database and you'll need to either qualify all table references with a database name or issue a USE *db_name* statement to specify a default database.

mysql can be run interactively. You can also use it in batch mode to execute statements that are stored in a file if you redirect the input of the command to read from that file. For example:

```
% mysql -u sampadm -p -h cobra.snake.net sampdb < my_sql_file
```

In interactive mode, when mysql starts, it displays a mysql> prompt to indicate that it's waiting for input. To issue a statement, type it in (using multiple lines if necessary) and then indicate the end of the statement by typing ';' (semicolon) or \g. mysql sends the statement to the server, displays the results, and then prints another prompt to indicate that it's ready for another statement. \G also terminates a statement, but causes statement results to be displayed vertically (that is, with one column value per output line).

mysql varies the prompt to indicate what it's waiting for as you enter input lines, as shown in the following table. The mysql> prompt is the primary prompt, displayed at the beginning of each statement. The other prompts are secondary prompts, displayed to obtain additional lines for the current statement.

Prompt	Meaning
mysql>	Waiting for the first line of a new statement
->	Waiting for the next line of the current statement
'>	Waiting for completion of a single-quoted string in the current statement
">	Waiting for completion of a double-quoted string in the current statement
`>	Waiting for completion of a quoted identifier in the current statement
/*>	Waiting for completion of /* ... */ comment (MySQL 5.0.6 and up)

The '> and "> prompts indicate that you've begun a single-quoted or double-quoted string on a previous line and have not yet entered the terminating quote. Similarly, `> indicates an unterminated quoted identifier. /*> indicates that the beginning /* but not the ending */ of a /*...*/ comment has been seen. Usually, you see these prompts when you've forgotten to terminate a string, identifier, or comment. If that's the case, to escape from string-collection mode, enter the appropriate matching quote or comment ending that is indicated by the prompt, followed by \c to cancel the current statement.

On Unix, when mysql is used in interactive mode, it saves statements in a history file. The name of this file is $HOME/.mysql_history by default, and it can be specified explicitly by setting the MYSQL_HISTFILE environment variable.

Some options suppress use of the history file. Generally, these are options that indicate non-interactive use of mysql, such as --batch, --html, and --quick.

On systems that support the Readline library, statements can be recalled from the command history and re-issued, either with or without further editing. Under Windows, Readline editing capabilities are not available, but Windows itself supports several editing commands, so they become available to mysql. For information about editing commands that work with Readline or on Windows, see Section 1.5.2.1, "Using the mysql Input Line Editor."

F.5.1 Standard Options Supported by mysql

```
--character-sets-dir    --host        --silent
--compress              --password    --socket
--debug                 --pipe        --user
--debug-check           --port        --verbose
--debug-info            --protocol    --version
```

```
--default-character-set    --set-variable
--help                     --shared-memory-base-name
```

--debug-check is available as of MySQL 5.1.21.

--debug-info has its standard effect as of MySQL 5.1.14. Before that, it also displays query result metadata; use --column-type-info as of 5.1.14 to display metadata.

mysql also supports the standard SSL options.

--silent and --verbose can be given multiple times for increased effect.

-I is a synonym for --help.

F.5.2 Options Specific to mysql

- --auto-rehash (*boolean*)

When mysql starts, it can hash database, table, and column names to construct a data structure that enables fast completion of names. You can type the initial part of a name when entering a statement and then press Tab. mysql will complete the name unless it's ambiguous; press Tab again to see the possible completions.

Name hashing is on by default, although it does not take effect until you have se-lected a default database. --skip-auto-rehash suppresses hash calculation, which enables mysql to start up more quickly, particularly if you have many tables.

If hashing has been disabled and you want to use name completion after starting mysql, you can use the rehash command at the mysql> prompt.

- --auto-vertical-output (*boolean*)

Uses vertical output style automatically for query results that exceed the terminal width. This option was introduced in MySQL 6.0.4.

- --batch, -B

Runs in batch mode. mysql displays query results in tab-delimited format (each row on a separate line with tabs between column values). This is especially conven-ient for generating output that you want to import into another program, such as a spreadsheet application. Query results include an initial row of column headings by default. To suppress these headings, use the --skip-column-names option.

- --column-names (*boolean*)

Displays column names as column headers in query results. Use --skip-column-names to suppress display of column names. You can also achieve that effect by speci-fying the --silent option twice.

- --column-type-info, -m (*boolean*)

Includes result set metadata with query output. This option was introduced in MySQL 5.1.14 (-m in 5.1.21.) Use --debug-info to get result set metadata before 5.1.14.

- `--comments, -c` (*boolean*)

  For statements that contain comments, includes these comments when the statements are sent to the server. By default, comments are stripped (same as specifying `--skip-comments`). This option was introduced in MySQL 5.0.52/5.1.23.

- `--database=db_name, -D db_name`

  Specifies the default database.

- `--delimiter=str`

  Sets the statement delimiter. The default delimiter is the semicolon (';').

- `--execute=stmt, -e stmt`

  Executes the statement and quits. You should enclose the statement in quotes to prevent your shell (command interpreter) from treating it as multiple command-line arguments. Multiple statements can be given; separate them by semicolons in the `stmt` value.

- `--force, -f` (*boolean*)

  Normally when `mysql` reads statements from a file, it exits if an error occurs. This option causes `mysql` to continue processing statements, regardless of errors.

- `--html, -H` (*boolean*)

  Produces HTML output.

- `--i-am-a-dummy` (*boolean*)

  This option is synonymous with `--safe-updates`.

- `--ignore-spaces, -i`

  Causes the server to ignore spaces between names of built-in functions and the '(' character that introduces the argument list. Normally, function names should be followed immediately by the parenthesis with no intervening spaces. This option causes function names to be treated as reserved words.

- `--line-numbers` (*boolean*)

  Displays line numbers in error messages. This is the default; to suppress line numbers, use `--skip-line-numbers`.

- `--local-infile` (*boolean*)

  Enables or disables LOAD DATA LOCAL. The LOCAL capability might be present but disabled by default. If LOAD DATA LOCAL results in an error, try again after invoking `mysql` with the `--local-infile` option. This option can also be used to disable LOCAL if it is enabled, for example, with `--disable-local-infile`.

  This option is ineffective if the server has been configured to disallow use of LOCAL.

- `--named-commands, -G` (*boolean*)

  Enables long forms of `mysql`'s internal commands at the beginning of any input line. If this capability is disabled with `--skip-named-commands`, long commands are allowed only at the primary prompt and disallowed at the secondary prompts. (That is, they are disallowed on second and subsequent lines of a multiple-line statement.)

- `--no-auto-rehash, -A`

  This option is deprecated in favor of `--skip-auto-rehash`. See the description for `--auto-rehash`.

- `--no-beep, -b` (*boolean*)

  Suppresses production of beeps when errors occur.

- `--no-named-commands, -g`

  This option is deprecated. See the description for `--named-commands`.

- `--no-pager`

  This option is deprecated in favor of `--skip-pager`. See the description for `--pager`.

- `--no-tee`

  This option is deprecated in favor of `--skip-tee`. See the description for `--tee`.

- `--one-database, -o`

  This option is used when updating databases from the contents of a binary log file. It tells `mysql` to update only the default database (the database named on the command line). Updates to other databases are ignored. If no database is named on the command line, no updates are performed.

- `--pager[=program]`

  The name of a paging program to use for displaying long query results one page at a time (for example, `/bin/more` or `/bin/less`). If *program* is missing, the paging program is determined from the value of the `PAGER` environment variable. Output paging is unavailable in batch mode, and does not work under Windows. Paging can be disabled with `--skip-pager`.

- `--prompt=str`

  Changes the primary prompt from `mysql>` to the string defined by *str*. The string can contain special sequences, as described in Section F.5.5, "`mysql` Prompt Definition Sequences."

- `--quick, -q`

  Normally `mysql` retrieves the entire result of a query from the server before displaying it. This option causes each row to be displayed as it is retrieved, which uses much less memory and may allow some large statements to be performed successfully that would fail otherwise. However, this option should not be specified for interactive use; if the user pauses the output or suspends `mysql`, the server continues to wait, which can interfere with other clients.

- `--raw, -r` (*boolean*)

Writes column values without escaping any special characters. This option is used in conjunction with the `--batch` option.

- `--reconnect` (*boolean*)

Automatically reconnects to the server if the connection is lost. Before MySQL 5.0.3, this option is enabled by default; disable it with `--skip-reconnect`.

Automatic reconnection can cause problems in some circumstances. For example, any currently active transaction is rolled back and the values of session variables are lost without an indication that this has happened.

- `--safe-updates, -U` (*boolean*)

This option places some limits on what you can do and can be beneficial for new MySQL users:

  - Updates (statements that modify data) are allowed only if the rows to be modified are identified by key values or if a `LIMIT` clause is used. This helps prevent statements that mistakenly change or wipe out all or large parts of a table.

  - Result sets produced by non-join retrievals are limited to one thousand rows unless a `LIMIT` clause is used. Retrievals that involve a join are disallowed if the optimizer estimates that it will need to examine more than one million rows. This helps prevent unintended generation of very large query results.

These limits can be changed by setting the `select_limit` and `max_join_size` variables.

- `--secure-auth` (*boolean*)

Prevents connecting to the server unless it supports the more secure password format introduced in MySQL 4.1.

- `--show-warnings` (*boolean*)

Automatically displays any warnings for each statement. This option was introduced in MySQL 5.0.6.

- `--sigint-ignore` (*boolean*)

Ignores `SIGINT` signals, typically sent by typing Control-C. Before MySQL 5.0.25, Control-C causes `mysql` to exit. As of 5.0.25, Control-C tells `mysql` to kill the current statement. `mysql` exits if the statement could not be killed or you enter another Control-C before the statement is killed. Using `--sigint-ignore` prevents `mysql` from interpreting Control-C as just described. This option was introduced in MySQL 5.0.2.

- `--skip-column-names, -N`

See the description for `--column-names`. The `-N` form of this option is deprecated.

- `--skip-line-numbers, -L`

  See the description for `--line-numbers`. The `-L` form of this option is deprecated.

- `--table, -t` (*boolean*)

  Produces output in tabular format, with values in each row delimited by bars and lined up vertically. This is the default output format when `mysql` is not run in batch mode.

- `--tee=file_name`

  Appends a copy of all output to the named file. Output copying can be disabled with `--skip-tee`. This option does not work in batch mode.

- `--unbuffered, -n` (*boolean*)

  After each statement, flushes the buffer used for communication with the server.

- `--vertical, -E`

  Prints query results vertically—that is, with each row of a query result displayed as a set of output lines, one column per line. (Each line consists of a column name and value.) The display for each row is preceded by a line indicating the row number within the result set. Vertical display format may be useful when a query produces very long lines.

  If this option is not specified, you can enable vertical display format for individual queries by terminating them with `\G` rather than with ';' or `\g`.

- `--wait, -w`

  Waits and retries if a connection to the server cannot be established.

- `--xml, -X` (*boolean*)

  Produces XML output.

F.5.3 Variables for `mysql`

The following `mysql` variables can be set using the instructions given in Section F.2.1.2, "Setting Program Variables."

- `connect_timeout`

  The number of seconds to wait before timing out when attempting to connect to the server. The default value is 0.

- `max_allowed_packet`

  The maximum size of the buffer used for communication between the server and the client. The default value is 16MB and the maximum is 1GB.

- max_join_size

  The row limit on the execution of joins if the --safe-updates option is given. The server rejects joins for which it believes it will need to examine more than max_join_size rows. The default value is 1,000,000.

- net_buffer_length

  The initial size of the buffer used for communication between the server and the client. This buffer can be expanded up to max_allowed_packet bytes long. The default value is 16KB.

- select_limit

  The limit on the number of rows returned by SELECT statements if the --safe-updates option is given. The default value is 1,000.

F.5.4 mysql Commands

In addition to enabling you to send SQL statements to the MySQL server, mysql implements several other commands internally. Each command must be given on a single line. Most of the commands have a long form consisting of a word, and a short form consisting of a backslash followed by a single letter. Commands in long form are not case sensitive. Commands in short form must be specified using the lettercase shown in the following list. A semicolon at the end of the line is unnecessary but allowed for long-form commands, but should be omitted for short-form commands.

If you have disabled named commands (for example, with the --skip-named-commands option), long command names are recognized only at the primary mysql> prompt.

- clear, \c

  Clears (cancels) the current statement. The current statement is the one that you are in the process of typing; this command does not cancel a statement that has already been sent to the server and for which mysql is displaying output.

- connect [*db_name* [*host_name*]], \r [*db_name* [*host_name*]]

  Connects (or reconnects) to the given database on the given host. If the database name or hostname is missing, the most recently used values from the current mysql session are used.

- delimiter *str*, \d *str*

  Sets the statement delimiter. The default delimiter is the semicolon ('; '). The stored program parser recognizes only the semicolon as the statement delimiter, so this command can be used to redefine the delimiter for mysql while defining a stored program. For an example, see Section 4.1, "Compound Statements and Statement Delimiters."

  It's best to avoid using backslashes in the delimiter because MySQL treats backslash as an escape character.

- edit, \e

  Edits the current statement. mysql attempts to determine what editor to use by examining the EDITOR and VISUAL environment variables. If neither variable is set, mysql uses vi. This option is unavailable under Windows.

- ego, \G

  Sends the current statement to the server and displays the result vertically.

- exit

  Same as quit.

- go, \g, ;

  Sends the current statement to the server and displays the result.

- help, \h, ?, \?

  Displays a help message describing the available mysql commands.

  If the help tables in the mysql database have been loaded, you can also use help to get server-side help: Use help contents to get a list of help categories, help *category* for help on a particular category, or help *keyword* for help about the particular keyword (such as SELECT or UPDATE). For instructions on loading the help tables, see Section A.4.4.4, "Installing or Upgrading Additional System Tables."

- nopager, \n

  Disables the pager and sends output to the standard output. This command is unavailable under Windows.

- notee, \t

  Stops writing to the tee file.

- nowarning, \w

  Stops automatically displaying any warnings generated by each statement. This command was introduced in MySQL 5.0.6.

- pager [*program*], \P [*program*]

  Sends output through the paging program specified by *program*, or through the program specified in the PAGER environment variable, if that variable is set and *program* is not given. This command is unavailable under Windows.

- print, \p

  Prints the current statement (the text of the statement itself, not the results obtained by executing it).

- prompt [*arguments*], \R [*arguments*]

  Redefines the primary `mysql>` prompt. Everything following the first space after the `prompt` keyword becomes part of the prompt string, including other spaces. The string can contain special sequences, as described in Section F.5.5, "`mysql` Prompt Definition Sequences." To revert the prompt to the default, specify `prompt` or `\R` with no arguments.

- quit, \q

  Quits `mysql`.

- rehash, \#

  Recalculates the information needed for database, table, and column name completion. See the description for the `--auto-rehash` option.

- source *file_name*, \. *file_name*

  Reads and executes the statements contained in the named file. For Windows filenames that include backslash ('\') pathname separators, double them or specify them using slash ('/') instead.

- status, \s

  Retrieves and displays status information from the server. This is useful if you want to check the server version, default database, whether the connection is secure, and so forth.

- system *command*, \! *command*

  Executes *command* using your default command interpreter. This command is unavailable under Windows.

- tee [*file_name*], \T [*file_name*]

  Copies output to the end of the named file.

- use *db_name*, \u *db_name*

  Selects the given database to make it the default database.

- warnings, \W

  Automatically displays any warnings generated by each statement. This command was introduced in MySQL 5.0.6.

F.5.5 `mysql` Prompt Definition Sequences

The `MYSQL_PS1` environment variable, the `--prompt` option, or the `prompt` command can be used to redefine the primary `mysql>` statement prompt that `mysql` prints. For example, to include the name of the default database in the prompt, use the `prompt` command as follows and then select different databases to see how the prompt follows the current selection:

```
% mysql
mysql> prompt \d>\_
PROMPT set to '\d>\_'
(none)> USE sampdb;
Database changed
sampdb> USE test;
Database changed
test>
```

The prompt keyword is followed by the prompt definition string. Within the definition, escape sequences that begin with backslashes indicate special prompt options. The \d and _ sequences signify the default database name and a space. (If you set the prompt using the environment variable or the --prompt option, you might find it necessary to double the backslashes when specifying the prompt string.) The following table shows the complete list of available options.

Sequence	Meaning
\c	Current input line number
\d	Default database name, or "(none)" if no database is selected
\D	Full date and time
\h	Current host
\l	Current delimiter (as of MySQL 5.0.25/5.1.12)
\m	Minute
\o	Month number
\O	Month name, three letters
\p	Current port number, socket filename, named-pipe name, or shared-memory name
\P	am or pm indicator for time values
\r	Hour (12-hour time)
\R	Hour (24-hour time)
\s	Second
\S	Semicolon
\t	Tab
\u	Current username, without hostname
\U	Current username, including hostname

Sequence	Meaning
\v	Server version
\w	Weekday name, three letters
\y	Year (two-digit)
\Y	Year (four-digit)
\'	Single quote
\"	Double quote
_	Space character
\	Space character (the sequence is backslash-space)
\\	Literal '\'
\n	Newline (linefeed)
\x	Literal 'x' for any 'x' not otherwise listed

F.6 `mysql.server`

`mysql.server` starts and stops the `mysqld` server by invoking `mysqld_safe`.
`mysql.server` is a shell script and is available on Unix.

  `mysql.server` understands a command-line argument of `start` or `stop`:

```
mysql.server start
mysql.server stop
```

  Normally, `mysql.server` is installed in a run-level directory on Unix systems that use
such directories under `/etc`. (The installed version typically is named `mysql` rather than
`mysql.server`.) The system starts the server by invoking the script with an argument of
`start` at system boot time. The system shuts down the server by invoking the script with
an argument of `stop` at system shutdown time. The script also can be invoked by hand
with the appropriate argument to start or stop the server.

F.6.1 Options Supported by `mysql.server`

Support by `mysql.server` for standard MySQL options is limited. It does not read any
standard options from the command line. Within the `[mysql.server]` group in option
files, it reads `basedir`, `datadir`, and `pid-file` options and passes them to `mysqld_safe`.
As of MySQL 5.0.40/5.1.17, an option of `service-startup-timeout=n` indicates how
long in seconds the script should wait for the server to start. The default value is 900. A
value of 0 means "do not wait" and negative values mean "wait forever."

F.7 `mysql_config`

The `mysql_config` utility is an aid to developing MySQL-based programs written in C. It can be invoked to obtain the proper flags needed to compile C source files or link in MySQL libraries:

```
mysql_config [options]
```

F.7.1 Options Specific to `mysql_config`

- `--cflags`

  Displays the include directory flags needed to access MySQL header files and other C compiler flags that might be necessary.

- `--embedded`, `--embedded-libs`

  These options are synonyms for `--libmysqld-libs`.

- `--include`

  Displays the include directory flags needed to access MySQL header files.

- `--libmysqld-libs`

  Displays the library flags needed to link in `libmysqld`, the embedded server library.

- `--libs`

  Displays the library flags needed to link in the client library.

- `--libs_r`

  Displays the library flags needed to link in the thread-safe client library.

- `--plugindir`

  Displays the default plugin directory. This option was introduced in MySQL 5.1.24/6.0.5.

- `--port`

  Displays the default TCP/IP port number.

- `--socket`

  Displays the default Unix socket file pathname.

- `--version`

  Displays the MySQL version string.

F.8 `mysql_install_db`

The `mysql_install_db` script creates the server's data directory, initializes the `mysql` database that contains the grant tables, and creates an empty `test` database:

```
mysql_install_db [options]
```

`mysql_install_db` populates the grant tables with initial accounts for the `root` and anonymous users. See Chapter 12, "General MySQL Administration," for details on these accounts and how to secure your installation by establishing passwords.

`mysql_install_db` is unavailable on Windows, but unnecessary because Windows distributions include a preinitialized data directory.

F.8.1 Standard Options Supported by `mysql_install_db`

`--help`   `--user`

`--help` is available as of MySQL 5.0.48/5.1.21.

On Unix, the `--user` option runs the server using the login account of the named user. This is useful for making sure that any directories and files created by the server are owned by this user if you run `mysql_install_db` as the Unix `root` user.

F.8.2 Options Specific to `mysql_install_db`

You can use the options mentioned in this section on the command line, and you can set the values for many of them by placing appropriate entries in the `[mysqld]` group of an option file. The script also reads the `[mysql_install_db]` option group, which is useful for options such as `--ldata` and `--force` that are understood only by `mysql_install_db` and not by `mysqld`.

`mysql_install_db` passes any unrecognized options to `mysqld`.

- `--basedir=dir_name`

  The pathname to the MySQL base directory.

- `--datadir=dir_name`, `--ldata=dir_name`

  The pathname to the MySQL data directory.

- `--force`

  Runs even if the current hostname cannot be determined. The IP number of the host will be used to create grant table entries instead, which means that to use client programs, you'll need to specify the IP number rather than the hostname except for connections to `localhost`.

- `--skip-name-resolve`

  Uses only IP numbers in the grant tables rather than hostnames. This option might be necessary if you don't have a working DNS server.

F.9 `mysqladmin`

The `mysqladmin` client communicates with the MySQL server to perform a variety of administrative operations. You can use `mysqladmin` to obtain information from or control the operation of the server, set passwords, and create or drop databases:

```
mysqladmin [options] command ...
```

F.9.1 Standard Options Supported by `mysqladmin`

`--character-sets-dir`	`--host`	`--silent`
`--compress`	`--password`	`--socket`
`--debug`	`--pipe`	`--user`
`--debug-check`	`--port`	`--verbose`
`--debug-info`	`--protocol`	`--version`
`--default-character-set`	`--set-variable`	
`--help`	`--shared-memory-base-name`	

`--debug-info` and `--debug-check` are available as of MySQL 5.1.14 and 5.1.21, respectively.

`--silent` causes `mysqladmin` to exit silently if it cannot connect to the server. The `--verbose` option causes `mysqladmin` to print more information for a few commands. `mysqladmin` also supports the standard SSL options.

F.9.2 Options Specific to `mysqladmin`

- `--count=n, -c n`

  The number of iterations to make when `--sleep` is given. If `--sleep` is given but `--count` is not, `mysqladmin` iterates forever (or until you interrupt it).

- `--force, -f` (*boolean*)

  This option has two effects. First, it causes `mysqladmin` not to ask for confirmation of the `drop db_name` command. Second, when multiple commands are specified on the command line, `mysqladmin` attempts to execute each command even if errors occur. Normally, `mysqladmin` exits after the first error.

- `--no-beep, -b` (*boolean*)

  Suppresses production of beeps when errors occur. This option was introduced in MySQL 5.1.17.

- `--relative, -r` (*boolean*)

  Shows the difference between the current and previous values when used with `--sleep`. Currently, this option works only with the `extended-status` command.

- `--sleep=n, -i n`

  Executes the commands named on the command line repeatedly with a delay of *n* seconds between each repetition.

- `--vertical, -E` (*boolean*)

  This option is like `--relative`, but displays output vertically.

- `--wait[=n], -w[n]`

  The number of times to wait and retry if a connection to the server cannot be established. The default value of *n* is 1 if no value is given. If *n* is specified after `-w`, there must be no intervening space or the value will not be interpreted correctly.

F.9.3 Variables for `mysqladmin`

The following `mysqladmin` variables can be set using the instructions given in Section F..2.1.2, "Setting Program Variables."

- `connect_timeout`

  The number of seconds to wait before timing out when attempting to connect to the server. The default value is 43,200.

- `shutdown_timeout`

  For `shutdown` commands, the number of seconds to wait for a successful shutdown. The default value is 3,600.

F.9.4 `mysqladmin` Commands

Following any options on the command line, you can specify one or more of the following commands. Each command name can be shortened to a prefix, as long as the prefix is unambiguous. For example, `processlist` can be shortened to `process` or `proc`, but not to `p`.

Several of these commands have an equivalent SQL statement, as noted in the descriptions. See Appendix E, "SQL Syntax Reference," for more information about the meaning of these statements.

- `create` *db_name*

  Creates a new database with the given name. This command is like the CREATE DATABASE *db_name* statement.

- `debug`

  Instructs the server to dump debugging information to the error log.

- `drop` *db_name*

  Removes the database with the given name, and any tables that may be in the database. `mysqladmin` asks for confirmation of this command unless the `--force` option was given. This command is like the DROP DATABASE *db_name* statement.

- `extended-status`

  Displays the names and values of the server's status variables. This command is like the SHOW STATUS statement.

- `flush-hosts`

  Flushes the host cache. This command is like the FLUSH HOSTS statement.

- `flush-logs`

  Flushes (closes and reopens) the log files. This command is like the FLUSH LOGS statement.

- `flush-privileges`

  Reloads the grant tables. This command is like the FLUSH PRIVILEGES statement.

- flush-status

  Clears the status variables. (This resets several counters to zero.) This command is like the FLUSH STATUS statement.

- flush-tables

  Flushes the table cache. This command is like the FLUSH TABLES statement.

- flush-threads

  Flushes the thread cache.

- kill *id,id,...*

  Kills the server threads specified by the given identifier numbers. If you specify multiple numbers, the ID list should contain no spaces so that it will not be confused for another command following the kill command. To find out what threads are currently running, use mysqladmin processlist. This command is like issuing a KILL statement for each thread ID.

- old-password *new_password*

  This command is like the password command except that it causes the password to be stored in the password-hashing format used prior to MySQL 4.1.

- password *new_password*

  Changes the password for the account that the server authenticates you as when you connect. (Being able to connect to the server using this account serves as verification that you know the current password.) The password will be set to *new_password*. This command is like the SET PASSWORD statement.

  On Unix, you can use either single quotes or double quotes in the mysqladmin command to quote the password if it contains characters that your command interpreter considers special. On Windows, you should use only double quotes. Windows command interpreters do not recognize single quotes as argument-quoting characters. If you use any single quotes, they become part of your password!

- ping

  Checks whether the MySQL server is running.

- processlist

  Displays a list of the currently executing server activity. This command is like the SHOW PROCESSLIST statement. With the --verbose option, this command is like SHOW FULL PROCESSLIST.

- refresh

  This command flushes the table cache and the grant tables, and closes and reopens the log files. If the server is a replication master server, the command tells it to delete the binary log files listed in the binary log index file and to truncate the index. If the server is a slave server, the command tells it to forget its position in the master binary log.

- reload

  Reloads the grant tables. This command is like the FLUSH PRIVILEGES statement.

- shutdown

  Shuts down the server.

- start-slave

  Starts a replication slave server. This command is like the START SLAVE statement.

- status

  Displays a short status message from the server.

- stop-slave

  Stops a replication slave server. This command is like the STOP SLAVE statement.

- variables

  Displays the names and values of the server's variables. This command is like the SHOW GLOBAL VARIABLES. (There is no support for SHOW SESSION VARIABLES because that wouldn't make any sense.)

- version

  Retrieves and displays the server version information string. This is the same information that is returned by the VERSION() SQL function. (See Appendix C, "Operator and Function Reference.")

F.10 mysqlbinlog

The mysqlbinlog program displays the contents of a binary log file in readable format:

mysqlbinlog [options] file_name ...

By default, mysqlbinlog reads local log files directly without connecting to a server. It is also possible to connect to a server and ask it to send log files over the connection. See the description for the --read-from-remote-server option.

The format of the binary log has changed from time to time. To avoid compatibility problems, you may find it necessary to use a version of mysqlbinlog that is at least as recent as your server version.

mysqlbinlog also can read relay log files created by replication slave servers because the binary and relay logs have the same format.

F.10.1 Standard Options Supported by mysqlbinlog

--character-sets-dir	--help	--protocol
--debug	--host	--socket
--debug-check	--password	--user
--debug-info	--port	--version

--character-sets-dir is available as of MySQL 5.0.3. --debug-check and --debug-info are available as of MySQL 5.1.21.

F.10.2 Options Specific to `mysqlbinlog`

- --base64-output[=*value*]

  Indicates when output should consist of BINLOG statements in base-64-encoded form. This option was introduced in MySQL 5.1.5 as a boolean option. As of 5.1.24, it takes argument values of auto (use base-64 only when necessary), always, or never. The default is auto if the option is not given; if given with no argument, the default is always.

- --database=*db_name*, -d *db_name*

  Extracts statements from the log file only for the named database. This option works only when reading local logs.

- --disable-log-bin, -D (*boolean*)

  Includes statements in the output that disable binary logging of the update statements in the log. This prevents the statements from being logged again when they are re-executed.

- --force-if-open, -F (*boolean*)

  Reads binary log files even if they were not closed properly (or are currently in use). This option was introduced in MySQL 5.1.15.

- --force-read, -f (*boolean*)

  This option controls what mysqlbinlog does when it reads an event from the binary log that it is unable to recognize. By default, it stops. If this option is enabled, mysqlbinlog continues after logging a warning and discarding the event.

- --hexdump, -H (*boolean*)

  Includes a hexadecimal/ASCII event dump in the output. This option was introduced in MySQL 5.0.16.

- --local-load=*dir_name*, -l *dir_name*

  The directory in which to create to create temporary data files for processing LOAD DATA LOCAL statements.

- --offset=*n*, -o *n*

  Skips the first *n* events in the log file.

- --position=*n*, -j *n*

  This option is deprecated in favor of --start-position.

- `--read-from-remote-server, -R` (*boolean*)

  Reads binary log files by making a network connection to a server and asking it to send the logs over the connection. To do this, use the `--read-from-remote-server` option and give the `--host`, `--password`, `--port`, `--protocol`, `--socket`, and `--user` options as necessary to specify connection parameters. Without `--read-from-remote-server`, those options are ignored.

- `--result-file=file_name, -r file_name`

  Writes output to the named file.

- `--server-id=n`

  Dumps only events created by the server with this ID. This option was introduced in MySQL 5.1.4.

- `--set-charset=charset`

  Includes a `SET NAMES` statement in the output. This option was introduced in MySQL 5.0.23/5.1.12.

- `--short-form, -s`

  Shows only the statements that are present in the log; omits any extra information in the log that is associated with the statements and does not show row-based events.

- `--start-datetime=date_time`

  Starts reading binary log events beginning with the first event that has a time at or later than the given `date_time` value. `date_time` should be specified in a legal `DATETIME` format in the time zone local to the host on which you run `mysqlbinlog`. Quote the value if necessary for your command interpreter.

- `--start-position=n`

  Starts reading binary log events at the given position in the first log file named on the command line.

- `--stop-datetime=date_time`

  Stops reading binary log events beginning with the first event that has a time at or later than the given `date_time` value. `date_time` should be specified in a legal `DATETIME` format in the time zone local to the host on which you run `mysqlbinlog`. Quote the value if necessary for your command interpreter.

- `--stop-position=n`

  Stops reading binary log events at the given position in the last log file named on the command line.

- `--to-last-log, -R` (*boolean*)

  When reading log files from a server (which requires the `--read-from-remote-server` option), this option causes binary log files to be read through the last log file of the server, rather than at the end of the last requested log file. `--to-last-log` can be used to make sure that you have obtained all binary log information from the server. (However, if you are sending the events to the same server to be processed, this can lead to an infinite loop.)

F.10.3 Variables for `mysqlbinlog`

The following `mysqlbinlog` variables can be set using the instructions given in Section F.2.1.2, "Setting Program Variables."

- `open_files_limit`

   The number of file descriptors to reserve. The default value is 64.

F.11 `mysqlcheck`

`mysqlcheck` is a client program for checking and repairing tables. It presents a command-line interface to the CHECK TABLE, ANALYZE TABLE, OPTIMIZE TABLE, and REPAIR TABLE statements. It's somewhat similar to `myisamchk`, but is used while the server is running and has some support for non-MyISAM tables. `mysqlcheck` works by sending administrative SQL statements to the server to be executed. This contrasts with `myisamchk`, which operates directly on table files and thus requires either that you coordinate table access with the server or stop the server.

All `mysqlcheck` options are supported for MyISAM tables. `mysqlcheck` also can check and analyze InnoDB tables.

`mysqlcheck` can be run in any of three modes:

```
mysqlcheck [options] db_name [tbl_name] ...
mysqlcheck [options] --databases db_name ...
mysqlcheck [options] --all-databases
```

In the first case, `mysqlcheck` checks the named tables in the given database. If no tables are named, `mysqlcheck` checks all tables in the database. In the second case, all arguments are taken as database names and `mysqlcheck` checks all tables in each one. In the third case, `mysqlcheck` checks all tables in all databases.

F.11.1 Standard Options Supported by `mysqlcheck`

`--character-sets-dir`	`--help`	`--shared-memory-base-name`
`--compress`	`--host`	`--silent`
`--debug`	`--password`	`--socket`
`--debug-check`	`--pipe`	`--user`
`--debug-info`	`--port`	`--verbose`
`--default-character-set`	`--protocol`	`--version`

`--debug-check` and `--debug-info` are available as of MySQL 5.1.21.

`mysqlcheck` also supports the standard SSL options.

F.11.2 Options Specific to `mysqlcheck`

`mysqlcheck` supports the following options to control how it processes tables. Following this list is a description of the equivalences between these options and the SQL statements to which they correspond.

- `--all-databases, -A` (*boolean*)

  Processes all tables in all databases.

- `--analyze, -a`

  Performs table analysis by issuing an ANALYZE TABLE statement. (For example, this analyzes the distribution of key values.) The results of the analysis can help the query optimizer perform index-based lookups and joins more quickly.

- `--all-in-1, -1` (*boolean*)

  Without this option, `mysqlcheck` issues separate statements for each table. This option causes `mysqlcheck` to group tables by database and name all tables within each database in a single statement.

- `--auto-repair` (*boolean*)

  If any tables to be checked are found to have problems, runs a second phase to repair them after the check phase has finished.

- `--check, -c`

  Issues a CHECK TABLE statement to check for errors. This is the default action if no action is specified explicitly.

- `--check-only-changed, -C`

  Checks only tables that have changed since they were last checked or that have not been closed properly.

- `--check-upgrade, -g`

  Checks whether tables are compatible with your currents version of MySQL and is useful after an upgrade. With `--auto-repair`, automatic table repair is attempted if incompatibilities are found. This option was introduced in MySQL 5.0.19/5.1.7.

- `--databases, -B` (*boolean*)

  Interprets all arguments as database names and checks all tables in each database.

- `--extended, -e` (*boolean*)

  Performs an extended table check. If used with `--repair`, uses a more extensive but slower repair method than is used for `--repair` by itself.

- `--fast, -F` (*boolean*)

  Checks only tables that have not been closed properly.

- `--fix-db-names` (*boolean*)

  Checks database names and converts them for name-encoding changes that were made between MySQL 5.0 and 5.1. This option was introduced in MySQL 5.1.7.

- `--fix-table-names` (*boolean*)

  Checks table names and converts them for name-encoding changes that were made between MySQL 5.0 and 5.1. This option was introduced in MySQL 5.1.7.

- `--force, -f` (*boolean*)

  Continues execution even if errors occur.

- `--medium-check, -m`

  Performs table checking using a method that is faster than `--extended` but slightly less thorough. This check mode should be sufficient for most circumstances.

- `--optimize, -o`

  Performs table optimization by issuing an OPTIMIZE TABLE statement.

- `--quick, -q` (*boolean*)

  For table checking, this option skips checking links in the data rows. Used with `--repair`, this option repairs only the index file and leaves the data file untouched. Giving this option twice is no different from giving it once, in contrast to `myisamchk`, which does behave differently when the option is specified twice.

- `--repair, -r`

  Performs table repair by issuing a REPAIR TABLE statement. This repair mode should correct most problems except the occurrence of duplicate values in an index that should contain only unique values.

- `--tables`

  Overrides `--databases` to cause any following arguments to be interpreted as table names.

- `--use-frm` (*boolean*)

  When used with `--repair`, performs a table repair operation that uses the table's .frm file to reinitialize the index file and to determine how to interpret the contents of the data file so that the indexes can be rebuilt. This can be useful if the index has become lost or irrecoverably corrupted. However, it should be treated as a last resort and should be used only if your current version of MySQL is the same as that used to create the table.

- `---write-binlog` (*boolean*)

  Writes ANALYZE TABLE, OPTIMIZE TABLE, and REPAIR TABLE statements to the binary log (which means that they will be sent to replication slaves). This option is enabled by default; use `--skip-write-binlog` to disable it. This option was introduced in MySQL 5.1.18.

The following tables show the relationship between `mysqlcheck`'s options and the SQL statements that it issues.

Table checking options (MyISAM and InnoDB tables only):

Options	Corresponding Statement
--check	CHECK TABLE *tbl_list*
--check-only-changed	CHECK TABLE *tbl_list* CHANGED
--extended	CHECK TABLE *tbl_list* EXTENDED
--fast	CHECK TABLE *tbl_list* FAST
--medium-check	CHECK TABLE *tbl_list* MEDIUM
--quick	CHECK TABLE *tbl_list* QUICK

For InnoDB tables, all options in the preceding table are treated as --check; InnoDB does not support different types of checks.

Table analysis options (MyISAM and InnoDB tables only);

Option	Corresponding Statement
--analyze	ANALYZE TABLE *tbl_list*

Table repair options (MyISAM tables only):

Options	Corresponding Statement
--repair	REPAIR TABLE *tbl_list*
--repair --quick	REPAIR TABLE *tbl_list* QUICK
--repair --extended	REPAIR TABLE *tbl_list* EXTENDED
--repair --use-frm	REPAIR TABLE *tbl_list* USE_FRM

Table optimization options (MyISAM tables only):

Option	Corresponding Statement
--optimize	OPTIMIZE TABLE *tbl_list*

F.12 mysqld

mysqld is the MySQL server. It provides database access to client programs, so it must be running or clients cannot use databases administered by the server. When mysqld starts, it opens network interfaces on which to listen and then waits for client connections. mysqld is multi-threaded and processes each client connection using a separate thread to provide concurrency among clients. Statements that write to the database are executed atomically; when the server begins executing such a statement, it will execute no other statement for the data involved until the current statement has finished. For example, no two clients can modify the same row in a table at the same time.

The usual invocation sequence is simply the server name followed by any desired options:

```
mysqld [options]
```

On Windows, a server can be installed to run as a service. For example, the server might be installed to run automatically at system startup time, or removed as a service as follows:

```
C:\> C:\mysql\bin\mysqld --install
C:\> mysqld --remove
```

The install command uses the full pathname to the server. If the server is installed in a different location, modify the pathname accordingly. The default service name is MySQL. You can provide a service name following the option:

```
C:\> C:\mysql\bin\mysqld --install service_name
C:\> mysqld --remove service_name
```

This enables multiple servers to be run under different service names. With no service_name argument or a service name of MySQL, the server uses MySQL as the service name and reads the [mysqld] group from the standard option files. With a service_name argument different from MySQL, the server uses that name as the service name and reads the [mysqld] and [service_name] groups from the standard option files.

You can also provide a --defaults-file option following the service name to specify an additional file of options for the server to read at startup time:

```
C:\> C:\mysql\bin\mysqld --install service_name --defaults-file=file_name
```

In this case, the service_name argument is not optional.

The preceding remarks about --install apply to --install-manual as well.

F.12.1 Standard Options Supported by mysqld

```
--character-sets-dir      --port                       --user
--debug                   --shared-memory-base-name    --verbose
--help                    --socket
```

The `--help` option by itself displays only a brief usage message. To see the full help message, use this command:

```
% mysqld --verbose --help
```

`mysqld` also supports the standard SSL options.

Note that although `--socket` is supported, the corresponding short form (`-S`) is not. On Windows, `--socket` sets the pipe name if the server supports named-pipe connections.

On Unix, if the `--user` option is given, it specifies the username or numeric user ID of the account to use for running the server. In this case, when the server starts, it looks up the user and group ID values of the account from the password file and then changes its user and group IDs to match. In this way, the server runs with the privileges associated with that user, not `root` privileges. (The server must be started as `root` for the `--user` option to be effective; it will not be able to change its user ID otherwise and a warning is issued.)

F.12.2 Options Specific to `mysqld`

The first list of options here describes general options. It is followed by lists of options specific to Windows, to InnoDB, and to replication.

- `--allow-suspicious-udfs` (*boolean*)

  Enables the server to load older user-defined functions (UDFs) that might define only the symbol corresponding to the function name and not any of the related standard support-routine symbols. This capability is disabled by default as a precaution against loading functions that might not be true UDFs. This option was introduced in MySQL 5.0.3.

- `--ansi, -a`

  Tells the server to use standard SQL behavior for certain types of syntax, rather than MySQL-specific syntax. This option can be used to make the server more standards-compliant.

  This option is equivalent to using the `--sql-mode` option with the `REAL_AS_FLOAT`, `PIPES_AS_CONCAT`, `ANSI_QUOTES`, `IGNORE_SPACE`, and `ONLY_FULL_GROUP_BY` mode values.

- `--basedir=dir_name, -b dir_name`

  The pathname to the MySQL installation directory. Many other pathnames are resolved in relation to this directory if they are given as relative pathnames.

- `--big-tables`

  Enables large result sets to be processed by saving all temporary results to disk rather than by holding them in memory. This avoids most "table full" messages that occur as a result of having insufficient memory to hold large result sets. This option is unnecessary now because the server automatically saves results to disk as required.

- `--bind-address=ip_addr`

  Binds to the given IP number. Normally, `mysqld` binds to the default IP number for the host on which the server is running. This option can be used to select an alternative address to bind to if the host has multiple addresses.

- `--bootstrap`

  This option is used by installation scripts when you first install MySQL.

- `--character-set-client-handshake` (*boolean*)

  Tells the server to use character set information provided by the client. This option is enabled by default; `--skip-character-set-client-handshake` causes the information to be ignored, which is the behavior in MySQL 4.0. This option was introduced in MySQL 5.0.13.

- `--character-set-filesystem=charset`

  Sets the `character_set_filesystem` system variable. This option was introduced in MySQL 5.0.19/5.1.6.

- `--character-set-server=charset, -C charset`

  The default server character set.

- `--chroot=dir_name, -r dir_name`

  Runs the MySQL server anchored to the given directory as its root directory. See the `chroot()` Unix manual page for more information on running in a `chroot()`-ed environment.

- `--collation-server=collation`

  The default server collation.

- `--concurrent-insert` (*boolean*)

  Enables concurrent inserts on MyISAM tables. If a MyISAM table has no holes in the middle, concurrent inserts add new rows at the end of the table while retrievals are being performed on the existing rows. This option is enabled by default. To disallow concurrent inserts, use `--skip-concurrent-insert`.

- `--core-file`

  Causes the server to generate a core file before exiting when a fatal error occurs.

- `--datadir=dir_name, -h dir_name`

  The pathname to the MySQL data directory.

- `--default-character-set=charset`

  This option is deprecated in favor of `--character-set-server`.

- `--default-collation=collation`

  This option is deprecated in favor of `--collation-server`.

- `--default-storage-engine=engine_name`

  The default table storage engine to use. The `engine_name` value should be the name of one of the storage engines that the server supports, such as MyISAM or InnoDB. (The value is not case sensitive.) If this option is not specified, the server uses MyISAM.

- `--default-table-type=engine_name`

  This option is deprecated in favor of `--default-storage-engine`.

- `--default-time-zone=tz_name`

  Sets the server's default time zone to `tz_name`. Time zone values are described in Section 12.10.1, "Configuring Time Zone Support." This option sets the `time_zone` system variable, not `system_time_zone`.

- `--delay-key-write=val`

  Sets the mode used by the server for handling delayed key writes for MyISAM files. `val` can be `ON` (delay key writes on a per-table basis, according to any `DELAY_KEY_WRITE` value specified when tables were created; this is the default), `OFF` (never delay key writes for any MyISAM table), or `ALL` (delay key writes for all MyISAM tables). `OFF` and `ALL` enforce a policy that is applied regardless of how individual tables were defined when they were created.

  It's common to run replication slave servers with `--delay-key-write=ALL` to obtain increased performance for MyISAM tables by delaying key writes no matter how the tables were created originally.

- `--des-key-file=file_name`

  The name of the file that holds DES keys for the `DES_ENCRYPT()` and `DES_DECRYPT()` functions. For a description of the format of this file, see the entry for `DES_ENCRYPT()` in Appendix C.

- `--enable-locking`

  This option is deprecated in favor of `--external-locking`.

- `--enable-pstack` (*boolean*)

  Enables symbolic stack printing when an error occurs.

- `--exit-info[=n], -T[n]`

  Causes the server to produce debugging information when it terminates. If *n* is specified after `-T`, there must be no intervening space or the value will not be interpreted correctly.

- `--external-locking` (*boolean*)

  Enables external locking (filesystem locking) for systems such as Linux, where external locking is off by default.

External locking is problematic because it doesn't work reliably on some systems, and if effective only for operations that just read tables, such as table checking. (See Section 14.1, "Performing Database Maintenance with the Server Running," for more information.)

- `--flush`

Causes the server to flush all tables to disk after each update. This reduces the risk of table corruption in the event of a crash but seriously degrades performance. Thus, it is useful only if you have an unstable system. This option applies only to MyISAM tables.

- `--gdb`

Sets up signal handlers that are useful for debugging with `gdb`.

- `--general-log` (*boolean*)

Enables the general log for the logging destinations selected by the `--log-output` option, or disables the log if given as `--skip-general-log`. This option was introduced in MySQL 5.1.12.

- `--init-connect=`*str*

Statements to be executed for each client when the client connects. The value should be one or more SQL statements, separated by semicolons. The statements are executed only for clients that do not have the SUPER privilege.

- `--init-file=`*file_name*

The name of a file of SQL statements to be executed at startup time. A relative filename is interpreted starting at the data directory. The file should contain one statement per line.

- `--isam` (*boolean*)

This option is obsolete because the ISAM storage engine was removed in MySQL 5.0. The option itself was removed in 5.1.14.

- `--language=`*lang_name*, `-L` *lang_name*

Displays error messages to clients in the specified language. *lang_name* is a value such as `english` or `german`, or the full pathname to the directory containing the language files.

- `--large-pages` (*boolean*)

Enables support for large memory pages. This option does not appear unless MySQL was compiled to allow this feature. This option was introduced in MySQL 5.0.3.

- `--lc-time-names=`*locale_name*

The locale for the `lc_time_names` system variable. This option was introduced in MySQL 5.0.42/5.1.18.

- **--local-infile** (*boolean*)

  Enables or disables LOAD DATA LOCAL. Invoke the server with --local-infile or --disable-local-infile to enable or disable LOCAL on the server side.

- **--log[=*file_name*], -l[*file_name*]**

  The general log contains information about client connections and SQL statements. As of MySQL 5.1.6, this option enables the general query log for the logging destinations selected by the --log-output option and optionally specifies a filename for file logging. Before 5.1.6, this option enables logging to a file. If *file_name* is not given, the log filename is HOSTNAME.log in the data directory, where HOSTNAME is the name of the server host. If *file_name* is given as a relative path, it is interpreted starting at the data directory. If *file_name* is specified after -l, there must be no intervening space or the value will not be interpreted correctly.

- **--log-bin[=*file_name*]**

  Enables the binary log. *file_name* specifies the basename for the binary log files. If not given, the log filename is HOSTNAME-bin.nnnnnn in the data directory, where HOSTNAME is the name of the server host and nnnnnn is a sequence number that the server increments by one each time it opens a new log file. If *file_name* is given as a relative path, it is interpreted starting at the data directory.

- **--log-bin-index=*file_name***

  Enables the binary log index file. If *file_name* is not given, the default name is the same as the basename of the binary log files, with an .index extension. If *file_name* is given as a relative path, it is interpreted starting at the data directory.

- **--log-error[=*file_name*]**

  The error log filename. If *file_name* is not given, the log filename is HOSTNAME.err in the data directory, where HOSTNAME is the name of the server host. If *file_name* is given as a relative path, it is interpreted starting at the data directory. If *file_name* is given as a name that has no extension, mysqld adds an extension of .err.

- **--log-isam[=*file_name*]**

  Enables index file logging. This is used only for debugging MyISAM operations. If you specify no name, the default is myisam.log in the data directory.

- **--log-long-format**

  Writes additional information to the binary log and slow-query log if those logs are enabled. This option is deprecated. Extra information is now the default for logging, which you can disable with the --log-short-format option.

- **--log-output[=*destinations*]**

  This option selects which output destinations to use for the general query log and slow-query log, if those logs are enabled. *destinations* is a list of comma-separated destination names. Allowable destinations are TABLE, FILE, and NONE.

If present, NONE disables logging and takes precedence over any other values. If this option is omitted or is given without a value, the default value is FILE (TABLE from MySQL 5.1.6 through 5.1.20).

--log[=*file_name*] enables the general query log for the selected output destinations and optionally specifies a filename for file logging. The --general-log or --skip-general-log option enables or disables the general query log without specifying a filename. The --log-slow-queries, --slow-query-log, and --skip-slow-query-log options have similar effects for the slow-query log.

The general_log or slow_query_log system variable can be set at runtime to enable or disable the respective log. The general_log_file or slow_query_log_file system variable can be set at runtime to change the name of the respective log file.

This option was introduced in MySQL 5.1.6. Before that, the destination is always logging to a file.

- --log-queries-not-using-indexes (*boolean*)

If the slow-query log is enabled, this option enables logging of queries to that log that do not use indexes.

- --log-short-format (*boolean*)

Writes less information to the binary log and slow-query log if those logs are enabled.

- --log-slow-admin-statements (*boolean*)

Administrative operations such as those performed by ALTER TABLE or OPTIMIZE TABLE might be slow, but by default are not logged to the slow-query logs. This option causes them to be logged if they are slow. It was introduced in MySQL 5.0.8.

- --log-slow-queries[=*file_name*]

As of MySQL 5.1.6, this option enables the slow-query log for the logging destinations selected by the --log-output option and optionally specifies a filename for file logging. Before 5.1.6, this option enables logging to a file. If no file is named, the default name is *HOSTNAME*-slow.log in the data directory, where *HOSTNAME* is the name of the server host. If *file_name* is given as a relative path, it is interpreted starting at the data directory.

- --log-tc=*file_name*

The pathname to the transaction coordinator log file (for XA transactions). This option is unused. It was introduced in MySQL 5.0.3.

- --log-tc-size=*n*

The size of the transaction coordinator log file. This option was introduced in MySQL 5.0.3.

- `--log-update[=file_name]`

  Turns on logging to the update log file. This option is deprecated; the update log was removed in MySQL 5.0, so `--log-update` enables the binary log if you haven't also given the `--log-bin` option.

- `--log-warnings[=n]`, `-W[n]`

  Writes certain non-critical warning messages to the error log. This option is on by default. You can give the option without a value to enable warnings, or with a value 0 or 1 to disable or enable warnings. You can give the option without a value twice or specify it with a value of 2 to enable logging of aborted connections or (as of MySQL 5.2.6) access-denied errors. If *n* is specified after `-W`, there must be no intervening space or the value will not be interpreted correctly.

- `--low-priority-updates` (*boolean*)

  Gives updates lower priority than retrievals.

- `--memlock` (*boolean*)

  Locks the server in memory if possible. This option is effective only systems such as Solaris that can lock processes in memory, and only if the server is run as `root`.

- `--myisam-recover[=level]`

  Enables automatic table repair for MyISAM tables. When the server opens a MyISAM table, it does a repair if the table is marked as crashed or was not closed properly when last used. *level* can be empty to disable recovery or a comma-separated list of one or more of the following values: BACKUP (create a backup of the table if the repair will change it), FORCE (force recovery even if more than a row of data will be lost), QUICK (quick recovery), or DEFAULT (recover without any of the other special handling; this is the same as specifying the option with no argument at all).

  It's a good idea to use this option if you run the server with the `--delay-key-write` option or have MyISAM tables configured to enable delayed index writes.

- `--ndbcluster` (*boolean*)

  Enables the NDBCLUSTER storage engine. If NDBCLUSTER is compiled in, it is enabled by default. If you don't use NDBCLUSTER tables, you can use `--skip-ndbcluster` to disable NDBCLUSTER, which saves memory.

- `--new`, `-n`

  This option was used in MySQL 4.0 to causes the server to use certain 4.1 behaviors. It is now unused.

- `--old` (*boolean*)

  Set the `old` system variable, which enables older behavior for some features. This option was introduced in MySQL 5.1.18.

- --old-passwords

  As of MySQL 4.1, the server supports a more secure password encryption method than previously. Existing accounts that have passwords encrypted the old way are still supported, but new passwords are encrypted using the new method. The --old-passwords option forces the old method to be used even when assigning new passwords. (This can be useful if you want to be able to downgrade the server or move the accounts to an older server.)

- --old-style-user-limits (*boolean*)

  MySQL accounts can have limits placed on their activities, as described in Section 12.3.1.5, "Limiting an Account's Resource Consumption." Before MySQL 5.0.3, limits were assessed separately per host from which the account connected if the account could be used to connect to the server from different hosts. As of 5.0.3, limits for an account are assessed ignoring which particular host the account connected from, but --old-style-user-limits can be used to enable the old method of assessing limits.

- --one-thread

  Causes the server to run using a single thread. This is used for debugging under Linux, which normally uses three threads at a minimum. This option is deprecated in favor of --thread_handling=one-thread as of MySQL 5.1.17.

- --pid-file=*file_name*

  When mysqld starts, it writes its process ID (PID) into a file. This option specifies the pathname of the PID file. The file may be used by other processes to determine the server's process number, typically for purposes of sending a signal to it. For example, mysql.server reads the file when it sends a signal to the server to shut down. If *file_name* is given as a relative path, it is interpreted starting at the data directory. This option has no effect for the embedded server.

- --safe-mode

  This option is like --skip-new, but disables even more things. You can try it if MySQL appears to be unstable or if complex statements seem to yield incorrect results.

- --safe-show-database (*boolean*)

  This option is obsolete. MySQL administrators should use the SHOW DATABASES privilege to manage access to database names.

- --safe-user-create (*boolean*)

  Disallows account creation by users who do not have INSERT access to the user grant table.

- `--safemalloc-mem-limit=n`

Simulates a memory shortage. The value represents the limit on the amount of memory available for allocation. This option can be used only if the server was built with the `--with-debug=full` option at configuration time.

- `--secure-auth` (*boolean*)

Prevents clients from connecting unless they use the more secure password format introduced in MySQL 4.1.

- `--secure-file-priv=dir_name`

Sets the `secure_file_priv` system variable, which restricts some file operations to the named directory. This option was introduced in MySQL 5.0.38/5.1.17.

- `--skip-grant-tables` (*boolean*)

Disables use of the grant tables for verifying client connections. This gives any client full access to do anything. It also disables the CREATE USER, DROP USER, RENAME USER, GRANT, REVOKE, and SET PASSWORD statements. You can tell the server to begin using the grant tables again by issuing a FLUSH PRIVILEGES statement or a `mysqladmin flush-privileges` command, or by restarting it without `--skip-grant-tables`.

- `--skip-host-cache`

Disables use of the hostname cache.

- `--skip-locking`

This option is deprecated in favor of `--skip-external-locking`. See the description for `--external-locking`.

- `--skip-name-resolve`

Suppresses hostname resolution. If this option is specified, the grant tables must specify hosts by IP number or as `localhost`.

- `--skip-networking`

This option disables TCP/IP connections. Only local clients can connect, and must do so using a non–TCP/IP interface. Unix clients can connect using a Unix socket file. Windows clients can connect using shared memory or a named pipe.

- `--skip-new`

Skips the use of new, possibly unsafe routines.

- `--skip-safemalloc`

Skips memory allocation checking. This option can be used only if the server was built with the `--with-debug=full` option at configuration time.

- `--skip-show-database`

By default, the SHOW DATABASES statement can be issued by any user. It displays all databases if the user has the SHOW DATABASES privilege, or those databases for which the user has some privilege otherwise. With the `--skip-show-database` option, the SHOW DATABASES statement can be used only by users who have the SHOW DATABASES privilege, in which case it displays all databases.

- `--skip-stack-trace`

Skips stack-trace printing when failure occurs.

- `--skip-symlink`

This option is deprecated in favor of `--skip-symbolic-links`. See the description for `--symbolic-links`.

- `--skip-thread-priority`

Normally, updates (statements that modify tables) run at a higher priority than statements that retrieve data. If that is undesirable, this option causes the server not to give different priorities to different types of statements.

- `--slow-query-log` (*boolean*)

Enables the slow-query log for the logging destinations selected by the `--log-output` option, or disables the log if given as `--skip-slow-query-log`. This option was introduced in MySQL 5.1.12.

- `--sql-bin-update-same` (*boolean*)

Yokes together `sql_log_bin` and `sql_log_update` so that setting one (with the SET statement) sets the other as well. This option is obsolete as of MySQL 5.0, when the update log no longer exists. The binary log should be used instead.

- `--sql-mode=mode_list`

This option modifies certain aspects of the server's behavior to cause it to act according to standard SQL, or to be compatible with other database servers or older MySQL servers. `mode_list` should be a comma-separated list of one or more mode values, or an empty string to clear the mode. The allowable mode values are given in the description of the `sql_mode` system variable in Appendix D, "System, Status, and User Variable Reference."

- `--symbolic-links` (*boolean*)

For Unix, this option enables symbolic linking for MyISAM table data and index files (using the DATA DIRECTORY and INDEX DIRECTORY table creation options). For Windows, it enables symbolic linking of database directories. These techniques are discussed in Chapter 11, "The MySQL Data Directory." Database symlinking support on Windows is enabled by default; use `--skip-symbolic-links` to disable it.

- `--sync-frm` (*boolean*)

Tells the server to synchronize each `.frm` file to disk when it is created. This option is enabled by default; use `--skip-sync-frm` to disable it.

- `--sysdate-is-now` (*boolean*)

As of MySQL 5.0.13, SYSDATE() returns the date and time at which it is invoked, whereas NOW() returns the time at which the statement began executing.

`--sysdate-is-now` causes `SYSDATE()` to behave like `NOW()`. This option was introduced in MySQL 5.0.20.

- `--tc-heuristic-recover=`*str*

  The strategy for recovering from crashed two-phase commits. The value can be `COMMIT` or `ROLLBACK`. This option is unused. It was introduced in MySQL 5.0.3.

- `--temp-pool` (*boolean*)

  With this option, the server uses a small set of names for temporary files, rather than creating a unique name for each file. This avoids some caching problems on Linux. This option is enabled by default; use `--skip-temp-pool` to disable it.

- `--timed_mutexes` (*boolean*)

  Causes the server to collect InnoDB mutex timing information. This option was introduced in MySQL 5.0.3.

- `--transaction-isolation=`*level*

  Sets the default transaction isolation level. The allowable *level* values are `READ-UNCOMMITTED`, `READ-COMMITTED`, `REPEATABLE-READ`, and `SERIALIZABLE`.

- `--tmpdir=`*dir_name*, `-t` *dir_name*

  The pathname of the directory to use for temporary files. The option value can be given as a list of directories, to be used in round-robin fashion. Under Unix, separate directory names by colons; under Windows or NetWare, separate them by semicolons.

- `--warnings[=`*n*`]`

  This option is deprecated in favor of `--log-warnings`.

F.12.2.1 Windows Options

The options in this section are available only for servers running under Windows. Service names and named-pipe names are not case sensitive. Shared-memory names are case sensitive.

- `--console` (*boolean*)

  Displays a console window for error messages.

- `--enable-named-pipe` (*boolean*)

  For MySQL servers that include named-pipe support, named-pipe connections are disabled by default. This option enables named-pipe connections. The default pipe name is `MySQL`. The name can be changed with the `--socket` option.

  Enabling named pipes may cause problems at server shutdown time. Test your system to make sure that this option works properly for you.

- `--install [`*service_name*`]`

  Installs the server as a service that runs automatically when Windows starts. If *service_name* is not given, the default service is named `MySQL`.

- `--install-manual [`*`service_name`*`]`

  Installs the server as a service that does not run automatically when Windows starts. You must explicitly start the service yourself. If *service_name* is not given, the default service is named `MySQL`.

- `--remove [`*`service_name`*`]`

  Removes the server as a service. If *service_name* is not given, the default service is named `MySQL`.

- `--shared-memory` (*boolean*)

  Enables support for shared-memory connections. The default shared-memory name is `MYSQL`. The name can be changed with the `--shared-memory-base-name` option.

- `--standalone`

  Runs the server as a standalone program rather than as a service.

F.12.2.2 InnoDB Options

The options in this section are specific to the InnoDB storage engine.

- `--innodb` (*boolean*)

  Enables the InnoDB storage engine. If InnoDB is compiled in, it is enabled by default. If you don't use InnoDB tables, you can use `--skip-innodb` to disable InnoDB, which saves memory.

- `--innodb_autoextend_increment=`*`size`*

  If the InnoDB shared tablespace is configured to be auto-extending, this option controls the increment size for extending it. The value is specified in megabytes. The default value is 8MB.

- `--innodb_data_file_path=`*`filespec_list`*

  The specifications for the InnoDB tablespace component files. The format of the option value is discussed in Section 12.6.3.1, "Configuring the InnoDB Tablespace."

- `--innodb_data_home_dir=`*`dir_name`*

  The pathname to the directory under which the InnoDB tablespace components are located.

- `--innodb_fast_shutdown` (*boolean*)

  Speeds up the server shutdown process; the InnoDB storage engine skips some of the operations that it performs normally.

- `--innodb_file_per_table` (*boolean*)

  If this option is enabled, InnoDB creates new tables with individual tablespace files. That is, each InnoDB table has an `.ibd` tablespace file located in its database directory. The shared tablespace is used only for the InnoDB data dictionary entry, not for data or index storage. The option is disabled by default.

- `--innodb_flush_log_at_trx_commit=n`

  This option has a value of 1 by default, which causes InnoDB log flushing when transactions are committed so that ACID properties are guaranteed. Setting the option to 0 reduces the amount of flushing to disk that InnoDB performs. However, this comes at a somewhat increased potential for losing a few of the most recent committed transactions if a crash occurs. The following table shows the possible values.

Value	Meaning
0	Write to log once per second and flush to disk
1	Write to log at each commit and flush to disk
2	Write to log at each commit, but flush to disk only once per second

- `--innodb_log_arch_dir=dir_name`

  This option is unused, and was removed in MySQL 5.1.21.

- `--innodb_log_archive=n`

  This option is unused.

- `--innodb_log_group_home_dir=dir_name`

  The pathname to the directory where the InnoDB storage engine should write its log files.

- `--innodb_max_dirty_pages_pct=n`

  The percentage of dirty pages that InnoDB allows in its buffer pool before it considers it necessary to flush the log to disk. Allowable values are from 0 to 100; the default is 90.

- `--innodb_safe_binlog`

  Following crash recovery by InnoDB, truncates the binary log to the last statement or transaction that was not rolled back.

- `--innodb_status_file` (*boolean*)

  Writes SHOW INNODB STATUS information to a file named innodb_status.*nnnnnn* in the data directory periodically. *nnnnnn* is the server process ID number. These status files are not removed except for clean shutdown. Periodically, you should remove those that no longer are needed.

F.12.2.3 Replication Options

The options in this section pertain to MySQL's replication capabilities.

Several replication options with names of the form `--master-xxx` are not described here. These were used on slave servers for specifying parameters for connecting to the master, but became deprecated as of MySQL 5.1 and were removed in 5.2. Instead, specify the parameters using the CHANGE MASTER statement.

The `--report-xxx` and `--show-slave-auth-info` options affect the output of SHOW SLAVE HOSTS on the master, as described in Appendix E.

- `--abort-slave-event-count=n`

  This option is used by the MySQL test suite for replication testing.

- `--binlog-do-db=db_name`

  Tells a replication master to log updates only for the named database. No other databases will be replicated. To log updates for multiple databases, repeat the option once for each database.

- `--binlog-ignore-db=db_name`

  Tells a replication master not to log updates for the named database. To ignore updates for multiple databases, repeat the option once for each database.

  Note that use of this option causes the binary log to contain no information that could be used for recovery of the named database if a crash occurs. To avoid this problem, use `--replicate-ignore-db` on the slave server instead.

- `--disconnect-slave-event-count=n`

  This option is used by the MySQL test suite for replication testing.

- `--init-rpl-role=val`

  Indicates the initial replication role; `val` can be master or slave. This option is used by the MySQL test suite for replication testing.

- `--init-slave=str`

  For a master replication server, this option specifies statements to be executed for each slave replication server when the slave connects. The value should be one or more SQL statements, separated by semicolons.

- `--log-slave-updates` (*boolean*)

  This option causes a replication slave to log updates that it receives from the master server to its own binary log. It's necessary to do this if the slave acts as a master to another server (that is, if you chain slave servers).

- `--master-info-file=file_name`

  For a replication slave, the name of the file that stores information about the current replication state. The contents of this file are the replication coordinates (master binary log filename and position), master host, username, password, port number, connection retry interval, and SSL option values. The default name for this file is `master.info` in the data directory. If `file_name` is given as a relative path, it is interpreted starting at the data directory.

- `--master-retry-count=n`

For a replication slave, the number of times to attempt a connection to a master server before giving up.

- `--max-binlog-dump-events=n`

This option is used by the MySQL test suite for replication testing.

- `--relay-log=file_name`

For a replication slave, this option specifies the basename of the relay log files. (The slave I/O thread stores updates read from the master in the relay log, and the SQL thread reads the relay log for statements and executes them.) By default, relay log filenames are `HOSTNAME-relay-bin.nnnnnn` in the data directory, where `HOSTNAME` is the name of the server host and `nnnnnn` is a sequence number that the server increments by one each time it opens a new log file.

- `--relay-log-index=file_name`

For a replication slave, the name of the relay log index file. The default name is `HOSTNAME-relay-bin.index` in the data directory, where `HOSTNAME` is the name of the server host. If `file_name` is given as a relative path, it is interpreted starting at the data directory.

- `--relay-log-info-file=file_name`

For a replication slave, the name of the relay log information file. The default name is `relay-log.info` in the data directory.

- `--replicate-do-db=db_name`

Tells a replication slave to replicate only the named database. To restrict replication to a set of databases, repeat the option once for each database.

- `--replicate-do-table=db_name.tbl_name`

Tells a replication slave to replicate only the given table, which should be named in `db_name.tbl_name` format. To restrict replication to a set of tables, repeat the option once for each table.

- `--replicate-ignore-db=db_name`

Tells a replication slave not to replicate the named database. To ignore multiple databases, repeat the option once for each database.

- `--replicate-ignore-table=db_name.tbl_name`

Tells a replication slave not to replicate the named table. To ignore multiple tables, repeat the option once for each table.

- `--replicate-rewrite-db=master_db->slave_db`

  Tells a replication slave to treat one database as another. Updates made to the original database *master_db* on the master server are replicated as updates to the database *slave_db* on the slave server. The rewrite applies only when *master_db* is the default database and only to statements that operate on tables in that database. When given on the command line, the option value should be enclosed within quotes to prevent the command interpreter from treating the '>' character as an output redirection operator. This option can be given multiple times. The server tries them in order and uses the first rule for which the *master_db* value matches.

  This option is applied before actions specified by other `--replicate-xxx` options are tested, so if you use it, those options should use *slave_db* as the database name.

- `--replicate-same-server-id` (*boolean*)

  If this option is enabled, the server will not skip replication events that contain its own server ID. This option is disabled by default to prevent replication loops, but can be enabled in certain special circumstances.

- `--replicate-wild-do-table=pattern`

  Tells a replication slave to replicate only tables with names that match the given pattern. To restrict replication to a set of patterns, repeat the option once for each pattern.

- `--replicate-wild-ignore-table=pattern`

  Tells a replication slave not to replicate tables with names that match the given pattern. To ignore multiple patterns, repeat the option once for each pattern.

- `--report-host=host_name`

  Reports to the master server that the slave server host is *host_name*.

- `--report-password=pass_val`

  Reports to the master server that the slave server account password is *pass_val*.

- `--report-port=port_num`

  Reports to the master server that the slave server port is *port_num*.

- `--report-user=user_name`

  Reports to the master server that the slave server account name is *user_name*.

- `--rpl-recovery-rank=n`

  This option is not used.

- `--server-id=n`

  The replication server ID value. The value must be in the range from 1 to $2^{32}-1$ and it must be unique among communicating replication servers.

- `--show-slave-auth-info` (*boolean*)

  Causes a master server to display slave server usernames and passwords in the output of the SHOW SLAVE HOSTS statement.

- `--skip-slave-start`

  Causes the server not to start the slave threads automatically. They must be started manually by issuing a START SLAVE statement.

- `--slave-allow-batching` (*boolean*)

  Sets the `slave_allow_batching` system variable. This option was introduced in MySQL 5.2.5.

- `--slave-load-tmpdir=dir_name`

  The pathname to the directory used by a slave server for processing LOAD DATA statements. If this option is not specified, it defaults to the value of `--tmpdir`.

- `--slave-skip-errors=error_list`

  The list of errors that a slave server should ignore rather than suspending replication if they occur. (However, it's usually better to determine what is causing problems so that you can resolve them rather than using this option to ignore them.) A value of `all` means all errors should be ignored. Otherwise, the value should be a list of one or more error numbers separated by commas.

- `--sporadic-binlog-dump-fail` (*boolean*)

  This option is used by the MySQL test suite for replication testing.

F.12.3 Variables for `mysqld`

To see the full help message that displays the system variable values that `mysqld` will use by default, use this command:

```
% mysqld --verbose --help
```

To see what system variable values the currently executing `mysqld` is using, use this command:

```
% mysqladmin variables
```

You can also check the current system variable values by issuing a SHOW VARIABLES statement. Individual system variables are described in Appendix D. System variable values can be set at startup time using the instructions given in Section F.2.1.2, "Setting Program Variables." In addition, many system variables can be modified dynamically; for more information, see Section 12.5.1, "Setting and Checking System Variable Values," and the entry for the SET statement in Appendix E.

F.13 `mysqld_multi`

The `mysqld_multi` script makes it easier to run several `mysqld` servers on a single host. It enables you to start or stop servers, or determine whether they are running:

```
mysqld_multi [options] command server_list
```

command is one of `start`, `stop`, or `report`. The *server_list* argument indicates which servers you want to manipulate. For further instructions on using `mysqld_multi`, see Section 12.11.4, "Using `mysqld_multi` for Server Management."

F.13.1 Standard Options Supported by `mysqld_multi`

```
--help        --silent       --verbose
--password    --user         --version
```

`--silent` and `--verbose` are available as of MySQL 5.0.2.

`mysqld_multi` passes the `--user` and `--password` option values to `mysqladmin` when it needs to stop servers or determine whether they are running.

F.13.2 Options Specific to `mysqld_multi`

- `--config-file=file_name`

  As of MySQL 5.0.42/5.1.18, this option is deprecated; use the standard `--defaults-extra-file` option instead. For earlier versions, this option names the option file from which to read to obtain options for the servers that `mysqld_multi` manipulates; without `--config-file`, `mysqld_multi` reads `/etc/my.cnf` and the `.my.cnf` file in your home directory to obtain server options. (`mysqld_multi` reads the standard option files for its own options. This option does not change that behavior.)

- `--example`

  Displays a sample option file that demonstrates option file groups suitable for use with `mysqld_multi`.

- `--log=file_name`

  The name of the log file where `mysqld_multi` should log its actions. Output is appended to the log if it already exists. The default log file is named `mysqld_multi.log` in the data directory. To disable logging, use `--no-log`.

- `--mysqladmin=file_name`

  The pathname to the `mysqladmin` binary you want to use. This can be useful if `mysqld_multi` cannot find `mysqladmin` by itself, or if you want to use a particular version.

- `--mysqld=file_name`

  The pathname to the `mysqld` binary you want to use. This can be useful if `mysqld_multi` cannot find `mysqld` by itself, or if you want to use a particular version. It is allowable to specify a pathname to `mysqld` or `mysqld_safe` as the value of this option.

- `--no-log`

  Displays log output rather than writing it to a log file. If you want to see output on the screen, you must use this option, because the default is to log to a file.

- `--tcp-ip`

  By default, `mysqld_multi` attempts to connect to a server using a Unix socket file. This option causes the connection attempt to use TCP/IP instead. It can be useful when a server is running but its socket file has been removed, in which case the server will be accessible only via TCP/IP.

F.14 `mysqld_safe`

`mysqld_safe` starts the `mysqld` server and monitors it:

`mysqld_safe [options]`

If the server dies, `mysqld_safe` restarts it. `mysqld_safe` is a shell script and is available on Unix. There is also a compiled version that can be used on NetWare.

F.14.1 Standard Options Supported by `mysqld_safe`

`--help`

`--help` is available as of MySQL 5.0.3.

F.14.2 Options Specific to `mysqld_safe`

Options that may be used with `mysqld` may also be used with `mysqld_safe`, which simply passes them to `mysqld`. In addition, `mysqld_safe` understands the following options of its own:

- `--basedir=dir_name`

  The pathname to the MySQL base directory.

- `--core-file-size=n`

  Limits the size of core files to n bytes if the server crashes.

- `--datadir=dir_name`

  The pathname to the MySQL data directory.

- `--err-log=file_name`

  This is the old form of the `--log-error` option.

- --ledir=*dir_name*

The directory in which to look for the server. (It's taken to be the location of the "libexec" directory.)

- --log-error=*file_name*

The file to use for the error log. Relative names are interpreted with respect to the directory from which mysqld_safe was invoked. If this option is not specified, the default error log is *HOSTNAME*.err in the data directory, where *HOSTNAME* is the name of the current host.

- --mysqld=*file_name*

The path to the mysqld program.

- --mysqld-version=*suffix*

The value of this option is a suffix string. If the option is given, the suffix is added to the basename mysqld, with a dash in between, to produce the name of the server that mysqld_safe should start.

- --open-files=*n*, --open-files-limit=*n*

The number of file descriptors that mysqld should reserve.

- --pid-file=*file_name*

The name of the mysqld process ID file.

- --port=*port_num*

The port number on which the server should listen for TCP/IP connections.

- --port-open-timeout=*n*

How long in seconds the server should wait for its TCP/IP port to become available at startup. The default is 0 (no wait). This option was introduced in MySQL 5.0.19/5.1.5.

- --skip-kill-mysqld

Do not try to kill any currently running mysqld process before starting a new one. This can be useful if you are running multiple instances of a given mysqld binary. If is effective only on Linux.

- --skip-syslog

Specifies that error output should not be sent to syslog; a log file is used instead. The default is to use a log file. This option was introduced in MySQL 5.1.20.

- --socket=*file_name*

The pathname of the Unix socket file.

- --syslog

Specifies that error output should be sent to syslog, for systems that have the logger program. This option was introduced in MySQL 5.1.20.

- `--syslog-tag=tag`

  When error output is sent to `syslog`, messages from `mysqld_safe` and `mysqld` are tagged with the program name as a prefix. The `--syslog-tag` option modifies the prefix to be `mysqld_safe-tag` and `mysqld-tag`, respectively. This option was introduced in MySQL 5.1.21.

- `--timezone=tz_name`

  Sets the server system time zone to `tz_name`. This might be useful if the server doesn't determine the system time zone automatically.

- `--user=user_name`, `--user=uid`

  The username or numeric user ID of the account to use for running the server.

F.15 `mysqldump`

The `mysqldump` program writes the contents of database tables into text files. These files can be used for a variety of purposes, such as database backups, moving databases to another server, or setting up a test database based on the contents of an existing database.

By default, output for each dumped table consists of a `CREATE TABLE` statement that creates the table, followed by a set of `INSERT` statements that load the contents of the table. If the `--tab` option is given, the table contents are written to a data file as tab-separated values, one line per row, and the table-creation SQL statement is written to a separate file.

`mysqldump` can be run in any of three modes:

```
mysqldump [options] db_name [tbl_name] ...
mysqldump [options] --databases db_name ...
mysqldump [options] --all-databases
```

In the first case, `mysqldump` dumps the named tables in the given database. If no tables are named, `mysqldump` dumps all tables in the database. In the second case, all arguments are taken as database names and `mysqldump` dumps all tables in each one. In the third case, `mysqldump` dumps all tables in all databases. If `--databases` or `--all-databases` is used, the output contains `CREATE DATABASE IF EXISTS` and `USE` statements preceding the statements for the tables in each database.

One common way to use `mysqldump` is as follows:

```
% mysqldump db_name > backup_file
```

The backup file should be imported back into MySQL with `mysql` rather than with `mysqlimport`:

```
% mysql db_name < backup_file
```

`mysqldump` ignores and does not dump the `INFORMATION_SCHEMA` database, even if you name it explicitly on the command line.

F.15.1 Standard Options Supported by `mysqldump`

`--character-sets-dir`	`--password`	`--socket`
`--compress`	`--pipe`	`--user`
`--debug`	`--port`	`--verbose`
`--default-character-set`	`--protocol`	`--version`
`--help`	`--set-variable`	
`--debug-check`	`--host`	
`--debug-info`	`--shared-memory-base-name`	

`--debug-info` and `--debug-check` are available as of MySQL 5.0.32/5.1.14 and 5.1.21, respectively.

mysqldump also supports the standard SSL options.

F.15.2 Options Specific to `mysqldump`

The following options control how mysqldump operates. Section F.15.3, "Data Format Options for mysqldump," describes options that may be used in conjunction with the `--tab` option to indicate the format of data files.

- `--add-drop-database` (*boolean*)

  Adds a DROP DATABASE IF EXISTS statement before each CREATE DATABASE statement. This option was introduced in MySQL 5.0.7.

- `--add-drop-table` (*boolean*)

  Adds a DROP TABLE IF EXISTS statement before each CREATE TABLE statement.

- `--add-locks` (*boolean*)

  Adds LOCK TABLE and UNLOCK TABLE statements around the set of INSERT statements for each table.

- `--all, -a` (*boolean*)

  This option is deprecated in favor of `--create-options`.

- `--all-databases, -A` (*boolean*)

  Dumps all tables in all databases. This option also causes the dump output to include CREATE DATABASE IF NOT EXISTS and USE statements for each database.

- `--all-tablespaces, -Y` (*boolean*)

  Dumps all tablespaces. This option was introduced in MySQL 5.1.6.

- `--allow-keywords` (*boolean*)

  Allows for the creation of column names that are keywords.

- `--apply-slave-statements` (*boolean*)

  This option is used in conjunction with `--dump-slave`. It causes the dump output to include STOP SLAVE before the CHANGE MASTER statement and START SLAVE at the end. This option was introduced in MySQL 6.0.4.

- --comments, -i (*boolean*)

  Includes additional informational comments in the output, such as the `mysqldump` version, which tables each set of `INSERT` statements applies to, and so forth. This open is enabled by default; disable it with `--skip-comments`.

- --compact (*boolean*)

  Generates more concise output that does not include comments, including version-specific comments that set system variables. This option also enables the `--skip-add-drop-table`, `--skip-set-charset`, `--skip-disable-keys`, and `--skip-add-locks` options.

- --compatible=*mode*

  This option causes `mysqldump` to modify its output to be compatible with standard SQL, other database servers, or older versions of MySQL server. The *mode* value specifies a compatibility mode. It can be given using one or more of the following values as a comma-separated list.

Option	Compatibility Meaning
ANSI	ANSI-compatible
DB2	Compatible with DB2
MAXDB	Compatible with MaxDB
MSSQL	Compatible with MS SQL Server
MYSQL323	Compatible with MySQL 3.23
MYSQL40	Compatible with MySQL 4.0
ORACLE	Compatible with Oracle
POSTRESQL	Compatible with PostgreSQL
NO_FIELD_OPTIONS	Suppress MySQL-specific column-related options
NO_KEY_OPTIONS	Suppress MySQL-specific index-related options
NO_TABLE_OPTIONS	Suppress MySQL-specific table-related options

  This option has no effect if you connect with `mysqldump` to a server older than MySQL 4.1.0.

- --complete-insert, -c (*boolean*)

  Writes `INSERT` statements that name each column to be inserted.

- --create-options (*boolean*)

  Includes additional information in the `CREATE TABLE` statements that `mysqldump` generates, such as the storage engine, the beginning `AUTO_INCREMENT` value, and so forth. This is the information that you can specify using *table_option* values in the CREATE TABLE syntax. (See Appendix E.)

This option is enabled by default; use `--skip-create-options` to disable it.

- `--databases`, `-B` (*boolean*)

Interprets all arguments as database names and dumps all tables in each database. This option also causes the dump output to include CREATE DATABASE IF NOT EXISTS and USE statements for each database.

- `--delayed-insert` (*boolean*)

Writes INSERT DELAYED statements rather than INSERT statements. If you are loading a dump file for MyISAM tables into another database and you want to minimize the impact of the operation on other statements that may be taking place in that database, `--delayed-insert` is helpful for achieving that end.

- `--delete-master-logs`

Deletes the binary log files on the server and begins a new one by issuing a FLUSH MASTER statement after generating the dump output. Don't use this option unless you're sure you want the existing binary logs to be wiped out. This option enables `--master-data`.

- `--disable-keys`, `-K` (*boolean*)

Adds ALTER TABLE ... DISABLE KEYS and ALTER TABLE ... ENABLE KEYS statements to the output, to disable updates to non-unique indexes while INSERT statements are being processed. This speeds up index creation for each MyISAM table by causing it to happen all at once after the table is loaded.

- `--dump-date` (*boolean*)

Adds a comment indicating the dump date to the end of the output. This option was introduced in MySQL 5.0.52/5.1.23.

- `--dump-slave[=n]`

This option is like `--master-data`, but is used for dumping a replication slave server and produces a CHANGE MASTER statement in the output that indicates the binary log coordinates of the slave's master, not those of the slave itself. See the description of `--master-data` for a description of how the option argument is used. The `--dump-slave` option was introduced in MySQL 6.0.4.

- `--events`, `-E` (*boolean*)

Includes events in the dump output. This option was introduced in MySQL 5.1.8.

- `--extended-insert`, `-e` (*boolean*)

Writes multiple-row INSERT statements. These can be loaded more efficiently than single-row statements.

- `--first-slave, -x` (*boolean*)

  This option is deprecated in favor of `--lock-all-tables`.

- `--flush-logs, -F` (*boolean*)

  Flushes the server log files before dumping tables. By default, the logs are flushed for each database to create a checkpoint. This makes it easier to perform restore operations because you know that binary log files created after the checkpoint time were made after the backup for a given database. In conjunction with `--lock-all-tables` or `--master-data`, the logs are flushed only after all tables have been locked. This option requires the `RELOAD` privilege.

- `--flush-privileges` (*boolean*)

  If the dump includes the `mysql` database, includes a `FLUSH PRIVILEGES` in the output after dumping that database. This option was introduced in MySQL 5.0.26/5.1.12.

- `--force, -f` (*boolean*)

  Continues execution even if errors occur.

- `--hex-blob` (*boolean*)

  Dumps `BINARY`, `VARBINARY`, and `BLOB` columns as hexadecimal constants. For example, with this option, `mysqldump` writes `"MySQL"` as `0x4D7953514C`.

- `--ignore-table=`*db_name*`.`*tbl_name*

  Skips dump output for the named table. To ignore multiple tables, repeat the option once for each table. This option was introduced in MySQL 5.0.3.

- `--include-master-host-port` (*boolean*)

  For the `CHANGE MASTER` statement in output produced with `--dump-slave`, includes `MASTER_HOST` and `MASTER_PORT` options that specify the hostname and port number of the slave's master. This option was introduced in MySQL 6.0.4.

- `--insert-ignore` (*boolean*)

  Writes `INSERT IGNORE` statements rather than `INSERT` statements. This option was introduced in MySQL 5.0.6.

- `--lock-all-tables, -x` (*boolean*)

  Uses `FLUSH TABLES WITH READ LOCK` to lock all tables across all databases. This option disables `--single-transaction` and `--lock-tables`.

- `--lock-tables, -l` (*boolean*)

  Uses `LOCK TABLES ... READ LOCAL` obtain locks for all tables being dumped before dumping them. This option is good for MyISAM tables because a `READ LOCAL` lock enables concurrent inserts to proceed while the dump is in progress. For InnoDB and Falcon tables, `--single-transaction` is preferable.

- `--log-error=file_name`

Writes warning and error messages to the end of the named file. This option was introduced in MySQL 5.0.42/5.1.18.

- `--master-data[=value]`

This option helps make a backup that can be used to set up a a slave server. With this option, `mysqldump` sends a `SHOW MASTER STATUS` statement to the server to get its current binary log filename and position, and uses the results to write a `CHANGE MASTER` statement to the output that contains the same filename and position. The effect is that when you load the dump file into a slave server, it synchronizes the slave to the proper replication coordinates of the dumped server to begin replicating at the point when the dump was made. This option has no effect unless the server has binary logging enabled.

By default, the `CHANGE MASTER` statement is written in non-commented form. `--master-data` takes an optional value to explicitly control commenting of the statement. A value of 1 produces a non-commented statement, and a value of 2 produces a commented statement.

`--master-data` requires the `RELOAD` privilege. This option automatically enables `--lock-all-tables` if `--single-transaction` is not given.

- `--no-autocommit` (*boolean*)

Writes the `INSERT` statements for each table within a transaction. The resulting output can be loaded more efficiently than executing each statement in autocommit mode.

- `--no-create-db, -n` (*boolean*)

Causes `CREATE DATABASE` statements not to be written. (Normally, these are added to the output automatically when `--databases` or `--all-databases` are used.)

- `--no-create-info, -t` (*boolean*)

Causes `CREATE TABLE` statements not to be written. This is useful if you want to dump just table data.

- `--no-data, -d` (*boolean*)

Causes table data not to be written. This is useful if you want to dump just the `CREATE TABLE` statements.

- `--no-tablespaces, -y` (*boolean*)

Causes tablespaces not to be dumped. This option was introduced in MySQL 5.1.14.

- `--opt`

Optimizes table dumping speed and writes a dump file that is optimal for reloading speed. This option turns on whichever of the following options are present in your version of `mysqldump`: `--add-drop-table`, `--add-locks`, `--create-options`, `--disable-keys`, `--extended-insert`, `--lock-tables`, `--quick`, and `--set-charset`. This option is enabled by default; use `--skip-opt` to disable it.

■ `--order-by-primary` (*boolean*)

Dumps table rows in order of the primary key or the first unique index if there is one. This produces sorted dump output for each table at a cost in performance.

■ `--quick, -q` (*boolean*)

By default, `mysqldump` reads the entire contents of a table into memory and then writes it out. This option causes each row to be written to the output as soon as it has been read from the server, which is much less memory intensive. However, if you use this option, you should not suspend `mysqldump`. Doing so causes the server to wait, which can interfere with other clients.

■ `--quote-names, -Q` (*boolean*)

Quotes table and column names by enclosing them within backtick ('`') characters. This is useful if names are reserved words or contain special characters. `--quote-names` is enabled by default; use `--skip-quote-names` to disable it.

■ `--replace`

Writes REPLACE statements rather than INSERT statements.

■ `--result-file=`*file_name*`, -r `*file_name*

Writes output to the named file. This option is intended for Windows, where it prevents conversion of linefeeds to carriage return/linefeed pairs.

■ `--routines, -R` (*boolean*)

Includes stored functions and procedures in the dump output. This option was introduced in MySQL 5.0.13.

■ `--set-charset` (*boolean*)

Writes a SET NAMES `charset` statement to the output, where `charset` is `utf8` by default. The character set can be changed using the `--default-character-set` option. The `--set-charset` option is enabled by default; use `--skip-set-charset` to disable it.

■ `--single-transaction` (*boolean*)

This option enables consistent dumps of InnoDB and Falcon tables. The idea is that all the tables are dumped within a single transaction. `mysqldump` uses the REPEATABLE READ transaction isolation level to produce a consistent dump without causing other clients to block. (For non-transactional tables, changes might still occur during the dump operation.) This option disables `--lock-all-tables`.

- `--skip-opt`

This option has the opposite effect of `--opt`, which is enabled by default.

- `--tab=dump_dir`, `-T dump_dir`

This option causes `mysqldump` to write two files per table, using `dump_dir` as the location for the files. The directory must already exist. For each table `tbl_name`, a file `dump_dir/tbl_name.txt` is written containing the data from the table, and a file `dump_dir/tbl_name.sql` is written containing the CREATE TABLE statement for the table. You must have the FILE privilege to use this option.

By default, data files are written as newline-terminated lines consisting of tab-separated column values. This format may be changed using the options described under Section F.15.3, "Data Format Options for `mysqldump`."

The effect of the `--tab` option can be confusing unless you understand exactly how it works:

- Some of the files are written on the server host and some are written on the client host. `dump_dir` is used on the server host for the `*.txt` files and on the client host for the `*.sql` files. If the two hosts are different, the output files are created on different machines. To avoid any uncertainty about where files will be written, it is best to run `mysqldump` on the server host when you use this option so that all files are created on the same machine.

- The `*.txt` files will be owned by the account used to run the server, and the `*.sql` files will be owned by you. This is a consequence of the fact that the server itself writes the `*.txt` files, whereas the CREATE TABLE statements are sent by the server to `mysqldump`, which writes the `*.sql` files.

- `--tables`

Overrides `--databases` to cause any following arguments to be interpreted as table names.

- `--triggers` (*boolean*)

Includes triggers in the dump output. Triggers are included by default; to exclude them, use `--skip-triggers`. This option was introduced in MySQL 5.0.11.

- `--tz-utc` (*boolean*)

Sets the time zone to UTC after connecting to the server and include a SET TIME_ZONE='+00:00' statement in the output. The effect is to suppress conversion to and from the local time zone when dumping and reloading data so that TIMESTAMP values do not change if the reload occurs in a time zone different from the dump. This option is enabled by default but can be disabled with `--skip-tz-utc`. This option was introduced in MySQL 5.0.15.

- `--where=where_expr, -w where_expr`

  Dumps only rows selected by the WHERE condition given by `where_expr`. You should enclose the condition in quotes to prevent your command interpreter from treating it as multiple command-line arguments.

- `--xml, -X`

  Generates output in XML format rather than as a set of SQL statements.

F.15.3 Data Format Options for `mysqldump`

If you specify the `--tab` or `-T` option to generate a separate data file for each table, several additional options apply. You might need to enclose the option value in appropriate quoting characters. These options are analogous to the data format options for the LOAD DATA statement. See the entry for LOAD DATA in Appendix E.

- `--fields-enclosed-by=char`

  Specifies that column values should be enclosed within the given character, usually a quote character. The default is to not enclose column values within anything. This option precludes the use of `--fields-optionally-enclosed-by`.

- `--fields-escaped-by=char`

  Specifies the escape character for escaping special characters. The default is no escape character.

- `--fields-optionally-enclosed-by=char`

  Specifies that column values should be enclosed within the given character, usually a quote character. The character is used for non-numeric columns. The default is to not enclose column values within anything. This option precludes the use of `--fields-enclosed-by`.

- `--fields-terminated-by=str`

  Specifies the column value separation character or characters to use for data files. By default, values are separated by tab characters.

- `--lines-terminated-by=str`

  Specifies the character or characters to write at the end of output lines. The default is to write newlines.

F.15.4 Variables for `mysqldump`

The following `mysqldump` variables can be set using the instructions given in Section F.2.1.2, "Setting Program Variables."

- max_allowed_packet

  The maximum size of the buffer used for communication between the server and the client. The default value is 24MB and the maximum is 1GB.

- net_buffer_length

  The initial size of the buffer used for communication between the server and the client. This buffer may be expanded up to max_allowed_packet bytes long. The default value is slightly less than 1MB.

F.16 mysqlhotcopy

The mysqlhotcopy performs efficient backups of databases and tables. It works only for MyISAM and ARCHIVE tables. mysqlhotcopy is a Perl script. It requires that you have DBI support installed (not surprising, given that it was originally written by Tim Bunce, one of the creators of DBI). mysqlhotcopy works on Unix and NetWare, but not Windows.

mysqlhotcopy connects to the server on the local host. It sends table flushing and locking statements to the server for each table to be copied, and then copies the table files to another location to make a backup. This ensures that outstanding table modifications have been flushed to disk and that the server won't try to further modify the table while it is being copied. (Essentially, mysqlhotcopy implements the protocol described in Section 14.1, "Performing Database Maintenance with the Server Running." This protocol serves to tell the server to leave the designated tables alone while you're working directly with the table files.)

This program can be invoked in a number of ways. The general invocation syntax is as follows:

```
mysqlhotcopy [options] db_name[./regex/] [new_db_name | dir_name]
```

For example, to make a copy of the database db_name named db_name_copy under the data directory, use this command:

```
% mysqlhotcopy [options] db_name
```

To copy the db_name database to a directory named db_name under the /tmp directory instead, do this:

```
% mysqlhotcopy [options] db_name /tmp
```

More examples are provided in the online documentation, available with this command:

```
% perldoc mysqlhotcopy
```

F.16.1 Standard Options Supported by `mysqlhotcopy`

```
--debug      --host       --port       --user
--help       --password   --socket
```

The `--host` option, if given, is intended *only* for specifying the name of the local host. Normally, `mysqlhotcopy` tries to connect to the local server using a Unix socket file. It connects over TCP/IP instead if you specify the actual hostname or IP number of the server using the `--host` option. The `--port` option may be used in this case to specify a port number other than the default. For `--password`, the password value is not optional.

F.16.2 Options Specific to `mysqlhotcopy`

- `--addtodest`

  Instead of renaming the target directory if it already exists, just adds backup files to it.

- `--allowold`

  If the target directory already exists, renames it by adding a suffix of `_old`. If the copy fails, the renamed directory is restored to the original name. If the copy operation succeeds, the renamed directory is deleted, unless the `--keepold` option is also given.

- `--checkpoint=db_name.tbl_name`

  Writes a checkpoint record to the given table, which should have been created in advance with this structure:

  ```
  CREATE TABLE tbl_name
  (
      time_stamp  TIMESTAMP NOT NULL,
      src         VARCHAR(32),
      dest        VARCHAR(60),
      msg         VARCHAR(255)
  );
  ```

  `src` is the source database name, `dest` is the destination directory pathname, and `msg` indicates success or failure of the copy operation.

- `--chroot=dir_name`

  Use this option when `mysqld` runs in a `chroot` jail. The directory name is the base directory of the jail.

- `--dryrun, -n`

  "No execution" mode. `mysqlhotcopy` reports what actions it would take to perform the command, without actually doing them. This is useful for checking whether `mysqlhotcopy` will do what you expect, particularly when you're learning how to use it.

- `--flushlog`

Flushes the logs after all the tables have been locked and before copying them. This has the effect of checkpointing them to the time of the copy operation.

- `--keepold`

If the previous target directory exists, renames it by adding a suffix of `_old` prior to making a new copy. This option implies `--allowold`.

- `--method=copy_method`

The method to use for copying files. A value of `cp` uses the `cp` program. Experimental support for an `scp` method is also available. In this case, the `copy_method` value should be the entire `scp` command to use, and the destination directory must already exist. The `scp` method may result in your tables being locked for a much longer time than a local copy due to the extra time required to copy the files over the network. To avoid this problem, make the backup locally, and then copy it to the remote host after `mysqlhotcopy` finishes.

- `--noindices`

Causes index files not to be copied. (If you need to use the backup files later to recover the tables, you can re-create the indexes by using the files with `myisamchk --recover` for MyISAM tables.)

- `--quiet, -q`

Causes the program to produce no output except when errors occur.

- `--record_log_pos=db_name.tbl_name`

Before copying tables, causes `mysqlhotcopy` to issue SHOW MASTER STATUS and SHOW SLAVE STATUS statements and record the results in the given table, which should have been created in advance with this structure:

```
CREATE TABLE tbl_name
(
    host            VARCHAR(60) NOT NULL,
    time_stamp      TIMESTAMP NOT NULL,
    log_file        VARCHAR(32) NULL,
    log_pos         INT NULL,
    master_host     VARCHAR(60) NULL,
    master_log_file VARCHAR(32) NULL,
    master_log_pos  INT NULL,
    PRIMARY KEY (host)
);
```

The results from SHOW MASTER STATUS are recorded in the `log_file` and `log_pos` columns. This information provides replication coordinates for the binary log; if the backup host is a replication master server, a slave should begin from these coordinates if it is initialized from the backup files as a slave of the master. The results from SHOW SLAVE STATUS are recorded in the `master_host, master_log_file`, and `master_log_pos` columns; they can be used if the backup host is a replication slave server and you want to initialize another slave of the same master from the backup files.

- `--regexp=pattern`

Copies all databases having names that match the given regular expression. The final argument of the command should be the directory where you want to copy the databases.

- `--resetmaster`

Resets the binary log by issuing a `RESET MASTER` statement after all the tables have been locked and before they are copied.

- `--resetslave`

Resets the information in the `master.info` file by issuing a `RESET SLAVE` statement after all the tables have been locked and before they are copied.

- `--suffix=str`

This option is used when making a copy of databases into the database directory. Each new database directory name is the same as the original with the given suffix added.

- `--tmpdir=dir_name`

The pathname of the directory in which to create temporary files. The default is to use the directory named by the `TMPDIR` environment variable, or `/tmp` if that variable is not set.

F.17 `mysqlimport`

The `mysqlimport` client program is a bulk loader for reading the contents of text files into existing tables. It functions as a command-line interface to the LOAD DATA SQL statement, and is an efficient way to enter rows into tables:

```
mysqlimport [options] db_name file_name ...
```

The `db_name` argument specifies the database that contains the tables into which you want to load data. The tables to load are determined from the filename arguments. For each filename, any extension from the first period in the name is stripped off and the remaining basename is used as the name of the table into which the file should be loaded. For example, `mysqlimport` will load the contents of a file named `president.txt` into the `president` table.

`mysqlimport` reads data files only. It is *not* intended for reading SQL-format dump files produced by `mysqldump`. Use `mysql` to read such files instead.

F.17.1 Standard Options Supported by `mysqlimport`

`--character-sets-dir`	`--help`	`--shared-memory-base-name`
`--compress`	`--host`	`--silent`
`--debug`	`--password`	`--socket`
`--debug-check`	`--pipe`	`--user`
`--debug-info`	`--port`	`--verbose`
`--default-character-set`	`--protocol`	`--version`

`--debug-info` and `--debug-check` are available as of MySQL 5.1.14 and 5.1.21, respectively.

`mysqlimport` also supports the standard SSL options.

F.17.2 Options Specific to `mysqlimport`

The following options control how `mysqlimport` processes input files. Section F.17.3, "Data Format Options for `mysqlimport`," describes options that may be used to indicate the format of the data in the input files.

- `--columns=col_list`

  Specifies the list of columns in the table to which columns in the data file correspond. Values in input rows will be loaded into the named columns, and other columns will be set to their default values. `col_list` is a list of one or more column names separated by commas.

- `--delete, -d` (*boolean*)

  Empties each table before loading any data into it.

- `--force, -f` (*boolean*)

  Continues loading rows even if errors occur.

- `--ignore, -i`

  When an input row contains a value for a unique key that already exists in the table, keeps the existing row and discards the input row. The `--ignore` and `--replace` options are mutually exclusive.

- `--ignore-lines=n`

  Ignores the first *n* lines of the data file. This can be used to skip an initial row of column labels, for example.

- `--local, -L` (*boolean*)

  By default, `mysqlimport` lets the server read the data file, which means that the file must be located on the server host and that you must have the FILE privilege. Specifying the `--local` option tells `mysqlimport` to read the data file itself and send it to the server. This is slower but works when you're running `mysqlimport` on a different machine than the server host, as well as on the server host even if you don't have the FILE privilege.

This option is ineffective if the server has been configured to disallow use of LOAD DATA LOCAL.

- `--lock-tables, -l` (*boolean*)

Locks each table before loading data into it.

- `--low-priority` (*boolean*)

Uses the LOW_PRIORITY scheduling modifier to load data into the table.

- `--replace, -r` (*boolean*)

When an input row contains a value for a unique key that already exists in the table, replaces the existing row with the input row. The `--ignore` and `--replace` options are mutually exclusive.

- `--use-threads=n`

Uses *n* threads to load files in parallel. This option was introduced in MySQL 5.1.7.

F.17.3 Data Format Options for `mysqlimport`

By default, `mysqlimport` assumes that data files contain newline-terminated lines consisting of tab-separated values. The expected format may be altered using the following options. You might need to enclose the option value in appropriate quoting characters. These options are analogous to the data format options for the LOAD DATA statement. See the entry for LOAD DATA in Appendix E.

- `--fields-enclosed-by=char`

Specifies that column values are enclosed within the given character, usually a quote character. By default, values are assumed not to be enclosed by any character. This option precludes the use of `--fields-optionally-enclosed-by`.

- `--fields-escaped-by=char`

Specifies the escape character used to escape special characters. The default is no escape character.

- `--fields-optionally-enclosed-by=char`

Specifies that column values may be enclosed within the given character, usually a quote character. This option precludes the use of `--fields-enclosed-by`.

- `--fields-terminated-by=str`

Specifies the character or characters that separate column values. By default, values are assumed to be separated by tab characters.

- `--lines-terminated-by=str`

Specifies the character or characters that terminate input lines. By default, lines are assumed to be terminated by newline characters.

F.18 mysqlshow

mysqlshow lists databases, tables within a database, or information about columns or indexes within a table. It acts as a command-line interface to the SHOW SQL statement:

```
mysqlshow [options] [db_name [tbl_name [col_name]]]
```

If no database name is specified, mysqlshow lists all databases on the server host. If a database name but no table name is specified, all tables in the database are listed. If database and table names are specified, but no column name is specified, it lists the columns in the table. If all the names are specified, mysqlshow shows information about the given column.

The final argument may contain the '%' and '_' SQL wildcard characters, which are treated the same way as for the LIKE operator. Output is limited to values that match the wildcards. If the final argument contains the '*' or '?' shell wildcard characters, they are treated as '%' and '_', respectively .

F.18.1 Standard Options Supported by mysqlshow

--character-sets-dir	--help	--shared-memory-base-name
--compress	--host	--socket
--debug	--password	--user
--debug-check	--pipe	--verbose
--debug-info	--port	--version
--default-character-set	--protocol	

--debug-info and --debug-check are available as of MySQL 5.1.14 and 5.1.21, respectively.

The --verbose option causes additional columns to be included in the output (tables per database, rows per table, and so forth). The option may be given multiple times.

mysqlshow also supports the standard SSL options.

F.18.2 Options Specific to mysqlshow

- --count (*boolean*)

  Includes the number or rows per table in the output. Counting the rows may be slow for some storage engines. This option was introduced in MySQL 5.0.6.

- --keys, -k (*boolean*)

  Shows information about table indexes in addition to information about table columns. This option is meaningful only if you specify a table name.

- --status, -i (*boolean*)

  Displays the same kind of table information displayed by the SHOW TABLE STATUS statement.

F.19 `perror`

`perror` displays error messages for error codes:

```
perror [options] [err_code] ...
```

You can use it to determine the meaning of errors returned by MySQL programs.

```
% perror 142
MySQL error:  142 = Unknown character set used
```

F.19.1 Standard Options Supported by `perror`

```
--help        --silent      --verbose      --version
```

The `--silent` option causes only the error message and not the code to be displayed. The default is `--verbose`, which displays both the code and the message.

`--info` and `-I` are synonyms for `--help`.

Symbols

A

C

D

M

O

Q

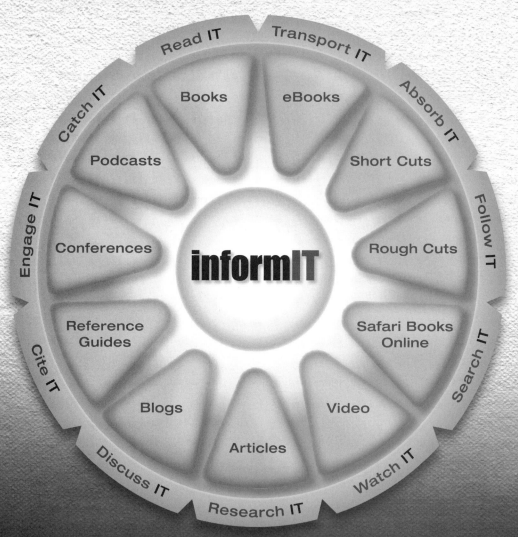

FREE Online Edition

Your purchase of **MySQL** includes access to a free online edition for 120 days through the Safari Books Online subscription service. Nearly every Addison-Wesley Professional book is available online through Safari Books Online, along with over 5,000 other technical books and videos from publishers such as Cisco Press, Exam Cram, IBM Press, O'Reilly, Prentice Hall, Que, and Sams.

SAFARI BOOKS ONLINE allows you to search for a specific answer, cut and paste code, download chapters, and stay current with emerging technologies.

Activate your FREE Online Edition at
www.informit.com/safarifree

> **STEP 1:** Enter the coupon code: XBH9-8DIH-PNZK-I4H7-FMAM.

> **STEP 2:** New Safari users, complete the brief registration form.
> Safari subscribers, just login.

If you have difficulty registering on Safari or accessing the online edition, please e-mail customer-service@safaribooksonline.com